THE LAW AND
HIGHER EDUCATION

THE LAW AND
HIGHER EDUCATION:
Cases and Materials on
Colleges in Court

Michael A. Olivas

Professor of Law, and Director
Institute for Higher Education Law and Governance
University of Houston

With the research assistance of
Idelma Saenz

CAROLINA
ACADEMIC
PRESS
POST BOX 51879
DURHAM
N. CAROLINA
27717

International Standard Book Number: 0-89089-364-0
Library of Congress Card Catalog Number: 89-62027

Carolina Academic Press
P.O. Box 51879
Durham, North Carolina 27717
(919) 489-7486

Printed in the United States of America

Table of Contents

Table of Cases

Preface

The study of higher education law, like that of its parent fields, higher education and law, is developing rapidly. In response to an administrative need to understand complex litigation and its effect upon the governance of institutions, knowledge of higher education law has become essential to anyone in a responsible position in higher education. In addition to the immediate, practical, and applied uses of law in college settings, there has emerged more systematic research on higher education law. Beginning with M. M. Chambers' seminal 1941 work, *The Colleges and the Courts*, scholars have mined the rich veins of litigation to contribute to an understanding of legal processes in postsecondary institutions.

However, this research, frequently published in law reviews and legal periodicals, rarely enriches the practice of administration. Attorneys and law professors rarely become college administrators, although most college administrators rely heavily upon counsel when making major policy decisions. Moreover, faculty in other fields become administrators, and there is little interaction in formal scholarly associations between legal researchers and academics. A veritable cottage industry has emerged to bridge the gap between litigation and administration and between scholar and practitioner, but the gap remains great.

Also great is the lack of consensus on what constitutes higher education law. As Paul Dressel and Lewis Mayhew noted more than a decade ago, higher education itself as a field of study "is an active, confused field, lacking many of the attributes of a discipline, yet demanding more disciplined effort." Surely the same must be said for the field's subspecialty, higher education law. More vexing, perhaps, is what constitutes the "law" of higher education law. While no definition is proffered here, the organization of the book suggests more than a narrow definition of law-as-litigation. Indeed, an expansive view is taken, revealing testing organizations, politicians, state agencies, the federal government, and institutions all to be actors in the legalization of the academy. Notably absent is any deliberate ideological attempt to comment upon whether the increased litigation is "good" or "bad" for the higher education enterprise. This omission is deliberate, not because I have no principled views in the matter, but because the questions are simply beyond the scope of this project.

In truth, however, the issue of whether the litigation chronicled here is too much or too little is crucial to the legitimacy of higher education law as a developing field of study. If legal scholarship in higher education were simply to take on a "body-count" cast, counting victories and losses, serving only to legitimate unprincipled administrative decisions, or advancing only theories of risk management, much would be lost in law's possibility for ensuring equitable treatment in a meritocracy. This scenario is unlikely to occur, as the increased resort to litigation has not always advantaged college administrators, who frequently lose in court. As many of these cases demonstrate, courts' views of students have changed, and more than one critic has decried the pendulum's swing to students.

When a more thorough review of higher education law is written, it will surely address the crucial issue of the proper role of law in the academy. Fifteen years ago, in *Higher Education as a Field of Study*, Dressel and Mayhew noted, "An almost new component of the field of higher education covers legal provisions, legal interpretations and the implications for higher education of precedent and legislated and administrative law." This case book is an attempt to provide a teaching tool that reflects the extraordinary growth in "the law of higher education" and the corollary rise in scholarship and commentary on higher education law and governance.

As in any casebook, I chose cases to reflect major themes and issues, and they form the core of the text. Additional materials were selected from exceptional scholarship, commentary, and news coverage of legal issues bearing upon higher education. I consulted widely with colleagues to identify the most significant cases and materials for inclusion, with their pedagogical value in mind: would they help students understand the complex relationships between institutions of higher education and society? To this end, I considered cases with interesting facts but less precedential value, anomalous cases since disregarded but providing a unique insight into a judge's thinking, news accounts of fascinating cases or developments to reveal how law arises in U.S. society, and insights from scholars and practitioners who have thought about these issues. I edited with a heavy hand, and refer readers to the complete opinions; all extraneous footnotes and citations have been deleted without notice, and all deletions from the text have been noted with asterisks. In addition, some obvious cases were not included, either because they were extensively incorporated into cited cases or because space limitations necessitated the choice.

I gained renewed admiration for authors who had produced excellent casebooks, and I read through dozens, in order to understand the thread of logic, the flow of ideas, and the organizing principles employed by authors. Two principles struck me, and I have tried to appropriate them for my own work. First, the best casebooks, to my way of thinking, treated a few large ideas extremely well: there is no room for purebred foxes, and no room for hedgehogs. Students appreciate several large ideas, organized around meaningful principles, and the field of higher education law has evolved to the point that many cases exist for choosing among important issues. Second, the authors evidently made hard choices about including reference materials, and chose to incorporate enough to refer students to additional sources, but were judicious in their selections. The least interesting books to me when I was a law student and doctoral student, and to me today as a law professor, were those that indiscriminately included notes or ephemeral commentary, or that seemed to include rote string-cites.

This book is intended for classroom use or for general legal reference. It is not intended to serve as a manual or substitute for legal counsel. Persons not having access to a law library may find it useful for reading edited cases, but I deliberately chose not to write a treatise, or to include reference materials on every case. Several exceptional treatises exist (most notably William Kaplin's *The Law of Higher Education* and Matthew Rapp's 4 volume *Education Law*), and many excellent sources are incorporated by reference throughout the book. In the spirit of full disclosure, I acknowledge that the book's central purpose is to teach. One last thought on the best textbooks, or for that matter, the best writing. For my tastes, the best writing on almost any topic shows enthusiasm and care. Cases can seem bloodless, dry recitations of facts, even when the underlying issue is important to the participants, who may feel passionately about their stake in the matter.

Higher education cases are often a proxy for larger societal themes—particularly race relations, fairness in the treatment of women, and the rise of the modern administrative state. Students in higher education law courses have an understanding of their subject matter, one almost unique in their curriculum; they may never have drafted a will, been a criminal defendant, purchased property, or committed a tort, but they are students, and will have ideas about their own status. As a result, I have been the fortunate beneficiary of much student thinking on this topic, and I hope I have met the high expectations students properly have for their course materials. I welcome advice and comments from persons who use this text, as well as suggestions for inclusions in subsequent editions.

Acknowledgements

This book has been in the works since 1983, when I discovered to my dismay that Harry Edwards and Virginia Nordin would not be supplementing or updating their useful work, *Higher Education & the Law*, published in 1979 by the Institute for Educational Management, with three annual supplements. For several years, colleagues and I squirreled away copies, trading them like bootleg concert tapes or valuable baseball cards, or purchasing them back from our students. When this proved impossible, we secured permission from IEM to photocopy the Edwards-Nordin text, paying royalties and photocopying costs. This was an unsatisfactory state of events.

Finally, a seminar on teaching education law at the Association of American Law Schools' annual meeting convinced me that the only way to meet the needs of students in this area was to write a casebook myself. Professors Bill Kaplin and Gail Sorenson, the speakers at that seminar, deserve my thanks for the encouragement and valuable assistance they have provided me since then. Similarly, Monique Westin Clague, James Brooks, Laura Rothstein, and Mark Rothstein provided help in recommending cases and materials or advice in editing. My dean, Robert Knauss, provided me with administrative support for the Institute I direct, while University Counsel Scott Chafin and UH Law Professor Steve Huber have been excellent colleagues and sounding boards for these ideas. At the Institute, I thank Carolyn Winter, Juanita Stewart, and Deborah Jones for their staff assistance, and many research assistants and students who helped in various ways with the research for the book: Sandi Vera, Ramana Jones, Kay Denison, Sarah Klein-Tower, Ha Cao, and Melissa Kral. Idelma Saenz became a valued collaborator for her extraordinary service, and I acknowledge her as a virtual co-author in this enterprise. At Carolina Academic Press, Keith Sipes and Mayapriya Long were excellent sources of encouragement.

Rev. Msgr. Leonard J. Fick, my major professor at the Pontifical College Josephinum, first encouraged me as a student to become involved in college administration, and in the twenty years since I took his advice, I have always considered my actions by his exacting norms and written with his critical encouragement in mind. To my parents, Sabino Olivas, III and Clara Olivas, I offer this as an anniversary gift. To them and to my wife, Augustina Reyes, I gratefully dedicate this book.

THE LAW AND
HIGHER EDUCATION

Chapter 1

The Legal Governance of Higher Education

Lewis Thomas, "The Governance of a University"

Long ago, in the quiet years before World War II, being chairman of the Department of Medicine (or the Department of Physiology, or Surgery, or whatever) in an American medical school was pretty much like being head of the English department over in the main part of the university. From year to year, the medical school remained the same size, in the same aging buildings. The university shared a fixed portion of its general endowment with the medical school. The latter did its best to secure extra money of its own, but never great sums, from affluent alumni or their patients. The medical school's budget was a fairly steady sum of money from one year to the next. The main difference between running a major department in the two parts of the university was that many of the key faculty members—the professors—in the clinical departments of the medical school were not paid a salary by either the university or the medical school. These men had their own offices elsewhere in the city where they conducted a private practice and earned their livelihood. The holding of a professorial appointment on the medical school faculty was a mark of professional distinction, carrying some assurance that patients would be referred to the physician-teacher's care for diagnosis or treatment by other doctors, and the physician-teacher did quite well.

At the time I reached the low rungs of the academic ladder, ready to try my hand at science, money for research had to be scraped together in very small sums, enough to buy rabbits and mice and minor supplies. Technicians were rare personages, to be found only at the benches of the senior-most professors. It was taken for granted that I would be responsible for preparing my own bacteriological media, washing and sterilizing my own glassware, and looking after whatever animals were involved in my experiments. For the first two years of my work at the Thorndike, the costs of all the supplies came to $500 a year, this from a special endowment called the Wellington Fund, which had been bequeathed to the laboratory years earlier.

After the war, the federal government made the decision that science was useful and important, and research within the medical schools became a much more serious business. As a result, the differences between the management of the medical school departments and their counterparts elsewhere in the university became sharper. While the English department continued to lead its more or less steady existence, assured of a fixed complement of tenure and nontenure positions for its faculty, and equally assured of a steady but very modest fixed income from the university's endowment to pay its costs, the medical school departments, and some of the science departments within the university proper, began to explode. An individual faculty member in, say,

3

the Department of Microbiology, an expert on the streptococcus or meningococcus, could now file an application for a government grant to support his laboratory, purchase supplies and new instruments needed for the pursuit of some new ideas, pay part or all of his own salary, and hire one or two technicians. A few years later, whole departments came under grant support, with money enough to recruit new faculty members, provide fellowship funds for increasing numbers of Ph.D. candidates as well as postdoctoral fellows, even money to build new laboratory quarters. And later still, in the 1950s and throughout most of the sixties, the federal research funds arrived in bundles large enough to renovate most of the buildings in existing medical schools and to build more than a score of brand-new schools.

I served as the dean of one medical school, New York University, during the period of rapid expansion and at another, Yale, during the time when the funds were reduced, not yet to a trickle, but to a thin, even flow. Both experiences brought me closer to the inner workings of the modern university than I had ever been before. Being a professor in a medical school is a good way to find out how these highly specialized institutions and their connected hospitals function, but the university itself seems a remote place, almost nonexistent. Being a dean is different: you get to look inside.

The governance of academic institutions has been considered and reconsidered, reviewed over and over by faculty committee after committee, had more reports written about it than even the curriculum, even tenure. Nothing much ever comes of the labor. How should a university be run? Who is really in charge, holding the power? The proper answer is, of course, nobody. I know of one or two colleges and universities that have actually been tightly administered, managed rather like large businesses, controlled in every detail by a president and his immediately surrounding bureaucrats, but these were not really very good colleges or universities to begin with, and they were managed this way because they were on the verge of running out of money. In normal times, with institutions that are relatively stable in their endowments and incomes, nobody is really in charge.

A university, as has been said so many times that there is risk of losing the meaning, is a community of scholars. When its affairs are going well, when its students are acquiring some comprehension of the culture and its faculty are contributing new knowledge to their special fields, and when visiting scholars are streaming in and out of its gates, it runs itself, rather like a large organism. The function of the administration is solely to see that the funds are adequate for its purposes and not overspent, that the air is right, that the grounds are tidy—and then to stay out of its way.

To function in accordance with its design and intentions, a university must be the most decentralized of all institutions.

This is not easy to do, and it is a surprise that it works, by and large, as well as it does. The risk of politics is always there, and there can be nothing so confusing and aimless as academic politics, or, sometimes, so bitter and recriminatory. The remark was once made, attributed to the California politician Jesse Unruh, that the trouble with university politics, the thing that makes it so different and more potentially damaging than the ordinary politics of state government, is that "the stakes are so low." There is some truth to this. In real life, nothing much is to be gained through the temporary leadership of a committee or *ad hoc* group out to reform the curriculum or change the parking rules or get rid of the president or whatever. The leader, even if successful, is not likely to emerge from victory with a higher salary or more space for his office or laboratory, and he runs a greater risk of not changing anything or, at the most, acquiring the reputation of a disturber of other people's peace.

The worst of all jobs is that of the dean. He carries, on paper, the responsibility for the tranquillity, productivity, and prestige of all the chairmen of the departments within his bailiwick, and when things go wrong at the outskirts, in the laboratories of an individual faculty member or the cubicle of a graduate student, the blame is swiftly transported toward the center, past the desks of the senior faculty, past the chairman's secretary (who is usually the person running the day-to-day affairs of the department), and straight on to the dean.

The actual power of a dean to do anything much is marginal at best and, even at that best, dangerous if he tries to use it. In the major research universities, and especially those with medical schools, the money for running the departments is money generated by the individual faculty members and their students. In good times, this money cascades over the dean's head, arranges itself in rivulets that flow past the chairman's office out into the individual budgets of the faculty. In this circumstance, the faculty members are convinced that the university is run by their efforts, is forever in debt to each of them for its sustenance, and owes them a strict and accurate accounting for every dollar of the funds brought in through their efforts. The dean, in this environment, is there in order to serve the professors, and they, in turn, are paid salaries to serve the junior faculty, who actually do the research for which the grants are made, and the students, who help in this work.

The principal usefulness of academic committees is in getting people to know each other. You get to know your colleagues very well indeed when you sit with them for a couple of hours once a week, to talk, say, about the grading of faculty by students. It is possible to learn more about the substance, the inner resources, and the reliability of a man or a woman in this way than by going off on a canoe trip in white water. You learn quickly who is to be trusted and who is to be worried about.

The main function of committees, and the one most likely to affect in an enduring way the quality and future destiny of the university, is the nomination of faculty members for promotion to tenure rank. This is the single area in which the dean can exert real power, since selecting the membership of tenure committees is, in most places, the prerogative of the dean. If he has an idea that Associate Professor Smith would be a likely prospect for a permanent appointment, good for the future name of the university, he can choose a search committee likely to come down on Smith's side—or at least he can avoid appointing members likely to hold prejudices against Smith or Smith's field. In some universities, the faculty are aware of the dean's power in this matter and mistrust him, and therefore insist that the tenure committee must be a standing committee not subject to a change in its membership by the dean's whim.

The principal task of the administrators—the president, the provost, and the deans—after making sure that the proper systems are in place for keeping track of the money and generating reliable reports to the outside world in accounting for all funds, is to Let Nature Take Its Course. At any rate, this is the main part of the job in an established university with a distinguished name and a good record. Not to meddle is the trick to be learned. The university is perhaps the greatest of all social inventions, a marvel of civilization, a product of collective human wisdom working at its best. A good university doesn't need to be headed as much as to be given its head, and it is the administrator's task—not at all an easy one—to see that this happens. The temptations to intervene from the top, to reach in and try to change the way the place works, to arrive at one's desk each morning with one's mind filled with exhilarating ideas for revitalizing the whole institution, are temptations of the devil and need resisting with all the strength of the administrator's character.

Hands off is the safest rule of thumb. The hands of trustees, the state legislature, the alumni, the federal granting bureaucracies, the national professional and educational societies, and most of all the administrators, must be held off, waving widely from a distance maybe but never touching the mechanism. I would as soon take command of a platoon of scuba divers and swim into a coral reef with the notion of making improvements in its arrangements for living as I would undertake revision in the ecosystem of a university. It needs a lot of leaving alone, and a lot of spontaneous, natural evolution.

A medical school is an anomaly within a university and works differently, sometimes placing the whole institution at risk for its principles. Medical schools are constantly having hands laid on them, from all sides, hands carrying money or threatening to take money away, other hands twisting the head of this part of the university and turning it in a direction skewed to one side, aimed at immediate service to the community, also aimed in the direction of money, money carrying the guarantee of something tangible delivered quickly in return. This is not the habit of the universities. Not to say that universities do not seek money, they do so day and night, but not, generally, with the promise of a service or a product.

I have lived most of my professional life in one medical school after another, and have a deep affection and admiration for these institutions, but I can see that some things are wrong with them and are beginning to go wronger still. If I were the president of a major university I would not want to take on a medical school, and if it already had one, I would be lying awake nights trying to figure out ways to get rid of it.

At the beginning, having a medical school was no great responsibility for a university, no trouble at all, and nice for the prestige of the whole place. Medical schools were small affairs by today's standards, a hundred students or fewer per class: two years of basic biomedical science taught by faculty who usually added strength to the university's resources for scientific research and teaching, and a small and relatively inexpensive clinical faculty for the last two years, most of whom made their own living in private practice and cost the university nothing for their services. The teaching hospitals were autonomous institutions, supported by the local community, managed as separate corporate entities unrelated to the university and maintained either as voluntary or municipal (or county) institutions. Medicine was a solidly respected career, intellectually rewarding if not famous for being lucrative; the applicants for admission were adequate in number to fill the classes, but not much in excess of that number. The medical school was often located in another part of town—sometimes in another, distant part of the state—from the rest of the university, which, most of the time, was oblivious to its existence.

The great change began in the years immediately after World War II, with the expansion of extramural research programs of the National Institutes of Health. During the mid-1950s I was a member of what was then referred to as the "Senior Council" of the NIH, the National Advisory Health Council, which reported directly to the Surgeon General of the U.S. Public Health Service and was supposed to set policy. We had the time of our lives. Everything seemed possible. The Congress was fascinated by the possibilities that lay ahead in medical research, and Senator Lister Hill and Congressman John Fogarty were powerful figures who had already started to build their legislative careers on medical science. The medical schools of the country were of a mind to begin expanding their scientific facilities, and there was money all around. Dr. Frederick Stone, executive secretary for the council, was a skilled and ambitious bureaucrat, and Dr. James Shannon, the director of NIH, knew exactly where he wanted NIH to go and how to lead it to its destiny, which involved strengthening the nation's capacity for medical science by building research into the daily, central, and essential functions of the American medical schools.

In retrospect, it can be seen that the expansion of NIH and the recruitment of medical facilities for implementing the national mission of NIH represented one of the most intelligent and imaginative acts of any government in history, and NIH itself became, principally as the result of Shannon's sheer force of will and capacity to plan ahead, the greatest research institution on earth. Only one thing went wrong, a mistake no one involved in the early years envisioned: research became more expensive than anyone would have guessed. While NIH selected for excellence and picked the strongest universities and their medical schools for the effort, it became at the same time the accepted idea that *every* faculty member of *every* medical school in the country must be a working scientist with a grant from NIH and a laboratory at his disposal. As an inevitable result, the merit system for recruiting and promoting faculty members in the medical schools would henceforth be determined, in large part or in whole, by research productivity and papers published.

With this stimulus, the emergence of the modern medical center, now known at some universities as the Health Sciences Center, or some such term, began. Today, these creations dominate the scene at many universities. They are typically located at or near the edge of the campus, immense structures built around the core of a huge hospital, swarming with clinics, diagnostic laboratories, special buildings for rehabilitation, mental health, retardation, geriatrics, heart disease, cancer, stroke, and any number of other categorical programs that have, at one time or another down the years, caught the interest of one or another congressional committee. The central hospital is usually designated as the "university hospital"; sometimes the university owns it outright, or otherwise has contractual arrangements which give the university the key right to designate its own faculty as members of the hospital's professional staff, usually with their incomes provided by the hospital.

Most of these new medical centers are of great value to the communities around their doors, and many of them can fairly be regarded as national, even international, resources for the most skilled and specialized health care to be found anywhere. There is no question as to their excellence—indeed, they have had the effect of raising the professional standards for medical and nursing care across the country.

The only question—and now it is a question causing anguish for both medical school and university administrators—concerns their relevance to the university mission. The question did not arise so often in the years when the medical centers were being built, or in the years when there seemed to be plenty of money to meet their costs of upkeep. But now, in the 1980s, with demands for retrenchment in all governmental programs and outcries everywhere against the rising costs of medical care, particularly hospital costs, the relationship between these hospitals and their parent medical schools, and of both to their fiscal guardians, the universities, is becoming increasingly strained and uncomfortable.

Meanwhile, during the past ten or fifteen years, the medical schools themselves have undergone a great expansion. Not only has the number of schools in the country increased by 50 percent, the number of medical students in many schools has doubled, or more than doubled. This happened during a period when both the federal government and many state legislatures believed that we were short of doctors, and the schools were paid by capitation, a sort of bounty, for each student added to the entering classes. Now, with the federal cutbacks already launched, including sharp reductions in low-interest student loans, many of the medical schools are barely escaping bankruptcy. As for the students already in the system, and those now planning to enter it, the cost of medical education is becoming so high that only those backed by affluent families can pay their way. The annual tuition alone in the medical schools of private universities is already close to $10,000 for most, and rising above $20,000 in some. The state schools are considerably cheaper, but their costs are also rising steeply.

The universities themselves are now at risk. Step by step, they have assumed— probably without anyone realizing the magnitude of each step—the ultimate control and ultimate responsibility for a large sector of the nation's health-care system. The annual budget of some medical schools matches or exceeds the operating budget of all the rest of the university. The rosters of tenured faculty and the commitment to graduate and postdoctoral education have become disproportionately greater in many medical schools. And now, with the sure prospect of reductions in the funds flowing from Washington to support the medical schools, it is the universities and the trustees who will have to decide where to make the inevitable cuts. Most universities live chancily from year to year, depending heavily on contributions from their alumni and philanthropic friends, sailing close to the wind. It is not within their conceivable resources to pick up deficits of any size, and the medical school deficits are soon likely to become of great size indeed.

Somehow or other, the medical centers will have to do a better job of sorting out their component parts. The medical school faculties carry responsibilities for teaching, research, and patient care, and are largely dependent on the hospitals for their income. As integral parts of the universities, the medical schools ought not to be in the business of running immense hospitals, any more than the law schools should be running the local court system or the business schools operating the town's major corporations and banks. The teaching hospitals cannot divorce themselves completely from the medical schools with which they are affiliated, but they should be recognized and supported by society for what they are—complex and costly institutions which are indispensable not only for the local community but for the whole country, some of them indeed for the whole world.

(Chapter 16, *The Youngest Science: Notes of a Medicine-Watcher* (New York: Viking, 1983). Reprinted by permission.)

————

Lewis Thomas, perhaps our most thoughtful commentator on medicine and science in society, ascribes organic qualities to the university, and his view of a college as a "community of scholars" is grounded in an appreciation of the history of education. Paul Goodman's *The Community of Scholars* (New York: Random House, 1962) and John Millett's *The Academic Community* (New York: McGraw-Hill, 1962) also exemplify this perspective. Like a prism refracting light differently depending upon how you hold it up for viewing, higher education can appear differently. For Herbert Stroup and many other sociologists, colleges are essentially bureaucracies (*Bureaucracy in Higher Education*, New York: Free Press, 1966), and no student confronting course registration today is likely to be dissuaded from this view. To Victor Baldridge, universities are indisputably political organizations (*Power and Conflict in the University*, New York: John Wiley, 1971), as they also appear to Clark Kerr (*The Uses of the University*, Cambridge: Harvard University Press, 1982) and Burton Clark (*The Higher Education System*, Berkeley: University of California Press, 1983). To critics, higher education is stratified by class (Randall Collins, *The Credential Society*, New York: Academic Press, 1979), resistant to legal change (Harry Edwards, *Higher Education and the Unholy Crusade Against Governmental Regulation*, Cambridge: Institute for Educational Management, 1980), and in need of fundamental restructuring (Paulo Freire, *Education for Critical Consciousness*, New York: Seabury Press, 1973). As many observers would insist, all are equally close to the truth or truths, depending upon which truth is being refracted. The cases in this book reveal many truths and, often frustratingly, few answers. As the next cases reveal, legal considerations can pare governance issues down to essentials: What is a college?

What is a College?

The first case contains two elements that reappear throughout higher education law: the legal character of a college and race. Both elements are fugue-like in their way, weaving throughout cases, legislation, and regulations in higher education. As will be seen in successive chapters, these themes will be considered in more detail. P.S. The entering freshman class of Rice University in 1989–90 was nearly 25% minority.

Coffee v. Rice University
408 S.W.2d 269 (1966)

COLEMAN, Justice.

This is a suit brought by William Marsh Rice University, and the Trustees thereof, for the purpose of securing an interpretation of the organic instruments by which the institution was created that the Trustees, in the exercise of their discretion, are free to accept as students qualified applicants without regard to color and to charge tuition to those able to pay the same. In the alternative, the University requested the court to apply the equitable doctrines of Cy Pres and deviation if such action was found to be necessary in order that students might be admitted without regard to color and that tuition might be charged those able to pay the same.

After a trial before a jury the court entered a judgment granting the requested relief, and certain former students of the University, intervenors herein, have perfected an appeal to this Court.

By an instrument dated May 13, 1891, and acknowledged on May 16, 1891, William Marsh Rice gave to James A. Baker, Jr., E. Raphael, C. Lombardi, J.E. McAshan, F.A. Rice and A.S. Richardson, as Trustees, a promissory note in the sum of $200,000.00 payable at his death. This instrument recited the terms of the note verbatim, and provided that the money donated should be an endowment fund, the interest, income, issues and profits of which should forever be donated "to the instruction of the white inhabitants of the City of Houston, and State of Texas, through and by the establishment and maintenance of a Public Library and Institute for the Advancement of Literature, Science and Art, to be incorporated as hereinafter provided, and to be known by such name as the said parties of the second part (Trustees) may in their judgment select."

This instrument then directed the Trustees to incorporate "forthwith for the purpose of carrying out the uses, intents, and purposes of this trust." The next paragraph provided:

"*THIRD*:   That as soon as the said Public Library and Institute for the Advancement of Science and Art shall have been incorporated, as herein contemplated, then the said *Institute*, through and by its Board of Trustees hereinafter named, shall accept from the said parties of the second part, the Endowment Fund of Two Hundred Thousand Dollars."

The instrument proceeded to appoint as Trustees of the Institute William Marsh Rice and the same people who were Trustees under the trust indenture; provided life tenure; reserved to William Marsh Rice the right to fill vacancies arising during his lifetime; providing that all trustees be inhabitants of the City of Houston, Texas; reserving to William Marsh Rice, "during his natural life," the right to make all decisions in the event he disagreed with the other Trustees.

Numbered Paragraph SEVENTH reads:

"The Endowment Fund, herein mentioned, including all future endowments, donations and bequests that may hereafter be made to the said Institute, not otherwise provided, shall be devoted to the following objects, and purposes, to-wit:

"A. To the establishment and Maintenance of a Free Library, Reading Room, and Institute for the Advancement of Science and Art.

"B. To provide, as soon as the fund will warrant such an expenditure, for the establishment and maintenance of a thorough polytechnic school, for males and females, designed to give instructions on the application of Science and Art to the useful occupation of life; the requirements for admission to which shall be left to the discretion of the Board of Trustees.

"C. Said Library, Reading Room, Scientific Departments, and Polytechnic School, and the instruction, benefits and enjoyments to be derived from the Institute to be free and open to all; to be non-sectarian and non-partisan, and subject to such restrictions only, as in the judgment of the Board of Trustees will conduce to the good order and honor of the said Institute."

The Trustees were expressly forbidden "ever to permit any lien, encumbrance, debt or mortgage to be placed upon any of the property, or funds, belonging now, or that may hereafter belong to said Institute; * * * "

They were given "full authority" to formulate and enforce such by-laws, rules and regulations, for the government of the affairs of said Institute as in their judgment they may deem proper.

The last paragraph reads:

"*THIRTEENTH*:   It is expressly provided that one-tenth of the increase of the Endowment Fund, herein mentioned, shall be set apart as a Sinking Fund, which may be used in the discretion of the Board of Trustees for betterments and improvements of the Institute."

On the 18th day of May, 1891, the charter of the Institute was signed and acknowledged by all of the Trustees except William Marsh Rice. The trust instrument was quoted verbatim in the charter. There was evidence that both the trust instrument and the charter were prepared by E. Raphael, who was not then practicing law. At that time William Marsh Rice resided in New York, although he had previously lived in Texas for a number of years.

Since the trust indenture and the corporate charter were prepared by E. Raphael at the direction of William Marsh Rice at about the same time and each refer to the other, the instruments must be construed together.

The name of the corporation, established by the charter, was the William M. Rice Institute for the Advancement of Literature, Science and Art.

Article Two (2) of the Corporate Charter reads:

"The objects, intents, and purposes of this Institution are declared to be the establishment and maintenance, in the City of Houston, Texas, of a Public Library, and the maintenance of an Institute for the Advancement of Literature, Science, Art, Philosophy and Letters; the establishment and maintenance of a Polytechnic school; for procuring and maintaining scientific collections; collections of chemical and philosophical apparatus, mechanical and artistic models, drawings, pictures and statues; and for cultivating other means of instruction for the white inhabitants of the City of Houston, and State of Texas, to, for, and upon the uses, intents, and purposes, and upon the trusts, and subject to the conditions and restrictions contained in a deed which is in form, substance and words as follows * * * ."

After quoting the trust instrument the charter provided that the "office" of the Institute shall be established and remain in the City of Houston, Texas. It provided for a board of seven trustees, naming them, and provided that the "corporation powers of this Institute" shall be managed and exercised by them. The charter then in general terms granted the corporation power "to execute the trusts and powers mentioned in and intended to be created by" the trust indenture quoted, and to hold the endowment with the increase and profits thereof, "including all endowments, donations, and bequests at any time to be made to the said Institute, subject to the conditions and restrictions created in said deed, and to, for and upon the uses, intents, and purposes expressed and provided." The corporation, "and the Board of Trustees thereof," were authorized "to do and perform all and every act and thing whatever, and to carry out and accomplish all and every trust, intent and purpose provided to be done, carried out or accomplished, in and by the aforesaid deed * * * and * * * to receive all and every endowment, donation and bequest made to it, and to appropriate the same to the uses, intents, and purposes contemplated herein and in said deed."

Article EIGHT (8) provides: "The said Institute has no capital stock."

William Marsh Rice died in 1900. His will was not admitted into evidence, however it was stipulated that by its terms the residue of his estate passed to Rice Institute, and that in the will he stated it as his desire that his nephew, William Marsh Rice, Jr., be elected to the Board of Directors of William Marsh Rice Institute and stated his hope that he would take an interest in the prosperity and success of the Institute. He also stated in his will his desire that E. Raphael should act in the capacity of secretary of the Institute as long as he wished to and felt an interest in the success of the purpose for which said Institute was formed.

At the time of the trial of this case none of the original Trustees were living and no letters could be produced written by Mr. William Marsh Rice concerning his plans for Rice Institute. During the years after the corporation was formed before the death of William Marsh Rice, there were no buildings and no functioning institution. The minutes of the Board of Trustees show some twelve meetings during this period, two of which were attended by William Marsh Rice. These minutes reflect that he wrote letters and sent telegrams to the Trustees for the purpose of conducting the business of the Institute, but none of them were found.

Our task in this case is not unlike that of the court in William Buchanan Foundation v. Shepperd, where the court summarized the general rules of construction by which we must be guided:

"The cardinal principle to be observed in construing a trust instrument is to ascertain the settlor's intent with the view of effectuating it.

"Also it is the intention of the settlor at the time of the creation of the trust that is determinative.

"The rules of construction for deeds, wills and other instruments are also applicable for the construction of trust instruments. In Pugh v. Mays, it is stated: 'The general rule for construing deeds is that announced in Hancock v. Butler, as elementary, and applicable alike to written instruments generally, and that is, every part of a deed should be harmonized and given effect to, if this can be done; but if it is found that there is in the instrument inherent conflict of intention, *then the main intention, the object of the grant being considered, shall have controlling influence.*'

"It is elementary that if a written instrument is unambiguous the construction of it is for the court to determine from the terms of the instrument itself.

"Parol or extrinsic evidence may be admitted to aid in construing a trust instrument only if the instrument is ambiguous or uncertain, and only to explain and not to contradict, the instrument, but also on the other hand, in case of doubt or ambiguity, parol, extraneous, or extrinsic evidence may be considered in order to ascertain the settlor's intention, and may be proper in order to illuminate the circumstances surrounding the execution of the instrument and the settlor's conception or understanding of any ambiguous words employed by him therein. Also where the trust instrument is indefinite, ambiguous, uncertain or inconsistent, the court can, or must, consider the surrounding circumstances in determining just what the intention of the donor was, or the meaning of the instrument."

* * *

It should be noted that a question arises, from this language, as to whether the library, scientific departments and polytechnic school are considered integral parts of the Institute, or whether they are to be considered as separate projects to be supported by the Institute from the endowment committed to its care. Is the Institute to be "free and open to all," or is it the "instruction, benefits, and enjoyments" to be derived from the Institute that are to be free and open to all? The Institute is variously described as one for the advancement of Science and Art, or for the advancement of Literature, Science and Art, or for the advancement of Literature, Science, Art, Philosophy and Letters. That these phrases are descriptive of the purpose of the institution, rather than merely a reference name, is clear from a consideration of the writings in their entirety.

While the motivating factor leading to the establishment of the trust was the donor's desire to promote the education of the white inhabitants of the City of Houston, and State of Texas, the dominant purpose of the trust was to establish a free library and an educational institution, the primary aim of which was to contribute to the advancement of human knowledge in the fields of literature, science, art, philosophy and letters. Subsidiary purposes were to be the establishment and maintenance of a polytechnic school, scientific collections, and collections of chemical and philosophical apparatus, mechanical and artistic models, drawings, pictures, and statues, as well as such other means of more directly instructing the white inhabitants of Houston and Texas, as the Trustees might devise.

The institute was repeatedly mentioned in the trust instrument and the corporate charter. The name given the corporation is revealing. The Institute was to be incorporated and the endowment fund was to be managed by the Trustees of the corporation. After provision is made for the establishment and maintenance of the Library and Institute, the Polytechnic School is to be established. A sinking fund was provided for "betterments and improvements" of the Institute. The office of the Institute is to remain in Houston. It must also be noted that the word "Institute" is used in the charter to refer to the corporation. Nevertheless, it is our opinion from a consideration of all provisions of the instruments that the dominant purpose of the donor was to create an educational institution primarily devoted to research and original work calculated to expand the boundaries of human knowledge, the benefits of which would accrue only indirectly to the white inhabitants of Houston and Texas. By reason of the subsidiary purposes and the authority to provide "other means of instruction" the Trustees were given great discretion in formulating the vehicle by which the purposes of the donor were to be accomplished. It should also be noted that the polytechnic school, museums, and "other means of instruction," with the exception of the Library, probably were intended to be functioning components of the Institute, since they were to be established, financed, and managed by the corporation, and the sinking fund was to be established for improvements and betterments of the Institute.

Judicial note may be taken of the fact that in 1891, when the trust instrument was signed, the University of Texas had been in operation only eight years, and that the number of students attending institutions of higher learning in Texas was small. At that time the opportunities for free education at the college level were limited. The amount of research and creative work being carried out in science and the liberal arts could not have been significant. The number of people qualified by education to do such work was undoubtedly small. The need for such an institution in this State was apparent.

Webster's International Dictionary, 2nd Edition, defines the word "institute" as: "an institution; an organization for the promotion of learning, philosophy, art, science, or the like, as a society, academy, college, technical school, * * * ." It defines "university" as: "an institution organized for teaching and study in the higher branches of learning, and empowered to confer degrees in special departments, as theology, law, medicine, and the arts, * * * . In the United States a university typically comprises a college and one or more graduate or professional schools; but the term is sometimes loosely used."

While the word "university" does not appear in the trust instrument or the charter, it seems clear that an "Institute for the Advancement of Literature, Science and Art" might well be a university. Clearly the Trustees of the corporation were empowered by the donor with the authority to make of the Institute a university of the first class so long as the general purposes and intents disclosed in the trust instrument were accomplished.

* * *

While a reasonable construction of the trust instruments requires the conclusion that the donor intended to benefit the white inhabitants of the City of Houston and State of Texas primarily, reason compels the further conclusion that the instruction, benefits, and enjoyments of the Institute were not intended to benefit them solely. Expanded knowledge in the field of science in the nature of things cannot be excluded from a segment of our society. The selection of a university as the most suitable instrument through which the purpose of the donor could be accomplished was the action of the Trustees, not the donor. It was not required by the terms of the trust, which might have been complied with literally by establishing a foundation to assist scholars, scientists, artists and writers financially; by establishing museums, and art galleries; and by establishing a polytechnical school. We cannot say that the donor had a fixed purpose to establish a university to which students would be admitted free, and from which Negroes would be excluded. It is equally clear, however, that the establishment of such an institution was within the discretionary power of the Trustees.

Nevertheless, to consider the instrument in light of the conditions prevailing at the time was executed, the fact of segregation of the races cannot be ignored. In 1891 in the State of Texas the segregation of races in public educational institutions was required by law, and such segregation was the invariable custom in private institutions. As a practical matter at that time a school was either a school for white children or one for Negro children. Bearing in mind the expressed intent to instruct the white inhabitants of Texas, the Trustees, when they established an educational institution to which students were to be admitted, understood that Negro students were to be excluded without specific instructions to that effect.

It also follows that, while the injunction that the instruction, benefits, and enjoyment derived from the Institute were to be free and open to all was not a specific instruction that no tuition be required of students of Rice University, it was the expression of a general philanthropic intent which the Trustees properly carried into effect by adopting a policy of requiring no tuition. Since these policies were adopted by the Trustees as their interpretation of the intention of the donor, and since these policies have been consistently followed for fifty years without a question being raised as to their propriety, this Court would not be justified in adopting a construction of the instrument different from that of the Trustees designated by the donor to carry out his purposes unless compelled by the clear language of the trust instrument.

While we have concluded as a matter of law from the language of the trust instruments that the primary purpose of the donor was to establish an educational institution of the first class, the careful trial judge submitted the question to the jury, which found as a fact that such was his primary purpose. Complaint is made that the Court erred in the submission of this issue. Evidence was admitted which supports the jury's answer, and, in view of our construction of the instrument, the submission of such an issue could not have resulted in the entry of an improper judgment.

In answer to special issues submitted to them, the jury found that William Marsh Rice intended that the funds given the Institute be used for the instruction and improvement of white inhabitants only, but that it is impossible or impracticable under present conditions to carry out said intent.

The jury also found that William Marsh Rice intended that the benefits to be derived from the Institute were to be free of tuition, but that it is impossible or impracticable under present conditions to carry out said intent.

There is no contention that the answers made by the jury to these issues are not supported by the evidence produced at the trial.

Testimony was produced at the trial of this case from the Chancellors and Presidents of most of the universities located in the State of Texas. This testimony, with no material inconsistency or contradiction, established that under present conditions no university that discriminates in the selection of teachers or students on the basis of race could attain or retain the status of a university of the first class because it could not recruit the necessary faculty, and would be at a disadvantage in seeking grants for research from foundations and the government. It was established that it would be impossible to carry on significant research in the field of science without such assistance since the cost of necessary facilities and equipment is prohibitive. It was established that Rice University has attained a position of eminence in selected scientific fields, but has not reached this position in the humanities and literature.

It was also established that the costs of operating a university increased slowly before the Second World War and have increased astronomically since that time. There was testimony that a professor drawing a salary of $7,500.00 at the University of Texas in 1946 would be paid $20,000.00 today; that the costs of equipment required in a professional engineering school have increased not only because of the general increase in prices, but also because new kinds of equipment have been devised. To maintain a library, books that cost $2.50 have to be replaced at $7.50. The number and variety of scientific and professional books and journals necessary for a graduate school have increased greatly. The cost of operating a graduate program is much greater per student than that of the undergraduate program, and Rice University could not possibly maintain its position if it curtailed its graduate program. There was testimony that the greatest educational need in Texas today is for an increase in the facilities for, and quality of, the graduate programs offered. There was testimony that in order to become a university of the first class, Rice University needs to expand its graduate programs in the humanities and liberal arts. There was testimony that Rice was unable to fill teaching positions authorized in 1963 costing $177,965.00 because of budgetary limitations. The evidence shows that the cost per student at Rice University has increased from $286.00 in 1940 to $2,737.00 in 1964. There was testimony that in the fiscal year ending June 30, 1963, Rice sustained a deficit of $150,000.00, and that for the year 1964 a deficit of $560,367.00 was anticipated. While it was shown that there was no deficit in 1963 considering cash flow because a sum in excess of the deficit was allocated to a contingency fund, this was not true with regard to the anticipated future deficits. There was testimony that the failure of Rice University to charge tuition impaired its ability to secure foundation grants. There was testimony that if the institution continued to operate on a deficit basis it could not maintain its program and position in the academic world, and that it would be impossible for a poor university to stay great. There was direct testimony that the typical tuition charged a graduate student thirty years ago was $400.00, but that this tuition today approximates $2,000.00, and that Rice University will be severely handicapped in its effort even to maintain its position of preeminence in the field of technology and science if it does not charge tuition.

While it is well known that Rice University is one of the most richly endowed schools in the South, it is a matter of common knowledge that for some years costs have been increasing faster than the rate of return on invested capital. If Rice University is denied all sources of revenue other than gifts and income from the endowment fund, it is entirely reasonable to conclude that it will inevitably, in the course of time, fall behind those schools receiving large percentages of their operating revenue from tuition or tax sources. The remarkable achievements in science, which have occurred since the death of William Marsh Rice and which make necessary the use of extremely expensive atomic and electronic equipment by educational institutions engaged in scientific research necessary in order to maintain a competitive position in the educational world, could not have been foreseen, and were not foreseen by him. There was a question of fact as to whether it is impossible or impractical to carry out the purpose of William Marsh Rice that the benefits to be derived from the Institute be free of tuition. The jury's determination of this issue of fact is conclusive on this Court since it is supported by evidence.

The judgment entered by the trial court is supported by our construction of the trust instruments, the evidence, the facts found by the jury, and the applicable rules of law. It is, therefore, affirmed.

———

As might be expected, many colleges have sought to reconstitute trusts when institutional missions changed substantially, or when events required reconsideration of the original terms. See E. Johnson and K. Weeks, "To Save a College: Independent College Trustees and Decisions on Financial Exigency, Endowment Use, and Closure," *Journal of College and University Law*, 12 (1986), 455–88. Colleges have also resisted efforts to reconstitute trusts if officials felt the original purposes were meritorious. *Shapiro v. Columbia Union National Bank and Trust Co.*, 576 S.W. 2d 310 (1979) (private trust for male students did not constitute state action, and public colleges not required to consider female students for awards).

———

Fountain Gate Ministries v. City of Plano
654 S.W.2d 841 (Tex. App. 5 Dist. 1983)

SPARLING, Justice.

This is an appeal from a permanent injunction. On motion by appellee, the City of Plano, the trial court enjoined appellant, Fountain Gate Ministries, Inc., from specific activities which were allegedly in violation of the Plano zoning ordinance. In eleven points of error, Fountain Gate claims that the zoning ordinance is unconstitutionally vague and overbroad; that its enforcement infringes upon Fountain Gate's freedoms of religion and speech and violates the First Amendment establishment clause; that there was no evidence, or insufficient evidence, that the ordinance is related to a compelling state interest; that there is insufficient evidence to support the court's conclusion that Fountain Gate's prohibited activities are not a permitted use of church under the ordinance; and finally, that the injunction itself was imprecise and overbroad. We overrule all of appellant's points of error, and affirm.

Zoning Ordinance: Exceptions and Prohibitions

In 1978 Fountain Gate purchased 21 acres located in the City of Plano, Texas. On that property Fountain Gate operated a church, an academy, and allegedly, a college. The property is zoned "SF-2" which is restricted to single family residences with several exceptions: notably, a "church and rectory" and a "school, public, or parochial." "Church and rectory" is defined by ordinance as:

> A place of assembly and worship by a recognized religion including synagogues, temples, churches, instruction rooms, and the place of residence for ministers, priests, rabbis, teachers, and directors of the premises.

"School, public or parochial," is defined by ordinance as:

> A school under the sponsorship of a public or religious agency having a curriculum generally equivalent to public elementary or secondary schools, but not including private or trade or commercial schools.

The SF-2 zoning ordinance specifically prohibits the land to be used for a boarding house, rooming house, child care center, and college or university. "College or University" is defined by ordinance as:

> "an institution established for educational purposes and offering a curriculum similar to the public school, or an accredited college or university, but excluding trade and commercial schools."

When a property use is proscribed under the terms of the SF-2 zoning ordinance, the prohibition may be waived by the Plano city council if they approve a special use permit. Fountain Gate applied for a special use permit to operate a college or university, but the permit was denied by the city council. Fountain Gate then took the position that a special use permit was not necessary because the operation of a college was already permitted under the terms of the SF-2 zoning ordinance. More particularly, Fountain Gate avers that the "college" activities are so closely related to the "church" activities that the college falls within the "church & rectory" exception to the SF-2 zoning ordinance. Fountain Gate does not contend that a traditional college or university is improperly prohibited under the Plano SF-2 zoning ordinance.

The Injunction

It is apparent that the trial court conceded that Fountain Gate is a "recognized religion" as that term is used in the "church or rectory" definition, because the court specifically refused to enjoin any activities that would fall within the "church," "rectory" or "parochial school" category. Fountain Gate does not allege that the parochial school activities are substantially impaired.

By the terms of the injunction, Fountain Gate was specifically prohibited from using its premises for: (1) maintaining dormitories, (2) offering courses of study, (3) conferring a degree, (4) allowing overnight guests, (5) offering academic credit, (6) soliciting students to enroll, (7) using the cafeteria, (8) maintaining a faculty to teach courses, (9) maintaining a day care center or (10) maintaining any office activity. The prohibition of each of these activities was carefully phrased in the injunction so that it would not infringe upon the right of Fountain Gate to carry on activities that are permitted under SF-2 zoning. For example, all prohibited academics were limited to those over the 12th grade level, thus, prohibiting only that which was included in the "college or university" category, and leaving untouched the academy, which arguably is permitted by the "school, public or parochial" exception. Likewise, the lodging provision of the injunction specifically excluded ministers, directors and teachers from the prohibition, thereby taking it out of the "rectory" definition. The other provisions had similar language limiting their scope.

* * *

Is the Ordinance Constitutional?

In five points of error, Fountain Gate challenges the constitutionality of the zoning ordinance. It claims that it impairs the freedoms of religion and speech, that it is constitutionally overbroad and vague, and that it violates the establishment clause of the first amendment. Fountain Gate does not contend, however, that the operation of a college, *per se*, is an activity protected by the first amendment.

Fountain Gate argues that the ordinance is facially overbroad and unconstitutional because it prohibits the exercise of rights guaranteed by the first amendment. Thus, Fountain Gate relies upon *Schad v. Mt. Ephraim*, in its argument that this court should consider how the detrimental impact of the ordinance would affect the expressive activities *on others* as well as its own activities in determining its constitutionality. We disagree because unlike the injunction in *Schad*, this injunction does not prohibit a first amendment freedom, but rather colleges and universities.

As previously noted, the injunction is couched in terms to carefully avoid prohibiting any activity falling within a "church or rectory" category. In "Findings of Fact and Conclusions of Law," the trial court made the following findings which we hold to be supported by the evidence.

* * *

C. The College

9. The College is an institution operated by Fountain Gate which offers an advanced two-year or four-year course of study for adults on a continuous basis throughout the year. Successful completion of the two or four year curriculum of the College results in the conferral of a degree by the College.

10. Enrollment in the College is open to any person regardless of his or her denomination, religious affiliation, or geographic location. Approximately seventy-five percent (75%) of all students who have been admitted to the College were not members of the Church at the time of enrollment.

11. Students wishing to enroll in the College must submit an application, pay an application fee, and provide evidence of high school completion or its equivalent.

12. Students attending the College are required to pay tuition for each hour of curriculum credit for which they enroll or register. In 1981–82, the tuition charged for a full-time student (i.e., twelve hours or more per trimester) was $300 per trimester.

13. The College employs a full-time faculty and staff to operate the College and administer to the non-academic needs of the students.

* * *

Thus, the trial court properly concluded that the above enumerated activities were that of a college, and not of a church. We have found no case, and none is cited, that includes the existence or location of colleges within the purview of the first amendment.

We hold that the operation of a college is not protected as an exercise of freedom of speech or freedom of religion within the first amendment.[3]

Because we determine that the only restrictions placed on Fountain Gate emanate from zoning against colleges—and related child care centers, rooming houses, or boarding houses—we find no issues of constitutional dimensions. We therefore over-rule points of error three, four, five, eight and nine.

Is the State Interest Served by the Ordinance?

Fountain Gate next complains that there is no evidence, or alternatively, insufficient evidence, that the ordinance is related to a compelling state interest. We disagree. The City of Plano has had a comprehensive plan for development since 1963 which provides for the health, safety and general welfare of the public. The present zoning ordinance is the principal means of implementing that comprehensive plan.

Zoning ordinances are a valid exercise of the City's police powers. Further, the good of the community shall prevail when in conflict with private interests.

As previously held, Fountain Gate's activities that are prohibited by the ordinance are not protected by the first amendment; therefore, Plano does not have the burden to justify the prohibition of activities as did the city in *Schad*. Because the adoption of a zoning ordinance by a city's governing body is an exercise of its legislative discretion, it is *presumed* to be valid.

Further, the party contesting the ordinance has an "extraordinary burden" to show that the ordinance is invalid. In the absence of proof by Fountain Gate that the ordinance is *not* related to a compelling state interest, we presume it to be valid. We overrule points of error six and seven.

Is the Evidence Insufficient?

In points of error ten and eleven, Fountain Gate contends that the evidence is insufficient to support the trial court's conclusion that the prohibited activities are not a church or rectory, or do not constitute an activity permitted by the ordinance. Again, we disagree. Fountain Gate fails to identify any finding of fact which is unsupported by evidence, and indeed, a perusal of the record reveals sufficient evidence to support all findings.

The findings, in turn, support the conclusions that the various prohibited activities are not a church or rectory. The dormitories house twenty-five college students and are capable of accommodating up to sixty-five students. Further, friends or guests of Fountain Gate may, for a fee, reside in the dormitory. The full-time students are required to eat in the cafeteria, but anyone, whether affiliated with Fountain Gate or not, may eat there for the price of a meal. Finally, a day-care-center is maintained, primarily to care for the children of the college students.

Fountain Gate argues that because the prohibited activities are usually conducted in separate buildings, therefore the SF-2 Zoning ordinance permits their existence under the provision which would allow an "accessory building" which is customarily incidental to the main structure. We disagree. These activities are incidental to the structure containing the business of a college, not a church.

---

3. We distinguish this from the freedom to choose teaching *content*.

We hold that the trial court correctly concluded that the prohibited activities were not the activities of a church or rectory. Accordingly, we overrule points of error ten and eleven.

All points of error are overruled and the case is affirmed.

Jansen, doing business as White Hotel v. Atiyeh
743 P.2d 765 (Or. App. 1987)

DEITS, Judge.

Plaintiffs, Ashland area motel and hotel operators, taxi drivers and caterers, sought declaratory and injunctive relief against defendant Oregon State Board of Higher Education (Board) acting by and through Southern Oregon State College (SOSC). Plaintiffs' complaint alleged that defendant exceeded its authority in providing housing, food and transportation to groups attending the Shakespearean Festival whose members are not fully matriculated students of SOSC. The Board contends that none of the disputed activities exceed its authority. The court held that at least some parties had standing to contest all of the issues and granted partial injunctive relief.

The Board challenges the court's ruling concerning the services for non-SOSC students and out-of-state students at SOSC. Plaintiffs cross-appeal, challenging the court's rulings concerning the Board's authority to furnish services to non-State Board of Higher Education students attending educational institutions located within Oregon and the hotel and motel operators' lack of standing to challenge the Board's housing of participants in the Elderhostel and Senior Venture programs at SOSC.

SOSC is located in Ashland, which hosts the annual Oregon Shakespearean Festival, a series of theatrical performances and related events extending from early spring until late fall. The festival is a nonprofit corporation unaffiliated with SOSC or the Board. In the early 1980's, SOSC administrators began implementing a plan to increase revenues by making their dormitory facilities available to groups of people meeting certain qualifications. In order to qualify to use SOSC facilities, a group must include more than 15 persons and must have an educational objective. In order to meet the educational requirement the group must be:

> "A gathering of a group of individuals with the purpose of learning new skills, sharing insights or exploring specific problems relating to a defined subject, issue, discipline, or profession...."

SOSC does not necessarily offer the groups either on- or off-campus organized instruction. The educational objective of the groups typically consists of exposure to or discussion of the plays presents by the Shakespearean Festival.

When SOSC decided to offer its facilities for use by the groups, it became necessary to renovate some of the resident halls. Most of the costs of renovation were raised through issuance of Article XI-F(1) bonds. Plaintiffs argue that the use of facilities constructed or renovated with the bonds is inconsistent with the provisions of Article XI-F(1) of the Oregon Constitution and the requirements of ORS 351.160(1).

Article XI-F(1) authorizes the issuance of revenue bonds "to finance the cost of buildings and other projects for higher education, and to construct, improve, repair, equip, and furnish buildings and other structures for such purpose, and to purchase or improve sites therefor." ORS 351.160(1), which was enacted to carry out the provisions of Article XI-F(1), provides:

> "The board of higher education may undertake the construction of any building or structure for higher education when, in the judgment of the board, it appears that the building or structure will be wholly self-liquidating and self-supporting from revenues to accrue from the operation thereof and from gifts, grants or building fees, and from unobligated revenues of buildings or projects of like character. The board may enter into contracts for the erection, improvement, repair, equipping and furnishing of buildings and structures for dormitories, housing, boarding, offstreet motor vehicle parking facilities and other *purposes for higher education* pursuant to Article XI-F(1) of the Oregon Constitution, ORS 351.160 to 351.190, 351.350 to 351.460, 351.480 and 351.490." (Emphasis supplied.)

Plaintiffs argue that SOSC's use of its facilities for non-SOSC students does not satisfy the requirement that the facilities be used for purposes of "higher education."

Plaintiffs are correct that buildings constructed or improved with proceeds of Article XI-F(1) bonds must be used *for* purposes of "higher education." Thus, the crucial issue in this case is whether SOSC's policy of allowing the groups to use the facilities is within the definition of "higher education."

The terms are not defined in the statutes, nor are they exact terms, because they do not communicate a precise meaning. Whether the term is interpretive or delegative depends upon whether it embodies "complete expressions of legislative meaning," or expresses "noncompleted legislation that the agency is given delegated authority to complete." In view of the broad general authority that the legislature has given to the Board to manage the higher education system of the state, we conclude that the term is delegative and that the Board has the authority to define the terms "higher education." The legislature has granted the Board the authority to "[s]upervise the general course of instruction * * * and the research, extension, educational and other activities" of each institution under its control. It may "[m]aintain cultural and physical development services" of its institutions.

It may appoint and employ presidents, teachers and employees of its entities, set fees for enrollment, confer degrees, and prescribe qualifications for admission into its institutions. In addition, the Board may adopt regulations and policies relating to certain matters without complying with the rulemaking provisions of the Administrative Procedures Act.

The Board also has been delegated broad authority over the management of property:

> "The State Board of Higher Education may:

> "(1) Control and provide for * * * the custody and occupation of the * * * buildings * * * belonging to each and all the institutions, departments or activities under the control of the [board].

> "(2) Manage, control and apply all property of whatever nature given to or appropriated for the use, support or benefit of any or all of the institutions, departments or activities under the control of the [board].

> "(3) Erect, improve, repair, maintain, equip and furnish buildings, structures and lands for higher education.

"(4) [C]ontrol, * * * manage, operate, lease, lend, invest, improve and develop any and all property, real or personal:

" * * *

"(b) * * * for the benefit of any of the institutions, departments or activities under the control of the board * * * ."

We conclude that the legislature has delegated to the Board the authority to interpret the term "higher education." We also conclude that the Board's interpretation in this instance was within its discretion and is not inconsistent with the constitutional or statutory provisions. As noted above, the statutory scheme relating to higher education contemplates that the system may offer more than traditional formal degree programs. The Board may maintain "cultural development services," as well as offer "extension" activities, in its instructions. SOSC has decided that only groups having an educational mission may use its facilities. That use is within those contemplated by the legislative scheme.

* * *

Philip Crosby Associates v. Florida State Board of Independent Colleges
506 So. 2d 490 (Fla. App. 5 Dist. 1987)

JOHNSON, Jr., W.C., Associate Judge.

Philip B. Crosby Associates, Inc., (Crosby) appeals a final order from the State Board of Independent Colleges and Universities (Board) based on a petition for declaratory statement. The order ruled that Crosby was not required to be licensed by the Board because they did not offer academic degrees or college credit. The Board also ruled that Crosby could not use the term "college" to describe its teaching program.

Crosby is a management consulting firm which assists its clients in improving the quality of their products and services. An unincorporated division of the company, known as Quality College, maintains classroom facilities in Winter Park, Florida, and conducts seminars on the quality improvement process. It does not furnish or offer to furnish a degree or instruction leading toward college credit or an academic degree beyond the secondary level.

On July 31, 1985, Crosby received a letter from the Board notifying Crosby that no private college or university may operate in Florida or use the words "college" or "university" in its name without prior express authority from the Board. Crosby responded and at a September 1985 meeting of the Board it was informally determined that Crosby's Quality College did not require licensure. The question of whether it could use the word "college" in its name was left open and unresolved.

Crosby thereafter filed a formal petition for declaratory statement and a hearing was held. On December 13, 1985, the Board issued a final order and ruled as follows:

> 3. That PCA is not required to obtain licensure from the Board for the activities of its Quality College Division because the division does not furnish or offer to furnish any sort of academic degree beyond the secondary level or college credit. Its activities do not fall within the definition

of a 'college' in section 246.021(1), Florida Statutes (1983), nor is it 'operating in Florida' as that term is used in Rule 6E-1.03(8) and 6E-1.03(1), Florida Administrative Code.

4. PCA is not, however, entitled to use the term 'college' with respect to the activities of its Quality College division.

The Board was proceeding under section 246.121(1), (2), Florida Statutes, which provides:

(1) The designated use of the title, 'college' or 'university' in combination with any series of letters, numbers, or words shall be restricted in this state to degree-granting colleges accredited as defined in s.246.021(1) or licensed under ss.246.011-246.151 or such colleges as were in active operation and using such designation on April 1, 1970, except with respect to branches or divisions of the parent corporation.

(2) Effective October 1, 1982, no person alone or in concert with others may use the term 'university' or 'college' as part of the name or other designation of any nonpublic college in this state without authorization from the Board. However, no public college licensed under ss.246.011-246.151 on October 1, 1982, shall be required to change its name to comply with this subsection. The Board shall adopt rules for authorizing nonpublic colleges to use the term 'university' or 'college' as part of their names or designations, which rules shall consider the qualification of the institution to award degrees and may include minimum standards similar to those prescribed by law for licensing.

The overall issue on appeal is whether the Board correctly denied Crosby the use of the name "college." The Board has interpreted section 246.121, to mean that only degree-granting institutions which are accredited, licensed, or exempt because they were in active operation and using the term on April 1, 1970, are eligible to use the word "college." The Board in this case itself determined that it had no jurisdiction over Crosby because its activities did not fall within the statutory definition of those that the Board is empowered to regulate.

Statutes should be construed in light of the manifest purpose to be achieved by the legislation. The cardinal rule of statutory construction is that a statute should be construed so as to ascertain and give effect to the legislative intent expressed in the statute. When a statute is susceptible of and in need of interpretation or construction, it is axiomatic that courts should endeavor to avoid giving it an interpretation that will lead to an absurd result.

The Board's interpretation would prohibit the use of "college" and its counterpart "university" by any other person or entity for any other purpose. Such an interpretation of the statute would mean that the Roman Catholic College of Cardinals would be required to seek permission of the Board before it could convene in Florida and that permission would have to be denied based on the Board's precedent in this case. All the businesses and shops that surround the University of Florida and call themselves "College" or "University" would have to change their names. There could be no Kiddie College day care centers or preschools. Barber colleges and the Ringling Brothers Clown College likewise would be in violation of the law. Anheuser Busch could no longer sell University of Budweiser t-shirts to students on spring break.

Of course, all these entities could apply for permission from the Board for relief from its rule in advance of using it. The prior restraint aspects and dangers of such a situation are obvious. It is worth noting in this regard that this case was initiated because a Board member happened to see the Quality College sign while driving through downtown Winter Park. What has followed is frightening in its implications. Will the Board next decide it needs a force of investigators patrolling the state to locate and investigate the word "college" or "university"? And, will that lead to a determination that it has the power to summarily terminate any use that it has not authorized?

This court concludes that the Board has misinterpreted the statute and that Crosby's arguments and position are well founded and should be sustained. This court finds 1) that the Board had no jurisdiction over Crosby and 2) that the Board has erroneously interpreted section 246.121, Florida Statutes (1983) and as a consequence has exceeded its authority. We do not reach the constitutional issues raised in light of this holding.

The final order of the State Board of Independent Colleges and Universities is accordingly,

REVERSED.

Hacker v. Hacker
522 N.Y.S.2d 768 (Sup. 1987)

ETHEL B. DANZIG, Justice:

Plaintiff Ruth Hacker moves this court to punish defendant Seymour Hacker for contempt of court for willfully disobeying a judgment of this court which incorporates a separation agreement between the parties—particularly those portions which require the payment of child support,—and for failing to post security as ordered by this court. Plaintiff further seeks permission to enter judgment against the defendant in the sum of $6,600 together with interest, costs and disbursements and for an assessment of reasonable counsel fees for the defendant's failure to obey the prior mandates of this court.

That portion of plaintiff's motion which seeks to punish defendant for contempt for failing to satisfy prior money judgments entered by plaintiff relating to arrears in child support is denied, defendant having annexed to his opposition paper documentation showing that these judgments have been paid in full and that Satisfactions of Judgment have been received and filed by this court.

Defendant was also directed by Order of the Honorable Stanley S. Ostrau dated August 27, 1985 to post a surety bond in the sum of $5,000 to insure future compliance with his child support obligations. This bond was admittedly never filed. However, any judgment for arrears in child support that this court may grant on this motion will necessarily be the last such possible judgment, since it covers the time period up to and including the daughter's emancipation. Accordingly, to direct the defendant to file a bond at this time would serve no purpose. In addition, it appears to this court that plaintiff's main concern here is the issue of the child support payments and not the pursuit of the issue of contempt.

Accordingly, that portion of the motion seeking to hold defendant in contempt is denied.

Plaintiff further seeks leave to enter a judgment against the defendant in the sum of $6,600 which she claims represents 44 weeks of child support for the period November 2, 1984 through October 2, 1985 at $150 per week which remains unpaid. There is no dispute between the parties that any obligation defendant may have had to pay child support for the parties' daughter Emily definitely terminated on October 2, 1985, the date of Emily's 22nd birthday, in accordance with the terms of Article III, subdivision 2 of the parties' separation agreement. This section provides in relevant part, that

> "an Emancipation event shall be deemed deferred beyond the twenty-first (21) birthday of a Child *only if, and so long as a Child pursues college education with reasonable diligence and on a normally continuous basis*, and in no event beyond the twenty-second (22) birthday of a Child."

The real dispute here focuses upon whether or not Emily's attendance at The Neighborhood Playhouse located at 340 East 54th Street, New York, New York constituted the pursuit of a college education as contemplated by the Separation Agreement.

Defendant claims that Emily's attendance at The Neighborhood Playhouse—a professional acting school—can in no way be considered equivalent to the pursuit of a college education within the meaning and intent of the parties under the agreement, and, therefore, that he was not obligated to pay child support for the period from September 1984 through October 2, 1985 while Emily was attending classes there. He points out that he, nonetheless, paid Emily's tuition at The Neighborhood Playhouse which was not required by the separation agreement, in order to "encourage the artistic development of [his] child," but that he was not obligated to pay child support to the plaintiff for this period of time. Moreover, defendant seeks a refund of $1,200 in child support for the eight week period from September 2, 1984 through November 2, 1984 during which he made payments and when, he claims, Emily's attendance at The Neighborhood Playhouse "was carefully concealed from [him]."

Plaintiff argues that The Neighborhood Playhouse is a recognized school for the pursuit of theatrical training and is approved by The New York State Education Department. She annexes a copy of the School's bulletin to her papers and points to the requirements that a student be 18 and be a high school graduate or its equivalent as evidence that the Playhouse tracks the age and prior educational requirements of a college.

Plaintiff further contends that Emily was interested in acting at a very early age, while she and the defendant were still living together, and that it was envisioned that Emily would try to pursue an acting career through educational and other means. She argues, therefore, that it was her intention and, she believes, the intention of her former husband when signing the separation agreement that the provision in issue would "provide for the support of [our] children should they determine to go on to study education at any level."

Neither party, or the court has been able to find much legal treatment of the term "college." Education Law § 2, subd. (2) defines the term "college" to include "universities and other institutions for higher education *authorized to confer degrees*." (underlining supplied). In the case of *Matter of Kelly*, Chief Judge Irving Lehman, writing the majority opinion, found that

"The word 'college' is not a word of art which, by common understanding, has acquired a definite, unchanging significance in the field of education. Its meaning varies with its context. Though at times it is used to denote any institution of higher learning, including institutions for professional or post-graduate study, it is frequently used, perhaps I should say ordinarily used, in this country, to denote, an 'undergraduate' school for instruction in liberal arts *having a course of study commonly requiring four years for completion and leading to a bachelor's degree.*" (underlining supplied)

Plaintiff annexed to her papers definitions of the term 'college' from Black's Law Dictionary and the American College Dictionary published by Random House. While she quotes from part of the Black's definition in her affidavit, she fails to address the other portion of the definition which states in relevant part:

"In the most common use of the word, it designates an institution of learning (usually incorporated) which offers instruction in the liberal arts and humanities and in scientific branches, *but not in the technical arts or those studies preparatory to admission to the professions.*" (underlining supplied.) (Black's Law Dictionary, Revised Fourth Ed., p. 329).

It appears from the brochure that The Neighborhood Playhouse fits into the category of an institution which offers instruction "in the technical arts or those studies preparatory to admission to the professions," which Black's specifically excludes under its definition of college.

In brief, it does not appear that the common definition of the term "college" has changed much since Judge Lehman spoke for the Court of Appeals in 1941. While The Neighborhood Playhouse is no doubt a well-recognized school with a distinguished faculty training its students in the theatre arts, it does not lead to a degree, which appears to be a significant factor in the definitions of the term "college." Thus, after much deliberation, this Court finds that The Neighborhood Playhouse is not a "college" as contemplated by the terms of the parties' separation agreement.

Emily attended several institutions since her graduation from high school, including UCLA for a short time and The Neighborhood Playhouse. There is no dispute that Mr. Hacker paid Emily's tuition at these schools so that she could pursue her chosen field of study. However, during the time she attended The Neighborhood Playhouse, she was not pursuing a "college education," and, therefore, defendant was not required to pay child support for the period from September 1984 through October 2, 1985.

Therefore, plaintiff's motion to enter judgment against defendant for arrears in child support for the 44 week period from November 2, 1984 through October 2, 1985 is denied. Based on the court's finding herein, plaintiff's motion for attorneys fees is also denied. Further, this Court finds that defendant is entitled to a refund of $1,200 for child support payments he made to plaintiff for the eight week period from September 2, 1984 through November 2, 1984 when Emily was attending The Neighborhood Playhouse.

London v. Department of Health and Rehabilitative Services

502 So. 2d 57 (Fla. App. 2 Dist. 1987)

HALL, Judge.

Diane London appeals a final order of the Department of Health and Rehabilitative Services reducing the amount of her food stamp benefits. We affirm in part and reverse in part.

On November 5, 1985, HRS notified London that her monthly food stamp benefits would be reduced from $115 to $10 for a five-month period beginning December 5, 1985. HRS stated as its reason for the reduction its inclusion of London's $2,353.46 Florida Guaranteed Student Loan as unearned income for purposes of determining the amount of food stamp benefits for which London is eligible.

On January 2, 1986, London filed a request for a hearing with the Office of Public Assistance Appeals. A hearing was held, and on February 27, 1986, the hearing officer filed a final order affirming the reduction of London's food stamp benefits. The hearing officer cited as the basis of the order a Department of Agriculture regulation allowing only student loans to be used at institutions of higher education to be excluded from consideration as income in determining food stamp eligibility and benefits. Institution of higher education is defined as "any institution which normally requires a high school diploma or equivalency certificate for enrollment, including but not limited to colleges, universities, and vocational or technical schools at the post-high school level." Because London intended to use her student loan to attend a college which does not require its students to have high school diplomas or equivalency certificates, the Sunstate College of Hair Design, the hearing officer affirmed HRS's inclusion of the loan as part of London's income.

In this appeal London argues that the high school diploma requirement in the definition of *institution of higher education* does not pertain to vocational or technical schools. We disagree. The plain and clear language of 7 C.F.R. § 271.2 does not exclude any of the types of schools listed from the high school diploma or equivalency certificate requirement. Rather, the types of schools listed are only listed as examples of institutions requiring a high school diploma or equivalency certificate. It is the requirement of proof of completion of a high school education that is the gist of the definition of *institution of higher education*.

Although we disagree with London's argument in this appeal, there is a basis for partially reversing the reduction of London's food stamp benefits. On December 23, 1985, Congress passed the Food Security Act of 1985, which, among other things, amended the Food Stamp Act of 1977. It was in pursuance of this latter act that the regulations referred to previously were enacted. In the Food Security Act of 1985, Congress replaced the term *institution of higher education* with *institution of postsecondary education*. The House Committee report explains that this change in terms was intended to also allow the exclusion of educational loans to be used at institutions of postsecondary education that do not require high school diplomas as prerequisites for attendance from consideration as income in determining the amount of food stamp benefits for which an individual is eligible. The effective date of the 1985 act was December 23, 1985; thus, as of that date London could exclude her student loan to the extent it was used for tuition and mandatory fees from consideration as part of her income for purposes of determining the amount of her food stamp benefits.

HRS argues that because the Department of Agriculture did not issue its regulations implementing the changes of the Food Security Act until August 22, 1986, London's case is not affected by those changes. We disagree. The power of an agency to promulgate substantive regulations derives from the statutory authority granted the agency by Congress. The Food Security Act provides that the Secretary of Agriculture "shall establish uniform national standards of eligibility . . . for participation by households in the food stamp program in accordance with the provisions of this section." As we have noted, the provisions of that section contain the change of the term *institution of higher education* to *institution of postsecondary education* and the House Committee report explains the Congressional intent behind that change. The Agriculture regulations of August 22, 1986, add nothing new to that explanation.

Accordingly, this cause is remanded for recalculation of London's food stamp benefit as of December 23, 1985.

Beth Rochel Seminary v. Bennett
825 F.2d 478 (D.C. Cir. 1987)

BUCKLEY, Circuit Judge:

The Department of Education interprets the Higher Education Act of 1965 to require that institutions desiring to participate in federal programs for student financial aid either receive or be about to receive accreditation from a nationally recognized accrediting body, or show that credits earned by its students are accepted, upon transfer and enrollment, by at least three accredited institutions. Appellant applied for qualification under the Act on the basis of assurances received from three accredited institutions that its credits would be accepted on transfer.

The Department initially approved the request and disbursed funds to appellant. Subsequently, on learning that appellant's students did not actually enroll at one of the three institutions, the Department disqualified appellant from all student financial aid programs without a hearing. It also demanded that appellant return all federal funds already received. The district court granted the Department's motion for summary judgment, and we affirm. We hold that the Department's construction of the statute is reasonable and reject appellant's assertion of a due process right to a hearing.

I. BACKGROUND

Beth Rochel Seminary, a non-profit seminary for Jewish women with a campus in Monsey, New York, has not sought accreditation because the main accrediting body recognized by the Department of Education, the Association of Advanced Rabbinical and Talmudic Schools, accredits only male institutions. Under Title IV of the Higher Education Act of 1965, as amended ("Act"), non-accredited post-secondary schools like Beth Rochel may participate in federal financial aid programs for students only if their "credits are accepted, on transfer, by not less than three institutions which are so accredited, for credit on the same basis as if transferred from an institution so accredited." ("Three institutional certification" or "3-IC")

Beth Rochel applied for 3-IC status and identified three accredited institutions of higher education which, it asserted, accepted its academic credits on the same basis as credits from other accredited institutions: Touro College, Adelphi University, and Marywood College. When the Department contacted these institutions, all three responded that they had offered transfer admission with academic credit to Beth Rochel students. On November 17, 1980, the Department certified Beth Rochel under section 1141(a)(5)(B) for a period of three years. The Department's certification letter stated that "[t]he institution remains eligible *only* while it continues to meet all statutory and regulatory requirements...."

Beth Rochel students became eligible for federal financial aid, and the school received $52,268 in federal funds which it disbursed to the eligible students. The Chief of the College Eligibility Unit within the Department's Office of Postsecondary Education, Joseph M. Hardman, subsequently asked Touro College whether Beth Rochel students had actually enrolled at Touro following their admission with academic credit. Norman Twersky, Dean of Admissions of Touro College, responded on November 9, 1981, that although the Beth Rochel students had been offered admission with credit for their work at the Seminary, none had registered at Touro.

Citing that information, the Department then informed Beth Rochel that it "has not satisfied the statutory requirements for institutional eligibility, and in fact has never been an eligible institution to apply for student financial assistance." On July 23, 1982, the Department also requested that Beth Rochel "prepare a check in the amount of $52,268 payable to the [United States Department of Education]" to return financial aid funds inappropriately received.

Beth Rochel filed its complaint in the district court seeking review of the Department's withdrawal of financial aid certification. On motions for summary judgment, the district court held for the government.

II. DISCUSSION

The critical fact, whether Beth Rochel students enrolled or attended classes at Touro College, is not in dispute. The case therefore turns on the meaning of the phrase "on transfer" in section 1141(a)(5)(B). Beth Rochel contends that the phrase does not require that its transferring students actually register and attend classes at all three accredited institutions, as the Department asserts, but merely that they be admitted to study by three accredited institutions willing to accept the academic credits they earned at Beth Rochel. We disagree.

The term "on transfer" is not crystal clear. We do not have to decide, however, whether it is sufficiently clear to admit no other construction than that reached by the Department of Education. Rather, because the Department of Education is the agency charged with the administration of section 1141(a)(5)(B), and because we find that its construction is at least reasonable, we defer to the Department's conclusion that the statute requires actual enrollment by students transferring from the unaccredited institution seeking 3-IC status.

A large part of Beth Rochel's arguments before this court has focused on what Beth Rochel believes are the general purposes of the statutes:

> The 3IC [sic] method was intended by Congress to broaden the availability of federal financial aid funds to include students attending non-traditional or specialized postsecondary institutions like Beth Rochel Seminary. The purpose of the provision was solely to ensure that the unaccredited institutions seeking

eligibility for their students to participate in student aid programs be of acceptable academic quality. Beth Rochel meets this criterion.

Beth Rochel further argues that as the Act makes no reference to enrollment, the Department may not impute such a requirement. Because students are free at any time to decide *not* to enroll in a particular institution after they and their credits have been accepted for transfer, appellant maintains that the Department's construction has the effect of "shift[ing] the focus of the statute from the decision by the accredited institution to the subsequent decision by the applicable students."

There can be no doubt that appellant offers a reasonable interpretation of the statutory language. That language, however, is subject to more than one interpretation as the construction placed on it by both the Department and the district court amply testifies. Therefore, as Beth Rochel has failed to point to any evidence that "Congress has directly spoken to the precise question at issue," we are required to defer to the Department's permissible construction of the Act.

In addition to advancing its own interpretation of the phrase "on transfer," Beth Rochel contends that the Department's construction works a change in policy. Beth Rochel points to no instance, however, in which the Department accepted a school's 3-IC application merely on the basis of three accredited institutions' acceptance with credit of that school's students. Therefore none of the Department's prior 3-IC actions cited by Beth Rochel is inconsistent with the view that "on transfer" means "actually on transfer." It is true that, after its experience with Beth Rochel, the Department modified its 3-IC verification forms to inquire whether students from schools seeking 3-IC certification had actually enrolled and attended classes at three accredited institutions. This is easily and reasonably explained as a departmental response to the events leading to this litigation and does not suggest a change from prior understanding of the phrase "on transfer."

Finally, Beth Rochel argues the Department violated its right to notice and hearing pursuant to 20 U.S.C. § 1094 (1982) and regulations promulgated thereunder, as well as Beth Rochel's right to a hearing pursuant to the due process clause of the Fifth Amendment to the Constitution. Section 1094 permits the Secretary of Health and Human Services to terminate the eligibility of "an otherwise eligible institution" only after notice and a hearing on the record. The Secretary has issued a regulation strictly interpreting the term "otherwise eligible institution" as used in section 1094. The regulation provides that a right to notice and hearing "does not apply to a determination that . . . [a]n institution of higher education fails to meet the statutory definition set forth in section . . . 1201 of the Higher Education Act."

Beth Rochel emphasizes that the term "determination" in section 668.71(c) really means "*initial* determination." As the determination challenged here is not the initial decision granting Beth Rochel 3-IC status, but rather the Department's subsequent finding that Beth Rochel's factual representations were inaccurate, appellant contends that section 668.71 does not apply and its right to notice and hearing under section 1094(b) does.

We find the argument unpersuasive. The regulation does not state that the notice and hearing right is inapplicable only to an *initial* determination. Moreover, Beth Rochel can point to no clear Department practice favoring a narrow construction of section 668.71 at the expense of the regulation's clearly broad language. Although the circumstances of this case are unique and the Department has never before done exactly what it did here, no one has suggested an agency has no discretion reasonably to interpret its prior rules and decisions to reach the unique circumstances that seem inevitably to arise in each case. Such an approach would make it impossible for the Department to apply general rules to specific situations and is therefore untenable.

Appellant's due process argument also fails. Although it invokes the principles of *Goldberg v. Kelly*, and *Mathews v. Eldridge*, Beth Rochel does not dispute the critical fact that none of its students had registered or attended classes at Touro College when its certification was withdrawn. No constitutional right to a hearing arises where the dispositive facts are not in dispute. As a fact-finding hearing would have served no practical purpose, one was not required by the due process clause of the Fifth Amendment to the Constitution. In any event, Beth Rochel presented its arguments at length in its correspondence with the Department, and there is every indication that its views were adequately considered.

III. Conclusion

The judgment of the district court is affirmed in all respects. Beth Rochel Seminary remains indebted to the federal government for the $52,268 in federal funds it received as the result of inappropriate 3-IC certification.

So ordered.

For another example of the problems arising under the "3 letters of credit rule," with respect to tribal colleges, see M. Olivas, "The Tribally Controlled Community College Assistance Act of 1978: The Failure of Federal Indian Higher Education Policy," *American Indian Law Review*, 9 (1982), 219–52. In this instance, tribal colleges were required to be "institutions of higher education," but few of the colleges were able to negotiate the accreditation test of the "institution" definition, or to avail themselves of the statutory exceptions to the requirement.

The Establishment of Private Colleges

Frederick Rudolph, in explaining the differences between private and public colleges, noted the blurred lines between church and state in the establishment of colonial colleges in the United States:

> These many purposes, whether at the oldest of the colonial colleges or at the youngest, were carried out with varying degrees of success. Obviously several of the colleges were barely able to prove their existence before the American Revolution gave a new twist to their fortunes. Uniformity, whether of performance or of organization and spirit, never characterized the colonial colleges. Variety carried the day, as the relations between college and state and between college and church certainly made clear. Harvard, William and Mary, and Yale, for example, were creatures as much of the state as of the established churches they were intended to serve. And whether they should be thought of as state colleges or as church colleges is a problem in semantics that is perhaps best resolved by calling them state-church colleges.
>
> As such, they were clearly recognized as being engaged in a relationship of mutual obligation and responsibility with the state. Harvard was supported by

the [Massachusetts] General Court from the moment of its birth; it relied on such support long past the colonial period. In 1652 and 1653 the General Court donated 2,000 acres of land to the college, and the next year it ordered a tax levy of £100 in its support. But the state's responsibility went beyond economic assistance. Under the administration of Nathaniel Eaton, Harvard fell into such straits that the General Court began an investigation and effectively closed the college for a year by dismissing Eaton from his post. Having done so, the General Court fulfilled its obligations to Harvard the next year by assigning the Charlestown Ferry rents to the college, a source of revenue that continued in one form or another for the next two hundred years. In 1725 when the corporation elected to the presidency a leading liberal Congregationalist, he declined the position after sounding out the General Court and finding himself extremely obnoxious to the conservatives there. In 1737 the General Court awarded to the church at Marblehead £140 as a bit of balm for losing its minister, Edward Holyoke, to the presidency of Harvard.

At William and Mary a similar pattern of strong ties with the state prevailed. The main street of colonial Williamsburg, Duke of Gloucester Street, extended from the capitol building at one end to the college at the other; such an arrangement was both convenient and symbolic. For variety of financial support nothing compared with the generosity of Virginia to its college. The 1693 charter privileges of William and Mary put a tobacco tax at its disposal and "brought the entire land system of the colony into the hands of a collegiate land office." George Washington, for example, received his commission as county surveyor from the president of the college. In 1693 the college was awarded the returns from an export duty on skins and furs; in 1759 it enjoyed the fruits of a tax on peddlers.

Yale, which for a long time was tossed around by a squabbling legislature, in the end built up a firm and useful relationship with the state. It early discovered that the state could be helpful in other than direct subsidies. *The American College and University* (New York: Vintage, 1962), pp. 13–14.

However, it was the *Dartmouth College* case that first clarified the evolving distinction between the two sectors.

Trustees of Dartmouth College v. Woodward
4 Wheaton (U.S.) 518 (1819)

The opinion of the court was delivered by MARSHALL, Ch. J.:

This is an action of trover, brought by the trustees of Dartmouth College against William H. Woodward, in the State Court of New Hampshire, for the book of records, corporate seal, and other corporate property, to which the plaintiffs allege themselves to be entitled.

A special verdict, after setting out the rights of the parties, finds for the defendant, if certain acts of the legislature of New Hampshire, passed on the 27th of June, and on the 18th of December, 1816, be valid, and binding on the trustees without their assent, and not repugnant to the constitution of the United States; otherwise, it finds for the plaintiffs.

The Superior Court of Judicature of New Hampshire rendered a judgment upon this verdict for the defendant, which judgment has been brought before this court by writ of error. The single question now to be considered is, do the acts to which the verdict refers violate the constitution of the United States?

* * *

The title of the plaintiffs originates in a charter dated the 13th day of December, in the year 1769, incorporating twelve persons therein mentioned, by the name of "The Trustees of Dartmouth College," granting to them and their successors the usual corporate privileges and powers, and authorizing the trustees, who are to govern the college, to fill up all vacancies which may be created in their own body.

The defendant claims under three acts of the legislature of New Hampshire, the most material of which was passed on the 27th of June, 1816, and is entitled, "an act to amend the charter, and enlarge and improve the corporation of Dartmouth College." Among other alterations in the charter, this act increases the number of trustees to twenty-one, gives the appointment of the additional members to the executive of the state, and creates a board of overseers, with power to inspect and control the most important acts of the trustees. This board consists of twenty-five persons. The president of the senate, the speaker of the house of representatives of New Hampshire, and the Governor and Lieutenant-Governor of Vermont, for the time being, are to be members ex officio. The board is to be completed by the Governor and council of New Hampshire, who are also empowered to fill all vacancies which may occur. The acts of the 18th and 26th of December are supplemental to that of the 27th of June, and are principally intended to carry that act into effect.

We are next led to the inquiry, for whose benefit the property given to Dartmouth College was secured. The counsel for the defendant have insisted that the beneficial interest is in the people of New Hampshire. The charter, after reciting the preliminary measures which had been taken, and the application for an act of incorporation, proceeds thus: "Know ye, therefore, that we, considering the premises, and being willing to encourage the laudable and charitable design of spreading Christian knowledge among the savages of our American wilderness, and, also, that the best means of education be established, in our province of New Hampshire, for the benefit of said province, do, of our special grace," etc. Do these expressions bestow on New Hampshire, any exclusive right to the property of the college, any exclusive interest in the labors of the professors? Or do they merely indicate a willingness that New Hampshire should enjoy those advantages which result to all from the establishment of a seminary of learning in the neighborhood? On this point we think it impossible to entertain a serious doubt. The words themselves, unexplained by the context, indicate that the "benefit intended for the province" is that which is derived from "establishing the best means of education therein"; that is, from establishing in the province Dartmouth College, as constituted by the charter. But, if these words, considered alone, could admit of doubt, that doubt is completely removed by an inspection of the entire instrument.

The particular interests of New Hampshire never entered into the mind of the donors, never constituted a motive for their donation. The propagation of the Christian religion among the savages, and the dissemination of useful knowledge among the youth of the country, were the avowed and the sole objects of their contributions. In these, New Hampshire would participate; but nothing particular or exclusive was intended for her.

*   *   *

The opinion of the court, after mature deliberation, is, that this is a contract, the obligation of which cannot be impaired without violating the constitution of the United States. This opinion appears to us to be equally supported by reason, and by the former decisions of this court.

We next proceed to the inquiry whether its obligation has been impaired by those acts of the legislature of New Hampshire to which the special verdict refers.

The majority of the trustees of the college have refused to accept this amended charter, and have brought this suit for the corporate property, which is in possession of a person holding by virtue of the acts which have been stated.

It can require no argument to prove that the circumstances of this case constitute a contract. An application is made to the crown for a charter to incorporate a religious and literary institution. In the application, it is stated that large contributions have been made for the object, which will be conferred on the corporation as soon as it shall be created. The charter is granted, and on its faith the property is conveyed. Surely in this transaction every ingredient of a complete and legitimate contract is to be found.

The points for consideration are:

1. Is this contract protected by the constitution of the United States?

2. Is it impaired by the acts under which the defendant holds?

*   *   *

It is, then, an eleemosynary, and, as far as respects its funds, a private corporation.

Do its objects stamp on it a different character? Are the trustees and professors public officers, invested with any portion of political power, partaking in any degree in the administration of civil government, and performing duties which flow from the sovereign authority?

That education is an object of national concern, and a proper subject of legislation, all admit. That there may be an institution founded by government, and placed entirely under its immediate control, the officers of which would be public officers, amenable exclusively to government, none will deny. But is Dartmouth College such an institution? Is education altogether in the hands of government? Does every teacher of youth become a public officer, and do donations for the purpose of education necessarily become public property, so far that the will of the legislature, not the will of the donor, becomes the law of the donation? These questions are of serious moment to society, and deserve to be well considered.

Doctor Wheelock, as the keeper of his charity-school instructing the Indians in the art of reading, and in our holy religion; sustaining them at his own expense, and on the voluntary contributions of the charitable, could scarcely be considered as a public officer, exercising any portion of those duties which belong to government; nor could the legislature have supposed that his private funds, or those given by others, were subject to legislative management, because they were applied to the purposes of education. When, afterwards, his school was enlarged, and the liberal contributions made in England, and in America, enabled him to extend his cares to the education of the youth of his own country, no change was wrought in his own character, or in the nature of his duties. Had he employed assistant tutors with the funds contributed by others, or had the trustees in England established a school with Dr. Wheelock at its head, and paid salaries to him and his assistants, they would still have been private tutors; and the fact that they were employed in the education of youth could not have converted them into public officers, concerned in the administration of public duties, or have given the legislature a right to interfere in the management of the fund. The trustees, in whose care that fund was placed by the contributors, would have been permitted to execute their trust uncontrolled by legislative authority.

Whence, then, can be derived the idea that Dartmouth College has become a public institution, and its trustees public officers, exercising powers conferred by the public for public objects? Not from the source whence its funds were drawn; for its foundation is purely private and eleemosynary. Not from the application of those funds; for money may be given for education, and the persons receiving it do not, by being employed in the education of youth, become members of the civil government. Is it from the act of incorporation?

From the fact, then, that a charter of incorporation has been granted, nothing can be inferred which changes the character of the institution, or transfers to the government any new power over it. The character of civil institutions does not grow out of their incorporation, but out of the manner in which they are formed, and the objects for which they are created. The right to change them is not founded on their being incorporated, but on their being the instruments of government, created for its purposes. The same institutions, created for the same objects, though not incorporated, would be public institutions, and, of course, be controllable by the legislature. The incorporating act neither gives nor prevents this control. Neither, in reason, can the incorporating act change the character of a private eleemosynary institution.

* * *

From the review of this charter, which has been taken, it appears that the whole power of governing the college, of appointing and removing tutors, of fixing their salaries, of directing the course of study to be pursued by the students, and of filling up vacancies created in their own body, was vested in the trustees. On the part of the crown it was expressly stipulated that this corporation, thus constituted, should continue forever; and that the number of trustees should forever consist of twelve, and no more. By this contract the crown was bound, and could have made no violent alteration in its essential terms, without impairing its obligation.

By the revolution, the duties, as well as the powers, of government devolved on the people of New Hampshire. It is admitted, that among the latter was comprehended the transcendent power of parliament, as well as that of the executive department. It is too clear to require the support of argument, that all contracts, and rights, respecting property, remained unchanged by the revolution. The obligations, then, which were created by the charter to Dartmouth College, were the same in the new that they had been in the old government. The power of the government was also the same. A repeal of this charter at any time prior to the adoption of the present constitution of the United States, would have been an extraordinary and unprecedented act of power, but one which could have been contested only by the restrictions upon the legislature, to be found in the constitution of the state. But the constitution of the United States has imposed this additional limitation, that the legislature of a state shall pass no act "impairing the obligation of contracts."

It has been already stated that the act "to amend the charter, and enlarge and improve the corporation of Dartmouth College," increases the number of trustees to twenty-one, gives the appointment of the additional members to the executive of the state, and creates a board of overseers, to consist of twenty-five persons, of whom twenty-one are also appointed by the executive of New Hampshire, who have power to inspect and control the most important acts of the trustees.

On the effect of this law, two opinions cannot be entertained. Between acting directly, and acting through the agency of trustees and overseers, no essential difference is perceived. The whole power of governing the college is transferred from trustees appointed according to the will of the founder, expressed in the charter, to the executive of New Hampshire. The management and application of the funds of this eleemosynary institution, which are placed by the donors in the hands of trustees named in the charter, and empowered to perpetuate themselves, are placed by this act under the control of the government of the state. The will of the state is substituted for the will of the donors in every essential operation of the college. This is not an immaterial change. The founders of the college contracted, not merely for the perpetual application of the funds which they gave, to the objects for which those funds were given; they contracted also to secure that application by the constitution of the corporation. They contracted for a system which should, as far as human foresight can provide, retain forever the government of the literary institution they had formed, in the hands of persons approved by themselves. This system is totally changed. The charter of 1769 exists no longer. It is reorganized; and re-organized in such a manner as to convert a literary institution, moulded according to the will of its founders, and placed under the control of private literary men, into a machine entirely subservient to the will of government. This may be for the advantage of this college in particular, and may be for the advantage of literature in general, but it is not according to the will of the donors, and is subversive of that contract, on the faith of which their property was given.

In the view which has been taken of this interesting case, the court has confined itself to the right possessed by the trustees, as the assignees and representatives of the donors and founders, for the benefit of religion and literature. Yet it is not clear that the trustees ought to be considered as destitute of such beneficial interest in themselves as the law may respect. In addition to their being the legal owners of the property, and to their having a freehold right in the powers confided to them, the charter itself countenances the idea that trustees may also be tutors with salaries. The first president was one of the original trustees; and the charter provides, that in case of vacancy in that office, "the senior professor or tutor, being one of the trustees, shall exercise the office of president, until the trustees shall make choice of, and appoint a president." According to the tenor of the charter, then, the trustees might, without impropriety, appoint a president and other professors from their own body. This is a power not entirely unconnected with an interest. Even if the proposition of the counsel for the defendant were sustained; if it were admitted that those contracts only are protected by the constitution, a beneficial interest in which is vested in the party, who appears in court to assert that interest; yet it is by no means clear that the trustees of Dartmouth College have no beneficial interest in themselves.

But the court has deemed it unnecessary to investigate this particular point, being of opinion, on general principles, that in these private eleemosynary institutions, the body corporate, as possessing the whole legal and equitable interest, and completely representing the donors, for the purpose of executing the trust, has rights which are protected by the constitution.

It results from this opinion, that the acts of the legislature of New Hampshire, which are stated in the special verdict found in this cause, are repugnant to the constitution of the United States; and that the judgment on this special verdict ought to have been for the plaintiffs. The judgment of the State Court must therefore be reversed.

Rudolph calculated the effect of the *Dartmouth College* case in these terms: "The decision discouraged the friends of strong state-supported and state-controlled institutions ... [and] by encouraging [private] college-founding and by discouraging public support for higher education, probably helped to check the development of state universities for half a century" (p. 211).

Significant federal legislation that affected public higher education in the 18th and 19th centuries included the Northwest Ordinance of 1787, the Morrill Act of 1862, the Hatch Act (1887), and the second Morrill Act (1890). The Northwest Ordinance required new states in the Union to provide public higher education with proceeds from the sale of public lands. The Morrill Land-Grant College Act established funding sources for the study of agricultural and technical (mechanical) education. Many states used the money, also from the sale of public lands, to establish new institutions, to convert existing private colleges, or to restructure components of public colleges. The Hatch Act of 1887 furthered agricultural research, initiated by the 1862 Morrill Act, by allocating federal funds for agricultural experiment stations. The second Morrill Act (1890) provided federal funding for agricultural, engineering, and natural sciences research; it also established black agricultural colleges. In the twentieth century, governmental programs for higher education increased in number, in amounts of money distributed, and in emphases. The College Work Study Program (1935), the GI Bill (1944), and the Higher Education Act of 1965 all reflected federal commitments to student financial aids and grant programs. Research funds were channeled through multiple programs, including the Smith-Lever Act of 1914 and the National Defense Education Act of 1958. Facilities programs included many Public Works Administration projects, the Higher Education Facilities Act (1963), and the Higher Education Act of 1965.

It was the states, though, that established the many institutions. By the 1950s, the post-World War II baby boom had begun, and the burgeoning elementary and secondary enrollments portended a "Tidal Wave" of college students, even if college attendance rates remained constant. Not only did states begin to increase the size of their public colleges, they increased the number by building new ones and by reconstituting private or municipal institutions into state colleges. The period between 1966 and 1974 saw more than one new public community college open each week, more than doubling the existing number of institutions. In addition, states moved energetically to centralize their control and governance of institutions. Between 1958 and 1964, more than half the states had moved to establish a state higher education board or coordinating agency. See R. Berdahl, *Statewide Coordination of Higher Education* (D.C.: American Council on Education, 1971). Ohio is a good example of the legal consequences of the growth patterns.

Fenn College v. Nance

210 N.E. 2d 418 (1965)

LYBARGER, Judge.

This is an action brought under favor of Chapter 2721 of the Revised Code of Ohio for a declaratory judgment with respect to certain questions in the administration of trusts. The plaintiffs invoke not only the inherent jurisdiction of the Court, sitting in equity, but also the provisions of R.C. Sec. 2107.46 which permit fiduciaries to seek directions of the Court respecting trust property, and R.C. Sec. 2307.21 relating to class actions of common or general interest to many persons when it is not practical to bring all of them before the court.

The plaintiffs are Fenn College (hereafter called "Fenn"), a non-profit corporation of Ohio, and the Trustees and Members of Fenn.

The defendants Nance, Bartunek, Johnson, Smith, Lambright, Silverstein, Chase, Sloan and Taft are the Trustees of The Cleveland State University (hereafter referred to as "CSU"), a state university created December 18, 1964 by authority of R.C. Chapter 3344. William B. Saxbe is Attorney General of Ohio. The defendants, The Young Men's Christian Association of Cleveland, Ohio, The Distribution Committee of The Cleveland Foundation, The Cleveland Electric Illuminating Company, The White Motor Company, George P. Bickford and Thomas F. Patton are donors to Fenn College in times past and representatives of the class of such donors who are too numerous to be included herein.

The petition states that Fenn and the Trustees of CSU have entered into an Agreement and Plan of Transition (hereafter called the "Agreement") by the terms of which the facilities, faculty and staff of Fenn will serve as a nucleus for the establishment of CSU; Fenn will convey to the State of Ohio as a gift the land and buildings of Fenn's present campus, and transfer to the Trustees of CSU all of Fenn's furniture, fixtures and equipment. The Trustees of CSU will pay Fenn $260,000, maintain a "Fenn College of Engineering" as part of the new university, and continue to offer, wherever feasible, the so-called Fenn Plan for Cooperative Education. After the Agreement is consummated Fenn will cease to operate a college and by amended articles of incorporation become "Fenn Educational Foundation," with the purpose of wide support of educational, literary, charitable and scientific activities and projects.

The plaintiff prays that the Court (a) recognize the representative capacity of the defendant donors to defend on behalf of all donors to Fenn as a class; (b) declare that Fenn and the Trustees of CSU have full power to enter into said Agreement; (c) authorize performance of the Agreement; (d) decree that all assets to be transferred are the absolute property of Fenn and that donors over the years have no interest or claims therein and are precluded from any cause of action against Fenn or its Trustees or Members for voting to consummate or for consummating the Agreement or for bringing Fenn's academic functions to a close; (c) authorize Fenn to cease functioning as an academic institution; (f) assure that all assets of Fenn remaining after the said transfer are Fenn's absolute and exclusive property, free of any claims of past donors; (g) declare that after the Effective Date as defined in the Agreement Fenn is free to amend its articles of incorporation to continue as "Fenn Educational Foundation."

* * *

December 18, 1964 the General Assembly of Ohio created Cleveland State University. R.C. Chapter 3344 vests government of CSU in nine trustees (defendants herein), gives them authority to accept donations of lands, moneys and other personal property and hold the same in trust for the university, and enter into agreements incidental to its operation. Section 2 of H 2 (130 v Pt. 2) also made this specific grant of authority:

"Subject to rules and regulations adopted by the Ohio Board of Regents, the board of trustees of Cleveland State University may enter into and fulfill contracts and agreements with the board of trustees of Fenn college for the transfer of lands, buildings, and equipment of Fenn college to the state for the use of Cleveland State University."

With the proposal to create CSU, and now with its establishment as a university supported by the State of Ohio, it has become obvious that Fenn's financial contributions have been curtailed. It is a logical conclusion of fact from the evidence that, with Fenn lacking an adequate endowment, depending largely on student fees and facing rising costs of operation, the change of functions by Fenn and the adoption of active educational functions by CSU is highly desirable not only from the standpoint of both but also because it is in the public interest in promoting the cause of education in northeastern Ohio. It will make possible a strong university built upon the foundation laid by Fenn and having a much higher potential in the field of public education in the future.

The Court has studied the Agreement and Plan of Transition and finds that it is carefully drawn fully to protect the interests of Fenn and CSU and to accomplish the transition between the two institutions in an efficient manner.

Granted that present conditions suggest the desirability of the Agreement, and that its terms are fair in every respect, a pertinent legal question is whether Fenn has authority to make a contract transferring most of its physical assets and merging its faculty, staff and facilities with those of another institution?

As a non-profit corporation Fenn has the wide general authority granted it in R.C. Chapter 1702. The Court need not belabor the fact that Fenn, under R.C. 1702.12 may make donations for "charitable, scientific, literary, or educational purposes." It may "sell, exchange, transfer, and dispose of property of any description." It may make contracts and do all lawful things incidental to its general purposes. Fenn's Articles of Incorporation give it broad purposes and plenary power to accomplish them. R.C. 1702.39 specifically gives a corporate body such as Fenn power to transfer any assets "without the necessity of procuring authorization from the court." Since the transfer here involves by far the larger part of Fenn's assets and the change of Fenn's name and functions, Fenn has complied with the requirements of R.C. 1702.39 as a corporation not for profit and has also complied with the express requirements of R.C. 1713.25 in giving more than thirty days actual notice to each Trustee of a special meeting of the Board, at which meeting more than a majority of said Board of 34 members attended and voted for such changes without a single dissenting vote. Finally, the 105th General Assembly, as noted above, gave statutory authority to the Trustees of CSU specifically to make a contract with Fenn such as is now embodied in the Agreement.

The evidence establishes that the Ohio Board of Regents, in the exercise of the authority granted in R.C. Chapter 3333, has approved the Agreement and found it to be in accord with its regulations, as contemplated by Sec. 2 of H 2 (130 v Pt. 2).

It is abundantly clear that Fenn has full and complete legal authority and its Trustees and Members ample discretion to enter into the Agreement and thereby transfer most of its assets to CSU. It need not even have resorted to the Court to have such action sanctioned.

May Fenn legally carry on by changing its name to "Fenn Educational Foundation" and by modifying its purposes and powers as proposed in amended articles of incorporation, appended to its petition as Exhibit 2? The answer is an unequivocal "yes." R.C. 1702.38 gives such authority to Fenn, as a corporation not for profit and R.C. 1713.25 dealing with changes of name and functions of a college was fully complied with in the meeting of September 14, 1965 as pointed out above, and as noted hereafter equity sanctions it. The evidence establishes that under its new name Fenn will carry on as a non-profit corporation supporting worthy educational, literary, charitable and scientific endeavors.

But what of Fenn's donors of past years? Do they have any present interest in Fenn's assets? May any givers be heard to complain that the carrying out of the Agreement and the subsequent change of name and program of Fenn violate either the spirit or the terms of their donations? In spite of the fact that the representative general donors in their answers have disclaimed any interest in Fenn's property, and that those who have made gifts for specific purposes have almost unanimously waived the observance by Fenn of their former conditions, the litigants deserve an answer to the questions just raised.

There is nothing more certain in life than change. As a wise man has said: "New occasions teach new duties; time makes ancient good uncouth." What is reasonable and helpful today may not remain so with the passing of the years. No man can accurately anticipate the needs of the next generation. Equity has long recognized this, and in dealing with trusts, both private and charitable, has not hesitated to exercise its inherent power over the administration of trusts in order to perpetuate the purposes of settlors in the face of changed conditions. This has been especially true as to charitable trusts. In Gearhart v. Richardson, the Ohio Supreme Court said:

> "Charitable trusts are entitled to a liberal and favorable consideration and will receive a more liberal construction than is allowable to private trusts or in cases of gifts to private individuals."

Now two doctrines have been developed in equity to aid in sustaining trusts under altered circumstances, *cy pres* and *deviation*. Cy pres means "as nearly as may be." The doctrine is a simple rule of judicial construction, designed to aid the court to ascertain and carry out, as nearly as may be, the intention of a donor of a gift to provide for the future. It is properly applied only where it is or has become impossible beneficially to apply the property left by the donor in the exact way in which he has dedicated it to be applied, and it can only be applied beneficially to similar purposes by different means.

Deviation is sanctioned by a court of equity to permit a departure from the terms of a trust where compliance is impossible or illegal, or where changed circumstances, not known or anticipated by a donor, would defeat or substantially impair the purposes of the trust.

In the instant case it is clear that the doctrine of deviation should be applied (1) to declare that in view of altered circumstances Fenn is fully justified in changing the form of its corporate existence while still carrying on the broad educational purposes of its charter; and (2) to make it clear that the transfer of assets and facilities to or for the use by CSU is a justified departure from the original object of generous gifts made in the past by so many, but not a material change in the charitable uses intended by such donors, and that therefore no donor may complain or hereafter have any cause of action against Fenn, its Trustees or Members growing out of the execution or carrying out of the Agreement.

The right of an educational institution to transfer its property to another such institution has not been passed on before in Ohio. There are, however, numerous Ohio cases which have applied the doctrine of deviation to permit changes affecting educational institutions.

* * *

The Court concludes that Fenn is fully justified not only by statute but also under the equitable doctrine of deviation (1) in amending its charter to change its name, modify its purposes and alter its program of operation as proposed; (2) in transferring its property to or for the use of CSU as called for in the Agreement, and (3) in taking all steps necessary and incidental to effectuating the Agreement. Finally it is clear that those who have been so generous to Fenn in the past have the assurance that their charitable intents will be perpetuated, and, although they have no legal title or interest in any of Fenn's assets, that their donations will continue to advance the cause of education.

For the above reasons the Court grants the prayer of the plaintiffs' petition and has this day rendered a declaratory judgment accordingly.

Cleveland, the largest city in Ohio, did not have a public institution until 1962, when the Cuyahoga Community College was established; as the *Fenn College* case noted, Cleveland State University was established in December 1964. For a detailed study of the issues surrounding higher education politics in Ohio during this period, see M. Olivas, "State Law and Postsecondary Coordination: The Birth of the Ohio Board of Regents," *Review of Higher Education*, 7 (1984), 357–95; J. Millett, *Politics and Higher Education* (University, Alabama: University of Alabama Press, 1974).

Private Colleges and State Action

The tug of war between states and private colleges has existed in the U.S. since the first colleges were chartered, and there are hundreds of cases illustrating the tension between the two sectors, and an increasing attempt by state legislatures to "regulate" private colleges, particularly in areas of consumer protection and in other general welfare areas. See "Md. Seeking More Control Over Private Colleges," *Washington Post*, 24 February 1988, B1, B3; D. Breneman and C. Finn, eds., *Public Policy and Private Higher Education* (D.C.: Brookings, 1978). Taxation and accreditation most directly affect these relationships, as several cases reflect.

Powe v. Miles
407 F.2d 73 (1968)

FRIENDLY, Circuit Judge:

This appeal from the dismissal of a complaint under the Civil Rights Act, 42 U.S.C. § 1983, by students at Alfred University, some of them in the New York State College of Ceramics, demands analysis of the elusive concept of "state action," recently characterized as "the most important problem in American law." It requires us to consider this in the context not of racial discrimination, to which Professor Black limited his discussion, but of First Amendment rights. Our labors have at least convinced us of the wisdom of Mr. Justice Clark's observation in Burton v. Wilmington Parking Authority, criticized at the time for failing to provide adequate guidance:

> "Only by sifting facts and weighing circumstances can the nonobvious involvement of the State in private conduct be attributed its true significance."

I.

Alfred University began in 1836 as a "select school," which developed into Alfred Academy, chartered in 1843. The Academy was incorporated as a private university by the New York Legislature in 1857. Its charter provides for government by a board of 33 self-perpetuating trustees. All are private individuals. It now has four colleges, the Liberal Arts College, the Graduate School, the School of Nursing, and the New York State College of Ceramics. The last stems from a state school of clay-working and ceramics which New York founded at Alfred in 1900. When New York established a State University in 1948, it provided that the University should include not only state-operated institutions but also "statutory or contract colleges" like that at Alfred, to wit, "Colleges furnishing higher education, operated by private institutions on behalf of the state pursuant to statute or contractual agreements."[2] At the same time the Legislature directed that, subject to higher state authority, "the state university trustees shall be responsible for: (a) The over-all central administration, supervision and co-ordination of state-operated institutions and statutory or contract colleges in the state university," and also added what is now § 357 of the Education Law providing that:

> "Statutory or contract colleges shall continue to be operated pursuant to the provisions of this chapter [the 1948 Act] but such colleges shall be subject to the general supervision and control of the state university trustees."

In 1950 the provisions of the Education Law dealing specifically with the New York State College of Ceramics were recast in light of the establishment of the State University; we set them forth in the margin.

Although the record does not contain the contract between the State and Alfred University with respect to the Ceramics College, the testimony of President Miles furnishes many significant details. The State pays all the direct expenses of the College (sometimes hereafter CC). In addition it pays a stipulated sum per credit hour for courses taken by CC students in "the private sector," with a corresponding payment by the latter for instruction CC gives students in other colleges. The State reimburses Alfred for a pro rata share of the entire administrative expense of the University

---

2. For those unfamiliar with New York's education system, an explanation of nomenclature may be useful. There has long been in existence the "University of the State of New York." This is a university without walls; the term is used to include all secondary and higher educational institutions incorporated in the state and subject to general regulation by the Board of Regents and the Commissioner of Education. Not until 1948 did New York establish a State University in the ordinary sense. Some theretofore private institutions were taken over, the statutory or contract colleges were included, and new public colleges were founded.

including the salaries of the President, the Dean of Students, and other general officers, utilities and overhead.

The dean and faculty of CC are hired and gain tenure in the same way as the dean and faculty of other colleges at Alfred. On retirement they can opt between the state retirement plan and the Alfred plan but in fact all take the latter. While § 355-a(1) of the Education Law generally authorizes the state university trustees to classify and allocate all professional employees of the state university, it excepts "those of the New York state colleges * * * administered by Cornell University and Alfred University," which are authorized, subject to state approval, to allocate professional and other employees at their contract colleges. The two universities are to classify each professional or non-professional employee of the contract colleges within two grade schedules laid down in the statute. Maximum and minimum salaries, and a maximum annual increment, are specified for each grade. Further detailed provisions govern other aspects of the remuneration of all state university employees, regulating identically the contract colleges and the state-operated institutions.

The state's last annual appropriation for CC was $1,800,000. This was 20.75% of the total Alfred budget. There are some 550 students and 40 faculty members in CC, as compared with University totals of 1800 and 140. As indicated, CC students take some courses in the Liberal Arts College; indeed this is an important reason for having CC at Alfred. The reverse is true in lesser degree.

II.

In recent years students at Alfred, like those at many other universities, have engaged in protests and demonstrations, sparked in particular by opposition to the war in Vietnam and commitment to improving relations between black and white citizens. Fully recognizing the propriety of such action, the University issued a Policy on Demonstrations effective January 1, 1968.

The events giving rise to this suit took place on May 11, 1968. We summarize them as follows:

Alfred has for several years sponsored an annual Parents Day, on which the parents of students are invited to visit the campus and attend various gatherings. Since the founding of an Army ROTC unit on campus in 1952, a military review has been scheduled as one of the Parents Day activities. Held on the university's football field, the review allows the parents to see the cadet corps in marching maneuvers and serves as the occasion for the presentation of awards to cadets who have excelled in the military science program. During the week prior to the 1968 Parents Day on Saturday, May 11, several Alfred students, members of the SDS chapter on campus, met to discuss the possibility of staging a demonstration during the ceremonies. They considered the event an appropriate occasion for demonstration because there had recently been controversy over the requirement that each male student at Alfred participate in the ROTC program during his freshman and sophomore years and the assembly of parents would furnish a large audience to witness the expression of views. The students did not confer with the Dean of Students about their plan to demonstrate or give his office the 48-hour prior notice required by the Policy on Demonstrations. There was testimony that two of the students attempted unsuccessfully to meet with President Miles during that week, but apparently the President was informed only that this related to "the matter of compulsory ROTC on the campus" and not that it concerned a planned demonstration. By Thursday evening these students had agreed among themselves that they would demonstrate at the military review on Saturday. When they met Saturday morning, they were joined by several other students and one faculty member, their number totaling sixteen.

Just before the ROTC ceremony was scheduled to begin on Saturday morning, several hundred parents and school officials had assembled in the grandstand at the football field. Four or five feet in front of the grandstand, straddling the 50-yard line, a reviewing stand had been erected in which military and other officials were to sit and review the cadets' march. To one side of this stand was a small table bearing trophies and awards to be presented to honored cadets. On the field itself red flags marked out the line of march that would be taken by the 500 cadets participating in the program.

After the stands had filled, the "adjutant's call" was sounded and the band began to march onto the field. The sixteen demonstrators entered from the end, walking single-file down the sideline four feet in front of the reviewing stand between the stand and the cadets then assembling on the field. Carrying signs that advocated scholarships for black students, the teaching of Negro history, an end to compulsory ROTC, and peace in Vietnam, the demonstrators marched once or twice down the sideline and then came to rest directly before the stands facing the audience and holding their signs for maximum visibility. Shouts were exchanged between the demonstrators and the spectators; the plaintiffs testified that their presence was greeted with boos and hisses from parts of the grandstand and clapping from other parts. At no time, however, did the onlookers indicate an intention to interfere physically with the demonstration. About five minutes after the demonstrators entered the field, when the Dean of Students concluded that they intended to remain indefinitely where they were, he announced by microphone from the press box at the top of the grandstand that their actions were in violation of the demonstration guidelines and requested them to "conform" by "removing" themselves from the field. Eight of the student demonstrators obeyed this announcement by moving past the end of the grandstand, where they sat on the sidelines with their signs for the remainder of the event; seven students and the faculty member stayed where they were. The Dean repeated his request four times, twice to the students and twice to the faculty member. He then declared those disobeying his order to be "provisionally suspended" from the university, and informed them that they could pick up the charges against them at his office that afternoon and that a hearing would be held the following morning. The eight persisting demonstrators remained in their places, seating themselves for a few moments but rising again at the playing of the Star Spangled Banner that began the presentation of awards. A second faculty member joined them, and they remained standing before the reviewing stand for the duration of the ROTC parade, about 45 minutes, holding their signs at chest level and occasionally raising them above their heads. The demonstrators were thus a direct obstacle to the vision of those in the reviewing stand and in the lower tiers of the grandstand.

* * *

No attempt was made to accost the demonstrators at the end of the event, nor was there any interference with their leaving the field.

The hearing for the seven students before the faculty-student review board was adjourned to May 20 at their request; when it resumed, they were represented by counsel. The board recommended to President Miles that the students "be separated forthwith from the University." The President modified this by suspending them for the remainder of the semester and for the first semester of 1968–69, with leave to apply for readmission in January 1969. He made arrangements to allow them to take final examinations off campus and receive credit for the courses then being taken.

III.

The seven students thus suspended brought this action late in August, 1968, in the District Court for the Western District of New York. Four are students at the Liberal Arts College, three at the New York State College of Ceramics. Alleging violation of the Civil Rights Act, 42 U.S.C. § 1983, they invoked the court's jurisdiction under 28 U.S.C. § 1343(3) and sought temporary and final injunctions compelling Alfred to reinstate them for the fall semester and preventing it from imposing penalties on students for exercising their right of free speech, a judgment declaring the Policy on Demonstrations to be void, and damages. The action was tried by Judge Curtin as on final hearing, with commendable dispatch. He concluded, in a thoroughly reasoned opinion, that plaintiffs had failed to show action "under color of any State law, statute, ordinance, regulation, custom or usage" as required by 28 U.S.C. § 1343(3), and dismissed the complaint for want of federal jurisdiction. We expedited the appeal.

Appellants' primary position is that there was state action in the suspension of all seven students; the defendants deny there was such action in any. Not being imprisoned by this formulation of the issue, we shall first consider the situation of the liberal arts students. If we should find state action with respect to them, the case of the CC students would be *a fortiori*; if we do not, the status of the latter must be separately examined.

IV.

We perceive no sufficient basis for holding that the University's action with respect to the liberal arts students comes within the district court's jurisdiction to enforce the Civil Rights Act. To be sure, on a strictly literal basis, whatever Alfred University does is "under color of" the New York statute incorporating it. But this is also true of every corporation chartered under a special or even a general incorporation statute, and not even those taking the most extreme view of the concept have ever asserted that state action goes that far. Appellants' claims are rather that Alfred performs a "public function," that it is subject to state regulation in many respects, that it receives government aid in addition to the support of CC, and finally that the interrelations between CC and the rest of the University are so intimate as to deprive the latter of the private character it might otherwise have.

Appellants' "public function" argument seeks to fuse a number of lines of authority, none of which is applicable here.

* * *

[T]he fact that New York has exercised some regulatory powers over the standard of education offered by Alfred University does not implicate it generally in Alfred's policies toward demonstrations and discipline.

The amount of aid Alfred receives from the State other than for the Ceramics College is small. President Miles thought state and federal aid, excluding scholarships to students and the provision for CC, was only a hundred or two hundred thousand dollars a year, as against the total budget of $6.8 million. This is a long way from being so dominant as to afford basis for a contention that the state is merely utilizing private trustees to administer a state activity. We perceive no basis for holding that the grant of scholarships and the financing of CC imposes on the State a duty to see that Alfred's overall policies with respect to demonstrations and discipline conform to First and Fourteenth Amendment standards so that state inaction might constitute an object of attack. Whether this would be true if Alfred were to adopt discriminatory admission policies is a different question we need not here decide.

So far as concerns the liberal arts students, there remains only the argument based on the presence of the New York State College of Ceramics on the Alfred Campus. The contention has two additional facets. The first is that since the President and the Dean of Students allegedly act as agents of the State with respect to CC students— a claim we will examine in the next section of this opinion—they should be regarded as so acting with respect to all. Griffin v. Maryland is relied upon in this connection. But, in sharp contrast to the situation of the deputy sheriff in *Griffin*, there is no reason why the liberal arts students should regard the President and the Dean of Students as arms of the State in conduct concerning them. The other facet is that if we should hold there was state action with respect to the CC students, it would be impracticable to have different rules for the two groups. Perhaps so, but that would be Alfred's problem. Whether or not it decided to establish the same policies for students outside CC as for those within it, its choice and the administration of the policies chosen for the former would be private action. We do not have at all a case where the wholly state-supported activity is so dominant that the private activity could be deemed to have been swallowed up.

V.

The question whether the action of President Miles in establishing the guidelines and of the Dean of Students in enforcing them with respect to students in the New York State College of Ceramics constitutes state action is a rather close one. The argument against it begins with the assertion that what is decisive is the nature of the actor, not of those who are acted upon; we accept this as a good starting point, although only as that. The argument continues that here the actors were officers selected by the private board of trustees, paid in largest part by funds other than the state grant for CC, and bearing no outward indicia of state office. Moreover, the demonstration forbidden in this case occurred on private property, not in the state-provided buildings of the Ceramics College. Alfred relies also upon New York decisions holding, with respect to similar contract colleges at Cornell University, that the university cannot resist tort claims upon the basis of the State's sovereign immunity, and that the State is not liable for the university's torts or breaches of contract.

We find such decisions of little value. An agent is normally liable for his own torts and does not have his principal's immunity. If New York chooses not to consider itself liable in tort or contract for the acts of its contract colleges, that is its affair. The question whether it has so far involved itself in the operation of the New York State College of Ceramics that acts of its delegates constitute action "under color of any State law, statute, ordinance, regulation, custom or usage" is a different one, whose resolution depends upon federal law. No one would question for a moment that the establishment of discriminatory admission policies for CC by the Alfred University trustees—not simply against blacks but against Jews or redheads—would constitute state action, although similar policies in the other colleges might not. As against this we recognize that discrimination may stand somewhat differently, because of the peculiar offensiveness of the state's taxing all citizens for objectives from the benefits of which a particular category is arbitrarily excluded or disadvantaged.

We hold that regulation of demonstrations by and discipline of the students in the New York State College of Ceramics at Alfred University by the President and the Dean of Students constitutes state action, for the seemingly simple but entirely sufficient reason that the State has willed it that way. The very name of the college identifies it as a state institution. In part I of this opinion we have extensively reviewed the statutes making the college an integral part of the State University; it suffices here to cite Education Law § 6102, whereby Alfred University maintains discipline and determines educational policies with respect to the State College "as the representative of the state university trustees." We see no reason why the State should not be taken at its word. The statutory provisions are not mere verbiage; they reflect the Legislature's belief that the citizens of New York would demand retention of State control over an educational institution wholly supported by State money. If the discipline had been administered by the Dean of CC, all of whose salary is paid by the State, because of acts of CC students in the State-owned buildings, the existence of state action would hardly be doubted. We do not think a different result is justified because here the CC students were demonstrating on another part of the campus, which the State's payments on their behalf entitled them to enter for proper purposes, and the authority was exercised by delegates of the State who also have other roles. While even as to the CC students the President and the Dean of Students may lack the symbolic tie with the state furnished by the deputy sheriff's badge in Griffin v. Maryland, or the public building in Burton v. Wilmington Parking Authority, the students of the New York State College of Ceramics can properly regard themselves as receiving a public education and entitled to be treated by those in charge in the same way as their counterparts in other portions of the State University. If the State wanted Alfred's policy on demonstrations changed for the CC students, mere order of the State University trustees would suffice; no general legislation would be needed, as it would be if the State desired to control the policy for other students. However one characterizes Alfred's relationship to the State with respect to the New York State College of Ceramics, it is much closer than that of an independent contractor. The State furnishes the land, buildings and equipment; it meets and evidently expects to continue to meet the entire budget; it requires that all receipts be credited against that budget, and in the last analysis it can tell Alfred not simply what to do but how to do it. The confiding of certain duties to private individuals no more insulates the State under these circumstances than in Kerr v. Enoch Pratt Free Library. While it may well be that the principle of Burton v. Wilmington Parking Authority would not require a finding of state action or, in any event, of unconstitutional state action if the coffee shop involved in that case dismissed a waitress without notice and hearing or refused to rent a private dining room to the local branch of the Communist Party, the State's relation to the New York State College of Ceramics goes far beyond that of landlord and tenant. The control of these student protests by the President and the Dean of Students on behalf of the State is an instance of positive state involvement, whether obvious or not.

* * *

Coleman v. Wagner College
429 F.2d 1120 (1970)

IRVING R. KAUFMAN, Circuit Judge:

This case presents an interesting variation on the familiar theme of state action. A not uncommon method of establishing the presence of state action is to show that a private organization has undertaken to perform functions peculiarly "public" in nature and traditionally entrusted to the state. When a state acquiesces in the governing of a town by a private company or permits a political party to control a primary election, it may expect to be held responsible for the acts of those performing state functions. The approach to state action pressed upon us in this case is the converse of the public function doctrine. The state has intervened in the performance of a function traditionally entrusted to private organizations, the maintenance of internal order by private universities. By so doing, we are told, it has subjected the imposition of disciplinary sanctions by private colleges and universities to scrutiny under the fourteenth amendment.

Having put the question presented to us in perspective, we now distill the following factual account from the complaint, affidavits and testimony at a hearing held to determine whether an order to show cause and a temporary restraining order should be issued. The basic outline follows countless similar scenarios enacted on college campuses across the country. In April 1970, the twenty-four plaintiffs were students at Wagner College, a privately supported college affiliated with the Lutheran Church and located on Staten Island in New York City. All were members of "Black Concern," a campus organization devoted to furthering the interests of blacks and other ethnic group students at Wagner. The incident which occasioned their expulsion commenced shortly before noon on April 23, when a group of students including the plaintiffs visited the office of Dean Haas, Dean of the College, for the purpose of arranging a meeting with Wagner's President, Dr. Davidson. Dean Haas made an effort to communicate with Dr. Davidson but was unsuccessful. At no time while they were present in his office, the students tell us, was Dean Haas physically restrained, nor did he request that they depart or threaten disciplinary measures.

Other members of the college's staff, however, seem to have viewed the students' presence in Dean Haas's office in a different light. Dean of Students Maher, who apparently had primary responsibility for student discipline, requested the plaintiffs to vacate the office, and at 12:45 p.m. they were warned that unless they did so within ten minutes they would be suspended. The students, nevertheless, failed to leave Dean Haas's office. At 4:00 p.m. Dean Maher stated in writing that all students in the office were suspended for the remainder of the year; that Dean Haas's detention by the students would be referred to the police if he were not freed immediately; and that the students would be expelled if they did not leave the office within an hour.

Dean Haas testified that Maher's statement was passed in to the office together with a copy of the rules and regulations for the maintenance of public order adopted by the college following the enactment of New York State Education Law. This section required every college in the State of New York to file with the regents and the commissioner of education "rules and regulations for the maintenance of public order on college campuses." And "[t]he penalties for violations of such rules and regulations [were to] be clearly set forth therein" and could include "suspension, expulsion or other appropriate disciplinary action" for student violators. Colleges which failed to file such rules and regulations lost their eligibility for state aid to education.

Despite Dean Maher's warning, the plaintiffs refused to leave Dean Haas's office. We are also told that Dean Haas remained until 7:15 p.m., and before his departure, allegedly granted the students permission to utilize the office for a meeting with their attorneys. This meeting was concluded at about 10:00 p.m., and the students then left the office.

The College, thereafter, proceeded to carry out its ultimatum. On April 25, the twenty-four plaintiffs and three other students who had been present in the office received notices of expulsion. The notices did not specify the college rule the students were alleged to have violated, though they did set forth the procedures for an appeal to the Faculty Counsel. The students were required to leave the Wagner campus by 5:00 p.m. April 27, a deadline prior to the time the Faculty Counsel could hear their appeals.

After failing to convince the College to stay the order requiring them to depart from the campus, twenty-four of the expelled students brought this action in the Eastern District of New York. The students alleged that the procedures employed by the college in issuing the expulsion orders did not comport with the requirements of due process. Moreover, based upon allegations of college hostility toward black students and its failure to expel white students who had engaged in similar demonstrations, the expulsions were claimed to have been in violation of the equal protection clause of the fourteenth amendment. The complaint sought injunctive relief ordering the college to reinstate the students pending a hearing, to conform its hearing procedures to the requirements of due process, and to refrain from racially discriminatory expulsions. After a hearing which appears to have been restricted to the question of state responsibility for the imposition of disciplinary sanctions by Wagner College, the district court declined to issue an order to show cause and a temporary restraining order and, *sua sponte*, dismissed the complaint for want of jurisdiction.

On appeal, the students do not urge that all of the actions of the administrative staff of Wagner College, an institution affiliated with a religious denomination and supported almost entirely by private funds, are actions of the state. Perhaps this is so because we rejected a similar contention in Powe v. Miles. Instead, the appellants seize upon Judge Friendly's dictum in *Powe* that "[s]tate action would be * * * present [in a case involving campus demonstrations] if New York had undertaken to set policy for the control of demonstrations in all private universities." By enacting section 6450, they argue, the state legislature did undertake to set policy for dealing with campus demonstrations and, in fact, became involved with the regulation of the very activity by which the plaintiffs claim to have been unjustly injured—the imposition of disciplinary sanctions for offenses against the public order on college campuses.

The appellants' interesting argument is not without some support. In several instances, public regulation of private organizations has been adjudged a basis for a finding of state action. The Supreme Court has determined that a privately-owned and publicly-regulated transit company's practice of broadcasting radio programs on its buses and trolleys was susceptible to challenge as a "state" action. The Public Utilities Commission of the District of Columbia, the regulatory agency involved in *Pollak*, licensed and closely supervised Capital Transit's service. The Commission had, in fact, granted specific approval to the challenged practice. Similarly, a political party required to perform certain significant duties by law and to conform its internal organization to statutory standards was not permitted to evade the fourteenth amendment's proscription of racial segregation in the conduct of primary elections.

But, this case differs in material respects from the cited cases. Neither the New York legislature, the regents, nor the commissioner of education ever granted approval to the particular conduct sought to be challenged, as had the Public Utilities Commission in *Pollak*. Nor, in our view, was Wagner College's expulsion of twenty-four students for participation in a campus demonstration as closely tied to traditional governmental functions as was the conduct of primary elections by the Democratic party of Texas in Smith v. Allwright. Moreover, it appears to us that the "regulation" of college discipline embodied in section 6450 appears almost devoid of meaningful content. Colleges are not required to secure approval of rules and regulations drafted pursuant to the section but merely to file them with the designated officials. The statute does not proscribe specific activities or types of conduct as violations of the public order of the campus. No penalty is designated; although college officials are required to have the sanction of ejection (and, in the case of students and faculty members, an "appropriate disciplinary action") at their disposal, they are not required to use it. One wonders whether rules and regulations consisting solely of the statement that any individual guilty of a transgression against the public order of the campus shall be required to give the Dean of the College a rose and a peppercorn on Midsummer's Day would satisfy the literal command of the statute in all respects. Read in this manner, the statute does little more than call upon the college administrators to reconsider the problem of student discipline and to place the results of this reconsideration on record with certain officials of the State of New York. If the statute is applied in accordance with its literal meaning, regulations filed pursuant to its provisions and disciplinary proceedings instituted pursuant to these regulations are the product and responsibility of private individuals and not of the state.

We are, however, cognizant of the possibility that the statute may have been intended, or may be applied, to mean more than it purports to say. More specifically, section 6450 may be intended or applied as a command to the colleges of the state to adopt a new, more severe attitude toward campus disruption and to impose harsh sanctions on unruly students. The Governor's Memorandum approving section 6450 referred to an "intolerable situation on the Cornell University Campus" and spoke of "the urgent need for *adequate* plans for student-university relations." Several other bills pending in the New York legislature while section 6450 was under consideration suggest that the statute was enacted in an atmosphere of hostility toward unruly student demonstrators and of resolve to make disruption costly for the participants. If these considerations have merit and section 6450 was intended to coerce colleges to adopt disciplinary codes embodying a "hard-line" attitude toward student protesters, it would appear that New York has indeed "undertaken to set policy for the control of demonstrations in all private universities" and should be held responsible for the implementation of this policy. Since we cannot resolve this question on the record before us, we conclude that the district court acted too hastily in dismissing the complaint and, consequently, remand for a further hearing at which the plaintiffs may introduce evidence to establish that section 6450 represents a meaningful state intrusion into the disciplinary policies of private colleges and universities.

Of the factors to be explored on remand, several would seem of particular importance. Most significant are the actions of the state officials with whom the rules and regulations are to be filed. If these officials were to regard their function as more than a ministerial task, and, as an illustration, believed themselves empowered to prevent regulations from being filed because of substantive "inadequacies," or exercised any other influence upon the content of regulations filed pursuant to section 6450, they would provide strong indicia of state action. Less obvious in its significance is the attitude of the college administrators required to draft regulations by the statute. We would ordinarily be loath to suggest that state action can arise from a private individual's mistaken notion that his acts have the imprimatur of the state. A reasonable and widespread belief among college administrators, however, that section 6450 required them to adopt a particular stance toward campus demonstrators would seem to justify a conclusion that the state intended for them to pursue that course of action. And this intent, if present, would provide a basis for a finding of state action. We discern several possible means of determining the attitude of college administrators toward the effect of the statute. The universal adoption of noticeably more stringent standards governing student disruption following the statute's enactment or an attempt by administrators to attribute the imposition of harsh penalties to the command of the state would give support to the contention that the statute constitutes significant state intervention in the area of campus discipline.

Reversed and remanded for proceedings consistent with this opinion.

While there are institutions that are decidedly public, and those that are decidedly private, and those (as in the *Alfred University* case) that are simultaneously both, many colleges fall in between—often requiring plaintiffs to establish "state action" for reaching a private institution, or to circumvent a defense by a public institution that it is a "state agency" with sovereign immunity. For a review of these issues, see W. Kaplin, *The Law of Higher Education* (San Francisco: Jossey-Bass, 1986) and P. Swan, "The Eleventh Amendment Revisited: Suits Against State Government Entities and Their Employees in Federal Courts," *Journal of College and University Law*, 14 (1987), 1–57.

Religion and Higher Education

Another fugue running through the materials is religion, which remains, unsurprisingly, a matter of considerable litigation in several higher education settings. *Bob Jones* represents the quintessential case in the area, fusing issues of race, the religious mission of a college, and the legal character of a college. For a primer on higher education and religion, a pattern emerges from cases in each chapter: religious issues arise in cases of academic freedom, faculty hiring and firing, recognition of student groups, affirmative action, and regulation by the state. See P. Moots and E. Gaffney, *Church & Campus* (Notre Dame: University of Notre Dame Press, 1979); F. Dutile and E. Gaffney, *State and Campus: State Regulation of Religiously Affiliated Higher Education* (Notre Dame: University of Notre Dame Press, 1984).

Bob Jones University v. United States
461 U.S. 574 (1983)

Chief Justice BURGER delivered the opinion of the Court.

We granted certiorari to decide whether petitioners, nonprofit private schools that prescribe and enforce racially discriminatory admissions standards on the basis of religious doctrine, qualify as tax-exempt organizations under § 501(c)(3) of the Internal Revenue Code of 1954.

I

A

Until 1970, the Internal Revenue Service granted tax-exempt status to private schools, without regard to their racial admissions policies, under § 501(c)(3) of the Internal Revenue Code, and granted charitable deductions for contributions to such schools under § 170 of the Code.

On January 12, 1970, a three-judge District Court for the District of Columbia issued a preliminary injunction prohibiting the IRS from according tax-exempt status to private schools in Mississippi that discriminated as to admissions on the basis of race. Thereafter, in July 1970, the IRS concluded that it could "no longer legally justify allowing tax-exempt status [under § 501(c)(3)] to private schools which practice racial discrimination." At the same time, the IRS announced that it could not "treat gifts to such schools as charitable deductions for income tax purposes [under § 170]." By letter dated November 30, 1970, the IRS formally notified private schools, including those involved in this litigation, of this change in policy, "applicable to all private schools in the United States at all levels of education."

On June 30, 1971, the three-judge District Court issued its opinion on the merits of the Mississippi challenge. That court approved the IRS's amended construction of the Tax Code. The court also held that racially discriminatory private schools were not entitled to exemption under § 501(c)(3) and that donors were not entitled to deductions for contributions to such schools under § 170. The court permanently enjoined the Commissioner of Internal Revenue from approving tax-exempt status for any school in Mississippi that did not publicly maintain a policy of nondiscrimination.

The revised policy on discrimination was formalized in Revenue Ruling 71–447, 1971–2 Cum. Bull. 230:

> "Both the courts and the Internal Revenue Service have long recognized that the statutory requirement of being 'organized and operated exclusively for religious, charitable, ... or educational purposes' was intended to express the basic common law concept [of 'charity']. ... All charitable trusts, educational or otherwise, are subject to the requirement that the purpose of the trust may not be illegal or contrary to public policy."

Based on the "national policy to discourage racial discrimination in education," the IRS ruled that "a [private] school not having a racially nondiscriminatory policy as to students is not 'charitable' within the common law concepts reflected in sections 170 and 501(c)(3) of the Code."

The application of the IRS construction of these provisions to petitioners, two private schools with racially discriminatory admissions policies, is now before us.

B

No. 81–3, Bob Jones University v. United States

Bob Jones University is a nonprofit corporation located in Greenville, S.C. Its purpose is "to conduct an institution of learning ..., giving special emphasis to the Christian religion and the ethics revealed in the Holy Scriptures." The corporation operates a school with an enrollment of approximately 5,000 students, from kindergarten through college and graduate school. Bob Jones University is not affiliated with any religious denomination, but is dedicated to the teaching and propagation of its fundamentalist Christian religious beliefs. It is both a religious and educational institution. Its teachers are required to be devout Christians, and all courses at the University are taught according to the Bible. Entering students are screened as to their religious beliefs, and their public and private conduct is strictly regulated by standards promulgated by University authorities.

The sponsors of the University genuinely believe that the Bible forbids interracial dating and marriage. To effectuate these views, Negroes were completely excluded until 1971. From 1971 to May 1975, the University accepted no applications from unmarried Negroes, but did accept applications from Negroes married within their race.[5]

Following the decision of the United States Court of Appeals for the Fourth Circuit in *McCrary v. Runyon*, prohibiting racial exclusion from private schools, the University revised its policy. Since May 29, 1975, the University has permitted unmarried Negroes to enroll; but a disciplinary rule prohibits interracial dating and marriage. That rule reads:

"There is to be no interracial dating.

"1. Students who are partners in an interracial marriage will be expelled.

"2. Students who are members of or affiliated with any group or organization which holds as one of its goals or advocates interracial marriage will be expelled.

"3. Students who date outside of their own race will be expelled.

"4. Students who espouse, promote, or encourage others to violate the University's dating rules and regulations will be expelled."

The University continues to deny admission to applicants engaged in an interracial marriage or known to advocate interracial marriage or dating.

Until 1970, the IRS extended tax-exempt status to Bob Jones University under § 501(c)(3). By the letter of November 30, 1970, that followed the injunction issued in *Green v. Kennedy*, the IRS formally notified the University of the change in IRS policy, and announced its intention to challenge the tax-exempt status of private schools practicing racial discrimination in their admissions policies.

After failing to obtain an assurance of tax exemption through administrative means, the University instituted an action in 1971 seeking to enjoin the IRS from revoking the school's tax-exempt status. That suit culminated in *Bob Jones University v. Simon*, in which this Court held that the Anti-Injunction Act of the Internal Revenue Code, 26 U.S.C. § 7421(a), prohibited the University from obtaining judicial review by way of injunctive action before the assessment or collection of any tax.

Thereafter, on April 16, 1975, the IRS notified the University of the proposed revocation of its tax-exempt status. On January 19, 1976, the IRS officially revoked the University's tax-exempt status, effective as of December 1, 1970, the day after the University was formally notified of the change in IRS policy. The University

---

5. Beginning in 1973, Bob Jones University instituted an exception to this rule, allowing applications from unmarried Negroes who had been members of the University staff for four years or more.

subsequently filed returns under the Federal Unemployment Tax Act for the period from December 1, 1970, to December 31, 1975, and paid a tax totalling $21 on one employee for the calendar year of 1975. After its request for a refund was denied, the University instituted the present action, seeking to recover the $21 it had paid to the IRS. The Government counterclaimed for unpaid federal unemployment taxes for the taxable years 1971 through 1975, in the amount of $489,675.59, plus interest.

The United States District Court for the District of South Carolina held that revocation of the University's tax-exempt status exceeded the delegated powers of the IRS, was improper under the IRS rulings and procedures, and violated the University's rights under the Religion Clauses of the First Amendment. The court accordingly ordered the IRS to pay the University the $21 refund it claimed and rejected the IRS's counterclaim.

The Court of Appeals for the Fourth Circuit, in a divided opinion, reversed. Citing *Green v. Connally* with approval, the Court of Appeals concluded that § 501(c)(3) must be read against the background of charitable trust law. To be eligible for an exemption under that section, an institution must be "charitable" in the common-law sense, and therefore must not be contrary to public policy. In the court's view, Bob Jones University did not meet this requirement, since its "racial policies violated the clearly defined public policy, rooted in our Constitution, condemning racial discrimination and, more specifically, the government policy against subsidizing racial discrimination in education, public or private." The court held that the IRS acted within its statutory authority in revoking the University's tax-exempt status. Finally, the Court of Appeals rejected petitioner's arguments that the revocation of the tax exemption violated the Free Exercise and Establishment Clauses of the First Amendment. The case was remanded to the District Court with instructions to dismiss the University's claim for a refund and to reinstate the IRS's counterclaim.

C

No. 81–1, Goldsboro Christian Schools, Inc. v. United States

Goldsboro Christian Schools is a nonprofit corporation located in Goldsboro, N.C. Like Bob Jones University, it was established "to conduct an institution or institutions of learning . . . , giving special emphasis to the Christian religion and the ethics revealed in the Holy scriptures." The school offers classes from kindergarten through high school, and since at least 1969 has satisfied the State of North Carolina's requirements for secular education in private schools. The school requires its high school students to take Bible-related courses, and begins each class with prayer.

Since its incorporation in 1963, Goldsboro Christian Schools has maintained a racially discriminatory admissions policy based upon its interpretation of the Bible.[6] Goldsboro has for the most part accepted only Caucasians. On occasion, however, the school has accepted children from racially mixed marriages in which one of the parents is Caucasian.

---

6. According to the interpretation espoused by Goldsboro, race is determined by descendance from one of Noah's three sons—Ham, Shem, and Japheth. Based on this interpretation, Orientals and Negroes are Hamitic, Hebrews are Shemitic, and Caucasians are Japhethitic. Cultural or biological mixing of the races is regarded as a violation of God's command.

* * *

II

A

In Revenue Ruling 71–447, the IRS formalized the policy, first announced in 1970, that § 170 and § 501(c)(3) embrace the common-law "charity" concept. Under that view, to qualify for a tax exemption pursuant to § 501(c)(3), an institution must show, first, that it falls within one of the eight categories expressly set forth in that section, and second, that its activity is not contrary to settled public policy.

Section 501(c)(3) provides that "[c]orporations . . . organized and operated exclusively for religious, charitable . . . or educational purposes" are entitled to tax exemption. Petitioners argue that the plain language of the statute guarantees them tax-exempt status. They emphasize the absence of any language in the statute expressly requiring all exempt organizations to be "charitable" in the common-law sense, and they contend that the disjunctive "or" separating the categories in § 501(c)(3) precludes such a reading. Instead, they argue that if an institution falls within one or more of the specified categories it is automatically entitled to exemption, without regard to whether it also qualifies as "charitable." The Court of Appeals rejected that contention and concluded that petitioners' interpretation of the statute "tears section 501(c)(3) from its roots."

It is a well-established canon of statutory construction that a court should go beyond the literal language of a statute if reliance on that language would defeat the plain purpose of the statute:

> "The general words used in the clause . . ., taken by themselves, and literally construed, without regard to the object in view, would seem to sanction the claim of the plaintiff. But this mode of expounding a statute has never been adopted by any enlightened tribunal—because it is evident that in many cases it would defeat the object which the Legislature intended to accomplish. And it is well settled that, in interpreting a statute, the court will not look merely to a particular clause in which general words may be used, *but will take in connection with it the whole statute . . . and the objects and policy of the law. . . .*"

Section 501(c)(3) therefore must be analyzed and construed within the framework of the Internal Revenue Code and against the background of the congressional purposes. Such an examination reveals unmistakable evidence that, underlying all relevant parts of the Code, is the intent that entitlement to tax exemption depends on meeting certain common-law standards of charity—namely, that an institution seeking tax-exempt status must serve a public purpose and not be contrary to established public policy.

This "charitable" concept appears explicitly in § 170 of the Code. That section contains a list of organizations virtually identical to that contained in § 501(c)(3). It is apparent that Congress intended that list to have the same meaning in both sections. In § 170, Congress used the list of organizations in defining the term "charitable contributions." On its face, therefore, § 170 reveals that Congress' intention was to provide tax benefits to organizations serving charitable purposes. The form of § 170 simply makes plain what common sense and history tell us: in enacting both § 170 and § 501(c)(3), Congress sought to provide tax benefits to charitable organizations, to encourage the development of private institutions that serve a useful public purpose or supplement or take the place of public institutions of the same kind.

Tax exemptions for certain institutions thought beneficial to the social order of the country as a whole, or to a particular community, are deeply rooted in our history, as in that of England. The origins of such exemptions lie in the special privileges that have long been extended to charitable trusts.

More than a century ago, this Court announced the caveat that is critical in this case:

> "[I]t has now become an established principle of American law, that courts of chancery will sustain and protect . . . a gift . . . to public charitable uses, *provided the same is consistent with local laws and public policy. . . .*"

When the Government grants exemptions or allows deductions all taxpayers are affected; the very fact of the exemption or deduction for the donor means that other taxpayers can be said to be indirect and vicarious "donors." Charitable exemptions are justified on the basis that the exempt entity confers a public benefit—a benefit which the society or the community may not itself choose or be able to provide, or which supplements and advances the work of public institutions already supported by tax revenues. History buttresses logic to make clear that, to warrant exemption under § 501(c)(3), an institution must fall within a category specified in that section and must demonstrably serve and be in harmony with the public interest. The institution's purpose must not be so at odds with the common community conscience as to undermine any public benefit that might otherwise be conferred.

B

We are bound to approach these questions with full awareness that determinations of public benefit and public policy are sensitive matters with serious implications for the institutions affected; a declaration that a given institution is not "charitable" should be made only where there can be no doubt that the activity involved is contrary to a fundamental public policy. But there can no longer be any doubt that racial discrimination in education violates deeply and widely accepted views of elementary justice. Prior to 1954, public education in many places still was conducted under the pall of *Plessy v. Ferguson*; racial segregation in primary and secondary education prevailed in many parts of the country. This Court's decision in *Brown v. Board of Education* signalled an end to that era. Over the past quarter of a century, every pronouncement of this Court and myriad Acts of Congress and Executive Orders attest a firm national policy to prohibit racial segregation and discrimination in public education.

An unbroken line of case following *Brown v. Board of Education* establishes beyond doubt this Court's view that racial discrimination in education violates a most fundamental national public policy, as well as rights of individuals.

> "The right of a student not to be segregated on racial grounds in schools . . . is indeed so fundamental and pervasive that it is embraced in the concept of due process of law."

In *Norwood v. Harrison*, we dealt with a nonpublic institution:

> "[A] private school—even one that discriminates—fulfills an important educational function; *however, . . . [that] legitimate educational function cannot be*

isolated from discriminatory practices.... [D]iscriminatory treatment exerts a pervasive influence on the entire educational process."

Congress, in Titles IV and VI of the Civil Rights Act of 1964, clearly expressed its agreement that racial discrimination in education violates a fundamental public policy. Other sections of that Act, and numerous enactments since then, testify to the public policy against racial discrimination.

The Executive Branch has consistently placed its support behind eradication of racial discrimination. Several years before this Court's decision in *Brown v. Board of Education*, President Truman issued Executive Orders prohibiting racial discrimination in federal employment decisions, and in classifications for the Selective Service. In 1957, President Eisenhower employed military forces to ensure compliance with federal standards in school desegregation programs. And in 1962, President Kennedy announced:

"[T]he granting of Federal assistance for ... housing and related facilities from which Americans are excluded because of their race, color, creed, or national origin is unfair, unjust, and inconsistent with the public policy of the United States as manifested in its Constitution and laws."

These are but a few of numerous Executive Orders over the past three decades demonstrating the commitment of the Executive Branch to the fundamental policy of eliminating racial discrimination.

Few social or political issues in our history have been more vigorously debated and more extensively ventilated than the issue of racial discrimination, particularly in education. Given the stress and anguish of the history of efforts to escape from the shackles of the "separate but equal" doctrine of *Plessy v. Ferguson*, it cannot be said that educational institutions that, for whatever reasons, practice racial discrimination are institutions exercising "beneficial and stabilizing influences in community life," or should be encouraged by having all taxpayers share in their support by way of special tax status.

There can thus be no question that the interpretation of § 170 and § 501(c)(3) announced by the IRS in 1970 was correct. That it may be seen as belated does not undermine its soundness. It would be wholly incompatible with the concepts underlying tax exemption to grant the benefit of tax-exempt status to racially discriminatory educational entities, which "exer[t] a pervasive influence on the entire educational process." Whatever may be the rationale for such private schools' policies, and however sincere the rationale may be, racial discrimination in education is contrary to public policy. Racially discriminatory educational institutions cannot be viewed as conferring a public benefit within the "charitable" concept discussed earlier, or within the congressional intent underlying § 170 and § 501(c)(3).

C

Petitioners contend that, regardless of whether the IRS properly concluded that racially discriminatory private schools violate public policy, only Congress can alter the scope of § 170 and § 501(c)(3). Petitioners accordingly argue that the IRS overstepped its lawful bounds in issuing its 1970 and 1971 rulings.

Yet ever since the inception of the Tax Code, Congress has seen fit to vest in those administering the tax laws very broad authority to interpret those laws. In an area as complex as the tax system, the agency Congress vests with administrative responsibility must be able to exercise its authority to meet changing conditions and new problems.

* * *

Guided, of course, by the Code, the IRS has the responsibility, in the first instance, to determine whether a particular entity is "charitable" for purposes of § 170 and § 501(c)(3). This in turn may necessitate later determinations of whether given activities so violate public policy that the entities involved cannot be deemed to provide a public benefit worthy of "charitable" status. We emphasize, however, that these sensitive determinations should be made only where there is no doubt that the organization's activities violate fundamental public policy.

On the record before us, there can be no doubt as to the national policy. In 1970, when the IRS first issued the ruling challenged here, the position of all three branches of the Federal Government was unmistakably clear. The correctness of the Commissioner's conclusion that a racially discriminatory private school "is not 'charitable' within the common law concepts reflect in ... the Code" is wholly consistent with what Congress, the Executive, and the courts had repeatedly declared before 1970. Indeed, it would be anomalous for the Executive, Legislative, and Judicial Branches to reach conclusions that add up to a firm public policy on racial discrimination, and at the same time have the IRS blissfully ignore what all three branches of the Federal Government had declared. Clearly an educational institution engaging in practices affirmatively at odds with this declared position of the whole Government cannot be seen as exercising a "beneficial and stabilizing influenc[e] in community life," and is not "charitable," within the meaning of § 170 and § 501(c)(3). We therefore hold that the IRS did not exceed its authority when it announced its interpretation of §170 and §501(c)(3) in 1970 and 1971.

* * *

III

Petitioners contend that, even if the Commissioner's policy is valid as to nonreligious private schools, that policy cannot constitutionally be applied to schools that engage in racial discrimination on the basis of sincerely held religious beliefs. As to such schools, it is argued that the IRS construction of § 170 and § 501(c)(3) violates their free exercise rights under the Religion Clauses of the First Amendment. This contention presents claims not heretofore considered by this Court in precisely this context.

This Court has long held the Free Exercise Clause of the First Amendment to be an absolute prohibition against governmental regulation of religious beliefs. As interpreted by this Court, moreover, the Free Exercise Clause provides substantial protection for lawful conduct grounded in religious belief. However, "[n]ot all burdens on religion are unconstitutional. . . . The state may justify a limitation on religious liberty by showing that it is essential to accomplish an overriding governmental interest."

On occasion this Court has found certain governmental interests so compelling as to allow even regulations prohibiting religiously based conduct. In *Prince v. Massachusetts*, for example, the Court held that neutrally cast child labor laws prohibiting sale of printed materials on public streets could be applied to prohibit children from dispensing religious literature. The Court found no constitutional infirmity in "excluding [Jehovah's Witness children] from doing there what no other children may do." Denial of tax benefits will inevitably have a substantial impact on the operation of private religious schools, but will not prevent those schools from observing their religious tenets.

The governmental interest at stake here is compelling. As discussed in Part II-B, *supra*, the Government has a fundamental, overriding interest in eradicating racial discrimination in education—discrimination that prevailed, with official approval, for the first 165 years of this Nation's constitutional history. That governmental interest substantially outweighs whatever burden denial of tax benefits places on petitioners' exercise of their religious beliefs. The interests asserted by petitioners cannot be accommodated with that compelling governmental interest, and no "less restrictive mean," are available to achieve the governmental interest.

IV

The remaining issue is whether the IRS properly applied its policy to these petitioners. Petitioner Goldsboro Christian Schools admits that it "maintain[s] racially discriminatory policies," but seeks to justify those policies on grounds we have fully discussed. The IRS properly denied tax-exempt status to Goldsboro Christian Schools.

Petitioner Bob Jones University, however, contends that it is not racially discriminatory. It emphasizes that it now allows all races to enroll, subject only to its restrictions on the conduct of all students, including its prohibitions of association between men and women of different races, and of interracial marriage. Although a ban on intermarriage or interracial dating applies to all races, decisions of this Court firmly establish that discrimination on the basis of racial affiliation and association is a form of racial discrimination. We therefore find that the IRS properly applied Revenue Ruling 71–447 to Bob Jones University.[32]

The judgments of the Court of Appeals are, accordingly,

Affirmed.

Sheldon Jackson College v. State
599 P.2d 127 (1979)

MATTHEWS, Justice.

The final sentence of article VII, section 1 of our state constitution prohibits the payment of money from public funds "for the direct benefit of any religious or other private educational institution." The question in this case is whether Alaska's tuition grant program violates this provision.

The tuition grant program awards Alaska residents attending private colleges in Alaska an amount generally equal to the difference between the tuition charged by the student's private college and the tuition charged by a public college in the same area, not to exceed $2,500.00 annually. The student is required to apply the entire amount of the grant towards his or her tuition.

---

32. Bob Jones University also argues that the IRS policy should not apply to it because it is entitled to exemption under § 501(c)(3) as a "religious" organization, rather than as an "educational" institution. The record in this case leaves no doubt, however, that Bob Jones University is both an educational institution and a religious institution. As discussed previously, the IRS policy properly extends to all private schools, including religious schools. The IRS policy thus was properly applied to Bob Jones University.

In May of 1976 the attorney general issued an opinion declaring tuition grants to be invalid as a direct benefit to private schools in violation of article VII, section 1. The Department of Administration then stopped paying tuition grants. Appellant Sheldon Jackson College, a private educational institution, filed suit to enjoin the department's termination order, but agreed to dismiss the suit without prejudice when a proposition to amend article VII, section 1, to permit tuition grants was placed on the ballot to be voted on in the general election of November, 1976.

The ballot proposition was rejected by the voters 64,211 to 54,636. Sheldon Jackson then renewed its lawsuit and another private university, Inupiat University of the Arctic, filed a complaint in intervention. The superior court concluded that the tuition grant program provides direct benefits to private educational institutions and thus violates article VII, section 1. Summary judgment was thereupon granted in favor of the state. We affirm.

I

The minutes of the Alaska Constitutional Convention show that an unsuccessful motion was made to delete entirely the direct benefit prohibition of article VII, section 1. The proponent of the motion argued that the state constitutional provisions prohibiting the establishment of religion and prohibiting spending public funds for private purposes, were sufficient to accomplish the objectives of the direct benefit clause. By rejecting this proposal the convention made it clear that it wished the constitution to support and protect a strong system of public schools. Other authorities have also suggested that a constitutional provision barring aid to all private schools serves to enforce the separation of church and state without requiring executive or judicial inquiry into the sectarian affiliation of particular schools, and furthermore disengages the state from the undesirable task of withholding benefits solely on the basis of religious affiliation.

At the same time, in expressly rejecting alternative language that would have prohibited "direct *or indirect* benefits," the delegates to Alaska's Constitutional Convention made it abundantly clear that they did not wish to prevent the state from providing for the health and welfare of private school students, or from focusing on the special needs of individual residents. Article VII, section 1, was thus designed to commit Alaska to the pursuit of public, not private, education, without requiring absolute governmental indifference to any student choosing to be educated outside the public school system.

The Alaska Constitution is apparently unique in its express ban only on "direct" benefits. However, in construing state constitutional provisions that prohibit "support" for private schools, or state and federal proscriptions against the establishment of religion, the courts have frequently resorted to a distinction between "direct" and "incidental" benefits. Though the distinction may at times appear more "metaphysical" than precise, the analyses found in these decisions are helpful in determining generally the type of government action intended to be prohibited by article VII's direct benefit clause. The following generalizations can be drawn from these authorities.

First, constitutional provisions governing aid to private schools have generally been perceived as requiring neutrality rather than hostility from the state; thus the breadth of the class to which statutory benefits are directed is a critical area of judicial scrutiny. For example, though the police and fire protection afforded a private school may provide the school with quite direct benefits, as when a campus fire is extinguished, such benefits are provided without regard to status and affiliation, and have universally been presumed to be constitutional. Conversely, a benefit flowing only to private institutions, or to those served by them, does not reflect the same neutrality and non-selectivity.

A second central criterion in determining the constitutionality of a state aid program, is the nature of the use to which the public funds are to be put. As is apparent from the convention debate, the core of the concern expressed in the direct benefit prohibition involves government aid to *education* conducted outside the public schools. Though any state assistance that relieves the burden on a private school to provide for the health and welfare of its students will free the school to concentrate its funds on its private educational mission, numerous delegates voiced their understanding that the direct benefit clause would not bar such incidental support. An analogous distinction has frequently been drawn in establishment clause cases, where the pertinent inquiry is whether a statute impacts "essentially secular educational functions" that are separable from the school's religious instruction.

Third, in determining whether a school is directly benefitted by public funds, a court must consider, though not in isolation, the magnitude of the benefit conferred. A trivial, though direct, benefit may not rise to the level of a constitutional violation, whereas a substantial, though arguably indirect, benefit may.

Finally, while a direct transfer of funds from the state to a private school will of course render a program constitutionally suspect, merely channeling the funds through an intermediary will not save an otherwise improper expenditure of public monies. The courts have expressly noted that the superficial form of a benefit will not suffice to define its substantive character.

II

The foregoing observations are readily applicable to the present case. First, the class primarily benefitted by the tuition grant program consists only of private colleges and their students. Though the appellants characterize the statute as merely equalizing the positions of private and public university students, effectively the chief beneficiaries are the private colleges themselves. Unlike a statute that provides comparable dollar subsidies to all students, Alaska's tuition grant program is not neutral, inasmuch as the only incentive it creates is the incentive to enroll in a private college. Subsidy programs suffering from similar deficiencies have been repeatedly struck down under a variety of state constitutional provisions, as well as under the Federal Constitution.

Second, the public funds expended under AS 14.40.776 constitute nothing less than a subsidy of the education received by the student at his or her private college, and thus implicate fully the core concern of the direct benefit provision. While the program may be motivated, as was stated in the preface to the statute as it was originally passed, by the desire to "help retain qualified students in Alaska," such a laudable purpose cannot escape article VII's mandate that Alaska pursue its educational objectives through public educational institutions.

Furthermore, the magnitude of benefits bestowed under the tuition grant program is quite substantial. For the last year in which the tuition grants were paid, 1975–76, Sheldon Jackson received approximately six hundred thousand dollars from the program. The grants were then $1,850 for each eligible student, and for the 1976–77 school year the grants were to be $2,500. According to Sheldon Jackson it has

suffered "a substantially diminished capacity" to function as an educational institution as a result of the termination of the tuition grant program, as reflected in a
reduction of students, faculty, income and curriculum offerings. Inupiat University
claims a similar impairment of function.

Finally, though the tuition grants are nominally paid from the public treasury
directly to the student, the student here is merely a conduit for the transmission of
state funds to private colleges. Before the state will deliver a check to the student,
the latter must certify under oath and under penalty of perjury that he or she will
pay it over to the college. Simply interposing an intermediary "does not have a cleansing
effect and somehow cause the funds to lose their identity as public funds. While the
ingenuity of man is apparently limitless, the Court has held with unvarying regularity
that one may not do by indirection what is forbidden directly."

Based on the foregoing we have no difficulty in concluding that the tuition grant
program is in its effect a direct benefit to private educational institutions and therefore
violates article VII, section 1, of our constitution. Though Sheldon Jackson points out
that several courts have upheld tuition grant programs involving college students, and
that aid programs involving colleges have more readily been found constitutional than
similar programs involving elementary and secondary schools, the cited decisions rely
on the *de minimis* degree of church control in the benefitted sectarian colleges. Such
reasoning obviously has no application with respect to article VII's direct benefit
prohibition, which bans aid to all private educational institutions, including those
with no religious affiliation.

Sheldon Jackson also argues that the direct benefit clause was not meant to apply
to colleges and universities, but only to primary and secondary private educational
institutions. We see no basis for this contention. Both the plain language of the
constitution and the minutes of the constitutional debate indicate that all private
educational institutions were meant to be included. The judgment is AFFIRMED.

Witters v. Washington Department of Services for the Blind

474 U.S. 481 (1986)

Justice MARSHALL delivered the opinion of the Court.

The Washington Supreme Court ruled that the First Amendment precludes the State
of Washington from extending assistance under a state vocational rehabilitation assistance program to a blind person studying at a Christian college and seeking to
become a pastor, missionary, or youth director. Finding no such federal constitutional
barrier on the record presented to us, we reverse and remand.

I

Petitioner Larry Witters applied in 1979 to the Washington Commission for the
Blind for vocational rehabilitation services pursuant to Wash. Rev. Code § 74.16.181
(1981). That statute authorized the Commission, *inter alia*, to "[p]rovide for special
education and/or training in the professions, business or trades" so as to "assist
visually handicapped persons to overcome vocational handicaps and to obtain the
maximum degree of self-support and self-care." Petitioner, suffering from a progressive eye condition, was eligible for vocational rehabilitation assistance under the terms

of the statute. He was at the time attending Inland Empire School of the Bible, a private Christian college in Spokane, Washington, and studying bible, ethics, speech, and church administration in order to equip himself for a career as a pastor, missionary, or youth director.

The Commission denied petitioner aid. It relied on an earlier determination embodied in a Commission policy statement that "[t]he Washington State constitution forbids the use of public funds to assist an individual in the pursuit of a career or degree in theology or related areas," and on its conclusion that petitioner's training was "religious instruction" subject to that ban. That ruling was affirmed by a state hearings examiner, who held that the Commission was precluded from funding petitioner's training "in light of the State Constitution's prohibition against the state directly or indirectly supporting a religion." The hearings examiner cited Wash. Const., Art. I, § 11, providing in part that "no public money or property shall be appropriated for or applied to any religious worship, exercise or instruction, or the support of any religious establishment," and Wash. Const., Art. IX, § 4, providing that "[a]ll schools maintained or supported wholly or in part by the public funds shall be forever free from sectarian control or influence." That ruling, in turn, was upheld on internal administrative appeal.

Petitioner then instituted an action in state superior court for review of the administrative decision; the court affirmed on the same state-law grounds cited by the agency. The State Supreme Court affirmed as well. The Supreme Court, however, declined to ground its ruling on the Washington Constitution. Instead, it explicitly reserved judgment on the state constitutional issue and chose to base its ruling on the Establishment Clause of the Federal Constitution. The court stated:

> "The Supreme Court has developed a 3-part test for determining the constitutionality of state aid under the establishment clause of the First Amendment. 'First, the statute must have a secular legislative purpose; second, its principal or primary effect must be one that neither advances nor inhibits religion...; finally, the statute must not foster "an excessive government entanglement with religion." ' To withstand attack under the establishment clause, the challenged state action must satisfy each of the three criteria."

The Washington court had no difficulty finding the "secular purpose" prong of that test satisfied. Applying the second prong, however, that of "principal or primary effect," the court held that "[t]he provision of financial assistance by the State to enable someone to become a pastor, missionary, or church youth director clearly has the primary effect of advancing religion." The court, therefore, held that provision of aid to petitioner would contravene the Federal Constitution. In light of that ruling, the court saw no need to reach the "entanglement" prong; it stated that the record was in any case inadequate for such an inquiry.

We granted certiorari, and we now reverse.

II

The Establishment Clause of the First Amendment has consistently presented this Court with difficult questions of interpretation and application. We acknowledged in *Lemon v. Kurtzman*, that "we can only dimly perceive the lines of demarcation in this extraordinarily sensitive area of constitutional law." Nonetheless, the Court's opinions in this area have at least clarified "the broad contours of our inquiry," and are sufficient to dispose of this case.

We are guided, as was the court below, by the three-part test set out by this Court in *Lemon*. Our analysis relating to the first prong of that test is simple: all parties concede the unmistakably secular purpose of the Washington program. That program was designed to promote the well-being of the visually handicapped through the provision of vocational rehabilitation services, and no more than a minuscule amount of the aid awarded under the program is likely to flow to religious education. No party suggests that the State's "actual purpose" in creating the program was to endorse religion, or that the secular purpose articulated by the legislature is merely "sham."

The answer to the question posed by the second prong of the *Lemon* test is more difficult. We conclude, however, that extension of aid to petitioner is not barred on that ground either. It is well-settled that the Establishment Clause is not violated every time money previously in the possession of a State is conveyed to a religious institution. For example, a State may issue a paycheck to one of its employees, who may then donate all or part of that paycheck to a religious institution, all without constitutional barrier; and the State may do so even knowing that the employee so intends to dispose of his salary. It is equally well-settled, on the other hand, that the State may not grant aid to a religious school, whether cash or in-kind, where the effect of the aid is "that of a direct subsidy to the religious school" from the State. Aid may have that effect even though it takes the form of aid to students or parents. The question presented is whether, on the facts as they appear in the record before us, extension of aid to petitioner and the use of that aid by petitioner to support his religious education is a permissible transfer similar to the hypothetical salary donation described above, or is an impermissible "direct subsidy."

Certain aspects of Washington's program are central to our inquiry. As far as the record shows, vocational assistance provided under the Washington program is paid directly to the student, who transmits it to the educational institution of his or her choice. Any aid provided under Washington's program that ultimately flows to religious institutions does so only as a result of the genuinely independent and private choices of aid recipients. Washington's program is "made available generally without regard to the sectarian-nonsectarian, or public-nonpublic nature of the institution benefited," and is in no way skewed towards religion. It is not one of "the ingenious plans for channeling state aid to sectarian schools that periodically reach this Court." It creates no financial incentive for students to undertake sectarian education. It does not tend to provide greater or broader benefits for recipients who apply their aid to religious education, nor are the full benefits of the program limited, in large part or in whole, to students at sectarian institutions. On the contrary, aid recipients have full opportunity to expend vocational rehabilitation aid on wholly secular education, and as a practical matter have rather greater prospects to do so. Aid recipients' choices are made among a huge variety of possible careers, of which only a small handful are sectarian. In this case, the fact that aid goes to individuals means that the decision to support religious education is made by the individual, not by the State.

Further, and importantly, nothing in the record indicates that, if petitioner succeeds, any significant portion of the aid expended under the Washington program as a whole will end up flowing to religious education. The function of the Washington program is hardly "to provide desired financial support for nonpublic, sectarian institutions." The program, providing vocational assistance to the visually handicapped, does not seem well-suited to serve as the vehicle for such a subsidy. No evidence has been presented indicating that any other person has ever sought to finance religious education or activity pursuant to the State's program. The combination of these factors, we think, makes the link between the State and the school petitioner wishes to attend a highly attenuated one.

On the facts we have set out, it does not seem appropriate to view any aid ultimately flowing to the Inland Empire School of the Bible as resulting from a *state* action sponsoring or subsidizing religion. Nor does the mere circumstance that petitioner has chosen to use neutrally available state aid to help pay for his religious education confer any message of state endorsement of religion. Thus, while *amici* supporting respondent are correct in pointing out that aid to a religious institution unrestricted in its potential uses, if properly attributable to the State, is "clearly prohibited under the Establishment Clause," because it may subsidize the religious functions of that institution, that observation is not apposite to this case. On the facts present here, we think the Washington program works no state support of religion prohibited by the Establishment Clause.

III

We therefore reject the claim that, on the record presented, extension of aid under Washington's vocational rehabilitation program to finance petitioner's training at a Christian college to become a pastor, missionary, or youth director would advance religion in a manner inconsistent with the Establishment Clause of the First Amendment. On remand, the state court is of course free to consider the applicability of the "far stricter" dictates of the Washington state constitution. It may also choose to reopen the factual record in order to consider the arguments made by respondent. We decline petitioner's invitation to leapfrog consideration of those issues by holding that the Free Exercise Clause *requires* Washington to extend vocational rehabilitation aid to petitioner regardless of what the state constitution commands or further factual development reveals, and we express no opinion on that matter.

The judgment of the Washington Supreme Court is reversed, and the case is remanded for further proceedings not inconsistent with this opinion.

It is so ordered.

Warder v. Board of Regents of the State of New York
423 N.E.2d 352 (1981)

COOKE, Chief Judge.

Petitioners, proposed trustees of the Unification Theological Seminary, challenge as arbitrary the denial of a provisional charter by the Board of Regents. The Seminary, an educational institution in Barrytown, New York, is sponsored and financially supported by the Holy Spirit Association for the Unification of World Christianity ("Unification Church"), a religious organization incorporated in California in 1961. Since 1975, the Seminary has offered a two-year graduate program of religious education. Seeking incorporation and the authority to confer Master of Religious Education degrees, petitioners applied to the Board of Regents and Commissioner of Education for a provisional charter. Following a lengthy investigation of the Seminary, its sponsor and the educational program offered, the application was denied.

A review of the proceedings is necessary in order to evaluate petitioners' claims. The provisional charter application was submitted in April, 1975. The State Education Department reviewed the application, investigated the Seminary and, in June, 1976, the Deputy Commissioner of Higher and Professional Education issued a report favorable to the Seminary but recommending that action be deferred in light of pending and anticipated investigations of the parent organization. In the fall of 1976, in accordance with Education Department practice, the Seminary was evaluated by two independent consultants. The consultants, while noting certain areas of concern, recommended approval. By February, 1977, the office of counsel for the State Education Department, the Deputy Commissioner of Higher and Professional Education and the Commissioner of Education had recommended approval of the application, which was then forwarded to the Board of Regents for action at the February, 1977 meeting. No action was taken at that time.

In March of that year, legislative resolutions cited recently publicized concern about the policies and practices of the Unification Church and requested the Board of Regents to delay its decision pending investigation. The matter was deferred again following the April meeting of the board, at which Regents Yavner and Griffith, during debate, expressed concern about provisional charter approval, in light of unresolved questions as to faculty and programs and the charges against the Unification Church of involvement with the South Korean government and Korean Central Intelligence Agency (KCIA). They were also concerned about charges that the church and its leaders engaged in or encouraged brain-washing and deceptive practices. Yavner commented critically on the book containing the religious tenets of the church and was of the opinion that it was a political as well as a religious document. Griffith went further to express disapproval of the purposes and activities of the church, which he felt were incompatible with the principles of our society. Yavner moved to delay a decision pending further review by a committee of Regents appointed by the board. The motion carried and Regents Genrich, who would have granted approval and voted against delay, and Yavner together with Bongiorno, another Regent, were appointed to the committee.

Petitioners, dissatisfied with the progress on the Seminary application, commenced an article 78 proceeding in July, 1977 to compel a decision. The proceeding was dismissed upon a determination that the delay was not unreasonable.

In mid-November, 1977, the Regents committee issued a preliminary progress report summarizing the information it had obtained. As to the academic questions, the report summarized the reports of the original consultants and another independent consultant, all of which found the program, facilities and administration adequate. As to the related issues, the committee as yet had found no evidence of a link between the Seminary and the Korean government or KCIA, or of brainwashing at the Seminary or by members of the Unification Church. The committee noted that further investigation by it was necessary because pending investigations by other governmental agencies had not been completed. Furthermore, information obtained by the committee raised questions concerning the Seminary's stability, financing plan and dependence upon the Unification Church as its source of income, and the church's alleged policy of deception in fundraising and recruitment. The Seminary was to be questioned on these matters and given an opportunity to respond.

Petitioners thereafter were requested to furnish affidavits concerning KCIA involvement, recruitment and fundraising techniques of the Unification Church and an audited financial statement from the church. The Education Department, under the direction of the committee, issued a staff report on December 7, 1977, which noted that it was still awaiting responses to some of the questions raised in the previous report. The staff also had confirmed that the Unification Church of New York, Inc., the organization upon which the Seminary was to rely for financial support through a lease arrangement, had become inactive, having transferred the majority of its assets and liabilities to the California organization. A request was outstanding for the submission of an alternative financing plan. The staff stated that evidence, in the form of affidavits and statements from former church members, was available concerning deceptive practices used by church members in fundraising and recruitment but that there was no evidence of advocacy of illegal activities by leaders of the church or petitioners or at the Seminary and no evidence that the Seminary, petitioners or Unification Church were involved with the KCIA.

Before the December, 1977 meeting of the Board of Regents, petitioners were provided with copies of and invited to respond to the information that had been received by the committee. The December meeting produced a decision to defer action on the application in light of the receipt of additional allegations against the church and Seminary, including representations of deception concerning the Seminary program and noncompliance with admissions and program requirements established by the Seminary. Petitioners were also informed that the financial statement of the Unification Church, the substituted lessee of Seminary property, was inadequate and were again requested to submit a statement in audited form.

Petitioners were informed on December 19 that a review team from the Education Department would visit the Seminary on December 20 to review its records. Following that visit, the Education Department and Regents committee recommended that the application be denied. The findings were that the Seminary had represented itself through brochures and transcripts as having degree-granting status, that the student records showed that some graduates had not completed the number of credits or courses represented by the Seminary to be required, that admissions requirements set up by the Seminary, such as submission of GRE scores, letters of recommendation, and undergraduate transcripts, had not been enforced and that no audited financial statement for the Unification Church had been submitted.

Petitioners were given the opportunity to respond to the committee report and submitted denials of and explanations for the perceived deficiencies, including oversight, program evolution and practical difficulties. The Board of Regents, at the January, 1978 meeting, again deferred action to allow the Education Department to consider petitioners' response. The Education Department and Regents committee issued a final report in February, which addressed issues disputed in petitioners' response, found the explanations inadequate to remove concern over the deficiencies and adhered to its recommendation for denial. At the February meeting of the board, that body voted unanimously to deny the application based on the findings and conclusions of the Regents committee reports.

Petitioners commenced the second article 78 proceeding challenging the determination as arbitrary on numerous grounds, including bias, administrative abuse and the application of imprecise standards. Respondents' motion for summary judgment was granted and the petition dismissed. Petitioners appealed this judgment and the judgment in the first article 78 proceeding to the Appellate Division. That court affirmed both judgments, concluding that the delay in the decision was not unreasonable and that no constitutional rights had been violated by the investigation or determination. Petitioners were granted leave to appeal to this court.

Petitioners maintain that the Board of Regents determination should be annulled as arbitrary because it represents an abuse of the administrative process and the violation of petitioners' substantive and procedural rights, and because the statutes, rules and regulations under which the Board of Regents acted are unconstitutionally vague. Finally, petitioners urge that summary judgment was improper on this record. Their contentions are not persuasive.

It is well settled that in reviewing administrative action a court may not substitute its judgment for that of the agency responsible for making the determination, but must ascertain only whether there is a rational basis for the decision or whether it is arbitrary and capricious. Deference to the judgment of the agency, when supported by the record, is particularly appropriate when the matter under review involves a factual evaluation in the area of the agency's expertise. These principles in mind, it is concluded that the determination to deny has a rational basis.

The Education Department discovered serious inconsistencies between the Seminary's practice and the method by which it represented it would operate. Student records did not accurately reflect work done and admissions and program standards set up by the Seminary were not adhered to or were changed without publication or notification to the department. The erroneous impression was given that the Seminary had degree-granting status. The records at the very least evidenced inadequate administration. Although the Seminary explained certain inconsistencies, neither the department nor the board was bound to adopt the explanations as sufficient to dispel the impression of poor administration and conduct of the academic program. Finally, following the discovery that the original sponsoring organization had become inactive and a new organization had been substituted, the Seminary failed to submit audited financial statements for the substituted organization as requested. Thus, the Seminary failed to satisfy the board of its financial resources. These deficiencies rationally could be considered contrary to the standards necessary for charter approval.

Unable to challenge the determination on the basis of the findings, petitioners mount a broad-based attack on the entire decision-making process as abusive and unlawful and urge that the findings were contrived to mask the board's predetermined decision to deny the provisional charter.

*   *   *

It is here urged that the board transgressed permissible limits when it delayed decision beyond February, 1977 to engage in a broad investigation of the policies and practices of the Seminary and its sponsor, even after the favorable recommendations of the Education Department and consultants. Acceptance of this argument in the face of the record would place an unwarranted restriction on the board's power to discharge its responsibility to the people of this State. The board was not bound by the initial recommendations of the Education Department and the consultants. Areas of concern in the Seminary program identified in the consultants' reports, such as the extent of faculty accessibility and unclear program objectives and intent, reasonably and justifiably could prompt a request by the board for further study and evaluation. In addition, at the time the application was first submitted to the board for action, substantial public concern about the practices of the Seminary's sponsoring organization had been voiced by State and Federal legislators, members of the clergy and others. Reports of KCIA involvement, brainwashing and encouragement of deceptive fundraising and recruitment practices were widespread. The board had a right to investigate the serious allegations of illegal or unethical conduct on the part of the Seminary sponsors and determine whether the Seminary participated in or encouraged such conduct.

Petitioners do not and cannot dispute that the board validly could deny a provisional charter to an institution that engaged in "brainwashing" and deception. That the broad investigation revealed no evidence of such practices does not mean that it was improperly undertaken in the first instance. The board cannot now be faulted because it discharged its responsibility for ensuring ethical educational programs of quality and in the process discovered serious deficiencies in the conduct of the academic program.

* * *

It follows that a determination based not on a dispassionate review of facts but on a body's prejudgment or biased evaluation must be set aside. But a mere allegation of bias will not suffice. There must be a factual demonstration to support the allegation of bias and proof that the outcome flowed from it. Here, there is neither.

True, two Regents expressed strong opposition to charter approval for the Seminary during the April, 1977 board meeting, noting the charges of political activity, brainwashing and deception. But it was at that same meeting that these Regents requested further investigations. Only one, Regent Yavner, became a committee member. Of the two other members, one was equally outspoken in favor of charter approval. The reports from that committee were frank with respect to the lack of evidence found to substantiate the charges. The Regents' comments, in the context in which they were made and in the light of subsequent actions of the committee and the board, do not evidence an inability on the part of the particular Regents or the whole board to make an unbiased evaluation of the application once all the facts were in. Nor is a question of fact raised as to bias by the isolated statement allegedly made by an unnamed member of the December, 1977 review team that the controversy was political rather than academic and that the team had come to "find" a basis for the decision about to be made by the board. The source of this statement is unnamed and the facts upon which the statement was based are undisclosed. Such a bare assertion does not establish a fact question warranting denial of summary judgment.

Petitioners also maintain that the statutes, rules and regulations under which the board acted are unconstitutionally vague and lacking in objective standards. This court has not hesitated to annul a determination predicated on rules and regulations that allow wholly subjective decisionmaking without adequate "safeguards against the exercise of arbitrary power or simple unfairness." Here, however, no such unrestrained power is evident. Rather, the scheme for provisional charter approval is integrated with that for program registration and provides sufficiently objective standards to enable meaningful judicial review. It must be remembered that in the area of determining qualifications for educational institutions, where the nature and quality of programs necessarily will vary, precise criteria cannot be expected or demanded. The statutes and regulations at issue here offer sufficiently concrete guidelines and standards for judging an applicant to prevent the unfettered or arbitrary exercise of discretion.

The record reveals that no material factual question has been raised by petitioners concerning bias or an abuse of the administrative process. Petitioners were not denied due process by the procedures employed. Summary judgment was properly granted.

Accordingly, the orders of the Appellate Division should be affirmed, with costs.

State ex rel. McLemore v. Clarksville School
636 S.W.2d 706 (1982)

BROCK, Justice.

The Clarksville School of Theology is a postsecondary degree-granting school of theology which has not complied with the requirements for degree-granting institutions established by the Tennessee Higher Education Commission pursuant to the Postsecondary Education Authorization Act of 1974. The Attorney General, as authorized and directed by T.C.A., § 49–3924, brought this action for declaratory and injunctive relief seeking to prohibit the Clarksville School of Theology from granting degrees until it shall meet the requirements of the Act.

The School contends that application of the Act to it would deprive it of its right of free exercise of religion, guaranteed by the First Amendment to the Constitution of the United States and by Art. I, Section 3, of the Tennessee Constitution. The School alleges that its budget will not permit it to meet the criteria of the Act and that it will be forced out of business if required to do so; it alleges further that, if it is not permitted to grant degrees, enrollments of students will decline so greatly that it will be forced out of business. The State contends that the granting of degrees is a purely secular activity and in no way affects the free exercise of religion by the appellants and, therefore, that the School should be required to comply with the law.

Upon an earlier appeal in this case, we remanded the cause to the trial court for further development of the facts. Upon the remand, a full evidentiary hearing was conducted, resulting in a well documented and detailed finding of fact and conclusions of law contained in a memorandum opinion filed by Judge Boaz, which, in pertinent part, we adopt as a part of this opinion, and is as follows:

. . .

"At said hearing there was a full development of facts with an extensive explanation of the procedure under the regulations of the State Postsecondary Education Commission as applied to similarly situated institutions, as well as an explanation of the study procedure, the courses covered and not covered, and the degrees awarded by the defendant School.

"In general, the Tennessee Higher Education Commission, according to the proof, followed the standards approved and in use by the Southern Association of Colleges and Schools, but the application was somewhat less stringent. The Act went into effect on July 1, 1975, and in October, 1975, the Clarksville School of Theology was sent an application form, and eventually, an application was filed by the defendant School on January 15, 1976. The application was denied on January 22, 1976, but the defendant School was permitted to complete its 25th year and it was agreed, according to the correspondence between the Commission and the defendant School, that the defendant would cease operation at that time. The defendant School has, however, continued to operate and to issue postsecondary degrees without approval of the Tennessee Higher Education Commission and in violation of the Act.

"The defendant School offered proof, through its President of 28 years, as to the program of study followed by its students and the degrees offered by the Clarksville School of Theology. He testified that the purpose of the institution was to help many preachers, especially Baptist, who had never had the opportunity to receive a theological degree. He stated that the School granted a Bachelor of Theology, a Master of Theology, and a Doctor of Theology. For the Bachelor's degree, for example, he stated that the applicant must (1) have faith, (2) must be a pastor or evangelist, (3) must complete a 'synthetic Bible study' and write a thesis of 30,000 words. He further stated that the School teaches only religion, that no science, mathematics or any other such course was offered. He stated that a Bachelor of Theology degree, for example, cost $25 at enrollment, $320 tuition and $30 for a cap and gown. He admitted that the students must attend only three 'seminars' on March 3, June 6, and October 10, this being the only classroom attendance required. He testified that the School must grant education degrees, or the students would not attend. Two additional witnesses testified they would not have attended the Clarksville School of Theology unless degrees were granted. It was shown, incidentally, that last year the School had 80 students and that the largest budget in one year had been $37,000.00. The President of the defendant School testified that it was a non-profit School, that the receipts from tuition were used to maintain the buildings of the defendants.

"It seems to the court that the first question to resolve is whether or not the Postsecondary Education Authorization Act of 1974 was intended to apply to the defendant School. Under Tennessee Code Annotated, § 49–3902, the purpose of the Act is stated as: to provide for the protection, education, and welfare of the citizens of the state of Tennessee, its postsecondary educational institutions and its standards, by: (a) establishing minimum standards concerning the quality of education, ethical and business practices, health and safety, and fiscal responsibility, to protect against substandard, transient, unethical, deceptive, or fraudulent institutions and practices; and (b) authorizing the granting of degrees, diplomas, certificates or other educational credentials by postsecondary education institutions and prohibiting the granting of false or misleading educational credentials.... It would seem that it was the intent of the legislature to include the defendant School, and, there being no words in the Act which would specifically exclude the defendant School, it is held that the Act does apply.

"The most important question and the one most difficult to resolve, due to its delicate nature, is the question of whether or not applying the Act to the defendant School would infringe upon defendant's right to the free exercise of religion as protected by the State and Federal Constitutions.

"The Act sets out the minimum requirements before a postsecondary educational institution will be issued the necessary authorization to operate. Only those institutions so authorized may issue educational credentials or degrees. The Act makes no attempt to regulate or control the religious beliefs, practices or teachings of any institution. The defendant School insists that it cannot operate unless it can issue educational degrees. However, it is not made to appear by the proof that issuing educational degrees is a religious tenet of the defendants, nor that the operation of the School is prompted or required by religious beliefs. In fact, the School is inhibited in no way by the Act as far as religion is concerned, the Act only proscribing the issuance of educational credentials by those institutions failing to meet the minimum requirements. The court holds, therefore, that applying the Act to defendant School does not violate the free exercise of religion clause of the Constitution, State or Federal.

"The School, as its President admits, has not and cannot meet the requirements of the Act, and yet it insists on the right to issue educational credentials, including a Bachelor of Theology, a Master of Theology and a Doctor of Theology. It is the inescapable conclusion of the court that these are false or misleading educational credentials, as specifically prohibited in (b) of T.C.A., § 49–3902.

"In view of the above decision, an injunction should issue prohibiting the defendants from issuing any further educational degrees."

If the Act placed a burden upon the free exercise of religion by the defendants or posed a threat of entanglement between the affairs of the church and the state, the state would be required to show that "some compelling state interest" justified the burden and that there exists no less restrictive or entangling alternative.

We conclude, however, that this Act places neither a direct nor indirect burden upon the free exercise of religion by the defendants nor threatens an entanglement between the affairs of church and state. As the Chancellor noted in his memorandum opinion, above quoted, the Act does not regulate the beliefs, practices or teachings of any institution; it merely sets forth minimum standards which must be met in order for an institution to be authorized to issue degrees. Moreover, the evidence shows that the granting of degrees is a purely secular activity. It is only this activity that brings the School under the regulation of the Act.

*   *   *

As noted by the Chancellor, no proof has been offered in this case that operation of the Clarksville School of Theology is required by religious beliefs of the defendants; but, if such were the case, the application of this Act would only prohibit the granting of degrees by them and would not interfere with the content or methods of instruction. The School can choose to not comply with the Act and yet may continue to train ministers as it chooses; such noncompliance with the Act will simply prohibit the School from granting degrees.

*   *   *

It is established in the evidence that granting a degree is not a part of the Clarksville School of Theology's religious beliefs and is not considered by it to be religious activity. Indeed, the President and founder of the School testified that getting a degree was not a tenet of faith followed by the School. Nevertheless, the School contends that application of the statute to it has an indirect effect on its religious activity of educating ministers. It contends that the effect confronts it with two choices: (1) If it continues to award degrees, it would have to comply with the Tennessee Higher Education Commission regulations which, it contends, it cannot and would not be able to do and, thus, would have to close its doors or (2) if it stopped awarding degrees, no one would desire to attend the School and, again, it would slowly cease to exit. Therefore, the School claims that the Act indirectly prohibits it from carrying on the religious activity of training ministers.

Nevertheless, the fact remains that the State is merely regulating the awarding of educational degrees. The supposed predicament of the School is not a result of the state's regulation of its religious function of *training ministers* but of its pre-eminent role of *awarding degrees* which is, as conceded by its President and founder, a purely secular activity.

The reliance of the appellants upon *Sherbert v. Verner, Wisconsin v. Yoder,* and *McDaniel v. Paty* is misplaced. In each of these cases, the effect of the state law was to impose an indirect burden upon the right of free exercise of religion. For example, in *Sherbert* the South Carolina statute forced the citizen to choose between her right to receive unemployment benefits and her right to practice her religion by keeping Saturday as the Sabbath. Said the court:

> "The ruling forces her to choose between following the precepts of her religion and forfeiting benefits, on the one hand, and abandoning one of the precepts of her religion in order to accept work, on the other hand. Government imposition of such a choice puts the same kind of burden upon the free exercise of religion as would a fine imposed against appellant for her Saturday worship."

The statute here under consideration does not require any individual to violate religious convictions. The Clarksville School of Theology does not claim as a tenet of its religion that its ministers should receive academic degrees. Thus, no *Sherbert, Yoder*, or *McDaniel* type of dilemma is posed in the instant case.

We find no constitutional infirmity in the statute; the decree of the trial court is affirmed. Costs incurred on appeal are taxed against the appellants.

On occasion, religious factionalism involves colleges in legal entanglements. *World Teacher Seminar v. Iowa District Court for Jefferson County* involved one such internecine war over the direction of Maharishi International University, 406 N.W.2d 173 (Iowa, 1987), and at the University of Houston in 1984, two religious factions went to court after a schism to determine which was the group entitled to use the religion center facilities for meetings and worship. The case was settled, but only after the University was brought into the case by both sides.

The Establishment of Public Colleges and State Agency

Because many institutions were established before the rise of state agency doctrines, it is not always a simple matter to discover whether a state agency principle applies to a public institution. Often, some state laws or regulations will make it clear, but equally often, the statutes or regulations are silent on the issue. In *Sprague v. University of Vermont*, the Court found the University of Vermont to be a "state agency," subject to the state's open meeting law, Public Records Law, and Fair Employment Practices Act, but not subject to the Administrative Procedure Act. See A. Bonfield, *State*

Administrative Rule Making (Boston: Little, Brown and Co., 1986); L. Glenny and T. Dalglish, *Public Universities, State Agencies, and the Law* (Berkeley: Center for Research and Development in Higher Education, 1973).

Goss v. San Jacinto Junior College
588 F.2d 96 (1979)

INGRAHAM, Circuit Judge:

This case arose out of the non-renewal of the teaching contract of an untenured public junior college instructor. Mrs. Patsy Goss brought suit against San Jacinto Junior College, the Board of Regents, certain administrators and faculty members, and the President, Dr. Thomas Spencer, in his individual capacity, alleging that she was denied renewal of her contract in retaliation for her exercise of First Amendment rights. A jury verdict was rendered and judgment entered in favor of Mrs. Goss and against the junior college and its president. Mrs. Goss was awarded $23,400 in back pay. Finding that the appellants' jurisdictional, constitutional, and evidentiary arguments are without merit, we affirm the entry of judgment.

Mrs. Goss was hired by San Jacinto Junior College in 1966 as an untenured history instructor. She had earned a bachelor of arts degree from Texas Christian University and a master of arts degree from the University of Texas. She was then enrolled in a doctoral degree program at the University of Houston. Her contract with San Jacinto Junior College was renewed annually for six years.

During those six years, Mrs. Goss participated in the formation of a local chapter of the National Faculty Association, the college division affiliate of the National Education Association, and initiated efforts to organize a local chapter of the Texas Junior College Teachers Association. She also campaigned on behalf of her husband, Dr. Allen Goss, in his bid for a seat on the San Jacinto Junior College Board of Regents.

On April 5, 1972, Mrs. Goss was advised in writing by Dr. Spencer that the Board of Regents had voted not to renew her teaching contract for the coming academic year, because of declining enrollment and the poor evaluation of her work. A hearing was convened by the Board of Regents at Mrs. Goss' request, after which the Board affirmed its decision.

Mrs. Goss filed a complaint on November 22, 1972, alleging that the non-renewal of her teaching contract was in retaliation for her exercise of First Amendment rights in violation of 42 U.S.C. § 1983 (1970). San Jacinto Junior College reinstated Mrs. Goss in the fall of 1974. The action proceeded to a trial by jury in the summer of 1976. The jury found that Mrs. Goss' contract had not been renewed for the 1972–73 and 1973–74 academic years because of her involvement in teacher associations and/or the Board of Regents election. She was awarded $23,400 in compensatory damages for lost employment.

Appellants contend that the district court lacked subject matter jurisdiction under both 28 U.S.C. § 1331 (1970) and 28 U.S.C. § 1343 (1970).

Appellants first argue that the amount in controversy is insufficient to support federal question jurisdiction under § 1331(a). Mrs. Goss sought $40,000 in compensatory damages in her complaint. The test of the sufficiency of a pleading for jurisdictional amount is well-established:

> [T]he sum claimed by the plaintiff controls if the claim is apparently made in good faith. It must appear to a legal certainty that the claim is really for less than the jurisdictional amount to justify dismissal. The inability of plaintiff to recover an amount adequate to give the court jurisdiction does not show his bad faith or oust the jurisdiction.

Thus, appellants' assertion of defenses to the amount claimed will not destroy federal question jurisdiction. Since Mrs. Goss sought reinstatement to a position with an annual salary in excess of $10,000, it was far from a "legal certainty" at the time the complaint was filed that Mrs. Goss would not have been entitled to more than $10,000. Jurisdiction was proper under § 1331.

Alternatively, jurisdiction was proper under 28 U.S.C. § 1343 (1970). Appellants argue that San Jacinto Junior College is not a "person" under 42 U.S.C. § 1983 (1970), and that, therefore, jurisdiction is lacking under § 1343. The recent Supreme Court decision in *Monell v. Dept. of Social Services of City of New York* held that local government entities and local independent school boards are "persons" for purposes of § 1983. Such persons are not entitled to an immunity defense "when execution of a government's policy or custom, whether made by its lawmakers or by those whose edicts or acts may fairly be said to represent official policy, inflicts the injury."

Although the district court did not have the benefit of *Monell*, the court's jury instructions comport with the reasoning of *Monell*. After charging the jury that a "ban on the right of teachers to express political opinions and engage in political activities is inconsistent with the First Amendment," the court stated that "[t]he execution of any such policy or practice through a denial for reemployment . . . would be prohibited." In answers to interrogatories, the jury found that the Board of Regents voted not to renew Mrs. Goss' teaching contract on the recommendation of Dr. Spencer, because of Mrs. Goss' constitutionally protected activity. As President of the Junior College, Dr. Spencer is surely one "whose edicts or acts may fairly be said to represent official policy." Since the requirements of *Monell* were satisfied by the court's instructions and the jury findings, no purpose would be served by remanding the case for reconsideration.

Appellants argue that even if the district court had jurisdiction, the Eleventh Amendment bars the award of damages against San Jacinto Junior College under *Edelman v. Jordan*. *Edelman* held that while states and state officials are protected by the Eleventh Amendment, mere "political subdivisions" of the state do not enjoy Eleventh Amendment immunity. The issue here is whether San Jacinto Junior College is to be treated as an arm of the state or a "political subdivision." The nature of the entity under state law guides our decision. Addressing the same issue in *Hander v. San Jacinto Junior College*, we held that San Jacinto Junior College is an independent "political subdivision" as a matter of Texas statutory and common law. *Hander* leaves no doubt that this appellant has no Eleventh Amendment immunity.

The district court had jurisdiction over the subject matter of this lawsuit under 28 U.S.C. §§ 1331 and 1343 (1970). San Jacinto Junior College is not immune from damages under the Eleventh Amendment. There is sufficient evidence to support the jury findings that the Board of Regents discharged Mrs. Goss because of her First Amendment activity rather than the quality of her teaching or the enrollment at the junior college. Accordingly, we affirm the district court's entry of judgment.

Krynicky v. University of Pittsburgh

742 F.2d 94 (1984)

BECKER, Circuit Judge.

These consolidated appeals present the question whether the recent Supreme Court decisions in effect overruled this court's decision in *Braden v. University of Pittsburgh*, which held that the University of Pittsburgh (and by implication Temple University) are "state actors" for purposes of 42 U.S.C. § 1983.

The district courts reached differing results. In *Krynicky* the district court concluded that the *Lugar* trilogy had undermined *Braden*, and held that, because the Commonwealth of Pennsylvania had not participated with the University of Pittsburgh in making the faculty tenure decision challenged by Krynicky, the University's decision was not subject to the constraints of the fourteenth amendment. In *Schier* the district court reached the opposite result, holding that *Braden* was still controlling, and that the Commonwealth had so far insinuated itself into the operation of Temple University that the institution was subject to the mandates of the fourteenth amendment in connection with Schier's claim of retaliatory discharge.

Because we believe that *Braden* has not been overruled by the *Lugar* trilogy, we reverse in *Krynicky* and affirm in *Schier*.

I. *FACTUAL AND PROCEDURAL HISTORY*

A. *Krynicky*

Harry Krynicky, an Assistant Professor of English at the University of Pittsburgh, brought suit against the University and various administrative officials under 42 U.S.C. § 1983, alleging that he had a "property" and "liberty" interest in his employment contract within the meaning of the fourteenth amendment, and that the University infringed those interests when it failed to notify him in a timely fashion of its decision to deny him tenure. In addition, Krynicky alleged that the tenure process generally denied him due process, and that the decision to deny him tenure was made in retaliation for his outspoken criticism of the University administration and his unorthodox teaching methods. The linchpin of Krynicky's claim for purposes of this appeal is that the University's actions were taken "under color of state law" within the meaning of § 1983 because of the relationship between the Commonwealth of Pennsylvania and the University.

The University and the individual defendants moved for summary judgment, but did not contest the existence of state action in the motion. The district court granted the motions in part. Defendants then amended their answer to assert that there was no state action as required by § 1983, and again moved for summary judgment. The district court thereupon granted the motion as to the remaining claims, stating that the reasoning of *Rendell-Baker* and *Blum* essentially superseded the Third Circuit's analysis in *Braden*, and that, therefore, *Braden* did not control. The court held that "the receipt of revenue from the state, membership of state nominees on the University's Board of Trustees, and statutory recognition that the University is part of the state's system of higher education are not sufficient to make the University's employment policies state decisions."

B. *Schier*

Rosemary Schier, who was an employee of Temple University Hospital from September 1979 through September 3, 1981, brought suit against the University alleging that during the course of her employment, she was discriminated against on grounds of her sex, and that her supervisor had sexually harassed her, had retaliated against her for having filed internal complaints, and had forced her to sign a resignation memorandum. Schier sought relief under 42 U.S.C. § 1983 and under Title VII of the Civil Rights Act of 1964.

At the close of discovery, Temple moved for summary judgment on all claims, asserting that the Title VII claim was time-barred and that Schier had not presented any facts to support her claim that Temple had acted under color of state law for the purposes of § 1983. The district court granted summary judgment on Schier's Title VII claim, but denied Temple's motion on the § 1983 claim, holding that, under the symbiotic relationship test for state action articulated in *Burton v. Wilmington Parking Authority*, the state had a sufficiently close relationship with Temple that actions taken by Temple were subject to constitutional scrutiny under section 1983. In reaching its decision, the district court considered the applicability of the *Lugar* trilogy to its decision, but concluded that *Blum* and *Rendell-Baker* did not overrule *Burton*, and that, therefore, the Third Circuit's opinion in *Braden* was still good law. However, recognizing that another district court in the circuit had reached the opposite result in the *Krynicky* case, the court certified for interlocutory appeal pursuant to 28 U.S.C. § 1292(b) the question "whether, for the purposes of 42 U.S.C. § 1983, acts performed by employees of a statutorily designated 'state-related' institution of higher education such as Temple University constitute 'state action.'" We agreed to hear the appeal.

II. *DISCUSSION*

A. *The State Action Requirement and the State Action Tests*

The fifth and fourteenth amendments protect individuals only from governmental action. In order for Krynicky or Schier to benefit from these constitutional protections, they must show that the alleged violations of due process and freedom of speech are "fairly attributable to the state." The "state action requirement" preserves "individual freedom by limiting the reach of federal law and federal judicial power" and avoids "imposing on the state, its agencies or officials, responsibility for conduct for which they cannot fairly be blamed."

The requirement of section 1983 that the challenged activity be taken "under color of state law" has been treated as identical to the "state action" element of the fourteenth amendment. What constitutes sufficient state participation to attribute activity to the state under section 1983 has proved to be an extremely difficult question. It has variously been characterized as "murky waters," "obdurate," and a "protean concept."

The Supreme Court to date has not developed a uniform test for ascertaining when state action exists and has stated that no such unitary test is possible. Instead, the Court has adopted a number of approaches whose application depends upon the circumstances. The Court has suggested that lower courts investigate carefully the facts of each case. Two of the approaches are relevant to these appeals: the "symbiotic relationship" test and the "nexus" test.[4]

---

4. The other tests are the "public function" test and the "state compulsion" test. "Public

In *Burton v. Wilmington Parking Authority*, the Supreme Court found state action where there was a "symbiotic relationship" between the acting party and the state. The Court held that state action exists when:

> The State has so far insinuated itself into a position of interdependence with ...[the acting party] that it must be recognized as a joint participant in the challenged activity, which, on that account, cannot be considered to have been so "purely private" as to fall without the scope of the Fourteenth Amendment.

In *Jackson v. Metropolitan Edison Co.*, the Court held that state action may also exist when the state becomes sufficiently involved in the particular challenged activity. The Court suggested that in considering the state action issue, the "inquiry must be whether there is a sufficiently close nexus between the state and the challenged action of the...entity so that the action of the latter may be fairly treated as that of the State itself."

In *Braden v. University of Pittsburgh*, we confronted the question whether the University of Pittsburgh acted under the color of state law with respect to a claim almost identical to that of Ms. Schier. We rejected Pitt's contention that *Jackson* had overruled *Burton*, stating:

> Based on a review of the Supreme Court's opinion in *Jackson*, we believe that that decision would not preclude application of the precepts of *Burton* here, *should the appropriate state-private relationship exist*. Instead of overruling *Burton*, the *Jackson* Court merely distinguished the earlier opinion, finding "absent in [Jackson] the symbiotic relationship presented in *Burton*..."

Based on the provisions of University of Pittsburgh-Commonwealth Act, we concluded that Pennsylvania had so far insinuated itself into a position of interdependence with the University of Pittsburgh that there was a symbiotic relationship between the two, and we therefore held that the actions of the University could fairly be attributed to the state for purposes of satisfying the state action requirement of section 1983.

Unless *Braden* has been overruled by the Supreme Court's recent *Lugar* trilogy, it is binding precedent for the proposition that the University of Pittsburgh and the Commonwealth of Pennsylvania are involved in a "symbiotic relationship," and therefore, that the actions of the University are actions taken under color of state law for purposes of section 1983. Moreover, since the Temple University-Commonwealth Act, which sets out the relationship between Temple and the State, is virtually identical to University of Pittsburgh-Commonwealth Act, which was the basis for our conclusion in *Braden* that Pitt and the Commonwealth have a symbiotic relationship, there can be no doubt that, if *Braden* has not been overruled, it requires the conclusion that the actions of Temple, like Pitt, are actions taken under color of state law.

Pitt and Temple make two arguments in support of their contention that *Braden* has been overruled:

---

function" analysis has been applied in three different situations: first, when the government, after performing a particular function, attempts to avoid its constitutional obligations by transferring the function to a private entity; second, in cases involving the exercise of powers, such as the supervision of elections that are almost always carried out by government; and third, in the first amendment context to determine if private property is the functional equivalent of a municipality. The "state compulsion" analysis has been used in cases where the state, by its law, has compelled a particular act.

(1) the *Lugar* trilogy overruled or, at a minimum, limited *Burton v. Wilmington Parking Authority* to its facts, and therefore *Braden*, which relies on *Burton*, is no longer good law; and

(2) even if the symbiotic relationship test remains viable, the *Lugar* trilogy has clarified that test and, as a result, it is now clear that the Third Circuit in *Braden* misapplied *Burton* when it concluded that a symbiotic relationship existed between Pitt and the Commonwealth.

We consider these arguments in turn.

B. *The Impact of the Lugar Trilogy on Burton*

* * *

[T]he Supreme Court in the *Lugar* trilogy clearly treated the symbiotic relationship test as a viable framework of analysis, but concluded that *Burton* was inapposite to the factual scenarios of those cases. The only indicia of state involvement in *Rendell-Baker* and *Blum* were financial assistance and routine state regulation. By comparison, in *Burton* the state was much more intertwined with the Eagle Coffee Shop: the shop was located in a state-owned building; the state maintained the facility and made all necessary repairs; and the coffee shop and the state conferred mutual benefits on each other because of their location. Thus, we reject Temple and Pitt's assertion that *Rendell-Baker* and *Blum* eliminate the *Burton* symbiotic relationship test.

C. *The Impact of the Lugar Trilogy on Braden*

Alternatively, Pitt and Temple argue that *Blum* and *Rendell-Baker* preclude the finding of a symbiotic relationship unless it can be shown that the state benefits financially from the activities of the defendant. Such a financial relationship was present in the *Burton* case, but was not proved in *Braden*, and was not, the defendants contend, demonstrated here. Thus, the defendants argue that although *Burton* may still be good law after the *Lugar* trilogy, *Braden* has implicitly been overruled and we should find that there is no symbiotic relationship in the cases of Pitt and Temple.

It is true that the Supreme Court in *Blum* and *Rendell-Baker* focused on the financial relationship between the defendants and the State, but that was because the financial relationship was the only significant form of state influence over the defendants in those cases. The Court concluded that merely proving the existence of the limited type of financial relationship present in those cases was not sufficient to establish the requisite symbiotic relationship. By way of contrast, the Court in *Burton* emphasized the complete intermingling of state and private actions that were present in that case as grounds for its conclusion that a symbiotic relationship existed. The court referred to [facts] that the state-owned Parking Authority financially benefited from renting to the coffee shop, but the Court also emphasized that the coffee shop was located in a building owned and operated by the State. It is apparent from the opinion that this second factor is at least as important as the financial relationship.

The Commonwealth's interrelationship with Pitt and Temple in these cases is more closely analogous to the complete intermingling of state and private actors found in *Burton* than to the relatively minimal interrelationship between the State and the defendants in *Blum* and *Rendell-Baker*. An examination of the statutes that create and define the Commonwealth's relationship with Pitt and Temple demonstrates this fact. Since the two statutes are virtually identical, we will refer specifically only to the University of Pittsburgh statute.

To begin with, the statute was enacted to save the Commonwealth the expense of creating an additional state college. In addition, the statute changes the name of the University of Pittsburgh to "The University of Pittsburgh—Of the Commonwealth System of Higher Education." Consonant with this linkage, the legislature declares it to be the purpose of the Act to extend the opportunities for higher education in the Commonwealth "by establishing University of Pittsburgh as an *instrumentality* of the Commonwealth to serve as a State-related institution in the Commonwealth System of higher education." This same section also provides:

> That the Commonwealth of Pennsylvania recognizes University of Pittsburgh as an integral part of a system of higher education in Pennsylvania, and that it is desirable and in the public interest to perpetuate and extend the relationship between the Commonwealth of Pennsylvania and University of Pittsburgh for the purpose of improving and strengthening higher education by designating University of Pittsburgh as a State-related university.

The statute also furnishes the "nuts and bolts" of this linkage. It provides that one-third of the University's trustees are to be selected by the Commonwealth, and that the Governor of Pennsylvania, the Mayor of the City of Pittsburgh, and the Superintendent of the Department of Public Instruction are trustees ex officio. The Act provides that the Commonwealth will make annual appropriations to the University, to be used as specified by the state, and that the appropriated funds must be kept in a specific account. The state may further set tuition and fee schedules for Pennsylvania students in the annual appropriation act.

The Act also mandates that the University "file with the General Assembly and with the Auditor General of the Commonwealth, a statement setting forth the amounts and purposes of all expenditures made from both the Commonwealth Appropriation Account and other University accounts during the fiscal year." The statute entitles the University to benefit from all Commonwealth programs for capital development, and creates a state tax exemption for income derived from bonds issued by the University and loans secured by its mortgages. Finally, the Chancellor of the University must file annually a report of all University activities, "instructional, administrative and financial," with the Board of Trustees who "shall transmit [the report] to the Governor and to the members of the General Assembly."

The logic of *Rendell-Baker* and *Blum* is that state contributions to otherwise private entities, no matter how great those contributions may be, will not of themselves transform a private actor into a state actor. In the cases of Pitt and Temple, to the contrary, the issue is not whether the level of state contributions has reached a magic figure necessary to effect this transformation, but rather the affirmative state act of statutorily accepting responsibility for these institutions. This fact, above all, marks the difference between these two institutions and those discussed by the Supreme Court in *Rendell-Baker* and *Blum*.

In addition, unlike the school in *Rendell-Baker* and the nursing home in *Blum*, Temple and Pitt are not merely private contractors with the state. Not only do they receive present financial support, but also the state has committed itself to future financial aid and sets an annual appropriation policy and tuition rate. There is nothing to indicate that the state could not discontinue its support of the New Perspectives School or the American Nursing Home at any time by the simple means of not renewing their contracts. By contrast, it would require a legislative enactment to disentangle Temple and Pitt from the Commonwealth, and the idea that legislative appropriations to these institutions might be severely curtailed is unrealistic. Furthermore, neither of the institutions in *Rendell-Baker* or *Blum* had to submit to state-sponsored audits or make yearly reports to the State Assembly. Finally, unlike the institutions in *Blum* and *Rendell-Baker*, one-third of the Trustees of Pitt and Temple are now appointed by the state. Temple and Pitt are not merely "private contractors performing services for the government"; they not only receive funding and are subject to routine state regulations, but are instrumentalities of the state, both in name and in fact.

In sum, we see nothing in either *Blum* or *Rendell-Baker* that conflicts with *Braden* or its rationale, and, therefore, we conclude that the Supreme Court did not overrule our decision in *Braden*.[12]

III. CONCLUSION

We hold that the Supreme Court's recent decisions in the so-called *Lugar* trilogy do not overrule either the Supreme Court's decision in *Burton v. Wilmington Parking Authority* or our opinion in *Braden v. University of Pittsburgh*. Therefore, we are bound by Third Circuit precedent to hold that a "symbiotic relationship" exists between the Commonwealth of Pennsylvania on the one hand and Pitt and Temple on the other. Actions taken by those two institutions are, therefore, actions taken under color of state law and are subject to scrutiny under section 1983. Consequently, we will reverse the judgment of the district court in *Krynicky v. University of Pittsburgh* and affirm the judgment of the district court in *Schier v. Temple University*, and will remand both cases for further proceedings consistent with this opinion.

Wynne v. Shippensburg University of Pennsylvania
639 F. Supp. 76 (M.D. Pa. 1985)

CONABOY, District Judge.

We consider here the motion of Defendant Shippensburg University (hereinafter Shippensburg) to dismiss this complaint as to it for failure to state a claim upon which relief can be granted pursuant to Rule 12(b)(6) of the Federal Rules of Civil Procedure. This motion was briefed in timely fashion as was the opposing brief of Plaintiff Robert M. Wynne, formerly a tenured faculty member at Shippensburg. Thus, this motion is now ripe for decision. For the reasons which follow, we shall grant the motion.

This is essentially a wrongful termination action brought under the guise of 42 U.S.C. § 1983—the federal statute which provides a remedy for those persons whose federally protected rights are violated by persons acting under color of state law— 28 U.S.C. § 1343 and the 14th Amendment to the United States Constitution.

Plaintiff alleges that he had taught at Shippensburg from August 24, 1970 until what he claims was his *sudden* termination on August 17, 1984. He further alleges that he had acquired tenured status in May of 1973 and, thus, acquired a property interest in his position which cannot be extinguished without due process of law (i.e.

---

12. Temple and Pitt also argue that, under state law precedent, the state courts have declared them to be private entities despite their statutory relationship with the state. * * *

adequate notice of the reason for his dismissal and an opportunity to be heard in opposition to said dismissal). Finally, he alleges that a collective bargaining agreement was in force between the Commonwealth of Pennsylvania and the Association of Pennsylvania State College and University Faculty which provided that tenured faculty members could not be terminated without just cause.

Shippensburg does acknowledge the fact that Plaintiff Wynne enjoyed tenured status but denies that his termination was sudden or that he had no opportunity to oppose it. Shippensburg's position was stated concisely as:

> ... Plaintiff had been continually advised of his position being in jeopardy, and plaintiff had been evaluated negatively repeatedly, with respect to his teaching performance.
>
> ... Plaintiff was also given several opportunities to present reasons, either in person or in writing, why the termination should not take place.

Defendant Shippensburg's motion to dismiss this case is based on two premises: (a) that Shippensburg is a state agency and, thus, is not susceptible to suit under § 1983 because it is not a "person" within the meaning of that statute; or (b) that the 11th Amendment to the United States Constitution, as delineated in *Hans v. Louisiana* and its progeny, precludes lawsuits against a state or its agencies by its own citizens.

I. May Shippensburg be characterized as a "person" within the meaning of 42 U.S.C. § 1983?

Shippensburg's first defense is predicated on the fact that it would answer the question above in the negative. *Rochester v. White* is cited for the proposition that "... federal courts have long recognized that neither the Commonwealth nor its agencies are "persons" within the meaning of § 1983." This begs the questions, however, of whether Shippensburg University is a state agency.

Plaintiff Wynne argues that the term "person" "... extends to such entities as corporations and municipalities..." and "... Universities are among the entities which have been held to be 'persons' (citations omitted)." It is, therefore, obvious that, to answer this question of whether Shippensburg is a "person" or "state actor" under § 1983, we must first determine whether Shippensburg may be appropriately characterized as a state agency. This leads directly to Defendant's second argument.

II. May Shippensburg be characterized as a state agency which is immune to suit in federal court due to immunity conferred by the 11th Amendment?

This question is to be resolved under a very different standard from that used in deciding whether an entity is a "person" or "state actor" under § 1983. The parties agree that the test to be utilized in determining whether an agency is an "arm of the state" or state agency for 11th Amendment purposes was first announced in *Urbano v. Board of Managers of New Jersey State Prison*. We note that the *Urbano* test has been utilized recently to resolve a similar dispute by Judge Caldwell in *Braderman v. Pennsylvania Housing Finance Agency*. We think it plain that the *Urbano* test is the appropriate standard to apply here.

The briefs of the parties frame an interesting question as to whether the current Pennsylvania State Universities—Shippensburg included—remain state agencies in the aftermath of the enactment of 24 P.S. § 20–2001–A *et seq.*, the statute which has transformed the former state colleges into state universities. Plaintiff admits that it was clear prior to the passage of said statute that the state colleges were state agencies. Plaintiff admits, too, that *Skehan v. Board of Trustees of Bloomsburg State College*, a case relied upon by Defendant Shippensburg, stood for the very proposition that the state colleges of Pennsylvania were agencies of the state. Plaintiff alleges, however, that the passage of 24 P.S. § 20–2001–A *et seq.* has robbed *Skehan* of its vitality and that "the 1982 legislative enactment which transformed 'Shippensburg State College' into the present 'Shippensburg University' substantially altered the relationship between the Commonwealth of Pennsylvania and the University."

Plaintiff then asserts:

> The test for determining whether or not an entity is an agency of the state for Eleventh Amendment purposes has been set out and explained in *Urbano.*... Several factors are to be considered:
>
> ...Local law and decisions defining the status and nature of the agency involved in its relations to the sovereign are factors to be considered, but only one of a number that are of significance. Among the other factors, no one of which is conclusive, perhaps the most important is whether, in the event plaintiff prevails, the payment of the judgment will have to be made out of the state treasury; significant here also is whether the agency has the funds or the power to satisfy the judgment. Other relevant factors are whether the agency is performing a governmental or proprietary function; whether it has been separately incorporated; the degree of autonomy over its operations; whether it has the power to sue and to be sued and to enter into contracts; whether its property is immune from state taxation, and whether the sovereign has immunized itself from responsibility for the agency's operations.

In the reply brief of Defendant Shippensburg there is no quarrel with the Plaintiff's position that the factors mentioned in *Urbano* should be resorted to in an effort to determine whether Shippensburg is a state agency. Defendant Shippensburg does state, however, that "it has properly invoked Eleventh Amendment immunity, when the relevant (Urbano) factors are considered...." It remains for this Court to examine the facts of this case with respect to these factors in order to determine the status of Shippensburg University. If Shippensburg is an "arm of the state" with respect to the weight of the *Urbano* factors, then it enjoys 11th Amendment immunity from suit in federal court. We shall sequentially analyze these factors as they affect this case.

A. Local Law and Decisions Defining the Status and Nature of Shippensburg University in its Relation to the Commonwealth of Pennsylvania.

Plaintiff contends:

> The statutory scheme is apparently too new for authoritative state court decisions on the sovereign immunity issue, but the enabling legislation itself is helpful in understanding the relationship between Shippensburg University and the Commonwealth. Unlike its predecessor state college, Shippensburg University is a part of a "body corporate and politic" which is "independent of the Department of Education."

Plaintiff also points out that this new system is governed by a 16 member Board of Governors which appoints a chancellor and a president who are charged with overseeing the day-to-day operation of state universities. He also notes that planning and coordinating the development and operation of the system is a responsibility which lies with the Board of Governors and not with the Secretary of Education.

While this data seems to suggest that Shippensburg is sufficiently independent of Commonwealth control to be denied the status of a state agency, Plaintiff has neglected to include language from the same statute he cites which is less supportive of his position. As Defendant points out in its reply brief: "24 P.S. § 20–2002–A(a) provided, *inter alia*, that the State System of Higher Education is 'a body corporate and politic constituting a *public corporation and government instrumentality*'...." Moreover, there is a Pennsylvania decision subsequent to the enactment of the statute which transformed the state colleges into state universities which deals with the question of whether the Commonwealth System of Higher Education is a state agency. While said decision—*Pennsylvania Industries for the Blind and Handicapped v. Commonwealth of Pennsylvania, State System of Higher Education*—does not go directly to the seminal question in the case *sub judice*, it provides strong evidence that the Courts of Pennsylvania are likely to construe 24 P.S. §§ 20–2001 *et seq.* as continuing to provide that the various state universities are state agencies. The Commonwealth Court held that the various state universities are required to comply with § 2409.1 of the Administrative Code of Pennsylvania which mandates that the Commonwealth purchase products and services "from non-profit making agencies for the handicapped without competitive bidding, if furnished at fair market price."

We find that *Pennsylvania Industries* likely heralds a trend in the Courts of Pennsylvania to require state universities to comply with the regulations generally intended to govern the operation of state agencies. We find, too, that the clear language of the statute which conferred university status on the former state colleges denoting these new universities to be part of a "public corporation and government instrumentality" strongly indicates that the legislature intended that these fledgling universities be so closely associated with the state as to remain the state agencies they clearly were in terms of *Skehan*, supra. Most significantly, we find that the first *Urbano* factor—the weight of local law and decisions—is in favor of Defendant's position that it is a state agency.

B. Source of Funds to Satisfy Judgment

The *Urbano* Court characterized this inquiry as the most significant in the determination of whether any organization is a state agency. It is not disputed here that some degree of funding for the state universities is provided by the Commonwealth. The Plaintiff argues:

> Any impact of a judgment against Shippensburg University upon the Commonwealth of Pennsylvania will be indirect, at best. It does not matter for 11th Amendment purposes that the entity in question receives "a significant amount of money from the state."

The Plaintiff also points out that Shippensburg has authority to accept funds from "foundations, corporations, or any other source."

Nevertheless, it stands to reason that any judgment rendered against Shippensburg or any of its sister universities will result in a drain upon the treasury of Pennsylvania since the state has undertaken primary responsibility for funding these entities. This is true because 24 P.S. § 20–2002–A(b) provides: "As successor institutions to the State Normal Schools, appropriations for their operation are *ordinary expenses of government*, requiring only a majority vote of each House of the General Assembly. *The State System of Higher Education shall have the same preferred status for appropriations as is enjoyed by its constituent institutions.*" This language makes it plain that Shippensburg and the Commonwealth of Pennsylvania are inextricably linked financially and that the Commonwealth does not supply monies to Shippensburg out of periodic spasms of benevolence but, rather, out of a statutorily imposed, continuing obligation.

Plaintiff suggests that " . . . In a 'close case,' it may be necessary to go 'beyond the statutory language and examine the operational structure of the agency and the relationship to the Commonwealth.' " Our examination of *Blake*, supra, indicates that the explanation of the *Blake* Court regarding the import of a state satisfying a judgment incurred by an organization resides more in the reason for the state's contribution than in the level of said contribution. The *Blake* Court stated:

> . . . Although we recognize that the exact percentage of the state contribution is not determinative of eleventh amendment immunity, the nature and size of those funds may be probative.
>
> . . . .
>
> For eleventh amendment purposes, the nature of the state's obligation to contribute may be more important than the size of the contribution.
>
> . . . a court should consider whether the state, in making the contribution, is acting in the role of a sovereign or is contributing in some other capacity.

Since Plaintiff himself concedes that public education has traditionally been a governmental function and since, in this Court's view, 24 P.S. §§ 20–2001(A) *et seq.* are permeated with indications that the legislature's intent was to create state controlled as opposed to state subsidized universities, we find that any contribution Pennsylvania would make toward satisfying a judgment entered against Shippensburg in this context would be pursuant to a governmental function and, thus, would be an exercise of sovereignty in terms of *Blake*. In light of this determination we conclude that the state, because of its statutory duty to provide continuing financial support to Shippensburg would, at the least, contribute to the satisfaction of any judgment against Shippensburg and would do so out of its sovereign responsibility. Therefore, we find that the "source of funds" and "government as opposed to proprietary" factors announced in *Urbano* and clarified in *Blake* weigh in the Defendants' favor in this case.

C. Separate Incorporation

The language of the legislature in 24 P.S. § 20–2002–(A)(a) does denominate the state universities as separate corporations but also, as we have previously noted, describes them as a "public corporation and government instrumentality." We think this language ambiguous enough to preclude this Court from finding unequivocally that these universities are truly separately incorporated or, on the strength of the language alone, "arms of the state." However, we do think that, considering the state's *obligation* to provide some degree of funding to Shippensburg and the power vested in the Governor of Pennsylvania to unilaterally determine who is on Shippensburg's Board of Governors, a conclusion that Shippensburg and its sister universities are corporations separate and distinct from the Commonwealth of Pennsylvania would border on the ludicrous.

D. Degree of Autonomy

This issue has been discussed in several respects above and—in view of the Defendant Shippensburg's partial dependency upon state funds, the obviously pervasive control the Governor of Pennsylvania exerts over its operations by his decisions as to who sits on the Board of Governors, and the fact that the Commonwealth Court of Pennsylvania indicated in *Pennsylvania Industries* that the state can limit the ability of Shippensburg and its sister universities to enter into contracts—we must find that the weight of the evidence here indicates that Shippensburg is not sufficiently autonomous to escape characterization as a state agency.

E. Sovereign Immunity from the Agency's Operation

This Court is aware that, while Pennsylvania has abolished sovereign immunity with respect to eight carefully delineated areas in which state representatives are prone to commit torts, it has not statutorily abolished Commonwealth immunity with respect to the acts or omissions of the employees of state universities. What import we can derive from this fact will necessarily involve an exercise in assumptions that we think it unwise to undertake. Thus, we find that this factor is neutral as regards support to the parties to this dispute.

III.

In summation, we find that, by applying the *Urbano* factors to this lawsuit as urged by Plaintiff Wynne, the conclusion is compelled that Shippensburg is an "arm" or an *alter ego* of the Commonwealth of Pennsylvania and, therefore, immune from suit in federal court by virtue of the immunity afforded such entities by the 11th Amendment. See *Pennhurst State School Hospital v. Halderman*, which states in pertinent part:

> This Court's decisions thus establish that "an unconsenting State is immune from suits brought in federal courts by her own citizens as well as by citizens of another state." There may be a question, however, whether a particular suit in fact is a suit against a State. It is clear, of course, that in the absence of consent a suit in which the State or one of its agencies or departments is named as the defendant is proscribed by the Eleventh Amendment. . . .

Since we have previously found that Shippensburg University is a state agency by virtue of the degree of control exercised over it by the Commonwealth of Pennsylvania, and since we have determined that Pennsylvania has not waived its Eleventh Amendment immunity, we now declare that this lawsuit may not be maintained against Defendant Shippensburg University.

This Court has an additional concern. We wonder about the efficacy of trying this case when it is apparent from the pleadings that an arbitrator has been assigned to this controversy who is empowered to award Plaintiff much of the relief he seeks here. Mindful of the traditional deference federal courts show the arbitration process in the labor context—and this case is essentially a dispute as to whether procedures outlined in a collective bargaining agreement were followed—we direct that this case be closed until such time as the arbitrator rules on Plaintiff's grievance pursuant to the provisions of the collective bargaining agreement between his union and Shippensburg University.

Autonomy of Public Institutions

The autonomy accorded public colleges and universities to govern themselves is directly proportional to the terms of statutory establishment and the subsequent reach of legislation. Thus, in states where extraordinary independence was conferred upon trustees (such as in Michigan or California), considerable autonomy has been established and generally respected by courts. The University of Michigan, under this reasoning, could not be compelled by the State Legislature to relocate a university hospital from Ann Arbor to Detroit. *Sterling v. Regents*, 68 N.W. 253 (1896). The University of Nebraska similarly fought off legislative efforts to affect university personnel and gift policies, including line-item vetoes by the governor. *Board of Regents v. Exxon*, 199 Neb. 146, 256 N.W.2d 330 (1977). Arizona State University fended off a legislative attempt to include university employees in the State Civil Service System. *ASU v. Arizona Department of Administration*, 151 Ariz. 450, 728 P.2d 669 (1986). And Ohio State University was found not to be a state "agency" for purposes of Ohio's Administrative Procedure Act. *Board of Trustees v. Ohio Department of Administrative Services*, 429 N.E.2d 428 (1981).

This book is also replete with cases holding the opposite, where states exert substantial legislative and administrative authority over public institutions. Indeed, public institutions may lose their autonomy by their silence, if they acquiesce in legislative actions that affect them, as occurred in *University of Utah v. Board of Examiners*, which held, "In those early days the Regents [understandably] were not disposed to tell the legislature to leave them alone. They weren't taking any chance on offending Santa Claus.... The University enjoyed and thrived on its dependence on the Legislature, but lately it seeks a change. It chooses to declare that independence, which the institution never had had, and which has never, prior to the bringing of this action, been asserted. After these 50 years of acquiescence it is difficult to understand this sudden quest for independent control." 295 P.2d 348, 366–68 (1956).

In a comparative study of 20th century legislation affecting colleges in several states, Lois Fisher concluded:

> the number of higher education laws and the number of control laws passed per decade from 1900 to 1979 increased over time, especially during the last twenty years studied. However, there was a parallel increase in flexibility legislation, and there was no statistically significant variability in the ratio of control to flexibility legislation over the period studied. Moreover, the surge in the number of higher education laws passed during the 1960s and 1970s is associated with the increase in all laws passed in the sample states and with the unprecedented growth of the higher education enterprise during that time. Thus we may conclude... that the increase in the number of higher education laws of all kinds reflects growth and not a change in the tendency of state legislatures to interfere in or to reduce the autonomy of colleges and universities.

"State Legislatures and the Autonomy of Colleges and Universities," *Journal of Higher Education*, 59 (1988), 133–62.

Moore v. Board of Regents
407 N.Y.S.2d 452 (1978)

JASEN, Judge.

Presented for our review on this appeal is the issue whether the Board of Regents, through the Commissioner of Education, has the power to deny registration of doctoral degree programs offered by the State University of New York on the ground that they do not satisfy academic standards prescribed by the commissioner.

Appellants, the Chancellor and Trustees of the State University of New York and certain professors and doctoral students in the History and English Departments of the State University of New York at Albany, commenced this action seeking a declaration that the Trustees of the State University constitute the body charged with the operation of university programs, courses and curricula, thus invalidating the directive of the commissioner denying registration of doctoral programs in history and English, as made in excess of his powers. Special Term granted summary judgment to respondents, the Board of Regents and the Commissioner of Education, holding that respondents do possess the power to review academic programs offered by the State University to determine whether such programs should be registered. Insofar as Special Term viewed appellants' action as an article 78 proceeding to review the determination of the commissioner denying registration of appellants' programs, the court concluded that, as to the history program, judicial review was barred by the Statute of Limitations. Although finding appellants' proceeding timely as to the English program, Special Term nonetheless concluded that there existed a rational basis for the commissioner's determination. On appeal, the Appellate Division unanimously affirmed. Before this court, appellants do not raise the rationality of the commissioner's determination, but, rather, limit their challenge to the power of respondents to require registration of programs offered by the State University.

We hold that the Education Law does empower the Board of Regents, acting through the Commissioner of Education, to require registration of doctoral degree programs offered by the State University and to deny registration to those programs it determines to be academically deficient.

To place the current dispute between the Regents and the State University in proper perspective, a brief review of the historical evolution of these bodies is appropriate. When first created by the Legislature, the Regents of the University of the State of New York succeeded to the powers of the governors of Kings College, which was then renamed Columbia College. This grant of power endowed the Regents with full authority to govern and manage any college established in New York, all such institutions to be deemed part of the University of New York. Subsequently, however, the Legislature altered the role of the Regents by granting to a board of trustees of Columbia College autonomous control over the operation of the college. Concomitantly, this act endowed all colleges established in New York with the same rights and privileges vested in the trustees of Columbia College. As a result, the Regents underwent a metamorphosis, the effect of which was to clothe it with a broad policy-making function over higher education in New York, leaving the day-to-day operation of the colleges to their own governing bodies.

With the advent of the State University of New York, however, the Regents became enmeshed in the day-to-day operation of this semi-independent educational corporation. To alter this governing structure, the Legislature subsequently vested in the

Board of Trustees of the State University the same power to administer the day-to-day operations of the State University as trustees of private institutions of higher education had been granted. Viewed in this historical perspective, the issue in the instant case can be framed as whether the Regents, as a policy-making body, possesses the power to require registration of doctoral degree programs or whether control over the offering of such programs lies within the ambit of the Trustees of the State University.

At the outset, we note that a critical function of the Regents is its preparation, once every four years, of a master plan "for the development and expansion of higher education" in New York. This plan includes public as well as private institutions. The 1972 master plan, prepared by the Regents, and approved by the Governor, recognized the need for strengthening graduate programs and recommended that "institutions should withdraw those programs which, upon evaluation, prove to be (a) inactive or underenrolled, (b) of marginal quality and which cannot be strengthened by sharing resources with other institutions, and (c) below the minimum standards set by Commissioner's Regulations." Separate and apart from the policy recommendations concerning graduate programs contained in the 1972 master plan, section 210 of the Education Law specifically gives the Regents the power to "register domestic and foreign institutions in terms of New York standards."

It is true that read literally section 210 speaks only of the registration of domestic and foreign institutions and is silent as to the registration of particular programs offered by such institutions. However, we do not believe the power of registration granted to the Regents need be construed so narrowly. Section 210 must not be read in isolation, but with an awareness of the full range of powers granted to the Regents. Particularly significant in this regard is the power of visitation provided in section 215 of the Education Law. This section authorizes the Regents or the Commissioner of Education to "visit, examine into and inspect, any institution in the university" and to "require, as often as desired, duly verified reports therefrom giving such information and in such form as the regents or the commissioner of education shall prescribe." In the event that an institution violates "any law or any rule of the university," the Regents is empowered to "suspend the charter or any of the rights and privileges of such institution."

We see no reason why sections 210 and 215 should not be read together as the statutory authority for the power of the Regents to require registration of doctoral degree programs offered by institutions of higher education in New York. If the Regents, in the first instance, has the power to register institutions "in terms of New York standards," and the power to suspend the rights and privileges of an institution violating "any rule or law of the university," it would not appear unreasonable to conclude that the Regents also possesses the power to deny the registration of doctoral degree programs which it believes do not conform with standards set for institutions of higher education. Of course, the standards for registration set by the Regents must not be arbitrary or capricious, either in the abstract or in application to specific programs. To hold that the Regents is empowered to require registration of doctoral degree programs is not to insulate such administrative action from judicial scrutiny.

Of critical importance to the effectuation of the Regents' powers is the legislative function with which it has been endowed: that is, to determine the educational policies of the State and to "establish rules for carrying into effect the laws and policies of the state, relating to education, and the functions, powers, duties and trusts conferred or charged upon the university and the education department." Implementing this power, the Regents, based upon the policy recommendations made in the 1972 master plan, established a rule providing the Commissioner of Education with authority to promulgate regulations governing the registration of courses of study in colleges, as well as in professional, technical and other schools. Acting upon this mandate, the commissioner promulgated a regulation requiring the registration of "[e]very curriculum creditable toward a degree offered by institutions of higher education."

To effectuate this registration requirement, the commissioner also promulgated a regulation setting forth standards to be employed in the determination whether to grant or deny the registration of degree programs offered by all institutions of higher education, both private and public. This regulation provided, *inter alia*, that "[e]ach member of the academic staff shall have demonstrated by his training, earned degrees, scholarship, experience, and by classroom performance or other evidence of teaching potential, his competence to offer the courses and discharge the other academic responsibilities which are assigned to him."

In reviewing the qualifications of the faculty of the English and History Departments at the State University of New York at Albany to offer doctoral programs, the commissioner, based upon reports submitted by the site visitation team and program evaluation committee, as well as upon the recommendation of the doctoral council, determined that the faculty in these departments were not sufficiently productive or prominent to support a doctoral program and, therefore, declined to register the programs. Indicia of faculty productivity or prominence relied upon by the commissioner focused upon the extent of research and publications credited to members of the faculty of the doctoral programs evaluated. Concerning the history program, the report of the visitation team concluded that the department was not widely known and that "[w]ith one outstanding exception * * * the members of the department, individually and collectively [did] not represent the kind of prominent scholars to whom one refers undergraduates in all parts of the country for graduate training." Similarly, the report of the visitation team evaluating the English program concluded "that in general the members of the department are not recognized nationally by appointment to national honorary bodies, MLA committees, or editorial boards."

In concluding that the Commissioner of Education did not act in excess of his powers in denying registration of these programs based upon this criteria, we reject, at the outset, appellant's contention that the power of the Regents is limited pursuant to chapter 388 of the Laws of 1961 to supervision and approval of the State University Trustees' master plan. The purpose of that legislation was not to exempt the State University from the authority of the Regents. On the contrary, the Legislature sought merely to place the State University on the same footing as private institutions of higher education in New York: that is to grant the trustees of the State University the same power to govern the day-to-day operations of the State University as trustees of private institutions possessed. It was intended to have, and in fact had, no effect on the broad policy-making function exercised by the Regents over both private and public institutions of higher education in New York.

In exercising this function, the Regents recommended in its 1972 master plan the withdrawal of academically deficient programs. Moreover, as previously discussed, sections 210 and 215 of the Education Law must be interpreted to empower the Regents to register degree programs as well as the institutions themselves in terms of New York standards. These standards, promulgated as regulations by the Commissioner of Education, provide the necessary authority for the commissioner's determination to deny the registration of the English and History doctoral programs offered by the State University of New York at Albany.

We also reject appellants' contention that standards for the registration of educational programs were never promulgated. This argument is premised upon the conclusion that the standards employed in the determination of the commissioner to deny registration were those contained in position paper 19, a document published by the Regents recommending the evaluation of all doctoral programs in the State to ensure that only programs of high academic caliber be continued. We would agree that the recommendations contained in position paper 19 did not, upon publication, acquire the status of regulations promulgated by the Commissioner of Education. But that is not to say that the recommendations made in position paper 19 could not have been considered by the commissioner in his determination to deny registration in the present case, together with the essential standards contained in the regulation which he had promulgated.

As a word of caution we add that the power of the Regents is not unbridled. Its function is one of an overseer: a body possessed of broad policy-making attributes. In its broadest sense, the purpose of the Regents is "to encourage and promote education," a purpose which must be realized only through the powers granted to the Regents by the Legislature. In the absence of a specific grant of power by the Legislature, the Regents cannot transform section 207 of the Education Law, the fountainhead of the Regents' rule-making power, into an all-encompassing power permitting the Regents' intervention in the day-to-day operations of the institutions of higher education in New York. Were this provision interpreted otherwise, it would run afoul of the constitutional prohibition against the Legislature's delegation of lawmaking power to other bodies. In view, however, of the specific powers granted by the Legislature to the Regents previously discussed, we believe that, in the present case, section 207 operates as a means for the effectuation of independent powers, rather than as their source.

Accordingly, the order of the Appellate Division should be affirmed, without costs.

Regents of the University of Michigan
v. State of Michigan
419 N.W.2d 773 (Mich. App. 1988)

WALSH, Presiding Judge.

Plaintiff, the body corporate known as the Regents of the University of Michigan, appeals from a circuit court order denying its motion for summary judgment under GCR 1963, 117.2(3), now MCR 2.116(C)(10), and granting summary judgment under GCR 1963, 117.2(1), now MCR 2.116(C)(8), to defendant, the State of Michigan. Defendant cross-appeals from a circuit court order denying defendant's motion for partial accelerated judgment. At issue on appeal is the constitutionality of 1982 P.A. 512, which amended the Civil Rights Act (CRA). On cross-appeal, defendant challenges plaintiff's standing to raise certain constitutional challenges to Act 512.

The CRA prohibits discriminatory practices, policies and customs in the exercise of rights based on religion, race, color, national origin, age, sex, height, weight and marital status. Article 4 of CRA addresses the issue of discrimination by educational institutions. Act 512 amended § 402 of Article 4 by adding the requirement that educational institutions, which include public universities, shall not

"(f) Encourage or condone legally required discrimination against an individual on the basis of race or color by knowingly making or maintaining after April 1, 1984, an investment in an organization operating in the Republic of South Africa. This subdivision shall not apply to a private educational institution.

"(g) Encourage or condone religious discrimination or ethnic discrimination by knowingly making or maintaining after February 1, 1983, an investment in an organization operating in the Union of Soviet Socialist Republics."

Plaintiff is the constitutional body corporate known as the Regents of the University of Michigan. The Constitution confers on plaintiff, as it does on the controlling boards of the other institutions of higher education established by Michigan law and authorized to grant baccalaureate degrees, the "general supervision of its institution and the control and direction of all expenditures from the institution's funds." Candidates for membership on the eight-member Board of Regents are nominated at the state convention of each political party. The regents, whose eight-year terms are staggered, are elected at the state general election. They are subject to recall and to removal by impeachment.

On July 15, 1983, plaintiff commenced this action seeking a declaratory judgment that Act 512 is unconstitutional. Plaintiff's principal challenge was that Act 512 contravenes Const. 1963, art. 8, § 5 in attempting to restrict plaintiff's authority to control and direct expenditures of the university's funds. Attached to plaintiff's complaint was a copy of an April 15, 1983, resolution of the regents whereby, subject to limited exceptions, the chief financial officer of the university was directed to divest the university of its interest in investments in shares of corporate stock and other equities of organizations operating in the Republic of South Africa. Also attached to plaintiff's complaint were lists of university investments in companies doing business in the Union of Soviet Socialist Republics and the Republic of South Africa. The market values of such investments as of June 30, 1983, were $17,756,507.90 and $51,636,241.54, respectively. Each of the listed companies doing business in the U.S.S.R. also did business in South Africa. The parties both moved for summary judgment. The circuit court rejected each of plaintiff's challenges to Act 512 and granted summary judgment to defendant. We reverse.

In the Constitution of 1850, provision was first made for the election of regents of the University of Michigan. In addition, in language largely echoed in the 1908 and present constitutions, the Constitution of 1850 conferred on the regents "the general supervision of the University, and the direction and control of all expenditures from the university interest fund."

*   *   *

The issue of the extent to which legislative action may, if at all, permissibly impinge on the authority granted to the governing boards of Michigan's state universities is not new to the jurisprudence of our state. The Michigan Supreme Court has repeatedly affirmed the constitutional independence and exclusive authority of art. 8, § 5 boards in the face of attempted legislative encroachment. The courts have clearly interpreted the Constitution as conferring general fiscal autonomy on the university boards.

In this case, the circuit court found that Act 512 does not contravene art. 8, § 5 because it does not impinge on the "expenditure" of university funds but only on the "investment" of those funds. We agree with plaintiff that reliance on selected dictionary definitions offers an insufficient basis for the constitutional adjudication demanded by this case. As plaintiff additionally notes, any investment of funds entails what even the circuit court would be constrained to agree is the incidental expenditure of funds. And, as noted *supra*, the appellate courts have interpreted art. 8, § 5 as conferring general fiscal autonomy on the university boards.

In the instant case, the circuit court found that there is no violation of art. 8, § 5 "when an enactment of the Legislature under its police power would impose limitations or requirements on the Regents' actions *not within the educational sphere*." (Emphasis in original.) The court's reasoning that Act 512 was "a valid exercise of the police power" was as follows:

> "If the Legislature can provide for labor peace, for some measure of tort recovery and for indemnification of injured workers under the remedial principles of the workers' compensation laws, this Court holds that the Legislature can likewise provide for freedom from any and all vestiges of racial, religious and ethnic discrimination that have long injured our society."

We are persuaded that, in contrast to the cases on which the circuit court relied, the controversy in this case does not revolve around a public policy clearly established in Michigan.

* * *

All agree that the clearly established public policy of our state strictly prohibits racial and religious discrimination in the exercise of civil rights. It is also beyond dispute that the apartheid system of South Africa is repugnant to our common sense of morality and justice. Neither the people nor the Legislature, however, have clearly declared that Michigan public policy prohibits investment of public funds in organizations operating in South Africa. Act 512 is directed solely at educational institutions. The Legislature has not prohibited all investment of public funds in organizations operating in South Africa. Such investment of public employees' pension funds, for example, has not been prohibited. While Act 512 has not been the Legislature's only statement concerning investments in South Africa, we find that the investment standards contained in Act 512 do not yet reflect "a clearly established public policy" in this state.

The circuit court found that university autonomy is limited to "the educational sphere." We do not read the *Employment Relations Comm.* case as restricting university autonomy to a strictly "educational sphere." In any event, we agree with plaintiff that the distinction, if any, between the "educational" and "noneducational" spheres of a major research university is indistinct and often indiscernible. The Constitution contains no "educational sphere" limitation.

In *Regents of the University of Michigan v. Employment Relations Comm.*, the Supreme Court agreed with this Court that "within the confines of the operation and the allocation of funds of the University, [the University] is supreme." Because Act 512 impermissibly encroaches on plaintiff's authority to allocate university funds, it violates Const. 1963, art. 8, § 5.

Defendant argues that Act 512 is a permissible exercise of legislative power under Const. 1963, art. 9, § 19, which provides:

"The state shall not subscribe to, nor be interested in the stock of any company, association or corporation, except that funds accumulated to provide retirement or pension benefits for public officials and employees may be invested as provided by law; and *endowment funds created for charitable or educational purposes may be invested as provided by law governing the investment of funds held in trust by trustees* and other state funds or money may be invested in accounts of a bank, savings and loan association, or credit union organized under the laws of this state or federal law, as provided by law."

This provision, however, does not confer on the Legislature general power to regulate university investments. Plaintiff concedes that, if the Legislature amended "the law governing the investment of funds held in trust by trustees" to mandate divestment by trustees in general, investment of university endowment funds would be governed thereby. Act 512 does not represent such an amendment.

We hold that, as applied to plaintiff, Act 512 is unconstitutional. Because we find that the act violates art. 8, § 5, we do not address the remaining challenges made by plaintiff. Nor do we address the standing issue raised on cross-appeal, since defendant concedes plaintiff's standing to challenge the statute under art. 8, § 5.

Reversed. No costs.

———————

Local Ordinances and Higher Education

While the large majority of cases arise under federal or state jurisdiction, colleges exist in towns and cities; as a result, there is a rich tradition of "town-gown" enmity reaching back to the earliest universities, and attempts by college towns to regulate students and institutions. In *Yale University v. Town of New Haven*, Yale's property was held to be tax-exempt (except where its leases generated more than $6,000). 71 Conn. 316, 42 A. 87 (1899). This issue persists, as the *Morgantown* case reveals, and as other cases throughout the book reveal. See "The Carrier Dome Controversy," *Change*, 20 (March/April 1988), 43–49 (dispute over taxation of Syracuse University athletic/entertainment facility); "City, University Reach Growth and Environment Pact in Santa Cruz," *NACUBO Business Officer*, April 1988, p. 21 (agreement to negotiate environmental impact study for university expansion plans).

In addition to taxation, land use regulation is a widespread fact of regulatory life for colleges. Many of these zoning laws are enacted to regulate fraternal organizations, although on occasion an area becomes gentrified, and new regulations are enacted in traditional fraternity communities. In Salt Lake City, the city council passed extensive legislation in 1987, regulating zoning, alcohol consumption, "supervision by authorities" of the colleges, and security provisions, including a requirement that the houses hire police and "that a representative of at least thirty-five years of age from the hosting fraternity/sorority's house corporation be present at all times during such a gathering." S.L.C. Ordinance 45, 1987, Sec. 51–14–5 (1) (h).

———————

City of Morgantown v. West Virginia Board of Regents
354 S.E.2d 616 (W.Va. 1987)

BROTHERTON, Justice:

The City of Morgantown filed a declaratory judgment action in the Circuit Court of Kanawha County in July, 1985, asking whether the Board of Regents was required to collect the City's two-percent amusement tax on the sale of tickets to entertainment events such as carnivals, basketball and football games, and big time entertainers, which are open to the general public. Judge Canady of the Circuit Court of Kanawha County granted summary judgment to the Board of Regents, from which the City now appeals. We agree with the circuit court that the events sought to be taxed are not conducted for private profit, and therefore affirm.

The legislature granted cities the power to levy amusement taxes in W.Va. Code § 8–13–6 (1984). It reads, in pertinent part:

> Every municipality shall have plenary power and authority to levy and collect an admission or amusement tax upon any public amusement or entertainment conducted within the corporate limits thereof *for private profit or gain*. The tax shall be levied upon the purchaser and added to and collected by the seller with the price of admission, or other charge for the amusement or entertainment. The tax shall not exceed two percent of the admission price or charge, but a tax of one cent may be levied and collected in any case.

In order to uphold the summary judgment, we must find that there is no genuine issue of material fact as to whether sports and entertainment events sponsored by West Virginia University are conducted "for private profit or gain."

The City of Morgantown relies to a large extent on depositions taken of various University employees that indicate that the West Virginia University Department of Intercollegiate Athletics is a separate, self-supporting unit and that money generated by sports activities does not go directly to the support of the academic function of the University. The City also points out that these receipts do not go into the general revenue fund, but are sequestered in special revenue accounts, and that the State collects consumers sales tax on them. The Board of Regents counters that there is no "private" party that stands to gain from profits generated by West Virginia University's athletic or entertainment events; that the legislature and this Court have recognized that West Virginia University exercises a governmental (as opposed to private) function when it sponsors athletic contests, and that special revenue funds are nonetheless State funds. Further, the Board of Regents asserts that imposition of the sales tax on certain state activities is expressly authorized by W.Va. Code § 11–15–2(7), and that such authorization does not convert a public function to private status.

The appellant cites two cases that have sustained taxes on football ticket receipts. The first is *Allen v. Regents of Univ. Sys. of Ga.*, in which the United States Supreme Court sustained a federal ten percent admissions tax on tickets to University of Georgia and Georgia Tech football games. That case focused on whether the federal exaction would unconstitutionally burden a governmental activity of the state. The Court assumed that public education was a governmental function, and that athletic contests were an integral part of the program of public education conducted by the State of Georgia. It concluded that the State of Georgia was conducting a business "having the incidents of similar enterprises usually prosecuted for private gain," and that even if education was an essential governmental function, funds generated by conducting a business enterprise were nonetheless subject to federal taxation. This case supports the City of Morgantown's argument to the extent that it finds that two universities were conducting a business enterprise "for gain" in the form of their athletic programs. It also compares such programs to "enterprises usually prosecuted for private gain." It does not, however, hold that the football games sponsored by Georgia universities were *conducted* "for private profit or gain." It does not, therefore, compel us to accept the City of Morgantown's position.

The second case is *City of Boulder v. Regents of the Univ. of Colo.* There the City of Boulder sought a declaratory judgment regarding the validity of its admissions tax on charges made to attend public events sponsored by the University of Colorado. The Supreme Court of Colorado held that the City's ordinance was valid as applied to university football games, but invalid as applied to university lectures, dissertations, art exhibitions, concerts, and dramatic performances.[1] The statute in the Colorado case, however, imposed a tax on "admission to any place or event in the city that is open to the public," and made no reference to "private profit or gain." Thus the Colorado case, like the *Allen* case, did not address the issue before us.

Proceeds from athletic and entertainment events sponsored by West Virginia University are state funds held in special revenue accounts under W.Va. Code § 12–2–2 (1985). Special revenue accounts are state accounts kept separate from the general revenue due to a legislative determination that money generated by a particular activity should be allocated to a specific purpose. Such accounting does not remove the funds from the state treasury or destroy the public accountability of those who spend them.

This Court has held that admission fees collected by state educational institutions at athletic events are "public moneys." Similarly, we have observed that athletic programs are a proper and integral part of the education provided by state universities. We believe that the same is true of entertainment events such as concerts, lectures, exhibits, dramatic performances, and similar functions, the profits from which accrue to the benefit of a public university.

The City of Morgantown asks us to hold that such public moneys are collected for private profit or gain. The word "private" means "intended for or restricted to the use of a particular person or group or class of persons: not freely available to the public... belonging to or concerning an individual person, company, or interest." There is no individual person, company, or interest that stands to profit from university-sponsored events, and the profits therefrom are not "private."

In a case construing the term "private gain," Washington, D.C., had a statute providing that property used for educational purposes that was not used for private gain was exempt from taxation, and all other property used for educational purposes was to be taxed as any other property. The court in *District of Columbia v. Mt. Vernon Seminary* held that the seminary was not taxable under the statute even though operation of the school resulted in a profit. The court held:

> The term "private gain," as used in the statute, has reference only to gain
> realized by any individual or stockholder who has a pecuniary interest in the

---

1. The court went on to hold, however, that the City of Boulder could not force a state institution to collect such a tax.

corporation and not...to profits realized by the institution but turned back into the treasury or expended for permanent improvements....

If it had been intended to tax institutions earning a profit, i.e., having income in excess of expenditures, Congress would have used the word *profit* or the word *gain* instead of *private gain*.

The same is true in this case.

For the reasons discussed, we conclude that sports and entertainment events sponsored by West Virginia University are not conducted for private profit or gain, and are not subject to the amusement tax levied by the City of Morgantown. We find no genuine issue of material fact in this regard, and no error in the circuit court's application of the law. We therefore affirm the grant of summary judgment.

Affirmed.

United States v. City of Philadelphia
798 F.2d 81 (3d Cir. 1986)

SEITZ, Circuit Judge.

The City of Philadelphia, the Philadelphia Commission on Human Relations, and Barbara W. Mather, the Philadelphia City Solicitor, appeal from a final order of the district court granting summary judgment in favor of the United States of America ("The United States") and Temple University ("Temple"). The Philadelphia Lesbian and Gay Task Force, Lesbians and Gays at Penn, and a number of individuals (collectively "the Task Force") appeal from an order of the district court denying their motion to intervene as defendants. This court has jurisdiction over these appeals by virtue of 28 U.S.C. § 1291.

I.

A. *The Philadelphia Administrative Proceedings*

The Temple School of Law ("the Law School") operates a Placement Office that arranges interviews between its students and prospective employers. Approximately 100 employers accept the Law School's invitation to participate in this program each year, including the Judge Advocate General Corps of the Army, Navy, and Marine Corps (collectively "the J.A.G. Corps"). Participating employers select 75% of the students to be interviewed after screening their resumes; the remaining 25% are randomly selected by the Placement Office.

In the fall of 1982, two law students, Richard Brown and Loretta DeLoggio, sought interviews with the J.A.G. Corps; neither Brown nor DeLoggio was selected for an interview. Shortly thereafter, they each filed a complaint with the Philadelphia Commission on Human Relations ("the Commission"), alleging that the Law School had violated the Philadelphia Fair Practices Ordinance, Philadelphia Code §§ 9–1101 to 9–1110 ("the Ordinance"), because the Placement Office referred students to employment interviews conducted by the J.A.G. Corps while knowing or having reason to know that the Army, Navy, and Marine Corps do not accept homosexuals as members of the uniformed services.[1] The Commission subsequently issued its own complaint against the Law School, again alleging that it had violated the Ordinance by permitting the J.A.G. Corps to participate in the interviewing process conducted by the Placement Office.

A hearing on the Commission's complaint was held, at which the United States appeared as *amicus curiae* and argued that enforcement of the Ordinance against the Law School based on the hiring practices of the Army and Navy would violate the supremacy clause. The Commission, nonetheless, ordered the Law School to "cease and desist from allowing the use of its Placement Office facilities by the" J.A.G. Corps ("the Order"). In an opinion accompanying the Order, the Commission found that the Law School had committed three "unlawful employment practices": First, it had violated section 9–1103(A)(2) by "establishing, announcing and following the policy of permitting the use of its placement facilities" by representatives of the J.A.G. Corps; second, it had violated section 9–1103(A)(4) by "referring persons for employment" to the J.A.G. Corps; and third, it had violated section 9–1103(A)(7) by "aiding and abetting" the J.A.G. Corps in executing their policy of discriminating against persons based on their sexual orientation.[2]

B. *The District Court Proceedings*

Shortly after the Commission ordered the Law School to "cease and desist" from cooperating with the J.A.G. Corps, the United States filed a complaint in the district court alleging that the Ordinance, as applied to the Law School by the Commission, violated the supremacy clause. At the same time, Temple filed a complaint alleging that the Order violated both the supremacy clause and the first amendment.

---

1. Department of Defense Directive 1332.14 provides, in pertinent part, that:

    Homosexuality is incompatible with military service. The presence in the military environment of persons who engage in homosexual conduct or who, by their statements, demonstrate a propensity to engage in homosexual conduct seriously impairs the accomplishment of the military mission. The presence of such members adversely affects the ability of the Military Services to maintain discipline, good order, and morale; to foster mutual trust and confidence among service-members; to ensure the integrity of the system of rank and command; to facilitate assignment and worldwide deployment of servicemembers who frequently must live and work under close conditions affording minimal privacy; to recruit and retain members of the Military Services; to maintain the public acceptability of military service; and to prevent breaches of security.

2. The Ordinance provides, in pertinent part, that:

    (A) It shall be an unlawful employment practice:

    (2) For any...employment agency...to establish, announce or follow a policy of denying or limiting...the employment...opportunities, of any individual or group because of...sexual orientation....

    ....

    (4) For any employment agency because of a person's race, color, sex, religion, national origin, ancestry, age or handicap to:

    (a) fail or refuse to classify properly or refer for employment;

    (b) otherwise discriminate against any person.

    ....

    (7) For any person to aid, abet, incite, compel or coerce the doing of any unfair employment practice...or to attempt directly or indirectly to commit any act declared by this Chapter to be an unfair employment practice.

The United States and Temple subsequently filed motions for summary judgment. The Commission (and the other named defendants) opposed both motions, and filed a cross-motion for summary judgment. The district court held a hearing on these motions and, at its conclusion, granted summary judgment to the United States and Temple. The court essentially found that the Commission's order constituted an attempt to do indirectly what it was without power to do directly—i.e., "to regulate ... indirectly through Temple University the conduct of the United States, insofar as it adheres to its policy of discrimination against homosexuals." As a result, the district court entered an order prohibiting the Commission from "adjudicating any complaint or taking any adverse action under the [Ordinance] against any person, corporation, association or group based on the Commission's objection to the policy of the United States in discriminating on the basis of sexual orientation in its military recruitment efforts." It is this order that forms the basis for the Commission's appeal.

II.

In the brief opinion accompanying its order, the district court concluded that the supremacy clause prohibits any state or local agency "from interfering with or attempting to frustrate the willingness of private citizens or entities or public entities from participating with the United States to carry out a joint effort protected under the constitution." The Commission and the Task Force, together with the American Civil Liberties Union of Greater Philadelphia ("the A.C.L.U.") and the Lambda Legal Defense and Education Fund, Inc. ("Lambda"), take issue with this conclusion and contend that the district court improperly granted summary judgment to the United States and Temple.

A.

We emphasize, at the outset, that all parties to this action agree that the Commission cannot directly prohibit the military from recruiting persons on whatever terms it deems appropriate. They sharply disagree, however, as to whether the City of Philadelphia, acting through the Commission, may legally prohibit Temple from making its Law School placement services available to the J.A.G. Corps because of the military's policy of discriminating on the basis of sexual orientation.

The task presently before us, then, is to determine whether the Ordinance, as applied to the Law School by the Order, "*conflicts* with Congressional legislation or with any discernible Congressional policy." While ostensibly a question of governmental immunity, this issue is perhaps "best understood as posing an issue essentially of federal preemption." Viewed in this light, the Order "conflicts" with federal law if, and to the extent that, it "stands as an obstacle to the accomplishment and execution of the full purposes and objectives of Congress."

In conducting this inquiry, we remain mindful of the fact that "[a]n unexpressed purpose of Congress to set aside statutes of the states regulating their internal affairs is not lightly to be inferred and ought not to be implied where the legislative command, read in the light of its history, remains ambiguous."

B.

Congressional legislation authorizing military recruiting falls into two categories. First, there is the general Congressional directive that the respective branches of the military "shall conduct intensive recruiting campaigns to obtain enlistments." Second, there is the long-standing Congressional policy of encouraging colleges and universities to cooperate with, and open their campuses to, military recruiters. This legislation, with certain exceptions not relevant here, prohibits the "expenditure of defense funds at institutions of higher learning when recruiting personnel of the Armed Forces are barred by policy or where the institution, as a matter of policy, eliminates ROTC."

We believe that only one reasonable conclusion can be drawn from this legislation: Congress considers access to college and university employment facilities by military recruiters to be a matter of paramount importance. In other words, we think that Congress views such access an integral part of the military's effort to conduct "intensive recruiting campaigns to obtain enlistments." This conclusion is buttressed by the legislative history of these provisions. For example, a committee report accompanying the DDA Act of 1973 states, in pertinent part, that "the Committee believes that [the] national interest is best served by colleges and universities which provide for the full spectrum of opportunity for various career fields, including the military field through the Reserve Officers Training Corps program, and by the opportunity for students to talk to all recruiting sources, including military recruiters."

Given this interpretation of the funding prohibitions contained in the DDA Acts of 1971 and 1973, and the NASAA Act of 1969, it is obvious that the Commission's Order conflicts with a "discernible Congressional policy." The Order absolutely prohibits the cooperation that Congress intended this legislation to engender and, as a result, military recruiters are denied the access that Congress deemed critical to their ability to conduct "intensive recruiting campaigns."

Nonetheless, the Supreme Court has cautioned that " 'a mere conflict in words is not sufficient'; the question remains whether the 'consequences [of the state regulation] sufficiently injure the objectives of the federal program to require nonrecognition.' " We interpret this statement to mean, in the present circumstances, that if the Order does not significantly impair the military's ability to recruit doctors, lawyers, and other skilled personnel, the fact that it conflicts with Congress' policy of promoting on-campus recruiting by the military would not permit us to invalidate the Order.

In support of its motion for summary judgment, the government introduced two declarations from Lieutenant General Edgar A. Chavarrie, the Deputy Assistant Secretary of Defense for Military Personnel and Force Management, which illustrate the scope of military recruiting in the City of Philadelphia. For example, in his original declaration, Chavarrie stated that the military currently recruits approximately 5,000 persons per year from Philadelphia; he also stated that there are about 840 students enrolled in Reserve Officer Training Corps ("R.O.T.C.") programs at 23 Philadelphia-area colleges and universities. In his supplemental declaration, Chavarrie stated that of the 95 officers recruited by the Navy from Philadelphia-area colleges and universities in 1984, approximately 47% or 45 officers were recruited from contacts established on campus. These 45 officers included 2 doctors, 12 naval aviators, and 11 nuclear propulsion engineers—all skills that are, according to Chavarrie, in short supply throughout the Armed Forces. Chavarrie also stated that, during the last three years, 98% of the Navy's nuclear propulsion engineers were recruited from on-campus contacts. Finally, in the same declaration, Chavarrie stated that, based on these statistics, campus recruiting represents the most effective way to fill the critical shortage of persons possessing these important skills.

Even viewing this evidence in the light most favorable to the Commission, we believe that the government has demonstrated, in the words of the Supreme Court, that the Order has "the potential to frustrate" effective recruiting of skilled personnel in the Philadelphia area. Thus, we reject the A.C.L.U.'s assertion that, given the present record, the concerns expressed by Temple and the government are "too speculative to support pre-emption."

We likewise reject the suggestion by the Commission, the A.C.L.U., and the Task Force that we should not consider the effect of the Order on military recruiting outside the context of the Law School's Placement Office. We believe that it is appropriate to consider the Order's effect on military recruiting on Temple's campus generally, as well as its impact on military recruiting on other college and university campuses throughout the City, and the possibility that other jurisdictions may adopt a similar interpretation of their anti-discrimination ordinances. We cannot conceive of any reason why the Commission would prohibit the military from recruiting lawyers at Temple, yet permit it to recruit doctors or engineers at the University of Pennsylvania. Nor can we conceive of any reason why other jurisdictions with similar laws would adopt a construction different from that adopted by the Commission. Rather, these considerations simply underscore the fact that the Order has "the potential to frustrate" effective military recruiting, both in Philadelphia and throughout the nation.

Finally, while we agree with the A.C.L.U., the Task Force, and Lambda, that, under the DDA Act of 1973 and its predecessor legislation, each college and university retained the "absolute right to determine whether it desires to have any association with the military forces of its country, and this includes the right to determine whether it desires to permit military recruiters . . . on its campus," we do not believe that this detracts from our conclusions that Congress considers on-campus recruiting to be an integral part of its military recruiting policy, and that the Order significantly impairs the military's ability to recruit the skilled personnel it requires.

We conclude, therefore, that the Order conflicts with a clearly discernible Congressional policy concerning military recruitment on the campuses of this nation's colleges and universities. It follows, then, that the Commission cannot enforce the Ordinance against Temple with respect to the latter's decision to make its placement facilities available to the J.A.G. Corps.

In reaching this conclusion we freely concede that the issues raised by the Commission are difficult given the traditional importance of the City's interest, under its police power, in eradicating employment discrimination. But our conviction that the Order cannot stand is highlighted by one critical fact: in most (if not all) of the reported cases involving questions of governmental immunity, it was at least theoretically possible for the persons involved to comply with both the state and federal policies involved.

* * *

IV.

Accordingly, the order of the district court granting summary judgment to Temple and the United States will be affirmed. Likewise, the order of the district court denying the motion of the Task Force to intervene will be affirmed.

Consortia and Interinstitutional Governance

Colleges cooperate in many ways, by participating in exchanges, by grouping together for professional solidarity, by forming consortia for various purposes, by agreeing to accept student credits from similar colleges, and by dozens of other formal and informal means. Some of these are historical ties, such as "feeder schools" whose students go on to transfer at cooperating institutions, while others are secured through legislative mechanisms, such as the Education Commission of the States (ECS) or the Western Interstate Commission on Higher Education (WICHE).

Two of the most formal means are accreditation and athletics, devices by which institutions recognize each other as legitimate and by which intercollegiate athletics are governed. Because accreditation is the formal, legal means by which colleges exist, several cases on this issue have been included earlier. Unaccredited institutions, unless they can avail themselves of alternative means for recognition (such as the 3-letters-of-credit rule), are ineligible for federal aid and most states' aid programs. As the *Marjorie Webster* case reveals, there are antitrust implications in the collective activity of accrediting—whether for general collegiate recognition purposes or for more specialized purposes, such as law or medical schools.

Marjorie Webster Junior College v. Middle States Association

139 U.S. App. D.C. 217, 432 F.2d 650 (1970),
cert. denied, 400 U.S. 965 (1970)

BAZELON, Chief Judge:

Middle States Association of Colleges and Secondary Schools, Inc., is a voluntary nonprofit educational corporation, the successor to an unincorporated association of the same name established in 1887. Its general purposes are to aid and encourage the development of quality in secondary schools and institutions of higher education located within its geographical domain (New York, New Jersey, Pennsylvania, Delaware, Maryland, and the District of Columbia) or outside of the continental United States. Chief among its activities is that of accrediting member institutions and applicants for membership. Marjorie Webster Junior College, Inc., is a proprietary junior college for women located in the District of Columbia. In 1966, it applied to Middle States for accreditation. Relying upon a policy statement of the Federation of Regional Accrediting Commissions of Higher Education, and upon its own past practice, Middle States refused to consider Marjorie Webster for accreditation because the latter was not "a nonprofit organization with a governing board representing the public interest." Following this refusal Marjorie Webster brought suit to compel its consideration for accreditation without regard to its proprietary character. The District Court found Middle States' refusal to consider proprietary institutions of higher education for accreditation a violation of § 3 of the Sherman Act and of the developing common law regarding exclusion from membership in private associations; in addition, it found that Middle States' activities in the field of accreditation were sufficiently under the aegis of the Federal Government as to make applicable the limitations of the Due Process Clause; and that to deny accreditation to all proprietary institutions solely by reason of their proprietary character was arbitrary and unreasonable, in violation of the Fifth Amendment. Concluding, finally, that continued denial of consideration for accreditation would result in irreparable injury to Marjorie Webster, the District Court enjoined Middle States from denying Marjorie Webster accreditation solely because of its proprietary character, and ordered it to accredit Marjorie

Webster if it should otherwise qualify for accreditation under Middle States' standards. On the application of Middle States, we stayed the District Court's order pending our determination of this appeal. For the reasons hereafter set forth, we conclude that the Sherman Act is not applicable to Middle States' conduct as indicated by the present record; that the circumstances are not such as to warrant judicial interference with the accreditation and membership policies of Middle States; and that, assuming the Due Process Clause to be applicable, Marjorie Webster has not sustained its burden of showing the irrationality of the policy in question as applied to bar consideration of Marjorie Webster for accreditation. Accordingly, we reverse the judgment of the District Court.

I.

Appellee strongly urges, and the court below concluded, that once it be determined that appellee is engaging in "trade," restraint of that "trade" by appellant's conduct is subject to the limitations of the Sherman Act. If this were the ordinary case of a trade association alleged to have transgressed the bounds of reasonable regulation designed to mitigate the evils afflicting a particular industry, this reasoning might be conclusive. But in our view, the character of the defendant association, and the nature of the activities that it regulates, require a finer analysis.

Despite the broad wording of the Sherman Act, it has long been settled that not every form of combination or conspiracy that restrains trade falls within its ambit. For the language of the Act, although broad, is also vague; and in consequence of that vagueness, "perhaps not uncalculated, the courts have been left to give content to the statute, and in the performance of that function it is appropriate that courts should interpret its word in light of its legislative history and of the particular evils at which the legislation was aimed." The Act was a product of the era of "trusts" and of "combinations" of businesses and of capital organized and directed to control of the market by suppression of competition in the marketing of goods and services, the monopolistic tendency of which had become a matter of public concern.

"The Court in *Apex* recognized that the Act is aimed primarily at combinations having commercial objectives and is applied only to a very limited extent to organizations, like labor unions, which normally have other objectives."

That appellant's objectives, both in its formation and in the development and application of the restriction here at issue, are not commercial is not in dispute. Of course, when a given activity falls within the scope of the Sherman Act, a lack of predatory intent is not conclusive on the question of its legality. But the proscriptions of the Sherman Act were "tailored * * * for the business world," not for the non-commercial aspects of the liberal arts and the learned professions. In these contexts, an incidental restraint of trade, absent an intent or purpose to affect the commercial aspects of the profession, is not sufficient to warrant application of the antitrust laws.

We are fortified in this conclusion by the historic reluctance of Congress to exercise control in educational matters. We need not suggest that this reluctance is of such depth as to immunize any conceivable activity of appellant from regulation under the antitrust laws. It is possible to conceive of restrictions on eligibility for accreditation that could have little other than a commercial motive; and as such, antitrust policy would presumably be applicable. Absent such motives, however, the process of accreditation is an activity distinct from the sphere of commerce; it goes rather to the heart of the concept of education itself. We do not believe that Congress intended this concept to be molded by the policies underlying the Sherman Act.

II.

The increasing importance of private associations in the affairs of individuals and organizations has led to substantial expansion of judicial control over "The Internal Affairs of Associations not for Profit." Where membership in, or certification by, such an association is a virtual prerequisite to the practice of a given profession, courts have scrutinized the standards and procedures employed by the association notwithstanding their recognition of the fact that professional societies possess a specialized competence in evaluating the qualifications of an individual to engage in professional activities. The standards set must be reasonable, applied with an even hand, and not in conflict with the public policy of the jurisdiction. Even where less than complete exclusion from practice is involved, deprivation of substantial economic or professional advantages will often be sufficient to warrant judicial action.

The extent of judicial power to regulate the standards set by private professional associations, however, must be related to the necessity for intervention. Particularly when, as here, judicial action is predicated not upon a legislative text but upon the developing doctrines of the common law, general propositions must not be allowed to obscure the specific relevant facts of each individual case. In particular, the extent to which deference is due to the professional judgment of the association will vary both with the subject matter at issue and with the degree of harm resulting from the association's action.

With these factors in mind, we turn to consider the harm appellee will suffer by virtue of the challenged exclusion. We note in this regard that denial of accreditation by Middle States is not tantamount to exclusion of appellee from operating successfully as a junior college. It has been, and without regard to accreditation by appellant will remain, accredited by the District of Columbia Board of Education, and licensed to award the Associate in Arts degree. The record indicates that appellee's listing in the major publications available for use by high school guidance counsellors (and often, by students and their families) does not depend upon its accreditation by appellant. Appellee's lack of accreditation does not appear to render it, or its students, ineligible to receive federal aid. Appellee's students seeking to transfer to four-year colleges at the completion of their programs are not necessarily barred from obtaining credit for their studies because of the unaccredited status of the institution. We recognize, as the trial court found, that lack of accreditation may be a not insignificant handicap to appellee both in the effect that such lack may have on students considering application for admission, and in the loss of the substantial benefits that the accreditation process itself has upon the institution under study. But appellee has operated successfully as a junior college since 1947. Although it suffered a decline in applications for admission in the years immediately preceding the instant suit, this decline was shared by the other women's institutions in the District of Columbia. In the last year for which figures were introduced, it received over 100 more applications than Mount Vernon Junior College, the institution receiving the second highest number. We do not believe, therefore, that the record supports the conclusion that appellee will be unable to operate successfully as a junior college unless it is considered for accreditation by appellant.

* * *

We do not conclude, nor does appellant even suggest, that competition from proprietary institutions is anything but wholesome for the nonprofit educational establishment. We merely find that, so far as can be discerned from the present record, appellant does not wield such monopoly power over the operation of educational institutions that its standards for accreditation may be subject to plenary judicial review; and that in light of the substantial latitude that must accordingly be allowed appellant in setting its criteria for accreditation, appellee's exclusion solely on the basis of its proprietary character is not beyond the bounds of appellant's allowable discretion.

III.

What has been said above should also dispose of so much of appellee's argument as is based upon the Due Process Clause. We may assume, without deciding, that either the nature of appellant's activities or the federal recognition which they are awarded renders them state action subject to the limitations of the Fifth Amendment. If so, however, the burden remains with appellee to show the unreasonableness of the restriction, not simply in the abstract but as applied specifically to it. We need not decide here the precise limits of those circumstances under which governmental action may restrict or injure the activities of proprietary educational institutions. For the reasons already discussed, we conclude that appellee has failed to show that the present restriction was without reasonable basis. Accordingly, it must be upheld.

Reversed.

Bennett v. State Bar of Nevada

746 P.2d 143 (Nev. 1987)

GUNDERSON, Chief Justice:

The petition before us seeks a waiver [Sup. Ct. Rules, Rule 51, subd. 3.] (SCR 51(3)) and requests this court to allow petitioners to be admitted as members of the State Bar of Nevada. Petitioners graduated from the Nevada School of Law (the school), formerly Old College School of Law, in 1985, 1986 and 1987, and all but one have successfully completed the Nevada bar examination since graduation. The Board of Governors of the State Bar of Nevada does not oppose the petition.

In 1984, the Nevada School of Law sought a waiver of SCR 51(3) which requires that an applicant for examination for a license to practice as an attorney in this state have received a law degree from an institution accredited by the American Bar Association (ABA). In January, 1985, this court denied the request for a general waiver or modification of SCR 51(3). Nevertheless, we granted conditional relief to graduates of the school based upon our findings and conclusions. Specifically, based upon the record and our inspection of the school, we determined that despite its inauspicious beginnings and initial shortcomings, the school had made impressive strides toward academic credibility. Moreover, the school represented to the satisfaction of the court that it would have its physical plant, library, faculty, student admission practices, and student support services in condition to enable it, in good faith, to apply for ABA provisional accreditation by the fall of 1985. Accordingly, this court ordered that in the event the school achieved ABA provisional accreditation by August 31, 1988, such accreditation would be accepted as proof that any student graduating before accreditation has received an education "functionally equivalent" to that provided by an ABA-accredited school. Additionally, pending the granting of such accreditation, the court allowed the school's graduates to sit for the bar examination, conditioned upon the completion of certain corrective courses on or before the time of the school's accreditation. The successful examinees' admission to the State Bar of Nevada, however, was to be deferred until the ABA granted provisional accreditation to the school.

The school subsequently took various steps to overcome the deficiencies identified in our 1985 order. In September, 1986, the school applied to the ABA for provisional accreditation. An ABA inspection team examined the school during the week of November 15, 1986, and reported its findings to the Accreditation Committee for the Section of Legal Education and Admissions of the ABA (the Committee) on March 19, 1987. On April 28, 1987, the Committee denied the school's application for provisional accreditation.

In May, 1987, the school's trustees attempted to donate the school and its assets to the University of Nevada. Unable to convince the University to accept the gift or to overcome the school's substantial operating debt, the school's trustees voted to close the school after a ten-month "wind-down" period. Consequently, petitioners will be unable to satisfy the condition precedent to their admission to practice law in Nevada, i.e., that the school achieve ABA provisional accreditation by August 31, 1988. Petitioners now contend that waiver of SCR 51(3) is appropriate, in spite of the ABA's denial of accreditation to the school, since the record as a whole demonstrates that the education received at the school was substantially similar or functionally equivalent to that provided at an ABA-accredited school. We agree.

The purpose of the educational requirement embodied in SCR 51(3) is to promote high standards of competence among members of the State Bar of Nevada. To evaluate an applicant's legal education effectively and expeditiously, without imposing an excessive burden on our resources, this court has elected to utilize the accreditation resources of the ABA. On the other hand, we must ensure that applicants are treated fairly and that any qualification for admission to the bar "must have a rational connection with the applicant's fitness or capacity to practice law." Accordingly, we have recognized exceptions and waived the application of SCR 51(3) "whenever it can be demonstrated that the rules operate in such a manner as to deny admission to a petitioner arbitrarily and for a reason unrelated to the essential purpose of the rule." Stated another way, if an applicant proves to this court that the education received at a law school not accredited by the ABA is nonetheless functionally equivalent to an education provided at an ABA-approved school, and the applicant has otherwise complied with all requirements of the law relative to admission to the State Bar of Nevada, the objective of SCR 51(3) has been met and a waiver of the rule may be appropriate.

In the present case, the Nevada School of Law took several steps since 1985 to improve the legal education offered and to overcome the deficiencies identified in our previous order. Specifically, the school provided supplemental courses to its graduates, extensively improved its facilities, increased its library collection from 34,000 hardbound volumes to 71,853 hardbound and microform volumes, hired a full-time library director holding J.D. and M.L.S. degrees, increased its full-time faculty to twelve, and established an employment placement office. The only deficiency identified in our order of 1985 which has not been remedied is the achievement of financial stability.

The report issued by the ABA's Accreditation Committee likewise recognizes several noteworthy achievements. Indeed, in critical areas, the Committee's report can be read to support the proposition that the education received by petitioners was functionally equivalent to an education offered at an ABA-accredited school. We note that the Committee's report encompasses far more than just educational factors. Indeed, in determining whether the school could operate in the future as a viable law school, the Committee directed its inquiry for the most part of financial and budgetary considerations. Ten of the fifteen findings and conclusions of the Committee focus primarily on the lack of financial stability and on factors related indirectly, at best, to the quality of the legal education offered. Of the remaining five findings, No. 6 concerns the calibre of students admitted in the fall of 1986. This finding, however, is immaterial to this petition since these students are not presently before the court. Moreover, the remaining four findings, Nos. 4, 8, 9 and 10, do not conclusively demonstrate that the education received by petitioners was not functionally equivalent to that received at an ABA-accredited institution.

Finding No. 4 concerns the perceived inability of the school to attract full-time professors based on the current budget and the projected budgets for the next five years. This finding, however, looks mainly to the future. With respect to the *current* faculty, the inspection team's report notes: "The educational credentials of the current faculty are good in terms of academic background, representing a number of excellent law schools. The professional experience of some of the current faculty is broad." Similarly, although Finding No. 8 indicates that "overall academic rigor" has been low, the Committee concludes that "[c]lassroom teaching was judged by the site team to range from good to marginal." None of the teaching observed by the on-site inspection team was unacceptable. Although the teaching may not have been exceptional, it was in every respect adequate.

Finding No. 9 states that "[b]ar results have been mixed." The Committee notes that the "pass rate of Old College graduates on the Nevada bar exam has been about 69 percent . . . well below the 91 percent pass rate of the nearest California law school." This finding, more than any other, is subject to varied interpretations depending on the utilization and application of the variables. Broken down by year, the school represents that 67% passed in 1985, 77% in 1986, and 71% in 1987. Moreover, the school correctly suggests that it is misleading to compare the school's pass rate with the pass rate of the McGeorge School of Law only. We are not convinced that the pass rate of graduates of McGeorge School of Law, whose graduates historically have performed exceptionally well on both the California and Nevada bar examinations, is uniquely representative or standard of an acceptable pass rate. Indeed, we are persuaded that comparing Nevada School of Law to McGeorge, in support of denying accreditation to Nevada School of Law, was patently inappropriate. In this regard, we note that the Nevada School of Law's pass rate compared favorably with the pass rate for graduates from four ABA-approved California law schools commonly attended by Nevada students: University of San Diego (73%); California Western (63%); Loyola of Los Angeles (60%); and Whittier (28.5%). Indeed, the school's pass rate exceeded the pass rate for twenty-seven other ABA-accredited schools whose graduates sat for the same bar examinations. Thus, while the school's pass rate may not compare favorably with that of McGeorge School of Law, it nonetheless evidences that petitioners received an education sufficient to enable them successfully to pass the bar, and to practice law and advise clients as capably as graduates from many schools accredited by the ABA.

Finding No. 10 concludes that the school's conditions were inadequate to attract and retain a competent faculty. This finding, however, is based on the unproven assumption that funding would have remained unavailable in the future. Further, it does not negate the inspection team's and the Committee's findings that "the current faculty are good in terms of academic background..." and that their teaching was good to marginal.

Based on the foregoing, we conclude that petitioners are entitled to relief. Accordingly, we hereby waive the requirements of SCR 51(3) as to the above-named petitioners who have successfully passed the bar examination and otherwise complied with the rules for admission of the Supreme Court of Nevada.

IT IS HEREBY ORDERED that petitioners will be admitted as members of the State Bar of Nevada with all privileges relating thereto, upon complying with any and all remaining requirements of law relative to such admission.

———————

Although accreditation associations are not governed by purely constitutional requirements, state agency law may require a basic, fundamental fairness. *Medical Institute of Minnesota v. National Association of Trade and Technical Schools*, 817 F.2d 1310 (1987). For a review of accreditation policies and acceptable procedures, see W. Kaplin, "Accrediting Agencies' Legal Responsibilities: In Pursuit of the Public Interest," *Journal of Law and Education*, 12 (1983), 87–114; K. Young et al., *Understanding Accreditation* (San Francisco: Jossey-Bass, 1983); D. Neal, ed. *Consortia and Interinstitutional Cooperation* (New York: Macmillan, 1988).

Another major area of interinstitutional governance is intercollegiate athletics, and, like *Marjorie Webster*, antitrust activities are implicated in the arrangement. In *NCAA v. Board of Regents*, a detailed history of the National Collegiate Athletic Association is recounted, including the establishment of a rival consortium (College Football Association), which had negotiated its own college football television contract. The district court found that the NCAA constituted a "classic cartel," and the Supreme Court agreed. Since the decision, there has been a shift in individual athletic conference cooperative arrangements as well, with the most powerful university programs choosing to go their own way in negotiating media broadcast contracts. See K. Rowe, "*NCAA v. Board of Regents*: A Broadening of the Rule of Reason," *Journal of College and University Law*, 11 (1984), 377–97; W. Kirby, "Federal Antitrust Issues Affecting Institutions of Higher Education: An Overview," *Journal of College and University Law*, 11 (1984), 345–76.

———————

NCAA v. Board of Regents
of the University of Oklahoma
468 U.S. 85 (1984)

Justice STEVENS delivered the opinion of the Court.

The University of Oklahoma and the University of Georgia contend that the National Collegiate Athletic Association has unreasonably restrained trade in the televising of college football games. After an extended trial, the District Court found that the

NCAA had violated § 1 of the Sherman Act and granted injunctive relief. The Court of Appeals agreed that the statute had been violated but modified the remedy in some respects. We granted certiorari, and now affirm.

I

The NCAA

Since its inception in 1905, the NCAA has played an important role in the regulation of amateur collegiate sports. It has adopted and promulgated playing rules, standards of amateurism, standards for academic eligibility, regulations concerning recruitment of athletes, and rules governing the size of athletic squads and coaching staffs. In some sports, such as baseball, swimming, basketball, wrestling, and track, it has sponsored and conducted national tournaments. It has not done so in the sport of football, however. With the exception of football, the NCAA has not undertaken any regulation of the televising of athletic events.

The NCAA has approximately 850 voting members. The regular members are classified into separate divisions to reflect differences in size and scope of their athletic programs. Division I includes 276 colleges with major athletic programs; in this group only 187 play intercollegiate football. Divisions II and III include approximately 500 colleges with less extensive athletic programs. Division I has been subdivided into Divisions I-A and I-AA for football.

Some years ago, five major conferences together with major football-playing independent institutions organized the College Football Association (CFA). The original purpose of the CFA was to promote the interests of major football-playing schools within the NCAA structure. The Universities of Oklahoma and Georgia, respondents in this Court, are members of the CFA.

History of the NCAA Television Plan

In 1938, the University of Pennsylvania televised one of its home games. From 1940 through the 1950 season all of Pennsylvania's home games were televised. That was the beginning of the relationship between television and college football.

On January 11, 1951, a three-person "Television Committee," appointed during the preceding year, delivered a report to the NCAA's annual convention in Dallas. Based on preliminary surveys, the committee had concluded that "television does have an adverse effect on college football attendance and unless brought under some control threatens to seriously harm the nation's overall athletic and physical system." The report emphasized that "the television problem is truly a national one and requires collective action by the colleges." As a result, the NCAA decided to retain the National Opinion Research Center (NORC) to study the impact of television on live attendance, and to declare a moratorium on the televising of football games. A television committee was appointed to implement the decision and to develop an NCAA television plan for 1951.

The committee's 1951 plan provided that only one game a week could be telecast in each area, with a total blackout on 3 of the 10 Saturdays during the season. A team could appear on television only twice during a season. The plan also provided that the NORC would conduct a systematic study of the effects of the program on attendance. The plan received the virtually unanimous support of the NCAA membership; only the University of Pennsylvania challenged it. Pennsylvania announced that it would televise all its home games. The council of the NCAA thereafter declared

Pennsylvania a member in bad standing and the four institutions scheduled to play at Pennsylvania in 1951 refused to do so. Pennsylvania then reconsidered its decision and abided by the NCAA plan.

During each of the succeeding five seasons, studies were made which tended to indicate that television had an adverse effect on attendance at college football games. During those years the NCAA continued to exercise complete control over the number of games that could be televised.

From 1952 through 1977 the NCAA television committee followed essentially the same procedure for developing its television plans. It would first circulate a questionnaire to the membership and then use the responses as a basis for formulating a plan for the ensuing season. The plan was then submitted to a vote by means of a mail referendum. Once approved, the plan formed the basis for NCAA's negotiations with the networks. Throughout this period the plans retained the essential purposes of the original plan. Until 1977 the contracts were all for either 1- or 2-year terms. In 1977 the NCAA adopted "principles of negotiation" for the future and discontinued the practice of submitting each plan for membership approval. Then the NCAA also entered into its first 4-year contract granting exclusive rights to the American Broadcasting Cos. (ABC) for the 1978–1981 seasons. ABC had held the exclusive rights to network telecasts of NCAA football games since 1965.

The Current Plan

The plan adopted in 1981 for the 1982–1985 seasons is at issue in this case. This plan, like each of its predecessors, recites that it is intended to reduce, insofar as possible, the adverse effects of live television upon football game attendance. It provides that "all forms of television of the football games of NCAA member institutions during the Plan control periods shall be in accordance with this Plan." The plan recites that the television committee has awarded rights to negotiate and contract for the telecasting of college football games of members of the NCAA to two "carrying networks." In addition to the principal award of rights to the carrying networks, the plan also describes rights for a "supplementary series" that had been awarded for the 1982 and 1983 seasons, as well as a procedure for permitting specific "exception telecasts."

In separate agreements with each of the carrying networks, ABC and the Columbia Broadcasting System (CBS), the NCAA granted each the right to telecast the 14 live "exposures" described in the plan, in accordance with the "ground rules" set forth therein. Each of the networks agreed to pay a specified "minimum aggregate compensation to the participating NCAA member institutions" during the 4-year period in an amount that totaled $131,750,000. In essence the agreement authorized each network to negotiate directly with member schools for the right to televise their games. The agreement itself does not describe the method of computing the compensation for each game, but the practice that has developed over the years and that the District Court found would be followed under the current agreement involved the setting of a recommended fee by a representative of the NCAA for different types of telecasts, with national telecasts being the most valuable, regional telecasts being less valuable, and Division II or Division III games commanding a still lower price. The aggregate of all these payments presumably equals the total minimum aggregate compensation set forth in the basic agreement. Except for differences in payment between national and regional telecasts, and with respect to Division II and Division

III games, the amount that any team receives does not change with the size of the viewing audience, the number of markets in which the game is telecast, or the particular characteristic of the game or the participating teams. Instead, the "ground rules" provide that the carrying networks make alternate selections of those games they wish to televise, and thereby obtain the exclusive right to submit a bid at an essentially fixed price to the institutions involved.

The plan also contains "appearance requirements" and "appearance limitations" which pertain to each of the 2-year periods that the plan is in effect. The basic requirement imposed on each of the two networks is that it must schedule appearances for at least 82 different member institutions during each 2-year period. Under the appearance limitations no member institution is eligible to appear on television more than a total of six times and more than four times nationally, with the appearances to be divided equally between the two carrying networks. The number of exposures specified in the contracts also sets an absolute maximum on the number of games that can be broadcast.

Thus, although the current plan is more elaborate than any of its predecessors, it retains the essential features of each of them. It limits the total amount of televised intercollegiate football and the number of games that any one team may televise. No member is permitted to make any sale of television rights except in accordance with the basic plan.

Background of this Controversy

Beginning in 1979 CFA members began to advocate that colleges with major football programs should have a greater voice in the formulation of football television policy than they had in the NCAA. CFA therefore investigated the possibility of negotiating a television agreement of its own, developed an independent plan, and obtained a contract offer from the National Broadcasting Co. (NBC). This contract, which it signed in August 1981, would have allowed a more liberal number of appearances for each institution, and would have increased the overall revenues realized by CFA members.

In response the NCAA publicly announced that it would take disciplinary action against any CFA member that complied with the CFA-NBC contract. The NCAA made it clear that sanctions would not be limited to the football programs of CFA members, but would apply to other sports as well. On September 8, 1981, respondents commenced this action in the United States District Court for the Western District of Oklahoma and obtained a preliminary injunction preventing the NCAA from initiating disciplinary proceedings or otherwise interfering with CFA's efforts to perform its agreement with NBC. Notwithstanding the entry of the injunction, most CFA members were unwilling to commit themselves to the new contractual arrangement with NBC in the face of the threatened sanctions and therefore the agreement was never consummated.

Decision of the District Court

After a full trial, the District Court held that the controls exercised by the NCAA over the televising of college football games violated the Sherman Act. The District Court defined the relevant market as "live college football television" because it found that alternative programming has a significantly different and lesser audience appeal. The District Court then concluded that the NCAA controls over college football are those of a "classic cartel" with an "almost absolute control over the supply of college football which is made available to the networks, to television advertisers, and ultimately to the viewing public. Like all other cartels, NCAA members have sought and achieved a price for their product which is, in most instances, artificially high. The NCAA cartel imposes production limits on its members, and maintains mechanisms for punishing cartel members who seek to stray from these production quotas. The cartel has established a uniform price for the products of each of the member producers, with no regard for the differing quality of these products or the consumer demand for these various products."

The District Court found that competition in the relevant market had been restrained in three ways: (1) NCAA fixed the price for particular telecasts; (2) its exclusive network contracts were tantamount to a group boycott of all other potential broadcasters and its threat of sanctions against its own members constituted a threatened boycott of potential competitors; and (3) its plan placed an artificial limit on the production of televised college football.

In the District Court the NCAA offered two principal justifications for its television policies: that they protected the gate attendance of its members and that they tended to preserve a competitive balance among the football programs of the various schools. The District Court rejected the first justification because the evidence did not support the claim that college football television adversely affected gate attendance. With respect to the "competitive balance" argument, the District Court found that the evidence failed to show that the NCAA regulations on matters such as recruitment and the standards for preserving amateurism were not sufficient to maintain an appropriate balance.

Decision of the Court of Appeals

The Court of Appeals held that the NCAA television plan constituted illegal *per se* price fixing. It rejected each of the three arguments advanced by NCAA to establish the procompetitive character of its plan. First, the court rejected the argument that the television plan promoted live attendance. noting that since the plan involved a concomitant reduction in viewership the plan did not result in a net increase in output and hence was not procompetitive. Second, the Court of Appeals rejected as illegitimate the NCAA's purpose of promoting athletically balanced competition. It held that such a consideration amounted to an argument that "competition will destroy the market"—a position inconsistent with the policy of the Sherman Act. Moreover, assuming *arguendo* that the justification was legitimate, the court agreed with the District Court's finding "that any contribution the plan made to athletic balance could be achieved by less restrictive means." Third, the Court of Appeals refused to view the NCAA plan as competitively justified by the need to compete effectively with other types of television programming, since it entirely eliminated competition between producers of football and hence was illegal *per se*.

Finally, the Court of Appeals concluded that even if the television plan were not *per se* illegal, its anticompetitive limitation on price and output was not offset by any procompetitive justification sufficient to save the plan even when the totality of the circumstances was examined. The case was remanded to the District Court for an appropriate modification in its injunctive decree.

II

There can be no doubt that the challenged practices of the NCAA constitute a "restraint of trade" in the sense that they limit members' freedom to negotiate and enter into their own television contracts. In that sense, however, every contract is a restraint of trade, and as we have repeatedly recognized, the Sherman Act was intended to prohibit only unreasonable restraints of trade.

It is also undeniable that these practices share characteristics of restraints we have previously held unreasonable. The NCAA is an association of schools which compete against each other to attract television revenues, not to mention fans and athletes. As the District Court found, the policies of the NCAA with respect to television rights are ultimately controlled by the vote of member institutions. By participating in an association which prevents member institutions from competing against each other on the basis of price or kind of television rights that can be offered to broadcasters, the NCAA member institutions have created a horizontal restraint—an agreement among competitors on the way in which they will compete with one another. A restraint of this type has often been held to be unreasonable as a matter of law. Because it places a ceiling on the number of games member institutions may televise, the horizontal agreement places an artificial limit on the quantity of televised football that is available to broadcasters and consumers. By restraining the quantity of television rights available for sale, the challenged practices create a limitation on output; our cases have held that such limitations are unreasonable restraints of trade. Moreover, the District Court found that the minimum aggregate price in fact operates to preclude any price negotiation between broadcasters and institutions, thereby constituting horizontal price fixing, perhaps the paradigm of an unreasonable restraint of trade.

Horizontal price fixing and output limitation are ordinarily condemned as a matter of law under an "illegal *per se*" approach because the probability that these practices are anticompetitive is so high; a *per se* rule is applied when "the practice facially appears to be one that would always or almost always tend to restrict competition and decrease output." In such circumstances a restraint is presumed unreasonable without inquiry into the particular market context in which it is found. Nevertheless, we have decided that it would be inappropriate to apply a *per se* rule to this case. This decision is not based on a lack of judicial experience with this type of arrangement, on the fact that the NCAA is organized as a nonprofit entity, or on our respect for the NCAA's historic role in the preservation and encouragement of intercollegiate amateur athletics. Rather, what is critical is that this case involves an industry in which horizontal restraints on competition are essential if the product is to be available at all.

As Judge Bork has noted: "[S]ome activities can only be carried out jointly. Perhaps the leading example is league sports. When a league of professional lacrosse teams is formed, it would be pointless to declare their cooperation illegal on the ground that there are no other professional lacrosse teams." What the NCAA and its member institutions market in this case is competition itself—contests between competing institutions. Of course, this would be completely ineffective if there were no rules on which the competitors agreed to create and define the competition to be marketed. A myriad of rules affecting such matters as the size of the field, the number of players on a team, and the extent to which physical violence is to be encouraged or proscribed, all must be agreed upon, and all restrain the manner in which institutions compete.

Moreover, the NCAA seeks to market a particular brand of football—college football. The identification of this "product" with an academic tradition differentiates college football from and makes it more popular than professional sports to which it might otherwise be comparable, such as, for example, minor league baseball. In order to preserve the character and quality of the "product," athletes must not be paid, must be required to attend class, and the like. And the integrity of the "product" cannot be preserved except by mutual agreement; if an institution adopted such restrictions unilaterally, its effectiveness as a competitor on the playing field might soon be destroyed. Thus, the NCAA plays a vital role in enabling college football to preserve its character, and as a result enables a product to be marketed which might otherwise be unavailable. In performing this role, its actions widen consumer choice—not only the choices available to sports fans but also those available to athletes—and hence can be viewed as procompetitive.

Broadcast Music squarely holds that a joint selling arrangement may be so efficient that it will increase sellers' aggregate output and thus be procompetitive. Similarly, as we indicated in *Continental T.V., Inc. v. GTE Sylvania Inc.,* a restraint in a limited aspect of a market may actually enhance marketwide competition. Respondents concede that the great majority of the NCAA's regulations enhance competition among member institutions. Thus, despite the fact that this case involves restraints on the ability of member institutions to compete in terms of price and output, a fair evaluation of their competitive character requires consideration of the NCAA's justifications for the restraints.

Our analysis of this case under the Rule of Reason, of course, does not change the ultimate focus of our inquiry. Both *per se* rules and the Rule of Reason are employed "to form a judgment about the competitive significance of the restraint." A conclusion that a restraint of trade is unreasonable may be

> "based either (1) on the nature or character of the contracts, or (2) on surrounding circumstances giving rise to the inference or presumption that they were intended to restrain trade and enhance prices. Under either branch of the test, the inquiry is confined to a consideration of impact on competitive conditions."

* * *

[T]he NCAA television plan on its face constitutes a restraint upon the operation of a free market, and the findings of the District Court establish that it has operated to raise prices and reduce output. Under the Rule of Reason, these hallmarks of anticompetitive behavior place upon petitioner a heavy burden of establishing an affirmative defense which competitively justifies this apparent deviation from the operations of a free market. We turn now to the NCAA's proffered justifications.

IV

Relying on *Broadcast Music*, petitioner argues that its television plan constitutes a cooperative "joint venture" which assists in the marketing of broadcast rights and hence is procompetitive. While joint ventures have no immunity from the antitrust laws, as *Broadcast Music* indicates, a joint selling arrangement may "mak[e] possible a new product by reaping otherwise unattainable efficiencies." The essential contribution made by the NCAA's arrangement is to define the number of games that may be televised, to establish the price for each exposure, and to define the basic terms of each contract between the network and a home team. The NCAA does not, however, act as a selling agent for any school or for any conference of schools. The selection of individual games, and the negotiation of particular agreements, are matters left to the networks and the individual schools. Thus, the effect of the network plan is not to eliminate individual sales of broadcasts, since these still occur, albeit subject to fixed prices and output limitations. Unlike *Broadcast Music*'s blanket license covering broadcast rights to a large number of individual compositions, here the same rights are still sold on an individual basis, only in a noncompetitive market.

The District Court did not find that the NCAA's television plan produced any procompetitive efficiencies which enhanced the competitiveness of college football television rights; to the contrary it concluded that NCAA football could be marketed just as effectively without the television plan. There is therefore no predicate in the findings for petitioner's efficiency justification. Indeed, petitioner's argument is refuted by the District Court's finding concerning price and output. If the NCAA's television plan produced procompetitive efficiencies, the plan would increase output and reduce the price of televised games. The District Court's contrary findings accordingly undermine petitioner's position. In light of these findings, it cannot be said that "the agreement on price is necessary to market to product at all." In *Broadcast Music*, the availability of a package product that no individual could offer enhanced the total volume of music that was sold. Unlike this case, there was no limit of any kind placed on the volume that might be sold in the entire market and each individual remained free to sell his own music without restraint. Here production has been limited, not enhanced. No individual school is free to televise its own games without restraint. The NCAA's efficiency justification is not supported by the record.

Neither is the NCAA's television plan necessary to enable the NCAA to penetrate the market through an attractive package sale. Since broadcasting rights to college football constitute a unique product for which there is no ready substitute, there is no need for collective action in order to enable the product to compete against its nonexistent competitors. This is borne out by the District Court's finding that the NCAA's television plan *reduces* the volume of television rights sold.

V

Throughout the history of its regulation of intercollegiate football telecasts, the NCAA has indicated its concern with protecting live attendance. This concern, it should be noted, is not with protecting live attendance at games which *are* shown on television; that type of interest is not at issue in this case. Rather, the concern is that fan interest in a televised game may adversely affect ticket sales for games that will not appear on television.

* * *

VI

Petitioner argues that the interest in maintaining a competitive balance among amateur athletic teams is legitimate and important and that it justifies the regulations challenged in this case. We agree with the first part of the argument but not the second.

Our decision not to apply a *per se* rule to this case rests in large part on our recognition that a certain degree of cooperation is necessary if the type of competition that petitioner and its member institutions seek to market is to be preserved. It is reasonable to assume that most of the regulatory controls of the NCAA are justifiable means of fostering competition among amateur athletic teams and therefore procompetitive because they enhance public interest in intercollegiate athletics. The specific restraints on football telecasts that are challenged in this case do not, however, fit into the same mold as do rules defining the conditions of the contest, the eligibility of participants, or the manner in which members of a joint enterprise shall share the responsibilities and the benefits of the total venture.

The NCAA does not claim that its television plan has equalized or is intended to equalize competition within any one league. The plan is nationwide in scope and there is no single league or tournament in which all college football teams compete. There is no evidence of any intent to equalize the strength of teams in Division I-A with those in Division II or Division III, and not even a colorable basis for giving colleges that have no football program at all a voice in the management of the revenues generated by the football programs at other schools. The interest in maintaining a competitive balance that is asserted by the NCAA as a justification for regulating all television of intercollegiate football is not related to any neutral standard or to any readily identifiable group of competitors.

The television plan is not even arguably tailored to serve such an interest. It does not regulate the amount of money that any college may spend on its football program, nor the way in which the colleges may use the revenues that are generated by their football programs, whether derived from the sale of television rights, the sale of tickets, or the sale of concessions or program advertising. The plan simply imposes a restriction on one source of revenue that is more important to some colleges than to others. There is no evidence that this restriction produces any greater measure of equality throughout the NCAA than would a restriction on alumni donations, tuition rates, or any other revenue-producing activity. At the same time, as the District Court found, the NCAA imposes a variety of other restrictions designed to preserve amateurism which are much better tailored to the goal of competitive balance than is the television plan, and which are "clearly sufficient" to preserve competitive balance to the extent it is within the NCAA's power to do so. And much more than speculation supported the District Court's findings on this score. No other NCAA sport employs a similar plan, and in particular the court found that in the most closely analogous sport, college basketball, competitive balance has been maintained without resort to a restrictive television plan.

Perhaps the most important reason for rejecting the argument that the interest in competitive balance is served by the television plan is the District Court's unambiguous and well-supported finding that many more games would be televised in a free market than under the NCAA plan. The hypothesis that legitimates the maintenance of competitive balance as a procompetitive justification under the Rule of Reason is that equal competition will maximize consumer demand for the product. The finding that consumption will materially increase if the controls are removed is a compelling demonstration that they do not in fact serve any such legitimate purpose.

VII

The NCAA plays a critical role in the maintenance of a revered tradition of amateurism in college sports. There can be no question but that it needs ample latitude to play that role, or that the preservation of the student-athlete in higher education adds richness and diversity to intercollegiate athletics and is entirely consistent with the goals of the Sherman Act. But consistent with the Sherman Act, the role of the NCAA must be to *preserve* a tradition that might otherwise die; rules that restrict output are hardly consistent with this role. Today we hold only that the record supports the District Court's conclusion that by curtailing output and blunting the ability of member institutions to respond to consumer preference, the NCAA has restricted rather than enhanced the place of intercollegiate athletics in the Nation's life. Accordingly, the judgment of the Court of Appeals is

Affirmed.

It is interesting to note that in intercollegiate athletics, many of the rules have been drafted essentially to protect the institutions from excessive wrongdoing and from each other's wrongdoing. The best example is the highly codified NCAA rules governing college recruiting, and the invocation of the "death-penalty" for institutions (such as Southern Methodist University) found to have engaged in extraordinary improprieties. See R. Smith, "The National Collegiate Athletic Association's Death Penalty: How Educators Punish Themselves and Others," *Indiana Law Journal*, 62 (1986–87), 985–1059; "NCAA Presidents Panel, Unable to Agree on Reforms, Proposes Few Rules Changes," *Chronicle of Higher Education*, 8 April 1987, 35–36. States have gotten into the act, as in Texas, where revelations about SMU and other Southwest Conference athletic violations prompted the legislature in 1987 to enact legislation governing violations of collegiate athletic association rules:

CHAPTER 131. VIOLATION OF COLLEGIATE ATHLETIC ASSOCIATION RULES

Section		Section	
131.001.	Definitions	131.004.	Cause of Action by Institution
131.002.	Adoption of Rules	131.005.	Defenses
131.003.	Cause of Action by Regional Collegiate Athletic Association	131.006.	Damages
		131.007.	Distribution of Damage
		131.008.	Attorney's Fees and Costs

* * *

§ 131.003. Cause of Action by Regional Collegiate Athletic Association

A person who violates a rule of a national collegiate athletic association adopted by this chapter is liable for damages in an action brought by a regional collegiate athletic association if:

(1) the person knew or reasonably should have known that a rule was violated; and

(2) the violation of the rule is a contributing factor to disciplinary action taken by the national collegiate athletic association against:

(A) the regional collegiate athletic association;

(B) a member institution of the regional collegiate athletic association; or

(C) a student at a member institution of the regional collegiate athletic association.

*   *   *

§ 131.004. Cause of Action by Institution

person who violates a rule of a national collegiate athletic association adopted by this chapter is liable for damages in an action brought by an institution if:

(1) the person knew or reasonably should have known that a rule was violated; and

(2) the violation of the rule is a contributing factor to disciplinary action taken by the national collegiate athletic association against the institution or a student at the institution.

Trustees

As has become evident in several cases, trustees hold the legal authority granted by their college's original charter, whether it arises from articles of incorporation or from enabling legislation. The case of Antioch's law school articulates these issues of where authority resides, made more interesting by the long distance between Antioch's home campus in Yellow Springs, Ohio and the law school in Washington, DC.

The struggle continued to 1988, when the law school ostensibly graduated its final class. However, the D.C. School of Law, its successor, is negotiating with the D.C. city government to become a unit of the University of the District of Columbia (U.D.C.). For a review of trustee issues, see P. Haskell, "The University as Trustee," *Georgia Law Review*, 17 (1982), 1–80.

Sometimes, trustees have a legal obligation to listen to grievances. A group brought suit under a Texas constitutional procedure called "Remonstrance," and the court held that the remonstrance provision required the board of trustees to hear and consider the grievance (brought over the issue of tenure). However, the board was not required to adopt the petition, only to "consider" it. *PEACE v. El Paso County Community District*, 678 S.W. 2d 94 (Tex. App. 8 Dist. 1984). See New Jersey State College Governing Boards Association, *Self-Governance and Accountability: Implementing the State College Autonomy Law, 1986–1987*.

Cahn and Cahn v. Antioch University
482 A.2d 120 (D.C. App. 1984)

TERRY, Associate Judge:

This case presents what we hope is the last chapter of an acrimonious dispute between Antioch University and the former deans of its law school. The former deans contend that the trial court erred in not awarding them damages for lost salary as faculty members under their employment contract. Antioch University argues in its cross-appeal that appellants breached the fiduciary duty which they owed to the University. As damages, the University seeks to recover the expenses it incurred in *In re Antioch University*, under the bad-faith exception to the American rule on attorney's fees. The University also contends that it is entitled to recover $8,000 which appellants paid to two attorneys out of University funds without authorization.

We hold that the trial court erred in concluding that the Cahns owed a fiduciary duty to the students and clients of the law school. As employees of Antioch University, the Cahns' only fiduciary duty was owed to the University. We therefore hold that the University is entitled to recover the $8,000 which it seeks as damages for the Cahns' breach of that duty, and to that extent we reverse the judgment of the trial court and remand the case for modification of the judgment in favor of the University. In all other respects, however, we affirm the judgment below, thereby rejecting not only the Cahns' salary claims but also the University's claim for attorney's fees and litigation expenses.

I. Procedural History

In November 1979 Edgar S. Cahn and Jean Camper Cahn, co-deans of the Antioch School of Law, filed a complaint against Antioch University seeking "(1) a declaration that the law school [was] an entity independent of and separate from the University, or, alternatively, (2) a judgment that the law school [could] conduct its fiscal and administrative affairs without 'interference' from the University, with injunctive relief and continuing supervision of the court to enforce [the] judgment." After a lengthy hearing on the parties' cross-motions for preliminary injunctions, the trial court entered an order in favor of the University directing, in part, that

> the Co-Deans and responsible administrative personnel of the Antioch School of Law transfer to the Central Business Office of Antioch University in Yellow Springs, Ohio, all funds received in connection with the operation of the Antioch School of Law....

That same day the Cahns received a letter from William Birenbaum, president of the University, terminating their employment by Antioch University "in any role whatsoever...." The trial court's order granting the University's motion for a preliminary injunction was affirmed by this court.

In October 1980 the Cahns amended their complaint to include a claim for breach of contract. Specifically, the Cahns alleged that their "termination...was unlawful and in violation of their contracts as members of the faculty, University practices and prevailing academic standards and practices." The University in turn filed an amended counterclaim against the Cahns in which it sought to recover (1) $250,000 in damages on a breach of fiduciary duties claim, (2) $8,000 for unauthorized legal services paid by the Cahns out of University funds, (3) $2,331 for gardening and landscaping services performed on the Cahns' personal residence, (4) $5,000 for salary advanced to Edgar Cahn in 1979, (5) $2,206 for money refunded to the Cahns by two airlines for several unused plane tickets which had been purchased with University funds, and (6) $2,070.40 for "double payment of wages from the spring of 1979." Following a three-day trial without a jury, the court took the matter under advisement.

In its findings of fact and conclusions of law, issued three months later, the court ruled that the Cahns had not breached any of their fiduciary duties toward the University. With respect to the Cahns' breach of contract claim, the court determined that the Cahns "held separate and distinct positions as members of the faculty" and that the "action taken by [them] which provided sufficient cause to discharge them as administrators [did] not provide *de facto* a sufficient basis for discharging them as members of the faculty prior to the expiration of the employment period." Nevertheless, the court concluded that since the Cahns had not taught during the 1979–1980 academic year, they had not suffered any damages from lost salary due to their improper termination as members of the faculty. The court did, however, award them damages for the loss of fringe benefits from January 12 through June 30, 1980. The court also held that the Cahns "were not entitled to notification of non-reappointment as faculty by December 15 because they failed to prove by a preponderance of the evidence that they were members of the faculty bargaining unit and therefore had rights under the collective bargaining agreement or that the University had agreed on a policy binding on [it] and applicable to the school of law to give notification of non-reappointment by December 15 to law school faculty not members of the bargaining unit." The University and the Cahns bring these cross-appeals.

II. THE EVIDENCE AT TRIAL

A. *The Breach of Contract Claims*

On December 16, 1971, Dr. James Dixon, who was then the president of Antioch College, appointed the Cahns "Professor[s] of law and Co-Dean[s] of the Antioch School of Law." On July 3, 1973, President Dixon reappointed them co-deans for a one-year term. A form accompanying their letters of appointment designated their positions as "administrative." In July of 1974 the Cahns were both offered three-year appointments, but they declined the offer, saying that they would not accept any appointment in excess of one year. They continued as co-deans for the next three years under annual reappointments. Pursuant to a reorganization of the College in 1977, the Cahns were appointed "co-provosts of the Antioch School of Law" for the 1977–1978 academic year, and reappointed co-provosts for the subsequent year. They were not given any written notification of reappointment for 1979–1980, their last year at the law school.

Edgar Cahn testified that from the outset he and his wife served as members of the faculty. He stated that they never received any repudiation of their 1971 appointments as professors of law and that the only risk which they associated with the litigation against the University was that they would lose their positions as deans. If this were to occur, Mr. Cahn testified, they would "simply walk in the next day as faculty member[s] and try to work together as a community." When asked whether this reversion to faculty status was guaranteed in any document, Cahn replied, "It was based on an explicit agreement that did not have to be reduced and to my knowledge was not reduced to writing." Edgar Cahn further testified that even though the University's last letters of appointment provided that he and his wife could be terminated for financial reasons, the University would still have had "to deal with [their] rights as faculty members which would be for a remuneration scale appropriately agreed to by the collective bargaining agreement...."

Patricia Eames, a member of the law school faculty during the 1978–1979 and 1979–1980 academic years, testified about the law school's policy on notice of non-reappointment. She stated that during her tenure notice of non-renewal would be given to a faculty member by March 15 of his first year or December 15 of his second year of teaching. This policy applied to both members and non-members of the collective bargaining unit, provided that they were on the faculty. Eames stated that the faculty "asked the deans to initiate legal proceedings to prevent the university from letting the law school go down the drain." The faculty assumed that if the legal battle was lost, the Cahns would lose their positions as deans, but it never anticipated that by bringing that action the Cahns would also jeopardize their positions as faculty members.

Professor James P. Dixon, the former president of Antioch University (then Antioch College) responsible for the appointment of the Cahns as co-deans and professors of law at the law school, testified that he never entered into any agreement with the Cahns regarding residual faculty status. He said that in appointing them professors of law, he was bestowing an academic title upon them which "carried ... the connotation of rank ... and scholarly status within the legal profession," but that their teaching "was not a primary consideration" in their appointment as deans.

William M. Birenbaum, who replaced President Dixon in 1976, testified that during his presidency no dean or provost connected with the University had achieved faculty status by virtue of teaching while holding the position of provost or dean. President Birenbaum stated that the personnel policies affecting the law school faculty were expressed in the collective bargaining agreement. That agreement did not cover the Cahns since, as members of management, "they were front-line negotiators ... so they could hardly be covered by the documents conferring rights upon themselves." Birenbaum explained that when he wrote in his letter of dismissal to the Cahns that their employment was "terminated in any role whatsoever," he did not intend to sever their connection as members of the faculty because they had never been faculty members in the first place.

Ronald E. Pollack, the Cahns' successor as dean of the Antioch School of Law, testified that after his appointment as dean, he sought and was granted faculty status at a full meeting of the faculty. Dean Pollack stated, however, that "[t]he faculty status conferred upon [him] by the faculty did not confer any greater status with regard to protection of the job than [he] had from the president's appointment." He explained that, as dean, he represented management and that the December 15 deadline for notice of non-reappointment would not apply to him because he was not covered by the collective bargaining agreement. Dean Pollack further testified that the law school never adopted the model policy of the American Association of University Professors regarding notification of non-reappointment and that the revised pre-tenure appointment policies found in the University's personnel manual and apparently applicable to all campuses did not affect the law school.

B. *The Breach of Fiduciary Duty Claims*

In May 1979 the University found itself in a severe financial crisis. As the trial court found, "[t]he payroll of the entire University, including the School of Law, went unpaid and the University was without resources to pay substantial outstanding debts to creditors, including debts in connection with law school operations." At a meeting on May 18 and 19, the law school Board of Governors adopted a resolution directing the law school management to take all steps to insure that all of its fiduciary obligations [were] discharged. This include[d] proper disposition of all restricted funds whether received from private or public sources. The management [was] further directed to identify the fiduciary obligations of the law school both as to amount and source, of the measures taken to satisfy these obligations, and to make a written report thereof to the Executive Committee [of the Board of Governors] at its June meeting.

In response to the resolution, the Cahns engaged the services of Professor Terence J. Anderson of the University of Miami School of Law, an expert in such matters, who prepared four memoranda "approach[ing] the problem from different perspectives." The text of the resolution, meanwhile, was communicated by telegram to President Birenbaum.

On June 2, after rejecting a proposal that it declare bankruptcy, the University's Board of Trustees resolved to impose stringent fiscal limitations on University operations during the summer. The Board directed the University's various units to maintain accounts on a cash basis, with weekly reporting, and to transfer all cash promptly to the University in Ohio. The minutes of the law school Board of Governors meeting on June 25 describe what happened next:

> Mr. Poirier [the chairman of the Board's Executive Committee] opened the conference with a report of a telephone call he had received from an agitated President Birenbaum who alleged that the Law School was not in compliance with the Board of Trustees' resolution requiring all University units to transfer all cash to the University. The President said that, unless the Law School complied with this resolution, he would "pull their plug" at the end of the month. Though Mr. Poirier denied the allegation, the President "ordered" Mr. Poirier to inform Co-Deans Cahn of his intended action.

After discussing the financial difficulties the law school was encountering with the University, the Board agreed to make a final decision on the appropriate course to follow after Inez Reid, one of its members, had an opportunity to discuss the situation with President Birenbaum.

On June 28 John W. Cummiskey, the chairman of the Board of Governors, wrote to President Birenbaum and informed him that the law school was depositing all funds received from federal grants in bank accounts in the District of Columbia and that it would not be transferring such funds to Yellow Springs. He also sought an accounting from the University for restricted funds previously transferred to Yellow Springs to make sure that all obligations chargeable to those funds were met, and that those funds were used for no other purpose. The University's grave financial condition remained unabated throughout the summer. On September 4, as the trial court found, President Birenbaum "apparently advised the managers of units in disagreement with policies of the University administration that they could seek separation if they so chose." On September 20 Mr. Cummiskey wrote to the chairman of the University's Board of Trustees, Douglas Ades, to advise him that the law school had decided to accept President Birenbaum's offer.

Meanwhile, on September 14, the Cahns received a letter from Charles Docter, an attorney whom they had retained that summer pursuant to the Board of Governors' directive, advising them to file a preemptive Chapter XI proceeding for the law school under the Bankruptcy Act. Mr. Docter explained that he had "analyzed . . . certain questions concerning the exact nature of the entity of Antioch School of Law and . . . concluded . . . that there [was] enough of an entity or unincorporated association to permit a filing of a Chapter XI." His letter continued:

> We [his firm] would, of course, agree with you that if we felt that the matter with the University could be negotiated shortly after and during the litigation which you apparently now intend to file that this would be the appropriate course. However, our advice has been based upon the assumption that you believe the filing of a Chapter XI under the old Act or a Chapter 11 under the new Code by the University is eminent [*sic*]. . . . [A] chapter proceeding filed by the University gives the Law School no choice other than to protect itself now by the prompt filing of a Chapter XI. The Law School's lack of options is further heightened by the ABA's efforts to remove accreditation.

On September 23 the Board of Governors adopted a resolution whereby it decided

> to do all things necessary to protect the financial viability of the School of Law and to insure that it retains the resources and capacity to discharge fully its obligations to students, clients, employees, creditors and funding sources. . . .

Toward these ends the Board authorized its chairman

> to designate a team fully empowered to open discussions with the University to explore ways to best achieve those ends including seeking corporate insulation, affiliation, independence, deferred withdrawal or immediate severance. . . .

On October 9 John W. Karr, another attorney whom the Cahns had consulted, advised them by letter that in view of the Board's September 23 resolution, "the conservative course" to follow would be "to preserve the *status quo ante* by insulating the assets against any attempt by the University summarily to assume control of them. . . ." Mr. Karr went on to say that the University's "summary invasion" of the law school's assets, particularly its cash assets, would make it impossible for the law school "to fulfill contractual obligations both to students and to various government agencies from which grants ha[d] been obtained. Even more significant," Mr. Karr stated, was "the certainty that any depletion of these assets [would] make it impossible to meet obligations to the approximately 1,000 indigent persons who [were] currently" the Urban Law Institute's clients. Thus Mr. Karr proposed that the Cahns "place all of the law school's assets into a trustee's account, leaving the cash available, of course, to meet the school's obligations to faculty, staff, and creditors as they [arose]." Such an account was opened in a local bank, with Karr as trustee.

The University's Board of Trustees met on October 27 and adopted two resolutions with regard to the law school. The first, a general resolution, passed in public session, included a statement reaffirming the Board of Trustees' commitment to the welfare of the law school. The second resolution was approved during an executive session. It directed the president to "[instruct] the Co-Deans . . . to account for all funds received since the date of the last complete accounting and to transfer to the Central Office all funds on hand or under the control of the administration of the School of Law. . . ." This resolution concluded by stating that "as soon as practicable" after the law school had complied with University policies, the president would "arrange a meeting between the Board's Standing Committee on the School of Law and the Board of Governors [of the law school] to reassess the relationship between the Board of Governors and the Board of Trustees. . . ."

On November 1 a Mailgram was sent to the Cahns containing the substance of the October 27 resolution. Mr. Cummiskey responded with a Mailgram on November 5 requesting that implementation of the University's demands be deferred pending a meeting of the Board of Governors. President Birenbaum denied this request by telegram on November 8 and instructed the Cahns to comply with the October 27 resolution's directives by November 9. When the Cahns failed to do so, the University on November 9 notified various District of Columbia banks holding University funds that it had revoked the authority of its employees at the law school to dispose of any of these funds. On November 13 the Cahns filed suit against the University. At a meeting of the law school Board of Governors on November 15, the Board resolved, by a vote of five to four, to support both the maintenance of the lawsuit and the Cahns' refusal to turn over law school funds to the University. Four days later the Board of Trustees adopted a resolution dissolving the Board of Governors. The Cahns were fired on January 11, 1980.

III. The Issues on Appeal

A. *The Arguments of the Parties*

The Cahns present two arguments on appeal. First, they contend that the trial court erred, as a matter of law, in holding that they were not entitled to any back pay for the period remaining under their faculty contract after they were fired. Second, they argue that the University's failure to notify them by December 15, 1979, that they would not be reappointed resulted in the automatic renewal of their faculty contracts for another year. They contend that this notice deadline was established through custom and usage and that the trial court erred in holding that they were not entitled to receive any notice.

* * *

If a case is tried to the court, as this one was, we "may review both as to the facts and the law, but the judgment may not be set aside except for errors of law unless it appears that the judgment is plainly wrong or without evidence to support it." This means that a trial court's findings of fact will not be disturbed unless they are clearly erroneous. The question before this court "is not whether [we] would have made the findings the trial court did, but whether 'on the entire evidence [we are] left with the definite and firm conviction that a mistake has been committed.' "

* * *

In so ruling the court erred. The Cahns owed a fiduciary duty not to the students and clients of the law school, but to the University which paid their salaries.

The legal relationship between the University and the Cahns was that of employer and employee, or principal and agent. An agency has been defined as

> the fiduciary relation which results from the manifestation of consent by one person to another that the other shall act on his behalf and subject to his control, and consent by the other so to act.

This relation "implies that the principal has reposed some trust or confidence in the agent, and the agent or employee is bound to the exercise of the utmost good faith, loyalty, and honesty toward his principal or employer."

In their roles as deans and provosts of the law school, the Cahns were entrusted with, and given access to, University funds. In managing these funds, they owed a fiduciary duty to the University.[21] They had ample reason to be concerned about the adverse effect that the University's possible declaration of bankruptcy might have on funds the law school received from grants and contracts with federal agencies. This concern, however, did not cloak them with fiduciary responsibilities toward the law school's students and clients. Notwithstanding the harmful repercussions which a bankruptcy filing might have had on the law school as an entity, the Cahns' only fiduciary obligations were to the University. It was the University, not the law school, which hired the Cahns.

Furthermore, the record supports the trial court's findings that, despite the "substantial functional autonomy" which the University's constituent units had, the "ultimate authority for fiscal affairs at the law school [had] always been vested in the Board of Trustees...." Although the law school Board of Governors enjoyed substantial autonomy from the central administration in academic, administrative, and fiscal matters, the routine practice before the May 1979 financial crisis was to transfer most restricted funds received from federal grants for use in connection with the law school to the University's central offices in Ohio. When the University found itself confronted with virtual insolvency in May and June, it imposed further stringencies on the expenditure of funds and required regular weekly accounting by all of its units. In flagrant violation of these restrictions, and without University authorization, the Cahns spent $8,000 from University funds in seeking legal advice from attorneys Docter and Karr. Their expenditure of this money was a breach of their fiduciary duty to the University.[23] The court's finding that, in doing so, they acted in good faith is irrelevant, for good faith is not a defense to a claim for damages based on a breach of fiduciary duty. The University is thus entitled to recover the $8,000 from the Cahns.

It is the American rule on attorney's fees, not the more narrowly drawn rules of fiduciary law, which governs this aspect of the case. Under the exception to the American rule on which the University relies, good faith is a defense; indeed, the University must affirmatively show that the Cahns acted in bad faith before it can prevail on this claim. Given the trial court's findings, the University cannot do so. However misguided or misdirected the Cahns' attempts to protect the law school may have been, the trial court, after considering all the evidence, found that they had "acted...out of a genuine concern for, and commitment to, the survival of the law school and the perpetuation of its service to clients and students." There was evidence to support this finding; hence it was not clearly erroneous. We therefore hold that the University cannot recover the $81,391.

IV. CONCLUSION

We affirm the judgment of the trial court except to the extent that it denied the University's claim against the Cahns for $8,000 in damages for breach of their

---

21. In its order granting the University's motion for a preliminary injunction, the court found that the Cahns "concede[d] that legal title to all assets of the law school [was] vested in the University, with the Management of those assets entrusted to the Board of Trustees."

23. The trial court specifically found:

> The corporate charter of Antioch University, Inc., vests responsibility for all property of the University in the University's Board of Trustees. The University has, in its accounts, consistently treated assets, liabilities, revenues, and expenditures of the school of law as belonging to the University.

fiduciary duty. The case is remanded to the trial court with directions to amend its judgment as to that one claim by awarding the University $8,000 in damages, plus such interest and costs as the law may permit. The judgment shall otherwise remain unchanged.

Affirmed in part, reversed in part, and remanded.

Closing a College

As the opening section noted, establishing a college is a complicated legal matter; so is closing a college. Although colleges close regularly (from 1970 to 1982, 167 closed, 50 merged with other colleges, and 20 were reconstituted as state colleges), the business of closing a college leaves many loose ends, including the distribution of assets, transition for affected students, arrangements for former students' records, pension provisions for staff, and other legal matters. See E. Johnson and K. Weeks, "To Save a College: Independent College Trustees and Decisions on Financial Exigency, Endowment Use, and Closure," *Journal of College and University Law*, 12 (1986), 455–88; F. Vecchione, "Chapter 11 of the Bankruptcy Code as an Alternative to Closing or Merger," *Journal of College and University Law*, 8 (1981–82), 1–19.

Nasson College v. New England Association of Schools and Colleges
16 B.C.D. 1299 (1988)

Frederick A. JOHNSON, Bankruptcy Judge.

MEMORANDUM OF DECISION

Nasson College, the Plaintiff, is a reorganized Chapter 11 debtor operating as a post-secondary educational institution in Springvale, Maine. The Defendant, the New England Association of Schools and Colleges, Inc. (NEASC), is a voluntary, self-governing organization whose members are accredited institutions. Among its functions NEASC undertakes to evaluate schools and colleges for accreditation. The Council on Postsecondary Accreditation (COPA) appeared as *amicus curiae*, filed a brief and argued orally.

During the administration of the Chapter 11 case and before confirmation, NEASC terminated the accreditation of Nasson.[1] Nasson now complains, in Count I of its complaint, that termination of accreditation was a violation of the automatic stay of Section 362(a)(3) of the Bankruptcy Code, because it was "an act to obtain possession of property of the estate or . . . to exercise control over property of the estate." Nasson also alleges that NEASC's refusal to reinstate Nasson's accreditation is in violation of a specific order of this court.

In Count II of its complaint Nasson asserts that NEASC is a governmental unit, and that it terminated Nasson's accreditation solely because Nasson filed for relief

---

1. Nasson's Board of Trustees acceded to the termination of accreditation. The court was unaware of the termination until this adversary proceeding was filed.

under Chapter 11. Nasson argues that NEASC's actions are discriminatory and pro-scribed by Section 525(a) of the Code.

Nasson seeks a "permanent mandatory injunction" ordering the NEASC to restore accreditation to Nasson as it existed on the date of filing for Chapter 11 relief. It also seeks a ruling that the NEASC is in contempt of the automatic stay and an order of this court, and, therefore, is subject to sanctions, including damages and costs.

Both parties have moved for summary judgment under Rule 56 of the Federal Rules of Civil Procedure, made applicable to bankruptcy proceedings by Bankruptcy Rule 7056. The court has reviewed the affidavits and exhibits submitted by the parties, parts of the voluminous records on file in the case and carefully considered the arguments of counsel. As a result, the court concludes that Nasson is entitled to summary judgment.

FACTS

The material facts are not in dispute. Nasson College was incorporated by a Private and Special Act of the Maine Legislature in 1909 and has operated as a private, four-year, liberal arts college. It became a member of NEASC in 1960 and was accredited at the time it filed its Chapter 11 petition.

Faced with declining enrollment and increasing costs, Nasson filed for relief under Chapter 11 of the Bankruptcy Code on November 4, 1982. Nasson continued to offer educational programs and activities through the second semester of the 1982–83 school year.

By letter of November 22, 1982, NEASC, by its Commission on Instruction of Higher Education (Commission), informed the school that the Commission was con-cerned about the fiscal stability of the school and requested (or ordered) that "Nasson College, show cause in writing by January 21, 1983, why the commission should not recommend termination of its accreditation." The letter stated that the Commission did not want "to prejudge the situation at Nasson College," but that they were concerned.

Nothing further occurred regarding accreditation until the Board of Trustees of the college, at a meeting held on April 25, 1983 voted:

> That Nasson College, as of May 1, 1983 shall cease operations... (recognizing that, as a practical matter, the college must now cease its educational programs if the college is to retain any possibility of carrying out an educational program in the future)....

During the April 25, 1983 meeting the President of Nasson, Dr. Schick, talked by phone with an official of NEASC.

On the same date, April 25, 1983, the Commission met and voted to recommend to the Executive Committee "that the accreditation status of Nasson College as an educational institution be terminated effective May 2, 1983." Certain conditions were provided for the protection of students nearing graduation. The school was notified of the Commission's action by letter dated April 27, 1983. The letter stated that the reason for the Commission's action was that:

> the trustees of Nasson College have voted to cease instructional programs and other institutional operations effective after commencement exercises to be held on May 1, 1983. Because only institutions offering instruction may be accredited,

membership status will cease effective with the conclusion of educational activities.

The Commission's letter explained that Nasson had a right to appeal and contained a copy of NEASC's appeal policy and procedures.

On May 10, 1983, the Executive Committee of NEASC voted:

> that the accreditation of Nasson College be terminated effective May 2, 1983, with the stipulation that accreditation will be maintained for degree-granting purposes for those students enrolled at Nasson in the Spring of 1983 with thirty-six (36) hours or less remaining to earn their Nasson degree.

At a meeting of Nasson's Board of Trustees held on May 25, 1983, the Trustees, in effect, agreed with NEASC's decision. No appeal from the decision was taken by Nasson, nor was the termination of accreditation brought to the court's attention by Nasson or by the Creditors' Committee, which, at the time, was very zealous in protecting the estate's property.

Although educational activities ceased at the end of the 1982–83 school year, the Board of Trustees continued to meet and the office of the Registrar remained open on an "as needed" basis to handle students' transcripts and other business. One dean, one principal business officer and three other members of the school's staff remained on the payroll.

On September 18, 1984, the Creditors' Committee of Nasson, which had been very active throughout, filed a "liquidation plan" for Nasson College. The plan was finally confirmed by this court on November 9, 1984, and by the District Court on November 16, 1984. The plan was modified by an order of this court dated November 21, 1984. That modification was to provide for the reorganization or "reconstitution" of Nasson as a college by use of a "reduced core" campus.

On December 10, 1984, an agreement between the Creditors' Committee, Nasson and Edward P. Mattar, of Worcester, Massachusetts, was executed. Mr. Mattar is experienced in the educational field, having operated a very successful college in Massachusetts for many years. The agreement provided for the retention by the reorganized Nasson of several buildings and other essential assets.

The agreement was conditioned upon Mattar's receipt from the State of Maine, or the appropriate agency thereof, written assurances that Nasson's charter and degree granting authority remain in full force and effect, or a final order of the Bankruptcy Court containing findings that such charter and degree granting authority have not been revoked, and that Nasson's Board of Trustees remained duly constituted.

On February 12, 1985, a hearing was conducted, after notice, on the joint motion of the Creditors' Committee and Edward P. Mattar III "Regarding Consummation of Second Amended Plan of Reorganization." As a result of that hearing an order was prepared for the Court's approval and signature. The order was signed by this court on March 8, 1985, and docketed the same day. The order, as pertinent here, contained the following language:

> 5. That the Debtor has maintained continuous operations since the petition date, and the Debtor may continue all operations as a college with full degree-granting authority, powers, licenses, privileges, and *accreditations* in and to the same extent as it enjoyed as of the date of the petition, November 4, 1982.

As previously noted in footnote 1, *supra*, the court was unaware of the termination of Nasson's accreditation by NEASC as of May 1, 1983. Further, not being an academician, the court was not fully cognizant of the significance of accreditation. The court has reviewed the tape recording of the hearing of February 12, 1985, which resulted in the Order of March 8, 1985, and not once during that hearing was accreditation mentioned. The minutes of the meetings of the Board of Trustees of the College, which were admitted as an exhibit for the purpose of re-establishing continuity of the Board, did, of course, contain discussions of the school's loss of accreditation. It was not necessary for the court to study these minutes until this proceeding was under way. As a consequence, at the time of the March 8, 1985 Order the court was unaware of the school's accreditation problem.

In September of 1985, the reorganized Nasson College resumed educational programs and activities. Its new officers and trustees immediately attempted to resolve the question of the college's accreditation with NEASC. NEASC has insisted that Nasson's accreditation was terminated in 1983, and that it must now apply for accreditation *de novo* and submit to the accreditation process. This adversary proceeding, commenced by Nasson, resulted.

PROPERTY OF THE ESTATE

Count I of Nasson's Complaint presents the issue of whether "accreditation" is property of the estate. Nasson asserts that it clearly is, and that NEASC violated the automatic stay of Section 362(a) by terminating Nasson's accreditation. It argues that the termination constituted an "act to obtain possession of property of the estate or of property from the estate or to exercise control over property of the estate."

This issue is one of first impression. No reported decision has been cited by the parties in support of their position and the court has found none.

Section 541 of the Code deals with property of the estate. It provides:

> (a) The commencement of a case . . . creates an estate. Such estate is comprised of all the following property, wherever located and by whomever held:
>
> (1) [A]ll legal or equitable interests of the debtor in property as of the commencement of the case.
>
> . . .
>
> (c)(1) [A]n interest of the debtor in property becomes property of the estate . . . notwithstanding any provision in an agreement, transfer instrument, or applicable nonbankruptcy law—
>
> (A) that restricts or conditions transfer of such interest by the debtor; or
>
> (B) that is conditioned on the insolvency or financial condition of the debtor, on the commencement of a case . . . and that effects or gives an option to effect a forfeiture, modification, or termination of the debtor's interest in property.

The legislative history of Section 541 informs us:

> The bill determines what is property of the estate by a simple reference to what interests in property the debtor has at the commencement of the case. This includes all interests, such as interests in real or personal property, tangible and intangible property, choses in action, causes of action, rights such as copyrights, trademarks, patents, and processes, contingent interests and future interests, whether or not transferable by the debtor.

Congress intended a broad range of property to be included in the estate. There are, however, outer boundaries of the bankruptcy estate. The Supreme Court in *Whiting Pools*, did not decide what, or where, those outer boundaries are.

Certainly, in determining what is property of the estate, a determination must first be made as to what is property. Is accreditation, a status, property of the estate? The court concludes that it is not.

Some guidance is offered by the Accreditation Handbook published by the Commission on Institution of Higher Education. The Commission is responsible for formulating and maintaining standards of accreditation for institutions such as Nasson. "Accreditation is a status granted to an educational institution or a program that has been found to meet or exceed stated criteria of educational quality."

This status, although it has value to the institution, is in essence, held in the nature of a trust for the Commission and the public, and assures the educational community, the public, and interested agencies that the institution has clearly defined objectives which meet criteria published by the Commission. The status is not permanent. The institution must continuously comply with the requirements for accreditation. Failure to comply would jeopardize the integrity of the accreditation process and tend to mislead prospective students and others who rely upon accreditation in making important decisions.

Accreditation may not be bought, sold, pledged, or exchanged; it may not be liquidated by a trustee in bankruptcy, or distributed to creditors. Accreditation will not be found on a balance sheet or scheduled as an asset on the debtor's bankruptcy schedules. Although it may enhance the value of goodwill it is not goodwill. An institution may have control of its activities and property which affect accreditation; but, it has no control over its status as an accredited institution. In seeking and accepting accreditation and membership in NEASC it placed control of its status in the association. This lack of control and lack of other attributes or property leads the court to conclude that accreditation is not property, and, therefore, is not property of the estate within the meaning and intent of Section 541 of the Bankruptcy Code.

*   *   *

The court agrees with the case cited, that NEASC is not a governmental unit within the meaning and intent of the Code.

Further, it is clear from the exhibits in this proceeding that Nasson's accreditation was terminated because it ceased to offer educational programs after May 1, 1983, a necessary requirement of accreditation, and not solely because of its filing of its Chapter 11 petition.

An appropriate order will be entered.

———————

Death reports of colleges may sometimes be exaggerated. Wilson College was slated for extinction in 1979, until a judge in Pennsylvania's Orphans' Court reconstituted the college's trust, replaced the board, and enjoined them from closing the institution. *Zehner v. Alexander*, 3 Franklin County L.J. (Orphans' Ct., PA. 1979). In 1988, a group of faculty, students, and alumni filed suit to prevent Loretto Heights College of Denver from merging with Regis College; and a 1985 plan to close a public agricultural college in Nebraska was changed by the legislature in 1988. "Groups File Lawsuit to Stop College's Closing," *Chronicle of Higher Education*, 6 April 1988, A8; "Neb. Legislature Revives College Slated for Closure," *Chronicle of Higher Education*, 4 May 1988, A24.

Chapter 2
Academic Freedom

Although academic freedom is often used as a claimed defense against retribution for a variety of speech and conduct, it is a concept that is often poorly understood and ill defined. It is rooted in European traditions and in the recognition that "institutions of higher education are conducted for the common good . . . [and] the common good depends upon the free search for truth and its free exposition . . . " (1940 Statement of Principles on Academic Freedom, American Association of University Professors). The AAUP in its Statement of Principles defines academic freedom as follows:

Academic Freedom

(a) The teacher is entitled to full freedom in research and in the publication of the results, subject to the adequate performance of . . . other academic duties; but research for pecuniary return should be based upon an understanding with the authorities of the institution.

(b) The teacher is entitled to freedom in the classroom in discussing [the subject], but . . . should be careful not to introduce into [any] teaching controversial matter which has no relation to [the] subject. Limitations of academic freedom because of religious or other aims of the institution should be clearly stated in writing at the time of the appointment.

(c) The college or university teacher is a citizen, a member of a learned profession, and an officer of an educational institution. When [a professor] speaks or writes as a citizen, [he or she] should be free from institutional censorship or discipline, but [their] special position in the community imposes special obligations. As a person of learning and an educational officer, [he or she] should remember that the public may judge the profession and institution by [their] utterances. Hence [they] should at all times be accurate, should exercise appropriate restraint, should show respect for the opinions of others, and should make every effort to indicate that [they are] not an institutional spokes[person].

The search for truth through academic freedom requires that scholars be protected in posing new, controversial, and even unpopular ideas through their teaching and research, and publication of their research. The tradition of academic freedom has been translated into practice by several means, particularly constitutional interpretations of first amendment penumbral rights, including freedom of inquiry, freedom of thought, and freedom to teach. These rights of academic freedom are most clearly articulated by Justice Douglas in *Griswold v. Connecticut*:

> The association of people is not mentioned in the Constitution nor in the Bill of Rights. The right to educate a child in a school of the parents' choice— whether public or private or parochial—is also not mentioned. Nor is the right

133

to study any particular subject or any foreign language. Yet the First Amendment has been construed to include certain of those rights. * * * [T]he State may not, consistently with the spirit of the First Amendment, contract the spectrum of available knowledge. The right of freedom of speech and press includes not only the right to utter or to print, but the right to distribute, the right to receive, the right to read ... and freedom of inquiry, freedom of thought, and freedom to teach ... indeed the freedom of the entire university community. * * * Without those peripheral rights the specific rights would be less secure.

First amendment protection requires the requisite state action to be present, and may provide minimal protection for faculty in private institutions. Therefore, protection of academic freedom in private institutions must come either through state constitutional protections that reach private institutions, or through contract principles. Contract law may provide the basis for protection where AAUP Principles on Academic Freedom and Tenure or other customs or practices are adopted expressly or by implication in the contract of employment. More recently, there has been a trend towards explicitly providing for academic freedom protection in faculty contracts resulting from collective bargaining or other organized labor activity.

The cases in this chapter on academic freedom are organized into five zones of activity. The first is activities occurring in the classroom and in the laboratory, the zone of activity considered to be the heart of the academic mission. Activities in this zone relate to teaching (what is taught, who may teach, how one may teach, and the right to hear) and research (what can be researched, publication and disclosure of research, how research may be conducted, and who may do research). The second zone includes activities inherent in being a "citizen of the academy." These activities involve how a faculty member behaves within and with respect to the institution itself, other than classroom and research activities. The third zone covers activities of a faculty member as a citizen of the larger community. In this third zone, the freedoms do not differ substantially from those freedoms provided to all other citizens.

In all cases, there will be a balancing of interests. It should be noted that because it may be the protection of freedom of the academy, rather than the individual freedom of a faculty member that is at stake, there is sometimes tension between the faculty member and the academic institution in balancing these interests. Tensions may also arise when interests of other faculty members and students conflict with academic freedom claimed by faculty members. Increasingly, public and private colleges have claimed their own *institutional* academic freedom protections, drawing upon principles of institutional autonomy and freedom from state interference in academic affairs. This characterization is the fourth zone of this chapter. Concerns for national security or corporate interests are additional external considerations that can make the balancing even more problematic in some cases. This fifth zone is the least-settled area of academic freedom, and promises to provide much of the litigation and legislation in years to come.

Sweezy v. New Hampshire
354 U.S. 234 (1957)

Mr. Chief Justice WARREN

The ultimate question here is whether the investigation deprived Sweezy of due process of law under the Fourteenth Amendment. For the reasons to be set out in this opinion, we conclude that the record in this case does not sustain the power of the State to compel the disclosures that the witness refused to make.

* * *

The investigation in which petitioner was summoned to testify had its origins in a statute passed by the New Hampshire legislature in 1951. It was a comprehensive scheme of regulation of subversive activities. There was a section defining criminal conduct in the nature of sedition. "Subversive organizations" were declared unlawful and ordered dissolved. "Subversive persons" were made ineligible for employment by the state government. Included in the disability were those employed as teachers or in other capacities by any public educational institution. A loyalty program was instituted to eliminate "subversive persons" among government personnel. All present employees, as well as candidates for elective office in the future, were required to make sworn statements that they were not "subversive persons."

* * *

Under state law, [a joint resolution of the state legislature] was construed to constitute the Attorney General as a one-man legislative committee.

[The Attorney General or staff could call witnesses, but could not hold the witness in contempt although the Attorney General could obtain aid from the court in doing so.]

Petitioner was summoned to appear before the Attorney General on two separate occasions. On January 5, 1954, petitioner testified at length upon his past conduct and associations. He denied that he had ever been a member of the Communist Party or that he had ever been part of any program to overthrow the government by force or violence.

During the course of the inquiry, petitioner declined to answer several questions. * * * He declared he would not answer those questions which were not pertinent to the subject under inquiry as well as those which transgress the limitations of the First Amendment. * * *

The Attorney General again summoned petitioner to testify on June 3, 1954. There was more interrogation about the witness' prior contacts with Communists. * * *

[A]t the second hearing... petitioner refused to answer questions concerning the Progressive Party, and its predecessor....

The Attorney General also... [asked about] a lecture [delivered in 1954] to a class of 100 students in the humanities course at the University of New Hampshire. This talk was given at the invitation of the faculty teaching that course. Petitioner had addressed the class upon such invitations in the two preceding years as well. He declined to answer [questions about the subject and content of the lecture]. * * *

Petitioner adhered in this second proceeding to the same reasons for not answering he had given in his statement at the first hearing. He maintained that the questions were not pertinent to the matter under inquiry and that they infringed upon an area protected under the First Amendment.

* * *

[Mr. Sweezy was held in contempt by the Superior Court and the order was affirmed by the New Hampshire Supreme Court.]

There is no doubt that legislative investigations, whether on a federal or state level, are capable of encroaching upon the constitutional liberties of individuals. It is particularly important that the exercise of the power of compulsory process be carefully circumscribed when the investigative process tends to impinge upon such highly sensitive areas as freedom of speech or press, freedom of political association, and freedom of communication of ideas, particularly in the academic community.

* * *

According to the [New Hampshire Subversive Activities Act], a person is a "subversive person" if he, by any means, aids in the commission of any act intended to assist in the alteration of the constitutional form of government by force or violence. The possible remoteness from armed insurrection of conduct that could satisfy these criteria is obvious from the language. The statute goes well beyond those who are engaged in efforts designed to alter the form of government by force or violence. The statute declares, in effect, that the assistant of an assistant is caught up in the definition. This chain of conduct attains increased significance in light of the lack of a necessary element of guilty knowledge in either stage of assistants. The State Supreme Court has held that the definition encompasses persons engaged in the specified conduct " . . . whether or not done 'knowingly and willfully. . . . ' " The potential sweep of this definition extends to conduct which is only remotely related to actual subversion and which is done completely free of any conscious intent to be a part of such activity.

The statute's definition of "subversive organizations" is also broad. An association is said to be any group of persons, whether temporarily or permanently associated together, for joint action or advancement of views on any subject. An organization is deemed subversive if it has a purpose to abet, advise or teach activities intended to assist in the alteration of the constitutional form of government by force or violence.

The situation before us is in many respects analogous to that in *Wieman v. Updegraff*. The Court held there that a loyalty oath prescribed by the State of Oklahoma for all its officers and employees violated the requirements of the Due Process Clause because it entailed sanctions for membership in subversive organizations without scienter. A State cannot, in attempting to bar disloyal individuals from its employ, exclude persons solely on the basis of organizational membership, regardless of their knowledge concerning the organizations to which they belonged.

* * *

The sanction emanating from legislative investigations is of a different kind than loss of employment. But the stain of the stamp of disloyalty is just as deep. The inhibiting effect in the flow of democratic expression and controversy upon those directly affected and those touched more subtly is equally grave. Yet here, as in *Wieman*, the program for the rooting out of subversion is drawn without regard to the presence or absence of guilty knowledge in those affected.

The nature of the investigation which the Attorney General was authorized to conduct is revealed by this case. He delved minutely into the past conduct of petitioner, thereby making his private life a matter of public record. The questioning indicates that the investigators had thoroughly prepared for the interview and were not acquiring new information as much as corroborating data already in their possession. On the great majority of questions, the witness was cooperative, even though he made clear his opinion that the interrogation was unjustified and unconstitutional. Two subjects arose upon which petitioner refused to answer: his lectures at the University of New Hampshire, and his knowledge of the Progressive Party and its adherents.

The state courts upheld the attempt to investigate the academic subject on the ground that it might indicate whether petitioner was a "subversive person." What he taught the class at a state university was found relevant to the character of the teacher. The State Supreme Court carefully excluded the possibility that the inquiry was sustainable because of the state interest in the state university. There was no warrant in the authorizing resolution for that. The sole basis for the inquiry was to scrutinize the teacher as a person, and the inquiry must stand or fall on that basis.

* * *

The State Supreme Court thus conceded without extended discussion that petitioner's right to lecture and his right to associate with others were constitutionally protected freedoms which had been abridged through this investigation. These conclusions could not be seriously debated. Merely to summon a witness and compel him, against his will, to disclose the nature of his past expressions and associations is a measure of governmental interference in these matters. These are rights which are safeguarded by the Bill of Rights and the Fourteenth Amendment. We believe that there unquestionably was an invasion of petitioner's liberties in the areas of academic freedom and political expression—areas in which government should be extremely reticent to tread.

The essentiality of freedom in the community of American universities is almost self-evident. No one should underestimate the vital role in a democracy that is played by those who guide and train our youth. To impose any strait jacket upon the intellectual leaders in our colleges and universities would imperil the future of our Nation. No field of education is so thoroughly comprehended by man that new discoveries cannot yet be made. Particularly is that true in the social sciences, where few, if any, principles are accepted as absolutes. Scholarship cannot flourish in an atmosphere of suspicion and distrust. Teachers and students must always remain free to inquire, to study and to evaluate, to gain new maturity and understanding; otherwise our civilization will stagnate and die.

* * *

In our view, the answer is clear. No one would deny that the infringement of constitutional rights of individuals would violate the guarantee of due process where no state interest underlies the state action. Thus, if the Attorney General's interrogation of petitioner were in fact wholly unrelated to the object of the legislature in authorizing the inquiry, the Due Process Clause would preclude the endangering of constitutional liberties. We believe that an equivalent situation is presented in this case. The lack of any indications that the legislature wanted the information the Attorney General attempted to elicit from petitioner must be treated as the absence of authority. It follows that the use of the contempt power, notwithstanding the interference with constitutional rights, was not in accordance with the due process requirements of the Fourteenth Amendment.

* * *

The judgment of the Supreme Court of New Hampshire is *reversed.*

* * *

Mr. Justice FRANKFURTER, whom Mr. Justice HARLAN joins, concurring in the result.

For me this is a very different case from *Watkins v. United States*. This case comes to us solely through the limited power to review the action of the States conferred upon the Court by the Fourteenth Amendment. Petitioner claims that respect for liberties guaranteed by the Due Process Clause of that Amendment precludes the State of New Hampshire from compelling him to answer certain questions put to him by the investigating arm of its legislature. Ours is the narrowly circumscribed but exceedingly difficult task of making the final judicial accommodation between the competing weighty claims that underlie all such questions of due process.

* * *

The New Hampshire Supreme Court, although recognizing that . . . inquiries [about petitioners' lectures] "undoubtedly interfered with the defendant's free exercise" of his constitutionally guaranteed right to lecture, justified the interference on the ground that it would occur "in the limited area in which the legislative committee may reasonably believe that the overthrow of existing government by force and violence is being or has been taught, advocated or planned, an area in which the interest of the State justifies this intrusion upon civil liberties." According to the court, the facts that made reasonable the Committee's belief that petitioner had taught violent overthrow in his lecture were that he was a Socialist with a record of affiliation with groups cited by the Attorney General of the United States or the House Un-American Activities Committee and that he was co-editor of an article stating that, although the authors hated violence, it was less to be deplored when used by the Soviet Union than by capitalist countries.

When weighed against the grave harm resulting from governmental intrusion into the intellectual life of a university, such justification for compelling a witness to discuss the contents of his lecture appears grossly inadequate. Particularly is this so where the witness has sworn that neither in the lecture nor at any other time did he ever advocate overthrowing the Government by force and violence.

Progress in the natural sciences is not remotely confined to findings made in the laboratory. Insights into the mysteries of nature are born of hypothesis and speculation. The more so is this true in the pursuit of understanding in the groping endeavors of what are called the social sciences, the concern of which is man and society. The problems that are the respective preoccupations of anthropology, economics, law, psychology, sociology and related areas of scholarship are merely departmentalized dealing, by way of manageable division of analysis, with interpenetrating aspects of holistic perplexities. For society's good—if understanding be an essential need of society—inquiries into these problems, speculations about them, stimulation in others of reflection upon them, must be left as unfettered as possible. Political power must abstain from intrusion into this activity of freedom, pursued in the interest of wise government and the people's well-being, except for reasons that are exigent and obviously compelling.

These pages need not be burdened with proof, based on the testimony of a cloud of impressive witnesses, of the dependence of a free society on free universities. This means the exclusion of governmental intervention in the intellectual life of a university.

It matters little whether such intervention occurs avowedly or through action that inevitably tends to check the ardor and fearlessness of scholars, qualities at once so fragile and so indispensable for fruitful academic labor. One need only refer to the address of T.H. Huxley at the opening of Johns Hopkins University, the Annual Reports of President A. Lawrence Lowell of Harvard, the Reports of the University Grants Committee in Great Britain, as illustrative items in a vast body of literature. Suffice it to quote the latest expression on this subject. It is also perhaps the most poignant because its plea on behalf of continuing the free spirit of the open universities of South Africa has gone unheeded.

> "In a university knowledge is its own end, not merely a means to an end. A university ceases to be true to its own nature if it becomes the tool of Church or State or any sectional interest. A university is characterized by the spirit of free inquiry, its ideal being the ideal of Socrates—'to follow the argument where it leads.' This implies the right to examine, question, modify or reject traditional ideas and beliefs. Dogma and hypothesis are incompatible, and the concept of an immutable doctrine is repugnant to the spirit of a university. The concern of its scholars is not merely to add and revise facts in relation to an accepted framework, but to be ever examining and modifying the framework itself.

> . . . .

> "Freedom to reason and freedom for disputation on the basis of observation and experiment are the necessary conditions for the advancement of scientific knowledge. A sense of freedom is also necessary for creative work in the arts which, equally with scientific research, is the concern of the university.

> . . . .

> " . . . It is the business of a university to provide that atmosphere which is most conducive to speculation, experiment and creation. It is an atmosphere in which there prevail 'the four essential freedoms' of a university—to determine for itself on academic grounds who may teach, what may be taught, how it shall be taught, and who may be admitted to study." The Open Universities in South Africa 10–12. (A statement of a conference of senior scholars from the University of Cape Town and the University of the Witwatersrand, including A. v. d. S. Centlivres and Richard Feetham, as Chancellors of the respective universities.)

I do not suggest that what New Hampshire has here sanctioned bears any resemblance to the policy against which this South Africa remonstrance was directed. I do say that in these matters of the spirit inroads on legitimacy must be resisted at their incipiency. This kind of evil grows by what it is allowed to feed on. The admonition of this Court in another context is applicable here. "It may be that it is the obnoxious thing in its mildest and least repulsive form; but illegitimate and unconstitutional practices get their first footing in that way, namely, by silent approaches and slight deviations from legal modes of procedure."

White v. Davis
533 P.2d 222 (S. Ct. Cal. 1975)

TOBRINER, Justice.

Do the state and federal Constitutions permit police officers, posing as students, to enroll in a major university and engage in the covert practice of recording class discussions, compiling police dossiers and filing "intelligence" reports, so that the police have "records" on the professors and students? Is this "intelligence gathering" by the police covering discussions in university classes and in public and private meetings of university-sponsored organizations constitutionally valid when such reports "pertain to no illegal activity or acts"? The complaint in the present action challenges this practice of police surveillance as violative of the federal and state constitutional guarantees of freedom of speech, assembly, privacy and due process of law.

We conclude that the allegations of the complaint state a prima facie violation of freedom of speech and of assembly as well as of the state constitutional right of privacy. As we shall explain, a host of decisions of both the United States Supreme Court and of this court firmly establish the constitutionally enshrined status of freedom of speech and freedom of association in our nation's universities and colleges. Although the covert surveillance at issue here does not directly prohibit the exercise of protected rights in this realm, it is by now black letter First Amendment law that government activity which even indirectly inhibits the exercise of protected activity may run afoul of the First Amendment proscriptions. Given the delicate nature of academic freedom, we visualize a substantial probability that this alleged covert police surveillance will chill the exercise of First Amendment rights.

In light of this potentially grave threat to freedom of expression, constitutional authorities establish that the government bears the responsibility of demonstrating a compelling state interest which justifies such impingement and of showing that its purposes cannot be achieved by less restrictive means. At this stage of the proceedings, however, defendant has demonstrated no such justification; indeed, because the case arises upon the sustaining of a demurrer, defendant has yet even to file an answer in this litigation. Accordingly, we think that the demurrer should not have been sustained.

Moreover, the surveillance alleged in the complaint also constitutes a prima facie violation of the explicit "right of privacy" recently added to our state Constitution. As we point out, a principal aim of the constitutional provision is to limit the infringement upon personal privacy arising from the government's increasing collection and retention of data relating to all facets of an individual's life. The alleged accumulation in "police dossiers" of information gleaned from classroom discussions or organization meetings presents one clear example of activity which the constitutional amendment envisions as a threat to personal privacy and security. Though the amendment does not purport to invalidate all such information gathering, it does require that the government establish a compelling justification for such conduct. Once again, because the case arises after the sustaining of a demurrer, the government has not yet proffered any justification for the alleged covert information network and police dossiers. Consequently, the demurrer should have been overruled on this basis as well.

Accordingly, we reverse the judgment and remand for a trial on the merits.

1. *The allegations of the complaint.*

Plaintiff Hayden White, a professor of history at the University of California at Los Angeles and a resident taxpayer of the City of Los Angeles, instituted this taxpayer's suit against defendant Edward M. Davis, Chief of Police of the City of Los Angeles, seeking to enjoin the alleged illegal expenditure of public funds in connection with the police department's conduct of covert intelligence gathering activities at UCLA. The complaint alleges that with the authorization of Chief Davis, members of the Los Angeles Police Department, serving as "secret informers and undercover agents," have registered as students at UCLA, have attended classes held at the university and have submitted reports to the police department of discussions occurring in such classes. The complaint also alleges that the undercover police agents have joined university-recognized organizations, have attended public and private meetings of such organizations and have made reports on discussions at such meetings. The reports of these undercover agents are allegedly maintained by the police department in files, "commonly designated as 'police dossiers.' " Finally, the complaint alleges that the reports and dossiers compiled by the police pursuant to these covert surveillance activities "pertain to no illegal activity or acts."

Asserting that the expenditure of public funds for such operation is illegal because such activity "inhibits the exercise of freedom of speech and assembly, and abridges the right of due process of law and of privacy" in violation of the federal and state Constitutions, the complaint sought to enjoin the police department from expending funds for such activities in the future.

* * *

In United States v. United States District Court, the United States Supreme Court recently rejected a contention—somewhat analogous to that proposed in the instant case—that governmental intelligence operations in "domestic security" cases were immune from Fourth Amendment proscriptions, holding that the traditional constitutional guarantees could not be disregarded.

Unlike these past cases involving the limits on police surveillance prescribed by the constitutional "search and seizure" provisions, the instant case presents the more unusual question of the limits placed upon police investigatory activities by the guarantees of freedom of speech. As discussed below, this issue is not entirely novel; to our knowledge, however, the present case represents the first instance in which a court has confronted the issue in relation to ongoing police surveillance of a *university community*.

Our analysis of the limits imposed by the First Amendment upon police surveillance activities must begin with the recognition that with respect to First Amendment freedoms "the Constitution's protection is not limited to direct interference with fundamental rights." Thus, although police surveillance of university classrooms and organizations meetings may not constitute a direct prohibition of speech or association, such surveillance may still run afoul of the constitutional guarantee if the effect of such activity is to chill constitutionally protected activity.

* * *

As a practical matter, the presence in a university classroom of undercover officers taking notes to be preserved in police dossiers must inevitably inhibit the exercise of free speech both by professors and students. In a line of cases stretching over the past two decades, the United States Supreme Court has repeatedly recognized that to compel an individual to disclose his political ideas or affiliations to the government is to deter the exercise of First Amendment rights. Thus, for example, in NAACP v. Alabama, the Supreme Court struck down a court order requiring the NAACP to disclose its membership lists, declaring: "It is hardly a novel perception that compelled disclosure of affiliation with groups engaged in advocacy may constitute [an] effective . . . restraint on freedom of association. . . . Inviolability of privacy in group association may in many circumstances be indispensable to preservation of freedom of association, particularly where a group espouses dissident beliefs."

* * *

In like manner, covert police surveillance and intelligence gathering may potentially impose a significant inhibiting effect on the free expression of ideas. As the United States Supreme Court only recently observed: "Official surveillance, whether its purpose be criminal investigation or ongoing intelligence gathering, risks infringement of constitutionally protected privacy of speech."

The threat to First Amendment freedoms posed by any covert intelligence gathering network is considerably exacerbated when, as in the instant case, the police surveillance activities focus upon university classrooms and their environs. As the United States Supreme Court has recognized time and again: "The vigilant protection of constitutional freedoms is nowhere more vital than in the community of American schools." "Our Nation is deeply committed to safeguarding academic freedom, which is of transcendent value to all of us and not merely to the teachers [and students] concerned. That freedom is therefore a special concern of the First Amendment which does not tolerate laws that cast a pall of orthodoxy over the classroom.... The classroom is peculiarly the 'marketplace of ideas.' The Nation's future depends upon leaders trained through wide exposure to that robust exchange of ideas which discovers truth 'out of a multitude of tongues, [rather] than through any kind of authoritative selection.'"

In the past, threats to academic freedom have generally arisen from governmental conduct involving significantly less intrusion into the academic community than posed by the police activities at issue in the instant case.

* * *

In *Sweezy* a state attorney general, in the course of a far-reaching investigation into subversive activities, asked Sweezy, a college professor, several questions about the contents of a guest lecture Sweezy had delivered to a class at the University of New Hampshire. Sweezy refused to answer any questions about the lecture on the ground that such inquiries violated his First Amendment rights, but a state court held the professor in contempt. On appeal, the United States Supreme Court reversed the contempt order, and, in two separate opinions, emphasized in strong language the grave dangers presented by governmental intrusion into the contents of classroom discussion.

Chief Justice Warren, writing for four justices, declared: "The essentiality of freedom in the community of American universities is almost self-evident.... To impose any strait jacket upon the intellectual leaders in our colleges and universities would imperil the future of our Nation.... Scholarship cannot flourish in an atmosphere of suspicion and distrust." Justice Frankfurter, in a concurrence joined by Justice Harlan, was even more emphatic: "These pages need not be burdened with proof... of the dependence of a free society on free universities. *This means the exclusion of governmental intervention in the intellectual life of a university. It matters little whether such intrusion occurs avowedly or through action that inevitably tends to check the ardor and fearlessness of scholars, qualities at once so fragile and so indispensable for fruitful academic labor....* [I]n these matters of the spirit inroads on legitimacy must be resisted at their incipiency."

The police investigatory conduct at issue unquestionably poses at least as debili-
tating a threat to academic freedom as that presented by the governmental inquiry
in *Sweezy*. According to the allegations of the complaint, which for purposes of this
appeal must be accepted as true, the Los Angeles Police Department has established
a network of undercover agents which keeps regular check on discussions occurring
in various university classes. Because the identity of such police officers is unknown,
no professor or student can be confident that whatever opinion he may express in
class will not find its way into a police file. If the after-the-fact inquiry conducted in
Sweezy threatened to cast a pall of orthodoxy over classroom debates, the covert
presence of governmental agents within the classroom itself must cast a deeper shadow.

The crucible of new thought is the university classroom; the campus is the sacred
ground of free discussion. Once we expose the teacher or the student to possible
future prosecution for the ideas he may express, we forfeit the security that nourishes
change and advancement. The censorship of totalitarian regimes that so often condemns developments in art, science and politics is but a step removed from the inchoate
surveillance of free discussion in the university; such intrusion stifles creativity and
to a large degree shackles democracy.

*　*　*

As we have discussed above, the facts alleged in the instant complaint demonstrate
police surveillance activity which is likely to pose a substantial restraint upon the
exercise of First Amendment rights in university classes and organization meetings.
In view of this significant potential chilling effect, the challenged surveillance activities
can only be sustained if defendant can demonstrate a "compelling" state interest
which justifies the resultant deterrence of First Amendment rights and which cannot
be served by alternative means less intrusive on fundamental rights.

*　*　*

In the instant case, defendant's burden of justification is very heavy indeed. Not
only does the alleged covert intrusion into university classes and meetings pose a
grave threat to the freedom of expression necessary for the preservation of the university as we know it today, but the complaint also alleges that the information
gathered by the undercover police officers "pertains to no illegal activity or acts."
Because this case arises upon the sustaining of a demurrer, defendant has as yet given
no explanation or justification for the alleged surveillance; indeed, defendant has yet
to file any answer at all in this case. Thus, inasmuch as we have determined that the
complaint does demonstrate a prima facie violation of First Amendment rights, the
trial court erred in sustaining defendant's demurrer. The judgment must accordingly
be reversed and the case remanded for a trial on the merits.

*　*　*

Conclusion

As far as we are aware, the extensive, routine, covert police surveillance of university
classes and organization meetings alleged by the instant complaint are unprecedented
in our nation's history. The dangers implicit in such police operations, however, have
long been understood.

*　*　*

The motto of one of the great universities—Stanford University—is "The wind of
freedom blows," but the air of its classrooms would be befouled indeed by the presence

of secret police. In the course of classroom debate some thoughts will be hazarded only as the trial balloons of new theories. Yet such propositions, that are tentative only, will nevertheless be recorded by police officers, filtered through the minds of the listening informers, often incorrectly misstated to their superiors and sometimes maliciously distended. Only a brave soul would dare to express anything other than orthodoxy under such circumstances. But the classroom of the university should be a forum of free expression; its very function would largely be destroyed by the practices described in the complaint before us.

The judgment is reversed.

Academic Freedom in Classroom Teaching and Research Laboratories

Hammond v. Brown
323 F. Supp. 326 (N.D. Ohio 1971)

WILLIAM K. THOMAS, District Judge.

Each of these actions seeks declaratory and injunctive relief, and each is founded on 42 U.S.C. § 1983.

* * *

Also requested is an order to expunge a written report presented by the Special Grand Jury to the Honorable Edwin W. Jones, Judge of the Common Pleas Court of Portage County, at the same time the indictments were secretly returned.

The indictments grow out of events of May 1 through May 4, 1970, that took place on and off the campus of Kent State University in Kent, Ohio. Dealing with those events on October 4, 1970, the President's Commission on Campus Unrest issued a "Special Report—The Kent State Tragedy." The Special Grand Jury Report, the validity of which is an issue in this case, attempts to chronicle the same events. The issues in these cases, as this court sees them, neither require nor permit a general factual inquiry, and this court makes no independent findings as to what transpired during those four days in May in the Kent community.

However, it is material to record that responsive to a request of the Mayor of Kent, Ohio's Governor James A. Rhodes on the evening of May 2, 1970, dispatched units of Ohio National Guardsmen to duty in Kent, Ohio to assist the local authorities. Apparently martial law was not declared. On the afternoon of May 4, 1970, confrontations involving students and Ohio National Guardsmen climaxed on Blanket Hill in the vicinity of Taylor Hall on the university campus. Ohio National Guardsmen shot and killed four students and wounded nine other students.

* * *

Representative of the contentions of both complaints is this quote from the *Hammond* complaint:

The making of the indictments, together with the [Special Grand Jury] Report was a bad-faith use of the State's legal machinery with the purpose of inhibiting the exercise of free speech and has caused and will continue to cause, unless nullified and expunged, significant chilling effect on speech that cannot be avoided by future state court adjudication.

*   *   *

All plaintiffs in the *Adamek* case, 32 in number, are professors at Kent State University. The complaint charges that First, Fifth, Sixth and Fourteenth Amendment rights are violated by the issuance of the Report. It stresses that First Amendment Rights (including academic freedom) have been jeopardized by the indictment of fellow plaintiff Professor Thomas Lough. His indictment charges him with inciting to riot on May 4, 1970.

*   *   *

A further claim resting on 42 U.S.C. § 1983 (1964) is in a proposed conclusion of law of the non-indicted *Adamek* plaintiffs. It reads:

Those non-indicted plaintiffs who are members of the faculty at Kent State University have been subjected by defendants to deprivation of rights protected by the first, sixth, and fourteenth amendments to the Constitution of the United States by reason of the fact that they have been criticized by an official accusatory body of the State of Ohio for performance of their professional duties at Kent State University.

The proposed conclusion of law continues:

Criticism of said plaintiffs for overemphasizing dissent in the classroom and teaching the negative side of our institutions of government constitutes an invasion of freedom of speech effected in a manner violative of due process of law. *   *   *

This proposed conclusion of law stems from Part IX of the Report of the Special Grand Jury that begins by saying:

We find that the major responsibility for the incidents occurring on the Kent State University campus on May 2nd, 3rd, and 4th rests clearly with those persons who are charged with the administration of the university. To attempt to fix the sole blame for what happened during this period on the National Guard, the students or other participants would be inconceivable. The evidence presented to us has established that Kent State University was in such a state of disrepair, that it was totally incapable of reacting to the situation in any effective manner. We believe that it resulted from policies formulated and carried out by the University over a period of several years, the most obvious of which will be commented on here.

Part IX continues:

The administration at Kent State University has fostered an attitude of laxity, over-indulgence, and permissiveness with its students and faculty to the extent that it can no longer regulate the activities of either and is particularly vulnerable to any pressure applied from radical elements within the student body or faculty.

The first example the Grand Jury gives is the "delegation of a disciplinary authority under a student conduct code which has proven totally ineffective." After devoting several paragraphs to this first example, the Report then states:

> A second example of where the University has obviously contributed to the crisis it now faces is the overemphasis which it has placed and allowed to be placed on the right to dissent. Although we fully recognize that the right of dissent is a basic freedom to be cherished and protected, we cannot agree that the role of the University should be to continually foster a climate in which dissent becomes the order of the day to the exclusion of all normal behavior and expression.

The Report continues:

> We received the impression that there are some persons connected with the University who believe and openly advocate that one has a duty rather than a right to dissent from traditionally accepted behavior and institutions of government. This is evident by the administrative staff in providing a forum and available facilities for every "radical group" that comes along and the "speakers" that they bring to the campus.

After critically referring to certain student organizations that received official recognition from the University, the Report continues:

> A further example of what we consider an over-emphasis on dissent can be found in the classrooms of some members of the University faculty. The faculty members to whom we refer teach nothing but the negative side of our institutions of government and refuse to acknowledge that any positive good has resulted during the growth of our nation. They devote their entire class periods to urging their students to openly oppose our institutions of government even to the point of where one student who dared to defend the American flag was ridiculed by his professor before his classmates.
>
> We do not mean to suggest that these faculty members represent a majority of the faculty at Kent State University. To the contrary, we suspect that they form a small minority of the total faculty, but this does not mean that their presence should be ignored.

The Report does not identify this assumed "small minority of the total faculty." Since no faculty members are specifically identified and since the Report's reference to the faculty as a class does not either generally or specifically charge violation of any criminal offense, the claim of the *Adamek* plaintiffs based on the Fifth and Sixth Amendments is untenable.

The claimed violation of First Amendment rights violative of Due Process presents a different matter. Let us assume a member of the Kent State faculty reads the Grand Jury's criticism of "over-emphasis on dissent . . . in the classrooms of some members of the University faculty" and the Report's comment that this dissent "becomes the order of the day to the exclusion of all normal behavior and expression." He may reasonably believe that people in the Kent community (university and city) who have read Parts VIII and IX of the Report, may well think the Report may refer to him. People in the community may well believe that a particular faculty member is one of the "small minority of the total faculty" who depart from "all normal behavior and expression."

A Report of the Special Grand Jury, an official accusatory body of the community, that criticizes faculty members for "over-emphasis on dissent," thus seeking to impose norms of "behavior and expression," restricts and interferes with the faculty members' exercise of protected expression. The record reveals that this is happening.

Impairment of First Amendment freedom of expression is directly resulting from the Special Grand Jury Report. This is disclosed by candid and credited testimony of members of the faculty who appeared as witnesses. Because of the Report instructors have altered or dropped course materials for fear of classroom controversy. For example, an assistant professor of English, after reading the Report, "scratched three poems" from her outline in her Introduction to Poetry course. The poems are "Politics" by William Butler Yeats, "Prometheus" by Lord Byron, and "Dover Beach" by Matthew Arnold.

In "Politics," Yeats writes "And maybe what they say is true/of war and war's alarms."

A university professor may add or subtract course content for different reasons. But when a university professor is fearful that "war's alarm," a poet's concern, may produce "inflammatory discussion" in a poetry class, it is evident that the Report's riptide is washing away protected expression on the Kent campus.

Other evidence cumulatively shows that this teacher's reaction was not isolated. The Report is dulling classroom discussion and is upsetting the teaching atmosphere. This effect was described by other faculty witnesses. When thought is controlled, or appears to be controlled, when pedagogues and pupils shrink from free inquiry at a state university because of a report of a resident Grand Jury, then academic freedom of expression is impermissibly impaired. This will curb conditions essential to fulfillment of the university's learning purposes.

Issued by a Grand Jury purporting to act under the color of state law, the Report is not protected by the First Amendment as suggested by Attorney General Brown. "The freedom of speech and of the press...is...secured to all *persons* by the Fourteenth against abridgment by a state." Freedom of speech is a personal liberty that cannot be abridged by any arm of the state. An arm of the state, in this instance a grand jury, cannot corporately assert the freedom of speech that each of its members personally may exercise. Such a doctrine would permit any arm of the state to neutralize and cancel out protected personal freedoms and liberties.

Part IX of the Report, exemplified by the quoted excerpts, abridges the exercise of protected expression by the plaintiffs who are members of the Kent State University faculty and other persons of the same class on whose behalf the *Adamek* plaintiffs bring their action. Imposed under the color of state law, Part IX of the Report is determined and declared to deprive these parties of rights guaranteed under the Constitution in violation of 42 U.S.C. § 1983 (1964).

* * *

In accordance with this opinion and said findings of fact and conclusions of law, it is ordered:

1. Each of the declarations herein made shall be ordered into effect.

2. Defendant Clerk of Courts of Portage County, Lucy S. DeLeone, is ordered as follows:

a. With reference to any copies of the Special Grand Jury document (Plaintiff Hammond's Exhibit 1) that exist in the files or records (pending or closed) of the Common Pleas Court of Portage County, defendant DeLeone shall separate and retain Entry on Special Grand Jury, pages 1, 2, and 3 together with that upper portion of page 4 that includes the caption and the first two narrative paragraphs through the 16th line of typing. The remainder of any Report of the Special Grand Jury (balance of page 4 and pages 5 through 18) shall be physically expunged and destroyed.

So much time has passed since the Kent State University, Jackson State University, and Texas Southern University shootings, that many students will not remember the incidents, unless they see the famous photo or hear Neil Young's classic song, "Ohio." For a review of the extraordinary occurrences, see R. O'Neil, *No Heroes, No Villains* (San Francisco: Jossey-Bass, 1973). Readers today may find it odd that a professor was moved to delete classic poetry from her course. In the K–12 setting, however, the U.S. Supreme Court refused in 1987 to review a lower court decision, upholding the firing of a high school teacher in Lincoln County, Kentucky for showing an R-rated movie (*Pink Floyd's The Wall*) to her class of 14–18 year old students. *Fowler v. Board of Education*, 819 F.2d 657 (1987).

As indicated in an earlier note concerning the *Fowler* case, courts treat college professors differently than they treat schoolteachers. In an article exploring the "Three Faces of Academic Freedom," Mark Yudof delineates three dimensions of academic freedom: faculty autonomy, government expression, and institutional claims to autonomy. "The second face of academic freedom is not primarily rooted in a concern for the advancement of knowledge or for critical thinking; rather, it is rooted in a fear that government may press its advantage in universal and compulsory public schools and indoctrinate children to particular ideologies by overwhelming competing points of views. In other words, this face of academic freedom is designed more to curb government expression than it is to promote professional autonomy.... The second face will be turned toward primary and secondary schools, the first face will turn only toward the universities." M. Yudof, "Three Faces of Academic Freedom," *Loyola Law Review*, 32 (1987), 831–58.

In a case that drew considerable media attention, the U.S. Supreme Court struck down a Louisiana creationism law ("The Balanced Treatment for Creation-Science and Evolution Science in Public School Instruction Act") that required teachers "either to [exclude] the theory of evolution from public school classrooms or [to present] a religious viewpoint that rejects evolution in its entirety. The act violates the establishment clause of the first amendment because it seeks to employ the symbolic and financial support of government to achieve a religious purpose." *Edwards v. Aguillard*, 107 S. Ct. 2573 (1987). This case promises little direct effect upon college curricula, unless a state legislature chooses to enact a postsecondary equivalent; the Louisiana law also barred discrimination against creationists teaching in colleges. The dissent by Justice Scalia would have upheld the statute as intended to protect the academic freedom of schoolchildren.

Who May Teach and What is Taught

The issue of who may teach is extremely complex, both for its more philosophical tenets—those that involve academic freedom concepts and professional autonomy—

Campus of Kent State University, Kent, Ohio, 1970

and for its more quotidian aspect in the personnel context, which can often involve employment-related issues, including tenure and terms of employment. In its first meaning, the issue of who may teach becomes caught up in attendant political issues, especially when the appointment of professors takes on larger ideological significance or gets cast in larger symbolic terms. Chapter 3, "The Law and Faculty," treats several such cases, where tenure, misconduct, and intellectual property matters are essentially veiled academic freedom issues, while chapter 1 included several of these issues, particularly in the context of religion and institutions of higher education.

Nonetheless, there is a growing body of cases and commentary on the narrower concept of who may teach, in its legal and policy dimensions. This section includes several cases of older and more recent vintage, and a sampler of political and religious issues that bear directly upon this dimension of academic freedom.

Furumoto v. Lyman

362 F. Supp. 1267 (N.D. Cal. 1973)

RENFREW, District Judge.

* * *

I. STATEMENT OF FACTS

On January 18, 1972, shortly after 11:00 A.M., approximately fifteen people, including plaintiffs, entered Room 127, McCullough Building, on the Stanford University campus, where a scheduled quiz in a course on electrical engineering was being given under the supervision of Professor William Shockley. The racial or ethnic composition of the group was mostly non-Caucasian. Although plaintiffs were registered Stanford students it is not clear that all members of the group were Stanford students. The group's sole purpose was to condemn Shockley's view of genetics while demanding that he debate one Cedric Clark publicly. The intrusion was a planned event, with the members of the group acting in concert.

* * *

The action of the intruders effectively prevented the students in Shockley's electrical engineering class from taking the scheduled quiz.

* * *

Plaintiffs' first cause of action is based on 42 U.S.C. § 1983 and claims a deprivation of civil rights and privileges under color of state law. Plaintiffs claim that defendants denied them exercise of their First Amendment rights.

* * *

The complaint claims that Professor Shockley's writings are racist, "highly offensive" to anyone opposing racism, and "antagonize and anger" those in opposition. These claims upon analysis simply amount to vehement disagreement with another person's exercise of his First Amendment rights, not a statement of a claim under § 1983. The hearing officer's finding that Shockley did contribute to the continuation of the debate in his classroom does not suggest any deprivation of plaintiffs' civil rights.

*   *   *

A. *Plaintiffs' First Amendment Rights*

Although it is not entirely clear from plaintiffs' complaint, one element of their claim seems to be that defendants punished them for their expression of opposition to racism, thus denying them their rights under the First Amendment.

That the plaintiffs as students retained their First Amendment rights upon entering the University is clear beyond question.

*   *   *

At the oral argument on this motion, counsel for plaintiffs put forward the position that in academic life a professor must debate his views publicly if challenged. While this Court would agree that this may be desirable as a part of intellectual responsibility to consider opposing views and respond to them, that responsibility cannot extend to mandate public debating. Such a requirement would in itself be a potential inhibitor of academic freedom, since many individuals simply do not have the personality or talents to perform comfortably and adequately in oral debating. Such a requirement, if widely adopted, could drive otherwise qualified and valuable scholars from academic life. Professor Shockley thus had a First Amendment right to choose the medium for his response to his challengers or indeed even whether to respond at all. Plaintiffs cannot justify their actions by claiming that Professor Shockley would otherwise have been able to avoid a public debate.

*   *   *

D. *Support of Racism*

Plaintiffs claim that defendants supported racism by affording Professor Shockley a forum and academic respectability while punishing plaintiffs for their actions in opposition to racism. In a decision following New York Times Co. v. Sullivan, the Supreme Court has held that:

> "... absent proof of false statements knowingly or recklessly made by him, a teacher's exercise of his right to speak on issues of public importance may not furnish the basis for his dismissal from public employment."

That reasoning appears equally applicable here as to Professor Shockley's right to express his particular views with which plaintiffs disagree. Again, it must be remembered that the record is uncontroverted that at no time prior to January 18, 1972, did Professor Shockley ever lecture on or even discuss his theories of eugenics and dysgenics in the course in electrical engineering which plaintiffs disrupted. In this case, then, unless plaintiffs could meet the *Pickering* criteria with respect to Shockley's views, they could not begin to make a case that defendants supported racism by giving him a position. With respect to theoretical work, in contrast to factual description, a showing of falsity would be extremely difficult if not conceptually impossible.

Since Professor Shockley's views have not been shown by plaintiffs to fall outside the First Amendment and the scope of academic freedom, defendants cannot be charged with racism for giving him an academic position.

*   *   *

CONCLUSION

This case and this opinion have necessarily involved a review of society's legal response to the campus unrest of the past decade.

* * *

[T]he principle is established that a university cannot survive if it becomes a political arena in which direct action is justifiable in terms of personal moral codes. The President's Commission on Campus Unrest has expressed this idea:

"Academic institutions must be free—free from outside interference, and free from internal intimidation. Far too many people who should know better—both within university communities and outside them—have forgotten this first principle of academic freedom. The pursuit of knowledge cannot continue without the free exchange of ideas."

Plaintiffs' action against the Stanford Trustees and Professor Shockley is dismissed for failure to state a claim upon which relief can be granted. As to the remaining defendants their motion for summary judgment is granted.

Professor Shockley, a Nobel Prize-winning scientist, sought permission to teach a human genetics course, and was denied permission by Stanford to do so. W. Turner, "Stanford Vetoes Shockley Course," *New York Times*, 2 May 1972, Sec. 1A at p. 9.

There has been an ugly rise in campus race-baiting, raising serious questions about conflicting rights in campus discourse. At Dartmouth, four students associated with the *Dartmouth Review*, an avowedly conservative magazine, were suspended for a year after publishing a series of articles and harassing a black professor. A campus committee charged them with disorderly conduct, harassment, and invasion of privacy. See "4 Conservative Students at Dartmouth Say They'll Appeal Penalties Imposed After Incident with Black Professor," *Chronicle of Higher Education*, 23 March 1988, p. A34. In another acrimonious racial matter, a black professor at the University of Massachusetts was forced out of the Afro-American Studies department after he accused his colleagues of anti-semitism. The professor, a convert to Judaism, was reassigned to the university's Department of Judaic Studies. "Action at Massachusetts U. Raises Censorship Cry," *New York Times*, 29 May 1988, p. Y12.

Cary v. Board of Education of the Adams-Arapahoe School District
427 F. Supp. 945 (1977)

MATSCH, District Judge.

This case has been submitted on stipulated facts with both plaintiffs and defendants moving for summary judgment.

AGREED FACTS

Each of the plaintiffs is a senior high school English teacher employed by the defendant school district under a tenure system established by state statute. The plaintiffs have taught or are teaching elective courses designated as "Contemporary Literature," "Contemporary Poetry," and "American Masters" for eleventh and twelfth grade students, using contemporary literature and poetry as course material.

Three of the plaintiffs have structured these courses to permit the students to select almost all of the material to be read, individually. The others teach the same courses but assign most of the reading, with some electives. All of these teachers use group and class discussion of the books and poems read by the students.

* * *

In January, 1975, the defendants formed a committee of teachers, students, parents and school board members, called the "High School Language Arts Text Evaluation Committee" to review text material. That committee met publicly, solicited comments from the public, and submitted a report on January 6, 1976. A minority report was also submitted.

At a regularly scheduled public meeting on January 12, 1976 the defendants, by a majority vote, approved a list of 1275 textbooks for use in the high schools and they disapproved the following ten books:

> *A Clockwork Orange* by Anthony Burgess
>
> *The Exorcist* by William P. Blatty
>
> *The Reincarnation of Peter Proud* by Max Ehrlich
>
> *New American Poetry* by Donald Allen
>
> *Starting from San Francisco* by Lawrence Ferlinghetti
>
> *The Yage Letters* by William Burroughs and Allen Ginsberg
>
> *Coney Island of the Mind* by Lawrence Ferlinghetti
>
> *Kaddish and Other Poems* by Allen Ginsberg
>
> *Lunch Poems* by Frank O'Hara
>
> *Rosemary's Baby* by Ira Levin

Each of these books had been included in reading lists used by the plaintiffs in their courses and none of them has been ordered removed from the school libraries.

The parties agreed that these ten books are not legally obscene; that they do not represent any system of thought or philosophy; and that the exclusion of these books could not be considered to be an abuse of discretion or otherwise contrary to any constitutional standards applicable to an appropriate decision-maker.

On January 13, 1976, the school board issued a memorandum, directing that the subject ten books "will not be purchased, nor used for class assignment, nor will an individual be given credit for reading any of these books." That memorandum also cautioned that any materials not included in the approved list of books could be used in the subject courses only with prior approval of the Division of Instructional Services. At all times the plaintiffs and defendants have followed a policy of permitting students, with parental approval, to request alternatives to assignments of material which offends them.

The Aurora Education Association (AEA), a non-profit Colorado corporation, acting as the representative of all teachers employed in the defendant school district, conducted negotiations with the school board, resulting in a collective bargaining agreement, dated February 13, 1976, effective for the years 1975–1978. One item of disagreement during those negotiations was the issue of final authority on matters relating to curriculum and selection of instructional material. The initial AEA proposal provided for final determination of questioned materials by a committee of the Teachers Advisory Council. It also provided that the recommendations of the Teachers Advisory Council could be rejected by the school board only for "good and just cause shown."

That proposal was rejected and the provisions agreed upon in the signed agreement include the following:

> *Academic Freedom*—The parties seek to educate young people in the democratic tradition, to foster a recognition of individual freedom and social responsibility, to inspire meaningful awareness of and respect for the Constitution and the Bill of Rights.
>
> Freedom of individual conscience, association, and expression will be encouraged and fairness in procedures will be observed both to safeguard the legitimate interests of the schools and to exhibit by appropriate examples the basic objectives of a democratic society as set forth in the Constitution of the United States and the State of Colorado.
>
> The final responsibility in the determination of the above rests with the Board.

Article V, "Board Rights," at pages 7–8 of the agreement, provides that the board shall have the right to "[d]etermine the processes, techniques, methods and means of teaching any and all subjects."

The collective bargaining agreement includes a grievance procedure, with non-binding arbitration.

Each of the plaintiffs is an active member of the AEA. Mr. Bridgeman is now on leave from his teaching duties to serve as president of that organization.

The professional judgment of the plaintiffs is that the ten excluded books should be available for use in teaching the subject courses.

The defendants agree that the following activities by the plaintiffs would be a violation of the January 13, 1976 directive:

> (a) Adding any of the subject textbooks to the reading list in their courses;
>
> (b) Assigning the reading of any of the subject textbooks;
>
> (c) Giving any student any credit in courses for reading any of the subject textbooks;
>
> (d) Reading aloud or causing to be read aloud any of the subject textbooks in the classroom during class time; or
>
> (e) Discussing with students in the classroom during class time any of these materials at such length so as to amount to a constructive assignment of the materials.

* * *

Certainly there is no language in the First Amendment or in any other provision of the Constitution which explicitly recognizes a specific freedom to teach. Underlying the entire Constitution is the philosophy that communicated thought must be protected from governmental control. The First Amendment references to freedom of speech and of the press are designed to assure the free exchange in the general marketplace of ideas. Academic freedom, it can be argued, is the adaptation of those specific constitutional rights to protect communication in the classroom as a special market place of ideas.

* * *

Most of the discussion of academic freedom, including Justice Brennan's observation above, has been in the context of higher education. Chief Justice Warren wrote that "[t]he essentiality of freedom . . . is almost self-evident" and "[t]o impose any strait jacket upon the intellectual leaders in our colleges and universities would imperil the future of our Nation." These and many other statements from the Supreme Court reflect such a widely held belief and traditional view that it is unlikely that a board of regents or other public authority would even attempt to deny a college professor the authority and responsibility to select the materials to be used in his classes. Such an attempt would quite clearly be a case within federal question jurisdiction.

It is not so clear that there is a constitutional basis for the claimed right which would establish such jurisdiction in the context of high school education. Plaintiffs have cited two opinions which recognize some degree of academic freedom at the high school level in circumstances similar to those of the present case.

In *Parducci v. Rutland*, the trial court held that a high school teacher's dismissal for assigning a Kurt Vonnegut story to her English class, contrary to the instruction of the school board, constituted an unwarranted invasion of her First Amendment right to academic freedom. The court's analysis began with Justice Brennan's statement on academic freedom in *Keyishian, supra*. Assuming, without discussing, its applicability to the high school classroom, the court noted that "[t]he right to academic freedom . . . like all other constitutional rights, is not absolute and must be balanced against the competing interests of society." The trial judge then proceeded to decide whether the subject short story was appropriate reading for high school students. Finding that the story was neither inappropriate nor a cause of disruption to the educational process, the court concluded that the plaintiff's right to academic freedom had been infringed.

In *Keefe v. Geanakos*, the appellate court held that a high school teacher was entitled to a preliminary injunction preventing a discharge hearing because he was likely to prevail on his claim that academic freedom entitled him to assign reading of an *Atlantic Monthly* magazine article and to discuss its use of a controversial word in his English class of senior students. As in *Parducci*, the existence of academic freedom in high school was assumed although "some measure of public regulation" was also recognized. Again, as in *Parducci*, the specific controversy was resolved by the court's findings that the article was scholarly and thought-provoking; that the article, when properly understood, would reject rather than suggest use of the controversial word; and that the controversial word was hardly unknown to students in their last year of high school.

Parducci and *Keefe* are of limited value here, for two reasons. First, the existence of the constitutional right of academic freedom in the high school context is not self-evident. Secondly, assuming there is jurisdiction by virtue of some constitutional protection, I reject the approach that this kind of controversy can be resolved by a judicial review of the quality or character of the communications involved. The courts must not assume the role of arbiters of the appropriateness of material for use in a classroom. To force parents, teachers, students, administrators and school boards to obey the dictates of a judge would be wholly inimical to the interests of a free society and it would be yet another step toward the authoritarianism of a judicial oligarchy. The institutional role of the court is to determine whether the Constitution controls who has the authority to choose in a given context, and what are the constitutional limitations on the power of the decision-maker. The quality of the decision is irrelevant.

The cases cited by defendants are also of limited value. In *President's Council v. Community School Board*, the court held that a school board's decision to remove a book from junior high school libraries did not violate the First Amendment rights of either teachers or students. The court did not deny that academic freedom is a recognizable right in high school. It simply found that the intrusion of the board upon any First Amendment right was minuscule because the book was readily available in other libraries, and teachers were not precluded form discussing it in class or assigning it for outside reading. Consequently, there was no showing of a curtailment of freedom of speech or thought. *President's Council* does nothing to determine the question of the applicability of academic freedom to high school, and it is factually distinguishable from the present case.

* * *

While the eloquent statements of the Supreme Court may have been made in the context of higher education, and even there may be technically characterized as dicta, that does not destroy their importance in providing a philosophical guidance in this case.

* * *

In addressing a specific issue involving academic freedom, it is necessary to consider the purpose of the particular educational process in which it arises. The question is best phrased by asking whether the course objectives and the skill levels of the students are characterized as being within the implantation or indoctrination stage; or whether the teachers and students involved have become a part of the open, participatory community. In this case, that question was answered by the board of education when the students were given the freedom of choice as to these courses. Consequently, the claims of the plaintiffs do generate a substantial question arising under the First and Fourteenth Amendments to the United States Constitution and this court has jurisdiction.

ACADEMIC FREEDOM

This case involves the issue of academic freedom in its purest form. The plaintiffs are not seeking to avoid restriction of any rights which they share with all other citizens. They are asserting a freedom peculiar to their positions as teachers. While such a right has been recognized here, for jurisdictional purposes, as a specific application of the general freedom of communication protected by the First Amendment, it is now important to acknowledge limitations in its scope and the manner of its exercise.

* * *

The teacher's liberty is not a license, either as formalized authority or as an undisciplined freedom, and limitations on the manner of its exercise are required to achieve the purpose of academic freedom. Because that purpose is the protection of open communication as a fundamental requirement for a free society, the correlative rights of the other participants in the educational enterprise must be recognized. For a teacher to abuse the prestige or authority of his position to advance his own personal views or suppress those of a student, parent, or any other member of the community would be as stifling to the goal of free exchange and inquiry as an infringement on the teacher's own liberty. The point is illustrated in *Knarr v. Board of School Trustees,* *supra,* in which the court held that a school board can terminate a teacher for abuse of his teaching position by using his classroom "as his personal forum" and belittling students who challenge his opinions.

Additionally, there must be a sufficient stability in the structure of the enterprise to permit orderly interaction. That students' freedom of speech and expression in the academic context cannot be exercised in a manner which interferes with the work of the schools or with the rights of other members of the school community was clearly expressed by the Supreme Court in *Tinker v. Des Moines School Dist.* A teacher's liberty to teach is subject to the same limitation. That was the basis for the decision in *Peterson v. School District*, in which I held that a teacher could be discharged for the use of an innovative graffiti exercise which turned into a verbal personal attack upon the junior high school principal.

These limitations on the exercise of academic freedom can be summarized with the observation that this freedom must always be tempered by professional responsibility. The only justification for restricting this individual freedom is that the particular conduct or activity is inconsistent with or counterproductive to the objective of producing effective citizens. It is the same constitutional purpose of maintaining a society of ordered liberty which creates both the right and the responsibility.

CONCLUSION

The collective bargaining agreement is the central fact in this case. That is what alters the controversy from the abstraction of academic freedom to the specific commitment of a contractual obligation. Through the AEA the teachers in the defendant school district have elected to surrender their individual freedom of professionalism for the security of protectionism by collective action and a group contract. In so doing,they have voluntarily submitted themselves to the employer-employee model of the teacher's relationship to the school board for everything which is within the scope of the contract and that includes the authority to control communication through the assignment of reading material.

But for the bargained agreement, the plaintiffs would prevail here. The selection of the subject books as material for these elective courses in these grades is clearly within the protected area recognized as academic freedom. Additionally, the school board's policy directive of January 13, 1976, prohibiting the use of any material not included in the list of 1275 books without first obtaining approval of the Division of Instructional Services is the kind of broad prior restraint which is particularly offensive to First Amendment freedom.

Because of the bargained agreement, the plaintiffs' claims must be denied. Whatever may be the scope of the protection of the First and Fourteenth Amendments for a freedom to communicate with students, directly in classroom speech or indirectly through reading assignments, such protection does not present a legal impediment to the freedom to contract. Thus, a teacher may bargain away the freedom to communicate in her official role in the same manner as an editorial writer who agrees to write the views of a publisher or an actor who contracts to speak the author's script. One can, for consideration, agree to teach according to direction.

The combination of teachers into bargaining units with the coercive power of group action is a contradiction of the kind of individual freedom protected by the First Amendment. Conformity to the consensus of a peer group is the essence of a labor organization, and if teachers seek to enjoy the benefits of such concert they must respect the contract which results from the bargaining process and the rights which it gives to the employer.

* * *

ORDERED, that the defendants' motion for summary judgment is granted, and judgment shall enter for the defendants with costs to be taxed.

Kay v. Board of Higher Education
of the City of New York
18 N.Y.S. 2d 821 (1940)

McGEEHAN, Justice.

* * *

If there were only one person in the world who knew anything about philosophy and mathematics and that person was Mr. Russell, the taxpayers might be asked to employ him without examination, but it is hard to believe, considering the vast sums of money that have been spent on American education, that there is no one available, even in America, who is a credit both to learning and to public life. Other universities and colleges, both public and private, seem to be able to find American citizens to employ and to say that the College of the City of New York could not employ a professor of philosophy by an examination of some sort, is an assumption by the Board of Higher Education of the power which was denied to them by the People of the State of New York in the constitution and no Legislature and no board can violate this mandate.

* * *

The petitioner contends that the appointment of Bertrand Russell has violated the public policy of the state and of the nation because of the notorious immoral and salacious teachings of Bertrand Russell and because the petitioner contends he is a man not a good moral character.

It has been argued that the private life and writings of Mr. Russell have nothing whatsoever to do with his appointment as a teacher of philosophy. It has also been argued that he is going to teach mathematics. His appointment, however, is to the department of philosophy in City College.

In this consideration I am completely dismissing any question of Mr. Russell's attacks upon religion, but there are certain basic principles upon which this government is founded. If a teacher, who is a person not of good moral character, is appointed by any authority the appointment violates these essential prerequisites. One of the prerequisites of a teacher is good moral character. In fact, this is a prerequisite for appointment in civil service in the city and state, or political subdivisions, or in the United States. It needs no argument here to defend this statement. It need not be found in the Education Law. It is found in the nature of the teaching profession. Teachers are supposed not only to impart instruction in the classroom but by their example to teach the students. The taxpayers of the City of New York spend millions to maintain the colleges of the City of New York. They are not spending that money nor was the money appropriated for the purpose of employing teachers who are not of good moral character. However, there is ample authority in the Education Law to support this contention.

The contention of the petitioner that Mr. Russell has taught in his books immoral and salacious doctrines is amply sustained by the books conceded to be the writings of Bertrand Russell, which were offered in evidence. It is not necessary to detail here the filth which is contained in the books. It is sufficient to record the following: from "Education and the Modern World," pages 119 and 120: "I am sure that university life would be better, both intellectually and morally, if most university students had temporary childless marriages. This would afford a solution of the sexual urge neither restless nor surreptitious, neither mercenary nor casual, and of such a nature that it need not take up time which ought to be given to work." From "Marriage and Morals," pages 165 and 166: "For my part, while I am quite convinced that companionate marriage would be a step in the right direction, and would do a great deal of good, I do not think that it goes far enough. I think that all sex relations which do not involve children should be regarded as a purely private affair, and that if a man and a woman choose to live together without having children, that should be no one's business but their own. I should not hold it desirable that either a man or a woman should enter upon the serious business of a marriage intended to lead to children without having had previous sexual experience." ("The peculiar importance attached, at the present, to adultery, is quite irrational." From "What I Believe," page 50.)

The Penal Law of the State of New York is a most important factor in the lives of our people. As citizens and residents of our city we come within its protective scope. In dealing with human behavior the provisions of the Penal Law and such conduct as therein condemned must not be lightly treated or completely ignored.

*   *   *

Where it so acts as to sponsor or encourage violations of the Penal Law, and its actions adversely affect the public health, safety and morals, its acts are void and of no legal effect. A court of equity, with the powers inherent in that court, has ample jurisdiction to protect the taxpayers of the City of New York from such acts as this of the Board of Higher Education.

Assuming that Mr. Russell could teach for two years in City College without promulgating the doctrines which he seems to find necessary to spread on the printed pages at frequent intervals, his appointment violates a perfectly obvious canon of pedagogy, namely, that the personality of the teacher has more to do with forming a student's opinion than many syllogisms. A person we despise and who is lacking in ability cannot argue us into imitating him. A person whom we like and who is of outstanding ability does not have to try. It is contended that Bertrand Russell is extraordinary. That makes him the more dangerous. The philosophy of Mr. Russell and his conduct in the past is in direct conflict and in violation of the Penal Law of the State of New York. When we consider how susceptible the human mind is to the ideas and philosophy of teaching professors, it is apparent that the Board of Higher Education either disregarded the probable consequences of their acts or were more concerned with advocating a cause that appeared to them to present a challenge to so-called "academic freedom" without according suitable consideration of the other aspects of the problem before them. While this court would not interfere with any action of the board in so far as a pure question of "valid" academic freedom is concerned, it will not tolerate academic freedom being used as a cloak to promote the popularization in the minds of adolescents of acts forbidden by the Penal Law. This appointment affects the public health, safety and morals of the community and it is the duty of the court to act. Academic freedom does not mean academic license. It is the freedom to do good and not to teach evil. Academic freedom cannot authorize a teacher to teach that murder or treason are good. Nor can it permit a teacher to teach directly or indirectly that sexual intercourse between students, where the female is under the age of eighteen years, is proper. This court can take judicial notice of the fact that students in the colleges of the City of New York are under the age of eighteen years, although some of them may be older.

Academic freedom cannot teach that abduction is lawful nor that adultery is attractive and good for the community. There are norms and criteria of truth which have been recognized by the founding fathers. We find a recognition of them in the opening words of the Declaration of Independence, where they refer to the laws of nature and of Nature's God. The doctrines therein set forth, which have been held sacred by all Americans from that day to this, preserved by the Constitution of the United States and of the several states and defended by the blood of its citizens, recognizing the inalienable rights with which men are endowed by their Creator must be preserved, and a man whose life and teachings run counter to these doctrines, who teaches and practices immorality and who encourages and avows violation of the Penal Law of the State of New York, is not fit to teach in any of the schools of this land. The judicial branch of our government under our democratic institutions has not been so emasculated by the opponents of our institutions to an extent to render it impotent to act to protect the rights of the people. Where public health, safety and morals are so directly involved, no board, administrative or otherwise, may act in a dictatorial capacity, shielding their actions behind a claim of complete and absolute immunity from judicial review. The Board of Higher Education of the City of New York has deliberately and completely disregarded the essential principles upon which the selection of any teacher must rest. The contention that Mr. Russell will teach mathematics and not his philosophy does not in any way detract from the fact that his very presence as a teacher will cause the students to look up to him, seek to know more about him, and the more he is able to charm them and impress them with his personal presence, the more potent will grow his influence in all spheres of their lives, causing the students in many instances to strive to emulate him in every respect.

* * *

Considering Dr. Russell's principles, with reference to the Penal Law of the State of New York, it appears that not only would the morals of the students be undermined, but his doctrines would tend to bring them, and in some cases their parents and guardians, in conflict with the Penal Law, and accordingly this court intervenes.

The appointment of Dr. Russell is an insult to the people of the City of New York and to the thousands of teachers who were obligated upon their appointment to establish good moral character and to maintain it in order to keep their positions. Considering the instances in which immorality alone has been held to be sufficient basis for removal of a teacher and mindful of the aphorism "As a man thinketh in his heart, so he is," the court holds that the acts of the Board of Higher Education of the City of New York in appointing Dr. Russell to the Department of Philosophy of the City College of the City of New York, to be paid by public funds, is in effect establishing a chair of indecency and in doing so has acted arbitrarily, capriciously and in direct violation of the public health, safety and morals of the people and of the petitioner's rights herein, and the petitioner is entitled to an order revoking the appointment of the said Bertrand Russell and discharging him from his said position, and denying to him the rights and privileges and the powers appertaining to his appointment. Settle final order accordingly.

Cooper v. Ross

472 F. Supp. 802 (E.D. Ark. 1979)

FINDINGS OF FACT

In September 1969, Little Rock University was merged into the University of Arkansas, an educational institution of the State of Arkansas. Defendant G. Robert Ross was appointed Chancellor of the University of Arkansas at Little Rock (UALR or University) in January 1973. Defendant C. Fred Williams was named head of the History Department at the University in May 1973. The remaining defendants are all members of the University of Arkansas Board of Trustees. All defendants are sued only in their official capacities.

Grant Cooper was employed as an assistant professor of history at the University for the 1970–71 academic year. He was reappointed as assistant professor for the 1971–72, 1972–73 and 1973–74 academic years.

Cooper did not have tenure. The Faculty Handbook provided that:

> A non-tenure appointment may be terminated effective at the end of an academic or fiscal year as the case may be at the option either of the individual or the University.

During the fourth year of teaching at the rank of assistant professor, a faculty member was normally considered for promotion to associate professor. Promotion would automatically confer tenure. Alternatively, the teacher could be retained at the rank of assistant professor without tenure, or he could be notified that he would not be reappointed. The Faculty Handbook provided that one who had been a faculty member for two or more years was entitled to at least one year's written advance notice if he was not going to be recommended for reappointment.

Prior to the spring of 1973 there were no established procedures and no specific standards for faculty evaluation and promotion purposes, either University-wide or within the History Department. Beginning in the spring of 1973 the Ross administration instituted a policy of merit pay increases and required periodic faculty evaluations.

Cooper became a member of the Progressive Labor Party (PLP) in June or July 1973. In mid-July 1973, at the beginning of the second summer school session, Cooper informed his classes in World Civilization and American Civilization that he was a communist and a member of the PLP, and that he taught his courses from a Marxist point of view. Other History Department members and Chancellor Ross learned of the statements shortly thereafter.

At registration for the fall 1973 term, Williams questioned Cooper about his statements to his classes and suggested to Cooper that it was inappropriate for him to announce his personal point of view to his classes. Bedford Hadley, Dean of the Division of Social Science, similarly discussed the matter with Cooper. Cooper was, however, not directed to discontinue the practice.

On September 20, 1973, *Essence*, an "underground" student newspaper, carried an article about Cooper and his statements to his summer school classes. On September 26, 1973, substantially the same article appeared on the front page of the *Arkansas Gazette*, a newspaper with statewide circulation. The articles apparently reported that Cooper had been ordered by the University not to state his personal political views in the classroom. Thereafter, Cooper became the subject of considerable public controversy and for several weeks the case received daily newspaper and television coverage.

On October 8, 1973, twenty-three state legislators, as individuals, filed suit in state court against Cooper, Chancellor Ross, and the Trustees of the University, to enjoin Cooper's further employment at the University. The suit was predicated on Ark. Stat. Ann. §§ 41–4111 and 41–4113 (1964). Section 41–4113(c) provided,

> No person who is a member of a Nazi, Fascist or Communist society, or any organization affiliated with such societies, shall be eligible for employment by the State of Arkansas, or by any department, agency, institution, or municipality thereof.

On approximately October 2, October 9, and October 23, 1973, Cooper participated in public forums sponsored by Students for Action and the PLP regarding the use by another UALR faculty member of *The Unheavenly City* by Edward Banfield as a required textbook. Cooper publicly criticized the book as racist and unscientific and argued that the book should not be required course material and should be banned from the University campus.

On October 3, 1973, Cooper met with Chancellor Ross at the latter's request. They discussed the statements Cooper made to his classes, Cooper's political beliefs and how these affected his teaching of his courses. They also discussed Cooper's statements about the Banfield book.

A second meeting was held on October 29, 1973, and the same general issues were discussed. At the conclusion of the discussion Ross inquired whether, if instructed by the University, Cooper would teach his courses from an objective point of view and refrain from identifying his own beliefs to his classes. Cooper responded that he felt it would be intellectually dishonest if he did not state his own beliefs, that he could not be entirely objective toward other points of view, and that if he were ordered not to teach from a Marxist point of view he would feel compelled to resist the order. At no time in either meeting were any other factors relating to Cooper's performance as a teacher discussed.

On November 7, 1973, Cooper was notified by Williams that he was not recommending Cooper's reappointment and that Cooper's 1974–75 appointment would be a terminal appointment.

Cooper requested and was granted a conference at which Williams explained his decision not to recommend Cooper's further employment. Cooper then requested and received a written list of reasons for the non-reappointment recommendation. The reasons given were as follows:

* * *

Over a period of some three years, a variety of irregularities have been brought to your attention. These include:

a. Questionable grading procedures and problems involving evaluation of students.

b. Student complaints about meeting and conducting scheduled classes.

The Dean of the Division of Social Science, who was a former chairman of the History Department, has stated that during the past three years he has received more student complaints about your teaching responsibilities than has been received on any other faculty member in the division.

Students have repeatedly indicated that your courses did not cover the subject area as described in the University catalog; that you failed to adhere to the required text materials in assignments, lectures or discussion and your attitude toward those materials discouraged their use.

Changing, in a unilaterial [sic] manner, the content and scope of a course required by the general faculty for graduation.

Your attempts to restrict the academic freedom of others in the academic community which reflects a lack of restraint and does not show proper respect for the opinion of others in the academic setting. Specifically, your statements about banning a book on the UALR campus.

You have indicated either a lack of awareness or concern for a well known and respected statement of the American Association of University Professors in a "1940 Statement of Principles and Interpretive Comments" on academic freedom and tenure. Paragraph "C" of that document, in reference to the college or university teacher, includes the following statements:

"As a man of learning and an educational officer, he (the teacher) should remember that the public may judge his profession and his institution by his utterances."

These reasons have led me to conclude that your professional development in scholarly endeavors and classroom instruction have not been satisfactorily demonstrated and, therefore, your appointment as assistant professor should not be renewed. I feel confident that a more qualified person can be readily employed as an assistant professor.

* * *

Reason 6 referred, in part, to a handout Cooper used in his World Civilization course in the fall semester of 1973. This handout stated the proposition: "The history of all hitherto existing society is the history of class struggles." The handout attributed the statement to Marx and Engels and indicated Cooper's agreement with it. Students were assigned to write a term paper on a subject of their choosing to test the proposition.

Reason 7 referred to Cooper's public comments about the Banfield book.

* * *

Cooper requested that his case be reviewed by the Senate Standing Committee on Academic Tenure, as provided in the UALR Faculty Handbook. There was, however, at that time no such committee in existence. Therefore, the UALR faculty assembly created an ad hoc committee to review Williams's recommendation not to reappoint Cooper. In May 1974 the committee conducted hearings at which Cooper and his attorneys were present and were allowed to question the University witnesses. Cooper was not permitted to present witnesses. Because this was the first such review in the history of UALR, there was considerable confusion regarding the purpose and function of the committee. The committee initially agreed that its purpose was not to consider the merits of the decision, but only to consider its procedural adequacy, *i.e.*, whether the procedural requirements set out in the handbook regarding notice and hearings in non-reappointment cases had been complied with. In fact, however, there was some discussion of the reasons for the non-reappointment decision.

In a cryptic report the committee concluded that the decision not to recommend Cooper's reappointment was "the result of adequate consideration in terms of the relevant standards of the institution." However, the committee also reported that many of its members expressed "deep concern" about "the ambiguities in the eight stated reasons for non-reappointment, the quality of the evidence and documentation submitted by the History Department, the timing of the non-reappointment announcement, and the generally unprofessional administration of this matter."

* * *

The fact that Cooper was a communist and a member of the PLP and publicly stated both in and out of the classroom that he was a communist and a member of the PLP were substantial or motivating factors in the decision not to renew his appointment.

Other factors also played some part in the decision not to renew Cooper's appointment, including evaluations of his teaching performance by the department chairman and other members of the History Department faculty, and the manner in which he expressed his criticism of the Banfield book.

However, the same non-reappointment decision would not have been made had it not been for the fact that Cooper was a communist and a member of the PLP and publicly acknowledged these facts. The factors relied on by the University, considered individually or collectively, would not alone have caused the nonrenewal of Cooper's contract.

The University, through the History Department, prescribed the general subject matter for each course in the department. For the World Civilization course, which was divided into multiple sections taught by different teachers, there was general agreement among the department faculty on the text to be used in the course and on the periods of history to be covered each semester. Beyond this, each instructor had considerable latitude in organizing and presenting the material. Specifically, there were no department standards or policies requiring that this course, or any other course, be taught from an objective or any other specific point of view. Different faculty members taught their courses from different points of view.

Cooper substantially covered the subject matter of his courses. The record does not support the University's position that the fact Cooper professed to teach his courses from the Marxist point of view necessarily limited his coverage of the prescribed subject matter. Similarly, the handout distributed to Cooper's World Civilization course in the fall term of 1973 is not alone sufficient to establish that the course deviated in content and scope from the prescribed curriculum. There is simply no evidence of what in fact was covered in his courses other than Cooper's testimony that he covered the prescribed course material.

Cooper did not use his classes to proselytize students for membership in the PLP. In fact, he encouraged students to challenge and dispute his views.

* * *

When a non-tenured teacher alleges that he was not rehired in violation of his First Amendment rights, he bears the initial burden of establishing that his conduct was constitutionally protected and that this protected conduct was a "substantial factor" or a "motivating factor" in the school's decision not to reappoint him. If this burden is sustained, the school then has the burden of showing by a preponderance of the evidence that it would have reached the same non-reappointment decision even in the absence of the protected conduct.

* * *

It is evident that the bare announcement of Cooper's personal views did not materially or substantially disrupt his classes. In fact, it caused remarkably little concern until the matter was publicized by the media. The subsequent public reaction is not the kind of disruption that can be balanced against a teacher's right to free expression. The Court does not imply that it was desirable or even appropriate for Cooper to have informed his classes of his personal beliefs, except to note that the college classroom is peculiarly suited to the "robust exchange of ideas." The Court concludes only that, at least in the context of a university classroom, Cooper had a constitutionally protected right simply to inform his students of his personal political and philosophical views.

The Court is persuaded that this protected conduct was a substantial or motivating factor in the decision not to reappoint Cooper. Several factors point to this conclusion including the timing of the nonrenewal decision, the fact that during the three years prior to his joining the PLP Cooper was never informed that the University was seriously concerned about his performance as a teacher, the fact that Chancellor Ross's October 1973 meeting with Cooper focused almost exclusively on the matter of his beliefs, and the fact that prior to Cooper no full-time faculty member had ever been non-reappointed or dismissed from UALR.

More significant and more disturbing to the Court, however, is the political furor which followed the newspaper reports about Cooper, particularly the action filed by certain state legislators to remove Cooper from the University. The Supreme Court has emphasized the importance of maintaining our universities free of political intervention.

* * *

Clearly, the University was under considerable public and political pressure to discharge Cooper. Although the University contested the state lawsuit and joined with Cooper in challenging the Arkansas statutes as unconstitutional, this does not compel the conclusion that it remained unswayed by external influences. Rather, for a variety of reasons it could well have determined that the prudent course was to publicly contest the suit while privately resolving the problem by non-reappointment.

Cooper having established that protected activity was a substantial or motivating factor in his non-reappointment, the burden shifted to the University to show that it would have reached the same decision even in the absence of the protected conduct.

* * *

However, in a case such as this one, when there has been a substantial claim that the decision was in derogation of First Amendment rights, the paucity of supporting evidence implies that the reasons given by the University were hastily prepared, make-weight reasons which do not fully reflect its true motivation. The Court concludes, therefore, that the University failed to sustain its burden of proving by a preponderance of the evidence that Cooper would not have been reappointed absent his protected conduct.

Several of the University's contentions require more detailed consideration because they pose very difficult constitutional questions. The University argues that Cooper's political philosophy was relevant to its nonrenewal decision because he interjected his beliefs into the classroom not only by merely announcing that he was a communist and a member of the PLP, but also by announcing that he intended to teach, and by actually teaching, from the Marxist point of view. The University contends that along with its right to determine the curriculum and subject matter to be taught, it is the University's prerogative to determine that material should be presented from an objective point of view or from any other particular point of view. The ultimate question thus posed is whether Cooper's decision to teach his courses from a Marxist point of view was constitutionally protected so that if in fact this motivated his non-reappointment, his rights were violated.

* * *

The present case is particularly difficult because it involves a fundamental tension between the academic freedom of the individual teacher to be free of restraints from the university administration, and the academic freedom of the university to be free of government, including judicial, interference.

Case law considering the extent to which the First Amendment and academic freedom protect a teacher's choice of teaching methodology is surprisingly sparse and the results are not entirely consistent.

The Court concludes, however, that this sensitive and difficult issue need not be reached in this case. At the time Cooper was notified he would not be reappointed he was not informed that the fact that he taught his classes from a Marxist point of view was one reason for the decision. This suggests this reason was an afterthought and not in fact a motivating factor in the discharge. The only one of the written reasons given to Cooper which is arguably related is reason 6. At trial, the University attempted to prove that because Cooper taught from the Marxist point of view, he deviated from the prescribed subject matter. However, there was little or no evidence that Cooper did not substantially cover the material. Furthermore, it is clear that there were no established standards or policies requiring that World Civilization or any other course be taught from any particular point of view or by any particular method. Different faculty members taught their courses from different points of view. Other than his express announcement of his point of view to his classes in the summer of 1973, Cooper's approach to his courses was substantially the same as it had been during his three previous years at UALR without objection. It is clear that other members of the History Department were aware from the time he joined the department that Cooper personally shared the Marxist interpretation of history and economics. The Court thus concludes as a matter of fact that had Cooper not become a member of the PLP and announced his personal beliefs to his classes, he would have been rehired, notwithstanding his Marxist viewpoint toward the teaching of history.

If Cooper's nonrenewal had in fact been motivated by his teaching methods, the Court would be inclined to invoke this doctrine. However, in view of the conclusion that the decision was not so motivated, this need not be done. The Court also need not decide the more difficult question whether, should it so choose, a university may constitutionally prohibit teaching from a Marxist point of view.

Cooper's comments about the Banfield book raise other potentially sensitive questions about academic freedom on a university campus. The University contends that Cooper's criticisms of the book were unprofessional and that this was a legitimate consideration in the nonrenewal decision. It is clear that a teacher's out of class statements on matters of public concern are entitled to considerable constitutional protection. Nevertheless, a teacher's rights are not absolute and must be balanced against the interests of the state as an employer. Thus, some cases have held that a university teacher's out of class statements are unprotected and may properly be the basis of a nonrenewal decision when the statements are such that they reflect adversely on the teacher's professional competence and judgment. It is, however, the Court's opinion that had it not been for his other clearly protected conduct, Cooper would have been reappointed, regardless of what he said about the Banfield book. It is therefore unnecessary to decide whether his comments were unprofessional and properly subject to consideration by the University in making the non-reappointment decision.

In summary, the Court concludes that Cooper's membership in the PLP and his public acknowledgment of his beliefs, both inside and outside the University classroom, were protected conduct under the First and Fourteenth Amendments. The Court finds that this protected activity was a substantial or motivating factor in the University's decision not to reappoint Cooper. The University failed to prove by a preponderance of the evidence that the same non-reappointment decision would have been made absent Cooper's exercise of First Amendment rights.

Ollman v. Toll

518 F. Supp. 1196 (D.C. Md. 1981)

ALEXANDER HARVEY, II, District Judge:

Bertell Ollman, the plaintiff in this civil action, is a Marxist. He has here sued various representatives of the University of Maryland under 42 U.S.C. § 1983, claiming that in 1978 he was rejected for the position of Professor and Chairman of the Department of Government and Politics at that College Park campus of the University because of his political beliefs and associations. Named as defendants are John S. Toll, President of the University of Maryland, Wilson H. Elkins, the past President of the University, and the University's Board of Regents. As relief, plaintiff seeks an injunction which would require the University to appoint him as Professor and Chairman of the Department in question, back pay, compensatory and punitive damages, attorneys' fees and other relief.

In opposing the plaintiff's claims for relief, the defendants assert that plaintiff's political beliefs were not a substantial or motivating factor in the decision of the President of the University not to appoint him as Chairman of one of its major departments and as a Professor with tenure. Defendants further contend that if plaintiff's Marxism were found to be a substantial factor in President Toll's rejection of defendant for the position, the President would have reached the same decision as to plaintiff's employment at the University even in the absence of plaintiff's political beliefs. It is further contended that defendants Elkins and the Board of Regents were not responsible for any violation of plaintiff's constitutional rights because the ultimate decision was made by President Toll on July 20, 1978 and not by the other named defendants.

* * *

After considering a list of approximately 100 persons during the final three months of 1977, the Search Committee by early January of 1978 had not come up with a likely candidate to recommend for the position. Dr. Bertell Ollman, the plaintiff, was at the time an Associate Professor of the Department of Politics at New York University (hereinafter "N.Y.U."). His name was not on the original lengthy list which the Search Committee had considered. However, in early January, three members of the Committee suggested plaintiff's name for the position, and the Committee ultimately recommended him and one other candidate for the position. The other candidate was Dr. Robert T. Holt, who is a Professor of the Department of Political Science at the University of Minnesota and presently Chairman of that Department.

* * *

Under the By-laws of the Board of Regents, it was the President who had the final authority to appoint a person Chairman of a Department. However, it was the practice that all recommendations for faculty appointments to be made by the President would first come to the Vice President of Academic Affairs for review. In the spring of 1978, Dr. R. Lee Hornbake had occupied this post for some eighteen years. He regularly reviewed recommendations of this sort from the Chancellor, and in turn, made recommendations to the President before final action was taken.

In the spring of 1978, Dr. Wilson H. Elkins had been President of the University of Maryland for some twenty-four years. He had previously announced his retirement effective June 30, 1978, and Dr. John S. Toll had been selected to replace him as President, commencing on July 1, 1978, Dr. Toll had been President of the State University of New York at Stony Brook, New York, for some thirteen years. During the spring of 1978, he was finishing up his term at the Stony Brook campus and was, of course, not then responsible for affairs of the University of Maryland.

Acting with some urgency between early January and late February, 1978, the Search Committee for the Department of Government and Politics recommended both Dr. Holt and Dr. Ollman for appointment as Chairman of the Department. In a meeting with Provost Polakoff, the same members of the Committee who had initially suggested plaintiff's name urged that he be selected for the position. The Provost agreed and, after reviewing the matter with the Chancellor and receiving his concurrence, telephoned plaintiff on March 3, 1978 and offered the post to him, provided that the President approved the appointment. When he had originally reviewed the qualifications of the candidates, Chancellor Gluckstern had rated Dr. Holt over Dr.

Ollman, but he was later persuaded by the Provost that the position should be offered to Dr. Ollman.

More than six weeks then elapsed before Chancellor Gluckstern forwarded his recommendation to Dr. Hornbake and Dr. Elkins. Various steps were taken during that period to have the files on the recommended appointment put in proper form for submission to the President. Meanwhile, on April 18, 1978, an article appeared in *The Diamondback*, the campus newspaper, reporting that plaintiff, a Marxist, was being recommended for appointment as Chairman of the Department of Government and Politics. This first press report led in the following weeks to a veritable storm of publicity relating to the appointment. Articles appeared in Baltimore and Washington newspapers as well as in *The Diamondback*, discussing the fact that a Marxist was being considered for this important position. The publicity evoked considerable comment by both public officials and private citizens, and the Ollman matter quite rapidly became a cause célèbre. The Governor, legislators, alumni, members of the faculty, members of the Board of Regents and private citizens raised questions concerning the propriety of the proposed appointment. Members of the faculty and other supporters of plaintiff viewed the Ollman affair as a question of academic freedom and urged President Elkins to promptly appoint plaintiff to the position in question. Suit was threatened if the appointment was not made at once. Some of those who opposed the appointment based their objections on plaintiff's qualifications to be Chairman of this important department at the University. Others took the flat position that a Marxist should not occupy the post.

When the formal papers eventually reached Dr. Hornbake and were reviewed by him, he was disturbed by certain irregularities which he concluded had occurred in the search procedures. The more he looked into the matter, the more concerns he had. After further study of the file and discussions with various faculty members, Dr. Hornbake eventually recommended to President Elkins that plaintiff not be appointed. Meanwhile, the publicity and controversy over the appointment continued. Since late April, President Elkins had been aware that if the appointment was rejected by him, a suit in federal court would be filed against him by Dr. Ollman.

By this time it was late May of 1978, a very busy time of the year for a University President. To complicate matters even further, President Elkins was scheduled to retire effective June 30. Fearing that if he went along with the recommendation of Dr. Hornbake he would be involved in lengthy litigation which would come to trial after his retirement, President Elkins decided to seek the help of the Board of Regents. At a meeting of the Board of Regents on June 16, 1978, he stated that he was bringing the matter to the Board because of unusual circumstances surrounding the appointment. Dr. Elkins informed the Board that he was not inclined to support the appointment but that he was asking the Board itself to make the final decision. After some discussion, the Board concluded that it did not have sufficient information on the matter at that time. The Board decided to meet with counsel, secure counsel's advice and then decide on its further course of action. Before the Board would legally have been able to act on the appointment, it would have been necessary to change its By-laws, which provided that only the President had the authority to approve or disapprove an appointment of this sort. Between June 16 and June 30, 1978, which was the last day that President Elkins was in office, the Board had the matter under study, receiving advice from an Assistant Attorney General of the State. At a meeting of the Board held on June 21, the Board formally requested President Elkins to give the Board a written report on the matter before he left office. It was decided that upon receipt of this report, the Board would then consider what further action it should take.

President Elkins left office without having acted on the appointment. On June 30, as requested, he submitted to the Board his written report, together with pertinent materials from Chancellor Gluckstern, Provost Polakoff and the Search Committee. On July 1, 1978, defendant Toll assumed his new duties as President of the university and was confronted immediately with the Ollman matter. After considering the posture of the appointment at that time, he decided that he alone should make the final decision. He so advised the Board, which concurred in that decision since it was in keeping with the existing By-laws. At a later meeting held on July 18, the Board formally reaffirmed the President's authority to act on the Ollman appointment.

After discussing the matter with Dr. Hornbake and reviewing all documents in University files, President Toll decided that he would not rely merely on information in the files but would himself make an independent investigation of the qualifications of the plaintiff to be Chairman of the Department of Government and Politics. He held an open meeting with members of the Department on July 11, 1978, soliciting their views. Various Professors and other faculty members presented their comments both *pro* and *con* concerning the appointment of plaintiff to this position. Most favored the appointment but one-third of those present opposed it, including two former Chairmen of the Department and the Acting Chairman. On his own, President Toll had prepared a list of political science experts and others for consultation, and in early July, President Toll personally communicated with these individuals. Most of the persons on this so-called "referee list" were political scientists, and many were persons known and respected by President Toll. Some of the comments were favorable to Dr. Ollman but most were unfavorable.

Finally, on July 20, 1978, President Toll announced his decision. In a prepared statement, he said that after appropriate consultation and review, he had decided not to approve the appointment of plaintiff for the position of Professor and Chairman of the Department of Government and Politics at the University of Maryland at College Park. President Toll stated that his decision had been based on his own evaluation of whether or not the proposed candidate was the best qualified person for the position. His decision was announced at a special meeting of the Board of Regents held on the morning of July 20, 1978.

On August 1, 1978, this civil action was filed. Plaintiff contends that defendant Toll's stated reason for disapproving the appointment was a mere pretext and that defendant Toll was actually motivated to reject plaintiff because of his Marxist beliefs. With reference to his claim against President Elkins, plaintiff asserts that this defendant refused to decide whether or not to confirm plaintiff's appointment, because of plaintiff's Marxism, and that such refusal amounted to a violation of plaintiff's rights under § 1983. As to the Board of Regents, it is also contended that this defendant refused to take action to confirm plaintiff's appointment because of legally impermissible reasons.

II

The applicable legal principles

It is well established that a state university may not refuse to employ a prospective member of its faculty if the decision is made by reason of the exercise by the applicant of constitutionally protected First Amendment rights. Marxist or Communist beliefs, like other political beliefs, are protected under the First and Fourteenth Amendments, and such beliefs or one's association with others holding them is protected activity for which a state may not impose civil disabilities such as exclusion from employment by a state university.

* * *

In this case, the Court is called upon first to determine whether the plaintiff has satisfied his initial burden of proving that his beliefs were constitutionally protected and that these beliefs were a substantial or motivating factor in the decision of one or more of the defendants not to hire him as Professor and Chairman of the Department of Government and Politics at the University of Maryland. Secondly, if plaintiff has satisfied his initial burden, the Court must determine whether the defendants have shown by a preponderance of the evidence that they would have made the same decision even in the absence of the constitutionally protected beliefs of the plaintiff. Thirdly, and related to each of these questions, is whether the reasons given by one or more of the defendants for refusing to hire the plaintiffs were pretextual.

III

The claim against defendant Toll

(a) Plaintiff's burden

Quite clearly, plaintiff has satisfied the first part of the burden placed upon him in a case of this sort. Dr. Ollman was a Marxist and was known for professing those political beliefs. Whether or not plaintiff's Marxist beliefs are popular ones and whether or not they have the approval of other citizens of this country, they are entitled to the full protection of the First Amendment. No more direct assault on academic freedom can be imagined than for school authorities to refuse to hire a teacher because of his or her political, philosophical or ideological beliefs.

* * *

The second portion of plaintiff's burden is a much more difficult one. Plaintiff must go beyond proving that his Marxism was a factor in his rejection. To be entitled to the relief he seeks, plaintiff in this case has the burden of showing that his beliefs or associations were a substantial or motivating factor in the decision of one or more of the defendants that he would not be hired at the University of Maryland. It is this issue to which the great bulk of the evidence in this case has been directed.

Although plaintiff has contended that President Elkins and the Board of Regents played a part in rejecting him for employment at the University, it is abundantly clear that President Toll and only President Toll made the final decision which is being challenged. Moreover, under the By-laws of the Board of Regents, only President Toll was legally authorized to make the decision after July 1, 1978, and no decision either way was made before that date. Therefore, it is the reasons given by President Toll for acting as he did which must be examined critically and in detail before the Court can determine whether plaintiff has met his burden of proving that his Marxism was a substantial or motivating factor in his rejection.

(b) President Toll's review of the matter

Most of the voluminous evidence in the case related to events that occurred before President Toll assumed his duties at the University on July 1, 1978. These facts are of course relevant, because many of the events occurring in the first six months of 1978 were later brought to the attention of President Toll when he assumed office on July 1, 1978 and reviewed extensive University files relating to the matter. But, much more significant are the critical events that occurred between July 1, when President Toll took office, and July 20, when he announced that he would not appoint plaintiff to the position in question. A detailed examination of these events in particular is necessary for this Court to determine whether plaintiff has met his burden in this case.

President Toll had first heard of the Ollman matter while he was still at Stony Brook. A letter dated March 23, 1978 and marked "PERSONAL AND CONFIDEN-TIAL" was addressed to and received by him. Although unsigned, the letter was written on stationery of the University of Maryland's Department of Government and Politics, and purported to be submitted on behalf of a group of faculty of the Department. Attached to the letter was the Curriculum Vitae of the plaintiff. This letter informed defendant Toll that there was a vacancy in the Department and that certain persons were trying to bring in the plaintiff and have his appointment confirmed before defendant arrived on the scene. It was suggested in the letter that the appointment might slip through in the shuffle during the change of presidency and be made irrevocable before defendant Toll took office.

* * *

[Alerted by this letter, Dr. Toll investigated the procedures and became troubled by both the procedures and the result.]

Included in the file before him were letters to Chancellor Gluckstern from Dr. Martin C. McGuire, Chairman of the Search Committee, recommending both Professor Robert T. Holt and plaintiff for the position. Dr. McGuire's letter of February 21, 1978, which attached a copy of Professor Holt's Curriculum Vitae (hereinafter "C.V."), stated that Professor Holt had been "enthusiastically" endorsed by the Search Committee as a candidate for Chairman of the Department of Government and Politics. Dr. McGuire stated that Professor Holt had "a superb record as a scholar," "a proven track record as an administrator" and that he would "be most adept" at bringing research grant money into the Department. Dr. McGuire's shorter letter of February 24, 1978, which attached a copy of plaintiff's C.V., stated that plaintiff had been "warmly" endorsed by the Committee as a candidate for the position. Although stating that plaintiff was "a world renowned student of Marx" who had "captured the imagination" of the Search Committee, Dr. McGuire made no mention of any administrative experience of plaintiff nor of any experience he had in obtaining research grants.

When he read these letters and the attached C.V.'s, President Toll concluded that Holt appeared to be a much stronger candidate than Ollman. He wondered why an offer had not been made to Holt. Dr. Holt had been promoted in 1964 to a full professorship in the Department of Political Science at the University of Minnesota, which, according to Dr. McGuire's letter, was one of the top six political science departments in the nation. Unlike plaintiff, Holt had been on the original list of 100 names that had been compiled by the Search Committee. Holt's C.V. indicated that he was a top flight scholar, that he had published extensively in recognized journals and that he had considerable administrative experience. Furthermore, Holt had experience in research development. President Toll felt that it was important for the University of Maryland to have as Chairman of the Department of Government and

Politics an individual who would know how to obtain research grants and develop graduate research programs. Since the Department at Maryland was a large one and since the University occupied a unique location so close to the seat of the national government in Washington, D.C., President Toll believed that one of the important missions of the Department was to develop strong graduate research programs.

President Toll also noted that Professor Holt had, between 1976 and 1978, been a member of the Council of American Political Science Association (APSA), the leading professional association for political scientists in the nation. In President Toll's mind, election to such a position was a recognition of national achievement by a professor's colleagues and particularly by those interested in research in political science. Recognizing that Professor Holt was a leading candidate for the position, the Search Committee had speeded up its procedures since Holt had to know before mid-March whether the offer would be made to him. Although the deadline was that of Holt, the Committee, in acting with urgency, had recommended Ollman to the Provost.

During his long weekend review of these files, President Toll also studied plaintiff's C.V. and other materials submitted in support of the Chancellor's recommendation of plaintiff for the appointment. Unlike the other leading candidates, plaintiff was not at the time a full Professor but merely an Associate Professor at N.Y.U. President Toll noted that plaintiff's principal contribution as a scholar was his book entitled *Alienation: Marx's Conception of Man in Capitalist Society*, published in 1971. This was recognized as plaintiff's major work, but it was apparently based in substantial part on his 1967 doctoral dissertation. Information contained in the files before him did not indicate to President Toll that plaintiff possessed the administrative experience to be Chairman of a large Department such as this one. Many of the letters of recommendation contained statements to the effect that the author of the letter had little knowledge of plaintiff's experience in this regard.

Although his impressions of plaintiff's qualifications for the position and of those of other candidates were merely tentative ones, President Toll concluded, before returning to the Maryland campus on July 5, that it would be necessary for him to investigate the matter further. He recognized that both the Provost and the Chancellor had recommended the appointment. But President Toll had serious doubts whether his approval of the Chancellor's recommendation would result in the best appointment that could reasonably be made, and he had enough concerns that he felt he should check further. He decided to secure additional expert opinions on plaintiff's qualifications, both from within the University and from outside. He also decided that he himself would read plaintiff's publications and use the knowledge gained thereby as background for his discussions with the experts with whom he would consult.

President Toll's approach to this appointment was consistent with the practice he had followed in making appointments at Stony Brook as to which he had had concerns. On those occasions, he had solicited views from knowledgeable persons outside the University. Moreover, he himself had often been called by representatives of other universities and asked for his appraisal of the qualifications of candidates who had applied for positions at such institutions.

* * *

[As was his practice, Toll sought the advice of others whose judgment he had relied upon in the past, including colleagues he had known from his previous employment at the University of Maryland. Almost all of the external reviews were negative about Ollman's scholarship and professional standing. Toll met with members of the Department, at which time it became clear to him that there were sharply divided views, apparently along old guard/young guard lines; the search committee that had recommended Ollman was more representative of the newer and younger members of the Department, and favored the avowed Marxist Ollman.

There had been a number of procedural irregularities in the search process, and this meeting with Toll appeared to convince him that the entire matter was improper. He seemed particularly impressed with several of the more senior members of the Department, who opposed Ollman's appointment. Some of the senior professors had not originally opposed Ollman, but after reading more of his scholarship and discussing the matter more thoroughly, they came to different conclusions, and did oppose him for the position.

The final blow was the significant opposition from the senior academic officer of the University, who had expressed doubts all along, but who prepared his own assessment of the procedures and Ollman's scholarship, and recommended to Toll that Ollman not be offered the position. Toll relied greatly upon this recommendation, and announced to the Board of Regents in July, 1978 (his first month as President) that he would not appoint Ollman to be department chair.]

(d) *Discussion*

On the record here, this Court finds and concludes that plaintiff has not met his burden of proving that his Marxist beliefs were a substantial or motivating factor in President Toll's decision not to appoint him as Professor and Chairman of the Department of Government and Politics at the University of Maryland. What must be determined here is the real reason for the adverse decision. The evidence in this case indicates that the reasons assigned by President Toll in his statement of July 20 and in his testimony were the true motivating factors for his decision. President Toll did not base his decision on plaintiff's Marxist beliefs. Rather, he acted as he did because it was his considered judgment that plaintiff did not possess the qualifications to develop the Department of Government and Politics in the manner in which President Toll thought it should develop.

The evidence indicates that the reasons assigned by President Toll for his decision were sincere ones, that there was an adequate factual basis for the conclusions reached and that he had fairly and conscientiously reviewed the entire matter before reaching his decision. Whether or not this Court might agree with President Toll concerning the direction which the Department should take and the qualifications of a Chairman to lead the Department in that direction, it is not for this Court to substitute its judgment for that of the University's Chief Executive Officer, so long as a legally impermissible reason was not the substantial or motivating factor.

Even if this Court were to conclude (as it has not) that plaintiff had carried his initial burden and had proved that his political beliefs were a motivating factor in President Toll's decision, the result in this case would still be the same. For the reasons stated at length herein, this Court finds and concludes that defendants have shown by a preponderance of the evidence that President Toll would have reached the same decision as to plaintiff's employment even in the absence of the protected beliefs. As the Supreme Court there explained, the rule of causation in a case such as this one should not focus solely on whether the plaintiff's protected activity played a part in the decision not to hire him. In *Mt. Healthy*, the Supreme Court pointed out that if such an approach were adopted, a person like plaintiff would be placed "in a better position as a result of the exercise of constitutionally protected conduct than he would have [otherwise] occupied.... The constitutional principle at stake is sufficiently vindicated if such an employee is placed in no worse a position than if he had not engaged in the conduct." Whether or not plaintiff was a Marxist and whether or not that fact had significance to President Toll, plaintiff did not in President Toll's judgment possess the qualifications for the position. Defendants have thus here met their burden of showing that plaintiff would not have been hired in any event.

In contending that he has met his burden of proof in this case, plaintiff asserts that President Toll's decision was influenced by improper comments made by public officials and others. Plaintiff relies on statements that a Marxist should not be appointed as Chairman of the Department at Maryland made by the Governor, by legislators, by private citizens, by several members of the faculty and of the Board of Regents, and by newspaper columnists. It is further contended that President Toll acted as he did because he feared that the University's budget would be cut if a Marxist were appointed to an important position such as this one.

The evidence in the case does not support these contentions. President Toll was certainly aware of the widespread comment which this recommendation had evoked. He was also fully aware of the fact that his decision concerning this appointment could not and should not be based on plaintiff's political beliefs. Following careful study and analysis of all the factors, President Toll made the ultimate decision based on his honest appraisal of plaintiff's qualifications for the particular position.

Plaintiff argues that President Toll succumbed to the pressure brought upon him and his predecessor, President Elkins, resulting from the continuing adverse comments and publicity during the three-month period after the matter became public knowledge. But, there was also pressure brought by persons and organizations favoring the appointment. The American Association of University Professors announced in April that if Dr. Ollman was rejected for the position, the University would be sued. Various members of the faculty supported such a suit, including Dr. Hardin of the Search Committee who spoke to various attorneys and urged that press coverage should be pushed. Plaintiff himself held a press conference in Washington on July 17, stating that if he was not appointed immediately, suit would be filed. Plaintiff correctly points out that many of the opponents of the appointment improperly based their opposition on the legally impermissible ground that plaintiff was a Marxist. But equally unsound comments were made by certain proponents who, without detailed knowledge of plaintiff's qualifications for the appointment, took the position early in the controversy that any rejection would necessarily have to be based on plaintiff's Marxist beliefs. As the Supreme Court emphasized in the *Mt. Healthy* case, a person like plaintiff should not, merely because of his political beliefs, be able to insulate himself from review and prevent his prospective employer from assessing his qualifications and reaching an employment decision based on all the pertinent facts.

President Toll recognized the outside pressure from both proponents and opponents of the appointment. He resolutely refused to yield to the blandishments of either side, and made the decision based on the facts as he saw them. He was an experienced Chief Executive Officer of a State institution and was fully capable of focusing on the essentials and making a decision based on his own professional judgment.

Plaintiff also relies heavily on facts in the record indicating that appointments of this sort were in the usual case routinely and speedily approved by the President of the University after recommendations had been received from both the Provost and the Chancellor. But the Ollman matter was unique, and what may have been done before or after in other cases has little relevance here. Certainly, there had never before 1978 been an appointment like this one faced by a President of the University. Indeed, it is difficult to believe that anything approaching a matter as controversial and publicized as this one could ever occur in the future. A badly divided Department was involved. There were irregularities in the search procedure, which had initially been speeded up but later, after an offer had been made and accepted, slowed down so that the deficiencies could be corrected. There were press reports concerning the appointment before the Chancellor's recommendation had even been received by the President. There were threats of suit before the President had even had an opportunity to review the matter. Most important of all, President Elkins was scheduled to retire shortly after the matter was presented to him for a decision. Because of these unique facts, little weight will be given to the manner in which previous appointments had been handled by President Elkins.

In any event, it was President Toll and not President Elkins who made the ultimate decision. What President Elkins may or may not have done in other cases was of little concern to President Toll, who acted on the basis of his own investigation of the matter as well as on the basis of facts contained in the materials turned over to him by the retiring President.

Plaintiff challenges the manner in which President Toll conducted his own independent review of the appointment. Plaintiff claims that President Toll relied on persons unqualified to give an opinion about him, that Toll intentionally asked such persons misleading questions, that he falsified or modified their responses in his notes, and that he ignored relevant evidence contained in his own files. There is no support in the record for these extreme charges. On the contrary, this Court finds from the evidence that President Toll conducted his investigation of the appointment in a fair and open-minded manner. The outside referees were fairly selected by him, the questions he asked them were proper, and his notes accurately recorded their comments. Indeed, those referees who testified at the trial, either in person or by way of deposition, corroborated in substantial part the testimony and notes of President Toll concerning the statements made by them in early July of 1978. Where there are differences between President Toll's version and the testimony of these individuals, this Court will credit President Toll's account as contained in his notes. These notes were made contemporaneously with the conversations in July of 1978 while the testimony of the individuals themselves was based on their recollections stated in depositions taken a year or more later.

In seeking to sustain his burden in this case, plaintiff places heavy reliance on evidence in the record that distinguished scholars recommended his appointment for the position. But there is substantial evidence in the record to the contrary furnished by other distinguished political scientists. And the impartiality and timing of those who wrote letters supporting plaintiff is subject to question. Plaintiff himself supplied the names of a number of the political scientists who wrote letters to the Search

Committee recommending him for the position. At least one of the letter writers knew when he recommended plaintiff, that a conditional offer had already been made and that plaintiff had already accepted.

* * *

Plaintiff contends that the evidence produced shows that he is well qualified for the position in question. But it is not for this Court to second guess the decision made by President Toll by weighing the evidence and determining whether plaintiff has the necessary qualifications for the position.

* * *

VI

Pretextuality

One of plaintiff's principal arguments in this case is that the reasons given by all defendants for acting as they did were pretextual and that plaintiff's Marxism was the real reason why he was rejected by the University. Plaintiff has characterized the actions taken by President Toll between July 1 and July 20, 1978 as a "charade," and the reasons stated by him and by President Elkins for rejecting the appointment have been called "sham."

These charges raise a substantial issue of credibility in this case. For this Court to find in favor of the plaintiff here, it would have to reject large portions of the testimony given under oath in open court by President Toll, by President Elkins and by Vice President Hornbake. This the Court will not do.

Rather than rejecting as unworthy of belief the testimony of President Toll, President Elkins and Vice President Hornbake, this Court will give full credit to what was said on the stand by each of these three key witnesses, particularly insofar as each of them described their motivations for acting as they did. The testimony of each of the three supports and corroborates that of each one of the others. Furthermore, extensive other evidence in the case, both exhibits and in-court testimony, supports the versions of these events described by each of these three in open court.

Moreover, this Court, in viewing and hearing these three witnesses and in considering their many years of experience in the field of higher education, found each of the witnesses to be impressive in a distinctly different way. Dr. Toll impressed the Court as a man of great integrity, who, as an experienced chief executive officer of a university should do, did not shirk from the unpleasant task of making a difficult decision. Dr. Elkins had served this very large state university for twenty-four years before his retirement on June 30, 1978. He had been a Rhodes scholar at Oxford, had presided over the tremendous growth of the University since 1954, and was hardly the sort of man who would give sham reasons for acting as he did. Dr. Hornbake had been the Academic Vice President of the University for eighteen years and had previously filled many important positions related to matters of higher education. His experience played an important part in the decisions he reached, and his calm and judicious demeanor in answering questions on both direct and cross-examination was hardly that of a dissembling witness.

Plaintiff's case is built essentially on unwarranted inferences derived from actions and statements of President Toll, Dr. Elkins and Vice President Hornbake. But the actions taken by each of these three men were conscientious and responsible ones, their views were honestly held, and their motives were clearly and sincerely stated in their testimony. The circumstantial evidence relied upon by plaintiff simply does not support his contention that President Toll, Dr. Elkins and Dr. Hornbake all had sinister and concealed motives for rejecting him for the position, particularly in view of the weight this Court has given to their sworn testimony in this case.

VII
Summary

There was a massive record in this case, and the parties have locked horns on a myriad of conflicting issues. When the welter of conflicting evidence is weighed and considered, the Court's decision may be summarized in a few brief sentences. First, the final decision concerning the appointment of the Chairman of the Department of Government and Politics at the University of Maryland was in 1978 committed exclusively to the judgment of the President of the University. Secondly, the decision in this case was made honestly and conscientiously by President Toll alone for reasons which he believed would promote his goal of improving the standing of the University. Thirdly, this decision was not based upon plaintiff's political beliefs. President Toll so testified, and this Court has accepted that testimony.

* * *

Conclusion

For the reasons stated, judgment will be entered in favor of the defendants, with costs.

———————

The case against Ollman's appointment was upheld upon appeal. The appeals court reviewed the extensive record, and found that there were "legitimate academic considerations" for denying the appointment. They did concede "that a different set of findings could have been made on the written record before us." 704 F.2d 139 (1983).

———————

Lansing Community College v. Association
for Higher Education
409 N.W.2d 823 (Mich. App. 1987)

SULLIVAN, Judge.

Defendant Lansing Community College Chapter of the Michigan Association for Higher Education appeals as of right from an opinion and order of the Ingham Circuit Court which vacated an arbitration award. We reverse.

Ronald P. Byrum, a member of the defendant association, was employed by plaintiff Lansing Community College as an associate professor of psychology from 1975 until May 15, 1984, when he was discharged primarily for allegedly smoking marijuana with his students at his condominium. Through the defendant, his bargaining representative, Byrum filed a grievance contesting his discharge pursuant to the terms of the parties' collective bargaining agreement. Byrum alleged, inter alia, that the college discharged him without "just cause" in violation of article VI.T.1 of the agreement, which states, "No faculty member shall be reprimanded, demoted, or discharged without just cause."

Pursuant to the grievance procedure, the dispute was submitted to an arbitrator, who received the following evidence: In November, 1983, W. Heater, chairperson of the social science department at the community college, received an anonymous letter from one of Professor Byrum's students. The letter informed Heater that Byrum had distributed drugs in a psychology class and conducted "bazaar [sic] pot parties disguised as a college class."

Consequently, C. Alvarado, an undercover Lansing police officer, enrolled in Professor Byrum's Altered States of Consciousness class, which began in January, 1984. Alvarado testified that during the last week of February, 1984, Byrum informed the class that the next meeting would be held in his condominium. Apparently, Byrum also told Alvarado that marijuana would be distributed at that class.

Alvarado attended the next "class" at Byrum's condominium during the evening of March 4, 1984, with J. Martin, an Eaton County deputy sheriff. Alvarado testified that both Byrum and his students were smoking marijuana from a pipe and that Byrum even offered a student his own pipe, containing a "special blend." Eventually, Alvarado and Martin signalled a surveillance crew stationed outside to enter and secure Byrum's arrest.

S. Abdo, a member of the surveillance crew, testified that Byrum admitted to him that all the marijuana at the party belonged to him, rather than to the students. However, at the hearing, Byrum denied that any marijuana was smoked in his presence. He testified that he tried to dissuade his students from smoking the pipes, as he suspected the pipes contained marijuana. He claimed that neither of the pipes confiscated belonged to him.[2]

The arbitrator issued her opinion and order on September 3, 1985, in which she found that Byrum committed the marijuana-related offenses with which he was charged, and did so under work-related conditions. However, she further found that Byrum's conduct was not so grave a violation of professional obligations as to constitute just cause supporting the sanction of discharge. In arriving at this conclusion, the arbitrator considered several mitigating factors, including Byrum's good record with the college, the facts that the students enrolled in the college are adults who are not necessarily influenced by Byrum's personal conduct and that Byrum "condoned" rather than "advocated" marijuana, the college's failure to promulgate rules on faculty drug use, and the college's approval of the course.[3] The arbitrator determined that dismissal was too harsh a penalty, and awarded Byrum reinstatement without back pay. The fifteen months lost by Byrum prior to the order was considered a disciplinary suspension.

* * *

I

The first issue is whether the circuit court erred in vacating the award upon the basis that the award was beyond the contractual authority of the arbitrator.

Labor arbitration is, of course, a product of contract and an arbitrator's authority to resolve a dispute arising out of the appropriate interpretation of a collective bargaining agreement is derived exclusively from the contractual agreement of the parties.

---

2. Byrum was tried in Ingham Circuit Court in August, 1984, on charges of distribution, possession, and use of marijuana. He was acquitted on all three counts.

3. The arbitrator reasoned that since the college approved the course, it must have suspected from the course's title what it entailed.

Consequently, it is well settled that judicial review of an arbitrator's decision is limited; a court may not review an arbitrator's factual findings or decision on the merits. Rather, a court may only decide whether the arbitrator's award "draws its essence" from the contract. If the arbitrator, in granting the award, did not disregard the terms of his employment and the scope of his authority as expressly circumscribed in the arbitration contract, judicial review effectively ceases.

Here, in vacating the arbitration award, the circuit court stated in pertinent part:

> "Apart from and independent of the public policy rationale, the Court believes the Arbitrator exceeded her authority as well. The clear implication of Art VI.T.1 is that the College, by the language of the CBA [Collective Bargaining Agreement], retained the authority and discretion to terminate an employee as long as it was for just cause. The retention of that authority is a term of the CBA which Arbitrator Kahn was required to adhere to. There is no question that the type of criminal conduct which Arbitrator Kahn found Prof. Byrum to have engaged in would be sufficient cause for discharge. Consequently, the Court believes that she erred and exceeded her authority by finding that even though he was involved in such conduct, discharge was not justified."

Article VI.T.1 of the agreement, to which the court referred, states in part: "No faculty member shall be reprimanded, demoted, or discharged without just cause." Article VIII.C.4.a provides that any grievance, not previously resolved, may be submitted to an arbitrator. Article VIII.A.1 defines a grievance as "an alleged violation, misinterpretation, or misapplication of a specific article or section of this agreement and/or the board's personnel policies." Article VIII.C.4.b provides:

> "The power of the arbitrator shall be limited to the interpretation or application of this agreement, and he/she shall have no power to alter, add to, or subtract from the terms of this agreement as written. The decision of the arbitrator shall be binding on all parties involved."

Professor Byrum's grievance charged an alleged violation of Article VI.T.1, the just cause provision. The arbitrator determined that the misconduct did not constitute just cause for dismissal and, thus, acted pursuant to her power described in Article VIII.C.4.b, above, to "interpret and apply the agreement." The arbitrator was not prohibited from considering mitigating factors in arriving at her conclusion and did not exceed her contractual authority in doing so.

Moreover, in finding to the contrary, the circuit court relied on its own interpretation of the collective bargaining agreement and its own conclusion that the marijuana-related activities did constitute just cause for dismissal. In making its own just cause determination, the circuit court exceeded its authority. As stated, judicial review of a labor arbitration award is very limited and the reviewing court must not substitute its judgment for that of the arbitrator in questions of contract interpretation. In reviewing the award, the circuit court was limited to deciding whether the arbitrator acted within her authority. The court's failure to defer to the arbitrator's interpretation of the agreement was error. The parties bargained for the arbitrator's construction of the just cause provision of the contract and, subject to the discussion ahead, they are bound by it.

II

The second issue is whether the circuit court erred in vacating the arbitrator's award upon the alternative basis that it violated public policy. Although this jurisdiction does recognize a public policy exception to the usual deference given to an arbitrator's award, we are not persuaded that the instant award violated public policy.

* * *

Because no case within this jurisdiction has vacated an arbitrator's award as violative of public policy, the parameters of the exception are unclear. Defendant maintains the exception would apply only where the arbitrator affirmatively orders a party to commit an illegal act. Defendant consequently reasons that the exception would be inapplicable to the instant facts because the action which the award mandates, reinstating Professor Byrum, is not contrary to law. By contrast, plaintiff asserts that the award was contrary to the well-defined public policy against illegal drug use, particularly that by a teacher with his students.

* * *

Rather, we are of the opinion that, complying with the requirements of *W.R. Grace*, a reviewing court may overturn an award if the underlying contract, as interpreted by the arbitrator, violates a well-defined and dominant public policy. Additionally, an award which itself violates such a public policy may be vacated by the reviewing court. In determining if an award itself violates public policy, the court must consider each case on its own set of facts and must pay special attention to the actual ramifications of the award, which must not be contrary to the public interest protected by the public policy at issue. Here, the arbitrator interpreted the collective bargaining agreement and found that Professor Byrum's conduct constituted just cause to support a suspension without pay but not the sanction of permanent dismissal. Contrary to the circuit court's holding, neither the agreement, as so interpreted, nor the award violates the well-defined public policy against the use of illegal narcotics. The arbitrator merely interpreted the agreement as providing violators such as Professor Byrum a second chance at employment following the imposition of a form of punishment less severe than permanent discharge. Based on the facts of the case, the arbitrator obviously found that Professor Byrum was still capable of teaching at the community college level. We are unpersuaded that Byrum's return to the college is contrary to public interest. Any other holding would be based upon a general consideration that similar violators might never again be worthy of pursuing their chosen profession. Such a supposed public interest, *W.R. Grace, supra*, is, of course, an insufficient basis upon which to invoke the public policy exception.

Reversed and remanded for further proceedings not inconsistent with this opinion.

The *Lansing Community College* case, like the *Cary* case, indicates the extent to which collective bargaining policies impact upon the governance of education, particularly in personnel issues. While the predominance of unionized faculty are in public schools and community colleges, chapter 3, "The Law and Faculty," includes several significant higher education cases in which more senior institutions in the private sector were involved. It should be noted that the fact pattern in *Lansing* would, in all likelihood, have warranted discharge in most circumstances. Faculty misconduct outside class is treated more thoroughly in chapter 3, as well as later in this chapter, "Citizen of the Academy." For a review of these issues, see S. Olswang, "Union Security

Provisions, Academic Freedom and Tenure: The Implications of *Chicago Teachers Union v. Hudson*," *Journal of College and University Law*, 14 (1988), 539–60.

The cases that follow straddle several areas of higher education law, including those affecting academic freedom (particularly the right to speak and to hear), immigration and nationality law, legislation, and constitutional law. These cases, edited primarily for their academic freedom dimensions, do not actually turn on purely constitutional grounds, and the incomplete court in *Abourezk* leaves uncertain the contours of this particular issue, who outside the country may teach in U.S. institutions.

Kleindienst v. Mandel
408 U.S. 753 (1972)

Mr. Justice BLACKMUN delivered the opinion of the Court.

The appellees have framed the issue here as follows:

> "Does appellants' action in refusing to allow an alien scholar to enter the country to attend academic meetings violate the First Amendment rights of American scholars and students who had invited him?"

* * *

Ernest E. Mandel resides in Brussels, Belgium, and is a Belgian citizen. He is a professional journalist and is editor-in-chief of the Belgian Left Socialist weekly La Gauche. He is author of a two-volume work entitled Marxist Economic Theory published in 1969. He asserted in his visa application that he is not a member of the Communist Party. He has described himself, however, as "a revolutionary Marxist." He does not dispute . . . that he advocates the economic, governmental, and international doctrines of world communism.

Mandel was admitted to the United States temporarily in 1962 and again in 1968. On the first visit he came as a working journalist. On the second he accepted invitations to speak at a number of universities and colleges. On each occasion, although apparently he was not then aware of it, his admission followed a finding of ineligibility under § 212(a)(28), and the Attorney General's exercise of discretion to admit him temporarily, on recommendation of the Secretary of State, as § 212(d)(3)(A) permits.

On September 8, 1969, Mandel applied to the American Consul in Brussels for a nonimmigrant visa to enter the United States in October for a six-day period, during which he would participate in a conference on Technology and the Third World at Stanford University. He had been invited to Stanford by the Graduate Student Association there. The invitation stated that John Kenneth Galbraith would present the keynote address and that Mandel would be expected to participate in an ensuing panel discussion and to give a major address the following day. The University, through the office of its president, "heartily endorse[d]" the invitation. When Mandel's intended visit became known, additional invitations for lectures and conference participations came to him from members of the faculties at Princeton, Amherst, Columbia, and Vassar, from groups in Cambridge, Massachusetts, and New York City, and from others. One conference, to be in New York City, was sponsored jointly by the Bertrand Russell Peace Foundation and the Socialist Scholars Conference; Mandel's assigned subject there was "Revolutionary Strategy in Imperialist Countries."

Mandel then filed a second visa application proposing a more extensive itinerary and a stay of greater duration.

On October 23 the Consul at Brussels informed Mandel orally that his application of September 8 had been refused. This was confirmed in writing on October 30.

* * *

The Department of State in fact had recommended to the Attorney General that Mandel's ineligibility be waived with respect to his October visa application. The Immigration and Naturalization Service, however, acting on behalf of the Attorney General, see 28 U.S.C. § 510, in a letter dated February 13, 1970, to New York counsel stated that it had determined that Mandel's 1968 activities while in the United States "went far beyond the stated purposes of his trip, on the basis of which his admission had been authorized and represented a flagrant abuse of the opportunities afforded him to express his views in this country." The letter concluded that favorable exercise of discretion, provided for under the Act, was not warranted and that Mandel's temporary admission was not authorized.

Mandel's address to the New York meeting was then delivered by transatlantic telephone.

In March Mandel and six of the other appellees instituted the present action against the Attorney General and the Secretary of State. The two remaining appellees soon came into the lawsuit by an amendment to the complaint. All the appellees who joined Mandel in this action are United States citizens and are university professors in various fields of the social sciences. They are persons who invited Mandel to speak at universities and other forums in the United States or who expected to participate in colloquia with him so that, as the complaint alleged, "they may hear his views and engage him in a free and open academic exchange."

Plaintiff-appellees claim that the statutes are unconstitutional on their face and as applied in that they deprive the American plaintiffs of their First and Fifth Amendment rights. Specifically, these plaintiffs claim that the statutes prevent them from hearing and meeting with Mandel in person for discussions in contravention of the First Amendment.

* * *

We have almost continuous attention on the part of Congress since 1875 to the problems of immigration and of excludability of certain defined classes of aliens. The pattern generally has been one of increasing control with particular attention for almost 70 years now, first to anarchists and then to those with communist affiliation or views.

III

It is clear that Mandel personally, as an unadmitted and nonresident alien, had no constitutional right of entry to this country as a nonimmigrant or otherwise.

* * *

The case, therefore, comes down to the narrow issue whether the First Amendment confers upon the appellee professors, because they wish to hear, speak, and debate with Mandel in person, the ability to determine that Mandel should be permitted to enter the country or, in other words, to compel the Attorney General to allow Mandel's admission.

IV

In a variety of contexts this Court has referred to a First Amendment right to "receive information and ideas":

* * *

The Government ... argues that exclusion of Mandel involves no restriction on First Amendment rights at all since what is restricted is "only action—the action of the alien in coming into this country."

* * *

The rights asserted here, in some contrast, are those of American academics who have invited Mandel to participate with them in colloquia, debates, and discussion in the United States. In light of the Court's previous decisions concerning the "right to receive information," we cannot realistically say that the problem facing us disappears entirely or is nonexistent because the mode of regulation bears directly on physical movement.

* * *

The Government also suggests that the First Amendment is inapplicable because appellees have free access to Mandel's ideas through his books and speeches, and because "technological developments," such as tapes or telephone hook-ups, readily supplant his physical presence. This argument overlooks what may be particular qualities inherent in sustained, face-to-face debate, discussion and questioning. While alternative means of access to Mandel's ideas might be a relevant factor were we called upon to balance First Amendment rights against governmental regulatory interests—a balance we find unnecessary here in light of the discussion that follows in Part V—we are loath to hold on this record that existence of other alternatives extinguishes altogether any constitutional interest on the part of the appellees in this particular form of access.

V

Recognition that First Amendment rights are implicated, however, is not dispositive of our inquiry here. In accord with ancient principles of the international law of nation-states, the Court [has] held broadly, as the Government describes it, ... that the power to exclude aliens is "inherent in sovereignty, necessary for maintaining normal international relations and defending the country against foreign encroachments and dangers—a power to be exercised exclusively by the political branches of government. ... " Since that time, the Court's general reaffirmations of this principle have been legion. The Court without exception has sustained Congress' "plenary power to make rules for the admission of aliens and to exclude those who possess those characteristics which Congress has forbidden." ...

"[O]ver no conceivable subject is the legislative power of Congress more complete than it is over" the admission of aliens.

* * *

[The Appellees argue that the First Amendment right should prevail at least where there is not governmental justification for failing to grant the waiver.]

Appellees' First Amendment argument would prove too much. In almost every instance of an alien excludable under § 212(a)(28), there are probably those who would wish to meet and speak with him. The ideas of most such aliens might not be so influential as those of Mandel, nor his American audience so numerous, nor the planned discussion forums so impressive. But the First Amendment does not protect only the articulate, the well known, and the popular. Were we to endorse the proposition that governmental power to withhold a waiver must yield whenever a bona fide claim is made that American citizens wish to meet and talk with an alien excludable under § 212(a)(28), one of two unsatisfactory results would necessarily ensue. Either every claim would prevail, in which case the plenary discretionary authority Congress granted the Executive becomes a nullity, or courts in each case would be required to weigh the strength of the audience's interests against that of the Government in refusing a waiver to the particular alien applicant, according to some as yet undetermined standard. The dangers and the undesirability of making that determination on the basis of factors such as the size of the audience or the probity of the speaker's ideas are obvious. Indeed, it is for precisely this reason that the waiver decision has, properly, been placed in the hands of the Executive.

Appellees seek to soften the impact of this analysis by arguing, as has been noted, that the First Amendment claim should prevail, at least where no justification is advanced for denial of a waiver.

The Government would have us reach this question, urging a broad decision that Congress has delegated the waiver decision to the Executive in its sole and unfettered discretion, and any reason or no reason may be given.

This record, however, does not require that we do so, for the Attorney General did inform Mandel's counsel of the reason for refusing him a waiver. And that reason was facially legitimate and bona fide.

*   *   *

We hold that when the Executive exercises this power negatively on the basis of a facially legitimate and bona fide reason, the courts will neither look behind the exercise of that discretion, nor test it by balancing its justification against the First Amendment interests of those who seek personal communication with the applicant. What First Amendment or other grounds may be available for attacking exercise of discretion for which no justification whatsoever is advanced is a question we neither address nor decide in this case.

Reversed.

Mr. Justice DOUGLAS, dissenting.

*   *   *

Can the Attorney General under the broad discretion entrusted in him decide

that one who maintains that the earth is round can be excluded?

that no one who believes in the Darwinian theory shall be admitted?

that those who promote a Rule of Law to settle international differences rather than a Rule of Force may be barred?

that a genetic biologist who lectures on the way to create life by one sex alone is beyond the pale?

that an exponent of plate tectonics can be barred?

that one should be excluded who taught that Jesus when he arose from the Sepulcher, went east (not up) and became a teacher at Hemis Monastery in the Himalayas?

I put the issue that bluntly because national security is not involved. Nor is the infiltration of saboteurs. The Attorney General stands astride our international terminals that bring people here to bar those whose ideas are not acceptable to him. Even assuming, *arguendo*, that those on the outside seeking admission have no standing to complain, those who hope to benefit from the traveler's lectures do.

Thought control is not within the competence of any branch of government. Those who live here may need exposure to the ideas of people of many faiths and many creeds to further their education. We should construe the Act generously by that First Amendment standard, saying that once the State Department has concluded that our foreign relations permit or require the admission of a foreign traveler, the Attorney General is left only problems of national security, importation of heroin, or other like matters within his competence.

*   *   *

In a confusing turn of events, *Kleindienst v. Mandel* was substantially overturned in *Reagan v. Abourezk*, 108 S.Ct. 252 (1987). In a *per curiam* decision, the "judgment below is affirmed by an equally divided court." (Neither Justices Blackmun nor Scalia took part, and Justice Kennedy had not yet been confirmed.) This action upheld the decision by the U.S. Court of Appeals for the D.C. Circuit, in which the State Department was denied use of 8 U.S.C. § 1182(a)(27) to exclude alien members of the Communist party merely upon their membership; subsection (27) permits such exclusion only for "activities," not mere affiliation. The upshot is that foreign lecturers will not be excludable solely due to their organizational memberships, without independent evidence that they would engage in activities harmful to the national interest. 785 F. 2d 1043 (1987). See also "Ideological Exclusion," *Academe* (March/April 1988), 79–80 (summarizing developments in ideological exclusion provisions).

Harvard Law School Forum v. George P. Schultz

633 F. Supp. 525 (D. Mass. 1986)

SKINNER, District Judge.

Facts.

The facts in this case are not in dispute. In August, 1985, the plaintiff Harvard Law School Forum invited Zuhdi Labib Terzi to participate in a debate on "Prospects for Peace in the Middle East" with Professor Dershowitz. Terzi is the Permanent Observer of the PLO at the United Nations ("UN") and the highest ranking member of the PLO in the United States. Professor Dershowitz is said to be an outspoken member of the Harvard Law School faculty and a well-known pro-Israeli activist. Plaintiff Roth arranged the debate and the Forum agreed to sponsor it, scheduling it for October 31, 1985.

The parties agree that Terzi, as a member of the PLO, is an excludable alien under federal immigration law. 8 U.S.C. § 1182(a)(28)(F). The excludability of a member of the PLO is not dependent on any demonstration by the State Department that admission of the individual to this country would pose a security threat. 22 U.S.C. § 2691(c). However, the Attorney General may, "in his discretion," grant a waiver allowing an excludable alien into the country temporarily. 8 U.S.C. § 1182(d)(3). Such waivers are subject to conditions as prescribed by the Attorney General. 8 U.S.C. § 1182(d)(6).

The United States, as host country of the UN, has entered into the "UN Headquarters Agreement." In Section 11 of the Headquarters Agreement, the United States agreed not to impede the transit to and from the UN Headquarters of members of Observer Missions to the UN. As a result, the Attorney General, on advice from the Secretary of State, has granted a waiver of excludability to allow PLO Observer Mission personnel access to the UN headquarters, even though such individuals are excludable under immigration law.

* * *

In opposition to the plaintiff's motion, the defendant has submitted the declaration of Alan L. Keyes, Assistant Secretary of State for International Organization Affairs. In his declaration, the Assistant Secretary sets forth the United States' policy toward the PLO generally and toward Terzi's travel requests. The Assistant Secretary states that the United States has consistently refused to recognize or negotiate with the PLO as long as the PLO does not recognize Israel's right to exist and does not accept certain UN Security Council resolutions.

* * *

The issue in this case in whether the Secretary of State can constitutionally deny the travel request of a UN Observer on the basis of the Observer's intention to participate in a political debate with American citizens. Although the Secretary's proffered reason for denying the request involves the executive's policy of not affording recognition to the PLO, the case is not a challenge to that policy. A determination of the constitutionality of the Secretary's conditioning of a waiver of excludability under 8 U.S.C. § 1182(d) does not impinge upon the executive's conduct of foreign relations simply because the individual at issue is a member of a nonrecognized foreign entity.

Moreover, despite the Secretary's argument to the contrary, *Kleindienst v. Mandel* and its progeny strongly indicate that this case is judicially reviewable. In *Mandel*, the Court determined that where Congress had provided a waiver procedure in the statutory scheme governing excludability of aliens, the courts could determine whether the executive's decision not to grant such a waiver was supported by a "facially legitimate and bona fide" reason. Although the Court did not explicitly address the political question doctrine, the case suggests that the federal courts have some role in enforcing constitutional restraints on the executive's implementation of the statutory scheme enacted by Congress.

* * *

The Secretary is obliged to justify the denial of Terzi's travel request with a facially legitimate and bona fide reason in the face of plaintiffs' assertion of their First Amendment rights to participate in a debate with Terzi.

The justification the Secretary offers for the denial of Terzi's travel request is that if the Secretary were to allow Terzi to participate in political activity outside of the limited area in which he is presently allowed to travel and publicly speak, he would be undermining the United States' policy of not lending legitimacy to the PLO. Thus, the Secretary concedes that his reason is based on Terzi's proposed participation in a political debate with American citizens.

Although the Secretary's reason appears to be bona fide, it is not facially legitimate. The Secretary's justification is directly related to the suppression of a political debate with American citizens. If plaintiffs in this case desired to interact with Terzi in a social setting, the Secretary would allow such interaction. Because they desire to hear his views on the politics of the Middle East in a political forum, they are denied access to him. The Secretary's decision on the travel request at issue is therefore based on the content of the discussions and interaction Terzi would have with those outside the geographic limitation. The Secretary's actions are completely at odds with the First Amendment's protection of political debate and our "national commitment to the principle that debate on public issues should be uninhibited, robust and wide open, and that it may well include vehement, caustic, and sometimes unpleasantly sharp attacks on government and public officials."

The speech at issue in this case is at the heart of what was intended to be protected by the First Amendment:

> Whatever differences may exist about interpretations of the First Amendment, there is practically universal agreement that a major purpose of that Amendment was to protect the free discussion of governmental affairs.

This speech is no less protected because the listeners' and debater's First Amendment rights are asserted. The Secretary's proffered reason for denying Terzi's travel request is not facially legitimate because it is related to the suppression of protected political discussion. Accordingly, even under the limited review contemplated by *Mandel*, I conclude that it is likely that the Secretary's actions will be adjudged unconstitutional.

Finally, I must consider the balancing of the public interest. It may well be that the public interest will, in some respect, be adversely affected by affording a forum to a PLO representative whose policies are in conflict with those of the United States and indeed are anathema to many citizens. The public interest in preserving free and open debate on precisely such subjects, however, must be regarded as of overwhelming priority, as mandated by the First Amendment, and as being at the heart of our survival as a free people.

Plaintiffs' motion for a preliminary injunction is ALLOWED. The Secretary's motion to dismiss or in the alternative for summary judgment is DENIED.

"The Limits of Academic Freedom"

Louis Dubose and David Denison
The Texas Observer, December 4, 1987, pp. 2–4.

* * *

Consider now the case of Jim Smith, until very recently the director of the Bureau of Business Research at the University of Texas in Austin. Smith holds a Ph.D. in economics from Southern Methodist University and was once the chief economist for the Union Carbide Corporation in Danbury, Connecticut. Not the kind of man who would run into trouble with the likes of Bill Clements, Jim Smith's misfortune was to displease a few members of the state's Democratic establishment—and to be working for university administrators who handle political pressure as if it were a hot dish out of the oven.

Smith is the kind of economist you might expect at something called a bureau of "business research." He looks at statistical data and economic indicators and operates under the not-too-unusual assumption that what is good for Texas business will be good for us all. As director of the bureau, which operates under the authority of UT's graduate school of business (although it is funded by the legislature outside of the university budget), Smith wrote the *Texas Business Review*, a six-page bi-monthly publication analyzing the Texas economy.

Since his arrival in September of 1986, Smith has been responsible for a year's worth of issues of the *Texas Business Review*. But this autumn found him in a particularly feisty mood, judging from what he wrote in the October edition. Under the headline "The Texas Economy: Full Steam Ahead," Smith wrote what can only be described, at least from our perspective, as a highly peculiar piece of economic analysis. He began by saying that consumer confidence remained high and that this was good news for the Texas economy. He pointed out that total employment in the state went up by 97,000 (seasonally adjusted) from June to July and that the unemployment rate had dropped to 8.3 percent. He explained why he chose to focus on total employment and "not to waste much time looking at the rate of unemployment." Here he went into an esoteric explanation to the effect that Texas has a higher proportion of people who want to work, and if that proportion (the labor force participation rate) were at the nationwide level, "there would not be a single unemployed person in the state, and every newspaper, radio and television station in the world would be running feature stories on the 'miracle' of the Texas economy." (So much for "focusing" on the 8.3 percent of the workforce currently out of a job.)

Smith couldn't resist taking a poke at the state legislature's recent efforts, saying, "They gave us a record tax increase for any state, which we did not need. . . . " Nor did he approve of Senator Lloyd Bentsen's efforts in Washington to push a bill to address the trade deficit problem—a bill Smith sees as "protectionist" legislation. "The dependence of the Texas economy on exports is such that over 100,000 people could lose their jobs if the trade bill . . . is enacted," Smith wrote. "It is very difficult to understand why the primary sponsor of the trade bill is the senior senator from Texas," he added, with a little touch of acerbity that turned out to be more costly than he might have expected.

In the first week of October, Smith received a letter (a copy of which also went to university president Bill Cunningham) from Tom Scott, executive assistant to Lieutenant Governor Bill Hobby. Under Hobby's letterhead, Scott pointed out a factual error in Smith's report, having to do with the amount of money that would go into a "rainy day fund" in the case of future budget surpluses, and went on to complain that Smith's remark in the *Business Review* that a tax increase was unnecessary was unsubstantiated. "I object to your use of this publication to espouse personal beliefs that are not buttressed by any analysis, thoughtful or otherwise," wrote Scott.

At about the same time, a UT official responded to a call from Senator Lloyd Bentsen's office with a note to Bentsen's press secretary Jack DeVore that said Smith had had "several other complaints" about his October article and that Smith would be willing to talk with Bentsen's office about his comments on the trade bill. Smith says he got a note from UT official Gerald Hill during this time that said "I've got one hot Senator on my hands."

"The next thing I knew, I was called onto the carpet of the Dean's office, being lectured about the strong importance of avoiding editorializing in the *Texas Business Review*," says Smith, referring to a Monday, October 12, meeting with Bob Witt, the dean of the graduate school of business. Witt pointed to the comment about Bentsen's trade bill as an example of the kind of editorializing that he said was "inconsistent with the policy" of the publication.

On Thursday of that week, Smith was informed that he was expected in Dean Witt's office the next day, and after a meeting with Witt on Friday, Smith was out of a job. That weekend Smith had his wife type his resignation letter, which was accepted by the Dean's office on Monday, October 19. Ironically, it was the same day the stock market crashed—a Black Monday indeed for the relentlessly optimistic economist who had written articles over the past months entitled "The Texas Economy: Growth Continues," and "The Texas Economy: Full Steam Ahead," and in the current December issue, "The Texas Economy: Rolling Right Along."

Dean Bob Witt says of Smith: "He was not fired; he was not asked to resign." The article with the comment about Bentsen's trade bill, Witt says, "had nothing to do with it." But Smith speaks of being "ordered to resign," and sees the incident as a "fairly strong attack on either academic freedom or the First Amendment," depending on how one looks at it. He suspects that the negative reaction from Bentsen's office had something to do with Dean Witt's decision. His comment on Bentsen's trade bill "got [Bentsen aide Jack] DeVore going through the roof," he says, and Dean Witt "is a person who doesn't like to be bothered."

Bentsen's press aide Jack DeVore claims he didn't even see the issue of the *Texas Business Review* in question but that he was aware that Smith had made earlier comments on Bentsen's trade bill in a speech in Beaumont. "I wanted a chance to straighten him out," DeVore said, because in his view a comment that the bill would cost Texans jobs showed "utter ignorance about what Senator Bentsen's bill would do." So he called a "personal friend" at UT (he will not say who he called) to ask about Smith's remarks. DeVore's friend responded with a note saying that Smith would be happy to talk to him and attached a copy of the letter Smith received from Hobby's assistant, Tom Scott. DeVore said he didn't know Smith had resigned until he heard about it from a reporter who called him for a comment.

Dean Witt says he was aware a call had been made from Bentsen's office but that no one from Bentsen's office spoke with him directly. Of his final meeting with Smith he says that he reviewed Smith's performance and "at that point in time, Jim elected to resign."

Smith's letter of resignation, entitled "Request for Reclassification," does not read like the work of a man anxious to move on voluntarily. He cites "ever rising amounts of administrative matters," in asking that he be allowed to relinquish the position of Director of the Bureau of Business Research, but closes with the sentence, "I would be grateful for the opportunity to remain in the position of Chief Economist as long as possible." As of now, he will not be Chief Economist past January. He will be a lecturer in the business school this spring and as of May 31 he will need a new job.

As evidence that he did not intend to leave his job at the Bureau of Business Research, Smith tells of meeting with Dean Witt twice in July to discuss his future. He says Witt reassured him about his position at the Bureau. So in September Smith finally moved his family to Austin from Connecticut where they had remained since Smith had left Union Carbide the year before. Then, as Smith puts it, "Six weeks later I got bounced."

Dean Witt and university president Bill Cunningham both hint darkly that there is more to this story than there seems to be but that they are prevented from discussing it by university policies against disclosure of certain personnel matters. The news story in the *Austin American-Statesman*, whose obeisant reporters can always be trusted to reflect the university administrators' outlooks, reported that "it is believed" that Smith's consistently optimistic reports on the Texas economy "cost him credibility and undercut his job standing." The *Statesman* story added that Smith's upbeat reports "reportedly" were criticized by "some business leaders and other Texas economists."

President Cunningham insists that he was not consulted in advance about Smith's ouster (to do otherwise would suggest that Witt had considered getting rid of Smith before his "resignation"). Cunningham says he talked with Witt only after Smith resigned on October 16. "As far as I know, Jim resigned and Bob accepted it," concludes Cunningham. Aside from unspecified secret information about personnel matters, Witt offers only the view that Smith was not adequately handling the management and administrative functions of his directorship in explaining his differences with Smith.

This is all pretty transparent. If Smith's management skills were at issue why did everything come to a head in the first two weeks of October, just when Hobby's and Bentsen's offices were complaining about Smith's "editorializing"? If Smith's resignation was voluntary why does he insist he was "bounced"? All the evidence that has been made public suggests that it was the university that decided it was time for Smith to go, and that they simply buckled from the heat they were getting from Democrats who didn't like the conservative analysis and commentary served up by Dr. Smith.

We would readily agree with Democrats—if they are out there somewhere—who would fault Smith's economic writings for painting a picture that obscures or ignores the economic crisis that is very real to thousands of working (and unemployed) Texans. But to suggest that Smith should somehow present an "objective" picture of the Texas economy is an insult to his standing as a thinker and a scholar, and it is an insult to the greater academic community. Smith, as much as any professor on campus, ought to have the right to present his view of the world as he sees it, without interference from meddling administrators.

*   *   *

©*The Texas Observer*, reprinted with permission.

The remaining issues in this section include a sampling of external influences that have direct bearing upon who is allowed to teach in higher education. From among the array of possible influences, two are represented—religion and government. While both are represented more thoroughly elsewhere, the more narrow dimension of religious and governmental restrictions upon who may teach has become increasingly evident.

Chapter 1, "The Legal Governance of Higher Education," incorporated commentary and cases concerning the unique intersection of secular higher education and religious tenets; chapter 3, "The Law and Faculty," treats tenure in religiously affiliated institutions, including the case of Rev. Charles Curran at Catholic University. Another series of incidents involving a Catholic theologian, Professor Daniel Maguire of Marquette University, specifically concerns who may teach.

He signed a *New York Times* advertisement that appeared on October 7, 1984, in which he and several co-signers called for "candid and respectful discussion" on the issue of abortion, and encouraged Catholic "priests, religious, theologians, and legislators" to discuss and dissent from the official hierarchy on this matter. Prior to the publication of the October ad, Professor Maguire had accepted offers to teach summer courses or lecture in 1985 at four Catholic colleges, all of which then cancelled their invitations to him.

These incidents, chronicled in "Academic Freedom and the Abortion Issue," *Academe* (July-August 1986) 1a–13a, exemplify the tensions inherent in sectarian colleges, which the 1940 *Statement of Principles on Academic Freedom and Tenure* finessed: "Limitations of academic freedom because of religious or other aims of the institution should be clearly stated in writing at the time of the appointment." In 1970, an Interpretive Comment was added: "most church-related institutions no longer need or desire the departure from the principle of academic freedom implied in the 1940 *Statement*, and we do not now endorse such a departure." Although these clauses were designed to protect faculty rights, the incidents at several religiously affiliated colleges have reconstituted these protections into institutional freedoms. See the special issue of *Academe* on "Religious Education & Academic Freedom" (January-February 1988).

As in the *Aguillard* case, where creationism was at issue, there are overarching tenets in religious higher education that affect and, in some instances, shape inquiry and eligibility to teach. In the Catholic faith, the papal *magisterium*, or infallibility in matters of faith, has presented problems of concurrence and applicability. In 1960, the American Association of Theological Schools adopted many of the AAUP principles, with the provision, "[so] long as the teacher remains within the accepted constitutional and confessional basis of his school he should be free to teach, carry on research and to publish . . . [and] a concept of freedom appropriate to theological schools will respect this confessional loyalty, both in institutions and in their individual members." Although this was modified slightly in 1976, it remains substantially intact. For additional scholarship on this issue, see J. Annarelli, *Academic Freedom and Catholic Higher Education* (Westport: Greenwood Press, 1987).

Of course, Catholics are not the sole denomination engaged in intensive religious dissents over orthodoxy. In 1987, Missouri Baptist College, Mercer University, and Southwestern Baptist Theological Seminary were involved in acrimonious turmoil over academic freedom and faculty appointments. To maintain orthodoxy in its teaching ranks, Southwestern Baptist Theological Seminary in Ft. Worth, Texas, requires that all its faculty abide by the 1963 Baptist Faith and Message Statement, which incorporates principles of academic freedom "limited by the preeminence of Christ, the authoritative nature of the Scriptures and the distinct purposes for which the seminary exists. These suppositions obviously involve doctrinal as well as lifestyle guidelines." Oral Roberts University established a law school (since transferred to the Christian Broadcast University), which required all faculty to take an oath of Christian loyalty, while Brigham Young University's law school accreditation process prompted the bar and accrediting associations to revise their procedures for approving religiously affiliated legal education. See A. Cassou and R. Curran, "Secular Orthodoxy and Sacred Freedoms: Accreditation of Church-Related Law Schools," *Journal of College and University Law*, 11 (Winter 1984), 293–322.

In 1985, a long-standing practice was ruled unconstitutional in Texas public colleges. "Bible Chairs" were non-tenured positions where religious denominations selected and paid for the professorships. In Opinion JM-352, the Texas Attorney General ruled:

> [If a church were the source of either the naming or financing of a religion teacher] it would involve the potential for and the appearance of advancing, endorsing, or favoring religion. [Moreover, a] system whereby university faculty members are either nominated or salaried by religious organizations involves the type of intimate continuing relationship between government and religion which is prohibited by the Establishment Clause. [This would create an excessive entanglement.] . . . [T]he donors may not be permitted to exercise control or influence over the religious studies course or professors. Also, a university . . . must structure the selection of teachers for such courses in a manner which does not differ from the way in which it selects teachers for all of its other academic courses . . . higher education must receive somewhat different treatment than lower division schools. . . . [C]ollege students are presumed to be less impressionable and less susceptible to religious indoctrination than are elementary and secondary students.

See also "Texas Attorney General Rules Colleges Must Drop 'Bible Chair' Instructors," *Chronicle of Higher Education*, 12 August 1987, pp. 19–20; "U. of Texas Allows Bible Chairs for One Semester," *Chronicle of Higher Education*, 23 September 1987, p. 29.

A number of influences upon or threats to academic freedom arise in the intersection between public or private colleges and governments: examples thread their way through each chapter. However, government affects higher education curricula less often than is the case in elementary and secondary education. See M. Yudof, *When Government Speaks* (Berkeley: University of California Press, 1983). Nonetheless, state legislatures do decide curricular requirements. In Texas, the Higher Education Code requires all public college students to satisfy government or political science and an American or Texas history course [Sec. 51.301–.302], and extensively determines the acceptable courses for schoolteacher and administrator licensing. The news story that follows is unusual, inasmuch as community colleges rarely involve classified contracts for the military.

"Electronic Warfare in CTC Curriculum,"

Nancy Stancill, *Houston Chronicle*, December 20, 1987, Sec. 1, pp. 1, 4.

A community college here is conducting secret classes for the U.S. Army to teach selected Fort Hood officers how to jam, confuse or destroy Soviet communications equipment and how to counter such tactics from the Soviets.

Central Texas College has been teaching classified electronic-warfare courses under contract with Fort Hood since the early 1980s, said Alvin Ornstein, executive deputy chancellor for CTC.

Several military officials and experts said it is unusual for such a sensitive area to be taught by a public community college or any other non-military contractor.

But Ornstein said the college merely provides qualified instructors—usually retired military personnel—to teach "doctrine and principles developed by the U.S. Army for this important function."

The course work is classified secret, and the instructors and most participants must have secret security clearances, according to the contract between CTC and Fort Hood. The Chronicle obtained a copy of the contract document—which is not classified—through the federal Freedom of Information Act.

Ornstein said he can describe the classes only in general terms.

"When we discuss capabilities, techniques and procedures involving specific pieces of equipment or battlefield applications, we are in a very classified arena which cannot be disclosed," he said. "I can't tell you what the details of the course consist of. I'd be violating the Espionage Act."

Several Texas higher education officials said they were surprised to hear that CTC is teaching electronic warfare. But they said that they are aware the public community college does extensive military education contracting.

"As a private citizen, my natural impulse is to question why the Department of Defense is not teaching the course," said Hal Daugherty, chairman of the Texas Higher Education Coordinating Board and an El Paso banker. "I question why the Army would contract something like that out."

"It sounds fairly exotic," said Sam Carroll, a member of the coordinating board from San Antonio. "It doesn't sound like we'll find out about it, because I doubt if we can get security clearance to examine the curriculum."

"I don't know of any community college that does this," Carroll said. "Because something is different doesn't mean it's necessarily wrong, but I do need it clarified."

Capt. Tim Vance, a Fort Hood media relations officer, said the post contracts with CTC because it is "much more cost effective" than assigning a senior non-commissioned officer to teach it or sending officers away to school.

Brad Rose, a Fort Bliss spokesman, said the El Paso-area Army installation does not teach electronic warfare. He said officials there were not aware of any Army electronic-warfare instruction handled by a civilian contractor.

"The majority of schoolhouse education in electronic warfare is done by in-house military personnel," he said. "The contracting portion comes in the repair of the equipment."

Jan Bodanyi, a Pentagon spokesman, said, "There's really no overarching policy on training for electronic warfare." She said different branches of the military handle it differently but that such training can be quite sensitive.

For example, she said, electronic warfare would be used to foil the guidance and sensor systems of missiles. If a missile were headed toward a U.S. target, she said, military personnel could send out "chaff" or metal material to confuse it or direct an electronic beam so that enemy radar would become blinded.

Electronic-warfare equipment and techniques also can be used to jam the radar in enemy planes, hobble large-scale data processing systems and disable telephone networks.

Bodanyi said instruction usually includes two components—learning how to operate electronic-warfare equipment and having a separate discussion of tactics. "When do you jam a missile, and when do you outrun it?" she offered as an example of a tactical discussion.

The Fort Hood contract outlines three different courses being taught by CTC— an 80-hour electronic-warfare staff officer course for battalion-level officers, a 40-hour course geared mostly for junior-level officers and a four-hour course for unit-level officers. In the four-hour course, it is left up to unit officials to determine whether the students should have a secret security clearance.

"The level of classification is secret only," Ornstein said. If the classes were highly sensitive, he added, they would be classified top secret. Military classifications range in sensitivity from confidential to secret to top-secret.

The courses are taught several times during the year, and CTC will be paid $64,033 this year under the contract. During the fiscal year that ended in September, CTC taught electronic-warfare courses to 101 Fort Hood officers, Ornstein said.

Ornstein said CTC teaches electronic warfare only at Fort Hood and would like to compete for electronic-warfare contracts at other military installations. But the college has never had the opportunity to do so because other military installations have not sought contractors.

Master Sgt. Wallace Ross, a spokesman for the Electronic Security Command at Kelly Air Force Base in San Antonio, said there are no civilian contractors for electronic-warfare subjects at ESC.

"I find it unusual that it's going through a civilian college," he said of electronic-warfare courses taught by CTC.

Previously, said Ornstein, Fort Hood used military personnel to teach electronic-warfare courses.

"The decision to allow a civilian contractor to teach these courses was based on the availability of personnel to teach them, the costs involved and the demonstrated ability to provide this type of training," he said. "If we didn't do it, someone else would do it."

Ornstein, a retired Army colonel, added: "Fort Hood has always been part of our community. It has always been our policy to serve the military in whatever way we can to assist the armed forces in accomplishing their mission."

Currently, CTC spokesman Bill Alexander said, the college holds $6.1 million in annual contracts with Fort Hood to teach academic and military occupational skills courses ranging from early childhood education to food service instruction.

CTC, part of a Killeen-based education consortium called the American Educational Complex, holds multiple federal contracts to teach at military bases and posts in the United States and around the world. Since September, [1987] Alexander said, the AEC has won nearly $40 million in new contracts for military instruction over the next several years.

Ornstein said only a fraction of CTC courses are classified.

CTC receives no state money for teaching the electronic-warfare courses at Fort Hood but last spring submitted materials to the coordinating board for a new associate in applied science degree program in electronics communications operations. The degree program incorporated electronic-warfare course elements.

The coordinating board staff looked askance at the degree program, which would train radio-intelligence operators and electronics intelligence operations specialists, saying it would meet only military needs.

CTC officials said, however, that they were submitting the degree materials only for coordinating board files and have not sought state funding for such a program.

State auditors are completing a review of how CTC keeps its state funding separate from the federal and local funds it takes in. Results are expected in January [1988]. The audit was spurred by revelations that the college was spending more than $1 million yearly on travel, using a travel agency owned by the college president's daughter and reimbursing the chancellor $33,000 for taxicab rides taken during a 17-month period.

©*Houston Chronicle*. Reprinted with permission.

American University officials were stunned when 18 members of Congress wrote them a letter asking why the university had dropped an experimental course on "The Politics of Non-Violence," taught by the columnist Colman McCarthy.

The letter noted that the university was chartered by Congress in the 1890's. It also noted that the course was very popular, that several Congressional aides had taken it, and that two signers of the letter had addressed the class.

Said university president Richard Berendzen, "If this is not a form of intimidation, I don't know what is. It certainly smacks of intrusion into academic and personnel decision-making. Maybe they're overreacting, but some faculty members are worried about their research grants and students about financial aid."

University officials said the course had been discontinued because of academic concerns, including the fact that Mr. McCarthy allowed students to grade themselves. As a result, 94 percent of them received A's.

Although chartered by Congress, the university has no legal ties to the government. Said a top administrator: "We're sitting around stunned. This kind of thing just doesn't happen."

An aide to one lawmaker who signed the letter said no intimidation was intended. "We don't have any power to do anything, other than express concern," he said.

©*Chronicle of Higher Education*, November 12, 1986, p. 23. Reprinted with permission.

How It Shall Be Taught

The third element of Justice Frankfurter's "four essential freedoms," to determine how subjects shall be taught, has generated much litigation and commentary. Moreover, it is clear from who-may-teach cases (*Ollman*, for example) that who teaches is virtually indistinguishable from how-it-shall-be-taught. Was the opposition to Professor Ollman due to his administrative inexperience, his Marxist ideology and scholarship, or his dogmatic teaching style? Is the disparaging evaluation of teaching an abridgment of teaching freedom? The cases that follow in this section reveal a range of extramural influences upon pedagogy and subject matter. They are considered in somewhat of a chronological order, to discern if there has been a developing pattern in the law of academic freedom concerning teaching style.

Edward Jervey v. Charles Martin, Jr. et al.

336 F. Supp. 1350 (1972)

DALTON, District Judge.

Order on Ruling on the Defendants' Motion to Dismiss

* * *

The amended complaint alleges that the plaintiff, Dr. Edward D. Jervey, was denied a raise of twelve hundred dollars for the 1968–69 school year as a reprisal by President Charles K. Martin and the members of the Board of Visitors of Radford College for Dr. Jervey's exercise of his First Amendment right to free speech. It appears that Dr. Martin, in his role as President of Radford College had recommended to the Board of Visitors that Dr. Jervey's salary be raised from $11,500 to $12,700 for the 1968–69 academic year. However, the plaintiff alleges that this recommendation was rescinded and Dr. Jervey's salary increase denied when Dr. Martin and the Board of Visitors became aware of a letter written by Dr. Jervey to the editor of *Redbook*, a national magazine.

In that letter, which appeared in *Redbook*'s letter-to-the-editor section, Dr. Jervey had praised the author of an article on premarital sex which had appeared in a prior edition of that magazine. Dr. Jervey indicated in the letter that he intended to use some of the author's comments in his teaching, and he signed the letter in a manner which identified him as a professor at Radford College. Dr. Jervey alleges that as a result of the letter to *Redbook*, Dr. Martin and the Board of Visitors also excluded him from eligibility for summer school teaching and for eligibility to serve as a class sponsor. Dr. Jervey alleges that President Martin has imposed other restrictions, both social and academic, upon him and his wife as a result of the *Redbook* letter.

The defendants, in support of their claim that the plaintiff has not set forth a claim upon which relief can be granted, contend that the raise in question was entirely discretionary with the Board of Visitors. In effect, it appears to this court that the defendants take the position that under the laws of the State of Virginia, the Board has absolute discretion in determining the salary which an employee of Radford College will receive. As a state institution, Radford College is administrated in accordance with the provisions of the Code of Virginia concerning colleges and universities. Specifically, Section 23–155.7 of the Code of Virginia describes the powers and duties of the Radford College Board of Visitors. That section reads in part as follows:

> The board shall control and expend the funds of the College and any appropriation hereafter provided, and shall make all needful rules and regulations concerning the College, appoint the president, who shall be its chief executive officer, and *all professors, teachers and agents, and fix their salaries*, and generally direct the affairs of the College. (emphasis added)

The defendants contend that the granting of raises which are based on individual performance is a matter solely within the province of the Board of Visitors, and the federal court, in the light of the public's interest in the administration of state colleges and universities, should refrain from interference with such discretionary administrative functions.

This court agrees with the defendants with respect to the wide discretion which is vested in the Board of Visitors of Radford College. Likewise, the court believes that great care and judicial discretion should be exercised when the federal courts are asked to interfere with the administration of our colleges and universities. On the other hand, it has been held by the court of appeals for this circuit that no matter how wide the discretion of the Board is, it cannot be exercised so as to arbitrarily deprive persons of their constitutional rights.

* * *

This court realizes that the Board of Visitors of Radford College does and should have wide discretion in managing that educational institution. However, this court feels that the Board of Visitors of a state university should not administratively penalize the exercise by a faculty member of his first amendment rights by use of the power granted by Section 23–155.7 of the Virginia Code. This is not to say that such action was done in this case, for that is a question for the jury; however, this court feels that the plaintiff's complaint does set forth a cause of action which is cognizable in the federal courts. Unlike the plaintiff in *Lewis*, supra, the plaintiff in the case at bar has set forth enough in his complaint to indicate the possibility of infringement; therefore, this court is of the opinion that the plaintiff should be allowed to proceed.

The defendants contend that no rights have been abused because the nature of a salary raise is such that the individual has nothing until the raise is granted. This may be true however, it is not the loss of the raise itself which is at issue. The right which allegedly is in danger is the first amendment right to freedom of speech and expression. It is this right which plaintiff alleges is endangered by the denial of a raise. This court feels that a denial without sufficient basis which is made to punish an individual for the expression of his views is constitutionally impermissible.

The defendants also contend that the letter in question could be used by the Board in other ways which would be constitutionally permissible. This court will not pass upon this contention at this point in the proceedings, but instead will consider this issue in deciding how the jury is to be instructed.

For the reasons given above the defendants' motion to dismiss for failure to state a claim upon which relief can be granted is overruled.

Max Lynch v. Indiana State University Board of Trustees
378 N.E. 2d 900 (1978)

LYBROOK, Presiding Judge.

Here, no genuine issues of material fact exist as both parties agree Lynch was employed to teach mathematics at the University Laboratory School at Terre Haute, which is operated by I.S.U. During the course of his employment, Lynch made a practice of reading Bible verses aloud to his mathematics students for several minutes at the beginning of each class hour. During several discussions between Lynch and I.S.U. officials, Lynch was admonished to cease his religious readings as the practice was violative of University policy and unlawful. At first Lynch agreed to discontinue the practice, but he subsequently informed I.S.U. officials that he intended to continue reading aloud from the Bible to his classes. I.S.U. advised Lynch that a Faculty

Dismissal Hearing would be held to consider his dismissal, and that he had a right to prepare and present a defense. The Faculty Dismissal Hearing Committee recommended Lynch's dismissal, and Lynch requested consideration by the I.S.U. Board of Trustees, which voted to affirm Lynch's dismissal from the faculty.

I.

Lynch claims that the trial court erred in finding that the reading of Bible verses, without comment, to his students was a violation of the students' constitutional rights. It is his contention that so long as his students were accorded the opportunity to absent themselves from the classroom to avoid hearing the Bible reading, he has preserved or at least not infringed upon their rights.

* * *

For the students in his mathematics classes, the indisputable effect of Lynch's Bible reading was the advancement or promotion of Lynch's particular religious views and practices. Peer pressure, fear of the teacher, concern about grades, and the alternative of standing outside the classroom in the hall, severely limit the freedom of a student to absent himself from class during a Bible reading. Additionally, Lynch's religious activity was being conducted while he was employed by the I.S.U. Board of Trustees, using public facilities, during class time.

We think that the alternative afforded Lynch's students to absent themselves from the classroom was not sufficient protection to their own constitutional rights in light of the supervisory position of control occupied by the teacher over student grading and conduct, coupled with peer pressure and disapproval which we feel would have a "chilling" effect at best and more likely, a coercive impact on the student's free exercise of their religious right.

II.

Next, Lynch asserts that the trial court's decision is contrary to law in that Lynch's dismissal violated his constitutional rights under the First and Fourteenth Amendments of the U.S. Constitution and Article 1, Sections 2 and 3 of the Indiana Constitution.

Lynch argues that I.S.U. has adopted a policy which is hostile to the free exercise of his religion in an area which is not proscribed by the Constitutions of the United States and the State of Indiana, thereby depriving Lynch of his employment based upon his religious beliefs.

Lynch cites *Torcaso v. Watkins* for the proposition that public positions cannot be withheld from persons because of their religious beliefs. Here, I.S.U. maintains that Lynch was not discharged because of his religious beliefs but only for his refusal to cease the religious act of oral Bible reading during school time.

It is Lynch's contention that he is compelled by his religious beliefs to read from his Bible in mathematics class. He asserts that he was never informed that as a condition of his employment he could not exercise his beliefs, but was informed he could not read his Bible only subsequent to his employment.

* * *

In order for the State to interfere with the practice of a legitimate religious belief, it must appear either that the State does not deny the free exercise of religious belief by its requirement, or that there is a State interest of sufficient magnitude to override the interest claiming protection under the Free Exercise Clause.

To allow Lynch to exercise his freedom to act, here, in reading the Bible aloud to his students would impinge upon his students' freedom to believe as they wish. Under the rule in *Cantwell*, which was reaffirmed in *Torcaso*, the concept of freedom to believe is an absolute right, and the freedom to act, in the nature of things, cannot be absolute. Thus when the exercise of his religious acts impinges upon the rights of his students to believe, then Lynch's rights must fall. A man cannot extend his religious freedom until it infringes upon another person's civil rights or constitutional liberties. The right to worship is not a right to disturb others in their worship.

Lynch was not discharged from I.S.U.'s employment because of his religious beliefs, but was terminated because of his activities of reading aloud from the Bible before each of his mathematics classes. Lynch was not deprived of his right to read aloud from the Bible before and after school at his home, in church and with friends. The record shows that I.S.U. advised Lynch that he must not consume the limited and valuable classroom time available for teaching mathematics by reading the Bible. This I.S.U. unquestionably had the right to do in order for the University to maintain religious neutrality and promote secular education.

* * *

Lynch's contention that the First and Fourteenth Amendments proscribe only *legislation* in respect to religion must also fall, as the Federal Courts have interpreted their language to forbid voluntary student initiated prayers and Bible readings even in the absence of state statutes or regulation, where the resolution of a school board authorizing Bible reading and encouraging group recitation of the Lord's Prayer, was held to be the act of a political subdivision of a state government and hence violative of the Establishment Clause. Later in *Goodwin v. Cross Country School*, the Federal Court considered three religious activities challenged by petitioner Goodwin. While it upheld the participation of local clergy in baccalaureate services because such services were not held on a school day nor was student attendance required, the Court found that a voluntary, student initiated program of Bible reading and recitation of the Lord's Prayer along with a program for distribution of Gideon Bibles in the school system were clearly of religious character violative of the Establishment Clause where the programs used tax-supported facilities and took advantage of compulsory public school attendance, all with the permission of school authorities.

For the State of Indiana or I.S.U. to have ordered Lynch or his students to participate in religious activities would clearly have violated the Establishment Clause of the U.S. Constitution's First Amendment, as well as Article 1, § 2 of the Indiana Constitution, both set out above.

* * *

The Establishment Clause, then, stands at least for the proposition that when government activities touch on the religious sphere, they must be secular in purpose, evenhanded in operation, and neutral in primary impact.

While the State has not directly participated in the act of Bible reading by Lynch, it placed him in the position of authority from which he might express his religious views during a part of the curricular day, involving young people whose presence is compelled by law, hence utilizing the prestige, power, and influence of school authority.

Thus had I.S.U. permitted Lynch to continue the Bible readings, it would have violated its religious neutrality mandated by the Establishment Clause of the First Amendment, allowed infringement upon the religious freedoms of its students, and failed to promote the secular goal of instruction in mathematics for which Lynch was employed. The I.S.U. Board of Trustees was justified in acting, pursuant to IC 1971, 20–12–1–2, to discharge Lynch after his refusal to cease his religious activities in the classroom.

Finding no genuine issue of fact, we affirm the trial court's award of summary judgment in favor of I.S.U.

Affirmed.

Martin v. Parrish

805 F.2d 583 (5th Cir. 1986)

EDITH HOLLAN JONES, Circuit Judge:

Whether a publicly employed college teacher is constitutionally protected in the abusive use of profanity in the classroom is the most significant issue presented by this appeal. We hold that the constitution does not shield him and therefore AFFIRM the judgment of the district court.

I. BACKGROUND

Appellant Martin was an economics instructor at Midland College in Midland, Texas. Appellees are the president, vice president, dean and trustees of the college. The dean and vice president originally disciplined Martin in 1983, following a formal student complaint regarding Martin's inveterate use of profane language, including "hell," "damn," and "bullshit," in class. Martin was warned orally and in writing that should his use of profanity in the classroom continue, disciplinary action requiring suspension, termination or both would be recommended. Heedless of the administrators' concerns, Martin continued to curse in class, using words including "bullshit," "hell," "damn," "God damn," and "sucks." Two students filed written complaints concerning Martin's speech in the classroom on June 19, 1984, which included the following statements: "the attitude of the class sucks," "[the attitude] is a bunch of bullshit," "you may think economics is a bunch of bullshit," and "if you don't like the way I teach this God damn course there is the door." Following notice of this outburst, the dean initiated actions to terminate Martin, which culminated, following several administrative steps, in approval by the college's board of trustees.

Martin's subsequent § 1983 lawsuit alleged deprivation of his first amendment right of free speech, abridgement of an alleged right of academic freedom, and denials of due process and equal protection. The jury found in Martin's favor on issues pertaining to free speech and equal protection and awarded damages, but denied his due process claim. The district court granted judgment n.o.v. to the defendants, finding no evidentiary support for the equal protection allegations and concluding that Martin's profanity was not constitutionally protected. Martin appeals all but the due process claim.

II. ANALYSIS

Appellant asserts his language was not obscene, but only profane and as such enjoys constitutional protection unless it caused disruption.[2] We find this argument an incomplete and erroneous expression of pertinent first amendment jurisprudence.

The constitution protects not simply words but communication, which presupposes a speaker and a listener, and circumscribes this protection for purposes which enhance the functioning of our republican form of government. The "rights" of the speaker are thus always tempered by a consideration of the rights of the audience and the public purpose served, or disserved, by his speech. Appellant's argument, by ignoring his audience and the lack of any public purpose in his offensive epithets, founders on several fronts.

Connick v. Myers recently explained the limits of first amendment protection of speech afforded public employees like Martin. The Supreme Court reiterated that the goal of such protection is to prevent suppression of such employees' participation in public affairs and "chilling" of their freedom of political association. It is limited to speech on matters of "public concern," otherwise, government would be hobbled in its regulation of employment conditions, and public employees would enjoy an immunity from the consequences of their speech not shared by anyone in the private sector. If the offending speech does not bear upon a matter of public concern, "it is unnecessary for us to scrutinize the reasons for [the] discharge." Moreover, "whether an employee's speech addresses a matter of public concern must be determined by the content, form, and context of a given statement...."

There is no doubt that Martin's epithets did not address a matter of public concern. One student described Martin's June 19, 1984, castigation of the class as an explosion, an unprovoked, extremely offensive, downgrading of the entire class. In highly derogatory and indecent terms, Martin implied that the students were inferior because they were accustomed to taking courses from inferior, part-time instructors at Midland College. The profanity described Martin's attitude toward his students, hardly a matter that, but for this lawsuit, would occasion public discussion. Appellant has not argued that his profanity was for any purpose other than cussing out his students as an expression of frustration with their progress—to "motivate" them—and has thereby impliedly conceded his case under *Connick*.

Ignoring that his audience consisted of students also led to Martin's undoing. Indecent language and profanity may be regulated in the schools and over the public airwaves. The policies leading to affirmation of some speech restrictions in these circumstances support the college's termination of Martin. In *Bethel*, the Supreme Court affirmed disciplinary action against a high school senior who, against the advice of teachers and in violation of school rules, gave a sexually explicit and vulgar speech to a student assembly.

Bethel admittedly involved a high school audience and it may be suggested that its justification for speech restraints rests largely on this fact. Nevertheless, we view the role of higher education as no less pivotal to our national interest. It carries on the process of instilling in our citizens necessary democratic virtues, among which are

---

2. Appellant also argues vigorously that he has a first amendment right to "academic freedom" that permits use of the language in question. It is, however, undisputed that such language was not germane to the subject matter in his class and had no educational function. Thus, as in *Kelleher v. Flawn*, we find it unnecessary to reach this issue.

civility and moderation. It is necessary to the nurture of knowledge and resource-fulness that undergird our economic and political system. Repeated failure by a member of the educational staff of Midland College to exhibit professionalism de-grades his important mission and detracts from the subjects he is trying to teach. The school officials uniformly made this point at trial, testifying that use of profanity in the classroom is unprofessional and hinders instruction. Parrish, the college pres-ident, emphasized that it is vital for the teacher to have respect for the students, especially when he is in an authority role. Parrish further observed that a teacher's conduct can strongly influence the students, even at the college level. Indirectly con-firming these views, one student described Martin's outpouring as unprofessional and stated that he had lost interest in economics as a result of Martin's belittling comments. Another student expressed his reticence to asking questions in class for fear of Martin's ridicule. To the extent that Martin's profanity was considered by the college admin-istration to inhibit his effectiveness as a teacher, it need not be tolerated by the college any more than Fraser's indecent speech to the Bethel school assembly.

* * *

[W]e hold that the students in Martin's classroom, who paid to be taught and not vilified in indecent terms, are subject to the holding of *Pacifica*, which, like *Cohen*, recognizes that surroundings and context are essential, case-by-case determinants of the constitutional protection accorded to indecent language. Martin's language is unprotected under the reasoning of these cases because, taken in context, it constituted a deliberate, superfluous attack on a "captive audience" with no academic purpose or justification.

Were Martin an assistant district attorney who repeatedly used profanity in the courtroom, we have no doubt that he could be terminated for unprofessional behavior. Were he a member of Congress, such language could result in censure. For the foregoing reasons, we conclude his status as a college teacher is no less sensitive to the use of such language than that of a courtroom lawyer or member of Congress.

Martin also challenges the district court's judgment n.o.v. on the issue of equal protection. We have reviewed the record and find that Martin failed to introduce evidence that he had been treated differently from other similarly situated persons, or even that there were others similarly situated. The district court correctly held for the defendants on this point.

The judgement of the district court is AFFIRMED.

ROBERT MADDEN HILL, Circuit Judge, concurring in the judgment.

I concur in the judgment because I believe that *Connick v. Myers* controls this case. I write separately, however, because I cannot agree with the majority's unnecessary dicta extending the rationale of *Pacifica*, *Bethel*, and *Pico* to a university setting.

* * *

The majority indicates that the profane nature of Martin's words precludes a finding that a matter of public concern is involved. The use of profane words by themselves, in my opinion, does not preclude a finding that an employee's speech addresses a matter of public concern. Instead, as *Connick* indicates, the record *as a whole* must be examined. Looking at Martin's comments as a whole, I agree with the majority's conclusion that they do not address a matter of public concern. While some of Martin's comments in isolation could be construed as challenging the attitude of the class in its approach to economics, the derogatory nature of the comments overall convinces me that no matter of public concern is involved. For the same reason, I agree with the majority that the question of Martin's first amendment right to "academic freedom" does not need to be reached in this case. While some of the comments arguably bear on economics and could be viewed as relevant to Martin's role as a teacher in motivating the interest of his students, his remarks *as a whole* are unrelated to economics and devoid of any educational function. Thus, I agree with the majority that Martin's discharge did not violate his first amendment rights.

Although I would end the analysis at this point, the majority proceeds to focus on the audience that Martin was addressing, and, citing three Supreme Court cases involving high schools and young children, concludes that the rationale of those cases is equally applicable to a college or university setting. I do not feel it is necessary to reach this issue; furthermore, an examination of the three cases involved raises questions about the majority's conclusion.

* * *

Ultimately, as the majority implicitly concedes earlier in its opinion, it is up to the courts and not the Midland College faculty to determine whether the first amendment rights of Martin have been infringed. The majority's approach, however, would appear to preclude a court from reviewing the judgment of an administrator that the use of profanity by a faculty member in the course of his teaching was undesirable because it would lower the "esteem" of the institution. The majority indicates that we must defer to school officials in "all but the most sensitive constitutional areas." I fail to see a more sensitive constitutional area, however, than an individual's first amendment rights. The majority's citations from various Supreme Court cases do not convince me that their position is correct.

The largest problem in my view with the majority's extension of cases like *Bethel* and *Pico* is that the majority does not give sufficient weight to the differences between the high school instructional setting involved in the cases it cites, and the college instructional setting involved in this case. The purpose of education through high school is to instill basic knowledge, to lay the foundations to enable a student to learn greater knowledge, and to teach basic social, moral, and political values. A college education, on the other hand, deals more with challenging a student's ideas and concepts on a given subject matter. The college atmosphere enables students to rethink their views on various issues in an intellectual atmosphere which forces students to analyze their basic beliefs. Thus, high school is necessarily more structured than college, where a more free-wheeling experience is both contemplated and needed. What might be instructionally unacceptable in high school might be fully acceptable in college.

* * *

Lovelace v. Southeastern Massachusetts University
793 F.2d 419 (1st Cir. 1986)

[The U.S. Court of Appeals for the First Circuit upheld a summary judgment, finding that Professor Lovelace had no protected due process property interests, and that any liberty interest he had was not infringed by his non-renewal.]

Plaintiff claims that the real reason his contract was not renewed and his grievances were rejected or interfered with is because he refused to inflate his grades or lower his expectations and teaching standards. He contends that, in response to student complaints that homework assignments were too time consuming and that plaintiff's courses were too hard, defendants first threatened not to renew plaintiff's contract unless he appeased the students and then carried out their threat when plaintiff refused to lower his standards. This, plaintiff says, interfered with his academic freedom which, plaintiff maintains, is protected by the first amendment.

It is important to note what plaintiff's first amendment claim is and to separate speech from action. Plaintiff has not contended that he was retaliated against simply because he *advocated* that the university elevate its standards. Indeed, plaintiff would be hard pressed to support such a claim in view of the February 11, 1983 memorandum from Dean Ward which plaintiff placed in the record. The memo indicates that as a result of consultations with plaintiff about the student complaints, the Dean concluded upgrading of the lower level computer courses was warranted. Far from manifesting hostility towards voiced concerns about educational matters, the memo suggests a spirit of receptivity to faculty concerns. Plaintiff's complaint instead is that he was retaliated against when he refused to *change* his standards.

We will assume for purposes of this opinion that plaintiff's refusal to lower his standards was a substantial motivating factor in the decision not to renew his contract. We nevertheless conclude that plaintiff has failed to state a constitutional claim.

Whether a school sets itself up to attract and serve only the best and the brightest students or whether it instead gears its standard to a broader, more average population is a policy decision which, we think, universities must be allowed to set. And matters such as course content, homework load, and grading policy are core university concerns, integral to implementation of this policy decision.

To accept plaintiff's contention that an untenured teacher's grading policy is constitutionally protected and insulates him from discharge when his standards conflict with those of the university[2] would be to constrict the university in defining and performing its educational mission. The first amendment does not require that each nontenured professor be made a sovereign unto himself.

Nor do we find that *Hillis v. Stephen F. Austin State University* or the other cases on which plaintiff relies require a different result in the circumstance of the present case. In *Hillis*, a teacher, who had been directed to give a specified student a B grade, claimed his refusal to do so was protected by the first amendment and that his subsequent contract nonrenewal was in retaliation for the refusal. Similar to the present case, two distinct matters were potentially at issue: 1) whether plaintiff's *speech* in protesting the directive was protected and 2) whether plaintiff's *action* in disobeying the directive was protected. The court noted this speech/action distinction

---

2. It is true that plaintiff contends that his grading policy was in fact in accordance with the university's published criteria. We think, however, that it must be university officials—and not either an untenured teacher in his first year at the university or a federal court—which must be the judge of that, at least in the context of the constitutional claim plaintiff assets.

Plaintiff also contends that the Federation Agreement guaranteed him academic freedom and this guaranty was violated by the university's alleged action in attempting to coerce plaintiff to alter grades. If that were so, plaintiff at most would state a contract claim, not a constitutional one.

(the grade incident "involved plain insubordination as one component, and *arguably* included Hillis' first amendment—protected criticism as another") (emphasis added), and, we think, implied—though did not decide—that the former component—the insubordination in refusing to grade as directed—would not be protected. In any event, because the court concluded that the grading incident was not a substantial motivating factor in the decision not to renew Hillis' contract, the court never decided whether Hillis' activity was protected, and thus the case does not assist plaintiff.

Having found no merit in any of plaintiff's arguments, we affirm the district court judgment.

Denny Carley v. Arizona Board of Regents
737 P.2d 1099 (Ariz. App. 1987)

EUBANK, Presiding Judge.

OPINION

This appeal is from a superior court judgment affirming a decision of Northern Arizona University President Eugene M. Hughes to deny the renewal of a teaching contract to the appellant Denny Carley. Carley raises the following issues on appeal: (1) whether his right to academic freedom was violated because student evaluations were utilized as the primary tool to determine his teaching effectiveness, (2) whether President Hughes abused his discretion by rejecting the findings of the majority of the Academic Freedom and Tenure Committee and (3) whether there was substantial evidence to support the President's decision. We find no infringement upon Carley's right to academic freedom and further find that President Hughes' decision was not an abuse of discretion and is supported by the record.

FACTS

In 1983–84 Carley was in his fifth year as an untenured assistant professor of art at Northern Arizona University (NAU). The Art Department Committee on Faculty Status reviewed material supplied by Carley in support of his request for continued retention and in addition considered several years of student evaluations. By a three-to-two vote, the committee recommended that Carley not be retained as a faculty member.

In accordance with university policies, the Art Department chairman, Dr. Don Bendel, reviewed the committee's recommendation and made his recommendation to Dr. Charles Aurand, Dean of the College of Creative Arts. Dr. Bendel disagreed with the committee and recommended that Carley be retained. Dr. Aurand then made a recommendation that Carley not be retained to Dr. Joseph W. Cox, Vice-President for Academic Affairs. Dr. Cox in turn recommended that President Hughes uphold the recommendations of the Art Department Committee on Faculty Status and Dean Aurand not to retain Carley. On May 29, 1984, President Hughes concurred in the recommendations for non-retention and informed Carley that he was being offered a terminal contract for the 1984–85 academic year.

Carley requested that Dr. Hughes review his decision. He was subsequently informed that Dr. Hughes had made his review and reaffirmed his original decision. Carley then appealed Dr. Hughes' decision to the NAU Committee on Academic

Freedom and Tenure alleging violations of his constitutional rights to freedom of speech, press, association, academic freedom and substantive due process.

The Academic Freedom and Tenure Committee met on February 2 and 3, 1985, and by a six-to-three vote found that Carley's rights to academic freedom and due process had been violated and recommended that he be retained in his position at NAU. Both the majority and minority reports of the committee were submitted to President Hughes. President Hughes reviewed these reports and in addition considered a legal opinion from the Board of Regents' counsel, memoranda from counsel for NAU and counsel for Carley, and a transcript of Carley's hearing before the Committee on Academic Freedom and Tenure. He adopted the findings of the minority report and again reaffirmed his decision that Carley's contract for 1984–85 was a terminal contract.

* * *

ACADEMIC FREEDOM

Carley's basic premise is that he was engaged in a constitutionally protected activity and that this activity was a motivating factor in the university's decision not to rehire him. He contends that the university must show that he would have been terminated notwithstanding the protected activity, citing *Mt. Healthy City School District Board of Education v. Doyle.*

The activities which Carley identifies as "protected speech" are his teaching methods. He characterizes himself as being a "demanding teacher contrary to some student expectations" and represents one of his teaching methods as frequently leaving his classes unattended during appointed meeting times in order to teach students to be more self-reliant. He further describes his methods as emphasizing independent student work in order to reflect the expectations which students will encounter in the business world. Carley contends that, because student evaluations were critical of those methods, the students are challenging his exercise of academic freedom. Thus, he concludes that the student evaluations cannot be used as the primary basis for failing to renew his contract because they infringe on a protected activity.

Carley cites several cases in support of his contention that teaching methodology is part of his "academic freedom" right. However, our review of the cases indicates that each involved conduct closely identified with speech content rather than teaching methods.

For example, Carley relies on *Keyishian v. Board of Regents,* in which the court was dealing with a New York law under which the "utterance of any treasonable or seditious word or words . . . " was grounds for dismissal, as well as questions of Communist Party membership. Similarly, in *State Board for Community Colleges and Occupational Education v. Olson,* also cited by Carley, the court stated that the "principle [of academic freedom] finds its source in the belief that teachers should be free to engage in the exchange of *diverse ideas on controversial topics. . . . " Olson* involved the cancellation of a student newspaper, finding that such closure did *not* "abridge the constitutionally protected aspects of [her] teaching function." She was still free to utilize other means for "presentation of the idea-content of her journalism courses. . . . "

In *Kingsville Independent School District v. Cooper,* also cited by Carley, the court considered a history teacher's presentation of post-Civil War Reconstruction history through a role-playing technique which evoked strong student feelings on racial issues. The school board declined to renew her teaching contract because there had been parent complaints about this teaching method. Again, like *Keyishian* and *Olson,* the case involved the discussion of controversial topics and the presentation of controversial course materials. The court found that the speech was protected and could not be used as a basis for non-renewal unless the classroom discussions "clearly overbalance[d] [her] usefulness as an instructor. . . . " In neither *Keyishian, Olson* nor *Cooper* was termination or nonrenewal of employment based only upon classroom teaching techniques. Speech content was clearly at issue. Unlike those cases, specific communications are not at issue here.

Various courts have expressed their reticence to intervene in academic decision making by a university concerning retention of teaching personnel. This reluctance is based on the belief that such decisions are best made by those who have expertise in education.

Challenges to institutional decisions to deny tenure to faculty for reasons relating to teaching methods, course content and grading policies have been notably unsuccessful. For example, in *Hetrick v. Martin*, a state university declined to renew the appointment of a nontenured faculty member because of disapproval of her "pedagogical attitude," as evidenced by teaching styles and techniques. The court expressly refused to recognize teaching methods as protected speech, holding:

> Whatever may be the ultimate scope of the amorphous 'academic freedom' guarantee to our nation's teachers and students . . . , it does not encompass the right of a nontenured teacher to have her teaching style insulated from review by her superiors when they determine whether she has merited tenured status. . . .

Similarly, in *Clark v. Holmes*, the court upheld the nonrenewal of a nontenured instructor for reasons related to the structure of his course content. The court stated "we do not conceive academic freedom to be a license for uncontrolled expression at variance with established curricular contents and internally destructive of the proper functioning of the institution."

In *Lovelace v. Southeastern Massachusetts University*, a faculty member contended that his right of academic freedom was violated when he was denied tenure because he refused to lower his standards and change his grading policies. Student complaints concerning his policies were considered by the university. The court held that, even if he were fired for refusing to lower his standards, he failed to state a constitutional claim. Finding that the first amendment does not require that a teacher be made a sovereign to himself, the court held that the university, not the individual faculty member, had the right to set policy on course content, homework load and grading policy. The court particularly noted that the teacher was not denied employment for voicing an opinion concerning these policies, but for refusing to comply with existing policies. This was distinguishable from a protected speech claim.

* * *

The Supreme Court recently spoke on the issue of academic freedom in *Regents of the University of Michigan v. Ewing*. While student retention rather than teacher retention was at issue, the principles set forth are applicable to both situations. After noting its reluctance to encroach on the prerogatives of educational institutions and its commitment to the academic freedom of those institutions, the court commented in footnote 12:

> Academic freedom thrives not only on the independent and uninhibited exchange of ideas among teachers and students [citations omitted], but also, and somewhat

inconsistently, on *autonomous decision making by the academy itself* [citations omitted]. Discretion to determine, on academic grounds, who may be admitted to study, has been described as one of "the four essential freedoms" of a university.

Sweezy v. New Hampshire, cited in *Ewing*, expressly includes among the "four essential freedoms of the university," the freedom "to determine for itself on academic grounds who may teach. . . . "

The record is clear that Carley was not denied a contract because of expressing unpopular opinions or otherwise presenting controversial ideas to his students. Rather, the University concluded that he was not an effective teacher. It was apparently their professional opinion that his methodology was not successful. Academic freedom is not a doctrine to insulate a teacher from evaluation by the institution that employs him. Thus, we conclude that the decision not to retain Carley, even if based, in part, upon student evaluation expressing disapproval of his teaching methods, did not violate his first amendment rights.

Carley has contended it was wrong to evaluate his teaching effectiveness primarily by student evaluations. The use of student evaluations as a consideration in assessing teaching fitness has been upheld without discussion in a number of cases. Carley has cited no authority that relying *primarily* or *solely* on student evaluations would be impermissible. We have found none.

Based on our review of the record, including student evaluations, we find substantial evidence to support President Hughes' decision.

The record in this matter shows that President Hughes relied on a committee decision of Carley's own peers that he should not be renewed and similar recommendations from the dean of his college and the vice-president for academic affairs. Further, President Hughes reviewed his original decision at Carley's request. He also reviewed the factual findings of the majority and minority of the Committee on Academic Freedom and Tenure, the transcript of the hearing, and sought input from counsel for both parties and independent counsel. The record demonstrates diligence in reaching what appears to have been a difficult decision. It is precisely this type of decision which is best left to the academic community rather than to a court.

We find that President Hughes did not act in an arbitrary or capricious manner nor in abuse of his discretion. We therefore affirm the decision of the trial court.

Melvin Baker v. Lafayette College
532 A. 2d 399 (Pa. 1987)

ZAPPALA, Justice.

* * *

On or about May 19, 1976, the Appellant accepted a position as an Assistant Professor in the Art Department of Lafayette College (College). The written contract term was for two years commencing with the Fall term of 1976 although the Appellant believed he had a commitment for two two-year contracts to be followed with tenure. Furthermore, his contract incorporated and included *The Faculty Handbook*.

Between May and June of 1977, internal problems arose within the Art Department and with the behavior of its chairman. As a result of alleged behavioral problems of the department chairman, the Appellant had frank and open discussions with the College's staff, including the President, the Provost, the Assistant Provost, and the College physician. The Appellant was assured that all conversations would be held in strict confidence. However, at a later date, the Appellant learned that the department chairman had been advised of the substance of these conversations. Further investigation of the chairman resulted in the College physician recommending psychiatric and psychological counseling for the department chairman.

On July 15, 1977, the department chairman wrote his first evaluation of the Appellant. In this report, the chairman critiqued each course taught by the Appellant as well as his overall job performance. On October 31, 1977, the chairman authored his second evaluation in which he expressed disappointment and dissatisfaction with Appellant's overall job performance, his failure to improve such performance, and his failure to live up to his projected performance. In this second evaluation, the department chairman recommended that Appellant not be reappointed. Neither of these evaluations were forwarded to the Appellant.

On December 13, 1977, the Appellant was informed that he would not be reappointed because economic factors required a decrease in the staffing of the Art Department. The Appellant then advised the provost that he would not appeal this determination and requested that no further review be conducted as had occurred after another teacher's termination. Notwithstanding, the dean of the Tyler School of Art of Temple University (Tyler) visited the College. Although the provost indicated that the purpose of the dean's visit was to evaluate the Art Department, the dean indicated in his report that the purpose of his visit was to evaluate a faculty member of the Art Department and the facts surrounding his termination.

*   *   *

Applying these well established legal principles to the present case, it is clear that none of the statements are defamatory. Exhibit A is the first evaluation, directed to the provost by the department chairman. In this report, the department chairman first outlines his review of the various courses taught by the Appellant, including the Appellant's adherence to the written course descriptions, and the overall success of the course. In at least two instances, the chairman concludes that the courses taught by the Appellant were no worse than previously. On the whole, this evaluation is just that, an evaluation of the work performance of the Appellant for the first academic year. Exhibit B presents an evaluation of Appellant's second semester. Like Exhibit A, it presents the chairman's opinion as to the continued value of the Appellant to the Art Department and the College. Although Exhibit B does not portray the Appellant in glowing terms, the substance of the report includes frank opinion void of innuendo. Thus, we must conclude as both lower courts have previously, that neither Exhibit A nor B are capable of defamatory meaning.

Exhibit C is the memorandum from the department chairman to the provost. This memorandum was written after the Appellant had been notified that his appointment would not be renewed but before the end of his final academic year. The Appellant complains that the following language is defamatory:

> I consider [his wife's presence in Professor Baker's studio classes] to be an extraordinary, peculiar, and academically deplorable arrangement. Nevertheless, since Mel has been notified that he will not be reappointed to the faculty next year, I have decided to overlook it, just as I have overlooked so many other

questionable things that have occurred in the art department during the past three years.

In discussing why the aforementioned statements are actionable, the Appellant states only that "the third document . . . contained critical comments concerning Baker." He then argues that these words are actionable because the chairman had no right to evaluate him since it was already determined that the Appellant's appointment would not be renewed. While the Appellant's argument may raise an issue regarding the continued consent to an evaluation of his work under *The Faculty Handbook*, we need not reach that argument if these statements cannot be considered defamatory. As with Exhibits A and B, the department chairman is merely expressing his personal opinion that having Mrs. Baker in the classroom during class is "deplorable." Since the above-quoted language does not appear to be based upon any undisclosed facts, but rather specifically disclosed facts, we conclude that such language is not susceptible to any defamatory meaning.

Appellant contends that Exhibit D, the letter from the dean of Tyler to the provost, likewise defames him. Specifically, the Appellant contends the following statements defamed him:

> Professor Baker seems, from the reports I received, to be less successful at meeting these requirements than the other studio faculty member. His attitude, as reported by Professor Gluhman, would seem to be almost cavalier in his dealings with the students, i.e. no regular hours, no outside assignments, a general attitude that the best way to build a program is by giving high grades. Although he was brought in originally to develop the sculpture and three-dimensional design program, he does not seem to have interest in three-dimensional design. His primary interest lies in the area of figurative modeling, but the results of his class as shown in examples provided for me, seem ordinary at best.

As with Exhibit C, before we reach the consent argument, we must analyze the above statements to determine whether they are capable of defamatory meaning. Like the previous Exhibits, it is unclear as to why these statements are defamatory. It appears that the dean is expressing his conclusions based upon his investigation of the Art Department. Within this statement, the dean provided the very facts he relied upon to reach his conclusions. Based upon his perceived needs of the Department and the College, he concludes that the Appellant is expendable. On its face nothing in this report is defamatory.

Finally, the [Appellant] argues that the College breached his employment contract by not evaluating his performance in "good faith." Since the College was aware of the chairman's distaste for the Appellant, the Appellant argues that the College was responsible to conduct an independent review of the Appellant's performance based upon "his teaching record, professional growth and service to the College."

As in all aspects of life, no procedure is fool proof. In our judicial system we have various appeals to review lower court determinations alleged to be improper or unwise. The purpose of appellate review is to correct any prior wrongdoings. Likewise, *The Faculty Handbook* sets forth review procedures. In accordance with these procedures, the Appellant appealed to the president of the College and ultimately to the board of trustees. We would be hard-pressed to conclude that the College acted in bad faith when it followed the required review procedures. This Court has no jurisdiction to review the factual determinations of a college's governing body unless it can be clearly demonstrated that that body violated its own procedures.

Judgment affirmed.

Natthu S. Parate v. Edward Isibor, et al.

Unpublished opinion, United States District Court, Middle District of
Tennessee, Nashville Division (August 1987)

Judge HIGGINS:

On April 4, 1986, the plaintiff, Natthu S. Parate, brought this action against Edward I. Isibor, individually and in his official capacity; Michael Samuchin, individually and in his official capacity; Tennessee State University (TSU) and the Board of Regents of the State University and Community College System of Tennessee. On June 25, 1986, the plaintiff filed a second amended complaint substituting the president of TSU and the Chancellor of the Board of Regents, in their official capacities, as defendants in lieu of TSU and the Board of Regents. Jurisdiction was invoked pursuant to 28 U.S.C. § 1343 and 28 U.S.C. § 1331. The plaintiff brought this civil action pursuant to 42 U.S.C. § 1983, together with pendent state law claims.

On April 25, 1986, the defendants filed a motion to dismiss, asserting that the applicable statute of limitations had expired on the plaintiff's cause of action. After a hearing on both the motion to dismiss and the plaintiff's motion for a preliminary injunction, the Court made its findings of fact and conclusions of law and entered an order dated June 5, 1986, denying both motions. On October 7, 1986, the defendants Isibor and Samuchin, in their individual capacities, filed a motion for summary judgment. On October 21, 1986, all the defendants in their official capacities moved for summary judgment or dismissal. An amended motion for summary judgment or dismissal was filed by the defendants in their official capacities on October 22, 1986.

By order entered December 2, 1986, the motions were referred to the Magistrate for consideration and submission of proposed findings of fact and recommendations for disposition. On January 23, 1987, the Magistrate's Report and Recommendation (Report) was filed.

The plaintiff was a nontenured professor at TSU in the Civil Engineering Department of the School of Engineering and Technology. The plaintiff alleges that the defendants Isibor and Samuchin, while acting under color of state law, engaged in conduct which violated his right to academic freedom and due process under the First and Fourteenth Amendments. At the hearing on the plaintiff's motion for a preliminary injunction, this Court framed the issues presented in the plaintiff's complaint as follows:

First, whether the First and Fourteenth Amendments to the Constitution of the United States afforded the plaintiff the right to refuse to change a grade he had assigned to a student despite the direction of his superiors to do so.

Second, if, so, whether the actions and conduct of the individual defendants in the winter of 1983 and particularly in March of 1983, violated the plaintiff's rights.

Third, whether the subsequent actions and conduct of the individual defendants constitute retaliatory measures because of the assertion of a protected interest.

Finally, whether the plaintiff's contract was not renewed because of the exercise of a constitutionally protected right.

The Magistrate recommended that the plaintiff's claims under the First and the Fourteenth Amendments be dismissed.

The plaintiff filed his objections to the Report on February 2, 1987. The defendants, in their official capacities, filed a response to the plaintiff's objections to the Report on February 13, 1987. The defendants Isibor and Samuchin, in their individual capacities, filed a response to the plaintiff's objections to the Report on February 17, 1987.

The plaintiff divides his objections to the Magistrate's Report into three categories: the plaintiff's liberty interest; the grade change incident; and the classroom incident. The Court notes that the objections of the plaintiff raise no new issues not already considered by the Magistrate.

First, the plaintiff objects to the Magistrate's determination with regard to his liberty interest by contending that the Magistrate set forth facts which demonstrate a substantial and direct interference by the defendants with the plaintiff's right to freely pursue his teaching profession at TSU. In his objections, the plaintiff asserts that the "defendants' interference was not pursuant to legitimate, supervisory authority; rather, it was arbitrary, malicious, unreasonable and motivated by the plaintiff's exercise of his constitutional right to academic freedom." The plaintiff further objects to the Magistrate's conclusion "that an individual must be totally precluded from entering into a profession or from obtaining employment elsewhere for a liberty interest violation to exist is not warranted under the case law." The plaintiff further contends that his liberty interest clearly was violated by the defendants' actions which meet the "shocks the conscience" test. The objections to the Magistrate's determination of the plaintiff's liberty interest must be meritorious to show a deprivation of due process.

In this light, it is well recognized that a person may not be deprived of life, liberty, or property without due process of law. The first step for the Court is to determine whether the plaintiff's claimed interest is entitled to protection and second whether the defendants violated the process due the plaintiff. The Sixth Circuit has determined that "[f]reedom to choose and pursue a career, 'to engage in any of the common occupations of life,' qualifies as a liberty interest which may not be arbitrarily denied by the State." In *Wilson v. Beebe*, the Sixth Circuit enumerated two types of substantive due process: (1) official acts that are unreasonable and arbitrary and cause a deprivation of a substantive right specified in the Constitution, or (2) an official act that "may not take place no matter what procedural protections accompany them." The plaintiff claims a violation by the defendants of both kinds of substantive due process.

Two factors to consider in determining if there has been governmental interference (a substantive due process violation) with the plaintiff's freedom to pursue his teaching career are: (1) the nature and seriousness of the infringement, and (2) the strength of the justification given. In this instance, the plaintiff was terminated at the end of a one-year contract. He was not a tenured professor and was subject to termination without cause. Simply because the defendants did not renew his contract does not mean that the plaintiff is precluded from pursuing his career. He is not being denied his choice of career. Furthermore, the plaintiff has not demonstrated that the defendants brought false charges against him that "might seriously damage his standing and associations in his community" or that impose a "stigma or other disability" that forecloses freedom to take advantage of other employment opportunities. The Court concludes that there has been no substantial infringement with the plaintiff's right to pursue his career. He remains free to seek employment.

With regard to the second factor, the manner in which the defendants terminated the plaintiff was within the contractual bounds of his employment contract. The justification for the plaintiff's termination was the expiration of the one-year contract. The Court finds that his termination from TSU did not foreclose his freedom to take advantage of other employment opportunities. The Court further finds that the justification given for the plaintiff's termination is well-founded and supported by his one-year written contract.

The plaintiff further contends his liberty interest was violated because the defendants' conduct toward the plaintiff while he was employed at TSU would "shock the conscience." The Court agrees with the Magistrate's determination that "the conduct of defendants, while unprofessional, nonetheless does not rise to the 'shocks the conscious' level, that is, unconscionable, egregious, and conduct not tolerated by society." The plaintiff must realize "a citizen does not suffer a constitutional deprivation every time he is subject to the petty harassment of a state agent." A substantive due process violation is generally not found

> unless the governmental conduct is sufficiently severe, sufficiently disproportionate to the need presented and so deliberate and unjustified a misuse of [authority] as to transcend the bound of ordinary tort law and establish a deprivation of constitutional right.

The Court finds nothing in the record to support the assertion of the plaintiff that the defendants arbitrarily and unreasonably interfered with his substantive due process liberty interest to freely and fully pursue his profession. The Court therefore finds that the plaintiff's objections regarding his liberty interest are without merit and adopts and approves the Magistrate's findings and recommendation that the plaintiff's claims under the Fourteenth Amendment be dismissed.

The plaintiff addresses the grade change incident as his next objection. He bases his claim to be free in his assignment of grades on the First Amendment guarantee of academic freedom. He asserts that the defendants' actions were unjustified, arbitrary, unreasonable and in no way a legitimate exercise of their authority to supervise the plaintiff's assignment of grades. The plaintiff's rationale which he alleges supports his claim to a First Amendment right of academic freedom in this regard is flawed.

The Court finds that the Magistrate was correct in his analysis of the issues in this action. The Court agrees with the Magistrate that the First Amendment right to academic freedom does not include the right to be free from or override administrative authority. An instructor is subject to supervision and control by his supervisor. There is no dispute about the fact that a professor does enjoy certain constitutionally protected First Amendment rights denominated as "academic freedom." It is well established that a teacher does not surrender constitutionally protected rights of freedom of expression and association as a condition of public employment. However, this Court does note that not all of a professor's academic activity constitutes protected First Amendment rights.

The Magistrate was correct when he stated "[a] nontenured teacher, such as the plaintiff, may be dismissed or denied tenure for any reason, or no reason at all, and has no recourse unless such dismissal or denial abridges the teacher's exercise of a constitutionally protected right." For a First Amendment claim to exist, the plaintiff must first establish that his "speech" is constitutionally protected expression.

The concept of "academic freedom" is recognized as protected First Amendment speech. The roots of academic freedom based on First Amendment rights have their origins in the protection against the infringement of a teacher's freedom concerning classroom content and the method of teaching that content. These two components of classroom content and method form the substantive analysis of academic freedom rights. To determine if the speech is protected classroom content or teaching method "a balance between the interests of the teacher, as a citizen, in commenting upon matters of public concern and the interest of the State, as an employer, in promoting the efficiency of the public services it performs through its employees" must be established. The refusal of the plaintiff to change the grade of a student does not constitute a "teaching method" which is a constitutionally protected right. Therefore, the Court finds in this action that a refusal to change a grade does not rise to the level of a constitutionally protected First Amendment right. Since the plaintiff had no First Amendment right, the issue of whether or not a discharge might be [predicated] on the exercise of a First Amendment right does not need to be addressed.

The Court finds the plaintiff's First Amendment claim to be without merit and adopts and approves the Magistrate's findings and recommendation.

The plaintiff's third objection to the Report is predicated on the Magistrate's conclusion that the "defendants' actions on October 4, 1985, did not violate the plaintiff's First Amendment rights" and that the "[p]laintiff was not protected by the First Amendment from monitoring and inquiry into his competence as a teacher." (Report at pp. 17, 19.) The plaintiff contends that the classroom incident of October 4, 1985, was not an attempt by the defendants to observe, review or evaluate the plaintiff's competence as a teacher and was not a legitimate exercise of the defendants' supervisory functions. The plaintiff alleges that the defendants' actions violated the plaintiff's First Amendment right to academic freedom.

The requisite test in the classroom situation for a violation of the plaintiff's First Amendment rights is whether the defendants' actions "cast a pall of orthodoxy over the classroom." The Court agrees with the Magistrate's conclusion that the defendants' actions on October 4, 1985, did not violate the plaintiff's First Amendment rights.

*   *   *

This Court does note that the behavior of the defendants, Isibor and Samuchin, was unprofessional and offensive. However, this one incident of unprofessional and offensive behavior is not a First Amendment constitutional violation. It may rise to the level of a tort of defamation but defamation is not cognizable under § 1983.

The Court finds the plaintiff's First Amendment claims to be without merit and adopts and approves the Magistrate's findings and recommendation.

The Court concludes that all of the plaintiff's objections are without merit. The Court therefore adopts and approves the Report in its entirety. The defendants' motions for summary judgment are granted. The plaintiff's claims under 42 U.S.C. § 1983 are dismissed with prejudice. The plaintiff's pendent state law claims are dismissed without prejudice.

An appropriate order will be entered.

Two important cases concerning grading, among other issues, are included in chapter 4, "Students and the Law"—*Horowitz* and *Ewing*. Both arose over students' classroom performance, and the decisions have defined the contours of student due process in academic matters. As is evident in the cases addressing how a subject may be taught, these disputes arise in a variety of guises, including faculty hiring, dismissal, evaluation, professional misconduct, and grading practices. Two recent cases promise to elaborate the extent to which a professor conducts class: *McConnell* and *Keen*.

In *McConnell v. Howard*, 818 F.2d 58 (D.C. Cir. 1987) a tenured professor at Howard University was dismissed after he refused to continue teaching a class in which a student had called him a racist; McConnell argued that the incident compromised his "moral authority" to teach. This case, which McConnell lost in his second trial, appears in chapter 3. In *Keen v. Penson*, a professor was demoted one rank after refusing to change a student's F grade. Professor Keen had insisted three times that a student in his class apologize for questioning course requirements; the student apologized three times in writing. An investigation cleared the student, and the chancellor ordered Keen to change the grade to a C. Civ. Action 87–C–1092 (E.D. Wisc. 20 August 1987).

In *Lewis v. Chicago State College*, a court held: "A professor's value depends upon his creativity, his rapport with students and colleagues, his teaching ability, and numerous other intangible qualities which cannot be measured by objective standards." *Lewis v. Chicago State College*, 299 F. Supp. 1357, 1359 (N.D. Ill. 1969). See also *Peters v. Middlebury College*, 409 F. Supp. 857 (D. Vt. 1976); *Lovelace v. Southwestern Massachusetts University*, 793 F.2d 419 (1st Cir. 1986); *Levi v. University of Texas at San Antonio*, 840 F.2d 277 (5th Cir. 1988). Absent extraordinary circumstances, such as those posed by the *Keen* case, faculty will be held to have near-total discretion in awarding grades and conducting classes.

The Right to Hear

The fourth dimension of Justice Frankfurter's "essential freedoms," the freedom to determine who may be admitted to study, is treated both in the section on institutional academic freedom, as well as in chapter 4, "Students and the Law." Nonetheless, while the right-to-hear pervades much of the higher education body of law, it warrants discrete treatment as well, in the context of academic freedom. Often, the variety of student activities that regularly occur on campus supplements formal coursework, such as a professional conference, a speaker lecturing on an important topic, or a film shown to the public in conjunction with a class. Professors regularly assign these activities to students, or urge them upon their classes.

Brooks v. Auburn University
412 F.2d 1171 (5th Cir. 1969)

BELL, Circuit Judge:

This appeal involves a decree of the district court restraining the president of Auburn University, Dr. Harry M. Philpott, from barring the scheduled appearance and speech on the Auburn campus of the Reverend William Sloan Coffin.

* * *

The record demonstrates that Auburn had no rules or regulations governing speaker eligibility. The practice was for the Public Affairs Seminar Board, an officially chartered student-faculty board, to pass on requests from student groups to invite speakers. Funds were allocated to the Board by the university from student fees for use in obtaining speakers. The Human Affairs Forum wrote the Board under date of November 13, 1968 requesting $650.00 needed for honorarium and expense purposes in bringing Reverend Coffin, Chaplain at Yale University, to Auburn for a speaking engagement on February 7, 1969. The Board, at a formal meeting on November 20, 1968, approved the request. The approval was communicated in writing to the chairman of the Human Affairs Forum by letter dated November 21, 1968.

Dr. Philpott then notified the Public Affairs Seminar Board that the Reverend Coffin would not be allowed to speak on the Auburn University campus because he was a convicted felon and because he might advocate breaking the law. These reasons had not previously been invoked at Auburn to bar a speaker.

* * *

Attributing the highest good faith to Dr. Philpott in his action, it nevertheless is clear under the prior restraint doctrine that the right of the faculty and students to hear a speaker, selected as was the speaker here, cannot be left to the discretion of the university president on a pick and choose basis. As stated, Auburn had no rules or regulations as to who might or might not speak and thus no question of a compliance with or a departure from such rules or regulations is presented. This left the matter as a pure First Amendment question; hence the basis for prior restraint. Such a situation of no rules or regulations may be equated with a licensing system to speak or hear and this has been long prohibited.

It is strenuously urged on behalf of Auburn that the president was authorized in any event to bar a convicted felon or one advocating lawlessness from the campus. This again depends upon the right of the faculty and students to hear. We do not hold that Dr. Philpott could not bar a speaker under any circumstances. Here there was no claim that the Reverend Coffin's appearance would lead to violence or disorder or that the university would be otherwise disrupted. There is no claim that Dr. Philpott could not regulate the time or place of the speech or the manner in which it was to be delivered.

* * *

[Supreme Court] decisions have fashioned the principle that the constitutional guarantees of free speech and free press do not permit a State to forbid or proscribe advocacy of the use of force or of law violation except where such advocacy is directed to inciting or producing imminent lawless action and is likely to incite or produce such action.

There was no claim that the Coffin speech would fall into the category of this exception.

Affirmed.

Brown v. Board of Regents of the University of Nebraska

669 F. Supp. 297 (D. Neb. 1986)

URBOM, District Judge.

"Hail Mary" is a movie depicting the birth of Jesus Christ in a contemporary setting. It was chosen, scheduled and advertised for showing at the Sheldon Film Theater, a state-operated art theater on the University of Nebraska campus. The showing was canceled because of its controversial content, and the issue now is whether the cancellation has denied the plaintiffs a constitutional right to see the film.

I conclude that it has.

* * *

II. FACTUAL BACKGROUND

The Sheldon Film Theater is owned and operated by the University of Nebraska-Lincoln and housed within the Sheldon Memorial Art Gallery. The Gallery is a museum of art, where film as an art form is exhibited for the public by the theater. Films that are not typically shown at commercial theaters in Lincoln, Nebraska, are selected for viewing. The wide variety of films shown include American independent, contemporary foreign, classic American and foreign, experimental, and documentary films. The operating expenses of the theater are paid by admission fees, University funds, and donations. Occasionally, organizations are permitted to rent the theater to show films.

The ultimate authority for selection of works of art rests with the Director of the Sheldon Memorial Art Gallery, George Neubert, but Neubert has largely delegated the responsibility for film selection to Dan Ladely, Director of the Sheldon Film Theater. Typically, Neubert's input into the decision-making is limited to signing film requisition forms, informally and infrequently discussing with Ladely upcoming films and making some suggestions about films to be shown. The one exception to the rule that Ladely chooses the films is that once a year the Friends of the Sheldon Theater, a group of donators, vote on a selected list of approximately fifty films.

Ladely selected "Hail Mary" because it was the most recent film directed by Jean-Luc Godard. At the time, Ladely was only "slightly aware" of the controversy surrounding the film's contemporary picturing of the birth of Christ. Ladely ordered the film "Hail Mary" on approximately December 27, 1985, and included it in the *Winter-Spring, 1986 Film Schedule* for showing on Thursday, May 29, 1986, through Sunday, June 1, 1986. On about January 13 the schedule was delivered to the press, to Friends of Sheldon Film Theater, and to patrons within the theater.

On about January 26, 1986, the *Lincoln Sunday Journal-Star* printed the scheduled dates for the running of the film. On about January 28 Ladely received four phone calls from individuals opposing the presentation of the film. One of them was from Senator Bernice Labedz, a member of the Nebraska legislature, who had received several citizens' expressions of disapproval of the film. Senator Labedz had not seen the film, but had read reviews of it. In her call to Ladely, the senator articulated two reasons for wanting the film not to be shown: (1) it blasphemed the Blessed Virgin Mary and the birth of Christ, accordingly, its content offended the senator's religious precepts and (2) exhibition of the film might result in demonstrations by others who disagreed with the religious content of the film. Senator Labedz testified of her telephone conversation with Ladely:

"[T]he year prior to the time I was talking to him, there was a big controversy on the floor [of the legislature] whether or not the Sheldon Art Gallery should be closed, and I said that I didn't want to see them have that type of trouble; that there would be some very difficult times on the floor and that I myself would introduce a resolution then—Not waiting for the budget, I was going to introduce a resolution within the next week or so objecting to the film, and hoping that I would get the support of the senators on the floor, at least 25 of them, showing our objections to the film. And I said—But I did not want to call President Roskens, whom I consider a very personal friend of mine, or Chancellor Massengale, whom I consider a friend."

In response to the question of whether she had suggested in any way that the University budget might be affected by showing the film, Senator Labedz replied:

"No, I did not. I said that there was a—unless he took it for granted that the resolution would do that. He did not—I did not tell him what I would introduce in the resolution, I just said I would introduce a resolution objecting to the film being shown at the University."

On January 29 Ladely responded in writing to the senator's concerns. He wrote that the film was not intended to be "blasphemous, inflammatory or prejudiced against the Catholic Church and its followers" and included several reviews of the film. Ladely also corresponded with Senator Don Wesely in the hope that Wesely could dissuade Labedz from further attempts to ban the film. Ladely also informed Neubert of Senator Labedz's phone call and of Ladely's subsequent written response. Neubert told Ladely to "handle" the "touchy" situation. However, later that day Neubert informed Ladely that the chancellor's office had expressed concern regarding Ladely's letters to Senators Labedz and Wesely and Ladely was directed to obtain Neubert's approval before officially communicating with any senator in the future. In addition, Neubert ordered Ladely to cancel the film because it was "offensive to a segment of society and did not merit the efforts it would take to defend it." In the thirteen years in which Ladely has been employed by the University, his decision to present a film had never before been overruled.

*   *   *

III. FIRST AMENDMENT RIGHT TO RECEIVE INFORMATION AND IDEAS

When the Supreme Court of the United States gives voice to an issue, I am obliged to be guided by its path as precisely as I can determine its direction. *Board of Education, Island Trees Union Free School District No. 26 v. Pico* provided an occasion for guidance, but the justices pointed in all directions. No less than seven separate written opinions addressed the issue of whether the members of a board of education could constitutionally remove from a high school and junior high school library books the board had characterized as "Anti-American, Anti-Christian, Anti-Sem[i]tic, and just plain filthy." The Court of Appeals had remanded the case for a trial on the merits and the Supreme Court affirmed. The plurality opinion found the First Amendment rights of the students infringed by the removal of books from the library shelves, reasoning that the First Amendment not only fosters individual self-expression but ensures public access to the "spectrum of available knowledge." Consequently, it said, an inherent corollary of the rights of free speech and press is the right to receive information and ideas, and the right to receive ideas necessarily inures from the sender's constitutional right to disseminate ideas. Moreover, it declared that the right to receive ideas is fundamental to "the *recipient*'s meaningful exercise of his own rights of speech, press, and political freedom."

*   *   *

At trial, Neubert gave three reasons for cancelling the film: (1) controversy surrounding the film, (2) the likelihood of a demonstration by those opposing the film, and (3) the political climate. I conclude that the pivotal factor was a combination of (1) and (3): controversy within the political climate. The Sheldon Film Theater has exhibited many controversial films; there was nothing unique about having a controversy. It was not the fact of controversy that caused the cancellation of "Hail Mary." It was that the prospect of a religious battle in the uneasy political setting of the time—already pencilled in by prior legislative cuts and underlined by an individual senator's warnings—threatened the peace and stability of the Sheldon Gallery. Even if the cause had been only the fact of controversy, however, cancellation would not have been justified, because action taken by an arm of the state merely to avoid controversy from the expression of ideas is an insufficient basis for interfering with the right to receive information. In the decision to cancel the film, Neubert's foremost concern was not that the Gallery and its collections would be damaged by demonstrators. That consideration was not highlighted in Neubert's testimony, and he did not even mention it in his letter to the Board of Trustees of the Nebraska Art Association outlining the reasons for the film's cancellation. Furthermore, in *Tinker*, the Supreme Court rejected the contention that the action of school authorities was reasonable because it was premised upon the fear of a disturbance.

*   *   *

When the senator demanded the banning of the film, Neubert felt compelled to withdraw from the chilly political winds. The legislature had previously reduced state funding and Neubert, not unreasonably, concluded that further budget cuts might be forthcoming were he to disregard the legislator's wishes. The constitution interjects safeguards against just this type of governmental influence. The effect of such unauthorized use of political power is obvious and the precedent is untenable.

> "What is at stake is the right to receive information and to be exposed to controversial ideas—a fundamental First Amendment right. If [the film] can be banned by those opposed to [the] ideological theme, then a precedent is set for the removal of any such work."

*   *   *

Here, the facts show only slight involvement of the government as an educator on a college campus—slight because the theater showings are for the public at large and are no part of the academic program of the university—and direct intrusion by the government as a sovereign. Senator Labedz was not merely speaking out as a private citizen; she purposely used her position as a legislator who had a hand on the financial throat of the Sheldon Gallery to prevent the showing of the film. This case is a stronger case for the plaintiffs than the *Pico* case was for its plaintiffs.

IV. SHELDON FILM THEATER AS A PUBLIC FORUM

The First Amendment not only safeguards free speech and press, but public places for purposes of expressive activity. A constitutional right of access to a public forum is guaranteed to all. However, this concept of equal access does not attach to government property which is not a public forum.

* * *

The reasons stated in *Perry* are equally applicable to this case. The Sheldon Film Theater has not consented to unrestricted access by the general public to its auditorium and facilities. Permitting the Friends of the Sheldon Film Theater, once a year, to choose from a selected list of films and organizations to infrequently rent the theater, does not evidence relinquishment of editorial control over the selection of the films presented. Consequently, the theater may not be characterized as a public forum.

Since the Sheldon Film Theater fits within the third category of public forums, reasonable limitations may be placed on expression. However, the Supreme Court clearly indicated that the restrictions may not suppress expression. This court has previously determined that the Sheldon Film Theater unconstitutionally canceled "Hail Mary" because of an unnerving campaign to suppress its content because it was at odds with a public official's religious views.

* * *

V. CONCLUSION

The decision to cancel the film "Hail Mary" was not independent of state involvement; rather, were it not for the intervention of a state legislator, the film would have been presented as scheduled. University students were denied the right to receive the controversial ideas expressed in the film "Hail Mary" because its content was officially characterized as offensive. Since the expression was unconstitutionally suppressed, the film "Hail Mary" must be reinstated in the Sheldon Film Theater schedule.

* * *

The relief will take the form of a declaration that the action of George Neubert in cancelling the film was a denial of the plaintiffs' right under the First Amendment of the Constitution of the United States to receive information and ideas, declaring null and void that decision, enjoining the defendant and those participating with him from preventing the making, showing, and presentation of the film by the Sheldon Film Theater, and awarding the plaintiffs' attorney's fees and expenses.

VII. ADDENDUM

I add two observations by way of addendum. Neither makes any difference to my decision.

First, I have viewed "Hail Mary." It is what critics have called it. From time to time its parts are dull, beautiful, incomprehensible, brave, shallow, penetrating, vulgar, demeaning and, no doubt, blasphemous for some and inspirational for others.

Second, a petition signed by many people has come to my office. It is not in evidence and I have no reason to think that any of the attorneys or parties know of it. I have made a point of not counting the names or seeing whether I know any of them. Lawsuits are not matters for resolution by petition. It is the Constitution that must govern the disposition of this case and no vote of the people can affect a right guaranteed by it, unless it is one amending the Constitution itself.

Academic Freedom in Research and Publications

As with classroom teaching, academic freedom's application to research and publication has dimensions including what may be studied, how it can be studied, and who may undertake research. Similarly, the issues can travel together or travel under different guises: Chapter 3, "The Law and Faculty," contains a number of instances where there are mixed tenure/academic freedom issues, while other cases in the book detail a number of significant restrictions upon research.

In "God, Galileo and Government: Toward Constitutional Protection for Scientific Inquiry," *Washington Law Review*, 53 (1978), 349–404, Delgado and Millen suggest that the right to undertake research is fundamental, but that state interests may be superior, if the restrictions are narrowly tailored. They cite research that may provoke psychological injuries, stigmatize, erode the ideals of equality, inhibit reproductive freedom, risk violence, or cause other harms. Cases included in this section include instances where scholars have succeeded in protecting their research, and instances where they have not prevailed. As is often the case, important interests collide.

U.S. v. Doe
460 F.2d 328 (1972)

COFFIN, Circuit Judge.

This is an appeal by Samuel Popkin from an order of the district court holding him in civil contempt for refusing to answer certain questions propounded to him by a federal grand jury in Massachusetts. An assistant professor of government at Harvard University, Popkin has written numerous articles on the war in Indochina. He contends first that he should not be forced to respond without a demonstration by the government of the relevance of both the general inquiry and the specific questions. He urges also that he should be excused from answering those questions by virtue of a scholar's First Amendment privilege not to divulge his sources of information insofar as those sources are confidential and supply him with information relating to his field.

* * *

The government argues that the scholar's privilege is a creature not to be found in the province of jurisprudence; that the closest analogue, a reporter's privilege, recognized by the Ninth Circuit in Caldwell v. United States, has been otherwise uniformly rejected by the courts; and that even if *Caldwell* was correctly decided, appellant falls outside its compass, his relationship with his sources not being so intimate as in *Caldwell*, nor covered by the special canopy of free press, and the grand jury being engaged in a specific rather than a general investigation. Appellant discounts the lack of precedent as stemming from the past absence of efforts to invade a scholar's privilege. He claims to serve a public interest fully as vital as that served by a reporter, which interest would be as grievously imperilled by a forced disclosure of his sources, absent a showing of compelling need by the government.

* * *

For perspective, it is important to recognize what has not been and could not successfully be argued here. Appellant could not, for example, cite his discomfort in being asked to testify about others. Although the discomfort is real, it is shared by all grand jury witnesses. Indeed, a witness called before a grand jury investigating

Although both parties have cast their arguments in these broad terms, the substantiated rationale of appellant and the questions put by the grand jury do not, in our opinion, quite meet head on. The overwhelming majority of appellant's affidavits from other scholars lay stress on the importance of a two-way communication between participants in decision making (or those affected) and scholars. The asserted importance of non-disclosure of a network of sources lies in the necessity for a continued flow of inside information to the sphere of scholarly reporting, assessment, and criticism, a flow made particularly important by the selective and self-serving release of information by other, particularly higher, officials. In short, the thrust of the asserted privilege bears on the right of the scholar not to disclose the identities of his "contacts and sources," those officials and non-governmental actors within the purview of his specialty whose actions, knowledge, and views give him the primary data for his work. The reason for the claimed privilege lies not in the importance of protecting the officials and other sources *per se* but in the importance of preserving the flow of their communications via scholars to the public domain.

This underlying rationale falls short of immunizing a scholar from testifying about conversations with those who are not his sources. Of course a scholar may also be an official or such a participant in an activity that he is also a sensitive source. But to the extent that a scholar qua scholar is asked about statements made to him by other scholars we do not conceive of him as in any different position from that of a doctor asked about his conversations with other doctors, or a lawyer about his talks with other lawyers. Nor is there reason to believe that scholars, as opposed to public officials, will lose their jobs and thus their usefulness as sources if the contents of their conversations are revealed to a grand jury. And while we acknowledge that scholars customarily discuss their work with colleagues and in doing so may perhaps violate confidences, a privilege which would give comprehensive protection to such collateral discussions would make scholars a uniquely privileged class in the broadest sense.

We therefore conclude that the two questions seeking the names of persons interviewed who gave him knowledge of participants in the Pentagon Papers study should be answered, at least to the extent that the persons were not government officials or other participant-sources.

* * *

What this analysis does not dispose of is the remaining group of questions seeking appellant's opinion concerning who might have possessed the Pentagon Papers generally or in Massachusetts and the persons with whom he talked who gave him a basis of that opinion. Appellant had candidly testified that, while he had no knowledge of possession in Massachusetts, he had formed opinions over the years as to persons he thought had had access to the Papers. This kind of inquiry, at least in the present posture of this case, does not appeal to the author of this opinion. Appellant in his brief has asserted that he knows of no case where a witness has been held in contempt for refusing to give an opinion. Nor do I. In the long run, the quest for opinions would not be a useful investigative tool. If appellant were forced to answer, scholar-sleuths would in the future think long and hard before admitting to an opinion, and grand juries would be without workable means for forcing them to do so.

* * *

The generality of the opinion questions here, the apparent basis for the opinion being pursued, and the idea of using one scholar to speculate about the sources of others' work, without any showing of strong need therefor, are repugnant to me. In my view, even apart from constitutional claims, we should exercise our supervisory power to state that in this circuit scholars ought not to go to prison for refusing to give their opinions or beliefs based on casual and retrospective reflections on similarities of content. But while my brothers agree that the opinion questions were improper, their objection is a narrower formal one. Accordingly, at present we simply disapprove the questions as asked.

* * *

ALDRICH, Chief Judge (concurring).

Perhaps I am old-fashioned, but I was taught that a scholarly study was valuable to the extent that it disclosed its sources. How does Popkin know that he, and hence his public, is not being hornswoggled by a "source"? Is there great public worth in a book, the reference table of which consists of a bare curriculum vitae of the author?

The answer may be yes, and may be no. I am tempted to wonder, though I hope uncharacteristically, if too much is not being asked of the First Amendment. Hearst could consider Walter Winchell so valuable to it that it was willing to agree that, in case of a libel suit, it would pick up the tab and not require him to divulge his source. Is the public so interested in research that the government finds itself with a similar, although diminished in scope, contract of immunity from disclosure with every Ph.D.? If so, we believe it should be in very narrow limits. Happily this case does not call for them to be defined.

Dow Chemical Co. v. Allen

672 F.2d 1262 (7th Cir. 1982)

FAIRCHILD, Senior Circuit Judge.

At issue in this case is whether a private corporation, Dow Chemical Company, threatened with possible government cancellation of certain herbicides it manufactures, may compel through administrative subpoenas University of Wisconsin researchers to disclose all of the notes, reports, working papers, and raw data relating to on-going, incomplete animal toxicity studies so that it may evaluate that information with a view toward possible use at the cancellation hearings. The administrative law judge, at the request of Dow and over the objection of the Office of General Counsel of the Environmental Protection Agency, issued such subpoenas, but the district court refused to enforce them. We affirm the judgment of the district court and hold that the present facts do not warrant forced disclosure of the university research information.

I. Background

This case arises out of four research studies at the University of Wisconsin involving the dietary ingestion by rhesus monkeys of a chemical compound, 2,3,7,8—tetrachlorodibenzo-p-dioxin (TCDD).

* * *

2. Academic Freedom

A point not discussed by the district court, but presented by the State of Wisconsin as *amicus* on appeal, is that the instant dispute touches directly upon interests of academic freedom. Essentially, the State argues that scholarly research is an activity which lies at the heart of higher education, that it comes within the First Amendment's protection of academic freedom, and therefore judicially authorized intrusion into that sphere of university life should be permitted only for compelling reasons, which do not exist here. In response, Dow asserts simply that "[t]he First Amendment interests at stake in this case are no greater than those involved in the ordinary case of enforcement of a subpoena *duces tecum*." We think this issue sufficiently important to merit our discussion.

"Academic freedom, though not a specifically enumerated constitutional right, long has been viewed as a special concern of the First Amendment."

* * *

The precise contours of the concept of academic freedom are difficult to define. One First Amendment scholar has written "[t]he heart of the system consists in the right of the individual faculty member to teach, carry on research, and publish without interference from the government, the community, the university administration, or his fellow faculty members." We think it clear that whatever constitutional protection is afforded by the First Amendment extends as readily to the scholar in the laboratory as to the teacher in the classroom.

Of course academic freedom, like other constitutional rights, is not absolute, and must on occasion be balanced against important competing interests.

* * *

Case law considering the standard to be applied where the issue is academic freedom of the university to be free of governmental interference, as opposed to academic freedom of the individual teacher to be free of restraints from the university administration, is surprisingly sparse. But what precedent there is at the Supreme Court level suggests that to prevail over academic freedom the interests of government must be strong and the extent of intrusion carefully limited.

* * *

In the present case, the administrative subpoenas by their terms would compel the researchers to turn over to Dow virtually every scrap of paper and every mechanical or electronic recording made during the extended period that those studies have been in progress at the university. The ALJ's decision would have further obliged the researchers to continually update Dow on "additional useful data" which became available during the course of the proceedings. These requirements threaten substantial intrusion into the enterprise of university research, and there are several reasons to think they are capable of chilling the exercise of academic freedom. To begin with, the burden of compliance certainly would not be insubstantial. More important, enforcement of the subpoenas would leave the researchers with the knowledge throughout continuation of their studies that the fruits of their labors had been appropriated by and were being scrutinized by a not-unbiased third party whose interests were arguably antithetical to theirs. It is not difficult to imagine that that realization might well be both unnerving and discouraging. Indeed, it is probably fair to say that the character and extent of intervention would be such that, regardless of its purpose, it would "inevitably tend to check the ardor and fearlessness of scholars, qualities at once so fragile and so indispensable for fruitful academic labor." In addition, the researchers could reasonably fear that additional demands for disclosure would be made in the future. If a private corporation can subpoena the entire work product of months of study, what is to say further down the line the company will not seek other subpoenas to determine how the research is coming along? To these factors must be added the knowledge of the researchers that even inadvertent disclosure of the subpoenaed data could jeopardize both the studies and their careers. Clearly, enforcement of the subpoenas carries the potential for chilling the exercise of First Amendment rights.

We do not suggest that facts could not arise sufficient to overcome respondents' academic freedom interests in the . . . studies. Nor do we say that a waiver of the protection afforded by the First Amendment is impossible. If, for example, Dr. Allen, Mr. Van Miller, or other researchers were likely to testify about the . . . studies at the cancellation hearing, there might well be justification for granting at least partial or conditional enforcement of the subpoenas. Of course, we need not decide that question now. For present purposes, our point is simply that respondents' interest in academic freedom may properly figure into the legal calculation of whether forced disclosure would be reasonable. . . . Based on the facts before us which, among other things, show that potentially probative evidence will not be available from the studies for months or years to come, that Dow will not be confronted by information from the studies at the cancellation hearing, and that present 25 ppt and 5 ppt study data cannot be used to test the validity of the 500 ppt study, we conclude there is little to justify an intrusion into university life which would risk substantially chilling the exercise of academic freedom. The district court could correctly have taken this factor into consideration in deciding that enforcement of the subpoenas would be unreasonable. We regard it as additional reason for affirming the judgment appealed from.

Wright v. Jeep Corp.
547 F. Supp. 871 (1982)

JOINER, District Judge.

MEMORANDUM OPINION AND ORDER

This case deals for the first time with the conflict between the need for evidence in the administration of justice and the desire of a researcher not connected with the litigants to avoid being imposed upon at the whim of litigants. It deals with a person who has become a public figure as a result of a research project yet wants to remain essentially anonymous so far as the administration of justice is concerned. Finally, it deals with an effort by this court to provide information essential to the fair determination of litigation and to protect researchers who have that information and who might otherwise be burdened.

All of this comes before the court on appeal from the United States Magistrate's order to quash a subpoena duces tecum to a non-party expert.

FACTS

Dr. Richard Snyder, the non-party respondent, is a professor and research scientist at the Highway Safety Institute of the University of Michigan. He is the principal author of the 1980, 152 page report, "On-Road Crash Experience of Utility Vehicles," published by the Institute. The report was the result of a research project and study by the Highway Safety Institute for the Insurance Institute for Highway Safety. The study concludes that utility vehicles, particularly the Jeep CJ-5, experience a disproportionately high roll over rate in accidents.

Jeep Corporation, a defendant in the above personal injury action, seeks to subpoena

> [a]ny and all research data, memoranda, drafts, correspondence, lab notes, reports, calculations, moving pictures, photographs, slides, statements and the like pertaining to the on-road crash experience of utility vehicles study by the Highway Safety Research Institute of the University of Michigan for the Insurance Institute for Highway Safety in which [Prof. Snyder] participated.

It is Jeep's position that the study is likely to be used by the plaintiff in the action and that the material requested in the subpoena is necessary to judge the validity of the conclusions reported and for the defense in that action.

* * *

Professor Snyder's claim for exemption asserts a right to refuse to give or produce evidence under the first amendment for the reason that he is a researcher and a writer and claims that a denial of this right would have a chilling effect on researchers and writers. The court agrees that the subpoena provides sufficient government action to raise the constitutional question in this case. However, the court does not believe that compelling Professor Snyder to testify violates any first amendment rights. The protection of the first amendment is designed to afford the right to write and to speak. It does not give a right to withdraw material written and published from public scrutiny, nor does it give a right to refuse to disclose facts discovered as a result of observations that are relevant in making a judgment as to the correctness of the researcher's published conclusions. The respondent argues that compelling him to produce his records and research data will chill other writers and researchers. The possibility of being subpoenaed to testify exists for everyone. At any time a person can see something or hear something that will cause him or her to be subpoenaed to testify. Every person, within limits, is subject to a subpoena to tell about or produce information about what he or she saw or heard. In many respects Professor Snyder is no different than any other witness who may be called upon to give evidence.

* * *

The limited protection given reporters and writers from providing testimony under the first amendment is given to preserve the flow of information from sources to these persons. This is clearly different from the situation before the court. When confidential sources are involved, the courts are concerned about not jeopardizing the flow of information from a third person. The requirement of disclosure of the identity of that third person may be sufficiently burdensome that he, or she, or others might choose not to provide information to a reporter. In the present case the court's concern is in balancing the minimal chance that compelling Dr. Snyder to testify or produce his underlying data would cause him to abandon research and writing as against the needs of the justice system to use basic research information, the results of which the researcher has placed in the public domain. As discussed above, the conclusion is clear that the exemption claimed is not justified. The court is not persuaded that the possibility of being subpoenaed will sufficiently chill writers and researchers to warrant a special exemption from the duty to provide evidence.

Not all subpoena cases have gone against researchers. In 1987, a New York Supreme Court refused to order a researcher from the Mt. Sinai Medical School to reveal data on tobacco research, in a case substantially similar to Professor Snyder's in *Jeep Corp*. Like Snyder, this researcher was not a party to the pending litigation or a witness or consultant. New York State recognizes a certain "expert privilege," and the court recognized the academic freedom issue, after balancing the "unreasonable burden that production of the data would have placed upon the researchers." *In the Matter of the Application of R. J. Reynolds Co.*, Sup. Ct. N.Y. County, 10 July 1987.

Moreover, not all these right-to-research cases arise in a court or subpoena context. In 1986, Rev. Terrance A. Sweeney resigned from the Jesuit order rather than disclose his research data to his religious superiors. For a research project on the Catholic hierarchy's attitudes toward celibacy and women priests, Sweeney had surveyed all U.S. bishops. When the Jesuits insisted he turn over his questionnaire's data—to which 145 of the 312 bishops had responded—he refused to comply. "Jesuit Priest Resigns Over a Questionnaire," *New York Times*, 24 August 1986, p. 14.

As is seen in many cases, both the litigants may be professors in the same institution, and the university sides with the party whose interests are consistent with the institutional interest at stake. In a case it found to be frivolous litigation, a court reviewed a professor's claim to have been denied his property interest in the listing of his name as senior author in a co-authored work: "If war is the extension of diplomacy by other means, this suit—like other litigation a form of Warfare—is the extension of academic politics by other means." *Weinstein v. University of Illinois*, 811 F.2d 1091 (7th Cir. 1987). In considering Weinstein's academic freedom claim, Judge Easterbrook referred to academic freedom as "that equivocal term," and dismissed the claim: "[The plaintiff] makes a first amendment argument in passing, but he was not fired on account of the political slant of his views, he was fired for not having any views, at least none recently in print."

How Research Can Be Conducted

This area of the law, which includes the quintessential dimensions of academic freedom, is at the intersection of academic research autonomy and the public interests in play: who governs research? In a provocative book on the topic, *Governing Science and Technology in a Democracy* (Knoxville: University of Tennessee Press, 1986), political scientist Malcolm Goggin suggests a useful framework for asking who should govern:

> Ours is a society of plural interests, each with competing claims and each claim with a certain degree of validity and legitimacy. . . .
>
> This leads to the question of who should govern science and technology. Who has a legitimate case for control over the direction and funding of research and development, and what arguments are used to justify and legitimize a claim? As a framework for answering this question, we introduce the notion of a science

and technology policy system, consisting of congressional committees and sub-committees, industry, and the university as *patrons*; the scientists and technologists as *providers*; and expert and non-expert citizen *consumers* as the people who benefit from, and are exposed to the risks and harms of, basic and applied research and technological development and deployment. Each party has a claim to be represented at the bargaining table where policies for science and technology are formulated and adopted. And the bargaining takes place in the context of a decision environment that includes elements of the national political economy, such as the federal technoscience agencies, interest groups, power wielders, labor unions, public opinion, the media, and many more. (pp. 44–45)

Goggin's "policy system," of course, includes legal mechanisms of legislation, regulation, and litigation. These competing interests, however, do not always align as "research" versus "the public," as each dimension has its inherent tensions and refractions. While regulation of research has increased at the federal, state, and local levels, litigation has been surprisingly rare in this area, at least rare on the narrow issue of how research may be conducted.

Two exceptions have been the recent flurry of cases in which potentially toxic or hazardous research has been challenged, and community ordinances in college towns to restrict genetics research and testing of chemical warfare agents; the most prominent examples have been Jeremy Rifkin's attempts to prevent atmospheric testing of genetically engineered microorganisms, and the Cambridge, Massachusetts, city actions on recombinant DNA in 1976 and chemical-engineering agents in 1984. (Sheldon Krimsky's chapter in the Goggin book, "Local Control of Research Involving Chemical Warfare Agents" is a case study of this issue.) Other instances incorporating these issues of how research can be conducted are included in sections on faculty misconduct, research regulation, and student research and due process.

California Agrarian Action Project v. Regents of the University of California

Superior Court, Alameda County, Unpublished Opinion, Conclusions and Judgment (18 November 1987), No. 516427–5

On January 17, 1979, Plaintiffs filed their Complaint for Injunctive and Declaratory Relief. Ultimately, a Second Amended Complaint for Injunctive and Declaratory Relief was filed and served on September 4, 1979, and has served as the operative pleading upon which this matter has proceeded. The following conclusions of fact and law, and orders of judgment refer to the causes of action as described in the Second Amended Complaint.

I. FIRST CAUSE OF ACTION ("GIFT OF PUBLIC FUNDS," CAL. CONST., ART. XVI, § 6):

On April 2, 1987, Plaintiffs requested dismissal with prejudice of the First Cause of Action pursuant to Code Civ. Proc. § 581(e). Dismissal was entered on April 8, 1987. Accordingly, this Cause is no longer before the Court.

II. SECOND CAUSE OF ACTION ("BREACH OF PUBLIC TRUST," CAL. CONST. ART. IX, § 9):

* * *

After oral argument and consideration of the pleadings and all documents filed relating to this motion, the Court entered its MEMORANDUM OF DECISION AND ORDER on March 20, 1986, granting Defendants' motion and now enters the following conclusions of law pursuant thereto:

1. Under article IX, § 9 of the California Constitution, the University of California is a public trust, established by the People of California, and administered by defendant Regents.

2. The Regents of the University of California is a corporation established pursuant to Article IX, section 9, of the California Constitution which administers the University of California.

3. Defendant Regents' responsibilities include, among other matters, the allocation, disposition and management of appropriations enacted by the state Legislature and approved by the Governor and of the resources acquired and/or developed by means of these funds.

4. The concept of a "public trust" has insufficient legal or other history to enable the Court to assign any enforceable meaning to the phrase. Accordingly, the Court finds that the "public trust" section of article IX, § 9, does not create a private right of action upon which plaintiffs may challenge defendants' conduct.

III. THIRD CAUSE OF ACTION ("HATCH ACT," 7 U.S.C. § 361a-i):

Defendants' motions for judgment on the pleadings, summary judgment, and/or summary adjudication on the Third Cause of Action were heard in Department 20 on October 10, and October 26, 1984.

At further proceedings on November 9, 1984, this Court informed counsel of its intent to deny defendants' motions for judgment on the pleadings and summary judgment, but to grant certain of defendants' motions for summary adjudication. (The Court formally issued these rulings on March 20, 1986.)

At further proceedings on January 15, 1985, the Court granted Plaintiffs' request to re-open discovery regarding the Third Cause of Action. Thereafter, and prior to commencement of trial of this cause, defendants offered certain factual stipulations, in which Defendant-Intervenor has joined. Plaintiffs' Exhibits P-5019 and P-5020 thus comprise the evidentiary record upon which judgment is awarded in the Third Cause of Action.

The Court's conclusions of law in this cause are reached upon consideration of the oral arguments and pleadings filed (as well as incorporated by reference or judicially noticed) relating to defendants' motions for judgment on the pleadings, summary judgment and/or summary adjudication.

A. *Conclusions of Fact:*

1. The Regents of the University of California is a corporation established pursuant to Article IX, section 9, of the California Constitution which administers the University of California.

2. The Regents operate, as part of the University, the California Agricultural Experiment Station which has principal branches at the University's Berkeley, Riverside and Davis campuses, and operates Field stations in other parts of the State.

3. The California Agricultural Experiment Station is administered through the Office of the University's Vice-President-Agriculture and Natural Resources.

4. The California Agricultural Experiment Station is the "State agricultural experiment station" for the State of California within the meaning of the Hatch Act of 1887 as amended, and receives federal appropriations annually pursuant to the Act.

5. Hatch Act appropriations are applied to the majority of research projects undertaken by the California Agricultural Experiment Station and amount to approximately three percent of the total budget of the Station.

6. In evaluating and selecting which research projects receive funds from the Hatch Act, the University has no process designed to ensure consideration of each legislatively expressed interest, with primary consideration given to the small family farmer.

B. *Conclusions of Law:*

1. Plaintiffs have a right of action to enforce the Hatch Act, as amended, in that:

   a. The Superior Court is a court of original jurisdiction with full power to hear and determine actions for injunctive and declaratory relief; and,

   b. A taxpayer has a right of action to enforce the federal Hatch Act in California courts pursuant to California Code of Civil Procedure section 526a; and,

   c. Plaintiffs have a right of action under 42 U.S.C. section 1983 in that they are within the class of intended beneficiaries of the Hatch Act, as amended, which creates enforceable rights; and,

   d. There is no need to determine whether a right of action is expressed in, or implied by, the Hatch Act, as amended, in that plaintiffs have a right to enforce the Act under state law as well as an express right of action to enforce the Act under 42 U.S.C. section 1983.

2. The statutory terms and legislative history of the Hatch Act, as amended, as interpreted in light of the Agricultural Research, Extension, and Teaching Policy Act of 1977, as amended, including the Congressional directive embodied in 7 U.S.C. section 2266(a), and the cognate terms and legislative history of Morrill Act of 1862 and the Smith-Lever Act of 1914, require that the defendant, when approving of, and allocating Hatch Act funds to its Hatch-funded projects, consider the extent to which the interests of all of the Congressionally intended beneficiaries will be favorably or unfavorably served by its agricultural research projects, and require that in that process, primary consideration shall be given to the interests of the small family farmer.

3. The express Congressional purposes of promoting a sound and prosperous agriculture and rural life, and the improvement of rural life, are intended to be furthered by research projects that have those direct objectives, and indirectly, by such projects that are intended to preserve and foster the small family farm system of agricultural production.

4. The express Congressional purpose that agricultural research projects contribute to maximizing the welfare of the consumer is intended to be furthered by research projects that are directed to that objective, as well as such projects that have the objectives of promoting a sound and prosperous agriculture and rural life and that contribute to the maintenance of maximum employment.

5. In order to implement the Act in accordance with such Congressionally intended purposes, defendant must establish and supervise an administrative process designed

to insure that the foregoing considerations take place thus seeking to assure that defendants' agricultural research program is operating in furtherance of the Congressionally intended purposes.

6. Because the expressed Congressional purposes, at least in part, may be competing or conflicting, all such interests need not be furthered by each such research project; a project may properly serve the interests of one or more intended beneficiary groups even at the arguable expense of other such groups.

7. The conclusions of law set forth in paragraphs two through seven are also applicable to such state funds as are provided to comply with the terms of section 3(d) of the Hatch Act, as amended, 7 U.S.C. section 361c(d).

8. Because in evaluating and selecting which research projects receive funds from the Hatch Act, defendant has no process designed to ensure consideration of each legislatively expressed interest, defendant is administering the Act in violation of the requirements of the Act as stated in paragraphs two through seven above.

Who May Conduct Research

Legal aspects of this dimension of academic freedom include several inchoate issues, similar to others in this chapter. Issues explicitly involving the eligibility of scholars to conduct their research have included government controls upon foreign nationals involved in access to supercomputing facilities and superconductivity research data, tax policy and its implications for university research and development activities, corporate involvement in university research and restrictions for trade-secrets or other intellectual property, and FBI surveillance of foreign scholars' library records. In 1987, details about the FBI's "Library Awareness Program" became public, highlighting frequent government requests for library users' records. "Libraries Are Asked by F.B.I. to Report on Foreign Agents," *New York Times*, 18 September 1987, pp. 1, 22. Thirty-six states have passed statutes to ensure confidentiality of library records, and university libraries have often insisted that any request for library records be made under an applicable state freedom of information act. Placing these requests in the open has successfully deflected several of these inquiries.

In Texas District Court, Travis County (Austin), Harold Nelson, a sociology professor at Pan American University, filed suit in 1987, to challenge the denial by the governor of Nelson's travel voucher reimbursement for a trip to a health conference in Nicaragua. Citing a Texas statute that requires the governor to approve state reimbursement for foreign travel, the governor and his state director for budget and planning denied the request (which had been approved by PAU officials) due to "political circumstances in Nicaragua [which] require that I decline your request for approval to that country on official business of the State of Texas." "Gov. Clements of Texas Faces Lawsuit for Denying Professor Right to Attend Meeting in Nicaragua," *Chronicle of Higher Education*, 11 November 1987, p. A29.

A Citizen of the Academy

Earlier cases involving academic freedom included the dimensions of protections afforded scholars in their classrooms, labs, and research. As citizens of the academy, faculty are also deemed by AAUP principles to be "a member of a learned profession and an officer of an educational institution"; unadjusted for its archaic gender references, this provision reads: "When he speaks or writes as a citizen, he should be free from institutional censorship or discipline, but his special position in the community imposes special obligations. As a man of learning and an educational officer, he should remember that the public may judge his profession and his institution by his utterances. Hence he should at all times be accurate, should exercise appropriate restraint, should show respect for the opinions of others, and should make every effort to indicate that he is not an institutional spokesman." There is also an interpretive comment on the provision, adopted in 1940:

> If the administration of a college or university feels that a teacher has not observed the admonitions of Paragraph (c) of the section on Academic Freedom and believes that the extramural utterances of the teacher have been such as to raise grave doubts concerning his fitness for his position, it may proceed to file charges under Paragraph (a)(4) of the section on Academic Tenure. In pressing such charges the administration should remember that teachers are citizens and should be accorded the freedom of citizens. In such cases the administration must assume full responsibility and the American Association of University Professors and Association of American Colleges are free to make an investigation.

These are two additional glosses on the principles. In 1964, a position on extramural utterances was added: "The controlling principle is that a faculty member's expression of opinion as a citizen cannot constitute grounds for dismissal unless it clearly demonstrates the faculty member's unfitness for his position. Moreover, a final decision should take into account the faculty member's entire record as a teacher and scholar." The 1966 Statement on Professional Ethics also addresses the responsibilities of professors: "As a member of his community, the professor has the rights and obligations of any citizen. He measures the urgency of these obligations in the light of his responsibilities to his subject, to his students, to his profession, and to his institution. When he speaks or acts as a private person he avoids creating the impression that he speaks or acts for his college or university. As a citizen engaged in a profession that depends upon freedom for its health and integrity, the professor has a particular obligation to promote conditions of free inquiry and to further public understanding of academic freedom." For a review of these issues, see S. Slaughter, "Academic Freedom and the State: Reflections on the Uses of Knowledge," *Journal of Higher Education*, 59 (1988), 241–62.

Pickering v. Board of Education
391 U.S. 563 (1968)

Mr. Justice MARSHALL delivered the opinion of the Court.

I.

In February of 1961 the appellee Board of Education asked the voters of the school district to approve a bond issue to raise $4,875,000 to erect two new schools. The proposal was defeated. Then, in December of 1961, the Board submitted another bond proposal to the voters which called for the raising of $5,500,000 to build two new schools. This second proposal passed and the schools were built with the money raised by the bond sales. In May of 1964 a proposed increase in the tax rate to be used for educational purposes was submitted to the voters by the Board and was defeated. Finally, on September 19, 1964, a second proposal to increase the tax rate was submitted by the Board and was likewise defeated. It was in connection with this last proposal of the School Board that appellant wrote the letter to the editor (which we reproduce in an Appendix to this opinion) that resulted in his dismissal.

Prior to the vote on the second tax increase proposal a variety of articles attributed to the District 205 Teachers' Organization appeared in the local paper. These articles urged passage of the tax increase and stated that failure to pass the increase would result in a decline in the quality of education afforded children in the district's schools. A letter from the superintendent of schools making the same point was published in the paper two days before the election and submitted to the voters in mimeographed form the following day. It was in response to the foregoing material, together with the failure of the tax increase to pass, that appellant submitted the letter in question to the editor of the local paper.

The letter constituted, basically, an attack on the School Board's handling of the 1961 bond issue proposals and its subsequent allocation of financial resources between the schools' educational and athletic programs. It also charged the superintendent of schools with attempting to prevent teachers in the district from opposing or criticizing the proposed bond issue.

The Board dismissed Pickering for writing and publishing the letter. Pursuant to Illinois law, the Board was then required to hold a hearing on the dismissal. At the hearing the Board charged that numerous statements in the letter were false and that the publication of the statements unjustifiably impugned the "motives, honesty, integrity, truthfulness, responsibility and competence" of both the Board and the school administration. The Board also charged that the false statements damaged the professional reputations of its members and of the school administrators, would be disruptive of faculty discipline, and would tend to foment "controversy, conflict and dissension" among teachers, administrators, the Board of Education, and the residents of the district. Testimony was introduced from a variety of witnesses on the truth or falsity of the particular statements in the letter with which the Board took issue. The Board found the statements to be false as charged. No evidence was introduced at any point in the proceedings as to the effect of the publication of the letter on the community as a whole or on the administration of the school system in particular, and no specific findings along these lines were made.

The Illinois courts reviewed the proceedings solely to determine whether the Board's findings were supported by substantial evidence and whether, on the facts as found, the Board could reasonably conclude that appellant's publication of the letter was "detrimental to the best interests of the schools." Pickering's claim that his letter was protected by the First Amendment was rejected on the ground that his acceptance of a teaching position in the public schools obliged him to refrain from making statements about the operation of the schools "which in the absence of such position he would have an undoubted right to engage in." It is not altogether clear whether the Illinois Supreme Court held that the First Amendment had no applicability to appellant's dismissal for writing the letter in question or whether it determined that the particular statements made in the letter were not entitled to First Amendment protection. In any event, it clearly rejected Pickering's claim that, on the facts of this case, he could not constitutionally be dismissed from his teaching position.

II.

To the extent that the Illinois Supreme Court's opinion may be read to suggest that teachers may constitutionally be compelled to relinquish the First Amendment rights they would otherwise enjoy as citizens to comment on matters of public interest in connection with the operation of the public schools in which they work, it proceeds on a premise that has been unequivocally rejected in numerous prior decisions of this Court.

*   *   *

An examination of the statements in appellant's letter objected to by the Board reveals that they, like the letter as a whole, consist essentially of criticism of the Board's allocation of school funds between educational and athletic programs, and of both the Board's and the superintendent's methods of informing, or preventing the informing of, the district's taxpayers of the real reasons why additional tax revenues were being sought for the schools. The statements are in no way directed towards any person with whom appellant would normally be in contact in the course of his daily work as a teacher. Thus no question of maintaining either discipline by immediate superiors or harmony among coworkers is presented here. Appellant's employment relationships with the Board and, to a somewhat lesser extent, with the superintendent are not the kind of close working relationships for which it can persuasively be claimed that personal loyalty and confidence are necessary to their proper functioning. Accordingly, to the extent that the Board's position here can be taken to suggest that even comments on matters of public concern that are substantially correct, such as statements (1)–(4) of appellant's letter, may furnish grounds for dismissal if they are sufficiently critical in tone, we unequivocally reject it.

We next consider the statements in appellant's letter which we agree to be false. The Board's original charges included allegations that the publication of the letter damaged the professional reputations of the Board and the superintendent and would foment controversy and conflict among the Board, teachers, administrators, and the residents of the district. However, no evidence to support these allegations was introduced at the hearing. So far as the record reveals, Pickering's letter was greeted by everyone but its main target, the Board, with massive apathy and total disbelief. The Board must, therefore, have decided, perhaps by analogy with the law of libel, that the statements were *per se* harmful to the operation of the school.

*   *   *

[The] question whether a school system requires additional funds is a matter of legitimate public concern on which the judgment of the school administration, including the School Board, cannot, in a society that leaves such questions to popular vote, be taken as conclusive. On such a question free and open debate is vital to informed decision-making by the electorate. Teachers are, as a class, the members of a community most likely to have informed and definite opinions as to how funds allotted to the operation of the schools should be spent. Accordingly, it is essential that they be able to speak out freely on such questions without fear of retaliatory dismissal.

*   *   *

What we do have before us is a case in which a teacher has made erroneous public statements upon issues then currently the subject of public attention, which are critical of his ultimate employer but which are neither shown nor can be presumed to have in any way either impeded the teacher's proper performance of his daily duties in the classroom or to have interfered with the regular operation of the schools generally. In these circumstances we conclude that the interest of the school administration in limiting teachers' opportunities to contribute to public debate is not significantly greater than its interest in limiting a similar contribution by any member of the general public.

IV.

The public interest in having free and unhindered debate on matters of public importance—the core value of the Free Speech Clause of the First Amendment—is so great that it has been held that a State cannot authorize the recovery of damages by a public official for defamatory statements directed at him except when such statements are shown to have been made either with knowledge of their falsity or with reckless disregard for their truth or falsity.

* * *

In sum, we hold that, in a case such as this, absent proof of false statements knowingly or recklessly made by him, a teacher's exercise of his right to speak on issues of public importance may not furnish the basis for his dismissal from public employment.

Roseman v. Indiana University of Pennsylvania
520 F.2d 1364 (1975)

VAN DUSEN, Circuit Judge.

This is a timely appeal from a September 24, 1974, judgment of the United States District Court for the Western District of Pennsylvania. The plaintiff, Roseman, was an associate professor in the Foreign Languages Department of Indiana University of Pennsylvania for the academic years beginning September of 1969 and 1970. Her contract was not renewed for the academic year beginning in September of 1971. Her complaint, filed December 20, 1973, alleged that the non-renewal violated her right to a pre-termination hearing, was in retaliation for her exercise of protected speech, and penalized her for her religious beliefs. She sought reinstatement, injunctive relief, and damages. The district court found for the defendants on all counts. We affirm.

* * *

The plaintiff's freedom of speech claim requires somewhat more extended discussion. The Committee on Merit and Tenure of the Faculty evaluated the plaintiff's performance at a meeting on March 20, 1970, and called several shortcomings to the plaintiff's attention. The Committee indicated at that time that it would meet again for a further discussion of the non-tenured staff. Shortly thereafter, a controversy arose within the Foreign Languages Department. Plaintiff apparently thought that Faust, the Acting Chairman of the Foreign Languages Department and a defendant in this action, may have suppressed the application of one Hyde for chairmanship of the Department. The district court found that Faust had committed no impropriety. The Findings indicate that plaintiff never made an investigation of the facts and her complaint was first made after the deadline for receiving applications had passed. Notwithstanding, on April 5, 1970, the plaintiff complained to the Dean of the College of Arts and Sciences of the University, McGovern, about what she believed to have been Faust's wrongful suppression of the Hyde application, and later repeated these charges at a May 5, 1970, meeting of the teaching staff of the Foreign Languages Department at the invitation of Dean McGovern, who specifically invited the plaintiff to explain them. She did so; the faculty nevertheless gave a vote of confidence to Faust. On May 12, the Committee on Merit and Tenure, of which Faust was a member, decided not to renew the plaintiff's contract by a vote of ten affirmatives and one abstention. This decision was subsequently ratified by University officials.

The district court expressed concern, which we share, over the "close proximity of the meeting of May 12, 1970, to the faculty meeting of May 5, 1970, at which plaintiff had voiced her complaints as to Mr. Faust." The district court found, however, that "there were adequate work-related reasons for not renewing plaintiff's contract," which language is supported by Findings 34 and 45, reading as follows:

> 34. Plaintiff was non-renewed because of her work practices which created administrative hardships and delays, her inadequate classroom performance and her failure to get along amicably in the department.

*   *   *

The parameters defining protected speech for state employees were set forth by the Supreme Court in *Pickering v. Board of Education.* "The problem in any case," the Court said, "is to arrive at a balance between the interests of the teacher, as a citizen, in commenting upon matters of public concern and the interest of the State, as an employer, in promoting the efficiency of the public services it performs through its employees." The communication for which Pickering, a high school teacher, had been discharged was a letter written to a "local newspaper in connection with a recently proposed tax increase." Pickering's letter "was critical of the way in which the Board [of Education] and the district superintendent of schools had handled past proposals to raise new revenue for the schools." The Court found some of the statements in Pickering's letter to be true and others, while not malicious, to be false, but it found all of them to be protected:

*   *   *

The communications made by the plaintiff in the case before us differ from Pickering's in two crucial respects. In the first place, Roseman's expressions were essentially private communications in which only members of the Foreign Languages Department and the Dean of the College of Arts and Sciences were shown by the plaintiff to have had any interest. Pickering's letter to the editor, urging the electorate with respect to a pending tax proposal, was, by contrast, a classic example of public communication on an issue of public interest. In *Pickering*, as in other cases, the Supreme Court inquired into the public nature of a communication in determining the degree of First Amendment protection. As Roseman's communications were made in forums not open to the general public and concerned an issue of less public interest than Pickering's, the First Amendment interest in their protection is correspondingly reduced.

The second respect in which Roseman's communications differ from Pickering's is in their potentially disruptive impact on the functioning of the Department. Pickering's attacks were on a remote superintendent and school board; in contrast, Roseman's called into question the integrity of the person immediately in charge of running a department which, it is fair to assume, was more intimate than a school district. The district court found that "plaintiff's attacks upon Faust's integrity in a faculty meeting would undoubtedly have the effect of interfering with harmonious relationships with plaintiff's superiors and coworkers." In making this finding, the district court reflected a similar concern expressed by the Supreme Court, which noted that Pickering's statements were "in no way directed towards any person with whom [Pickering] would normally be in contact in the course of his daily work as a teacher." Because of this, Pickering's case raised "no question of maintaining either discipline by immediate superiors or harmony among coworkers." The same obviously cannot be said of Roseman's faculty meeting accusations directed at the Acting Chairman of her Department.

For reason of these distinctions between the plaintiff's communications and the communications at issue in *Pickering*, we have concluded that the plaintiff's communications fall outside the First Amendment's protection. Because they do, the University did not deny the plaintiff her First Amendment rights, even if it considered her statements in making its non-renewal decision.

Richard Aumiller v. University of Delaware
434 F. Supp. 1273 (1977)

MURRAY M. SCHWARTZ, District Judge.

I. THE FACTS

Aumiller first came to the University of Delaware in February 1972, as a graduate student in the Department of Theatre. In 1973, he was employed part-time as an aide to Professor Lawrence Wilker, then Manager of the University Theatre. Dr. Wilker took a leave of absence the following academic year and recommended that Aumiller be hired as his replacement, which in fact occurred. Aumiller was rehired for the 1975–76 academic year when Dr. Wilker officially left the University to become permanent director of the Grand Opera House in Wilmington, Delaware.

About a month after Aumiller initially arrived at the University of Delaware in 1972, he joined an organization called the Gay Community. Aumiller is himself homosexual in sexual orientation and preference. As a graduate student he held no office in the organization. However, shortly after he became a faculty member in September, 1974, he was asked by members of the Gay Community to serve as their faculty advisor, an invitation which Aumiller accepted. Although the University requires every campus organization to have a faculty advisor, Aumiller's decision to serve in this capacity was purely voluntary.

* * *

In October 1975, Ms. Janice deBlieu, a "campus stringer" from the Wilmington News Journal, decided to research a possible article on the Gay Community at the University of Delaware. In order to contact a representative from the Gay Community, she called one of the numbers listed in an advertisement placed by the organization in the campus newspaper, the Review. Unbeknown to her, the number she dialed was the telephone number of Aumiller's residence. The person who answered the phone (who was not Aumiller) was unwilling to have his full name appear in a newspaper article on the Gay Community, but suggested that the reporter contact Aumiller. Ms. deBlieu subsequently interviewed Aumiller at his on-campus office in Mitchell Hall, and attended a Gay Community meeting. Following the interview and meeting, Ms. deBlieu twice telephoned Aumiller to ask some additional questions. During the first phone call, Ms. deBlieu also attempted to arrange for a photographer from the newspaper to take plaintiff's picture. Aumiller indicated to her that he was extremely busy, and had no time to pose for pictures during the day. He suggested, however, that if the photographer were present at play rehearsal that evening at the University Theater, he perhaps could take Aumiller's picture then.

The actual interview and subsequent telephone conversations covered a variety of subjects relating to the Gay Community. Ms. deBlieu also asked Aumiller a number of questions concerning the views of homosexuals on certain issues. In response Aumiller indicated that he could not speak for all homosexuals, but could give only his own views. Aumiller showed no reluctance in speaking to Ms. deBlieu, nor did he try to discourage her in any way from using his name in the article. Nevertheless, it is clear that the impetus for the article came exclusively from Ms. deBlieu and Aumiller did nothing to seek her out.

As discussed more fully *infra*, the parties differ significantly over the impression the November News Journal article creates in the mind of a reader. What must first be addressed is whether Aumiller intended to create the impression that he was speaking for the University and whether that was Ms. deBlieu's understanding. Aumiller did not request that he be identified in any particular way in the article....

Thus, both participants in the interview fully agree that Aumiller neither intended to foster nor in fact fostered the impression that he was speaking as an official University spokesman. The Court adopts this as its finding, for defendants have been unable to produce any evidence, other than by reference to the article itself, that Aumiller intended to portray himself as an official spokesman.

* * *

The November 2 News Journal article by Ms. deBlieu set in motion a series of events which eventually formed the basis for this litigation. These events perhaps can be analyzed most productively by focusing on the three most demonstrable responses by the administration, especially President Trabant: (1) the meeting between Trabant and Aumiller on November 4, 1975; (2) the decision by Trabant on December 22, 1975, not to sign a new contract for Aumiller if one were presented; (3) the decision by Trabant in May, 1976, to reject Aumiller's grievance petition. It is important to note at each of these stages the opinions and justifications which form the basis for the decision taken. Perhaps more significantly, the Court finds clear and specific subtle and not so subtle changes in those justifications as the drama was played out from November, 1975, to May, 1976.

D. *The Meeting of November 4, 1975*

After reading the November 2 News Journal article, President Trabant dictated a letter to Samuel Lenher, a defendant herein and Chairman of the Board of Trustees. That letter, dated November 4, 1975, is set out in full below:

* * *

"I have scheduled an appointment with Mr. Aumiller. I am going to tell him that as President of the University I am effronted [sic] by his statements and the signs which are in his office; that I had no knowledge that he was a gay when he was hired; that I really don't care what he does in his bedroom, but when he insists on making public information of it, I find that shocking and of harm to the University. Therefore, his actions and statements must be extremely conservative and that his position at the University will be reviewed at the year's end to determine whether he will continue in our employ or not.

"If you have thoughts and advice on this matter, of course I would be very pleased to receive them."

On the same day Trabant summoned Aumiller to his office to discuss the News Journal interview and article.

* * *

When Aumiller finished speaking, Trabant advised him they were on a "conflict course" because the majority of Delawareans did not share his views on homosexuality, nor would they in his lifetime. Aumiller asked the President point blank if the President wanted him to stop speaking out. The President responded indirectly by saying that Delaware was "like a small pond, and a small wind can raise large waves on a small pond."

* * *

In summary, the Court finds that in light of the letter to Lenher and the conversation with Aumiller, as of November 4, 1975, three major themes guided Trabant's responses to the July Bulletin and November News Journal articles: (1) his concern that Aumiller's "evangelistic endeavor" would attract homosexuals, both students and others, to the campus; (2) his concern that Aumiller's statements would cause "harm and embarrassment" to the University; (3) his belief that Aumiller's statements were "shocking" and an "effront" [sic] to him, personally, and to the University.

* * *

E. *The Decision Not to Renew Aumiller's Contract*

At a meeting with Provost Campbell on December 10, 1975, little more than one month after the meeting with Aumiller, President Trabant told the Provost that he would not sign a contract for Aumiller for the 1976–77 academic term, if one were presented to him.

* * *

Provost Campbell renewed his suggestion that some alternate way to accomplish the same end be selected, i.e., a budgetary reason for not renewing Aumiller's contract. To his credit, President Trabant would not accede in this, indicating that he had no desire to disguise the "true reason" for his decision. Thus, by December 22, 1975, Trabant had made his decision not to renew Aumiller's contract, if it were presented for his signature.

If one compares the statements made by Trabant at his November 4 meeting with the reasons presented in December, there is a striking change in the focus of Trabant's concerns. Most obvious is the absence of any reference at the December meetings to the purported affront to the University and to Trabant by the newspaper articles. What previously had elicited such a strong reaction from Trabant in November apparently had faded into relative unimportance. Instead, primary emphasis was placed on the thesis that Aumiller had advocated experimentation with homosexuality for nonhomosexual undergraduates and therefore should not be rehired. The question of the legal sufficiency of Trabant's concerns is discussed *infra*, but the Court would be remiss if it did not comment on one of the President's conclusions. I cannot find a scintilla of evidence in any of the newspaper articles to support the inference that Aumiller was on a campaign to convert heterosexuals to homosexuality.

* * *

F. *The Grievance Proceeding*

In January 1976, Aumiller filed a three-part grievance under the Collective Bargaining Agreement between the University of Delaware and the Delaware Chapter of the American Association of University Professors (AAUP). He contended: (1) that the University was required to provide him with notice of non-renewal no later than December 15, 1975; (2) that Hansen's letter of January 6, 1976 was insufficient in its form because the University was required to give him a statement of reasons for the non-renewal; and (3) that the reasons for non-renewal violated the University's policy on "academic freedom" as set forth in the Faculty Handbook.

On March 12, 1976, following extensive hearings on the Aumiller grievance, the University's Arts and Science Senate Committee on Academic Freedom and Responsibility ruled in Aumiller's favor on all *three* grievances and recommended that he be given a one-year contract for the 1976–77 academic year, as well as a contract for the 1976 Summer Festival of the Arts.

* * *

The University Appeals Committee concurred with the Senate Committee, ruled in Aumiller's favor on all three grievances and recommended Aumiller's reappointment for the 1976–77 school year.

The final step in the grievance process is the President of the University. The decision of the University Appeals Committee is only advisory to the President. President Trabant rejected the recommendation of the Appeals Committee and denied Aumiller's three grievances in a written decision dated May 24, 1976. After explaining why he did not feel that Aumiller's statements were covered by the principle of academic freedom, he opined that even if this were the case, Aumiller's actions were improper:

> "Based upon all the evidence available to me, it is my opinion that Mr. Aumiller, through his actions and statements, indicated erroneously that the University . . . condones and sanctions homosexuality for undergraduates. As a private citizen, Mr. Aumiller has the right to advocate unpopular and controversial causes. But he has no right to use his position at the University to foster and promote what most Americans and most Delawareans consider an aberrant lifestyle.

* * *

> "I recognize and respect the free speech rights of a faculty member as guaranteed by the First Amendment. Clearly, a faculty member should exercise his rights as a citizen, but in doing so he should be mindful of the interests of the University in maintaining public confidence in its ability to carry out the public duties which have been entrusted to it. In my opinion, Mr. Aumiller's actions and statements reflected adversely upon the University and tended to bring discredit to it."

Accordingly, this Court finds nothing in these newspaper articles to support the contention of the defendants that Aumiller abused his position at the University to create the inference that the University fully supported and encouraged those who adopt a homosexual lifestyle. The clear emphasis in each article is on an examination of how homosexuals adapt to life in a predominately [sic] heterosexual society. Aumiller appears as one example of a homosexual and his statements are directed towards educating readers of the article to an acceptance of homosexuals as equals and to the demythologization of certain stereotypes commonly applied to homosexuals. The articles simply do not support the inferences suggested by the defendants.

* * *

III. AUMILLER'S RIGHT TO FREEDOM OF EXPRESSION
The Applicable Standard

There can be little dispute that the decision not to renew Aumiller's contract was precipitated primarily by the three newspaper articles and the circumstances surrounding their publication. Accordingly, the proper framework for evaluating whether defendants' actions violated Aumiller's constitutional rights is to examine what limitation, if any, the University of Delaware may impose on the exercise of its employees' First Amendment rights.

* * *

Defendants have attempted to cast Aumiller as a misguided and manipulative individual, who intentionally or recklessly sought to intertwine the University in his own personal beliefs and views in a number of ways for the expressed purpose of conferring on them added credence. The record in this case is completely contrary to the Aumiller portrait painted by defendants. Aumiller neither sought out publicity on his own nor engaged in public acts. Aumiller did not surreptitiously manage to slip into his conversation with the two reporters the nature of his affiliation with the University or that he was the faculty advisor to the Gay Community; such information was reasonably related to the overall scope of the interviews. Aumiller never specifically requested to be identified by his University title; such identification was the choice of the reporters who spoke to him. Aumiller had no master plan to create the appearance of University sanction by conducting the interviews in his office and permitting his picture to be taken at the University Theatre. Aumiller acted in a manner reasonably related to his role as faculty advisor to the Gay Community, and acted in a manner that advisors to any other student organization apparently can act without fear of reprisal. The selection of these locations was not premeditated as suggested by defendants, but was fortuitous, dictated by concerns of time and convenience. In the one instance where confusion might have arisen—the possibility of students in the play being photographed with Aumiller—Aumiller took the necessary measures to ensure that the confusion did not arise.

Unquestionably there are certain circumstances in which a faculty member can take unfair advantage of his University affiliation or of the University's facilities. This, however, is not such a case. Aumiller neither sought to create the false impression that he was speaking on behalf of the University or that the University endorsed his views nor did he set out to exploit the facilities of the University to add credence to his personal views.

The Court fully recognizes that homosexuality is an extremely emotional and controversial topic and that Aumiller's opinions on the subject quite likely represent a minority view. But this unpopularity cannot justify the limitation of Aumiller's First Amendment rights by the University of Delaware. Indeed, the fundamental purpose of the First Amendment is to protect from State abridgement the free expression of controversial and unpopular ideas. The premise of the free speech clause is "that the best test of truth is the power of the thought to get itself accepted in the competition of the market [of ideas]." The decision not to renew Aumiller's contract because of his public statements contravenes these most basic teachings of the First Amendment and cannot be tolerated.

* * *

The Court holds that Aumiller is entitled to reinstatement for the 1976–77 academic term. Since the term is at an end, the primary manifestation of this relief will be in the form of his salary for the year, which he would have earned but for the constitutional violation. This amount, as agreed by the parties, totals $12,454.

In a letter dated January 25, 1977, plaintiff's counsel for the first time suggested reinstatement for the 1976–77 academic term would be inadequate to vindicate plaintiff's rights, in view of the fact that by the time the matter had been decided, Aumiller would be able to serve little if any of that term in his former position. Counsel then suggested that a more appropriate remedy would be reinstatement for the 1977–78 school year. The Court is not convinced that the reinstatement for the 1976–77 term is inadequate, since relief of this nature is intended only to place the plaintiff in the same position he would have occupied if the incident had not occurred. Certainly if Aumiller chooses to apply for a position at the University for the 1977–78 academic year, defendants cannot discriminate against him on the basis of this lawsuit or the exercise of his First Amendment rights. Concededly the experiential value of teaching during the 1976–77 term irretrievably has been lost; nonetheless the Court does not view the circumstances of this case as warranting what would be a novel and extraordinary remedy of reinstatement in a future year, for an individual who had no property interest in future employment.

VII. CONCLUSION

Judgment in this case will be granted in favor of plaintiff Aumiller, the Court having found that defendants, by their action in not renewing Aumiller's contract for the 1976–77 academic term because of his statements on the subject of homosexuality which appeared in three newspaper articles and the circumstances surrounding their publication, violated his right of freedom of expression as guaranteed by the First Amendment. There was no evidence that Aumiller's statements impeded his performance of his daily duties, substantially disrupted the University, violated an express need for confidentiality, or disrupted his working relationship with his superiors. Nor were defendants able to demonstrate that Aumiller intentionally or recklessly made false statements which reflected adversely on the University. Accordingly, it was concluded that defendants' interest in promoting the efficiency of the public services it performs through its employees does not outweigh Aumiller's interest in commenting upon matters of public concern.

In view of defendants' failure to demonstrate by a preponderance of the evidence that Aumiller would not have been rehired for the 1976–77 academic term had there been no violation of his First Amendment rights, [he is] entitled to an order granting reinstatement for the 1976–77 academic term and to back pay for that term totalling $12,454. Defendants further will be ordered to remove any reference to this incident from Aumiller's employment records held by the University and to make no reference to such incident in connection with any employment inquiries received concerning Aumiller.

In addition, defendants, the University of Delaware and President Trabant are jointly and severally liable to Aumiller for his emotional distress, embarrassment and humiliation resulting from the violation of his constitutional rights and will be ordered to pay Aumiller $10,000 in compensatory damages. Finally, because President Trabant demonstrated a malicious or wanton disregard for Aumiller's constitutional rights by his actions, he will be ordered to pay to Aumiller punitive damages in the amount of $5,000.

Submit Order on notice.

Mt. Healthy City School District Board of Education
v. Doyle
429 U.S. 274 (1977)

Mr. Justice REHNQUIST delivered the opinion of the Court.

* * *

Doyle was first employed by the Board in 1966. He worked under one-year contracts for the first three years, and under a two-year contract from 1969 to 1971. In 1969 he was elected president of the Teachers' Association, in which position he worked to expand the subjects of direct negotiation between the Association and the Board of Education. During Doyle's one-year term as president of the Association, and during the succeeding year when he served on its executive committee, there was apparently some tension in relations between the Board and the Association.

Beginning early in 1970, Doyle was involved in several incidents not directly connected with his role in the Teachers' Association. In one instance, he engaged in an argument with another teacher which culminated in the other teacher's slapping him. Doyle subsequently refused to accept an apology and insisted upon some punishment for the other teacher. His persistence in the matter resulted in the suspension of both teachers for one day, which was followed by a walkout by a number of other teachers, which in turn resulted in the lifting of the suspensions.

On other occasions, Doyle got into an argument with employees of the school cafeteria over the amount of spaghetti which had been served him; referred to students, in connection with a disciplinary complaint, as "sons of bitches"; and made an obscene gesture to two girls in connection with their failure to obey commands made in his capacity as cafeteria supervisor. Chronologically the last in the series of incidents which respondent was involved in during his employment by the Board was a telephone call by him to a local radio station. It was the Board's consideration of this incident which the court below found to be a violation of the First and Fourteenth Amendments.

In February 1971, the principal circulated to various teachers a memorandum relating to teacher dress and appearance, which was apparently prompted by the view of some in the administration that there was a relationship between teacher appearance and public support for bond issues. Doyle's response to the receipt of the memorandum—on a subject which he apparently understood was to be settled by joint teacher-administration action—was to convey the substance of the memorandum to a disc jockey at WSAI, a Cincinnati radio station, who promptly announced the adoption of the dress code as a news item. Doyle subsequently apologized to the principal, conceding that he should have made some prior communication of his criticism to the school administration.

Approximately one month later the superintendent made his customary annual recommendations to the Board as to the rehiring of nontenured teachers. He recommended that Doyle not be rehired. The same recommendation was made with respect to nine other teachers in the district, and in all instances, including Doyle's, the recommendation was adopted by the Board. Shortly after being notified of this decision, respondent requested a statement of reasons for the Board's actions. He received a statement citing "a notable lack of tact in handling professional matters which leaves much doubt as to your sincerity in establishing good school relationships." That general statement was followed by references to the radio station incident and to the obscene-gesture incident.

The District Court found that all of these incidents had in fact occurred. It concluded that respondent Doyle's telephone call to the radio station was "clearly protected by the First Amendment," and that because it had played a "substantial part" in the decision of the Board not to renew Doyle's employment, he was entitled to reinstatement with back pay.

* * *

We are thus brought to the issue whether, even if that were the case, the fact that the protected conduct played a "substantial part" in the actual decision not to renew would necessarily amount to a constitutional violation justifying remedial action. We think that it would not.

A rule of causation which focuses solely on whether protected conduct played a part, "substantial" or otherwise, in a decision not to rehire, could place an employee in a better position as a result of the exercise of constitutionally protected conduct than he would have occupied had he done nothing. The difficulty with the rule enunciated by the District Court is that it would require reinstatement in cases where a dramatic and perhaps abrasive incident is inevitably on the minds of those responsible for the decision to rehire, and does indeed play a part in that decision—even if the same decision would have been reached had the incident not occurred. The constitutional principle at stake is sufficiently vindicated if such an employee is placed in no worse a position than if he had not engaged in the conduct. A borderline or marginal candidate should not have the employment question resolved against him because of constitutionally protected conduct. But that same candidate ought not to be able, by engaging in such conduct, to prevent his employer from assessing his performance record and reaching a decision not to rehire on the basis of that record, simply because the protected conduct makes the employer more certain of the correctness of its decision.

This is especially true where, as the District Court observed was the case here, the current decision to rehire will accord "tenure." The long-term consequences of an award of tenure are of great moment both to the employee and to the employer. They are too significant for us to hold that the Board in this case would be precluded, because it considered constitutionally protected conduct in deciding not to rehire Doyle, from attempting to prove to a trier of fact that quite apart from such conduct Doyle's record was such that he would not have been rehired in any event.

In other areas of constitutional law, this Court has found it necessary to formulate a test of causation which distinguishes between a result caused by a constitutional violation and one not so caused. We think those are instructive in formulating the test to be applied here.

* * *

While the type of causation on which the taint cases turn may differ somewhat from that which we apply here, those cases do suggest that the proper test to apply in the present context is one which likewise protects against the invasion of constitutional rights without commanding undesirable consequences not necessary to the assurance of those rights.

Initially, in this case, the burden was properly placed upon respondent to show that his conduct was constitutionally protected, and that this conduct was a "substantial factor"—or, to put it in other words, that it was a "motivating factor" in the Board's decision not to rehire him. Respondent having carried that burden, however, the District Court should have gone on to determine whether the Board had shown by a preponderance of the evidence that it would have reached the same decision as to respondent's reemployment even in the absence of the protected conduct.

In *Givhan v. Western Line Consolidated School District*, 439 U.S. 410 (1979), an additional protection was afforded public employees, that of private views, expressed *privately*. Justice Rehnquist held, "The First Amendment forbids abridgment of the 'freedom of speech.' Neither the Amendment itself nor our decisions indicate that this freedom is lost to the public employee who arranges to communicate privately with his employer rather than to spread his views before the public. We decline to adopt such a view of the First Amendment."

Is the Speech a Matter of Public Concern?

Connick v. Myers
461 U.S. 138 (1983)

Justice WHITE delivered the opinion of the Court.

In *Pickering v. Board of Education*, we stated that a public employee does not relinquish First Amendment rights to comment on matters of public interest by virtue of government employment. We also recognized that the State's interests as an employer in regulating the speech of its employees "differ significantly from those it possesses in connection with regulation of the speech of the citizenry in general." The problem, we thought, was arriving "at a balance between the interests of the [employee], as a citizen, in commenting upon matters of public concern and the interest of the State, as an employer, in promoting the efficiency of the public services it performs through its employees." We return to this problem today and consider whether the First and Fourteenth Amendments prevent the discharge of a state employee for circulating a questionnaire concerning internal office affairs.

I

The respondent, Sheila Myers, was employed as an Assistant District Attorney in New Orleans for five and a half years. She served at the pleasure of petitioner Harry Connick, the District Attorney for Orleans Parish. During this period Myers competently performed her responsibilities of trying criminal cases.

In the early part of October 1980, Myers was informed that she would be transferred to prosecute cases in a different section of the criminal court. Myers was strongly opposed to the proposed transfer and expressed her view to several of her supervisors, including Connick. Despite her objections, on October 6 Myers was notified that she was being transferred. Myers again spoke with Dennis Waldron, one of the First Assistant District Attorneys, expressing her reluctance to accept the transfer. A number of other office matters were discussed and Myers later testified that, in response to Waldron's suggestion that her concerns were not shared by others in the office, she informed him that she would do some research on the matter.

That night Myers prepared a questionnaire soliciting the views of her fellow staff members concerning office transfer policy, office morale, the need for a grievance committee, the level of confidence in supervisors, and whether employees felt pressured to work in political campaigns. Early the following morning, Myers typed and copied the questionnaire. She also met with Connick who urged her to accept the transfer. She said she would "consider" it. Connick then left the office. Myers then distributed the questionnaire to 15 Assistant District Attorneys. Shortly after noon, Dennis Waldron learned that Myers was distributing the survey. He immediately phoned Connick and informed him that Myers was creating a "mini-insurrection" within the office. Connick returned to the office and told Myers that she was being terminated because of her refusal to accept the transfer. She was also told that her distribution of the questionnaire was considered an act of insubordination. Connick particularly objected to the question which inquired whether employees "had confidence in and would rely on the word" of various superiors in the office, and to a question concerning pressure to work in political campaigns which he felt would be damaging if discovered by the press.

Myers filed suit under 42 U.S.C. § 1983, contending that her employment was wrongfully terminated because she had exercised her constitutionally protected right of free speech. The District Court agreed, ordered Myers reinstated, and awarded back pay, damages, and attorney's fees. The District Court found that although Connick informed Myers that she was being fired because of her refusal to accept a transfer, the facts showed that the questionnaire was the real reason for her termination. The court then proceeded to hold that Myers' questionnaire involved matters of public concern and that the State had not "clearly demonstrated" that the survey "substantially interfered" with the operations of the District Attorney's office.

Connick appealed to the United States Court of Appeals for the Fifth Circuit, which affirmed on the basis of the District Court's opinion. Connick then sought review in this Court by way of certiorari, which we granted.

II

For at least 15 years, it has been settled that a State cannot condition public employment on a basis that infringes the employee's constitutionally protected interest in freedom of expression. Our task, as we defined it in *Pickering*, is to seek "a balance between the interests of the [employee], as a citizen, in commenting upon matters of public concern and the interest of the State, as an employer, in promoting the efficiency of the public services it performs through its employees." The District Court, and thus the Court of Appeals as well, misapplied our decision in *Pickering* and consequently, in our view, erred in striking the balance for respondent.

* * *

In *Pickering*, the Court held impermissible under the First Amendment the dismissal of a high school teacher for openly criticizing the Board of Education on its allocation of school funds between athletics and education and its methods of informing tax-payers about the need for additional revenue. Pickering's subject was "a matter of legitimate public concern" upon which "free and open debate is vital to informed decision-making by the electorate."

Our cases following *Pickering* also involved safeguarding speech on matters of public concern. The controversy in *Perry v. Sindermann* arose from the failure to rehire a teacher in the state college system who had testified before committees of the Texas Legislature and had become involved in public disagreement over whether the college should be elevated to 4-year status—a change opposed by the Regents. In *Mt. Healthy City Board of Ed. v. Doyle*, a public school teacher was not rehired because, allegedly, he had relayed to a radio station the substance of a memorandum relating to teacher dress and appearance that the school principal had circulated to various teachers. The memorandum was apparently prompted by the view of some in the administration that there was a relationship between teacher appearance and public support for bond issues, and indeed, the radio station promptly announced the adop-tion of the dress code as a news item. Most recently, in *Givhan v. Western Line Consolidated School District*, we held that First Amendment protection applies when a public employee arranges to communicate privately with his employer rather than to express his views publicly. Although the subject matter of Mrs. Givhan's statements were not the issue before the Court, it is clear that her statements concerning the School District's allegedly racially discriminatory policies involved a matter of public concern.

Pickering, its antecedents, and its progeny lead us to conclude that if Myers' ques-tionnaire cannot be fairly characterized as constituting speech on a matter of public concern, it is unnecessary for us to scrutinize the reasons for her discharge. When employee expression cannot be fairly considered as relating to any matter of political, social, or other concern to the community, government officials should enjoy wide latitude in managing their offices, without intrusive oversight by the judiciary in the name of the First Amendment. Perhaps the government employer's dismissal of the worker may not be fair, but ordinary dismissals from government service which violate no fixed tenure or applicable statute or regulation are not subject to judicial review even if the reasons for the dismissal are alleged to be mistaken or unreasonable.

*   *   *

We do not suggest, however, that Myers' speech, even if not touching upon a matter of public concern, is totally beyond the protection of the First Amendment. "[T]he First Amendment does not protect speech and assembly only to the extent it can be characterized as political. 'Great secular causes, with smaller ones, are guarded.' " We in no sense suggest that speech on private matters falls into one of the narrow and well-defined classes of expression which carries so little social value, such as obscenity, that the State can prohibit and punish such expression by all persons in its jurisdiction. For example, an employee's false criticism of his employer on grounds not of public concern may be cause for his discharge but would be entitled to the same protection in a libel action accorded an identical statement made by a man on the street. We hold only that when a public employee speaks not as a citizen upon matters of public concern, but instead as an employee upon matters only of personal interest, absent the most unusual circumstances, a federal court is not the appropriate forum in which to review the wisdom of a personnel decision taken by a public agency allegedly in reaction to the employee's behavior.

* * *

Myers' questionnaire touched upon matters of public concern in only a most limited sense; her survey, in our view, is most accurately characterized as an employee grievance concerning internal office policy. The limited First Amendment interest involved here does not require that Connick tolerate action which he reasonably believed would disrupt the office, undermine his authority, and destroy close working relationships. Myers' discharge therefore did not offend the First Amendment. We reiterate, however, the caveat we expressed in *Pickering*: "Because of the enormous variety of fact situations in which critical statements by . . . public employees may be thought by their superiors . . . to furnish grounds for dismissal, we do not deem it either appropriate or feasible to attempt to lay down a general standard against which all such statements may be judged."

Our holding today is grounded in our longstanding recognition that the First Amendment's primary aim is the full protection of speech upon issues of public concern, as well as the practical realities involved in the administration of a government office. Although today the balance is struck for the government, this is no defeat for the First Amendment. For it would indeed be a Pyrrhic victory for the great principles of free expression if the Amendment's safeguarding of a public employee's right, as a citizen, to participate in discussions concerning public affairs were confused with the attempt to constitutionalize the employee grievance that we see presented here. The judgment of the Court of Appeals is

Reversed.

Justice BRENNAN, with whom Justice MARSHALL, Justice BLACKMUN, and Justice STEVEN join, dissenting.

Sheila Myers was discharged for circulating a questionnaire to her fellow Assistant District Attorneys seeking information about the effect of petitioner's personnel policies on employee morale and the overall work performance of the District Attorney's Office. The Court concludes that her dismissal does not violate the First Amendment, primarily because the questionnaire addresses matters that, in the Court's view, are not of public concern. It is hornbook law, however, that speech about "the manner in which government is operated or should be operated" is an essential part of the communications necessary for self-governance the protection of which was a central purpose of the First Amendment. Because the questionnaire addressed such matters and its distribution did not adversely affect the operations of the District Attorney's Office or interfere with Myers' working relationship with her fellow employees, I dissent.

* * *

Such extreme deference to the employer's judgment is not appropriate when public employees voice critical views concerning the operations of the agency for which they work. Although an employer's determination that an employee's statements have undermined essential working relationships must be carefully weighed in the *Pickering* balance, we must bear in mind that "the threat of dismissal from public employment is . . . a potent means of inhibiting speech." If the employer's judgment is to be controlling, public employees will not speak out when what they have to say is critical of their supervisors. In order to protect public employees' First Amendment right to voice critical views on issues of public importance, the courts must make their own appraisal of the effects of the speech in question.

* * *

The Court's decision today inevitably will deter public employees from making critical statements about the manner in which government agencies are operated for fear that doing so will provoke their dismissal. As a result, the public will be deprived of valuable information with which to evaluate the performance of elected officials. Because protecting the dissemination of such information is an essential function of the First Amendment, I dissent.

Through 1983 and the *Connick* decision, several professors won cases in which their unpopular actions had caused them to be fired, but the record was mixed. In *Starsky v. Williams*, 353 F. Supp. 900 (1972), an untenured professor who missed classes in order to attend an off-campus rally was reinstated when the court held that the board and president impermissibly dismissed him: "The Board fails to distinguish those circumstances in which Professor Starsky spoke as a professional, under circumstances where the interests of the school balanced First Amendment interest sufficiently to warrant a narrower professional standard of speech, from those circumstances in which [he] spoke publicly as a citizen and had the right to the same broad constitutional protection afforded every citizen ... and the major emphasis in the charges is so clearly based upon protected ideology, that this court must conclude that the primary reason for the discipline of Professor Starsky is grounded in his exercise of his First Amendment rights in expressing unpopular views." In *Peacock v. Board of Regents*, 510 F.2d 1324 (9th Cir. 1975), a suit against the same Regents, the court treated a tenured faculty dismissal quite differently. Professor Peacock had disagreed with his dean, and was removed as department chair and then removed as a tenured professor, with only a post-suspension hearing. The court upheld the dismissal, citing a "common law of the campus" for the proposition that an administrative appointment was at-will. In *Strasny v. Board of Trustees of Central Washington University*, 647 P.2d 496 (Wash. App. 1982), a professor who ignored specific warnings that he not leave the country to lecture, causing him to miss classes, was found to be insubordinate. His request to travel was not an academic freedom issue, since the denial was grounded in his teaching obligations to students.

Connick significantly changed the contours of public employees' status to dissent, either publicly or privately. Within a year of *Connick*, five cases brought by college professors on *Pickering* grounds had all been lost by the professors. As one example, *Landrum v. Eastern Kentucky University*, 578 F. Supp. 241 (D.C. Ky. 1984), held that *Pickering* cases "would have been different under *Connick*": "In frankness, the court must state that it reads *Connick* as deliberately intended to narrow the scope of [*Pickering* cases], even though they were not expressly overruled. A careful study of all these decisions leads to the inevitable conclusion that the First Amendment in the employment context is now to be more narrowly interpreted to give greater scope to the legitimate rights of governmental entities as employers, and also to reduce the burdens on the courts caused by the burgeoning of litigation initiated by the decision upon which plaintiff relies here."

Ferrara v. Mills

781 F.2d 1508 (11th Cir. 1986)

HATCHETT, Circuit Judge:

In this civil rights action a public school teacher contends that school administrators assigned him an inferior teaching schedule in retaliation for his criticism of school policies. The district court granted summary judgment for the school administrators. We affirm.

FACTS

Lawrence J. Ferrara, the appellant, has been employed with the Palm Beach County School Board, Palm Beach, Florida, as a teacher since 1965. He has taught in the social studies department of John I. Leonard Community High School in Lake Worth, Florida, since 1970. Traditionally, he taught eleventh and twelfth grade American history and political science courses between 6:45 a.m. and 2:15 p.m. on school days.

* * *

In January, 1980, Ferrara spoke out against the high school's use of collegiate registration, a procedure through which students are permitted to choose their subjects and teachers. At a meeting of the high school faculty in the spring of 1981, the faculty expressed general disapproval of collegiate registration and recommended to Principal John Munroe that the practice be discontinued. Consistent with this recommendation, Munroe abolished collegiate registration.

Later that term, on June 10, 1981, at Ferrara's request, Munroe and Ferrara met "to discuss several items regarding the assignment of [Ferrara's] subjects for the coming 1981–82 school year." Ferrara reiterated his request to teach a newly instituted advanced history course and expressed his disapproval of the practice of filling teacher vacancies within the social studies department with physical education teachers and athletic coaches. Ferrara expressed particular displeasure at the fact that one of the physical education teachers assigned to teach a social studies course was not certified in the field of social studies, and suggested that such out-of-field placement of teachers contributes to "civic illiteracy."

Sometime after the June, 1981, meeting, Munroe assigned Ferrara to teach elective courses to ninth and tenth graders between 9:45 a.m. and 5:15 p.m., rather than the required courses which he had traditionally taught to eleventh and twelfth graders between 6:45 a.m. and 2:15 p.m.

* * *

"Follow[ing] the required procedures," Ferrara solicited the assistance of Thomas Mills, the superintendent of schools for Palm Beach County. Dissatisfied with Mills's decision not to alter his schedule, Ferrara took his grievance to the Palm Beach County School Board. The school board also declined to intervene. Thereafter, Ferrara allegedly became inflicted with severe headaches, psoriasis, insomnia, and other stress-related disorders and, consequently, was not able to work for the remainder of the 1981–82 school year.

On July 29, 1982, pursuant to 42 U.S.C.A. § 1983 and the first and fourteenth amendments to the Constitution, Ferrara filed this action.

* * *

CONTENTIONS OF THE PARTIES

Ferrara challenges the district court's entry of summary judgment in favor of the school administrators on two grounds. First, he argues that disputed issues of material fact exist as to the time, place, manner, and context of his speech. Second, he contends that the district court erred in imposing upon him the undue burden of affirmatively proving that his speech related to matters of interest to the community at large, rather than imposing upon the school administrators the burden of proving that the speech related only to matters of personal interest to him.

The school administrators argue that the time, manner, and context of Ferrara's speech illustrate that the speech related only to Ferrara's course assignments, a matter not of public concern, but of interest only to Ferrara.

ISSUES

The issues which we address are: (1) whether the district court correctly allocated the relevant burdens of proof, and (2) whether Ferrara's speech related to matters of public concern.

* * *

DISCUSSION

Because of some confusion in this area of the law, we begin our discussion with an outline of the analytic framework which gives definition to our consideration of Ferrara's first amendment claim.

I. Analytic Framework

A.

[1] To prevail on his claim that the school administrators infringed upon his first amendment right to freedom of speech, Ferrara must establish prima facie that his speech (1) is constitutionally protected, and (2) was a substantial or motivating factor in the decision to alter his teaching assignments. If Ferrara is successful in making this initial showing, the burden then shifts to the school administrators to show by a preponderance of the evidence that they would have altered Ferrara's teaching assignments even in the absence of his protected speech.

The Supreme Court's most recent explication of the *Mt. Healthy* test is found in *Connick v. Myers*. The Supreme Court announced in *Connick* that the question of whether a public employee's speech is constitutionally protected turns upon whether the speech related to matters of public concern or to matters of merely personal interest to the employee. "Whether an employee's speech addresses a matter of public concern must be determined by the content, form, and context of a given statement, as revealed by the whole record."

* * *

[2] If the employee's speech cannot fairly be characterized as constituting speech on a matter of public concern, the inquiry is at an end. With that circumstance present, we need not proceed to determine whether the employee's speech was a substantial or motivating factor in the adverse employment decision.

[3] If, however, the employee's speech is determined to relate to a matter of public concern and to have been a substantial or motivating factor in the adverse employment

decision, the inquiry focuses upon whether the adverse employment decision was justified.

The fact that an employee is retaliated against for exercising constitutionally protected speech does not *automatically* render the disciplinary action unconstitutional. A public employee's free speech rights are not absolute. The employee's interest must be weighed against that of the state to determine which is more compelling in a given situation.

In weighing the competing interests, we must consider such factors as (1) whether the nature of the employer's public responsibilities are such that a close working relationship is essential, (2) the manner, time, and place of the speech, and (3) the context within which the speech was made.

[5] The manner, time, and place of the employee's speech are factors to be weighed in the *Pickering* balance of the employer's and employee's competing interests. These factors are not, however, relevant at the first level of the analysis. The *Pickering* balance is not triggered unless it is first determined that the employee's speech is constitutionally protected. If the employee's speech does not relate to matters of public concern, then the employee has no first amendment interest against which the employer's interest need be weighed.

*   *   *

The degree of public interest in a public employee's speech is yet another factor which is relevant only in the context of the *Pickering* balance of the employer's interest in the efficient operation of the public office against the employee's constitutionally protected right to freedom of speech.

[7] Thus, the burden of proof is not, as Ferrara argues, upon the school administrators to demonstrate that Ferrara's speech related only to matters of personal interest to him. Rather, the burden of proof is, in the first instance, upon Ferrara to demonstrate, by resort to the content, form, and context of his speech, that the speech related to matters of public concern.

*   *   *

Having considered the content, form, and context of Ferrara's speech, we conclude that it cannot fairly be characterized as constituting speech on a matter of public concern. The school administrators are entitled to judgment as a matter of law on the first amendment claim. Accordingly, we affirm the district court's entry of summary judgment in favor of the school administrators.

Is the Speech Protected?

Franklin v. Stanford University
218 Cal. Rptr. 228 (Cal. App. 6 Dist. 1985)

AGLIANO, Associate Justice.

This appeal by plaintiff H. Bruce Franklin challenges the judgment of the trial court upholding plaintiff's dismissal by his former employer, Leland Stanford Junior University. The underlying dispute dates back to a time of protest against the Vietnam war. More specifically, it concerns plaintiff's conduct on February 10, 1971. He was then, as he described himself, a leader of the local anti-war movement, his stature deriving partly from his tenured position as an associate professor of English. This action, filed August 15, 1972, challenges his dismissal from that position. Plaintiff's major contentions are that his conduct was protected by the First Amendment and the University regulations authorizing his discharge were unconstitutionally vague. We reject these contentions and the others discussed below.[3]

Procedural History

On March 22, 1971, University President Lyman filed charges with the Faculty Advisory Board of the Academic Council against plaintiff, alleging he had engaged in activities which constituted a "substantial and manifest neglect of duty and a substantial impairment of his performance of his appropriate functions" within the University in violation of the Statement of Policy on Appointment and Tenure at Stanford University and the Stanford Policy on Campus Disruption.

The charges alleged four incidents:

1. On January 11, 1971, plaintiff participated in disruptive conduct which prevented Ambassador Henry Cabot Lodge from speaking at a public program at the University (Lodge incident).

2. On February 10, 1971, at a rally at White Memorial Plaza to discuss methods of protesting the Vietnam War, plaintiff intentionally "urged and incited students and other[s] . . . to [disrupt University functions] and specifically to shut down a University computer facility known as the Computation Center" (White Plaza speech).

3. Later on February 10, 1971, following disruption at the Computation Center, plaintiff significantly interfered with a police order to disperse by inciting those present to disobey it (Computation Center incident).

4. On the evening of February 10, 1971, at a rally in the Old Union Courtyard, plaintiff "intentionally urged and incited students and other persons to engage in conduct calculated to disrupt activities of the University . . . and which threatened injury to individuals and property" (Old Union speech).

Upon plaintiff's request, a seven-member Faculty Advisory Board evaluated the charges in accordance with the University's tenure agreement. Following 33 days of hearing in which 111 witnesses testified, the Board, on January 5, 1972, issued a detailed decision in which it (1) declined to sustain the charge regarding the Lodge incident; (2) unanimously sustained the charge regarding the White Plaza speech; (3) sustained the charges regarding the Computation Center incident and Old Union speeches by a 5–2 vote; and (4) by the same 5–2 vote recommended plaintiff's dismissal. President Lyman and the Board of Trustees of the University accepted the recommendation and discharged plaintiff effective August 31, 1972.

Plaintiff filed this action seeking reinstatement, declaratory relief, back pay and damages.

---

3. We do not here decide that First Amendment free speech principles apply to Stanford or any private institution. The Faculty Advisory Board which recommended plaintiff's termination committed the University in this case to affording him the same constitutional protection as that available were he employed by a state school. For purposes of this appeal and the motions under review, Stanford has adopted the position that the outcome is the same whether it is viewed as a private or public employer. We thus review Stanford's action as if it were state action.

On January 4, 1978, the trial court determined the University's standard for dismissal was not unconstitutionally vague and plaintiff's conduct during the White Plaza speech and the Computation Center incident was not constitutionally protected. However, the court did not sustain the charge relating to the "Old Union Speech." Since the trial court could not determine whether the University would have imposed the same penalty based on two of the three charges, on September 1, 1978, the case was remanded to the University for such determination.

The Faculty Advisory Board conducted further proceedings without redetermining the facts found by the 1972 board. On May 30, 1980, the Advisory Board unanimously recommended plaintiff's dismissal be reaffirmed. The Board of Trustees accepted the recommendation and reaffirmed plaintiff's dismissal on July 14, 1980.

The case returned to the trial court on November 18, 1980, for review. The court concluded the proceedings were proper, there was no abuse of discretion in the Advisory Board's determination that either of the two charges was serious enough to merit dismissal, and entered judgment in favor of defendants.

Plaintiff's timely appeal followed.

* * *

Facts

Both incidents occurred on February 10, 1971. The second ensued from the first, but both are set in a broader context. There was unrest at Stanford about the war in Indochina and the University's role in U.S. involvement. On January 11, 1971, a speech on campus by Ambassador Henry Cabot Lodge was disrupted. Proceedings by the Stanford Judicial Council against several students due to this disruption were in progress.

Several arson attempts and false alarms occurred on the evening of Saturday, February 6. The rumored invasion of Laos was officially confirmed on Sunday, February 7. That evening about 600 persons attended an antiwar benefit in Dinkelspiel Auditorium. Leaflets were circulated to the crowd, including one by an antiwar group called "The Inquisition" which described a war-simulation program by the Stanford Research Institute run at the school's Computation Center and advocated immediate end to war research at the Center. The Center was evacuated that evening due to a bomb threat. After the gathering at Dinkelspiel, about 100 windows were broken on campus, including windows on two University police cars when they trained spotlights on a group throwing rocks.

On Monday, February 8, a noon rally at White Memorial Plaza on campus was attended by about 800 persons. Then, about 150 persons blocked a room in which members of the Stanford Board of Trustees were meeting. The group dispersed after the Sheriff declared an unlawful assembly and deputy sheriffs arrived. Later that day the police dispersed two other assemblies and maintained a presence on campus that evening.

At 8 p.m., on Tuesday, February 9, a three-hour meeting in Dinkelspiel Auditorium was attended by about 800 persons. Plaintiff was present throughout the following events. An open discussion was guided by a chairman. Information was received regarding protest activities in other areas. Proposals were sought regarding positions to take and demands to make, and finally, proposals were sought for implementation.

Several written demands were announced. "The Inquisition" demand centered on publicizing and prohibiting use of the Computation Center and any other Stanford facilities for military research. Plaintiff spoke in response to a question concerning the connection between United States involvement in Indochina and local demands for action. His point was that multi-national corporations represented by the Stanford Board of Trustees were the architects of a planned Pacific Basin empire of which the war was just a part. He called for discussion of that "consciousness," contending that if persuasive, then "we ought to take some very effective action here on the University" rather than only to lie down in front of military trains. Others then spoke to develop the connection as plaintiff had suggested. Three demands were approved by majority vote, namely: (1) the United States should get out of Southeast Asia, (2) all political prisoners should be freed, and (3) the University should end its participation in the war.

The discussion moved on to implementation of the demands. A speaker recommended shutting down the University by a strike. Another suggested a strike at the Computation Center because it was vulnerable to power loss. The first speaker responded that the Computation Center power supply need not be hit, but the workers could be stopped somehow. A majority favored a strike to include the Computation Center as a target. They then agreed on a plan of action, consisting of a noon rally the following day to initiate a roving strike to close down as many buildings as they could reach and an exploratory march to the Computation Center after that evening's meeting. Plaintiff joined the march to the Computation Center that evening.

On Wednesday, February 10, a noon rally at White Memorial Plaza was attended by about 700 people, including plaintiff. Some suggested that the antiwar protest should be directed at writing letters to Congress and generating community support. Others characterized these speakers as counter-insurgents. There were reminders that the purpose of the rally was to decide what to strike, not whether to strike. Nevertheless, other speakers continued to make other proposals for action, such as sending money to the Pathet Lao or marching in protest the following day.

Plaintiff made what proved to be the last speech of the rally. He concluded his speech by urging that the people take the action of shutting down the University Computation Center. Thereafter a vote was taken on whether to "put down" the Computation Center or the Hoover Institute, and the majority voted for the Computation Center.

Provost Miller was informed the demonstrators were converging on the Computation Center and shortly before 1 p.m., he ordered the building closed. Doors, windows, and gates were locked; handwritten notices were posted on the doors. Two campus police were stationed at the front door. The computer was kept running.

About 100 to 200 demonstrators arrived outside the Center shortly after 1 p.m. A back door was forced open about 1:15 p.m. and a number of people entered through that door, opening other entrances as they occupied the building. At 1:20 p.m., power to the building and the computer was cut off by pulling a master switch near the back door. About 100 to 200 demonstrators occupied the building. Some forced open the doors of the machine room and wires were pulled out on one unit. About $800 of physical damage was done on the premises, disregarding the loss of computer time.

Plaintiff did not immediately join those he had exhorted. Instead, he went to his 1:15 class and since only 7 of the 150 registered students were present, he moved the class to the area outside the Computation Center, where he remained as an observer outside the Center.

Bruce Wiggins, Stanford's Director of Public Safety, and C.D. Marron of the Santa Clara County Sheriff's Office toured the occupied building. At about 3 p.m., they met with representatives of the University's administration and also Sergeant Tamm and Captain Rosa of the Sheriff's Office. Wiggins announced throughout the building a declaration of trespass. No demonstrators departed, although they conferred amongst themselves and decided to leave voluntarily when the police arrived. Officers Marron, Tamm, and Rosa returned to the building about 4 p.m. to attempt to persuade the occupants to leave voluntarily and heard demands that the war-simulation program be removed from the Center. The officers returned again with the information that the Stanford Research Institute work had been stopped, but the occupants demanded a written statement to that effect from the University President.

Soon after 4 p.m., C.D. Marron announced through a bullhorn that the congregation both within and outside the building was an unlawful assembly which should disperse to avoid arrest. There was no immediate response, but as the first platoon of uniformed police arrived and entered the Computation Center, the occupants cleared out without any arrests, some remaining outside the Center. While Marron verified the building was unoccupied, the police formed a two-deep "skirmish line." Marron walked around outside the building, repeating his order to disperse.

It was at this time the second incident occurred. A double line of police was facing the crowd which consisted of demonstrators and observers, including members of the faculty. Clusters of demonstrators heckled the police from about ten feet away. Marron gave the crowd three or four orders to move a wider area away from the Computation Center. Not everyone heard these orders or knew how far back to move. Those who were already farther from the police began to disperse.

Plaintiff reacted to this new order with about three minutes of words and action. He first approached Sergeant Tamm and vigorously challenged the legality of the order to disperse. The crowd shouted support. He also claimed a right to remain as a faculty observer. Tamm disagreed on both points. Plaintiff looked around and saw Dean Lincoln Moses, a faculty observer about to leave. Plaintiff was aware some others were leaving in response to the orders. Plaintiff approached Mr. Moses, shouting to him that he should remain as a faculty observer because the assembly was not illegal and because a police charge and brutality were imminent. Moses halted and began to follow plaintiff, who turned back through the crowd in the direction of the police line, about 50 feet away. He continued to shout that the order to disperse was illegal and that the people had a right to remain. He confronted Tamm face-to-face, loudly disputing the legality of the dispersal order and insisting on his right to remain as a faculty observer. He was aware of a crowd forming around them. There was an attempt by other officers to seize plaintiff, who was then spirited away by his comrades. Then the police charged the crowd.

The Speech Incidents Were Not Constitutionally Immune From Employer Discipline

A public employee cannot be disciplined or discharged for expressive conduct protected by the First and Fourteenth Amendments. Whether the employee's conduct is deemed protected against disciplinary action depends upon a balancing of the interests of the employer and the employee involved in the particular speech incidents.

* * *

Plaintiff ignores *Pickering* and relies on cases such as *Brandenburg v. Ohio* which held: "[T]he constitutional guarantees of free speech and free press do not permit a State to forbid or proscribe advocacy of the use of force or of law violation except where such advocacy is directed to inciting or producing imminent lawless action and is likely to incite or produce such action." *Brandenburg* was concerned with establishing a boundary for the imposition of criminal punishment on speech, however, and identifies speech unprotected by the Constitution in that context.

* * *

The government as an employer is entitled to expect more of its employees than merely noncriminal conduct. We conclude, in light of *Pickering,* that *Brandenburg* is not the controlling test.

* * *

It is clear that the constitutional freedom to speak does not license a teacher to substantially disrupt and interfere with the normal operations of his or her employer, whether they be instruction, research, or administration. Expressive conduct which may not justify criminal or civil liability may be the subject of employer discipline. Plaintiff's expressive conduct in our view was well out of constitutional bounds. Speech which results in disruption, which materially interferes with school activities, or impairs discipline is not constitutionally protected against an employer's response. That description fits plaintiff's White Plaza speech and his interference with the police dispersal order at the Computation Center.

* * *

Plaintiff goes on to attack the Faculty Board's interpretation of the University regulations for its reliance on "a web of largely unwritten rules as tough and living as the British Constitution." We need not discuss whether campus traditions proscribed plaintiff's conduct, however, because the written regulations did so.

Plaintiff asserts there is other evidence apart from the words of the University's regulations which make them vague as applied. He argues that other speakers at the White Plaza and Old Union rallies used similar language without being disciplined; that in prior years other faculty members were involved in sit-ins without discipline; and that faculty members who engaged in violent conduct were subject to lesser discipline. These equal protection arguments have no place in analyzing the clarity of a written regulation; in any event most of this evidence was not presented to the 1972 Faculty Board or the trial court when each ruled on the vagueness argument. He also attempts to demonstrate by affidavits of other faculty members that his discipline had a chilling effect on First Amendment rights. We question whether the vagueness of a regulation could be proved by the opinion of experts or lay witnesses; in any event, these affidavits do not address this issue and are irrelevant.

School regulations need not be spelled out with the precision of a criminal code. We find the Stanford regulations at issue constitutionally clear as interpreted by the Faculty Advisory Board to apply to plaintiff's conduct.

The judgment is affirmed.

Kemp v. Ervin

651 F. Supp. 495 (N.D. Ga. 1986)

Horace T. WARD, District Judge.

I. FACTUAL STATEMENT

This case originated with the filing by the plaintiff of an action against the defendants under 42 U.S.C. § 1983 for monetary damages, attorneys' fees and for declaratory and injunctive relief. The plaintiff was at all times relevant to her lawsuit an Assistant Professor of English (and for a time Coordinator of the English Component) in the Division of Developmental Studies at the University of Georgia. The defendants originally included the Board of Regents of the University System of Georgia, but prior to trial the Board of Regents was dismissed as a party. The defendants at the time of trial and judgment consisted of two administrators at the University of Georgia. One defendant is Dr. Leroy Ervin, Director of the Division of Developmental Studies and Assistant Vice President for Academic Affairs. The other defendant is Dr. Virginia Trotter, who served as the Vice President of Academic Affairs for the University of Georgia.

Plaintiff contends that she was deprived of her employment and other employment benefits because of the exercise of the freedom of speech rights secured to her by the First and Fourteenth Amendments of the Constitution of the United States. The plaintiff demanded a jury trial and the case was tried before a court and jury, with the trial time covering approximately six weeks. The jury determined that the plaintiff's first amendment rights of free speech were violated in the job actions taken against her and that both defendants were involved.

In its verdict, the jury awarded the total of $2,579,681.95 in terms of compensatory and punitive damages. In specific details, the compensatory damages awarded against both defendants were as follows: $79,680.95 as lost wages, $200,000 for mental distress, and $1.00 for loss of professional reputation. Punitive damages were awarded against defendant Trotter in the amount of $1.5 million dollars and against defendant Ervin in the amount of $800,000.

It was the contention of the plaintiff that defendants Ervin and Trotter took several adverse employment actions against her in violation of her constitutional rights to freedom of speech secured by the first amendment. Specifically, plaintiff contended that she was relieved of all committee chairmanships, demoted from the position as Coordinator of the English component, and was ultimately terminated from her position as a nontenured professor in retaliation for engaging in protected speech activities. Among the speech activities asserted by the plaintiff were the following: participation in a student disciplinary hearing concerning an obscene phone call made to her by a student, protest to her supervisors and others because of the exiting of nine student athletes who had not met exit qualifications, and participation in an administrative hearing in which she challenged her removal as English Coordinator.

To the contrary, defendants denied that any of the employment actions taken with respect to the plaintiff were in retaliation for her exercise of protected free speech, or that her speech activities constituted a substantial or motivating factor in any of the employment decisions taken with regard to the plaintiff. Defendants further contend that there was a factual basis for all employment decisions made regarding the plaintiff, and that these actions would have been taken without regard to plaintiff's outspokenness. Also, defendant Virginia Trotter contended that she was not directly involved in any of the employment decisions taken with regard to the plaintiff.

Only a small portion of the evidence presented at the long trial will be set out here. Other significant portions will be dealt with in a limited manner hereinafter in this Opinion as various legal issues are discussed. The plaintiff, who held an Ed.D. degree from the University of Georgia at the time of her severance, had been employed as a teacher in the Division of Developmental Studies at the University from 1976 until the non-renewal of her contract at the conclusion of the 1982–83 academic year. She served as an English instructor, was promoted to the rank of assistant professor in 1980, and served as the coordinator of the English component within the Department until her removal from that position in February 1982. Dr. Leroy Ervin, as Director of the Division of Developmental Studies, was the plaintiff's immediate supervisor. The Division of Developmental Studies at all times relevant to the issues raised in this case was not a part of or supervised by any of the regular academic departments or schools of the University of Georgia. Dr. Ervin reported directly to Dr. Virginia Trotter, who was his supervisor.

The Division of Developmental Studies was not one of the regular academic units of the University of Georgia, and was established and maintained for the purpose of being an educational unit to which incoming high school graduates who were not ready or who could not meet the qualifications for regular University admission would be admitted. These students generally remained in Developmental Studies until they met the requirements to enter the regular college program. Rather than being promoted to the regular college program, they were "exited" from Developmental Studies if they met the requirements. Otherwise, they were dismissed from the University. On occasion, certain students who were enrolled in regular college programs were admitted to Developmental Studies for brief periods of time to participate in certain courses. The Division of Developmental Studies consisted of three main components: Mathematics, English and Reading, together with research and counseling services. Each of the three units was headed by a coordinator.

In the fall of 1982 the plaintiff insisted on bringing a student before the student disciplinary hearing to determine whether he had made an obscene phone call to her, and participated in the hearing. For various reasons, Dr. Ervin sought to persuade the plaintiff from pressing the charges before the student judiciary. Shortly thereafter, the plaintiff was removed from the chairmanship of the Promotion and Tenure Committee. Around the conclusion of the fall 1981 quarter, nine (9) student athletes were "exited" from the developmental studies program into the regular University curriculum, though each had received a "D" in English during their fourth quarter. Simultaneously, at least one non-athlete student who had received a "D" in English during the fourth quarter was dismissed from the University. The nine athletes were administratively exited by defendant Trotter by virtue of authority vested in her as Vice President of Academic Affairs.

It is clear from the evidence that the exiting of the nine students was in contravention of University policy that required that students within the program achieve a minimum grade of "C" in English during the fourth and final quarter of the program. A number of faculty members decided to protest this decision, and the plaintiff was in the forefront of the protest. Plaintiff drafted a strong proposed letter to be directed to defendant Trotter and openly stated her views to the committee. An ad hoc faculty committee met with defendant Trotter as a part of the protest. Although a member of the committee, the plaintiff was unable to attend. Shortly after plaintiff's participation in the faculty protest of the exiting of the nine students, defendant Ervin removed her from the position as Coordinator of English in the division, which led to a change in her contract from 12 months to 9 months. Thereafter, the plaintiff pursued an administrative grievance within the University of Georgia seeking redress for her removal from the position of Coordinator of the English component. At the hearing she was represented by Mr. Larry Blount, a member of the University of Georgia School of Law faculty. Defendant Trotter appointed a hearing tribunal, consisting of herself and two other vice presidents, to hear the plaintiff's complaint. There is conflict in the evidence as to what the authority of the tribunal was, and as to the nature of plaintiff's appeal. It is clear that the plaintiff's perception of her endeavor was that she was seeking a review of the merits of her grievance in an effort to have the action of defendant Ervin changed. The tribunal simply reviewed the procedure which defendant Ervin applied to effect plaintiff's removal and found that the procedure was appropriate. Following the hearing and as a result of a telephone conversation with plaintiff's attorney, Dr. Trotter prepared a written memorandum in which she underlined the statement that Dr. Kemp "is threatening to go public." The evidence further reveals that defendant Ervin attended the hearing before the tribunal, at which time he demonstrated his disagreement and hostility toward plaintiff's presentation. During the latter part of the summer of 1982, defendant Ervin notified Dr. Kemp in writing that he was recommending that her contract of employment not be renewed for the academic year 1983–84. One witness testified that Dr. Ervin told her that he was going to get rid of the plaintiff. Dr. Ervin denied that he made this statement.

Testimony of Dr. Trotter at a prior hearing was read into the record in which she testified about her knowledge and concurrence with the action taken by Dr. Ervin. She stated that his recommendation to nonrenew plaintiff's contract was reviewed and approved by her. Although Dr. Ervin did not specifically testify that he asked for the approval or concurrence of Dr. Trotter, he testified that he informed her of his decision to remove Dr. Kemp from English Coordinator and to recommend nonrenewal of her employment contract with the University prior to taking those actions. Also, the plaintiff introduced certain notes made by Dr. Trotter in relation to the ad hoc committee meeting. These notes were highly critical of Dr. Kemp, a matter that was not the subject matter of the meeting.

The evidence in the record supports a finding of various aspects of preferential treatment given to revenue producing athletes (scholarship athletes), particularly in the relaxing of admission standards and, to some extent, efforts to maintain their enrollment for extended periods of time during their period of eligibility. Plaintiff testified that, during a dispute about a student athlete, defendant Ervin inquired of her as to whom did she think was more important to the University—a star basketball player or the plaintiff.

The defendants contended that there was no causal connection between the employment actions taken regarding the plaintiff and her outspokenness as to student athletes or otherwise. The defendants submitted evidence in an effort to show that they would have demoted and dismissed Dr. Kemp notwithstanding her exercise of first amendment rights. Defendants sought to prove that the plaintiff did not participate in research, was insubordinate and had difficulty in getting along with her peers and others. Defendants further sought to show that there was no reasonable likelihood that she would be tenured and that the fair thing to do, from an academic point of view, was to nonrenew her contract at the finding that the plaintiff's research efforts might not have satisfied the University requirement for research as a tenure requirement, there was testimony that it should have been considered as a scholarly activity. Also, the evidence showed widespread disagreement as to the research required of members of the faculty in Developmental Studies, as this was primarily a teaching unit. While the evidence is sufficient to support a finding that the plaintiff was often caustic and argumentative, it was conceded by the defendants that she was an excellent English teacher.

II. DISCUSSION AND CONCLUSIONS OF LAW

* * *

With the aim in mind of clearly focusing on the central issue in the case and to eliminate possible jury confusion, the court gave an instruction which the defendants now say was inadequate. In this regard, the court instructed the jury as follows:

> The jury is to bear in mind that this is a free speech case and that the central issue to be decided is whether the plaintiff was retaliated against because of her exercise of protected speech activities. The guidelines to be used by the jury in determining this issue are set forth hereinafter in these instructions. While many relevant facts and circumstances must be considered by the jury in reaching a decision on the central issue, there are many other issues which are not to be decided in this case. The jury is not called upon to render a decision as to whether it is right or wrong to give preferential treatment to scholarship athletes and other students or on the merits of the admission policies regarding these particular students.

The jury was further instructed in detail regarding the issues for its determination. The court now determines that when the above-quoted language from the instructions to the jury is reviewed and evaluated in the context of the total instructions given, it is neither misleading nor incomplete.

* * *

As far as the court is aware, this might be the largest amount of punitive damages of record in a § 1983 case involving public employees or officers (particularly university administrators). Reported cases reveal instances of higher awards of punitive damages in other civil rights cases involving claims against major business corporations. The court can only speculate as to what reasons prompted the jury to arrive at the size of the punitive damages award. There was ample evidence from which the jury could have determined that the plaintiff was chastised for speaking out against a long-standing and well-entrenched practice (preferential treatment to athletes) which was beyond the business of an English teacher in developmental studies. This thought is certainly raised by the statement attributed to Dr. Ervin to the plaintiff as to whether she considered herself as important to the University as a star basketball player. The jury certainly had no understanding as to Eleventh Amendment considerations and the coverage of § 1983 with regard to who would be responsible for paying the award. It might be that the jury thought that there was insurance or that others would be equally responsible for the debt. It is most probable that the violation of free speech in the context of the volatile subject of preferential treatment to athletes was a consideration by the jury.

* * *

The aim and purpose of the jury with regard to its punitive damages award was clearly in order given the facts and circumstances of the case. It was designed to be a message that was loud and clear and far reaching in scope. Unfortunately, the reach and coverage of the award far out distance the aim and purpose, and exceed the limit of punitive damages in the context of this case. The amount of the punitive damages award was and is shockingly excessive. Further, to the extent that its weight is to be borne solely by the defendants in their personal capacities, it is oppressive.

* * *

Professor Kemp succeeded as no professional plaintiff before her. After winning her case, including $2.57 million, a settlement was negotiated, in which she collected approximately $80,000 in back pay, approximately $600,000 for mental distress, $400,000 in punitive damages, and $1.00 for damages to her reputation. In addition, on July 1, 1986, she was reinstated to her position as co-director in developmental studies, and to a tenure-track position in which she has the traditional 7 years to earn tenure.

Is the Speech a Substantial or Motivating Reason?

Hamer v. Brown
831 F.2d 1398 (8th Cir. 1987)

McMILLIAN, Circuit Judge.

Hamer was hired by SAU-Tech in 1978 as director of the Environmental Academy. Later, he was also named director of the Public Administrative and Technical Services Division (PATSD). In February 1982, Hamer was removed as director of the Environmental Academy but continued as director of PATSD.

In March 1982, a committee of the Arkansas Fire Prevention Commission (committee) came to SAU-Tech to investigate complaints made by firefighters who had attended training sessions at the Arkansas Fire Training Academy (AFTA). AFTA is located at and administered by SAU-Tech and provides training to firefighters throughout the state. Allegations of mismanagement of AFTA facilities and misuse of AFTA funds by SAU-Tech prompted the investigation.

The committee asked Hamer to talk with them privately about his perception of problems with the SAU-Tech administration. Hamer told the committee that there was a problem with the way SAU-Tech was using AFTA money; he stated that the SAU-Tech administration was "moving money around to make the place look nice while technical programs went underfunded." Hamer also told the committee that the SAU-Tech administration indiscriminately fired people that it did not like and then created documents to justify the firing.

A day or two after Hamer met with the committee, he was approached in the cafeteria by Vice Chancellor Gary Oden. Oden asked Hamer if he had talked to the committee and what he had said to them. Hamer responded that he did not wish to discuss the matter with Oden. Hamer contends that he was treated less favorably by Vice Chancellor Oden and Chancellor George Brown after they became aware that he had talked to the committee. He concedes, however, that in April 1982 (a month after he spoke with the committee), his contract was renewed for the school year August 1, 1982 to May 31, 1983.

In January and February 1983, several reports critical of the relationship between AFTA and SAU-Tech were issued, including a final recommendation from the committee that AFTA be removed from SAU-Tech. The most serious charge—misuse of funds by the SAU-Tech administration—was not substantiated. On April 29, 1983, Chancellor Brown presented Hamer with a terminal contract for the 1983–84 school year, which provided: "This contract is terminal and will not be renewed beyond the end of the current school year, June 20, 1984." Brown told Hamer the contract was not being renewed because PATSD had a low enrollment and further that PATSD's continued existence depended on program growth and development in the near future.

Enrollment in PATSD had steadily declined from a high of 682 students in 1978–79 to only 152 students in 1982–83. During the same period, overall enrollment at SAU-Tech had increased substantially.

* * *

Courts, in reviewing challenges to discharges based on alleged violations of freedom of speech rights, have applied a three-step analysis. A court must determine whether: (1) the plaintiff established that he or she engaged in protected activity, *Pickering*, (2) the plaintiff established that the protected activity was a substantial or a motivating factor in the action taken against him or her, *Mt. Healthy*, and (3) the employer demonstrated that the same action would have been taken in the absence of the protected activity. *Givhan.*

In determining whether speech is constitutionally protected, the court must first consider whether the speech involves a matter of public concern. In the present case, the district court held that Hamer's speech was not protected because it involved only internal campus matters, i.e., the administration and facilities at SAU-Tech, and did not concern the general public.

The Supreme Court has held that a public employee's speech is protected activity when he or she speaks "as a citizen upon matters of public concern," but not when he or she speaks "as an employee upon matters only of personal interest." Not all matters which transpire within a government office nor every criticism directed at a public official by a public employee are matters of public concern. "Whether an employee's speech addresses a matter of public concern must be determined by the content, form, and context of a given statement, as revealed by the whole record."

> When employee expression cannot be fairly considered as relating to any matter of political, social, or other concern to the community, government officials should enjoy wide latitude in managing their offices, without intrusive oversight by the judiciary in the name of the First Amendment. Perhaps the government employer's dismissal of the worker may not be fair, but ordinary dismissals from government service which violate no fixed tenure or applicable statute or regulation are not subject to judicial review even if the reasons for dismissal are alleged to be mistaken or unreasonable.

Applying the above principles to Hamer's speech, we hold that the district court erred in holding that Hamer's speech did not relate to a matter of public concern. Hamer's speech related to the expenditure of public funds and the proper functioning of a state-supported entity and his comments were made in response to a request by a committee which was authorized to investigate the relationship between SAU-Tech and AFTA.

Having determined that Hamer's speech involved a matter of public concern, next we must balance the interest of Hamer, as a citizen, in commenting upon such matters against the interest of SAU-Tech, as an employer, in rendering efficient educational service through its employees. This court has considered the following factors in making this determination: (1) the need for harmony in the office or the workplace; (2) whether the government's responsibilities require a close working relationship between the plaintiff and co-workers; (3) whether the speech in question has caused or could cause the relationship to deteriorate; (4) the time, manner and place of the speech; (5) the context in which the dispute arose; (6) the degree of public interest in the speech; and (7) whether the speech impeded the employee's ability to perform his or her duties.

The district court held that the interest of SAU-Tech in the efficient operation of its campus, which required a harmonious relationship between the division directors and the administration, outweighed Hamer's interest in complaining about the administration. Memorandum opinion at 664. The district court further found that Hamer's complaints to the committee impeded his ability to perform his duties. We do not agree.

As we held above, the proper expenditure of funds and the implementation of programs by a state educational institution is a matter of public concern and also a matter of public interest. The record reflects that SAU-Tech's administration of AFTA was a matter of public interest and controversy; the presence of an investigating committee is indisputable evidence of this. Hamer's speech was also given at an appropriate time and place and in an appropriate manner. The committee asked Hamer to talk with them privately about his general perception of issues under investigation regarding SAU-Tech's administration and policy. The generality of Hamer's remarks about administration policy was consistent with the purpose for which he was invited to talk with the investigators. We reject SAU-Tech's argument that Hamer's speech was not protected because he spoke about matters and problems for which he did not have responsibility and which had not been brought to the attention of the administration. An employee may not be limited to speaking only about those matters which relate directly to his or her job nor may an employer require an employee to discuss with the employer matters which would otherwise be constitutionally protected before speaking publicly.

SAU-Tech insists, however, that Hamer's speech seriously undermined the working relationship between division directors and the SAU-Tech administration. We rejected a similar argument as too broad. We held that a teacher's relationship with a school administrator was not of such a personal and intimate nature that certain forms of criticism of the superior by the teacher would seriously undermine the effectiveness of the working relationship between them. There is no evidence in the present case that Hamer's position involved a close personal or intimate relationship with the SAU-Tech administrators. Moreover, from the record it is not clear that Hamer's criticism was directed at his immediate supervisor or at any particular person or persons.

While we recognize that even such general criticism may detract from the desired harmony and cohesion in an educational institution, such a result is not sufficient to defeat an employee's interest in speaking out on matters of public concern.

We next consider whether Hamer's protected speech was a substantial or motivating factor in the termination of his contract. The district court found that the refusal to renew Hamer's contract was because of the decline in PATSD enrollment from 1980 to 1982; this decline occurred prior to March 1982 when Hamer made his statements to the committee. The district court also found that Hamer had failed to recruit students for PATSD, that the obstacles that Chancellor Brown allegedly placed in the path of increased enrollment in the division occurred after the decision had been made not to renew Hamer's contract, and that no action was taken against Hamer for one year after his statements to the committee. The district court also found that Chancellor Brown did not know that Hamer had talked to the committee until the termination appeal process and thus had no reason to retaliate against him.

We hold that the district court did not clearly err in holding that Hamer's speech was not a substantial and motivating factor in the termination of his contract. There was undisputed evidence that there had been a marked and persistent decline in enrollment in PATSD. Hamer's allegations do not explain the enrollment decline because the actions Chancellor Brown allegedly took to obstruct enrollment in PATSD took place after the decision to terminate Hamer's contract had already been made. Although there was disputed evidence that SAU-Tech terminated Hamer at the earliest possible time following his speech, the district court credited the testimony of the SAU-Tech administrators and concluded that Hamer's speech was not a motivating or substantial factor in SAU-Tech's refusal to renew his contract.

Because we hold that Hamer failed to establish a causal relationship between his protected speech and the termination of PATSD and his contract of employment, Hamer's claim that his First Amendment rights were violated must fail.

Accordingly, the judgment of the district court is affirmed.

Honore v. Douglas
833 F.2d 565 (5th Cir. 1987)

POLITZ, Circuit Judge:

Stephan L. Honore appeals an adverse summary judgment, rejecting his claims that the termination of his employment as a member of the faculty of the Thurgood Marshall School of Law of Texas Southern University (TSU) violated his due process and first amendment rights. For the reasons assigned we vacate and remand.

Background

Honore was employed as an assistant, then associate, professor of law by TSU from June 1, 1974 until May 31, 1984. After serving four academic years, 1974–1978, Honore was granted three consecutive one-year leaves of absence to serve in the Peace Corps. He returned to full-time teaching in 1981, continuing until TSU declined to grant tenure status and terminated him three years later.

In 1981 when Honore returned to the law school after service with the Peace Corps, the Rank and Tenure Committee of the law school recommended that he be promoted to associate professor and recognized as having tenure, based on his four years of teaching and three years of authorized leave. When Honore was first employed in 1974, controlling University regulations provided for tenure at the end of seven years. The record indicates that this regulation was interpreted as being self-effective and automatic. There was a dispute whether a period of authorized leave would be accruable time. Honore was promoted, but the TSU regents did not extend tenure. Because Honore was then a member of the Rank and Tenure Committee, he maintained that he chose not to contest the disputed tenure question at that time.

In 1978 University regulations affecting tenure were changed to delete the provision allowing automatic vesting of tenure after seven years' service. The provisions of the 1978 manual require the law school and university representatives to address a petition for tenure initially, with the Board of Regents retaining ultimate decisional authority. Those provisions further require notification of the nontenured faculty member, by May 31 of the sixth probationary year, that the seventh year will be the final year of employment unless tenure is sought and secured.

On February 13, 1983, the dean of the law school notified Honore that the next year would be his last unless he became tenured. Insisting that he had automatic tenure under the 1974 regulations, Honore sought formal confirmation of that status. The faculty Rank and Tenure Committee unanimously recommended tenure. The dean objected to Honore's tenure, and the Board of Regents rejected the application. Honore sought review by a faculty hearing committee which received sworn testimony and documentary evidence, including the testimony of Honore, the dean, the former legal counsel for the university who had drafted the 1978 regulations at issue, as well as other members of the faculty tenure committee. The faculty hearing committee recommended that Honore be granted tenure. Its recommendation was rejected, however, by the TSU president and regents.

The record reflects that following his return from the Peace Corps assignment, Honore was active and vocal in law school affairs; and he was directly involved in a number of disputes with the dean. Prior to and about the time of the February 1983 tenure-notice letter, Honore had protested actions by the dean, signed grievance letters, and participated in a meeting of 18 of the 22 members of the faculty where 12, including Honore, expressed a lack of confidence in the dean. The other six abstained from voting. Among items of controversy were the law school admissions policy, the size of the student population, administration of the school budget, and the failure to certify graduates for the Texas bar examination in a timely fashion.

Following the rejection of his tenure petition, Honore filed the instant suit seeking equitable and monetary relief, alleging due process and first amendment violations, and pendent state-law claims. Shortly prior to trial the court considered the matter on motion for summary judgment, found no genuine issue of material fact, and concluded that defendants were entitled to judgment as a matter of law. Honore appeals.

Analysis

The court may terminate litigation by rendering a summary judgment where no genuine issue of material fact exists and the moving party is entitled to judgment as a matter of law. Fed. R. Civ. P. 56(c). Once the moving party makes the initial showing, negating any disputed, material fact, the party opposed to the motion must offer evidence reflecting the existence of one or more genuine issues of material fact. The bare allegations of the pleadings will not suffice.

[1] Honore made no specific response in opposition to defendants' motion, but he had previously offered various admissions of the parties and the transcript of the testimony and arguments before the faculty hearing committee. Summary judgment disposition is inappropriate if the evidence before the court, viewed as a whole, could lead to different factual findings and conclusions. It is not the function of the trial judge, in ruling on a motion for summary judgment, to weigh evidence, assess credibility, or determine the most reasonable inference to be drawn from the evidence. Those are functions of the trier of fact.

We consider the appeal using these rules for guidance, resolving all factual uncertainties and making all reasonable inferences in favor of the nonmoving party.

Due Process

[2] We find no merit in Honore's claim of a denial of procedural due process. He received adequate notice and was given a fair opportunity to be heard. The Board of Regents retained ultimate decisional authority, and its rejection of the hearing committee's recommendation did not vitiate the adequacy of the process.

However, despite this finding of procedural adequacy, we do not agree with the trial court's rejection of the substantive due process claim. To reach the jury with his substantive due process claim, Honore must demonstrate a genuine issue of material fact about his protected property interest (entitlement to vested tenure) and the university's arbitrary or capricious deprivation of that interest.

[3] The trial court concluded that Honore had presented insufficient evidence to create a genuine issue relating to his claim to automatic tenure. It found that Honore had offered no evidence to support his claim of legitimate entitlement to automatic tenure other than an ambiguous "impression of support" from the dean of the law school. The court stated that Honore had not contended that the 1974 regulations, arguably providing for automatic tenure, applied to his case; and it concluded that his 1983 petition formally seeking a declaration of tenure belied his alleged understanding that automatic tenure vested in 1981.

We disagree with these conclusions. In his pleadings Honore made repeated references to regulations in force when he began work in 1974. He claimed the benefit of those regulations. The transcript before the faculty hearing committee contains sufficient evidence to create a jury issue that Honore was claiming automatic tenure under the regulations in effect in 1974, that those regulations were self-effectuating, vesting automatic tenure after seven years of teaching, and that authorized leave time counted as teaching time. Under that scenario, if it be accepted, after Honore taught for four years, was on authorized leaves of absence for three years, and returned to work in 1981 for the eighth year, he was entitled to tenure.

The transcript also contains the testimony of the former counsel for the university, an attorney who drafted the 1978 regulations which changed the tenure requirements. He attested to the nonretroactivity of the 1978 regulations and stated that the earlier regulations controlled the rights of those hired prior to 1978. That witness, a member and former chairman of the faculty tenure committee, was of the opinion that Honore was vested with tenure upon his return from the Peace Corps assignment. Honore testified that it was not until 1983 that he became aware of the 1978 regulations which had been adopted while he was away. He maintains that his first notice came when he received the February 1983 letter from the dean. He testified that he applied to the Rank and Tenure committee solely for administrative recognition of the tenure previously acquired in 1981. The record reflects genuine issues of material fact regarding these matters. Resolution of these factual disputes will involve credibility assessments. Such evaluations may not be made in a summary judgment setting.

We are persuaded that Honore has created a genuine issue concerning his "legitimate claim of entitlement" based on "mutually explicit understandings." He has offered sufficient evidence to reach the trier of fact on the claim that the 1974 regulations created a reasonable understanding that tenure would automatically vest in 1981 if he continuously remained on the law school faculty.

Moreover, the record contains indicators of arbitrary and capricious deprivation. The dean of the law school conceded that he told Honore that his teaching performance was adequate. Honore testified that neither the dean nor any other law school authority ever questioned his teaching performance. He supported his academic credentials with activities generally accepted as reflective of legal scholarship. In addition to publication of writings in legal journals, those activities included beginning a law review program at TSU, training TSU law students for moot court competition, chairing two faculty committees, and, most significantly, establishing a research and writing program designed to assist minority law students at TSU and teaching a similar course at Washburn University. This testimony, alone or in combination with circumstantial evidence of impermissible retaliatory motive (discussed *infra*), creates a genuine issue of material fact as to the arbitrary and capricious nature of Honore's dismissal.

[4] We are mindful of the Supreme Court's admonishment in *Bishop v. Wood* that a federal court is generally not the appropriate forum in which to review the multitude of personnel decisions that are made daily by public agencies. This measure of judicial restraint, however, does not require slavish deference to a university's arbitrary deprivation of a vested property right. Honore is entitled to a jury resolution of his substantive due process claim.

First Amendment

Honore contends that he was dismissed in retaliation for the exercise of his first amendment right to free speech. Regardless of the tenure issue, he could not be discharged for that reason. To establish this claim, Honore must show that his activity was protected by the first amendment and that the protected activity was a substantial and motivating factor in the decision to deny him tenure. Once this is done the defendants must show "by a preponderance of the evidence that [they] would have reached the same decision," without consideration of the protected activity.

[5] The trial court found that Honore's speech embraced subjects of public concern which were protected by the first amendment. That factual finding is amply supported by the record, clearly sufficient to erect the disputed-fact bar to summary judgment. It may be that the defendants will be able to establish a basis for terminating Honore completely [absent] the free speech elements. The record before us contains conflicting evidence. The defendants rely on the dean's affidavit, which proclaims innocence of improper motivation. Honore offered the testimony of a tenure committee member that the dean originally supported his tenure. Further, the dean testified that he changed his mind about Honore, a change which occurred contemporaneously with Honore's open challenges to the dean's administration of the law school. At the core of the matter are both credibility assessments and issues of motive and intent.

* * *

The record before us contains sufficient conflicting evidence about material facts to present jury issues. Honore has adequately challenged the underlying facts upon which the summary judgment motion rests.

The summary judgment is VACATED and the matter is REMANDED to the district court for further proceedings consistent herewith.

As is detailed in chapter 3, "The Law and Faculty," tenure-by-default circumstances rarely occur, due to more carefully drafted tenure policies in most colleges. *Honore* is interesting, as it is the only reported case where a professor loses on procedural grounds, but wins (at least a remand) on substantive first amendment grounds. On remand, the court is to determine whether his protected speech was the substantial or motivating reason for his dismissal. In *Selzer v. Fleisher,* the same issue was considered by a jury, when a political scientist was recommended for tenure, but once it was discovered that he had assisted the CIA, his department reversed their decision and denied him tenure. Members of the department were found to have deprived him of his associational rights. In dissent, Judge Kaufman argued that Selzer's CIA contacts were inherently disruptive in *Pickering*'s terms, and that the committee was justified in not recommending him for tenure. 629 F.2d 809 (1980).

After the National Science Foundation formally apologized to a geologist for falsely alleging he had been a CIA agent, he settled a suit against the agency. In the $20,000 settlement, the NSF conceded that agency staff had conveyed the false allegations to peer review panelists considering the geologist's research proposals. "NSF Apologizes to Geologist Who Accused It of Spreading CIA Rumor," *Chronicle of Higher Education,* 16 December 1987, p. A17; "Suit on Rumor of Tie to C.I.A. Brings Apology to Geologist," *New York Times,* 5 December 1987, p. 9.

On the Issue of Remedies

In *Southside Public Schools v. Hill,* 827 F.2d 270 (8th Cir. 1987), teachers who wrote to the Arkansas Department of Education to complain about programs for mainstreaming handicapped children were fired or retaliated against. The court held that their correspondence was protected speech and a matter of public concern. In addition, the court found their charges to be accurate, and determined that they were "exercising their rights as citizens." In a similar higher education case at the University of Houston, an employee of a federally funded student program, who complained about the program to a federal program officer and was constructively dismissed, was found to have been wrongfully discharged in violation of his *Pickering* rights.

The remedy for "whistleblowers" is not always clear. In *Hill,* the parties agreed to damages, while in the University of Houston case, the plaintiff won back pay. In *Reeves v. Claiborne County Board,* 828 F.2d 1096 (5th Cir. 1987), an administrator held to have been wrongfully dismissed for testifying against the superintendent and school board in a colleague's lawsuit was ordered reinstated. The issue of reinstating wrongly dismissed employees has been deemed mandatory in some settings, as in *Allen v. Autauga County Board of Education,* 685 F.2d 1302 (11th Cir. 1982), and deemed preferable in other settings, *TSTA/NEA v. El Paso Community College District,* 730 F.2d 258 (5th Cir. 1984). For a series of charges and countercharges on an NIH-funded project, see the series of stories in *Science & Government Report,* 1988. In *Hale and Hale v. Walsh,* an untenured history professor at Idaho State University was found to have been wrongfully dismissed after a series of strenuous disagreements with students, faculty, and administrators. After applying *Pickering* and *Connick*, the Idaho Appeals Court held that his speech and activities were protected matters of public concern, and that he had been fired as a result of exercising his rights. He also met the *Mt. Healthy* requirement that he prove that the decision not to rehire him would have been reached even in the absence of the protected speech. On remand to the trial court for determining remedies (damages and/or reinstatement), the appeals court held:

> The district court gave two reasons for refusing reinstatement—the revival of old antagonisms and a jury award that "more than compensates the plaintiff for any damages he has suffered as a result of the jury's determination that there was misconduct on the part of defendants." The first does not weigh heavily against reinstatement. The second is problematic in this case. The court stated that the plaintiff received an award that "more than" compensated the plaintiff. If this was a determination that the monetary award of the jury exceeded the damages suffered by the plaintiff it would be a valid consideration in determining if there should be reinstatement. If there was an excessive award, reinstatement would place the plaintiff in a better position than he would have enjoyed had he not engaged in constitutionally protected conduct. However, if the award is not excessive, the award of adequate damages would not weigh heavily against reinstatement. The trial court's finding is not sufficient to make a determination on this issue. Moreover, the district court failed to make a finding as to whether Hale engaged in inappropriate and opprobrious conduct so that reinstatement would be inequitable. The court did say that reinstatement would "cause further conflicts within the internal departmental affairs of the Department of History and foster further conflicts between the finding of the trial court—at least so far as it relates to Hale's chairmanship of the history department—is supported by the record. For example, the unrebutted testimony of the Dean of the College of Education was to the effect that his department chairman and members of his faculty "would avoid, frankly, in any way that they could, having to deal with the Department of History, and with Dr. Hale specifically." Reinstatement could still be inappropriate, depending upon the court's findings as to the root causes for such anticipated future conflicts.
>
> Moreover, it is our view that the trial judge should be free to consider separately the question of Hale's reinstatement as a member of the teaching faculty and as chairman of the history department. The two positions involve separate and distinct responsibilities. Each requires different characteristics, abilities, associations and working relationships. A person suitable to one position may be incapable of handling the other. Thus, we will not presume to dictate the outcome of this issue to the trial court.

Thomas Hale and Margaret Hale v. Mary Ellen Walsh, Court of Appeals of Idaho, Slip Opinion No. 14927, July 28, 1987.

Conduct Toward Colleagues: Academic Freedom Privilege

In re Dinnan
661 F.2d 426 (1981)

THOMAS A. CLARK, Circuit Judge:

The instant action arises from a suit brought by Maija Blaubergs against the Board of Regents of the University of Georgia and others. This suit alleges, *inter alia*, that she was unlawfully denied promotion to the rank of associate professor and that her employment had been unconstitutionally terminated. During the course of discovery, on April 18, 1980, the deposition of Professor James A. Dinnan was taken. This deposition related to his service on the College of Education Promotion Review Committee that considered Blaubergs' application for promotion during the 1979–80 academic year. When asked how he voted on the application, Dinnan refused to answer.

The appellee then filed a motion for an order compelling discovery. After a hearing on the issue, the court ordered the appellant to testify. The deposition continued on May 23, 1980, and Dinnan reiterated his refusal to answer any question regarding his vote. The appellee thereupon filed a motion for the imposition of contempt sanctions against Dinnan. On June 2, 1980, the court held a hearing to consider the appellee's motion, and informed Dinnan that it intended to proceed against him at a hearing the next day.

The court heard the appellant's arguments on June 3, and thereafter held him in contempt. He was ordered to pay a fine of one hundred dollars per day for thirty days and if he persisted in his defiance of the court order he was to report for a ninety-day term of imprisonment. However, the order was framed to allow an immediate cessation of the fine and imprisonment if Dinnan came forward with the desired information. A motion to stay sentence was denied, and a notice of appeal filed. Immediately thereafter, Dinnan filed a motion under 28 U.S.C. § 2255 alleging an illegal sentence and a denial of due process. The motion was denied on the basis that this was a civil, not a criminal, proceeding and that there was adequate notice. Notices of appeal from the court's order compelling discovery and from the court order finding him in contempt have been consolidated in the instant action.

The appellant argues that the instant case is one of "academic freedom." We, however, are unable to accept this characterization and, indeed, believe that any such view of the present case requires a gross distortion of its facts.

This case simply involves the law of evidence; there are no issues of constitutional dimension raised. The appellant is claiming a privilege, *i.e.*, a right to refrain from testifying, that heretofore has not been considered or recognized by any court. The issue before this court then is whether the privilege claimed by the appellant should be endorsed by this circuit.

We hold that no privilege exists that would enable Professor Dinnan to withhold information regarding his vote on the promotion of the appellee. This result is required on the basis of fundamental principles of law and sound public policy.

* * *

Bearing in mind that there has been a notable hostility on the part of the judiciary to recognizing new privileges and that the public policy served by a new privilege must transcend the normally dominant truth-seeking considerations, we turn to the privilege claim brought forth in the instant case. The appellant argues that the new privilege is necessary to protect two important societal interests, "academic freedom" and the "secret ballot." We find neither argument to be even slightly persuasive; we will examine the former contention first.

The appellant urges us to establish an evidentiary privilege in the instant case in order that "academic freedom" might be protected. The appellant construes the term "academic freedom" to include more than it does. Unquestionably, academic freedom is one of the paramount values of this Republic. However, if the concept is expanded too far it can cause other important societal goals (such as the elimination of discrimination in employment decisions) to be frustrated. Indeed, if the concept were extended as far as the appellant argues, it would rapidly become a double-edged sword threatening the very core of values that it now protects.

Academic freedom is "of transcendent value to all of us and not merely to the teachers concerned." Time after time the Supreme Court has upheld academic freedom in the face of government pressure. However, in all those cases there was an *attempt to suppress ideas by the government*. Ideas *may be suppressed just as effectively by denying tenure as by prohibiting the teaching of certain courses*. Quite bluntly, this Court feels that the government should stay out of academic affairs. However, these issues are not presented in the instant case. Here a *private* plaintiff is attempting to enforce her constitutional and statutory rights in an employment situation. Therefore, the reasoning behind the cited cases simply does not apply here.

* * *

Here the allegation is that the appellee *was discriminated against*, precisely the situation that the Third Circuit envisioned in *Kunda v. Muhlenberg College* in which courts should intervene. Thus, the authority relied upon by the appellant does not, upon close scrutiny, support his position.

The appellant is frustrating the appellee's attempt to vindicate an alleged infringement of her statutory and constitutional rights. Though the case is one involving an alleged case of sex discrimination, admittedly a cause of action not especially favored by some groups at the present time, its implications are staggering. Using the appellant's logic, if a tenure committee attempted to stop the promotion of all faculty members who were not pro-abortionists, a right-to-life music professor's attempt at discovery could be barred by the concept of "academic freedom." Likewise, a physicist's application might be sabotaged because he opposed the cession of the Panama Canal where such a position was not favored by the committee. In all these cases, "academic freedom" would shield the tenure committee from having to reveal its votes, even though the decisions had nothing to do with any academic grounds. In every one of these scenarios, the rights of the applicant would be infringed upon, but "academic freedom" would serve to obstruct the vindication of these rights. This possibility is a much greater threat to our liberty and academic freedom than the compulsion of discovery in the instant case.

Though we recognize the importance of academic freedom, we must also recognize its limits. The public policy of the United States prohibits discrimination; Professor Dinnan and the University of Georgia are not above that policy. To rule otherwise would mean that the concept of academic freedom would give any institution of higher learning a *carte blanche* to practice discrimination of all types.

The appellant further claims that there is a common law privilege designed to protect the secret ballot, and that since Dinnan's vote was made by secret ballot it is protected. This claim is unconvincing. The only cases which the appellant cites deal either with the political process or with labor union elections (which are sufficiently close to the political process to justify their inclusion within that category). This alone effectively distinguishes those cases from that before the court at the present time. In the instant case we simply have an employment decision, which by no stretch of the imagination deserves the protection that is accorded to individual participation in the political process.

* * *

The appellant essentially argues that an institution of higher learning has the untrammeled right to grant tenure to whomever it pleases. He maintains that an evidentiary privilege is necessary to protect this right. Dinnan contends that the university decision-makers will be inhibited in making tenure decisions if there is a possibility that committee members will be required to reveal their votes. We do not believe that this justifies the creation of a new privilege. We fail to see how, if a tenure committee is acting in good faith, our decision today will adversely affect its decision-making process. Indeed, this opinion should work to reinforce responsible decision-making in tenure questions as it sends out a clear signal to would-be wrongdoers that they may not hide behind "academic freedom" to avoid responsibility for their actions.

* * *

E.E.O.C. v. University of Notre Dame

715 F.2d 331 (1983)

COFFEY, Circuit Judge.

The University of Notre Dame Du Lac appeals from an order granting enforcement of an administrative subpoena *duces tecum* issued by the Equal Employment Opportunity Commission ("EEOC") requiring the University to produce the personnel files of certain faculty members in the University's Department of Economics. We reverse and remand.

I.

On May 21, 1980, Oscar T. Brookins filed a charge with the EEOC alleging that the University had unlawfully discriminated against him on the basis of race in denying him a tenured position in the University's Economics Department.

* * *

In investigating Brookins' charge of unlawful racial discrimination, the EEOC sent the University an eight-part questionnaire demanding *inter alia* the following: (1) "Describe in detail your tenure practices in the University of Notre Dame"; (2) "[I]dentification by name and race, of persons responsible for reviewing the qualifications of candidates for tenured positions"; (3) "Identify by name, race, and job title the individual(s) making up the tenure committees for the economics department from January 1, 1980 to June 1, 1980"; (4) Construct a chart detailing the name, race and employment history of each member of the University Economics Department; (5) "Furnish copies of the personnel records of the Charging Party [Brookins]."

The University complied with each of the requests for information and documents with the exception of the EEOC's request that the University furnish copies of the personnel records of the charging party, Brookins. In a February 6, 1981 letter to the EEOC, the University's assistant general counsel offered to allow an EEOC investigator to visit the University to personally review Brookins' personnel files, but refused to permit the EEOC to make copies of the file on the grounds that the file was "so voluminous, and because so much of it is of such a confidential nature...."

On February 19, 1981, the EEOC demanded from the University not only the personnel files of Brookins but also the personnel files of all teaching personnel in the Economics Department. In response to the EEOC's latest demand for the personnel files of the Economics Department, the University offered to produce the files, subject to the EEOC signing an agreement requiring that they maintain the confidentiality of the information contained in the personnel files. The EEOC refused to sign the nondisclosure agreement, and then the EEOC issued an administrative subpoena *duces tecum* requiring the University to provide "copies of the complete personnel records of [the] charging party Oscar T. Brookins, and all other teaching personnel in the Economics Department for the period January 1, 1980 to the present."

* * *

The University did not comply with the subpoena and, on March 16, 1982, the EEOC filed an application in district court for an order to show cause why the subpoena should not be enforced.

The University objected to the EEOC subpoena on three grounds. First, the University argued that the personnel files in question contained peer review evaluations which were made with the assurance and expectation that the evaluations would remain confidential, and therefore the peer review evaluations were protected from disclosure by a qualified academic privilege.

* * *

Before turning to our discussion of the appropriate balance to be arrived at in this case it is important to emphasize that the University is seeking only to assert a qualified privilege, rather than an absolute privilege. The University does not argue that the personnel files of the Economics Department faculty members who were involved in the relevant tenure decisions should be shielded in their entirety from disclosure. Rather, the University merely asserts that it should be allowed to delete from the files the names and any and all identifying features of the academicians who participated in the respective tenure peer reviews.

* * *

Moreover, it is evident that confidentiality is absolutely essential to the proper functioning of the faculty tenure review process. The tenure review process requires that written and oral evaluations submitted by academicians be completely candid, critical, objective and thorough in order that the University might grant tenure only to the most qualified candidates based on merit and ability to work effectively with colleagues, students, and the administration. For these reasons, academicians who are selected to evaluate their peers for tenure have, since the inception of the academic tenure concept, been assured that their critiques and discussions will remain confidential. Without this assurance of confidentiality, academicians will be reluctant to offer candid and frank evaluations in the future.

The importance of confidentiality to decision-making processes is recognized throughout the American institutional, administrative and judicial processes. The Supreme Court recognized the importance of confidentiality, *albeit* in the jury deliberation context, when Justice Cardozo wrote that "[f]reedom of debate might be stifled and independence of thought checked if jurors were made to feel that their arguments... were to be freely published to the world." In its adoption of Exemption 5 to the Freedom of Information Act which protects the decision-making process of governmental agencies, Congress recognized that " 'frank discussion of legal or policy matters' in writing might be inhibited if the discussions were made public; and that the 'decisions' and 'policies formulated' would be poorer as a result." Just as a limited executive privilege is necessary for the executive branch of our government to function properly, and as confidential judicial and jury deliberations are essential to preserve the integrity of those processes, confidentiality is equally critical in the faculty tenure selection process, in order that only the best qualified educators become the "lifeblood" of our institutions of higher learning.

There are, however, factors weighing in favor of disclosure of some of the contents of the peer review files. If an academic freedom privilege could be used to totally prohibit disclosure of tenure review records, the privilege could be used as a shield to hide evidence of discrimination. The integrity of the truth-seeking process would be impaired and Congress' goal of eradicating discrimination would be frustrated.

Likewise the EEOC's investigatory powers must not be frustrated in order that it might substantiate meritorious claims and conciliate when appropriate, and reject non-meritorious claims. Moreover, the important interests of academic excellence might well be frustrated if tenure decisions were allowed to be made on other than lawful grounds.

It is clear that both parties before us have significant and substantial interests at stake. After weighing the respective interests, we recognize in this case a qualified academic freedom privilege protecting academic institutions against the disclosure of the names and identities of persons participating in the peer review process thereby reaffirming long-standing policies of academic institutions. In so holding, we join other courts in recognizing a limited academic freedom privilege in the context of challenges to college or university tenure decisions. For example, in *Gray v. Board of Higher Education*, the court recognized a qualified academic freedom privilege, but held that under the circumstances, the plaintiff's need for the privileged information outweighed the college's interest in keeping the information confidential. We recognize the qualified privilege here because it is likely that "the privilege will in fact protect [the] relationship in the factual setting of [this] case."

Having determined that the district court erred in refusing to recognize a qualified privilege protecting against the disclosure of the identities of the academicians participating in the peer review process, we remand this case to the district court and direct the court to issue an order implementing the procedures that follow. Before producing the personnel files sought by the EEOC, the University should be permitted to redact the name, address, institutional affiliation, and any other identifying features (e.g., publications, professional honors received, or any other material which could be used to identify the particular academician) of the reporting scholar from the evaluations found in each of the files. After completing the redaction procedures outlined above, the University should, since it volunteered to do so originally, produce the redacted files and, in addition, the original unredacted files to the district court.

The district court shall then review the files, *in camera,* to determine whether the redactions are reasonably necessary to prevent disclosure of the identity of the scholar or scholars providing the evaluation. Should the court determine that the redactions are reasonably necessary to prevent disclosure of the identity of the evaluating scholar, then the redacted files should be turned over the EEOC and the unredacted files returned to the University.

If, after receiving the redacted files, the EEOC believes that it is necessary to seek more information from the unredacted files, the EEOC must then make a particularized showing before the court as to its need for further disclosure in any one or more of the files produced. In this respect, the EEOC will be required to make a substantial showing of "particularized need" for relevant information, a burden similar to that imposed on a party seeking disclosure of grand jury materials.

Before determining whether to compel disclosure of materials covered by the qualified privilege, the court must apply a balancing test to determine whether the need of the party seeking disclosure outweighs the adverse effect such disclosure would have on the policies underlying the privilege. Under the "particularized need" standard, "a party's need varies in proportion to the degree of access he has to other sources of information he seeks." A party must conduct thorough and exhaustive discovery to exploit each and every possible source of information prior to seeking those materials protected by the qualified privilege. "Exploratory" searches will not be condoned. Similarly, the mere fact that certain information may be relevant or useful does not establish a "particularized need" for disclosure of information. The party seeking disclosure of the privileged information must show a "compelling necessity" for the *specific* information requested.

In addition to the foregoing general rules regarding "particularized need," the court will also be required to consider factors unique to the context of faculty tenure denial. Once the basis for faculty tenure denial is determined it may be easier for the EEOC to demonstrate a "particularized need" for the identity of one or more evaluating academicians because then the court could determine whether the material sought was relevant to the discrimination claim and unavailable elsewhere. For example, if the University contends that in fact Brookins was denied tenure based on his peer evaluations and the EEOC is able to make a particularized showing that an evaluation was not supported by legitimate non-discriminatory reasons or that an evaluator is likely to have displayed racial animus against Brookins or other individuals, disclosure of the particular evaluator's identity may be warranted. We foresee that the identities of the scholars would be released only under the most limited circumstances. Any particularized showing in this regard would have to be supported by specific material contained in the redacted peer review files or probative evidence obtained through other investigatory means such as the thorough and exhaustive discovery mandated above. If, however, the University could demonstrate that its decision was motivated by reasons separate and distinct from those addressed by the peer reviewers, such as unsatisfactory student evaluations as alleged by Mr. Brookins, there would be little or no need for the identities of the peer reviewers.

*   *   *

The restrictions and limitations we have placed on the access to the records in question here are necessary not only to preserve the integrity of academic freedom at stake, but also to prevent those who would use this case as authority to invade other confidential relationships from doing so absent the most compelling circumstances.

* * *

Since *In re Dinnan* was decided by the Fifth Circuit and denied by the Supreme Court, 457 U.S. 1106 (1982), over a dozen federal, state, and county courts have ruled on the "academic freedom privilege" defense to quash *subpoenae* or to consider evidentiary privileges in discovery proceedings. To date, the privilege has only been successfully raised (albeit partially) in the *Notre Dame* case, although *Gray v. Board of Higher Education*, 692 F.2d 901 (2d Cir. 1982), *Kahn v. Superior Court*, 233 Cal. Rptr. 662 (6th Dist. 1987), and *Cockrell v. Middlebury College*, Vermont Supreme Court, No. 86–142, November 6, 1987 all acknowledge the concept. Neither *Gray* nor *Kahn* allowed the qualified privilege, and the *Cockrell* court remanded for a better record:

> "The overriding dilemma created by a conflict between a privilege and discovery is that immediate discovery may effectively render impossible appropriate protection for confidentiality before questions as to the availability of any such privilege can be examined in light of the facts of the particular case.
>
> If the issues in a given case relate to discrimination denominated invidious for being based on race, sex or national origin, confidentiality may have to yield in some measure. Other issues call for other balances, if any such privilege is to be justified by circumstances. None of that is possible on the record before us. It may be that after examination it will be decided that the Vermont common law ought not to recognize even a conditional privilege of confidentiality as part of academic freedom, but the opportunity to make that determination ought not to be destroyed by the too-early, unexamined exercise of discovery.
>
> Part of the judicial process, if there is to be any such privilege, will be to develop procedures for its orderly exercise, with fairness to all parties. This Court has had to do just that in similar circumstances relating to First Amendment privileges and the press. The possible presence of a qualified privilege such as urged here would require that before a plaintiff can insist on his discovery rights, he is burdened with the obligation to demonstrate to the trial court the specific need for the matter sought to be discovered, its relevance, and the existence or non-existence of other available sources for the same information.
>
> It should also be pointed out that it is possible for parties to contract to make certain matters privileged in their relationship. The plaintiff is here seeking employment rights under a contract with the College. It may be of significance for the trial court to examine that contract with respect to its provisions relating to the tenure process in order to determine whether confidentiality is, through established custom or contract, a part of that process.
>
> The inquiry posed by the certification in this case asks this Court to say it was error for the lower court to fail to recognize a qualified privilege protecting from disclosure the confidential deliberations of academic tenure review committees and associated documentation. We are not prepared to do so without the development of a factual record. The order of this Court will provide for the reversal of the existing discovery order, pending performance by the plaintiff of his burden to establish factually his right to discovery."

It can be expected that litigation on this aspect of conduct toward colleagues will continue to increase, in personnel matters and privacy issues generally. In addition to federal dimensions posed by EEOC or other federal enforcement or investigation powers, state open records or privacy legislation will continue to affect the qualified academic freedom privilege.

Apart from the context of personnel matters or tenure reviews, conduct toward colleagues rarely rises to litigation. The *Weinstein* case, involving attribution of credit in publication, is one such case, as is the *Dong* litigation, essentially a dispute over allegations of fraud in research. In the context of inciting others to unlawful action, the *Franklin* case was excerpted in this chapter; in a similar vein, heckling of speakers, a Northwestern University professor was reprimanded in 1985 for her actions at a campus lecture. Professor Barbara Foley had heckled Nicaraguan rebel Adolfo Calero, preventing him from speaking, and saying he would be "lucky to get out of here alive." A faculty committee that reviewed the incident determined that she had violated campus principles on academic freedom. Although her tenure committee recommended that she be granted tenure, the provost denied her tenure, and a faculty committee subsequently charged that the tenure recommendations "were scripts played to an empty theater." "Panel Finds No Violation of Academic Freedom in Northwestern Case; Provost's Role Criticized," *Chronicle of Higher Education*, 28 January 1987, p. 16.

Conduct Toward Students Outside Class

Unreasonable conduct in the classroom or toward students enrolled in class has the obvious potential of interfering with the students' education experience. One type of conduct that constitutes such an unreasonable interference is sexual harassment. Federal prohibition against sexual harassment is found in regulations under Title IX of the Education Amendments of 1972; many institutions are adopting institutional policies on sexual harassment regardless whether their institutions fall under Title IX mandates. (Since the 1988 Civil Rights Restoration Act, most institutions will be reached by Title IX.)

The following is conduct prohibited under federal law and under many university policies:

> unwelcome sexual advances, requests for sexual favors, and other verbal or physical conduct of a sexual nature ... when submission ... is ... either explicitly or implicitly a term or condition of [grades or academic progress] or such conduct has the purpose or effect of unreasonably interfering with an individual's work performance or creating an intimidating, hostile or offensive [educational] environment. 29 C.F.R. § 1604.11.

Because the recipient is the party deciding what is unwelcome, it is essential that faculty members be sensitive to the possibility that faculty behaviors will be interpreted differently by different individuals. Sexual harassment is an issue for which litigation as a means of resolving complaints is usually undesirable for all parties. Even "willing" relationships between faculty and students may create problems, particularly where the student is enrolled in a class taught by that faculty member. Problems arise from the resulting perception that the student involved in the relationship may be at an advantage compared to students who are not so involved, and the clear disparities in power between faculty and students.

One writer recently reviewed college policies concerning sex between faculty and students, and concluded:

> The rules universities fashion should ban all relationships in which the teacher is in a position to evaluate the student officially; such relationships are presumptively problematic. Other relationships require officials to decide whether the interests of the student are threatened. In making such a decision, universities should strive to protect the student's freedom—both her freedom from pressure to enter a relationship, and her freedom to enter a relationship when no such pressure exists. P. DeChiara, "The Need for Universities to Have Rules on Consensual Sexual Relationships Between Faculty Members and Students," *Columbia Journal of Law and Social Problems*, 21 (1988), 137–62.

Alexander v. Yale University
631 F.2d 178 (2d Cir. 1980)

LUMBARD, Circuit Judge:

[Appellants are] five women who were students at Yale University ... [They] alleged in their complaint that Yale was violating Title IX of the Education Amendments of 1972, 20 U.S.C. § 1681, et seq., and H.E.W.'s Title IX regulations, by refusing to consider seriously women students' complaints of sexual harassment by male faculty members and administrators. They argue that the district court erred ... in failing to grant the relief requested—an order enjoining Yale to institute a procedure for receiving and investigating complaints of sexual harassment—because Price failed to prove that she was sexually harassed. We affirm the judgment of the district court for Yale as to all of the plaintiffs.

I.

Section 1681 of Title IX (hereinafter "Title IX") states:

> No person in the United States shall, on the basis of sex, be excluded from participation in, be denied the benefits of, or be subjected to discrimination under any education program or activity receiving Federal financial assistance. . . .

Under the authority of § 1682, H.E.W. requires educational institutions receiving federal assistance to "adopt grievance procedures providing for prompt and equitable resolution of student and employee complaints alleging any action which would be prohibited by this part." 45 C.F.R. § 86-8(b).

In an amendment complaint filed on November 15, 1977, three female students, two female graduates, and one male professor at Yale alleged that Yale's "failure to combat sexual harassment of female students and its refusal to institute mechanisms and procedures to address complaints and make investigations of such harassment interferes with the educational process and denies equal opportunity in education" in violation of Title IX and H.E.W.'s regulation. The plaintiffs sought as relief (1) a declaratory judgment that Yale's policies and practices regarding sexual harassment violate Title IX and (2) an order enjoining Yale, among other duties, "to institute and continue a mechanism for receiving, investigating, and adjudicating complaints of sexual harassment, to be designed and implemented under the supervision" of the district court.

The plaintiffs sought that relief on behalf of themselves and the class, which they purported to represent, of those Yale students and faculty members "who are disadvantaged and obstructed in their educational relations" by Yale's failure to combat sexual harassment. More specifically, they sued on behalf of (1) female students who have had to choose between tolerating sexual demands from "men in positions of authority at Yale" or sacrificing "any educational opportunity, benefit or chance to grow or advance educationally"; (2) female students who "are subject to the discriminatory atmosphere adverse to their educational development created by the practice of such sexual harassment"; and (3) all faculty members "whose professional effectiveness in teaching and in engaging in the pursuit of knowledge with students is seriously impaired by that contamination of the faculty/student relationship created by defendant's tolerance of said sexual pressures."

Additionally, each plaintiff alleged an injury which was "the result of a pattern, practice, and policy of defendant, its officers, agents, and employees, of neglecting and refusing to consider seriously complaints of sexual harassment of women students, with the effect of actively condoning continued sexual harassment of female students by male faculty members and administrators." Thus:

Ronni Alexander, a 1977 graduate of Yale College, alleged that she "found it impossible to continue playing the flute and abandoned her study of the instrument, thus aborting her desired professional career," because of the repeated sexual advances, "including coerced sexual intercourse," by her flute instructor, Keith Brien. Alexander further alleged that she attempted to complain to Yale officials about her harassment, but "was discouraged and intimidated by unresponsive administrators and complex and *ad hoc* methods."

Margery Reifler, a member of the Class of 1980, alleged that Richard Kentwell, coach of the field hockey team, "sexually harassed" her while she was working as that team's manager, and that she "suffered distress and humiliation... and was denied recognition due her as team manager, all to her educational detriment." Reifler further alleged that she "wanted to complain to responsible authorities of defendant about said sexual harassment but was intimidated by the lack of legitimate procedures and was unable to determine if any channels for complaint about sexual harassment were available to her."

Pamela Price, a member of the Class of 1979, alleged that one of her course instructors, Raymond Duvall, "offered to give her a grade of 'A' in the course in exchange for her compliance with his sexual demands," that she refused, and that she received a grade of "C" which "was not the result of a fair evaluation of her academic work, but the result of her failure to accede to Professor Duvall's sexual demands." She further alleges that she complained to officials of Yale who failed to investigate her complaint and told her that "nothing could be done to remedy her situation."

Lisa Stone, a member of the Class of 1978, alleged that her discussions with a woman student who had been sexually harassed and the absence of an "established, legitimate procedure" for complaints of such harassment caused her "emotional distress," deprived her of "the tranquil atmosphere necessary to her pursuit of a liberal education," and put her "in fear of her own associations with men in positions of authority at Yale."

Ann Olivarius, a 1977 graduate, alleged that the absence of a procedure for complaining about sexual harassment "forced [her] to expend time, effort and money in investigating complaints herself, preparing them to be presented to responsible officials of defendant, and attempting to negotiate the complexities of *ad hoc* 'channels.' " Olivarius further alleged that she was "subjected to threats and intimidation from individuals involved in her investigations and was given no protection or encouragement by responsible officials of defendant."

Then District Judge Newman, upon the opinion of Magistrate Latimer, dismissed all the plaintiffs but Price in an order entered on December 21, 1977. The court dismissed Stone and Olivarius on the ground that they had not asserted claims "of personal exclusion from a federally funded education program or activity or of the personal denial of full participation in the benefits of such a program or activity in any measurable sense." Believing that "[n]o judicial enforcement of Title IX could properly extend to such imponderables as atmosphere or vicariously experienced wrong," the court held that Stone and Olivarius "advance[d] no persuasive claim that they have been deprived of cognizable Title IX rights." The court dismissed Alexander, although she alleged a "personal experience of sexual harassment," on the ground that her graduation mooted her claim for equitable relief absent the "sheer conjecture" that she might someday wish to resume her flute studies. The court dismissed Reifler, although she too alleged a personal experience of sexual harassment, because she had not complained to anyone at Yale.

... [T]he court concluded that Reifler's claim "that general university inertia should be equated with policy and has 'the effect of actively condoning ... sexual harassment' is simply not adequate to show that Yale acted to deny her any right"; and the court further held that "the concept of mere *respondeat superior* appears ill-adapted to the question of Title IX sex discrimination based on harassment incidents." As to Price, the court held that "academic advancement conditioned upon submission to sexual demands constitutes sex discrimination in education," and it therefore refused to dismiss Price.

* * *

After the trial of Price's claim, Judge Burns found that "the alleged incident of sexual proposition did not occur and the grade of 'C' which Miss Price received on the paper submitted to Professor Duvall and the grade of 'C' which she received in his course did not reflect consideration of any factor other than academic achievement." Accordingly, although the district court agreed that Yale's procedures for handling complaints of sexual harassment were inadequate, it refused to enjoin Yale to establish a different procedure, concluding, "[I]t does not follow that, if Yale University failed to articulate appropriate procedures to deal with such a claim, a plaintiff who can show neither an improper advance nor the injury she claimed has a grievance to be redressed by this court." The district court therefore entered judgment for Yale, and the five female plaintiffs (hereinafter "appellants") brought their appeal.

II.

We first consider the claims raised by Olivarius, Stone, Alexander and Reifler. We find that the district court should be affirmed as to these plaintiffs because none of them presents a justiciable case or controversy.

In order to proceed with suit in the federal courts, a party seeking relief must establish both that he or she has suffered a "distinct and palpable injury," * * * and that "the exercise of the Court's remedial powers would redress the claimed injury."

* * *

The injury must be suffered personally by the party invoking the court's assistance, and the relief requested must redound to that party's personal benefit.

These requirements are often said to be the prerequisites for "standing" to bring suit. It is also mandatory that they be satisfied throughout the course of adjudication by the courts. This "time element of standing" comes under the rubric of mootness doctrine.

* * *

A party's case or controversy becomes moot either when the injury is healed and only prospective relief has been sought or when it becomes impossible for the courts, through the exercise of their remedial powers, to do anything to redress the injury. We find that none of the claims brought by these four plaintiffs satisfies the prerequisites of justiciability.

Olivarius's claim on appeal from her dismissal presents the weakest case for justiciability. Her allegation that she spent her own time and money investigating women students' complaints of sexual harassment because Yale refused to do so, and that Yale gave her "no protection or encouragement" when she "was subjected to threats and intimidation from individuals involved in her investigations," fails to state the "distinct and palpable injury to [herself]" that is the first requirement of standing. . . . Olivarius spent her time and money upon her own volition. The allegation that Yale failed to protect and encourage her in her investigations does not allege an injury, for it does not allege that Olivarius was hurt—in any way—by Yale's failure. Accordingly, we affirm the dismissal of her complaint.

As for the other plaintiffs, including Price, whose claim we discuss below, their graduations appear to prevent the courts both from addressing the predominant injury relied upon—deprivation of an educational environment free from condoned harassment—and from awarding the relief requested—an order directing Yale to institute effective procedures for receiving and adjudicating complaints of sexual harassment. None of these plaintiffs at present suffers from the alleged injury. Nor would the grant of the requested relief aid these plaintiffs in the slightest. Thus their claims appear moot.

It is perhaps more important to note that, as Yale's counsel has assured us in brief and oral argument, Yale in fact has adopted a set of procedures for hearing such complaints. The procedures were proposed by a committee consisting of faculty, administrators and students, in a report published March 1979, following a year of careful study specifically limited to the problems involved in structuring procedures appropriate for consideration of student complaints of sexual harassment. Furthermore, Yale's counsel has also assured us that although the procedures were originally designed only to receive and consider claims of sexual harassment occurring at Yale College, their jurisdiction has since been expanded to afford consideration of claims by those who suffer harassment while participating in any program sponsored by the University. We have no reason to doubt that the procedures now in effect will tend to alleviate the "atmosphere of inequality" alleged by plaintiffs in this suit. Thus, it appears that the major relief sought in this suit has already been granted.

Nothing more need be said about the complaint brought by Stone. It was based solely upon the fear of association with male faculty and administrators and the general atmosphere of tolerance or condonement of sexual harassment. Graduation has entirely mooted her claim. There is nothing a complaint procedure or any other remedy can do now to redress her alleged injuries. Therefore the exercise of federal court power to pass on her claim "would be gratuitous and thus inconsistent with the Art. III limitation."

Both Alexander and Reifler, however, allege additional personal injuries. Nevertheless, what remains of their claims does not seem sufficient to justify judicial action. Their alleged injuries are too speculative. Alexander asserts that sexual harassment by her flute instructor in a University-sponsored music program deterred her from a successful career as a flutist. Needless to say, this is a highly conjectural claim. Reifler claims that sexual harassment by her field hockey coach caused her to leave the team and fail to receive a varsity letter. What harm she has suffered as a result is not specified.

In a Title IX suit, it is the deprivation of "educational" benefits which, once proven, allows the courts to afford relief. The statute recognizes that loss of educational benefits is a significant injury, redressable by law. Where the alleged deprivation, however, relates to an activity removed from the ordinary educational process, a more detailed allegation of injuries suffered as a result of the deprivation is required. This is not to say that exclusion of all members of one sex from all extra-curricular activities would not give rise to palpable injuries which could be redressed by the courts. Rather, when such activities are involved, more specific allegations as to harm suffered are necessary to assure "that concrete adverseness which sharpens the presentation of issues upon which the court so largely depends..." and to assure that the exercise of the courts' remedial powers may be designed to redress the alleged injuries.

Moreover, it is difficult to imagine what relief a court could possibly award Reifler and Alexander. No money damages have been requested, and as already noted, graduation has mooted their claims for grievance procedures. As the district court remarked, there is nothing left that a court could do to redress Alexander's injury "absent sheer conjecture that [she] may in the future wish to resume study in a field allegedly abandoned at Yale because of 'sexual demands' by her tutor." In appellants' brief on appeal a suggestion has been made that a court might award Reifler a varsity letter, yet we do not believe that such a possibility warrants judicial scrutiny, particularly when the alleged injury is so uncertain. Because we do not believe that the courts should indulge in speculation of the sort required here, we also affirm the dismissal of the complaints of Alexander and Reifler.

We thus agree with the district court that only plaintiff Price presented a justiciable claim for relief under Title IX. That claim, however, was tried and dismissed. We now turn to her assertions on appeal.

III.

The district court found that Price failed at trial to prove that her alleged sexual harassment had in fact occurred. Price argues that, her failure to prove the incident of harassment notwithstanding, the district court should have enjoined Yale to adopt a complaint procedure such as H.E.W. requires, because the gravamen of her complaint is that she was deprived of an institutional grievance procedure that would promptly and equitably have resolved her claim. She also argues that the district court erred in refusing to certify her suit as a class action, in limiting the evidence at her trial to that relevant to her own alleged harassment, and in refusing to reopen the record after trial to receive testimony of one who supposedly could verify her allegation. We disagree. As Price failed to prove her case, she failed to prove any perceptible harm and therefore she lacks standing to attack Yale's failure to establish a complaint procedure, and she is not a proper representative of the purported class.

* * *

We affirm the judgment for Yale as to all of the plaintiffs.

Board of Trustees of Compton Junior College District v. Stubblefield

16 C.A. 3d 820, 94 Cal. Rptr. 318 (1971)

* * *

Reduced to its simplest terms, defendant's contention on appeal is that the trial court erred as a matter of law in holding that defendant's conduct constituted sufficient grounds for dismissal.

Although there was some conflict in the evidence, the conduct in which the trial court found the defendant to have engaged was amply established by competent testimony.

That conduct viewed objectively as well as when viewed in the light of logical inferences to be drawn therefrom was unquestionably, as we shall see, well within even the most restricted definition of "immoral conduct" as that term is used generally or as it is used in Education Code section 13403.

The evidence of defendant's conduct which the trial court found to be true, a finding which is not assailed by defendant on appeal, can be briefly summarized as follows.

After teaching a class on the night of January 28, 1969, defendant drove a female student, and member of that class, in his car to a location on a side street near Compton College and parked. The location is in an area of industrial construction and was not lighted.

At some time after defendant parked, a Los Angeles County Deputy Sheriff spotted defendant's car. The car appeared to the deputy to be abandoned and he went to investigate. When the deputy illuminated defendant's car with his headlights and searchlight, defendant then sat up. When the deputy approached defendant's car, illuminating the interior with his flashlight, he observed that defendant's pants were unzipped and lowered from the waist, exposing his penis. The student was nude from the waist up, and her capri pants were unzipped and open at the waist.

The deputy orally identified himself as a police officer. In addition, he was wearing a yellow raincoat with a badge on the chest and a helmet bearing a sheriff's emblem. Defendant recognizing that the deputy was a police officer, threw open the left car door, nearly striking the deputy, and shouted, "Get the hell away from me, you dirty cop."

As the deputy was standing behind the still open left door, defendant shifted the car into reverse, accelerated rapidly backward, knocking the deputy to the pavement and causing minor injuries to the deputy and damage to his clothing.

Defendant then drove away. The deputy pursued defendant in his patrol car with his red lights flashing, and his siren and searchlight on; during the chase defendant drove at speeds between 80 and 100 miles per hour and refused to yield until the student, by persuasion and by attempting to force the steering wheel to the right, caused defendant to stop.

The legislative scheme for discharging permanent employees of a school district essentially gives the governing board in the first instance the power to suspend and discharge or retain such employee against whom charges have been made under the applicable provisions of section 13403 of the Education Code. When the employee demands a hearing, the board can either rescind its action or ask the superior court to conduct such hearing. Thus, in these cases the court conducts what in other areas of the civil service would be an administrative hearing.

Whether this rather unique procedure amounts to superior court review of an administrative determination, or an ordinary decision of the superior court, the scope of our review is the same. We must determine only whether the findings and conclusions of the trial court, as a matter of law, lack support in the record.

* * *

It would seem that, as a minimum, responsible conduct upon the part of a teacher, even at the college level, excludes meretricious relationships with his students and physical and verbal assaults on duly constituted authorities in the presence of his students.

Defendant quickly calls to our attention the recent pronouncement of our Supreme Court in Morrison v. State Board of Education.

In that case the court held that the revocation of a teaching credential upon grounds of "immoral and unprofessional conduct and acts involving moral turpitude" could not be supported by evidence limited to a showing that on one occasion three years in the past, while under severe stress, the teacher had engaged in an undescribed but noncriminal private act "of a homosexual nature" with a consenting adult. The court concluded that, " * * * the State Board of Education can revoke a life diploma or other document of certification and thus prohibit local school officials from hiring a particular teacher only if that individual has in some manner indicated that he is unfit to teach. Thus an individual can be removed from the teaching profession only upon a showing that his retention in the profession poses a significant danger of harm to either students, school employees, or others who might be affected by his actions as a teacher."

Defendant contends that Morrison prohibits his discharge because the evidence adduced against him concerned only his conduct and did not expressly demonstrate how that conduct rendered him unfit to teach. We do not agree with defendant's broad interpretation of that case.

Morrison does not appear to substantially alter the fundamental considerations traditionally applied to cases involving the dismissal of a teacher or the revocation of a teacher's credential for "immoral conduct." Consistent with previous cases, the court in its analysis of the conduct placed paramount importance on the *possible* impairment of teaching ability and relationships with students and clearly recognized the power of governmental employers to maintain proper discipline in the particular governmental service.

* * *

The clear import of that decision, then, is that a teacher may be discharged or have his certificate revoked on evidence that either his conduct indicates a potential for misconduct with a student or that his conduct while not necessarily indicating such a potential, has gained sufficient notoriety so as to impair his on-campus relationships.

There is no requirement that both the potential and the notoriety be present in each case.

While in this case no evidence was offered which directly dealt with notoriety, the very fact that a police officer, in the course of his official duties, easily discovered defendant and his companion, demonstrates the tenuous security from public attention provided by the front seat of defendant's automobile. Moreover, upon detection, defendant chose to assault the police officer and attempt an escape through dark city streets at high speeds thereby ultimately insuring further public attention.

Finally, "unfitness to teach" in terms of an indication that defendant was "more likely than the average adult male to engage in any untoward conduct with a student" can be inferred from the very conduct itself. Defendant's actions in this case speak louder than any words of a psychiatrist. The potential, evidence of which was found lacking in *Morrison*, was overtly manifested here.

The integrity of the educational system under which teachers wield considerable power in the grading of students and the granting or withholding of certificates and diplomas is clearly threatened when teachers become involved in relationships with students such as is indicated by the conduct here.

The findings and conclusions of the trial court are amply supported by the record.

A final matter under review in this section is the issue of faculty writing letters of recommendation for students. The issue of faculty letters for faculty has been alluded to in the section on the defense of "academic freedom privilege." However, on rare occasions, a tort issue may arise when a faculty member writes a defamatory letter in the tenure review process; in a 1982 Illinois case, the court found that even when defamatory statements were made, no liability arose unless the writer knew the remarks were either false, or acted in reckless disregard of their veracity. *Colson v. Steig*, 433 N.E. 2d 246 (1982).

While such a common-law approach to privilege is often extended in such circumstances, a recent case left the matter unsettled in the instance of faculty writing for students. In *Burt v. Board of Regents*, a faculty member was asked to write a letter in support of his former student's job application; he wrote that Burt's work had been "well below average," but that he "might serve adequately" in some field of medicine other than his ostensible specialty. The professor won at trial, but the Tenth Circuit Court of Appeals reversed, predominantly on issues of whether the professor could be sued out of state. Before the U.S. Supreme Court could hear the case, Burt dropped the litigation. Therefore, the issue was unsatisfactorily resolved, although it appears that traditional defamation standards obtain. *Burt v. Board*, 757 F.2d 242 (10th Cir. 1985), vacated and dismissed sub nom. *Connolly v. Burt*, 106 S. Ct. 1372 (1986).

Faculty as Citizens in Society

In earlier sections, several cases indicated the extent to which the larger society affects faculty while carrying on teaching and research responsibilities. Faculty research has been sought by grand juries and by defense counsel; colleagues have sued colleagues for hiring and firing; former students have sued faculty for writing lukewarm letters of reference; former colleagues have accused each other of fraudulent research. Occasionally, faculty encounter threats to academic freedom in contexts that do not derive from teaching or research dimensions. A large proportion of these cases have been loyalty oath or dissent cases, where governmental investigations to ferret out subversives or dissidents have focused upon intellectuals.

In *No Ivory Tower: McCarthyism and the Universities* (New York: Oxford University Press, 1986), historian Ellen Schrecker identified hundreds of instances in which universities collaborated with federal and state investigations into allegedly subversive beliefs and Communist party membership, in the 1940s and 1950s. For example, the Rapp-Coudert Committee in New York held hearings in 1940, which led to 31 professors being dismissed, and Washington state legislators hauled a dozen professors in for hearings into "subversive activities" in 1948; a faculty committee fired three of the professors and placed three others on probation. Unfortunately, the AAUP was in disarray during this period. Both Schrecker and Walter Metzger attribute this to the personal failures of the AAUP general secretary, who had become virtually incapacitated and overwhelmed with his professional responsibilities. "Ralph Fuchs and Ralph E. Himstead: A Note on the AAUP in the McCarthy Period," *Academe* (November-December 1986), 29–35.

More contemporary examples of governmental spying upon colleges include the FBI surveillance of library users, and widespread FBI and CIA investigations into campus-based political activities opposing U.S. involvement in Vietnam and Central America. "F.B.I. Contradicted on Surveillance of Policy Foes," *New York Times*, 14 February 1988, p. Y23; "The F.B.I.'s Invasion of Libraries," *The Nation*, 9 April 1988. More detail on these activities is included elsewhere, particularly in chapter 3.

Slochower v. Board of Education
350 U.S. 551 (1956)

Mr. Justice CLARK delivered the opinion of the Court.

This appeal brings into question the constitutionality of § 903 of the Charter of the City of New York. That section provides that whenever an employee of the City utilizes the privilege against self-incrimination to avoid answering a question relating to his official conduct, "his term or tenure of office or employment shall terminate and such office or employment shall be vacant, and he shall not be eligible to election or appointment to any office or employment under the city or any agency." Appellant Slochower invoked the privilege against self-incrimination under the Fifth Amendment before an investigating committee of the United States Senate, and was summarily discharged from his position as associate professor at Brooklyn College, an institution maintained by the City of New York. He now claims that the charter provision, as applied to him, violates both the Due Process and Privileges and Immunities Clauses of the Fourteenth Amendment.

On September 24, 1952, the Internal Security Subcommittee of the Committee on the Judiciary of the United States Senate held open hearings in New York City. The investigation, conducted on a national scale, related to subversive influences in the

American educational system. At the beginning of the hearings the Chairman stated that education was primarily a state and local function, and therefore the inquiry would be limited to "considerations affecting national security, which are directly within the purview and authority of the subcommittee." Professor Slochower, when called to testify, stated that he was not a member of the Communist party, and indicated complete willingness to answer all questions about his associations or political beliefs since 1941. But he refused to answer questions concerning his membership during 1940 and 1941 on the ground that his answers might tend to incriminate him. The Chairman of the Senate Subcommittee accepted Slochower's claim as a valid assertion of an admitted constitutional right.

It had been alleged that Slochower was a Communist in 1941 in the testimony of one Bernard Grebanier before the Rapp-Coudert Committee of the New York Legislature. Slochower testified that he had appeared twice before the Rapp-Coudert Committee, and had subsequently testified before the Board of Faculty relating to this charge. He also testified that he had answered questions at these hearings relating to his Communist affiliations in 1940 and 1941.

Shortly after testifying before the Internal Security Subcommittee, Slochower was notified that he was suspended from his position at the College; three days later his position was declared vacant "pursuant to the provisions of Section 903 of the New York City Charter."

Slochower had 27 years' experience as a college teacher and was entitled to tenure under state law. Under this statute, appellant may be discharged only for cause, and after notice, hearing, and appeal. The Court of Appeals of New York, however, has authoritatively interpreted § 903 to mean that "the assertion of the privilege against self incrimination is equivalent to a resignation." Dismissal under this provision is therefore automatic and there is no right to charges, notice, hearing, or opportunity to explain.

The Supreme Court of New York, County of Kings, concluded that appellant's behavior fell within the scope of § 903, and upheld its application here. The Court of Appeals, by a divided court, affirmed. We noted probable jurisdiction because of the importance of the question presented.

Slochower argues that § 903 abridges a privilege or immunity of a citizen of the United States since it in effect imposes a penalty on the exercise of a federally guaranteed right in a federal proceeding. It also violates due process, he argues, because the mere claim of privilege under the Fifth Amendment does not provide a reasonable basis for the State to terminate his employment. Appellee insists that no question of "privileges or immunities" was raised or passed on below, and therefore directs its argument solely to the proposition that § 903 does not operate in an arbitrary or capricious manner. We do not decide whether a claim under the "privileges or immunities" clause was considered below, since we conclude the summary dismissal of appellant in the circumstances of this case violates due process of law.

The problem of balancing the State's interest in the loyalty of those in its service with the traditional safeguards of individual rights is a continuing one. To state that a person does not have a constitutional right to government employment is only to say that he must comply with reasonable, lawful, and nondiscriminatory terms laid down by the proper authorities.

* * *

[T]he State must conform to the requirements of due process. In *Wieman v. Updegraff*, we struck down a so-called "loyalty oath" because it based employability solely on the fact of membership in certain organizations. We pointed out that membership itself may be innocent and held that the classification of innocent and guilty together was arbitrary. This case rests squarely on the proposition that "constitutional protection does extend to the public servant whose exclusion pursuant to a statute is patently arbitrary or discriminatory."

* * *

At the outset we must condemn the practice of imputing a sinister meaning to the exercise of a person's constitutional right under the Fifth Amendment. The right of an accused person to refuse to testify, which had been in England merely a rule of evidence, was so important to our forefathers that they raised it to the dignity of a constitutional enactment, and it has been recognized as "one of the most valuable prerogatives of the citizen." We have reaffirmed our faith in this principle recently in *Quinn v. United States*. In *Ullmann v. United States*, decided last month, we scored the assumption that those who claim this privilege are either criminals or perjurers. The privilege against self-incrimination would be reduced to a hollow mockery if its exercise could be taken as equivalent either to a confession of guilt or a conclusive presumption of perjury.

* * *

It is one thing for the city authorities themselves to inquire into Slochower's fitness, but quite another for his discharge to be based entirely on events occurring before a federal committee whose inquiry was announced as not directed at "the property, affairs, or government of the city, or . . . official conduct of city employees." In this respect the present case differs materially from *Garner*, where the city was attempting to elicit information necessary to determine the qualifications of its employees. Here, the Board had possessed the pertinent information for 12 years, and the questions which Professor Slochower refused to answer were admittedly asked for a purpose wholly unrelated to his college functions. On such a record the Board cannot claim that its action was part of a bona fide attempt to gain needed and relevant information.

Without attacking Professor Slochower's qualification for his position in any manner, and apparently with full knowledge of the testimony he had given some 12 years before at the state committee hearing, the Board seized upon his claim of privilege before the federal committee and converted it through the use of § 903 into a conclusive presumption of guilt. Since no inference of guilt was possible from the claim before the federal committee, the discharge falls of its own weight as wholly without support. There has not been the "protection of the individual against arbitrary action" which Mr. Justice Cardozo characterized as the very essence of due process.

This is not to say that Slochower has a constitutional right to be an associate professor of German at Brooklyn College. The State has broad powers in the selection and discharge of its employees, and it may be that proper inquiry would show Slochower's continued employment to be inconsistent with a real interest of the State. But there has been no such inquiry here. We hold that the summary dismissal of appellant violates due process of law.

The judgment is reversed and the cause is remanded for further proceedings not inconsistent with this opinion.

Keyishian v. Board of Regents
385 U.S. 589 (1967)

Mr. Justice BRENNAN delivered the opinion of the Court.

Appellants were members of the faculty of the privately owned and operated University of Buffalo, and became state employees when the University was merged in 1962 into the State University of New York, an institution of higher education owned and operated by the State of New York. As faculty members of the State University their continued employment was conditioned upon their compliance with a New York plan, formulated partly in statutes and partly in administrative regulations, which the State utilizes to prevent the appointment or retention of "subversive" persons in state employment.

Appellants Hochfield and Maud were Assistant Professors of English, appellant Keyishian an instructor in English, and appellant Garver, a lecturer in philosophy. Each of them refused to sign, as regulations then in effect required, a certificate that he was not a Communist, and that if he had ever been a Communist, he had communicated that fact to the President of the State University of New York. Each was notified that his failure to sign the certificate would require his dismissal. Keyishian's one-year-term contract was not renewed because of his failure to sign the certificate.

* * *

Our Nation is deeply committed to safeguarding academic freedom, which is of transcendent value to all of us and not merely to the teachers concerned. That freedom is therefore a special concern of the First Amendment, which does not tolerate laws that cast a pall of orthodoxy over the classroom. "The vigilant protection of constitutional freedoms is nowhere more vital than in the community of American schools." The classroom is peculiarly the "marketplace of ideas." The Nation's future depends upon leaders trained through wide exposure to that robust exchange of ideas which discovers truth "out of a multitude of tongues, [rather] than through any kind of authoritative selection." In *Sweezy v. New Hampshire*, we said:

> "The essentiality of freedom in the community of American universities is almost self-evident. No one should underestimate the vital role in a democracy that is played by those who guide and train our youth. To impose any strait jacket upon the intellectual leaders in our colleges and universities would imperil the future of our Nation. No field of education is so thoroughly comprehended by man that new discoveries cannot yet be made. Particularly is that true in the social sciences, where few, if any, principles are accepted as absolutes. Scholarship cannot flourish in an atmosphere of suspicion and distrust. Teachers and students must always remain free to inquire, to study and to evaluate, to gain new maturity and understanding; otherwise our civilization will stagnate and die."

We emphasize once again that "[p]recision of regulation must be the touchstone in an area so closely touching our most precious freedoms... [f]or standards of permissible statutory vagueness are strict in the area of free expression.... Because First Amendment freedoms need breathing space to survive, government may regulate in the area only with narrow specificity." New York's complicated and intricate scheme plainly violates that standard. When one must guess what conduct or utterance may lose him his position, one necessarily will "steer far wider of the unlawful zone...." For "[t]he threat of sanctions may deter... almost as potently as the actual application of sanctions." The danger of that chilling effect upon the exercise of vital First Amendment rights must be guarded against by sensitive tools which clearly inform teachers what is being proscribed.

The regulatory maze created by New York is wholly lacking in "terms susceptible of objective measurement." It has the quality of "extraordinary ambiguity" found to be fatal to the oaths considered in *Cramp* and *Baggett v. Bullitt*. "[M]en of common intelligence must necessarily guess at its meaning and differ as to its application...." Vagueness of wording is aggravated by prolixity and profusion of statutes, regulations, and administrative machinery, and by manifold cross-references to interrelated enactments and rules.

We therefore hold that § 3021 of the Education Law and subdivisions 1(a), 1(b) and 3 of § 105 of the Civil Service Law as implemented by the machinery created pursuant to § 3022 of the Education Law are unconstitutional.

[L]egislation which sanctions membership unaccompanied by specific intent to further the unlawful goals of the organization or which is not active membership violates constitutional limitations.

Measured against this standard, both Civil Service Law § 105, subd. 1(a), and Education Law § 3022, subd. 2, sweep overbroadly into association which may not be proscribed. The presumption of disqualification arising from proof of mere membership may be rebutted, but only by (a) a denial of membership, (b) a denial that the organization advocates the overthrow of government by force, or (c) a denial that the teacher has knowledge of such advocacy. Thus proof of nonactive membership or a showing of the absence of intent to further unlawful aims will not rebut the presumption and defeat dismissal. This is emphasized in official administrative interpretations. For example, it is said in a letter addressed to prospective appointees by the President of the State University, "You will note that... both the Law and regulations are very specifically directed toward the elimination and nonappointment of 'Communists' from or to our teaching ranks...." The Feinberg Certificate was even more explicit: "Anyone who is a *member* of the Communist Party or of any organization that advocates the violent overthrow of the Government of the United States or of the State of New York or any political subdivision thereof cannot be employed by the State University." This official administrative interpretation is supported by the legislative preamble to the Feinberg Law, § 1, in which the legislative concludes as a result of its findings that "it is essential that the laws prohibiting persons who are *members* of subversive groups, such as the communist party and its affiliated organizations, from obtaining or retaining employment in the public schools, be rigorously enforced."

Thus § 105, subd. 1(c), and § 3022, subd. 2, suffer from impermissible "overbreadth." They seek to bar employment both for association which legitimately may be proscribed and for association which may not be proscribed consistently with First Amendment rights. Where statutes have an overbroad sweep, just as where they are vague, "the hazard of loss or substantial impairment of those precious rights may be critical," since those covered by the statute are bound to limit their behavior to that which is unquestionably safe. As we said in *Shelton v. Tucker*, "The breadth of legislative abridgment must be viewed in the light of less drastic means for achieving the same basic purpose."

We therefore hold that Civil Service Law § 105, subd. 1(c), and Education Law § 3022, subd. 2, are invalid insofar as they proscribe mere knowing membership without any showing of specific intent to further the unlawful aims of the Communist Party of the United States or of the State of New York.

The judgment of the District Court is reversed and the case is remanded for further proceedings consistent with this opinion.

Reversed and remanded.

Mr. Justice CLARK, with whom Mr. Justice HARLAN, Mr. Justice STEWART and Mr. Justice WHITE join, dissenting.

* * *

The majority says that the Feinberg Law is bad because it has an "overbroad sweep." I regret to say—and I do so with deference—that the majority has by its broadside swept away one of our most precious rights, namely, the right of self-preservation. Our public educational system is the genius of our democracy. The minds of our youth are developed there and the character of that development will determine the future of our land. Indeed, our very existence depends upon it. The issue here is a very narrow one. It is not freedom of speech, freedom of thought, freedom of press, freedom of assembly, or of association, even in the Communist Party. It is simply this: May the State provide that one who, after a hearing with full judicial review, is found to have wilfully and deliberately advocated, advised, or taught that our Government should be overthrown by force or violence or other unlawful means; or to have wilfully and deliberately printed, published, etc., any book or paper that so advocated *and to have personally* advocated such doctrine himself; or to have wilfully and deliberately become a member of an organization that advocates such doctrine, is prima facie disqualified from teaching in its university? My answer, in keeping with all of our cases up until today, is "Yes"!

I dissent.

Joseph Little v. City of North Miami
805 F.2d 962 (11th Cir. 1986)

PER CURIAM:

CORRECTED OPINION

This case involves alleged civil rights violations. Appellant brought an action against multiple defendants in the United States District Court for the Southern District of Florida alleging *inter alia* five violations of 42 U.S.C. § 1983 (1981). The District Judge dismissed the civil rights claims for failure to state a claim upon which relief could be granted. Because we conclude that appellant's first amendment and procedural due process claims state causes of action cognizable under Section 1983, we reverse.

I.

BACKGROUND

For the purpose of evaluating the sufficiency of a complaint, we must accept the facts pleaded as true and construe them in the light most favorable to appellant. Appellant is a member of the Florida Bar Association and a professor of law at the University of Florida. Prior to October, 1983, appellant represented the Florida Defenders of the Environment in two Florida state court civil actions. This representation was on a *pro bono publico* basis with the approval of the University of Florida. The City of North Miami was an intervening party in the second lawsuit and was represented by Jennifer Hurst Kroner, an attorney employed by Simon, Schindler and Hurst, P.A. This state litigation involved the constitutionality of state appropriation for the purchase of land owned by the City of North Miami.

On October 11, 1983, the city Council of North Miami adopted Resolution No. R83–65 which states: "the Council of the City of North Miami hereby censures Professor Joseph W. Little for improper use of public funds to represent private parties in litigation against the State and against the interests of the City of North Miami." This resolution was passed and read aloud at a public meeting without notice to appellant and without verification that the assertions were truthful. Copies of R83–65 were circulated to twenty persons, including the president of the University of Florida, the dean of the University of Florida College of Law, the chairman and members of the Florida Board of Regents, the members of the Florida Legislature representing Dade County, and the Florida State Auditor General.

As a result of the passage and publication of the resolution, governmental investigations were undertaken and appellant claims he "suffered damage to his reputation, his employment relations, and mental and emotional pain and distress." Appellant does not assert that his employment has been terminated or that he has been denied tenure. Nevertheless, appellant brought an action against the city of North Miami, the mayor and council members, the attorney who prepared the resolution and the legal professional association who employed her. The complaint sought damages for five alleged constitutional violations and five pendant state law claims. As indicated, the district court dismissed the federal claims pursuant to Fed. R. Civ. P. 12(b)(6) without prejudice for appellant to seek redress for his state claims in state court. We have distilled the federal claims down to four issues and shall analyze them seriatim in order to determine whether appellant set forth sufficient facts which would entitle him to relief. For the reasons that follow, we reverse the ruling of the district court with respect to appellant's first amendment and procedural due process claims.

II.

ANALYSIS

* * *

In this case, the act which allegedly infringed upon appellant's first amendment rights is the resolution adopted by a local governmental body—the City Council of North Miami. As indicated, "local government bodies . . . can be sued directly under § 1983 for monetary, declaratory, and injunctive relief where . . . the action that is alleged to be unconstitutional implements or executes a policy statement, ordinance, regulation, or decision officially adopted and promulgated by that body's officers." Viewing the facts in the light most favorable to appellant, it appears that the City Council decided that appellant was guilty of culpable conduct and decided to publicly censure him as punishment. Because we conclude that the resolution in question can be fairly characterized as "*a decision officially adopted and promulgated*" by the City Council of North Miami, we conclude that the minimum requirements for imposing municipal liability have been alleged.

Second, unlike a Section 1983 claim based on an alleged bill of attainder, a Section 1983 action premised on an infringement of First Amendment rights does not require a legislative act having the force of law. The only requirement is an action "*under color of state law*" which inhibits the exercise of protected rights. When an infringement of first amendment rights is alleged, the deprivation of a property interest is irrelevant.

By representing the Florida Defenders of the Environment, himself and others in state litigation, appellant was engaging in a "form of political expression" entitled to First and Fourteenth Amendment protection. This protection not only extends to prohibitions on prior restraints of speech; it also forbids the imposition of retaliatory sanctions designed to punish the legitimate exercise of First Amendment rights.

Viewed in the light most favorable to appellant, appellant's complaint asserts that the City Council of North Miami, acting under the color of Florida law, adopted and disseminated an official resolution publicly censuring appellant in retaliation for appellant's representation of an adverse party in state litigation, thereby subjecting appellant to official investigation and intentionally placing appellant in potential criminal, professional, social, political and economic jeopardy without any justification. A municipality, like any state governmental entity, may not retaliate against an individual because of that person's legitimate use of the courts. Thus, we conclude that under the facts as alleged, appellant's First Amendment claim states an action cognizable under Section 1983. Accordingly, the decision of the district court dismissing this claim is reversed.

* * *

The district court evidently construed appellant's complaint as alleging nothing more tangible than injury to personal reputation due to the fact that appellant could not allege deprivation of employment. As the district court observed, "[t]he allegations in the Complaint are devoid of any suggestion of a deprivation of a tangible, economic interest. The University has not fired the [appellant]. They have not denied him tenure.

There is no indication that the [appellant] has sought employment elsewhere only to meet with closed doors."

With all due respect, we disagree with the district court's construction of appellant's complaint. It alleges that the City Council of North Miami, without affording appellant notice or a hearing, passed a resolution which has "embarrassed [appellant] in his personal life" and "[degraded] him in his employment." Based upon the liberal principles of notice pleading, we conclude that appellant has sufficiently alleged injury to his business reputation. We see no reason why an attorney is not entitled to property or liberty interests in his or her business (professional) reputation/goodwill when the same rights have been extended to other businesses. Accordingly, we reverse the decision of the district court dismissing appellant's Section 1983 based on alleged procedural due process violations.

CONCLUSION

We AFFIRM the dismissal of appellant's Section 1983 claims based on alleged violations of the Sixth Amendment and the prohibition against bills of attainder. We REVERSE the dismissals of appellant's First Amendment and procedural due process claims and REMAND these issues for further proceedings.

Institutional Academic Freedom

There can be no doubt that academic freedom norms protect institutions, as seen throughout cases excerpted in this chapter, especially when university personnel are threatened by outsiders who seek to pierce institutional autonomy veils. However, in recent cases, colleges have raised their own academic freedom defenses against outsiders (particularly students or applicants), in the form of institutional academic freedom. Matthew Finkin has characterized the issue as "a desire in search of a legal theory. The institutional desire is to be left alone. It calls to mind the condition von Humboldt sought for the German university . . . freedom and solitude. It also reminds us that, at certain points, university autonomy *is* a necessary condition for freedom of teaching and inquiry . . . [the] elemental infirmity in the theory of 'institutional' academic freedom lies in its refusal to admit of distinctions. The desire is laudable— but the theory claims too much." "On 'Institutional' Academic Freedom," *Texas Law Review*, 61 (1983), 817–57.

Cases including institutional academic freedom dimensions include several excerpted or treated elsewhere. *Bakke*, of course, is a student admissions case; *Schmid* and *Tate* are campus access cases; *Widmar, Bob Jones*, and *Cuesnongle* are religion cases. The excerpts in this section are presented to consider their institutional academic freedom claims.

Regents of the University of California v. Bakke
438 U.S. 265 (1978)

POWELL, Justice.

Petitioner simply has not carried its burden of demonstrating that it must prefer members of particular ethnic groups over all other individuals in order to promote better health-care delivery to deprived citizens. Indeed, petitioner has not shown that its preferential classification is likely to have any significant effect on the problem.

C

The fourth goal asserted by petitioner is the attainment of a diverse student body. This clearly is a constitutionally permissible goal for an institution of higher education. Academic freedom, though not a specifically enumerated constitutional right, long has been viewed as a special concern of the First Amendment. The freedom of a university to make its own judgments as to education includes the selection of its student body. Mr. Justice Frankfurter summarized the "four essential freedoms" that constitute academic freedom:

> "It is the business of a university to provide that atmosphere which is most conducive to speculation, experiment and creation. It is an atmosphere in which there prevail 'the four essential freedoms' of a university—to determine for itself on academic grounds who may teach, what may be taught, how it shall be taught, and who may be admitted to study."

Our national commitment to the safeguarding of these freedoms within university communities was emphasized in *Keyishian v. Board of Regents*:

> "Our Nation is deeply committed to safeguarding academic freedom which is of transcendent value to all of us and not merely to the teachers concerned. That freedom is therefore a special concern of the First Amendment. . . . The Nation's future depends upon leaders trained through wide exposure to that robust exchange of ideas which discovers truth 'out of a multitude of tongues, [rather] than through any kind of authoritative selection.' "

The atmosphere of "speculation, experiment and creation"—so essential to the quality of higher education—is widely believed to be promoted by a diverse student body. As the Court noted in *Keyishian*, it is not too much to say that the "nation's future depends upon leaders trained through wide exposure" to the ideas and mores of students as diverse as this Nation of many peoples.

Thus, in arguing that its universities must be accorded the right to select those students who will contribute the most to the "robust exchange of ideas," petitioner invokes a countervailing constitutional interest, that of the First Amendment. In this light, petitioner must be viewed as seeking to achieve a goal that is of paramount importance in the fulfillment of its mission.

It may be argued that there is greater force to these views at the undergraduate level than in a medical school where the training is centered primarily on professional competency. But even at the graduate level, our tradition and experience lend support to the view that the contribution of diversity is substantial. In *Sweatt v. Painter*, the Court made a similar point with specific reference to legal education:

> "The law school, the proving ground for legal learning and practice, cannot be effective in isolation from the individuals and institutions with which the law interacts. Few students and no one who has practiced law would choose to study in an academic vacuum, removed from the interplay of ideas and the exchange of views with which the law is concerned."

Physicians serve a heterogeneous population. An otherwise qualified medical student with a particular background—whether it be ethnic, geographic, culturally advantaged or disadvantaged—may bring to a professional school of medicine experiences, outlooks, and ideas that enrich the training of its student body and better equip its graduates to render with understanding their vital service to humanity.

Ethnic diversity, however, is only one element in a range of factors a university properly may consider in attaining the goal of a heterogeneous student body. Although a university must have wide discretion in making the sensitive judgments as to who should be admitted, constitutional limitations protecting individual rights may not be disregarded. Respondent urges—and the courts below have held—that petitioner's dual admissions program is a racial classification that impermissibly infringes his rights under the Fourteenth Amendment. As the interest of diversity is compelling in the context of a university's admissions program, the question remains whether the program's racial classification is necessary to promote this interest.

* * *

D

In enjoining petitioner from ever considering the race of any applicant, however, the courts below failed to recognize that the State has a substantial interest that legitimately may be served by a properly devised admissions program involving the competitive consideration of race and ethnic origin. For this reason, so much of the California court's judgment as enjoins petitioner from any consideration of the race of any applicant must be reversed.

State v. Schmid
423 A.2d 615 (1980)

HANDLER, J.

While distributing political literature on the campus of Princeton University, defendant Chris Schmid, a member of the United States Labor Party, was arrested and charged by the University with trespass upon private property. He was subsequently convicted under the State's penal trespass statute. On this appeal he challenges the conviction on the grounds that it stems from a violation of his federal and state constitutional rights to freedom of speech and assembly.

* * *

II

Defendant asserts initially that his conviction in this case violated his rights under the First Amendment to the United States Constitution. The First Amendment was designed by its framers to foster unfettered discussion and free dissemination of opinion dealing with matters of public interest and governmental affairs. It embraces the freedom to distribute information and materials to all citizens, a freedom "clearly vital to the preservation of a free society." The guarantees of the First Amendment are effectuated against potential state interference through the Fourteenth Amendment by limiting the extent to which states can restrict individuals in the exercise of rights of speech and assembly. The First Amendment, however, does not similarly protect rights of speech and assembly against interference or impairment by private individuals. The Amendment imposes no limitations upon "the owner of private property used nondiscriminatorily for private purposes only," even though such use may trench upon the speech and assembly activities of other persons.

It is clear that public colleges and universities, as instrumentalities of state government, are not beyond the reach of the First Amendment. A public college or university, created or controlled by the state itself, is an arm of state government and, thus, by definition, implicates state action.

A private college or university, however, stands upon a different footing in relationship to the state. Such an institution is not the creature or instrument of state government. Even though such an institution may conduct itself identically to its state-operated counterparts and, in terms of educational purposes and activities, may be virtually indistinguishable from a public institution, a private college or university does not thereby either operate under or exercise the authority of state government. Hence, the state nexus requirement that triggers the application of the First Amendment is not readily met in the case of a private educational institution.

Notwithstanding the primary thrust of the First Amendment against state governmental interference with expressional freedoms, the guarantees of this Amendment may under appropriate conditions be invoked against nongovernmental bodies. In particular settings, private entities, including educational institutions, may so impact upon the public or share enough of the essential features of governmental bodies as to be engaged functionally in "state action" for First Amendment purposes. The more focused inquiry therefore must be turned to those circumstances that can subject an entity of essentially nongovernmental or private character to the requirements imposed by the First Amendment.

One test of such state action involves the presence of an interdependent or symbiotic relationship between the private entity and the state government. This standard was utilized in *Burton v. Wilmington Parking Auth.*, in which the Supreme Court held that a privately-owned restaurant which leased premises in a government-owned and government-maintained parking garage was subject to the Equal Protection Clause of the Fourteenth Amendment; the restaurant thus could not refuse to serve blacks. The Court stressed that the parking facility was essentially a government building engaged in a governmental purpose and that the State and the restaurant mutually benefited from their "joint participation" in the operation.

Another basis for determining the existence of state action is the extent of direct governmental regulation of the private entity. This standard was applied in *Public Utilities Comm'n v. Pollak*, wherein the Supreme Court held that the First and Fifth Amendments to the federal Constitution were applicable to a policy decision made by a private transit company operating in the heavily-regulated field of public transportation because that decision was subject to approval by a governmental agency. The governmental regulation or control standard, however, is fairly difficult to administer as a means for positing state action. The Supreme Court has stated that the mere fact that a business is subject to extensive state regulation will not in and of itself convert the actions of that business entity into state action. There must be demonstrated a "sufficiently close nexus" between the state regulation and the allegedly unconstitutional actions of the regulated business entity before it can be said that those actions emanate from or can be attributed to state government.

Both of these approaches for ascertaining state action have been followed in challenges to the actions of private colleges or universities as violative of First Amendment rights. Among the factors most often marshaled to show state action are that the institution received government funds, that the institution was performing a governmental function by providing education, that it was state-accredited or state-chartered or was otherwise highly regulated by the state, that the college derived economic benefit from tax exemptions, that it indirectly enforced governmental laws, or, in some instances, that the college had been built on formerly public lands. For the most part, however, such challenges have failed.

The record reveals that Princeton University, though privately owned and controlled, is involved in a continuous relationship with the State. The University is a state-accredited educational institution; it participates in and receives, as do other public and private educational institutions, the advantages of certain State programs. Its property and buildings on the central campus, with the exception of its ice skating and hockey facility and its campus parking lots, are tax-exempt. The University also receives state-budgeted funds through *The Independent College and University Assistance Act*, N.J.S.A.18A:72B–15 *et seq*. In addition, according to the stipulations of the parties, the University Security Department, some of whose employees are deputized to make arrests under the laws of New Jersey, is primarily responsible for providing security services for the entire University community.

Nonetheless, this congeries of facts does not equate with state action on the part of Princeton University. Princeton University is, indisputably, predominantly private, unregulated and autonomous in its character and functioning as an institution of higher education. The interface between the University and the State is not so extensive as to demonstrate a joint and mutual participation in higher education or to establish an interdependent or symbiotic relationship between the two in the field of education.

Moreover, the degree of State regulation does not evince a "close nexus" between the State and Princeton University's policies, particularly with regard to the public's access to the University campus and facilities and, even more particularly, with regard to either the distribution of political literature or other expressional activities on University property. Furthermore, the resort by Princeton University to the State's trespass laws to protect its own rights of property does not constitute state action for First Amendment purposes. In the absence of a protectable First Amendment right in the individual, the property owner's recourse to appropriate and otherwise neutral penal sanctions to protect its legitimate interests does not constitute action by the State nor clothe the property owner with a state identity for First Amendment purposes.

Although Princeton University is thus not subject to First Amendment obligations by virtue of a joint relationship with or direct regulation by the State, there remains to be considered still another standard for determining First Amendment applicability, *viz*, the "public function doctrine." Even though a private entity is not engaged in "state action," it may nevertheless be required to honor First Amendment rights if its property is sufficiently devoted to public uses. Arguably, there are a broad public invitation and wide use of University property that serve to encourage expressional rights and are conducive to the educational goals of Princeton University. Nevertheless, it must be recognized that the public uses and expressional activities that are permitted by the University are subordinate to its overall educational policies. In this sense, while the invitation to the public is broad, it is not truly "open-ended" or for "any and all purposes." Therefore, although Princeton University's *raison d'etre* is more consonant with free speech and assembly principles than a shopping center's purposes might be, the attachment of First Amendment requirements to the University by virtue of the general public's permitted access to its property would still be problematic.

If we were to examine whether Princeton University has in the pervasive and all-inclusive sense of *Marsh v. Alabama*, undertaken to act as a local government body, the applicability of the First Amendment remains doubtful. The nature of college community life as determined by Princeton University, even with its residential characteristics, would not seem to invest the University with the fundamental attributes of a government substitute or surrogate in the manner deemed critical for positing state action in *Marsh v. Alabama*.

A private educational institution such as Princeton University involves essentially voluntary relationships between and among the institution and its students, faculty, employees, and other affiliated personnel, and the life and activities of the individual members of this community are directed and shaped by their shared educational goals and the institution's educational policies. The public's invitation to use college facilities is incident to the educational life of the institution and must comport and be integrated with its educational endeavors. It is dubious therefore whether Princeton can or should be regarded as a quasi-governmental enclave or the functional equivalent of a "company town," which has all of the characteristics of a municipality, for First Amendment purposes.

In attempting to pull together these diverse strands of constitutional doctrine, it is apparent that First Amendment principles as applied to the owners of private property are still evolving. The precise question in this case has not been definitively resolved or even clearly foreshadowed by extant decisional authority. Furthermore, invoking First Amendment strictures against private property owners, as has been noted, necessarily engenders countervailing concerns for legitimate private property rights. In this case, the difficulty of the decisional task and the uncertainty of its solution posed by this consideration are further compounded because the private property is an educational institution. Such institutions, in addition to their own protectable private property interests, are committed to the achievement of important societal educational objectives which are generally consistent with First Amendment purposes. While these purposes may temper the protections accorded private property, the legitimate and genuine property interests of educational institutions should not be denuded because of the apparent coincidence between the goals of higher education and the First Amendment.

We are thus confronted with strong crosscurrents of policy that must be navigated with extreme care in reaching any satisfactory resolution of the competing constitutional values under the First Amendment in this case. These concerns persuade us to stay our hand in attempting to decide the question of whether the First Amendment applies to Princeton University in the context of the present appeal. Defendant, moreover, has presented compelling alternative grounds for relief founded upon the State Constitution, which we now reach.

III

Defendant asserts that under the State Constitution he is afforded protection of his expressional rights even if it is not clear that the First Amendment would serve to grant that protection. The United States Supreme Court has recently acknowledged in the most clear and unmistakable terms that a state's organic and general law can independently furnish a basis for protecting individual rights of speech and assembly.

The view that state constitutions exist as a cognate source of individual freedoms and that state constitutional guarantees of these rights may indeed surpass the guarantees of the federal Constitution has received frequent judicial expression.

On numerous occasions our own courts have recognized the New Jersey Constitution to be an alternative and independent source of individual rights. Mr. Justice Brennan in his oft-cited piece in 90 *Harv. L. Rev.* drew support for this proposition from *State v. Johnson*, wherein Justice Sullivan had observed that although the New Jersey constitutional provision relating to searches and seizures was identical to the federal Fourth Amendment provisions, " 'we have the right to construe our State constitutional provision in accordance with what we conceive to be its plain meaning.' "

The guarantees of our State Constitution have been found to extend to a panoply of rights deemed to be most essential to both the quality of individual life and the preservation of personal liberty.

Most recently, this Court recognized through Chief Justice Wilentz that freedom of the press, intimately associated with individual expressional and associational rights, is strongly protected under the State Constitution, state statutory enactments, and state decisional law. The United States Supreme Court itself has acknowledged that the First Amendment, which implicates this important freedom, does not accord to it the degree of protection that may be available through state law.

A basis for finding exceptional vitality in the New Jersey Constitution with respect to individual rights of speech and assembly is found in part in the language employed. Our Constitution affirmatively recognizes these freedoms, *viz*:

> Every person may freely speak, write and publish his sentiments on all subjects, being responsible for the abuse of that right. No law shall be passed to restrain or abridge the liberty of speech or of the press....

> The people have the right freely to assemble together, to consult for the common good, to make known their opinions to their representatives, and to petition for redress of grievances.

*   *   *

We conclude, therefore, that the State Constitution furnishes to individuals the complementary freedoms of speech and assembly and protects the reasonable exercise of those rights. These guarantees extend directly to governmental entities as well as to persons exercising governmental powers. They are also available against unreasonably restrictive or oppressive conduct on the part of private entities that have otherwise assumed a constitutional obligation not to abridge the individual exercise of such freedoms because of the public use of their property. The State Constitution in this fashion serves to thwart inhibitory actions which unreasonably frustrate, infringe, or obstruct the expressional and associational rights of individuals exercised under Article I, paragraphs 6 and 18 thereof.

*   *   *

Accordingly, we now hold that under the State Constitution, the test to be applied to ascertain the parameters of the rights of speech and assembly upon privately-owned property and the extent to which such property reasonably can be restricted to accommodate these rights involves several elements. This standard must take into account (1) the nature, purposes, and primary use of such private property, generally, its "normal" use, (2) the extent and nature of the public's invitation to use that property, and (3) the purpose of the expressional activity undertaken upon such property in relation to both the private and public use of the property. This is a multifaceted test which must be applied to ascertain whether in a given case owners of private property may be required to permit, subject to suitable restrictions, the reasonable exercise by individuals of the constitutional freedoms of speech and assembly.

Even when an owner of private property is constitutionally obligated under such a standard to honor speech and assembly rights of others, private property rights themselves must nonetheless be protected. The owner of such private property, therefore, is entitled to fashion reasonable rules to control the mode, opportunity and site for the individual exercise of expressional rights upon his property. It is at this level of analysis—assessing the reasonableness of such restrictions—that weight may be given to whether there exist convenient and feasible alternative means to individuals to engage in substantially the same expressional activity.

* * *

IV

The application of the appropriate standard in this case must commence with an examination of the primary use of the private property, namely, the campus and facilities of Princeton University. Princeton University itself has furnished the answer to this inquiry in expansively expressing its overriding educational goals, *viz*:

> The central purposes of a University are the pursuit of truth, the discovery of new knowledge through scholarship and research, the teaching and general development of students, and the transmission of knowledge and learning to society at large. Free inquiry and free expression within the academic community are indispensable to the achievement of these goals. The freedom to teach and to learn depends upon the creation of appropriate conditions and opportunities on the campus as a whole as well as in classrooms and lecture halls. All members of the academic community share the responsibility for securing and sustaining the general conditions conducive to this freedom.

* * *

Free Speech and peaceable assembly are basic requirements of the University as a center for free inquiry and the search for knowledge and insight. . . . No one questions that Princeton University has honored this grand ideal and has in fact dedicated its facilities and property to achieve the educational goals expounded in this compelling statement.

In examining next the extent and nature of a public invitation to use its property, we note that a public presence within Princeton University is entirely consonant with the University's expressed educational mission. Princeton University, as a private institution of higher education, clearly seeks to encourage both a wide and continuous exchange of opinions and ideas and to foster a policy of openness and freedom with respect to the use of its facilities. The commitment of its property, facilities, and resources to educational purposes contemplates substantial public involvement and participation in the academic life of the University. The University itself has endorsed the educational value of an open campus and the full exposure of the college community to the "outside world," *i.e.*, the public at large. Princeton University has indeed invited such public uses of its resources in fulfillment of its broader educational ideals and objectives.

The further question is whether the expressional activities undertaken by the defendant in this case are discordant in any sense with both the private and public uses of the campus and facilities of the University. There is nothing in the record to suggest that Schmid was evicted because the purpose of his activities, distributing political literature, offended the University's educational policies. The reasonable and normal inference thus to be extracted from the record in the instant case is that defendant's attempt to disseminate political material was not incompatible with either Princeton University's professed educational goals or the University's overall use of its property for educational purposes. Further, there is no indication that even under the terms of the University's own regulations, Schmid's activities in any way, directly or demonstrably "disrupt[ed] the regular and essential operations of the University" or that in either the time, the place, or the manner of Schmid's distribution of the political materials, he "significantly infringed on the rights of others" or caused any interference or inconvenience with respect to the normal use of University property and the normal routine and activities of the college community.

Without necessarily endorsing any of the foregoing conclusions, the University nevertheless contends that its solicitation regulation was properly invoked against Schmid in this case because it requires that there be a specific invitation from on-campus organizations or students and a specific official authorization before an individual may enter upon University premises even for the purpose of exercising constitutional rights of speech and assembly. It points out that Schmid failed to obtain such permission. The University stresses the necessity for and reasonableness of such a regulation.

In addressing this argument, we must give substantial deference to the importance of institutional integrity and independence. Private educational institutions perform an essential social function and have a fundamental responsibility to assure the academic and general well-being of their communities of students, teachers and related personnel. At a minimum, these needs, implicating academic freedom and development, justify an educational institution in controlling those who seek to enter its domain. The singular need to achieve essential educational goals and regulate activities that impact upon these efforts has been acknowledged even with respect to public educational institutions. Hence, private colleges and universities must be accorded a generous measure of autonomy and self-governance if they are to fulfill their paramount role as vehicles of education and enlightenment.

In this case, however, the University regulations that were applied to Schmid contained no standards, aside from the requirement for invitation and permission, for governing the actual exercise of expressional freedom. Indeed, there were no standards extant regulating the granting or withholding of such authorization, nor did the regulations deal adequately with the time, place, or manner for individuals to exercise their rights of speech and assembly. Regulations thus devoid of reasonable standards designed to protect both the legitimate interests of the University as an institution of higher education and the individual exercise of expressional freedom cannot constitutionally be invoked to prohibit the otherwise noninjurious and reasonable exercise of such freedoms. In these circumstances, given the absence of adequate reasonable regulations, the required accommodation of Schmid's expressional and associational rights, otherwise reasonably exercised, would not constitute an unconstitutional abridgment of Princeton University's property rights. It follows that in the absence of a reasonable regulatory scheme, Princeton University did in fact violate defendant's State constitutional rights of expression in evicting him and securing his arrest for distributing political literature upon its campus.

We are mindful that Princeton University's regulatory policies governing the time, place, and manner for the exercise of constitutionally-protected speech and associational rights have been modified substantially since the events surrounding Schmid's arrest and now more fully and adequately define the nature of these restrictions. As we have indicated, the content of such regulations, recognizing and controlling the right to engage in expressional activities, may be molded by the availability of alternative means of communication. These current amended regulations exemplify the approaches open to private educational entities seeking to protect their institutional integrity while at the same time recognizing individual rights of speech and assembly and accommodating the public whose presence nurtures academic inquiry and growth. As noted, however, these regulations were not in place when the University interfered with Schmid's reasonable efforts to communicate his political views to those present on its campus in April 1978. Hence, Schmid suffered a constitutional impairment of his State constitutional rights of speech and assembly and his conviction for trespass must therefore be undone.

Accordingly, for the reason set forth, the judgment below is reversed.

Commonwealth v. Tate
432 A.2d 1382 (1981)

ROBERTS, Justice.

On March 27, 1976, appellants were arrested on the campus of Muhlenberg College and charged with the summary offense of defiant trespass, when they refused to discontinue the peaceful distribution of leaflets outside a college building in which Clarence Kelley, then Director of the Federal Bureau of Investigation, was speaking at a public symposium on crime prevention. Appellants were convicted at a magistrate's hearing on August 11, 1976, and fined $25.00 each plus court costs. They appealed their convictions to the Court of Common Pleas of Lehigh County. Following a trial de novo without a jury, appellants were found guilty of defiant trespass and ordered to pay fines of $50.00 each plus court costs. On appeal, the Superior Court affirmed without opinion, with Judge Hoffman noting his dissent. We granted allowance of appeal. In light of the affirmative defense provided by the trespass statute, and Article I, sections 7 and 20, of the Pennsylvania Constitution, we conclude that these defiant trespass convictions cannot stand. Hence we reverse.[2]

Muhlenberg College is a private institution of higher education located in Allentown and charted by the Commonwealth of Pennsylvania. The event at which appellants were arrested was a symposium planned and presented by the Board of Associates of Muhlenberg College, a civic group which regularly uses the college's facilities to present a series of programs for the benefit of the community. The March 27, 1976,

---

2. Because we decide this case under our state Constitution, we need not reach appellants' claim that their convictions are also barred by the First Amendment to the United States Constitution.

symposium was entitled "Citizens' Crusade Against Crime." It was held primarily in the Seegers Student Union Building of the college and featured F.B.I. Director Clarence Kelley, a public figure of national repute, as its principal speaker.

The symposium had been publicized in newspapers and advertised in handbills as being open to the public. In one newspaper account, the president of the Muhlenberg Board of Associates gave the following description of the program: "The symposium has been designed to provide the springboard for an on-going cooperative community effort exploring, evaluating, and implementing practical ways and means for personal and group involvement in crusade against crime. . . . [W]e invite and encourage every concerned citizen to join us on March 27." A registration fee of $4.00 was requested of those attending the symposium, with attendance limited to the first five hundred registrants.

Appellants, who were not Muhlenberg students, were all members of the Lehigh-Pocono Committee of Concern (LEPOCO), a local non-violent anti-war organization. When members of LEPOCO read of Director Kelley's scheduled appearance, they decided to distribute leaflets to members of the public attending his speech. Through the leaflets, LEPOCO wished to protest the denial by Mr. Kelley, in a personally signed letter, of their request under the federal Freedom of Information Act, for information maintained in F.B.I. files concerning LEPOCO and its members. Further, LEPOCO wished to point out to the public the incongruity of Director Kelley's appearance at a crime prevention symposium in light of then-recent public revelations concerning criminal activities by the F.B.I. which were prominent in the news media. The symposium was the site of Director Kelley's first public appearance in the Allentown area.

On Friday, March 26, the day before the symposium, some members of LEPOCO went to the Muhlenberg campus and attempted to distribute leaflets explaining to students why LEPOCO felt it necessary to be present on the following day to communicate its views on Director Kelley and the F.B.I. At that time they were stopped and informed that they would not be permitted to distribute leaflets on the campus grounds since they did not have a permit from the college to do so. The LEPOCO members then attempted to obtain a permit for the following day, but their request was summarily refused.

Appellants and other members of LEPOCO arrived at the Muhlenberg campus on the morning of the symposium and twice attempted to distribute their leaflets to persons entering and leaving the symposium. Both times, at the request of college officials, members of the Allentown Police Department escorted the LEPOCO leafletters to a public sidewalk located approximately forty yards from the entrance to the main symposium building. No arrests were made on either occasion.

Appellants attempted to distribute their leaflets a third time at the close of the symposium that afternoon. They stood about forty feet from the entrance to the student union building and quietly distributed their leaflets. They engaged in no disorderly conduct, carried no signs, used no loud or offensive language, and made no attempt to enter any of the college buildings. They blocked no building entrances and did not attempt to force their leaflets upon unwilling passersby. They received no complaints from any members of the public regarding their presence on campus.

Nonetheless, the Allentown Chief of Police personally instructed appellants that they would be arrested if they did not leave the campus, because they did not have permission from the college to distribute their leaflets and had not paid the $4.00 registration fee for the symposium. Appellants replied that they wished not to attend the symposium but merely to distribute their leaflets peacefully. Upon appellants' refusal to leave the campus grounds until they had completed their leafletting, the Allentown police arrested the five appellants and removed them to police headquarters, where they were served with citations for the summary offense of defiant trespass and released on their own recognizance.

* * *

Although privately supported, Muhlenberg College serves in many respects as a community center for Allentown, maintaining upon its campus a United States Post Office station, a public cafeteria, an information and sales booth for tickets to public events, and a federal book depository library, which is required "to be maintained so as to be accessible to the public." All of these facilities are located within a few hundred yards of the site of appellants' arrest. It was established at trial that other members of the public who, like appellants, did not choose to attend the symposium, were present without incident on the Muhlenberg campus on March 26, 1976. Moreover, according to the testimony of the college president, Muhlenberg had "no policy about off-campus visitors," and "a lot of people walk[ed] the campus."

The college did have a requirement that any person from off campus wishing to distribute materials or offer materials for sale secure the permission of the college beforehand. The only difference between appellants and the other members of the public on the college grounds on the day of the symposium was that appellants attempted to distribute leaflets relating to the symposium without having received permission to do so from the college. As stated earlier, appellants had sought a permit on the previous day but had been refused. The record does not reveal what standards, if any, were applicable to the granting or denial of such permission. It appears, however, from the testimony of the college president, that the college believed itself entitled to exercise its discretion arbitrarily.

Thus at issue is whether the college's standardless permit requirement constitutes a lawful condition with which appellants were obligated to comply or otherwise face prosecution and conviction as defiant trespassers. Here we are faced with an educational institution which holds itself out to the public as a community resource and cultural center, allows members of the public to walk its campus, permits a community organization to use its facilities as a forum for a public official of national importance, and at the same time arbitrarily denies a few members of the public the right to distribute leaflets peacefully to the relevant audience present at that forum. In these circumstances, we are of the view that the Constitution of this Commonwealth protects appellants' invaluable right to freedom of expression against the enforcement, by state criminal statute, of the college's standardless permit requirement.

In 1776, more than a decade before the adoption of the Federal Constitution, this Commonwealth set forth in Article XII of the Declaration of Rights of its first Constitution the principle "[t]hat the people have a right to freedom of speech, and of writing, and publishing their sentiments. . . . " The Pennsylvania Constitution of 1790 further articulated this affirmative guarantee in language which is preserved in Article I, section 7, of our present Constitution:

> "The free communication of thoughts and opinions is one of the invaluable rights of man, and every citizen may freely speak, write, and print on any subject, being responsible for the abuse of that liberty. . . . "

So, too, the framers of our first Constitution recognized the complementary rights of assembly and petition, which are safeguarded today through Article I, section 20 of our present Constitution:

> "The citizens have a right in a peaceable manner to assemble together for their common good, and to apply to those invested with the power of government for redress of grievances or other proper purposes, by petition, address or remonstrance."

It is well settled that a state may provide through its constitution a basis for the rights and liberties of its citizens independent from that provided by the Federal Constitution, and that the rights so guaranteed may be more expansive than their federal counterparts.

* * *

Mindful of both this Commonwealth's great heritage of freedom and the compelling language of the Pennsylvania Constitution, we likewise hold that, in certain circumstances, the state may reasonably restrict the right to possess and use property in the interests of freedom of speech, assembly, and petition.

To determine whether the appropriate circumstances exist here, we must balance the college's right to possess and protect its property against appellants' rights of expression in light of the compatibility of that expression with the "activity of [the] particular place at [the] particular time." On this record, it is clear that the balance must be struck in appellants' favor.

* * *

At the same time, Muhlenberg College, as a private institution, was by no means powerless to control the access of members of the public to the area in front of its student union building on the day of the symposium. Here, however, there existed only a vague requirement of "permission," governed by no articulated standards.

Through public advertisements, the Board of Associates assembled a public audience on the Muhlenberg College campus to hear F.B.I. Director Kelley present his views. In these circumstances, the college could not, consistent with the invaluable rights to freedom of speech, assembly, and petition constitutionally guaranteed by this Commonwealth to its citizens, exercise its right of property to invoke a standardless permit requirement and the state's defiant trespass law to prevent appellants from peacefully presenting their point of view to this indisputably relevant audience in an area of the college normally open to the public. Because appellants complied with all "lawful conditions" for access to the premises, their convictions may not stand.

Accordingly, the judgments of sentence are reversed and appellants discharged.

Widmar v. Vincent

454 U.S. 263 (1981)

Justice POWELL delivered the opinion of the court.

This case presents the question whether a state university, which makes its facilities generally available for the activities of registered student groups, may close its facilities to a registered student group desiring to use the facilities for religious worship and religious discussion.

I

It is the stated policy of the University of Missouri at Kansas City to encourage the activities of student organizations. The University officially recognizes over 100 student groups. It routinely provides University facilities for the meetings of registered organizations. Students pay an activity fee of $41 per semester (1978–1979) to help defray the costs to the University.

From 1973 until 1977 a registered religious group named Cornerstone regularly sought and received permission to conduct its meetings in University facilities. In 1977, however, the University informed the group that it could no longer meet in University buildings. The exclusion was based on a regulation, adopted by the Board of Curators in 1972, that prohibits the use of University buildings or grounds "for purposes of religious worship or religious teaching."

Eleven University students, all members of Cornerstone, brought suit to challenge the regulation in the Federal District Court for the Western District of Missouri. They alleged that the University's discrimination against religious activity and discussion violated their rights to free exercise of religion, equal protection, and freedom of speech under the First and Fourteenth Amendments to the Constitution of the United States.

Upon cross-motions for summary judgment, the District Court upheld the challenged regulation. It found the regulation not only justified, but required, by the Establishment Clause of the Federal Constitution. Under *Tilton v. Richardson*, the court reasoned, the State could not provide facilities for religious use without giving prohibited support to an institution of religion. The District Court rejected the argument that the University could not discriminate against religious speech on the basis of its content. It found religious speech entitled to less protection than other types of expression.

The Court of Appeals for the Eighth Circuit reversed. Rejecting the analysis of the District Court, it viewed the University regulation as a content-based discrimination against religious speech, for which it could find no compelling justification. The court held that the Establishment Clause does not bar a policy of equal access, in which facilities are open to groups and speakers of all kinds. According to the Court of Appeals, the "primary effect" of such a policy would not be to advance religion, but rather to further the neutral purpose of developing students' "social and cultural awareness as well as [their] intellectual curiosity."

We granted certiorari. We now affirm.

* * *

On one hand, respondents' First Amendment rights are entitled to special constitutional solicitude. Our cases have required the most exacting scrutiny in cases in which a State undertakes to regulate speech on the basis of its content. On the other hand, the state interest asserted here—in achieving greater separation of church and State than is already ensured under the Establishment Clause of the Federal Constitution—is limited by the Free Exercise Clause and in this case by the Free Speech Clause as well. In this constitutional context, we are unable to recognize the State's interest as sufficiently "compelling" to justify content-based discrimination against respondents' religious speech.

IV

Our holding in this case in no way undermines the capacity of the University to establish reasonable time, place, and manner regulations. Nor do we question the right of the University to make academic judgments as to how best to allocate scarce resources or "to determine for itself on academic grounds who may teach, what may be taught, how it shall be taught, and who may be admitted to study." Finally, we affirm the continuing validity of cases, *e.g., Healy v. James,* that recognize a university's right to exclude even First Amendment activities that violate reasonable campus rules or substantially interfere with the opportunity of other students to obtain an education.

The basis for our decision is narrow. Having created a forum generally open to student groups, the University seeks to enforce a content-based exclusion of religious speech. Its exclusionary policy violates the fundamental principle that a state regulation of speech should be content-neutral, and the University is unable to justify this violation under applicable constitutional standards.

For this reason, the decision of the Court of Appeals is

Affirmed.

Justice STEVENS, concurring in the judgment.

As the Court recognizes, every university must "make academic judgments as to how best to allocate scarce resources." The Court appears to hold, however, that those judgments must "serve a compelling state interest" whenever they are based, even in part, on the content of speech. This conclusion apparently flows from the Court's suggestion that a student activities program—from which the public may be excluded,—must be managed as though it were a "public forum." In my opinion, the use of the terms "compelling state interest" and "public forum" to analyze the question presented in this case may needlessly undermine the academic freedom of public universities.

Today most major colleges and universities are operated by public authority. Nevertheless, their facilities are not open to the public in the same way that streets and parks are. University facilities—private or public—are maintained primarily for the benefit of the student body and the faculty. In performing their learning and teaching missions, the managers of a university routinely make countless decisions based on the content of communicative materials. They select books for inclusion in the library, they hire professors on the basis of their academic philosophies, they select courses for inclusion in the curriculum, and they reward scholars for what they have written. In addition, in encouraging students to participate in extracurricular activities, they necessarily make decisions concerning the content of those activities.

Because every university's resources are limited, an educational institution must routinely make decisions concerning the use of the time and space that is available for extracurricular activities. In my judgment, it is both necessary and appropriate for those decisions to evaluate the content of a proposed student activity. I should think it obvious, for example, that if two groups of 25 students requested the use of a room at a particular time—one to view Mickey Mouse cartoons and the other to rehearse an amateur performance of Hamlet—the First Amendment would not require that the room be reserved for the group that submitted its application first. Nor do I see why a university should have to establish a "compelling state interest" to defend its decision to permit one group to use the facility and not the other. In my opinion, a university should be allowed to decide for itself whether a program that illuminates the genius of Walt Disney should be given precedence over one that may duplicate material adequately covered in the classroom. Judgments of this kind should be made by academicians, not by federal judges, and their standards for decision should not be encumbered with ambiguous phrases like "compelling state interests."

Thus, I do not subscribe to the view that a public university has no greater interest in the content of student activities than the police chief has in the content of a soapbox oration on Capitol Hill. A university legitimately may regard some subjects as more relevant to its educational mission than others. But the university, like the police officer, may not allow its agreement or disagreement with the viewpoint of a particular speaker to determine whether access to a forum will be granted. If a state university is to deny recognition to a student organization—or is to give it a lesser right to use school facilities than other student groups—it must have a valid reason for doing so.

In this case I agree with the Court that the University has not established a sufficient justification for its refusal to allow the Cornerstone group to engage in religious worship on the campus. The primary reason advanced for the discriminatory treatment is the University's fear of violating the Establishment Clause. But since the record discloses no danger that the University will appear to sponsor any particular religion, and since student participation in the Cornerstone meetings is entirely voluntary, the Court properly concludes that the University's fear is groundless. With that justification put to one side, the University has not met the burden that is imposed on it by *Healy*.

Nor does the University's reliance on the Establishment Clause of the Missouri State Constitution provide a sufficient justification for the discriminatory treatment in this case. As I have said, I believe that the University may exercise a measure of control over the agenda for student use of school facilities, preferring some subjects over others, without needing to identify so-called "compelling state interests." Quite obviously, however, the University could not allow a group of Republicans or Presbyterians to meet while denying Democrats or Mormons the same privilege. It seems apparent that the policy under attack would allow groups of young philosophers to meet to discuss their skepticism that a Supreme Being exists, or a group of political scientists to meet to debate the accuracy of the view that religion is the "opium of the people." If school facilities may be used to discuss anticlerical doctrine, it seems to me that comparable use by a group desiring to express a belief in God must also be permitted. The fact that their expression of faith includes ceremonial conduct is not, in my opinion, a sufficient reason for suppressing their discussion entirely.

Accordingly, although I do not endorse the Court's reasoning, I concur in its judgment.

Bob Jones University v. U.S.
461 U.S. 574 (1983)

BURGER, C.J.

* * *

III

Petitioners contend that, even if the Commissioner's policy is valid as to nonreligious private schools, that policy cannot constitutionally be applied to schools that engage in racial discrimination on the basis of sincerely held religious beliefs.[28] As to such schools, it is argued that the IRS construction of § 170 and § 501(c))(3) violates their free exercise rights under the Religion Clauses of the First Amendment. This contention presents claims not heretofore considered by this Court in precisely this context.

This Court has long held the Free Exercise Clause of the First Amendment to be an absolute prohibition against governmental regulation of religious beliefs. As interpreted by this Court, moreover, the Free Exercise Clause provides substantial protection for lawful conduct grounded in religious belief. However, "[n]ot all burdens on religion are unconstitutional.... The state may justify a limitation on religious liberty by showing that it is essential to accomplish an overriding governmental interest."

On occasion this Court has found certain governmental interests so compelling as to allow even regulations prohibiting religious based conduct. In *Prince v. Massachusetts*, for example, the Court held that neutrally cast child labor laws prohibiting sale of printed materials on public streets could be applied to prohibit children from dispensing religious literature. The Court found no constitutional infirmity in "excluding [Jehovah's Witness children] from doing there what no other children may do." Denial of tax benefits will inevitably have a substantial impact on the operation of private religious schools, but will not prevent those schools from observing their religious tenets.

The governmental interest at stake here is compelling. As discussed in Part II-B, *supra*, the Government has a fundamental, overriding interest in eradicating racial discrimination in education[29]—discrimination that prevailed, with official approval, for the first 165 years of this Nation's constitutional history. That governmental interest substantially outweighs whatever burden denial of tax benefits places on petitioners' exercise of their religious beliefs. The interests asserted by petitioners cannot be accommodated with that compelling governmental interest, and no "less restrictive means," are available to achieve the governmental interest.

IV

The remaining issue is whether the IRS properly applied its policy to these petitioners. Petitioner Goldsboro Christian Schools admits that it "maintain[s] racially discriminatory policies," but seeks to justify those policies on grounds we have fully discussed. The IRS properly denied tax-exempt status to Goldsboro Christian Schools.

Petitioner Bob Jones University, however, contends that it is not racially discriminatory. It emphasizes that it now allows all races to enroll, subject only to its restrictions on the conduct of all students, including its prohibitions of association between

---

28. The District Court found, on the basis of a full evidentiary record, that the challenged practices of petitioner Bob Jones University were based on a genuine belief that the Bible forbids interracial dating and marriage. We assume, as did the District Court, that the same is true with respect to petitioner Goldsboro Christian Schools.

29. We deal here only with religious *schools*—not with churches or other purely religious institutions; here, the governmental interest is in denying public support to racial discrimination in education. As noted earlier, racially discriminatory schools "exer[t] a pervasive influence on the entire educational process," outweighing any public benefit that they might otherwise provide.

men and women of different races, and of interracial marriage.[31] Although a ban on intermarriage or interracial dating applies to all races, decision of this Court firmly establish that discrimination on the basis of racial affiliation and association is a form of racial discrimination. We therefore find that the IRS properly applied Revenue Ruling 71–447 to Bob Jones University.[32]

The judgments of the Court of Appeals are, accordingly.

Affirmed.

Cuesnongle v. Ramos
835 F.2d 1486 (1st Cir. 1987)

Facts and Proceedings

In August, 1980, a strike of non-teaching employees occurred at Universidad Central de Bayamon (UCB) in Puerto Rico. UCB is a coeducational, private, non-profit Catholic University, conducted under the auspices of the Order of Dominican Fathers. Classes had been scheduled to start on August 16th, but did not in fact begin until August 25th. Although courses continued with what was later described as "relative normalcy," several classes had to be cancelled for lack of professors as a result of the labor dispute. After the strike ended, eight students, claiming breach of contract, filed complaints before the Council of Higher Education. When these complaints were dismissed, the students filed claims with the Puerto Rican Department of Consumer Affairs (DACO), invoking a consumer protection law that had been enacted to regulate product liability and contract protection for consumer services. The alleged breaches of contract included changing the opening dates for classes, reducing student services, altering class and course schedules, discharging employees, suspending students, substituting professors, refusing to allow a student assembly, and refusing to reimburse registration fees.

UCB raised numerous objections to DACO's jurisdiction over the matter, among them that DACO was barred by the doctrine of separation of church and state from adjudicating the case. When its objections were overruled, UCB voluntarily withdrew from the DACO administrative hearing without offering any evidence. UCB reasoned that any further involvement on its part could have been interpreted as a submission to DACO's authority and as a waiver of UCB's constitutional rights.

Following the hearing, on October 28, 1981, DACO reaffirmed its jurisdiction over the students' contract actions, and dismissed all of the complaints except one. As to that single complaint, DACO ordered the return of $217 in registration fees to one student, Froilan Montfort Seijo.

In contrast to the other complainants, Montfort had crossed the picket lines and tried to attend classes. When at first it seemed that no classes were going to take

---

31. This argument would in any event apply only to the final eight months of the five tax years at issue in this case. Prior to May 1975, Bob Jones University's admissions policy was racially discriminatory on its face, since the University excluded unmarried Negro students while admitting unmarried Caucasians.

32. Bob Jones University also argues that the IRS policy should not apply to it because it is entitled to exemption under § 501(c)(3) as a "religious" organization, rather than as an "educational" institution.

place, Montfort attempted to withdraw his registration, but was advised not to do so by the Registrar's Office, by whom he was assured of an imminent normalization of classes. When classes were resumed, two of the five courses for which Montfort had registered were cancelled. One of those cancelled was a graduation prerequisite for Montfort. There is also some evidence that teachers and sections were changed occasionally in those of Montfort's classes that remained. Unlike the other complainants, Montfort was at no time suspended by the University; in DACO's words, he was merely "hindered from attending classes." DACO ruled that Montfort, having paid his registration fees, expected to be rendered some services in accordance with the University Catalogue. With the "understand[ing]" that such Catalogue was the "Law among the Parties" for contractual purposes, DACO applied certain articles of the Civil Code of Puerto Rico and concluded that because Montfort had fully complied with his portion of the "obligation" between the parties, he had the "right to demand compliance or the resolution of the obligation" from UCB.

On November 5, 1981, UCB filed before DACO a Motion for Reconsideration, in which it reiterated its jurisdictional arguments. In a further submission on November 16th, UCB focused on the absence of statutory authority for DACO's actions, on DACO's alleged misreading of the Catalogue "contract," and on DACO's alleged misinterpretation of the facts.

Before the motion for reconsideration was decided, the President and trustees of UCB filed suit in the federal district court in Puerto Rico in December of 1981, seeking nullification of DACO's ruling and an injunction preventing DACO from further interference in the University's affairs. UCB alleged at least three separate grounds for relief: first, that DACO's actions violated the free exercise clause of the First Amendment and the parallel section of the state constitution, because of excessive government entanglement with a religious institution; second, that, assuming there was no constitutional violation, DACO's organic statute did not provide the agency jurisdiction over claims involving universities; and third, that even if DACO did have statutory jurisdiction over the University which was not constitutionally barred, and assuming that the Catalogue could be construed as a contract between university and student to which the consumer protection law would apply, that DACO nonetheless misread that Catalogue to provide for liability in this case, *i.e.*, that DACO erred in its contract interpretation.

The District Court for the District of Puerto Rico granted summary judgment for the University on October 27, 1982. Without addressing what we shall herein denominate the "statutory" and "contract" claims, the district court decided that UCB had suffered a violation of its First Amendment free exercise rights as a result of DACO's "excessive entanglement in the university's affairs."

This court, on August 10, 1983, reversed the holding of the district court, ruling that the UCB was not a true parochial school for First Amendment purposes, and that the decisions which prompted DACO's actions were "totally unrelated to any religious aspects of UCB's mission."

We noted, however, that there was a possible infringement upon UCB's free *speech* rights, insofar as there exists a "zone of First Amendment protection for the educational process." The constitutional issue was identified as: "whether and to what extent a university, engaged in the highly important and complex enterprise of teaching, should properly be subject to state regulation by an administrative body established to protect consumers from defective products and . . . 'undesirable practices.' "

We suggested that constitutional concerns might be particularly implicated because DACO was "subject to review only for errors of law and findings not supported by substantial evidence," and because the system grants administrative control to "a less than judicial body [DACO]" which is not "specialized" or "particularly qualified" in the area. We upheld the district court's injunction preventing DACO from enforcing its judgment, and remanded the case to the district court to permit UCB to amend its complaint to reflect the "freedom of educational process" issue.

On September 27, 1983, UCB amended its complaint to allege that DACO had "meddl[ed] in plaintiffs' educational . . . affairs," in violation of UCB's freedom of speech, freedom of association, and due process rights. The state "contract" and "statutory" claims remained as express, albeit minor, portions of the complaint. In addition to a request that DACO's order of reimbursement be annulled, UCB also asked for additional relief in the form of an injunction "permanently enjoining, forbidding and restraining defendants from interfering, meddling, encroaching or entangling with or in the internal affairs and educational process and mission of Plaintiffs."

On the basis of submitted stipulated facts, the district court denied UCB's petition on December 21, 1984. The court began its analysis by addressing the statutory issue of DACO's jurisdiction. It correctly identified that issue as whether students *qua* students are "consumers" of "services" "within the purview of the statute." Though the consumer protection statute does not itself provide definitions of either of these terms, the legislative history suggested that "services" should be used "as it is understood in the consensus of the Puerto Rican community," and that this determination had to be made on a case-by-case basis, in light of the specific circumstances of each case. The district court held that "under ordinary circumstances and conditions a person matriculating at a university establishes a contractual relationship with the university," and that the terms of the contract "are expressed in the university's charter and the promulgated regulations governing student conduct." Thus, the court decided that DACO did have statutory jurisdiction to resolve contract disputes between the university and its students.

The district court acknowledged that the university was protected by a constitutional guarantee of a certain degree of academic and institutional freedom, but decided that no absolute rule could be devised to measure the violation of that freedom in every case. The court properly confined its First Amendment analysis to the narrow facts of this case, namely, the $217 reimbursement to Montfort. While agreeing with this court that DACO had misinterpreted the "contract" in the Catalogue, the district court nonetheless found no constitutional violation in DACO's actions. It noted that "[t]he agency's misapplication of the standard in the analysis of the contractual relationship cannot be confused with the infringement of the First Amendment rights even when it may give the impression of such infringement." The court concluded that the reimbursement order itself could not be characterized as a "governmental surveillance, control, and regulation over the internal affairs of the UCB" which would constitute a violation of the university's academic freedom. It further decided that UCB's rights were not violated, as the university had asserted, merely by the "concrete intervention of the agency . . . [in] ascertaining the breach of an obligation of a university toward its students." The court expressly declined to enjoin DACO from future adjudications involving UCB, rejecting the university's argument that the threat of more extensive intrusions had to be addressed. The district court decided that it need not embark down this postulated slippery slope, noting that it "should not attempt to test the operation of a law under every conceivable set of circumstances," and that it would not analyze hypothetical or conjectural injuries. UCB then filed its second appeal to this court.

Instead of deciding the constitutional issue on appeal, we determined that the best course of action was to certify the unclear issues of state law for resolution by the Supreme Court of Puerto Rico. We noted our reluctance to subject the statute to constitutional scrutiny without a definitive interpretation of it from that court. The certified questions were as follows:

> a. Does the Department of Consumer Affairs (DACO) Organic Act apply without qualification or restriction to private, primarily non-sectarian, nonprofit colleges and universities in Puerto Rico?
>
> b. If said act does not so apply generally to such colleges and universities, does it nevertheless apply to the DACO ruling in this case that a student, who because of a campus strike suffered the cancellation of two of his classes, was entitled to a refund of his registration fees of $217, under penalty of fine for noncompliance?

* * *

Because the Supreme Court of Puerto Rico declined to answer the state law questions, we could invoke *Pullman* abstention, sending the case to the state trial court for resolution of the questions we had earlier certified. In addition, the state courts could determine whether, under the civil law contract doctrine of the Commonwealth, DACO properly interpreted the university Catalogue, which was found to be the "contract" between the parties.

Nevertheless, we decline to order the district court to abstain. We do so for two principal reasons. First, we heed the Supreme Court's warning that "because of the delays inherent in the abstention process and the danger that valuable federal rights might be lost in the absence of expeditious adjudication in the federal court, abstention must be invoked only in 'special circumstances.' " It is too late in the day to ensure that this adjudication be expeditious, but that is hardly a reason to prolong it further still. This $217 controversy is now almost seven years old; it has been in the federal courts since 1981. It has been the source of much confusion and stasis. Our decision not to abstain is, thus, in part "a concession to the shortness of life."

* * *

The Academic Freedom Claim

Our first task in the constitutional analysis is to assess the injury that UCB is alleged to have suffered. While the university does contend that the reimbursement to Montfort itself violates a First Amendment right, it has taken great pains to assert that this injury is trivial compared to the greater harm it has suffered. UCB contends that the constitutional violation consists of DACO's very adjudication of the contract claims which were presented. UCB's requested relief consists of enjoining the agency from "interfering, meddling, encroaching or entangling with or in the internal affairs and educational process and mission of [UCB]."

It is eminently clear from appellants' briefs that the interference complained of consists not of the "final result" of DACO's resolutions, "but rather the whole process of entertaining, reviewing, and adjudging each claim." But we fail to see the basis for appellants' claim that this adjudication *ipso facto* constitutes a violation of First Amendment rights to academic freedom regardless of DACO's resolution of the claims.

The heart of UCB's constitutional argument is that *any* administrative adjudication of claims of this nature against the university is an abridgment of academic freedom. UCB makes its claim very explicit: "[T]he Executive does not have power, authority or jurisdiction to review *any* matter concerning private Academia." This argument is completely unsupported by law. The university is properly subject to numerous administrative regulatory schemes which do not implicate First Amendment concerns. Some of the most obvious examples include intervention of the Treasury Department in affairs of income, taxation and property, and regulation by the Department of Labor of employee matters.

UCB offers scant explanation of how DACO adjudication *per se* might infringe upon academic freedom. It argues that such regulatory action compels the university to disclose testimony and documentation concerning the disputed claims. UCB complains that it is "forced to defend its actions at a quasi-judicial hearing," and that it has "an obligation to disclose to DACO the rationale and thought process behind its academic policies."

UCB argues that such obligations of disclosure threaten an excessive "entanglement" in academic affairs. Those cases do not support appellants' contentions. In *NAACP* and *Buckley*, the government required organizations to disclose lists of members or contributors. The Court ruled that such disclosure, unless outweighed by a compelling government interest, cannot withstand First Amendment scrutiny. But the court made clear that the First Amendment interest involved in both those cases was the privacy of association and belief. UCB had presented no evidence to demonstrate that DACO adjudication of contract claims would implicate these interests. We are unpersuaded that any comparable interest exists that would forbid disclosure of information regarding class schedules, faculty composition, and enrollment fees. In any event, DACO has not *compelled* UCB to disclose anything, thus further distinguishing this case from *NAACP* and *Buckley*, where the state demanded production of documents.

In *Surinach*, DACO itself had subpoenaed financial data from religious institutions. We ruled there that such disclosure of "extremely detailed information about the expenditure of funds of these Catholic schools" had the potential for substantially infringing the schools' free exercise rights, because it constituted an impermissible entanglement under the teachings of *Lemon v. Kurtzman* and *Walz v. Tax Commission*. The instant case does not involve the "entanglement" element of free *exercise* doctrine; it involves a purported right of academic freedom. We decline to construct a new "entanglement" rule in addition to that used in freedom of religion cases. Such a rule might virtually preclude any state regulation of private universities.

We find, therefore, that adjudication over the contract claims without more is insufficient to establish a First Amendment claim against the agency. We prefer to evaluate each claim on a case-by-case basis. If a university is able to show that any particular decision, order, or compelled procedure of the agency impermissibly intrudes upon the academic freedom protected by the First Amendment, it may be afforded relief in federal court. It may be, as we suggested in our prior opinion, that because of its lack of expertise in the area DACO might be insufficiently zealous in protecting the First Amendment interests that will invariably arise incident to its adjudication of university matters. If such is the case, the university will have recourse to either the federal or state judiciary for vindication of its rights of academic freedom. In this particular case, however, we agree with the district court that the specific action taken by DACO here does not constitute an abridgement of those rights. UCB was not compelled to disclose any matters which would harm associational or speech rights, and the reimbursement of $217 itself threatens no protected interest of the appellants.

Conclusion

Our disposition here is ironic. Appellant may well be correct that DACO misread the University Catalogue to guarantee tuition reimbursement when classes are cancelled. UCB may also be correct that DACO's organic statute does not provide that agency jurisdiction over university matters. Yet after six years of litigation, UCB's federal claims have been finally rejected. We regret that we have had to reach this point in a case where a simple contract interpretation might have resolved the controversy.

It may be that the university can still appeal DACO's decision in the Montfort case to the state courts for resolution of the state law claims. But if that option is foreclosed by the statute of limitations, UCB is without relief in a case where there exists a serious dispute over the agency's substantive decision. Such is the legacy of *Pennhurst*, in light of the decision of the Supreme Court of Puerto Rico.

The judgment of the district court is affirmed. Each party to bear its own costs.

Academic Freedom for Students and Others on Campus

Students regularly invoke first amendment protection, with mixed results. Several of these cases are included in chapter 4, "Students and the Law," particularly concerning rights to free expression and associational rights. In *Rosenfeld v. Ketter*, 820 F.2d 38 (2d Cir. 1987), a law student was suspended due to his presence at a campus protest. Prior to the protest, the university had indicated its intention to suspend any student participating in the activity; the court held that this warning constituted adequate notice. The court also found that his first amendment rights were not violated because he could have expressed his views virtually anywhere else off campus. His suspension was affirmed.

As has been seen in several cases where faculty held administrative positions, neither faculty positions nor administrative responsibilities offer clear security. In 1985, an administrator at the University of California's Lawrence Livermore National Laboratory was demoted from his position as director of weapons research, after he publicly disagreed with other lab scientists, including Edward Teller, a prominent science adviser to the White House, on the efficacy of the Star Wars program. Roy Woodruff appealed his demotion to the university, which held that he had been improperly demoted. The university restored him to a directorship at the lab. W. Board, "In from the Cold at a Top Nuclear Lab," *New York Times*, 27 December 1987, p. E-14.

"New Papers Reveal FBI Surveillance at Duquesne U."

Michael W. Hirschorn

The Federal Bureau of Investigation conducted surveillance of political activity at Duquesne University in December 1983 as part of a five-year, nationwide investigation into groups opposed to United States policy in Central America, new documents obtained by a New York lawyers' group reveal.

The documents, obtained under the Freedom of Information Act, provide new details about a massive investigation by the bureau of the politically left-leaning Committee in Support of the People of El Salvador, or CISPES, that grew to include surveillance of more than 100 liberal and left-wing anti-Administration groups.

The outlines of that investigation, which was ended in 1985 after the bureau found no evidence of criminal wrongdoing, were first revealed in more than 1,300 pages of internal F.B.I. correspondence obtained in January by the lawyers' group, the Center for Constitutional Rights, on behalf of CISPES.

Those files revealed that the F.B.I. had conducted surveillance of students, faculty, or administrators on at least 18 campuses. The files provided a rare insight into how the bureau conducts surveillance of left-leaning campus groups and individuals active in opposing Administration policies.

Because only about 30 percent of the files were released and many pages were heavily censored, the full nature and extent of that surveillance could not be determined, however.

The new files provide an in-depth account of Catholic church services at the Duquesne University chapel on December 11, 1983.

The services featured speeches by two Salvadoran refugees, a man and a woman, during the homily portion of the mass.

The CISPES office here allowed a reporter to examine the files on the condition that the names of those identified in them would not be published without permission.

According to the files, the refugees indicated that they were illegal aliens [sic] in the United States and had been helped by the church sanctuary movement, which protects illegal immigrants from deportation.

Speaking through an interpreter, the refugees, according to a report filed by a Pittsburgh-based F.B.I. agent, "discussed the oppressiveness of the current Salvadoran government" and talked about being the targets of Salvadoran "government death squads."

Speculation About Break-in

The files released did not give any indication of whether the bureau had taken any action against the refugees who spoke at the church.

The new files, which included specific information about monetary transactions made by the Dallas office of CISPES, have also renewed speculation that the F.B.I. may have staged a break-in at the CISPES headquarters in Dallas. Those allegations were first aired more than a year ago on the CBS Evening News by a former F.B.I. informant, Frank Varelli.

The files released last week also show that the F.B.I. investigated the activities of Iranian students in the United States who are opposed to the Khomeini regime.

The nature of that investigation and its connection to political activity on Central American issues could not be determined.

The new files are from the Dallas field office of the F.B.I., which apparently headed up the CISPES investigation.

Only 10 percent of the Dallas files requested by the Center for Constitutional Rights were released, and the F.B.I. has said it has halted its processing of requests for the remaining CISPES material, pending an internal review of the CISPES investigation. The majority of the CISPES files have yet to be released.

50 Field Offices

Margaret Ratner, a spokeswoman for the Center for Constitutional Rights, called the internal review a ploy to prevent the release of embarrassing documents. "Are we expected to believe that the Federal Bureau of Investigation does not have the resources to photocopy a set of files in order to comply with their obligations under the Freedom of Information Act?" she asked.

The remaining documents apparently include information on file at the more than 50 F.B.I. field offices involved in the CISPES investigation. Those files, especially from cities like Boston, where there has been heavy opposition to the Administration's policies in Central America, are likely to provide more detailed evidence of the bureau's surveillance on college and university campuses, a CISPES official said last week.

© Michael W. Hirschorn, *Chronicle of Higher Education*, 23 March 1988, p. A16, reprinted with permission.

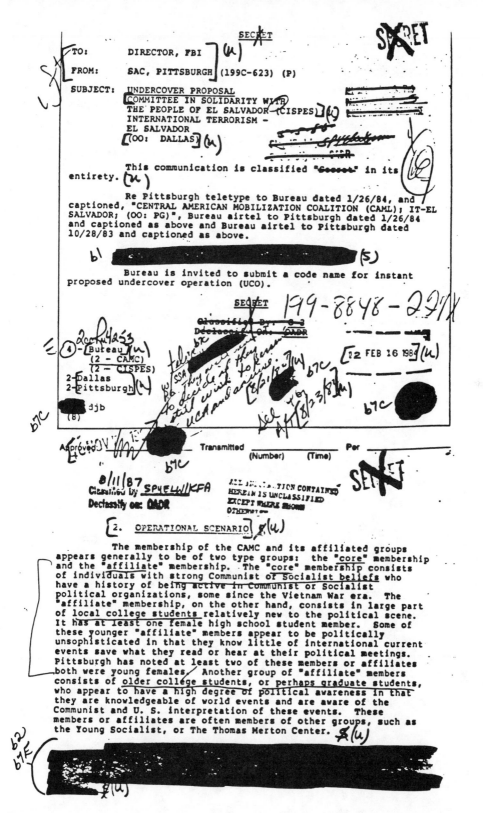

SECRET

TO: DIRECTOR, FBI

FROM: SAC, PITTSBURGH (199C-623) (P)

SUBJECT: UNDERCOVER PROPOSAL
         COMMITTEE IN SOLIDARITY WITH
         THE PEOPLE OF EL SALVADOR (CISPES)
         INTERNATIONAL TERRORISM -
         EL SALVADOR
         (OO: DALLAS)

         This communication is classified "Secret" in its
entirety.

         Re Pittsburgh teletype to Bureau dated 1/26/84, and
captioned, "CENTRAL AMERICAN MOBILIZATION COALITION (CAML); IT-EL
SALVADOR; (OO: PG)", Bureau airtel to Pittsburgh dated 1/26/84
and captioned as above and Bureau airtel to Pittsburgh dated
10/28/83 and captioned as above.

         Bureau is invited to submit a code name for instant
proposed undercover operation (UCO).

SECRET

ALL INFORMATION CONTAINED
HEREIN IS UNCLASSIFIED
EXCEPT WHERE SHOWN
OTHERWISE

2. OPERATIONAL SCENARIO

         The membership of the CAMC and its affiliated groups
appears generally to be of two type groups: the "core" membership
and the "affiliate" membership. The "core" membership consists
of individuals with strong Communist or Socialist beliefs who
have a history of being active in Communist or Socialist
political organizations, some since the Vietnam War era. The
"affiliate" membership, on the other hand, consists in large part
of local college students relatively new to the political scene.
It has at least one female high school student member. Some of
these younger "affiliate" members appear to be politically
unsophisticated in that they know little of international current
events save what they read or hear at their political meetings.
Pittsburgh has noted at least two of these members or affiliates
both were young females. Another group of "affiliate" members
consists of older college students, or perhaps graduate students,
who appear to have a high degree of political awareness in that
they are knowledgeable of world events and are aware of the
Communist and U. S. interpretation of these events. These
members or affiliates are often members of other groups, such as
the Young Socialist, or The Thomas Merton Center.

Two pages of internal FBI documents detailing Bureau surveillance of campus groups. Obtained
by Freedom of Information Act (FOIA) request. Reprinted by permission of Center for Constitutional Rights.

Chapter 3

The Law and the Faculty

Tenure and Promotion Issues

As was evident in several cases concerning academic freedom, faculty tenure is often at issue in academic litigation. The academic custom and usage of tenure derive from the 1940 AAUP *Statement of Principles on Academic Freedom and Tenure* (unedited from its archaic gender references):

Academic Tenure

(a) After the expiration of a probationary period, teachers or investigators should have permanent or continuous tenure, and their service should be terminated only for adequate cause, except in the case of retirement for age, or under extraordinary circumstances because of financial exigencies. In the interpretation of this principle it is understood that the following represents acceptable academic practice:

1. The precise terms and conditions of every appointment should be stated in writing and be in the possession of both institution and teacher before the appointment is consummated.

2. Beginning with appointment to the rank of full-time instructor or a higher rank, [a] the probationary period should not exceed seven years, including within this period full-time service in all institutions of higher education; but subject to the proviso that when, after a term of probationary service of more than three years in one or more institutions, a teacher is called to another institution it may be agreed in writing that his new appointment is for a probationary period of not more than four years, even though thereby the person's total probationary period in the academic profession is extended beyond the normal maximum of seven years. [b] Notice should be given at least one year prior to the expiration of the probationary period if the teacher is not to be continued in service after the expiration of that period. [c]

3. During the probationary period a teacher should have the academic freedom that all other members of the faculty have. [d]

4. Termination for cause of a continuous appointment, or the dismissal for cause of a teacher previous to the expiration of a term appointment, should, if possible, be considered by both a faculty committee and the governing board of the institution. In all cases where the facts are in dispute, the accused teacher should be informed before the hearing in writing of the charges against him and should have the opportunity to be heard in his own defense by all bodies that pass judgment upon his case. He should be permitted to have with him an adviser of his own choosing who may

act as counsel. There should be a full stenographic record of the hearing available to the parties concerned. In the hearing of charges of incompetence the testimony should include that of teachers and other scholars, either from his own or from other institutions. Teachers on continuous appointment who are dismissed for reasons not involving moral turpitude should receive their salaries for at least a year from the date of notification of dismissal whether or not they are continued in their duties at the institution. [e]

5. Termination of a continuous appointment because of financial exigency should be demonstrably bona fide.

In addition, the *1940 Statement* has been elaborated upon by the 1970 *Interpretive Comments*, keyed to the provisions in brackets:

Both the protection of academic freedom and the requirements of academic responsibility apply not only to the full-time probationary as well as to the tenured teacher, but also to all others, such as part-time faculty and teaching assistants, who exercise teaching responsibilities.

[a] The concept of "rank of full-time instructor or a higher rank" is intended to include any person who teaches a full-time load regardless of his specific title.

[b] In calling for an agreement "in writing" on the amount of credit for a faculty member's prior service at other institutions, the *Statement* furthers the general policy of full understanding by the professor of the terms and conditions of his appointment. It does not necessarily follow that a professor's tenure rights have been violated because of the absence of a written agreement on this matter. Nonetheless, especially because of the variation in permissible institutional practices, a written understanding concerning these matters at the time of appointment is particularly appropriate and advantageous to both the individual and the institution.

[c] The effect of this subparagraph is that a decision on tenure, favorable or unfavorable, must be made at least twelve months prior to the completion of the probationary period. If the decision is negative, the appointment for the following year becomes a terminal one. If the decision is affirmative, the provisions in the 1940 *Statement* with respect to the termination of services of teachers or investigators after the expiration of a probationary period should apply from the date when the favorable decision is made.

The general principle of notice contained in this paragraph is developed with greater specificity in the *Standards for Notice of Nonreappointment*, endorsed by the Fiftieth Annual Meeting of the American Association of University Professors (1964). These standards are: Notice of nonreappointment, or of intention not to recommend reappointment to the governing board, should be given in writing in accordance with the following standards:

(1) *Not later than March 1 of the first academic year of service*, if the appointment expires at the end of that year; or, if a one-year appointment terminates during an academic year, at least three months in advance of its termination.

(2) *Not later than December 15 of the second academic year of service*, if the appointment expires at the end of that year; or, if an initial two-year appointment terminates during an academic year, at least six months in advance of its termination.

(3) At least twelve months before the expiration of an appointment after two or more years in the institution.

Other obligations, both of institutions and individuals, are described in the *Statement on Recruitment and Resignation of Faculty Members*, as endorsed by the Association of American Colleges and the American Association of University Professors in 1961.

[d] The freedom of probationary teachers is enhanced by the establishment of a regular procedure for the periodic evaluation and assessment of the teacher's academic performance during his probationary status. Provision should be made for regularized procedures for the consideration of complaints by probationary teachers that their academic freedom has been violated. One suggested procedure to serve these purposes is contained in the *Recommended Institutional Regulations on Academic Freedom and Tenure*, prepared by the American Association of University Professors.

[e] A further specification of the academic due process to which the teacher is entitled under this paragraph is contained in the *Statement on Procedural Standards in Faculty Dismissal Proceedings*, jointly approved by the American Association of University Professors and the Association of American Colleges in 1958. This interpretive document deals with the issue of suspension, about which the 1940 *Statement* is silent.

The 1958 *Statement* provides: "Suspension of the faculty member during the proceedings involving him is justified only if immediate harm to himself or others is threatened by his continuance. Unless legal considerations forbid, any such suspension should be with pay." A suspension which is not followed by either reinstatement or the opportunity for a hearing is in effect a summary dismissal in violation of academic due process.

The concept of "moral turpitude" identifies the exceptional case in which the professor may be denied a year's teaching or pay in whole or in part. The statement applies to that kind of behavior which goes beyond simply warranting discharge and is so utterly blameworthy as to make it inappropriate to require the offering of a year's teaching or pay. The standard is not that the moral sensibilities of persons in the particular community have been affronted. The standard is behavior that would evoke condemnation by the academic community generally.

The cases that comprise this chapter establish the definition of tenure, including its legal contours—property interests, liberty interests, and contract principles—as well as the procedural norms that have evolved. Several cases have been chosen to illustrate the exceptions to tenure or acceptable reasons for dismissing tenured faculty. Where possible, cases include instances both where courts upheld institutions and where dismissals were held to be invalid. The final cases explore the effects of seniority, "tenure density," and collective bargaining upon tenure policies, and illustrate the various remedies available to faculty found to have been discriminated against in tenure and promotion.

A number of the discrimination cases rely upon Title VII of the Civil Rights Act of 1964 (42 U.S.C. 2000e); before it was amended in 1972 (by Pub. L. No. 92-261, § 2, 86 Stat. 103, (1972), colleges and universities had not been covered by Title VII. See Yurco, "Judicial Recognition of Academic Collective Interests: A New Approach to Faculty Title VII Litigation," *Boston University Law Review*, 60 (1980), 473. The leading case for establishing the rules of Title VII is *McDonnell Douglas Corp v. Green*, 411 U.S. 792 (1973), which clarified the burden of proof. Plaintiffs can establish *prima facie* Title VII eligibility if they are a member of a Title VII protected class, applied for a position for which they were qualified, were rejected, and the employer hired someone less well qualified. If the *prima facie* case is established, the burden of proof shifts to the institution to pose either a legitimate exception (such as a bona fide occupational qualification) or another nondiscriminatory rationale for not hiring the plaintiff. If a sufficient reason is offered, the burden reverts to plaintiffs to prove the rationale is pretextual, and that the true reason was discriminatory. Despite the growing number of cases, the contours of *McDonnell Douglas* criteria are not always clear, as they include both objective criteria (Ph.D., experience, etc.) and subjective standards (scholarly excellence, collegiality).

In addition, if the adverse action is alleged to be retaliatory (usually a dismissal or first amendment matter), the burden of proof issues become increasingly important. In *Ruggles v. California Polytechnic State University*, 797 F.2d 782 (9th Cir. 1986), the court of appeals held:

> a plaintiff would satisfy her prima facie case by showing that but for her protected activities the position would not have been eliminated or someone else would not have been hired. * * * [this] requires a plaintiff to show only that she did not get the job because of her protected activities.
>
> We hold that [this] standard is more appropriate than the first for retaliation claims arising in the failure-to-hire context. This standard requires a plaintiff to show that the position for which she applied was eliminated or not available to her because of her protected activities. Her "adverse employment decision" is the closing of the job opening to her and the loss of opportunity even to compete for the position. The plaintiff need not show that she would have obtained the job, a showing that would be nearly insurmountable at the prima facie state and involves factors better marshalled and presented by the defendants. Accordingly, we hold that in the failure-to-hire context involving a claim of retaliation, the plaintiff meets her prima facie burden by showing that 1) she engaged in protected activities, 2) the position was eliminated as to her, and 3) the position was eliminated as to her because of the protected activities.
>
> At this point, consistent with the *McDonnell Douglas* analysis, the burden of production shifts to the defendant to articulate some legitimate, nondiscriminatory reason for the "adverse employment decision." If the defendant is successful, the plaintiff must then prove by a preponderance of the evidence that the proffered reasons are pretexts for retaliation or that a discriminatory reason more likely motivated the employer's action.
>
> If the plaintiff succeeds at this point, a presumption is created that the adverse employment decision was the product of retaliatory intent. The defendant may rebut this presumption by showing by a preponderance of the evidence that the adverse action would have been taken even in the absence of discriminatory or retaliatory intent. This final stage in the allocation of proof allows a defendant to show that the plaintiff would not have been hired, or would have been fired,

regardless of the retaliatory motives of the employer. This is essentially a question of causation, the courts having recognized that a plaintiff garners a windfall if she receives the panoply of Title VII compensatory remedies without proof that she would have obtained the job. Engaging in protected activities or protected conduct should not put the plaintiff in a better position than she would be in otherwise. This rule of causation has been applied to employment decisions involving First Amendment claims of protection, as well as to discrimination claims under Title VII. It applies equally to retaliation claims under Title VII.

In chapter 5, "Affirmative Action in Higher Education," this topic is considered in greater detail. Issues of affirmative action in faculty matters, student admissions, and institutional characteristics remain the most persistently troubling features of higher education. Title VII arises in several of the cases that follow, and forms a substantial part of the common law of tenure.

Perry v. Sindermann
408 U.S. 593 (1972)

Mr. Justice STEWART delivered the opinion of the Court.

From 1959 to 1969 the respondent, Robert Sindermann, was a teacher in the state college system of the State of Texas. After teaching for two years at the University of Texas and for four years at San Antonio Junior College, he became a professor of Government and Social Science at Odessa Junior College in 1965. He was employed at the college for four successive years, under a series of one-year contracts. He was successful enough to be appointed, for a time, the cochairman of his department.

During the 1968–1969 academic year, however, controversy arose between the respondent and the college administration. The respondent was elected president of the Texas Junior College Teachers Association. In this capacity, he left his teaching duties on several occasions to testify before committees of the Texas Legislature, and he became involved in public disagreements with the policies of the college's Board of Regents. In particular, he aligned himself with a group advocating the elevation of the college to four-year status—a change opposed by the Regents. And, on one occasion, a newspaper advertisement appeared over his name that was highly critical of the Regents.

Finally, in May 1969, the respondent's one-year employment contract terminated and the Board of Regents voted not to offer him a new contract for the next academic year. The Regents issued a press release setting forth allegations of the respondent's insubordination. But they provided him no official statement of the reasons for the nonrenewal of his contract. And they allowed him no opportunity for a hearing to challenge the basis of the nonrenewal.

The respondent then brought this action in Federal District Court. He alleged primarily that the Regents' decision not to rehire him was based on his public criticism of the policies of the college administration and thus infringed his right to freedom of speech. He also alleged that their failure to provide him an opportunity for a hearing violated the Fourteenth Amendment's guarantee of procedural due process. The petitioners—members of the Board of Regents and the president of the college—denied that their decision was made in retaliation for the respondent's public criticism and argued that they had no obligation to provide a hearing. On the basis of these bare pleadings and three brief affidavits filed by the respondent, the District Court granted summary judgment for the petitioners. It concluded that the respondent had "no cause of action against the [petitioners] since his contract of employment terminated May 31, 1969, and Odessa Junior College has not adopted the tenure system."

The Court of Appeals reversed the judgment of the District Court. First, it held that, despite the respondent's lack of tenure, the nonrenewal of his contract would violate the Fourteenth Amendment if it in fact was based on his protected free speech. Since the actual reason for the Regents' decision was "in total dispute" in the pleadings, the court remanded the case for a full hearing on this contested issue of fact. Second, the Court of Appeals held that, despite the respondent's lack of tenure, the failure to allow him an opportunity for a hearing would violate the constitutional guarantee of procedural due process if the respondent could show that he had an "expectancy" of re-employment. It, therefore, ordered that this issue of fact also be aired upon remand. We granted a writ of certiorari, and we have considered this case along with *Board of Regents v. Roth*.

I

The first question presented is whether the respondent's lack of a contractual or tenure right to re-employment, taken alone, defeats his claim that the nonrenewal of his contract violated the First and Fourteenth Amendments. We hold that it does not.

For at least a quarter-century, this Court has made clear that even though a person has no "right" to a valuable governmental benefit and even though the government may deny him the benefit for any number of reasons, there are some reasons upon which the government may not rely. It may not deny a benefit to a person on a basis that infringes his constitutionally protected interests—especially, his interest in freedom of speech. For if the government could deny a benefit to a person because of his constitutionally protected speech or associations, his exercise of those freedoms would in effect be penalized and inhibited. This would allow the government to "produce a result which [it] could not command directly." Such interference with constitutional rights is impermissible.

We have applied this general principle to denials of tax exemptions, unemployment benefits, and welfare payments. But, most often, we have applied the principle to denials of public employment. We have applied the principle regardless of the public employee's contractual or other claim to a job.

Thus, the respondent's lack of a contractual or tenure "right" to re-employment for the 1969–1970 academic year is immaterial to his free speech claim. Indeed, twice before, this Court has specifically held that the nonrenewal of a nontenured public school teacher's one-year contract may not be predicated on his exercise of First and Fourteenth Amendment rights. We reaffirm those holdings here.

In this case, of course, the respondent has yet to show that the decision not to renew his contract was, in fact, made in retaliation for his exercise of the constitutional right of free speech. The District Court foreclosed any opportunity to make this showing when it granted summary judgment. Hence, we cannot now hold that the Board of Regents' action was invalid.

But we agree with the Court of Appeals that there is a genuine dispute as to "whether the college refused to renew the teaching contract on an impermissible basis—as a reprisal for the exercise of constitutionally protected rights." The respondent has alleged that his nonretention was based on his testimony before legislative committees and his other public statements critical of the Regents' policies. And he has alleged that this public criticism was within the First and Fourteenth Amendments' protection of freedom of speech. Plainly, these allegations present a bona fide constitutional claim. For this Court has held that a teacher's public criticism of his superiors on matters of public concern may be constitutionally protected and may, therefore, be an impermissible basis for termination of his employment.

For this reason we hold that the grant of summary judgment against the respondent, without full exploration of this issue, was improper.

II

The respondent's lack of formal contractual or tenure security in continued employment at Odessa Junior College, though irrelevant to his free speech claim, is highly relevant to his procedural due process claim. But it may not be entirely dispositive.

We have held today in *Board of Regents v. Roth*, that the Constitution does not require opportunity for a hearing before the nonrenewal of a nontenured teacher's contract, unless he can show that the decision not to rehire him somehow deprived him of an interest in "liberty" or that he had a "property" interest in continued employment, despite the lack of tenure or a formal contract. In *Roth* the teacher had not made a showing on either point to justify summary judgment in his favor.

Similarly, the respondent here has yet to show that he has been deprived of an interest that could invoke procedural due process protection. As in *Roth*, the mere showing that he was not rehired in one particular job, without more, did not amount to a showing of a loss of liberty. Nor did it amount to a showing of a loss of property.

But the respondent's allegations—which we must construe most favorably to the respondent at this stage of the litigation—do raise a genuine issue as to his interest in continued employment at Odessa Junior College. He alleged that this interest, though not secured by a formal contractual tenure provision, was secured by a no less binding understanding fostered by the college administration. In particular, the respondent alleged that the college had a *de facto* tenure program, and that he had tenure under that program. He claimed that he and others legitimately relied upon an unusual provision that had been in the college's official Faculty Guide for many years:

> "*Teacher Tenure*: Odessa College has no tenure system. The Administration of the College wishes the faculty member to feel that he has permanent tenure as long as his teaching services are satisfactory and as long as he displays a co-operative attitude toward his co-workers and his superiors, and as long as he is happy in his work."

Moreover, the respondent claimed legitimate reliance upon guidelines promulgated by the Coordinating Board of the Texas College and University System that provided that a person, like himself, who had been employed as a teacher in the state college and university system for seven years or more has some form of job tenure. Thus, the respondent offered to prove that a teacher with his long period of service at this particular State College had no less a "property" interest in continued employment than a formally tenured teacher at other colleges, and had no less a procedural due process right to a statement of reasons and a hearing before college officials upon their decision not to retain him.

We have made clear in *Roth* that "property" interests subject to procedural due process protection are not limited by a few rigid, technical forms. Rather, "property" denotes a broad range of interests that are secured by "existing rules or understandings." A person's interest in a benefit is a "property" interest for due process purposes if there are such rules or mutually explicit understandings that support his claim of entitlement to the benefit and that he may invoke at a hearing.

A written contract with an explicit tenure provision clearly is evidence of a formal understanding that supports a teacher's claim of entitlement to continued employment unless sufficient "cause" is shown. Yet absence of such an explicit contractual provision may not always foreclose the possibility that a teacher has a "property" interest in re-employment. For example, the law of contracts in most, if not all, jurisdictions long has employed a process by which agreements, though not formalized in writing, may be "implied." Explicit contractual provisions may be supplemented by other agreements implied from "the promisor's words and conduct in the light of the surrounding circumstances." And, "[t]he meaning of [the promisor's] words and acts is found by relating them to the usage of the past."

A teacher, like the respondent, who has held his position for a number of years, might be able to show from the circumstances of this service—and from other relevant facts—that he has a legitimate claim of entitlement to job tenure. Just as this Court has found there to be a "common law of a particular industry or of a particular plant" that may supplement a collective-bargaining agreement, so there may be an unwritten "common law" in a particular university that certain employees shall have the equivalent of tenure. This is particularly likely in a college or university, like Odessa Junior College, that has no explicit tenure system even for senior members of its faculty, but that nonetheless may have created such a system in practice.

In this case, the respondent has alleged the existence of rules and understandings, promulgated and fostered by state officials, that may justify his legitimate claim of entitlement of continued employment absent "sufficient cause." We disagree with the Court of Appeals insofar as it held that a mere subjective "expectancy" is protected by procedural due process, but we agree that the respondent must be given an opportunity to prove the legitimacy of his claim of such entitlement in light of "the policies and practices of the institution." Proof of such a property interest would not, of course, entitle him to reinstatement. But such proof would obligate college officials to grant a hearing at his request, where he could be informed of the grounds for his nonretention and challenge their sufficiency.

Therefore, while we do not wholly agree with the opinion of the Court of Appeals, its judgment remanding this case to the District Court is

Affirmed.

Board of Regents v. Roth
408 U.S. 564 (1972)

Mr. Justice STEWART delivered the opinion of the Court.

In 1968 the respondent, David Roth, was hired for his first teaching job as assistant professor of political science at Wisconsin State University-Oshkosh. He was hired for a fixed term of one academic year. The notice of his faculty appointment specified that his employment would begin on September 1, 1968, and would end on June 30, 1969. The respondent completed that term. But he was informed that he would not be rehired for the next academic year.

The respondent had no tenure rights to continued employment. Under Wisconsin statutory law a state university teacher can acquire tenure as a "permanent" employee only after four years of year-to-year employment. Having acquired tenure, a teacher is entitled to continued employment "during efficiency and good behavior." A relatively new teacher without tenure, however, is under Wisconsin law entitled to nothing beyond his one-year appointment. There are no statutory or administrative standards defining eligibility for re-employment. State law thus clearly leaves the decision whether to rehire a nontenured teacher for another year to the unfettered discretion of university officials.

The procedural protection afforded a Wisconsin State University teacher before he is separated from the University corresponds to his job security. As a matter of statutory law, a tenured teacher cannot be "discharged except for cause upon written charges" and pursuant to certain procedures. A nontenured teacher, similarly, is protected to some extent *during* his one-year term. Rules promulgated by the Board of Regents provide that a nontenured teacher "dismissed" before the end of the year may have some opportunity for review of the "dismissal." But the Rules provide no real protection for a nontenured teacher who simply is not re-employed for the next year. He must be informed by February 1 "concerning retention or nonretention for the ensuing year." But "no reason for non-retention need be given. No review or appeal is provided in such case."

In conformance with these Rules, the President of Wisconsin State University-Oshkosh informed the respondent before February 1, 1969, that he would not be rehired for the 1969–1970 academic year. He gave the respondent no reason for the decision and no opportunity to challenge it at any sort of hearing.

The respondent then brought this action in Federal District Court alleging that the decision not to rehire him for the next year infringed his Fourteenth Amendment rights. He attacked the decision both in substance and procedure. First, he alleged that the true reason for the decision was to punish him for certain statements critical of the University administration, and that it therefore violated his right to freedom of speech. Second, he alleged that the failure of University officials to give him notice of any reason for nonretention and an opportunity for a hearing violated his right to procedural due process of law.

The District Court granted summary judgment for the respondent on the procedural issue, ordering the University officials to provide him with reasons and a hearing. The Court of Appeals, with one judge dissenting, affirmed this partial summary judgment. We granted certiorari. The only question presented to us at this stage in the case is whether the respondent had a constitutional right to a statement of reasons and a hearing on the University's decision not to rehire him for another year. We hold that he did not.

I

The requirements of procedural due process apply only to the deprivation of interests encompassed by the Fourteenth Amendment's protection of liberty and property. When protected interests are implicated, the right to some kind of prior hearing is paramount. But the range of interests protected by procedural due process is not infinite.

The District Court decided that procedural due process guarantees apply in this case by assessing and balancing the weights of the particular interests involved. It concluded that the respondent's interest in re-employment at Wisconsin State University-Oshkosh outweighed the University's interest in denying him re-employment summarily. Undeniably, the respondent's re-employment prospects were of major concern to him—concern that we surely cannot say was insignificant. And a weighing process has long been a part of any determination of the *form* of hearing required in particular situations by procedural due process. But, to determine whether due process requirements apply in the first place, we must look not to the "weight" but to the *nature* of the interest at stake. We must look to see if the interest is within the Fourteenth Amendment's protection of liberty and property.

"Liberty" and "property" are broad and majestic terms. They are among the "[g]reat [constitutional] concepts... purposely left to gather meaning from experience.... [T]hey relate to the whole domain of social and economic fact, and the statesmen who founded this Nation knew too well that only a stagnant society remains unchanged." For that reason, the Court has fully and finally rejected the wooden distinction between "rights" and "privileges" that once seemed to govern the applicability of procedural due process rights. The Court has also made clear that the property interests protected by procedural due process extend well beyond actual ownership of real estate, chattels, or money. By the same token, the Court has required due process protection for deprivations of liberty beyond the sort of formal constraints imposed by the criminal process.

Yet, while the Court has eschewed rigid or formalistic limitations on the protection of procedural due process, it has at the same time observed certain boundaries. For the words "liberty" and "property" in the Due Process Clause of the Fourteenth Amendment must be given some meaning.

II

"While this Court has not attempted to define with exactness the liberty... guaranteed [by the Fourteenth Amendment], the term has received much consideration and some of the included things have been definitely stated. Without doubt, it denotes not merely freedom from bodily restraint but also the right of the individual to contract, to engage in any of the common occupations of life, to acquire useful knowledge, to marry, establish a home and bring up children, to worship God according to the dictates of his own conscience, and generally to enjoy those privileges long recognized... as essential to the orderly pursuit of happiness by free men." In a Constitution for a free people, there can be no doubt that the meaning of "liberty" must be broad indeed.

There might be cases in which a State refused to reemploy a person under such circumstances that interests in liberty would be implicated. But this is not such a case.

The State, in declining to rehire the respondent, did not make any charge against him that might seriously damage his standing and associations in his community. It did not base the nonrenewal of his contract on a charge, for example, that he had been guilty of dishonesty, or immorality. Had it done so, this would be a different case. For "[w]here a person's good name, reputation, honor, or integrity is at stake because of what the government is doing to him, notice and an opportunity to be heard are essential." In such a case, due process would accord an opportunity to refute the charge before University officials. In the present case, however, there is no suggestion whatever that the respondent's "good name, reputation, honor, or integrity" is at stake.

Similarly, there is no suggestion that the State, in declining to re-employ the respondent, imposed on him a stigma or other disability that foreclosed his freedom to take advantage of other employment opportunities. The State, for example, did not invoke any regulations to bar the respondent from all other public employment in state universities. Had it done so, this, again, would be a different case. For "[t]o be deprived not only of present government employment but of future opportunity for it certainly is no small injury. . . . " The Court has held, for example, that a State, in regulating eligibility for a type of professional employment, cannot foreclose a range of opportunities "in a manner . . . that contravene[s] . . . Due Process," and, specifically, in a manner that denies the right to a full prior hearing. In the present case, however, this principle does not come into play.

To be sure, the respondent has alleged that the nonrenewal of his contract was based on his exercise of his right to freedom of speech. But this allegation is not now before us. The District Court stayed proceedings on this issue, and the respondent has yet to prove that the decision not to rehire him was, in fact, based on his free speech activities.

Hence, on the record before us, all that clearly appears is that the respondent was not rehired for one year at one university. It stretches the concept too far to suggest that a person is deprived of "liberty" when he simply is not rehired in one job but remains as free as before to seek another.

III

The Fourteenth Amendment's procedural protection of property is a safeguard of the security of interests that a person has already acquired in specific benefits. These interests—property interests—may take many forms.

* * *

Just as the welfare recipients' "property" interest in welfare payments was created and defined by statutory terms, so the respondent's "property" interest in employment at Wisconsin State University-Oshkosh was created and defined by the terms of his appointment. Those terms secured his interest in employment up to June 30, 1969. But the important fact in this case is that they specifically provided that the respondent's employment was to terminate on June 30. They did not provide for contract renewal absent "sufficient cause." Indeed, they made no provision for renewal whatsoever.

Thus, the terms of the respondent's appointment secured absolutely no interest in re-employment for the next year. They supported absolutely no possible claim of entitlement to re-employment. Nor, significantly, was there any state statute or University rule or policy that secured his interest in re-employment or that created any legitimate claim to it. In these circumstances, the respondent surely had an abstract concern in being rehired, but he did not have a *property* interest sufficient to require the University authorities to give him a hearing when they declined to renew his contract of employment.

IV

Our analysis of the respondent's constitutional rights in this case in no way indicates a view that an opportunity for a hearing or a statement of reasons for nonretention would, or would not, be appropriate or wise in public colleges and universities. For it is a written Constitution that we apply. Our role is confined to interpretation of that Constitution.

We must conclude that the summary judgment for the respondent should not have been granted, since the respondent has not shown that he was deprived of liberty or property protected by the Fourteenth Amendment. The judgment of the Court of Appeals, accordingly, is reversed and the case is remanded for further proceedings consistent with this opinion.

It is so ordered.

In *Perry v. Sindermann*, the Court relied partially upon the state agency rules, promulgated to regularize tenure in public colleges. Most states have similar agencies and either statutes or rules for tenure. While the rules in Texas suggested de facto tenure for Professor Sindermann, the statute in Wisconsin worked against Professor Roth in his case. The following story shows how tenure can live or die by the legislative sword.

"Governor's Veto Saves Colorado Tenure System—For the Time Being"

Scott Jaschik, *Chronicle of Higher Education*, 20 May 1987, p. 21.

The Governor of Colorado last week saved the tenure system for faculty members at the state's community colleges and six of its four-year institutions by vetoing a bill that would have abolished it. But legislators may well succeed in negating his action in the next month.

The bill vetoed by Gov. Roy Romer, a Democrat, would have revoked the Higher Education Due Process Act. The act, instituted in 1975, established requirements that governing boards must follow to remove faculty members after their third year of employment.

Faculty leaders, angry that the tenure rules were under attack, acknowledged they were having trouble mounting a lobbying campaign to save them because many teachers were either grading papers or were away on summer vacation.

The act covers all of the state's community colleges as well as Adams State, Fort Lewis, Mesa, Metropolitan State, and Western State Colleges and the University of Southern Colorado. Tenure systems for other public colleges in the state are set by governing boards.

Amended a Technical Change

The move to abolish the act came as the Senate was preparing for a final vote on a technical change in the law. A Senator then proposed an amendment that would simply eliminate the act, and that version of the bill passed in both of the Republican-controlled houses.

The Assistant Attorney General then issued an opinion saying the bill violated the state constitution because the final bill was not consistent with the title of the bill, which dealt with the technical change.

Thereupon Governor Romer vetoed the bill, but did not comment on the merits of abolishing the 1975 act. Instead, he said such a move would be too important a change to occur without a full legislative review. He said he had some concerns about the present tenure system, but would not elaborate on them.

The sponsors of the amendment then introduced their plan as a new bill. It was passed by a committee in the House last week and was expected to begin gaining momentum in the Senate this week.

Governing boards of the colleges now covered by the act have endorsed the new bill. But faculty members at the institutions are confused and angry, some of them said.

Some Major Changes

Houston G. Elam, president of the Consortium of State Colleges in Colorado, which governs Adams State, Mesa, Metropolitan State, and Western State Colleges, stressed that faculty members would still be covered by some due-process regulations if the new bill became law.

The consortium's Board of Trustees has pledged that the current system would remain in place until the 1988–89 academic year, he said.

At that time, he said, some major changes would be considered. He said the practice of awarding tenure after three years might be changed to the more standard practice of awarding it after six years.

Charles E. Allbee, president of the Faculty Senate at Metropolitan State, said faculty members would like to maintain the statutory tenure system because, without it, it would be easy for governing boards to change the system from time to time.

"It's very unsettling because we just don't know what will happen," he said.

Political observers here said the political climate made it probable that the act would be revoked. Governor Romer is considered unlikely to wage a protracted fight over the issue with the Republican legislative leaders, they said, because he badly needs their cooperation on other issues that are more important to him.

Reprinted with permission.

In a reaction to threatened faculty layoffs in British colleges, members of Parliament have insisted upon an academic freedom provision, to be included in a bill that would abolish tenure. The House of Commons voted to abolish tenure in April 1988, but in May 1988, the House of Lords refused to accede to the bill unless it were amended to guarantee that affected faculty would not be dismissed for espousing unpopular ideas. "In a Rare Rebellion, British Lords Demand Academic-Freedom Law," *Chronicle of Higher Education*, 1 June 1988, pp. A1, A43.

The Contours of Tenure

Liberty, Property, and Contract Interests

Wellner v. Minnesota State Junior College Board
487 F.2d 153 (1973)

STEPHENSON, Circuit Judge.

Minnesota State Junior College Board (the Board) appeals following an adverse final order in a 42 U.S.C. § 1983 action brought against the Board by Gary A. Wellner, a nontenured faculty member of Metropolitan State Junior College (Metro). Wellner alleged that he was deprived of procedural due process since the Board did not afford him a hearing prior to its decision not to reappoint him as a Metro faculty member. The trial court in an unreported opinion, held that certain "racist" charges made against Wellner, which were placed in his file, and the attendant stigma involved in the Board's failure to reappoint him constituted "a deprivation of his interest in liberty," within the meaning of Board of Regents of State Colleges et al. v. Roth, and Perry v. Sindermann; and that Wellner therefore was entitled to a prior hearing.

The trial court determined at the time it rendered its order that "a hearing held now could not adequately reflect the actual circumstances surrounding the making of the racist charges against plaintiff and the decision not to reappoint him for the 1971–1972 year." It therefore assessed back pay against the Board; ordered the Board to appoint Wellner at the beginning of the next quarter or semester to a position of equal rank, responsibility and salary to that which he held at Metro during the 1970–1971 academic year, but at a Minnesota State Junior College other than Metro because of the "tensions and problems which would result from him working there"; and further ordered the Board to expunge from its records all matter relating to Wellner's "actions or attitudes toward black people which indicate that he holds a bias or prejudice against them."

We affirm in part and reverse in part and remand this cause with directions.

In its opinion and order the trial court found: that Minnesota Stat. Ann. § 136.62 (1967) authorizes Metro to appoint, reappoint and not reappoint nontenured faculty members without giving reasons or affording a hearing; that Dr. Robert W. Jensen, Metro's president, appointed Wellner to the Metro faculty during the 1969–1970 academic year as a physical education instructor and wrestling coach; that pursuant to the recommendation of the Faculty Review Committee (Committee), Dr. Jensen reappointed Wellner for the next academic year; that although Wellner applied for the position of permanent athletic director, Dean of Students, Dr. James P. Lund, appointed an outsider, Grover Garvin; that Wellner was heavily burdened with extra work, which he was forced to assume in order to keep his job; that problems arose during the 1970–1971 academic year between Wellner and other faculty members, which triggered Dr. Lund to recommend to Dr. Jensen in writing that Wellner not be reappointed "because of 'lack of cooperation and the ill feelings that have developed in the Athletic Department as a result of Mr. Wellner's attitude and actions' "; that other anti-Wellner material was gathered by Dr. Lund and placed in Wellner's file at Metro which charged Wellner with having a hatred toward blacks; that during the same period the Committee recommended to Dr. Jensen that Wellner be reappointed; that Dr. Lund in a memorandum to Dr. Jensen recommended to the contrary; and that Dr. Jensen decided not to reappoint Wellner.

The trial court concluded that the accusations contained in the adverse memoranda were without foundation in fact, and that "[t]hey consist of conclusions and mental impressions which are readily explainable when one considers that they were made at the direction of Dr. Lund" who was the superior of the authors of the memoranda. Insofar as the racist charges were concerned, the trial court found that there was no evidence of any kind to sustain or lend veracity to such charges. It determined that "[t]he evidence shows that the presence of the written racist charges in [Wellner's] file at Metro clearly reduces and diminishes his chances to obtain another teaching position since it is likely that his prospective employers will have access to such file."

The principal question presented by this appeal is whether the record supports the trial court's determination that Wellner had been deprived of an interest in liberty entitling him to a hearing pursuant to the dictates of *Roth* and *Sindermann*.

In Harnett v. Ulett, we interpreted *Roth* as determining "that absent some sort of statutory tenure or contractual rights, a public employee has no interest cognizable at law necessitating due process protection unless a showing is made that the government conduct likely will ... impose a stigma upon the employee that will foreclose future opportunities to practice his chosen profession."

Both *Roth* and *Sindermann* subscribe to the view that although a person may have "no 'right' to a valuable governmental benefit and even though the government may deny him the benefit for any number of reasons, there are some reasons upon which the government may not rely." " '[W]here a person's good name, reputation, honor, or integrity is at stake because of what the government is doing to him, notice and an opportunity to be heard are essential.' "

* * *

The record discloses that subsequent to its decision to recommend reappointment, the Faculty Review Committee received written anti-Wellner memoranda from Dr. Lund, together with written charges of racism from the Black Student Union. Additional material adverse to Wellner had been collected by Dr. Lund from Garvin and Gardner, along with a letter addressed to Lund from the Black Student Union Basketball Team, which contained more racist charges. Dr. Lund placed the material into Wellner's activity file which ultimately came into Dr. Jensen's custody. Despite this new information, the Committee adhered to its original recommendation. Dr. Jensen nevertheless refused to follow the Committee's suggested action and informed Wellner in writing that he would not be reappointed. Dr. Jensen testified that Wellner's requested review of the decision was denied and that the decision would stand without a hearing.

Our examination of this record convinces us that no mistake has been made. There is ample evidence to support the trial court's finding that the presence of racist charges against Wellner were the principal cause of his non-reappointment and this deprived Wellner of an interest in liberty which entitled him to a prior hearing, despite his nontenured status.

We turn then to the nature of the trial court's remedy. We agree with that portion of its order which in effect states that Wellner is entitled to receive the salary he would have received had he been reappointed, unless and until he is lawfully discharged. We also agree with that portion of the trial court's order which directs the Board to expunge from its records all written matter which indicates that Wellner holds a bias or prejudice toward blacks. However, the trial court erred when it determined not to order a hearing and instead ordered the board to reappoint Wellner to a similar teaching position. As we noted earlier, the trial court reasoned that "a hearing held now could not adequately reflect the actual circumstances surrounding the making of the racist charges."

We acknowledge that this latter point is troublesome. Nevertheless, we are governed by *Roth* and *Sindermann* which dictate that upon the requisite showing of deprivation of an interest in liberty the appropriate remedy is a hearing ordered by the trial court. That is, in such a case due process requires that a party be given notice of the charges against him and a reasonable chance to be heard. The Supreme Court in *Roth* observed:

> "The purpose of such notice and hearing is to provide the person an opportunity to clear his name. Once a person has cleared his name at a hearing, his employer, of course, may remain free to deny him future employment for other reasons."

We deem it inappropriate in this case to do more than follow the requirement. The trial court chose to go further and erred in so doing.

The final order of the trial court is therefore affirmed in part and reversed in part. We affirm that portion of the order requiring the Board to compensate Wellner for lost wages and to expunge from its records the material adverse to Wellner. We also affirm the assessment of costs against the Board, not including attorney's fees. We reverse that portion of the order which directs Wellner to be reemployed. The cause is remanded to the trial court with directions to order an administrative hearing before the Board in accordance with due process requirements as noted in this opinion.

Affirmed in part, reversed in part and remanded with directions.

Brandt v. Board of Cooperative Education Services
820 F.2d 41 (1987)

FEINBERG, Chief Judge:

This appeal concerns whether appellant Wayne Brandt, after his dismissal as a public school teacher, was entitled to a name-clearing hearing pursuant to 42 U.S.C. § 1983 based on the presence of allegedly false and defamatory charges in his personnel file. In October 1980, the Board of Cooperative Educational Services, Third Supervisory District, Suffolk County, New York (the Board), appointed Brandt as a substitute teacher of autistic children at the James E. Allen Learning Center operated by the Board. Brandt's students were 16 to 19 years old with I.Q. scores ranging from 10 to 25. In a series of meetings held in March and April 1981, appellees—the Board; Edward J. Murphy, the Superintendent of Schools; and Dominick Morreale, the principal of the Learning Center—charged Brandt with various acts of sexual misconduct involving his students. Despite pressure from appellees, Brandt refused to resign. His demand for a hearing to clear himself of the charges was denied. He was discharged in April 1981, in the middle of his term.

* * *

The district court ruled that, in order for Brandt to establish his liberty interest, he had to prove that the sexual allegations about him were false and that there was actual disclosure of them to individuals other than those involved in the investigation. Finding that Brandt was unable to prove actual disclosure of the allegations, the district court granted summary judgment to appellees and dismissed Brandt's complaint. This appeal followed.

A government employee's liberty interest is implicated where the government dismisses him based on charges "that might seriously damage his standing and associations in his community" or that might impose "on him a stigma or other disability that foreclose[s] his freedom to take advantage of other employment opportunities." For example, charges that the employee is guilty of dishonesty or immorality are stigmatizing because they call into question the person's "good name, reputation, honor, or integrity." In addition, the charges against the employee must be made "public" by the government employer, and the employee must allege that the charges are false. Where the employee's liberty interest is implicated, he is entitled under the due process clause to notice and an opportunity to be heard.

The issue before us is whether the district court properly granted summary judgment to appellees based on its ruling that Brandt must prove that appellees had actually disclosed false allegations of sexual misconduct. As a preliminary matter, it is not clear whether the district court ruled that Brandt had to prove the falsity of the charges in order to establish his right to a name-clearing hearing or only in order to establish damages. While we do not take issue with the latter proposition, we have no doubt that the former is erroneous. The Supreme Court has required only that a plaintiff raise the issue of falsity regarding the stigmatizing charges—not prove it—in order to establish a right to a name-clearing hearing. Here, Brandt satisfied that requirement by alleging in his complaint that the charges were false. The truth or falsity of the charges would then be determined at the hearing itself. If Brandt had to prove the falsity of the charges before he could obtain a hearing, there would be no need for the hearing.

Appellees do not contest that point but they argue that under Bishop, no liberty interest is implicated where there has been no public disclosure of the reasons for the discharge. Brandt has conceded that appellees have disclosed the charges against him only to those involved in the investigation. Brandt argues, however, that the presence of the charges in his personnel file satisfies the "public disclosure" requirement because there is a likelihood that these charges may be disclosed in the future. He claims that prospective employers will want to know about his qualifications as a teacher, will gain access to the file and "will most certainly not hire him" when they learn of the charges.

It is important to emphasize that we are reviewing a grant of summary judgment. If there was any genuine issue of material fact before the district court, then the grant of summary judgment was improper. At the conference before Judge Wexler in November 1986, the Board did not stipulate that it would never disclose the charges to Brandt's prospective employers. The Board's counsel stated that he believed the Board's policy was to not disclose but Brandt vigorously contested this representation. Thus, there was a genuine issue of fact regarding the likelihood of disclosure to Brandt's prospective employers. The question now is whether the likelihood of such disclosure is material to Brandt's claim, and we conclude that it is.

The Supreme Court set forth the "public disclosure" requirement in Bishop. In that case, the reasons for the employee's termination were communicated orally to the employee in private, and prior to litigation, the reasons had not been made public. With respect to the impact on the discharged employee's future employment opportunities, the Court concluded that despite termination, the employee "remain[ed] as free as before to seek another" job where there had been no public disclosure of the reasons for the discharge. The Court also concluded that because the communication was not made public, "it cannot properly form the basis for a claim that [the employee's] interest in his 'good name, reputation, honor, or integrity' was thereby impaired."

Similarly, in Gentile, this court held that the discharged government employee failed to establish that she had been deprived of a liberty interest because there had been no public disclosure of the reasons for her discharge. The reasons had been disclosed to plaintiff through letters and conferences in private, and there was no claim that these communications were ever published to potential employers by the defendant governmental unit.

Thus, where the reasons for an employee's termination are kept private, it is clear that the "public disclosure" requirement has not been met and there has been no violation of the employee's liberty interest. Neither Bishop nor Gentile, however, involved the placement of stigmatizing charges in the personnel file of the discharged employee. More important, the "public disclosure" requirement set forth in Bishop and Gentile is not a self-defining concept. The purpose of the requirement is to limit a constitutional claim to those instances where the stigmatizing charges made in the course of discharge have been or are likely to be disseminated widely enough to damage the discharged employee's standing in the community or foreclose future job opportunities. In determining the degree of dissemination that satisfies the "public disclosure" requirement, we must look to the potential effect of dissemination on the employee's standing in the community and the foreclosure of job opportunities. As a result, what is sufficient to constitute "public disclosure" will vary with the circumstances of each case.

In this case, we consider the effect on Brandt's future job opportunities since that is the harm he contends will result from dissemination of the reasons for his discharge. If Brandt is able to show that prospective employers are likely to gain access to his personnel file and decide not to hire him, then the presence of the charges in his file has a damaging effect on his future job opportunities. Brandt need not wait until he actually loses some job opportunities because the presence of the charges in his personnel file coupled with a likelihood of harmful disclosure already place him "between the devil and the deep blue sea." In applying for jobs, if Brandt authorizes the release of his personnel file, the potential employer would find out about the allegations of sexual misconduct and probably not hire him. If he refuses to grant authorization, that, too, would hurt his chances for employment. Thus, Brandt, unlike the employee in Bishop, would not be "as free as before to seek another" job.

Courts of appeals for other circuits have similarly concluded that the public disclosure requirement has been satisfied where the stigmatizing charges are placed in the discharged employee's personnel file and are likely to be disclosed to prospective employers.

We hold, therefore, that it was error for the district court to grant summary judgment to appellees, and to deny Brandt the chance to substantiate his claim that future employers are likely to gain access to his personnel file and refuse to hire him.

State ex rel. McLendon v. Morton
249 S.E.2d 919 (1978)

MILLER, Justice:

Relator, Vonceil McLendon, an Assistant Professor at Parkersburg Community College, seeks this original writ of mandamus against the West Virginia Board of

Regents and Ben L. Morton, its Chancellor. Her claim is based on the fact that she was denied a due process hearing in connection with the College's decision not to grant her tenure. We agree and issue the writ.

Relator bases her right to a due process hearing on the ground that the Board of Regents' tenure standards set out in its Amended Policy Bulletin No. 36 establish certain objective criteria which, if met, bestow a property interest sufficient to require that she be afforded a procedural due process hearing before tenure can be denied. The respondents, the Board of Regents and the Chancellor, deny that their tenure policy confers any property interest.

Tenure for teachers in State-supported colleges and universities is controlled by Amended Policy Bulletin No. 36 (herein Bulletin), effective July 1, 1974, entitled "Policy Regarding Academic Freedom and Responsibility, Appointment, Promotion, Tenure and Termination of Employment of Professional Personnel."

The authority of the Board of Regents to adopt the Bulletin is not questioned in this case. Notwithstanding any implication that may be found in *State ex rel. Kondos v. West Virginia Board of Regents*, the broad language contained in W. Va. Code, 18–26–8, placing " ... the general determination, control, supervision and management of the financial, business and educational policies and affairs of all state colleges and universities ... ", together with similar language found in W. Va. Code, 18–26–13b, relating to community colleges, compels the conclusion that the Board of Regents is authorized to set standards for the hiring, tenure and dismissal of teachers at State colleges and universities. This power was explicitly recognized in *Sheppard v. West Virginia Board of Regents*.

Section 8A of the Bulletin makes clear that tenure is intended to ensure academic freedom by protecting faculty members against capricious dismissal. Tenure is not granted automatically, "but shall result from action by the West Virginia Board of Regents upon the recommendation of the president following consultation with the department concerned." Obviously, and as is the case here, tenure is considered first by the college. Parkersburg Community College implemented the Board's tenure policy by its own Policy Regulation No. 4P–36–03, which provides that "applications and/or nominations for tenure shall be filed with the chairman of the College Wide Tenure Committee." The regulations also provide for an evaluation process.

Of considerable significance is Section 8C of the Bulletin, which makes tenure available to all full-time employees who hold the rank of Assistant Professor or above. Equally significant is Section 9C of the Bulletin, which sets forth the maximum time periods within which the tenure decision must be made by the institution: "The maximum period of probation shall not exceed seven years; and at the end of six years any non-tenured faculty member will be given notice in writing of tenure, or offered a one-year written terminal contract of employment. ... "

These are the relevant provisions in regard to eligibility for tenure. It is clear from Section 11 of the Bulletin that once tenure is obtained, a faculty member cannot be dismissed except for six specified reasons, and is entitled to formal hearing procedures with the right to appeal to the Board of Regents. These procedural rights do not apply to a non-tenured teacher unless he is dismissed during the term of his annual contract.

I

THE NATURE OF THE INTEREST

Both parties agree that the question of whether Professor McLendon is entitled to any procedural due process upon rejection of her application for tenure must be answered by determining whether she has some protected interest created by Amended Policy Bulletin No. 36.

We are cited *Board of Regents v. Roth, Perry v. Sindermann,* and our own cases of *Waite v. Civil Service Commission* and *North v. West Virginia Board of Regents,* as establishing the guidelines for determining a protected interest.

Each of these cases announces the rule that a protected interest, in the sense that its withdrawal requires some procedural due process protection, can be either a liberty or property interest. Admittedly, no claim of a liberty interest is at stake in this case, as Professor McLendon does not assert that the denial of her tenure arose out of her exercise of some constitutionally protected right, such as freedom of speech, or that the denial was based upon some charge which involved her reputation, honor or integrity.

The issue thus narrows to whether she had some property interest by virtue of the Bulletin and the regulations surrounding tenure. We acknowledged in *Waite* that *Roth* formulated a property interest broader than the traditional concept of real and personal property:

> "It is clear from the Supreme Court decision in *Roth* that the Constitution protects property interests beyond the traditional concept of real or personal property. The Court indicated that a benefit which merits protection as a property interest must be one to which there is more than a 'unilateral expectation.' Rather, there must exist rules or understandings which allow the claimant's expectations to be characterized as 'a legitimate claim of entitlement to [the benefit.]"

We also recognized in *Waite* that our analysis of liberty and property interests was hinged to our constitutional due process standard, West Virginia Constitution, Article III, Section 10. Consequently, while we may utilize the teachings of the United States Supreme Court in its due process cases, we are not constrained by identicality so long as we do not diminish our State standard below the federal standard.

We find no United States Supreme Court case involving tenure which is precisely in point with the present case.

* * *

On several occasions this Court has entertained mandamus to require the granting of an application where the applicant met the eligibility standards. Although the rationale of a property entitlement was not used, it is clear that this basic substantive principle was involved. These cases focused on the arbitrary and capricious nature of the actions of the public official, which is nothing more than an alternative way of finding a lack of procedural due process.

In considering the tenure program of Parkersburg Community College, along with the Board of Regents' policy on tenure, it is clear that the sixth year of a teacher's employment marks the critical time. The decision on tenure must be made by the end of that year. The College's policy regulations provide the right to apply for tenure and establish a detailed evaluation and review procedure with fixed time periods for action. The regulations require a recommendation by the College Wide Tenure Committee to the President by November 20. This time period obviously integrates with the Board of Regents' requirement for timely notice to teachers of their non-retention.

On the basis of these regulations, Professor McLendon, a full-time employee with the rank of Assistant Professor in her sixth teaching year, filed for tenure. The application was processed by the tenure committee and culminated with a letter from the President of the College denying tenure. The letter gave no reasons for the denial of tenure and she was offered a one-year termination contract.

We conclude that Professor McLendon had more than a unilateral expectation of tenure. With her rank of Assistant Professor, six years of teaching service and full-time employment in academic teaching, she met the eligibility criteria to make application for tenure. This does not mean, however, that she was automatically entitled to obtain tenure status. Both the Board's Bulletin and the College's regulations indicate that teaching competency is a further criterion for obtaining tenure. Competency involves an evaluation of a teacher's total professional skills. It is the basic substantive issue once the objective eligibility requirements are met.

However, satisfying the objective eligibility standards for tenure gave Professor McLendon a sufficient entitlement so that she could not be denied tenure on the issue of her competency without some procedural due process.

II

THE DEGREE OF PROTECTION AFFORDED

Syllabus Point 5 of *Waite v. Civil Service Commission* enunciates the following standards for considering the extent of due process protection afforded where a property interest is sought to be deprived:

> "The extent of due process protection affordable for a property interest re-
> quires consideration of three distinct factors: first, the private interests that will
> be affected by the official action; second, the risk of an erroneous deprivation
> of a property interest through the procedures used, and the probable value, if
> any, of additional or substitute procedural safeguards; and finally, the govern-
> ment's interest, including the function involved and the fiscal and administrative
> burdens that the additional or substitute procedural requirement would entail."

Waite involved a temporary suspension of a civil service classified employee and acknowledged the more general rule for due process protection set forth in *North*, where, in the pertinent part of Syllabus Point 2, we stated:

> "First, the more valuable the right sought to be deprived, the more safeguards
> will be interposed. Second, due process must generally be given before the
> deprivation occurs unless a compelling public policy dictates otherwise. Third,
> a temporary deprivation of rights may not require as large a measure of pro-
> cedural due process protection as a permanent deprivation."

North dealt with the expulsion of a fourth-year medical student and relied in part on the procedural due process analysis in *Goss v. Lopez*, which involved a suspension of up to ten days of public high school students.

If we apply the *Waite* formulation here, it is apparent that the private interest affected is of considerable importance to the teacher. Tenure once acquired is a substantial right. It ensures that the teacher cannot be dismissed except for the defined reasons which are set out in the Bulletin and then not until a full due process hearing has been held. The Board's Bulletin recognizes tenure is inextricably tied to academic freedom. We cannot blind ourselves to the fact that tenure is a paramount professional and economic goal for a teacher. Thus, it is a valuable property interest.

Under the second standard, there are currently no orderly procedures or protections that exist for one who meets the objective standards for tenure eligibility but is denied tenure. The risk of erroneous or capricious denial of tenure is apparent in light of the lack of any safeguards that would diminish this margin of error.

The final factor is the state interest in avoiding the increased fiscal and administrative burden resulting from procedural due process requirements. A state college or university has a substantial interest in determining that only competent and dedicated teachers are afforded the security of tenure, but this interest is not diminished by affording some procedural due process after the decision to deny tenure has been made.

Prior to a teacher reaching tenure eligibility status, a state college can decide not to renew the annual teaching contract and thereby terminate the teacher without the necessity of any reasons or hearing. We cannot help but assume that after several years with the college, a teacher's qualifications and merits would be well known to the administration so that it could sever the incompetent teacher prior to his obtaining tenure eligibility.

While we recognize that a procedural due process hearing may entail some additional burden to the college, we cannot measure the quality of due process solely by the economic burden it may impose.

We also recognize that the determination of a teacher's qualifications is not limited to a narrow inquiry into his academic credentials, but encompasses a wide spectrum of qualities, not all of which may have the same significance. There is obviously a need to permit a latitude of discretion as the issue cannot be framed with mathematical precision or exactitude. What should not be tolerated is a wholly arbitrary and capricious selection process where the competent are turned aside in favor of those less qualified.

We conclude that minimal procedural due process necessitates a notice of the reasons why tenure is not extended and a hearing with an opportunity to submit evidence, relevant to the issues raised in the notice. The hearing tribunal should be unbiased. If the teacher demonstrates that the reasons are wholly inadequate or without a factual basis, the administration would be required to show the contrary. Because academic personnel are involved, we do not believe that the right to retained counsel at the hearing is obligatory unless the parties agree.

The factual issues at such hearing fall into two categories. First, whether the objective eligibility standards of full-time teaching employment, rank and time in service have been met. The second is whether the adverse decision with respect to her teaching competency was arbitrary and capricious or lacked any factual basis.

For the foregoing reasons, a writ of mandamus is awarded compelling the respondents to grant the relator a hearing in accordance with the principles set forth herein.

Writ awarded.

Upadhya v. Langenberg
834 F.2d 661 (7th Cir. 1987)

EASTERBROOK, Circuit Judge.

The University of Illinois hired Kamleshwar Upadhya in 1984 as an assistant professor of engineering. He was appointed to the tenure track, with a decision to be made no later than fall 1988, the beginning of his fifth year. Upadhya believes that the University committed itself to give him the full five years to demonstrate his professional skills.

The University evaluates each professor on the tenure track annually, and after evaluating Upadhya in June 1986 the University decided not to renew his contract. As the Statutes of the University require, Upadhya received a terminal appointment, expiring on August 31, 1987. He filed this suit under 42 U.S.C. § 1983, contending that his discharge violated the Due Process Clause of the fourteenth amendment. The district court held a trial and issued a permanent injunction compelling the University to "continue [Upadhya] in his present position in this employ until it has given him constitutionally sufficient due process of law with relation to his termination."

The Due Process Clause of the fourteenth amendment applies only to deprivations of "life, liberty, or property." Upadhya maintains, and the district court held, that his job is "property." The district court apparently concluded that once the University hires a professor, it may not let the professor go without providing an adversarial hearing. This is the effect of the injunction, which does not distinguish between the initial five-year period and an indefinite (tenured) appointment. We have held, however, that professors on the tenure track at the University of Illinois lack a property interest in receiving tenure. To the extent the district court thought that an initial appointment carries with it the right to remain until dismissed after an adversarial hearing, its decision is inconsistent with settled law.

* * *

Upadhya contends, and the district court found, that the professors who recruited him promised him five years to prove himself, and that this promise creates a property interest despite the Statutes and our holdings in *McElearney* and *Weinstein*.

Upadhya's claim is based on his understanding of what was said to him, rather than on the words the University used or a reading of its Statutes. The three writings do not promise him five years' employment; the Statutes make it clear that no one with whom Upadhya dealt had the authority to make such a promise. Giving a paper, moving from one city to another, and similar activities are common among assistant professors and do not negate the Statutes. Neither do vague statements about how long Upadhya could expect to serve before a final decision. Such statements—no doubt accurate depictions of the practices—do not transmute probabilities into entitlements. We held as much in *McElearney*. A misunderstanding of one's entitlements, even if reasonable, does not enlarge those entitlements.

We accept the district court's finding that Upadhya believed that his appointment ran for five years and that no one expressly told him otherwise. The court also found that Upadhya did not receive or read the Statutes that would have disabused him— though Upadhya signed a document expressly incorporating these readily-available Statutes, making them part of the contract under Illinois law. Upadhya's belief is still just a "unilateral expectation." It cannot be a "legitimate claim of entitlement" unless backed up by a promise. (Given the parol evidence rule, Upadhya would face hurdles in relying on even an express oral promise, for he uses it to vary the terms of three subsequent writings; more, Illinois treats the Statutes as "laws," which may forbid variances by subordinate officials of the state. We need not consider whether Upadhya has adequate replies to these difficulties.)

The district court found that agents of the University expressly promised Upadhya he would have a five-year term. The record does not support this conclusion.

* * *

[O]nly the President may vary the usual terms of appointment, and that requires a special writing. The district court did not find that McNallan and Danyluk had apparent authority to bind the University, and they did not; Upadhya negotiated with Wu, the Department Head, not with McNallan and Danyluk. And when Wu made Upadhya a written offer by letter on July 30, Wu identified five years as the outer limit, not as a guarantee. To the extent the district court found that Upadhya expected to have five years to raise money and conduct research, its findings accord with the evidence; to the extent the court found that the University promised Upadhya he could not be dismissed before five years were up, its findings are clearly erroneous.

Upadhya misunderstood the difference between the maximum and the minimum times before a decision. Dr. Wu did not draw this difference to his attention, probably because in the great majority of cases there is none. Upadhya did not read the Statutes that spelled out the rules; anyway, the Statutes are written for lawyers rather than metallurgists. Whether or not the University treated Upadhya well, unless unilateral expectations are enough to create a property interest, Upadhya cannot prevail.

A brief note about *Vail*, on which the district court principally relied. We concluded in *Vail* that a high school football coach had a "property" interest in the job for two years, even though his contract covered but one year. The coach had been given an express oral promise of renewal for the second year, after full consideration and decision by the Board of Education. This was enough, we said, to create a property interest. It should be clear by now that Upadhya does not come within the holding of *Vail*: he did not obtain an express promise that five years would be his minimum term, and any implication to that effect was unauthorized by the President and Board of Trustees of the University—the only persons who could bind the University to such contracts. *Vail* distinguished *McElearney* on these grounds, concluding that "the [University of Illinois'] explicit rules governing tenure in *McElearney* suggest that any reliance to be based on a supposed entitlement . . . by virtue of the informal assurances McElearney received would be unreasonable." So McElearney's were; so Upadhya's were. We are left with a misunderstanding: Upadhya thought he had a five-year term, but this belief cannot be derived from a fair reading of the writings and statements in the record. Upadhya lacked property interest in the renewal of his appointment, and the University therefore was not required to give him notice or an opportunity for a hearing.

Reversed.

Manes v. Dallas Baptist College

638 S.W.2d 143 (Tex. App.–, Dallas 1982, writ ref'd n.r.e.)

AKIN, Justice.

Dr. Charles Manes appeals from a summary judgment granted against him in his suit for breach of his employment contract with Dallas Baptist College. Dr. Manes was discharged by the College's Board of Trustees for alleged insubordination. Dr. Manes then sued alleging that he was terminated without cause, in breach of his employment contract. The College moved for summary judgment, which was granted, on the ground that the contract provided for common law arbitration. Because the trial judge improperly construed the employment contract, we reverse the judgment and remand for trial.

The crucial language in the contract provided:

> Tenured faculty may be terminated for incompetence or moral turpitude or insubordination or unethical conduct or financial exigency of the college, and then only after due process.
>
> . . . .
>
> In every case of termination of a tenured faculty member the faculty member shall be informed in writing of the specific circumstances upon which his/her termination is based. The faculty member will be provided the opportunity to appeal to the Campus Administration. *The action taken by the Board of Trustees shall be final.* [Emphasis added]

Our review of this summary judgment is limited to deciding what interpretation to give the provision that "the action taken by the Board of Trustees shall be final." The College urges that "final" means not subject to judicial redetermination; in other words, this language was in effect an agreement for common law arbitration which precludes litigation of the issues decided in arbitration by the college trustees. Dr. Manes contends, on the other hand, that "final" means only that the trustee's action was the last step in the College's internal grievance procedure before he could resort to the courts but that it did not otherwise affect his right to judicial review. We hold that the contract does not provide for common law arbitration but that whether grounds existed for termination is subject to judicial redetermination. Thus, summary judgment was improperly granted.

* * *

Dr. Manes' employment contract provided for a hearing before the College's Board of Trustees. If the Board of Trustees was considered to be an arbitrator, the effect would be to allow one of the parties to act as judge in its own case. Such a result is totally inconsistent with the theory of arbitration. The contract plainly establishes only a procedure for internal administrative remedies and cannot be considered as an agreement to arbitrate. Summary judgment was thus improper because the College failed to establish as a matter of law that the contract provided for common law arbitration.

Additionally neither party pleaded ambiguity of the contract in the trial court. If a contract is so worded that it can be given a definite and certain legal meaning, it is not ambiguous. When a contract is susceptible to a legal meaning, construction of the written instrument is one of law for the court. Since allowing the College to act as an arbitrator in its own dispute is inconsistent with the theory of arbitration, the College's contention that the contract provides for common law arbitration constitutes an unreasonable reading of the contract. The only possible reading of the contract is that it establishes a procedure for administrative review of disputes between the College and its employees. This allows for possible resolution of disputes without the necessity of judicial intervention, but it does *not* preclude judicial intervention. Dr. Manes was required to exhaust these administrative remedies before he could seek a judicial determination of his complaint, and he did so. Because the contract provided only for a procedure for administrative review and the College failed to establish as a matter of law that the parties entered into common law arbitration, the summary judgment must be reversed and the cause remanded.

SPARLING, Justice, dissenting.

I cannot agree that a reasonable construction of the employment contract contemplates a judicial determination of the merits of appellant's termination. Accordingly, I dissent.

This case does not concern the judicial review of a public institution as a matter of administrative law, but rather the review of the action of a private institution as a matter of contract law. Academic freedom does not inherently require a more liberal construction of rights under a teacher's contract of employment than the construction of contractual rights of any other wage earner. "Tenure" is a status defined by contract, vesting only those rights provided by contract and no right to arbitration exists without language so specifying.

Majority implies that the summary judgment was granted on the ground that the contract provided for common law arbitration, yet "arbitration," by word or inference, is nowhere mentioned by the court in the judgment. Majority presumes that the summary judgment must have been based upon a finding of arbitration because the College's Motion for Summary Judgment, in one part, referred to the action of the Executive Committee of the Board of Trustees as "common law arbitration." The word "arbitration" was used when the College urged the court to construe the word "final" in the employment contract as precluding a judicial determination of insubordination. I would hold that the College properly presented the issue of the construction of the employment contract to the court by Motion for Summary Judgment, although it was improperly labelled as "arbitration." In *Albritton v. Henry S. Miller Co.*, this court held that Rule 166-A(c) allows issues to be "expressly presented" by all summary judgment evidence presented to and considered by the court, even if the motion fails to specifically set forth the issue. In *Stark v. Morgan*, this court held that summary judgment may be granted on *any* ground set forth in the motion. Therefore, if the *issue* is properly presented, the trial court is not bound by the label chosen by the College in describing that issue.

I would hold that the plain and intelligible language of the contract of employment does not provide for arbitration, but rather provides a system of administrative "due process" which is a prerequisite to termination. It is immaterial that the final decision was made by the College, if those were the terms upon which the parties agreed.

* * *

Price v. Oklahoma College
of Osteopathic Medicine and Surgery
733 P.2d 1357 (Okla. App. 1986)

BRIGHTMIRE, Judge.

This might be called the case of the unwelcome acceptance. The ultimate issue for resolution is whether the trial judge erred when he dismissed the tenured professor's petition seeking declaratory relief in the form of a judicial determination that plaintiff had entered into a valid teaching contract with osteopathic medical school for the 1984–85 school year. We hold he did and reverse.

I

The essential facts are undisputed. In 1974 plaintiff, Dr. James T. Price, was appointed by the Oklahoma College of Osteopathic Medicine and Surgery to the position of Associate Professor of Pathology "with tenure."[1] Each year the college sent him a letter setting out the salary and other terms of his employment for the ensuing academic year and requesting that his acceptance be indicated by signing on a designated line and returning it to the college. Dr. Price complied with the request annually, sometimes "under protest" as he did in 1982 and sometimes with explanation of his objections as he did in 1983 and 1984. The 1982 protest, for instance, was aired in a grievance hearing before a review committee and narrative minutes of the hearing show that the committee proceeded on the premise that a valid 1982–83 contract existed and restricted its concern to the merits of the protest. Certainly no one suggested his criticism of administrative policies and procedures, written below his acceptance of the 1983 appointment letter, was to be treated as a counteroffer.

But in 1984, something different happened. In June Dr. Price received the usual appointing letter from the college administration. And, as usual, he signed it, added a protest note and returned it to the college. The letter is reproduced below:

Dr. Price received the following letter dated June 29, 1984, from Dr. Barson:

"Dear Dr. Price:

Your reply is considered as non-acceptance of the Board of Regents' appointment action of June 14, 1984. Accordingly, your voluntary decision to terminate employment will be reported to the Board at their next meeting.

Sincerely,

/s/

John Barson, Ed.D.

President"

By letter dated July 2, 1984, the professor responded this way:

"Dear Dr. Barson:

I am somewhat puzzled by your letter of 29 June 1984 that addresses my "non-acceptance" on the contract which I signed as accepting and delivered to your personnel office on 29 June.

I did sign as accepting this contract while protesting what I believe are violations of our previous contract on the part of the institution. I did this to specifically preserve options of grievance during the contract year 1984–1985.

I consider that you, serving for the Board of Regents, have offered a contract that was completed in agreement, by my returning the signed contract on the day specified.

Sincerely,

/s/

James T. Price, Ph.D.

Associate Professor"

---

1. "Tenure" in the academic community commonly refers to status granted, usually after probationary period, which protects teacher from dismissal except for serious misconduct, incompetence, financial exigency, or change in institutional programs.

Finally Dr. Price received the following epistle, dated July 6, 1984, from the college president:

"Dear Dr. Price:

As follow-up to my correspondence dated June 29, 1984, I wish to inform you that the Board of Regents, at its meeting on July 5, 1984, took note of your signed protest of the terms of an employment contract offered you by the Board of Regents on June 14, 1984. By approved motion, the Board of Regents declared the budget position of Associate Professor of Pathology (# 12110) which you occupied during FY 1983–84, to be vacant due to the absence of a valid contract.

In accordance with Board action, you should proceed to remove your personal effects from your office. College separation procedure requires clearance with the Physical Plant, Library, Audiovisual Department, your department supervisor, Dr. Robert Ritter, and any other unit which has issued you working materials or equipment, in order to complete our records and assure proper return of College-owned items.

Sincerely,
/s/
John Barson, Ed.D.
President"

This lawsuit was filed by the banished prof on July 17, 1984, against the college and its Board of Regents. After stating the operative facts the plaintiff asked the court to (1) declare that a legally binding contract of employment for the fiscal year 1984–85 was created when he signed the offering letter and returned it to the college personnel office on June 29, 1984; (2) determine that plaintiff is due his salary in accordance with the rules and regulations of the college; and (3) award his costs and a judgment for his attorney fee expense.

Defendants filed an answer September 18, 1984, in which they admitted the allegations of fact but denied most of the conclusions stated, including plaintiff's claim of being entitled to the relief requested.

Plaintiff moved for a judgment on the pleadings October 9, 1984. The motion was briefed by the parties and apparently overruled by the court. On July 10, 1985, defendants moved for a summary judgment stating that no material fact was in dispute and therefore they were entitled to judgment. While this motion was being briefed plaintiff moved for a summary judgment on the same grounds and fortified his request with a couple of affidavits. These motions were heard August 15, 1985. The trial court held that the protest written by plaintiff below his signature on the appointing letter "qualified his acceptance" and such "qualified acceptance of Defendants' offer of employment was a new offer for an employment contract which was not accepted by the Defendants," citing 15 O.S. 1981 § 71. Based on these legal hypotheses defendants' motion for summary judgment was sustained, plaintiff's lawsuit "dismissed," and each party ordered to pay his own attorney fees.

The professor appeals asserting that his post-acceptance declamation—"signed under protest"—rather than having a legal effect on the executed employment contract, merely preserved a grievance for potential rectification through proper school-sponsored channels.

II

The dispositive issue may be framed thus: If the acceptance of an offer is carried out in accordance with the directions of the offeror, does notification of offeror—by note written on the margin of the offeror's document below the offeree's signature—that the offeree signs or accepts the offer under protest, amount to a condition or qualification which has the legal effect of altering the terms of the offer thus transforming the acceptance into a counter proposal?

In defense of the trial court's conclusion—that the protest did just that—defendants rely on the law pertaining to the type of acceptance it takes to create an enforceable contract, namely, the provisions of 15 O.S. 1981 § 71. It reads:

> "An acceptance must be absolute and unqualified, or must include in itself an acceptance of that character, which the proposer can separate from the rest, and which will include the person accepting. A qualified acceptance is a new proposal."

The gist of defendants' argument is that plaintiff's "signed under protest" statement was a qualification of his acceptance because he, "in effect, responded to OCOMS' offer by stating that he accepts the offer of employment but not at the salary offered." And, defendants add, salary is a material term of the offer. The case of *Swanson v. McCall* is tendered as decisional support for the legal theory.

Surely just to state the facts and the foregoing law is sufficient to demonstrate the lack of merit in defendants' position. While one may qualify an acceptance as an act of protest, a mere protest does not in itself qualify an acceptance. And that is all we have here—an unqualified acceptance of the proffered appointment followed by a protest based on a perceived error in fixing the amount of salary agreed on.

* * *

The college's offering letter recited the terms of the appointment and then specified the mode and manner of acceptance, namely, "by signing and returning one copy of this letter to the office of Personnel Services no later than June 29, 1984." Further down on the page was a signature line above which was this statement by the plaintiff to Dr. Barson: "I accept the responsibilities of the appointment *under the terms outlined above*." Thus, when Dr. Price signed on the designated line he complied with the first essential and when he returned a copy of the letter to the designated office he met the second requirement at which point a binding contract came into being. No mention was there of any conditional or qualified acceptance or change of terms, but on the contrary there was only an unequivocal and specific acceptance of each and every term of the college's offer. The protest language did not in tenor or letter alter or purport to alter any term of the offer; it merely articulated the offeree's opinion that one term of the offer—the salary—had not been determined in accord with "present and past personnel policies." Execution of the acceptance was precisely in the manner directed by the offeror. The note added below the acceptance was a precative protest not substantially unlike he had written on the acceptance letter in prior years. The notation amounted to no more than saying I don't like your offer, I don't think it's right or fair, but I accept it. That and nothing more.

Under these circumstances, we hold that the trial judge erred in granting defendants a summary judgment.

III

We further hold it to be an undisputed fact that a valid contract of continued tenured employment was made between OCOMS and Dr. Price on June 29, 1984. Dr. Barson's letters of response on same date and on July 6 described a wrongful repudiation of the agreement by the defendants and an unlawful termination of Dr. Price's tenured professorial position without just cause. The action is, therefore, remanded to the trial court with directions to determine what relief plaintiff is entitled to and to grant him a judgment that is consistent with the conclusions of this court and such other relief as he may be entitled to under the pleadings, the law, and the evidence.

University of Minnesota v. Goodkind
399 N.W.2d 585 (Minn. App. 1987)

LANSING, Judge.

The University of Minnesota appeals from an order granting summary judgment to a tenured professor on a breach of contract claim. The University contends the trial court erred in incorporating the Dental School Constitution into the employment agreement, erred in refusing to incorporate the Dental School Administrative Policy 15 (hiring policy), and improperly directed the University to appoint the professor chair of the Department of Fixed Prosthodontics. We affirm, as modified, the trial court's award of summary judgment to the professor.

FACTS

Dr. Richard Goodkind has been a faculty member of the University of Minnesota School of Dentistry since 1966. He is currently a member of the Department of Removable Prosthodontics. In September 1982 the Dean of the Dental School, Dr. Richard Oliver, appointed a search committee to screen and recommend candidates for the position of chairperson of the Department of Fixed Prosthodontics. That position was to be vacant due to retirement at the end of the 1982–83 academic year. Dr. Goodkind applied for the position. In May 1983 the search committee recommended Dr. Goodkind as the only candidate. Between May and September 1983, Dean Oliver decided not to recommend Goodkind to the president of the University. Dean Oliver listed four reasons for his decision:

1. Dr. Goodkind had limited experience in teaching prosthodontics to pre-doctoral students.

2. There were differences in educational goals between Drs. Oliver and Goodkind with respect to the predoctoral program in Fixed Prosthodontics and the assessment of the relative capabilities of predoctoral students and graduate dentists.

3. Dr. Goodkind lacked administrative experience in budget and personnel management.

4. Dr. Oliver had significant doubt that he and Dr. Goodkind could work together smoothly and constructively.

Dean Oliver then appointed Dr. Harvey Colman as "acting" department chairperson. Dr. Colman had been an applicant for the position, but his application was rejected by the screening committee. Although Dr. Colman's appointment was temporary, it was not until early 1985 that Dean Oliver appointed another search committee to screen candidates for the permanent appointment.

In September 1983 Dr. Goodkind filed a formal grievance with the dental school. The grievance was referred to the Academic Freedom and Responsibility Appeals Committee of the University. The committee reviewed the complaint and concluded that it did not have jurisdiction to hear it. Dr. Goodkind then filed suit in federal court in January 1984. In January 1985 the federal district court dismissed Dr. Goodkind's breach of contract suit, without prejudice, for lack of jurisdiction.

Goodkind then filed this suit in January 1985 in Hennepin County District Court. The University moved for summary judgment in August 1985. That motion was denied in October 1985. A settlement conference was scheduled for November and later continued to December 1985. The conference was unsuccessful, and both parties subsequently filed motions for summary judgment. Those motions were heard and judgment entered in favor of Goodkind in June 1986.

The district court found that the language of the Dental School Constitution met the unilateral contract formation criteria set out by the Minnesota Supreme Court in *Pine River v. Mettille.* The constitution contained specific procedures for hiring department chairpersons which the court found "directly related to plaintiff's employment as professor in the Dental School." Specifically, the constitution directed that "heads or chairpersons of a department *shall* be selected" (emphasis supplied) from those recommended by the search committee. The court found that by failing to appoint Dr. Goodkind, the only person recommended by the search committee, Dean Oliver (and the University) breached this contract.

The court rejected the University's claim that Administrative Policy 15 also applied to the employment contract. That policy provides, "[i]n the event that the Dean does not find the recommended candidates acceptable, a request may be made that the search be broadened or extended, or that a new search committee be appointed." The policy also provides that temporary appointments may be made by the Dean for one, two, or three years following the recommendations of a search committee, but "[i]n no case shall such a position be filled for more than one (1) year without filing a hiring plan and conducting the required search for the position."

The trial court granted summary judgment in favor of Dr. Goodkind. It also awarded him back pay based on the augmentation he would have received as department chair and ordered the University to appoint him chair of the Department of Fixed Prosthodontics.

ISSUES

1. Did the trial court err in including the Dental School Constitution and excluding Administrative Policy 15 as part of Dr. Goodkind's contract with the University?

2. Did the trial court err in finding the University breached its contract with Dr. Goodkind?

3. What is the appropriate remedy for Dr. Goodkind?

ANALYSIS

I

Dr. Goodkind is a tenured faculty member at the University of Minnesota. As a tenured faculty member, he has a contract with the University which is governed by the tenure code. The University characterizes this contract as a written bilateral document. However, they also acknowledge that it does not contain all of the conditions which make up the employment agreement.

Courts have recognized that where faculty tenure agreements do not set forth the full terms and conditions of employment, employment policies, rules and regulations of the college or university become part of the employment contract between the college and the faculty member. Similarly, a university policy of nondiscrimination has been found to be a part of the contract between a professor and a university. And, "a university's policies, rules and regulations relating to faculty members are a part of the employment contract, as a matter of law."

The process by which the policies, rules and regulations are incorporated in the employment agreement is similar to the basic legal principles of contract formation and modification. The trial court found the principles in *Pine River State Bank v. Mettille* to control Dr. Goodkind's employment relationship with the University. *Pine River* is factually dissimilar in that it dealt with the discharge procedure in an employment manual given to an at-will employee. However, *Pine River* does create a structure for applying contract modification principles which can be applied in analyzing the effect of the Dental School Constitution and Administrative Policy 15 on Dr. Goodkind's employment agreement.

The constitution was approved by the Board of Regents in June 1979. It sets forth the purpose and powers of the Dental School. It also established the authority, duties and responsibilities of the Dean, the faculty and the various departments and councils of the Dental School.

Administrative Policy 15 was adopted by the Dental School Council on Administration in August 1980 to comply with the Rajender Consent Decree. The Rajender Consent Decree was entered in federal court in 1980 as the result of a discrimination in hiring suit. Under the settlement agreement, each department of the University promulgated a policy which would ensure faculty and staff hiring practices which would not discriminate against women. However, the policy is acknowledged not only to prevent discrimination, but as the general hiring policy for the University. Administrative Policy 15 is the hiring policy for the Dental School.

Pine River establishes a four-part test for formation of a contract by terms arising after employment has begun: The terms must be (a) definite in form, (b) communicated to the offeree, (c) accepted by the offeree, and (d) enforceable by reason of adequate consideration.

(a) *Definite in Form*

The University claims that both the language and the stated intent of the constitution make it merely a general policy statement which is not sufficiently specific for contract language. Goodkind claims the applicable sections are very specific:

Article VI, Section G:

Recommendations for candidates to be Head(s) or Chairperson(s) of a Department shall be made to the President of the University by the Dean. *The candidates shall be selected from among those recommended by a Search Committee appointed by the Dean.*

Article II, Section B:

The Dean shall have the final authority to make recommendations to the President on appointment * * * of Head(s) or Chairperson(s) of Departments *following duly constituted consultative procedures in the School.*

Adding the emphasis noted above, the trial court declared the language to be specific enough to be part of a contract.

We agree. The quoted language has specificity similar to the handbook language in *Pine River.*

* * *

The University concedes that if the constitution and Policy 15 are a contract, then Goodkind has furnished consideration by continuing his employment for several years after they were adopted. We agree.

We are satisfied that the Dental School Constitution and Administrative Policy 15 are part of Dr. Goodkind's employment contract with the University.

II

Breach of Employment Contract

The trial court found that a breach of Dr. Goodkind's employment agreement occurred when the University failed to appoint him as the only person recommended by the search committee to the chair of the Fixed Prosthodontics Department. The court reached this determination by applying only the provisions of the Dental School Constitution. Because we conclude that Administrative Policy 15 is also a part of Goodkind's employment agreement, the provision on appointment of individuals recommended by the search committee is subject to some latitude, rather than the absolute terms contained in the Dental School Constitution.

We do not see the provisions of Administrative Policy 15 as conflicting with the constitution. The two documents can be read to be consistent with each other. Although only qualified candidates recommended by the search committee can be appointed, if the dean does not find the recommended candidates acceptable, a request may be made that the search be broadened or extended, or that a new search committee be appointed. However, even with this additional latitude, the undisputed evidence shows that the agreement was breached.

* * *

We cannot find that Dr. Goodkind is absolutely entitled to appointment. We note that he is a candidate in the renewed search and may be successful. However, we cannot overlook the fact that from September 1983 to the present Dr. Goodkind is the only person who was eligible for a term of more than one year. He was the only candidate recommended by the search committee. Because he is the only candidate who could fill the position and because the University's actions in not following their own regulations and policies prevented him from assuming this position, we believe that he is entitled to augmentation damages from July 1983 to the present, and affirm the trial court's award of damages.

Gertler v. Goodgold

487 N.Y.S.2d 565 (A.D. 1 Dept. 1985)

SULLIVAN, Justice Presiding.

Defendants appeal from the denial of their motion to dismiss the complaint or, alternatively, for summary judgment dismissing the complaint.

Plaintiff, a practicing physician and tenured faculty member in the Department of Rehabilitation Medicine of New York University School of Medicine, instituted this action against New York University, the New York University Medical Center, which includes the School of Medicine, and three medical doctors who are faculty members and administrators of the School of Medicine, whom he claims have, through a series of related incidents, "sought, without justification, to undermine [his] career and deprive him of the basic benefits and privileges of his academic tenure." He seeks to enjoin the relocation of his office within the Medical Center's Institute of Rehabilitation Medicine and to recover compensatory and punitive damages totalling $4,150,000.

Alleging that the University is "obligated to provide adequate amenities and fair administrative conduct and decisions to provide [plaintiff] with 'full freedom in research and in the publication of results,' " the complaint sets forth four causes of action—breach of contract, intentional interference with contractual relations, intentional interference with prospective economic advantage, and *prima facie* tort. It further alleges that through a pattern of discrimination plaintiff has been deprived of five supposed contractual concomitants of his tenure, *viz.*, adequate space for research, fair teaching assignments, non-discriminatory treatment, cooperation in allowing and promoting research grants under discernible procedures, and adequate grievance procedures fairly administered under reasonably certain standards. Defendants deny that those so-called contractual concomitants are elements of any contract, and point to the University's by-laws and other governing documents for a general description of the actual attributes of academic tenure.

In both the complaint and affidavit submitted in opposition to the motion plaintiff alleges that the pattern of discriminatory acts began with the denial of teaching assignments in 1973, when Dr. Goodgold, one of the three individual defendants herein, became director of research at the Institute of Rehabilitation Medicine. Although he still had his research and a staff to assist him, plaintiff alleges, defendants gradually began to deprive him of all his academic perquisites. For instance, Dr. Goodgold would often fail to notify him of scheduled meetings at which presentations were to be made for research funding; on other occasions he was given such short notice that he was unable to prepare adequately. As a result he was not given the opportunity to compete for grants on an equal basis with other staff members. In 1980 Dr. Goodgold allegedly attempted to prevent him from completing the application process for one grant and then, by a series of maneuvers, was able to undermine the application. In late 1980 and early 1981, according to plaintiff, defendants, without any prior discussion, withdrew their consent to a grant which had been approved by the National Institute of Health (NIH). At that time plaintiff filed an unsuccessful grievance, the review procedures of which he describes as a parody of due process.

In 1983 Dr. Goodgold allegedly effectively thwarted plaintiff's efforts to participate jointly in another NIH grant.

Plaintiff contends that this pattern of contractual breaches culminated in Dr. Goodgold's demand on April 2, 1984 that he and his five-person staff vacate, within 30 days, approximately 1720 square feet of office and work space they had occupied for the past 12 years on the second floor of the Medical Center's Institute of Rehabilitation Medicine to take less space on a part-time basis on the ground floor. Plaintiff was permitted, however, to keep his 1633 square feet of laboratory space. This relocation, he claims, will deprive him of the opportunity to conduct the advanced experiments in which he is engaged. Patients who furnish data for studies could not be seen, and his staff would certainly leave him. Thus, plaintiff contends, relocation would render meaningless his ability to research or teach—a basic tenet of academic freedom and the rationale underlying the tenure contract.

Three weeks after the demand that he vacate, plaintiff commenced this action and simultaneously sought *pendente lite* relief barring the relocation of his work space. Special Term denied the request for a preliminary injunction, and this court affirmed. In the interim defendants moved to dismiss the complaint for failure to state a cause of action and lack of subject matter jurisdiction, and on the further ground that plaintiff's claims are time-barred. In the alternative defendants sought summary judgment. Special Term denied the motion. Since we believe that the complaint fails to state a cause of action, we reverse and dismiss.

While the complaint recites a litany of academic and administrative grievances couched in terms of a violation of a contractual right to tenure or a tortious interference with that right, it is significantly devoid of any reference to the contractual basis of these privileges of tenure. For example, the main focus of the complaint is plaintiff's claim of a right to office space. This was the subject of his unsuccessful motion for a preliminary injunction. Yet, there is nothing in the complaint or the record to show that tenure guarantees a faculty member any office at all, much less space of his own choosing. As a matter of academic practice, according to the record, efforts are made to provide a faculty member with office space for his immediate needs, but offices are not awarded on the basis of seniority, experience or credentials.

Plaintiff premises his asserted contractual rights on the proposition that the notion of tenure is instinct with the obligation to provide faculty members with adequate research facilities, as well as other benefits commensurate with their position. While tenure is a concept of some elasticity and, no doubt, the source of many rights, it cannot be the wellspring of every conceivable academic amenity and privilege. Nor can the University's academic and administrative prerogatives be impliedly limited by custom, or by a strained theory of contractual construction. "[I]mplied promises are to be cautiously and not hastily raised." Indeed, the Court of Appeals has noted that "a promise can be implied only where we may rightfully assume that it would have been made if attention had been drawn to it . . . and that it is to be raised only to enforce a manifest equity, or to reach a result which the unequivocal acts of the parties indicate they intended to effect." This case is precisely the instance where such an assumption may not be made. The University has never expressly, by contract or otherwise, obligated itself to provide the amenities plaintiff claims, and thus has not relinquished its authority to make its own academic judgments and to administer and allocate its resources. The benefits which plaintiff seeks are undoubtedly perquisites of faculty life, but they are not contract entitlements. . . .

A Reasonable Expectation of Continued Employment, Tenure by Default, Defacto Tenure

Soni v. University of Tennessee

513 F.2d 347 (1975)

PHILLIPS, Chief Judge.

Dr. Raj P. Soni, a mathematics professor at the University of Tennessee, filed a complaint in the District Court alleging that he was denied procedural due process when the University failed to renew his teaching contract without giving him adequate notice or a hearing. District Judge Robert L. Taylor, sitting without a jury, held that Dr. Soni was entitled to a due process hearing and to back pay from the date of contract termination until the University provided such a hearing. The University appeals. We affirm.

Jurisdiction is invoked under 28 U.S.C. §§ 1331 and 1343(3).

Dr. Soni was born and reared in India. He attended an Indian university from which he received a Bachelor of Arts degree and a Master of Arts degree in mathematics. For several years Dr. Soni taught mathematics at the college level in India, and in 1959 he came to the United States to obtain his Ph.D. degree in mathematics from Oregon State University, which he received in 1963.

In September 1967, Dr. Soni joined the Mathematics Department of the University of Tennessee as a Visiting Associate Professor. At this time, Dr. Soni's teaching experience at the college level included six years as an instructor in India and one year as an Associate Professor at Oregon State University.

On several occasions during the 1967–1968 school year, Dr. Soni discussed with the then head of the Department of Mathematics, Professor John H. Barrett, the question of his being granted a permanent position at the University. At that time Dr. Soni was concerned about the permanency of his job status with the University and was interested in having a decision made one way or the other. As a result of these discussions, it was agreed between Dr. Soni and Professor Barrett that his visiting appointment would be extended for the 1968–1969 school year, and that a decision about a permanent appointment would be made in the fall of 1968.

On October 3, 1968, Professor Barrett issued "A recommendation for consideration by Professors and Associate Professors (with tenure)" regarding Dr. Soni and his wife, Mrs. Kusum Soni:

> "I recommend that Professor Raj Soni be offered an Associate Professorship with tenure.
>
> . . .
>
> Shortly after he arrived, he and I agreed that a two-year visiting position would be appropriate and that during this time we would consider him for a permanent position.
>
> . . .
>
> Since it is not possible for two people in the same family to have tenure in the same department, there is no question of tenure for Mrs. Soni. However, I recommend that we express our intention to keep her on the staff permanently."

Later that month Dr. Donald J. Dessart, who was appointed Acting Head of the Department of Mathematics when Professor Barrett became ill, called a special meeting of the Department's tenured faculty solely to consider approving Dr. Soni for a permanent appointment. At the meeting on October 29, 1968, Professor Dessart summarized the contents of Professor Barrett's memorandum recommending tenure for Dr. Soni. During the ensuing discussion, Professor Dessart pointed out that Dr. Soni was not a citizen of the United States and, consequently, could not be appointed formally to a permanent position in view of a University regulation and a state law, T.C.A. § 49-1303, providing that although aliens could be appointed to temporary positions at the University, they could not receive permanent appointments.

Because of the state law, the University regulation, and Dr. Soni's foreign citizenship, no formal vote was taken at the meeting on appointing Dr. Soni to a permanent faculty position with the University. Instead, Dr. Soni was changed from a Visiting Associate Professor to an Associate Professor for the 1969–1970 school year. Immediately following the special meeting, Dr. Soni was congratulated by those faculty members who had attended and was assured by his colleagues that the action taken at the meeting had been favorable.

Shortly thereafter, Dr. Soni received a letter dated October 29 from Professor Dessart stating in part as follows:

> [I]t was recommended that you be appointed an associate professor without tenure. . . . The question of recommending tenure will be considered by a similar departmental group at the time you become a citizen of the United States. In addition, it was recommended that you receive the full benefits of participation in TIAA/CREF at the first feasible opportunity. . . .

The TIAA/CREF is a financial retirement program at the University that was restricted at that time to "permanent type personnel."

In contrast to the congratulations of his colleagues, the October 29 letter seemed unfavorable and indefinite to Dr. Soni, and accordingly he sought out Professor Dessart for an explanation. Professor Dessart informed Dr. Soni that state law prohibited a grant of tenure to aliens, but he also gave assurances that the meeting in fact had been favorable, that the faculty wanted Dr. Soni to stay at the University, and that Dr. Soni's prospects with the University were good. According to Dr. Soni, he also was told that he would be treated like any other tenured professor.

Satisfied that his nontenured status was a matter of form necessitated by a technical state law, Dr. Soni purchased a home in the Knoxville area and stopped looking for employment elsewhere. He continued teaching at the University through the 1971–1972 school year, and on December 15, 1971, he became a naturalized United States citizen. During this time Dr. Soni was given no reason to believe that he was not a permanent member of the faculty. As stated above, Dr. Soni was permitted to participate in the University retirement program, which was ordinarily available only to permanent personnel. He attended departmental meetings and voted on tenure for other teachers, and he received further verbal assurances from his colleagues.

On March 8, 1972, however, Dr. Soni was notified that his appointment would be terminated as of August 31, 1973, because his performance as a teacher and as a research mathematician had "not been of the quality we expect of our tenured staff."

He was never granted a due process hearing as provided by the University's tenure policy.

1) *Reasonable Expectation of Continued Employment*

Judge Taylor found as a fact that despite Dr. Soni's awareness of the disqualifying statute,[1] "there existed sufficient objective evidence to vest in plaintiff a cognizable property interest in the form of a reasonable expectation of future and continued employment," within the meaning of Board of Regents v. Roth and Perry v. Sindermann.

The District Court further held that the University "objectively acted toward plaintiff in such a manner as to reasonably lead him to believe that he was a person with a relative degree of permanency in the academic community of this University. Upon acquiring this property interest, it cannot be terminated without procedural due process."

On the record before us, these findings cannot be held clearly erroneous, but to the contrary are supported by substantial evidence. Based on his findings, Judge Taylor correctly concluded that Dr. Soni's employment could not be terminated without notice and a hearing before an appropriate tribunal.

Appellants contend, however, that Dr. Soni could not have acquired a reasonable expectation of continued employment because the University of Tennessee had a well-established tenure system that would have prevented any expectancy from arising in a professor who had not been granted formal tenured status. We do not find this argument convincing. The Supreme Court has stated that a legitimate expectancy of continued employment "is particularly likely in a college or university . . . that has no explicit tenure system even for senior members of its faculty, but that nonetheless may have created such a system in practice." The Court did not say, as it easily could have, that a reasonable expectancy cannot arise in the context of a formal tenure system. The existence of such a system is but one factor for the trial court to consider in analyzing the due process claim of a formally nontenured professor.

In this case, we believe that Judge Taylor properly considered all of the circumstances of the employment relationship and correctly concluded that Dr. Soni "had a viable understanding that his employment would continue on a permanent basis with the Department of Mathematics, notwithstanding the statement contained in the October 29 correspondence that [Dr. Soni's] position was one without tenure."

* * *

The power to sue grants to the University the right to recover a money judgment. Consent to be sued inescapably subjects the University to the hazard of having a money judgment rendered against it.

---

1. This statute, T.C.A. § 49-1303, provides in part as follows:

> 49-1303. *Aliens as teachers—Advocating overthrow of government.*—It shall be unlawful for the trustees of the University of Tennessee, the state board of education, or any local board of education, or any other person to employ any superintendent, principal, teacher, tutor, supervisor, or other person to have in any way the custody and care of students of the public educational institutions of this state who is not a citizen of the United States of America; provided that nothing in this section shall be construed to prohibit arrangements whereby professors and teachers who are citizens of other nations may be employed on a temporary basis on the faculties of colleges, universities or public schools in Tennessee. . . .

The District Court did not pass on the constitutionality of this statute, and the issue is not before us now. We simply note that the validity of § 49-1303 is open to question.

We, therefore, conclude that the eleventh amendment does not bar the money judgment against the University in this case.

Accordingly, the judgment of the District Court is affirmed. The costs of this appeal are taxed against the University of Tennessee.

Willens v. University of Massachusetts
570 F.2d 403 (1978)

BOWNES, Circuit Judge.

Plaintiff Willens appeals from a summary judgment in favor of defendant on her denial of tenure claim. We are presented with three issues: (1) did the district court err in finding that plaintiff had no valid contract right to tenure; (2) did the court properly find that plaintiff had not been denied due process; and (3) did the court abuse its discretion in refusing to amend or alter the judgment?

If the court correctly determined that there was no genuine issue as to any material fact, and properly applied the appropriate legal standards, the judgment will be affirmed.

THE CONTRACT CLAIM

Plaintiff alleged below that she had established a right to tenure at the University of Massachusetts under a theory of de facto tenure. There was, however, uncontroverted sworn testimony that the University had not adopted the de facto tenure system alleged by plaintiff. Having thus established that there was no genuine issue on this material fact, the court entered summary judgment against plaintiff. We find no error. The district court, in finding no evidence to support plaintiff's allegation, also noted that the University's highly structured system of de jure tenure argued against a parallel system of de facto tenure. In the absence of any credible evidence to the contrary, we affirm.

The district court found that plaintiff forwarded only the de facto tenure system argument to support her contract claim to tenure. Plaintiff now raises before us for the first time a theory of estoppel *in pais*. While we need not consider this argument on appeal, we do observe that plaintiff has not cited any act or omission taken by the University upon which she could have *reasonably* relied. The sole basis for plaintiff's claim lies in the original May 1, 1967, letter of hire which indicated that she would receive two years' credit toward tenure and that her tenure decision year would be 1970–1971. This statement by the University, which was later corrected by the University prior to any time at which plaintiff's rights could have been prejudiced, is no basis for equitable estoppel. The record before us includes a copy of the Notification of Personnel Action for 1970–1971, which plaintiff signed on June 22, 1970, acknowledging her assent to the terms of the reappointment, which clearly states that her tenure decision year is 1972–1973. Subsequent forms similarly indicate this as the tenure decision year. In the absence of fraud, and none is alleged here, plaintiff is bound by the terms of that agreement. While plaintiff may have been confused by the inconsistent information she had received from the University administration, she could not reasonably have interpreted such information as indicating that she had unofficially been awarded tenure. As has been noted, the University of Massachusetts does not have a de facto tenure policy and plaintiff did not receive any affirmative notice that she had been awarded tenure. Either by virtue of an implied waiver or estoppel, plaintiff is foreclosed from maintaining that she remained at her teaching post at the University unwittingly believing that her tenure decision year was 1970–1971.

THE DUE PROCESS QUESTION

The district court ruled that plaintiff, as a year-to-year employee, enjoyed no property right to continued employment and that she had been denied no liberty interest by the University's refusal of tenure.

To prevail on her property claim, plaintiff would have to demonstrate that under state law she had a claim of entitlement to tenure which matured by 1970–1971. The district court specifically found that, because there was no de facto tenure system at the University, plaintiff had no right to tenure under Massachusetts law. Lacking a claim of entitlement under state law or justifiable expectations based on institutional practice, plaintiff has no property interest sufficient to invoke the Fourteenth Amendment's guarantee to due process.

Plaintiff alleges that her liberty interest has been infringed by the very denial of tenure itself and because of the stigma of being implicitly labelled "unscholarly." The district court found that neither allegation was such a stigma that it would trigger due process rights. The court observed that the reasons given by the University in denying plaintiff tenure were uncontradicted by her and did not involve any charge of dishonesty or moral turpitude. We agree with the court that the reasons given by the University, *viz.*, lack of scholarly publication during the eleven years since receiving her Masters degree and the duplication of her specialization within the French Department are not of the genre to pin a "badge of infamy" upon plaintiff. The Ninth Circuit has held that a label of inadequate performance on the part of an employee generally does not constitute an infringement of one's liberty interest. We need not adopt such a comprehensive rule to conclude that plaintiff's liberty interest has not been impaired in this case. Due process does not protect an individual from essentially neutral evaluations that do not cast aspersions on her ability to perform her duties competently. Moreover, in this case, the University in no way publicized its decision.

The reasons given by the University for denying plaintiff tenure were uncontroverted. There being no genuine controversy as to the facts, we agree with the district court that the reasons were not arbitrary or capricious. We, therefore, need not and do not reach the question of whether a claim to substantive due process can stand in the absence of a finding of a constitutionally protected property or liberty interest.

Hill v. Talladega College
502 So. 2d 735 (Ala. 1987)

TORBERT, Chief Justice.

Linda Hill, Belinda G. Heglar, and Howard L. Rogers were employed as teachers at Talladega College, a private institution, under employment contracts with a term of one year, extending from August 1984 to August 1985. In May 1985, they received letters terminating their employment with the college. The letter to Hill is typical of these letters:

"Dear Dr. Hill:

"By now you have been apprised of a number of changes taking place at the College. As a result, I have been instructed to inform you that your services at the College shall no longer be required. It is with deep regret and sincere appreciation of your contributions that this step is taken. Please be advised that such action is consistent with policies established by the Board of Trustees.

"Attached, you will find procedures for your clearance, if you have not already completed the process.

> Sincerely,
> s/Joseph E. Thompson
> Joseph E. Thompson
> Academic Dean"

Shortly after receiving these letters, the teachers filed separate suits against the college and its president, Paul B. Mohr, Sr., alleging a breach of their employment contracts and wrongful termination. The court granted summary judgment for the defendants in each case, and the plaintiffs appealed. We have consolidated these three cases for the purpose of writing one opinion. We affirm the judgment of the trial court in each of these cases.

The primary issues raised by the plaintiffs on this appeal all concern the effect to be given the *Procedural Standards in Faculty Dismissal Proceedings* promulgated by the American Association of University Professors (AAUP). These standards establish relatively elaborate procedural safeguards that must be followed before a professor can be fired. These procedures are to be followed "[w]hen reason arises to question the fitness of a college or university faculty member who has tenure or whose term appointment has not expired. . . . "

The plaintiffs argue that these standards were incorporated within their employment contracts and that the college's failure to follow these procedures gives rise to a claim for breach of contract and wrongful termination. In essence, the plaintiffs assert that the standards apply to their cases because the standards, by their terms, apply to any non-tenured teacher "whose term appointment has not expired." In view of the fact that the receipt of their termination letters preceded their contracts' August expiration dates, the plaintiffs insist that a genuine issue of material fact was established in support of their cases, precluding the trial court's grant of summary judgment in favor of the defendants.

The AAUP standards are neither expressly a part of, nor referenced in, the plaintiffs' written contracts of employment. However, the plaintiffs argue that references to these standards in a faculty handbook and other college documents operate to incorporate the AAUP guidelines within their formal contracts of employment. We need not consider here, however, the plaintiffs' many arguments in support of this theory. Like the trial court, we feel that these standards are inapplicable to the facts of this case, even if the standards were incorporated within the contracts at issue. Assuming, therefore, but not deciding, that the AAUP standards are a part of the plaintiffs' contracts, we will proceed with our analysis of this case.

Initially, we note that our review of a trial court's ruling on a motion for summary judgment is limited to the same factors that were considered by the trial court in making its decision. Our reasoning, however, is not limited to that applied by the trial court. "[T]he judgment of the trial court will be upheld if the court's holding is correct, despite the fact that our reasons are different from those stated by the trial court." Accordingly, we will turn to the materials that were before the trial court when it ruled on the motions and to the precedent and rules of law that we hold applicable to this case.

It is well established that "[s]ummary judgment is appropriate in a breach of contract action where the contract is unambiguous and the facts undisputed."

We hold that the contracts in these cases, including the AAUP standards "incorporated" therein for the purposes of this decision, are unambiguous as a matter of law. Specifically, it is clear from the title of the standards and the language contained in their provisions that the standards apply only to *dismissals* of college or university faculty members. Moreover, we think it self-evident that the ordinary meaning of the word "dismissal" forecloses the application of these standards to this case, as the following discussion will show.

By definition, tenured faculty are entitled to continuing employment, and a "dismissal" obviously takes place whenever tenured teachers are fired. On the other hand, the nature of a term contract is far different. Such a contract will by definition lapse at the completion of the time for performance, and the teacher serving under such a contract generally has no legally enforceable entitlement to continued employment beyond the contract's stated term. Assuming that all obligations under such a contract are performed, the parties cannot be said to have been "dismissed" when their respective performances have been completed. The contract simply matures and dies, and the parties are then free to do as they please. The only time a party may properly be said to have been "dismissed" under a term contract is when that contract is cancelled before its stated termination date. Only in that situation are the contractual expectations of the parties disturbed.

Therefore, we think it clear in both logic and law that the AAUP dismissal standards apply to term contracts only when the "dismissal" represents an attempt to cancel an established, ongoing contractual relationship. We think that is the plain meaning of the statement that the standards will apply to a faculty member "whose term appointment has not expired." If the obligations under the term appointment are fulfilled, then the standards are not implicated. Each party has gotten what he bargained for, and neither has "dismissed" the other.

There is no genuine issue of material fact as to whether the plaintiffs were "dismissed" in this case. They were not. While the plaintiffs refer repeatedly in their brief to their May "terminations" and treat these letters as though they cancelled the existing contracts, the evidence presented to the trial court is to the contrary. The affidavits of Paul B. Mohr, the president of the college, unequivocally state that each of the plaintiffs was paid in full for his or her services under the contracts, and Mohr further characterizes each of these letters as a "notice of non-renewal." In short, it appears from Mohr's affidavits that the effect of the letters was to inform the plaintiffs that they would not be re-hired for the next academic year, and not that the plaintiffs were "dismissed" from the existing contracts. Additional documents and affidavits characterizing the college's actions as giving notice of non-renewal also appear in the record. Moreover, none of the plaintiffs' answering affidavits denies or contradicts either Mohr's statements or this other evidence in this regard.

In summary, we find that the AAUP standards are unambiguous as a matter of law; that they apply only to "dismissals," as that word is commonly applied; and that no such "dismissal" occurred in this case. Rather than being "dismissed," the plaintiffs were instead given notice of non-renewal of their term contracts. Therefore, there appears to be no genuine issue of material fact regarding this issue, and the plaintiffs could not recover on their complaint as a matter of law. The "contracts" the plaintiffs so vigorously champion have not been breached on the instant facts.

* * *

Plaintiff Rogers also contends on this appeal that he is a tenured faculty member. Thus, he claims he is entitled to the AAUP dismissal procedures on this ground as well as those advanced above. Rogers claims that, although he was not the recipient of "formal" tenure, he had achieved "de facto" tenured status, largely as a result of his being employed for 10 years at the college and his reliance on an additional group of AAUP standards.

The faculty handbook noted earlier also states that the college's tenure policies would conform with a provision of the *Principles of Academic Freedom and Tenure* of the AAUP. This provision, as reproduced in the faculty handbook, provides that

> "[b]eginning with appointment to the rank of full-time instructor or a higher rank, the probationary period should not exceed seven years, including within this period full-time service in all institutions of higher education; but subject to the proviso that when, after a term of probationary service of more than three years in one or more institutions, a teacher is called to another institution it may be agreed in writing that his new appointment is for a probationary period of not more than four years, even though thereby the person's total probationary period in the academic profession is extended beyond the normal maximum of seven years."

Rogers argues that this provision was also incorporated within his contract. Therefore, he asserts that his employment for over ten years establishes a genuine issue of material fact—whether he had de facto tenure—and he argues that the trial court erred in granting summary judgment on this issue. We disagree.

We note initially that the AAUP standard at issue here is not absolute on its face. It does not unequivocally state that tenure shall be granted after seven years of employment; rather, it states that tenure *should* be granted after seven years, and it later refers to seven years as the "normal" maximum probationary period. Therefore, we are not convinced that this statement alone would create an expectation that tenure would be granted after seven years of service.

Moreover, unlike that portion of the faculty handbook which arguably incorporates intact the AAUP dismissal standards, that portion of the handbook noting the tenure provision promulgated by the AAUP contains additional and unambiguous limiting language. Two caveats appear on the same page with the cited reference:

1) "Permanent tenure is extended only to persons who are specifically elected by the Board [of Trustees]...."

2) "It should be understood that the acquisition of tenure or of promotion at Talladega College is not automatic after seven years of teaching...."

As noted previously, summary judgment is proper where the contract is unambiguous and the facts are not in dispute. Assuming, without deciding, that this additional AAUP standard was also incorporated into the plaintiff's contract, we hold that the proposed contract unambiguously provides that such tenure could be granted only by specific action on the part of the Board of Trustees, and that the "seven year" provision is, by its terms, a non-mandatory provision, especially as limited by the subsequent caveat. Thus, no "de facto" tenure as such could arise under the terms of this "contract." The trial court was therefore correct in granting summary judgment against Rogers, there being no evidence before it of any specific action with respect to Rogers's tenured status on the part of the Board of Trustees.

We think the above discussion resolves the issues relating to the plaintiffs' contract claims. Of necessity, it also disposes of their claims for wrongful termination. If there was no breach of the underlying contracts, then no "terminations" occurred, and, thus, no causes of action for "wrongful termination" arose. The trial court, therefore, was not in error in granting summary judgment on these claims.

Likewise, the plaintiffs' argument that President Mohr acted in his individual capacity, and not as an agent of the college, is also foreclosed by the above analysis. If no cause of action arose on the facts set forth in the court below, then Mohr's personal liability is not an issue. The trial court, therefore, did not err in granting summary judgment in favor of Mohr.

We have carefully considered the other arguments and issues advanced by the plaintiffs, and we find that they are either without merit or are resolved by the discussion set forth above.

For the foregoing reasons, we affirm the three judgments of the trial court.

AFFIRMED.

Honore v. Douglas
833 F.2d 565 (5th Cir. 1987)

Politz, Circuit Judge.

Background

Honore was employed as an assistant, then associate, professor of law by TSU from June 1, 1974 until May 31, 1984. After serving four academic years, 1974–1978, Honore was granted three consecutive one-year leaves of absence to serve in the Peace Corps. He returned to full-time teaching in 1981, continuing until TSU declined to grant tenure status and terminated him three years later.

In 1981 when Honore returned to the law school after service with the Peace Corps, the Rank and Tenure Committee of the law school recommended that he be promoted to associate professor and recognized as having tenure, based on his four years of teaching and three years of authorized leave. When Honore was first employed in 1974, controlling University regulations provided for tenure at the end of seven years. The record indicates that this regulation was interpreted as being self-effective and automatic. There was a dispute whether a period of authorized leave would be accruable time. Honore was promoted, but the TSU regents did not extend tenure. Because Honore was then a member of the Rank and Tenure Committee, he maintained that he chose not to contest the disputed tenure question at that time.

In 1978 University regulations affecting tenure were changed to delete the provision allowing automatic vesting of tenure after seven years' service. The provisions of the 1978 manual require the law school and university representatives to address a petition for tenure initially, with the Board of Regents retaining ultimate decisional authority. Those provisions further require notification of the nontenured faculty member, by May 31 of the sixth probationary year, that the seventh year will be the final year of employment unless tenure is sought and secured.

On February 13, 1983, the dean of the law school notified Honore that the next year would be his last unless he became tenured. Insisting that he had automatic tenure under the 1974 regulations, Honore sought formal confirmation of that status. The faculty Rank and Tenure Committee unanimously recommended tenure. The dean objected to Honore's tenure, and the Board of Regents rejected the application. Honore sought review by a faculty hearing committee which received sworn testimony and documentary evidence, including the testimony of Honore, the dean, the former legal counsel for the university who had drafted the 1978 regulations at issue, as well as other members of the faculty tenure committee. The faculty hearing committee recommended that Honore be granted tenure. Its recommendation was rejected, however, by the TSU president and regents.

The record reflects that following his return from the Peace Corps assignment, Honore was active and vocal in law school affairs; and he was directly involved in a number of disputes with the dean. Prior to and about the time of the February 1983 tenure-notice letter, Honore had protested actions by the dean, signed grievance letters, and participated in a meeting of 18 of the 22 members of the faculty where 12, including Honore, expressed a lack of confidence in the dean. The other six abstained from voting. Among items of controversy were the law school admissions policy, the size of the student population, administration of the school budget, and the failure to certify graduates for the Texas bar examination in a timely fashion.

Following the rejection of his tenure petition, Honore filed the instant suit seeking equitable and monetary relief, alleging due process and first amendment violations, and pendent state-law claims. Shortly prior to trial the court considered the matter on motion for summary judgment, found no genuine issue of material fact, and concluded that defendants were entitled to judgment as a matter of law. Honore appeals.

* * *

However, despite this finding of procedural adequacy, we do not agree with the trial court's rejection of the substantive due process claim. To reach the jury with his substantive due process claim, Honore must demonstrate a genuine issue of material fact about his protected property interest (entitlement to vested tenure) and the university's arbitrary or capricious deprivation of that interest.

The trial court concluded that Honore had presented insufficient evidence to create a genuine issue relating to his claim to automatic tenure. It found that Honore had offered no evidence to support his claim of legitimate entitlement to automatic tenure other than an ambiguous "impression of support" from the dean of the law school. The court stated that Honore had not contended that the 1974 regulations, arguably providing for automatic tenure, applied to his case; and it concluded that his 1983 petition formally seeking a declaration of tenure belied his alleged understanding that automatic tenure vested in 1981.

We disagree with these conclusions. In his pleadings Honore made repeated references to regulations in force when he began work in 1974. He claimed the benefit of those regulations. The transcript before the faculty hearing committee contains sufficient evidence to create a jury issue that Honore was claiming automatic tenure under the regulations in effect in 1974, that those regulations were self-effectuating, vesting automatic tenure after seven years of teaching, and that authorized leave time counted as teaching time. Under that scenario, if it be accepted, after Honore taught for four years, was on authorized leaves of absence for three years, and returned to work in 1981 for the eighth year, he was entitled to tenure.

The transcript also contains the testimony of the former counsel for the university, an attorney who drafted the 1978 regulations which changed the tenure requirements. He attested to the nonretroactivity of the 1978 regulations and stated that the earlier regulations controlled the rights of those hired prior to 1978. That witness, a member and former chairman of the faculty tenure committee, was of the opinion that Honore was vested with tenure upon his return from the Peace Corps assignment. Honore testified that it was not until 1983 that he became aware of the 1978 regulations which had been adopted while he was away. He maintains that his first notice came when he received the February 1983 letter from the dean. He testified that he applied to the Rank and Tenure Committee solely for administrative recognition of the tenure previously acquired in 1981. The record reflects genuine issues of material fact regarding these matters. Resolution of these factual disputes will involve credibility assessments. Such evaluations may not be made in a summary judgment setting.

We are persuaded that Honore has created a genuine issue concerning his "legitimate claim of entitlement" based on "mutually explicit understandings." He has offered sufficient evidence to reach the trier of fact on the claim that the 1974 regulations created a reasonable understanding that tenure would automatically vest in 1981 if he continuously remained on the law school faculty.

Moreover, the record contains indicators of arbitrary and capricious deprivation. The dean of the law school conceded that he told Honore that his teaching performance was adequate. Honore testified that neither the dean nor any other law school authority ever questioned his teaching performance. He supported his academic credentials with activities generally accepted as reflective of legal scholarship. In addition to publication of writings in legal journals, those activities included beginning a law review program at TSU, training TSU law students for moot court competition, chairing two faculty committees, and, most significantly, establishing a research and writing program designed to assist minority law students at TSU and teaching a similar course at Washburn University. This testimony, alone or in combination with circumstantial evidence of impermissible retaliatory motive (discussed *infra*), creates a genuine issue of material fact as to the arbitrary and capricious nature of Honore's dismissal.

We are mindful of the Supreme Court's admonishment in *Bishop v. Wood* that a federal court is generally not the appropriate forum in which to review the multitude of personnel decisions that are made daily by public agencies. This measure of judicial restraint, however, does not require slavish deference to a university's arbitrary deprivation of a vested property right. Honore is entitled to a jury resolution of his substantive due process claim.

* * *

[The Court of Appeals, Politz, Circuit Judge, held that: (1) professor was not deprived of procedural due process rights; (2) genuine issue of material fact whether professor's substantive due process rights were violated precluded grant of summary judgment; and (3) genuine issue of material fact regarding whether professor was terminated on basis of exercise of free speech also precluded grant of summary judgment.]

Vacated and remanded.

———————

P. Carpenter v. Board of Education

514 N.Y.S.2d 264 (A.D. 2 Dept. 1987)

* * *

Memorandum by the Court.

It is undisputed that the petitioner served as a regular substitute teacher in the employ of the appellants beginning September 1, 1982. He became a probationary teacher on February 28, 1983, and continued to work in that capacity until his employment was terminated, effective February 27, 1985. It is also conceded that the petitioner had received tenure as a teacher in a different school district prior to his employment with the appellants. We agree with Special Term that under these circumstances the petitioner's probationary term expired on September 1, 1984. Since the appellants permitted him to continue to teach subsequent to that time, they acquiesced in his obtaining tenure.

Our conclusion that the petitioner's probationary term expired on September 1, 1984, is based upon the provisions of Education Law § 2509(1)(a). As a teacher who had previously been granted tenure by a different school district, the petitioner's probationary term could be no longer than two years, pursuant to the terms of that statute. Furthermore, pursuant to the construction placed upon that statute by the Commissioner of Education, with the approval of the Court of Appeals, the one-half year period of time during which the petitioner served as a regular substitute teacher must be counted as part of the two-year probationary term.

We reject the appellants' argument that the credit given to the petitioner on account of his service as a regular substitute teacher, commonly referred to as "Jarema credit," may not serve to lessen the petitioner's statutory two-year probationary term, although that credit would concededly serve to reduce an ordinary three-year term applicable to probationary teachers who, unlike the petitioner, had never received tenure with a different school district. Absolutely no distinction exists between ordinary probationary teachers, on the one hand, and probationary teachers who have previously been tenured on the other, which would rationalize a rule allowing the former class of teachers to benefit from "Jarema credit," but not the latter. Just this sort of irrational distinction would result if we were to accept the construction of the statute urged upon us by the appellants.

* * *

Lewis v. Loyola University of Chicago

500 N.E.2d 47 (Ill. App. 1 Dist. 1986)

McGillicuddy, J.

In June 1979, plaintiff was approached by defendant's search committee for consideration as chairman of the pathology department of defendant's Stritch School of Medicine. Negotiations ensued over several months. On September 20, 1979, Dean Clarence N. Peiss sent plaintiff a letter outlining the terms of an offer. The letter was written in the form of numbered paragraphs. It addressed staffing, salary (including an administrative stipend and practice plan supplement), departmental space allocations and funding, and tenure. Specifically, paragraph 8 included a commitment to recommend plaintiff for early tenure consideration at the first opportunity after his licensure by the Illinois State Board of Registration and Education. Dr. Lewis replied by letter with some questions and the negotiations continued.

On February 18, 1980, Dean Peiss sent plaintiff a second letter. The letter was in the same format as the letter of September 20, updating certain paragraphs and leaving others "as stated in the September 20, 1979 memo." In the February 18 letter, paragraph 8 read: "On the assumption that both you and the medical school administration will be satisfied in this relationship, I will propose early approval of tenure for you in September 1981." The letter also stated that if plaintiff accepted the offer, Dean Peiss would submit his recommendation to the committee on faculty appointments and a formal letter of appointment would be sent to him.

Plaintiff received the letter of appointment dated May 14, 1980. The letter was a one-page document listing plaintiff's teaching salary and administrative stipend, and appointing him as professor of pathology for the period July 1, 1980 through June 30, 1981. The letter of appointment incorporated by reference the faculty handbook included with the letter. The transmittal letter accompanying these documents detailed plaintiff's salary, including a supplement of $48,000 per year under the Loyola Medical Practice Plan (LMPP). Plaintiff accepted the chairmanship and signed the letter of appointment on June 19, 1980.

The following year plaintiff accepted a letter of appointment as professor of pathology for the period July 1, 1981 through June 30, 1982. In April 1982, Dean Peiss resigned to return to full-time teaching. On April 15, 1982, plaintiff was sent a letter of appointment for the period July 1, 1982 through June 30, 1983. On May 19, 1982, plaintiff received a letter relieving him of his duties as department chairman effective May 19, 1982, and, on May 25, plaintiff was advised that his 1982–83 faculty contract was terminal and that his appointment would not be renewed after June 30, 1983.

Dean Peiss failed to submit plaintiff's name for tenure consideration in September 1981. Plaintiff testified that in the fall of 1981, he received a telephone call from the dean who told him he had forgotten to present plaintiff's name for tenure. When plaintiff asked whether that made any difference, or whether there was a problem, Dean Peiss assured him that it was an oversight and plaintiff's name would be submitted for tenure the following year. Dean Peiss' testimony corroborated plaintiff's impression that Dean Peiss had been busy and had forgotten to submit the name. Although as department chairman, plaintiff could have submitted his own name for tenure consideration, he testified that he did not think it was his place to do so and further, that after being reassured by Dean Peiss that it would be done routinely at the next available opportunity, he believed there was no need to take any action himself.

* * *

In the instant case, the record discloses conversations, meetings and correspondence over a period of a year. It cannot seriously be argued that a form contract for a teaching position, albeit personalized with plaintiff's name and an additional sum described as compensation for administrative duties, embodied the complete agreement and understanding of the parties. Nothing in the form contract reflects the position plaintiff accepted, with its attendant considerations of staffing, long and short-term funding or physical space. Indeed, even the letter of transmittal, which defendant would also exclude from consideration, reflects part of plaintiff's compensation for participation in the LMPP, which is not covered in the formal letter of appointment.

In his letters to plaintiff, Dean Peiss stated that should plaintiff accept the offer as outlined, a formal letter of appointment would be forthcoming. We believe that this evidences the requisite intent that the letter of September 20, 1979, as modified by the letter of February 18, 1980, was part of the contract and not merely negotiation. We therefore agree with the trial court that the letters were properly considered as part of the employment contract.

Defendant next contends that the trial court's finding that plaintiff would have been tenured pursuant to the terms of the employment contract was manifestly erroneous. Defendant first argues that the letter of appointment and faculty handbook govern the granting of tenure and nothing in those documents constitutes a promise to plaintiff of tenure. Our determination above that the parties' contract includes the letters from Dean Peiss promising to recommend tenure in September 1981 renders further discussion of this argument unnecessary.

Defendant also maintains that even if the letters are part of the contract, those promises do not constitute a guarantee of tenure. Rather, defendant argues, they are expressions of goodwill and are not an enforceable promise creating a contractual obligation on the defendant's part to grant tenure.

It is undisputed that plaintiff was not tenured at the time of his termination, nor does plaintiff contend that Dean Peiss could have granted him tenure himself. The evidence adduced at trial, however, established that plaintiff's name was not submitted for tenure in 1981 solely because of an oversight, and that Dean Peiss, as the trial court noted in its order, acknowledged the error and pledged to correct it the following year. There was also testimony to the effect that objective criteria are used when considering whether to grant tenure and that plaintiff met those standards. Although defendant's provost, Richard Matre, testified that occasionally a dean's recommendation is denied tenure, he conceded that it was an uncommon situation. It is the province of the trial court, when sitting without a jury, to resolve disputed questions of fact and to determine the credibility of witnesses and the weight to be accorded their testimony, and we will not substitute our judgment thereon unless the opposite conclusion is clearly evident. Indeed, the trial court's findings will not be disturbed in a non-jury case where the testimony is contradictory unless those findings are contrary to the manifest weight of the evidence. We believe that the evidence detailed above amply supports the trial court's finding that plaintiff would have been tenured pursuant to the contract but for Dean Peiss' oversight. The court's finding was not against the manifest weight of the evidence.

Defendant also contends that the trial court's award of damages was speculative and improper. The proper measure of damages is the contract price, less what the employee earned or could have earned. In Illinois, however, the damages awarded upon breach of an employment contract are limited to such damages as plaintiff may have accrued up to the date of trial, and damages beyond that date are disallowed due to their speculative and uncertain nature. In the present case, the trial court awarded $36,492 for damages plaintiff sustained during the year ending June 30, 1984, and accruing up to the time of trial. These damages were properly awarded.

* * *

Here, plaintiff's losses subsequent to the date of trial are highly speculative for several reasons. The $100,000 awarded by the trial court apparently derives from the $48,000 faculty salary defendant paid plaintiff in the 1982–1983 academic year, and the $52,000 he received from the LMPP. The future faculty salary is speculative because plaintiff might have quit before reaching age 65; or defendant might have terminated his employment for cause or for financial exigency. Moreover, plaintiff's base teaching salary was subject to annual decreases, and there was no evidence that defendant uses faculty salary schedules, guaranteed pay increases, or Federal cost-of-living index adjustments. Instead, faculty salaries are negotiated annually depending on merit and budgetary considerations. Some tenured faculty receive raises, others receive reductions, and others remain the same. Any basis for determining plaintiff's teaching salary following the date of trial, therefore, is highly speculative.

* * *

In sum, we find that the evidence supports the trial court's finding that defendant breached its employment contract with plaintiff, and that the trial court properly entered judgment in the amount of $36,492 for damages incurred to the date of trial. We hold, however, that the trial court erred in awarding damages beyond the date of trial.

For the foregoing reasons, the judgment of the circuit court of Cook County is affirmed in part and reversed in part. The cause is remanded with directions to enter judgment in accordance with the holdings of this opinion.

Tenure and Race

Scott v. University of Delaware
455 F. Supp. 1102 (1978)

Stapleton, District Judge.

* * *

[Of] the 26 full time black faculty at the University since 1965 other than Dr. Scott, four were tenured or close to tenure at the time of trial. One other had left after she had been recommended for promotion. Three were visiting professors who stayed for only one year. One retired after being on the faculty for five years. Two left after three years service; two left after two years service; and five left after only one year of service. There is no evidence that any of these nine black faculty members left other than voluntarily.

Of the ten non-tenured blacks on the faculty at the time of trial, two were in their sixth year of service, three were in their fifth year of service; one was in her fourth year; two were in their third year; and two were in their second year.

II. THE DISPARATE TREATMENT CLAIM.

Relying primarily on *McDonald v. Santa Fe Trail Transportation Co.*, Dr. Scott asserts that because of his race he was denied an equal opportunity to qualify for a tenured faculty position at the University. In support of this contention he relies primarily upon evidence that other non-black professors were reevaluated for renewal in the third year of their initial contract and/or were renewed for additional periods and thus afforded greater opportunity to qualify for tenure. In order to make the comparison which plaintiff invites, further facts are necessary concerning Dr. Scott and several other faculty members.

A. *Scott.*

Scott began his service at the University in September of 1971. As of that date, his experience included eight years of teaching at a Canadian university and three years as a part-time graduate teaching assistant at Penn State. Scott acknowledges that at the time of the commencement of his service to the Sociology Department, he knew that teaching and scholarship were two of the three criteria considered in renewal and tenure decisions in the Sociology Department. He likewise acknowledges that he expected to be reviewed for possible renewal of his three year contract in the spring of 1973. I am confident that Dr. Scott had learned at least shortly after his arrival on campus of the departmental emphasis on scholarly research and publication.

In March of 1973 Dr. Scott was informed that he should complete his dossier for evaluation by April 16, 1973. On May 1, 1973, the Sociology Department faculty met. The faculty believed that there was inadequate evidence of research activity to be evaluated in the dossier, and Scott was asked to prepare an addendum regarding his scholarly achievements. On May 3, 1973, the faculty senior to Scott met and recommended a denial of renewal. On May 8, 1973, the full Sociology Department faculty met and voted against renewal 9 to 1, with 2 abstentions. As a result, Scott's service to the University was terminated when his contract expired after the 1973–4 year.

On May 9, 1973, Chairman Scarpitti wrote to Scott notifying him of the Department's recommendation and setting forth the reasoning which led to that recommendation. The letter stated in part:

> * * * It was the consensus of the department faculty that your performance in the areas of teaching and scholarship have been below the standard that we wish to maintain in the department. In the area of service we found your performance to be adequate, although here there was some mixed feeling. It is not the faculty's belief, however, that an adequate performance in the area of service is enough to compensate for perceived deficiencies in the areas of teaching and scholarship.

The letter then went on to comment on the perceived deficiencies in Scott's teaching effectiveness and scholarship. It spoke of persistent complaints by a large number of Dr. Scott's students about lack of preparation, class time wasted with extraneous discussion, and the inhibiting of expression of student opinion, etc. It also noted Scott's prior teaching experience and the faculty's view that he should have been able to demonstrate more teaching effectiveness than he had after ten years of teaching. On the subject of scholarship, the letter observed:

> The difficulty we perceive in your teaching is compounded by the faculty's elief that you do not show the necessary promise in research and publishing. Your scholarly activities in the two years you have been on our faculty have been very limited. Indeed, to this date, no specific research has been undertaken by you with the aim toward scholarly publication. Your plans for the future were found to be imprecise and generally inadequate.

The letter concluded with an offer by Scarpitti to do whatever he could to help Scott locate a new position.

In the fall of 1973, Scott underwent open heart surgery and was on sick leave for the entire first semester. He returned to teach Introduction to Sociology and American

Minorities in the spring of 1974. He left the University upon the expiration of his contract on August 31, 1974.

It is clear from the record that from September of 1971 until the time of his evaluation for contract renewal, Scott had undertaken very little in the way of research and had produced nothing by way of scholarly publication. Moreover, he had nothing of substance underway or planned at the time of the May 1973 decision on renewal. These deficiencies weighed heavily against him in the minds of most of the Sociology faculty.

Dr. Scarpitti had evaluated Scott's effectiveness as a teacher on two occasions prior to the renewal evaluation, once on November 29, 1971, and once on November 14, 1972. In 1971, Scott was assigned values of 4 on a scale of 10 for effectiveness as an undergraduate teacher and effectiveness as an undergraduate advisor. In 1972, values of 6 were assigned for those categories. While this was described as a "marked" improvement over the preceding year by the Chairman in his written comments, no member of the Sociology faculty received a lower grade in these categories in 1972.

During Scott's first year and the spring of his second, Chairman Scarpitti and other members of the faculty received numerous complaints from their advisees and other students of the kinds described in Scarpitti's letter. There was also a Student Government Association course evaluation in the fall of 1971, which rated Scott's "Social Problems" course. In that student evaluation, only 29% of the class responded (35 of 120). 45.5% of those responding believed that the lectures contained mainly irrelevant materials. 55.9% believed that the course had not contributed to their growth or development. 70.5% felt Scott, as a teacher, was "below average" or a "bummer." Finally, 81.2% said they would not recommend Scott as a professor.

With respect to service activity, the Chairman's evaluation in 1972 acknowledges that he was engaging in a great deal of service activity both on and off the campus. Among other activities Scott served as Chairman of the Education Committee of the Wilmington Branch of the NAACP.

*   *   *

F. Analysis.

The ultimate decision to be made in any racial discrimination case where the plaintiff makes a claim of disparate treatment is whether it is reasonable to infer from all the evidence that the challenged action was based in whole or in part upon race. Hence, the question is whether the non-renewal of Scott's contract or the failure to reevaluate him in his third year was based in whole or in part on his race. If the non-racially based reasons advanced for these actions (or failure to act) were in fact what occasioned them, there is no basis for liability on the disparate treatment claim. If they were mere pretext, however, for a racially motivated decision, relief must be fashioned.

This focus must be kept in mind in determining how much similarity between the situations of different faculty members make them "comparable" for purposes of applying the doctrine of McDonald and McDonnell Douglas. These cases speak of ways "to evaluate the evidence in light of common experience as it bears on the critical question of discrimination." The closer the situations of two employees of different races who are treated differently, the more compelling is the inference that race played a role in the disparate treatment. But the ultimate question is whether, drawing the reasonable inferences from all the evidence, it appears that the plaintiff was treated differently from other employees due to his race.

Based on all the evidence, I conclude that the failure of the University to renew Scott's contract resulted from the opinion of nine members of the Sociology Department that he was not, and would not develop into, an acceptable permanent professional colleague. This opinion was based primarily on what they considered to be a demonstrated lack of interest in pursuing the kind of scholarship, research and writing which they thought to be significant, and secondarily, on the view that one with the teaching experience which Scott had should have developed greater effectiveness in relating with students.

* * *

The uniform view, which I accept as an accurate reflection of the opinions which motivated the non-renewal decision, was that Scott was not the kind of "sociologist's sociologist" the department was looking for. He appeared to lack either the interest or discipline necessary to do the kind of research and publication that they were interested in and, indeed, Scott recognized this at the time. In February of 1973, for example, he told Professor James (who was then seeking a job at the University) that he did not feel his interests matched the University's and the Department's interests and that he did not perceive himself as writing the kind of scholarly journal articles that were required. While some of Scott's colleagues felt that his teaching had improved during his stay at the University, they believed it was substantially below what should be expected for the amount of his experience. Finally, while they acknowledged Scott's interest in community service, some considered the service concept to relate solely to making one's professional skills available to the community and did not feel that Scott was serving the community in the capacity of sociologist.

Besides the comparative evidence just discussed, plaintiff sets forth a list of miscellaneous supportive evidence indicating discrimination against Scott. I do not believe, however, that any of this evidence fairly leads to the conclusion that Scott was not renewed, or that he was not given an opportunity for improvement, for racial reasons. These pieces of evidence include the receipt by Scott of hate mail, some clearly racially motivated, a student complaint that Scott was seen lying drunk on the ground with a whiskey bottle in his hand, and a remark by Dr. DiRenzo of the Sociology Department at a 1971 faculty meeting referring to the hiring of Scott and using the words "window dressing." While some of this evidence is indicative of racial prejudice on the University campus, it does not suggest to me that Scott was a victim of racial discrimination by the University in its renewal process, or that he was treated differently than non-black faculty by the University.

Dr. Scott's disparate treatment claim is without merit.

III. THE DISPARATE IMPACT CLAIM.

Plaintiff asserts on behalf of the class that the employment practices of the University have had, and continue to have, a disparate impact upon blacks in the areas of hiring, contract renewal, promotion and tenure. This Court is asked to declare these practices to be in violation of Title VII of the Civil Rights Act of 1964, as amended, 42 U.S.C. § 2000e, et seq., and the Civil Rights Acts of 1886 and 1871, 42 U.S.C. §§ 1981 and 1983. The relief which plaintiff seeks is an order requiring that one of every three new faculty hires at all levels at the University (e.g. Assistant Professor, Associate Professor, etc.) shall be black until such time as blacks make up 12.5% of the total faculty.

Plaintiff makes two arguments in support of his claim of disparate impact. First, it is said that the University's use of a doctoral degree criterion has a disparate impact upon blacks which is not justified by the legitimate needs of the University. Second it is argued that, even assuming the validity of this educational degree criterion, the decentralization and subjectiveness of the decisional process in the areas of hiring, renewal, and advancement have the overall effect of putting black candidates at a disadvantage.

* * *

A. *The Ph.D. Or Its Equivalent Criterion.*

A "Ph.D. degree (or its equivalent)" is a prerequisite for appointment or promotion to most of the Assistant Professor, Associate Professor and Professor positions at the University. It is clear that this requirement currently has a disparate impact upon blacks. The black percentage of those holding Ph.D. degrees in the disciplines taught at the University is substantially lower than the black percentage of those holding Master's degrees and Bachelor's degrees in those disciplines. Thus, if the University utilized an inflexible Ph.D. requirement, it would necessarily affect blacks adversely. While the University does utilize an equivalency concept, this modification does not eliminate the disparate impact. I reach this conclusion because the black percentage of those either holding Ph.D. degrees in the relevant disciplines or possessing the kind of experience which the University accepts as equivalent is also undoubtedly less than the black percentage of those holding Master's and Bachelor's degrees or the equivalent in those disciplines.

The remaining questions are (1) whether the University has justified its degree requirement by showing that it has a "manifest relationship" to the responsibilities of a full time faculty member and, if so, (2) whether the plaintiff has shown that some other criterion or selection procedure with less of a disparate impact upon blacks would serve the University's legitimate interests as well.

* * *

[W]hile the "Ph.D. or its equivalent" requirement probably has a disparate impact upon blacks, I conclude (1) that this disparate impact is justified by the legitimate interest of the University in hiring and advancing persons who are likely to be successful in adding to the fund of knowledge in their chosen disciplines and effective in the teaching of graduate students in those disciplines, and (2) that plaintiff has suggested no alternative criterion or selection procedure which would serve that interest as well with less potential for adverse effect on blacks.

B. *Subjective And Decentralization In Hiring.*

(1) *The Title VII claim.*

The provisions of Title VII were not applicable to the University until March 24, 1972, the effective date of the 1972 Amendments to that Act. Thus, as far as the Title VII discrimination in hiring claim is concerned, the task is to determine whether the hiring practices of the University have had a disparate impact at any time between March of 1972 and the present.

Based on the record as a whole, I think it highly unlikely that the University's subjective employment criteria and its decentralized decision-making process have resulted in blacks being adversely affected by the selection process.

The evidence which tends to negate the first two possible explanations for the University's underutilization of black faculty inferentially supports the validity of the third explanation. Three other categories of evidence provide support for this hypothesis as well. First, plaintiff's lay witnesses who testified as to the University's reputation in the black community and as to the difficulties of attracting black faculty members prior to achieving a "critical mass" clearly established that black academics generally have not viewed the University as an appealing employment location. Second, defendants' witnesses testified to numerous individual recruiting efforts which terminated in a black opting for another employment opportunity despite an offer or clear interest from the University. Finally, there was the data from the applicant supplemental forms which tends to show a significant gap, at least during 1974 and 1975, between the black applicant rate and the black percentage of the relevant labor pool. Having concluded that evidence of the University's hiring needs did reach all segments of the relevant pool, including the black segment, this evidence tends to confirm that black preference is responsible for the disparity between the black proportion of the University's full time faculty and the black proportion of the pool from which they have come.

Based on all the evidence pertaining to the post-Act period, I conclude that the University's hiring practices did not adversely affect blacks during that period.

* * *

While the procedures used in the year preceding the adoption of the affirmative action program lacked some of the safeguards of the procedures in later years, given the productivity of the procedures utilized in the 1970–71 school year and the evidence of the preferences accorded blacks at that time, I am unwilling to conclude that these procedures had a disparate impact upon blacks.

C. Subjectivity and decentralization—renewal, promotion and tenure.

The University's tenure, promotion and renewal practices, like its hiring procedures, involve subjective criteria and decentralized decision making. As with hiring, it is difficult to imagine procedures in these areas for an institution of higher learning which would not have these two characteristics. As earlier detailed, however, the various departmental have substantially reduced the opportunity for discrimination by specifying how the more general criteria will be applied. Also as earlier noted, there is centralized review of departmental policy statements and of individual departmental recommendations. The limited evidence in the record reflecting the application of these procedures does not suggest that they have a disparate impact on blacks.

Dr. Siskin testified that, assuming a pool which is 2.55% black, the probability of finding two or less tenured black faculty members out of a total tenured faculty of 314 is 4.9%. It also appears that in 1976, 44.3% of the white faculty had tenure, while only 16.7% of the black faculty was tenured. These statistics have little probative value, however, in trying to assess whether the procedures for conferring tenure have a disparate impact. Tenure is almost always conferred upon people who are already on the University's faculty and who have been there for three to six years. Accordingly, one must look to the University faculty as the primary pool and consider the experiences of black faculty members as contrasted with those of non-blacks.

Of the twelve black full time faculty at the time of trial, two were tenured and two were on the verge of being tenured. Of the remaining eight black faculty members, only four had been on the faculty for three years. Of these four, Gregory and Miles had only Bachelor's degrees, and Farrow and Washington had only Master's degrees. Thus, every black faculty member with a doctorate and with three or more years of service at the University was tenured or near tenure. The only other black faculty members who have stayed at the University for more than three years in the past were Hilda Davis, a Ph.D. in Sociology, who had a special function in the Writing Center of the English Department, and Mary Farrell, who had only a Master's degree, and who was recommended for promotion (though not tenure) when she left the University in 1974. In addition, the University has attempted to hire Doctors Eubanks and Colson into tenured positions on its faculty.

The record on promotions is too sketchy to draw any inference. All we know is that there were some promotions of black faculty and that the EEOC found that two of the three blacks who became eligible for promotion between 1972 and 1975 were promoted.

Finally, with respect to renewals, there is no evidence of any black faculty member other than Dr. Scott who has not had his contract renewed. Indeed, no faculty member other than Dr. Scott is identified in the record as once claiming to be a victim of any racial discrimination in renewal, promotion or tenure at the University.

CONCLUSION

As a part of its continuing Affirmative Action Program, the University committed itself in 1975 to attempt to hire a substantial number of new minority faculty members by 1980. Thus far, its efforts in pursuit of that goal have not borne the hoped for fruit. This may counsel review and change by the University. I conclude, however, that neither this shortfall nor the disparity between the percentage of blacks on the faculty and the percentage of blacks in the available pool is attributable to unjustified employment practices which have a disparate impact against blacks. Absent such impact, there is no occasion for judicial intervention. Since I also conclude that plaintiff has not been subjected to disparate treatment because of his race, judgment will be entered for the defendants.

The litigation brought by Professor Scott is detailed in a fascinating book by La Noue and Lee, *Academics in Court: The Consequences of Faculty Discrimination Litigation* (Ann Arbor: University of Michigan Press, 1987), in a chapter entitled, "An 'Average' Sociologist of Race Relations." In 1973, Nolvert Scott underwent open heart surgery, and he was pursuing an appeal from the 1974 decision when he suffered a fatal heart attack. After his death, his attorneys continued the appeals, but the University of Delaware won on all counts in the appeals. In 1979, the U.S. Supreme Court declined to review the case, *cert. denied,* 444 U.S. 931 (1979). The authors note that one exception to the general rules favoring institutions in tenure cases is the relatively higher success rate of majority faculty in their litigation against historically black colleges. One of the reasons for this anomaly may be that black colleges have not always had the resources to secure the best counsel to defend themselves, while another reason is the difficulty of mustering statistical evidence to prove their cases. Majority institutions have relied upon small availability pools of minority doctorates (or in some fields, women degree-holders) as a major feature of their own defenses in academic discrimination cases.

J. Carpenter v. Board of Regents, University of Wisconsin System

728 F.2d 911 (1984)

PER CURIAM.

Dr. Joseph Carpenter brought this action under Title VII of the Civil Rights Act of 1964, 42 U.S.C. § 2000e, after he was denied tenure at the University of Wisconsin-Milwaukee ("UW-M"). He alleged that he was denied tenure, and consequently fired, because of his race, black. The case was tried without a jury on both disparate treatment and disparate impact theories, the disparate impact theory having been introduced only on the first day of the trial. The disparate treatment claim was dismissed at the close of the plaintiff's case and, after the trial, judgment was entered for defendant on the disparate impact claim. On appeal, Dr. Carpenter challenges only the adverse judgment with respect to the disparate impact claim. Because we find none of the factual findings of the district court to be clearly erroneous and, further, no legal errors appear in the record, the judgment is affirmed.

I. Background

The factual and historical circumstances leading to this litigation are described in admirable detail in the district court's seventy-one pages of findings. In fact, the district court's findings enlighten us thoroughly both on the history of the Afro-American Studies Department ("AASD" or the "Department") at UW-M and on the mechanics of obtaining academic tenure. Without in any way depreciating the value of extensive findings in facilitating appellate review, we will attempt to be more brief.

Carpenter was appointed to a tenure track position at UW-M in AASD in 1972. Carpenter had been awarded his Ph.D. in 1970 by Marquette University and from 1970 until his appointment at UW-M he served as an assistant professor and director of Afro-American Studies at Carthage College in Kenosha, Wisconsin. Although he had job offers at six other colleges and universities, Carpenter accepted the position at UW-M because he did not want to uproot his family from Milwaukee.

AASD was a relatively young department when Carpenter joined it. The Department was first established as the Afro-American Studies Center in 1969, largely due to pressure from the black student community to recognize the importance to our society of black culture and history. The Center offered several courses for credit but was also envisioned as a place to provide support services for black students and to serve as a black cultural center for the Milwaukee community. The conversion of the Center to an academic department in 1971 required a narrowing of the mission of the Center so that it could concentrate primarily on academic matters. However, UW-M maintained its policy of hiring only blacks as faculty members of AASD.

When Carpenter was appointed to the Department he was informed of the three-pronged test for achieving tenure at UW-M: the candidate must achieve a minimal level of competence and demonstrate a reasonable likelihood of future growth and performance in teaching, in research and scholarly writing and in service to the university community and to the larger community. At UW-M, as is apparently the case at most universities in the United States, faculty members were considered for tenure by the end of the seventh year of service. Because of certain peculiarities of Wisconsin law which required a full year's notice before termination, in practice a candidate was required to submit materials for tenure after five and a half years of service. At UW-M, if a faculty member failed to achieve tenure by the end of the seventh year, the faculty member was terminated.

The district court found that the three-pronged tenure test at UW-M, in the context of the seven year time rule, was not intended to discriminate against blacks. This finding is not challenged on appeal. The district court further found that UW-M did not foresee that the tenure practices might have a disparate impact on blacks or, more specifically, on black junior faculty at the AASD. In fact, the seven year rule was promulgated by the American Association of University Professors to protect its members from the possibility of delays in tenure decisions that could result in negative decisions occurring too late in a professor's career to allow a start at a new position. The district court also found that the three areas of competence covered by the test were related to the fulfillment of the basic function of the university.

The relative newness of the Department created significant additional responsibilities for Carpenter that were not borne by faculty members of other, more established, departments. For instance, Carpenter was required to do extensive work in curriculum development and even had to develop courses outside his areas of expertise. Further, the young age of the Department apparently required Carpenter to assume much heavier administrative duties than junior faculty in other departments. In fact, Dr. Carpenter served as Chairman of the AASD for the academic year 1975–76.

The position of the Department in the black community also contributed to Carpenter's increased responsibilities. The district court found that the special needs of black students in the predominantly white UW-M community required Carpenter to engage in a higher level of counselling and advising activities than young professors in the well-established, "white" departments. Carpenter also took it upon himself, admirably, to participate in community service activities such as membership on the Milwaukee Board of Election Commissioners and service for a neighborhood association.

These activities, some forced on Carpenter because of the absence of senior faculty and established courses at AASD, some caused by unique problems of black students at a predominantly white university and some voluntarily undertaken by him apparently curtailed the time available to him for scholarly work, one of the three areas in which proficiency was required to attain tenure. Carpenter, in 1974, requested that one or two years of his prior service be eliminated from the time counted toward tenure so he could defer his tenure application beyond the 1975–76 academic year when it would normally be made. This request was refused, purportedly because university regulations allowed no discretion as to the time when a faculty member must apply for tenure. We must presume, because of the negative finding below on the disparate treatment claim, that any increased responsibilities Carpenter had were not "heaped" upon him as part of a scheme to prevent black professors from gaining tenure.

Carpenter prepared his tenure materials for submission in accordance with university regulations. The materials were submitted to the AASD executive committee in early December, 1975 and the executive committee, on December 15, 1975, recommended to the Dean's office that tenure be granted. William Halloran, Dean of the College of Letters and Science (the "College"), of which AASD was a department, transmitted the recommendation to the executive committee of the Division of Professions. The latter committee unanimously recommended Carpenter be granted tenure.

After the executive committee of the Division of Professions made its recommendation, Carpenter's tenure application went back to the Dean's office for review. An associate dean, Nason Hall, was first to review the materials, and he advised his superior, Halloran, to review the submissions carefully because he thought there "was a problem." Halloran, after reading the materials, agreed that deficiencies in Carpenter's scholarly writing precluded him from supporting the application for tenure. Without going into detail, the record amply supports the district court's finding that Halloran, in good faith, felt that "the materials submitted as evidence of research and scholarship were not of sufficient quality to support a recommendation for Carpenter's tenure." Halloran, at the same time, considered Carpenter's record of teaching and service acceptable.

Without support from Halloran, Carpenter's application for tenure was effectively denied. Carpenter unsuccessfully appealed Halloran's decision to the top of the University of Wisconsin System. He also filed charges with the Wisconsin Equal Rights Division, the Equal Employment Opportunities Commission ("EEOC"), the Civil Rights Division of the Department of Health, Education and Welfare and the Office of Federal Contract Compliance Programs ("OFCCP") of the Department of Labor. Each of these agencies concluded that probable cause existed to believe that Carpenter's race was a factor in the tenure decision. The OFCCP concluded that Carpenter was a victim of disparate treatment. After receiving his right-to-sue letter from the EEOC, Carpenter brought this suit.

As noted, this suit was brought under both the disparate treatment and disparate impact theories of race discrimination. The district court held that Carpenter failed to prove his disparate treatment case; that finding is not challenged. The plaintiff claimed, however, that the district court erroneously failed to find that application of UW-M's three part tenure requirements (and the seven year rule) illegally made it more difficult for blacks to attain tenure.

In order to prevail on his "disparate impact" claim, Carpenter would have had to prove that the tenure requirements resulted in a disproportionate failure rate for black applicants. If he succeeded in proving this prima facie case, UW-M would then be required to prove that the tenure requirements were job related. If UW-M showed job relatedness then "it remain[ed] open to [Carpenter] to show that other tests or selection devices, without a similarly undesirable racial effect, would also serve the employer's legitimate interest in 'efficient and trustworthy workmanship.' Such a showing would be evidence that the employer was using its tests merely as a 'pretext' for discrimination."

Under the leading Supreme Court decisions on the subject, it is difficult to see how the district court could have found for Carpenter on a disparate impact theory. We have not found record evidence that would support a finding that blacks at UW-M were disproportionately denied tenure. Carpenter claims that such a disparate impact was proven by non-statistical, qualitative evidence. He claims his evidence shows it was "inevitable that the University's facially neutral tenure standards would have a disparate impact" on blacks because of the "many additional burdens in the teaching and service areas borne by the black Afro-American Studies junior faculty...." While a court may, in an appropriate case, project a disparate impact from non-statistical evidence, in this case we are not confident that such a racial effect would necessarily have occurred. We could only speculate that new departments with white faculties are not burdened in some comparable fashion or that employment of the usual tenure requirements would "inevitably" result in proportionately fewer blacks receiving tenure. In any event, we are unpersuaded that the district court's refusal to accept a disparate impact approach here was erroneous.

Even if we were to find that the evidence supported a finding of disparate impact, there is no question that UW-M has a legitimate business interest in ensuring that its tenured professors are competent in the three competency areas. Therefore, we have no difficulty in agreeing with the district court's conclusions that the tenure standards, as employed, are "job related." We further conclude, because Carpenter did not present evidence that different tenure standards would adequately serve UW-M's business interests, that no showing has been made that the tenure standards are a "pretext" for race discrimination.

We are left with the problem of the seven year rule. The district court found that UW-M's interests in competent tenured faculty could have been served just as well if tenure decisions were made later than the seventh year of service. Carpenter argues that the increased burdens borne by junior faculty in AASD were attributable to the racial characteristics of the faculty and clientele and that these increased burdens made it impossible for him to meet the scholarship competency requirement within seven years. In fact, in October, 1982, the executive committee of AASD recommended that the Dean grant leaves of absence to two black tenure track junior faculty so their "tenure clock" would stop running temporarily. The reason given for this request by the committee was that the faculty members "have had to face unusual difficulties during their probationary period as young black faculty members, given the range of countervailing pressures upon them."

But the district court found a fatal flaw in Carpenter's argument concerning the seven year rule: Carpenter did not prove that his failure to achieve the required level of scholarly competency was due to the application of the seven year rule. The district court viewed this as an essential element of the case: Carpenter had to prove that his failure to achieve tenure was due to the disparate impact of the seven year rule. We find the absence of proof on the amount of time left to Carpenter for scholarly work to be particularly disturbing. Perhaps the apparent lack of proof is due to the lateness of the decision to add the disparate impact theory to the case. In any event, Carpenter had not proven that the additional demands on his time materially diminished his capacity to demonstrate the required competency in scholarship. The record does not disclose that Carpenter lacked adequate time within the tenure period to prove himself a scholar. Therefore, we cannot conclude that Carpenter has met his burden of showing that the seven year rule had a disparate impact on him because of his race.

We agree with the district court that a plaintiff in a disparate impact case must show that he or she was really injured by the policy alleged to have had a disparate impact. For example, a plaintiff denied a promotion could not challenge a promotion test as discriminatory, if promotion was denied for a reason completely unrelated to the test, such as lack of experience. Here, the district court determined that Carpenter failed to prove that any tendency to discriminate inherent in the seven year rule or the tenure standards really affected him. He simply failed to prove that the practices of which he complained had the discriminatory effect of which he complained. Even if the refusal to waive the seven year rule may appear overly strict, on these facts Title VII provides no remedy.

This case would be more difficult if we were presented with a record which illustrated in detail the extra demands placed on Carpenter's time because he is black.

However, we have no idea how much time was available for scholarly work and how much time similarly situated white professors had available. We cannot conclude, on this record, that UW-M impeded Carpenter's quest for tenure because of his race or that there was not enough time left over to achieve the competency necessary to achieve tenure. For us to conclude that UW-M should have granted tenure would be to "replac[e] [the] university's judgment about academic employment with judgments made by the judiciary." When presented with an appropriate case, we may be required to make such judgments, but this is not the case.

For the reasons expressed above, we affirm the judgment of the district court.

Firing Faculty

Even if colleges do not entirely follow their own rules in tenure reviews, most courts will affirm tenure denials if there is no clear evidence of bad faith, or if the review process is in substantial compliance with the accepted procedures. *Stensrud v. Mayville State College*, 368 N.W.2d 519 (N.D. 1985); *Piacitelli v. Southern Utah State College*, 636 P.2d 1063 (Utah 1981); and *Smith v. State of North Dakota*, 389 N.W. 2d 808 (N.D. 1986), instances where incomplete or otherwise flawed procedures were conceded, all held for the colleges on "substantial compliance" or abstention grounds.

At Harvard Law School, a ⅔ positive vote by the faculty is required for a positive recommendation to the president. In 1987, after a vote of 30–8, sufficient for a recommendation, the president denied an appointment after convening an extraordinary external review panel and formal hearing. D. Kaplan, "Battle at Harvard Law Over Tenure," *National Law Journal*, 22 June 1987, pp. 3, 38. In another case, in 1988, after convening another panel and hearing, he denied a 29–20 positive vote, one that just fell short of the required ⅔. In both instances, there were widespread charges that both professors were denied tenure due to their politics. E. Adams, "Professor Denied Tenure at Harvard to Pursue Sex-Discrimination Claim," *National Law Journal*, 28 March 1988, p. 4.

Termination for Cause

Morgan v. American University
534 A.2d 323 (1987)

STEADMAN, Associate Judge:

Philip Morgan is a former faculty member at American University ("AU") whose teaching contract was "rescinded." Morgan brought an action for damages; the jury verdict was in favor of AU. He appeals from denial of his pretrial summary judgment and post-trial motions for judgment notwithstanding the verdict. The principal issues on appeal are: 1) whether the denial of a summary judgment motion is appealable after a full trial on the merits; and 2) whether the interpretation of the contract was properly left to the jury. We hold against the appellant on both issues and therefore affirm.

I. The Facts

In the spring of 1981, Morgan obtained a one-year appointment as a full-time, "tenure-track" faculty member at AU for the 1981–82 academic year. In the fall of 1981 and 1982 he applied for an additional year's appointment and was reappointed both times as he apparently had performed satisfactorily. For each reappointment he was required to detail his professional activities during the past year. Morgan's reappointment for the 1983–84 academic year was granted in April 1983. In July 1983, AU received an anonymous letter alleging that appellant was serving as a full-time professor at Golden Gate University (Norfolk/Richmond, Virginia) during the same times as his full-time appointments at AU. When confronted by AU with this accusation, Morgan conceded that he did hold a position at Golden Gate but contended that his duties there had not interfered with his AU responsibilities. AU reviewed Morgan's personnel files and found that none of the materials submitted by Morgan in support of the initial appointment or reappointments revealed his employment with Golden Gate. Contending that it never would have hired Morgan if he had disclosed his Golden Gate position, AU then "rescinded" Morgan's appointment for the 1983–84 year without affording Morgan any of the notice and hearing procedures specified in Section 19 of the Faculty Manual which was incorporated by reference into appellant's employment contract.

In his suit, appellant contended that his dismissal was a breach of contract because the situation that caused his termination, nondisclosure of outside employment, was within those Faculty Manual provisions that require certain procedures before AU may "for cause" terminate tenure-track faculty members. These procedures include written notice of the charges, a hearing before an elected faculty committee, a clear and convincing burden of proof on AU, right of appeal to the University Trustees and one year's separation pay if termination is upheld unless there is a finding of moral turpitude. In response, AU argued that appellant was not terminated but rather the contract was rescinded on the grounds that Morgan made material misrepresentations to AU in obtaining his appointment, thus eliminating any rights under the contract and Faculty Manual. Both parties, asserting that the Faculty Manual language and relevant case law supported their position as a matter of law, moved for summary judgment. Both motions were denied by Judge Bacon, the motions judge, who ruled that there were issues of material fact to be resolved. The case then proceeded to trial.

At trial, Judge von Kann devised a special verdict form to accommodate the parties' vastly different conceptions of what issues were pertinent to the case. Following a five-day trial and three days of deliberations, the jury returned unanimous verdicts on all questions, finding in pertinent part that AU had established the essential prerequisites to rescission and that Section 19's procedures did not apply to situations involving the ending of a full-time faculty member's employment for failure to disclose a full-time position at another university.

Appellant then filed a post-trial for judgment notwithstanding the verdict. He conceded that AU had proven the elements of rescission but argued that, as a matter of law, AU had abrogated or limited its common law right to rescission in this case by including Section 19 in the employment contract. In a carefully reasoned order, Judge von Kann rejected this claim. On appeal, Morgan continues to contend that both Judge Bacon at summary judgment and Judge von Kann in his post-trial order should have found the contract language unambiguous and that pursuant to Section

19, AU could not rescind or otherwise terminate appellant's employment without establishing "Cause" through the specified procedures.

*   *   *

III. Jury Contract Interpretation

We now turn to appellant's contention that the plain language of Section 19 of the Faculty Manual establishes its applicability to situations such as his as a matter of law. The language he relies on appears in subsection (a) of Section 19 entitled "Termination for Cause" which states that:

> The University reserves the right to terminate an appointment with continuous tenure, or of a probationary or special appointment before the end of the specified term, for adequate cause shown. Adequate cause for dismissal will be related, directly and substantially, to the fitness or performance of the faculty member in his or her professional capacity as a teacher or researcher or creative member of his or her professional field.

Morgan contends this language is unambiguous and is capable of only one clear and definite meaning; that it prohibits any termination of such faculty except after cause has been established by the procedures set forth in parts (b) - (g) of Section 19 without any exception permitting termination by way of rescission. Therefore he argues that the issue was correctly submitted to the jury and the trial court erred in not construing the contract itself and in not granting appellant judgment notwithstanding the verdict.

In *Best*, we held that

> if a contract is ambiguous, and the evidence supports more than one reasonable interpretation, the interpretation is a question of fact for the jury. But if the meaning of a contract is so clear that reasonable men could reach but one conclusion or no extrinsic evidence is necessary to determine the contract's meaning, then contract interpretation is a matter for the court.

In resolving this issue we note that it has been observed:

> [S]ome of the surrounding circumstances always must be known before the meaning of the words can be plain and clear; and proof of the circumstances may make a meaning plain and clear when in the absence of such proof some other meaning may also have seemed plain and clear.
>
> Furthermore, while extrinsic evidence of the parties' subjective intent may be resorted to only if the document is ambiguous, "extrinsic evidence may be considered to determine the circumstances surrounding the making of the contract so that it may be ascertained what a reasonable person in the position of the parties would have thought the words meant." Thus while the determination of whether or not a contract is ambiguous is a legal question, it follows that we should be mindful of the trial court's familiarity with the surrounding circumstances in reviewing its determination of this issue on the JNOV motion.

Within this framework of analysis, the specific question before us is this: can we say that a reasonable person, looking at the documents in context, would have to conclude that Section 19's language concerning terminations applies without a doubt to a situation where a faculty member is terminated by means of rescission for failing to inform a university that he or she holds a simultaneous position at another university? Judge von Kann concluded that sufficient ambiguity existed to submit this question to a jury. In his order denying appellant's JNOV motion he stated:

> A fair reading of Section 19(a) seems to indicate that the provisions of that Section are intended to govern termination based on a faculty member's inadequate performance of duties rather than misrepresentations made in the course of obtaining his employment in the first place. Certainly there is nothing in the language of Section 19 which expressly abrogates the University's normal right to rescind a contract based on material misrepresentation. There is no reason that such an abrogation would not be given effect if it had been plainly and unequivocally set forth in the agreement. For example, Dr. Morgan would definitely have been entitled to the benefits of Section 19 had that section contained a sentence such as the following: American University renounces its right to rescind a faculty member's employment on grounds that he or she made a material misrepresentation to the University in obtaining employment and agree that, before any faculty member may be terminated on such grounds, he or she shall be afforded the procedures set forth in this Section 19. Section 19 as it is now framed contains no provision of this sort.

* * *

It is important to recognize that the doctrine of misrepresentation and its concurrent remedy of rescission apply in this case because the misrepresentation was made prior to the formation of the contract. Therefore AU could argue that had it known of appellant's position at Golden Gate, it would never have entered the contract. On the other hand, if a faculty member engaged in no misrepresentation during negotiation of the contract but then subsequently, during the term took an outside position without disclosure to the University, rescission might be an inappropriate theory for termination. In that situation, not before us today, we express no opinion as to whether a faculty member would be entitled to the protections of Section 19.

Affirmed.

Community College Dist. 508 v. McKinley
513 N.E.2d 951 (Ill. App. 1 Dist. 1987)

Justice HARTMAN delivered the opinion of the court:

Plaintiff, Board of Trustees of Community College District 508 ("Board"), appeals from circuit court orders on administrative review which affirmed a hearing officer's reversal of a Board employee discharge ruling. The issues presented in this appeal include whether: (1) the hearing officer's ruling was a final administrative decision subject to administrative review; (2) the Board satisfied due process pre-termination hearing requirements; (3) the hearing officer's decision reversing the Board was against the manifest weight of the evidence; and (4) the discharged, tenured employee was entitled to back-pay.

Defendant, Ronald McKinley, was employed by the Board as a tenured full-time radiology instructor at Malcolm X. College from March 30, 1973, to December 23, 1981. His employment application and his annual employment contracts with the Board prohibited his accepting or continuing any "concurrent full-time [employment] position or positions equal to a full-time position" while he remained a full-time teacher. Full-time employment by the Board for a professor under Board rules was limited to 30 hours per week. The collective bargaining agreement between the Board and the teachers' union contained a similar provision. No definitions were set forth in either document of what was meant by "concurrent full-time position," or whether the same 30 hour rule was intended to be applied to the hours spent in outside employment, or whether the judgment of whether the outside employment was full- or part-time should be made by the outside employer. The only explanation of what was meant by part-time employment was an unofficial newspaper column authored by the then-chancellor of District 508, appearing in the Chicago Tribune of September 10, 1978, which stated that: "Outside employment is another 'right' that full-time faculty have won—up to 99 percent of a full-time outside job."

Evidence later presented to a hearing officer revealed the facts which follow. Subsequent to his employment by the Board, McKinley began working in the radiology department at Norwegian-American Hospital ("hospital") on December 16, 1977. Whether his hospital employment was for full-time or part-time employment was the subject of conflicting evidence. Between December 1977 and August 31, 1981, McKinley worked an average of 37.13 hours per week at the hospital. There was substantial evidence supporting his belief that he was actually a part-time employee: hospital employment guidelines defined full-time employment there as 75 or more hours per two week pay period; his application for hospital employment specified that he was to work 72 hours per two week pay period and his supervisor testified that he was expected to work only 70–72 hours per two week pay period; the head of the radiology department, his supervisor, stated that McKinley had been hired as a part-time employee specifically due to his teaching responsibilities; McKinley had replaced a previous part-time employee; and McKinley had received full-time benefits merely as an employment inducement because he was a high caliber employee. McKinley also worked about 1½ hours per week as a vocalist at a funeral home after 1976: two or three selections per service lasting five to seven minutes each, as needed.

Evidence which conflicted with, or contradicted, that set forth in the preceding paragraph was also introduced and considered by the hearing officer.

Board policies prohibiting full-time outside employment required employees to complete outside employment disclosure statements beginning in October 1978. McKinley filed disclosure statements on October 18, 1978, March 9, 1979, October 16, 1980, February 17, 1981, and August 20, 1981. He disclosed his employment by the funeral home on each of the statements, but disclosed his employment at the hospital only on the last statement, August 20, 1981, revealing employment of 16–20 hours per week. On August 31, 1981, McKinley voluntarily reduced his work period at the hospital to 20 hours per week.

In October 1981, plaintiff's director of labor relations ("director") noted McKinley's part-time employment and contacted the hospital for verification. McKinley requested that the hospital disclose only his then part-time employment; nevertheless, the hospital disclosed McKinley's entire employment record, first identifying it as full-time prior to August 31, 1981, but later changing the characterization to part-time.

Thereafter, the director recommended to the chancellor of District 508 that McKinley be discharged. The chancellor notified McKinley by letter on October 22, 1981, of his intention to recommend his discharge to the Board by reason of McKinley's violation of his employment contracts in working full-time for the hospital. The letter also stated that McKinley could meet with the director and discuss the charge prior to the chancellor's recommendation being made to the Board.

McKinley met with the director on October 23, 1981, and attempted to persuade him that his employment by the hospital had been merely part-time. The director thereafter reasserted his discharge recommendation to the chancellor, basing it on both McKinley's outside employment and on his false disclosure statements. The chancellor thereafter recommended McKinley's discharge to the Board.

On November 3, 1981, the Board adopted a resolution discharging McKinley, of which it notified him on November 4, 1981. McKinley requested and received a bill of particulars from the Board which specified that his "holding of positions equal to a full-time position with Norwegian-American Hospital and Griffin Funeral Home constitutes a direct violation of a specific condition of employment [and] . . . constitutes cause for . . . dismissal" and "false and intentional misrepresentations of . . . outside employment . . . constitutes cause for . . . dismissal as a faculty member." He was suspended without pay on December 23, 1981. Up to this point, no evidentiary hearing had taken place.

Meanwhile, on November 10, 1981, McKinley filed a written request for a post-termination hearing as provided by section 3B–4 of the Public Community College Act ("Act"). An independent hearing officer took evidence, heard witnesses and arguments on April 20 and May 17, 1982. On August 19, 1983, fifteen months later, the hearing officer ruled in McKinley's favor, reversing the Board's decision; the hearing officer did not then consider McKinley's alleged misrepresentations in making his ruling.

The Board sought circuit court administrative review of the hearing officer's decision on September 19, 1983. On June 20, 1984, the circuit court vacated the decision of the hearing officer and remanded the case for a determination of the misrepresentation issue. The hearing officer thereafter found that McKinley had falsified his outside employment disclosure statements but concluded that discharge was too harsh a punishment and accordingly ordered that McKinley be reinstated and that he "suffer no loss of pay due to his suspension."

On October 31, 1984, the Board filed a supplemental administrative review complaint. On March 7, 1986, the circuit court affirmed the hearing officer's decision holding that the Board's discharge procedures had violated McKinley's due process rights to a pre-termination hearing under *Cleveland Board of Education v. Loudermill* and, further, that his punishment by discharge was too severe. The Board's motion to reconsider was denied on September 8, 1986. In denying the latter motion the circuit court issued a 50 page order restating due process and harshness of penalty reasons contained in an earlier ruling by another judge. The court also ruled that the hearing officer's decision was not against the manifest weight of the evidence.

The Board appeals.

I.

A preliminary issue raised by the Board concerns whether the Board's discharge of McKinley, or the hearing officer's reinstatement of him, is the final administrative decision subject to review and therefore entitled to be held *prima facie* true and correct on administrative review. The Act provides that the Board's decision is final unless, under section 3B–4, the individual chooses to appeal that decision to a hearing officer, in which case the hearing officer's decision becomes the final administrative decision and must be accorded the statutory presumption of factual correctness. Additionally, the Act specifically provides that the "Administrative Review Law . . . shall apply to . . . all proceedings instituted for the judicial review *of final administrative decisions of a hearing officer* under section 3B–4." Accordingly, the Board's contention that the hearing officer's decision was not a final decision by an *administrative agency*, is unsupportable. The circuit court correctly so held.

II.

The Board next contends that the circuit court erred in holding that McKinley had been denied his pre-termination due process rights. Due process requires that notice and an opportunity to respond be given. The opportunity to defend one's self and to present reasons, either in person or in writing, why a proposed action is unwarranted is a fundamental requirement of due process. A tenured public employee, such as McKinley, is entitled to oral or written notice of the charges against him, an explanation of his employer's evidence, and an opportunity to defend himself against the charges. To require more, prior to termination, would be an unwarranted intrusion into the realm of the government's legitimate interest in quickly removing unsatisfactory employees.

In the case *sub judice*, the chancellor notified McKinley of the impending action against him and offered him the opportunity to meet with the director. McKinley accepted that opportunity and attempted to explain his previous employment and its non-disclosure to the director. This opportunity satisfied the *Loudermill* requirement that a tenured public employee be accorded at least an informal pre-termination opportunity to be heard.

The circuit court held that McKinley's due process rights had been violated because he had not had a pre-termination opportunity to respond to the charges to the Board itself, the actual decisionmaker. The court's interpretation of *Loudermill* as requiring such a pre-termination opportunity was too narrow. Neither employee in *Loudermill*, for example, was given any opportunity to respond to the "charges" against them until after they were discharged (one was discharged for lying on his employment application; the other for failing an eye examination). The Supreme Court's concern with the employees' rights stemmed from the complete denial of any pre-termination opportunity to be heard, and not from whether a pre-termination response was directed to the initial decisionmaker.

Accordingly, the circuit court erred in holding that McKinley was denied due process. His rights were preserved by his being given the opportunity to meet with the director prior to any Board action and on his then being given the statutorily authorized opportunity for a final hearing after his discharge by the Board.

III.

The Board asserts that McKinley's actions clearly warranted his discharge and that the contrary conclusion by the hearing officer was in error. The Board notes McKinley's outside employment and his failure to disclose that employment when so requested by the disclosure statements, arguing that each, independently, provided cause for discharge. The Board's conclusion, although correct in insisting that cause for discipline existed, is not dispositive under the facts of this case. Here, because of the statutory procedure prescribed by section 3B–4, the Board's decision is not that subject to administrative review; rather, it is present only as a procedural predecessor to the hearing officer's decision, which is the only decision that was before the court on administrative review.

Section 3B–4 of the Act directs the hearing officer particularly to "make a decision as to whether or not the tenured faculty member shall be dismissed." The hearing officer is thereby empowered not only to evaluate the facts in a given case, but he or she may also evaluate the propriety of dismissal. Toward that end, the hearing officer is authorized to conduct a full evidentiary hearing.

In Illinois, whether cause for an employee's discharge exists is to be determined by the administrative agency and will not be reversed unless arbitrary or unreasonable. Here, the decision made by a statutorily prescribed "disinterested hearing officer?" was the final agency decision, and cannot be overturned unless it was arbitrary or unreasonable. The hearing officer's decision was premised, in part, upon the absence of any definition specifically explaining what was meant by "outside full-time employment," according the Board leeway to apply it in any manner it chose but leaving the affected employee in doubt, and, in part, upon the Board's inconsistent treatment of prior outside employment infractions by other employees and evidenced by the hearing officer's conclusion that dismissal was too harsh a penalty and unwarranted.

* * *

It was the function of the hearing officer to determine whether the tenured employee's violations constituted cause for discharge, subject to judicial review.

Based upon the evidence before him, the findings and conclusions of the hearing officer were neither arbitrary nor unreasonable. The circuit court correctly affirmed his decision, and must itself be affirmed.

* * *

Under these circumstances, we hold that concept of an award of back pay by the hearing officer, as affirmed by the circuit court, is authorized by section 3B–4 of the Act.

We have already noted the protracted proceedings in the circuit court and before the hearing officer have extended to almost six years. Upon remand, consideration should be given by the Board as to how much delay was due to its own actions and those of the hearing officer, and how much was attributable to the actions of McKinley, aside from the statutorily sanctioned procedures followed. Upon McKinley's reinstatement, the Board should award appropriate back pay allowances as demonstrated by the record and provided for by its rules.

For the foregoing reasons, the decision of the circuit court on administrative review is affirmed, except for the due process pre-termination aspect thereof, erroneously based upon *Loudermill*, and the cause is remanded to the Board of Trustees of Community College District 508 for further action not inconsistent with the opinion herein expressed.

Affirmed and remanded with directions.

Sinnott v. Skagit Valley College
746 P.2d 1213 (Wash. App. 1987)

THOMPSON, Judge.

William Sinnott, a tenured welding instructor with Skagit Valley College, appeals the decision of the trial court affirming his dismissal. We affirm.

Mr. Sinnott challenged his employment discharge and was given a hearing before a hearing examiner and the College Dismissal Review Committee. The examiner and committee recommended dismissal to the Skagit Valley College Board of Trustees. The board adopted the recommendation and terminated Mr. Sinnott's employment for cause. On appeal the superior court upheld the dismissal, and Mr. Sinnott appeals that decision.

* * *

First Amendment Freedom of Speech

Mr. Sinnott first contends his dismissal impermissibly resulted from his having exercised his constitutionally protected right to speech. After discussing problems in the welding department with a reporter from the Skagit Valley Herald, Mr. Sinnott was summoned to the president's office and given a letter that conditioned his continued employment on his agreeing to stop making derogatory remarks about the welding program and other employees and cooperating in curriculum modification and team teaching. Mr. Sinnott again met with the president and, when he refused to sign the letter, his employment at the College was terminated for unprofessional conduct and insubordination.

In determining whether an employee's dismissal violates his constitutional right to free speech, the interest of the employee as a citizen in commenting on matters of public concern must be balanced against the interests of the state as employer in promoting efficiency of the public services it performs through its employees. Whether the matter is of public concern is determined by the content, form, and context of the given statement as revealed by the whole record. Employee grievances concerning internal policy or matters of personal interest are not protected under this theory. Appropriate state interests against which First Amendment rights of teachers must be balanced include, *e.g.*:

> (1) The need to maintain harmony among coworkers; (2) the need to curtail conduct impeding the teacher's proper and competent performance of his daily duties; (3) the need to prevent activities disruptive of the educational process and to provide for the orderly functioning of the university.

Finally, the inquiry into the protected status of speech is one of law, not fact. If a nonpermissible reason such as the exercise of First Amendment rights played a substantial part in the actual decision to dismiss, after the employee makes a showing of protected conduct and that conduct was a substantial or motivating factor, the burden shifts to the board to show by a preponderance of the evidence that it would have reached the same decision, even in the absence of the protected conduct.

Mr. Sinnott contends his dismissal was based on protected activity involving comments on matters of public concern regarding the proper operation of the welding program. The College answers Mr. Sinnott's conduct was not protected because his derogatory statements damaged the professional reputation of his colleagues, and though his discussions with the press were a factor in the termination decision, the decision would have been the same in the absence of that conduct.

The administrative record contains testimony by James Ford, president of Skagit Valley College, that in 1976 he called Mr. Sinnott into his office to discuss derogatory remarks Mr. Sinnott allegedly made about other faculty members. Thereafter, in 1976 and 1979, President Ford again had discussions and meetings with Mr. Sinnott concerning his repeated criticism of certain faculty members and use of inappropriate language. In April 1980, Mr. Sinnott alerted College officials to what he alleged was theft by the chairman of the welding department. The allegations were investigated by local authorities and dismissed for lack of evidence. Other College officials involved with the welding department and occupational education program testified that Mr. Sinnott had a history of repeated profanity and ongoing criticism of his supervisors and coworkers.

In February 1981, Mr. Sinnott received a letter from a superior advising him he needed to improve his professional conduct. The letter referred to repeated attempts by Mr. Sinnott to discredit other welding instructors and noted that his behavior was "nearing, or may have even reached, a level that is sufficiently unprofessional to warrant disciplinary action." Thereafter Mr. Sinnott was given a positive evaluation wherein it was noted he appeared to be meeting conditions for improvement previously outlined.

A note was placed in Mr. Sinnott's personnel file indicating written information concerning a January 1982 reprimand was in the Welding file. Additionally, according to the associate dean of occupational education, Mr. Sinnott's 1983 evaluation contained language critical of his lack of cooperation, but after a conference with Mr. Sinnott during which he promised to cooperate in the future, that language was deleted.

On January 27, 1984, the State Board for Community College Education reviewed the welding program and listed several deficiencies in its recommendations for improvement. After the review, Mr. Sinnott met with a reporter from the Skagit Valley Herald, and commented, *inter alia*, that the report was a "whitewash." Mr. Sinnott criticized inconsistent standards used to certify instructors and instructors' lack of sufficient course work in welding-related mathematics. Mr. Sinnott was reported to have accused College administrators of replacing a former welding advisory board with "members more to their liking." He was also quoted as saying he knew of at least two instances where students were given credits for welding courses they did not actually take.

Richard Nowadnick, Dean of Educational Services, testified to Mr. Sinnott's continuous profanity and criticism and the efforts of the College to put an end to it. Mr. Sinnott could not get along with the other instructor in the welding department, and two previous instructors left because of such problems. From May 1979 until July 1982, when Mr. Nowadnick retired, 10 memos were generated by Mr. Sinnott's conduct. The last memo warned Mr. Sinnott that if his unprofessional conduct continued, Mr. Nowadnick would recommend his employment be terminated. Mr. Nowadnick's successor, George Delaney, testified problems with Mr. Sinnott continued. In March 1984, just 1 month prior to the dismissal, Mr. Delaney met with Mr. Sinnott seeking his cooperation in implementing program changes suggested by the review committee. Mr. Sinnott's response was, "It won't work."

Joe Pederson, Associate Dean for Occupational Education, and Susan Tinker, his successor, testified concerning the same problems. One of the things noted by the review committee in 1984 was that the animosity between instructors was affecting their teaching. On April 6, 1984, a Skagit Valley Herald reporter met with the College president and other officials concerning Mr. Sinnott's comments to the press. On April 12, Mr. Sinnott was called to the president's office. He brought his union representative with him. At that time the College president gave Mr. Sinnott a letter outlining conditions to continued employment:

1) ...make no derogatory statements about institutional employees to students, other faculty members or the community;

2) ...make no derogatory statements to students, other faculty members or the community concerning the Welding program; [and]

3) ...fully cooperate in the Welding curriculum modification and, effective Fall 1984, ...team-teach a coordinated program with the other Welding instructor, as directed by the Associate Dean for Occupational Education.

That same day an article containing comments by Mr. Sinnott was published in the Skagit Valley Herald. On April 17, the College president and dean of education services again met with Mr. Sinnott and his union representative. Although Mr. Sinnott agreed to discuss the letter's third condition, he refused to agree to the first two. After Mr. Sinnott refused to sign the letter, he was given notice of his dismissal, based on unprofessional conduct and insubordination.

The first inquiry in addressing Mr. Sinnott's contention that talking to the press was an impermissible basis for dismissal is whether his speech amounted to comments on matters of public concern. We view the content, form, and context of his statements as revealed by the entire record.

Although we concur with the determination that:

an individual cannot bootstrap his individual grievance into a matter of public concern either by bruiting his complaint to the world or by invoking a supposed popular interest in all aspects of the way public institutions are run...,

we conclude the tone of the article was directed toward the comprehensiveness of the program review and did not necessarily contain expressions of disagreement with internal decisions of immediate supervisors. The quality of the program was of sufficient public concern when balanced against efficiency of public services to warrant protection. The balance of interests here is close, however, considering the need to maintain harmony among coworkers and to curtail conduct impeding proper and competent performance of duties.

The president acknowledged that although the meeting with the press was a factor in Mr. Sinnott's employment termination, it was not the sole or principal factor. It was merely the last straw. Thus, the question becomes whether the College has shown by a preponderance of the evidence that it would have reached the same decision in the absence of the protected conduct. Given the substantial testimony regarding Mr. Sinnott's lengthy history of criticism and profanity, and the College's efforts to deal with the problems, we conclude the College met its burden. Accordingly, Mr. Sinnott's dismissal did not violate his First Amendment right to freedom of speech, nor did the actions of the College represent a sufficiently chilling limitation.

Vagueness/Overbreadth

Mr. Sinnott contends "insubordination" and "unprofessional conduct" as used in the notice of dismissal are unconstitutionally vague. Under the vagueness doctrine, no prohibition can stand or penalty attach where an individual could not reasonably understand his contemplated conduct is proscribed. An administrative agency rule violates the first essential of due process of law if it forbids an act in terms so vague, persons of common intelligence must guess as its meaning and may differ in applying it. "Insubordination" has been defined as the willful refusal of a teacher to obey reasonable rules and regulations. Here, Mr. Sinnott's continued use of profane language and criticism of other instructors after repeated direction by his superiors did constitute insubordination within the plain meaning of the term.

*   *   *

Sufficient Cause

Finally, we examine whether the trial court erred in ruling the College had established just cause for termination. Although article 9, section 4 of the collective bargaining agreements sets forth examples of "sufficient cause," one of which includes "unprofessional conduct," sufficient cause is not defined by Washington statute. Mr. Sinnott contends that for sufficient cause to exist, the conduct complained of must substantially affect the performance and fitness of the member *as a teacher*. On the contrary, although a lack of fitness to teach is one basis for dismissing a teacher, it is not a requirement of sufficient cause. Moreover *Hoagland* and *Gaylord* can be distinguished on the basis that the conduct at issue there was carried on outside the teacher's profession.

A person has a legitimate expectation of freedom from arbitrary action, which means being treated consistent with the statute and policies covering his employment. Arbitrary and capricious action has been defined as willful and unreasoning action without consideration and in disregard of the facts and circumstances. The board had before it the entire record of the hearing and adopted the findings and conclusions of the hearing examiner with some revisions. The board's findings and conclusions made clear reference to the testimony and exhibits in the record; no willful or unreasoning action is apparent.

A decision is clearly erroneous if, although there may be evidence to support a finding, the reviewing court is "left with the definite and firm conviction that a mistake has been committed." The substantial evidence in the record regarding Mr. Sinnott's open criticism of the welding program and fellow instructors negates his assertion the action of the College was clearly erroneous.

The record supports the determination regarding insubordination and unprofessional conduct.

Many tenure review cases contain undercurrents of faculty members who simply did not get along with colleagues. Lack of collegiality may be pretextual, but that it played a role in dismissal is a difficult scenario to prove to a court. Moreover, even when it is proven, it will not likely serve to overturn a negative decision unless the behavior that gave rise is protected; see chapter 2, "Academic Freedom." In "Personality as a Criterion for Faculty Tenure," Perry Zirkel reviewed 85 cases involving issues of collegiality or other personality factors in denial of tenure. He found that two-thirds of these cases resolved conclusively held for defendant institutions, while plaintiff faculty fully prevailed in only 3 of 14 conclusive decisions. Zirkel argues, "Institutions should assiduously avoid the use of collegiality and other personality factors unless they are legitimately part of [clearly articulated] performance criteria." *Cleveland State Law Review*, 33 (1984–85), 223–44.

On occasion, departments become so badly divided that extraordinary measures must be taken to restore order. In 1985, the University of Utah placed its sociology department into "receivership," after faculty became embroiled in intramural disputes over departmental policy. The university took the steps after a faculty committee had issued a report that found a general "disruptive environment." The university had taken similar steps in an earlier imbroglio in the School of Education. K. Winkler, "University of Utah Puts Sociology Department in 'Receivership,'" *Chronicle of Higher Education*, 27 November 1985, p. 6.

"After Lengthy Hearings, Rutgers Faculty Panel Recommends Dismissal of Tenured Professor"

C. Mooney, *Chronicle of Higher Education*, 13 January 1988, pp. A11, 12.

After holding 46 days of hearings that lasted more than 250 hours, a faculty panel at Rutgers University has recommended the dismissal of a tenured chemistry professor accused of pressuring visiting Chinese scholars to work in his garden, filing fraudulent employment reports, and taking part in other unethical activities.

The 44-page report by the five-member panel signals the end of the university's dismissal hearings, a rarely used procedure that was considered especially lengthy and bitter for this case. It was so time-consuming that administrators at Rutgers hope it will encourage faculty members to back recommendations for a shorter dismissal process in the future.

But as far as the accused faculty member is concerned, the dismissal proceedings— designed to allow faculty members accused of wrongdoing to be judged by their faculty colleagues—failed miserably.

Joseph San Filippo, Jr., a Rutgers faculty member since 1971, maintains that certain professors and administrators at Rutgers have campaigned for his dismissal for years. He and his lawyer say Rutgers twisted his actions and even contrived allegations that were later dropped. Above all, they say, the panel refused to allow Mr. San Filippo to present his entire case once the proceedings began to drag on.

The university's Board of Governors must now sort through the myriad of charges and recommendations outlined in the faculty panel's report before it makes the final decision on whether to dismiss Mr. San Filippo.

Few Choose Senate Hearings

Under university policy, a faculty member charged with professional wrongdoing can ask to have his case heard—either publicly or privately—by a panel of faculty members selected by members of the university's Senate. Few faculty members choose to do so, according to university officials.

In its report, the faculty panel upheld most of the charges and recommended that Mr. San Filippo be dismissed for alleged actions he took in 1984 and 1985. In October 1986, Mr. San Filippo, who frequently works with Chinese graduate students, was accused by the university of pressuring two visiting Chinese scholars, Gao Hetian and Xiao Changhe, to perform garden work at his home. He also allegedly deducted $700 from each of their salaries for health insurance that was never provided and harassed them by threatening to force them to leave the country.

Mr. San Filippo was also accused of directing one of the scholars to identify himself as another person in order to receive medical benefits for injuries he received while working at Mr. San Filippo's home. He was also accused of allowing employees under his supervision to submit false time reports and to make inappropriate charges to university accounts.

The panel's report noted that Mr. San Filippo had an excellent research record and had brought more than $1 million in grants to the university. But, it concluded, "we find that Professor San Filippo has exploited, threatened and been abusive of individuals who have worked under him in a professional capacity."

Mr. San Filippo said he had requested the hearings because he did nothing unethical, and that he had been singled out for actions that other faculty members routinely take.

For example, he said that, like other faculty members, he routinely socializes with graduate students, but never pressured the two scholars to do work for him. As for charges of submitting fraudulent time reports, he said he had authorized an employee to submit a time report for a week she did no work because she was taking compensatory time off that she had accrued earlier—a common practice at the university.

"I've been waiting for two years to put on my response to these charges, and I still haven't had the opportunity to do so." Mr. San Filippo said.

Filed Several Grievances

Mr. San Filippo's attorney, Ira Goldberg, speculated that faculty members and administrators at Rutgers considered Mr. San Filippo an abrasive whistle-blower who often clashed with his colleagues and with the chemistry department's chairman, Robert S. Boikess. Mr. San Filippo has filed several grievances and lawsuits against the university. One grievance that protested the decision by Rutgers not to give him a merit raise was decided in his favor.

In a written decision issued in that case a year ago, an arbitrator wrote that while it was clear that Mr. San Filippo was "argumentative, abrasive, stubborn, lacks tact, and attracts controversy as easily as uncovered food attracts ants," it was also clear he was being treated unfairly by the university.

Mr. San Filippo's dismissal case is so complicated that even faculty union leaders are sharply divided over it. Among the few people who have taken his side is Wells H. Keddie, a union leader who is serving as a counselor to Mr. San Filippo in the case.

"There's nothing in the tenure regulations that say you have to be on wonderful terms with everybody," said Mr. Keddie. "If that were the case, a lot of my colleagues wouldn't be around, and some would say I shouldn't be around."

Reprinted with permission.

McConnell v. Howard University
818 F.2d 58 (D.C. Cir. 1987)

HARRY T. EDWARDS, Circuit Judge:

Alan McConnell brought an action in the District Court alleging that Howard University (the "University") breached certain clear contractual obligations when it terminated his appointment as a tenured faculty member without cause and without adhering to prescribed procedures. He also claimed that University officials had made certain defamatory statements about him. The District Court entered summary judgment in favor of Howard University. We agree that the defamation claim is without merit, and affirm that portion of the judgment. However, because the District Court applied erroneous legal theories in deciding the appellant's contract claims, and because there exist several disputed questions of fact material to those claims, we vacate that portion of the judgment and remand the case to the District Court for further proceedings.

* * *

The District Court viewed the Faculty Handbook as constituting the contract defining the parties' rights and obligations. The trial court found that, under the contract, Dr. McConnell's appointment could be terminated for neglect of professional responsibilities and that the teaching of assigned classes was a professional responsibility. The judge held that Dr. McConnell's "refusal to teach a class . . . must constitute a failure to meet a professional responsibility," and so Dr. McConnell was terminated for "cause." He further found "no provision of the contract giving [Dr. McConnell] any legal right to be excused from performance of his teaching duty." Finally, the trial judge found no "material evidence that [Dr. McConnell] was deprived of procedural rights guaranteed by the contract." Therefore, termination was proper under the contract.

The District Court went on to hold that, under the contract and general principles of adjudication, judicial review of the University's actions was limited and that the Board of Trustees' decision should be upheld "unless the Board's decision was arbitrary, or plaintiff has proffered evidence of improper motivation or irrational action." ("[T]he cases generally support the proposition . . . that a federal court should hesitate before significantly intruding in the administration of university affairs. . . . ") The court then found that the Board's decision was not "arbitrary" or "irrational," and that there was no evidence of improper motivation.

With regard to the defamation claim, the court found, in the alternative, that the allegedly defamatory statements were either "evaluative opinions" that were not "false" or that the University enjoyed a qualified privilege under *Greenya v. George Washington University* and that Dr. McConnell had not established a *prima facie* case of malice to overcome the privilege. Dr. McConnell appealed the grant of summary judgment.

II. THE BREACH OF CONTRACT CLAIMS

The appellant argues that summary judgment was inappropriate in this case because a number of material facts are in dispute. Moreover, he alleges that the District Court relied on improper legal theories in rendering its judgment. We agree. As will be shown below, using the correct legal framework, several disputed issues of fact must be resolved before a judgment may be rendered on the appellant's breach of contract claims.

A. *Introduction*

It is well established that, under District of Columbia law, an employee handbook such as the Howard University Faculty Handbook defines the rights and obligations of the employee and the employer, and is a contract enforceable by the courts. Our analysis of this case must, therefore, begin with an examination of the Faculty Handbook. The Faculty Handbook provides that, "subject to provisions in Section VI [specifying dismissal procedures], an appointment with indefinite tenure is terminable by the University only for cause or on account of extraordinary financial emergencies." Among the enumerated causes is "[n]eglect of professional responsibilities." The parties agree that Dr. McConnell enjoyed an appointment with indefinite tenure and that the sole ground for his dismissal was neglect of professional responsibilities. Thus, the relevant issues are whether Dr. McConnell, by failing to teach four classes, neglected his professional responsibilities, and, assuming that he did, whether the University followed the procedures set forth in the Faculty Handbook.

B. *Neglect of Professional Responsibilities*

The District Court apparently viewed the term "neglect of professional responsibilities" as if the words "neglect of" were interchangeable with the words "failure to meet." It held that "[i]t seems incontrovertible that the refusal to teach a class (flouting direct administration orders in the process) must constitute a failure to meet a professional responsibility." It is difficult to doubt the assertion that teaching assigned classes was part of McConnell's professional responsibilities and that, by not teaching assigned classes, McConnell failed to meet a professional responsibility. "Failure to meet professional responsibilities," however, is not the standard set forth in the Faculty Handbook for dismissal for cause; "*neglect* of professional responsibilities" is. Thus, the issue that must be resolved is whether Dr. McConnell's *failure* to teach assigned classes constituted *neglect* of his professional responsibilities.

Dr. McConnell contends that his failure to teach the classes did not constitute neglect of professional responsibilities. He maintains that the McNeil incident disrupted the class and that he needed to reestablish an appropriate teaching atmosphere before he could resume teaching. In essence, Dr. McConnell asserts that, had he persisted in attempting to teach the class without resolving the incident, he could not teach effectively, and would thus be neglecting his professional responsibilities by *continuing* to teach in such a situation. Dr. McConnell argues that the District Court erred in viewing his failure to teach as *per se* constituting cause for his dismissal.

We agree with the appellant. The term "neglect" necessarily implies an assessment as to whether Dr. McConnell's actions, given the entire factual context, were within the acceptable range of conduct within his professor. The Grievance Committee's findings suggest that Dr. McConnell's actions may well not have constituted a neglect of professional responsibilities. The Grievance Committee stated that, in its view, Dr. McConnell's decision not to teach the class was an attempt "to restore what [he] believed to be standard teacher-student relationships," and that "it is convincingly clear from the evidence presented that his departmental colleagues, including the Departmental Chairman, fail to view him as being professionally negligent."

At trial, Dr. McConnell should be allowed to present evidence that, under the facts and circumstances of this case, he acted within the bounds of reasonable behavior for a professor. Among the relevant issues are: (1) whether Dr. McConnell's reaction to the McNeil incident was a reasonable one; (2) whether Dr. McConnell took reasonable steps to resolve the incident; and (3) whether, under the circumstances, including Howard University's alleged lack of action to rectify the McNeil incident, McConnell acted reasonably in deciding not to teach the class until Ms. McNeil either dropped the class or apologized.

In short, we believe that the term "neglect of professional responsibilities," by its very words, includes a consideration of the reasonableness of Dr. McConnell's actions under the totality of the circumstances surrounding them. We also believe that the very concept of termination for "cause" necessarily includes the consideration of mitigating factors. In any event, it is clear that the terms "neglect of professional responsibilities" and "cause" certainly do not explicitly exclude the consideration of reasonableness and mitigating circumstances. So, at worst, the terms are ambiguous and must be construed in keeping with general usage and custom at the University and within the academic community.

In the instant case, the termination procedures set forth in the Faculty Handbook make sense only if the determination as to whether "cause" for termination exists includes an assessment of professional standards in the context of the particular facts and circumstances. The termination procedures include a hearing before a Grievance Committee composed of tenured faculty members. The Grievance Committee, after conducting the hearing, then prepares a report containing findings and recommendations for presentation to the Board of Trustees. The Board then decides whether to adopt the Grievance Committee's recommendations, or to conduct its own review of the record. Such a structure, with fact-finding and recommendations made by a panel of fellow professors, would make little sense if the only relevant issue was whether an established responsibility had not been fulfilled. The contract clearly contemplates an evaluation of a professor's actions according to the standards of the profession and a determination as to whether, given the facts and circumstances, the actions of the professor constituted cause for termination. A wooden exercise in single-issue fact-finding is simply not contemplated under this structure.

In viewing Dr. McConnell's failure to teach as *per se* constituting cause for his dismissal, the District Court foreclosed consideration of the reasonableness of the appellant's actions and possible mitigating circumstances. This was error.

C. Breach of the Contract by the University's Inaction

Dr. McConnell also presents an alternative theory supporting his decision not to teach the classes. He claims that Howard University had a duty to act to rectify incidents such as the September 6 incident involving Ms. McNeil. Dr. McConnell maintains that if the University was in breach of its obligations to him as a result of its actions (or inaction) in the wake of the McNeil incident, it cannot terminate his appointment for his subsequent decision not to teach the classes.

There is no specific language in the Faculty Handbook regarding the University's role in resolving student/teacher grievances. However, Dr. McConnell argues that this duty is implied by the nature of the University setting and the existence of the Howard University Code of Conduct and of the System of Judiciaries that has been set up to enforce the code. The Code of Conduct states that "[a] student may be disciplined for ... '[the] [o]bstruction or disruption of teaching ... or [of] other University activities." The Grievance Committee agreed with Dr. McConnell. It found that "[t]he right to teach and the responsibilities associated with it are deeply rooted in academic tradition and reinforced by various organizational structures in the academy." The Committee believed that "[a] teacher has the right to expect the University to protect the professional authority in teacher-student relationships."

At trial, Dr. McConnell should be allowed to demonstrate that the University owed him a contractual duty to protect his professional authority in the classroom and that the University's actions constituted a breach of that duty. In this regard, we find it notable that, although Dean Lane stated that "[t]he University strongly disapproves of the type of behavior attributed to Miss McNeil" and that "repetition of a similar incident on the part of the student [would not] be tolerated," the University apparently took no steps to address the incident. If it was powerless to do so, Dean Lane's statement that repetition of a similar incident would not be tolerated is curious. Furthermore, although Elementary Functions I was offered in multiple sections, the University evidently took no steps either to transfer Ms. McNeil to a different section, or to assign Dr. McConnell to a different section. The Grievance Committee's evaluation of the University's actions was blunt and damning: "No one representing the University seemed inclined to do anything except to prefer charges against Dr. McConnell."

If Dr. McConnell can show that the University owed him a duty to protect his professional authority, there is still an additional showing that must be made. He must also prove that, under the contract, the breach either relieved him of his obligation to teach or that the breach itself constituted a mitigating factor precluding the University from terminating his appointment for cause.

We cannot at this point offer a final assessment of the appellant's position with respect to the University's alleged inaction. But we find that he has presented a claim that easily withstands summary judgment. As this court noted in *Greene v. Howard University*, "[c]ontracts are written, and are to be read, by reference to the norms of conduct and expectations founded upon them. This is especially true of contracts in and among a community of scholars." Surely, "among a community of scholars," one who is assigned to teach must have some semblance of control over the classroom. If control is lost, learning invariably will be obstructed and the teacher will be unable to fulfill a professional responsibility. In such a situation, it seems quite clear that there are a number of issues to be resolved: (1) Has there been a significant breakdown in classroom discipline, i.e., such that teaching and learning are or may be impaired? (2) If so, does the fault lie with the students, the instructor, or both? (3) What is the role of the University in such a situation? and (4) If it has a role to play, has the University acted to protect the professional authority of the teacher and/or to restore order to the classroom?

On the facts of this case, the District Court must consider whether Dr. McConnell was due some support from the University that he did not receive in connection with a student disciplinary matter. This matter could not be resolved on summary judgment because the parties have vastly different views about the responsibility of the University under the contract to protect Dr. McConnell's professional authority in the classroom. The resolution of this issue—along with the resolution of the issues pertaining to reasonableness and mitigating circumstances—is essential to any determinations regarding "neglect of professional responsibilities" and "cause" to justify the termination of a tenured appointment.

D. *The University's Compliance with Procedures*

Dr. McConnell also claims that, assuming, *arguendo*, that there was cause for his dismissal, the University was bound by the Faculty Handbook to follow prescribed procedures. He points to a disputed issue of fact as to whether one procedural step— transmittal of the report of the Grievance Committee to the Board of Trustees— occurred.

* * *

Dr. McConnell maintains that, rather than transmitting the "full report of the

Grievance Committee," the President presented the Board with a two-page summary of the Grievance Committee's findings. In fact, Dr. Cheek, the President of the University, stated in his deposition that he did not think that he transmitted the full report to the Board. Howard University maintains that, in fact, the Board of Trustees did receive the report.

Failure to transmit the full report to the Board would clearly be at odds with the procedures set forth in the Faculty Handbook. Since the power to terminate the appointment of a tenured faculty member is subject to procedures set forth in the Faculty Handbook, it follows that this failure, if established at trial, would place Howard University in violation of its contract with McConnell. "[T]he University . . . is bound by the contracts it makes."

III. The Standard of Review Over The University's Decision

The foregoing analysis of Dr. McConnell's breach of contract claims assumes that the trial court's posture in reviewing these claims is no different than the posture a court would take in analyzing *any* breach of contract claim. Namely, the court is charged with interpreting the meaning of the contractual terms, and determining whether the facts establish that a party has breached those terms. Both the District Court and the appellee have advanced reasons why a court should not engage in its typical role in this case, and ought to take a more deferential stance toward Howard University's decision to terminate Dr. McConnell's tenured appointment at the University. These arguments are without merit.

*　*　*

Given the structure of the prescribed procedures, it appears that the Board of Trustees has tremendous leeway to reject findings of the Grievance Committee. If we were to adopt a view limiting judicial review over the substance of the Board of Trustees' decision, we would be allowing one of the parties to the contract to determine whether the contract had been breached. This would make a sham of the parties' contractual tenure arrangement.

On remand, the trial court must consider *de novo* the appellant's breach of contract claims; no special deference is due the Board of Trustees once the case is properly before the court for resolution of the contract dispute.

C. *The Special Nature of the University*

The appellee urges us to adopt the view of the District Court that "a federal court should hesitate before significantly intruding in the administration of university affairs, particularly in a three-cornered dispute between a professor, a student and a university." We find no support for this argument in this case. This is not a "three-cornered dispute"; rather, what is at stake are the contractual rights of Dr. McConnell. However, taking the point more broadly, we do not understand why university affairs are more deserving of judicial deference than the affairs of any other business or profession. Arguably, there might be matters unique to education on which courts are relatively ill equipped to pass judgment. However, this is true in many areas of the law, including, for example, technical, scientific and medical issues. Yet, this lack of expertise does not compel courts to defer to the view of one of the parties in such cases. The parties can supply such specialized knowledge through the use of expert testimony. Moreover, even if there are issues on which courts are ill equipped to rule, the interpretation of a contract is not one of them. We find no precedent in the District of Columbia for the District Court's view, nor do we find persuasive precedent in any other jurisdiction.

Howard University's reliance on *Gray v. Canisius College* is misplaced. In *Gray*, the discharged tenured professor's suit was not based on a breach of contract theory. Rather, the suit was premised on the theory that New York courts may compel corporations chartered in New York to fulfill obligations imposed by their internal rules, such as the termination procedures set forth in the Canisius College Manual. In contrast, Dr. McConnell's case raises a breach of contract claim.

The District Court erroneously relies on our decision in *Williams v. Howard University* as support for employing a deferential standard of review in the university context. In *Williams*, an applicant who had been denied admission to Howard University Medical College brought suit, alleging violations of his constitutional rights, as well as contract and tort claims. We affirmed the District Court's dismissal of the civil rights claim, finding no government action to deprive Williams of his rights. We then found that "Williams ha[d] adduced no evidence of a violated contractual right," and that Williams' tort claim was actionable only on a showing of "improper motivation or irrational action on the part of Howard." *Williams* did *not* hold that actions by Howard University allegedly in contravention of a *contract* were actionable only if the plaintiff could show improper motivation or gross arbitrariness. We find no basis in law or reason for applying such a standard to a case involving the rights and obligations of parties to a contract, whether or not the case arises in a university setting.

* * *

V. CONCLUSION

We recognize that this is an important case. The termination of a tenured faculty member's appointment is a serious matter. In this appeal, Dr. McConnell has asked this court to determine his rights under his employment contract with Howard University. He does not ask for special treatment, but merely wishes Howard University to be made to account for its actions under its contract with him. We think that Dr. McConnell has raised a number of arguments that, if proved, would entitle him to relief under this contract. With the guidance provided in this opinion, we remand the case to the District Court so that Dr. McConnell will have an opportunity to prove his case.

As stated more fully above, this case is to be tried *de novo*, just as with any other contract case. In order to prevail on the merits, Dr. McConnell must establish either that "cause" did not exist to terminate his appointment *or* that the prescribed internal procedures were not followed. As a matter of law, Howard University could only terminate Dr. McConnell's appointment under the contract if, in light of all the surrounding facts and circumstances and the prevailing professional norms, Dr. McConnell's failure to teach assigned classes constituted neglect of professional responsibility. Thus, Dr. McConnell may offer evidence that there were mitigating factors in his situation that would lead a reasonable professor to decide not to teach the classes. Dr. McConnell also may attempt to establish at trial that Howard University breached an obligation owed to him in the way it handled the incident involving Ms. McNeil, and that, under the contract, this breach would relieve Dr. McConnell of his duty to teach the classes.

Finally, Dr. McConnell can also seek to establish that the procedures used by Howard University did not comply with the contractual requirements. This would include evidence concerning whether or not the full report of the Grievance Committee was transmitted to the Board of Trustees.

So ordered.

At trial before a D.C. jury, McConnell lost in 1988. Civ. A. 85–0298–LFO, 1988 W.L. 4237 (D.D.C.). Not many instances have arisen in which tenured faculty have litigated dismissals for cause. In public schools, there have been significantly more cases, both because there are many more schoolteachers than college professors, and because courts are less tolerant of behavior before children. College students are presumed less vulnerable and more resilient. Occasionally, as in *Mitchell v. Pewitt Independent School District*, the behavior of a teacher is so extraordinary that he would probably be denied a teaching post in either setting. Herbert Mitchell, a twenty-year teacher who taught 9th grade science, threatened in class to kill a student. When he was dismissed for unprofessional conduct, he appealed his firing, alleging, among other defenses, that he had not been counseled concerning his mistake, and that he had not been given an opportunity to make amends. The Texas Commissioner of Education held that his death threats did not necessitate counseling or an opportunity for remediation. Tex. Comm. Dec. 186-R2-785, 20 August 1987. One likely area where an increasing number of for-cause dismissals will occur is sexual harassment, due to increasing awareness of the problem, as noted in several cases elsewhere in the book, and to the pervasiveness of the inappropriate behavior on campuses.

Seniority and Age Discrimination

Rehor v. Case Western Reserve University
331 N.E.2d 416 (1975)

Plaintiff, Charles F. Rehor, was a tenured professor of English at Case Western Reserve University in Cleveland, which institution of higher learning is the defendant in this lawsuit.

Plaintiff commenced employment at Cleveland College in 1929, teaching primarily in the fields of English and Journalism. Cleveland College became a part of Western Reserve University in 1942. From 1942 through June 30, 1967, plaintiff was employed under contract as a professor at Western Reserve University. Plaintiff was granted tenure by Western Reserve University prior to 1948. At all times during which plaintiff was a faculty member there the retirement age was 70 years.

In July 1967, a federation of Case Institute of Technology and Western Reserve University took place and was organized under the laws of Ohio as a corporation not for profit, known as Case Western Reserve University. Plaintiff continued under contract as a professor at defendant university from July 1, 1967, to his retirement on June 30, 1973.

Defendant assumed the employment contracts between former Western Reserve University and its faculty members, including plaintiff. After the federation, defendant began a review of the separate policies, rules and regulations of the two former institutions and the adoption of uniform policies, rules and regulations for defendant, its faculty, students and administration.

Two faculty committees of defendant reviewed the separate retirement policies of the two former institutions and recommended a uniform retirement policy. Case had a retirement age of 65 and Western Reserve's was 70. Notices of the activities of these committees were given to faculty members, and at least one public hearing for faculty members was held.

On April 16, 1969, defendant's Board of Trustees, duly acting through its executive committee, adopted a resolution amending defendant's faculty retirement policy, specifically as outlined and recommended by the *ad hoc* University Committee on Faculty Retirement in a memorandum to President Robert W. Morse, dated January 15, 1968.

The amended retirement policy provided that retirement of all faculty members was to be at age 65, subject to the following conditions: (a) Contributions by the university to its retirement pension program would cease at age 65; (b) upon reaching the designated age of 65, the faculty member would have the option of continued employment either full time or part time to age 68; (c) between the ages of 68 and 70 the faculty member could petition to be reappointed on a part-time or full-time basis, and, upon recommendation of the appropriate university committees, could be reappointed for a one-year or two-year period; and (d) reappointments on an annual basis only could be continued beyond age 70, these to be initiated only by the university committees.

This amended retirement policy was communicated to all faculty members, including plaintiff, in writing on April 6, 1970. Plaintiff was specifically advised in writing by defendant on June 2, 1970, that the date of his retirement would be June 30, 1973. On July 2, 1969, plaintiff executed an annual reappointment form for the academic year, July 1, 1969, to June 30, 1970. On July 6, 1970, plaintiff executed a reappointment form for the academic year, 1970–1971. On May 6, 1971, plaintiff executed a reappointment form for the academic year, 1971–1972. On May 17, 1972, plaintiff executed a reappointment form for the academic year 1972–1973, noting his objection to the retirement date of June 30, 1973. Each of these annual reappointment forms, signed by plaintiff after the adoption of defendant's amended retirement policy, provided for an increase of salary to plaintiff over the prior year.

Plaintiff was 68 years of age on September 5, 1972, and was retired as of June 30, 1973, in accordance with defendant's amended retirement policy. Pursuant to the terms of the amended retirement policy, plaintiff petitioned the appropriate faculty committee for a recommendation that he be reappointed beyond age 68. After committee consideration, no action was taken on that petition. Plaintiff also petitioned the president of defendant university by letter, dated July 19, 1971, for reappointment beyond age 68; this request was refused by the president in writing on September 22, 1971.

*   *   *

Academic tenure does not, in the manner expressed, vest a faculty member with the right to continued reappointment to the faculty, and we so hold. A vested right is a right fixed, settled, absolute, and not contingent upon anything. Such is not the case here.

The only signed documents evidencing the employment agreement between Professor Rehor and Case Western Reserve University are the annual reappointment forms, which appear as exhibits in the record. There are also 12 annual reappointment contracts in the record between Professor Rehor and former Western Reserve University. The annual reappointment forms do not state the components of tenure or of retirement. Likewise, they do not state faculty fringe benefits, perquisites of faculty appointment, or faculty standards. All of these matters are established by various policies, rules and regulations adopted by defendant and promulgated to its faculty.

It is agreed by plaintiff and defendant that a university's policies, rules and regulations relating to faculty members become a part of the employment contract as a matter of law. The trial court properly adhered to that principle. The Court of Appeals also agreed but, oddly, did not follow it in its decision.

Accordingly, we agree with defendant's first proposition of law and hold that the retirement policy of defendant established in its policies, rules and regulations— which includes the amended retirement policy adopted April 16, 1969—was part of the annual employment agreements between plaintiff and defendant after July 1, 1967.

Defendant urges, as its second proposition of law, that a university's grant of tenure to a faculty member does not preclude the university from thereafter changing the retirement age for all faculty members including the tenured faculty member, provided the change is reasonable and uniformly applicable.

This change in Case Western Reserve University's amended retirement policy was made upon the recommendation of its faculty, after study and open hearings; the amended retirement policy had a grandfather provision. When its retirement policy was amended, it also amended its pension plan to provide increased university contributions to Professor Rehor's retirement plan account. Professor Rehor's retirement age of 68, under the amended retirement policy, was well within the American Association of University Professors' suggested range of retirement ages from 65 to 70. Rehor's salary was increased annually in each year of his employment under Case Western Reserve University from September 1969 to June 1973. A representative of the association was an *ex officio* member of the committee that recommended the amended retirement policy. All the above facts indicate the reasonableness of the policy. Its uniform application is obvious. And no objection to the policy was ever raised by the American Association of University Professors, the plaintiff or any other faculty member after its adoption on April 16, 1969, until the spring of 1973.

We approve defendant's proposition of law No. 2, and reject the conclusion of law reached by the Court of Appeals, as stated in paragraph three of its syllabus, that:

> "Where a faculty member is awarded tenure by a university and the faculty bylaws of the university at that time state that the mandatory retirement age for faculty is 70 years, such provision in the faculty bylaws becomes a binding term of the faculty member's employment contract with the university, the faculty member has a vested right to be reappointed to the faculty to age 70, and the university cannot thereafter lower the faculty member's mandatory retirement age without abridging the employment contract."

Defendant, in his proposition of law No. 3, asserts that a university's bylaw, stating that the board of trustees shall from time to time adopt such rules and regulations governing the appointment and tenure of the members of the faculty as the board of trustees deems necessary, includes a reservation of the right to change the retirement age of the faculty.

* * *

Either the retirement policy set forth in Section IV of the university's Statement of Principles for Appointment, Tenure and Separation for the Guidance of Faculties is part of and protected by tenure, or it is not; and, if the retirement policy is a part of tenure, and we hold that it is, then the reserved right to change rules of tenure includes the right to change the retirement policy.

The fourth proposition of law advanced by defendant is to the effect that an employment contract between a university and a tenured faculty member may be amended by the parties in writing when supported by adequate consideration.

Defendant amended its retirement policy in 1969. This changed plaintiff's retirement age from 70 to 68 years with a right in plaintiff to be appointed beyond age 68 upon recommendation of a faculty committee. On July 6, 1970, after having been advised of the amended retirement policy and its specific application to him, plaintiff signed his 1970–1971 annual reappointment form which gave him a $500 salary increase. On May 6, 1971, plaintiff signed his 1971–1972 reappointment form, which also specified a $500 salary increase. Then, on May 17, 1972, plaintiff executed a 1972–1973 reappointment form which provided that it was a "[t]erminal appointment, with retirement on June 30, 1973," and it carried another $500 salary increase.

Thus, there was demonstrated adequate consideration for the amendment of the employment contract by the change in the retirement policy of the university.

CONCLUSION.

The trial court correctly concluded that the contract between the parties permitted defendant to change its retirement policy; further, that plaintiff had consented to that change and that there was not a breach of contract.

For the reasons stated above, the judgment of the Court of Appeals is reversed, and the judgment of the Court of Common Pleas is reinstated.

Judgment reversed.

Linn v. Andover-Newton Theological School

638 F. Supp. 1114 (D. Mass 1986)

TAURO, District Judge.

Dr. Edmund H. Linn, a tenured faculty member of defendant Andover-Newton Theological School, was fired at the age of 62, after 31 years of service. He, thereafter, brought this suit, claiming that his employment was terminated in violation of the Age Discrimination in Employment Act ("ADEA")[1] and in breach of plaintiff's employment contract with defendant. Presently at issue is plaintiff's renewed motion for partial summary judgment.

---

1. The Age Discrimination in Employment Act provides in pertinent part:
   It shall be unlawful for an employer—

   (1) to fall or refuse to hire or to discharge any individual or otherwise discriminate against any individual with respect to his compensation, terms, conditions, or privileges of employment, because of such individual's age.

29 U.S.C. § 623(a).

I.

The material facts are undisputed. On December 3, 1980, the executive committee of the defendant's board of trustees met, ordered the president to reduce the defendant's budget by at least $50,000, and appointed a four member faculty advisory committee to make recommendations with respect to the implementation of its order. On December 11, 1980, the faculty advisory committee met and recommended that the plaintiff be discharged. On December 23, 1980, the executive committee accepted the faculty advisory committee's recommendation to discharge the plaintiff. On December 29, 1980, the plaintiff received a letter from the president, giving him one-year's notice of his discharge. The executive committee's discharge of the plaintiff was approved by the full faculty of March 6, 1981, received and by the full board of trustees on May 6, 1981.

II.

Plaintiff has moved for summary judgment on Count 2 of the complaint, which alleges that plaintiff was terminated in violation of the terms of his contractual academic tenure rights. To prevail on this cause of action, plaintiff must establish that 1) a contract was in force between the parties, 2) the contract established the procedures to be followed in the event of plaintiff's discharge, and 3) these procedures were not followed by defendant in discharging plaintiff.

A.

It is uncontested that a contract was in existence between the two parties, and that the contract established procedures to be followed in the event of discharge. Defendant admits that the Andover-Newton Theological School Faculty Promotion and Tenure Policy ("FPTP") and the 1972 American Association of University Professors Recommended Institutional Regulations on Academic Freedom and Tenure ("1972 AAUP Regulations") were part of plaintiff's contract with the Andover-Newton Theological School. These documents contain provisions governing termination of a tenured faculty member.

> Where termination of an appointment with continuous tenure, or of a non-tenured appointment before the end of the specified term, is based on bona fide financial exigency or discontinuance of a program or department of instruction, Regulation 5 will not apply, but faculty members shall be able to have the issues reviewed by the faculty, or by an appropriate faculty committee (such as the faculty's grievance committee), with ultimate review of all controverted issues by the governing board.

Regulation 4(c), 1972 AAUP Regulations. Defendant claims that plaintiff's dismissal was pursuant to both a bona fide financial exigency and discontinuance of his position. Thus, Regulation 4(c) provides the relevant procedures governing plaintiff's discharge.

B.

Given the applicability of Regulation 4(c), the controlling question is whether its provisions were followed by defendant when discharging plaintiff.

It is undisputed that defendant did not give plaintiff any opportunity to participate in the deliberations of either the faculty advisory committee or the executive committee. Defendant's bottom line position is that Regulation 4(c) did not require the school to allow plaintiff to participate in any way at any stage of the deliberations.

This precise issue, however, has previously been decided in this case. In its opinion issued February 7, 1985, this court stated:

> This court interprets Regulation 4(c) as requiring that the faculty member facing termination be allowed to participate in the proceedings before the faculty group and the governing board. Without an opportunity to be heard, the faculty member in jeopardy would be unable to have the "issues reviewed" in any meaningful sense.... Even assuming that the plaintiff's termination was based upon financial exigency, therefore, the defendant failed to follow its own rules and regulations. Defendant has failed to present any arguments that were not pressed before the February 7, 1985 decision. Nevertheless, this court has reconsidered its former ruling, and has reached the same result. Regulation 4(c) states that faculty members "shall be able to have the issues reviewed" by a faculty committee and the governing board. That language clearly supposes that an aggrieved faculty person has a contractual right to request a review of his termination. To have any substance, the right to request review of an issue must carry with it a corollary right of the petitioner to present his point of view on the issue, whether in writing or in person. How else is the reviewing body able to know what is on the petitioner's mind, or why he requested a review? Here, defendant acted without any opportunity for plaintiff to be heard, in either a literal or figurative sense. In doing so, defendant breached Regulation 4(c).

CONCLUSION

The parties agree that the Andover-Newton Theological School FPTP and the 1972 AAUP Regulations were a part of the contract between plaintiff and defendant. The parties further agree that the 1972 AAUP Regulation 4(c) governed the procedures to be followed in terminating a tenured faculty member in instances of financial exigency or the elimination of a teaching position. This court finds that defendant violated Regulation 4(c) by failing to provide plaintiff any opportunity to participate in the review process. This court concludes, therefore, that plaintiff is entitled to summary judgment on Count 2 of the complaint, for breach of his employment contract by defendant.

AN ORDER WILL ISSUE.

Financial Exigency

AAUP v. Bloomfield College
129 N.J. Super. 249, 322 A.2d 846 (Ch. Div. 1974)

ANTELL, J.S.C.

This is an action for declaratory relief and specific performance with respect to the academic tenure of faculty members at Bloomfield College, a private institution of higher education licensed under the laws of the State of New Jersey. Plaintiff American Association of University Professors, Bloomfield College Chapter (hereinafter AAUP), is a labor organization within the meaning of the National Labor Relations Act, which has been certified and recognized by the National Labor Relations Board as the exclusive representative for collective bargaining on behalf of the college faculty. The individual plaintiffs include faculty members who seek clarification of their claimed tenured status and those whose service has been terminated and seek reinstatement to their former positions. Their periods of accumulated service range from 8 to 22 years. In addition to Bloomfield College, also named as defendants are Merle F. Allshouse, president of the college, and the individual members of the college board of trustees.

The legal basis of plaintiff's claim of tenure is to be found in the *Faculty Handbook* of the college under the heading of "Bloomfield College Policies on Employment and Tenure" (hereinafter "Policies"). This document forms an essential part of the contractual terms governing the relationship between the college and the faculty. Under paragraph C thereof

> Bloomfield College recognizes that tenure is a means to certain ends, specifically: (1) freedom of teaching and research and of extramural activities, and (2) a sufficient degree of economic security to make the profession attractive to men and women of ability. Freedom and security, hence tenure, are indispensable to the success of an institution in fulfilling its obligations to its students and to society.

Following a probationary period of seven years, which has been completed by all the individual plaintiffs, subparagraph C(3) provides:

> ... a teacher will have tenure and his services may be terminated only for adequate cause, except in case of retirement for age, or under extraordinary circumstances because of financial exigency of the institution.

Pertinent also is subparagraph C(6) of the "Policies" which provides:

> Termination of continuous appointment because of financial exigency of the institution must be demonstrably *bona fide*. A situation which makes drastic retrenchment of this sort necessary precludes expansion of the staff at other points at the same time, except in extraordinary circumstances.

On June 21, 1973 the board of trustees adopted Resolution R-58 which in material part resolved:

> ... [U]pon the recommendation of the Executive Committee, the President, the Dean of the College, and with the advice of the special Evaluation Committee for the reduction of faculty size due to financial exigency, and in accordance with the action of the Board on March 1 and the recommendation of the Academic Affairs Committee that thirteen faculty members be terminated in the reduction of faculty size due to financial exigency, the following persons be informed that they will be terminated as of June 30, 1974, and their duties for the 1973–74 academic year be defined to include no teaching, participation in College governance, or voting privileges....

> That every faculty member be informed on or before June 30, 1973 that all 1973–74 contracts are one-year terminal contracts. The Board of Trustees through its Academic Affairs Committee will call together from among the remaining 54 members of the faculty an evaluation committee to determine

what faculty members will remain at the College beyond June 30, 1974. This Committee to Define and Evaluate Personnel Needs will define personnel needs for the new academic program priorities which are set and the curricular revisions which are made, and will evaluate existing faculty members to determine their qualifications for meeting these needs. Their recommendations are to be made no later than November 30, 1973. All faculty members will be notified by December 15, 1973, as to their contract status for the 1974–75 academic year.

Acting thereunder, defendant Allshouse under date of June 29, 1973 notified 13 members of the faculty that it was his "unpleasant duty to inform you that the Board of Directors, at its meeting on June 21, 1973, took action to terminate your services as part of the reduction of the faculty size due to financial exigency." They were further advised:

Following the Board's action and in accordance with our prior oral conversation, this will serve to advise you formally that you have been relieved of all duties as a Bloomfield College faculty member; and, therefore, you will not be obliged to and will not perform any services for the College or participate in College governance after June 30, 1973.

The letter expresses the hope that the recipient

... understand the need for the College to take stern measures in a time of financial exigency despite the personal disappointment and anguish which are inevitably part of such a decision. You have made an invaluable contribution to the College, and I deeply regret that our present situation makes this action necessary.

On the same date all the remaining members of the faculty, tenured and non-tenured, were notified by letter memorandum that at the June 21 meeting the board of trustees "took action to the effect that every faculty member should be informed that all 1973-74 contracts are one-year terminal contracts." The letter continues:

The notice of termination does not necessarily imply that you will be terminated at the end of the 1973-74 academic year, but it provides a base from which each faculty member can negotiate a learning contract which meets both personal professional interests and College needs.

During the period between June 21, 1973 and the commencement of the school year in September 1973 the College engaged the services of 12 new and untenured teachers to serve on its faculty. Defendants assert that these were hired to replace others who were lost to the school over a period of time as the result of "normal attrition," not those who were terminated under Resolution R-58.

Among the roster of plaintiffs are included (1) those faculty members who received termination notices and seek reinstatement to their former positions, and (2) those whose employment was continued, but subject to one-year terminal contracts. The latter ask declaratory judgment that their tenured status is unaffected by the action of the board of trustees in adopting Resolution R-58. As is clearly implied by the excerpted documents, defendants justify the resolution on the basis of "financial exigency." The issue projected is whether the action accomplished by Resolution R-58 in abrogating tenure and terminating the employment of tenured faculty members at Bloomfield College was "demonstrably bona fide" as having been taken "under extraordinary circumstances because of the financial exigency of the institution." Complementary thereto is the question as to whether the circumstances were further "extraordinary" so as to allow at the same time for the hiring of 12 new teachers.

Bloomfield College is a small commuter-type institution tracing its origins to an academy founded in 1807 by the Presbyterian Church. It was established as the German Theological School in 1868 and is affiliated with the New Jersey Synod of the United Presbyterian Church. It serves a student body which has been described as ethnically mixed, presenting a low academic profile and embracing a large minority group representation. Students are drawn mainly from the lower middle and upper lower economic strata and for the most part are enrolled in the school's business and nursing departments.

Present annual tuition is $2,000, up from $1,330 in 1969. Enrollment for the present year, 1973–74, is 867, down from 1,069 in 1972. The portent of these figures lies in the fact that three-fourths of the school's financial support is derived from enrollment income.

Enrollment projections testimonially offered by college officials for 1974–75 range between 450 and 638. Those were given without factual foundation and are said to have been based upon unspecified "demographic studies." They are in curious contrast to the projected enrollment of 905 for the same period, gradually increasing to 1,030 during the school year 1978–79, which appears at page 17 of the Bloomfield College Presidents' Report dated March 1974. The discrepancy is rationalized by President Allshouse's explanation in part that to publish the bleak truth in his report would have disserved the interest of public relations and been damaging to college morale. Although in final form, it has been decided to withhold the report from public distribution for reasons of economy, not because of any errors in its content.

Although the decreased enrollment for the 1973–74 year was accurately forecast in the spring of 1973, the previous year's projection fell short of the actual enrollment by 131 students. This miscalculation was never explained, and is noted with interest for the reasons that the faculty reduction from 76 to 54 was deliberately brought about to achieve, supposedly, a 17 to 1 student-faculty ratio based upon anticipated enrollment for the 1973–74 school year. That this decision rested upon data of demonstrated unreliability is pertinent to a determination as to the college's good faith.

The reduction referred to was the combined result of discharging the 13 teachers, "normal attrition" to the extent of 21 teachers who left for various reasons between June 30, 1972 and August 31, 1973, and addition of the 12 newcomers between June 21 and September 30, 1973. Consideration was given to retaining the discharged faculty members instead of hiring new ones, but this alternative was rejected upon the belief, it is said, that the former would not fit in with proposed program innovations which were envisioned by the college as part of its overall rehabilitation. The changes were described in the evidence as "new directions," and were planned to set the college on a unique academic course. Their design was to reduce the number of majors and departments by bringing them all into 12 broad interdisciplinary areas in order to improve administration and curricular planning. The ultimate objective, so it was said, was to turn around the enrollment projection by (1) offering career oriented prospective students a firm liberal arts foundation, (2) enhancing the distinctiveness of attending Bloomfield for what it could offer as a small college, and (3) responding "very seriously" to the personal needs of the students.

Apart from the installation of a special freshman seminar and advisory program and greater emphasis on the development of evening and part-time enrollment of mature women and special groups, and possibly the improvement of administrative controls, the practical changes to be accomplished by the new directions were never clearly stated. Despite the references to interdisciplinary approaches, the basic disciplines still prevail, and whatever revisions may have been made are minor in nature. Notable also on the question of bona fides is the fact that the decision to install the new directions was not made until the fall of 1973, some months after the adoption of Resolution R-58 and after the institution of plaintiffs' suit. In any event, the result assertedly anticipated by the new programs are not now seen as attainable. Present projections forecast continued reductions in enrollment.

Turning to a consideration of the college's assets and liabilities, we note first that its budget for the 1972–73 school year was $3,652,000. For the year 1973–74 it is $3,397,000. The planned cash deficit for 1972 was $123,000 and for 1973 $191,000, with estimates that it will probably rise to $231,000 for the year. Between June 30, 1973 and March 31, 1974 it reached $145,000. By cash deficit is meant the amount by which the accounts payable and direct loans exceed available cash. In June 1973 its operating deficit, i.e., the amount by which current liabilities exceed current assets, was $368,000. In 1973 the college endowment fund was $945,000, reflecting a 21% decline from the previous year, of which 17.19% occurred between January 1 and March 31, 1973. Cash flow problems intensified around June 1973, with accounts payable accumulating to the point where some went back to February 1973, and were compounded by financing difficulties. Interest on loans rose from 8% to 11%, higher borrowing costs resulted from the college's loss of status as a prime lending risk some years ago, and the declining value of the endowment portfolio further restricted borrowing capacity. As the result of conferences—which were, coincidentally, carried on during the hearings and of which the court was kept aware—its bank will now determine its lending status on a week-to-week basis and will advance no funds other than those necessary to meet payrolls. Under these circumstances a freeze has been placed upon all expenses other than payroll.

It is recognized by the administration that existing mortgages could be recast in order to ease the cash situation, but this decision has been deferred for the reason that the ultimate costs would eventually increase the financial burden. The prospect of rising fixed costs, the built-in limitation on tuitions resulting from the economic character of the student body, and reductions of federal aid with no corresponding increases in state aid programs are additional negative factors. Lack of available scholarship aid is another deterrent to the college's financial reanimation. At present it can only put 4% of its budget into scholarships, a figure which should be as high as 15% to 17%. Help is needed from federal or other outside sources, and without such assistance the school is burdened by a "tuition-subsidy gap." It is believed that enrollment and tuition income will continue to decline for the following three reasons: (1) the pool from which the college has historically drawn in terms of age and economic background is itself being diminished, a widespread phenomenon; (2) inability to develop a sufficiently attractive academic program, and (3) costs. In addition, it is believed that the present location of the college in Essex County is not conducive to further growth for the reason that the area is already overburdened with educational facilities in terms of existing need.

The remaining significant asset of the college, in addition to its tuition income, the college property and its endowment fund, is the Knoll Golf Club. The Knoll is a property of 322 acres, having two golf courses, two clubhouses, a swimming pool and a few residences. It was purchased by the college around the end of 1966 or early 1967 with the intention of using it for the establishment of an educational plant. The purchase price was $3,325,000, and was paid for by $900,000 cash, a bank loan of $300,000 and a mortgage of $2,125,000. The $900,000 was provided as a gift to the college by the Presbyterian Church out of monies raised as part of its Fifty Million Dollar Fund, a fund-raising project conducted by the church. These monies are dedicated to purposes of educational capital development and cannot be used for any other purpose.

Conservative estimates as to the market value of The Knoll in its present condition lie between $5,000,000 and $7,000,000. The net yield to the college out of a $5,000,000 sale, after taxes and the liquidation of secured debts, would be around $1,536,000. At $7,000,000 the sale would yield $2,366,000. In addition, there would also be realized some $795,000 owing to the college's current operating fund as well as approximately $727,000, being the present value of the gift from the Fifty Million Dollar Fund, subject, of course, to the terms and restrictions of that benefaction.

Although the college does not carry The Knoll as a liability, the income received therefrom does not exceed what is necessary to meet carrying charges. It is required, however, to make substantial cash advances during the year to sustain the operation, and these, of course, are additional burdens upon its already strained cash position. At year's end 1972 and 1973 these advances totaled $263,000 and $269,000, respectively.

The salient economic features of this property in its present posture, therefore, are that it is altogether lacking in income-producing characteristics, that it compels some degree of cash diversion from the operating needs of the college, and that its sale would release sufficient cash to meet the college's immediate and reasonably foreseeable financial requirements.

Present plans for the future of The Knoll are uncertain. The one being most seriously entertained is the installation of a large development which would occupy 202.5 acres of land. Site plans and proposals show an 84-month building plan projecting 61 units of low-density housing, 240 units of luxury housing, 2 medium-rise buildings having 340 units, as well as medium-density townhouses and condominiums. Negotiations preliminary to necessary zoning applications are taking place, but even assuming zoning approval is obtained (a prospect which is by no means assured), a lead time of at least two years must precede actual construction. Needless to say, the successful completion of such a program would greatly enhance the value of The Knoll to the college as a sustaining asset, but it is obvious that retention of the property for long-term appreciation necessarily requires that the college forego the benefit of the improved cash position which would be realized from a near term sale.

Without question, the economic health of the college is poor. A more definitive diagnosis is that the problem is chiefly one of liquidity, a difficulty with which the college has been coping for many years. Although a recent audit shows $56,000 in cash as against accounts payable of $301,000, previous years' figures show that in

1968 there was only $808 against $985,000 in accounts payable, in 1971 $6,000 available against $1,247,000 in accounts payable, in 1972 $6,000 available as against $777,000, and as of June 30, 1973 $12,302 available as against $1,018,000. The college's dilemma is real, but not unique. Although financially beleaguered, as Mr. Ritterskamp, who testified on behalf of the college as an expert in the financing of higher education, said, "all private education is in financial trouble today."

Notwithstanding the problem of cash flow, Bloomfield College is a very substantial educational institution with a net worth of $6,600,000, reflecting assets of $12,600,000 and liabilities of $6,000,000, based upon book values which show The Knoll as an asset worth only $3,370,000. The college is by no means insolvent, even though it is difficult for it to meet obligations as they mature. Although its preference is to exploit The Knoll's long-term possibilities, its choices are by no means restricted to this course of action. The option of selling the property now is perhaps more realistic as a survival measure since it would supply immediate liquidity. Near-term infusion of needed cash could start an economic recovery leading the college at some future time to a firmer financial base from which to move into more speculative, more rewarding ventures of the kind now under consideration. While the program of development being investigated might eventually provide vast financial resources, they would not begin to benefit the college for many years during which it would presumably continue its penurious standards to the detriment of its standing as an educational institution.

Regardless, however, of what the future may offer, the sale of The Knoll as an available alternative to the abrogation of tenure is a viable one and fairly to be considered on the meritorious issues.

* * *

Conceding that the college is under financial stress, and that "something had to be done," it does not follow that the college's freedom of response extends to the unilateral revocation of a contractually protected employment status and the discharge of tenured teachers as a matter of unbridled discretion. Similarly, although it may be appropriate to inspect the available resources and alternatives open to the college, this does not imply authority on the part of the court to substitute its judgment for that of the trustees, to weigh the wisdom of their action, to modify wayward or imprudent judgments in their formulation of educational or financial policy, or to decide whether the survival of the institution remains "possible" by the choice of other courses of action. The trustees, after all, have the best insight into the college's problems and will have the continuing duty of determining and providing for its future priorities. Their considered judgment in matters of policy is not lightly to be displaced. Interests must be balanced, and while the court must refrain from interfering with the policy-making and administrative processes of the college, still, it is called upon to protect important contractual rights against excesses in the mobilization of administrative and policy-making powers.

In the interpretation of a contract it is the primary function of the court to ascertain and effectuate the intention of the parties. The contract must be construed as a whole, and the intention of the parties is to be collected from the entire agreement, having regard to the language chosen, the relations of the parties, the attendant circumstances and the objective they were trying to attain.

In our search for the controlling standard we are struck by the great plasticity of the raw material presented. The very concept of "exigency" changes before our eyes. Its meaning varies with the light of surrounding circumstances. To say that it connotes a state of pressing urgency, a time of crisis or immediate need, is meaningless without knowing the nature of the particular need, its relationship to the purposes of the institution, and what will be sacrificed by its nonfulfillment. One must cross the long gradient between starvation and appetite, between illness and discontent, between need and desire, and determine where one ends and the other begins. It is a process which involves a sequence of changing value judgments based upon altering proportions between costs and objectives. In this sense, the only definition of exigency which suits our needs is that offered by Webster as "such need or necessity as belongs to the occasion."

That the parties intended that this evaluation not be left to the college free of restraint is shown by their choice of preconditions (1) that the Board's action be demonstrably bona fide, (2) extraordinary circumstances, (3) that staff expansions in other areas not be undertaken except in "extraordinary circumstances."

* * *

The test best suited to effectuate the intent of the parties on judicial review of the college's action, therefore, is whether the action taken followed from the board's demonstrably bona fide belief, under honestly formulated standards, in the existence of a financial exigency and extraordinary attendant circumstances, and in the necessity for terminating tenured faculty members as a means of relieving the exigent condition. Interrelated therewith is the question of whether sufficient credible evidence of "exigency" and "extraordinary circumstances" exists as to provide a basis for the conclusions reached in the exercise of a reasonable and prudent judgment.

Except for policy differences touching upon the presumption of correctness and burden of proof, the test proposed is materially comparable to that used on judicial review of actions by governmental administrative agencies and in cases involving the discharge of tenured teachers for cause. Bearing in mind the fluidity of the considerations which must be woven together and the extremely severe restrictions which the college has accepted upon its authority to act, it would seem to provide a fair and workable control upon capricious action in the firing of tenured teachers for reason of financial exigency. Application thereof requires that we consider and make allowance for: the obligation incumbent upon the board of trustees to manage the business of the college, to appraise and project existing and future needs and resources and to act in the light of its own best judgment free of outside interference; its duty to honor solemnly undertaken tenure commitments, the objective data relating to the college's financial circumstances, its financial history, the authenticity of the financial threat; evaluations expressed by the board of trustees, the existence of real alternatives to the action taken, and the nature and extent of academic tenure itself. We must somehow orchestrate these dissonant and uncongenial values, rights, obligations, objective facts and subjective judgments into a unified standard by which to judge whether defendants have carried their extraordinary burden of proof in justification for the firing of tenured faculty members and the abrogation of tenure for others. We have done so.

The court concludes that the actions of Bloomfield College with respect to the tenured status of its faculty members in terminating the services of some and placing others on one-year employment contracts under the circumstances presented overflowed the limits of its authority as defined by its own Policies, and therefore failed to constitute a legally valid interruption in the individual plaintiffs' continuity of service. Whatever other motivations defendants might have had, they have failed to demonstrate by a preponderance of the evidence that their purported action was in good faith related to a condition of financial exigency within the institution. These conclusions are compelled by the following enumerated considerations:

(1) Although some financial relief might have been realized by discontinuing the services of the 13 faculty members, it has not been suggested how the college could possibly have been similarly benefited by placing the entire remaining faculty, including tenured personnel, on one-year terminal contracts. This startling action could have produced no immediate financial benefit, could not have been inspired by financial exigency, and can only be interpreted as a calculated repudiation of a contractual duty without any semblance of legal justification. It was a gratuitous challenge to the principle of academic tenure. Its clear implication of ulterior design and lack of sensitivity to the question of moral correctness reflect adversely upon the claimed bona fides of discharging the 13 faculty members for the same given reason.

(2) The hiring of 12 new faculty members between June 21 and September 30, 1973 (the period during which the action complained of took place) has not been justified by a showing of "extraordinary circumstances" as required by subparagraph C(6) of the Bloomfield College "Policies." The record is lacking, in fact, any evidence from which it can be determined what the financial consequences of these hirings were, whether they resulted in a savings to the college, and if so in what amount. The explanation that the newcomers were brought in to meet the demands of a modified curriculum is totally unacceptable. Although the testimony is richly festooned with references to "teaching-learning contracts," "interdisciplinary programs," "steady state," "new directions," and "career tracks," the phrases lack content of any value in understanding what the new program was all about. It was only topically delineated and no explanation was offered as to why the tenured faculty members could not meet its requirements. Further, the court is entirely unclear as to the dynamics by which the new directions program was expected to reverse the unfavorable enrollment prognosis. This is notable in view of the fact that the success which defendants claim was anticipated never, in fact, materialized. In any case, the new program was not inaugurated until the fall of 1973, some months after the adoption of Resolution R-58 and after the institution of this suit.

*　　*　　*

(3) The financial problem is one of liquidity, which, as the evidence demonstrates, has plagued the college for many years. The board chairman himself testified that he cannot "remember when financing was ever easy." Unless we are prepared to say that financial exigency is chronic at Bloomfield College, it is difficult to say how, by any reasonable definition, the circumstances can now be pronounced exigent.

Recognizing the right of the board of trustees to make its own business judgments as to how to improve cash flow, still, the yield from a sale of The Knoll has been conservatively estimated at between 1 ½ and 4 million dollars. Apart from the discontinuation of cash advances to the golf club, the immediate benefits which the college would realize from such a cash infusion has been described. What effect this would have on the school's long-term future is, of course, uncertain. However, it clearly enhances the probability that it will be able to continue as a college for the foreseeable future. This much certainly cannot be said of the expansive development program now being explored. By so commenting, we do not suggest that one or the other of the courses is to be preferred, but that the college's claim of financial exigency can be validated only in its role as an educational institution, not as the aspiring proprietor of high rise apartments, condominiums and luxury dwellings. Its desire to retain this investment for long-term appreciation is not a factor which the court may weigh in passing upon the existence of a financial exigency. Its immediate duty is to maintain its educational programs and refrain from acts of faithlessness toward the faculty members by whom it has been competently served. In this light the fact surrounding its economic existence cannot reasonably support its claim of demonstrably bona fide financial exigency.

* * *

For our purposes completion by the individual plaintiffs of their seven-year probationary periods constitutes full performance of their obligations in return for which they have been granted tenured status.

For the reasons given it is concluded that the individual plaintiffs who were terminated from their positions as faculty members of Bloomfield College are entitled to reinstatement under the terms and conditions of the "Bloomfield College Policies on Employment and Tenure." By way of declaratory relief it will further be adjudged that all plaintiffs serving as tenured faculty members of Bloomfield College prior to June 21, 1973 are now, and shall continue, on tenured status within the terms of the "Bloomfield College Policies on Employment and Tenure," and that the provisions of Resolution R-58 to the contrary, adopted on June 21, 1973 by the Bloomfield College Board of Trustees, as well as all administrative actions taken thereunder by defendants, are in all respects inefficacious.

_____

The *Bloomfield* case was affirmed, holding that the college had not successfully met its burden of proof. 346 A.2d 615 (1975). The situation eventually stabilized, and by 1988, the college enrolled 1,400 students.

_____

Pace v. Hymas
726 P.2d 693 (Idaho 1986)

BISTLINE, Justice.

On June 30, 1981, Lois Pace was laid off from her tenured faculty position with the University of Idaho on the grounds of a financial exigency. At the time she was discharged, Pace held the position of professor in the home economics program of the University's College of Agriculture. Pace was one of five members of a cooperative extension service offered by the University through the research and extension division of the College of Agriculture.

At the time of her discharge, Pace had 31 years' experience in her profession, the last nine being with the University of Idaho. Pace was the most experienced of the five members of the extension service program, but the only one laid off. When she was terminated, Pace was 54 years old; she could have voluntary retired with full benefits with only one more year of service.

After being discharged, Pace filed suit against the defendants. Pace's complaint alleges that the defendants denied Pace her due process rights in discharging her. The defendants answered Pace's complaint, denying liability and alleging several affirmative defenses.

A central issue in the case is whether there was a valid financial exigency to justify the defendants' decision to terminate Pace. The defendants argued there was; Pace argued there was not.

For ease in handling the case, the district court bifurcated the trial. The first part of the trial was to deal solely with the issue of whether or nor a *bona fide* financial exigency existed. The second part of the trial would deal with (1) whether her discharge based on the alleged financial exigency violated due process subject to a remedy pursuant to 42 U.S.C. § 1983, and (2) all the other issues in the case. The district court, in a pre-trial order, also ruled that the defendants would have the burden of proving that a financial emergency existed. Neither side objected to the district court's decision to bifurcate the trial, but the defendants did object to the district court's decision to place the burden of proving a financial exigency on them.

The first part of the trial, heard by the district court without a jury, commenced on November 5, 1984. The evidence introduced in this stage of the trial included the following: On April 10, 1981, the State Board of Education issued a declaration of financial exigency. The declaration included the University of Idaho's Agricultural Research and Cooperative Extension Service. On May 12, 1981, President Gibb informed Pace that because of the financial exigency, she would be laid off.

Pace was a tenured faculty employee. The University's faculty-staff handbook defines "tenure" as follows:

> A condition of presumed continuing employment that is accorded faculty members by the regents, usually after a probationary period, on the basis of an evaluation and affirmative recommendation by a faculty committee with concurrence by the faculty member's departmental administrator and college dean and by the president. *After tenure has been awarded, the faculty member's service can be terminated only for adequate cause*, the burden of proof resting with the University of Idaho, ... *or under conditions of financial exigency as declared by the Board*, or in situations where extreme shifts of enrollment have eliminated the justification for the existence of the position.

"Financial exigency" is defined by the Handbook as follows:

> A *demonstrably bona fide*, imminent financial crisis which threatens the viability of an agency, institution, office or department as a whole or one or more of its programs, or other distinct units, and which *cannot be adequately alleviated by means other than a reduction in the employment force.*

There is no dispute that these two definitions were a part of Pace's contract of employment.

The defendants do not argue that Pace was discharged for any reason other than the alleged existence of a financial exigency. Thus, the propriety of discharging her hinged on whether a financial exigency did exist.

In 1981, the Idaho legislature appropriated $12,197,600 for fiscal year 1982 for the Agricultural Research and Cooperative Extension Service (the "Service"). The Service had requested $12,610,500, which resulted in an alleged shortfall of $412,900. The fiscal year 1982 appropriation, however, was $773,100 greater than the 1981 appropriation.

House Concurrent Resolution No. 24, 1981 called for an "across-the-board" salary increase of seven percent. University officials did not treat this resolution as mandatory, because some university employees received more than a seven percent salary increase while others did not. The legislature appropriated $667,800 to fund the salary increase for the Service. The district court found that a portion of this amount could have been used to help alleviate the alleged financial crisis at the Service.

At the end of the 1981 fiscal year, a $383,500 surplus was discovered in the Service's budget. Of this amount, $135,000 was already committed to research projects and was not available for personnel costs. The purchase of word processing and other equipment took another $135,000 from the surplus. The remaining $112,000 of the surplus was totally uncommitted. This amount was used for costs other than personnel. The district court found that this amount could have been used to alleviate the Service's financial crisis. The evidence also showed increases in the Service's fiscal year 1982 budget.

The district court found that alternatives other than a reduction in personnel were not considered by the State Board of Education when it declared the financial exigency. The Board of Education was not informed of and "did not consider the dollar savings possible by freezing or reducing the increases in such budget areas as salary, travel, capital outlay, supplies, or equipment." The Board of Education also was never informed of the $383,500 surplus which existed at the end of fiscal year 1981 in deciding to declare the financial exigency.

Based upon these facts, the district court held that because of the definitions of "tenure" and "financial exigency," as found in the University of Idaho's faculty handbook, and which were part of Pace's contract, the defendants had failed to prove a *"demonstrably bona fide* financial exigency." Specifically, the court held that the defendants had "failed to prove that the financial crisis could not have been 'adequately alleviated by means other than a reduction in the employment force.' "

After entering findings of fact and conclusions of law, the district court certified its decision on the matter of financial exigency as final, and this Court granted the defendants' motion to appeal by certification. Subsequently, attorneys for the American Association of University Professors filed a motion, which was granted, to participate as *amicus curiae*.

The defendants raised eight issues on appeal. Six of these issues are raised prematurely because they involve matters yet to be decided in the second half of the bifurcated trial. The trial court's pretrial order made clear that the *only* issue it was deciding in the first half of the trial was whether a financial exigency existed in 1982 which justified the defendants' decision to terminate Pace. In deciding this issue, as mentioned above, the district court held that the burden of proving a financial exigency rested with the defendants. The two issues properly before this Court are, therefore, whether the district court erred in placing the burden of proof upon the defendants with respect to proving a demonstrably *bona fide* financial exigency, and whether there is substantial and competent evidence to sustain the district court's finding that no financial exigency existed at the time Pace was fired. Addressing these issues in that order, we hold that the district court did not err. We therefore affirm the district court.

* * *

Applying these cases to the facts here convinces us that the district court did not err. Pace introduced evidence, which was undisputed, that she was a tenured professor. Her contract, quoted above, specifically guaranteed her continued employment with the University of Idaho except in cases where adequate cause is shown or a financial exigency exists. The defendants do not argue that Pace was fired for adequate cause. Thus the only valid reason under Pace's contract for which she could be terminated was the existence of a financial exigency. "Financial exigency," as mentioned above, is defined in pertinent part by the University of Idaho's faculty-staff handbook as a "*demonstrably bona fide* imminent financial crisis...which cannot be adequately alleviated by means other than a reduction in the employment force." As developed below, this definition clearly placed the burden of proof of this issue on the defendants.

If the word "demonstrably" has any meaning at all, it must mean that the party *declaring* the exigency must be able to *demonstrate* the existence of a "*bona fide* imminent financial crisis...which cannot be adequately alleviated by means other than a reduction in the employment force." The alternative would require Pace to demonstrate the non-existence of such a financial crisis, an interpretation clearly at odds with basic grammar and common sense. Other considerations also confirm our holding that the burden of proving a financial exigency rested with the defendants.

It is the general rule that where evidence necessary to establish a fact lies peculiarly within the knowledge and competence of one of the parties, principles of fairness require that party to bear the burden of going forward with evidence on the issue. Applying this rule required the defendants to bear the burden of proving a financial exigency, because the numerous facts and considerations which went into the defendants' decision to declare a financial exigency were specially within their knowledge.

It is also the general rule that "where the defense to an action is of an affirmative nature, the defendant becomes the proponent, and has the burden to bear...." Here the defense to Pace's claim is financial exigency. This defense is affirmative in nature. Accordingly, applying this rule, the defendants also had the burden of proving a financial exigency.

The fact that Pace has the burden of proving a constitutional deprivation does not change our analysis. There is no dispute here that Pace has a property interest in her contract which is constitutionally protected by the due process clauses of both art. 1, § 13 of the Idaho Constitution and the Fourteenth Amendment to the United States Constitution. Thus, to prevail, Pace must still show that her dismissal violated due process.

The due process guaranteed Pace has both a procedural and a substantive component to it. Pace does not argue that she was denied procedural due process, only that she was denied substantive due process. Hence, in order to prevail, Pace has the burden of proving a substantive due process violation.

"Substantive due process" means "that state action which deprives [a person] of life, liberty, or property must have a rational basis—that is to say, the reason for the deprivation may not be so inadequate that the judiciary will characterize it as 'arbitrary.'" Accordingly, refining further Pace's burden of proof, to prevail...she must show that the decision to discharge her was arbitrary, capricious, or without a rational basis.

Pace has not yet had the opportunity to go forth with her proof—that part of the case is set for the second half of the bifurcated trial. The fact that the defendants have failed their burden of proving a financial exigency does not mean, in and of itself, that her discharge necessarily violated substantive due process. While the absence of a *bona fide* financial exigency certainly strengthens Pace's argument that the decision to discharge her—a breach of her contract—was arbitrary, capricious or without a rational basis, it is clear that this fact alone does not necessarily change Pace's burden of proof nor necessarily satisfy it, although it might, depending upon the facts of the case.

A review of case law on this issue sustains our analysis. In *Browzin*, the plaintiff, a college professor, was dismissed as a result of an alleged financial exigency. Plaintiff sued for breach of contract. Before trial plaintiff stipulated that a financial exigency existed at the time of his firing. Plaintiff argued that even though there was a financial exigency, the defendants breached his contract because his contract also required the defendants to make very effort to find the plaintiff a different job within the University.

The district court placed upon the plaintiff the burden of proving that the University had not made every effort to find plaintiff a different job within the University. Plaintiff did not object to this. The district court ruled against the plaintiff, holding that he had failed his burden of proof. The District of Columbia Court of Appeals affirmed the district court. With respect to the burden of proof issue, it noted that because plaintiff had not objected to having the burden placed upon him, it would not reverse the district court's decision of placing the burden upon plaintiff. Significantly, however, the court did state that had the issue been properly preserved, it would have disagreed with the district court's decision to place the burden upon the plaintiff. Said the court: "Ordinarily a litigant does not have the burden of establishing facts peculiarly within the knowledge of the opposing party. The University here was plainly in a far better position to know what efforts were or were not undertaken to find for [plaintiff] another post within the University." This analysis is consistent with ours.

* * *

Despite its nonapplicability, *Levitt*'s holding is *consistent* with our analysis. *Levitt* placed the burden of proving the alleged due process violation upon the plaintiffs. We have reaffirmed that principle here. As mentioned above, Pace still has the burden of proving a substantive due process violation. Requiring the defendants to prove a financial exigency does not contradict this holding.

Accordingly, we affirm the district court on this issue.

II. SUBSTANTIAL AND COMPETENT EVIDENCE EXISTS IN THE RECORD TO SUSTAIN THE DISTRICT COURT'S DECISION THAT THE DEFENDANTS HAVE FAILED THEIR BURDEN HERE

The second issue is whether the district court erred in ruling that the defendants failed their burden of proving a financial exigency. Finding no error, we affirm the district court on this issue.

* * *

[We] hold that there is substantial and competent evidence in the record to sustain the district court; accordingly, the district court's findings of an absence of a financial exigency are not clearly erroneous.

For ready convenience, we repeat the University's definition of financial exigency:

> A *demonstrably bona fide*, imminent financial crisis which threatens the viability of an agency, institution, office or department as a whole or one or more

of its programs, or other distinct units, and which *cannot be adequately alleviated by means other than a reduction in the employment force.*

As mentioned above, pertinent to this definition, the district court found the following:

(1) The declaration of financial exigency was based upon an alleged budget shortfall of $412,900. This shortfall was the difference between the Agricultural Extension Service's 1982 fiscal year budget request of $12,610,500 and the appropriation of $12,197,600, which it received.

(2) The $12,197,600 appropriation amount received by the Service for fiscal year 1982 was $773,100 greater than the Service's 1981 appropriation.

(3) The 1982 appropriation included $667,800 for a seven percent salary increase at the Service.

(4) At the end of fiscal year 1981, a carryover surplus of $383,500 was discovered. At least $112,000 of this amount was totally uncommitted.

(5) The State Board of Education, which declared the financial exigency, was not informed of this carryover surplus before deciding to declare the financial exigency.

(6) The Board also did not consider alternatives other than a reduction in personnel in declaring the financial exigency; options such as freezing or reducing budgeted increases in areas such as salary, travel, capital outlay, supplies, or equipment, were not considered.

(7) The Extension Service's 1982 budget provided for increased spending in all areas.

We have reviewed the evidence supporting these findings and hold that it is substantial, and do so after viewing the "record in its entirety." The evidence is reasonable and persuasive. It clearly shows that the defendants did not satisfy the requirements for proving a financial exigency; they did not demonstrate a "bona fide, imminent financial crisis... *which cannot be adequately alleviated by means other than a reduction in the employment force.*"

It is the University's own strict and rigorous definition of "financial exigency" which determines this issue today. That definition precludes the declaration of a financial exigency unless several significant hurdles are passed. The evidence clearly supports the district court's finding that the defendants failed in their burden to show that they had cleared the hurdles. Accordingly, for the foregoing reasons, we affirm the district court.

———————

Professor Pace was offered the opportunity to return to the University of Idaho, but opted for a cash settlement, structured to pay her a monthly sum for life. *Chronicle of Higher Education*, 28 January 1987, p. 2. Another woman who won, Nancy Shaw, settled after dropping her suit against the University of California at Santa Cruz. Although she had been recommended for tenure by her department and faculty review groups, the chancellor overturned the decisions. "Santa Cruz Professor Wins 5-year Battle for Tenure," *Chronicle of Higher Education*, 4 March 1987, p. 2. It is rare for universities to lose exigency cases, as the *Bloomfield* litigation is well known to college attorneys.

———————

Krotkoff v. Goucher College

585 F.2d 675 (1978)

BUTZNER, Circuit Judge:

This appeal arises from the termination of Hertha H. Krotkoff's position as a tenured professor at Goucher College. Krotkoff sued Goucher, alleging that it violated the tenure provision of her contract. The college asserts that it eliminated Krotkoff's position and terminated her contract as part of a general retrenchment prompted by severe financial problems. The district court submitted the following issues to the jury, placing the burden of proof on the college in each instance:

(1) Was Goucher entitled to read into its contract of tenure with Krotkoff the condition of financial exigency; (2) Did the Trustees reasonably believe that a financial exigency existed at Goucher; (3) Did Goucher reasonably use uniform standards in selecting Krotkoff for termination; and (4) Did the College fail to make reasonable efforts to find Krotkoff alternate employment at Goucher?

The court instructed the jury that it must find in favor of Goucher on all four issues for the college to prevail; conversely, it instructed that if the jury found in favor of Krotkoff on any one of the four issues, Krotkoff should recover damages. The jury returned a general verdict of $180,000 for Krotkoff, but the district judge, perceiving error, stated that he would grant a new trial.

Subsequently, upon the representations of the parties that no additional evidence could be presented at a new trial, the court entered judgment for the college notwithstanding the verdict. In the alternative, should the judgment be reversed on appeal, the court granted the college's motion for a new trial on the ground that "the jury's verdict was against the overwhelming weight of the evidence." Satisfied that the college has met the stringent requirements for a judgment notwithstanding the verdict, we affirm.

I

Krotkoff began teaching German at Goucher in 1962 and was granted "indeterminate tenure" in 1967. In June of 1975, the college notified Krotkoff that because of financial problems, it would not renew her 1975–76 contract when it expired on June 30, 1976. The college acknowledges that Krotkoff has at all times been a fine teacher and that the termination was not based on her performance or behavior.

Goucher is a private, liberal arts college for women in Towson, Maryland. Beginning in 1968–69, the college operated at a deficit each academic year through 1973–74. The deficit for 1973–74 was $333,561, and the total deficit from 1968–69 through 1973–74 was $1,590,965. By the end of the 1973–74 year, the college's expendable endowment, which was used to cover these deficits, amounted to less than one-half of the 1973–74 deficit. In 1974–75, as a result of a substantial reduction in expenditures, the college showed a meager surplus of $1,482. This was increased to $5,051 in 1975–76, but, partially as a result of a revision of the curriculum to attract more students, the deficit in 1976–77 was anticipated to be in excess of $100,000. The college's enrollment fell every year from 1969–70 through 1976–77, reducing revenue generated by tuition and fees, a major source of income.

This financial situation convinced the trustees that action was needed to insure the institution's future. After a review of the finances and curriculum, the board adopted a more aggressive investment policy to seek a higher rate of return on endowment and promoted rental of the auditorium and excess dormitory space. It also froze salaries, cut administrative and clerical staffs, and deferred maintenance.

As a part of its retrenchment, the college did not renew the contracts of 11 untenured and four tenured faculty members, including Krotkoff. These professors were selected largely on the bases of the dean's study of enrollment projections and necessary changes in the curriculum. In addition, the faculty elected a committee to review curricular changes suggested by the administration. Among the administration's proposals were elimination of the classics department and the German section of the modern language department which were staffed exclusively by tenured professors. The classics department was dropped, but the faculty committee recommended that the college continue a service program in German staffed by one teacher for students majoring in other disciplines who needed the language as a research skill. The administration accepted this recommendation.

The German faculty consisted of Krotkoff, who taught mostly advanced literature courses, and another tenured teacher, Sybille Ehrlich, who taught chiefly introductory language courses. The dean, concurring with the chairman of the department, recommended retention of Ehrlich primarily because she had more experience teaching the elementary language courses that would be offered in a service program and because she was also qualified to teach French. The president followed this recommendation.

The faculty grievance committee, to which Krotkoff then turned, applied the criteria by which the college faculty were regularly evaluated and recommended her retention. The committee, however, did not suggest that Ehrlich's appointment be terminated, and it did not address the problem of keeping both tenured professors. The president declined to accept the committee's recommendation, and the trustees sustained her decision. The president also rejected a suggestion that both teachers be retained by assigning Krotkoff to teach the German courses, dismissing an assistant dean, and designating Ehrlich as a part time French teacher and a part time assistant dean.

Goucher sent Krotkoff a list of all positions available for the next year. Krotkoff insisted that any new position carry her present faculty rank, salary, and tenure. She expressed interest in a position in the economics department, but the school declined to transfer her because the department's chairman estimated that she would need two to four years of training to become qualified.

In accordance with its notice of June 1975, the college terminated her appointment on June 30, 1976.

II

The primary issue is whether as a matter of law Krotkoff's contract permitted termination of her tenure by discontinuing her teaching position because of financial exigency.

The college's 1967 letter to Krotkoff granting her "indeterminate tenure" does not define that term. The college by-laws state:

> No original appointment shall establish "tenure," i.e., the right to continued service unless good cause be shown for termination. Reappointment as Professor or Associate Professor, after three years of service in either rank, or appointment or reappointment to any professional rank after five years of service as Instructor

or in any higher rank, shall establish tenure. The term "service" as used in this section shall mean instructional service in full-time appointments.

The by-laws also specify that the college may terminate a teacher's employment at age 65 or because of serious disability or cause. The parties agree that Krotkoff's appointment was not terminated for any of these reasons. Financial exigency is not mentioned in the by-laws, and the college concedes that it is not considered to be a ground of dismissal for cause.

The national academic community's understanding of the concept of tenure incorporates the notion that a college may refuse to renew a tenured teacher's contract because of financial exigency so long as its action is demonstrably bona fide.

* * *

[The] 1940 Statement of Principles on Academic Freedom and Tenure, developed by the Association of American Colleges and the American Association of University Professors, was later adopted by a number of professional organizations. With respect to the security afforded by tenure, the statement explains:

> After the expiration of a probationary period, teachers or investigators should have permanent or continuous tenure, and their services should be terminated only for adequate cause, except in the case of retirement for age, or under extraordinary circumstances because of financial exigencies.

> In the interpretation of this principle it is understood that the following represents acceptable academic practice:

> . . . .

> (5) Termination of a continuous appointment because of financial exigency should be demonstrably bona fide.

Probably because it was formulated by both administrators and professors, all of the secondary authorities seem to agree that it is the "most widely-accepted academic definition of tenure."

The reported cases support the conclusion that tenure is not generally understood to preclude demonstrably bona fide dismissal for financial reasons. In most of the cases, the courts have interpreted contracts which contained an explicit reference to financial exigency. In others, where the contracts did not mention this term, the courts construed tenure as implicitly granting colleges the right to make bona fide dismissals for financial reasons.

* * *

In sum, there was no evidence of a general understanding in the Goucher community that the tenured faculty had greater protection from dismissal for financial reasons than the faculty at other colleges. The Krotkoff-Goucher contract must be interpreted consistently with the understanding of the national academic community about tenure and financial exigency. Although Judge McGowan addressed a different factual situation in *Greene v. Howard University*, his comments are appropriate here:

> Contracts are written, and are to be read, by reference to the norms of conduct and expectations founded upon them. This is especially true of contracts in and among a community of scholars, which is what a university is. The readings of the market place are not invariably apt in this noncommercial context.

By defining Krotkoff's relationship with the college in terms of tenure, the contract did not exempt her from demonstrably bona fide dismissal if the college confronted financial exigency.

III

Having determined that Krotkoff's contract permitted termination of her employment because of financial exigency, we consider whether the district court erred in holding as a matter of law that the college did not breach this contract.

Krotkoff urges that the jury was entitled to assess the reasonableness of the trustees' belief that the college faced financial exigency. In support of this position, she emphasizes that the college had a large endowment and valuable land. She is entitled, she claims, to have a jury determine whether the trustees acted unreasonably in failing to secure judicial permission to invade these assets and whether the trustees should have sold land which they were holding for a better price.

Courts have properly emphasized that dismissals of tenured professors for financial reasons must be demonstrably bona fide. Otherwise, college administrators could use financial exigency to subvert academic freedom. [In *AAUP v. Bloomfield*,] the court concluded that Bloomfield College used its genuine financial difficulties as a subterfuge to achieve its goal of abolishing tenure at the institution. Since Bloomfield acted in bad faith, the court ordered it to reinstate the tenured teachers that it had dismissed.

Bloomfield, however, establishes that the trustees' decision to sell or retain a parcel of land was not a proper subject for judicial review:

> Whether . . . [the sale of land] to secure financial stability on a short-term basis is preferable to the long-term planning of the college administration is a policy decision for the institution. Its choice of alternative is beyond the scope of judicial oversight in the context of this litigation. Hence the emphasis upon the alternative use of this capital asset by the trial judge in reaching his conclusion that a financial exigency did not exist was unwarranted and should not have been the basis of decision. [Opinion by the appeals court.]

The same principle, we believe, should apply to the dissipation of an endowment. The reasonableness of the trustees' decision concerning the disposition of capital did not raise an issue for the jury. Stated otherwise, the existence of financial exigency should be determined by the adequacy of a college's operating funds rather than its capital assets.

Krotkoff has acknowledged that the trustees and other college officials did not act in bad faith. The evidence overwhelmingly demonstrates that the college was confronted by pressing financial need. As a result of the large annual deficits aggregating more than $1,500,000 over an extended period and the steady decline in enrollment, the college's financial position was precarious. Action undoubtedly was required to secure the institution's future. Because of Krotkoff's disavowal of bad faith on the part of the college and because of the unrefuted evidence concerning the college's finances and enrollment, we believe that this aspect of the case raised no question for the jury. The facts and all the inferences that properly can be drawn from them conclusively establish that the trustees reasonably believed that the college was faced with financial exigency. We therefore hold that with respect to this issue, the district court correctly entered judgment for the college notwithstanding the verdict.

IV

We turn next to Krotkoff's claim that the court properly submitted to the jury whether Goucher used reasonable standards in deciding not to retain Krotkoff and whether it made reasonable efforts to find her another position at the college.

The college asserts that neither of these issues is a proper subject for judicial review. It relies on a number of cases in which courts have evinced reluctance to oversee the decisions of college administrators or to intrude on the prerogatives of trustees. These cases, however, generally have involved the application of the fourteenth amendment to state institutions or the interpretation of statutes prohibiting racial or sexual discrimination. Since Goucher is a private college and Krotkoff does not allege the type of unlawful conduct proscribed by civil rights acts, the cases on which the college relies to forestall judicial inquiry are not dispositive.

Krotkoff's claims must be resolved by reference to her contract. This involves ascertaining, first, what contractual rights she had, and second, whether the college breached them. Viewing the evidence in the light most favorable to Krotkoff, as we must for purposes of this appeal, we believe that the district court correctly held that she was contractually entitled to insist (a) that the college use reasonable standards in selecting which faculty appointments to terminate, and (b) that it take reasonable measures to afford her alternative employment.

Neither the letter granting Krotkoff tenure nor the documents setting forth Goucher's policy concerning tenure mentions the procedural rights to which a faculty member is entitled when the college proposes to terminate her appointment for financial reasons. Therefore, we must examine again the academic community's understanding concerning tenure to determine the nature of this unique contractual relationship.

As we mentioned in Part II, the 1940 Statement on Academic Freedom and Tenure sanctions termination of faculty appointments because of financial exigency. But it also stipulates: "Termination of a continuous appointment because of financial exigency should be demonstrably bona fide." The evidence discloses that the academic community commonly understands that inherent in the concept of a "demonstrably bona fide" termination is the requirement that the college use fair and reasonable standards to determine which tenured faculty members will not be reappointed. The college's obligation to deal fairly with its faculty when selecting those whose appointments will be terminated is an attribute of tenure. Consequently, it is an implicit element of the contract of appointment.

Nevertheless, the evidence questioning the reasonableness of Goucher's procedures was insufficient to submit this issue to the jury. The necessity for revising Goucher's curriculum was undisputed. A faculty committee accepted elimination of the classics department and reduction of the German section of the modern language department as reasonable responses to this need. The only substantial controversy was whether the college should have retained Krotkoff or Ehrlich, both tenured professors. Nothing in Krotkoff's contract gave her precedence, and the college did not breach it by retaining Ehrlich instead of Krotkoff. Nor was the college under any contractual obligation to retain Krotkoff by demoting Ehrlich to part time teaching and part time administrative work. Therefore, the district court did not err in ultimately ruling for the college on this issue.

*   *   *

The evidence conclusively establishes that the college did not breach any contractual obligation concerning alternative employment. The constraints of tenure, rank, and pay that Krotkoff placed on alternative employment severely restricted the college's efforts to accommodate her. Apart from Ehrlich's position, the only vacancy in which she expressed interest was in the economics department. No evidence suggested that the head of that department or the president acted unreasonably in assessing the time and expense of retraining Krotkoff for this position or in deciding that her transfer would not be feasible. Again, we conclude that the district judge did not err in holding that the college was entitled to judgment on these issues.

The judgment is affirmed.

Graney v. Board of Regents of the University of Wisconsin

286 N.W.2d 138 (Wis. App. 1979)

DYKMAN, Judge.

Plaintiffs appeal from an order of the Dane County Circuit Court entered December 6, 1978, granting defendants' motion for summary judgment. The court's order dismissed plaintiffs' action seeking damages and declaratory and injunctive relief for seventeen University of Wisconsin System tenured faculty members laid off or terminated by the defendants.

The plaintiffs were tenured members of the University of Wisconsin System under sec. 37.31, Stats. (1971). In the spring of 1973, the Board of Regents determined that several campuses of the University of Wisconsin System were experiencing a financial exigency which required a layoff of several tenured faculty members throughout the system. In a letter dated April 4, 1973, the president of the university directed each chancellor at the state campuses to select tenured faculty members for layoff effective June, 1974. A letter of May 14, 1973, sent to each chancellor explained that these actions would be considered layoffs rather than terminations, so that the tenured faculty members could retain their tenure status and employment benefits if they were rehired. About May 15, 1973, each of the plaintiffs received notification that he or she would be laid off as of June 30, 1974, due to financial exigency existing at their campuses. The Board of Regents adopted a review procedure in which the plaintiffs' layoffs were reconsidered by a committee consisting of other faculty members. Although the reconsideration committees at each state campus, with the exception of UW–Platteville, voted to rescind the layoff decisions, the chancellors reinstated the layoffs and the Board of Regents affirmed the chancellors' decisions.

Plaintiffs moved for a preliminary injunction in federal district court, alleging deprivation of their tenure rights in violation of their rights of due process and free speech protected by the first and fourteenth amendment of the United States Constitution. The preliminary injunction was denied, and the Seventh Circuit Court of Appeals affirmed the district court decision. Plaintiffs brought this action in April, 1976.

Plaintiffs assert six causes of action: (1) that sec. 37.31, Stats. (1971), creates a contract between the state and tenured faculty members which was breached by the defendants; (2) that sec. 37.31 creates vested statutory rights which only the legislature, not the Board of Regents, can modify; (3) that the Board of Regents' power to terminate tenure rights because of a financial exigency may not be delegated to the president or chancellors of the university; (4) that the procedures used to terminate plaintiffs violated their due process rights under the fourteenth amendment to the United States Constitution and art. 1, secs. 1, 13 and 22 of the Wisconsin Constitution; (5) that the defendants unlawfully terminated the plaintiffs' contracts without adopting rules pursuant to secs. 37.31 and 227.13, Stats.; and (6) that the terminations abridged plaintiffs' contract rights in violation of art. 1, sec. 10 of the United States Constitution.

We find that the plaintiffs are precluded from bringing this action against the Board of Regents because of the doctrines of sovereign immunity and public officer civil immunity and because they failed to exercise their exclusive method of review through ch. 227 administrative procedures.

* * *

Section 37.31, Stats. (1971), limits defendants' authority to terminate tenured faculty to discharge for "cause." Discharge for "cause" under sec. 37.31 only includes reasons associated with efficiency and good behavior of tenured teachers. Since financial exigency is not a basis for "cause" under sec. 37.31, plaintiffs contend that defendants acted outside their scope of authority in discharging them.

The Board of Regents' authority to terminate employees for reasons of financial exigency is not expressly granted by the statutes.[5] However, this authority is implied under the general powers of the board for state universities governed by ch. 37, Stats. (1971), which provide that, "The board of regents shall possess all other powers necessary or convenient to accomplish the objects and perform the duties prescribed by law."

Defendants present facts in affidavits of university officials that in 1973, the legislature reduced the university budget for the following biennium and introduced a funding formula which tied budget levels to the number of actual student credit hours. A decline in enrollment at the campuses throughout the state resulted in a loss of instructional funds. In order to comply with the legislature's budgetary restrictions,

---

5. In ch. 335, Laws of 1973, the University of Wisconsin System was merged and a new charter was created. That bill, which became effective July 1, 1974, included a provision expressly authorizing the Board of Regents to terminate tenured faculty when a financial exigency exists.

> Notwithstanding ss. 36.13(4) and 36.15, the board may, with appropriate notice, terminate any faculty or academic staff appointment when a financial emergency exists. No person may be employed at the institution within 2 years to perform reasonably comparable duties to those of the person whose appointment was terminated without first offering such person a reappointment. The board, after consultation with the faculty and chancellor of each institution, shall adopt procedures to be followed in the event of termination under this section.

Plaintiffs contend that this subsequent express authorization indicates that the board previously had no power to terminate faculty for reasons of financial exigency. We are persuaded, however, that this is not a necessary conclusion. First, the bill which introduced this express power was part of an extensive merger bill which reorganized the university system and did not solely focus on the board's power to terminate. Second, in addition to articulating the board's authority to terminate, the statutory provision outlines the procedure to be implemented by the board and the rights of the terminated faculty.

Thus, the statute could be said to indicate the parameters of the Board of Regents' power in the newly merged system and to eliminate any prior ambiguity as to the method of exercising this power.

the Board of Regents determined that in addition to firing nontenured employees, it was necessary to lay off or terminate tenured faculty.

Several jurisdictions have recognized that educational governing boards possess an inherent authority to discharge tenured faculty for reasons of financial exigency which is distinct from the authority to discharge for cause.

The court in *Krotkoff* reconciled this power to terminate with the concept of tenure:

> A concept of tenure that permits dismissal based on financial exigency is consistent with the primary purpose of tenure. Tenure's "real concern is with arbitrary or retaliatory dismissals based on an administrator's or a trustee's distaste for the content of a professor's teaching or research, or even for positions taken completely outside the campus setting. . . . It is designed to foster our society's interest in the unfettered progress of research and learning by protecting the profession's freedom of inquiry and instruction." Dismissals based on financial exigency, unlike those for cause or disability, are impersonal; they are unrelated to the views of the dismissed teachers. A professor whose appointment is terminated because of financial exigency will not be replaced by another with more conventional views or better connections. Hence, bona fide dismissals based on financial exigency do not threaten the values protected by tenure.

Several of the cases listed above were decided on the bases of statutory interpretation of general board powers, interpretation of contract provisions, and general custom and understanding by the academic community of the concept of tenure. Nevertheless, these courts noted the existence of an inherent power to terminate for reasons of financial emergency.

Courts which based their decision solely on an inherent power to terminate for reasons of financial emergency in the face of a tenure protection statute cited sound educational policy and common sense in support of their conclusions.

* * *

The reasons cited by the courts which recognize the power of educational governing boards to terminate for financial exigency are more persuasive than those presented by the courts in Louisiana and New Hampshire. The Louisiana court's analysis is not clear and the New Hampshire statutory history is dissimilar to Wisconsin statutes governing tenure and the Board of Regents' powers.

In exercising their broad authority "to accomplish the objects and perform the duties prescribed by law," the members of the Board of Regents determined, in their discretion, that the legislature's grant of limited funds required the layoff or dismissal of tenured faculty members. The exercise of this discretion did not interfere with the protection afforded by the tenure statute against arbitrary dismissal of tenured faculty for personal reasons.

Since the members of the board exercised a discretionary power within the scope of their authority, plaintiffs must allege malicious, willful, or intentional misconduct by the board members in order to maintain a damage action against them as individuals. There is no such allegation in this case.

Order affirmed.

Milbouer v. Keppler

644 F. Supp. 201 (D. Idaho 1986)

RYAN, District Judge.

I. FACTS & PROCEDURE

This action arises from the discharge of plaintiff from her position as a tenured professor from Boise State University (BSU) following a declaration of financial exigency by the State Board of Education in June of 1982. Plaintiff filed an action against the named defendants in June of 1984, alleging breach of contract, wrongful discharge, and denial of substantive and procedural due process in violation of the fourteenth amendment of the United States Constitution and 42 U.S.C. § 1983. The action was originally brought in state court, but was removed to this court by an order dated December 3, 1984.

On November 19, 1985, co-defendants BSU, William Keppler, Richard Bullington, and John Keiser filed a Motion for Summary Judgment pursuant to Rule 56 of the Federal Rules of Civil Procedure. Defendant State Board of Education filed a Motion for Summary Judgment on November 20, 1985. Plaintiff's brief in opposition and defendants' reply briefs were subsequently filed. On September 3, 1986, this court heard oral argument on the Motions for Summary Judgment. All parties were represented by counsel.

II. STANDARD OF REVIEW

A party is entitled to summary judgment if there is no genuine issue of material fact, and if, after viewing the evidence and permissible inferences in the light most favorable to the adverse party, the moving party is entitled to prevail as a matter of law. When a motion for summary judgment is made and supported, the adverse party must set forth specific facts showing that there is a genuine issue for trial.

III. DISCUSSION

Plaintiff asserts that the defendants, by declaring a "financial exigency," which did not in fact exist, arbitrary and capriciously deprived her of employment at BSU, causing a breach of her employment and tenure contracts with the University.

When an instructor is discharged from a tenured position because of a financial crisis, the education institution has the burden of proving both of the following: (1) that a genuine financial exigency existed at the institution, and (2) that a uniform set of procedures were used by the institution in determining what faculty members would be discharged.

A. Financial Exigency

Financial exigency, as defined by the Idaho State Board of Education, is:

> [A] demonstrably bona fide, imminent financial crisis which threatens the viability of an agency, institution, office or department as a whole, or one or more of its programs, or other distinct units, and which cannot be adequately alleviated by means other than a reduction in the employment force. A state of financial exigency shall exist only upon Board declaration.

In July of 1981, BSU implemented University Policies 5500-B and 5501-B in the Faculty Handbook. Rule 5500-B adopted the Idaho State Board of Education definition of financial exigency, and Rule 5501-B set forth an appeals procedure for faculty members terminated as a result of the declaration of a "financial exigency" by the State Board of Education.

On June 14, 1982, Governor John Evans issued Executive Order 82-13 directing agencies of Idaho to submit to the governor plans for reducing budget expenditures for fiscal year 1983 by nine percent. In compliance with the executive order, the State Board of Education advised the State institutions of higher learning, including BSU, of the nine percent holdback and requested that the universities inform the State Board as to whether a financial exigency existed at their respective institutions.

On June 2, 1982, Defendant John Keiser testified before the State Board of Education that based upon a thorough investigation of the financial situation at BSU, a financial exigency did exist. The University subsequently submitted a Budget Reduction Plan to the State Board, which was approved on July 14, 1982. This Budget Reduction Plan included the termination of plaintiff from her tenured position.

The preponderance of the evidence shows that a genuine financial exigency existed at BSU in June of 1982. The University had suffered significant budget reductions as a result of previous budget holdbacks ordered by the governor in fiscal years 1980 through 1982. These holdbacks did not result in loss of faculty members at BSU. However, when the nine percent reduction was ordered in June of 1982 for fiscal year 1983, the University was forced to take the drastic step of dismissing faculty members, including plaintiff.

In response to defendants' Motions for Summary Judgment, plaintiff has submitted to this court a partial transcript from the district court proceedings in the case of *Pace v. Hymas,* in which Judge Ron Schilling found that a financial exigency did not exist at the University of Idaho in fiscal year 1982. This decision has recently been upheld by the Idaho State Supreme Court. The facts of the *Pace* decision have no bearing on the present case. *Pace* involved the termination of a University of Idaho faculty member from her position with the Agriculture and Extension Department. More importantly, the *Pace* decision involved a totally different fiscal year (1982) than the fiscal year 1983 in the present case.

Plaintiff also places emphasis on the fact that the University had a surplus of over $300,000 from fiscal year 1982. It is undisputed, however, that Defendant Keiser was directed to retain those funds in anticipation of further holdbacks. Such a holdback did occur in October 1982, leaving only some $27,000 "surplus" remaining. This amount was simply not enough to solve the severe and long-standing budgetary problems facing the University.

Having reviewed the evidence and permissible inferences in the light most favorable to the plaintiff, the court finds that the defendants are entitled to summary judgment on the issue of whether a financial exigency existed at BSU for fiscal year 1983. This holding is consistent with the decision in *Scholes v. Healas,* in which Judge McNichols also found that a genuine financial exigency existed at BSU during fiscal year 1983, justifying the removal of a tenured professor.

B. *Due Process Claims*

The second prong of the *Bignall* test requires the institution to prove that uniform procedures were used in determining what faculty members would be discharged as a result of financial exigency. Plaintiff asserts that the defendants implemented the

Budget Reduction Plan, in an arbitrary and capricious fashion, all in violation of her substantive and procedural due process rights.

1. *Substantive due process rights.*

Tenure does provide plaintiff with a property interest as set forth in the due process clause of the fourteenth amendment. There is no evidence in this case, however, indicating that the interest was taken in an arbitrary or capricious fashion. In formulating a plan for dealing with the budgetary cutbacks, Defendant Keppler, then Dean of the College of Arts and Sciences, looked at the following criteria: student-teacher ratios, enrollment trend analysis, number of majors, and total students serviced in career opportunities. Defendant made a three- to five-year analysis of the academic programs at BSU using the above criteria. Applying the standards specifically to the German language program, Defendant Keppler found that it was a low priority program. Student enrollment was extremely low and only three to four students had graduated from the program from 1980 to 1982.

In light of the low student participation, Defendant Keppler recommended that the German Department, and the Foreign Languages Department as a whole, be eliminated from the curriculum at BSU. The criteria evaluation and recommendation were consistent with University policy 5500-B. The number one criteria in determining removal of staff is the viability of essential university programs. In light of the low participation in the German program, it was apparent that it, and its staff, would have to be subordinated to other active and viable university programs. Plaintiff was not discriminately chosen for dismissal from the Foreign Language Department, as the entire department was eliminated and has yet to have been reinstated. Plaintiff also points to the fact that fifteen new faculty members were hired after her dismissal in 1982. However, these new faculty members were hired to fill vacancies in programs that were still a viable part of the University's curriculum. None of the new faculty members were hired to replace faculty that were laid off as a result of the budget crisis.

Plaintiff further points to the University's failure to reinstate her in another position in the University. BSU policy 5500-B, section II-C-1, provides that the University must "make a good faith effort to relocate any affected faculty member in a suitable vacant position within the University." The University must also "consider retraining as an alternative to layoff." Again, it is undisputed that the University complied with this regulation. Plaintiff was offered a part-time position within the English Department at BSU, which she turned down. She was also offered the possibility to retrain for a position as a linguistic specialist in the business field. The University requested and received approval of the Defendant State Board of Education to waive tuition and fees for plaintiff to enroll in a program which would train her in the field. She did temporarily enroll in such a program, but abandoned it for a period at a Florida university.

2. *Procedural due process claims.*

Plaintiff has also alleged violation of certain procedural due process rights; namely that she was not given adequate notice of her termination and was not given a fair appeals hearing.

In the context of a dismissal of a tenured professor, the minimum procedural elements include, (1) written notice of the reasons of the termination, and (2) an opportunity to rebut those reasons.

(a) *Notice.*

The State Board of Education approved the University Budget Reduction Plan on July 14, 1982. On July 15, 1982, Defendant Keiser sent a cable to plaintiff in Germany and a letter to plaintiff's address in Boise setting forth in detail the reasons for her termination. Defendant Keiser attached to the letter a copy of the Budget Reduction Plan, as well as copies of the University's policies on financial exigency and the appeals procedures applicable thereto. This letter certainly satisfied the requirements of procedural due process. Plaintiff would direct the court's attention to the faculty handbook of the University which provides that a tenured faculty member must be given thirty days notice in advance of a recommendation of layoff. Plaintiff points to the fact that she received her last paycheck on July 1st. She considers this to be the termination date because she would have received a check on August 1st if she was still actively employed with the University. The court agrees that plaintiff would have been paid on August 1, 1982, if she indeed was going to be retained. However, Defendant Keiser's letter clearly stated that plaintiff's termination was not effective until August 15, 1982. The purpose of notice is to allow a plaintiff an opportunity to prepare a case against the institution. The facts clearly indicate that the one-month notice given to plaintiff did give her an opportunity to submit a detailed letter explaining her grounds for appeal, and an opportunity to a full hearing before the appeals council.

(b) *Appeals hearing.*

BSU policy 5501-B sets forth the standards for appealing a termination for financial exigency. Plaintiff presents no evidence indicating that the University failed to comply with this policy. The policy provides that a plaintiff is entitled to a prompt hearing after filing a written request. It is undisputed, on August 5, 1982, plaintiff submitted a written appeal for a hearing. A hearing was promptly held August 9, 1982. Pursuant to the regulations, plaintiff was allowed to voice a response to the dismissal, to question Defendants Keppler, Keiser and Bullington, and to introduce exhibits on appeal. After hearing all of the evidence, the council ruled that there had not been a violation of the University regulations in the dismissal of the plaintiff.

Plaintiff has presented no particular facts raising a genuine issue as to the due process claims. The University adhered to all regulations and procedures in dismissing plaintiff, gave her sufficient notice of termination, and gave her a fair hearing on the matter. Summary judgment will be granted on the due process claims.

*　　*　　*

[The] court finds that the University officials are also immune from suit under the eleventh amendment because an action against the officials is, in this case, an action against the State. This decision would also bar plaintiff's claim for injunctive relief for reinstatement, which would also require disbursement of state funds for her salary, or at the least, cause such a shortfall of non-appropriated funds that state funds would have to be used to make up for the loss.

The court realizes that plaintiff originally brought her claim in state court, and that it was subsequently removed by order of this court on December 3, 1984. However, this does not diminish the force of eleventh amendment immunity. In the *Pennhurst* decision, the Supreme Court explicitly held that, "neither pendent jurisdiction nor any other basis of jurisdiction may override the eleventh amendment." In this case, removal jurisdiction cannot override the eleventh amendment immunity powers.

Based upon the foregoing and the court being fully advised in the premises,

IT IS HEREBY ORDERED that the defendants' Motions for Summary Judgment should be, and are hereby, GRANTED.

Some colleges have many persons who direct academic programs, teach classes, and otherwise resemble tenured or tenure-track professors in every way but formal eligibility or receipt of tenure. Several of the tenure-by-default and defacto-tenure cases are rooted in such lax institutional practices, while other such occasions are averted when the "professor" is appointed to a semi-secure status without formal status, usually through a series of continuing contracts or other quasi-contractual arrangements. Texas Southern University, when it altered its defacto-tenure policies in 1978, grandparented most of the eligible faculty to avoid the inevitable cases that would arise. *Honore v. Douglas,* which appeared earlier in this chapter, arose nonetheless. In *Yaakob v. Schwartz,* a lower court held that an assistant professor who had taught for 13 years had been constructively tenured; an appeals court held otherwise, striking down his "tenure," despite his apparent eligibility based upon express or implied recommendations to the board by the college's academic officials. 431 N.Y.S. 2d 47 (App. Div. 1980). In *Apte v. Regents,* the University of California was found to have acted arbitrarily by not considering all the available evidence in dismissal of a staff member: "In view of Apte's rank, years of service, and employment in multiyear programs, this exclusion of evidence crucial to his case assumes a degree of unfairness that constitutes arbitrary, capricious, or unreasonable action." *Apte v. Regents of University of California,* 244 Cal. Rptr. 312 (Cal. App. 1 Dist. 1988).

Program Discontinuance or Program Change

Browzin v. Catholic University of America
527 F.2d 843 (1975)

J. SKELLY WRIGHT, Circuit Judge:

Recent years have brought financial troubles to scores of the nation's colleges and universities. Numerous faculty members have lost their teaching jobs as the colleges cut back in an effort to eliminate their deficits. We deal here with a challenge to one such layoff.

Dr. Boris Browzin, the plaintiff and appellant, was hired by Catholic University in September 1962 as a professor in the School of Engineering and Architecture. In 1962 and succeeding years he taught a full load of courses, concentrating primarily in the field of Structures and the field of Soil Mechanics. In late 1969 the School of Engineering and Architecture was faced with a severe budget reduction, and the administration, in conjunction with the faculty, began considering retrenchment and reorganization of the school. The administration also took steps to cut back on the faculty, releasing some faculty members who were nontenured, and a few, including Browzin, who had achieved tenure. The Dean informed Browzin of this decision in a letter dated November 11, 1969. In it he stated that after a "detailed review of all of our current programs," he had identified certain areas in which the University had no great strength and could not hope to achieve strength under the new budgetary limitations. Two of those areas were Soil Mechanics and Hydrology, which were Browzin's particular responsibility. Consequently, those courses would no longer be offered after the 1969–70 academic year, and Browzin's appointment was to be terminated as of January 31, 1971—a date some 14 months after the letter giving notice of termination. The Dean emphasized that he was motivated by financial considerations alone in making the difficult termination decision. Browzin received a similar letter from the Provost of the University about a month later.

Browzin sued, charging that this termination breached his contract with Catholic University. Before trial the parties stipulated that Dr. Browzin was a highly qualified professor in the field of civil engineering, that he was a tenured professor, and that Catholic University was faced with a *bona fide* financial exigency at the time the termination occurred. They also stipulated that the standards which were to govern the case were to be found in the 1968 Recommended Institutional Regulations on Academic Freedom and Tenure, propounded by the American Association of University Professors (AAUP). It was, in effect, a stipulation that the 1968 Regulations had been adopted as part of the contract between Browzin and the University, an adoption entirely consistent with the Statutes of the University and the University's previous responses to AAUP actions.

Of particular relevance is Regulation 4(c), which provides in pertinent part:

> Where termination of appointment is based upon financial exigency, or bona fide discontinuance of a program or department of instruction, Regulation 5 [dealing with dismissals for cause] will not apply.... In every case of financial exigency or discontinuance of a program or department of instruction, the faculty member concerned will be given notice as soon as possible, and never less than 12 months' notice, or in lieu thereof he will be given severance salary for 12 months. Before terminating an appointment because of the abandonment of a program or department of instruction, the institution will make every effort to place affected faculty members in other suitable positions. If an appointment is terminated before the end of the period of appointment, because of financial exigency, because of the discontinuance of a program of instruction, the released faculty member's place will not be filled by a replacement within a period of two years, unless the released faculty member has been offered reappointment and a reasonable time within which to accept or decline it.

The case was tried to the court without a jury, and at the close of appellant's case the University moved for dismissal, contending that on the facts and the law presented he had shown no right to relief. The court granted the motion and this appeal ensued. Since the case turned on an interpretation of the AAUP's 1968 Regulations, the AAUP sought, and was granted, permission to appear before this court as *amicus curiae*. We conclude that the AAUP is fundamentally correct in its interpretation of most of the crucial portions of the Regulations, but we affirm the District Court's disposition of the case.

I

The major issue on this appeal centers upon the trial court's interpretation of the third sentence of Regulation 4(c): "Before terminating an appointment because of the abandonment of a program or department of instruction, the institution will make every effort to place affected faculty members in other suitable positions." Unlike the other three sentences of the Regulation, this sentence does not in terms speak to terminations based upon financial exigency; it speaks only of discontinuances of programs or departments of instruction. The District Court found this to be a crucial distinction, and held that the "suitable position" requirement does not apply to terminations resulting in any way from financial exigency. Since Browzin's termination did stem from the University's *bona fide* financial difficulties, the court ruled that the University had no obligation to seek another suitable position within the institution for him.

* * *

In sum, we are left with conflicting indications as to the meaning of the third sentence of Regulation 4(c). The overarching purpose of the tenure system—protection of academic freedom—as well as the supporting materials invoked by *amicus,* do tend strongly to suggest that the "suitable position" requirement was meant to apply to terminations based on financial exigency. But it remains hard to square this suggestion with the language used in framing Regulation 4(c): care is taken in the first, second, and fourth sentences to specify financial exigency along with program discontinuance; the third sentence, however, mentions only abandonment of a program or department in imposing the "other suitable position" requirement.

Fortunately, we are not required to resolve this apparent conflict between purpose and history on the one hand and the language of the Regulation on the other because there are other reasons which compel us to hold, regardless of the resolution of that conflict, that the "suitable position" requirement applied to the termination of Browzin's appointment. Financial exigency is in the case, but so is *abandonment of a program of instruction"*—a matter expressly covered by the third sentence of Regulation 4(c). The District Court focused so intently on the former factor, financial exigency, that it apparently overlooked the presence of the latter. Catholic University, as the parties stipulated, was indeed faced with *bona fide* financial difficulties, but it chose to meet its problems by discontinuing its courses in Soil Mechanics and Hydrology. This discontinuance was, according to the University's own version of the events, the immediate reason why Browzin lost his job. There really is no dispute that there was an abandonment of Browzin's program of instruction. The Dean's letter makes the point explicitly; the University's counsel conceded as much at trial; and the District Court, in other portions of its findings, expressly so found.

The third sentence of Regulation 4(c) must be read to apply here. It makes no difference that financial exigency loomed in the background. The University did discontinue Browzin's program of instruction. It was therefore under an obligation to make every effort to find him another suitable position in the institution.

II

The District Court's erroneous ruling that the third sentence was inapplicable does not necessitate reversal, however, for the court made an alternative finding. It ruled that even if the "suitable position" requirement applied, "the plaintiff's own evidence failed to prove a prima facie case that the University failed to make every effort to place him in another suitable position, or that such a suitable position existed. . . ." We are unable to conclude that this finding was clearly erroneous. Although Browzin testified that the school had held no meetings with him before the notice of termination in an effort to find a suitable alternative position, this testimony does not by any means preclude the possibility that the University engaged in such efforts. Indeed, there is evidence in appellant's own presentation in the District Court that the school administration undertook a "detailed review" of all programs and positions before it sent Browzin his notice of termination. Moreover, appellant chose to try the case on the theory that there was a suitable position available within the Department of Civil Engineering. His counsel stressed again and again that Browzin was not limited to Soil Mechanics and Hydrology, the terminated courses, but that he was equipped to teach in the continuing area of Structure Design. However, Browzin's own witness indicated that the Structural Design courses could be taught by several members of the faculty and were in fact being given at the time by another tenured professor two years Browzin's senior, a point finally conceded by appellant's counsel. Teaching Structural Design might have been a suitable position for Browzin, but it was by no means available at the time of his termination.

* * *

III

The only other substantial issue on this appeal stems from the fourth sentence of Regulation 4(c). It provides that "the released faculty member's place will not be filled by a replacement within a period of two years," unless the displaced member has an opportunity to accept the post himself. There is no question but that Browzin was never offered the opportunity to return to his former place at Catholic University. Another professor did, however, join the Department approximately a year and a half after Browzin left, hired to teach Water Resources. The evidence showed that Browzin had competence in two of the branches of Water Resources, namely Hydrology and Hydraulics, which relate specifically to design of structures meant to control the flow or retention of water. He did not, however, have any particular background in the third branch, Planning. The University wished to emphasize the Planning branch of the subject, focusing more on the question whether a certain structure should be built rather than how to build structures already decided upon. The University reasoned that it could attract more students this way, since the growing interest in protection of the environment was making the Planning emphasis especially attractive. It also believed that it had a greater chance of obtaining grants for studies with such an emphasis than for studies of the more traditional type. And there was some indication that an outside committee reviewing the school's accreditation in mid-1971 had been the impetus for creating the new post. In sum, it was a program calling for someone with a background and interests different from Browzin's, whereas the interests and background of the other professor matched its requirements quite well. Clearly it was a program significantly different from what Browzin had been teaching during his years with Catholic University. The District Court found as a fact that the other professor had not been hired to fill Browzin's place. We are unable to conclude that that finding was clearly erroneous.

Scheuer v. Creighton University

260 N.W.2d 595 (1977)

SPENCER, Justice.

This is an action for reinstatement of employment. Edwin G. Scheuer, Jr., was terminated as an assistant professor at the School of Pharmacy of Creighton University, on the ground of financial exigency in that school. The trial court dismissed his petition. Two questions are presented: (1) Should the contract be construed to require a showing of financial exigency on the part of the University as a whole or only as to the School of Pharmacy; and (2) whether a financial exigency existed within the meaning of that term as it is used in the contract between the parties. We affirm.

Edwin G. Scheuer, Jr., was a tenured assistant professor at the School of Pharmacy of Creighton University, Omaha, Nebraska. Creighton University is a private institution of higher education with its principal place of business in Omaha, Douglas County, Nebraska. Scheuer had been granted the status of a tenured member of the faculty of Creighton University in 1971.

The School of Pharmacy is one of four schools making up the Health Sciences Division of the University, the others being Medicine, Dentistry, and Nursing. Each of the four schools has its own Dean, with the Vice President for the Health Services being responsible for the entire Health Sciences Division.

Creighton University operates on a June 1 to May 31 fiscal year. The budget for each school year is prepared in the fall of the preceding year. The School of Pharmacy has three sources of income: Tuition and fees; income generated from clinical services; and federal funds. A large part of the federal funds received were "capitation funds," which represent a certain amount of federal funds given to health science schools for each student educated. These funds were contingent upon the school agreeing to a specified enrollment increase. Additionally, in the School of Pharmacy, the funds were further conditioned on the school expanding its clinical pharmacy program.

In the fiscal year 1975–1976, the School of Pharmacy received approximately $160,000 in federal "capitation funds." For this same fiscal year, the School of Pharmacy's entire budget was between $600,000 and $700,000. In spite of federal aid, the School of Pharmacy had operated at a deficit since 1971. These deficits and the federal funding have been as follows:

Fiscal Year	Deficit	Federal Funding
1971–72	$11,407	$ 76,580
1972–73	68,311	70,199
1973–74	40,353	83,615
1974–75	56,656	142,733
1975–76	56,000	159,782

In June of 1975, the Vice President for the Health Sciences Division learned the Division was facing a $900,000 deficit for the fiscal year 1975–1976, which had just begun. The School of Pharmacy was responsible for approximately $50,000 of that deficit. Later that same summer, he learned the entire Health Sciences Division was facing a reduction of funds for the year 1976–1977, in the amount of $2,000,000, and this sum was on top of the already expected loss of $900,000. Of the $2,000,000 loss in funds for the Division, approximately $160,000 of that loss was attributable to the School of Pharmacy as a result of the loss of "capitation funds."

Adding to the problems of the School of Pharmacy was the fact that it was moving into a new building in the spring of 1976. This move created $100,000 in additional expenses for the School of Pharmacy. There was no possibility of postponing the move since the expenses had already been accrued in the building. Also, the School of Pharmacy had made a commitment to the federal government to move into the building or else refund certain government grants. Additionally, the School of Pharmacy's accreditation depended upon its moving into the new facility.

The record indicates steps were taken to cut costs without impairing the essential goal of maintaining the integrity of the program in the School of Pharmacy. Cuts were made first in the area of nonsalary costs, such as equipment, traveling, and office supplies. A freeze was placed on faculty salaries. Steps were taken to terminate certain nonfaculty positions. These steps were not sufficient, so it then became necessary to reduce the faculty. After a review of the various positions and their relation to the program, it was found necessary to terminate four faculty members. One of them was the plaintiff. Plaintiff was chosen because the only course he taught was medicinal chemistry which could also be taught by a tenured faculty member who had seniority over him and who also could teach biochemistry which plaintiff had stated he could not teach.

On November 25, 1975, plaintiff was notified by letter from the President of the University that his appointment as a member of the faculty of the School of Pharmacy would terminate, effective December 1, 1976. The termination notice stated in part: "Because of financial exigencies which have arisen by reason of cut back in federal support of basic Health Sciences educational programs, the School of Pharmacy has been required to make cuts in its program. . . . After consultation with the Vice President for Health Sciences and with the Dean of Pharmacy, it has been determined that your position is one which is being abolished."

Both parties agree that termination procedures are governed by the Creighton University faculty handbook. The handbook provides: "The right of tenure may not be revoked except for cause. In general we understand by 'cause,' professional incompetence; medical-physical incapacity; substantial and manifest neglect of duty; grave misconduct (including inciting the immediate impairment of the institution's functions, or personally and physically causing such impairment); personal conduct substantially impairing the individual's performance of his appropriate functions within the University community; *and financial exigency on the part of the institution.* The burden of showing cause and of substantiating such a showing with a preponderance of the evidence is upon the institution. . . .

"*Where termination of appointment is based upon financial exigency, which may be considered to include bona fide discontinuance of a program or department of instruction or the reduction in size thereof,* faculty members affected may have the issued (sic) reviewed by the Academic Senate or Academic Council, or by the Faculty Grievance Committee, with ultimate review of controverted issues by the Board of Directors. In case of financial exigency, including discontinuance or reduction of a program or department of instruction, the faculty member concerned is to be given notice as soon as possible but never less than 12 months before termination; or, in lieu thereof, he may be given severance salary for 12 months.

"Before terminating an appointment because of discontinuance or reduction of a program or department of instruction, the university will make every effort to place affected faculty in other suitable positions. If an appointment is terminated before the end of the period or term of appointment because of financial exigency, the released faculty will not be replaced for two years thereafter unless the released faculty has been offered reappointment and a reasonable period during which to accept or decline this reappointment." The emphasized portions of the quotations above are the portions which are pertinent to the discussion herein.

It is undisputed that Creighton University as a whole was not in a real state of financial exigency. However, as set out hereafter, the testimony of its Treasurer might suggest otherwise. The trial judge found plaintiff's appointment could be terminated upon a showing of financial exigency in the School of Pharmacy. We approach the case on that premise. The District Court found the language contained in the faculty handbook "clearly defines 'financial exigency' as possibly being 'bona fide discontinuance of a program or department of instruction or the reduction in size thereof,'" and concluded that "'financial exigency' should be construed as requiring a determination within a particular college, rather than requiring consideration of the financial condition of the University as a whole." The District Court made no reference to the language "and financial exigency on the part of the institution."

Another section of the faculty handbook relied upon by the District Court in reaching its determination was a provision concerning dual appointments. The handbook states: "A faculty member may hold appointments in more than one department and/or school or college. Dual appointments may be set up when the chairman of the appropriate departments and the dean or deans, as the case may be, expressly request such an arrangement for the reason that it will help them discharge their educational and service responsibilities. One department or college or school should always be designated primary, within which the faculty member concerned will accrue time toward academic tenure. Tenure should obtain in only one department or school or college and shall refer only to the primary appointment. Whereas financial support for the salary of the faculty member may be derived from both departments, with the consent of both chairmen, it is understood that the chairman of the secondary department may withdraw support at the end of any defined budget period, and that the obligation for full-time support will then revert to the primary department." The court found "expressed in this provision of the contract a clear understanding that various departments—individually—shall be responsible for the salary of its faculty."

* * *

"In evidence of this recognition, the university endorses the *1940 Statement of Principles on Academic Freedom and Tenure* adopted and promulgated by the Association of American Colleges and Universities and by the American Association of University Professors. The university likewise endorses the *1958 Statement of Procedural Standards in Faculty Dismissal Proceedings* adopted and promulgated by these associations."

The 1940 statement provides: "After the expiration of a probationary period, teachers or investigators should have permanent or continuous tenure, and their service should be terminated only for adequate cause, except in the case of retirement for age, or under extraordinary circumstances because of financial exigencies. . . . Termination of a continuous appointment because of financial exigency should be demonstrably bona fide." "Financial exigency" is not defined in the statement.

The termination procedures contained in the faculty handbook closely parallel those proposed by the American Association of University Professors in its *1968 Recommended Institutional Regulations on Academic Freedom and Tenure*. The brief of amicus curiae suggests that the American Association of University Professors, hereinafter called AAUP, has since adopted its *1976 Recommended Institutional Regulations on Academic Freedom and Tenure*. This for the first time defines "financial exigency" as "an imminent financial crisis which threatens the survival of the institution as a whole and which cannot be alleviated by less drastic means."

* * *

The evidence supports a finding that plaintiff's termination was based upon a bona fide reduction in size of a program of instruction. For accreditation purposes and in order to obtain federal funding, the School of Pharmacy was required to emphasize its clinical pharmacy program. Medicinal chemistry, which plaintiff taught, was reduced to a 1 semester, 3 hour, course for freshman students. Another tenured faculty member, who had both rank and seniority over plaintiff, was qualified to teach medicinal chemistry as well as biochemistry. He assumed both these duties and plaintiff, who could teach only medicinal chemistry, was released. The record fully supports a finding the process used to select plaintiff for termination was not only fair and reasonable but tended to maintain the most viable and best overall program for the School of Pharmacy within the financial limits of that college.

We do not accept the 1976 recommendation of the American Association of University Professors defining "financial exigency" so as to limit that term to an imminent crisis which threatens the survival of the institution as a whole. This definition was adopted several years subsequent to the execution of the contract being interpreted herein. It has no probative value as to the meaning of the term at the time of the contract.

* * *

The rapidly changing needs of students and society demand that university administrators have sufficient discretion to retrench in areas faced with financial problems. Creighton University is a private institution. We can take judicial notice of the fact that many private universities are facing severe financial crunches. When we consider only a single area we get an idea of the problem. The record indicates energy costs for Creighton University in a relatively short time have risen from $200,000 per year to $1,200,000.

If we read the record correctly, Creighton as an institution has less than $2,000,000 of unrestricted general funds available every year. Common sense dictates that plaintiff's contention is untenable. To sustain it, we must hold no tenured employee in any college may be released until the institution exhausts its total assets or at the very least reaches the point where its very survival as an institution is in jeopardy.

We specifically hold the term "financial exigency" as used in the contract of employment herein may be limited to a financial exigency in a department or college. It is not restricted to one existing in the institution as a whole.

The evidence is fairly conclusive the School of Pharmacy was faced with a financial exigency for the fiscal year 1976–1977. It had been operating with a deficit for the past 5 years. The deficit for 1974–1975 and 1975–1976 had reached $56,000 for each year. The deficit faced for 1976–1977 was in excess of $200,000. This deficit would be more than three times greater than any previous deficit.

The Vice President for Financial Affairs, who was Treasurer of Creighton University, testified the University generally subsidized each college in the amount of 6 to 7 ½ percent of the budget for that college. This subsidy came from the University general fund, which is made up of endowment earnings, Jesuit net contributed income, and gift income from the public. These sources total approximately $1,750,000 a year.

To continue the existing pharmacy program, the University would have been required to more than double the subsidy for that college, to the detriment of its other schools. The Treasurer further testified Creighton University as a whole was in delicate financial position. While stating the University was not then in a state of financial exigency, he did state it was on the edge of financial exigency. It was his further testimony that Creighton's endowment is only ⅒th of what it should have for a private university of its size.

For the reasons discussed above, the judgment of the District Court is correct and should be affirmed.

Jimenez v. Almodovar

650 F.2d 363 (1981)

WYZANSKI, Senior District Judge.

Two professors, whose employment a public university had terminated solely because it eliminated their positions as unnecessary because of a *bona fide* change of its academic program, brought this 42 U.S.C. § 1983 action against the university, its president, and others on the ground that they, in terminating the plaintiffs' employment, deprived them of their property without the due process of law guaranteed by the Fifth or the Fourteenth Amendment to the United States Constitution. The plaintiffs appeal from a judgment for the defendants. The essential facts are undisputed.

The University of Puerto Rico is a public instrumentality created by Act No. 1 of January 20, 1966, as amended. 18 LPRA §§ 601–614. It operates a number of separate institutional units each having a substantial degree of academic and administrative autonomy. 18 LPRA §§ 603, 606. The Council on Higher Education is the governing board of the university system. 18 LPRA § 602(f)(1). Among the Council's duties is to pass on appeals taken against decisions of the president of the university. 18 LPRA § 602(e)(6).

Humacao University College until 1975 was a Regional College. Act No. 1 of January 20, 1966, 18 LPRA § 611(d), gave the University of Puerto Rico general jurisdiction of Humacao, but Humacao retained its separate academic faculty.

On January 14, 1972 the Council on Higher Education approved for the then Humacao Regional College a program for an associate degree in physical education and recreation to be conducted as a pilot program (hereafter called "the pilot program"), the duration of which was made dependent upon a subsequent evaluation.

The university on September 1, 1970 employed Maria L. Garcia-Feliciano as a temporary instructor and two years later assigned her to the pilot program. On August 15, 1972, the university gave the plaintiffs—Raul E. Medina Jimenez and Jorge H. Garofalo Pastrana—temporary appointments in the pilot program. On July 1, 1977 the then president of the University wrote to each of the three persons just named identical letters having the following text:

> In accordance with the powers granted me by the Law of the University of Puerto Rico, approved on 20 January 1966 in its Article 5C(8), I appoint you a permanent member of the University teaching staff by virtue of the dispositions of the said law in its Article 14B.

> This permanent appointment is effective as of 1 July 1977 and by the same you are incorporated in the group of regular collaborators which integrate the Institution.

In the pre-trial agreement in this case it has been stipulated that the foregoing July 1, 1977 letters appointed each of the plaintiffs "a tenured professor of the University of Puerto Rico."

On July 19, 1978 the current president of the university—the defendant Ismael Almodovar—wrote to each of the aforesaid three persons identical letters having the following text:

> At a meeting held on 11 July 1978, the Council on Higher Education decided to inactivate the Associate Degree Program in Physical Education of the Humacao University College. This decision results from a series of factors, among them, the slight enrollment which has been benefiting from the program, the evaluation of the program recently carried out and the recommendations of the Department's Director and of the College, Dr. Federico Matheu. As a result of the recent action, it is necessary to eliminate three of the five teaching positions of the Physical Education Department at the Humacao College, since the teaching activity in that Department will be reduced to one of services to the other teaching programs of the College.

> I am sorry to inform you that, after taking various objective factors into consideration, one of the positions to be eliminated will be the one currently occupied by you. As a result of this programmatic reduction we must do without your services as part of our College's teaching staff as of 15 August 1978.

> As was determined by the Council on Higher Education itself, we have communicated with the chancellors and directors of other institutional units with offerings in the field of physical education to explore the possibility of relocating in one of the units of the University System, with reference to those programs' needs, the professors harmed by this action. Should any such possibility turn up, we will communicate with you immediately. With the purpose of allowing us to offer the directors and chancellors information about you I would be obliged, if you think it convenient, that you send us your "curriculum vitae."

> * * *

Each of the two teaching positions of the Physical Education Department which were not eliminated was held by a professor senior to the three recipients of the aforesaid letter.

The plaintiffs do not question that the university in reducing the number of professors in the Physical Education Department "acted in good faith, exclusively for the reasons stated in the July 19, 1978 letter, and without any motive or intention to dismiss the plaintiffs on "personal grounds"—a term here used to include not only dismissals for cause, or for fault, or for deficiency of any kind, but also to include dismissals reflecting any superior's personal attitude toward a plaintiff or any other individual.

Nor do the plaintiffs question that if eliminations were justified, the university, in selecting for elimination the plaintiffs rather than the two professors who were not eliminated, acted in good faith, on the basis of an appropriate standard of seniority of service and not on "personal grounds," as above defined.

On July 26, 1978, the plaintiffs were given an informal hearing by Mr. Pedro Juan Barbosa, assistant to President Almodovar, whom the president, being ill, had designated as his representative for the hearing. Mr. Barbosa informed the plaintiffs that seniority was the only criterion on which the president had based his decision. He also invited them to set forth any grievances or challenges they might make against the decision under which their employment would terminate on August 15, 1978. None was raised by the plaintiffs at that time.

The plaintiffs have never appealed from the president's July 19, 1978 decision effective August 15, 1978 eliminating their positions and terminating their employment. It is inferable that they knew that such an appeal was available because, to the knowledge of plaintiff's counsel, their colleague Maria L. Garcia-Feliciano appealed, pursuant to 18 LPRA § 602(e)(6), the decision against her to the Council on Higher Education. The Council has ordered a full evidentiary hearing of her appeal before a hearing examiner, pursuant to Articles 6, 10, 11 and 12 of Chapter IX of its by-laws, but, in accordance with a stipulation of the parties, the Council stayed the hearing pending the outcome of the present action.

Meanwhile, President Almodovar had been seeking to secure positions within the university for the plaintiffs. On July 19, 1978, the very day he transmitted to the plaintiffs and Maria L. Garcia-Feliciano the termination letters, the president directed to each of the chancellors and directors of the other university colleges within the university an inquiry as to whether any position was available for any of the three professors being eliminated. The president pursued these inquiries by telegrams sent at a later date.

On August 2, 1978, the Aguadilla College of the University of Puerto Rico employed Maria L. Garcia-Feliciano, who was senior to the plaintiffs, at the same rank and salary she had enjoyed at Humacao University College.

On September 6, 1978, the president offered both the plaintiffs the only teaching position then available at the Carolina Regional College of the University of Puerto Rico. At the same time, the president offered to the plaintiff Medina Jimenez, and later offered to the other plaintiff, Garofalo, an administrative position at Humacao University College. Medina Jimenez accepted effective October 2, 1978 the teaching position at Carolina Regional College, with the same rank and salary he enjoyed at Humacao University College. He still holds that position. He has also received retroactively to August 15, 1978 his salary. The other plaintiff, Garofalo, did not accept any position then or later.

On April 5, 1979, the president of the university offered plaintiff Medina Jimenez a teaching position in Humacao University College—a position which was in every respect similar to the one he had previously held in that college, including tenure and rank, plus an administrative, tenured position as the administrator of the new sports facilities in said college. The president offered plaintiff Garofalo the position occupied by plaintiff Medina Jimenez in the Carolina Regional College "that will be left vacant by the latter in case he accepts the offer made to him." Both positions were to be occupied immediately, retroactively as of April 1, 1979. On August 11, 1979, Medina Jimenez declined the offer made to him, so the Carolina position did not become available to Garofalo.

On July 28, 1978, the plaintiffs filed in the district court a complaint alleging that the defendants had taken their property without due process of law and had denied them the equal protection of the laws, and seeking an injunction ordering the defendants "to continue the plaintiffs in their posts as tenured teaching staff of the

University of Puerto Rico" and a payment of "their back salaries in full." Without a jury, the district judge heard the evidence, made findings, and, dismissing the complaint, entered judgment for the defendants.

The plaintiffs appealed. Inasmuch as there is no significant difference in the status of the plaintiff Medina Jimenez and the plaintiff Garofalo, we shall, for convenience, hereafter address the opinion principally to Medina Jimenez's case and to his claim that the defendants deprived him of his property and his liberty without due process of law.

Medina Jimenez's principal contention is that the defendants deprived him of his *property* rights under Puerto Rican law, including his right under 18 LPRA § 613(c) not to be deprived of his position without a hearing in which charges are preferred and he has an opportunity to defend himself. We do best to reach that contention against a broad background.

* * *

[It] is a reasonable inference that when the Puerto Rican legislature enacted § 16 of Act No. 135, Laws of Puerto Rico, 1942, and Act No. 334, Laws of Puerto Rico, 1949 which are the sources of § 613 of 18 LPRA, the legislature, being aware of and intending to preserve the distinction drawn by the *1940 Statement of Principles on Academic Freedom and Tenure* between a dismissal for cause or other personal grounds and a dismissal for impersonal institutional reasons, had a purpose to limit what is now § 613(c) to *ad hominem* dismissals for cause, or other personal grounds.

So far as we know, there are no relevant regulations. The only University of Puerto Rico regulation cited to us has no bearing upon the issues in this case. It does not impose any duty upon the university, nor give a faculty member any right; on the contrary, it gives the university a right to impose upon a faculty member a duty to do a full week's work for a full week's pay.

Having concluded that the university had an implied right of *bona fide* unavoidable termination of the contracts of the tenured members of the faculty on the ground of change of academic program, and that such right could be exercised by a procedure different from the one set forth in 18 LPRA § 613(c), we now consider what procedure the university did afford the plaintiffs and examine it in the light of the *procedural* aspects of the due process clause. The plaintiffs, as they presumably knew, had the right to a hearing by an intramural administrative tribunal which was empowered to receive evidence, to direct that the university give the plaintiffs employment substantially equivalent to their last employment, and probably to award damages, 18 LPRA § 602(e)(6). The decision of the tribunal was subject to review by a Puerto Rican court which had even greater powers.

That procedure fully satisfied the *procedural* requirements of the due process clause. Indeed, the plaintiffs have not pointed to any alleged shortcoming of the procedure other than its failure to comply with 18 LPRA § 613(c).

It seems that the plaintiffs also contend that they were deprived of their property without *substantive* due process of law.

Perhaps the plaintiffs mean merely that they were deprived by the university of substantive due process because it did not follow its own regulations and 18 LPRA § 613(c). Violations of a university's own *procedural* regulations have been held, on the ground that they were violations of the university's own contracts, to be a deprivation of *substantive* due process. We are not required to express agreement or disagreement with that doctrine of substantive due process inasmuch as here the university did not violate its own regulations or any Puerto Rican statute impliedly included in the contract.

However, it may be that the plaintiffs are contending that they were deprived of substantive due process on one or more of the following grounds: that if the contract implied that the university had a right of *bona fide* unavoidable termination of the plaintiff's employment on account of change of academic program, then (1) the university in the instant case has not borne the burden of showing that its termination was "unavoidable" or (2) the contract includes an implied obligation that the university shall not make the termination of a tenured faculty member's employment effective (a) until a reasonable time after the university informs him of his impending dismissal and (b) until the university has for a reasonable time exercised its best efforts to place him in another suitable position equivalent to the one eliminated. We emphatically state that we express no opinion on the merits of those possible contentions; they raise questions of state contractual law, and, in addition, at least the first and perhaps all of those contentions raise a problem as to exhaustion of available state administrative remedies. We are not here exercising pendent or other jurisdiction over a purely local cause of action. We decide only such state contractual questions as are necessary to determine whether the plaintiffs have been deprived of their *procedural* rights of due process under the United States Constitution. If the university by terminating the plaintiffs' contracts failed to accord them only their substantive *contractual* rights, we are not concerned. A mere breach of contractual right is not a deprivation of property without *constitutional* due process of law. Otherwise, virtually every controversy involving an alleged breach of contract by a government or a governmental institution or agency or instrumentality would be a constitutional case.

There being no proof that the university's dismissal of the plaintiffs involved a stigma or reflection on their reputation, they were not deprived of their "liberty" in violation of the due process clause.

Inasmuch as on the undisputed facts the plaintiffs did not have a valid cause of action based on the alleged deprivation by the defendants of their due process rights, it is a moot question whether the trial judge erred in accepting *verbatim* the defendants' proposed findings. Likewise, it is a moot question whether the trial judge erred in considering without a jury the plaintiffs' equitable claim before a jury could find the facts in connection with the plaintiffs' legal claim.

Affirmed.

Brumbach v. Rensselaer

510 N.Y.S.2d 761 (A.D. 3 Dept. 1987)

CASEY, Justice.

Appeal from an order of the Supreme Court at Special Term (Walsh, Jr., J.), entered December 17, 1985 in Schenectady County, which, *inter alia*, granted defendant's motion for summary judgment dismissing the complaint.

Defendant employed plaintiff in a temporary capacity as a research associate in the School of Humanities and Social Sciences from January 12, 1981 to May 5, 1981. That spring, defendant posted a job opening for a tenure-track position of assistant professor/contract archaeologist in the public archaeology program for which it sought an applicant with a doctorate degree. Previously, defendant had employed a non-tenure-track position of research associate or lecturer to teach archaeology, but changed the classification to a tenure-track position at the suggestion of the chairman of its department of science and technology studies, who believed that the change to a full-time faculty position would strengthen the public archaeology program. Eleven men and one woman, plaintiff, applied. The position was formally offered to plaintiff for a three-year period commencing September 1, 1981 and ending June 30, 1984, by letter dated July 27, 1981, which fixed the salary at $16,000 for the 1981–1982 academic year with future salary increases dependent on plaintiff's ability to obtain sufficient contracts. Plaintiff accepted the position on August 23, 1981 at the salary fixed and was increased to $19,000 for the 1982–1983 academic year and to $21,000 for the following year. For all three years, plaintiff received favorable faculty evaluations.

On May 2, 1984, at a meeting of all tenured faculty in the department of science and technology studies, continuation of plaintiff's position and her further appointment were considered. After due discussion of the question, the faculty unanimously voted not to continue the position of assistant professor/contract archaeologist, but rather to pursue a new direction. Plaintiff was notified of this decision and offered a one-year terminal appointment beginning July 1, 1984 and ending June 30, 1985. Plaintiff accepted this appointment on May 22, 1984. Thereafter, defendant determined that plaintiff's position should be replaced with a part-time tenure-track position, emphasizing computer archaeology. This newly created position was posted. Plaintiff did not apply for this position and another person was appointed for one academic year.

Plaintiff commenced this action on or about December 1, 1984 for breach of contract, fraud and sexual discrimination. After issue was joined, Special Term granted defendant's motion for summary judgment dismissing all three causes of action for insufficiency, and plaintiff appeals. We agree with the determination of Special Term.

To sustain her cause of action for breach of contract, plaintiff relies on defendant's "Handbook for Academic Staff," in which it is stated, "If the result of the evaluation is satisfactory, it is normal for an assistant professor to be re-employed for a second three-year period." Despite the favorable evaluation received by plaintiff, the language of the handbook can in no way be construed as a contract binding defendant to renewal. Plaintiff was employed for the full time for which she had been hired and was paid accordingly. Defendant promised no more than that. At the expiration of her term, plaintiff became an employee at will. Significantly, defendant's handbook, in the same section on which plaintiff relies, also provides, "If such appointment is not renewed, the appointment terminates at the end of the period of appointment as stated in the letter of agreement." As held in O'Connor, the method of evaluating performance fairly as prescribed in the handbook does not impose express limitations on defendant's right to terminate. The handbook herein did not provide that plaintiff would not be terminated "without just and sufficient cause" so as to bring plaintiff within the limited exceptions to the termination of an at-will employee provided for in Weiner v. McGraw-Hill, Inc. The manner and method outlined above, which caused defendant to change direction in regard to plaintiff's position, indicates that defendant's needs and priorities as considered by the faculty involved were a prime consideration in the action defendant has taken, and that action was not arbitrary or unreasonable. Consequently, plaintiff has not demonstrated a cause of action for breach of contract in response to defendant's motion for summary judgment.

Plaintiff's cause of action for discrimination focuses only upon the injury she has incurred by virtue of the nonrenewal of her appointment. Plaintiff does not allege in her complaint that she was paid a lower salary than others performing similarly, that she was excluded from organizational meetings, that she was down-graded in evaluation and the like, or that she was subjected to disparate treatment in the nonrenewal of her appointment. In this regard, plaintiff's complaint is insufficient. In *Shapolsky v. Shapolsky*, it was pertinently stated that "it is still essential * * * that the pleading enable the defendant to determine the nature of the plaintiff's grievances and the relief [she] seeks in consequence of the alleged wrongs." By this standard, plaintiff has failed to plead a cause of action for discrimination on the basis of sex.

Plaintiff's cause of action for fraud is based on defendant's alleged misrepresentation that plaintiff's position was tenure-tracked. This alleged fraud relates directly to plaintiff's cause of action for breach of contract and, therefore, cannot be the predicate for a separate cause of action for fraud. Furthermore, the alleged misrepresentation is not of an existing fact, but rather one of a possible future contingency, which required the consideration of many factors before it occurred. The fraud cause of action is likewise legally insufficient. The order appealed from should in all respects be affirmed.

D'Andrea v. Adams
626 F.2d 469 (1980)

RANDALL, Circuit Judge:

This appeal concerns a controversy between Dr. Nicholas D'Andrea, a tenured assistant professor of geography at Troy State University (TSU) in Alabama, and four administrators (collectively referred to as the Administrators) of the school: Dr. Adams, President of TSU; Dr. Barnett, Chief Academic Dean; Dr. Long, Dean of the College of Arts and Sciences; and Dr. Tway, Chairman of the Department of History and Social Science. The issue on this appeal is whether the Administrators were within their rights in discharging Dr. D'Andrea for communicating information he possessed that suggested impropriety in the use of TSU funds to a legislative budget subcommittee that was engaged in reviewing funding of state agencies, including TSU. Dr. D'Andrea contends that his statements were protected by the first amendment. The Administrators contend that Dr. D'Andrea's statements were not constitutionally protected because they materially and substantially interfered with the performance of his duties and with the functioning of school programs, and because the statements were made with reckless disregard for their truth. Additionally, the Administrators contend that there was insufficient proof for the jury to conclude that defendants Tway and Long knew of Dr. D'Andrea's statements to the state legislature, and hence to conclude that they participated in his discharge in retaliation for those statements. Under proper instructions, the jury returned a verdict in Dr. D'Andrea's favor against all the Administrators. The trial court granted the Administrators' motion for judgment n. o. v., on the ground that Dr. D'Andrea's statements were not constitutionally protected and also on the ground that there was insufficient evidence to support a verdict against defendants Tway and Long. We reverse.

In November 1976, Dr. D'Andrea went to the Alabama Capital in Montgomery and spoke to a Mr. Kirkland, then an administrative assistant to the Lieutenant Governor, and to an examiner from the Alabama Department of Examiners of Public Accounts, who was engaged in an examination of TSU finances in preparation for budget subcommittee hearings in the state legislature regarding the funding of the school. At that time, Dr. D'Andrea conveyed to Mr. Kirkland and the examiner information he had received from other people, whom he identified, concerning assertedly improper uses of TSU funds. Whether the information was true, partially true, or wholly false cannot be determined from the record because the trial court pretermitted inquiry into that question. For purposes of this appeal, we assume the information was inaccurate. Apparently, TSU received a "clean bill of health" after the legislative examination of the school's finances and it received the appropriation it had sought. Dr. Adams in particular was commended for his management of the school.

In January 1977, Dr. D'Andrea was told that the geography program at the school was going to be discontinued, and that his services as a professor of geography would no longer be needed. The decision to eliminate the geography program was made at a meeting on January 13, 1977, attended only by the Administrators. Dr. D'Andrea exercised his right as a tenured faculty member under TSU's procedures to seek other employment at the school for which he was qualified. The Ad Hoc Committee on Credentials did not recommend placement in another position, and Dr. D'Andrea sought review of this decision by the Faculty Personnel Advisory Committee. Dr. D'Andrea received notice of the hearing, which indicated that, because of the Ad Hoc Committee's recommendation, termination of the geography program "would carry with it a termination of your tenured status at the University." The notice informed Dr. D'Andrea that the hearing would cover the decision to terminate the geography program and the recommendation that Dr. D'Andrea not be offered an alternative teaching position. After a hearing, at which Dr. D'Andrea was present and represented by an attorney, the Faculty Committee upheld the recommendation of the Ad Hoc Committee and the decision to terminate the geography program. Dr. D'Andrea was therefore out of a job.

Before the beginning of the fall semester, however, TSU determined that the decision to terminate the geography program had been precipitate, because geography instruction is a necessary component of the degree in elementary education offered by the school and because enrollment data for the fall semester apparently indicated a burgeoning interest in geography. The school therefore reinstated geography as a minor area of study and offered D'Andrea reemployment, which he accepted. In the meantime, however, Dr. D'Andrea had filed this action, alleging that the decision to terminate the geography program was in fact a retaliation against him for his statements to state officials concerning TSU finances, and as such violated his first amendment rights. The case was not mooted by reason of his reemployment, because he had been dismissed for a time and because he sought injunctive relief against future violations of his constitutional rights.

The jury was properly instructed that they could find for Dr. D'Andrea only (1) if he convinced them, by a preponderance of the evidence, that his contact with state officials was constitutionally protected and was a substantial or motivating factor in the decision to terminate the geography program, and (2) if the Administrators failed to convince them, using the same standard, that they would have terminated the geography program even absent Dr. D'Andrea's contact with state officials. The jury returned a verdict in favor of Dr. D'Andrea, and the judgment n. o. v. did not attack the jury's determination that the termination of the geography program was motivated by Dr. D'Andrea's contact with state officials and that the termination would not have occurred absent that conduct. Accordingly, there is no *Mt. Healthy* issue in this appeal.

The only questions we face are (1) whether there was sufficient evidence for a reasonable jury to conclude that on January 13 Tway and Long knew about Dr. D'Andrea's contact with state officials, and (2) whether, as a matter of law, Dr. D'Andrea's statements to those officials were protected by the first amendment.

In passing on the first question, we are guided by the standard of review for judgments n. o. v. enunciated in *Boeing Co. v. Shipman*. Considering all the evidence "in the light and with all reasonable inferences most favorable to" Dr. D'Andrea, our task is to decide whether Dr. D'Andrea presented "evidence of such quality and weight that reasonable and fair-minded [jurors] in the exercise of impartial judgment might reach different conclusions" with regard to the question whether Tway and Long knew about Dr. D'Andrea's statements when they attended the January 13 meeting at which all the Administrators agreed to terminate the geography program. "[I]t is the function of the jury as the traditional finder of the facts, and not the Court, to weigh conflicting evidence and inferences, and determine the credibility of witnesses."

Under the *Boeing* standard, there was sufficient evidence for a reasonable jury to conclude that all the Administrators discussed Dr. D'Andrea's statements to state officials when they met on January 13. Only the Administrators were present at the meeting. The jury's necessary finding that Dr. Adams and Dr. Barnett knew of the statements at that time is not challenged on this appeal. Dr. Tway was the last to arrive at that meeting. He testified as follows regarding his arrival at the meeting and the ensuing discussion:

> DR. TWAY: When I first went into the office Dr. Barnett and Dr. Long were sitting off to my right. I pulled my chair up to the front right-hand corner of the president's desk and he was rather off center behind his desk . . . I pulled my chair up to his desk and he said to me, "What are we going to do—what about D'Andrea?" . . . And I said, "Well, what about Dr. D'Andrea?" And he said— I don't attempt to quote verbatim, it is a long time back, but something in the sense, "Well, he is just not as loyal as a fellow ought to be." And I made no response to that. I had no reason to be in defense or complimentary of his loyalty. The conversation immediately turned to discussion which led me to respond to the president it's my impression that if a man has tenure he could only be dismissed from his position as such for moral turpitude, incompetency to perform the job, or being guilty of some criminal offense. I said I don't know of either moral turpitude or criminal offense of Dr. D'Andrea. I went on to say we would have difficulty convincing anyone that the man was incompetent since he had been runner-up once and perhaps more than once for the outstanding teacher award known as Ingles Award. No sooner had I made that comment than the four of us went into a discussion of the viability of the geography program, for which I presume I was called in there.

The jury thus had before it direct evidence that Dr. D'Andrea's loyalty to TSU was questioned in the presence of all the Administrators at the January 13 meeting. No witness offered an explanation of what Dr. Adams may have meant. Dr. Adams denied that he characterized Dr. D'Andrea as disloyal.

In addition to Dr. Tway's testimony, the jury had before it evidence tending to show that although the problem of low enrollment in the geography program—the reason asserted by defendants for the termination of the program—had been informally discussed by members of the school administration for several months before the January 13 meeting, that meeting was not planned in advance. Rather, everyone involved concedes that the meeting, lasting only about an hour, was convened on the spur of the moment. Although the problem of low enrollment was assertedly the sole reason for terminating the geography program, no enrollment statistics were available at the meeting. No faculty committees were consulted concerning that decision, although the evidence showed that there were several such committees whose responsibilities included advising on curricular changes.

Taking all the evidence into consideration, a reasonable jury could conclude that, despite the Administrators' denials, Dr. D'Andrea's statements to state officials were discussed by all the Administrators at the January 13 meeting. No issue was taken with the jury's conclusion that Drs. Adams and Barnett knew of the statements. The jury could reasonably have believed Dr. Tway's testimony that Dr. Adams raised the question of Dr. D'Andrea's loyalty, and disbelieved his testimony that—although he knew of nothing reflecting poorly on Dr. D'Andrea's character—he simply did not challenge or inquire about the president's assertion that Dr. D'Andrea, a professor in Dr. Tway's department, was disloyal. Finally, a jury could reasonably conclude that a major curricular revision would not normally have been instituted in such a hasty and indeliberate fashion, and that the decision to terminate the geography program was, under those circumstances, deliberately done with the acquiescence of all the Administrators for the purpose of penalizing Dr. D'Andrea for his statements to state officials. We therefore hold that the district court erred in concluding that there was insufficient evidence that at the January 13 meeting defendants Tway and Long knew about the statements made by Dr. D'Andrea to state officials.

We turn now to the fundamental issue on this appeal, which is whether Dr. D'Andrea's statements to state officials were protected by the first amendment.

* * *

Dr. D'Andrea may well have believed that his information was too insubstantial to justify a public accusation, yet substantial enough to warrant investigation by the budget subcommittee. Moreover, he may have been apprehensive that disclosure of the information and of his visit to Montgomery to administrative officials at TSU would result in his dismissal or other objectionable consequences. He was entitled to assume that his statements would be dealt with prudently; that the rumors he had heard would be investigated; and that if they appeared to have a factual foundation, the TSU officials involved would have an opportunity to respond to them.

As Judge Goldberg observed in *Porter v. Califano*, "*Pickering* states that the First Amendment requires the government not just to show that certain employee speech injures the government, but to show that the benefits of preventing the injury actually outweigh the profound benefits of free speech in this society." The Administrators have utterly failed to make such a showing. Accordingly, we hold that the entry of judgment n. o. v. by the district court was error.

After the favorable verdict and before entry of the judgment n. o. v., the trial court awarded Dr. D'Andrea attorney fees and expenses totalling $7,832.70 for the trial of the case, pursuant to 42 U.S.C. § 1988. That award is to be reinstated along with Dr. D'Andrea's favorable jury verdict.

Tenure Density

Coe v. Board of Regents of University of Wisconsin
409 N.W.2d 166 (Wis. App. 1987)

DYKMAN, Judge.

Susan Coe appeals from an order affirming the University of Wisconsin Board of Regents' decision not to hold a formal hearing to review the chancellor's denial of tenure. Coe contends that faculty members denied tenure have rights under Wis. Adm. Code sec. UWS chapter 3 (January, 1986) and that the chancellor of the University of Wisconsin-Stevens Point erroneously denied her tenure because he considered her department's tenure situation, a factor she contends is not enumerated in sec. UWS 3.06(1)(b). She also contends she was entitled to a contested case hearing before the board of regents regarding the denial of tenure. Because we conclude the chancellor properly applied the tenure criteria and that Coe has not met the requirements for a contested case hearing, we affirm.

The board of regents functions as the administrative agency in the university system and has "primary responsibility for governance of the system...." Pursuant to sec. 36.13(3), Stats. (1981–82), the board adopted sec. UWS chapter 3 relating to tenure and probationary appointments. Tenure is granted upon affirmative recommendation of the appropriate academic department and chancellor.

Coe was an assistant professor of social work in the Department of Sociology and Anthropology at UW-Stevens Point under a series of yearly probationary contracts beginning in 1976. Her 1976 appointment letter stated that tenure would be based on her performance and other factors including but not limited to a programmatic need in her department and the department's financial ability to add another tenured position. Subsequent appointment letters referred to these factors. In 1979, 1980 and 1981, Coe's department recommended that she be reappointed and granted early tenure. The chancellor did not grant early tenure, stating that the university prefers to defer tenure decisions until the last year of the probationary period. Section 36.13(2)(b) limits probationary appointments to seven consecutive academic years.

Academic year 1981–82 was Coe's "up or out" year; she had to become tenured or her employment with the university would terminate. In March 1982, her department's Retention and Tenure Committee voted to retain her for an eighth year and to grant tenure, despite the fact that her department was overtenured, or had a tenure density problem.[2] The chancellor decided not to renew Coe's employment or grant tenure, stating:

> Many factors contributed to my overall decision to not recommend tenure. Application of the university tenure management policy reveals that no tenurable position exists in [your department]. In fact, your department currently is tenured to the extent of 3.19 positions over that allowed by the policy. Your department recognized the fact and argued for an exception. Any exception must be based on strong and compelling reasons related to academic program and your individual qualifications and performance. You hold the minimum academic credentials for tenure for individuals teaching in social work. However, you do not hold the doctorate. Your scholarly activity, as evidenced by publication and regional and national professional service, is not outstanding. The need for instruction in social work is not a major priority of the institution. In fact, we have no major, minor or concentration in social work. In short, I found no strong and compelling reasons to recommend tenure.

After receiving the chancellor's reasons for denying tenure in accordance with sec. UWS 3.07(1)(a), Coe appealed the decision to the faculty appeals committee provided by sec. UWS 3.08(1). She claimed she was discriminated against because early tenure was granted to a male faculty member with the same starting date after the department was overtenured. She also claimed she was never given any indication that her performance was below tenure requirements. The committee upheld the chancellor's decision in December 1982. Coe then requested that the board appoint a regent to review her case. The appointed regent recommended that the board provide a hearing. An attorney and a TAUWF (The Association of University of Wisconsin Faculties) representative appeared on Coe's behalf when the board considered Coe's hearing request in November 1983. On December 9, 1983, the board denied Coe's request for a formal hearing and then denied her request for reconsideration. Coe petitioned for review under chapter 227, Stats. (1981–82). The trial court affirmed the board's decision.

TENURE CRITERIA

Coe argues she met the tenure criteria set forth in sec. UWS 3.06(1)(b) and that the chancellor erroneously considered her department's tenure density problem in denying her tenure. She argues that because tenure density is not an enumerated criterion, the chancellor exceeded his authority in considering it. The board contends the chancellor properly interpreted sec. UWS 3.06(1)(b) as permitting consideration of a department's tenure density in granting or denying tenure.

Section UWS 3.06(1)(b) provides:

Decisions relating to renewal of appointments or recommending of tenure shall be made in accordance with institutional rules and procedures which shall require an evaluation of teaching, research, and professional and public service

---

2. The tenure management policy establishes tenure density guidelines: "the current number of tenured faculty members in a given department [cannot] exceed 80% of the number of FTE faculty positions generated (according to a specific formula) by the projected student enrollment...." In departments which have exceeded 80%, tenure may be granted to a faculty member only after the department has made "compelling arguments" to justify an exception to the 80% limit.

and contribution to the institution. The relative importance of these functions in the evaluation process shall be decided by departmental, school, college, and institutional faculties in accordance with the mission and needs of the particular institution and its component parts. Written criteria for these decisions shall be developed by the appropriate institutional faculty bodies.

We independently review administrative action and our scope of review is identical to that given the trial court by sec. 227.20, Stats. (1981–82). The board's validly enacted administrative rules have the force and effect of law and are "subject to the same principles of construction as apply to the construction of statutes...."

[T]he interpretation by an administrative agency of its own regulation is entitled to controlling weight unless inconsistent with the language of the regulation or clearly erroneous. This rule of construction accords with the principle that "a construction which fosters the purpose of the rule is to be sought and is favored over a construction which will defeat the manifest object of the rule." An administrative agency knows the specific purposes of the regulations it has promulgated. Moreover, an agency has a certain expertise in the area it is called upon to regulate. Thus we believe that an agency is in the best position to interpret its own regulations in accordance with their underlying purposes. For this reason, in construing such regulations, we ordinarily defer to the adopting agency's interpretation.

The chancellor is the executive head of his or her institution and is responsible for administering board policies. Subject to those policies and in consultation with the faculty, the chancellor defines and administers "institutional standards for faculty peer evaluation and screening candidates for appointment, promotion and tenure...." Definition and administration of institutional standards requires interpretation of the board's rules. We reject Coe's characterization of the chancellor as an academic who lacks expertise to interpret the board's rules. The legislature views the chancellor as an administrator charged with implementing board policies. Given this recognition of the chancellor's expertise, we will defer to the chancellor's interpretation of sec. UWS 3.06(1)(b) unless it is inconsistent with the rule's language or clearly erroneous.

Construction of an administrative rule is a question of law and the primary source of construction is the rule's language. A rule is not ambiguous merely because the parties disagree as to its meaning. Ambiguity occurs when reasonably "well-informed" persons can understand the rule in two or more senses.

Section UWS 3.06(1)(b) is not ambiguous. It lists several performance factors to be considered in making tenure decisions, and assigns the task of balancing these factors, in light of the needs and mission of the particular institution, to the faculty. It also authorizes the faculty to establish written criteria for making such decisions.

As directed by sec. UWS 3.06(1)(b), the UW-Stevens Point faculty senate approved a policy statement on probationary and tenure appointments in April 1979. This statement introduced guidelines and procedures intended to assist in tenure management. The policy establishes tenure density as a criterion in determining whether a faculty member's position can be designated as a tenured position. The vice chancellor interpreted the policy as conditioning the availability of a tenured position upon institutional need, departmental ability to meet the tenure guidelines, and the faculty member's performance. The policy was in effect when Coe was recommended for early tenure in spring 1980. Because the written criteria developed under sec. UWS

3.06(1)(b) established tenure density as a relevant criterion, the chancellor did not err in considering it. We do not consider whether, in the absence of such written criteria, the chancellor may consider other, nonspecified nonperformance criteria. The chancellor's interpretation refers to the performance and nonperformance criteria set forth in the rule and the tenure management policy promulgated in accordance with the rule. We will therefore defer to his interpretation because it is consistent with the rule's language.

Coe interprets sec. UWS 3.06(1)(b) as requiring that tenure be granted to any faculty member who has fulfilled the individual performance requirements. This interpretation ignores the "relative importance" language of the rule. Coe suggests that she ought to have been granted tenure regardless of her department's ability to sustain another tenured position and then laid off because her department was overtenured. This is nonsensical. We cannot construe a rule in derogation of common sense, nor can we interpret a rule "so as to work an unreasonable or absurd result." Interpreting sec. UWS 3.06(1)(b) as granting automatic tenure regardless of institutional need yields an unreasonable result.

CONTESTED CASE HEARING

Coe argues she was entitled to a contested case hearing before the board regarding the denial of tenure. Section 227.064(1), Stats. (1981–82), provides:

> In addition to any other right provided by law, any person filing a written request with an agency for hearing shall have the right to a hearing which shall be treated as a contested case if:
>
> (a) A substantial interest of the person is injured in fact or threatened with injury by agency action or inaction;
>
> (b) There is no evidence of legislative intent that the interest is not to be protected;
>
> (c) The injury to the person requesting a hearing is different in kind or degree from injury to the general public caused by the agency action or inaction; and
>
> (d) There is a dispute of material fact.

Section 227.064(1) "afford[s] a hearing right to those who are not granted a specific right to a hearing by other statutory provisions or administrative rules."

The legislature and the board of regents have established procedures to govern faculty employment decisions. Sections UWS 3.07 and 3.08, promulgated by the board, apply to renewal of faculty appointments and granting of tenure. Neither section grants an appeal to or hearing before the board. Section 36.13(5), Stats. (1981–82), requires notice and a hearing for a just cause dismissal of a tenured or probationary faculty member prior to the end of a contract term. Neither existing statutes nor administrative rules grant a nonrenewed probationary faculty member a board hearing. A contested hearing is available if the faculty member satisfies the conditions specified in sec. 227.064(1)(a)-(d), Stats. (1981–82).

Coe claims a "substantial interest" in becoming tenured at the end of her probationary period and argues that a contested hearing is necessary to protect this interest. We disagree. Coe merely has a "unilateral expectation" of becoming tenured, not a "substantial interest." An employee's interest in continued employment is created and defined "by existing rules or understandings that stem from an independent source such as state law—rules or understanding that secure certain benefits and that support claims of entitlement to those benefits." Coe's interest in continued employment at UW-Stevens Point was created and defined by the terms of her employment under a series of probationary contracts. The appointment letters referred to nonperformance factors as criteria for tenure. The terms of Coe's probationary employment did not secure her interest in becoming tenured or create any legitimate claim to it. In the absence of a substantial interest in becoming tenured, the board was not required to provide a contested hearing. Coe has not satisfied sec. 227.064(1)(a), Stats. (1981–82).

There is no evidence that the legislature intended to protect Coe's interest in becoming tenured. The legislature requires a hearing when a tenured faculty member is dismissed or when a probationary faculty member is dismissed prior to the expiration of a contract. "Under the general rule of statutory construction, *expressio unius est exclusio alterius*, the express mention of one matter excludes other similar matters not mentioned." Having specified in sec. 36.13(5) when a hearing is required, the legislature intended to deny nonrenewed probationary faculty members a hearing. Coe has not satisfied sec. 227.064(1)(b).

Coe argues she was not notified that tenure density or other nonperformance criteria would be considered in the tenure decision. Her appointment letters stated that tenure would be based on performance and nonperformance factors including the tenure situation in her department. The chancellor found that the tenure management policy was distributed to all faculty members although Coe insists she never received a copy of it. The chancellor's finding that the policy was distributed to all faculty members required a credibility determination which a reviewing court may not disregard. Furthermore, notice was not required because Coe did not have a substantial interest in becoming tenured.

Order affirmed.

Sola v. Lafayette College
804 F.2d 40 (3d Cir. 1986)

I.

Janet Sola became an assistant professor of psychology at Lafayette College in 1976. In 1982 Sola applied for tenure at the college.

Tenure decisions at the college are governed by the college's Faculty Handbook and section 70 of the college Statutes. Under the procedures set forth by the personnel manuals, tenure determinations are first made by the Appointments, Promotions and Dismissals Committee (the "AP & D Committee"). After reviewing the record of the tenure candidate, which includes the recommendation of the department chairperson, the AP & D Committee makes a recommendation to the President. If the AP & D Committee's decision is adverse, the candidate may appeal the decision to the President of the college or request that the committee reconsider its recommendation. The President makes a final recommendation to the college's Board of Trustees.

The Faculty Handbook sets forth the following criteria for tenure decisions:

> Appointments and promotions are made on the basis of merit and in consideration of departmental and institutional characteristics. These latter include, but are not restricted to, enrollment trends, the need for a desirable mix of specialties, the tenure guidelines, the principles of Affirmative Action, economic priorities, and other relevant needs.

A major factor in the tenure decision is the recommendation of the department chairperson. Under the guidelines in the Faculty Handbook, the recommendation of the department chairperson is to include "a statement indicating his judgment as to the probable effect of the promotion or award of tenure to the candidate on other members of the department." At the time that Sola's tenure decision was rendered, the AP & D Committee was bound to a tenure quota in which not more than two-thirds of a department could be tenured faculty members, absent an exceptional "guideline breaking" candidate.

The Chairman of the Psychology Department, Dr. Howard Gallup, recommended that Janet Sola receive tenure. His recommendation, however, was not unqualified. He noted that a male professor, whom he viewed as stronger than Sola, would come up for tenure within the next three years, and that a decision on Sola's application should not jeopardize this professor's candidacy. If Sola had been granted tenure, the Psychology Department would have had the maximum number of tenured professors under the tenure quota.

The AP & D Committee voted preliminarily in favor of granting Sola tenure. The next day, however, the final vote was a tie, which resulted in a denial of tenure under college procedures.

Sola appealed the decision to the President of the college. An Advisory Committee was formed, consisting of three professors, one chosen by the provost, one by Sola, and the third by the other two professors. The Committee expressed its concern that the record did not have sufficient information to substantiate Dr. Gallup's comparison of the two professors and recommended that the tenure decision be reconsidered. After requesting further explanation from Gallup, the President affirmed the judgment of the AP & D Committee denying Sola tenure.

Subsequent to the final tenure decision, Sola filed complaints with the Pennsylvania Human Relations Commission and the Equal Employment Opportunity Commission, claiming that the decision was a result of gender-based discrimination. Both agencies dismissed the complaints as untimely. Sola then filed this diversity action in district court, alleging wrongful discharge, breach of contract, and intentional infliction of emotional distress.

The district court granted the defendants' motion for summary judgment. It held that the Pennsylvania Human Relations Act, [the "PHRA"], preempts a tort action for wrongful discharge based on alleged gender discrimination. Assuming that the Faculty Handbook constituted a contract, the court turned to Sola's contract claims. First, it found that the PHRA also bars a contract action when the claim is based on contractual provisions that provide the employee with the same protections as those contained in the PHRA. The court, however, did not address whether the PHRA is the exclusive remedy when a contract provides greater protections than the statute, finding that this issue was not raised by the plaintiff. Second, the court found no evidence supporting Sola's assertion that the tenure decision violated the procedural protections contained in the personnel manuals. In particular, it rejected her claim that Dr. Gallup's comparison was against college policy. Finally, the district court dismissed the intentional infliction of emotional distress claim because Sola did not allege any outrageous conduct on the part of the college.

Sola appeals the district court's order insofar as it dismisses her wrongful discharge and breach of contract claims. Our review is plenary. We must review the record and ascertain whether, resolving all doubts in favor of the nonmoving party, there are no genuine issues of material fact remaining for trial.

II.

Sola does not challenge the district court's decision that a wrongful discharge action based on gender discrimination is preempted by the PHRA. Rather, she contends that because the tenure quota adopted by the college violates public policy by threatening the principles of academic freedom, the tenure decision comes within the public policy tort of wrongful discharge.

The Pennsylvania courts have recognized a cause of action for wrongful discharge where an employee demonstrates that the termination violates a "clear mandate of public policy." Noting the reluctance of the courts to give this tort wide-ranging application, we have held that only a discharge in violation of a "significant and recognized public policy" constitutes a claim for wrongful discharge under Pennsylvania law.

The cases that have recognized wrongful discharge claims have involved infringements on statutory and constitutional rights. We are not persuaded that Sola's claim of a potential threat to the tenure system rises to the level of the public policy concerns that have been recognized in the previous wrongful discharge cases. In addition, there are significant policy concerns counseling against recognizing Sola's claim. We have expressed our reluctance to interfere with the internal operations of academic institutions absent direction from the legislature. Adoption of Sola's position would require us to evaluate the wisdom of the college's decision to limit the number of tenured professors on its faculty. Such an evaluation may threaten the college's institutional academic freedom. Thus, the implications of Sola's position may pose a greater threat to academic freedom than does the tenure quota. Accordingly, we find that as a matter of law, the college was entitled to summary judgment on the wrongful discharge claim.

III.

Sola presents three distinct breach of contract claims on appeal. The defendant has conceded for purposes of summary judgment that the Faculty Handbook and Statutes created a unilateral contract. Consistent with this concession, we will proceed to address Sola's claims. First, she contends that summary judgment was inappropriate because there are material issues of fact as to whether the college followed the procedures set forth in the handbook in rendering the tenure decision. Second, she argues that the district court erred in holding that the PHRA preempts a breach of contract claim based on an equal opportunity provision in the contract. Finally, Sola asserts that the district court erred in refusing to consider the affirmative action provisions of the handbook as providing a separate basis for her breach of contract claim.

A.

Sola contends that the college's customs and the Faculty Handbook create a unilateral contract right to a full, fair, impartial and substantiated tenure decision. The gravamen of her complaint is that the department chairman's comparison of her and the other professor violated this right.

As noted above, the guidelines in the Faculty Handbook explicitly authorize department chairpersons to consider the effect of an affirmative tenure decision on other members of the department. Thus, that Gallup compared Sola with another professor is not in itself a breach of contract. Sola asserts, however, that since the Advisory Committee found that the comparison was unsubstantiated, there was a material issue of fact as to whether there was a breach of contract.

After receiving the recommendation of the Advisory Committee, the President requested and received further explanation of the comparison from Dr. Gallup, and subsequently determined that the AP & D Committee's decision denying tenure should be affirmed. We will not insist on further actions by the college in this regard because we will "not substitute [our] judgment for that of the college with respect to the qualifications of faculty members for promotion and tenure."

Sola also asserts that Gallup's recommendation was in effect a request that the AP & D Committee reserve a tenure slot for the other professor, and that this request violated her right to a full and fair tenure determination. The tenure quota guidelines state that "ordinarily no more than two thirds of the faculty in any department shall hold tenure. . . . A department may exceed this two-thirds guideline if and only if the guideline-breaking candidate is an exceptionally valuable teacher-scholar." Sola argues Gallup's request forced her to prove that she was a "guideline breaking" candidate despite the fact that the department had not reached the tenure limit when her application was considered, and thus it violated the procedures set forth under the tenure quota system.

There is no evidence, however, that the AP & D Committee placed any weight on Dr. Gallup's request that a tenured position be reserved. In fact, the uncontroverted evidence shows that the Committee rejected this recommendation. Therefore, we conclude that there is no factual support for Sola's claim that she was denied the procedural protections of her contract.

* * *

In this case, the claim is that the college discriminated against Sola in breach of her employment contract.

We will assume without deciding that Sola is correct in her assertion that the PHRA does not preempt actions based on express contracts. We will further assume without deciding that the handbook's policy statement with regard to equal employment opportunity is sufficient to create a contractual right to be free from gender discrimination. These assumptions, however, do not lead to the conclusion that summary judgment was improper on this claim.

The record shows no factual support for the claim that Sola's gender played any role in the college's decision. Sola produced no evidence that she was denied tenure in part based on her gender. Rather, she claims that the college created an inhospitable atmosphere for women, that the tenure quota had a disparate impact on women, and that Gallup's preference for the other professor was an outgrowth of the old-boy network. In light of the substantial discovery material negating any reasonable inference of gender discrimination, Sola's allegations alone are insufficient to establish a material issue of fact. The defendants, therefore, were entitled to summary judgment on this claim.

C.

Finally, we consider whether the district court erred in finding that Sola did not raise the issue of whether the Faculty Handbook provided greater protections against discrimination than those provided in the PHRA. We agree that the complaint does not specifically allege a contract claim based on the statement that "[a]ppointments and promotions are made in conformity with the principles of Equal Opportunity and Affirmative Action." In her brief in opposition to summary judgment, however, Sola did raise the claim, albeit in the context of her wrongful discharge claim, that the denial of tenure violated affirmative action principles. Moreover, at the hearing on summary judgment, Sola's attorney explicitly stated that the college was contractually bound to consider the fact that Sola was a woman.

Although the record is not clear on this point, we find that Sola did raise the issue of whether the college breached the contract in failing to consider her gender as a positive factor. Under Rule 15 of the Federal Rules of Civil Procedure, leave to amend the complaint "shall be freely given when justice so requires." Although the trial court has discretion to deny such a motion, this discretion is tempered by the liberal mandate of the rule. The district court should have considered the affirmative action claims raised in the brief and at oral argument as a motion to amend the complaint. In this case, justice requires that the affirmative action claim be heard.

Therefore, we conclude that the district court erred in not considering Sola's affirmative action claim. Because the district court did not consider this claim, we express no opinion as to whether Pennsylvania would recognize a breach of contract claim based upon the handbook's statements expressing the college's adherence to affirmative action principles. Accordingly, we will remand for the district court to consider whether Sola's claim is cognizable under Pennsylvania law and for such further proceedings as may be appropriate.

Tenure and Collective Bargaining

Biggiam v. Community College Dist. No. 516
506 N.E.2d 1011 (Ill. App. 2 Dist. 1987)

Unverzagt, J.

* * *

We consider at the outset the issue we believe is foremost in this appeal: whether section 3B–5 of the Community College Tenure Act and/or the collective bargaining agreement to which the instant parties are subject create rights for faculty members only with respect to other faculty members, or whether such rights may be asserted over part-time instructors as well. The Board's contention is that such tenure rights as are provided for therein are applicable only as against faculty members, and the teachers' contention is that they are applicable as against part-time instructors as well.

"Article IIIB. Tenure" was added January 1, 1980, codifying the tenure rights of community college teachers. Section 3B–5 of the Community College Tenure Act provides:

> "If a dismissal of a faculty member for the ensuing school year results from the decision by the Board to decrease the number of faculty members employed by the Board or to discontinue some particular type of teaching service or program, notice shall be given the affected faculty member not later than 60

days before the end of the preceding school year, together with a statement of honorable dismissal and the reason therefor; *provided that the employment of no tenured faculty member may be terminated under the provisions of this Section while any probationary faculty member, or any other employee with less seniority, is retained to render a service which the tenured employee is competent to render.* In the event a tenured faculty member is not given notice within the time herein provided, he shall be deemed reemployed for the ensuing school year. For the period of 24 months from the beginning of the school year for which the faculty member was dismissed, *any* faculty member shall have the preferred right to reappointment to a position entailing services he is competent to render prior to the appointment of *any new* faculty member; *provided that no non-tenure faculty member or other employee with less seniority shall be employed to render a service which a tenured faculty member is competent to render.*"

Section 3B–1 of the Community College Tenure Act provides one definition which is pertinent here:

" 'Faculty Member' means a full time employee of the District regularly engaged in teaching or academic support services, but excluding supervisors, administrators and clerical employees."

Article X, par. A, of the collective bargaining agreement provides:

"A. Tenure shall be granted to faculty members in accordance with the Illinois Community College Act, Illinois Revised Statutes Chapter 103B–1, etc., and Appendix B of the Agreement, which includes tenure, evaluation of non-tenured faculty, dismissal of tenured faculty members for cause, and reduction in number of full-time faculty members. Where remedies are provided under said statute, they shall be the exclusive means of resolving complaints or questions concerning tenure, including but not limited to appointment, dismissal and retrenchment of tenured faculty. Such matters shall not be the subject of a grievance, except where the statute does not provide for such remedies."

"Appendix B" referred to above provides the following pertinent definitions:

" *Faculty Member'* means a full-time employee of the district regularly engaged in teaching or academic support services, but shall exclude supervisors, administrators and all supportive staff, including secretarial/clerical, data processing and physical plant staff.

* * *

'*Tenure*' means continuous contractual employment unless dismissed for adequate cause or due to a decision of the Board to decrease the number of faculty members employed by the Board or to discontinue some particular type of teaching service or program.

* * *

'*Full-Time Employment*' for the purpose of this tenure policy shall be defined as follows:

Faculty Members: Faculty members normally have a teaching load of at least 30 semester hour equivalents which equivalents shall include released semester teaching load hours for non-teaching duties. A teaching load of less than 30

THE LAW AND THE FACULTY

semester hour equivalents per school year shall not be considered full-time employment.

'*Seniority*' means the length of continuous full-time employment as a faculty member as defined herein since the last date of hire as a full-time faculty member. Conflicts in seniority among faculty members with the same beginning date of continuous employment shall be resolved on the basis of the earliest date when the initial full-time contract of employment was approved by the Board."

With regard to "Reduction in Number of Full-Time Faculty Members," Appendix B of the collective bargaining agreement provides:

"The provisions of Chapter 122, Section 103B–5, Illinois Revised Statutes shall be applicable with respect to the dismissal of a faculty member due to a decision by the Board of Trustees to decrease the number of faculty members employed by the Board of Trustees or to discontinue some particular type of teaching service or program.

Each tenured faculty member who is subject to dismissal due to a reduction in the number of faculty members employed by the Board of Trustees shall be given the opportunity prior to honorable dismissal to advise the Board of Trustees in writing of *any position(s), if any, held by non-tenured faculty members, or any other employees with less seniority, which such faculty member believes he/she is competent to fill*, together with the documentation upon which such belief is based. It shall be the responsibility of the Board of Trustees, acting on recommendations of the administrative staff, to determine whether or not the tenured faculty member is, in fact, *competent to render the services for the position or positions identified by the tenured faculty member.*"

Initially, the Board contends it is essential to bear in mind the distinction between a *position* and the *teaching of a particular course* in construing the Community College Tenure Act. It asserts the Community College Tenure Act was never intended to perpetuate teachers in positions where they are no longer needed nor to permit, under the guise of tenure, a teacher to move to a position for which he or she is unqualified under the terms of the collective bargaining agreement, nor to force a board of trustees to create or gerrymander a position where none exists in order to satisfy a tenured teacher's demand for continued employment after his or her position has been eliminated. It contends the legislature's use of the language "competent to render a service" in the Community College Tenure Act was not meant to supplant the concept of being *qualified to fill a position* as that concept has been applied in numerous cases interpreting section 24–12 of Article 24 of the School Code (the Teacher Tenure Law), with the concept advanced by the teachers below: *i.e.*, that the Community College Tenure Act's protection applies to any *course* that the protected faculty member is competent to teach or any other *identifiable service* which the faculty member is competent to render.

The primary rule of statutory construction is to ascertain and effectuate the legislature's intent. In doing so, a court looks first to the statutory language itself, and if the language is clear, the court must give it effect and should not look to extrinsic aids for construction. But where differing interpretations are proffered, legislative intent must be determined from the reasons for the enactment and the purposes to be thereby attained, as well as the meaning of the words enlarged or restricted according to their real intent.

Although the School Code has been found inapplicable to community college districts which operate under the authority of the Public Community College Act, when legislative intent is not clear it is proper to compare the statute in question with statutes concerning related subjects even though they are not strictly *in pari materia*. Accordingly, the teachers urge construction of section 3B–5 of the Community College Tenure Act consistent with that of the Teacher Tenure Law in the School Code (Ill. Rev. Stat. 1985, ch. 122, par. 24–12); that is, that the primary purpose of teacher tenure is to provide priority job protection to tenured teachers "as against employees of lower priority status." Thus, they assert that the phrase "employee with less seniority" as used in section 3B–5 of the Community College Tenure Act must be read to include part-time instructors even though they acknowledge part-time instructors are not considered "faculty members" as that term is defined in section 3B–1 of the Community College Tenure Act. They assert that to do otherwise "would turn the Act on its head" since the colleges would be "free to displace those employees enjoying statutory protection by utilizing the unprotected part-timers."

We believe the teachers' position on this issue ascribes a far broader purpose to the Community College Tenure Act than that intended by the legislature.

The teachers acknowledge that part-time instructors are not faculty members and have no job protection under the terms of section 3B–5 of the Community College Tenure Act, yet argue that such instructors fall within the meaning of "any other employee with less seniority" over whom tenured and nontenured teachers are to have job priority. Such argument necessarily presupposes that part-time instructors are employees capable of having seniority. It is clear, however, that part-time instructors do *not* accumulate seniority as that term is defined in Appendix B of the collective bargaining agreement and as so testified by Dr. Viola. Consequently, a part-time instructor cannot be considered to be "any other employee with less seniority."

Although it is true that words used in a statute should be given their plain, ordinary and commonly accepted meaning, a plain word, such as "employee," may be given a restricted meaning if such is indicated by the Act as a whole or by persuasive gloss of legislative history. Viewing the Community College Tenure Act as a whole, we think such a restricted meaning must be placed on the word "employee" here to mean "any other *tenured* employee with less seniority." Consequently, we conclude that one of the premises on which the court's judgment was based—*i.e.*, that the phrase "any other employee with less seniority" includes part-time instructors—was erroneous.

We next consider the extent of the "bumping" rights afforded under section 3B–5 of the Community College Tenure Act: Do they extend to "any course that the protected faculty member is competent to teach or any other identifiable service which the faculty member is competent to render," as asserted by the teachers, or are they limited to a "position" entailing services the protected faculty member is "competent to render," as asserted by the board?

The teachers argue the use of the phrase "competent to render [a service]" in section 3B–5 of the Community College Tenure Act provides evidence that a new and entirely different result was intended to be achieved by enactment of the Community College Tenure Act when that language is compared with the phrase "legally qualified [to hold a position]" in the Teacher Tenure Law in the School Code. The effect of such language in the Teacher Tenure Law has consistently been construed to mean that an honorably dismissed teacher who is not "legally qualified" to fill the position held by a probationary or less-senior tenured teacher has no right to have a school board "gerrymander" in order to create a position he could fill by taking only some of the different courses taught by other teachers in established teaching positions and combining them into one position comprised of several areas of instruction, all of which the dismissed teacher is qualified to teach.

"Position" was thus construed to mean that the tenured teacher had to be qualified to teach every course of which the teaching "position" consisted or, in terms of the instant cause, the teacher would have to be qualified as set forth in the college's "Qualifications to Teach."

This difference in the language, the teachers assert, shows the legislature intended to allow tenured community college faculty members job priority over not only non-tenured faculty members and less senior employees holding *positions* entailing services the tenured employee was competent to render, but priority over those merely teaching a *course* ["rendering a service"] which the tenured teacher was competent to render as well.

The Board counters that the legislative history of the Community College Tenure Act is not supportive of the teachers' contention that a new and different result was intended since opponents of the Community College Tenure Act attacked it primarily on the basis the proposed act was too similar to elementary and secondary tenure practices (as opposed to the more difficult to achieve university tenure), and that it diminished the power of the local college district boards to establish tenure policies as provided in section 3–32. Further, the Board asserts, use of the different terms ("legally qualified"/"competent to render a service") was necessary by virtue of the fact that primary and secondary teacher qualifications are determined in a centralized manner by the State Board of Education whereas the determination of faculty qualifications under the Public Community College Act is a decentralized process in that it is one of the individual community college's board's nondelegable discretionary powers.

* * *

The parties here collectively bargained in order to reach the agreement which specifically states that "Tenure shall be granted to faculty members in accordance with the Illinois Community College Act, Illinois Revised Statutes Chapter 103B–1, et seq., and Appendix B of this Agreement * * * ." We find nothing in the provisions of the collective bargaining agreement dealing with tenure which might be construed as a diminishment of the tenure rights afforded community college faculty members under the statute. As the teachers note, such a diminishment would be contrary to the provisions of the Educational Labor Relations Act.

Appendix B of the collective bargaining agreement supplements the provisions of section 3B–5 of the Community College Tenure Act. (Ill. Rev. Stat. 1985, ch. 122, par. 103B–5.) As emphasized in the excerpt from Appendix B concerning reduction in the number of full-time faculty members, those tenured members who are to be honorably dismissed are given the opportunity to notify the Board of "*any position(s)*, *held* by nontenured faculty members, or any other employees with less seniority which such faculty member believes he/she is *competent to fill....* " (Emphasis added.) The determination of whether such member is, in fact, "competent to render the services for the position or positions identified by the tenured faculty member" is the responsibility of the Board.

We find the provisions of Appendix B consistent with the essence of section 3B–5 which provides the tenured faculty member freedom from termination in a retrenchment while there are probationary or less-senior teachers being retained to render a service which the tenured faculty member is competent to render. In order to be "retained," one must currently be filling a position, and in order for the freedom from termination afforded tenured teachers to have any value, it must operate vertically within one's own academic discipline.

The collective bargaining agreement sets forth no specific policies concerning the faculty members' recall rights as set forth in the latter part of section 3B–5. The recall rights of tenured faculty members provided therein are consistent with the retention rights; to wit: " * * * a preferred right to reappointment to *a position* entailing services he is competent to render." The statute provides that *any* faculty member (including nontenured) shall have a preferred right to reappointment to a position as against any *new* faculty member, but tenured faculty members have a preferred right to reappointment to a position as against any nontenured or less senior employee.

For lack of any precedent on this issue, the Board provided us with a copy of an arbitration opinion and award which construed section 3B–5 of the Community College Tenure Act and which was consistent with its own interpretation. The teachers neither acknowledge nor object to the opinion. Nonetheless, it is an unreported opinion, and it may not be afforded any precedential value here.

We have, however, found merit in the Board's argument, and conclude that section 3B–5 does not warrant the interpretation advanced by the teachers that the right of tenured faculty members to bump nontenured or less senior employees includes the right to bump them from certain *courses* as opposed to the *positions* in the college curriculum which are held by them.

Accordingly, we find:

1) The court's judgment that Neil Newlon is entitled to bump from Speech 1200 teaching assignments first, any part-time instructor of that course and, second, any probationary or less-senior teachers whose course load consists solely of Speech 100, must be reversed. As such, that portion of the court's judgment concerning the compensation to be received by Newlon is moot.

2) The court's judgment that Robert Biggiam and James Moreland are entitled to bump any part-time instructors or probationary or less-senior teachers of welding must also be reversed. Again, the matter of compensation is moot.

3) The court's judgment that Judith Vagas is entitled to bump only in regard to counseling positions as per Article VIII, section B, of the collective bargaining agreement, and is not qualified under the "Qualifications to Teach" regarding psychology must be affirmed. That portion of the court's judgment entitling her to preference over part-time counseling positions is reversed.

4) The court's judgment that Jon Pigage was outside the protection of section 3B–5 of the Community College Tenure Act is reversed insofar as Pigage has recall rights as against any *new* faculty member as provided therein.

Remedies and Relief

Sweeney v. Board of Trustees of Keene State College
569 F.2d 169 (1978)

TUTTLE, Circuit Judge.

This appeal presents important issues relating to the existence of discrimination against women in the awarding of promotions and the fixing of salaries at Keene State College. Dr. Christine Sweeney, a faculty member in the Department of Education at Keene since 1969, failed twice in her efforts to achieve promotion to the rank of full professor before finally succeeding in 1976. Attributing her earlier failures to sexual bias, she seeks a backdating of her promotion to the date of her first attempt and an accompanying adjustment in her salary for the intervening years. In addition, the plaintiff alleges that sex discrimination accounts for the disparity between the average salaries of males and females on the Keene faculty and claims that she has been paid less than men who carry a substantially equal workload.

Dr. Sweeney has brought suit under Title VII of the 1964 Civil Rights Act, as amended by the Equal Employment Opportunity Act of 1972; the Equal Pay Act of 1963, as amended by the Education Amendments of 1972; Title IX of the Education, Amendments of 1972; Sec. 1983; and the Fourteenth Amendment to the United States Constitution. Named as defendants are Keene State College, its Board of Trustees, its president, and two former deans.

Following a four-day trial, the United States District Court for the District of New Hampshire ruled against Dr. Sweeney on the Equal Pay, § 1983, Fourteenth Amendment, and Title IX counts, but permitted her a partial recovery under Title VII. The district court found that Dr. Sweeney had been a victim of sex discrimination in her second effort to gain promotion and ordered her promotion backdated to 1975, with the appropriate back pay. The court also awarded the plaintiff attorneys' fees and costs of $17,766.56. Although the court specifically found a pattern of sex discrimination against females in hiring, promotion, and salaries, no injunction against further discrimination was issued.

In their appeal, the defendants seek to persuade this Court that the plaintiff's evidence was insufficient to prove a violation of Title VII. They further contend that Dr. Sweeney has failed to prove that a discriminatory motive accounted for her unsuccessful promotion attempt. Dr. Sweeney cross-appeals from certain adverse findings of fact and rulings of law, and particularly seeks reversal of the trial court's holding that she failed to prove sex discrimination as to her level of pay as an associate professor or professor. For the reasons discussed below, the judgment of the district court is affirmed.

I.

Keene State College, a division of the University of New Hampshire, is a small liberal arts college located in Keene, New Hampshire. Originally dedicated to the training of teachers, it presently grants bachelor's degrees in a variety of other fields as well as a master's degree in education. Dr. Sweeney earned a bachelor of education degree from Keene in 1943, a master of arts from Catholic University in 1956, and a Ph.D. from Catholic University in 1962. She taught at the primary and secondary levels from 1943 until 1960 and served as a graduate assistant at Catholic University in the 1961–62 school year. Appointed an instructor at Catholic University in 1962, Dr. Sweeney remained there until 1966, when she joined the faculty at Emmanuel

College as an assistant professor. She was promoted to the rank of associate professor at Emmanuel, effective in the fall of 1968, with an anticipated salary of $9,000, but left that school before the start of the 1968–69 academic year. In January, 1969 Dr. Sweeney was appointed an associate professor of education at Keene and received $5,000 for the spring semester. Her initial position was supervisor of student teaching, but she has subsequently assumed various other teaching responsibilities in the department of education. In addition to her course load, Dr. Sweeney has served on numerous college and department committees and on the Professional Standards Board for the State Board of Education. This summary of her credentials is by no means exhaustive but suffices to demonstrate that Dr. Sweeney possesses the education and experience typical of college teachers.

From the record it appears that Dr. Sweeney's career at Keene went smoothly until 1971. In the spring of that year, she was selected by a committee within her department to accompany a group of students to England the following fall. The trip was part of a student exchange program developed by the Department of Education, and Dr. Sweeney had been quite active in the program. At the time of the plaintiff's selection, a man was selected for a second fall trip and another woman was selected as an alternate. Final approval of the faculty advisors rested with Dean Clarence Davis, and he refused to permit Dr. Sweeney to make the trip, selecting the alternate instead. Although the dean refused to tell the plaintiff his reasons for this decision, he testified at trial that he had acted upon the recommendation of the coordinator of the program, a female, who had advised him that the alternate was better qualified.

Plaintiff attempted to convince the trial court that this decision resulted from sex discrimination by showing that no women have been selected for subsequent trips and that no men have been disapproved. However, the trial court specifically found that the dean's decision rested on factors other than sex discrimination. This fact finding is amply supported by the evidence, because a woman took Dr. Sweeney's slot and the unfavorable recommendation came from a woman. Nevertheless, the incident plays a role in later developments and is mentioned for that reason. Dr. Sweeney testified that the incident alerted her to the possible existence of sex bias on campus. More importantly, she feared that the refusal to permit her to make the trip would affect her later efforts to seek promotion.

In spite of the England incident, Dr. Sweeney was granted tenure in 1972 with no apparent difficulty. In the 1972–73 academic year, she sought promotion to the rank of full professor, the highest rank in the academic setting. Like many other colleges and universities, Keene employs a peer-review system for screening requests for tenure and promotion. These requests, initiated either by the faculty member or by the department chairman on behalf of the faculty member, are sent to the dean of the college, who, in turn, forwards the matter to the Faculty Evaluations Advisory Committee (FEAC), a five-member panel elected each year by the entire faculty from persons in the highest two academic ranks. The FEAC measures the record and qualifications of the applicant against the standards set forth in the faculty manual and makes a recommendation to the dean either for or against promotion. Although the FEAC functions in an advisory capacity, its recommendations are usually adopted by the dean. If the FEAC recommends promotion and the dean concurs, the request is sent to the Board of Trustees for final approval. If, however, the dean concurs in a negative FEAC recommendation, the applicant can seek reconsideration by the dean and the FEAC. If still unsuccessful, an appeal can be taken to the Faculty Appeals Committee

(FAC), also composed of elected faculty members. This panel's authority is limited to determining whether due process has been accorded or whether new evidence has been presented. The FAC presents its findings to the college president, who in turn submits any favorable recommendations to the Board of Trustees. The president expressed a reluctance to overturn an FEAC decision unless the FAC found arbitrary or unfair action.

The plaintiff was recommended for promotion by her department and its chairman, Dr. Paul Blacketor, during the 1972–73 school year. An all-male FEAC voted unanimously against promotion and Dean Davis concurred. Dr. Sweeney was given no reasons for the adverse decision. Upon the advice of Dean Davis, Dr. Sweeney secured letters of support from faculty members and persons outside Keene to assist the FEAC in its reconsideration, but to no avail. The plaintiff appealed to the FAC in July 1973, citing the lack of reasons as evidence of unfairness. In a letter to President Leo Redfern eight months later, the FAC stated that the FEAC had refused to explain its adverse decision and that Dean Davis had declined to discuss his disapproval of Sweeney for the England trip. Therefore, the committee could not determine whether the trip incident had influenced the FEAC decision. Giving Dr. Sweeney the benefit of the doubt on the question of unfairness, the FAC strongly recommended that Dr. Sweeney be considered by the current (1973–74) FEAC even though she herself had not initiated a new request for promotion during that academic year because of her pending appeal. The president declined to permit what he viewed as a short-circuiting of normal procedures and notified the FAC in April of 1974 of his decision. Shortly thereafter, Sweeney filed charges of sex discrimination with the New Hampshire Commission of Human Rights and the EEOC.

The plaintiff sought promotion again during the 1974–75 academic year. A new FEAC, entirely male, voted against her promotion and the dean once again concurred. This time, however, the dean informed the plaintiff by letter that the decision was based on her failure to meet the qualifications enunciated in the faculty manual and he quoted a portion of it to her.

Alleging sex discrimination in her second appeal to the FAC, Dr. Sweeney submitted additional information to that committee to counter each of the objections cited by Dean Davis. After examining her case, the FAC sent a lengthy letter to President Redfern decrying the unprofessional treatment of the plaintiff and insisting that she be given more detailed reasons for the adverse decision. The FAC, one of whose members was a woman, also stated that it had been unable to find evidence of sex discrimination.

As a result of this prodding by the FAC, President Redfern conferred with Dean Davis and former FEAC members to ascertain the grounds for her nonpromotion. The list of criticisms which the president conveyed to Dr. Sweeney included allegations that she had narrow, rigid, and old-fashioned views, tended to personalize professional matters, kept minutes of the graduate faculty meetings which fell below a professional caliber, and emphasized to her students the importance of maintaining an even height of window shades in a classroom. This meeting of the plaintiff and President Redfern, which occurred in November 1975, apparently marked the end of her second appeal.

Dr. Sweeney's third try for promotion, during the 1975–76 academic year, was successful. The FEAC, composed of four men and a woman, voted unanimously in her favor only a few months after the plaintiff's meeting with the president. Her promotion was effective July 1, 1976.

At trial, the plaintiff presented statistical evidence to substantiate her claim of sex discrimination. She and other witnesses testified about specific instances of allegedly sex-biased treatment. Experts in the areas of education and sex discrimination were also called to testify. In a lengthy opinion which contains a thorough review of the testimony and exhibits, the district court found that the evidence established a pattern of sex discrimination at Keene State College in hiring, promotion, and salaries. Applying the approach employed by the Supreme Court in *McDonnell Douglas Corp. v. Green*, the district court held that the plaintiff had established a prima facie case of sex discrimination in her second promotion effort in violation of Title VII and that the defendants had not rebutted her evidence. Based on the plaintiff's qualifications, length of time at Keene, and her rapport with her colleagues, the court believed that Dr. Sweeney would not have been promoted in her first try even if she had been a male. Although the court found that the defendants applied a double standard in salaries, hiring, and promotion, the court held that the plaintiff had failed to prove that her own salary was less than males with the same or similar qualifications and responsibilities. The district court also found that Keene's affirmative action program was ineffective.

II.

The defendants strenuously argue on appeal that Dr. Sweeney has provided insufficient proof of discriminatory motivation to support a finding of disparate treatment. We recognize that disparate treatment cases, such as this one, differ from disparate impact cases, such as *Griggs v. Duke Power Co.* We also recognize that proof of discriminatory motive is critical in a disparate treatment case. This is necessarily so because the gist of a disparate treatment claim is that an employee has been treated less favorably than others because of race, color, religion, sex, or national origin. What we reject is an effort by the defendants to elevate the quantum of proof to such a level that a litigant is necessarily doomed to failure.

The Supreme Court has never said that an individual plaintiff seeking to establish a claim of disparate treatment in violation of Title VII must present direct evidence of discriminatory intent. Even in *Washington v. Davis*, which held that discriminatory intent is an essential element of a claim based upon the equal protection clause of the Fourteenth Amendment, the Supreme Court recognized that circumstantial evidence was one means of proving purposeful discrimination. The Court stated in *Davis*:

> Necessarily, an invidious discriminatory purpose may often be inferred from the totality of the relevant facts, including the fact, if it is true, that the law bears more heavily on one race than another. It is also not infrequently true that the discriminatory impact...may for all practical purposes demonstrate unconstitutionality because in various circumstances the discrimination is very difficult to explain on nonracial grounds.

Particularly in a college or university setting, where the level of sophistication is likely to be much higher than in other employment situations, direct evidence of sex discrimination will rarely be available. The Congress was no doubt aware of this fact when it extended Title VII to colleges and universities for the first time in 1972. The legislative history contains numerous indications of Congress' concern for the status of women in academia. Statistical evidence presented to the Congress at that time made glaringly clear that "[w]hen they have been hired into educational institutions, particularly in institutions of higher education, women have been relegated to positions of lesser standing than their male counterparts." Legislative concern over this sexual imbalance is further evidenced in the passage of Title IX of the Education Amendment of 1972.

Of course, legislative sympathy for the plight of female college teachers does not alleviate Dr. Sweeney's obligation to prove herself the victim of sex discrimination in order to recover under Title VII. In fact, the difficulty of her task is underlined by the lack of cases in which plaintiffs have succeeded in similar challenges to sex discrimination in academia. Admittedly, most if not all of these female plaintiffs have lost. Whether the evidence presented in these cases fell significantly short of the evidence in this case we do not know. However, we voice misgivings over one theme recurrent in those opinions: the notion that courts should keep "hands off" the salary, promotion, and hiring decisions of colleges and universities. This reluctance no doubt arises from the courts' recognition that hiring, promotion, and tenure decisions require subjective evaluation most appropriately made by persons thoroughly familiar with the academic setting. Nevertheless, we caution against permitting judicial deference to result in judicial abdication of a responsibility entrusted to the courts by Congress. That responsibility is simply to provide a forum for the litigation of complaints of sex discrimination in institutions of higher learning as readily as for other Title VII suits.

A.

It is clear from *McDonnell Douglas Corp. v. Green* and *International Brotherhood of Teamsters v. United States* that an individual plaintiff who alleges disparate treatment because of her sex must prove that her unfavorable treatment was sexually premised. Both of those cases explore the nature of proof and the allocation of the burden of proof in cases alleging disparate treatment. Neither requires *direct* proof of discriminatory motive.

As we understand those cases, a plaintiff bears the initial burden of presenting evidence sufficient to establish a prima facie case of discrimination. The burden then shifts to the defendant to rebut the prima facie case by showing that a legitimate, non-discriminatory reason accounted for its actions. If the rebuttal is successful, the plaintiff must show that the stated reason was a mere pretext for discrimination. The ultimate burden of persuasion on the issue of discrimination remains with the plaintiff, who must convince the court by a preponderance of the evidence that he or she has been the victim of discrimination.

* * *

B.

Dr. Sweeney clearly showed that she was a member of a protected class within Title VII, that she was qualified for promotion, that she was rejected, and that others of her qualifications were promoted. She went further and presented statistical evidence which supports an inference of sex bias in promotion decisions. Most persuasive of the statistics was the fact that only four women in the entire history of Keene State College have achieved the rank of full professor. There have never been more than two women professors in any given academic year and this has occurred in only two years since 1968. In all other years since 1968, only one woman occupied the top rank. In contrast, the number of male professors has gone from ten in 1969–70 to 23 in 1975–76. A similarly striking discrepancy exists in the rank of associate professor. There were only three female associates in 1969–70 and six in 1975–76, while the males in that rank numbered 17 in 1969–70 and 35 in 1975–76. While women represent approximately 20% of the faculty, a figure which compares fairly favorably with the percentage of women in the applicable labor pool, males held slightly more than 90% of the full professor slots in 1969–1970 and 92% in 1975–76. In fact, there have been more male professors than male instructors every year since 1969–70, despite the defendants' insistence that entry to the top rank is a significant achievement reserved for the excellent few.

In spite of their overall percentage on the faculty, women presently outnumber men in the instructor level. While many of the women in these lower levels may be new faculty members, that still does not account for the striking imbalance in the upper ranks. Moreover, the evidence showed that while men had been appointed to the faculty as full professors on many occasions since 1969, no woman has ever been appointed initially above the rank of associate professor. This fact supports the district court's finding of a pattern of discriminatory hiring. Dr. Sweeney also showed that no female has ever been promoted to the highest rank without a terminal degree, while several male professors do not possess such a degree. This statistical evidence supports the district court's finding that a double standard was applied in promotion decisions. The evidence also showed that women were underrepresented in the English, Art, History, Biology, Psychology and Industrial Education Departments.

The defendant attempted to rebut these statistics by pointing to highly qualified men who remained in the lower ranks longer than Dr. Sweeney. While this evidence is informative, the district court was not required to find that it totally dispelled the inference of discrimination created by the other statistics. Likewise, evidence of males who failed to be promoted on their first try does not necessarily rebut the inference of the plaintiff's more striking statistics. At best, these tales of individual males' struggles account for the district court's conclusion that Dr. Sweeney would not have achieved promotion in her first effort even if she had been a male. It is true that the defendants were able to find instances where an individual male of superior qualifications encountered difficulties in reaching the level of professor. But these examples were countered by other situations where females fared worse. In short, the plaintiff did not prove the existence of a completely consistent pattern, but she offered sufficient evidence to sustain the district court's findings.

Nor can defendants hope to disprove a discriminatory pattern by claiming that they chose outstanding male faculty members for promotion, for "affirmations of good faith in making individual selections are insufficient to dispel a prima facie case of systematic exclusion." The scarcity of women in the upper ranks accounts for their frequent lack of representation on the FEAC and the FAC. The racial or sexual composition of a body which makes subjective evaluations has often been considered a factor in employment discrimination cases.

In addition to statistical evidence, Dr. Sweeney presented testimony concerning other instances from which sex discrimination could be inferred. An important part of her case centered around the ineffectiveness of Keene's affirmative action effort. Although a faculty committee drafted an affirmative action plan in 1973, no such plan was officially adopted until 1976. The current plan, in the form presented to the district court, does not even address the questions of salary and promotion. Moreover, the testimony reveals that the person who nominally served as affirmative action coordinator did virtually nothing to advance the rights of women on the Keene campus. He admitted as much in his own testimony.

Certainly the most striking evidence presented in this context concerned the affirmative action coordinator's response to Dr. Sweeney's filing of charges with the State Human Rights Commission. Not only did he attempt to get the plaintiff to answer the interrogatories sent to Keene by the Human Rights Commission, a measure which cannot be condoned, he also wrote to the president of Smith College for information on how that school had responded to a charge of sex discrimination because he was "concerned that that form of anarchy may creep north into our virgin territory."

Various witnesses also testified that in their opinion sex bias influenced promotion decisions at Keene. This bias may often be unconscious and unexpressed, but its potential for harm is greatest in reaching decisions on the basis of criteria which simply cannot be objectively measured or definitively stated.

From our careful review of all the evidence we conclude that the trial court's finding that sex discrimination impeded the plaintiff's second promotion effort was not clearly erroneous.

With regard to the court's finding against the plaintiff on the issue of salary discrimination, we likewise hold that the fact-findings were not clearly erroneous. Dr. Sweeney presented statistical evidence which demonstrated that the average salaries of women fell below those of men in each rank in almost every year. This evidence persuaded the district court that a pattern of sex discrimination in compensation existed. However, Dr. Sweeney did not offer any proof of what her salary would have been but for the discrimination. Nor did she explore deeply enough the various elements which influenced salary amounts so as to enable the district court to determine to what extent sex or other factors contributed to the amount of her compensation. From the record it is clear that merit, longevity, experience, and availability of funds all influenced the salary level. It is also certain that Keene State College has made no effort to standardize salary levels within a given rank or department. It is difficult to attribute a lower salary to any one factor in the absence of more particularized comparative evidence. Moreover, Dr. Sweeney's salary was lower than the female average, so the court could have inferred that her sex did not affect her pay.

Because we leave this fact-finding undisturbed, it is not necessary for us to reach the issue of whether the Equal Pay Act is applicable to this kind of case and whether it can be constitutionally applied to a state college.

Furthermore, in light of the fact-findings made by the district court, Dr. Sweeney would gain nothing from reversal of her § 1983 and Fourteenth Amendment claims or from a holding on the issue of whether Title IX creates an implied cause of action. Title VII suffices to make her whole to the extent she is entitled to relief. We express no opinion on these undecided issues.

We also affirm the award of attorneys' fees, costs, and expenses.

Kunda v. Muhlenberg College

463 F. Supp. 294 (E.D. Pa. 1978)

[Female college teacher brought action against her former employer, alleging that she was denied promotion and tenure because of her sex. The District Court, Huyett,

J., held that: (1) the female teacher established by a preponderance of the evidence that the college discriminated against her on the basis of sex by failing to promote her to the rank of assistant professor; (2) though the female teacher presented a prima facie case of discrimination in connection with the college's failure to grant her tenure, the college rebutted the prima facie case by a preponderance of the evidence when it articulated a legitimate, nondiscriminatory and job-related reason for the failure to grant tenure to plaintiff, namely, her lack of a masters degree; (3) the female teacher established by a preponderance of the evidence that she was subjected to disparate treatment because of her sex in that she received different counseling concerning the requirements for promotion than that received by males in her department; (4) the female teacher proved that the difference in treatment was the result of purposeful discrimination on the basis of sex, in violation of the Civil Rights Act of 1964; (5) even assuming that plaintiff made a prima facie showing of disparate impact on women in connection with the terminal degree requirement for tenure, the college rebutted the showing through evidence that the terminal degree requirement was closely related to the duties of a faculty member and served a legitimate need in an educational institution; (6) the denial of tenure to the teacher was not based on her sex.]

*　*　*

Even though the denial of tenure in itself was not sex-based, we believe that plaintiff was treated differently than male faculty members in that she was never counselled that the failure to obtain a masters degree would preclude her from being considered for tenure. Under the circumstances, plaintiff reasonably believed that a masters degree was not an exclusive requirement for tenure and that she could qualify for tenure by meeting one or both of the alternative criteria listed in the Faculty Handbook. In fact, as we have seen, the terminal degree requirement was applied uniformly and exclusively in all tenure decisions after 1970. Plaintiff argues that this difference in treatment constitutes a violation of Title VII.

It is not enough for plaintiff merely to show disparate treatment, however; she must also show that this disparate treatment was not the result of mere inadvertence, but instead constituted purposeful discrimination on the basis of sex. We have considered this question carefully and conclude, on the basis of several factors, that the disparate treatment accorded to plaintiff was motivated by discriminatory animus based upon sex. First, plaintiff initiated a number of discussions with Dean Secor and President Morey concerning her future at Muhlenberg and, although the opportunity was clearly present, neither man told plaintiff that her failure to obtain a masters degree would be a barrier to her advancement. Second, Dean Secor and President Morey knew or should have known that members of the Physical Education Department might reasonably believe that a masters degree was not necessary in view of the treatment of Professors Whispell and Flamish. In point of fact, Dean Secor's memorandum of June 26, 1973, which recorded his meeting with Ronald Lauchnor, demonstrates an awareness of this potential problem.

Finally, with respect to Dean Secor, statistical evidence was presented which strongly suggested that, in the areas of tenure recommendations, his decisions were related to a candidate's sex. This evidence is relevant to a finding of discriminatory motive in the failure to adequately counsel plaintiff concerning the importance of obtaining a masters degree. It was Dean Secor who took it upon himself to inform Messrs. Beidleman and Lauchnor of the necessity of obtaining a masters degree, while failing to impart the same information to plaintiff. Therefore, it is Dean Secor's intent which is important here. Evidence that, in other contexts, Dean Secor improperly used sex as a criterion is certainly relevant to show discriminatory intent in his failure adequately to counsel plaintiff.

Defendants have given no convincing reason for their failure to inform Mrs. Kunda of the necessity of obtaining a masters degree. We conclude that the disparate treatment accorded Mrs. Kunda with respect to counselling constitutes purposeful discrimination on the basis of sex. We further find that if Mrs. Kunda had been adequately counselled, she would have made every effort to obtain a masters degree.

*   *   *

III. *Relief*

Section 706(g) of Title VII, 42 U.S.C. § 2000e–5(g), provides a panoply of remedies that a district court may invoke where unlawful employment discrimination has been established, thus providing the court with the flexibility to devise a remedy to suit the violation. By granting to the district court wide latitude in fashioning remedies for employment discrimination, Congress intended that this discretion be used "to further transcendent legislative purposes." One such purpose is to make whole persons who have suffered injury on account of unlawful employment discrimination. As the cases have made clear, the remedies set forth in section 706(g) are not mandatory, but are to be used by the district court in its discretion in an attempt to secure complete justice to injured parties.

In providing an adequate remedy for plaintiff, we believe that the critical inquiry is to determine the position plaintiff would have been in had she not suffered the unlawful discrimination proven here. We believe that the purposes of Title VII will be adequately served only by answering this inquiry based upon all of the circumstances and then using our equitable powers to the extent necessary to make plaintiff whole. It is clear that "federal courts are empowered to fashion such relief as the particular circumstances of a case may require to effect restitution, making whole insofar as possible the victims of . . . discrimination."

We find here that plaintiff was discriminated against on the basis of sex when she was denied a promotion. She was initially considered for and denied promotion during the 1971–72 school year. However, these acts occurred prior to the effective date of the 1972 Amendments to Title VII and, even if we were to find that the denial was a product of sex discrimination, we would be powerless to create a remedy. Plaintiff was also considered for and denied a promotion the following year. Absent discrimination on the basis of sex, plaintiff would have been granted a promotion during the 1972–73 school year, effective September 1, 1973. Therefore, the appropriate relief for purposes of making plaintiff whole is to grant her a promotion to the position of Assistant Professor effective September 1, 1973.

We also find that the denial of an award of tenure to plaintiff was not based upon her sex, but rather was the result of the application of the sex-neutral terminal degree requirement. Therefore, we are not empowered to award plaintiff tenure.

Finally, we find that defendant intentionally discriminated against plaintiff on the basis of sex in failing to adequately counsel her concerning the necessity of obtaining a masters degree in order to be awarded tenure. Dean Secor and President Morey had ample opportunity to so inform Mrs. Kunda, especially during meetings with her in the late Spring of 1972 after promotion was initially denied. Had Mrs. Kunda been counselled in the same manner as male members of the Physical Education

Department, we find that she would have done everything possible to obtain a masters degree in order to further enhance her chances of obtaining tenure. Although it is of course impossible for us to know if Mrs. Kunda would have in fact been able to obtain her masters degree, she would have had the *opportunity* to do so. Therefore, in order to make plaintiff whole for the discrimination she suffered, we must somehow restore to her this "lost opportunity" to obtain the masters degree prior to being considered for tenure.

We believe that the only fair way to restore this opportunity to Mrs. Kunda is to provide that she be awarded tenure contingent upon obtaining her masters degree within two full school years. Our calculation is based upon the assumption that if she had been properly counselled by Dean Secor or President Morey in the Spring of 1972, she would have had two full school years—that is, through the summer of 1974—to obtain her masters degree. Since both Muhlenberg officials had a reasonable opportunity to counsel plaintiff adequately at that time, we believe that Spring, 1972 is an appropriate date upon which to base our calculation. If plaintiff is able to complete the requirements for her masters degree within this time period, then plaintiff should be granted tenure retroactive to September, 1975. This is the date that tenure would have been granted to plaintiff if she had not been subjected to unlawful sex discrimination.

In addition, plaintiff is granted reinstatement with full back pay. The award of these remedies is premised upon the assumption that plaintiff would have been granted tenure but for defendant's discriminatory acts. We are mindful that, even if plaintiff had been adequately counselled, she may not have been able to obtain a masters degree, nor, as a consequence, obtain tenure. However, it is due to defendant's discriminatory acts that we are forced to make such conjectures. We conclude that to deny plaintiff reinstatement and back pay would penalize plaintiff for defendant's actions and deprive plaintiff of a full and complete remedy for her discrimination.

In sum, we grant to plaintiff (1) reinstatement; (2) back pay, from the date of termination less amounts earned in the interim; (3) promotion to rank of Assistant Professor effective September, 1973; and (4) the opportunity to complete or substantially complete the requirements of a masters degree within two full school years of this Order and, if the masters degree is successfully achieved, an award of tenure effective September, 1975.

Brown v. Board of Trustees, Boston University
674 F. Supp. 393 (D. Mass. 1987)

SKINNER, D.J.

This case went to trial before a jury on Count I of the complaint and a verdict was returned to the plaintiff in the amount of $200,000. This verdict was accompanied by the jury's answer to a special interrogatory which reflected a finding that the plaintiff had been denied tenure because of sex-based discrimination. This finding is binding on the court with respect to its finding on the remaining counts of the complaint alleging claims under Title VII of the Civil Rights Act, 42 U.S.C. § 2000e and the state civil rights act, M.G.L. c. 151B, which were tried to the court.

The jury's finding is determinative of liability under these two statutes; there remains only considerations of the relief to be awarded. The plaintiff seeks reinstatement in tenured status as an associate professor of English, immediate promotion to a full professor, a paid sabbatical, and an order for the defendant to make retirement contributions equivalent to the contributions which would have been made had she been awarded tenure at the proper time. She seeks damages for emotional distress under M.G.L. c. 151B, an order requiring non-discriminatory treatment in future promotions and an order requiring public posting of the result in this case.

A. Reinstatement

The parties agree, correctly, that the question of reinstatement is addressed to the sound direction of the court. It is a fairly common remedy in non-academic situations. Because of the special responsibility of university trustees and the lifetime span of academic tenure, our court of appeals has warned us to be more circumspect in tenure cases than in other cases. But we are not to avoid our responsibilities under the statute out of undue deference to university administrations.

In my view, the statutory mandate to give complete relief would best be served by an order requiring reinstatement as a tenured associate professor in the absence of a compelling reason to the contrary. It would not appear from evidence in this case that Professor Brown would encounter such hostility on her return as would interfere with her productive life at the university. She apparently is well regarded by her academic colleagues. Insulation from retaliation by the administration can be provided by an appropriate order of this court. There seems little risk that Boston University will be stuck with an unqualified person on its faculty, judging from the evidence in the case, although there was some dispute as to the quality of her scholarship. This case is distinguishable in this respect from my resolution of this issue in Fields v. Clark University.

Accordingly, an order shall enter requiring the Trustees of Boston University to reinstate the plaintiff as an associate professor of English, with tenure.

B. Damages for Emotional Distress

In my opinion, damages for emotional distress may be recovered under M.G.L. c. 151. I do not read into these decisions any restriction to a case involving extreme conduct nor do I think that the distinction noted between sections 5 and 9 of c. 151B require treatment of privately instituted cases with respect to these damages that is any different than the treatment of cases instituted by MCAD.

The damages awarded in these cases have been very modest. Our court of appeals has approved of the award of substantial damages for emotional distress in an employment case brought under 42 U.S.C. § 1981, but there was evidence of harassment of the plaintiff for a period of years.

I would suppose the usual rules governing damages would apply. For instance, it is reasonably predictable that denial of tenure will cause the applicant emotional distress. I conclude that part of the emotional distress in this case was a facet of the plaintiff's highly strung personality and her highly developed expectations for herself. But it is also a general rule of damage that a defendant takes the plaintiff as she is, and takes the risk that she may be unusually susceptible to particular sorts of harm. On the other hand, denial of tenure is a well-known risk of academic life, and may be visited on extremely qualified applicants for a variety of reasons, including the quality of the competition, the need of the institution for the applicant's specialty and budgetary constraints. The defendant was also entitled to expect some degree of emotional preparedness for such an eventuality.

There were no extreme circumstances. In fact, the defendant offered to soften the blow by giving the plaintiff an additional three-year contract. The plaintiff, however, considered this an additional insult.

Testimony on emotional distress was offered by the plaintiff herself and her therapist, a psychologist, whom she had consulted for a variety of problems before the denial of tenure. There was evidence of a period of depression resulting from the denial of tenure. These two witnesses also extended the area of damage to the plaintiff's unsatisfactory relationship with her first child, who was born during the pendency of the tenure controversy. The plaintiff was then in the middle of an acrimonious dispute with her first husband, which led to a divorce. Many parents find difficulty with a first child under the best of circumstances. In the midst of this marital discord it is no surprise that the child was unhappy, a circumstance that in my view should not be charged to Boston University.

An award of damages for emotional distress is necessarily imprecise. I award damages in the amount of $15,000, with interest from the date of the filing of the complaint in accordance with the Massachusetts rule.

C. Other Claims for Relief

The plaintiff has requested various other benefits, such as immediate promotion to full professor, a year's paid sabbatical right off the bat upon reinstatement, additional payments into her pension fund, continued supervision and posting.

In my view, the extremely generous award of the jury plus reinstatement plus damages for emotional distress constitute sufficient relief in this case. Granting of a sabbatical and promotion to full professor would be an interference by the court in the administration totally unwarranted by the evidence in this case. No posting is required. This case has received extensive publicity locally and nationally, and particularly in the academic community. In an abundance of caution, however, I will include in this order a prohibition against future discriminatory conduct in general and in particular with reference to the plaintiff.

A final judgment shall be entered in accordance with the foregoing, and with the jury's award on Count I of the complaint. The plaintiff shall recover her reasonable attorneys' fees and expenses of suit.

The *Kemp v. Ervin* case, detailed in chapters 2 and 5, is the most widely publicized remedy, inasmuch as Jan Kemp was reinstated, had her tenure clock reset, and received a large monetary settlement. A trickle of other results has begun to result in a range of options for judges who find that colleges have acted discriminatorily toward faculty. At present, nearly all of these cases have involved women faculty successfully suing colleges that wrongfully discharged them. Christine Sweeney's case was vacated and remanded by the U.S. Supreme Court, with instructions to examine the burden of proof, in light of *Furnco v. Waters*, 438 U.S. 567 (1978). On remand, she won again, after the court of appeals again found Keene State College's reasons for not promoting her pretextual. 604 F.2d 106 (1st Cir. 1979).

In another first circuit case, *Fields v. Clark University* (1987), a college was ordered to reinstate a female professor, reconsider her for tenure in two years, and pay back-salary; although the appeals court agreed that sex discrimination had permeated the earlier process, it held that she should not be subject to another tenure review. The court ordered that a rehearing determine whether there were other nondiscriminatory reasons for the denial. In late 1987, Fields was attempting to settle the case. C. Grosso, "Sex Discrimination Suits Against Colleges Win Mixed Results," *Education Daily,* 16 November 1987, pp. 5–6.

Among the alternatives employed by courts have included full reinstatement or appointment to the next appropriate vacancy: *Hooper v. Jensen,* 328 S.E.2d 519 (W.Va. 1985); *Owen v. Rutledge,* 475 So. 2d 826 (Ala. 1985); *University of Alaska v. Geistauts,* 666 P.2d 424 (Alaska 1983); *Rutherford v. State Personnel Board,* 101 Cal. App. 3d 1, 1651 Cal. Rptr. 287 (1980); *Ofsevit v. Trustees of California State University and Colleges,* 21 Cal. 3d 763, 148 Cal. Rptr. 1, 582 P.2d 88 (1978). Of course, as LaNoue and Lee demonstrated in *Academics in Court,* even plaintiffs who technically win their cases do so at great personal and professional cost.

Faculty Research and Regulation

Universities have been the major stage upon which research in the United States is played. In a 1986 report, the U.S. General Accounting Office estimated that in fiscal year 1984, the six major federal agencies funding scientific research and development performed at U.S. universities allocated nearly $4.8 billion. *Federal Funding Mechanisms in Support of University Research* (GAO, 1986, p. 15). In addition, considerably more federal, state, corporate, and philanthropic support underwrites research in the sciences, humanities, and social sciences. The federal government is the undisputed impresario, providing nearly ⅔ of the $7.3 billion spent for all research activities on campuses in 1982. *Assessing Federal Funding Mechanisms for University Research* (GAO, 1986). These impressive figures do not take into account the many other auxiliary enterprises that fund faculty research, either off campus or in other industrial or university/industrial/non-profit settings. Although there has been a high mortality rate, many colleges also participate in "research parks," consortia, and joint ventures for high-technology research. Faculty research has indisputably become big business.

It has also become big legal business, especially in the regulatory scheme, and in the development of intellectual property law. The legal developments in this section include relatively few significant cases, but the paucity of litigation masks the extraordinary increase in legislation, regulation, and affiliated legal mechanisms governing research. Nearly every university with any government-funded research faculty has an office for sponsored programs or research foundation for administering grants and contracts, and each of these colleges has in place the required institutional review processes for reviewing student and faculty research: human subjects committees, institutional review boards, or other informed-consent mechanisms.

The rise in the administrative state of research reflects itself throughout this book, ranging from faulty tenure and first amendment issues to federal and state governance of higher education. This section includes cases and materials on research regulation, including federal tax issues; informed consent and ethical considerations; the law and biotechnology; and national security and secrecy of research data.

Research Regulation

" 'Research' means a systematic investigation designed to develop or contribute to generalizable knowledge." 45 C.F.R. § 46.102(e).

[Basic research is] "any original investigation for the advancement of scientific knowledge not having a specific commercial objective." I.R.C. § 44F(e)(3).

"The determination as to whether research is 'scientific' does not depend on whether such research is classified as 'fundamental' or 'basic' as contrasted with 'applied' or 'practical.' On the other hand, for purposes of the exclusion from unrelated business taxable income provided by Code section 512(b)(9) it is necessary to determine whether the organization is operated primarily for purposes of carrying on 'fundamental,' as contrasted with 'applied,' research." Treas. Reg. §§ 1.501(c)(3)-1(d)(5)(1).

"Critical technology" is defined by the Defense Department as: "classified and unclassified nuclear and non-nuclear unpublished technical data, whose acquisition by a potential adversary could make a significant contribution, which would prove detrimental to the national security of the United States, to the military potential of such country—[irrespective] of whether such technology is acquired directly from the United States or indirectly through another recipient, or whether the declared intended end-use by the recipient, is a military or nonmilitary use." 50 U.S.C. app. § 2404(d).

As is evident by the definitional differences in these four governmental treatments of research (for purposes of human subjects review, the tax code, business purposes, and national security, respectively), research has far-reaching legal dimensions. A sampler of government treatment of research issues includes:

- Freedom of Information Act (5 U.S.C. § 552). Trade secrets are narrowly drawn in Exemption Four of the FOIA. See *Public Citizen Health Research Group v. Food and Drug Administration*, 704 F.2d 1280 (D.C. Cir. 1983).

- Export Administration Amendments Act (50 U.S.C. app §§ 2401–20). The EAAA contains licensing provisions for technical and cryptographic data.

- The Department of State Munitions List, including the International Traffic in Arms Regulations, 22 C.F.R. §§ 120.1-130.17, covers strategic materials for ceramics and other metallurgical research data. See M. Lam, "Restrictions on Technology Transfer Among Academic Researchers," *Journal of College and University Law*, 13 (1986), 311–34; and C. Ramirez, "The Balance of Interests Between National Security Controls and First Amendment Interests in Academic Freedom," *Journal of College and University Law*, 13 (1986), 179–227.

- The Food and Drug Administration, Department of Agriculture, National Science Foundation Environmental Protection Agency, National Institutes of Health, and National Institutes for Mental Health, as well as other federal agencies, regulate biotechnological and other scientific research; the funding and regulation extend deep into research projects and laboratories. In addition, there has been a rise in the regulation of lab procedures, from treatment of animals to disposal of hazardous waste. "UT Health Center Reportedly Fined $5,000 for Hiding Animal Research," *Houston Chronicle*, 27 November 1987; C. Cordes, "Smaller Colleges Are Now Subject to Stiff Hazardous Waste Rules," *Chronicle of Higher Education*, 24 September 1986, p. 23.

Additional areas for future litigation will increasingly include intellectual property and taxation of research. The *IIT* case and other cases in this chapter show the extent to which law has permeated the research enterprise in U.S. labs.

———————

Illinois Institute of Technology
Research Institute v. U.S.
[USTC ¶ 9734] (Ct. Cl. 1985)

MILLER, Judge:

This is a suit for refund of taxes for the year 1976, allegedly erroneously collected under the unrelated business taxable income provisions of the 1954 Internal Revenue Code. The question at issue is whether or not the income from some of the plaintiff's research contracts for government and business was derived from trade or business unrelated to plaintiff's exemption as a corporation organized and operated exclusively for scientific purposes.

I.

Plaintiff, IIT Research Institute (hereinafter "IITRI"), was organized in 1936 by the Board of Trustees of Armour Institute of Technology (now known as the Illinois Institute of Technology) and is one of three independent not-for-profit research institutes formed before World War II. The first research institute was founded in 1927 from a department at the University of Pittsburgh; the second was founded in 1929 pursuant to the will of an industrialist. Following World War II, eleven additional research institutes were formed.

These research institutes were established to stimulate industrial growth and technological development by making research services available to industry on a contract basis. All of the not-for-profit research institutes have significant common characteristics, including: (1) they are separate organizations from the universities and other institutions which were instrumental in their creation; (2) they maintain their own full-time staff, facilities and management; (3) they exist primarily to perform research and development on a contract basis for government and industry; (4) they are multi-disciplinary in nature and serve a multiplicity of clients; (5) they have all received letters of exemption from the I.R.S. acknowledging them to be exempt under section 501 of the Code or its predecessor; and, (6) they all use income exceeding expenses to improve and expand operations and do not distribute any earnings to any private shareholder or other individual.

IITRI's research activities are divided into divisions corresponding to different disciplines or scientific and technological specialties, to wit: (1) Metals; (2) Chemistry and Chemical Engineering; (3) Mechanics of Materials; (4) Electronics; (5) Management and Computer Sciences; (6) Engineering Mechanics; (7) Life Sciences; and (8) Medical Sciences and Engineering. A research director heads each division of IITRI and is responsible for its day-to-day operations.

On March 31, 1941, plaintiff, then known as Research Foundation of Armour Institute of Technology, received a letter from the Internal Revenue Service ruling that it was tax exempt. Subsequently, on April 25, 1980, the I.R.S. acknowledged that plaintiff's tax exempt status under § 501(c)(3) of the Internal Revenue Code continued at least through its fiscal year ended August 31, 1977. Plaintiff's exemption was recognized under § 501(c)(3) as a corporation organized and operated exclusively for scientific purposes, no part of the earnings of which inures to the benefit of any private shareholder or individual. IITRI's tax exempt status is not challenged by the government in this litigation.

During 1976, the taxable year at issue, plaintiff carried on numerous research assignments of various types pursuant to contracts. Plaintiff normally handles in excess of 650 projects annually. Some projects are initiated as a result of decisions by plaintiff's officers or personnel that a particular investigation or study is deemed desirable or appropriate to pursue without outside sponsorship ("in-house contracts"). Other contracts are sponsored by entities outside of IITRI's organization, such as government agencies or industrial organizations. Some contracts are multi-sponsored, and any given contract can include both governmental and non-governmental sponsors. In certain instances, IITRI is a subcontractor of contractors with the government.

An agreement with an agency of the Federal government or with an agency of a state or local government generally is executed on a standard form contract devised by the governmental agency. An agreement with an industrial sponsor is usually executed on a standard form devised by IITRI, although variations and modifications of particular provisions are common in the case of contracts involving large sums. In some cases a contract may be specifically negotiated for a single research project. Approximately 85 percent of IITRI's research is conducted pursuant to contracts with federal or state government agencies.

The determinations as to which contracts to pursue are made by IITRI's Research Committee, composed of the directors of the various research divisions during weekly meetings. The Committee decides first whether to bid for a project and then determines how much to bid. A contract proposal is generally initiated by a research director interested in pursuing that particular line of research. In determining whether to bid on a contract the committee considers: (1) whether the staff is capable of performing the task; (2) the project's relationship to the development of the particular scientific field; and (3) the probability that IITRI's bid will be successful. The elements included in the price at which IITRI bids on the project includes the salaries of those employees who will be involved, the overhead, and a fee. The fee is designed to allow accumulations of surplus for reserves and also the increased cost of new equipment. Usually the fee IITRI charges the government is 6 percent of its direct costs on the project. The fee for industrial contracts tends to be higher than 6 percent. These procedures are followed by the Research Committee for all contracts and all divisions and do not vary according to sponsor nor any other distinction among contracts.

All of the plaintiff's income exceeding expenses from such projects is used to improve and expand its operations. IITRI's compensation to its personnel is reasonable and it does not distribute its earnings to any private shareholder or individual.

Patents may result from plaintiff's research. Such a patent may become the property of plaintiff or of the sponsor, depending upon the terms of the specific contract. In 1976, IITRI received gross royalty income of $260,021, primarily from the licensing of patents.

For its fiscal year ending in 1976, plaintiff's gross accrued revenue was $24,963,590 from government contracts and $3,575,440 from industrial contracts. On or about January 13, 1977, plaintiff filed Form 990, Return of Organization Exempt from Income Tax, for fiscal year 1976, which reported no unrelated business taxable income. On November 14, 1976, the Internal Revenue Service (I.R.S.) issued to plaintiff a statutory notice of deficiency asserting that IITRI had net unrelated business taxable income of $256,788.74, upon which unrelated business income tax of $109,758.59 was due. On January 30, 1980, IITRI paid the deficiency and on April 25, 1980,

IITRI filed its claim for refund. The Commissioner of Internal Revenue rendered no decision on plaintiff's claim and plaintiff filed this suit more than 6 months after filing its claim for refund.

To facilitate the trial of this case, the parties agreed that, of the approximately 650 contracts which plaintiff handles annually, 58 contracts were illustrative or representative (as to content) of IITRI's activities in 1976, and that the liability portion of this suit could be disposed of entirely by reference to those 58 contracts. For the purposes of this suit, defendant challenged 24 of these contracts as being substantially unrelated to plaintiff's exempt activity. The other 34 contracts, the government concedes, were substantially related to plaintiff's exempt activity and were non-taxable.

II.

I.R.C. § 501 provides that certain organizations shall be exempt from income tax. Subsection 501(c)(3) includes in the list of such exempt organizations "Corporations * * * organized and operated exclusively for * * * scientific * * * purposes * * * , no part of the net earnings of which inures to the benefit of any private shareholder or individual."

However, § 511 imposes a tax on the unrelated business taxable income of organizations otherwise exempt under § 501(c). Section 512(a)(1) defines "unrelated business taxable income" as "the gross income derived by any organization from any unrelated trade or business (as defined in § 513) regularly carried on by it, less the deductions allowed by this chapter."

For purposes of this tax, § 513(a) defines such "unrelated trade or business" to be:

> any trade or business the conduct of which is not substantially related (aside from the need of such organization for income or funds or the use it makes of the profits derived) to the exercise or performance by such organization of its charitable, educational, or other purpose or function constituting the basis for its exemption under section 501.

Section 513(c) in turn clarifies the meaning of "trade or business" as used in § 513(a) as follows:

> For the purposes of this section, the term "trade or business" includes any activity which is carried on for the production of income from the sale of goods or the performance of services. For purposes of the preceding sentence, an activity does not lose its identity as a trade or business merely because it is carried on within a larger aggregate of similar activities or within a larger complex of other endeavors which may, or may not, be related to the exempt purposes of the organization.

Treasury Regulation § 1.513.1(a) (1976), interpreting the language of § 513, sets out the following three part test to determine whether a tax exempt organization's activities generate income subject to the unrelated business tax:

> [G]ross income of an exempt organization subject to the tax imposed by section 511 is includable in the computation of unrelated business taxable income if: (1) It is income from trade or business; (2) such trade or business is regularly carried on by the organization; and (3) the conduct of such trade or business is not substantially related (other than through the production of funds) to the organization's performance of its exempt functions.

All three of these requirements must be met before an organization may be held to have unrelated business taxable income.

* * *

Thus, the apparent inconsistency between §§ 501(c)(3) and 511 must be resolved as follows:

(1) For any of its income to be exempt, an organization must still be organized and operated *exclusively* for a purpose set out in § 501(c)(3).

(2) The operation of an unrelated trade or business having the purpose of earning income for use in promoting the exempt purpose, need not be deemed to change the exclusive purpose of an exempt organization, but such income is taxable as unrelated income under § 511.

(3) If the exemption under § 501(c)(3) is conceded, then the decisive question is whether or not the challenged income is from trade or business substantially related to the carrying out of the exempt purpose and not whether it would serve an exempt purpose on its own.

Treasury Regulation § 1.513-1(a)(2) defines the term "substantially related" in I.R.C. § 513 as follows:

> (2) *Type of relationship required.* Trade or business is "related" to exempt purposes, in the relevant sense, only where the conduct of the business activities has causal relationship to the achievement of exempt purposes (other than through the production of income); and it is "substantially related," for purposes of section 513, only if the causal relationship is a substantial one. Thus, for the conduct of trade or business from which a particular amount of gross income is derived to be substantially related to purposes for which exemption is granted, the production or distribution of the goods or the performance of the services from which the gross income is derived must contribute importantly to the accomplishment of those purposes. * * *

Thus, if this regulation is valid (and neither party contends to the contrary), the conduct of the business activities which give rise to the challenged income must have a substantial "causal relationship" to the achievement of the exempt purpose, and the activities "must contribute importantly" to the accomplishment of the exempt purposes.

III

A.

The undisputed evidence is that plaintiff's exempt purpose is and has been since its inception to provide multidisciplinary scientific research for government and industry; that no income therefrom inured to any individual; that plaintiff received rulings from the I.R.S. that its income from such activities are exempt; that the nature of plaintiff's business has not changed in any way since it received its exemption; that the Service has never sought to revoke such rulings, and defendant does not contest plaintiff's exemption in this litigation. Under these circumstances, it is difficult to comprehend why the performance of some portion of such activities has no causal relationship and does not contribute as importantly to the accomplishment of plaintiff's exempt purpose as any other portion of its activities.

* * *

Defendant's contention that 11 of the 24 challenged projects were not scientific in nature has no support in the record.

The terms "science" and "scientific" are not defined in the Internal Revenue Code, Congress apparently having chosen to rely on the commonly understood meaning of the term. The *McGraw-Hill Dictionary of Scientific and Technical Terms* defines "science" as a "branch of study in which facts are observed, classified, and, usually, quantitative laws are formulated and verified; [or] involves the application of mathematical reasoning and data analysis to natural phenomenon." The *Random House Dictionary Of The English Language* defines "science" as "[k]nowledge, as of facts and principles, gained by systemic study." Thus, in the context of this litigation, "science" will be defined as the process by which knowledge is systematized or classified through the use of observation, experimentation, or reasoning.

The regulations under § 501(c)(3) also add meaning to the terms "scientific" and "scientific research" in the context of that statute, which neither party disputes, to wit Treas. Reg. § 1.501(c)(3)-1(d)(5):

(i) * * * For research to be "scientific," within the meaning of section 501(c)(3), it must be carried on in furtherance of a "scientific" purpose. The determination as to whether such research is "scientific" does not depend on whether such research is classified as "fundamental" or "basic" as contrasted with "applied" or "practical." * * *

(ii) Scientific research does not include activities of a type ordinarily carried on as incident to commercial or industrial operations, as, for example, the ordinary testing or inspection of materials or products or the designing or constructing of equipment, buildings, etc. * * *

Under any of these definitions, all 24 challenged contracts may properly be deemed scientific research, as they meet these criteria. The government has stipulated that virtually all of IITRI's contracts consisted of work performed by, and capable of being performed only by, qualified engineers and scientists with expertise in particular technological fields. Further, all plaintiff's expert scientific witnesses testified that there were no significant differences between the 24 contracts the government is challenging and the 34 contracts not being challenged, with respect to their nature, content, sophistication of the scientific research involved, or the scientific methodology or approach. This testimony was not disputed in any way by the government.

The testimony further indicated that IITRI was not involved in the commercialization of the products or processes developed as a result of its research. IITRI would only develop a project to the point where the research principles were established. At this point, the sponsors would make the principles available to different customers, usually in the form of newly developed products or equipment. Also, the evidence showed that IITRI did not conduct consumer or market research, social science research, or ordinary testing of the type which is carried on incident to commercial operations. IITRI's activities, therefore, cannot be said to run afoul of the "commercial operations" section of Treas. Reg. § 1.501(c)(3)-1(d)(5)(ii). The fact that research is directed towards solving a particular industrial problem does not necessarily indicate that the research is not scientific. See Treas. Reg. § 1.501(c)(3)-1(d)(5)(i) (1976) ("The determination as to whether such research is 'scientific' does not depend on whether such research is classified as 'fundamental' or 'basic' as contrasted with 'applied' or 'practical.' ")

The scientific nature of each of the 11 contracts challenged by the government as not scientific can be readily understood from a brief description thereof. Any of these contracts can be deemed to be scientific research because it either: 1) involved the use of observation or experimentation to formulate or verify facts or natural laws; 2) could only have been performed by an individual with advanced scientific or technical expertise; 3) added to knowledge within a particular scientific field; 4) involved the application of mathematical reasoning; and/or, 5) was an attempt to systematize or classify a body of scientific knowledge by collecting information and presenting it in a useful form.

(1) C6333: Water Quenching of Coke. This contract, sponsored by the U.S. Environmental Protection Agency, assessed the impact of clean and contaminated water quenching of coke by the steel industry on the total suspended particulate levels in and around coke plants. The contract was for research and development work to solve some of the pollution problems of the steel industry. For this contract, IITRI's task was to develop an analytical model to predict the ambient air quality impact of quench tower emissions. In substance, this was a mathematical model designed to predict particulate levels suspended in the air downstream as a result of using water in water scrubbing towers to quench air pollution and gases from coking operations.

The defendant contends that this project was taxable because IITRI simply co-ordinated the work of others on behalf of the Environmental Protection Agency. There is no evidence in the record to support this contention. Further the evidence indicated both that this project was substantially related to other scientific projects performed by IITRI relating to causes of environmental particulates, and not challenged by the I.R.S., such as a study of the effect of rocket exhaust particulates on citrus crops, and also that this project involved the development of a mathematical model by IITRI which is included within the ambit of "science."

* * *

IV.

In addition to the performance of scientific research for government and industry, the undisputed evidence warrants the conclusion that plaintiff also had the purpose of conducting scientific research and analysis and disseminating the result thereof. Looked at in this light, as one scientist witness expressed it, the individual contracts were "building blocks" in an evolving structure of knowledge, which enabled plaintiff to advance the scientific projects and fields of interest of the talented scientists on its staff.

Generally, each contract was part of a larger area of scientific research activity that had been and would continue to be conducted by IITRI. The Research Committee, when deciding whether or not to undertake a contract, would evaluate the nature, scope, and research content of the contract to ascertain whether these were consistent with IITRI's research objectives and capabilities. For example, IITRI's chemistry department, being interested in developing the field of odor research, by undertaking different contracts involving odors, IITRI's scientists hoped to add to their store of knowledge concerning the composition of odors and ultimately prove that there exists an odor spectrum similar to the electromagnetic spectrum. Thus, each contract in this area was designed to contribute importantly to the achievement of plaintiff's scientific purpose.

Typically, a scientist at IITRI would work on a number of projects within a particular area of science over a number of years. Within the same period of time and same area of expertise, the same personnel would conduct "in-house," and government and industrial contracts. The scientist would then be able to draw upon knowledge gained through this work and synthesize these findings into a paper or other type of presentation. The publishing of the results and theories derived from their work on specific contracts enhanced the reputation of the scientists at IITRI and that of the Institute itself within the scientific community. This scientific reputation furthered the scientific purpose of the Institute because government and industrial sponsors solicit IITRI's input in scientific matters on the basis of its reputation in specific scientific fields and opened new fields of inquiry for further research and publication.

Indeed, the government concedes in its brief that the 24 projects it contends are taxable "may have grown out of or engendered other activities substantially related to plaintiff's exempt purpose."

Accordingly, it is held that the 24 contracts are substantially related to IITRI's exempt purpose and the income therefrom is not taxable.

VI.

Plaintiff also contends that the unrelated business tax is inapplicable to it because, even if some of its contracts did not qualify for exemption, they were not part of any separable, regularly carried on trade or business, as required by Treas. Reg. § 1.513.1(a) but were at the most sporadic activities.

Defendant, on the other hand, would lump together all contracts not qualifying for exemption and label them as a regular business carried on in addition to its exempt business. In view of the decision already arrived at, it is unnecessary to decide this question herein.

Conclusion

For the above reasons, it is held that IITRI has not engaged in a trade or business substantially unrelated to its organization and operation for scientific purposes. Therefore, the Commissioner's imposition of the unrelated business income tax on certain of plaintiff's activities was erroneous, and plaintiff is entitled to a full refund of $109,758.59 with interest as provided for by law.

Informed Consent and Research Ethics

In *Bad Blood: The Tuskegee Syphilis Experiment* (New York: Macmillan, 1981), historian James Jones revealed a horrifying federally funded study of black men who had degenerative syphilis, and who were deliberately left untreated in order for researchers to observe the terminal stages of venereal disease. Following this and other evidence of extraordinary patient abuse, Congress amended the Public Health Service Act by enacting the National Research Service Award Act of 1974 (88 Stat. 342, regulations at 45 C.F.R. § 46.101-409). The regulations require that all federal research funding be governed by institutional review mechanisms for human subjects' protection and informed consent. See Delgado and Leskovac, "Informed Consent in

Human Experimentation: Bridging the Gap Between Ethical Thought and Current Practice," *U.C.L.A. Law Review,* 34 (1986), 67–130.

Complex medical malpractice cases are routine in academic hospitals and medical programs, and undoubtedly constitute a major portion of rising litigation in colleges and universities. See B. Rich, "Malpractice Issues in the Academic Medical Center," *Journal of College and University Law,* 13 (1986), 149–77. ("Without question they treat a disproportionate number of the poor and the acutely ill. They also bear the major responsibility for conducting medical research and training the health care practitioners of tomorrow. Given those heavy burdens, it is truly remarkable that their medical malpractice plight is not more severe than that which actually exists.") The cases that follow concern two of the more famous medical stories, the artificial heart and the drug DES.

Karp v. Cooley
493 F.2d 408 (1974)

BELL, Circuit Judge:

Medical history was made in 1969 when Dr. Denton A. Cooley, a thoracic surgeon, implanted the first totally mechanical heart in 47-year-old Haskell Karp. This threshold orthotopic cardiac prosthesis also spawned this medical malpractice suit by Mr. Karp's wife, individually and as executrix of Mr. Karp's estate, and his children, for the patient's wrongful death. Grounded on diversity jurisdiction, and thus Texas substantive law, novel questions concerning experimentation, as well as issues of informed consent, fraud, and negligence are presented. After nine days of trial and numerous ancillary proceedings outside the jury's presence, the district court in a carefully considered opinion directed a verdict for the defendant-appellees, Dr. Denton A. Cooley and Dr. Domingo S. Liotta. For reasons stated herein, we affirm.

ASSIGNMENTS OF ERROR

There are eleven asserted errors. In assignments one through four, the claim is made that the district court erred in directing a verdict for defendants on appellants' causes of action based on fraud and a lack of informed consent; point five objects to the directed verdict on appellants' claim of fraud, negligence, and gross negligence in the performance of the various surgical procedures; point six is a claim of negligence based on "human experimentation"; point seven claims fraud and negligence in connection with the heart transplant; point eight assigns error in the exclusion of certain records of Baylor Medical School; points nine and ten are objections to the exclusion of Dr. Michael DeBakey's testimony and to alleged in-chambers judicial "coercion"; and point eleven assigns error for the exclusion of a motion picture film of the Karp operation. Because of the nature of the questions presented here, we have outlined the evidence presented at the trial in some detail.

FACTS

There is no dispute that prior to entering St. Luke's Episcopal Hospital in Houston on March 5, 1969, Haskell Karp had a long and difficult ten-year history of cardiac problems. He suffered a serious heart attack in 1959 and was hospitalized approximately two months because of diffuse anterior myocardial infarction. He had incurred four heart attacks, thirteen cardiac hospitalizations and considerable medical care culminating in the insertion of an electronic demand pacemaker in May, 1968. Subsequent hospitalization in September and October, 1968 occurred, and finally the decision was made to seek the assistance of Dr. Cooley. Mrs. Karp telephoned Dr. Cooley on March 3, 1969, and it was agreed Mr. Karp would be in Houston by Wednesday, March 5.

MRS. KARP'S TESTIMONY

Mrs. Karp's testimony in relevant part was that at the time of his hospital admission March 5, Mr. Karp's physical condition was "as normal as any man in the courtroom" and that he was in no pain or discomfort. She testified Dr. Homer L. Beazley, a cardiologist, examined Mr. Karp on March 6 and on a daily basis after that. She said Dr. Cooley first saw Haskell Karp on Tuesday, March 11. She said Dr. Cooley recommended a heart transplant, but that Mr. Karp rejected this suggestion. She said Dr. Cooley next saw Mr. Karp about a week later when he began to talk about a "wedge procedure" and an aneurysm. She then testified that she next saw Dr. Cooley the day before Mr. Karp's surgery on April 3, 1969, although she admitted that Dr. Cooley had seen Mr. Karp the night before on April 2 when she was not present. Mrs. Karp testified Dr. Cooley came into the hospital room about 6:30 or 7:00 p.m. on April 3. As Mrs. Karp described this meeting:

> "When Dr. Cooley came in, he said, 'I have a paper[4] here for you to sign for Mr. Karp's surgery,' and I looked at him, and said, 'Why do you want to operate,' you know, 'tomorrow after keeping us here so long? Can you tell me about it?'

---

4. This consent form was prepared by Dr. Cooley and Mr. Henry Reinhard, Assistant Administrator of St. Luke's Episcopal Hospital, on April 3 especially for the Karp operation. While there is a conflict in the testimony between Mrs. Karp, Dr. Cooley, and Mr. Reinhard as to *when* Mr. Karp signed the form, there is no dispute that Mr. Karp signed it, and that both Mr. and Mrs. Karp's signatures were verified consequently by Mr. Reinhard. The consent form reads as follows:

CONSENT TO OPERATION

April 3, 1969

I, Haskell Karp, request and authorize Dr. Denton A. Cooley and such other surgeons as he may designate to perform upon me, in St. Luke's Episcopal Hospital of Houston, Texas, cardiac surgery for advanced cardiac decompensation and myocardial insufficiency as a result of numerous coronary occlusions. The risk of this surgery has been explained to me. In the event cardiac function cannot be restored by excision of destroyed heart muscle and plastic reconstruction of the ventricle and death seems imminent, I authorize Dr. Cooley and his staff to remove my diseased heart and insert a mechanical cardiac substitute. I understand that this mechanical device will not be permanent and ultimately will require replacement by a heart transplant. I realize that this device has been tested in the laboratory but has not been used to sustain a human being and that no assurance of success can be made. I expect the surgeons to exercise every effort to preserve my life through any of these means. No assurance has been made by anyone as to the results that may be obtained.

* * *

Signature s/ *Haskell Karp*
Haskell Karp

WITNESSES:

s/ Mrs. Haskell Karp

Mrs. Haskell Karp (wife)
s/ *Henry C. Reinhard, Jr.*

Henry C. Reinhard, Jr.

"And he said, 'Mr. Karp has taken a sudden turn for the worse. His aneurysm is about to burst. If we wait too long, we may not be able to get into his heart to repair anything.'

"He says, 'I still don't know whether we can even wait till tomorrow.'

"I said to him, 'You once told me, Dr. Cooley, that . . . you thought he needed a transplant.' I said, 'Do you still think that's the answer.'

"And Dr. Cooley said to me, 'Mrs. Karp, there is a donor heart that will be available and that we will use if there's that need for it.' . . .

"He says, 'Will you sign this now?' And I looked at my husband, and I guess he was in tears because I was shaking. And Dr. Cooley said to me, 'Don't worry about the shock element to your husband because I told him exactly what I told you now last night.'

"So then my husband said, 'Honey, he told me this last night.' He said, 'Go ahead. We'll sign the agreement.'

"And that's what happened. My husband signed it—. . . . Then he gave it to me to sign. And I says, 'I got to read it first.'

"And I started to go down it and I was glancing at the—it was all too bewildering and all of a sudden I came across come sort of a mechanical device, and I said, 'Dr. Cooley, what's this thing here that you have?' [sic]

"I said, 'what's mechanical device?'

"And he said, 'well you know, Mrs. Karp, when we operate on a heart we have to take the heart out of the body. So what we do is use what's commonly known as a heart lung machine and we attach the pipes from the machine to the different arteries that they sever to take the heart out. And this here keeps the flow of blood going through the body and the oxygen so that there will not be any damage to the body.'

"So he says the reason that he put that into the consent was because the one that they had in the operating room, I believe he said, worked for a matter of maybe two hours or something and this here one was a new model and it was proven in the laboratory, but he [sic] hasn't been used on a human being yet. But that this here should sustain him if he should die on the table. He says it would sustain him for at least thirty minutes in order to get the donor heart into my husband's body."

Mrs. Karp also testified that Dr. Cooley did not state that the device was any different from the heart-lung device ordinarily used for open heart surgery, stating that it was a "newer model" that had not been used before. She said Dr. Cooley told her there was a donor heart available in a nearby hospital, and that the mechanical device would be used for only 30 minutes while the donor was being prepared. Mrs. Karp said Mr. Reinhard came to the room early the next morning to verify the signatures. She also testified that Mr. Karp at the time of the April 3 meeting with Dr. Cooley was as normal as when he entered the hospital, that his physical appearance was the same and there was no appearance of pain; and that Mr. Karp was able to walk around the hospital even the morning of the operation. She said both Dr. Beazley and Dr. Cooley had said the wedge excision had a 70 per cent chance of success, and that Dr. Cooley had said that in his own personal experience he had less than a five per cent chance of failure and that it "seemed like it hardly ever failed."

DR. COOLEY'S TESTIMONY

Dr. Cooley testified that he first saw Mr. Karp on or about March 5, 1969 and that he recommended a heart transplant which Mr. Karp rejected, preferring "some alternative procedure." Dr. Cooley said tests then showed Mr. Karp had triple vessel disease where all three coronary arteries were occluded. He said electrocardiograms showed evidence of extensive scarring and damage and that his chest x-rays showed enormous cardiac enlargement. In addition, said Dr. Cooley, he had a pacemaker which was about to fail. Dr. Cooley said he estimated that Karp's chances of dying in the operating room as a result of the wedge procedure were approximately thirty per cent. He testified that as some three weeks passed, Mr. Karp grew increasingly impatient waiting for a donor's availability in the event the wedge excision failed. Dr. Cooley said it was the custom of medical doctors in the community to advise a patient of risks of surgery "within certain boundaries... but not every contingency can be explained to a layman about the threat and the risk of open heart surgery or the type of device which we are using, many of which are being used for the first time in a patient." About a week before the operation of April 4, 1969, Dr. Cooley said he began to discuss with Mr. Karp the possibility of another alternative "which I did not think was proper when he initially came to the hospital."

> "I told him we had no heart donor available, had no prospect of one... I told him that there was a possibility that we had a device which would sustain his life in the event that he would die on the operating table. We had a device which would sustain his life, hopefully, until we could get a suitable donor. I had told him that I did not know whether it would take a matter of hours or days, weeks, or maybe not at all, but it would sustain his life and give us another possibility of salvaging him through heart transplantation."

Dr. Cooley said he did not recall who was present when these discussions began. Dr. Cooley described his discussion of this device:

> "I told him that it was a heart pump similar to the one that we used in open-heart surgery; that it was a reciprocating-type pump with the membrane, in which the pumping element never became in contact with the bloodstream; that it was designed in such a manner that it would not damage the bloodstream or it would cause minimal damage to the bloodstream; that it would be placed in his body to take over the function of the dead heart and to propel blood throughout his body during this interim until we could have a heart transplant.... I told him this device had not been used in human beings; that it had been used in the laboratory; that we had been able to sustain the circulation in calves and that it had not been used in human beings. It had been used on the bench in what we call in vitro experiments, in vitro as opposed to in vivo. In vivo means using it in live or experimental animals. In vitro means using it in some type of testing device where you test the hydraulic factors concerned with the pump. I told him it had been tested in the laboratory, it had not been used in a human being, but I was confident that it would support his circulation.... I told him that we had been successful in keeping an animal alive for more than forty hours with the device, but that this was a calf. It was a 300-pound animal in which the demands on the pump were far greater than would be in the human body, and that I was reasonably confident that this device

would sustain his life until we could get a heart transplant. But no guarantees were made at all."

*   *   *

Asked by appellants' counsel whether he described it as a heart-lung pump similar to that used in other open heart surgeries, Dr. Cooley said, "I told him it was a pump. I didn't tell him it was a lung. I told him it was an artificial heart, that it was a pump which would replace temporarily the heart."

Dr. Cooley said he next discussed the operation with Mr. Karp the evening of April 2, 1969 at approximately 10:30 p.m. Dr. Cooley said he assured himself that Mr. Karp understood the gravity of his personal situation and the nature of the operation to be performed. Dr. Cooley said he does not recall whether Mrs. Karp was present during these conversations, and added that he was not present when Mrs. Karp signed the consent form and that he did not witness the signing of the consent form.

*   *   *

According to Dr. Hallman, the repair described above was done in the manner that cardiovascular surgeons normally go about performing this operation. However, Dr. Hallman said that due to the extensive scarring of the heart, there simply was not sufficient healthy heart muscle remaining to form an efficient pump to support Mr. Karp's life. Dr. Hallman, Dr. Keats and Dr. Cooley all testified that at this point, that is after the attempted resection, Mr. Karp was again faced with imminent death.

Dr. Cooley said that it took about 20 minutes to make the resection repair. He said that after the repair the clamp was taken off the ascending aorta to attempt to restart the myocardium. He stated that there was fibrillation and that he attempted an electrical countershock at least once. He stated that there was a sinus type or nodal rhythm at that point but that the rhythm contraction was too weak to support life due to the fact that there simply was too much scar tissue in the heart. Dr. Hallman testified that some thirty minutes elapsed between the end of the repair and the decision to remove the heart. Mr. Karp's heart was then removed and the mechanical device was inserted. Dr. Cooley said that the mechanical heart functioned very well and Mr. Karp responded to stimulation within 15 or 20 minutes after the incision was closed. His blood pressure was well sustained according to Dr. Cooley and he showed signs of cerebral activity. Dr. Keats said that Mr. Karp was amazingly well following the operation, that the records reflect that he was responding reasonably to commands within 20 minutes postoperatively. Dr. Keats testified that the endocracheal tube was removed about 1:20 a.m., and that he saw Mr. Karp some time the next morning at which time he was responsive and could communicate.

After the mechanical heart had been inserted, Dr. Cooley said he went to Mrs. Karp and told her that the wedge procedure had been unsuccessful; that he had proceeded with the use of the mechanical device and that they were going to try to get a donor. The transplant operation was performed on the morning of April 7, 1969, approximately 64 hours after the mechanical device had been implanted in Mr. Karp. He died the next day, April 8, 1969, some 32 hours after the transplant surgery.

*   *   *

THE PROSTHESIS

The record is virtually undisputed that the mechanical heart inserted in Haskell Karp was prepared by Dr. Liotta at the Baylor [College of Medicine] laboratories.

Ms. Susan Anderson, a lab technician at Baylor, described her work on this heart pursuant to Dr. Liotta's instructions. She testified that they had been making this type of pump in the lab for some six to eight months. She was not sure whether she actually made the same pump used in Haskell Karp but said it was the same type. She said several of the pumps of different sizes were made at Dr. Liotta's request one month before the Karp surgery. She said that Dr. Liotta had the composition of the mechanical device changed some three or four weeks before the Karp surgery, such as smoothing ragged inflow edges. She said that these pumps were the same type that were used in the Baylor experiments although the valves were tied more securely and they had a velour lining.

Asked by plaintiffs' counsel whether Dr. Michael DeBakey was developing a similar type pump, Dr. Cooley said Dr. DeBakey had used a univentricular pump that Dr. Cooley said carried only about 30 per cent of the circulation. Dr. Cooley said that he and Dr. Liotta had designed the biventricular pump used in Mr. Karp at St. Luke's. Dr. Cooley said that the mechanical device was tested in seven calves in the Baylor labs as well as in vitro [lab] experiments. Dr. Cooley said that he could not testify as to some of the details of these last three calf experiments because his notes were confiscated by Dr. DeBakey, but said that the results of all three experiments were encouraging. He said the third calf experiment was the most gratifying of all because "it demonstrated conclusively that the device was efficient and deserved application in humans." Dr. Cooley said he did not recall what either the first or second calf died from, how long they lived, whether there was urinary output, or whether the calves were able to eat or stand up. He said he recalled there was some urine output in the third calf, although it was low.

We first affirm the district court's directed verdict for defendants on the issues of informed consent and fraud.

INFORMED CONSENT

Suits charging failure by a physician adequately to disclose the risks and alternatives of proposed treatment are not innovations in American law. They date back a good half-century, and in the last decade have increased in number. The courts and commentators have not been in agreement on the substantive requirements or the nature of the proof required, but the Texas requirements are reasonably well-settled and stringent.

The root premise jurisprudentially is that "[e]very human being of adult years and sound mind has a right to determine what shall be done with his own body. . . ." Physicians and surgeons have a duty to make a reasonable disclosure to a patient of risks that are incident to medical diagnosis and treatment. True consent to what happens to one's self is the informed exercise of a choice, and that entails an opportunity to evaluate knowledgeably the options available and the risks attendant upon each. From these general principles, however, the focus in each individual case must necessarily relate back to what the physician said or failed to say and what the law requires him to say.[14]

---

14. The doctrinal label "informed consent" has been criticized for its emphasis on the patient's understanding and consent rather than the central issue, the physician's duty to inform the patient of the risks and consequences involved in the contemplated procedure. This has been said to result from the doctrine's original development from a battery theory rather than the more currently accepted theory of negligence.

The Texas standard against which a physician's disclosure or lack of disclosure is tested is a medical one which must be proved by expert medical evidence of what a reasonable practitioner of the same school of practice and the same or similar locality would have advised a patient under similar circumstances. Quoting from and with approval of Aiken v. Clary, the Texas Supreme Court said in *Wilson*:

> "The question to be determined by the jury is whether the defendant doctor in that particular situation failed to adhere to a standard of reasonable care. These are not matters of common knowledge or within the experience of laymen. Expert medical evidence thereon is just as necessary as is such testimony on the correctness of the handling in cases involving surgery or treatment. . . . 'Without the aid of expert medical testimony . . . a jury could not, without resorting to conjecture and surmise or by setting up an arbitrary standard of their own, determine that defendants failed to exercise their skill and use the care exercised by the ordinarily skillful, careful and prudent physician acting under the same or similar circumstances.' . . . The question is not what, regarding the risks involved, the juror would relate to the patient under the same or similar circumstances, or even what a reasonable man would relate, but what a reasonable *medical practitioner* would do. Such practitioner would consider the state of patient's health, the condition of his heart and nervous system, his mental state, and would take into account, among other things, whether the risks involved were remote possibilities or something which occurred with some sort of frequency or regularity. This determination involves medical judgment as to whether disclosure of possible risks may have such an adverse effect on the patient as to jeopardize success of the proposed therapy, no matter how expertly performed."

As we understand appellants' contention, it is that Mr. Karp was not told about the number of animals tested or the results of those tests; that he was not told there was a chance of permanent injury to his body by the mechanical heart, that complete renal shutdown could result from the use of the prosthesis, that the device was "completely experimental"; and that Dr. Cooley failed to tell Mr. Karp that Dr. Beazley had said Mr. Karp was not a suitable candidate for surgery. Nine physicians testified, but none suggested a standard of disclosure required by Texas law under these circumstances. Appellants argue Dr. Cooley himself set the standard requiring the disclosure of Dr. Beazley's evaluation. Texas law does permit the defendant doctor to establish the standard of disclosure, but Dr. Cooley's testimony says no more than that what is a reasonable medical practice is a question of medical judgment.

* * *

In the instant case it is difficult to determine exactly what injury appellants complain of as resulting from a lack of informed consent. Although not particularly well-developed in Texas cases, other jurisdictions have held (1) that an unrevealed risk that should have been made known must materialize; (2) the unrevealed risk must be harmful to the patient; and (3) causality exists only when disclosure of significant risks incidental to treatment would have resulted in the patient's decision against it.

The only expert testimony was that Mr. Karp was near death prior to the wedge excision operation. Mrs. Karp says she does not complain of the informed consent for the wedge excision. The only expert testimony was that death was also imminent after the wedge excision. There is no expert evidence that says as a reasonable medical probability the mechanical heart caused Karp's death. The expert testimony at best links the mechanical heart as only one of the "possible" but less likely causes of the secondary cause of death, renal failure.

Finally, there is no proof that Mr. Karp would *not* have consented to the operative procedures had the alleged undisclosed material risks been disclosed.

Appellants failed to produce substantial evidence establishing a medical standard as to what disclosures should have been made to Mr. Karp, any violation of that standard, or causation. Thus, the trial court properly directed a verdict for defendants on the informed consent question.

* * *

EXPERIMENTATION

Appellants contend that the trial court erred in directing a verdict on the issue of experimentation. They acknowledge that no Texas case has expressly dealt with a cause of action based on experimentation, but assert that our court's decision in Bender v. Dingwerth suggests that the decision as to what is actionable experimentation should be left to a jury. We do not agree.

A Texas court bound in traditional malpractice actions to expert medical testimony to determine how a reasonably careful and prudent physician would have acted under the same or similar circumstances, would not likely vary that evidentiary requirement for an experimentation charge. This conclusion is also suggested by the few reported cases where experimentation has been recognized as a separate basis of liability. The record contains no evidence that Mr. Karp's treatment was other than therapeutic and we agree that in this context an action for experimentation must be measured by traditional malpractice evidentiary standards. Whether there was informed consent is necessarily linked to the charge of experimentation, and Mr. Karp's consent was expressly to all three stages of the operation actually performed—each an alternative in the event of a preceding failure. As previously discussed, appellants have not shown an absence of Mr. Karp's informed consent. Causation and proximate cause are also requisite to an actionable claim of experimentation. Even if Dr. DeBakey's testimony, as discussed subsequently, were admitted and did establish a standard and a departure from that standard in using this prosthetic device, substantial evidence on causation and proximate cause simply is not reflected in the record. That alone would warrant the directed verdict on this issue.

Mink v. University of Chicago

460 F. Supp. 713 (1978)

GRADY, District Judge.

Plaintiffs have brought this action on behalf of themselves and some 1,000 women who were given diethylstilbestrol ("DES") as part of a medical experiment conducted by the defendants, University of Chicago and Eli Lilly & Company, between September 29, 1950, and November 20, 1952. The drug was administered to the plaintiffs during their prenatal care at the University's Lying-In Hospital as part of a double blind study to determine the value of DES in preventing miscarriages. The women were not told they were part of an experiment, nor were they told that the pills administered to them were DES. Plaintiffs claim that as a result of their taking DES, their daughters have developed abnormal cervical cellular formations and are exposed to an increased risk of vaginal or cervical cancer. Plaintiffs also allege that they and their sons have suffered reproductive tract and other abnormalities and have incurred an increased risk of cancer.

The complaint further alleges that the relationship between DES and cancer was known to the medical community as early as 1971, but that the defendants made no effort to notify the plaintiffs of their participation in the DES experiment until late 1975 or 1976 when the University sent letters to the women in the experiment informing them of the possible relationship between the use of DES in pregnant women and abnormal conditions in the genital tracts of their offspring. The letter asked for information to enable the University to contact the sons and daughters of the plaintiffs for medical examination.

The complaint seeks recovery on three causes of action. The first alleges that the defendants committed a series of batteries on the plaintiffs by conducting a medical experiment on them without their knowledge or consent. The administration of DES to the plaintiffs without their consent is alleged to be an "offensive invasion of their persons" which has caused them "severe mental anxiety and emotional distress due to the increased risk to their children of contracting cancer and other abnormalities." The second court is grounded in products liability and seeks to recover damages from defendant Lily premised on its manufacture of DES as a defective and unreasonably dangerous drug. Finally, the plaintiffs allege that the defendants breached their duty to notify plaintiffs that they had been given DES while pregnant and that children born from that pregnancy should consult a medical specialist. Throughout the complaint plaintiffs claim the defendants intentionally concealed the fact of the experiment and information concerning the relationship between DES and cancer from the plaintiffs.

Both defendants have moved to dismiss the complaint for failure to state a claim. We will deny the motions as to the first cause of action, and grant the motions as to the second and third causes of action.

* * *

Charitable Immunity

The University of Chicago claims it is immune under the doctrine of charitable immunity from any actionable claims stated by plaintiffs. We agree with the plaintiffs that it would be premature to decide the question of charitable immunity at this point. Even if the doctrine were to be applied to this case, it would not afford the hospital immunity from suit. The protection goes only to the funds available for recovery if liability is found.

The University argues that the law of charitable immunity as it existed in the 1950's when the experiment was conducted is the proper doctrine to apply to their actions. This argument is premised on a passage in *Darling v. Charleston Hospital*, the case which abolished the doctrine of charitable immunity in Illinois. The court in *Darling* stated that the decision was not to be applied retrospectively because charitable corporations would have relied on prior law as established in *Moore v. Moyle*, in deciding the extent of their insurance coverage.

Plaintiffs take the position that this case is strictly post-*Darling* and thus the retrospective limitation does not apply. We note at this time, without deciding the question, that the plaintiffs' position is not persuasive. Since the operative facts occurred in the 1950's, this case cannot be construed as strictly post-*Darling*. There-fore, it is possible, although we do not decide the question, that execution against the assets of the University would be limited by *Moore v. Moyle*, to the insurance proceeds.

The parties have not fully explored the question, and as previously noted it is not ripe for resolution at this time. The University does not deny that it has insurance coverage and therefore we will assume that in the event there is a judgment for plaintiffs, there will be insurance proceeds to satisfy it. Accordingly, the University's motion to dismiss on the basis of charitable immunity is denied.

Conclusion

The motions to dismiss of defendants University of Chicago and Eli Lilly & Co. are denied as to the plaintiffs' first cause of action. The first count states a claim for relief for battery and is not barred by the statute of limitations or the doctrine of charitable immunity. The defendants' motions to dismiss the second and third counts for failure to state a claim are granted. Plaintiffs are given until April 7, 1978, to amend the second and third counts of their complaint.

* * *

ON MOTION TO DISMISS AMENDED COMPLAINT

Plaintiffs have brought this diversity action on behalf of themselves and some 1,000 women who were given diethylstilbestrol ("DES") as part of a medical experiment conducted by the defendants, University of Chicago and Eli Lilly & Company, between September 29, 1950, and November 20, 1952. The drug was administered to plaintiffs during their prenatal care at the University's Lying-In Hospital as part of a double blind study to determine the values of DES in preventing miscarriages. Plaintiffs' complaint sought recovery on three causes of action. The first alleged that defendants committed a series of batteries by conducting a medical experiment on plaintiffs without their knowledge or consent. The second count was grounded in products liability and sought to recover damages from defendant Lily premised on its manu-facture of DES as a defective and unreasonably dangerous drug. Finally, plaintiffs alleged that defendants breached their duty to notify plaintiffs they they had been given DES while pregnant and that children born from that pregnancy should consult a medical specialist.

Defendants moved to dismiss the complaint. We denied their motion as to Count I, holding plaintiffs had stated a cause of action for battery. We granted the motion as to Counts II and III because of plaintiffs' failure to alleged physical injury to themselves caused by defendants' actions. Plaintiffs filed an amended complaint. They allege that many class members have been physically injured as a result of the DES experiment, as many have developed breast or other endocrine-related cancer as a result of their ingestion of DES. They allege that defendants' failure to notify members of the plaintiff class has caused the death of some members. Defendants again move to dismiss Count II of the complaint on the grounds plaintiffs have not alleged injury to themselves. In their memorandum in opposition to the motion to dismiss, plaintiffs ask us to reconsider our ruling that the named plaintiffs must allege physical injury to themselves, and ask that we allow the named plaintiffs to recover damages on behalf of the class members who have suffered the physical injuries alleged.

Upon reconsideration, we must abide by our original decision. The Supreme Court has recently addressed the precise issue before us. In *Simon v. Eastern Ky. Welfare Rights Org.*, the Court noted: "The individual respondents sought to maintain this suit as a class action on behalf of all persons similarly situated. That a suit may be a class action, however, adds nothing to the question of standing, for even named plaintiffs who represent a class 'must allege and show that they personally have been injured, not that injury has been suffered by other unidentified members of the class to which they belong and which they purport to represent.' " Thus, since plaintiffs have not alleged physical injury to themselves, we grant defendants' motion to dismiss Court II of the amended complaint.

* * *

Defendants' motions to dismiss Counts II and III of the amended complaint are granted.

The court dismissed the failure to notify and strict liability claims of the women, but it did find a battery in the "unconsented-to" pill taking, despite the apparent consent. The decision was affirmed by the Seventh Circuit, 727 F.2d 1112 (7th Cir. 1984). *Whitlock*, a more modern research issue, concerns the issue of a sophisticated and experienced research subject, informed consent, and the assumption of risk.

Whitlock v. Duke University
829 F.2d 1340 (4th Cir. 1987)

Leonard T. Whitlock, his former wife, Sandra H. Whitlock, and son, David K. Whitlock appeal the district court's granting of summary judgment in favor of the defendants, Duke University and Dr. Peter B. Bennett. Because we find no error in the action taken by the district court, we affirm.

Leonard Whitlock (Whitlock) brought this diversity action, seeking compensation for injuries he claims he suffered while participating in a simulated deep dive experiment conducted by the F.G. Hall Laboratory at Duke University. Peter B. Bennett, a Ph.D., is the director of that laboratory at Duke University. Mrs. Whitlock and their son David sued for loss of companionship resulting from Whitlock's injuries.

Whitlock is an experienced diver, with a college degree in oceanographic technology. He has worked in his field for many years and has participated in several diving programs. One such diving program was the Atlantis Series conducted by the F.G. Hall Laboratory at Duke University. The Atlantis program was a series of simulated deep dives to research high pressure nervous syndrome. These dives did not take place in water but were simulated through a hyper-baric chamber pressurized with a mixture of gases. Whitlock participated in the first of these dives, known as Atlantis I. Atlantis I lasted 18 days and reached a simulated depth of 1500 feet. Whitlock suffered no adverse effects from participation in Atlantis I. He was out of the country when the Atlantis II experiment was conducted. When he knew he would be returning to the

United States, Whitlock wrote to Dr. Bennett at Duke about the possibility of his inclusion in the Atlantis III experiment.

After being selected for the Atlantis III dive, Whitlock underwent pre-dive testing and training. Whitlock signed an informed consent form. That form listed as potential risks from compression such things as hearing loss, inflammation of the ears and sinusitis, difficulty getting the air pressure in the ears, sinuses, teeth, lungs and intestines to equal the increasing pressure outside the body, and lung collapse. The form stated that risks associated with decompression included decompression sickness which could cause death or disability, and the risks associated with exposure to simulated altitudes could cause the diver to become unconscious and seriously injured. It stated that equipment failure could lead to serious injury or death. Further, the form stated that because these kinds of experiments had not been performed in the past, there could exist other risks unknown at that time. The form advised that compensation would be paid only when the injury was caused by negligence.

The Atlantis III dive lasted for 43 days and reached a simulated depth of 2250 feet, a new world record. Following completion of the Atlantis III dive, Whitlock began to experience physical problems. He asserts that he suffered organic brain damage as a result of the dive.

Whitlock then brought this suit against Duke University and Dr. Bennett, head of the laboratory conducting the Atlantis dives, alleging they were liable for fraud, conspiracy to commit fraud, breach of their fiduciary duty, intentional infliction of emotional distress, negligent failure to warn of the risk of organic brain damage, violation of the federal regulation, 45 C.F.R. § 46.116, regulating human experimentation, strict liability for ultra-hazardous activity and strict liability for human experimentation. The district court thoroughly considered each of these claims in its opinion and decided in favor of the defendants on each count. Whitlock appeals, alleging numerous errors committed by the district court. His principal claim on appeal is that the district court erred in its conclusion that the defendants did not either fraudulently or negligently misrepresent or conceal from him the risk of organic brain damage.

In order to prove fraud under North Carolina law, Whitlock must show: (1) that the defendants made a representation of a material fact or concealed a material fact, (2) that such representation was false, (3) that the defendants knew that such representation was false or that the defendants made such a representation recklessly without any knowledge of its truthfulness, (4) that such representation was made with the intention that the plaintiff rely upon it, (5) that the plaintiff reasonably relied upon the false representation, and (6) that the plaintiff was injured.

A review of the record convinces us, as the district court was convinced, that Whitlock's claim for fraud must fail because he was a highly educated and quite sophisticated diver and admittedly knew that some form of permanent brain damage could result from this type of dive. Thus, Whitlock reasonably could not have relied upon any such fact which might have been represented or concealed. Since failure to prove an essential element of fraud is fatal, Whitlock's claim must fail under state law.

We also agree with the district court's finding that Dr. Bennett had no knowledge of a reasonably foreseeable risk of permanent organic brain damage in the Atlantis III dive and therefore could not have concealed such a fact from Whitlock, either fraudulently or negligently. In his deposition, Dr. Bennett stated that he had been involved with deep dive research since the 1960's and had seen no evidence of organic brain damage from such dives. He further stated that the possibility of organic brain damage was not contained in the informed consent form for Atlantis III because it was not a normal condition for experimental deep diving. Before the Atlantis III dive, Dr. Bennett was not aware of any information indicating that some divers suffered post-dive temporary or permanent neurological defects.

Whitlock sought to contradict Dr. Bennett's testimony, and thus avoid summary judgment in favor of the defendants, by relying upon part of his own deposition where he stated that medical studies conducted prior to Atlantis III revealed symptoms similar to those he suffered. Whitlock never submitted those studies or any similar medical evidence to the district court for consideration prior to the award of summary judgment in favor of the defendants. We agree with the district court that Whitlock's statement standing alone is insufficient to create a genuine issue of material fact as to fraudulent concealment by Dr. Bennett. We reject Whitlock's claim that we should consider the contents of depositions of his experts taken prior to the granting of summary judgment below but not submitted to the district court before summary judgment was entered. Whitlock merely referred to these experts' opinions in his own answers to interrogations and in his brief in opposition of defendants' motion for summary judgment. The district court did not err in declining to rely upon Whitlock's statements of what these depositions contained when the depositions themselves were not submitted to the district court. We also decline to consider these depositions on appeal because they properly were not considered by the district court.

We find no merit to Whitlock's claim that the defendants fraudulently concealed his post-dive injuries. Dr. Bennett stated in his deposition that he found no evidence of Whitlock's suffering from organic brain disease. Again, Whitlock relied upon the depositions of Drs. Youngblood and Ginsberg that he was in fact suffering from organic brain damage as a result of the dive. These are depositions that were never given to the district court.

We have reviewed Whitlock's other claims of error and find that the district court more than adequately discussed these claims. We find no reversible error in those raised on appeal. Because Whitlock's claims for relief fail on the merits, his former wife's and son's claims for loss of consortium must also fail.

The Law and Biotechnology

Since the 1950s, when the DES research was undertaken, extraordinary advances in molecular biology and the commercialization of academic science have predictably resulted in bizarre legal scenarios and, equally predictably, in social anti-research organizing and litigation. The *Chakrabarty* case, affording patent protection to live, human-made microorganisms, cleared the underbrush and accelerated the rush to commercialize biotechnology, including many academic laboratories.

Diamond v. Chakrabarty
447 U.S. 303 (1980)

Mr. Chief Justice BURGER delivered the opinion of the Court.

We granted certiorari to determine whether a live, human-made micro-organism is patentable subject matter under 35 U.S.C. § 101.

I

In 1972, respondent Chakrabarty, a microbiologist, filed a patent application, assigned to the General Electric Co. The application asserted 36 claims related to Chakrabarty's invention of "a bacterium from the genus *Pseudomonas* containing therein at least two stable energy-generating plasmids, each of said plasmids providing a separate hydrocarbon degradative pathway." This human-made, genetically engineered bacterium is capable of breaking down multiple components of crude oil. Because of this property, which is possessed by no naturally occurring bacteria, Chakrabarty's invention is believed to have significant value for the treatment of oil spills.

Chakrabarty's patent claims were of three types: first, process claims for the method of producing the bacteria; second, claims for an inoculum comprised of a carrier material floating on water, such as straw, and the new bacteria; and third, claims to the bacteria themselves. The patent examiner allowed the claims falling into the first two categories, but rejected claims for the bacteria. His decision rested on two grounds: (1) that micro-organisms are "products of nature," and (2) that as living things they are not patentable subject matter under 35 U.S.C. § 101.

Chakrabarty appealed the rejection of these claims to the Patent Office Board of Appeals, and the Board affirmed the Examiner on the second ground. Relying on the legislative history of the 1930 Plant Patent Act, in which Congress extended patent protection to certain asexually reproduced plants, the Board concluded that § 101 was not intended to cover living things such as these laboratory created micro-organisms.

The Court of Customs and Patent Appeals, by a divided vote, reversed on the authority of its prior decision in *In re Bergy*, which held that "the fact that micro-organisms . . . are alive . . . [is] without legal significance" for purposes of the patent law. Subsequently, we granted the Acting Commissioner of Patents and Trademarks' petition for certiorari in *Bergy*, vacated the judgment, and remanded the case "for further consideration in light of *Parker v. Flook*." The Court of Customs and Patent Appeals then vacated its judgment in *Chakrabarty* and consolidated the case with *Bergy* for reconsideration. After re-examining both cases in the light of our holding in *Flook*, that court, with one dissent, reaffirmed its earlier judgments.

The Commissioner of Patents and Trademarks again sought certiorari, and we granted the writ as to both *Bergy* and *Chakrabarty*. Since then, *Bergy* has been dismissed as moot, leaving only *Chakrabarty* for decision.

II

The Constitution grants Congress broad power to legislate to "promote the Progress of Science and useful Arts, by securing for limited Times to Authors and Inventors the exclusive Right to their respective Writings and Discoveries." Art. I, § 8, cl. 8. The patent laws promote this progress by offering inventors exclusive rights for a limited period as an incentive for their inventiveness and research efforts. The authority of Congress is exercised in the hope that "[t]he productive effort thereby fostered will have a positive effect on society through the introduction of new products and processes of manufacture into the economy, and the emanations by way of increased employment and better lives for our citizens."

The question before us in this case is a narrow one of statutory interpretation requiring us to construe 35 U.S.C. § 101, which provides:

"Whoever invents or discovers any new and useful process, machine, manufacture, or composition of matter, or any new and useful improvement thereof,
may obtain a patent therefor, subject to the conditions and requirements of this
title."

Specifically, we must determine whether respondent's micro-organism constitutes a
"manufacture" or "composition of matter" within the meaning of the statute.

III

In cases of statutory construction we begin, of course, with the language of the
statute. And "unless otherwise defined, words will be interpreted as taking their
ordinary, contemporary common meaning." We have also cautioned that courts
"should not read into the patent laws limitations and conditions which the legislature
has not expressed."

Guided by these canons of construction, this Court has read the term "manufacture"
in § 101 in accordance with its dictionary definition to mean "the production of
articles for use from raw or prepared materials by giving to these materials new forms,
qualities, properties, or combinations, whether by hand-labor or by machinery."
Similarly, "composition of matter" has been construed consistent with its common
usage to include "all compositions of two or more substances and . . . all composite
articles, whether they be the results of chemical union, or of mechanical mixture, or
whether they be gases, fluids, powders or solids." In choosing such expansive terms
as "manufacture" and "composition of matter," modified by the comprehensive "any,"
Congress plainly contemplated that the patent laws would be given wide scope.

The relevant legislative history also supports a broad construction. The Patent Act
of 1793, authored by Thomas Jefferson, defined statutory subject matter as "any new
and useful art, machine, manufacture, or composition of matter, or any new or useful
improvement [thereof]." The Act embodied Jefferson's philosophy that "ingenuity
should receive a liberal encouragement." Subsequent patent statutes in 1836, 1870,
and 1874 employed this same broad language. In 1952, when the patent laws were
recodified, Congress replaced the word "art" with "process," but otherwise left
Jefferson's language intact. The Committee Reports accompanying the 1952 Act
inform us that Congress intended statutory subject matter to "include anything under
the sun that is made by man."

This is not to suggest that § 101 has no limits or that it embraces every discovery.
The laws of nature, physical phenomena, and abstract ideas have been held not
patentable. Thus, a new mineral discovered in the earth or a new plant found in the
wild is not patentable subject matter. Likewise, Einstein could not patent his celebrated
law that $E = mc^2$; nor could Newton have patented the law of gravity. Such discoveries
are "manifestations of . . . nature, free to all men and reserved exclusively to none."

Judged in this light, respondent's micro-organism plainly qualifies as patentable
subject matter. His claim is not to a hitherto unknown natural phenomenon, but to
a nonnaturally occurring manufacture or composition of matter—a product of human
ingenuity "having a distinctive name, character [and] use." The point is underscored
dramatically by comparison of the invention here with that in *Funk*. There, the
patentee had discovered that there existed in nature certain species of root-nodule
bacteria which did not exert a mutually inhibitive effect on each other. He used that
discovery to produce a mixed culture capable of inoculating the seeds of leguminous

plants. Concluding that the patentee had discovered "only some of the handiwork of nature," the Court ruled the product nonpatentable:

> "Each of the species of root-nodule bacteria contained in the package infects the same group of leguminous plants which it always infected. No species acquires a different use. The combination of species produces no new bacteria, no change in the six species of bacteria, and no enlargement of the range of their utility. Each species has the same effect it always had. The bacteria perform in their natural way. Their use in combination does not improve in any way their natural functioning. They serve the ends nature originally provided and act quite independently of any effort of the patentee."

Here, by contrast, the patentee has produced a new bacterium with markedly different characteristics from any found in nature and one having the potential for significant utility. His discovery is not nature's handiwork, but his own; accordingly it is patentable subject matter under § 101.

* * *

It is, of course, correct that Congress, not the courts, must define the limits of patentability; but it is equally true that once Congress has spoken it is "the province and duty of the judicial department to say what the law is." Congress has performed its constitutional role in defining patentable subject matter in § 101; we perform ours in construing the language Congress has employed. In so doing, our obligation is to take statutes as we find them, guided, if ambiguity appears, by the legislative history and statutory purpose. Here, we perceive no ambiguity. The subject-matter provisions of the patent law have been cast in broad terms to fulfill the constitutional and statutory goal of promoting "the Progress of Science and the useful Arts" with all that means for the social and economic benefits envisioned by Jefferson. Broad general language is not necessarily ambiguous when congressional objectives require broad terms.

Nothing in *Flook* is to the contrary. That case applied our prior precedents to determine that a "claim for an improved method of calculation, even when tied to a specific end use, is unpatentable subject matter under § 101." The Court carefully scrutinized the claim at issue to determine whether it was precluded from patent protection under "the principles underlying the prohibition against patents for 'ideas' or phenomena of nature." We have done that here. *Flook* did not announce a new principle that inventions in areas not contemplated by Congress when the patent laws were enacted are unpatentable *per se*.

To read that concept into *Flook* would frustrate the purposes of the patent law. This Court frequently has observed that a statute is not to be confined to the "particular application[s] ... contemplated by the legislators." This is especially true in the field of patent law. A rule that unanticipated inventions are without protection would conflict with the core concept of the patent law that anticipation undermines patentability. Mr. Justice Douglas reminded that the inventions most benefiting mankind are those that "push back the frontiers of chemistry, physics, and the like." Congress employed broad general language in drafting § 101 precisely because such inventions are often unforeseeable.

To buttress his argument, the petitioner, with the support of *amicus*, points to grave risks that may be generated by research endeavors such as respondent's. The briefs present a gruesome parade of horribles. Scientists, among them Nobel laureates, are quoted suggesting that genetic research may pose a serious threat to the human race, or, at the very least, that the dangers are far too substantial to permit such research to proceed apace at this time. We are told that genetic research and related technological developments may spread pollution and disease, that it may result in a loss of genetic diversity, and that its practice may tend to depreciate the value of human life. These arguments are forcefully, even passionately, presented; they remind us that, at times, human ingenuity seems unable to control fully the forces it creates— that with Hamlet, it is sometimes better "to bear those ills we have than fly to others that we know not of."

It is argued that this Court should weigh these potential hazards in considering whether respondent's invention is patentable subject matter under § 101. We disagree. The grant or denial of patents on micro-organisms is not likely to put an end to genetic research or to its attendant risks. The large amount of research that has already occurred when no researcher had sure knowledge that patent protection would be available suggests that legislative or judicial fiat as to patentability will not deter the scientific mind from probing into the unknown any more than Canute could command the tides. Whether respondent's claims are patentable may determine whether research efforts are accelerated by the hope of reward or slowed by want of incentives, but that is all.

What is more important is that we are without competence to entertain these arguments—either to brush them aside as fantasies generated by fear of the unknown, or to act on them. The choice we are urged to make is a matter of high policy for resolution within the legislative process after the kind of investigation, examination, and study that legislative bodies can provide and courts cannot. That process involves the balancing of competing values and interests, which in our democratic system is the business of elected representatives. Whatever their validity, the contentions now pressed on us should be addressed to the political branches of the Government, the Congress and the Executive, and not to the courts.

We have emphasized in the recent past that "[o]ur individual appraisal of the wisdom or unwisdom of a particular [legislative] course . . . is to be put aside in the process of interpreting a statute." Our task, rather, is the narrow one of determining what Congress meant by the words it used in the statute; once that is done our powers are exhausted. Congress is free to amend § 101 so as to exclude from patent protection organisms produced by genetic engineering. Or it may choose to craft a statute specifically designed for such living things. But, until Congress takes such action, this Court must construe the language of § 101 as it is. The language of that section fairly embraces respondent's invention.

Accordingly, the judgment of the Court of Customs and Patent Appeals is

Affirmed.

————————

The *Moore* and *Hagiwara* cases in tissue research best illustrate the nexus among patient rights, researcher ethics, and commercial interests. These two examples are excerpted from N. Benjamin, "John Moore and the Commercialization of Biotechnology," IHELG Monograph 87–6 (Houston: IHELG, 1987), pp. 4–7. [Citations omitted.]

Diagnosed in September, 1976 as having a rare form of cancer known as "hairy-cell" leukemia, John Moore sought a second opinion the following month from specialist Dr. David Golde, head of the Hematology-Oncology Division of UCLA

Medical Center. Golde confirmed the diagnosis and recommended removal of the cancerous spleen, the standard treatment for the disease, as essential for Moore's survival. After signing a routine surgical consent form, Moore underwent a splenectomy on October 20, 1976. Over the course of the next seven years, he returned periodically for checkups, at each of which, he alleges, large quantities of blood were withdrawn from his body. When Moore's personal finances were depleted, Golde, presumably from NIH grant money, paid Moore's travel expenses.

On an April 11, 1983 visit, Moore alleges that the hospital for the first time requested that he sign a consent form authorizing research, apparently related to his leukemia virus, on his blood before it was withdrawn; he complied. On his next visit in September, 1983, he was presented with a similar form requesting consent for research. Moore claims that he asked if his blood had any commercial value but was told it did not and that the consent form was a procedural formality of the hospital. Moore nevertheless indicated on the form this time that he would not grant the university research rights to his body products. After he left, the hospital personnel contacted him several times in an effort to convince him to change his form. Suspicious, Moore sought legal counsel from a firm specializing in medical litigation.

Moore also asserts that he assumed that the research authorized by his signed consent form was for his personal medical benefit, and perhaps that of humanity in general, but not for the defendants' personal gain from exploitation of his cells. Although the defendants filed only general demurrers to all of Moore's complaints in state district court, this past summer in a letter to the editor of *Genetic Engineering News*, Golde explained his perception of the events, involving no bodily harm to, but only benefit for, Moore:

> The research we do not only helps society, but was also of direct benefit to Mr. Moore. From the Mo cell line we were able to diagnose his type of leukemia and also to isolate, for the first time, a virus referred to as HTLV-II. We informed Mr. Moore of the presence of the virus and appropriate follow-up research studies were done by us and by scientists at the National Institutes of Health to determine the nature of this virus and how it might affect him and his family.

The epidemiological study referred to included studies on his blood serum, which carried antibodies to the virus.

Moore contends that, through his attorneys' efforts, he learned for the first time that Golde and his co-inventor Shirley Quan had developed and patented the "Mo-Cell Line" (derived from "Moore"), U.S. Patent No. 4,438,032, from the apparently unique cells of his removed spleen without his knowledge or consent. The patent application was filed on January 30, 1981, and the patent, entitled "Unique T-Lymphocite Line and Products Derived Therefrom," was issued on March 20, 1984, with the inventors partially assigning rights to the Regents of the University of California, presumably in accordance with the institution's regulations. For most of this period, Golde continued to act as Moore's physician but, according to Moore, Golde never revealed the existence of the cell line or of the patent. Moore filed suit on September 11, 1984.

Moore asserts that, during the legal process of discovery, his attorney uncovered evidence that Golde had made a formal agreement for financial gain with a biogenetics company, Genentech, for commercial development of biologically valuable substances produced by the cell line. In addition, Moore claims that the University and Genetics

Institute in 1981 entered into a collaborative agreement; the University would grant an exclusive license to the cell line in return for $500,000.00 and other benefits for Golde and UCLA. Additionally, Sandoz, Inc., a pharmaceutical company, was to market world-wide products of the cell line. One reporter claimed that Genetics Institute funded $330,000.00 of research in Golde's laboratory during the period when it was attempting to acquire the license. Simultaneously, Golde contracted with Genetics Institute for only $750.00 to receive approximately two million dollars' worth of stock options, which Moore alleges that he exercised, in return for exclusive use of the cell line. Furthermore, the University of California's policy permits Golde and Quan to receive fifty per cent of the royalties collected from the licensing.

Moore insists that Golde never informed him of the research on or value of his "blood and bodily substances" and he requests, *inter alia*, restitution for the value of his contribution to the patent and for the commercial use of his cells.

Given the facts of this case, under existing law Moore has no established legal claim to property rights in his excised spleen, in the patent, or in commercial profits made from exclusive licensing agreements under the patent. In light of developing technology, of novel changes in the use and exploitation of human tissue that was once justifiably viewed as waste, but that has suddenly assumed a potentially great value, and of the policies underlying the doctrine of informed consent, however, this case of first impression does raise valid questions as to whether the law should be reexamined and modified to reach and equitably respond to the concerns raised by this suit. The case is pending as of Spring 1988.

Reprinted by permission.

In another matter, one that never resulted in a lawsuit, a Japanese researcher, Hideaki Hagiwara, in collaboration with another University of California researcher, UC-San Diego Professor Ivor Royston, combined cancerous lymphocytes taken from Hagiwara's mother with a UCSD-patented cell line. The resulting hybridoma had great commercial promise for eventual medical treatment of cancer patients. Unbeknownst to Royston, Hagiwara treated his mother with the new hybridoma, took tissue samples to Japan (where his father was the owner of a major research and pharmaceutical company), applied for a Japanese patent, and submitted papers on the discovery to professional journals in his name solely. When challenged, he claimed that he alone had secured the cells, with permission from his dying mother, and that this "permission" constituted a property right. The university asserted its own property interests, based upon its ownership of the patented cell line with which the hybridoma was produced. The result was less Dickensian than the fact pattern or plot, as they reached an agreement where UC retained the patent rights, but granted exclusive licensing rights to the Hagiwara company in exchange for royalties. See "Cell Lines from Human Patients: Who Owns Them?" *Clinical Research*, 33 (October 1985), 442.

In 1987, the Congressional Office of Technology Assessment determined, "No area of existing law definitely sets forth the rights held by an individual who provides [his or her own] tissues and cells to an academic or commercial researcher." *New Developments in Biotechnology: Ownership of Human Tissues and Cells* (GPO, 1987). For a review of these complex issues in other countries, see Beier et al., *BioTechnology and Patent Protection: An International Review* (OECD, 1985); *Foreign Sponsorship of U.S. University Research* (GPO, 1988). Harvard was awarded a patent in 1988 on the GP120 protein, a factor in basic research and testing on AIDS viruses. P. Hilts,

"Harvard Given Patent for AIDS-Test Protein," *Washington Post*, 18 February 1988, p. A14.

Inevitably, ethical considerations have been outstripped by the quickening pace of biotechnology research. The Vatican published a document in 1987, urging restrictions on *in vitro* fertilization, reproductive technology, and research on human genes, embryos, and fetuses. A growing cadre of legal/medical writers has also generated a torrent of scholarship and commentary on these issues, with the vast majority urging strict guidelines and responsible peer review for research on human subjects. See Leskovac and Delgado, "Protecting Autonomy and Personhood in Human Subjects Research," *Southern Illinois University Law Journal*, 11 (1987), 1147–58.

However, not all ethical dilemmas are posed by new technologies. In March, 1988 the Environmental Protection Agency was faced with a choice of whether or not to use data gathered from WW II Nazi experiments on the effects of toxic gas upon prisoners. EPA officials argued that despite the ethical problems posed and questionable research value, better research data would be impossible to gather for measuring toxic reactions. See *Chronicle of Higher Education*, 30 March 1988, p. A4; *Hyman v. Jewish Chronic Disease Hospital*, 258 N.Y.S. 2d 397 (1965) (terminal cancer patients unknowingly inoculated with cancer cells).

Fear of the unknown, and widespread publicity of known abuses, have led to what the Supreme Court in *Chakrabarty* termed the "gruesome parade of horribles." Particularly active in this movement has been the Washington, D.C.-based Foundation on Economic Trends, whose president, Jeremy Rifkin, has been highly visible and prominent in advocating for stricter controls upon genetic and biotechnological research. As the following case (in which the University of California was originally a co-defendant) demonstrates, there are formidable legal barriers to external groups in the polity. Although FOET lost this case, Rifkin has had his successes. For example, in 1987, following a similar suit filed against the Department of Defense, the DOD agreed to review the effect of its biological warfare research upon the environment. "Defense Department to Review Research on Biological Warfare," *Chronicle of Higher Education*, 4 March 1987, p. 12. See also Office of Technology Assessment, *Ownership of Human Tissues and Cells* (GPO, 1987).

Foundations on Economic Trends v. Thomas

661 F. Supp. 713 (D.D.C. 1986)

GESELL, District Judge.

Plaintiffs seek an order requiring the Environmental Protection Agency ("EPA") to modify the procedures under which it authorizes persons to release genetically engineered pesticides into the environment. They assert that EPA has erred in refusing to promulgate regulations requiring such persons to document their financial capability to redress and abate any potential harms that may result from such releases. Plaintiffs seek a ban on all releases until EPA has so acted. Defendants, who are various employees of EPA sued in their official capacity, have moved to dismiss or in the alternative for summary judgment. The issues have been fully briefed.

Background

Plaintiff Foundation on Economic Trends ("FOET"), of which plaintiff Jeremy Rifkin is president, is a private, non-profit organization which advocates limits on genetic engineering. Plaintiffs, invoking the Administrative Procedure Act ("APA"), petitioned EPA for agency rulemaking on May 7, 1986 under the Federal Insecticide, Fungicide and Rodenticide Act, as amended by the Federal Environmental Pesticide Control Act of 1972 and the Federal Pesticide Act of 1978 (collectively "FIFRA").

FIFRA requires pesticides to be registered by EPA. To qualify for registration, in part, a pesticide must function as intended without causing "unreasonable adverse effects on the environment." "Unreasonable adverse effects" are those which impose "any unreasonable risk to man or the environment, taking into account the economic, social, and environmental costs and benefits of the use of any pesticide." To obtain registration of a pesticide a company must furnish EPA with extensive data on the pesticide.

In order to produce the required data preliminary field tests of the pesticide in the environment are often required. Before such tests are conducted on any substantial scale, the person applying is required to obtain an "experimental use permit" and demonstrate the experiment will generate registration data and will not cause unreasonable adverse effects. EPA exercises broad continuing supervision over experimental uses to ensure the public safety.

Experimental use permits generally are not required for field tests involving less than ten acres of land. However, since 1984 EPA has required advance permission for release of genetically engineered microbial pesticides regardless of acreage affected, on the belief that because these pesticides can reproduce and spread beyond the application site, they may raise special testing concerns that need to be monitored. Before permitting experimental field use of such pesticides, EPA conducts a thorough review of the risks and benefits of the test, choosing on a case-by-case basis whether to grant or deny the application, impose special restrictions, or require additional data before action.

By letter dated May 7, 1986 plaintiffs petitioned EPA to promulgate, through appropriate rulemaking procedures, regulations establishing "minimum financial responsibility standards" to be required from applicants for experimental use permits, and to establish equivalent standards for permanent registration of such pesticides. Stating their concern with the agency's current procedures they urged that the risks posed by such releases, although still unquantified, are of potentially devastating proportions, and suggested that EPA "currently does not have an adequate program for assessing, controlling, and assuring remedial actions and accountability for the environmental risks presented by the deliberate releases of recombinant organisms."

In support of their proposal, plaintiffs pointed out that "[t]he demonstration of financial responsibility has been required in other situations involving much more finite risks to man and the environment" such as activities posing danger to water quality or involving toxic wastes. They also noted that FIFRA requires EPA to balance the risks and benefits of pesticides to both man and the environment, and argued that "[t]o the extent that an applicant company cannot demonstrate adequate financial responsibility, then the public health and environment is exposed to a risk for which there will be no redress in the event of resulting harm." Plaintiffs concluded that proof of financial responsibility "must, as a matter of sound public policy, be required" and that under FIFRA the EPA "has the inherent authority to require evidence of financial responsibility and to establish appropriate standards therefor."

EPA considered the petition and by letter dated June 2, 1986 indicated its rejection of it and its conclusion that there was no basis for the proposed rulemaking. EPA noted specifically that "without an explicit directive from Congress, we do not believe that as a general matter the Agency should become involved in the liability insurance aspects of pesticide use." After pointing out plaintiffs' recognition that Congress had expressly required financial responsibility standards in other areas of environmental concern, EPA noted that "[n]o such provision is contained in FIFRA" and therefore it "must conclude that the administrative imposition of financial responsibility requirements would be beyond congressional intent under FIFRA."

EPA also explained that plaintiffs had provided no basis for imposing greater strictures on the release of genetically altered pesticides than on more conventional pesticides. It pointed out that the petition failed to provide a rationale for treating genetically altered pesticide products differently from others and asserted that although "the unique characteristics" of such products "may warrant a somewhat different review process, we are not aware of any evidence which demonstrates that organisms mutated through recombinant DNA techniques are, as a class, inherently riskier than organisms mutated through other techniques or than conventional chemical products." Plaintiffs have submitted no further evidence subsequent to EPA's response. They continue to press the argument that EPA has recognized a risk difference through its policy of requiring permits for *all* experimental releases of genetically altered materials.

Standing

Under the judicial review provision of the APA, plaintiffs may sue if they are "adversely affected or aggrieved by agency action," which requires that they establish standing to sue under article III's case-or-controversy requirement and satisfy related prudential requirements. Thus plaintiffs must allege: 1) injury in fact; 2) which is "fairly traceable" to EPA's "allegedly unlawful conduct"; and 3) is "likely to be redressed by the requested relief." Prudentially they must overcome several general limits, against: 1) representation of the rights of third parties; 2) adjudication of "generalized grievances more appropriately addressed to the representative branches"; and 3) consideration of injuries which do not fall "within the zone of interests protected by the law invoked."

In assessing the standing issue the Court must assume the truth of plaintiffs' allegations and construe the complaint in plaintiff's favor.

The two plaintiffs assert separate injuries. FOET claims injury to its organizational activities. It is a private, non-profit organization actively involved, in part, with policy issues related to genetic engineering technology. It serves as a clearinghouse for public information on these issues, releases a variety of educational publications, participates in congressional hearings and in litigation, and has an active presence in the news media through its staff members. Its general message is that the hazards of genetic engineering are vastly underappreciated, and it has accordingly opposed on a variety of fronts the development of the technology. It claims EPA's failure to require applicants to provide information about their financial capacity to redress and abate possible harms arising from genetic releases, and particularly about their liability insurance coverage, hinders its educational and advocacy functions by depriving it of information about who will bear the costs of redressing and abating any such harms. It does not claim standing as a representative of its members or staff.

Jeremy Rifkin, its president, alleges injury to his use and enjoyment of "the environmental resources of the United States, including (but not limited to) parks and other recreational lands." This enjoyment is substantially dependent, he claims, on "the ecological and genetic diversity and biological integrity of thousands of wild plants and animals . . . and of many domesticated plants and animals, and the stability and viability of the biosphere which sustains them." EPA's refusal to promulgate financial responsibility standards, he asserts, threatens these environmental qualities by encouraging the deliberate release of novel, potentially hazardous organisms into the environment and failing to guarantee that any resulting harms will be redressed and abated. He also asserts EPA's failure to provide information on financial responsibility hampers his public role as an advocate on these issues.

Addressing first the main standing claim of the individual plaintiff, it is clear that his allegations meet the causation and redressibility requirements. He alleges EPA's refusal to require financial responsibility standards injures his use and enjoyment of the environment by: (1) allowing the release of potentially dangerous pesticides that would not be released if such standards were instituted; and (2) failing to guarantee that releasers will compensate and rectify any harms from such releases.

* * *

The injury alleged by the individual plaintiff is insufficient. Plaintiff's allegations are wholly abstract, suggesting that absent relief from this Court releases of genetically engineered pesticides by financially irresponsible parties may occur. Nowhere in the complaint do plaintiffs suggest that any person currently desires to make releases in a financially irresponsible manner. Moreover, there is no allegation that *any* releases of whatever nature will occur in the future. Indeed, the only two recently proposed releases have apparently been permanently barred by court and agency action. Presumably because no threatening releases have been identified, plaintiffs are unable to suggest with any specificity how any given release could cause noticeable, palpable harm to the national environment; whether any harm would occur to a part of the environment that the individual plaintiff regularly uses and enjoys, and the precise impact on him either economically or otherwise; and whether any proposed release would be allowed by EPA despite its careful review process.

The individual plaintiff has therefore alleged at most a hypothetical interest in changing an EPA policy that under conceivable circumstances might have detrimental effects. Such allegations are insufficient. This Circuit has recognized that "[t]he injury requirement will not be satisfied simply because a chain of events can be hypothesized in which the action challenged eventually leads to actual injury." Where a party such as the individual plaintiff "relies wholly on the threat of future injury, the fact that the party (and the court) can 'imagine circumstances in which [the party] *could* be affected by the agency's action' is not enough."

By contrast, the allegations of environmental injury judged adequate by the Supreme Court have been relatively limited in scope. In Sierra Club, the Court contemplated that users of a specific area of California wilderness could allege distinct and palpable injury from the proposed development plan at issue. SCRAP, although it involved an alleged injury that was "far less direct and perceptible," challenged a distinct action of an agency and alleged specific, perceptible and reasonably immediate harm to several aspects of the environment enjoyed by plaintiffs. The proposed standing theory, however, would allow any person to assert a generalized concern with EPA's regulatory activities, based on conjectural assumptions of undefined future actions by EPA and private parties and without challenging any given action or identifying any particular impact on the environment. This position is without support. The individual plaintiff's application for "a special license to roam the country in search of governmental wrongdoing and to reveal [his] discoveries in federal court" must be rejected.

FOET's standing claim is also without merit. FOET has standing as a organization if it alleges sufficient injury to its activities. The alleged injury to its informational and educational functions is insufficient because this interest is not "arguably within the zone of interests to be protected or regulated" by FIFRA. FIFRA was established to allow EPA to regulate pesticide use under carefully drawn requirements, and is not concerned with provision of safety information to the public at large. For the same reason, this alleged informational interest cannot support the individual plaintiff's standing.

Ripeness

Even if plaintiffs had standing the case would not be justiciable because their claims are not ripe. In *Abbott Laboratories v. Gardner,* which remains the "leading discussion of the doctrine," the Supreme Court explained that whether a claim is ripe depends on "the fitness of the issues for judicial decision" and "the hardship to the parties of withholding court consideration." The doctrine's "basic rationale is to prevent the courts, through premature adjudication, from entangling themselves in abstract disagreements," concerning "uncertain or contingent future events that may not occur as anticipated, or indeed may not occur at all." Based on the nature of the present challenge as described above, it is evident that judicial review at this stage would be wholly inappropriate; the dispute must be resolved, if at all, in a far more concrete factual setting. Plaintiffs have not countered this conclusion by a showing "that delay in adjudication would cause unusual hardship" sufficient to warrant adjudication, such as "serious injury to important constitutionally protected interests."

Laurel Heights Improvement Association v. University of California

238 Cal. Rptr. 451 (Cal. App. 1 Dist. 1987)

KING, Associate Justice.

In this case we hold that approval of an environmental impact report constitutes an abuse of discretion when the report provides an inadequate description of the project and provides insufficient discussion of project alternatives, and when there is no substantial evidence to support the conclusion that potential environmental impacts would be mitigated to a level of insignificance.

The Laurel Heights Improvement Association of San Francisco, Inc. (Association) appeals from an order denying a petition for writ of mandate challenging the approval of an environmental impact report (EIR) by respondent Regents of the University of California (Regents). The EIR involves the proposed relocation of University of California, San Francisco (UCSF) biomedical research facilities from their present location on the UCSF campus on Parnassus Avenue to a building in the nearby Laurel Heights neighborhood. The Association's petition, filed under the aegis of the California Environmental Quality Act (CEQA), contested the informational sufficiency of the EIR and challenged its conclusion that the project's anticipated significant environmental impacts—including the venting of toxic and radioactive substances into the atmosphere—would be mitigated to a level of insignificance. The trial court concluded the EIR complied with the provisions of CEQA and was properly approved. We disagree, and reverse the order denying the petition for writ of mandate.

This project has caused intense, heated debate in the Laurel Heights neighborhood. The debate has focused largely on whether research employing toxic chemicals, carcinogens and radioactive materials is too high-risk to be conducted in a densely populated residential neighborhood. This question, as well as the philosophical debate over the use of hazardous substances, are essentially matters of a political and social nature which, of course, are not before us. At the present time there is no legal prohibition on the type of research conducted by the Regents, nor is there a prohibition on its being conducted in areas of high population density. The value of research in biomedicine, microbiology, immunology and related fields is not disputed. Such activities are, however, subject to the stringent requirements of CEQA and especially the informational disclosure and the analytical discussion of an EIR. The limited question we decide in this case is whether the EIR at issue is in compliance with California's environmental protection statutes and administrative guidelines. In other words, we decide whether the Regents have provided the public, including the Laurel Heights community, with sufficient information concerning the project and an adequate analysis of its anticipated impact on the environment.

We scrutinize the EIR with the aid of familiar points of reference. "CEQA demonstrates a legislative intent to maintain 'a quality environment for the people of this state' and to regulate conduct 'found to affect the quality of the environment' . . . 'so that major consideration is given to preventing environmental damage, while providing a decent home and satisfying living environment for every Californian.' " CEQA "is to be interpreted broadly in order to afford the fullest protection to the environment consistent with the reasonable scope of the statutory language."

Generally, an EIR is an essential prerequisite of any project with a potential significant effect on the environment. The EIR is the "heart of CEQA," an "environmental 'alarm bell' whose purpose it is to alert the public and its responsible officials to environmental changes before they have reached ecological points of no return." An EIR is an "informational document" designed to inform "public agency decisionmakers and the public generally of the significant environmental effect[s]" of proposed projects. "The EIR identifies significant effects of a project on the environment, the way those effects can be mitigated or avoided, and the alternatives to the project." The document also helps to ensure that the project's proponents carefully consider the environmental effects and do not simply render a " 'post hoc rationalization' of a decision already made."

The EIR process involves the preparation of a draft EIR, which is released to the public for review and comment and is then evaluated in light of comments received. The agency proposing the project then prepares a final EIR incorporating comment and evaluation of the draft. Before approving the project the agency must certify it has considered the final EIR, and must make findings that the project's significant environmental effects have been avoided or mitigated, or that unmitigated effects are outweighed by the project's benefits.

A judicial review of the approval of an EIR does not pass upon the validity of the document's environmental conclusions, but only on its sufficiency as an informational document. Our standard of review is the same as the trial court's: whether the agency approving the EIR (here the Regents) abused its discretion, either by approving the document without proceeding in the manner required by law or by rendering an approval decision not supported by substantial evidence.

CEQA requires "an interactive process of assessment of environmental impacts... which must be genuine [and] open to the public, premised upon a full and meaningful disclosure of the scope, purposes, and effect" of a project. The reviewing court must determine that the EIR and its approval process has fully complied with the procedural requirements of CEQA, "since only in this way can the important public purposes of CEQA be protected from subversion."

B

The present campus of UCSF provides facilities for the Schools of Medicine, Nursing, Pharmacy and Dentistry. A long range development plan prepared in 1982 indicated serious space constraints at the Parnassus campus, and concluded there was a need to "develop space in University managed off-campus locations for academic and support activities currently located on campus where space can be released for essential needs...." These essential needs were defined to include classrooms, laboratories, and research.

To overcome the space constraints at Parnassus, the Regents acquired the former Firemen's Fund Insurance Company headquarters building, a spacious four-story office building at 3333 California Street in the Laurel Heights neighborhood. The Regent filed a Notice of Exemption with the State Secretary of Resources, declaring that the purchase of the site had no significant environmental effect, and was categorically exempt from CEQA and its EIR requirements "because it involves the acquisition and operation of the existing facilities and site and involves negligible or no expansion of use beyond that previously existing." The Regents informed the public that the building would be used for "administrative and academic" functions.

For reasons which we cannot ascertain from the record, the quoted portions of the Notice of Exemption were incorrect. We do not know if they were correct when the notice was filed, but were affected by later decisions of the Regents to relocate biomedical research units to Laurel Heights. In any event, the Regents' present plan is not to use the site as an office building as Firemen's Fund did. Nor do they plan to use it for what lay persons might understand to be administrative and academic functions. At some point the Regents decided to relocate certain administrative and basic science research units of the UCSF School of Pharmacy to Laurel Heights. The relocation of the research units include facilities which handle toxic chemicals, carcinogens and radioactive substances. Apparently because this relocation contemplated an element of potential environmental impact, the Regents then began the formal process under CEQA for the preparation of the EIR which is at issue before us.

The draft EIR prepared by the Regents defined the project under review as the "mov[ing of] the School of Pharmacy basic science research units from the UCSF Parnassus campus to Laurel Heights." In addition to the objective of relieving Parnassus space limitations, the draft EIR noted a secondary project objective of the consolidation of scattered Pharmacy School facilities into a single building. The draft EIR further revealed that the basic science research units included a number of research facilities which handled toxic chemicals, carcinogens and radioactive substances; the document indicated that toxic chemicals would be vented to the outside air through laboratory fume hoods, and that harmful exposure to hazardous materials could occur through worker negligence, accidents or unidentified risks.

The draft EIR identified a number of potential environmental impacts, including direct and cumulative impacts on air quality caused by the fume hood emissions, as well as impacts on human health from exposure to hazardous substances. The draft EIR also identified less significant impacts from noise, traffic congestion, and parking.

After a public hearing and a 45-day period for public review and comment, the Regents held a final public meeting to respond to comments received during the review period. The Regents adopted specific measures to mitigate the identified environmental impacts. The final EIR concluded the environmental impacts had been "reduced to a level of insignificance." The Regents certified the EIR and approved the Laurel Heights project.

The Association then filed the instant petition for writ of mandate to set aside the EIR's approval. The superior court denied the petition. In a lengthy statement of decision, the trial court concluded the Regents approved the EIR in the manner required by law and the Regents' approval of the EIR is supported by substantial evidence. This appeal ensued.

C

Three aspects of the EIR are dispositive of this appeal: the adequacy of the EIR's project description, the sufficiency of its discussion of project alternatives, and the validity of its conclusion that potential environmental impacts will be mitigated to a level of insignificance.

1. Project Description

An accurate project description "is the *sine qua non* of an informative and legally sufficient EIR." Needless to say the definition of the project defines the scope of environmental review. If an individual project is a component of a larger, ultimate project (a "multiple" or "phased" project), and is a necessary precedent for action on the larger project, the ultimate project must be described and analyzed in the EIR. The EIR must also discuss the cumulative impact on the environment of the current project and reasonably foreseeable probable future projects.

The Association argues the Laurel Heights relocation is a component of a large project contemplated at the facility, and the EIR fails to address the future anticipated projects and their cumulative impact. The record does reveal the contemplated movement of additional Parnassus research facilities to the Laurel Heights building. A portion of the Laurel Heights building is currently leased to the California Department of Transportation; the EIR indicates that after this lease expires in 1995, the Regents intend to occupy the entire building and use it as "a biomedical research facility, with cross-disciplinary programs from all the schools." There also is an indication of the Regents' intent to move additional programs resulting in the use of at least 80 percent of the building for units primarily related to biomedical research.

Under these circumstances the Laurel Heights project is a "phased" project within the meaning of CEQA. The Laurel Heights initial use cannot be considered apart from the planned ultimate goal of full use of the building for a biomedical facility. The EIR should have addressed the issue of the extent and cumulative impact of the anticipated future plans. Since it failed to do so, we must conclude the EIR's project description is legally inadequate under governing provisions of CEQA.

2. *Alternatives Discussion*

The Association next argues the EIR's discussion of project alternatives is inadequate under CEQA and its interpretive cases. An EIR must describe all reasonable alternatives to the project, including those which would reduce or eliminate adverse environmental effects and including the "no project" alternative.

* * *

The discussion of alternatives in this case comprises a total of three pages of the EIR. One page is given over to a discussion of the "no project" alternative; the remaining two pages discuss the project alternatives of relocating the School of Pharmacy science units to either other sites on the Parnassus campus or to off-campus sites at other UCSF facilities. One of these two pages is devoted to a map; the other contains the sole discussion of the project alternatives in two paragraphs containing a grand total of nine lines of text. The first paragraph recites that alternative sites on the Parnassus campus have not been evaluated as possible candidates for the location of the Pharmacy School facilities. The second, the EIR's entire discussion of the alternative of off-Parnassus locations other than Laurel Heights, reads in its entirety, "Currently the University has facilities at numerous other locations in the City of San Francisco, as shown in Exhibit V-1 [map]. None of these sites had space available of sufficient size to accommodate the School of Pharmacy units that are to be moved."

It is not possible to consider this discussion of project alternatives to be adequate. It is woefully inadequate.

* * *

We conclude the alternatives discussion of the EIR does not comply with the requirements of CEQA.

3. *Mitigation*

The Association argues there is no substantial evidence to support the Regents' finding that all significant environmental impacts are mitigated. The Association focuses primarily on the significant impacts arising from the venting of toxic chemicals and radioactive substances into the surrounding air. Review of the EIR compels the conclusion that the EIR both fails to present adequate information concerning these environmental impacts and fails to muster substantial evidence to support the Regents' finding of successful mitigation.

The EIR identifies a potential significant environmental impact on air quality and human health, caused by the expulsion into the air of toxic chemicals, carcinogens and radioactive substances through laboratory fume hoods. The potential harmful effects of the emissions of these toxic, carcinogenic and radioactive substances are said to be reduced by the dilution of the substances by large quantities of room air drawn into the laboratory fume hoods, and by the dispersion of the diluted substance by entry into the surrounding atmosphere and dissipation by wind.

The Regents adopted several mitigation measures, identified as placement of the fume hood exhaust stacks seven feet above the building roof, as required by law; the use of air flow gauges to ensure an adequate flow of air for dilution; the use of high efficiency particulate air (HEPA) filters for regulated carcinogens; six-month inspection of fume hoods to ensure compliance with Cal/OSHA requirements; and a request to the Bay Area Air Quality Management District to monitor surrounding air quality periodically. The final EIR concluded that these mitigation measures were adequate to mitigate the air quality and human health effects to a level of insignificance.

This determination is not supported by substantial evidence due to a number of significant deficiencies of the EIR. First, the document fails to estimate the quantities of toxic chemicals, carcinogens, and radioactive substances which will be emitted through the fume hoods. These categories of substances are highly dangerous to human health; yet the Regents propose to vent the substances in a residential area with no attempt at assessing the quantities involved, which the EIR admits can "vary considerably." Significant failure of quantification can lead to the invalidation of an EIR.

* * *

The Regents, by promising to measure air quality at Laurel Heights, have admitted such monitoring is technologically possible. Yet there is no explanation for the lack of such monitoring at Parnassus to assess more accurately the contamination of the air by the fume hood exhaust. The limitation of the Parnassus studies to soil and vegetation is both indeterminative and unexplained.

Finally, the Parnassus stacks are 15 stories high with a measured exhaust plume of 44 feet. The stacks at Laurel Heights are only seven feet higher than four stories, and are lower than surrounding residences. What is safe at Parnassus may not be safe at Laurel Heights: even the transfer of existing uses must be considered in light of the different stack height, specific topography, wind, and other local conditions. Even accepting the assertion that Parnassus research activity has been more extensive than that planned at Laurel Heights, the studies are insufficient. An EIR must analyze the project's impact on the affected area.

We conclude that the Regents' determination that the environmental impact of the fume hood emissions will be mitigated to insignificance is not supported by substantial evidence.

D

The Laurel Heights EIR was not prepared and approved in the manner prescribed by law because of the legal deficiency of its description of the project and its discussion of project alternatives. The approval decision was based on a conclusion of adequate mitigation of environment impacts which is not supported by substantial evidence. Accordingly, the approval of the EIR by the Regents was an abuse of discretion. In light of the fundamental nature of the defects noted above, the abuse of discretion must be considered prejudicial. The errors are not the sort of trivial lapses of procedure discussed in such cases such as *Dusek v. Redevelopment Agency*; the deficiencies go directly to the main purpose of the EIR as envisioned by CEQA. In particular, the failure of adequate disclosure of alternatives to the project invokes section 21005, which specifically declares that a violation of CEQA's information disclosure provisions "may constitute a prejudicial abuse of discretion . . . regardless of whether a different outcome would have resulted" from complete disclosure.

The citizens of the State of California, for good reason, have great pride in the University of California. It is often referred to as the greatest public university in the world. With public confidence in the integrity of so many of our governmental institutions being shaken so often in contemporary times, it is more important than ever that our public institutions, particularly those of higher education engaging in important research utilizing toxic chemicals, carcinogens and radioactive substances, conduct themselves in a manner to engender public confidence.

The Laurel Heights building was constructed and used for commercial office space. When the Regents purchased it they certified that "it involves the acquisition and operation of the existing facilities and site and involves negligible or no expansion of use beyond that previously existing." This lawsuit arose when the Regents later approved a legally inadequate EIR and one which makes no serious effort to comply with the law requiring a discussion of reasonable alternatives to the project. Even viewing the conduct of the Regents with regard to Laurel Heights in the manner most favorable to them, their actions appear to have been carried out in a most cavalier fashion.

Because our process of approval of public projects permits the agency that is the proponent of the project to be the body that approves the EIR for the project, the agency bears a special responsibility to the public to make decisions based upon the public interest, not based upon the agency's self-interest. The test here is not what is best for UCSF; it is whether the requirements of the law have been fulfilled by providing the public and the Regents with sufficient information about the project and an adequate analysis of its anticipated impact upon the environment. Under the circumstances reviewed above, we have no alternative but to conclude that the Regents have not met the requirement of CEQA for "an interactive process of assessment of environmental impact... which must be genuine [and] open to the public, premised upon a full and meaningful disclosure of the scope, purposes, and effect" of this project.

When this court conducted an initial hearing on the Association's writ petition, the Association requested that we halt the construction of the biomedical research facilities at the Laurel Heights site pending this decision. The Regents opposed this request because of their urgent need for space and requested that they be allowed to proceed with the construction in order to expedite their move to Laurel Heights upon receiving a ruling in their favor on the petition. We agreed to allow the Regents to proceed with the construction, making clear that they did so at their own risk since an adverse ruling could mean that an expenditure of public funds had been made to construct facilities which could not be utilized for the purpose for which they were being constructed. The fact that expenditures have now been made cannot affect our decision, which we must make based upon whether the Regents have complied with CEQA. The Regents recognized CEQA provides that a party continuing construction during an appeal does so at its own risk. Although as citizens and taxpayers we are obviously concerned with a possible waste of public funds, in our role as justices our concern is limited to whether there has been a failure to comply with the law.

DISPOSITION

For the reasons discussed above, the Association's petition for writ of mandate should have been granted. In light of this conclusion we need not reach the remaining issues raised by the Association.

The order denying the petition for writ of mandate is reversed. The cause is remanded to the trial court with instructions to grant the petition and set aside approval of the Laurel Heights EIR.

The University of California was also a defendant in an additional case in which the issue was research regulation and technology. Unlike the *FOET* case, the university partially lost this challenge. UC-Davis litigation considered the application of the 1862 Morrill Act, which established the federal land-grant university system of agricultural colleges. The case (*CAAP v. Regents*) appeared in the section "How Research May Be Conducted."

National Security Controls and Research Secrecy

The commentary and cases on higher education, secrecy, and national security are extensive, and likely to increase as more universities participate in Star Wars research programs. In a collection of essays entitled *National Security Controls and University Research* (Association of American Universities, 1987), Dale Corson surveyed the broad range of scientific communication issues, including visa controls, attempts to restrict foreign students from enrolling in crucial curricula, and restrictions on publishing. He summarized the importance of "the atmosphere for research" by noting:

> Science and engineering progress most rapidly with completely free communication. In most fields, among those at the frontiers, there is an international network of people who are in frequent communication about progress and about new ideas. There is frequent circulation of "preprints" of papers prior to publication or simultaneous with submission for publication. Graduate students participate in this free exchange of ideas. It builds an esprit and an enthusiasm that propels the field in vital ways. Restriction on these communication channels destroys the enthusiasm, and the spirit goes out of the work to a considerable degree. The pace of the research slows. It is vital that we keep our research fields vital. Our place in the world rests on the vitality of our science and technology. We cannot retreat behind an intellectual Maginot line without running the risk of having someone bypass us.

Several of these issues arise in the cases and commentary throughout this volume. This section includes two of the many issues inherent in national security and higher education research: National Security Division Directive No. 84 (1983), concerning government employees, and N.S.D.D. No. 189 (1985) specifying the rules governing "fundamental research." The *Nondisclosure Agreement* that is included in the Appendix is the fruit of N.S.D.D. 84, Executive Order 12356, and the slew of other civil and criminal provisions mentioned on the form. All governmental employees with access to classified data have been required to sign the agreement; elected officials are exempt. Nearly 2 million federal employees have signed the form (or its counterpart, standard form 189), and a similar form was held to be constitutional in *Snepp v. U.S.*, 444 U.S. 507 (1980). However, two federal employee unions filed suit in 1987 to enjoin use of such agreements. The federal government has continued to insist that employees sign, although one Republican senator has publicly urged all employees "to refrain from signing SF 189" until the issue over classified information policy is resolved. See "Government Drops Use of Secrecy Form," *Houston Post*, 22 August 1987, p. 4A; "Washington Feeling Insecure About Non-Secret Information," *New York Times*, 30 August 1987, p. E5; "Grassley to Civil Servants: Ignore Secrecy Pledge," *Washington Post*, 16 October 1987, p. A21. Another important issue has been N.S.D.D. 189, signed by the president in 1985:

National Policy on the Transfer of Scientific, Technical and Engineering Information
(N.S.D.D. 189, 1985)

I. *Purpose*

This directive establishes national policy for controlling the flow of science, technology, and engineering information produced in federally-funded fundamental research at colleges, universities, and laboratories. Fundamental research is defined as follows:

> " 'Fundamental research' means basic and applied research in science and engineering, the results of which ordinarily are published and shared broadly within the scientific community, as distinguished from proprietary research and from industrial development, design, production, and product utilization, the results of which ordinarily are restricted for proprietary or national security reasons."

II. *Background*

The acquisition of advanced technology from the United States by Eastern Bloc nations for the purpose of enhancing their military capabilities poses a significant threat to our national security. Intelligence studies indicates a small but significant target of the Eastern Bloc intelligence gathering effort is science and engineering research performed at universities and federal laboratories. At the same time, our leadership position in science and technology is an essential element in our economic and physical security. The strength of American science requires a research environment conducive to creativity, an environment in which the free exchange of ideas is a vital component.

In 1982, the Department of Defense and National Science Foundation sponsored a National Academy of Sciences study of the need for controls on scientific information. This study was chaired by Dr. Dale Corson, President Emeritus of Cornell University. It concluded that, while there has been a significant transfer of U.S. technology to the Soviet Union, the transfer has occurred through many routes with universities and open scientific communication of fundamental research being a minor contributor. Yet as the emerging government-university-industry partnership in research activities continues to grow, a more significant problem may well develop.

III. *Policy*

It is the policy of this Administration that, to the maximum extent possible, the products of fundamental research remain unrestricted. It is also the policy of this Administration that, where the national security requires control, the mechanism for control of information generated during federally-funded fundamental research in science, technology and engineering at colleges, universities and laboratories is classification. Each federal government agency is responsible for: a) determining whether classification is appropriate prior to the award of a research grant, contract, or cooperative agreement and, if so, controlling the research results through standard classification procedures; b) periodically reviewing all research grants, contracts, or cooperative agreements for potential classification. No restrictions may be placed upon the conduct or reporting of federally-funded fundamental research that has not received national security classification, except as provided in applicable U.S. Statutes.

———

Predictably, this revised policy has been widely criticized by university researchers and scientists. For a sense of the more thoughtful reviews of these policies, see the National Academy of Sciences, *Balancing the National Interest: U.S. National Security Export Controls and Global Economic Competition* (NAS, 1987) and the Association of American Universities, *Government Information Controls: Implications for Scholarship, Science and Technology* (AAU, 1988).

Not all disclosure issues arise from classified data roots. After a 1985 discovery that the CIA had secretly underwritten the research of several Harvard professors and an academic conference, the issue of mandatory disclosure of subsidized research activities was raised. "Bok Asks Disclosure of Agreements to Review Work Before Publication," *Chronicle of Higher Education*, 3 December 1986, p. 10. In the midst of the 1988 presidential campaign, corporate officials in Massachusetts were alleged to have pressured MIT Press officials to delay the publication of a book that they felt was detrimental to Massachusetts Governor Michael Dukakis; several of the chapters were written by employees of the bank. "MIT Press Says the Bank of Boston Pressured It to Delay Publishing a Book Involving Dukakis," *Chronicle of Higher Education*, 30 March 1988, pp. A23, 32.

———

U.S. v. Edler Industries
579 F.2d 516 (1978)

ELY, Circuit Judge:

Edler Industries, Incorporated, and Vernon Edler appeal from their convictions for exporting, without a license, technical data relating to articles on the United States Munitions List. Edler Industries was sentenced to pay a fine of $25,000. Vernon Edler received a two-year sentence, suspended on the condition that he serve ten weekends in a jail-type institution, remain on probation for five years, and donate 1200 hours of work to a charitable organization.

I.

Most of the facts are not seriously disputed. About 1950 Edler Industries began in Newport Beach, California, as a small machine shop and gradually evolved into a manufacturing and engineering firm in the aerospace industry. Vernon Edler, the founder and president of the corporation, guided the business affairs of the firm and had frequent contacts with its engineers and technicians. The corporation acquired expertise in tape wrappings, a process for creating durable lightweight materials by wrapping specially impregnated cloth around a form, further impregnating it with other materials, and curing it under pressure and heat. It also developed a capacity to produce carbon/carbon composites through application of some of the same techniques. Both types of materials have important applications for rocket and missile components, particularly in nozzles. Their light weight is valuable, and they are ablative, wearing away under the pressure and heat of the rocket exhaust at a predictable rate. Edler Industries worked on the Polaris and other government missile programs; consequently, its officers and employees were familiar with missile components.

The techniques utilized by Edler Industries do not constitute classified information, and they have various civilian uses. Carbon/carbon technology is, for example, utilized in the manufacture of golf club shafts.

French missile companies eager to master this technology first contacted Edler Industries in 1968. Edler and the Societe d'Etude de la Propulsion par Reaction negotiated an agreement for a technical assistance program. Edler then sought approval from the Office of Munition Control of the State Department (OMC). OMC denied the request, but Edler nevertheless continued to provide assistance.

In January 1974 Edler Industries reached an agreement with a second French firm, the Societe Europeene de Propulsion (SEP), for the provision of technical assistance and data related to a tape wrapping program. In March 1974 Edler executed a similar agreement with SEP for carbon/carbon materials. SEP engineers visited Edler's Newport Beach plant, and Edler employees toured SEP's missile and rocket plant in Bordeaux. Edler filed applications with OMC for licenses covering the two programs, stating that the agreements would not become effective without OMC approval. OMC again rejected the requests in October 1974 on the basis that the exportation of this particular technical knowledge contravened United States policy. Edler, despite its prior representation, began implementing the programs shortly after the execution of the agreements. By the time OMS issued its disapproval, the tape wrapping program was completed, and, in spite of OMC's action, Edler continued to fulfill its carbon/carbon agreement.

Employees of Edler Industries demonstrated to SEP the techniques they used and experimented with the application of those techniques to the different materials used by SEP in France. They observed and commented on the techniques employed by SEP. They produced sample pieces in configurations similar to those utilized in missiles but not specifically designed for any particular missile. SEP was engaged in the production of rockets, a fact known to Edler personnel. Only on one minor occasion was there any indication that SEP might use the information supplied by Edler for nonmilitary purposes. The witnesses at trial generally agreed that the technology furnished by Edler had direct missile applications.

II.

The Mutual Security Act of 1954 authorizes the President to control the "export and import of arms, ammunition, and implements of war, including technical data relating thereto." The President is expressly empowered to designate which articles, including relevant technical data, constitute arms, ammunition, and implements of war. Pursuant to this statute the Department of State has promulgated regulations to restrict the international traffic in arms. One of the regulatory requirements is that an exporter of arms first obtain a license for exportation from the State Department.

22 C.F.R. § 125.01 (1977) provides a three-part definition for the term "technical data." The only portion that is relevant here provides:

> "[T]echnical data" means: (a) Any unclassified information that can be used, or be adapted for use, in the design, production, manufacture, repair, overhaul, processing, engineering, development, operation, maintenance, or reconstruction of arms, ammunition, and implements of war on the U.S. Munitions List. . . .

Invoking the First Amendment, appellants emphasize the great potential breadth of the definition. The basic principles of the diesel engine, for example, constitute unclassified information that can be used in the manufacture of military trucks, which are included in category VII(d) of the U.S. Munitions List.

Export controls regulate the transmission of unclassified information by mail, hand carriage, participation in foreign symposia, and domestic plant visits. An exemption to the license requirement exists for published unclassified technical data, provided the exporter follows prescribed procedures. The person seeking publication, however, has the burden of obtaining governmental approval prior to publication. In the context of the regulatory framework, an expansive interpretation of technical data relating to items on the Munitions List could seriously impede scientific research and publishing and the international scientific exchange.

III.

The First Amendment protects at least some transmissions of information in a commercial context.

The contours of freedom of speech in the commercial realm are highly unsettled. Edler has advanced a colorable claim that the First Amendment furnishes a degree of protection for its dissemination of technological information. We deem it unnecessary in this case to resolve the precise scope of that protection. Assuming the full applicability of the First Amendment, invalidation of the federal controls on munitions is unwarranted because of the narrow statutory construction that we adopt.

Recognition that Edler may have constitutionally protected expression does not by itself define the extent of that protection. By regulating conduct, the Government may pursue its legitimate objectives even though incidental limitations upon expression may result.

> [G]eneral regulatory statutes, not intended to control the content of speech but incidentally limiting its unfettered exercise, have not been regarded as the type of law the First or Fourteenth Amendment forbade Congress or the States to pass, when they have been found justified by subordinating valid governmental interests, a prerequisite to constitutionality which has necessarily involved a weighing of the governmental interest involved.

The federal government undeniably possesses the power to regulate the international arms traffic. The President, under section 1934, has the authority to act for the United States in this respect. As a necessary incident to the power to control arms export, the President is empowered to control the flow of information concerning the production and use of arms. The authority to regulate arms traffic would be of negligible practical value if it encompassed only the exportation of particular military equipment but not the exportation of blueprints specifying the construction of the very same equipment.

A strict test applies when legislation, though directed toward the regulation of conduct, also restricts expression. Whenever government regulation impinges upon freedom of speech, "the power to regulate must be so exercised as not, in attaining a permissible end, unduly to infringe the protected freedom." It is for this reason that, when reviewing alleged First Amendment violations, courts have refused to countenance overly broad statutes.

As we have indicated, section 1934 and the definition of technical data are susceptible of an overbroad interpretation. Their expansive language may be construed to restrict not only the export of arms and information directly leading to the production of articles on the Munitions List, but also the interchange of scientific and technical information that of itself is without any substantial military application. A broad statutory reading, however, is neither necessary nor proper. In our opinion, technical data must relate in a significant fashion to some item on the Munitions List. Moreover, adequate notice to the potential exporter requires that the relationship be clear. The Senate Committee on Foreign Relations described section 1934 as allowing control of munitions, "including relevant technical data." Presumably, Congress intended that the technical data subject to control would be directly relevant to the production of a specified article on the Munitions List, not simply vaguely useful for the manufacture of arms.

* * *

We conclude, therefore, that section 1934 and the accompanying regulations prohibits only the exportation of technical data significantly and directly related to specific articles on the Munitions List. The prohibition includes the provision of technical assistance for the foreign manufacture of articles that, if manufactured domestically, would be on the Munitions List. If the information could have both peaceful and military applications, as Edler contends that its technology does, the defendant must know or have reason to know that its information is intended for the prohibited use. These limitations are necessary both to adhere to the purpose of the Act and to avoid serious interference with the interchange of scientific and technological information.

As construed, section 1934 and the regulations do not interfere with constitutionally protected speech. Rather, they control the conduct of assisting foreign enterprises to obtain military equipment and related technical expertise. So confined, the statute and regulations are not overbroad. For the same reasons the licensing provisions of the Act are not an unconstitutional prior restraint on speech.

One additional First Amendment argument is presented. This is that the Government may not constitutionally prohibit the exportation of Edler's technology because that technology is widely distributed in the United States. The District Court properly rejected Edler's position. Given the unquestionable legitimacy of the national interest in restricting the dissemination of military information, the claim of public availability in the United States is not a defense recognized by the Constitution. The State Department regulations, we should note, do grant a public availability defense, subject to certain conditions. Technical data is exempt from the export license requirements if it is both published and available to the general public. To claim such an exemption an exporter must comply with the certification standards contained in 22 C.F.R. § 125.22 (1977).

While, under the facts present here, the trial court correctly refused to recognize appellants' public availability defense, the court did not have the benefit of our interpretation of technical data. It rejected a second defense raised at trial by both appellants, which was that the information furnished by Edler Industries had a number of nonmilitary uses. We believe evidence concerning nonmilitary applications is relevant to the question of *scienter, i.e.,* whether a defendant knew or should have known that the recipient of the exported information would use the information to produce or operate Munitions List articles.

The District Court also refused to permit the defense to develop the proposition that the assistance given to SEP would not, of itself, suffice for the manufacture of rocket nozzle components. Any information that would in any way help in a process that led to the final product, the court stated, came under the definition of technical data. Such a reading of the statute and regulations is far too broad, as such evidence bears on the significance of the relationship between information and Munitions List items.

Accordingly, because the case was tried on an incorrect interpretation of the scope of section 1934 and the pertinent regulations, the judgments of conviction are reversed and the case is remanded for a new trial consistent with this opinion.

While the area of technology transfer remains muddled, several of the issues clarified by *Edler* were revised in the reauthorization of the International Traffic in Arms Regulations. For a comprehensive review of ITAR, and the various laws concerning national security and academic research, see M. Lam, "Restrictions on Technology Transfer Among Academic Researchers," *Journal of College and University Law*, 13 (1986), 311–34.

Faculty Misconduct and Conflicts of Interest

The terrain of faculty misconduct has been plowed in several sections, most notably in the treatment of tenured faculty dismissed for cause, while conflicts of interest have been foreshadowed in the commentary on the industrialization of academic science. This section focuses upon three dimensions of misconduct by faculty: sexual harassment of students, academic fraud and scientific misconduct, and conflicts of interest in academic research. While each of these issues has appeared regularly in higher education settings, the pace of litigation appears to have quickened, due to increased regulation and heightened institutional awareness of the extensive problems. Because many institutions have adopted AAUP principles for professional responsibility, the 1966 *Statement on Professional Ethics* (unedited for its archaic gender references) begins this section:

AAUP Statement on Professional Ethics

I. The professor, guided by a deep conviction of the worth and dignity of the advancement of knowledge, recognizes the special responsibilities placed upon him. His primary responsibility to his subject is to seek and to state the truth as he sees it. To this end he devotes his energies to developing and improving his scholarly competence. He accepts the obligation to exercise critical self-discipline and judgment in using, extending, and transmitting knowledge. He practices intellectual honesty. Although he may follow subsidiary interests, these interests must never seriously hamper or compromise his freedom of inquiry.

II. As a teacher, the professor encourages the free pursuit of learning in his students. He holds before them the best scholarly standards of his discipline. He demonstrates respect for the student as an individual, and adheres to his proper role as intellectual guide and counselor. He makes every reasonable effort to foster honest academic conduct and to assure that his evaluation of students reflects their true merit. He respects the confidential nature of the relationship between professor and student.

He avoids any exploitation of students for his private advantage and acknowledges significant assistance from them. He protects their academic freedom.

III. As a colleague, the professor has obligations that derive from common membership in the community of scholars. He respects and defends the free inquiry of his associates. In the exchange of criticism and ideas he shows due respect for the opinions of others. He acknowledges his academic debts and strives to be objective in his professional judgment of colleagues. He accepts his share of faculty responsibilities for the governance of his institution.

IV. As a member of his institution, the professor seeks above all to be an effective teacher and scholar. Although he observes the stated regulations of the institution, provided they do not contravene academic freedom, he maintains his right to criticize and seek revision. He determines the amount and character of the work he does outside his institution with due regard to his paramount responsibilities within it. When considering the interruption or termination of his service, he recognizes the effect of his decision upon the program of the institution and gives due notice of his intentions.

V. As a member of his community, the professor has the rights and obligations of any citizen. He measures the urgency of these obligations in the light of his responsibilities to his subject, to his students, to his profession, and to his institution. When he speaks or acts as a private person he avoids creating the impression that he speaks or acts for his college or university. As a citizen engaged in a profession that depends upon freedom for its health and integrity, the professor has a particular obligation to promote conditions of free inquiry and to further public understanding of academic freedom.

Reprinted with permission.

Sexual Harassment

Korf v. Ball State University
726 F.2d 1222 (1984)

COFFEY, Circuit Judge.

Dr. William E. Korf appeals the district court's decision granting summary judgment to the defendants in an action brought by Dr. Korf following his termination as a tenured Associate Professor of Music History and Musicology at Ball State University, Muncie, Indiana. On appeal Dr. Korf argues that the entry of summary judgment was an improper denial of his due process and equal protection claims, and his challenge to the defendants' qualified immunity. Dr. Korf also argues that the district court abused its discretion in denying him the opportunity to conduct further discovery and in holding that the Eleventh Amendment provides defendants with immunity from prospective and injunctive relief. We affirm.

I.

In February, 1981, Dr. Korf was informed by Lloyd Nelson, Dean of Ball State's College of Fine and Applied Arts, that certain of his current and former male students had accused him of sexual harassment. The students alleged that the harassment consisted of Dr. Korf's making unwelcomed sexual advances towards them and offering good grades contingent upon sexual involvement. Dean Nelson informed Dr. Korf that he intended to commence termination proceedings against him, and provided him the opportunity to resign. Dr. Korf denied the accusations and refused to resign. In accordance with established procedures, a committee was formed to investigate the charges. On April 2, 1981, the committee concluded that sufficient grounds existed to institute formal termination proceedings against Dr. Korf.

The president of Ball State, Dr. Robert P. Bell, reviewed the committee's recommendation and informed Dr. Korf of the committee's findings. Based on those findings, on April 24, 1981, Dr. Bell told Dr. Korf that formal termination proceedings were being commenced and that he had the right to a hearing before an *ad hoc* hearing committee, drawn from the University Senate Judicial Committee, to determine whether or not Dr. Korf should be removed from his position. Dr. Korf requested a hearing and the University complied with his request on May 20, 1981.

At that hearing, a student related the relationship he had had with Dr. Korf and testified that Dr. Korf gave him money and gifts in exchange for sexual acts. In addition, the student alleged that he was promised good grades. While denying that grades were involved, Dr. Korf admitted his sexual involvement with this student. The committee also heard testimony from three individuals and had statements of four other individuals who recounted Dr. Korf's sexual advances towards them while or after they were his students.

On May 21, 1981, the committee made the following findings:

> "Based on the evidence provided at the hearing on May 20, 1981, we find Dr. William E. Korf guilty of unethical conduct because he used his position and influence as a teacher to exploit students for his private advantage. The evidence indicates a pattern of behavior in which he frequently built a personal, friendly relationship, followed by sexual advances, often in his home.
>
> "This pattern was evidenced by the testimony of six (6) witnesses who were either present or submitted signed statements . . . and by two (2) individuals who made statements to the Affirmative Action Officer. . . . These eight (8) people are current or former students in one or more of Dr. Korf's classes.
>
> "We find insufficient evidence to support the allegation that Dr. Korf encouraged dishonest academic conduct."

The committee based its finding that Dr. Korf engaged in unethical conduct on paragraph 2 of the American Association of University Professors ("AAUP") Statement on Professional Ethics which was adopted by Ball State University in 1967 and published in its *Faculty Handbook*. Even though the committee found Dr. Korf guilty of unethical conduct, they recommended only that Dr. Korf be placed on a three-year period of probation, rather than discharged, because they did not feel that he had been provided "ample warning and opportunity for behavioral change."

Pursuant to established procedures, the Board of Trustees was presented with the hearing committee's report. After hearing arguments from University representatives and counsel for Dr. Korf on July 6, 1981, the Trustees agreed with the committee's finding of unethical conduct but refused to accept the committee's disciplinary recommendation of three years probation and directed that the committee's report and recommendations be returned to them for reconsideration. Upon reconsideration, the hearing committee, after a "close re-examination of the statement of ethics in the *Faculty Handbook*" and because of the realistic unenforceability of some of the proposed conditions of probation,[3] reversed its prior recommendation of probation and recommended that Dr. Korf be discharged from the University. Based upon this recommendation the Trustees terminated Dr. Korf's employment on July 24, 1981.

Dr. Korf initiated this action under 42 U.S.C. § 1983 on May 21, 1982, seeking both legal and equitable relief. The six-count complaint alleged violations of Dr. Korf's constitutional rights to substantive and procedural due process, equal protection, free speech, freedom of association, and privacy, along with state law claims for breach of his employment contract and infliction of emotional distress. The defendants filed a motion to dismiss alleging that: (1) they possessed immunity both under the Eleventh Amendment and the doctrine of qualified immunity; (2) none of Dr. Korf's constitutional rights were violated; and (3) Dr. Korf's employment contract was not breached and his emotional distress claim was insufficient. The motion was accompanied by an affidavit from the President of the Ball State University Board of Trustees delineating the basis for Dr. Korf's termination. Attached to the affidavit was the transcript of the formal hearing and all the exhibits presented. On August 5, 1982, Dr. Korf moved for a continuance to allow him to respond to the defendants' motion to dismiss until after discovery. Alternatively, he moved for an enlargement of time to respond to the defendants' motion. The court granted his alternative motion.

On March 11, 1983 the district court granted defendants summary judgment on Dr. Korf's constitutional and state law claims. The court concluded that Ball State University was an instrumentality of the State of Indiana for the purposes of the Eleventh Amendment and therefore the University, its Board of Trustees and the individual defendants in their official capacities were immune from suit under § 1983. Because the affidavits presented on Dr. Korf's behalf failed to provide any evidence sufficient to create a genuine question whether the individual defendants acted in bad faith, the court also ruled that the defendants were immune from § 1983 liability under the doctrine of qualified or "good faith" immunity.

The main question we must decide is whether or not the district court committed error in granting the defendants' motion for summary judgment. Dr. Korf contends that since there were disputed issues of material fact concerning his substantive due process and equal protection claims, summary judgment was improper. Dr. Korf also argues that even if he has not created genuine issues of material fact regarding these constitutional claims, the trial court erred by failing to grant him sufficient time to conduct the necessary discovery to prove that the University's regulations were applied against him arbitrarily.

* * *

III.

A. SUBSTANTIVE DUE PROCESS

Dr. Korf argues that the record contains issues of material fact as to "whether he could have had adequate notice" of Ball State's "asserted prohibition of consensual

---

3. The terms of the recommended probation were:

"1. He will not invite students to his home.

"2. He will not have students living in his home.

"3. He will hold no private meetings with any student without leaving his office, classroom or studio door open.

"4. He will be excluded from consideration for promotion.

"5. He will be ineligible for merit pay consideration.

"6. He will periodically be reviewed by appropriate administrators."

sexual relations between faculty members and students." Dr. Korf does not contend he was unaware of the University's proscription of unethical faculty conduct; rather, he argues that the AAUP Statement on Professional Ethics could not be reasonably interpreted to include what he labels "consensual sexual relationships" with students but which the Hearing Committee expressly found to be "unethical behavior of exploiting students for his private advantage."

In support of his opposition to defendants' summary judgment motion, Dr. Korf failed to allege any specific facts which would tend to create a genuine issue challenging the reasonableness of the interpretation given to the AAUP Statement of Professional Ethics, paragraph 2, by his faculty peers on the Hearing Committee. While Dr. Korf argues that he was not "adequately put on notice" because he was the first Ball State University faculty member ever disciplined for conduct such as his or, for that matter, any unethical conduct, the only logical basis for this argument is that if another professor had previously been dismissed for conduct similar to his, Dr. Korf would have *definitely* known that his conduct would warrant discipline. The plaintiff-appellant has failed to cite any caselaw setting forth a constitutional requirement that such notice be provided to would-be offenders. Common sense, reason and good judgment should have made him cognizant of the fact that his conduct could and would be cause for termination. One cannot be heard to complain that it is somehow unfair to be the first one disciplined under a particular law, rule or regulation since if that were the case, no new law, rule or regulation could ever be enforced.

Dr. Korf also alleges that other "private and consensual" faculty/student sexual relationships had occurred and were presently occurring at Ball State University and that no steps had ever been taken against the faculty members allegedly involved. This argument also misses the mark. First, despite Dr. Korf's repeated characterization of his conduct as "private and consensual," the faculty Hearing Committee found that he engaged in unethical behavior by "exploiting students for his private advantage." Therefore, "consensual" sexual activity is not at issue as it does not concern a fact which is "outcome determinative under the governing law." In any event, while there is no evidence that the young student Dr. Korf admitted having a sexual relationship with did not consent to engage in sexual activity with him, Dr. Korf's conduct is not to be viewed in the same context as would conduct of an ordinary "person on the street." Rather, it must be judged in the context of the relationship existing between a professor and his students within an academic environment. University professors occupy an important place in our society and have concomitant ethical obligations. The AAUP Statement on Professional Ethics makes this clear.

*   *   *

Furthermore, the Committee heard evidence of Dr. Korf's sexual advances towards seven students who refused his advances. One student recounted how he had to be "very assertive to get away from Dr. Korf's amorous advances." Such conduct certainly cannot be characterized as consensual sexual activity. Second, even if such alleged relationships between other faculty and students were relevant, all Dr. Korf has done is make bare assertions of faculty-student sexual relationships without any detailed information, much less supporting affidavits or proof. He must set forth *specific facts* in order to create a genuine issue of fact.

Dr. Korf further argues that it is significant that the AAUP Statement on Professional Ethics relied upon by the Board of Trustees as the basis for his termination does not make any reference to sexual conduct. While his observation that the statement does not specifically mention sexual conduct is correct, his conclusion regarding the omission's significance is misplaced and is contrary to reason and common sense. As is the case with other laws, codes and regulations governing conduct, it is unreasonable to assume that the drafters of the Statement on Professional Ethics could and must specifically delineate each and every type of conduct (including deviant conduct) constituting a violation. Nor have we been cited any case reciting that the language of the Constitution requires such precision.

* * *

In sum, Dr. Korf's arguments merely consist of generalized allegations disparaging the reasonableness of the interpretation given to the AAUP Statement by the Hearing Committee and the Board of Trustees. Our examination of the record reveals no "genuine issue of material fact" precluding disposition of his substantive due process claim by summary judgment. When the record is viewed in the light most favorable to Dr. Korf, his bald allegations do not meet that standard of proof necessary to create a genuine issue of material fact as to whether he "had adequate notice of the standard of conduct to which he was being held." The facts and circumstances clearly demonstrate that he should have understood both the standards to which he was being held and the consequences of his conduct. Dr. Korf merely asserts that he was not afforded notice and thereby contends that an issue of fact exists. This assertion alone is "insufficient to raise a factual issue." Because of Dr. Korf's failure to allege any specific facts in support of his alleged lack of notice his substantive due process claim was ripe for summary judgment since "there [was] no genuine issue as to any material fact...."

We also agree with the conclusions of law reached by the district court regarding the substantive due process issue and the court's express finding that "it cannot be seriously maintained that Dr. Korf's conduct was not clearly proscribed by University Regulations."

> "The claim that a person is entitled to 'substantive due process' means, as we understand the concept, that state action which deprives him of life, liberty, or property must have a rational basis—that is to say, the reason for the deprivation may not be so inadequate that the judiciary will characterize it as 'arbitrary.' "

We have no difficulty whatsoever concluding that Dr. Korf's termination was not "arbitrary" since the reasons for his termination were adequate. The University's interpretation of the AAUP Statement was entirely reasonable and rationally related to the duty of the University to provide a proper academic environment.

* * *

Brown v. California State Personnel Board

213 Cal. Rptr. 53 (Cal. App. 3 Dist. 1985)

BLEASE, Associate Justice.

Four years after discovery of allegations that associate professor Orie Brown made amorous overtures to two adult female students, officials of California State University at Sacramento (CSUS) filed charges of misconduct. They charged these acts (and three others), as "a series and pattern of sexual harassment of female students," were cause for dismissal and Brown was fired. The two remote acts and one other occurring in 1979 were upheld as justifying dismissal by the State Personnel Board (board). Brown appeals from a judgment denying him relief by way of a writ of mandate. We conclude that the extreme delay in filing these charges precludes their use as grounds of discipline and that the remaining ground of discipline is insufficient to sustain the charge made. We will reverse the judgment and direct Brown's reinstatement.

FACTS

The basis for the dismissal is unprofessional conduct and failure to perform the duties of his office, charged as "a series and pattern of sexual harassment of female students." The events sustaining the cause were alleged to be five in number, three of which it was alleged were accompanied by threats of retaliation or retaliation. CSUS admits that it "does not now, and never has had any rule, regulation, law or policy against faculty and students dating each other, or even living together or marrying one another." Thus, the claim of misconduct is not premised on the fact of the sexual overtures alone. Rather, it is the extensiveness of the conduct which impairs the teacher student relationship by threats of retaliation which is viewed by CSUS as rendering the matter actionable.

Brown was charged in 1981 with five instances of sexual harassment of his female students, in violation of Education Code section 89535, subdivisions (a), (b) and (f). The board found that allegations of two of the instances were baseless. Allegations that Brown had linked his conduct with retaliation or threats of retaliation were found not to be true. Of the remaining charges two of the instances were in 1975 and the remaining instance in 1979. The board did find that these three charges had merit, albeit in two cases only partial merit. This was found to be cause for dismissal as both unprofessional conduct and a failure to carry out the duties of his position.

At the outset of the board hearing Brown argued that two of the three incidents which form the basis of his dismissal should not be considered because the events in 1975 are too remote to serve as grounds of discipline. The board hearing officer rejected the contention that delay in prosecution of the charges could bar their use as a basis of dismissal. He said that if the evidence showed inability to defend as a result of the delay he would consider the claim. In his proposed decision the hearing officer reiterated the conclusion that no statute of limitation was applicable to failure to prosecute a misconduct claim against a CSUS employee. The hearing officer found the passage of time had prejudiced Brown with respect to defense of the two charges found not sustained but that there was no such prejudice regarding the 1975 incidents. A general description of the charges found substantiated by the board will suffice to set the analytical stage.

Brown taught courses in criminal law at CSUS in the spring of 1975. One of Brown's female students, Ms. H., accompanied him to his office after they had been drinking beer in the school cafeteria. Brown made a pass at her, embracing her and attempting to kiss her. She rejected his advances. Another female student, Ms. N., was discussing an extra credit paper with Brown in his office when he made comments on her attractive physical appearance. He made a pass at her, embracing her and attempting to kiss her. She pushed him away and left his office.

Neither student complained to school authorities concerning these incidents until a year later, in the spring of 1976, when Brown was being considered for promotion and tenure. Then the complaints came to the attention of Professor Melnicoe, the chairman of Brown's department. Melnicoe testified that, although he believed the complaints were relevant to Brown's fitness to teach, they were not mentioned in the promotion and tenure proceedings. He said that the charges were not pursued as disciplinary matters because of the reluctance of the complainants. Melnicoe did bring them to the attention of his administrative superiors but was instructed "not to go forward [with] anything because the complainants were unwilling to take any action at that time."

Brown testified that Melnicoe brought up the accusations prior to the award of promotion and tenure. He also testified that the school's rules provided that charges of misconduct were germane to the decision to grant or deny tenure and promotion. He testified that he was summoned before the faculty committee considering his application for tenure and promotion and questioned concerning the charges of Ms. N. and Ms. H. Thereafter, the committee recommended that he receive tenure and be promoted. The CSUS president accepted the recommendation. The board found that the Ms. H. and Ms. N. incidents had been "discussed by the faculty of the department at a meeting where [Brown's] promotion was being considered."

The final alleged incident of sexual harassment sustained by the board hearing officer occurred four years later. It concerned Ms. B. She was a student in two of Brown's courses in the fall of 1979. She had sought Brown out on two occasions to discuss with him personal problems unrelated to her coursework. Later, on October 15, 1979, she went to his office to discuss her difficulties in studying for mid-term examinations. While she was there Brown asked when his "date" was. Ms. B. said there was no date and noted Brown was a married man and a parent. As she was leaving Brown stated he would "sure like to make love to [her]." Ms. B. took this to be a proposition and was offended. She complained to another university professor who took her to Melnicoe.

Melnicoe took no immediate action. In January 1980 Ms. B. filed a Title 9 complaint with CSUS. An investigation was commenced by university authorities in March of 1980. A protracted review procedure culminated in the issuance of the notice of dismissal in June of 1981. The notice included Ms. B's charges as one of the alleged "series and pattern of sexual harassment of female students." The notice is the administrative pleading upon which the dismissal action which we review was predicated.

* * *

"In order to excuse delay, [the responsible party] must show exceptional circumstances prevented earlier action." That might be shown, for example, where the public agency lacks knowledge of the grounds of action. That is not the case here. The only excuse advanced by CSUS is the reluctance of the witnesses to the 1975 events to lodge a formal complaint. This is unpersuasive. If an overt sexual advance to a student while acting as a professor is unprofessional conduct that is so regardless of the subjective response of the student. Whether the student welcomes the advance, declines the offer, or is deeply affronted, is extraneous. Unprofessional conduct may be a breach of the rights of the particular student or students affected. However, with respect to the dismissal of a professor for cause, the administrative cause of action is not founded upon a private right of a particular student. It is founded on the right and duty of CSUS to deter misconduct with punishment, just as a criminal offense is a matter between the state and the offender, independent of the wishes of the victim of the offense. The disposition of the victim may be of interest in the exercise of discretion to prosecute or not to prosecute. However, when the election is made to forego prosecution the unreasonable delay that attends that election is not excused merely because the authorities have deferred to the wishes of the victim. It is just as unfair to let an employee "twist slowly in the wind" regardless of who the employer permits to hold the rope. CSUS attempts to bolster its argument by noting it has a "practice" to act only upon written complaint. That is not an excuse. A self-imposed constraint is no more a justification because it is delineated a practice than if it is discretionary. We note that when CSUS made up its mind to act it was able to persuade the formerly reluctant victims to participate.

In sum, we find no cognizable excuse for the delay of four years in initiating the disciplinary action concerning the 1975 events.

That leaves the issue of prejudice. CSUS did attempt to meet this burden. The board said: "[Brown] made no showing of injury as a result of the delay in the charges, nor could he do so. The only witnesses who testified about each of these incidents were the women involved and appellant. No one else could have testified, since appellant was alone with each woman at the time of the alleged harassment. None of their memories seemed to be dimmed by the passage of time. Thus, there was no injury, and the doctrine of laches does not apply." The board however did not go far enough. Assuming that we credit its determination of credibility, prejudice may also be established by detrimental reliance by the affected party upon the status quo. The record show such reliance. The tenure committees in 1976 advanced Brown to tenure in the face of the 1975 charges. The board found that the Ms. H. and Ms. N. incidents had been "discussed by the faculty of the department at a meeting where [Brown's] promotion was being considered." That is a circumstance which we must assume, in the absence of contrary proof by CSUS, led Brown to devote his energies to his employment with CSUS and perforce to forgo other employment opportunities. Nothing in the record supports an inference that Brown was without alternative prospects. Professor Melnicoe testified that Brown was a good teacher whose evaluations compared favorably with other faculty members. The loss of four years at the outset of an academic career is a considerable change of position in reliance upon the status quo. That works a sufficient prejudice to transform the unreasonable delay in this case into the bar of laches. Accordingly, the disciplinary action may not be founded upon the 1975 events.

III

That leaves intact the finding of a single sexual advance made in 1979 without threats of academic retaliation and tenders the question whether it alone supports the disciplinary action. We will answer in the negative because it does not support the charges upon which the disciplinary action was taken and they cannot be amended at this late date.

The notice of dismissal, the charging document filed by CSUS, alleged a linked set of events as the singular ground constituting the cause for discipline. It charged that "[t]he events upon which the . . . causes [e.g., unprofessional conduct] are based are a series and pattern of sexual harassment of female students by you, including harassment of: [Ms. N., H. and B. accompanied by threats or retaliation]. The finding of a single sexual advance to Ms. B., made without threat or retaliation, remaining after elimination of the 1975 charges from consideration, does not support that charge.

Manifestly a single instance does not constitute a series or a pattern. Nor was the act accompanied by retaliation as charged. That bears upon the question whether the advance impinged upon Brown's professional duties. We again note that CSUS admits that it "does not now, and never has had any rule, regulation, law or policy against faculty and students dating each other, or even living together or marrying one another." Accordingly, there is not substantial evidence to support the charge made. That conclusion compels Brown's reinstatement.

The discipline of an employee of the California State University and Colleges must be predicated upon a "statement of cause [*and*] the events or transactions upon which the causes are based...." The causes for discipline are set forth in Education Code section 89535 and include unprofessional conduct. The university initiates the disciplinary proceedings by giving a notice (the charging document) to the employee alleging the cause and events upon which discipline is based and takes the disciplinary "action." The action constitutes the university's judgment that the conduct, i.e. the alleged "events or transactions," meets CSUS's criteria of the alleged *cause* of discipline, e.g. unprofessional conduct, and that the respondent has engaged in it. Neither section 89539 nor any other provision of law permits the amendment of the charging document after CSUS has taken its disciplinary action.

Where, as here, the employee elects an appeal to the State Personnel Board, Education Code section 89539 governs both the grounds of appeal and (necessarily) the grounds upon which the board may act, here "that the employee did not do the *acts or omissions alleged* as the events or transactions upon which the causes are based...." This provision limits the board's authority to act (Ed. Code, § 89539) to the allegations of the charging document. Consequently, the board may not alter the charging document or take action upon a charge not made.

The judgment is reversed. The trial court shall issue a peremptory writ of mandamus directing the reinstatement of Brown and according him any other relief to which he may be entitled as a result of said reinstatement.

Additional cases have held that institutional codes of conduct do not need to spell out each actionable offense against the code, although procedural fairness must be observed throughout hearing processes. See *Cockburn v. Santa Monica Community College District*, 207 Cal. Rptr. 589 (Cal. App. 2 Dist. 1984) (instructor dismissed for embracing and kissing a student); *Strastny v. Board of Trustees of Central Washington University*, 647 P.2d 496 (1982) ("insubordination," "misconduct," and "violation of rules" are not impermissibly vague terms when used in a written code); *Naragon v. Wharton*, 572 F. Supp. 1117 (M.D.La. 1983) (instructor may be removed from teaching if involved in a sexual relationship with a student, even if the student is not enrolled in teacher's courses).

In elementary and secondary schools, standards governing teacher behavior are stricter and the guidelines more likely to be strictly enforced. For example, in *Tidwell v. Simms Independent School District,* the State Commissioner of Education denied an appeal from a Texas math teacher, dismissed after a showing that he had routinely used "vulgar" language in class, discussed sex and prostitution with junior high cheerleaders he was chaperoning, offered to pay students for posing nude, and fondled a student. The commissioner ruled, "Just cause exists where a teacher has indicated that he is likely to engage in conduct harmful to his students. The harm may be either physical or emotional.... No school district can allow its students to continue to be exposed to a teacher who may engage in such potentially harmful conduct." Tex. Comm. Dec. (Educ.), No. 174-R2-884, 22 September 1986.

Academic Fraud and Scientific Misconduct

In two recent books, *The Betrayers of Truth* by Broad and Wade (New York: Simon and Schuster, 1983) and *The Mismeasure of Man* by Stephen J. Gould (New York: Norton, 1981), readers are treated to considerable evidence that fraudulent research has a long-standing history, particularly when scientists have an ideological axe to grind or when intense competition leads to corner-cutting and deception. Most of the litigation in this area has included students caught cheating on exams or plagiarizing papers; several such instances are included in chapter 4.

As in other issues involving research, issues of academic fraud have been considered both by professional organizations and by government agencies. The AAUP *Statement on Professional Ethics*, included in the previous section, notes the obligation that a professor practice "intellectual honesty." The Association of American Universities issued a *Report on the Integrity of Research* in 1983, defining academic fraud as falsifying research findings, plagiarizing, abusing confidentiality, and knowingly violating research regulations and procedures. The Health Research Extension Act of 1985 (Pub. L. No. 99-158) requires the Public Health Service to establish an administrative process to review reports of scientific fraud; the National Science Foundation promulgated regulations in 1987 to take actions against researchers alleged to have committed scientific misconduct and their colleges even before a formal investigation has been completed; the final rules and regulations are printed in the July 1, 1987 *Federal Register* (Vol. 52, No. 126, pp. 24466–24470), and codified at 45 C.F.R. Part 689:

Title 45—Code of Federal Regulations—Public Welfare

CHAPTER VI—NATIONAL SCIENCE FOUNDATION

PART 689—MISCONDUCT IN SCIENCE AND ENGINEERING RESEARCH

Sec.

689.1 General policies and responsibilities.

689.2 Actions.

689.3 Role of awardee institutions.

689.4 Initial NSF handling of misconduct matters.

689.5 Investigations

689.6 Pending proposals and awards.

689.7 Interim administrative actions.

689.8 Dispositions.

689.9 Appeals.

Authority: Sec. 11(a) of the National Science Foundation Act of 1950, as amended (42 U.S.C. 1870(a)).

§ 689.1 General policies and responsibilities.

(a) "Misconduct" means (1) fabrication, falsification, plagiarism, or other serious deviation from accepted practices in proposing, carrying out, or reporting results from research; (2) material failure to comply with Federal requirements for protection of researchers, human subjects, or the public or for ensuring the welfare of laboratory animals; or (3) failure to meet other material legal requirements governing research.

(b) The NSF will take appropriate action against individuals or institutions upon a determination that misconduct has occurred under an NSF award. It may also take interim action during an investigation. Possible actions are described in section 689.2.

(c) NSF will find misconduct only after careful inquiry and investigation by an awardee institution, by another Federal agency, or by NSF. An "inquiry" consists of information-gathering and preliminary fact-finding to determine whether an allegation or apparent instance of misconduct warrants an investigation. An "investigation" is a formal examination and evaluation of relevant facts to determine whether misconduct has taken place or, if misconduct has already been confirmed, to assess its extent and consequences or determine appropriate NSF action.

(d) Before NSF makes any final finding of misconduct or takes any final action on such a finding, NSF will normally afford the accused individual or institution notice, a chance to provide comments and rebuttal, and a chance to appeal. In structuring procedures in individual cases, NSF may take into account procedures already followed by other entities investigating the same allegation of misconduct.

(e) Debarment, suspension, or termination of an award for misconduct will be imposed only after further procedures described in applicable debarment and suspension regulations. Nothing in these regulations shall preclude integrated and concurrent procedures under these regulations and the debarment and suspension regulations.

(f) The Division of Audit and Oversight (DAO) in the Office of Budget, Audit, and Control, oversees and coordinates NSF activities related to misconduct, conducts any NSF inquiries and investigations into suspected or alleged misconduct, and except where otherwise provided, speaks and acts for NSF with affected individuals and institutions. The Office of the General Counsel (OGC) advises DAO and represents NSF on any current or potential criminal prosecution, current or potential litigation, or significant legal questions that arise.

Eugene Dong, Jr. v. Board of Trustees of Stanford University
236 Cal. Rptr. 912 (Cal. App. 6 Dist. 1987)

[This fascinating case resembles nothing so much as a Dickens novel, notwithstanding its reference to Dostoyevski. It includes allegations of fraud, deceit, and other treacheries, but is included here for its additional value in understanding who may teach.

After an extended Dramatis Personae, the court summarizes a twisting set of facts: suspecting fraud, Professor Dong has reported his former colleague, Professor Lucas, to the Stanford authorities. Although the record concerning the allegations is unclear, it appears that Lucas may have committed fraud in his research, but it cannot be determined with certainty. Lucas accuses Dong of fraud in his own research, although this cannot be established, either. After the acrimony escalates, and after several investigations, everyone at Stanford understandably wishes to be rid of the matter.

Lucas has left. Dong persists, having notified federal officials of the allegations. He files suit on a variety of theories, including his own academic freedom.]

* * *

VI

Dong renews these arguments and adds others. He now contends (1) that the principle of academic freedom allowed him access to the Feigen committee report, for the purpose of advancing his own professional career by establishing "the existence of fraud in publicly-funded research"; and (2) that the University "restrained and chilled appellant's Academic Freedom right by erecting standardless administrative barriers, which were substantively irrational and applied to him in an arbitrary and discriminatory fashion."

These arguments presuppose that the University may be held liable in damages to a professor for refusing to divulge the contents of a disciplinary report concerning a fellow faculty member. We question the premise.

As we pointed out in *Kahn v. Superior Court*, the exact contours of academic freedom have not been fully delineated. In a concurring opinion in *Sweezy v. New Hampshire*, Justice Felix Frankfurter said this: "It is the business of a university to provide that atmosphere which is most conducive to speculation, experiment and creation. It is an atmosphere in which there prevail 'the four essential freedoms' of a university—*to determine for itself on academic grounds who may teach*, what may be taught, how it shall be taught, and who may be admitted to study." The quoted passage has found approval in subsequent opinions of the United States Supreme Court. That court has also suggested, albeit in contexts different from this case, that academic freedom is "a special concern of the First Amendment." But the high court has not yet addressed the extent of a university's autonomy in deciding "who may teach."

We are unwilling to allow that autonomy to be circumscribed by the views of a single professor, no matter how righteous he may be. In *Franklin v. Leland Stanford Junior University* a tenured professor, who disapproved of certain research then performed at the University, incited students forcibly to shut down the research facility. The University dismissed him. He challenged the dismissal in the trial court, and lost. This court affirmed the judgment. Among other things we held: "It is clear that the constitutional freedom to speak does not license a teacher to substantially disrupt and interfere with the normal operations of his or her employer, whether they be instruction, research, or administration."

In the same vein, the right to speak freely does not compel an audience to attend or to listen. The opportunity for critical inquiry and analysis, vigorous advocacy, and dialogue, all in the pursuit of truth, provides no guarantee that the truth (if it is that) will be discerned and accepted. Galileo's inquisitors, for example, refused to accept the fact that the earth circles the sun. Here the University may have had a duty to the federal government to investigate the possibility of fraudulent research accomplished at the expense of federal funds. It may have had an obligation to the public at large, and to itself, to maintain high ethical standards of research in its medical school. But it had no corresponding duty to Dr. Dong as an individual; the implied covenant of good faith and fair dealing does not compel an employer to accept the views of an employee, even if those views are correct.

Furthermore, it appears that by its own regulations the University owed to Dr. Lucas the right to notice and an opportunity to be heard. The University's Faculty Handbook contains a "Statement on Faculty Discipline," which provides in pertinent part that in disciplinary proceedings "that member shall first be notified, in confidence, of the charges against him and shall be given the opportunity of replying to them." A faculty member wishing to contest the charges may request a full hearing in private, and is entitled to be represented by counsel and to appear in person. These provisions are totally antithetic to the notion that an investigation must reach a certain outcome.

We cannot perceive that Dr. Dong's own academic freedom was otherwise curtailed. From all that appears in the record, Dr. Dong was at all times allowed to teach, to argue, to complain, and to pursue his own research; and he apparently is still employed at the University's medical school.

We cannot and do not express any opinion as to whether Dr. Lucas in fact did false research; that question is plainly beyond our ken. But even if we assume, for the sake of argument—an assumption purely hypothetical—that Dr. Dong was entirely correct in his assertions, we nevertheless conclude that he has no cause of action against the University on that ground. In the words of Fyodor Dostoyevski, "Men reject their prophets and slay them, but they love their martyrs and honour those whom they have slain." They do not, however, award them damages; publicity brings its own reward.

* * *

The judgment is affirmed.

The *Dong* case, in which one colleague accused the other of committing fraud, shows the extent to which these cases can deteriorate, and such cases are increasing. A similar case was settled in 1988 ("N.J. University Agencies to Settle a Lawsuit Filed by the Ex-Professor Charging Colleague with Fraud," *Chronicle of Higher Education*, 24 February 1988, pp. A15, 16); and a federal panel reprimanded two universities for not adequately supervising a researcher who performed fraudulent studies: "such institutions also have an obligation to ensure responsible science and to pursue diligently any allegation of scientific misconduct brought to their attention." ("2 Universities Chastised on Fraud Investigation," *Chronicle of Higher Education*, 3 June 1987, pp. 1, 7). Even when scientific misconduct is determined to have occurred, problems remain both for the colleagues who "blow the whistle" and undertake the investigation, and for the remedy to be applied to the wrongdoer. "Rights of 'Whistle Blowers' Must Be Protected in Science-Fraud Inquiries, Universities Told," *Chronicle of Higher Education*, 16 March 1988, pp. A13, 15); "NIH Upholds Misconduct Charges in Cornell Case," *Science and Government Report*, 15 March 1988, p. 6. For a review of how institutions should proceed in these instances, see Olswang and Lee, "Scientific Misconduct: Institutional Procedures and Due Process Considerations," *Journal of College and University Law*, 11 (1984), 51–63.

Conflicts of Interest

As with many of the issues in this chapter, faculty conflicts of interest reflect the increased commercialization of the academy, and the proliferation of problems inherent in the rise of big academic science. The agribusiness case in *CAAP v. Regents* included issues of trustees' conflicts of interest, but there have been relatively few occasions where the institution's faculty have commercial transactions with their institutions, or where laws prohibited these transactions. Public officials, both appointed and elected, are governed by a system of federal and state laws concerning financial disclosures, and in 1982 the state of California amended its regulations covering government officials (the California Fair Political Practices Commission) to include some public university researchers. See H. Leskovac, "Ties that Bind: Conflicts of Interest in University-Industry Links," *University of California, Davis Law Review*, 17 (1984), 895–923 and L. Jack, "Constitutional Aspects of Financial Disclosure Under the Ethics in Government Act," *Catholic University Law Review*, 30 (1981), 583–603. The California code was amended to read:

> (b) Disclosure shall be required under Government Code Section 87302 or any Conflict of Interest Code in connection with a decision made by a person or persons at an institution of higher education with principal responsibility for a research project to undertake such research, if it is to be funded or supported, in whole or in part, by a contract or grant (or other funds earmarked by the donor for a specific research project or for a specific researcher) from a nongovernmental entity, Ca. Admin, Code tit. 2, R. 18, 705.

Each affected institution has been required to draft a plan for reviewing the disclosure forms and evaluating possible conflicts. While the state regulatory system prompted this policy, many other states and institutions, including private institutions, have established policies for monitoring possible conflicts in research. A. Burke, "University Policies on Conflict of Interest and Delay of Publication," *Journal of College and University Law*, 12 (1985), 175–200. The story that follows is typical of the problems inherent in this field, particularly in technology transfer research.

U. of California Disputes State Auditor's Report that Professor Misused $500,000 for Company

The University of California at Los Angeles has taken issue with a state auditor's report that charges that a medical-school professor misused $500,000 in state funds.

In a report to the Legislature last month, the auditor said U.C.L.A. had "recovered" $500,000 from a professor who had used state money for a privately owned company that marketed technology originally developed in his campus laboratory.

U.C.L.A. administrators, while acknowledging that a small amount of money had been misused and eventually repaid, argue that the $500,000 was part of a mutual agreement transferring commercial rights to the technology from the university to the professor, Paul I. Terasaki.

The incident, which has been widely reported in California, brings to light the complications that arise out of technology-transfer arrangements, in which more colleges and universities are becoming involved.

Mr. Terasaki has been a pioneer in the field of tissue typing, developing inexpensive techniques to match human organs for transplants.

Since 1970, the university was one of two licensed producers of tissue-typing trays and other materials involved in organ transplant. When the field was deregulated and other industries became involved in production, the university decided to get out of the business, according to Albert A. Barber, vice-chancellor for research programs.

In 1984 the university entered into an agreement with a company set up by Mr. Terasaki, in which U.C.L.A. gave up any right to earnings from the technology in exchange for $500,000.

According to Mr. Barber, the state auditor's office received anonymous complaints about the agreement. Once notified, U.C.L.A. conducted its own audit and found few of the allegations credible, he said.

Nevertheless, the auditor's report contends that Mr. Terasaki had "violated university policies, procedures, and conflict-of-interest regulations by using state resources in support of his private commercial activities."

The report said Mr. Terasaki's company had used university furnishings and facilities rent-free, and that several employees of the company had remained on the university payroll after they were officially transferred to the private company.

In a statement, U.C.L.A. said the financial arrangement had had the full approval of university officials and the professor had not been intentionally involved in any wrongdoing.

Administrators agreed, however, that there had been "inappropriate payments" made to some university personnel who went to work for Mr. Terasaki's company. The amount involved—$13,178—was paid back, according to the statement.

Mr. Barber said the negotiated agreement was a "one-time settlement" meant to keep a distinguished scientist from working elsewhere. Mr. Terasaki was part of the delegation sent to treat victims of the Soviet nuclear accident at Chernobyl.

Mr. Barber said the university had agreed to the settlement, rather than negotiating for the possible royalties, because the technology was being developed elsewhere. "If there was intellectual property that was protected under a patent, we would have negotiated to receive royalties," he said.

Mr. Terasaki will continue to direct the medical school's tissue-typing laboratory. Mr. Barber said the university had set up a committee to oversee the activities of the laboratory, to avoid other conflict-of-interest charges.

© *Chronicle of Higher Education*, 12 August 1987, pp. 9, 14. Reprinted with permission.

Gross v. University of Tennessee

448 F. Supp. 245 (1978)

WELLFORD, District Judge.

In this civil rights and antitrust action, plaintiffs, former professors of medicine at the University of Tennessee Center for the Health Sciences (UTCHS), challenge their dismissals from their teaching and administrative posts. Drs. Gross and Grant were both full-time, tenured faculty members. In addition, Dr. Gross was Chairman of the Department of Otolaryngology. During the early part of 1977, both plaintiffs were suspended from the faculty at UTCHS, and Dr. Gross was removed from his position as department chairman as a result of their refusal to sign Medical Practice Income Agreements (MPIA), which was required of all full-time UTCHS faculty members. Plaintiffs were ordered reinstated without pay by this Court pending a hearing relating to their suspensions. On April 22, 1977, after a full hearing had been afforded plaintiffs, a seven-member faculty committee found that "adequate cause," as defined in UTCHS' *Faculty Handbook*,[2] existed for the termination of plaintiffs. This decision was appealed to the full Board of Trustees of the University, which sustained the terminations for cause, and also upheld Dean McCall's dismissal of Dr. Gross as department chairman in the middle of the academic year.

Since 1958, UTCHS has had a policy of limiting the outside income of professors in order to insure that they devote maximum energy to their teaching duties. The policy was in effect when both plaintiffs were initially hired at UTCHS. Dr. Farmer, now Chancellor, assumed the position of Dean in 1972. Upon learning that plaintiffs had not signed an income limiting agreement, Dr. Farmer informed plaintiffs that they would have to do so in order to remain on the faculty and maintain a private practice. This was delayed, however, due to the fact that the faculty was in the process of investigating new ways to handle income limiting agreements and receipt of patient revenue.

As a result of this investigation, the faculty voted in 1973 to retain income limiting agreements and approved a proposal to set up a professional corporation through which the income limiting agreements would be administered. A trust agreement was signed by all department chairmen, including Dr. Gross, which authorized the formation of the Faculty Medical Practice Corporation (FMPC). The faculty, through its department chairmen, signed an agreement with FMPC that required each faculty member to sign an MPIA every year. Having so agreed, plaintiffs refused throughout 1975 to execute an MPIA.

On January 22, 1976, Dean McCall, who replaced Dr. Farmer when Dr. Farmer became Chancellor, wrote letters to plaintiffs requiring that they sign MPIA's by January 23 or resign. Based on their signing MPIA's covering the period from March 15, 1976, to June 30, 1976, both plaintiffs were reappointed for the 1976–77 year and Dr. Grant was granted tenure.

The next year, however, plaintiffs refused to sign the MPIA. On January 1, 1977, Gross was relieved of his chairmanship for failing to have the members of his department sign MPIA's. Gross appealed this decision to the President of the University, stating that unresolved issues concerning rental of office space and the purchase of his equipment by FMPC were the reasons why he had not signed his MPIA. Dr. McCall conceded these two issues to Gross, who still refused to sign the agreement. Because of repeated refusals to sign the agreement when instructed, Dr. McCall suspended both plaintiffs on March 4, 1977.

Defendants have moved for summary judgment on all issues raised in the pleadings. Defendants have submitted briefs and affidavits in support of their position, and have filed as exhibits transcripts of the administrative hearings relating to plaintiffs' ter-

---

2. "*Procedures for Termination of Tenured, Special or Probationary Appointed Personnel.* The services of tenured faculty members, special or probationary appointed faculty members prior to the end of a specified term, may be terminated for (1) adequate cause; . . .

> (1) 'Adequate cause' for termination consists of incompetence or moral turpitude. Incompetence is a seriously unsatisfactory level or manner of performance of assigned duties. It may include or consist of willful neglect of duty or defiance of assigned duties."

UTCHS *Faculty Handbook*, § 5–5.

On March 21, 1977, a three-member committee of the Board of Trustees upheld Dean McCall's mid-year termination of Dr. Gross as Chairman of the Department of Otolaryngology.

minations. The Court has considered the briefs in the cause. No material issue of fact now appears to exist in the case, and defendants are entitled to judgment as a matter of law.

I. THE § 1983 CLAIM:

Defendant, University of Tennessee (U.T.), maintains that it is not a "person" within the purview of 42 U.S.C. § 1983, and that the claim under that section must be dismissed. The current weight of authority appears to be that state universities are not such "persons," and may not be sued under § 1983 because the university is a state agency or body corporate.

This Court has previously held that U.T. at Martin is a § 1983 person. The Court cited as authority *Soni v. Board of Trustees of University of Tennessee,* noting its reservation in holding that U.T. is a § 1983 person.

It should be noted that *Soni* did not hold that defendant here was in fact a person within the purview of § 1983. *Soni* decided that, assuming U.T. is a state agency, the state had waived Eleventh Amendment protection for U.T. by allowing it to sue and be sued in all courts. Since the *Soni* decisions, however, the Tennessee General Assembly has expressed its specific intent that the charter provision not be construed as an implied waiver of Eleventh Amendment protection for the University. Subsequent decisions of the Sixth Circuit cast some doubt, moreover, as to the continued vitality of *Soni.*

The Court sustains defendant's contention that the University of Tennessee is not a person within the purview of 42 U.S.C. § 1983. Although Dean McCall is a person for purposes of this section, the complaint does not contain sufficient allegations to charge him with personal liability. The § 1983 claim is accordingly dismissed.

II. THE § 1331 CLAIM:

Plaintiffs seek to amend their complaint to allege claims under 28 U.S.C. § 1331, for violations of their Fourteenth Amendment rights. Defendant apparently has no objection to the amendment, and the Court will, therefore, consider the substance of plaintiffs' constitutional claims.

a. *The Due Process Claim*:

Plaintiffs claim that they have a right, which is protected by the due process clause of the Fourteenth Amendment, to engage in the unlimited private practice of medicine outside of their teaching positions. It appears that although this point has been addressed in dicta in various decisions, it has never been squarely confronted in a reported case. The cases cited by defendants indicate that there is no constitutional right to engage in unlimited employment outside of a government position. Courts have noted that practice-limiting regulations are rationally related to the policy of requiring school personnel to devote full time to the duties for which they were employed.

Bearing in mind that federal courts are to play an extremely limited role in reviewing the merits of personnel decisions made by public agencies, the Court holds that plaintiffs have no constitutional right to engage in the unlimited private practice of medicine while holding a public position of employment. The Court further holds that the income limiting agreements utilized were rationally related to the espoused legitimate goals of fostering full-time devotion to teaching duties. The termination of plaintiffs by defendants for their refusal to sign the agreements infringed no constitutionally protected right of plaintiffs.

b. *The Equal Protection Claim:*

Plaintiffs claim that there are or may be members of the UTCHS faculty who have not signed MPIA's and yet have not been terminated by defendants. Disparate treatment of this sort has been held to constitute a violation of the Equal Protection Clause of the Fourteenth Amendment. It should be noted, however, that the transcripts of the administrative proceedings in this case do not bear out plaintiffs' contentions. Particularly in the testimony of Dean McCall, it is asserted, without refutation, that all members of the full-time faculty at UTCHS were required to, and did, sign an MPIA. In light of the weight of the evidence in the record to the contrary, plaintiff Gross' assertion that he has knowledge of one UTCHS faculty member who has not signed an MPIA is not sufficient to raise a material issue of fact. Defendants' motion is, accordingly, granted with respect to plaintiffs' equal protection claim.

III. NOTICE PROVISIONS:

Plaintiffs claim that they were entitled to twelve months notice prior to their terminations. This argument is derived from § 5–4 of the UTCHS *Faculty Handbook* which, in dealing with probationary employees, states: "If the individual has served two or more years at the University, such notice will be given no later than twelve months before the expiration of the appointment." Plaintiffs argue that as full-time tenured faculty members they should be entitled to as much notice as probationary employees. The termination proceedings against plaintiffs, however, were brought under the "Procedures for Termination of Tenured, Special or Probationary Appointed Personnel" which allow termination "*Prior to the end of a special term*" for adequate cause. The twelve month notice provisions were intended to apply to a probationary employee who was not being reappointed for reasons not amounting to adequate cause. Plaintiffs were therefore not entitled to twelve months notice prior to their dismissals, when the faculty committee found that adequate cause for their termination existed.

IV. ANTITRUST CLAIMS:

Defendants have moved for summary judgment on the antitrust claims on the grounds that (1) the University is immune from suit under the "state agency" doctrine, and (2) plaintiffs have failed to state a claim under the various sections of the antitrust statutes cited. The recent Supreme Court decision in *City of Lafayette, Louisiana, et al. v. Louisiana Power & Light Company*, casts some doubt on the applicability of the "state agency" doctrine to this particular type of regulation. This question is not necessary to a conclusion of this controversy, however, because plaintiffs, under the circumstances alleged in the complaint, have not demonstrated that they are entitled, as a matter of law, to any sort of relief under the antitrust statutes. The relationship between the parties was simply that of employee-employer and the antitrust allegations do not lie under these circumstances.

V. CONCLUSIONS:

While deciding in favor of defendants, it should be noted that at no time did the University ever question the qualifications or professional competence of plaintiffs, and this decision does not in any way impugn their integrity or professional competence. Although vigorously represented by capable counsel, plaintiffs have simply failed to demonstrate that they are entitled to any relief on any grounds asserted.

A summary judgment is granted for defendants on all grounds asserted.

Intellectual Property

Taken to its logical conclusion or natural extension, this section would dwarf the remainder of the book, and certainly the remainder of the chapter on faculty issues, inasmuch as various intellectual property dimensions permeate research and development activities. However, to keep the materials to a manageable level, only four large issues will be reviewed: how intellectual property issues arise in this setting, delay-in-publication issues, the contours of applicable federal law and state law, and a sampler of cases. While these issues arise in previous sections and recur in later sections, they are treated in this chapter as ancillary to faculty research.

To appreciate how intellectual property issues arise, no more striking example could be employed than the case of Ching-Wu (Paul) Chu, the physicist at the University of Houston generally credited with first synthesizing superconducting oxides.

In the Trenches of Science
J. Gleick, *New York Times Magazine,* 16 August 1987,
pp. 28–31, 55, 74, 77.

Certain American scientists wasted some time recently trying to make a superconductor out of the wrong element. They were chasing a phantom—a typographical error by the physicist Ching-Wu Chu. Certain American scientists believe that the error was no accident.

Chu stunned his colleagues and competitors in laboratories around the world last February by announcing the discovery of a new material that would make the phenomenon of superconductivity commercially feasible at last. But Chu refused to name the material before official publication of his discovery, weeks away. His claim set off a stampede. For experimenters struggling to take part, a hellish month followed—a month of tense days and sleepless nights. A practical superconductor, a material through which electricity flows without losing even the smallest fraction of its energy to resistance, would be a turning point in scientific history. Scientists were glimpsing a new age of electricity—a world of absurdly cheap power and trains floating in the grips of magnets. Enormous corporate interests were already at stake. Patent lawyers were chaperoning the research teams like pilot fish surrounding sharks.

So Chu's incomplete announcement was every scientist's nightmare: the breakthrough of a generation, and someone else had the secret formula. "It was gruesome," says Robert J. Cava, a member of a team at the American Telephone and Telegraph Company's Bell Laboratories, one of the major institutions near the forefront of the research. "There was a lot of pressure on us to figure out what was going on." The Bell researchers say they remained in the dark until the last days before publication, but other scientists heard a provocative rumor: that the esoteric element ytterbium was the key to the new superconductive material.

Ytterbium was indeed the element named in the manuscript that had been submitted by Chu's team, relative unknowns at the University of Houston, to Physical Review Letters, the premier journal for reporting breakthroughs in physics. But when the journal appeared on March 2, the final paper named a different element, yttrium.

Chu had pleaded with the journal for special handling, insisting on secrecy, fearful that the editors would leak. "Which we now know they did—like a sieve," says Arthur J. Freeman, a theoretical physicist at Northwestern University. "Only they leaked ytterbium instead of yttrium. I had heard for weeks that the material was ytterbium, and now I know where it came from."

As news of the yttrium-ytterbium affair spread through the scientific world, the journal's editors denied vehemently that they had divulged the secret. They privately expressed anger at Chu, suspecting an intentional deception on his part to mislead competing researchers. (Chu's friends share the suspicion. They have been retelling the joke about the king who leaves to his favorite knight the key to his queen's chastity belt, only to hear the knight gallop up behind him, shouting angrily, "It's the wrong key.") Chu, in turn, earnestly denies any deception. He explains the mistake as a typist's error, and anyway, he says, he corrected it two weeks before publication. "I don't understand why those people made such a big deal," he says. "Whether it's a typo or not—it *is* a typo, I have to say—why should they get so excited?"

"This is all supersensitive," says Myron Strongin, the journal editor responsible for sorting out a flood of superconductivity papers. "Everybody's uptight. It's of unique scientific importance. And they know Nobel Prizes are on the way."

The secrecy, the petulance, the jockeying for science's top prize, the raw displays of ego and ambition—all these have risen nakedly to the surface in recent months. For researchers, the Nobel Prize is certain, but the precise names it will honor are not. For industry, a patent battle likely to burn through the next decade will hinge on the events of this year.

Still, when these conflicts recede from memory, a story will remain of scientific discovery in its purest form. The heroes will be a few obsessive physicists driven to understand the strange, shimmering, electronic qualities of crystalline matter and who chose a path that their colleagues either scorned or overlooked. They blended intuition with experiment, mixing weeks and months of patient trial-and-error with an occasionally uncanny insight into structures too small to see.

Today, superconductivity is becoming a household word. The United States, Japan and the Soviet Union have all begun national programs meant to foster the years of engineering and development that will be needed to make a commercial reality out of the laboratory discoveries. The White House science adviser, William R. Graham, announcing the American program last month, contended that the rewards would be as rich as those that have flowed from the invention of the transistor and the integrated circuit. Yet only a year ago, superconductivity belonged to the obsessive few. It was a piece of scientific esoterica, tantalizing but obscure, for good reason. It seemed to be strictly a creature of the extreme cold near absolute zero.

Mercury, for example, is an ordinary conductor at room temperature—some small part of any electric current running through it is lost, converted by resistance into heat. In 1911, though, mercury also became the first superconductor. When cooled to 4 kelvins (452 degrees below zero Fahrenheit), or degrees Centigrade above absolute zero—the point at which all atomic motion stops—it suddenly lost all resistance.

Scientists slowly realized that the phenomenon might raise the possibility not only of cheap electrical generation and transmission but, also, of powerful magnets and levitation—because it is a peculiar characteristic of superconductors that they float calmly into the air when placed above a magnet.

But for most practical purposes, the necessity for extreme cold made superconductivity forbiddingly expensive. Just a few applications could justify the necessary cooling apparatus: magnetic resonance imaging machines used in diagnostic medicine, for example, and the powerful magnets that speed subatomic particles around an accelerator. The most exiting applications never passed the stage of drawings or prototypes. The Japanese National Railway made a levitating train, floating in a magnetic field above a metal rail and racing quietly at 300 miles an hour. A superconducting cable at Brookhaven National Laboratory on Long Island, though just 16 inches thick, proved capable of carrying one-eighth of all the electricity used by New York City on the hottest of hot days. These demonstrations led no further. But they showed what superconductivity could do.

The search for materials that become superconductors at warmer temperatures progressed slowly, sometimes proceeding by just tenths of a degree at a time, and by 1973 the temperature of superconductivity had been raised to 23 kelvins. But there progress stopped. Physicists would hear rumors of some improvement, and occasionally the rumors even reached print, setting off minor flurries of futile activity. By the 1980's, though, the field was dying. Many believed that science had reached nature's limit. Only a few kept looking for a high-temperature superconductor, a substance that would work its magic with less cooling or none at all. Ching-Wu Chu was one of those.

Chu, known to his friends by his baptismal name, Paul, is in his tiny office at the University of Houston, wearing, as usual, a long white lab coat over his jeans, his head framed by a rough helmet of black hair. He is speaking excitedly into the telephone, using one of the increasingly common languages of American physics— scientific Chinese, every fourth word an English technical term. In the laboratory a few feet to the left, the red glow of a furnace is visible; inside, a dark pebble of ceramic hardens at a temperature of 900 degrees Centigrade. Across the hall, Chu's colleague Pei-Herng Hor is also on the telephone, explaining for the 100th time the miracle of superconductivity—conduction with zero resistance, whether over a few feet of wire coiled in a magnet or over transmission lines spanning a continent. "Not *approaching* zero, it is zero. Yes. Yes. It can be 10,000 miles long and it's still zero." In the quest for this ultimate zero of electricity, Chu's team—barely a dozen men and women, nearly all immigrants, working with second-rank equipment—was among the few serious players remaining.

Chu was born in 1941, in China's Hunan Province, grew up in Taiwan and graduated from Cheng Kung University there in 1962. He came to New York to get a master's degree at Fordham University and then he moved to the University of California at San Diego, where he came under the magnetic influence of Bernd Matthias, the grand old man of superconductivity. For years, the German-born Matthias was directly or indirectly responsible for almost every improvement in the temperature at which materials become superconductors. If Chu later routinely scoured the world's scientific journals for hints of new materials, it was because Matthias had taught him to. Whenever Matthias learned of a promising substance, he made sure to get a sample and cool it down to the realm of absolute zero; so did Chu. Matthias once told his protégé that many of the best ideas come from dreams. In 1982, Chu work from a dream about sodium sulphide and, for the next two weeks, his team concocted every conceivable version of sodium sulphide. (Every one turned out to be useless.)

Chu also shared with his teacher an intuitive feeling for his esoteric substances. "Paul has beliefs which he can't walk up to a blackboard and prove to you, but, if you talk to him, you realize they come from deep experience," says Marvin Cohen, a theoretical physicist at the University of California at Berkeley. "He has an intimate relationship to his materials. It's different from the cold, analytical, machinelike style of some people in our field." A theorist in this quantum age thinks of substances abstractly and mathematically. "I don't know what color they are, I don't know whether they're heavy or light," Cohen says. "Paul knows the sizes of their atoms, how they act chemically, what kind of crystal structures they go into. He's accumulated these things."

In studying superconductivity, Chu took an unusual tack. Instead of staying with metals, which are natural conductors, he worked with oxides, compounds of metallic elements and oxygen, which generally conduct no electric current at all. A few oxide superconductors were known to exist, but their useful temperatures were unpromisingly low. Considering that they were oxides, though, Chu thought it was odd and interesting that these substances would be superconductors at all.

He told his wife last summer that he was giving himself three years: if he did not find a high-temperature superconductor by 1989, he would give up. Soon after, one day in November, he arrived at work and found on his desk a paper from *Zeitschrift für Physik*, a German journal. He glanced at the title—"Possible High T_c Superconductivity . . . "—and felt a physical shock. "God," he said, "we had worked so hard on the oxides, and there they got it."

A long stalemate with nature had ended, not in Chu's laboratory, but at the Zurich research center of the International Business Machines Corporation, where two scientists had made the breakthrough reported in *Zeitschrift*. They, too, were specialists in oxides: Karl Alex Müller, a gentlemanly Swiss physicist who had seemed to be nearing the end of a productive career, and J. Georg Bednorz, an experimentalist and an expert on materials. Their work was guided by Müller's intuitive feeling about oxides but was governed, day to day, by the relentless demands of trial and error, mixing powders in water, dropping them in acid, testing them at cryogenic temperatures. Sometimes, they found just a tiny change in molecular structure, a substitution of one atom for another at certain places in the patterns that make up crystals, turned a material into a conductor. But as far as superconductivity was concerned, progress was not just slow; it was nonexistent.

Then Bednorz came across a paper by some French chemists describing an oxide of copper mixed with two other elements, barium and lanthanum. The French had never cooled the substance to look for superconductivity. Bednorz and Müller did— and, on Jan. 27, 1986, they struck gold. As Bednorz cooled his sample, measuring a current passing through tiny wires attached to it, he discovered a sharp drop in resistance. By April, the two men had raised the record for a superconductor from 23 kelvins to 35—still 397 degrees below zero Fahrenheit. That was not warm enough for new practical applications, but it was warm enough to rekindle interest in superconductivity's future.

Müller and Bednorz made no announcement. They did not even tell scientists at other I.B.M. laboratories. They submitted a modest paper, not to Physical Review Letters, but to the German journal, which they knew would remain unread by most physicists. One reason for the two scientists' caution was that the history of super-conductivity had been littered with false alarms. Another was that Müller and Bednorz wanted to continue their work in peace. "We expected we would have a delay time of one or two years," Bednorz says. "Even at I.B.M. we didn't spread the preprint. We wanted to measure as much as possible without being pressed by competitors."

Chu's group had a routine: the researchers divided up the journals and were responsible for catching any news of even the remotest significance. "I told them you don't have to understand what you read, but come back and tell us what you think is exciting," Chu says. *Zeitschrift für Physik* is not an obscure journal, but at places like Bell Laboratories it went unnoticed. "It's not in our tea room library," said Bertram Batlogg, who rushed into the fray at Bell a month later. Chu, calling his staff together that morning last November, had a head-start.

Racing to confirm the Zurich discovery and advance it to practical temperatures, Chu called on the intuition that his mentor Matthias had tried to foster. Even with the Zurich recipe at hand, Chu was operating almost blind: no one knew exactly what the desirable crystal structure was, because four elements mixed together can produce dramatically different substances depending on how they are baked or how they are cooled. Müller and Bednorz had stumbled upon a particular crystal by an accident of preparation—a different structure from the one discovered by the French. "That was a kick of luck," Bednorz says.

Chu found that he could duplicate the accident, but his first samples of the material were unstable. One day they would prove to be superconductors; four days later, after reacting with water vapor and carbon dioxide in the air, these porous ceramics would once again be worthless. In the middle of this work, at a scientific meeting in Boston last Dec. 4, Chu gave a long-scheduled talk on an earlier oxide superconductor and, at the end, described his latest results with the new materials. Koichi Kitazawa, a physicist at the University of Tokyo, was in the audience. His group, too, had read the I.B.M. paper and begun a race to pursue its promise. After telephoning Tokyo for the latest data in his lab there, he told the Boston meeting about his results so far.

Chu took him aside and asked, "Is your sample stable?"

Kitazawa looked at him. "It depends," he said.

"Four days?" Chu said.

"Yes."

The word was out, Chu's group and the Tokyo group quickly learned how to stabilize the I.B.M. material. Scientists at Bell Laboratories invited Kitazawa to present his latest data there, and he did so—traditional scientific openness still outweighed the less familiar urge for competitive secrecy. Bell's scientists hastily assembled a team. Like Chu, they quickly confirmed the Zurich results.

But for all these groups and the many others who now entered the fray, the question was whether the hint contained in the Zurich discovery could be turned into still other materials that would act as superconductors at even higher temperatures. The difference between 23 kelvins and 35 was historically enormous, but for applications it was not enough. The next goal was 77 kelvins, the temperature that would allow liquid nitrogen to be used as a coolant. Liquid nitrogen is cheap—the supply is as abundant as air. Scientists casually pour it from thermos bottles or even from laboratory hoses into Styrofoam containers.

Each scientist who considered the possibility of a liquid-nitrogen temperature superconductor brought to the problem a different set of hunches and a different style of experimentation. As a first step, many substituted new elements for the atoms of barium in the Swiss compound. The Bell researchers immediately tried the closely related element strontium, and strontium worked. Chu did a further test, highly characteristic of his working habits. He placed samples of the I.B.M. material under high pressure, using a piece of equipment he calls his "bomb"—a custom-made lipstick-sized container capable of creating within it pressure 200,000 times that of the earth's atmosphere.

Chu had "squeezed" many materials over the years, knowing that pressure reduces the distances between atoms. Having squeezed earlier superconducting oxides, he knew what to expect: not much. In this case, however, he found that pressure dramatically raised the temperature of superconductivity, to 40 kelvins, then 52, then 57. There were even fleeting, transitory hints of declining resistance at temperatures above 70. Chu next tried substituting smaller atoms: strontium, and then calcium. With calcium, though, the temperature at which superconductivity occurred fell back down, to a discouraging 20 kelvins. "So we said we should do something else now— no hope with that kind of structure."

The materials he was working with were rough, filled with impurities and visible discolorations. Chu tried growing pure single crystals of the materials, but he quickly realized that he lacked the equipment and expertise to compete with the big laboratories. The question of impurity nagged at him. In his desk drawer he kept microscopic photographs from his work on an earlier oxide superconductor, barium lead bismuth oxide, and the photographs showed an eerie, cracked molecular landscape riven with chaotic fragmentation. He wondered about the electronic role of such flaws—"quantum mechanically, anything is possible," he says. And he wondered whether it was a mistake to look for a perfectly regular crystal. Some theorists had proposed that the strangely coordinated flow of electrons needed for superconductivity might be enhanced by complex molecular structures, one-dimensional chains, for instance, or two-dimensional sheets.

In January, looking over his data, he found one more crucial clue. The impure materials produced hints of superconductivity at high temperatures, but, as the experimenters cooled the samples, the materials were slow to reach zero resistance. When the researchers succeeded in making purer versions of these materials, however, even though superconductivity came more suddenly, the hints at the higher temperatures did not appear. One especially impure sample had come out of the furnace red on the outside instead of shiny black, and green, blue and white on the inside. It was clearly a mixture of different substances and different crystalline arrangements of substances that were otherwise chemically the same. Chu insisted that this bastard ceramic be tested, and it showed a faint signal that it contained some as-yet-undiscovered superconducting substance. "It gave us confidence something must be there," Chu says.

By now he had expanded his team to include a group at the University of Alabama, headed by his former student Maw-Kuen Wu. This time, the scientists tried a different substitution, again dictated by Chu's sense of atomic size: they mixed in the element yttrium for I.B.M.'s lanthanum. At first, the composition was all wrong. The furnace temperature had to be changed. But on Jan. 29, testing a sample at different temperatures, Wu saw the unmistakable drop in resistance at more than 90 kelvins, only 298 below zero Fahrenheit, the pen line on graph paper falling off a cliff. A few days later, after due consultation with his university's patent lawyers, Chu made his incomplete announcement.

"He caused Chu's disease—everybody was trying to duplicate it without knowing his results," says Theodore H. Geballe, a Stanford University authority on superconductivity. Even those who suspected that Chu's secret was yttrium—if not the rumored ytterbium—remained off the track; they made the mistake of trying to follow the composition described in the I.B.M. paper, eliminating the impurities that led Chu to an altogether new crystal structure. As one experimenter, Ivan Schuller of Argonne National Laboratory, put it afterward: "Everybody was trying to do the same thing, imitate what Bednorz and Müller did, and with hindsight that was the completely wrong thing to do. The yttrium compound is a very different sort of beast."

When Chu's March paper finally appeared, several groups succeeded over a single weekend in duplicating the yttrium material. Several succeeded in purifying the compound and identifying its precise structure; Bell Laboratories was the first to publish these results. Theorists struggled to understand a superconductor that performed at theoretically improbable temperatures. Experimenters found a dozen more compounds sharing the crystalline form of Chu's yttrium material. Chu and others began talking openly of the next grail, perhaps already in sight, a room-temperature superconductor. A joyous fever over superconductivity erupted at a historic, all-night special session of the American Physical Society in New York later in March. But the competitive bitterness began to come out as well. "The history is already a dangerous subject," says Robert Cava of Bell Laboratories. "There's lots of big egos in this game."

None of the contenders mentions the most famous award in physics, even privately. As one physicist put it, "There's a very old saying: One way not to get the Nobel Prize is to talk about it." Those who do talk about it warn against revisionism. Some accuse I.B.M. of trying to keep the prize exclusively for itself. Some accuse the University of Houston of trying to capitalize on an accidental discovery. Some accuse Bell Laboratories of trying to deflect attention from all other competitors. On advice of counsel, all remain silent about their patent applications; I.B.M., Houston and Bell are only three of the institutions honing their claims. In a few years, the prize committees and patent courts will make their judgments.

But Paul Chu will remember four tense and glorious weeks in February. "It's strange," he says, "yttrium and ytterbium, they both start with 'Y.' People kept on calling me and saying, 'Ytterbium's not working.' I just said, 'Oh? It's not working?'"

Reprinted with permission.

Unsurprisingly, University of Houston counsel have responded to these developments in superconductivity research with substantial legal resources and patent applications. Notwithstanding the legal counsel, an attorney unconnected to the university has sought all of Chu's studies and UH documents on the discoveries, under applicable provisions of the Texas Open Records Act, on the grounds that the findings "are not adequately protected." The apparent act of altruism was done "for himself, as a citizen and taxpayer, not for a client." "UH Requests Patent Information," *Houston Chronicle*, 29 November 1987, p. B3. In order to house the university's projects, the state legislature created the Texas Center for Superconductivity, and trustees have approved a new building. "Recent Breakthroughs in Superconductivity Lead to Rush for Commercial Applications," *Chronicle of Higher Education*, 17 June 1987, pp. 1, 4, 9. See also "U. of Houston Uses Texas-sized Persuasion to Keep Physicist from Defecting to Berkeley," *Chronicle of Higher Education*, 13 April 1988, pp. A1, 14.

The race to publish in this field and others where timing is essential has led to unusual publication problems. Since 1987, two new biweekly superconductor journals have appeared, *High T_c Update* and *Superconductors Update*, and, as the following story notes, international conferences on superconducting are even being videotaped for faster turnaround with reported results.

Race to Produce Superconducting Materials Stirs Concern over Publications and Patents

K. McDonald, *Chronicle of Higher Education*, 29 April 1987, pp. 6–8.

In a frantic scientific race that many believe will revolutionize 20th-century technology, hundreds of researchers around the world are rushing to produce new types of ceramic materials that, when cooled, lose all resistance to electricity.

Major discoveries are occurring so quickly that many become obsolete before they reach scientific journals, forcing scientists to get word of their latest results to colleagues in new, and sometimes controversial, ways. The rush to report the discoveries has also raised questions about who should be given credit for developing a new material and who should own the patent to it.

The ease and speed with which the unusual ceramics can be created in laboratories, and their widespread commercial importance, have in recent months produced an explosion in the number of "superconductors"—materials that conduct electricity without any loss in power.

Tremendous Increase in Volume

The surge of laboratory experiments has also produced a tremendous increase in the volume of theoretical research on superconductivity, which seeks to explain how the ceramics become superconducting at temperatures that promise to make energy-efficient electrical transmission, ultra-fast compact computers, and high-speed trains commercially feasible.

Ever since the first of the new ceramic superconductors was identified last year, the development of new materials that require less and less cooling to become superconducting has proceeded at a phenomenal rate.

From Houston to Beijing, "warm" superconductors have spilled forth daily from laboratories where research teams work around the clock to prepare reports of their findings, file patent applications for the new materials, and search for the ultimate superconductor—one that remains superconducting at room temperature but is flexible enough to be formed into electrical wires, magnets, and computer switches.

Limits of Communication Pressed

The rapid pace of discovery in this once-obscure field of physics is especially remarkable considering that advances in the discipline had usually been years or decades apart.

Now, with major developments coming only days or hours apart, the rush to report new advances and to stay informed of developments has pressed the limits of scientific communication as never before. Scientific journals that typically handle submissions in materials science, for example, are now jammed with papers waiting to be published.

Special Procedures Established

"I've been around here for 10 years in some capacity and I've never seen anything like this, not this continual volume," said Reid Terwilliger, assistant editor of *Physical Review Letters*, which has received about 100 articles on superconductivity in recent months.

To deal with the backlog, *Physical Review Letters* and *Physical Review B*, journals considered to be among the most prestigious for publications in the field, have established special procedures for submissions on superconductivity.

Last month, editors of two journals created review panels of scientists who could render rapid judgments on the merits of each submission to speed its publication.

Another departure from standard procedures of scientific publication—the use of a videotaped journal—was tested last month at an international meeting on superconductivity sponsored by the American Physical Society. The society, which publishes *Physical Review Letters* and *Physical Review B*, videotaped the meeting to expedite the communication of more than 50 scientific presentations.

'Video Journal' for $150

Proceedings from such meetings are generally printed in volumes that can take six months or more to publish. But by videotaping last month's meeting, within weeks the society provided a record of the seven hours of presentation in a "video journal" for $150.

"People are calling in every day," said a sales representative of the society in New York.

"I think a lot of people viewed that as a publication of sorts," said M. Brian Maple, a physics professor at the University of California at San Diego, who chaired the historic meeting, which was attended by thousands of physicists (*The Chronicle*, March 25).

The format was such a radical departure from the usual method of communicating results that Myron Strongin, one of the editors of *Physical Review Letters*, jokingly referred to the videotape during the meeting as *Physical Review V*—for video.

It served an important purpose. Scientists working on new superconducting materials say the pressure on them to accelerate the usual procedures of scientific publication has been unusually intense.

Making Certain of Credit

Not only do researchers want their results reported before they become obsolete, but they also want to make certain they are credited. Since the credit for a discovery is typically given to the person who submits results first, researchers aren't wasting any time in submitting them for publication.

"At the beginning of this mad rush, people were sending their manuscripts by express mail to the publishers of journals," said Alex Zettl, an associate professor of physics at the University of California at Berkeley.

"Things are coming down to the hour, not just the day. From a practical point of view, people are developing many of these things simultaneously."

Mr. Terwilliger said many of the recent submissions on superconductivity received by his journal had been hand-delivered by special couriers or brought into the editorial office by the authors themselves.

While those short cuts have significantly reduced the time to publication, scientists still complain that the weekly or monthly lags between issues have meant that journals have been unable to keep up with the rapid rate of scientific progress on superconductivity.

"Some of these developments become obsolete before the papers appear in print," said Mr. Maple, who keeps track of the new developments through preprints of journal articles sent to him by authors. Mr. Maple said he had three large notebooks filled with papers on new superconductors, and all of them "are filled with preprints rather than reprints."

"The preprints are an unofficial way of communicating among the community of people that have been working in this subject," he said. "But with the tremendous interest in industry in these materials, the community has been growing. It has gone well outside of those who initially started working on superconductivity."

Scientists say the rapid progress in their field has also forced them to place greater reliance on daily telephone conversations with their colleagues, on newspaper accounts, and on press releases to keep abreast of new results.

That bothers some researchers, who complain that, in the rush to stake claims to a discovery, some of their colleagues are being pressured to publicize their results before they have been thoroughly confirmed.

When Wayne State University scientists, for example, recently claimed that they had discovered a material that becomes superconducting at minus 27 degrees Fahrenheit or 240 degrees Kelvin—a major advance in temperature—some scientists complained it was deceptive, because the results could not be confirmed by the accepted methods of determining superconductivity. (The Wayne State scientists noted in their press release, however, that they had used an unconventional method to measure superconductivity.)

"No one has clearly demonstrated superconductivity at 240 degrees Kelvin," said Mr. Zettl. "So I think they were jumping the gun a little bit."

Could Bring Nobel Prize

Conclusively demonstrating superconductivity at 240 degrees Kelvin or at room temperature is considered to be a major achievement, something that, scientists say, could bring a Nobel Prize or a patent worth billions of dollars in licensing fees.

But it is also likely that such a development could bring neither.

The reason is that the new superconductors are all very similar in chemical composition. That similarity, patent experts note, could make it difficult to prove that a room-temperature superconductor is substantially different from the original ceramic materials that last year launched the race for high-temperature superconductors.

The credit for producing the first of those ceramics goes to two scientists from the International Business Machines Corporation in Zurich. Substantial increases in temperature from those "high temperature" superconductors, meanwhile, is generally credited to a team of researchers at the University of Houston and at the University of Alabama at Huntsville.

Legal Battles Anticipated

The scientists at I.B.M. and at Houston and Alabama are considered good bets for Nobel Prizes. Both groups have also submitted patent applications that seek licensing rights over a broad range of warm superconducting materials—materials that are now being produced by other researchers, many of whom are submitting similar patent claims.

"I'm sure there will be legal battles," said Mr. Maple.

While officials at the U.S. Patent and Trademark Office have not yet tallied the number of patent applications that have been received for new superconducting materials, some scientists believe they will be considerable, because of the large number of materials being produced and their economic importance.

"I think this will end up as one of the most valuable patents of all time," said Roy Weinstein, dean of natural sciences and mathematics at the University of Houston. He estimated that a broad patent covering all superconducting materials could generate as much as $50-billion in licensing fees over its 17-year lifetime.

To win a patent, applicants must prove to the patent office that their invention is novel, useful, and not obvious to someone skilled in the field related to the patent.

Stephen H. Atkinson, president of the Society of University Patent Administrators and director of technology licensing at the Harvard University medical school, suspects that much of the debate among inventors of the new superconductors is likely to center on proving their materials are novel and not obvious.

If the patent office rules that the early research by I.B.M. and the University of Houston group constituted a major advance in the development of the subsequent high-temperature superconductors, he said, it could award a broad patent covering all of those materials. Such a patent would be similar to one that was awarded to the University of California and Stanford University in 1980 for the general development of gene-splicing techniques.

Competing claims and a legal controversy over whether new forms of life could be patented delayed granting of the gene-splicing patent for seven years.

Niels J. Reimers, director of technology licensing at Stanford, doubts that patents for new superconducting materials will take as long. He said the lack of public controversy over the applications of superconductivity should keep the process from being held up unduly.

Competing claims, or interferences, that are likely to be made for similar superconductors by other researchers could hold up patent awards for two or more years, experts said. Rene D. Tegtmeyer, assistant commissioner for patents, said accelerated procedures that his office instituted recently to deal with interferences should significantly reduce such delays.

"Interferences that may have taken three or four years to resolve can be cut to one or two years," he said.

Competition from Abroad

Whoever wins the U.S. patent rights to license the new superconductors, Paul Ching-Wu Chu, a professor of physics at Houston who heads the Houston-Alabama team, predicts that industry here will face stiff competition from abroad in commercializing the new technology.

Japan has already formed a consortium of university, government, and industry researchers to accelerate the commercial uses of superconductors, he said, but no such coordinated activity is being contemplated in this country. "We still need more research in the development area," he said, "and we really have to do that in a coordinated way."

Reprinted with permission.

Speeding research findings into print has an opposite face, delay of publication. A 1985 study of research institutions' delay policies for allowing funding sponsors to review data before publishing showed delays of 30 days to over one year. The author summarized:

> In general, all respondents allow some form of delay of publication. Clearly, then, a reasonable delay is considered by institutions generally to be within the scope of free and open publication. Publication delay is confined to patent protection and pre-disclosed proprietary data, issues that are easily defined. Other types of intellectual property protection, such as trade secrets, do not appear in institutional policies as legitimate reasons for interfering with open dissemination of research results.

A. Burke, "University Policies on Conflict of Interests and Delay of Publication," *Journal of College and University Law,* 12 (1985), 175–200. On a publication delay of a different kind, the *New England Journal of Medicine* requires an embargo on news stories concerning its findings, to allow more thorough treatment of complex findings. When the Reuters News Service published a *NEJM* story before the allowed time, the *Journal* suspended Reuters from receiving its prepublication copies. "Medical Journal Suspends Agency," *Houston Chronicle,* 10 February 1988, sec. 1, p. 10.

International, federal, and state laws in this area are comprehensive and complex; in addition to copyright, these issues include patents, trademarks, trade secrets, and service marks. Moreover, even the traditional norms of these areas are changing, as in a 1988 U.S. Patent and Trademark Office decision to allow royalties to patent holders of new animal forms. On April 12, 1988, a patent was granted on a genetically engineered mouse, and nearly 2 dozen patents were pending for gene-spliced livestock and other animals. Under such a revised policy, royalties would be paid on the offspring of patented animals, rather than the traditional one-time fee. "U.S. Farmers to Face Patent Fees for Gene-Transformed Animals," *New York Times,* 7 February 1988, pp. Y1, 16; "Agency OKs Historic Patent on Genetically Affected Mouse," *Houston Chronicle,* 12 April 1988, sec. 1, p. 7.

The Patent System originates in Art. I, Section 8, Clause 8 of the U.S. Constitution, providing, "Congress shall have the Power . . . To promote the Progress of Science and useful Arts, by securing for limited Times to Authors and Inventors the exclusive Right to their respective Writings and Discoveries." Earl Kitner and Jack Lahr offer several definitions:

• "In its simplest terms a patent is an agreement between an inventor and the public, represented by the federal government: in return for a full public disclosure of the invention the inventor is granted the right for a fixed period of time to exclude others from making, using, or selling the defined invention in the United States. It is a limited monopoly, designed not primarily to reward the inventor (this may or may not follow), but to encourage a pubic disclosure of inventions so that after the monopoly expires, the public is free to take unrestricted advantage of the invention. Because there exists no duty to disclosure inventions, an incentive to disclose is embodied in the patent laws of the United States and most other industrial countries of the world.

The federal patent laws define the terms and conditions that must be met in order to take advantage of this contract offer, and both the federal patent laws and the federal antitrust laws define what can and cannot be done with this patent grant." *An Intellectual Law Primer*, pp. 10–11.

• "In copyright law, two primary requirements must be satisfied in order for a work to constitute copyrightable subject matter—it must be an 'original wor[k] of authorship' and must be 'fixed in [a] tangible medium of expression.' 17 U.S.C. § 102(a). The statute provides:

> (a) Copyright protection subsists, in accordance with this title, in original works of authorship fixed in any tangible medium of expression, now known or later developed, from which they can be perceived, reproduced, or otherwise communicated, either directly or with the aid of a machine or device.

The statute enumerates seven categories under 'works of authorship' including 'literary works,' defined as follows:

> 'Literary works' are works, other than audiovisual works, expressed in words, numbers, or other verbal or numerical symbols or indicia, regardless of the nature of the material objects, such as books, periodicals, manuscripts, phonorecords, film, tapes, disks, or cards, in which they are embodied. 17 U.S.C. § 101." C. Joyce, *Copyright Law*, p. 86.

• "A trade secret may consist of any formula, pattern, device or compilation of information which is used in one's business, and which gives him an opportunity to obtain an advantage over competitors who do not know or use it. It may be a formula for a chemical compound, a process of manufacturing, treating or preserving materials, a pattern for a machine or other device, or a list of customers. . . . A trade secret is a process or device for continuous use in the operation of the business. Generally it relates to the production of goods, as, for example, a machine or formula for the production of an article. . . . " *Restatement of Torts*, cited in *An Intellectual Law Primer*, p. 134.

Since the *Chakrabarty* case, Congress has acted to speed the transition of patentable discoveries to market, especially research conducted by universities and federal contractors. In 1980, the Patent and Trademark Amendments (Pub. L. No. 96-517) altered federal policy to enable colleges to retain patents on inventions that result from federally funded research; the government retains a royalty-free license to use the invention. In 1984, the law was amended by Pub. L. No. 98-620 to allow additional federal contractors to retain non-weapons patents, including certain plant varieties. Also in 1984, Pub. L. No. 98-622 established an alternative patent procedure, the Statutory Invention Registration. In 1986, Pub. L. No. 99-502, the Federal Technology Transfer Act enabled federal contractors to negotiate intellectual property rights more easily. Federal evaluations of these recent changes have indicated that the legislation has made technological transfer and university research much easier to administer and protect. *Patent Policy, Universities' Research Efforts Under Public Law 96–517* (U.S.G.A.O., 1986) and *Patent Policy, Recent Changes in Federal Law Considered Beneficial* (U.S.G.A.O., 1987).

States have also moved to govern intellectual property, particularly that which results from state-funded research programs at the states' public institutions. As noted earlier, California amended its ethics code to include certain faculty with possible conflicts of interest. Texas also amended its law, to allow faculty to hold equity positions in companies that are engaged in the commercialization of the faculty member's research (V.T.C.A. Education Sec. 51–912), and requires all public colleges to develop guidelines for regulating intellectual property policies (V.T.C.A. Education Code Sec. 51–680).

The states have also engaged in a wide variety of activities to fund technological research, to establish research sites and consortia, to allocate research equipment, and even to establish non-profit or profit subsidiaries. One survey of these activities concluded:

> "Can universities support research activities in an impartial scholarly manner and then participate in the commercialization of research results as competitors in a business environment? It is clear that universities are exploring this question and will experiment with different structures to combine these two goals. The success of such activities depends upon the expectations of the institutions. The universities that have chosen to reorganize their internal patent and licensing capabilities have already achieved increased disclosures and income from licenses. The universities that are currently trying to organize technology transfer entities outside the university structure may have difficulty finding a nonprofit structure that can be sufficiently entrepreneurial or a corporate structure that can compete with private business. Federal and State incentives have increased the odds for success, but whether universities will find it worth the effort and expense of being their own entrepreneurs is yet to be determined. *Trends in Technology Transfer at Universities* (Association of American Universities, 1988).

Copyright is an issue even more pervasive than other intellectual property transactions on campus. One scholar has noted, "Copyright is of increasing importance to college and university counsel. The question of ownership of copyrighted works prepared by faculty or students, questions of infringement through performance of copyrighted works or their use in the classroom, and the application of the fair use [doctrine] to educational uses of copyrighted materials in the classroom and in scholarly research are among the most likely situations in which copyright presents itself to the college and university counsel." D. Olson, "Copyright and Fair Use: Implications of *Nation Enterprises* for Higher Education," *Journal of College and University Law*, 12 (1986), 489–509.

Section 107 of the Copyright Act defines what constitutes "fair use":

> "Notwithstanding the provisions of section 106, the fair use of a copyrighted work, including such use by reproduction in copies or phonorecords or by any other means specified by that section, for purposes such as criticism, comment, news reporting, teaching (including multiple copies for classroom use), scholarship, or research, is not an infringement of copyright. In determining whether

the use made of work in any particular case is a fair use the factors to be considered shall include—

(1) the purpose and character of the use, including whether such use is of a commercial nature or is for nonprofit educational purposes;

(2) the nature of the copyrighted work;

(3) the amount and substantiality of the portion used in relation to the copyrighted work as a whole; and

(4) the effect of the use upon the potential market for or value of the copyrighted work."

A recent higher education case involving a common practice will illustrate the problems of copyright in the college setting: In 1982, nine publishing companies filed suit against New York University and several NYU professors, charging that the professors were photocopying and selling copyrighted works to students; the development of xerography and widespread availability of commercial photocopying facilities have led to such practices at practically every library and college in the country. In a consent decree agreed upon in 1983, NYU agreed to develop and employ a policy forbidding copyright violations and to put faculty on notice of appropriate practices for securing copyright permission. *Addison-Wesley Publishing Co. v. NYU*, 82 Civ. 8333 (S.D. N.Y., 1983). Most scholars of this field concede that copyright on campus is observed in the breach. G. Sorenson, "The Impact of the Copyright Law on College Teaching," *Journal of College and University Law*, 12 (1986), 509–43; R. Dreyfuss, "The Creative Employee and the Copyright Act of 1976," *University of Chicago Law Review*, 54 (1987), 590–647; R. Gorman, "Copyright and the Professoriate," *Academe*, 73 (September–October 1987), 29–33.

The cases that follow illustrate the range of intellectual property concerns in higher education, and it is clear that the volume will continue to grow, both as the technology to publish improves with desktop publishing and as software issues become more regularly tested in the courts.

Speck v. North Carolina Dairy Foundation
319 S.E.2d 139 (N.C. 1984)

MITCHELL, Justice.

The underlying issue controlling the result in this case is whether the plaintiffs acquired any interest in a secret scientific process at the time they discovered it while employed by the defendant North Carolina State University. We hold that they did not. Accordingly, we reverse the decision of the Court of Appeals.

The plaintiffs brought this action seeking to impose a constructive trust upon royalties received by the defendant North Carolina Dairy Foundation (hereinafter "Foundation") for its licensing of the use, under the trademark "Sweet Acidophilus," of a secret process discovered by the plaintiffs. In support of this claim, the plaintiffs alleged that throughout the 1960's and the early 1970's they developed a secret process for the use of lactobacillus acidophilus in dairy products which made the production and marketing of "Sweet Acidophilus" milk possible. They alleged that they developed the secret process while employed by the defendant North Carolina State University (hereinafter "University") and that the defendants learned of the process because of their fiduciary relationship with the plaintiffs. The plaintiffs further alleged that the defendants had breached their fiduciary duties to the plaintiffs.

The defendants' motions for summary judgment came on for hearing before Judge Farmer. After considering the pleadings, affidavits, pertinent discovery, briefs and arguments, Judge Farmer allowed summary judgment for the defendants.

The plaintiffs gave timely notice of appeal to the Court of Appeals from the entry of summary judgment. The Court of Appeals reversed and remanded the case to Superior Court, Wake County, for further proceedings. Judge Hedrick dissented, and the defendants gave notice of appeal of right to the Supreme Court.

Summary judgment for the defendants was proper only if the pleadings and evidence before the trial court taken in the light most favorable to the plaintiffs showed no genuine issue of material fact and that the defendants were entitled to judgment as a matter of law. We turn then to a review in such light of the pleadings and evidence before the trial court.

From 1957 until his retirement in June, 1979, the plaintiff, Dr. Marvin L. Speck, was a William Neal Reynolds Professor of Food Science and Microbiology at the University. He was engaged in this capacity in teaching and research on the use of high temperature for the pasteurization and sterilization of foods and the development of standards for attaining public health safety in processing treatments. In this capacity he also conducted research with micro-organisms used in food manufacturing— primarily lacticstreptococci, lactobacilli, and leuconostocs. As a part of such research, he conducted experiments and research with regard to the feasibility of developing a pleasant tasting milk containing lactobacillus acidophilus. Lactobacillus acidophilus is a bacteria that minimizes or eliminates certain undesirable micro-organisms in the human intestinal tract and is believed by many in the scientific community to contribute to more favorable digestion, improved general health and longevity.

Milk containing lactobacillus acidophilus has been produced for decades since the development in 1931 of a process for adding the bacteria to milk and has been known as acidophilus milk. This process caused the milk to have a sour flavor because it had to be heated to high temperatures for an extended period of time before the lactobacilli could be introduced. Additional work in improving such processes was done by scientists at Oregon State University around 1958. Their research appears to have been very similar to that conducted by the plaintiffs.

With the assistance of the plaintiff, Dr. Stanley E. Gilliland, who was at all pertinent times an Assistant Professor of Food Science at the University, the plaintiff Dr. Speck conducted research into methods of preparing acidophilus milk so as to eliminate the sour flavor. As a result of a course of research, experiments and study conducted at the University during the 1960's and 1970's, the plaintiffs ultimately developed new procedures and technology for the easy preparation and preservation of concentrates of lactobacillus acidophilus and a process by which the bacteria could be added to milk without causing the milk to have a sour flavor.

Dr. Speck informed Dr. William Roberts, head of the Department of Food Science at the University of the plaintiffs' discovery in a memorandum dated September 15, 1972 in which he said that there was nothing sufficiently novel about the process to "warrant the filing of a patent application on this product or means for its manufacture." He suggested the possibility of the use of a trademark and the licensing of dairies to use the trademark and the process discovered by the plaintiffs. Dr. Roberts suggested to Dr. Speck that he submit a proposal to the University's Patent Committee recommending that the licensing and marketing of acidophilus milk produced by the use of the secret process be handled through the Foundation.

The Foundation is a nonprofit corporation engaged in the support of research for the public good. From time to time it provides funds in support of research at the University. The Foundation and the University maintain a close relationship and the Vice-Chancellor of Foundations and Development of the University serves as the Secretary of the Foundation.

Dr. Speck submitted a proposal concerning acidophilus milk to the Patent Committee. Dr. Speck and Dr. Roberts were invited to appear before the Patent Committee at its meeting on October 19, 1972. The minutes of that meeting of the Patent Committee show that:

> Dr. Speck briefly outlined the background of his research and he and Dr. Roberts explained the way in which they proposed to get the product on the market. In general, they proposed to work through the North Carolina Dairy Foundation and employ a patent attorney to advise on the desirability of obtaining either a trademark or a copyright. Cost of the venture would be borne by the Dairy Foundation and a licensing of any trademark obtained would be handled through that organization. After a brief discussion by the Committee, which brought out that a patent application was not feasible, Mr. Conner moved that the request be approved and the motion was seconded by Dr. Bennett. Motion carried unanimously.

At the annual meeting of the Foundation on October 28, 1972, Dr. J.E. Legates, Dean of the School of Agriculture and Life Sciences of the University, made a presentation concerning Dr. Speck's discovery. The minutes of that meeting show that Dean Legates:

> stated that this new process had been taken before the Patent Committee of the University and, with the approval of President [of the Foundation] Davenport, the [University] Patent Committee was applying for a patent on [sic] a trademark for the product through the Dairy Foundation. Dean Legates said that any funds derived through the licensing of the trademark for the acidophilus milk would accrue to the Dairy Foundation and requested that the Board of Directors appropriate up to $3,000 to register the trademark and to develop a merchandising proposal for its promotion.

During this same meeting of the Foundation, which Dr. Speck attended, a motion was made for the President of the Foundation to appoint a committee composed of a producer, a processor, and a supplyman "to work with the appropriate people at the University to carry out this activity." The motion was passed.

In 1973, the Foundation requested that Dr. Speck work with Miles Laboratories, Inc. and other companies to explore possible arrangements for the manufacturing of the cultures to be used in producing the bacteria for acidophilus milk. The only question Dr. Speck raised in the initial stages of the preparations for production and marketing of the acidophilus milk was whether the ownership of the trademark "Sweet Acidophilus" would be in the name of the University or the name of the Foundation. On January 9, 1974, Dr. Speck called Dr. Rudolph Pate, Vice-Chancellor for Foundations and Development at the University and Secretary of the Foundation, to ask if it was not true that the Foundation would own the trademark. Dr. Pate informed him that this was correct.

During 1974, Dr. Speck, Dr. Roberts, Dean Legates and other University officials worked with the Foundation to find a licensee to market "Sweet Acidophilus" milk. All of these individuals were employed by and paid by the University at all times pertinent to this appeal. As a result of their efforts, an agreement was entered on December 18, 1974 between the Foundation, G.P. Gundlach & Company and Miles Laboratories, Inc., whereby G.P. Gundlach & Company agreed to handle marketing, product development and promotion of "Sweet Acidophilus" milk and Miles Laboratories, Inc. agreed to produce the lactobacillus acidophilus cultures.

The University sponsored a luncheon on April 18, 1975 to announce the development of "Sweet Acidophilus" milk. In a letter about the luncheon, Dr. Pate stated that:

> We believe that the development and franchising of this culture nationally are two very significant activities in food science and constitute notable accomplishments of the University.

In form letters about the luncheon, Dr. Pate also wrote that:

> North Carolina State University will review details of the development of a new acidophilus culture by its food scientists and the plans to merchandise this important new product throughout the nation at a special luncheon at the University Faculty Club, Friday, April 18, at 1:00 p.m. The Acidophilus culture is being marketed through a franchise arrangement by the North Carolina Dairy Foundation, Inc....

Dr. Speck wrote to Dr. Roberts on November 3, 1975 stating that he thought it was:

> Entirely proper for the Dairy Foundation to be selected for the commercial development and marketing of "SWEET ACIDOPHILUS" and to be the University's agent to receive any royalties from our development. In attending to the various legal aspects of this project (which was the first experience for a number of us) participation by the inventor in the royalties was overlooked. It would seem that now is an appropriate time to take care of this matter.

In a November 10, 1976 response to Dr. Speck from Dr. Clauston Jenkins, Assistant to the Chancellor and Legal Advisor to the University, the University denied that Dr. Speck had any right to share in the royalties. Dr. Speck replied by the memorandum dated December 3, 1976 renewing his request for a share in the royalties.

On January 23, 1978, the Chairman of the University's Patent Committee wrote a memorandum to Dr. Joab Thomas, Chancellor of the University, recommending the University consider making a one time payment to Dr. Speck of fifteen percent of the royalty income from the successful marketing of the "Sweet Acidophilus" trademark. He based his recommendation on the fact that others in the same department with Dr. Speck at the University had received, under the written Patent Policy of the University, fifteen percent of the royalty income from patents on their inventions. He suggested that the University adopt a similar approach to be applied to trademarks not covered by the written Patent Policy in order to prevent the possibility of the development of "hard feelings and tensions" within the faculty. No royalty income was paid to Dr. Speck. Approximately four years later, on December 11, 1981, the plaintiffs, Dr. Speck and Dr. Gilliland, instituted the present lawsuit.

The plaintiffs alleged in their complaint that the defendants learned of the secret process for the preparation and use of lactobacillus acidophilus in dairy products as a result of their fiduciary relationship with respect to the plaintiffs. The plaintiffs also alleged that the defendants breached their fiduciary duties by using the secret process to their own advantage. The plaintiffs further alleged that the defendants' violation of their fiduciary duties entitled the plaintiffs to a constructive trust on the proceeds from the secret process and from the trademark "Sweet Acidophilus" which was obtained by the defendant Foundation, since both represent "the culmination of the plaintiffs' ingenuity and efforts." We do not agree.

A confidential or fiduciary relationship exists in all cases where there has been a special confidence reposed in one who "in equity and good conscience is bound to act in good faith and with due regard to the *interests* of the one reposing confidence." If the plaintiffs never had any interest in the process which they developed while employed by the University, the defendants did not stand in a fiduciary relationship to the plaintiffs with regard to the process. Further, even if a fiduciary relationship existed between the parties, the defendants were required only to refrain from abusing the confidence placed in them by taking advantage to themselves *at the expense of the plaintiffs*. Therefore, the threshold issue to be resolved on this appeal is whether the plaintiffs acquired any interests cognizable in equity or at law at the time they developed the secret process in question. We hold that they did not.

The respective rights of employer and employee in an invention or discovery by the latter arise from the contract of employment. The fruit of the labor of one who is hired to invent, accomplish a prescribed result, or aid in the development of products belongs to the employer absent a written contract to assign. In such instances:

> If the employee fails to reach his goal the loss falls upon the employer, but if he succeeds in accomplishing the prescribed result then the invention belongs to the employer even though the terms of employment contain no express provision dealing with the ownership of whatever inventions may be developed.

In the instant case the plaintiffs' pleadings reveal that they developed the secret process for improved methods of preparation and preservation of concentrates of lactobacillus acidophilus while employed as teachers and researchers to engage *inter alia* in just such research and development for the University. At all times pertinent, the plaintiffs' salaries were paid by the University. Additionally, the plaintiffs candidly acknowledged during oral argument that the University was the place where they discovered the secret process and that the resources provided them for their research by the University enabled them to discover the process. Under these facts, the secret process developed through the research of the plaintiffs belonged to the University absent a written contract by the University to assign.

Regrettably, the plaintiffs in the instant case were not employed pursuant to a written contract detailing their duties as professors and researchers. It is clear, however, that the plaintiffs were permitted and encouraged by their employer the University to conduct the precise research which led to the discovery and perfection of the secret process. It is equally clear that the plaintiffs performed this work on their employer's time and using their employer's research resources and that they were paid a salary to do so. As it has been clearly stated:

It matters not in what capacity the employee may originally have been hired, if he be set to experimenting with the view of making an invention, and accepts pay for such work, it is his duty to disclose to his employer what he discovers in making the experiments, and what he accomplishes by the experiments belongs to the employer.

Further, the written Patent Policy of the University was not a written contract to waive the University's rights in the secret process or to assign all or any part of those rights to the plaintiffs. That policy merely assigns fifteen percent of the royalties from any *patent* obtained on an invention by an employee of the University to the inventor. The secret process developed by the plaintiffs was not patentable, and this fact was recognized by the plaintiffs at the time they discovered the process. The written Patent Policy adopted on November 16, 1973 by the defendant, The Board of Governors of The University of North Carolina, simply was silent as to trademarks and trade secrets. The defendant Board of Governors is responsible for the general control and management of the defendant University and fifteen other constituent institutions. There is no indication in the record on appeal that the defendant Board of Governors has ever authorized or approved an amendment to its written Patent Policy in any way to cover trademarks and trade secrets.

As the secret process in question belonged to the University immediately upon its discovery by the plaintiffs, the plaintiffs never possessed any interest cognizable in equity or at law to the process. Therefore, the defendants owed no fiduciary duty to the plaintiffs as a result of the plaintiffs' confidential revelation to the University of the secret process it already owned. Indeed, any fiduciary duty owed with regard to the secret process was owed by the plaintiffs to the University in its capacity as the employer who had employed them to develop the process.

The plaintiffs pointed out during oral arguments that the November 10, 1976 letter to Dr. Speck from Dr. Jenkins, Assistant to the Chancellor and Legal Advisor to the University, characterized the actions of the Patent Committee of the University as "returning" all rights to Speck after concluding that the secret process was not patentable "to dispose of as you saw fit." They pointed out that Dr. Jenkins then took the position that the plaintiffs had waived any rights they had in the secret process in favor of the Foundation. The plaintiffs argued that the position taken by Dr. Jenkins, together with arguments made by the defendants in their briefs on appeal, alleged certain facts pertaining to the relationship between the plaintiffs and the defendants which caused the principles of law previously discussed in this opinion to be inapplicable. The plaintiffs argued that, if the construction given the facts by Dr. Jenkins and the defendants was correct, the plaintiffs own or did own rights in the secret process and that any remaining questions are questions of fact which the plaintiffs were entitled to have resolved by a jury. We do not find this argument persuasive.

The correspondence and actions of the parties previously reviewed herein clearly reveal that the plaintiffs at all pertinent times held the correct opinion that the secret process they had discovered belonged to the University and that the University was merely waiving its rights in favor of the Foundation or using the Foundation as its agent for marketing. Dr. Speck's letter of November 3, 1975 reveals that he clearly held this opinion. The letters by Dr. Pate and the statements by Dean Legates during the meeting of the Foundation attended by Dr. Speck on October 28, 1972—both previously set forth herein—could only have tended to lead Dr. Speck to hold the same opinion.

In any event, the characterization of facts concerning prior relationships of the parties by one of them does not control in a lawsuit. If in equity and at law the plaintiffs had no right to the secret process, and we have held that they did not, efforts by the defendants to construe the facts after they had occurred could not give the plaintiffs that which equity and the law did not give them.

Finally, it is worthwhile to note that the University and the Foundation are not dedicated to making and retaining profits, but instead use their income for the good of the public by promoting and financially assisting scientific research for the common good. Acidophilus milk is viewed by many experts as promoting good health and increasing longevity and, thereby, as improving the human condition. Judge John J. Parker perhaps exhibited remarkable foresight and anticipated a case similar to the instant case when he wrote:

> It is unthinkable that, where a valuable instrument in the war against disease is developed by a public agency through the use of public funds, the public servants employed in its production should be allowed to monopolize it for private gain and levy a tribute upon the public which has paid for its production....

The decision of the Court of Appeals reversing summary judgment for the defendants is reversed. The case is remanded to the Court of Appeals with instructions to reinstate the summary judgment for the defendants entered by the trial court.

Williams v. Weisser

78 Cal. Rptr. 542 (Cal. App. 2 1969)

KAUS, Presiding Justice.

Defendant Weisser, who does business under the fictitious name of Class Notes, appeals from a judgment which enjoins him from copying, publishing and selling notes of lectures delivered by plaintiff in his capacity as an Assistant Professor of Anthropology at the University of California at Los Angeles ("UCLA"). The judgment also awards plaintiff $1,000.00 in compensatory and $500.00 in exemplary damages.

A joint pretrial restatement described the nature of the case as follows: "Plaintiff is Assistant Professor at UCLA in the Anthropology Department. Defendant does business in Westwood, California as Class Notes selling outlines for various courses given in UCLA. In 1965, defendant paid Karen Allen, a UCLA student, to attend plaintiff's class in Anthropology 1 to take notes from the lectures, and to type up the notes. Allen delivered the typed notes to defendant and defendant placed a copyright notice thereon in defendant's name, reproduced the typed notes, and sold and offered them for sale. Plaintiff objected. Defendant did not cease these activities until served with summons, complaint and temporary restraining order. Plaintiff seeks a permanent injunction, general damages, and punitive damages."

At the pretrial it was agreed that: "Defendant has used plaintiff's name in selling the publications here in question."

The judgment in plaintiff's favor was based on two grounds: 1. defendant infringed plaintiff's common law copyright in his lectures; and 2. defendant invaded plaintiff's privacy by the use of plaintiff's name.

On appeal defendant advances the following points:

1. The common law copyright in plaintiff's lectures presumptively belonged to UCLA. Defendant's efforts at the trial to show that a purported assignment of the rights of the university to plaintiff was not intended to be an assignment or, if it was, that it was made under a mistake of law, were erroneously cut off by a peremptory ruling that plaintiff was the owner of the copyright.

2. Even if plaintiff was the owner of the copyright the "general and unrestricted publication" of the "organization and content" of the lectures constituted a divestment of any such right.

3. Defendant's use of the notes was "a fair use and did not constitute a wrongful trading on, or actionable commercial abuse of, plaintiff's personality or reputation."

4. The evidence does not support the award of damages, compensatory or exemplary.

Certain preliminary observations are in order:

1. The product of the mind in which the plaintiff claims a copyright consists of the extensive notes which he had compiled before the beginning of the course, together with the oral expression at the time of delivery of the lectures, based on the notes, which delivery included charts and diagrams placed on the classroom blackboard. This is, therefore, not a case where the concrete expression of the "composition" consists solely of an intangible oral presentation. As far as this litigation is concerned, the chief importance of the oral presentation is that it provided defendant with access to plaintiff's work and with an argument that there had been a divestive publication.

2. Defendant does not dispute on this appeal that the lectures were properly the subject of a common law copyright. Below it was contended that they lacked originality, were "merely lightly embellished and thinly disguised paraphrasings of the works of others, both as to form and content" and were "wholly in the public domain." These contentions are now abandoned.

3. Substantial similarity between the lectures and the notes published by defendant is conceded.

Ownership Of Copyright

Plaintiff became employed by UCLA starting in July 1965. Defendant's relations with the university started in 1948 when he began to publish and sell to students what purported to be notes of various courses. In 1963 defendant and the university authorities agreed on certain ground rules as a condition to advertising in the Daily Bruin, the student newspaper. Friction arose between defendant and the administration. The matter culminated in a memorandum dated November 19, 1964, addressed to all members of the faculty.

At the trial Vice Chancellor Sherwood of UCLA appeared as one of plaintiff's witnesses. He testified, among other matters, to the following: He had served for eight years as a member of the faculty committee charged with the responsibility of approving manuscripts for publication by the University of California Press. If a professor's manuscript was thought to have commercial value, the university would sign a regular publisher's contract with the author, under which contract the professor would receive royalties at commercial rates. This was, to his knowledge, the practice throughout the United States.

In 1964 Vice Chancellor Sherwood and Vice Chancellor Young drafted the memorandum of November 19, 1964. This was done after a discussion with Mr. John Sparrow, counsel representing the university. The court's peremptory ruling to the effect that plaintiff, rather than the university, was the owner of the copyright came right after Sherwood, on cross-examination, had perhaps admitted that if it were the law of California that the copyright in a professor's lectures belongs to the university that might have somehow affected the November 19, 1964, memorandum. He did, however, point out that if such were the law, it would simplify his job immensely, since "a faculty member would not be able to leave the university for the university would have a right to his lectures and he could only go to another institution if he were in a position to turn his attention to a new subject."

During the argument that followed the ruling, counsel, although he perhaps was not required to do so, stated: " * * * I believe he would testify, and I offer by way of offer of proof, that this witness will further testify if allowed to do so that this letter was nothing more than a statement of his and Chancellor Young's understanding of California common-law."

After this offer of proof the court asked a few questions of the witness: " * * * I will just ask one more question on this subject, Dr. Sherwood. Whether it was rightly or wrongly the expression of the opinion of counsel, is this the policy that was followed by the university with respect to these lecture notes? THE WITNESS: It is. THE COURT: And that is what you intended? THE WITNESS: And that is what we intended."

If it were the law that, in the absence of evidence one way or another, UCLA rather than plaintiff is presumed to be the owner of the copyright to plaintiff's lectures or if the record contained any evidence that plaintiff had assigned his copyright to the university, the trial court's ruling would have been premature. For what it was worth, defendant was still developing his theory that the November 19 memorandum did not effectively transfer the university's copyright to plaintiff.

We are, however, convinced that in the absence of evidence the teacher, rather than the university, owns the common law copyright to his lectures. Since there was no evidence that plaintiff had assigned his copyright to the university, the entire question of whether the university had quitclaimed something it did not own was beside the point. Defendant was therefore not prejudiced by the ruling.

Defendant claims that the opposite is the law. His sole statutory authority is section 2860 of the Labor Code which reads as follows: "Everything which an employee acquires by virtue of his employment, except the compensation which is due to him from his employer, belongs to the employer, whether acquired lawfully or unlawfully, or during or after the expiration of the term of his employment."

It is obvious that a literal application of that section does not cover the present situation. The code speaks of things which the employee "acquires," not matters which he creates. In Burns v. Clark, the Supreme Court said that the section, then section 1985 of the Civil Code, was to be construed as "but an expression of the familiar principle that forbids an agent or trustee from using the trust property or powers conferred upon him for his own benefit, and which, in case of his doing so, requires him to account for the profits. * * * " Thus the section has been applied principally, though not exclusively, to unfair competition carried on by former employees with the use of trade secrets and the like. Even so it has been narrowly employed. We do not believe it applies here.

Defendant also claims that plaintiff is in the position of an employee for hire whose employment calls for the creation of a copyrightable work, or, perhaps, of an independent contractor who has been so commissioned. In such cases it is usually presumed that, unless a different intention is shown, the employer or commissioner is the owner of the copyright.

This contention calls for some understanding of the purpose for which a university hires a professor and what rights it may reasonably expect to retain after the services have been rendered. A university's obligation to its students is to make the subject matter covered by a course available for study by various methods, including classroom presentation. It is not obligated to present the subject by means of any particular expression. As far as the teacher is concerned, neither the record in this case nor any custom known to us suggests that the university can prescribe his way of expressing the ideas he puts before his students. Yet expression is what his lawsuit is all about. No reason has been suggested why a university would want to retain the ownership in a professor's expression. Such retention would be useless except possibly for making a little profit from a publication and for making it difficult for the teacher to give the same lectures, should he change jobs.

Indeed the undesirable consequences which would follow from a holding that a university owns the copyright to the lectures of its professors are such as to compel a holding that it does not. Professors are a peripatetic lot, moving from campus to campus. The courses they teach begin to take shape at one institution and are developed and embellished at another. That, as a matter of fact, was the case here. Plaintiff testified that the notes on which his lectures were based were derived from a similar course which he had given at another university. If defendant is correct, there must be some rights of that school which were infringed at UCLA. Further, should plaintiff leave UCLA and give a substantially similar course at his next post, UCLA would be able to enjoin him from using the material, which according to defendant, it owns.

No one but defendant, an outsider as far as the relationship between plaintiff and UCLA is concerned, suggests that such a state of the law is desirable.

Another strange consequence which would follow from equating university lectures with other products of the mind which an employee is hired to create is, that in order to determine just what it is getting, the university would have to find out the precise extent to which a professor's lectures have taken concrete shape when he first comes to work. Not even defendant suggests that a contract for employment implies an assignment to the university of any common law copyright which the professor already owns.

* * *

It is thus apparent that no authority supports the argument that the copyright to plaintiff's notes is in the university. The indications from the authorities are the other way and so is common sense.

* * *

After defendant was advised that plaintiff objected to the note taking in his class his conduct became extremely devious. According to Miss Allen, who was called as a witness by plaintiff, defendant called her and said that if she chose "to go to Doctor Williams' class from then on and take notes that [she] should not let [herself]—well, not reveal [herself] [a]s a note-taker." Although, under gentle leading by defendant's counsel, Miss Allen softened the impact of that statement under cross-examination, the trial court was entitled to accept the first version at face value.

Taking the evidence as a whole, the trial court was amply justified in concluding that defendant was not an innocent layman, caught in the complexities of the law, but a businessman who, for personal profit, was determined to pursue a certain course of action even if it meant riding roughshod over the rights of others.

The judgment is affirmed.

Weinstein v. University of Illinois
811 F.2d 1091 (7th Cir. 1987)

EASTERBROOK, Circuit Judge.

Many disputes may be compromised by converting the stakes to a common denominator such as money and splitting the difference. Few commercial disputes end up in court, because the disputants may readily compromise and move on. Other disputes are harder to resolve because they seem to involve principles for which no compromise is readily apparent. The result may be a private war. A dispute that would be resolved quickly in the commercial world may fester. We have such a dispute. It is about the order in which the names of an article's authors will be listed. The article is D.J. Belsheim, R.A. Hutchinson & M.M. Weinstein, *The Design and Evaluation of a Clinical Clerkship for Hospital Pharmacists*, 50 Am. J. Pharmaceutical Education 139–45 (1986). Weinstein believes that it should have been published as M.M. Weinstein, D.J. Belsheim & R.A. Hutchinson, *Etc.* According to Weinstein, the publication of the article with the names in the wrong order violated the due process clause of the fourteenth amendment.

I

Weinstein was an Assistant Professor of Pharmacy Administration in the College of Pharmacy of the University of Illinois at Chicago. According to his complaint, from which we take these facts, he proposed a clinical program for practicing pharmacists, who would operate for two weeks in a "clerkship" under the guidance of professors. Several efforts to obtain funding for such a program were unsuccessful. The University finally supplied funds from its own budget for a program in August 1983. The proposal to the University was made jointly by Weinstein, Belsheim (another assistant professor and Director of Continuing Education in the College of Pharmacy), and Hutchinson (Director of Pharmacy Practice at the University of Illinois Hospital, where the clerkship program would be carried out). All three participated in the program. Although Weinstein asserts that he supplied most of the ideas and did most of the work, he concedes that the three agreed to write jointly on the results. Weinstein believes that he had an agreement with Belsheim under which Weinstein would be the first-listed author of a paper describing the clerkship and the data obtained from questionnaires, while Belsheim would be lead author of a paper to be called "Teaching Problem Solving in a Post-Graduate Clinical Pharmacy Clerkship."

In January 1984 Weinstein gave Belsheim a draft. Belsheim was dissatisfied. The two disagreed about the subjects to be covered and the conclusions to be drawn. By

January 1985 Weinstein had completed another draft. One day he found the draft in Belsheim's wastebasket, with many editorial marks and sections snipped out. Belsheim denied doing more than making "notes" but shortly produced a new draft, revising both the text and the order of listing of authors. Weinstein did not like either the new order or the new text. Belsheim raised the matter with T. Donald Rucker, head of the Department of Pharmacy Administration in the College of Pharmacy. Rucker urged "that a ruling be sought from a representative group of peers; the College Executive Committee." Neither Belsheim nor Rucker asked the committee to act. Henri R. Manasse, Dean of the College, also offered some advice to Weinstein. He suggested further consultation among the authors but expressed impatience with their slow progress. He explained: "The work described in the present draft is a clear articulation of the accomplishments of this most important College endeavor and its results should be shared with our colleagues. . . . It should therefore be submitted for publication with all due haste." Three days later, on July 19, 1985, Belsheim submitted the article to the American Journal of Pharmaceutical Education. It was published in the Journal's Summer 1986 issue. Weinstein has sued Belsheim, Hutchinson, Manasse, Rucker, two other members of the faculty, the Trustees of the University, and the University itself, contending that they mutilated his work and stole the credit, denying him due process of law. He seeks a remedy under 42 U.S.C. § 1983. The district court dismissed the complaint under Fed. R. Civ. P. 12(b)(6) for failure to state a claim on which relief may be granted, concluding that the University owns the article and may do with it what it likes.

Weinstein says that the listing of names is no small matter. He is seeking a topic on which to write a dissertation and believes that the clerkship program would have been suitable, but that Belsheim's being listed as first author precludes it. (The record does not contain an affidavit or other evidence confirming that his thesis adviser would take this view, and if things are as Weinstein portrays them it is hard to see why the adviser would, but given the procedural posture of the case we must accept Weinstein's allegations.) He also believes that because the principal author is listed first, the appearance of his name in third place will diminish his accomplishments in the eyes of other professors—a significant problem because, as we discuss below, he is looking for a job. His attorney adds the point that academic departments sometimes use the number of citations to a scholar's work as one indication of the importance of that work in the profession. The principal citation services list articles by first author only, so that any citations to the Belsheim, Hutchinson & Weinstein article would be collected under Belsheim's name.

We shall assume, given the posture of the case, that Weinstein could make good his claims of injury-in-fact. We shall also assume that the acts of Belsheim, an employee of a state university, were taken "under color of state law," and that the letter of the Dean of the College of Pharmacy is the sort of decision that may be imputed to the University under *Pembaur v. City of Cincinnati*. None of these assumptions assists Weinstein unless the acts to which he objects have deprived him of "property," for the due process clause applies only to deprivations of "life, liberty or property," and Weinstein does not invoke the first two.

II

The district court concluded that the article was the University's property rather than Weinstein's because it was a "work for hire." The copyright law gives an employer the full rights in an employee's "work for hire," 17 U.S.C. § 201(b), unless a contract provides otherwise. The statute is general enough to make every academic article a "work for hire" and therefore vest exclusive control in universities rather than scholars. The University of Illinois, like many other academic institutions, responded to the 1978 revision of the copyright laws by adopting a policy defining "work for hire" for purposes of its employees, including its professors. According to the policy, which is a part of each professor's contract with the University, a professor retains the copyright unless the work falls into one of three categories:

(1) The terms of a University agreement with an external party require the University to hold or transfer ownership in the copyrightable work, or

(2) Works expressly commissioned in writing by the University, or

(3) Works created as a specific requirement of employment or as an assigned University duty. Such requirements or duties may be contained in a job description or an employment agreement which designates the content of the employee's University work. If such requirements or duties are not so specified, such works will be those for which the topics or content is determined by the author's employment duties and/or which are prepared at the University's instance and expense, that is, when the University is the motivating factor in the preparation of the work.

The district court held that Weinstein's work is covered by paragraph (3) because the University funded the clerkship program and because, as a clinical professor, Weinstein was required to conduct and write about clinical programs.

This interpretation of the University's policy collides with the role of the three categories as exceptions to a rule that faculty members own the copyrights in their academic work. A university "requires" all of its scholars to write. Its demands—especially the demands of departments deciding whether to award tenure—will be "the motivating factor in the preparation of" many a scholarly work. When Dean Manasse told Weinstein to publish or perish, he was not simultaneously claiming for the University a copyright on the ground that the work had become a "requirement or duty" within the meaning of paragraph (3). The University concedes in this court that a professor of mathematics who proves a new theorem in the course of his employment will own the copyright to his article containing that proof. This has been the academic tradition since Copyright law began, a tradition the University's policy purports to retain. The tradition covers scholarly articles and other intellectual property. When Saul Bellow, a professor at the University of Chicago, writes a novel, he may keep the royalties.

The University's copyright policy reads more naturally when applied to administrative duties. Perhaps the University forms a committee to study the appropriate use of small computers and conscripts professors as members. The committee may publish a report, in which the University will claim copyright. We do not say that a broader reading is impossible, but such a reading should be established by evidence about the deliberations underlying the policy and the course of practice—material that is neither in the record nor an appropriate basis on which to dismiss the complaint for failure to state a claim. We would be surprised if any member of the faculty of the College of Pharmacy treats his academic work as the property of the University. Dean Manasse, for example, has not submitted an affidavit stating that the faculty regularly obtains consent (or a transfer of copyright) from the University before publishing articles.

The record does not contain the contracts between the American Journal of Pharmaceutical Education and Professors Belsheim, Hutchinson, and Weinstein, but we venture a guess that each represented to the Journal that he owned the copyright and was empowered to transfer the copyright to the Journal. (The article as published carries the Journal's copyright notice rather than that of the authors or the University of Illinois.) Dean Manasse told Weinstein to *publish* the article, not to ask the University for permission to publish—permission that would have been essential if the University owned the copyright.

If the members of the University's faculty own the copyright interest in their scholarly articles, Weinstein has some "property." But did the University "deprive" him of this property without "due process"? Both "deprivation" and "due process" are problematic. If the University does not own the copyright, the article is covered by 17 U.S.C. § 201(a), which states that "[t]he authors of a joint work are coowners of copyright in the work." This provision applies to all works of joint authorship, and Weinstein concedes that the article in question is (and was supposed to be) a jointly written work. Each coowner of a copyright may revise the work (that is, make a derivative work) and publish the original or the revision. So far as copyright law is concerned, Belsheim was entitled to do what he did. Belsheim is answerable to Weinstein for Weinstein's share of any royalties, but Weinstein does not claim that Belsheim made off with the profits. Belsheim did not diminish any of Weinstein's property rights; neither did the University. The University did not make Belsheim's acts possible. It therefore did not "deprive" Weinstein of any property interest. Indeed it could not have done so. No amount of academic deliberation or hearings before the College Executive Committee could have diminished Belsheim's entitlement to revise the article. Perhaps the University could have threatened Belsheim with sanctions, such as a duty to teach boring subjects, to induce him to desist, but the due process clause does not require a state to impose penalties on those who exercise legal entitlements.

*　*　*

If war is the extension of diplomacy by other means, this suit—like other litigation a form of warfare—is the extension of academic politics by other means. Weinstein and Belsheim were unable to compromise, and Weinstein has dragged his fellow scholars and the University into the contest. His willingness, even eagerness, to sue his colleagues may be explained by the fact that the University has fired him.

Weinstein was an instructor from 1968 until 1980, when he was hired as an assistant professor, his first tenure-track position. Professors on the tenure track at the University of Illinois have contracts specifying that the professor has no expectation of renewal. From time to time the faculty evaluates the candidate, with the expectation that by the end of six years the candidate will be given tenure or be released. Weinstein's first formal evaluation, in 1983, was negative. He had not published anything in a refereed journal in three years and was told to shape up. He did not publish anything new by the spring of 1984, when the second review occurred. This review was negative too. Department head Rucker, who made the critical recommendation, wrote to Weinstein that his teaching and citizenship were adequate but that "In reviewing your role in research and scholarly activity...I find major weakness. Since September of 1980, you have not published a single article in a refereed journal. Moreover, your dossier list [sic] (with an incorrect citation) a 'Letter to the Editor' with the implication that it represented a contributed article when it did not. In addition, I see no evidence that any such manuscripts were even submitted for the purpose of publication." The

University gave Weinstein a terminal contract, expiring August 31, 1985. So by the time Dean Manasse told Weinstein to get a move on in publishing the article, Weinstein had already "perished" at the University of Illinois for lack of publication and was six weeks away from being unemployed.

Weinstein insists that his discharge violates the Constitution, which is absurd. He lacked a property interest in his position.[4] No set of facts entitled him to reappointment. *McElearney v. University of Illinois* holds that an untenured professor at the same university, employed under the same contract, lacked a property interest.

*   *   *

Weinstein ignored all of theses cases. The rule of law is clear enough that even a wilfully blind litigant cannot misunderstand.

Weinstein is litigating a defunct claim. He hasn't a chance; he never did; but he has put the University to some expense. This is frivolous litigation. Fed. R. App. P. 38 allows us to award attorneys' fees to parties who resist frivolous claims on appeal. The claim that the due process clause prevents Weinstein's discharge was so tenuous that an award of fees would have been appropriate in the district court. Once the district court forcefully drew Weinstein's attention to *McElearney*, further litigation was a waste of everyone's time. The University won *McElearney* once; it need not keep litigating and winning *McElearney* over and again.

Awards of attorneys' fees induce people to reconsider and ensure that refusals to surrender do not burden the innocent. They also protect the courts—and derivatively parties in other cases—from impositions on their time. The more time we must devote to sifting through the claims of people who neglected to do their own legal research, the less time is available to deal with the claims of litigants who have substantial, unresolved questions. It is therefore not dispositive that the University did not ask for attorneys' fees in this case. The court has an interest in the orderly conduct of business, an interest independent of the University's. Recent cases including *Reis, Clearing,* and *Dreis & Krump* award fees in the absence of requests, and an award is similarly appropriate here. The defendants are entitled to attorneys' fees for the time necessary to reply to Weinstein's attack in this court on his discharge. They have 15 days to file an appropriate statement with the clerk of this court.

Affirmed.

———————

<h1 style="text-align:center">J.D. Salinger v. Random House, Inc.</h1>
811 F.2d 90 (2d Cir. 1987)

JON O. NEWMAN, Circuit Judge:

This appeal presents the issue whether the biographer of a renowned author has made "fair use" of his subject's unpublished letters. The issue arises on an expedited appeal from an order of the District Court for the Southern District of New York (Pierre N. Leval, Judge) denying a preliminary injunction sought by the well-known writer, J.D. Salinger, against Ian Hamilton and Random House, Inc., the author and

---

4. He makes a first amendment argument in passing, but he was not fired on account of the political slant of his views. He was fired for not having any views, at least none recently in print.

publisher, respectively, of a book about Salinger and his writings. For reasons that follow, we conclude that a preliminary injunction should be issued.

Background

The plaintiff J.D. Salinger is a highly regarded American novelist and short-story writer, best known for his novel, *The Catcher in the Rye*. He has not published since 1965 and has chosen to shun all publicity and inquiry concerning his private life. The defendant Ian Hamilton is a well-respected writer on literary topics. He serves as literary critic of *The London Sunday Times* and has authored a biography of the poet Robert Lowell. In July 1983 Hamilton informed Salinger that he was undertaking a biography of Salinger to be published by Random House and sought the author's cooperation. Salinger refused, informing Hamilton that he preferred not to have his biography written during his lifetime. Hamilton nevertheless proceeded and spent the next three years preparing a biography titled *J.D. Salinger: A Writing Life*.

An important source of material was several unpublished letters Salinger wrote between 1939 and 1961. Most were written to Whit Burnett, Salinger's friend, teacher, and editor at *Story* magazine, and Elizabeth Murray, Salinger's friend. A few were written to Judge Learned Hand, Salinger's friend and neighbor in New Hampshire, Hamish Hamilton and Roger Machell, Salinger's British publishers, and other individuals, including Ernest Hemingway.

Ian Hamilton located most, if not all, of the letters in the libraries of Harvard, Princeton, and the University of Texas, to which they had been donated by the recipients or their representatives. Prior to examining the letters at the university libraries, Hamilton signed form agreements furnished by the libraries, restricting the use he could make of the letters without permission of the library and the owner of the literary property rights. The Harvard form required permission "to publish the contents of the manuscript or any excerpt therefrom." The Princeton form obliged the signer "not to copy, reproduce, circulate or publish" inspected manuscripts without permission.

By May 1986 Hamilton had completed a version of his biography. Salinger received a set of the galley proofs of this version (the "May galleys") and learned from the galleys and the footnote citations to his letters that the letters had been donated to university libraries. In response, he took two actions. First, he registered 79 of his unpublished letters for copyright protection. Second, he instructed his counsel to object to publication of the biography until all of Salinger's unpublished materials were deleted.

In response to Salinger's objection, Hamilton and Random House revised the May galleys. In the current version of the biography (the "October galleys"), much of the material previously quoted from the Salinger letters has been replaced by close paraphrasing. Somewhat more than 200 words remain quoted. Salinger has identified 59 instances where the October galleys contain passages that either quote from or closely paraphrase portions of his unpublished letters. These passages draw upon 44 of the copyrighted letters, 20 to Burnett, 10 to Murray, 9 to Hamish Hamilton, 3 to Judge Hand, 1 to Machell, and 1 to Hemingway.

On October 3, 1986, Salinger sued Ian Hamilton and Random House, seeking an injunction against publication of Hamilton's biography and damages. In addition to copyright infringement, the complaint alleged unfair competition and breach of contract. The unfair competition claim was based on instances in the biography where

Hamilton uses phrases such as "he states" or "he writes" to introduce close paraphrases of portions of Salinger's letters; Salinger claimed that readers would be deceived into thinking that they were reading Salinger's exact words. The breach of contract claim was based on the form agreements that Hamilton signed with the Harvard, Princeton, and University of Texas libraries. Salinger alleged that he was a third-party beneficiary of those agreements.

Judge Leval granted a temporary restraining order but subsequently issued an opinion denying a preliminary injunction. In the District Judge's view, the extent of copying of expressive material entitled to copyright protection was "minimal," amounting to "about 30 instances of the use of a word or a phrase or an image." Building on the premise that only such fragmentary copying of protected material was involved, Judge Leval concluded that "Hamilton's appropriations of copyrighted expressions are too minimal to subject Salinger to any serious harm," and that such use as Hamilton had made was "fair use" within the meaning of the Copyright Act, 17 U.S.C. § 107 (1982). Judge Leval rejected the unfair competition claim, finding "no showing of distortions that would give rise to a Lanham Act claim." He also rejected the contract claim, concluding that the library agreements are to be construed not to prevent all quotations but only "quotations and excerpts *that infringe copyright*." The claim therefore fell with the conclusion that the infringement claim was defeated by the defense of fair use. Judge Leval also noted that the letters in the Harvard and Texas libraries had not been directly quoted and that the Princeton form did not expressly forbid quotation.

The District Court granted a limited stay, which this Court extended pending an expedited appeal.

Discussion

Rulings on applications for a preliminary injunction are reviewed under an "abuse of discretion" standard. Misapplication of the appropriate legal principles constitutes grounds for overturning the denial or issuance of a preliminary injunction.

To a large extent the appropriate legal principles are not in dispute on this appeal, though their application is seriously contested. The author of letters is entitled to a copyright in the letters, as with any other work of literary authorship. Prior to 1978, unpublished letters, like other unpublished works, were protected by common law copyright, but the 1976 Copyright Act preempted the common law of copyright and brought unpublished works under the protection of federal copyright law, which includes the right of first publication among the rights accorded to the copyright owner. The copyright owner owns the literary property rights, including the right to complain of infringing copying, while the recipient of the letter retains ownership of "the tangible physical property of the letter itself." Having ownership of the physical document, the recipient (or his representative) is entitled to deposit it with a library and contract for the terms of access to it. As with all works of authorship, the copyright owner secures protection only for the expressive content of the work, not the ideas or facts contained therein, a distinction fundamental to copyright law and of special significance in determining whether infringement has occurred in a work of biography or other account of historical or contemporary events.

Central to this appeal is the application of the defense of "fair use" to unpublished works. Though common law, especially as developed in England, appears to have denied the defense of fair use to unpublished works, the 1976 Act explicitly makes all of the rights protected by copyright, including the right of first publication, subject to the defense of fair use. That fair use applies to unpublished works does not determine, however, the scope of the defense as applied to such works. Whatever glimmerings on that subject have appeared in cases decided before May 20, 1985, our guidance must now be taken from the decision of the Supreme Court on that date in *Harper & Row, Publishers, Inc. v. Nation Enterprises,* the Court's first delineation of the scope of fair use as applied to unpublished works.

The Court begins its discussion of fair use by considering the application of the doctrine to unpublished works. The Court observes that "fair use traditionally was not recognized as a defense to charges of copying from an author's as yet unpublished works," but that this "absolute rule" was "tempered in practice by the equitable nature of the fair use doctrine." The Court notes that, under the Copyright Revision Act of 1976, all of the rights protected by copyright, including the right of first publication, are subject to fair use, but explicitly rejects the contention, advanced by *The Nation,* that Congress "intended that fair use would apply *in pari materia* to published and unpublished works." "Under ordinary circumstances," the Court states, "the author's right to control the first public appearance of his undisseminated expression will outweigh a claim of fair use." This proposition was emphasized with respect to unpublished letters. Reckoning with *The Nation's* argument that fair use could permissibly be made of President Ford's unpublished memoirs because the imminent publication demonstrated that the author has no interest in nonpublication, the Court said, "This argument assumes that the unpublished nature of copyrighted material is only relevant to letters or other confidential writings not intended for dissemination," an assumption the Court went on to reject. Pertinent to our case is the fact that the Court underscored the idea that unpublished letters normally enjoy insulation from fair use copying.

After emphasizing the insulation of unpublished works from fair use under "ordinary circumstances," the Court considers in turn each of the four factors identified by Congress as "especially relevant," in determining whether a use is fair. Reflecting its earlier discussion, the Court gives special weight to the fact that the copied work is unpublished when considering the second factor, the nature of the copyrighted work.

Following the Supreme Court's approach in *Harper & Row,* we place special emphasis on the unpublished nature of Salinger's letters and proceed to consider each of the four statutory fair use factors. Application of these four factors points in Salinger's favor.

1. *Purpose of the use.* Hamilton's book fits comfortably within several of the statutory categories of uses illustrative of uses that can be fair. The book may be considered "criticism," "scholarship," and "research." The proposed use is not an attempt to rush to the market just ahead of the copyright holder's imminent publication, as occurred in *Harper & Row.* Whether Random House plans to "exploit the headline value of its infringement," as *The Nation* did, is not clear on the record thus far developed. Though no evidence has yet been presented on the advertising material as Random House plans to use, it is hard to believe that some emphasis will not be placed upon the fact that the book draws generously upon Salinger's unpublished letters.

We agree with Judge Leval that Hamilton's purpose in using the Salinger letters to enrich his scholarly biography weighs the first fair use factor in Hamilton's favor, notwithstanding that he and his publisher anticipate profits. However, we do not agree that a biographer faces a dilemma that entitles him to a generous application of the fair use doctrine. Judge Leval perceived the dilemma in these terms:

> To the extent [the biographer] quotes (or closely paraphrases), he risks a finding of infringement and an injunction effectively destroying his biographical work. To the extent he departs from the words of the letters, he distorts, sacrificing both accuracy and vividness of description.

This dilemma is not faced by the biographer who elects to copy only the factual content of letters. The biographer who copies only facts incurs no risk of an injunction; he has not taken copyrighted material. And it is unlikely that the biographer will distort those facts by rendering them in words of his own choosing. On the other hand, the biographer who copies the letter writer's expression of facts properly faces an unpleasant choice. If he copies more than minimal amounts of (unpublished) expressive content, he deserves to be enjoined; if he "distorts" the expressive content, he deserves to be criticized for "sacrificing accuracy and vividness." But the biographer has no inherent right to copy the "accuracy" or the "vividness" of the letter writer's expression. Indeed, "vividness of description" is precisely an attribute of the author's expression that he is entitled to protect.

* * *

In sum, we agree with the District Court that the first fair use factor weighs in Hamilton's favor, but not that the purpose of his use entitles him to any special consideration.

2. *Nature of the Copyrighted Work.* "The fact that a work is unpublished is a critical element of its 'nature.' " Salinger's letters are unpublished, and they have not lost that attribute by their placement in libraries where access has been explicitly made subject to observance of at least the protections of copyright law. In considering this second factor, we encounter some ambiguity arising from the Supreme Court's observation that "the *scope* of fair use is narrower with respect to unpublished works." This could mean either that the circumstances in which copying will be found to be fair use are fewer in number for unpublished works than for published works or that the amount of copyrighted material that may be copied as fair use is a lesser quantity for unpublished works than for published works. Some support for the latter view can be derived from the statement in *Harper & Row* that, though "substantial" quotations might be used in a review of a published work, the author's right to control first publication weighs against "such use" prior to publication. However, we think that the tenor of the Court's entire discussion of unpublished works conveys the idea that such works normally enjoy complete protection against copying any protected expression. Narrower "scope" seems to refer to the diminished *likelihood* that copying will be fair use when the copyrighted material is unpublished.

The District Judge considered the nature of the copyrighted work, especially its unpublished nature, primarily in rejecting the plaintiff's argument that fair use was inapplicable to unpublished works. However, in analyzing and weighing the fair use factors, Judge Leval gave no explicit consideration to this second factor. Since the copyrighted letters are unpublished, the second factor weighs heavily in favor of Salinger.

3. *Amount and Substantiality of the Portion Used.* It is with regard to this third factor that we have the most serious disagreement with the District Judge's legal

analysis, both as to the pertinent standard and its application. As to the standard, we start, as did Judge Leval, by recognizing that what is relevant is the amount and substantiality of the copyrighted *expression* that has been used, not the *factual content* of the material in the copyrighted works. However, that protected expression has been "used" whether it has been quoted verbatim or only paraphrased. We cannot be certain that Judge Leval included close paraphrases of the Salinger letters in his determination of the quantity of copyrighted material that has been used in the Hamilton biography. At one point in his decision, Judge Leval states that he has identified "approximately 30 letters from which Hamilton has taken, either by brief quotation or *paraphrase*, a few words of copyright protected material." At other points, however, his opinion suggests that only direct quotations have been counted. Noting that Hamilton had revised the May galleys "by eliminating and writing around most of the quoted matter" previously appearing in that version of the book, Judge Leval concluded that what Hamilton accomplished "was to reduce from a large number to fewer than 30 the instances of use of copyrighted expression."

* * *

In almost all of those instances where the quoted or paraphrased passages from Salinger's letters contain an "ordinary" phrase, the passage as a whole displays a sufficient degree of creativity as to sequence of thoughts, choice of words, emphasis, and arrangement to satisfy the minimal threshold of required creativity. And in all of the instances where that minimum threshold is met, the Hamilton paraphrasing tracks the original so closely as to constitute infringement.

We have carefully analyzed all 59 of the passages from Hamilton's book cited by Salinger as instances of infringing copying from 44 of his letters. Of these 44 letters, the Hamilton biography copies (with some use of quotation or close paraphrase) protected sequences constituting at least one-third of 17 letters and at least 10 percent of 42 letters. These sequences are protected, notwithstanding that they include some reporting of facts and an occasional use of a commonplace work or expression. Hamilton's use of these sequences "exceeds that necessary to disseminate the facts." Judge Leval found that "[i]n the rarest case a complete sentence was taken." That is true only with respect to material directly quoted. The material closely paraphrased frequently exceeds ten lines from a single letter. Even if in one or two instances the portions of the letters copied could be said to lack sufficient creativity to warrant copyright protection, there remains sufficient copying of protected material to constitute a very substantial appropriation.

The taking is significant not only from a quantitative standpoint but from a qualitative one as well. The copied passages, if not the " 'heart of the book,' " are at least an important ingredient of the book as it now stands. To a large extent, they make the book worth reading. The letters are quoted or paraphrased on approximately 40 percent of the book's 192 pages.

In sum, the third fair use factor weighs heavily in Salinger's favor.

4. *Effect on the Market.* The Supreme Court has called the fourth factor—effect on the market for the copyrighted work—"the single most important element of fair use." As Judge Leval recognized, the need to assess the effect on the market for Salinger's letters is not lessened by the fact that their author has disavowed any intention to publish them during his lifetime. First, the proper inquiry concerns the "potential market" for the copyrighted work. Second, Salinger has the right to change

his mind. He is entitled to protect his *opportunity* to sell his letters, an opportunity estimated by his literary agent to have a current value in excess of $500,000.

Proceeding from his conclusion that only a few fragments of the letters have been used in Hamilton's book, Judge Leval expressed the view that such use would have "no effect" on the marketability of the letters. Concluding as we do that substantial portions of the letters have been copied, we do not share the District Judge's view that marketability of the letters will be totally unimpaired. To be sure, the book would not displace the market for the letters. Indeed, we think it likely that most of the potential purchasers of a collection of the letters would not be dissuaded by publication of the biography. Yet some impairment of the market seems likely. The biography copies virtually all of the most interesting passages of the letters, including several highly expressive insights about writing and literary criticism. Perhaps few readers of the biography would refrain from purchasing a published collection of the letters if they appreciated how inadequately Hamilton's paraphrasing has renewed Salinger's chosen form of expression. The difficulty, however, is that some readers of the book will gain the impression that they are learning from Hamilton what Salinger has written. Hamilton frequently laces his paraphrasing with phrases such as "he wrote," "said Salinger," "he speaks of," "Salinger declares," "he says," and "he said." For at least some appreciable number of persons, these phrases will convey the impression that they have read Salinger's words, perhaps not quoted verbatim, but paraphrased so closely as to diminish interest in purchasing the originals.

The fourth fair use factor weighs slightly in Salinger's favor.

On balance, the claim of fair use as to Salinger's unpublished letters fails. The second and third factors weigh heavily in Salinger's favor, and the fourth factor slightly so. Only the first factor favors Hamilton. We seriously doubt whether a critic reviewing a published collection of the letters could justify as fair use the extensive amount of expressive material Hamilton has copied. However that may be, if fair use is to have a more "limited scope" with respect to unpublished works, it is not available with respect to the current version of Hamilton's proposed biography.

To deny a biographer like Hamilton the opportunity to copy the expressive content of unpublished letters is not, as appellees contend, to interfere in any significant way with the process of enhancing public knowledge of history or contemporary events. The facts may be reported. Salinger's letters contain a number of facts that students of his life and writings will no doubt find of interest, and Hamilton is entirely free to fashion a biography that reports these facts. But Salinger has a right to protect the expressive content of his unpublished writings for the term of his copyright, and that right prevails over a claim of fair use under "ordinary circumstances." Public aware-ness of the expressive content of the letters will have to await either Salinger's decision to publish or the expiration of his copyright, save for such special circumstances as might fall within the "narrower" scope of fair use available for unpublished works. Evidently, public interest in the expressive content of the letters of a well-known writer remains substantial even fifty years after his death. *See, e.g.,* "516 Pirandello Letters Donated to Princeton," *N.Y. Times,* Dec. 29, 1986, at C13, col. 1 (reporting the great interest in the donation of the unpublished letters of Luigi Pirandello to the Princeton Library fifty years after the playwright's death).

Since we conclude that the record establishes Salinger's entitlement to a preliminary injunction on his copyright claim, we need not consider at this stage of the litigation whether he is also entitled to relief by virtue of the library agreements.

Reversed and remanded with directions to issue a preliminary injunction barring publication of the biography in its present form.

As a final matter, it should be noted that as complicated as traditional publishing copyright is, the phenomenal growth of software and computer technology promises even more complex issues, because some computer programs could be patented or copyrighted. The predominance of literary and other artistic works in the law of copyright suggests an imperfect fit when confronted with computer programs and other technological features. In "Copyright and Software Technology Infringement," R. Nimmer and P. Krauthaus propose an alternative to considering copyright and infringement issues in piracy or unauthorized duplication terms, that of third-party rights:

> [The] interests of both the original developer and of the second, value-added user are important and protectible. The original author's protections are enhanced insofar as the alleged infringement encompasses important aspects of the original work and directly impacts markets into which the developer is likely to enter. The position of the second party is heightened to the extent that its use is selective and developmental. The original author's claim weakens to the extent that it would distort technology, development and control methods, operation and processes, rather than merely code idiosyncratic to the program. This balancing does not create certainty in analysis of software infringement, but certainty may be impossible to achieve. The balancing does provide for [a] decision based on relevant, not distorted or misdescribed factors. It provides a vehicle to expressly recognize and protect third party rights.

Indiana Law Journal, 62 (1986), 13–62.

EDUCOM, a consortium of colleges designed to coordinate appropriate policies for software uses in higher education, has promulgated a Code for Software and Intellectual Rights:

> Respect for intellectual labor and creativity is vital to academic discourse and enterprise. This principle applies to works of all authors and publishers in all media. It encompasses respect for the right to acknowledgment, right to privacy, and right to determine the form, manner, and terms of publication and distribution.
>
> Because electronic information is volatile and easily reproduced, respect for the work and personal expression of others is especially critical in computer environments. Violations of authorial integrity, including plagiarism, invasion of privacy, unauthorized access, and trade secret and copyright violations, may be grounds for sanctions against members of the academic community.

Using Software (EDUCOM, 1987).

Time is of the essence in perfecting patent claims. In *Griffith v. Kanamaru*, 816 F.2d 624 (1987), Professor Griffith delayed filing a complete claim to a diabetes treatment, and a competing claim was approved. The delay did not meet the required "reasonable diligence" test for the patent. On occasion, however, even delayed patent claims can prevail. In *Gould v. Quigg* (822 F.2d 1074 (Fed. Ct. 1987), a former graduate student successfully proved in 1987 that he was entitled to the patent for a laser designs, derived from his work as a student in the 1960s.

As was the case in *Gould, Hajiwara,* and *Weinstein,* attribution of proper credit is often difficult to establish. In *Wayne State University v. Bajkowski,* [U.S. District Court, N.D. Illinois, 1987 W.L. 12911 (June 19, 1987)], a member of a research team was enjoined by the U.S. District Court from revealing by any means the research data from a WSU project on cancer cells. The consent agreement required, among other restrictions, that Bajkowski not publish any of the research, and if the WSU team published, they would "accord defendant [his] attribution in accordance with custom in the academic scientific community."

University of Pittsburgh v. Champion Products, Inc.
686 F.2d 1040 (1982)

VAN DUSEN, Senior Circuit Judge.

This is an appeal from a final order of the district court, sitting without a jury, entering judgment for the defendant based upon a finding that the plaintiff's trademark infringement and unfair competition claims are barred by laches.

Because we believe that the district court erred in applying the doctrine of laches to bar plaintiff's claims for prospective injunctive relief, we will reverse that portion of the judgment and remand for further consideration of the facts and law underlying plaintiff's claim for future injunctive relief. In all other respects, the judgment of the district court will be affirmed.

I.

The historical facts of this case are set forth in detail in the district court's opinion. The University of Pittsburgh ("Pitt") is a non-profit Pennsylvania corporation, originally established in 1787, which has been operating under its present name since 1908. Shortly thereafter, Pitt adopted the panther as the mascot for its athletic teams. Since that time, Pitt has come to enjoy a widespread reputation for the excellence of its undergraduate, graduate and professional schools and, more recently, for its national calibre athletic programs. As a result, "University of Pittsburgh," "Pitt," "Panthers," and "Pitt Panthers" have become largely synonymous in the public mind. As the district court found, the names "University of Pittsburgh" and "Pitt" have been used by Pitt on its athletic uniforms for over 50 years. Further, at least since World War II, the Pitt bookstore has sold an array of clothing and novelty items bearing these names and various representations of the University seal and panther mascot.

Champion Products, Inc. ("Champion") is a New York corporation engaged in the business of manufacturing and marketing "soft goods," approximately 80% of which are imprinted with the names and/or symbols of schools, colleges, universities, and other entities or events. It is largely undisputed that Champion created and nurtured the imprinted soft goods industry and is now the premier manufacturer in the field with annual sales in excess of $100 million. By Champion's own testimony, the names or insignia of more than 10,000 schools, colleges and universities appear on Champion goods. Champion has developed this business to a point where it employs over 100 salesmen, maintains an extensive art department to update old designs and develop new ones, and spends in excess of $800,000 annually to advertise its products. There has been no allegation that Champion's goods are not of the highest quality. Champion does not now, and apparently never has, maintained any licensing arrangement with, or paid royalties to, any of the schools or colleges whose insignia it uses.

Although the testimony was not without confusion, the district court found that the relationship between Pitt and Champion began in 1936 when Champion began supplying Pitt with athletic uniforms bearing Pitt's name and marks. At approximately the same time, Pitt began carrying Champion-made Pitt soft goods in the campus bookstore. This arrangement continued until 1960. During the same period, Champion apparently also sold goods with the Pitt marks to others in the Pittsburgh area not affiliated with the University. Since 1946, Champion sold such goods to Shea's Sporting Goods store in Pittsburgh, a business not affiliated with the University, which in turn resold the goods to the general public. Pitt maintains that Shea's had an informal license agreement with the University to sell insignia goods to campus organizations but that Pitt had no knowledge of and never approved any other distribution of Pitt insignia goods. The question of knowledge aside, however, Pitt never objected to any action taken by Champion until the early stages of this litigation.

The mid-1970s marked a period of dramatic success and increased national exposure for the Pitt football team. Following the 1976 football season, the Pitt team was invited to play the University of Georgia for the unofficial national championship at the 1977 Sugar Bowl game in New Orleans. Upon returning from that game, the manager of Pitt's campus bookstore reported to her superiors that literally thousands of garments bearing various Pitt insignia were in evidence at the game. This report engendered discussions of the issue among university officials and culminated in a decision to register its name and marks under federal and state trademark laws and license their use by manufacturers. On August 4, 1980, Pennsylvania trademark registrations were issued to Pitt covering 29 marks or combinations, including eight for use on clothing. On December 18, 1980, Pitt contacted Champion, gave notice of its claim to the marks, and requested that Champion execute a license agreement. Champion refused.

On December 2, 1981, Pitt brought this action in state court, alleging (1) common law trademark infringement; (2) trademark infringement in violation of Pa. Stat. Ann. tit. 73, § 23 (Purdon 1971); (3) common law unfair competition; and (4) false designation of origin of goods under the Lanham Act, 15 U.S.C. § 1125(a) (1976). Champion removed the case the next day to the United States District Court for the Western District of Pennsylvania. On December 4, 1981, after a hearing, the court denied Pitt's request for a preliminary injunction. A bench trial on the issue of liability was held on December 10–11 and 14–17, 1981, and on January 7, 1982, the district court filed its findings of fact and conclusions of law holding the plaintiff's claims to be barred by laches. Pitt's motion to make additional findings of fact and amended conclusions of law was denied on January 18, 1982.

This appeal followed.

II.

The issue before this court—and the only issue discussed in the district court's opinion—is very narrow: has Champion carried its burden of establishing on these facts the affirmative defense of laches to a degree which must bar Pitt's claims in their entirety? Because laches is an equitable doctrine, its application is inextricably bound up with the nature and quality of the plaintiff's claim on the merits relevant to a prospective injunction. Consequently, while we must of necessity discuss the merits of the plaintiff's claim, we express no opinion on the ultimate question of precisely what has been proven on this record, nor on the availability or scope of the prospective injunctive remedy available, preferring not to venture into this expanding area of the law without the benefit of the district court's findings and conclusions on the issues raised by the application for such a prospective injunction.

A. *The Doctrine of Laches*

It is hornbook law that laches consists of two essential elements: (1) inexcusable delay in instituting suit, and (2) prejudice resulting to the defendant from such delay.

* * *

Here, the character and scope of the alleged infringement changed substantially over the years from a modest program of sales to students and local adherents of the university to a program of national sales aimed at servicing and capitalizing upon Pitt's emergence as a national college football power. While Pitt may have acquiesced in the former, it promptly objected to the latter. Thus, to the extent that any of the traditional trademark cases are apposite, this case is less analogous to *Anheuser-Busch* than to *Scott Paper Co. v. Scott's Liquid Gold, Inc.*, where the plaintiff objected to the defendant's long-standing, although admittedly junior, use of the name "Scott's" only after the defendant, whose marketing efforts had previously been limited to the greater Denver area, made a public offering of its stock and began nationwide advertising and marketing efforts.

Consequently, we reject Champion's contention that Pitt's delay alone has barred its right to prospective relief and hold that such a bar must depend upon the degree to which Pitt's delay may have prejudiced Champion.

C. *Detrimental Reliance By Champion*

Although the district court made four separate findings of fact concerning Champion's reliance on Pitt's inaction, Champion's position may be stated succinctly: "Champion created, developed and expanded the imprinted soft-goods industry with the full knowledge of Pitt who should not now be permitted to profit from the markets developed by Champion." While this argument is rhetorically attractive, we do not believe that this case is nearly so simple.

* * *

Champion has indeed developed a market in the sense of recruiting sales outlets, but again Champion was seeking outlets and developing goodwill for whatever Champion products were in demand in that area. The fact that greater Pittsburgh sales outlets were interested in Pitt-marked goods is not so much a result of Champion's effort as understandable local loyalty. As to buyers outside the area, the evidence appears to show that consumer demand increased in direct proportion to Pitt's football fortunes. If a potential Pitt goods customer indicated that it would prefer to stock Penn State or Princeton or Duke imprinted goods, for example, there is no evidence that Champion would feel compelled to push Pitt-marked products. While Champion has indeed developed the mechanism for producing and marketing these goods, the demand for goods with any given imprint is due not to the efforts of Champion but rather to the efforts of the school, team, movie producer, musical group, or whatever person or entity whose imprint is used and whose current popularity makes that imprint desirable.

The teaching of *Boston Hockey, NFL Properties*, and related cases is that, whatever the ultimate scope of protection afforded, the crucial element is consumer desire to associate with the entity whose imprint is reproduced. This desire is based on success or notoriety which, in turn, is a result of the efforts of that entity. Champion merely packages and exploits it. Champion's investment is in the industry in general, not in Pitt's marks in particular. We doubt that if Pitt closed its doors tomorrow—or, perhaps more to the point, discontinued football—Champion's losses would extend beyond existing inventory. This we hold to be insufficient to bar all relief.

III.

For the foregoing reasons, the judgment of the district court will be reversed insofar as it holds Pitt's claims for prospective injunctive relief to be barred by laches, and the case will be remanded for further proceedings concerning the scope of prospective injunctive relief, if any, and for such findings and conclusions as the district court may make on that subject, consistent with this opinion and such further evidence as may be produced on remand. We decline to determine on the present record the precise scope of prospective injunctive relief available in light of the developing case law in this area and its application to the relevant facts underlying this case as they may be supplemented on remand.

In all other respects, the judgment of the district court will be affirmed.

The parties will bear their own costs.

University and affiliated organizational trademarks and service marks have, as anyone who has shopped at a college bookstore knows, become big business. Even the National Collegiate Athletic Association (NCAA) permits its name to be used in selling a Japanese sports drink; in all, the various NCAA royalties total $2 million annually. "NCAA Earns $2-million a Year from Licensing the Use of Its Name and Trademark," *Chronicle of Higher Education*, 18 March 1987, p. 51. In 1984, Texas A&M University had licensed more than 250 different manufacturers and vendors to use its various symbols, ranging from the university seal to slogans associated with its athletic programs (for example, "Gig 'Em Aggies"). *Texas A&M University System v. University Book Store, Inc.*, 683 S.W.2d 140 (Tex. App. Waco 1984, writ ref'd n.r.e.). As the *Pitt* case indicated, if institutions do not protect their commercial interests, they may lose their claim. *University of Pittsburgh v. Champion Products*, 529 F. Supp. 464 (W.D. Pa. 1982), *aff'd in part, rev'd in part*, 686 F.2d 1041 (3d Cir. 1982), *cert. denied*, 459 U.S. 1079 (1982), *on remand*, 566 F. Supp. 711 (W.D. Pa. 1983). See C. Geier, "Protection of University Symbols," *Baylor Law Review*, 38 (1986), 661–86; S. Burshtein, "Collegiate Licensing in Canada and the Statutory Advantage," *Journal of College and University Law*, 12 (1985), 227–60.

Collective Bargaining

Since the first college faculties were unionized in the 1960s and 1970s, collective bargaining has become widespread in higher education. In a 1988 article, Joel Douglas compiled union data indicating that 830 of the 3,284 institutions in the U.S. (25%) were covered by faculty collective bargaining agreements; figures for non-faculty college employees are even higher. By 1984, nearly 200,000 faculty (27% of all faculty) were unionized. Of these, 83% were in public colleges, while 17% were in private institutions. Unionized public senior colleges total 220, private 4-year colleges total 69, public 2-year colleges total 524, and private 2-year colleges include 13. J. Douglas, "Professors on Strike: An Analysis of Two Decades of Faculty Work Stoppages, 1966– 85," *The Labor Lawyer*, 4 (1988), 87–101. He also reported that in the last two decades, there were 138 full-time college faculty strikes (or work stoppages), averaging almost 15 days each; the longest was 150 days at St. John's University in 1966.

Collective bargaining is governed by federal and state laws, although several states also authorize local boards of junior colleges (hence local laws) to govern labor. Twenty-six states and the District of Columbia have such authorizing legislation. J. Douglas and E. Kotch, *Directory of Faculty Contracts and Bargaining Agents in Institutions of Higher Education* (National Center for the Study of Collective Bargaining in Higher Education and the Professions, 1985), table 2.

While state or local laws, if they exist, govern the respective state or local institutions, the National Labor Relations Act (NLRA) governs faculty collective bargaining in private institutions. In 1951, the National Labor Relations Board decided that colleges would not fall under NLRB jurisdiction if their mission was "noncommercial in nature and intimately connected with the charitable purposes and educational activities." *Trustees of Columbia University*, 29 LRRM 1098 (1951). This refusal to assert jurisdiction remained in force until 1970, when the NLRB reversed itself in the *Cornell University* case (in which Syracuse University was also included). After reviewing the development of labor law trends in the 20 years that had passed, the NLRB noted, "we are convinced that assertion of jurisdiction is required over those private colleges and universities whose operations have a substantial effect on commerce to insure the orderly, effective and uniform application of the national labor policy." 183 N.L.R.B. 329 (1970). The board set a $1 million gross revenue test for its standard, a figure that would today cover even the very smallest colleges. In 1980, however, the NLRB decision to extend collective bargaining privileges to Yeshiva University faculty was overruled by the U.S. Supreme Court.

N.L.R.B. v. Yeshiva
444 U.S. 672 (1980)

Mr. Justice POWELL delivered the opinion of the Court.

Supervisors and managerial employees are excluded from the categories of employees entitled to the benefits of collective bargaining under the National Labor Relations Act. The question presented is whether the full-time faculty of Yeshiva University fall within those exclusions.

Yeshiva is a private university which conducts a broad range of arts and sciences programs at its five undergraduate and eight graduate schools in New York City. On October 30, 1974, the Yeshiva University Faculty Association (Union) filed a representation petition with the National Labor Relations Board (Board). The Union sought certification as bargaining agent for the full-time faculty members at 10 of the 13 schools. The University opposed the petition on the ground that all of its faculty members are managerial or supervisory personnel and hence not employees within the meaning of the National Labor Relations Act (Act). A Board-appointed hearing officer held hearings over a period of five months, generating a voluminous record.

The evidence at the hearing showed that a central administrative hierarchy serves all of the University's schools. Ultimate authority is vested in a Board of Trustees, whose members (other than the President) hold no administrative positions at the University. The President sits on the Board of Trustees and serves as chief executive officer, assisted by four Vice Presidents who oversee, respectively, medical affairs and science, student affairs, business affairs, and academic affairs. An Executive Council of Deans and administrators makes recommendations to the President on a wide variety of matters.

University-wide policies are formulated by the central administration with the approval of the Board of Trustees, and include general guidelines dealing with teaching loads, salary scales, tenure, sabbaticals, retirement, and fringe benefits. The budget for each school is drafted by its Dean or Director, subject to approval by the President after consultation with a committee of administrators. The faculty participate in University-wide governance through their representatives on an elected student-faculty advisory council. The only University-wide faculty body is the Faculty Review Committee, composed of elected representatives who adjust grievances by informal negotiation and also may make formal recommendations to the Dean of the affected school or to the President. Such recommendations are purely advisory.

The individual schools within the University are substantially autonomous. Each is headed by a Dean or Director, and faculty members at each school meet formally and informally to discuss and decide matters of institutional and professional concern. At four schools, formal meetings are convened regularly pursuant to written bylaws. The remaining faculties meet when convened by the Dean or Director. Most of the schools also have faculty committees concerned with special areas of educational policy. Faculty welfare committees negotiate with administrators concerning salary and conditions of employment. Through these meetings and committees, the faculty at each school effectively determine its curriculum, grading system, admission and matriculation standards, academic calendars, and course schedules.

Faculty power at Yeshiva's schools extends beyond strictly academic concerns. The faculty at each school make recommendations to the Dean or Director in every case of faculty hiring, tenure, sabbaticals, termination and promotion. Although the final decision is reached by the central administration on the advice of the Dean or Director, the overwhelming majority of faculty recommendations are implemented. Even when financial problems in the early 1970's restricted Yeshiva's budget, faculty recommendations still largely controlled personnel decisions made within the constraints imposed by the administration. Indeed, the faculty of one school recently drew up new and binding policies expanding their own role in these matters. In addition, some faculties make final decisions regarding the admission, expulsion, and graduation of individual students. Others have decided questions involving teaching loads, student absence policies, tuition and enrollment levels, and in one case the location of a school.

A three-member panel of the Board granted the Union's petition in December 1975, and directed an election in a bargaining unit consisting of all full-time faculty members at the affected schools. The unit included Assistant Deans, senior professors, and department chairmen, as well as associate professors, assistant professors, and instructors. Deans and Directors were excluded. The Board summarily rejected the University's contention that its entire faculty are managerial, viewing the claim as a request for reconsideration of previous Board decisions on the issue. Instead of making findings of fact as to Yeshiva, the Board referred generally to the record and found no "significan[t]" difference between this faculty and others it had considered. The Board concluded that the faculty are professional employees entitled to the protection of the Act because "faculty participation in collegial decision making is on a collective rather than individual basis, it is exercised in the faculty's own interest rather than 'in the interest of the employer,' and final authority rests with the board of trustees."

The Union won the election and was certified by the Board. The University refused to bargain, reasserting its view that the faculty are managerial. In the subsequent unfair labor practice proceeding, the Board refused to reconsider its holding in the representation proceeding and ordered the University to bargain with the Union. When the University still refused to sit down at the negotiating table, the Board sought enforcement in the Court of Appeals for the Second Circuit, which denied the petition.

Since the Board had made no findings of fact, the court examined the record and related the circumstances in considerable detail. It agreed that the faculty are professional employees under § 2 (12) of the Act. But the court found that the Board had ignored "the extensive control of Yeshiva's faculty" over academic and personnel decisions as well as the "crucial role of the full-time faculty in determining other central policies of the institution." The court concluded that such power is not an exercise of individual professional expertise. Rather, the faculty are, "in effect, substantially and pervasively operating the enterprise." Accordingly, the court held that the faculty are endowed with "managerial status" sufficient to remove them from the coverage of the Act. We granted certiorari, and now affirm.

There is no evidence that Congress has considered whether a university faculty may organize for collective bargaining under the Act. Indeed, when the Wagner and Taft-Hartley Acts were approved, it was thought that congressional power did not extend to university faculties because they were employed by nonprofit institutions which did not "affect commerce." Moreover, the authority structure of a university does not fit neatly within the statutory scheme we are asked to interpret. The Board itself has noted that the concept of collegiality "does not square with the traditional authority structures with which th[e] Act was designed to cope in the typical organizations of the commercial world."

The Act was intended to accommodate the type of management-employee relations that prevail in the pyramidal hierarchies of private industry. In contrast, authority in the typical "mature" private university is divided between a central administration and one or more collegial bodies. This system of "shared authority" evolved from the medieval model of collegial decisionmaking in which guilds of scholars were responsible only to themselves. At early universities, the faculty were the school. Although faculties have been subject to external control in the United States since colonial times, traditions of collegiality continue to play a significant role at many universities, including Yeshiva. For these reasons, the Board has recognized that principles developed for use in the industrial setting cannot be "imposed blindly in the academic world."

The absence of explicit congressional direction, of course, does not preclude the Board from reaching any particular type of employment. Acting under its responsibility for adapting the broad provisions of the Act to differing workplaces, the Board asserted jurisdiction over a university for the first time in 1970. Within a year it had approved the formation of bargaining units composed of faculty members. The Board reasoned that faculty members are "professional employees" within the meaning of § 2 (12) of the Act and therefore are entitled to the benefits of collective bargaining.

Yeshiva does not contend that its faculty are not professionals under the statute. But professionals, like other employees, may be exempted from coverage under the Act's exclusion for "supervisors" who use independent judgment in overseeing other employees in the interest of the employer, or under the judicially implied exclusion for "managerial employees" who are involved in developing and enforcing employer policy. Both exemptions grow out of the same concern: That an employer is entitled to the undivided loyalty of its representatives. Because the Court of Appeals found the faculty to be managerial employees, it did not decide the question of their supervisory status. In view of our agreement with that court's application of the managerial exclusion, we also need not resolve that issue of statutory interpretation.

Managerial employees are defined as those who "formulate and effectuate management policies by expressing and making operative the decisions of their employer." These employees are "much higher in the managerial structure" than those explicitly mentioned by Congress, which "regarded [them] as so clearly outside the Act that no specific exclusionary provision was thought necessary." Managerial employees must exercise discretion within, or even independently of, established employer policy and must be aligned with management. Although the Board has established no firm criteria for determining when an employee is so aligned, normally an employee may be excluded as managerial only if he represents management interests by taking or recommending discretionary actions that effectively control or implement employer policy.

The Board does not contend that the Yeshiva faculty's decisionmaking is too insignificant to be deemed managerial. Nor does it suggest that the role of the faculty is merely advisory and thus not managerial. Instead, it contends that the managerial exclusion cannot be applied in a straightforward fashion to professional employees because those employees often appear to be exercising managerial authority when they are merely performing routine job duties. The status of such employees, in the Board's view, must be determined by reference to the "alignment with management" criterion. The Board argues that the Yeshiva faculty are not aligned with management because they are expected to exercise "independent professional judgment" while participating in academic governance, and because they are neither "expected to conform to management policies [nor] judged according to their effectiveness in carrying out those policies." Because of this independence, the Board contends there is no danger of divided loyalty and no need for the managerial exclusion. In its view, union pressure cannot divert the faculty from adhering to the interests of the university, because the university itself expects its faculty to pursue professional values rather than institutional interests. The Board concludes that application of the managerial exclusion to such employees would frustrate the national labor policy in favor of collective bargaining.

This "independent professional judgment" test was not applied in the decision we are asked to uphold. The Board's opinion relies exclusively on its previous faculty decisions for both legal and factual analysis. But those decisions only dimly foreshadow the reasoning now proffered to the Court. Without explanation, the Board initially announced two different rationales for faculty cases, then quickly transformed them into a litany to be repeated in case after case: (i) faculty authority is collective, (ii) it is exercised in the faculty's own interest rather than in the interest of the university, and (iii) final authority rests with the board of trustees. In their arguments in this case, the Board's lawyers have abandoned the first and third branches of this analysis, which in any event were flatly inconsistent with its precedents, and have transformed the second into a theory that does not appear clearly in any Board opinion.

The controlling consideration in this case is that the faculty of Yeshiva University exercise authority which in any other context unquestionably would be managerial. Their authority in academic matters is absolute. They decide what courses will be offered, when they will be scheduled, and to whom they will be taught. They debate and determine teaching methods, grading policies, and matriculation standards. They effectively decide which students will be admitted, retained, and graduated. On occasion their views have determined the size of the student body, the tuition to be charged, and the location of a school. When one considers the function of a university, it is difficult to imagine decisions more managerial than these. To the extent the industrial analogy applies, the faculty determines within each school the product to be produced, the terms upon which it will be offered, and the customers who will be served.

The Board nevertheless insists that these decisions are not managerial because they require the exercise of independent professional judgment. We are not persuaded by this argument. There may be some tension between the Act's exclusion of managerial employees and its inclusion of professionals, since most professionals in managerial positions continue to draw on their special skills and training. But we have been directed to no authority suggesting that that tension can be resolved by reference to the "independent professional judgment" criterion proposed in this case. Outside the university context, the Board routinely has applied the managerial and supervisory exclusions to professionals in executive positions without inquiring whether their decisions were based on management policy rather than professional expertise. Indeed, the Board has twice implicitly rejected the contention that decisions based on professional judgment cannot be managerial. Since the Board does not suggest that the "independent professional judgment" test is to be limited to university faculty, its new approach would overrule *sub silentio* this body of Board precedent and could result in the indiscriminate recharacterization as covered employees of professionals working in supervisory and managerial capacities.

Moreover, the Board's approach would undermine the goal it purports to serve: To ensure that employees who exercise discretionary authority on behalf of the employer will not divide their loyalty between employer and union. In arguing that a faculty member exercising independent judgment acts primarily in his own interest and therefore does not represent the interest of his employer, the Board assumes that the professional interests of the faculty and the interests of the institution are distinct, separable entities with which a faculty member could not simultaneously be aligned. The Court of Appeals found no justification for this distinction, and we perceive none. In fact, the faculty's professional interests—as applied to governance at a university like Yeshiva—cannot be separated from those of the institution.

In such a university, the predominant policy normally is to operate a quality institution of higher learning that will accomplish broadly defined educational goals within the limits of its financial resources. The "business" of a university is education, and its vitality ultimately must depend on academic policies that largely are formulated and generally are implemented by faculty governance decisions. Faculty members enhance their own standing and fulfill their professional mission by ensuring that the university's objectives are met. But there can be no doubt that the quest for academic excellence and institutional distinction is a "policy" to which the administration expects the faculty to adhere, whether it be defined as a professional or an institutional goal. It is fruitless to ask whether an employee is "expected to conform" to one goal or another when the two are essentially the same.

The problem of divided loyalty is particularly acute for a university like Yeshiva, which depends on the professional judgment of its faculty to formulate and apply crucial policies constrained only by necessarily general institutional goals. The university requires faculty participation in governance because professional expertise is indispensable to the formulation and implementation of academic policy. It may appear, as the Board contends, that the professor performing governance functions is less "accountable" for departures from institutional policy than a middle-level industrial manager whose discretion is more confined. Moreover, traditional systems of collegiality and tenure insulate the professor from some of the sanctions applied to an industrial manager who fails to adhere to company policy. But the analogy of the university to industry need not, and indeed cannot, be complete. It is clear that Yeshiva and like universities must rely on their faculties to participate in the making and implementation of their policies. The large measure of independence enjoyed by faculty members can only increase the danger that divided loyalty will lead to those harms that the Board traditionally has sought to prevent.

We certainly are not suggesting an application of the managerial exclusion that would sweep all professionals outside the Act in derogation of Congress' expressed intent to protect them. The Board has recognized that employees whose decision-making is limited to the routine discharge of professional duties in projects to which they have been assigned cannot be excluded from coverage even if union membership arguably may involve some divided loyalty. Only if an employee's activities fall outside the scope of the duties routinely performed by similarly situated professionals will he be found aligned with management. We think these decisions accurately capture the intent of Congress, and that they provide an appropriate starting point for analysis in cases involving professionals alleged to be managerial.

Finally, the Board contends that the deference due its expertise in these matters requires us to reverse the decision of the Court of Appeals. The question we decide today is a mixed one of fact and law. But the Board's opinion may be searched in vain for relevant findings of fact. The absence of factual analysis apparently reflects the Board's view that the managerial status of particular faculties may be decided on the basis of conclusory rationales rather than examination of the facts of each case. The Court of Appeals took a different view, and determined that the faculty of Yeshiva University, "in effect, substantially and pervasively operat[e] the enterprise." We find no reason to reject this conclusion. As our decisions consistently show, we accord great respect to the expertise of the Board when its conclusions are rationally based on articulated facts and consistent with the Act. In this case, we hold that the Board's decision satisfies neither criterion.

Affirmed.

Since the decision not to entitle Yeshiva faculty to organize collectively, almost 60 private colleges have sought to decertify existing faculty unions or refused to bargain with faculty on *Yeshiva*-grounds. Seventeen faculty unions have been decertified, and an untold number of organizing efforts have been thwarted because of the decision or because of the absence of state-enabling legislation. See "High Court's 'Yeshiva'

Ruling on Faculty Unions Is Starting to Affect," *Chronicle of Higher Education*, 13 May 1987, pp. 16, 17, 25.

The decision, which affected only private colleges, has recently been applied to public institutions, such as the University of Pittsburgh. The State of Pennsylvania has a labor law (Public Employment Relations Act), which was construed in 1987 by a Pennsylvania Labor Relations Board hearing examiner to exclude faculty: "As the faculty of the University of Pittsburgh participate with regularity in the essential process which results in a policy proposal and the decision to [hold a union election] and have a responsible role in giving practical effect to insuring the actual fulfillment of policy by concrete measures, the faculty of the university are management level employees within the meaning of PERA and thereby are excluded from PERA's coverage." United Faculty and University of Pittsburgh; PLRB No. PERA-R-84-53-W, March 11, 1987.

In some instances, a court has found that *Yeshiva* criteria were not met, and ordered a college to recognize a faculty union. *NLRB v. Cooper Union*, 783 F.2d 29 (2d Cir. 1985), *cert. denied*, 107 S. Ct. 70 (1986). As noted, much more common has been the extension of *Yeshiva* to private colleges.

Boston University Chapter v. N.L.R.B.
835 F.2d 399 (1st Cir. 1987)

TORRUELLA, Circuit Judge.

The Boston University Chapter, American Association of University Professors (Union) has petitioned this court for review of an order of the National Labor Relations Board (Board). The Union seeks to reverse the Board's decision dismissing unfair labor practice charges filed by the Union against Boston University (University), alleging violation of Sections 8(a)(1) and (5) of the National Labor Relations Act (Act).

We do not address this issue from a *tabula rasa*. A brief recount of the pertinent background is thus appropriate.

Background

On October 18, 1974, the Union filed a petition for representation with the Board, seeking certification as the collective bargaining agent for a unit composed of all regular full-time faculty members at the University except for those in the Schools of Law, Dentistry and Medicine. The University objected to the appropriateness of the unit, alleging that the full-time faculty were excluded from coverage of the Act by virtue of either their supervisory or managerial status. Notwithstanding said objections the Board ordered and held an election in which a majority of those employees presumably eligible voted in favor of being represented by the Union. After various administrative proceedings were completed the Union was certified by the Board as the bargaining representative of the unit sought.

The Union's bargaining request was rejected by the University, leading to the filing of the unfair labor practice charges presently before us. The Board's summary process was invoked and on March 22, 1977 the Board concluded that the University had violated Sections 8(a)(1) and (5) of the Act, and ordered it to bargain with the Union. The University petitioned this Court for review and the Board cross-appealed for enforcement of its order. We affirmed the Board.

On July 11, 1978, the University petitioned the Supreme Court for a writ of certiorari. On February 20, 1980, while this petition was still pending, the Supreme Court decided *N.L.R.B. v. Yeshiva University*, a ruling which shall be discussed in further detail *post*, but which in substance holds that under given factual circumstances university faculty members shall be considered managerial employees excluded from coverage by the Act. On March 3, 1980, the University's petition was granted and the judgment of this court recalled and remanded for further consideration in light of the ruling in *Yeshiva*.

Upon our remand to the Board, it reopened the record and in turn remanded the proceedings to the administrative law judge (ALJ) for further action. An extensive hearing was held and a comprehensive opinion issued by the ALJ on June 29, 1984. The ALJ's recommended ruling included findings to the effect that all full-time faculty in the requested unit were managerial employees as described in *Yeshiva*, and in addition, that all those above the rank of instructor were also supervisors. He thus recommended dismissal of the unfair labor practice charge against the University. The Board affirmed the ALJ's rulings and adopted the recommended order dismissing the charge against the University.

The full circle was completed to this court with the filing by the Union of the present petition seeking review of the Board's dismissal.

Standards of review

Under the circumstances, the parameters of our scope of action are severely restricted. On the one hand, on questions of fact, the standard of review is confined by Section 10(f) of the Act, which establishes as conclusive those findings of fact which are "supported by substantial evidence on the record considered as a whole." Substantial evidence, of course, means "such relevant evidence as a reasonable mind might accept as adequate to support a conclusion."

A determination by the Board regarding supervisory or managerial status is a mixed question of law and fact. Such a ruling is nevertheless entitled to deference if it is "warrant[ed] in the record and [has] a reasonable basis in law."

Regarding the law applicable to this case, our judicial hands are tied by *Yeshiva*. The crux of that case is contained in the following passage:

> The controlling consideration in this case is that the faculty of Yeshiva University exercise authority which in any other context unquestionably would be managerial. Their authority in academic matters is absolute. They decide what courses will be offered, when they will be scheduled, and to whom they will be taught. They debate and determine teaching methods, grading policies, and matriculation standards. They effectively decide which students will be admitted, retained, and graduated. On occasion their views have determined the size of the student body, the tuition to be charged, and the location of a school. When one considers the function of a university, it is difficult to imagine decisions more managerial than these. To the extent the industrial analogy applies, the faculty determines within each school the product to be produced, the terms upon which it will be offered, and the customers who will be served.

The Court reasoned that the divided loyalty that would be present if the faculty unionized, would be "particularly acute for a university like Yeshiva, which depends on the professional judgment of its faculty to formulate and apply crucial policies constrained only by necessarily general institutional goals." The Court reemphasized this point when it said that "Yeshiva and like universities must rely on their faculties to participate in the making and implementation of their policies."

Is Boston University a "like university"?

The Board so found, and given the limitations of Section 10(f) and *Yeshiva*, we must forcefully agree.

In adopting the ALJ's conclusion that the department chairman and full-time faculty are managerial employees pursuant to *Yeshiva*, the Board noted that:

> [T]he faculty has absolute authority over such matters as grading, teaching methods, graduation requirements, and student discipline. Additionally, the faculty is the moving force and almost always effectively controls matriculation requirements, curriculum, academic calendars, and course schedules. The faculty also plays an effective and determinative role in recommending faculty hiring, tenure, promotions, and reappointments (Note 3—We particularly note their authority to effectively veto curriculum and personnel decisions).... That ultimate authority for decision making at the University rests with the president and board of trustees does not alter the fact that, in practice, faculty decisions on all those policy matters are effectuated in the great majority of instances. Nor does the fact that the administration occasionally has made and implemented policy decisions without faculty input detract from the collegial managerial authority consistently exercised by the faculty.

Although these findings by the Board are somewhat conclusory they track the Court's ruling in *Yeshiva* and are fully supported by the ALJ's decision and the record. We should note that in *Yeshiva*, the various schools composing that institution were also served by a central administrative hierarchy, led by a president as chief executive officer, with the ultimate authority being vested in a board of trustees. There is no doubt, however, that here, as in *Yeshiva*, in the promulgation of the University's principal business, which is education and research, the faculty's role is predominant, and "in any other context unquestionably would be [considered] managerial." The various differences pointed to by petitioners between *Yeshiva* and the present case are minor distinctions without substance. Given the constraints of Section 10(f) and *Yeshiva*, our further consideration of this matter is an unnecessary spinning of our judicial wheels.

The decision of the Board dismissing the unfair labor charges against the University is affirmed and the petition for review is denied.

N.L.R.B. v. Florida Memorial College

820 F.2d 1182 (11th Cir. 1987)

TUTTLE, Senior Circuit Judge:

This case is before the Court on the application of the National Labor Relations Board for enforcement of its order directing Florida Memorial College to bargain with the Union. The Board found that the College violated Sections 8(a)(1) and 8(a)(5) of the National Labor Relations Act, by refusing to bargain with the United Faculty of Florida, Florida Memorial College Chapter (the Union), which the Board certified as the exclusive bargaining representative for the College faculty. As we find that the Board correctly concluded that the College's faculty is not managerial or supervisory and is therefore not excluded from the application of the Act, we grant enforcement of the Board's order.

Florida Memorial is a private, nonprofit four-year liberal arts college located in the Miami area. The College is made up of six academic divisions: general studies, business administration, education, humanities, science and mathematics, and social sciences. Florida Memorial has a student body of approximately 1,000 students and employs approximately thirty-five to forty full-time faculty as well as a number of part-time adjunct faculty. The College is governed by a sixteen-member board of trustees which includes two non-voting faculty representatives.

In 1979, in response to the Union's representation petition, the regional director of the Board issued a Decision and Direction of Election for a bargaining unit made up of all full-time faculty members, professional librarians, and professional counselors employed at Florida Memorial. The unit excluded part-time faculty members, administrative staff, non-professional employees, guards, and supervisors, as defined in the Act. The Union carried the election 21 to 14 and was certified as the exclusive bargaining representative of the employees in the Unit.

In 1980, the College filed a unit clarification petition with the Board's Regional Director contending that under the Supreme Court's decision in *N.L.R.B. v. Yeshiva University*, the College's faculty members and professional dormitory counselors should be excluded from the Unit because of their managerial and/or supervisory status. The Regional Director conducted a hearing on this issue and then transferred the case to the Board for a decision. Based on its findings, the Board concluded that the faculty members and division chairpersons should not be excluded from the Unit as managerial employees and that the division chairpersons and resident managers should not be excluded as supervisors. Accordingly, the Board dismissed the College's petition.

After the Board's decision, the College continued to refuse to bargain. The Union then filed an unfair labor practice charge. The College admitted its refusal to bargain, but adhered to its position that it had no obligation to do so because the Board had erred in determining the bargaining unit. The Board found that the College had raised no novel issues and that it had indeed committed an unfair labor practice in refusing to bargain. The Board, which ordered the College to bargain with the Union, is now before this Court seeking enforcement of its order.

The National Labor Relations Act expressly excludes supervisors from coverage under the Act. While managerial employees are not similarly expressly excluded, the Supreme Court has held that the Act implies such an exclusion. Thus, under the Act both supervisors and managerial employees are exempt from coverage. The reasons for these "exemption[s] grow out of the same concern: That an employer is entitled to the undivided loyalty of its representatives." As such, if Florida Memorial's faculty members are properly categorized as supervisory or managerial employees under the Act then they must be excluded from the bargaining unit.

The Court has defined managerial employees as those who " 'formulate and effectuate management policies by expressing and making operative the decisions of their employer.' " In terms of a college faculty, the Court has said that "the relevant consideration is [the faculty's] effective recommendation or control rather than final authority." In *Yeshiva*, the seminal case in this field, the Court found that the faculty was managerial because of its pervasive authority in running the University. The Court adopted the Second Circuit's conclusion that the faculty at Yeshiva " 'in effect, substantially and pervasively operat[e] the enterprise.' " Conversely, the Court also noted that there "may be institutions of higher learning unlike Yeshiva where the faculty are entirely or predominantly non-managerial." We find that the faculty at Florida Memorial fits into this latter category. Against the backdrop of *Yeshiva*, we hold that the Board correctly found that the faculty was not managerial.

Unlike Yeshiva's faculty, which exercised absolute authority in academic matters and considerable authority in the non-academic sphere, the faculty at Florida Memorial asserts insufficient control in terms of almost every one of the relevant criteria examined by the Court in that case. Simply put, Florida Memorial's faculty lacks the managerial characteristics considered by the Court in *Yeshiva*. A comparison of the fact pattern in this case in light of the criteria considered in *Yeshiva* illustrates this conclusion.

In *Yeshiva*, the Court considered the faculty's authority in both the academic and non-academic spheres. In terms of academic matters, the Court noted that the faculty's authority was absolute. Speaking in terms of the faculty's involvement in academic matters, the Court stressed that:

> They decide what course will be offered, when they will be scheduled, and to whom they will be taught. They debate and determine teaching methods, grading policies, and matriculation standards. They effectively decide which students will be admitted, retained, and graduated. On occasion their views have determined the size of the student body, the tuition to be charged, and the location of a school.

Furthermore, in terms of decision-making at Yeshiva, not only were faculty decisions almost never vetoed, but the faculty, at times, overrode the decision of the administration.

In contrast to *Yeshiva*, the faculty at Florida Memorial lack a faculty-wide governing organization through which to formulate collective faculty input as to matters at the College. While there is a faculty council, this body apparently meets only once or twice yearly and then for the sole purpose of electing two faculty members to serve as non-voting delegates on the Board of Trustees. The absence of an effective faculty-wide governing organization is in distinct contrast to *Yeshiva* where the faculty within the substantially autonomous undergraduate and graduate schools met formally, and in some instances pursuant to written bylaws, to decide matters of institutional and professional concern.

As opposed to expressing its views through a collective decision-making body, the faculty's participation in decision-making at Florida Memorial occurs through representatives on several standing committees. These committees, however, are structured in such a manner as to significantly dilute the faculty members' participation. First of all, the faculty does not select which members will sit on these advisory committees. Rather, the Vice President of the College appoints faculty members to serve. Second, it is significant that these committees include a number of administrators and students. In fact, some of the committees are made up of a majority of nonfaculty participants. This amalgamation of membership dilutes the effectiveness of the faculty's input into the committees' recommendations. In this regard, Courts have held that such mixed committees do not indicate managerial authority on a faculty's behalf.

Beyond any participation the faculty may have in these committees, the record indicates the administration's willingness to disregard such committees' recommendations. The College's 1978 selection of a new academic dean illustrates this practice. While a search committee did submit a list of candidates for this position, the College president refused to examine it and instead instructed the committee to expand the list. Thereafter, a member of the president's cabinet added an additional candidate to the list. The president hired that candidate despite the fact that that person was the committee's fifth choice. In sum, the faculty not only lacks a method of participation through which to channel collective input but also the mechanism through which the faculty does exert input lacks effective influence in the decision-making process.

The specific decisions concerning the institution which the faculty made and which the court considered in *Yeshiva* are not similarly controlled by the faculty at Florida Memorial.

Unlike *Yeshiva*, the Florida Memorial faculty has no effective control over the curriculum offered. The overwhelming majority of courses follow the existing curriculum set forth in the college catalog. As the Board noted, there was no evidence that the faculty had any effective input into the preparation of this catalog. While individual faculty members may suggest new courses, addition of these courses to the curriculum requires the approval of either the academic council or the academic dean. However, as the council consists of a mixture of faculty and administrators, its influence is diluted in terms of its representativeness of the faculty's views. Furthermore, the record indicates that in the past, when faculty members have proposed new courses, the administration has played a significant role in the process between origination and implementation of new course proposals.

Although individual faculty members establish course content, determine their teaching methods, and grade their students, *Yeshiva* makes it clear that "professors may not be excluded [as managerial] merely because they determine the content of their own courses [and] evaluate their own students...." Moreover, at Florida Memorial, even these conceivably autonomous decisions are encroached upon by the administration. In grading students the faculty applies a grading system supplied by the academic dean's office. The faculty must also select textbooks in collaboration with the academic dean. Further, teaching loads, as well as adjustments necessitated by underenrollment or overenrollment of a given course, are within the discretion of the academic dean who makes the final decision as to whether outside help is needed or to open an additional section of a course.

The faculty's role with respect to policies affecting students is virtually nonexistent. Because the College has an open admissions policy, there is no faculty involvement in the admissions process. Further, the administration has set forth in the college catalog policies concerning student absence, probation, suspension, and expulsion. There is no evidence of general faculty involvement in either the development or implementation of these policies. Graduation requirements also are set forth in the catalog, and there is again no evidence of faculty input into these policies. Moreover, the only role played by a faculty member in applying the graduation standards is the ministerial role of the division chairperson who compares the student's record with these requirements. Thereafter, the academic dean and registrar must still approve each candidate. Further, although division chairpersons may make recommendations concerning students' requests to alter the requirements, the academic dean and the registrar must approve any such requests.

In *Yeshiva*, the Court considered the faculty's involvement in the non-academic sphere. The Court noted "that faculty members at Yeshiva also play a predominant role in faculty hiring, tenure, sabbaticals, termination and promotion." The same cannot be said at Florida Memorial. These and other relevant nonacademic matters are under the control of the administration, particularly the president and the academic dean.

With regard to hiring, faculty participation in the process is within the discretion of the president. Moreover, such participation has lacked any pattern of consistency. Search committees have been utilized on some occasions, yet when used, the president has at times circumvented their recommendations.

With respect to tenure and sabbaticals, the faculty is also without influence. First, there is no tenure for faculty at the college. With the exceptions of a few two-year contracts offered at the discretion of the administration, faculty contracts are for one year. Furthermore, these contracts contain a provision giving the College broad leeway in terminations. If faculty members refuse to obey college rules and regulations prescribed by the president, or refuse to continue to promote scholarship, as prescribed by the president, then sufficient cause exists for termination of their contracts. The absence of tenure speaks to the question of faculty input. Its absence removes an area in which the faculty could have theoretically had input. Furthermore, an absence of tenure tends to indicate to this Court that the faculty is nonmanagerial. Without the security of tenure it would seem less likely that faculty members would attempt to assert managerial authority on matters in contradiction to an administration armed with the power of termination.

In regard to sabbaticals, the faculty at Florida Memorial has not exercised any influence in the process. While the College has granted only one sabbatical in its history, the decision to do so was reached by the Board of Trustees based upon recommendations from the president and academic dean.

Similarly, decisions at the College concerning termination and promotion are largely under the control of the administration. With respect to termination or nonrenewal of faculty contracts, the president and the academic dean play the predominant roles. In 1978, for instance, the president unilaterally decided not to renew the contracts of four faculty members without advanced notice. Thereafter, the president asserted to the Academic Council his authority to do so as a privilege of his office.

In terms of promotions, the academic dean is responsible for making determinations. The academic dean has both accepted and rejected faculty chairpersons' recommendations in this process.

Finally, the Court in *Yeshiva* relied on the fact that faculty views on occasions had determined the size of the student body, the tuition to be charged, and the location of a school. At Florida Memorial each of these matters is determined by the administration which is solely responsible for establishing admissions policies and tuition, and which was responsible for establishing and locating the College's satellite facilities.

In sum, the record amply supports the Board's conclusion in this case that the faculty at Florida Memorial failed to meet the relevant criteria under *Yeshiva* and its progeny. Accordingly, the Board reasonably found that the faculty was not managerial and therefore not excluded from the application of the Act.

The second question at issue in this case was not before the Court in *Yeshiva*. It concerns, in part, the supervisory status of certain faculty members. The Board found that the College faculty division chairpersons and the College's two dormitory resident managers exercised insufficient supervisory authority to be considered supervisors under the Act. Recognizing the great deference awarded to the Board's decision when its conclusions are rationally based on articulated facts and consistent with the Act, we uphold the Board's decision on this matter.

In regard to the division chairpersons, the record indicates that their limited authority falls short of the level required to establish supervisory status. Their roles in the promotion and wage increase process, as well as their authority to resolve grievances and evaluate faculty members is effectively and frequently circumscribed by the administration. The Board's finding that the responsibilities of the division chairpersons incident to their normal faculty positions did not amount to supervisory as envisioned by the Act is supported by substantial evidence.

Furthermore, in regard to the resident managers, the Board also properly concluded that such persons were not supervisors under the Act. Here, too, their supervisory role is de minimis and is tempered by an administration which holds tight reins over their authority.

The Board's order will be ENFORCED.

———

Scholars and courts will continue to sort out the consequences of *Yeshiva* and its successors, and unless legislation is enacted at the federal level (to amend the NLRA, for instance) or in the states (to repeal "right to work" legislation), this issue will remain a major bone of contention between faculty and their institutions, both public and private. See C. Clarke, "The *Yeshiva* Case, an Analysis and an Assessment of Its Potential Impact on Public Universities," *Journal of Higher Education*, 52 (1981), 449–69; R. Birnbaum and D. Inman, "The Relationship of Academic Bargaining to Changes in Campus Climate," *Journal of Higher Education*, 53 (1984), 609–20; M. Estey, "Faculty Grievance Procedures Outside Collective Bargaining," *Academe* (May/June, 1986), 6–15. In 1988, office workers at Harvard voted to be represented by a union, suggesting that the white-collar unions may increase their efforts at organizing academic staff in private colleges. "How Labor Broadened Its Beachhead in the Ivy League," *New York Times*, 22 May 1988, p. E5.

Faculty in Religious Institutions

A case filed in February 1987, but not tried had by summer 1988, already generated its own legal literature, and before it is fully resolved, will certainly spawn more commentary: the matter of Rev. Charles E. Curran, Professor of Moral Theology at Catholic University of America, in Washington, D.C. *Curran v. Catholic University* (D.C. Superior Court, 1562–87). Professor Curran's right to teach moral theology at Catholic University was revoked by the Vatican, following a longstanding dispute over his published views in which he dissented from official Catholic teaching. The Vatican informed him that he "will no longer be considered suitable nor eligible to exercise the function of a Professor of Catholic Theology." Following a protracted series of letters and discussions (published in the *Chronicle of Higher Education*, 3 September 1986, pp. 44–47), he was removed from his tenured position at the university. Because Catholic University's canon law, theology, and philosophy departments are considered "ecclesiastical" and "pontifical," they require a commission or teaching license from the Vatican. The only other "Pontifical" college in the United States is the Pontifical College Josephinum, a Roman Catholic seminary in Worthington, Ohio, established in 1888. Thus, he found himself removed from his tenured faculty position and filed a civil suit, alleging a breach of contract in the wrongful discharge. In 1988, Catholic University moved to dismiss the case, on institutional academic freedom principles, claiming religious grounds. In April 1988, the D.C. court refused to dismiss the civil suit, leading the university to settle upon an arrangement where he could remain on the faculty "[with] alternative teaching assignments in an area within his professional competence." By May 1988, however, the settlement unraveled when the university insisted he sign a pledge not to "teach Catholic theology" in the proposed assignment to the Department of Sociology. For a review of the controversy, see "Catholic U. Professor, Barred from Teaching Theology, Vows to Fight," *Chronicle of Higher Education*, 3 September 1986, pp. 44–47; "No Imminent Threat to Catholic Colleges' Freedom Seen in Vatican Ban on Teacher," *Chronicle of Higher Education*, 8 October 1986, pp. 1, 14–15; "Catholic Colleges in U.S. Debate Academic Freedom Amid Disputes," *New York Times*, 8 October 1986, pp. Y1, 10; "Dissenting Catholic Theologian Preaches More Critical Approach to Moral Issues," *Chronicle of Higher Education*, 24 June 1987, pp. 4–6; "Curran Can Sue, Catholic U. Told," *Chronicle of Higher Education*, 13 April 1988, p. A2; "Controversial Catholic U. Professor Retains Tenure, but He Is Barred from Teaching in Theology Dept.," *Chronicle of Higher Education*, 20 April 1988, pp. A15, 24; "Theologian Rejects Catholic U. Proposal to Settle Suspension," *New York Times*, 18 May 1988, p. A21. See also M. Feeley, "The Dissent of Theology: A Legal Analysis of the *Curran* Case," *Hastings Constitutional Law Quarterly*, 15 (1987), 7–44; J. Andrews et al., "Church Licensed Professors: The Curran Controversy," *Journal of College and University Law*, 13 (1987), 375–95.

This complex case has arisen against a background of the Vatican's *Proposed Schema for a Pontifical Document on Catholic Universities*, a document that appears in the appendix. The document, if adopted, would affect the appointment of faculty at Catholic institutions; Articles 26.1-.3 propose:

> Article 26.1. All teachers who are to be chosen, nominated and promoted in accordance with the statutes are to be distinguished by academic and pedagogic ability as well as by doctrinal integrity and uprightness of life so that they may cooperate effectively to achieve goals of the university.
>
> 26.2. Teachers who lack these requirements are to be dismissed, observing the procedures established in the statutes or equivalent document.
>
> 26.3. In accordance with Article 19 of these norms, every Catholic university shall establish such a juridical procedure.

For reactions and commentary on the proposed schema, see "Catholic College and University Presidents Respond to Proposed Vatican Schema," *Origins*, 10 April 1986, 697–711; " 'Anti-Reformation' in Church Seen Threatening the Academic Freedom of Professors of Religion," *Chronicle of Higher Education*, 1 July 1987, pp. 9, 11; "New Catholic Law Is No Threat to Academic Freedom," *Chronicle of Higher Ed-*

ucation, 15 July 1987, p. 41; D. Maguire, "Can a University Be Catholic?" *Academe,* January–February 1988, pp. 12–16.

Professor Curran presumably would not have been found ineligible to teach in the English department for dissenting from Catholic doctrine. While the case wended its way to court, another Catholic institution found itself in court. Catholic University of Puerto Rico dismissed a tenured English faculty member when she remarried without having her first marriage annulled; CUPR argued that its procedures allowed it to dismiss her for "professional or personal conduct that violates the moral and doctrinal principles of the Catholic Church." She had been divorced when she was hired, and when she received tenure, but the university argued that her second marriage—without having the previous marriage dissolved—meant that she was not a practicing Catholic. See *Academe,* May–June 1987, pp. 33–38; "7 Institutions, Including a Catholic U. That Fired Teacher Who Remarried, Face AAUP Censure Vote," *Chronicle of Higher Education,* 17 June 1987, pp. 10–12.

Chapter 4

Students and the Law

The Legal Relationship Between Colleges and Students

Of all the areas included in the field of higher education law, one of the more commonly litigated and least understood is that of students and their legal relationship with the institution. Although there are many students (over 12.5 million in 1988), student litigants have been a disproportionately small percentage of the parties in higher education suits: a 1987 study of all the postsecondary litigation in Iowa revealed that only 11% of the higher education cases brought since 1847 were brought by students (faculty brought 31%), and a 1988 study in Texas revealed that students brought 31%, compared to 35% by faculty, of the cases since 1878. Lelia Helms, "Patterns of Litigation in Postsecondary Education: A Case Law Study," *Journal of College and University Law,* 14 (1987), 99–110; Margaret Lam, "Patterns of Litigation at Institutions of Higher Education in Texas, 1878–1988," (Houston: IHELG Monograph 88–8, 1988).

An obvious reason for the relatively small number of student cases has been the small likelihood of prevailing. William Kaplin has noted of this relationship:

> Traditionally, the law accorded postsecondary institutions extensive autonomy in their daily operations. The academic environment was thought to be delicate and complex. Outsiders such as lawyers or judges would, almost by definition, be ignorant of the special arrangements and sensitivities underpinning this environment. Academia could operate well, by this view, only when its traditional means of governance by consensus and collegiality was fully respected.

> The judiciary developed various doctrines that had the effect of protecting this academic autonomy. The college's relationship to its students was said to be parental in nature. Since the college acted *in loco parentis*, it could exercise virtually unchecked authority over students' lives. Students similarly could not rely on claims to constitutional rights. Constitutional constraints did not apply at all to private education, and attendance at public postsecondary institutions was considered a privilege and not a right. Being a "privilege," attendance could constitutionally be extended and was subject to termination on whatever conditions the institution determined were in its and the students' best interests. Occasionally courts did hold that students had some contract rights under an express or implied contractual relation with the institution, but typically the institution was given virtually unlimited power to dictate the contract terms, and the contract, once made, was construed heavily in the institution's favor.

* * *

The established patterns of deference to authority and tradition were also

599

increasingly irrelevant to many of the new students. The emergence of the stu-
dent-veteran; the loosening of the "lock-step" pattern of educational preparation, which led students directly from high school to college to graduate work;
and finally, the lowered age of majority—all combined to make the *in loco
parentis* relationship between institution and student less and less tenable. New
demands for professional credentials also made higher education an economic
necessity for many. Some students, such as the G.I. Bill veterans, had cause to
view higher education as an earned right.

W. Kaplin, "Law on the Campus, 1960–1985," *Journal of College and University
Law*, 12 (1985), 269–299.

The cases in this Chapter were chosen to include the range of legal relationships
between colleges and students, instances in which students and colleges prevailed,
and a chronology of the changes in the legal characterization of this relationship.
Throughout the Chapter, dozens of cases explore the legal relationship, even where
the litigation may be cited for another feature, such as admissions, grades, dismissals,
misconduct, recognition of student organizations, student fees, opportunities for forums, student athletes, and residency requirements. Increasingly, legal scholarship has
focused upon the presumptions inherent in the legal duties owed students, and as the
cases indicate, the reports of the death of *in loco parentis* may be premature:

> [A] trend in plaintiff claims suggests that students are asking for this doctrine
> which they once rejected. Many courts have responded to the onslaught of
> students' personal injury lawsuits by imposing liability upon colleges and uni-
> versities, often in extraordinary circumstances. This new liability is recognizable
> as a return to the old *in loco parentis*—indeed, some courts have gone so far
> as to make colleges the insurer of student safety. What distinguishes the *in loco
> parentis* of the 1980's is that it is limited to protection of student safety. Missing
> is the once complementary power of colleges to police and control students'
> morals—this having long been barred by constitutional and civil rights pro-
> tections.
>
> The development suggests one of two things. The first is that the student-
> college relationship may not be so one-sided in favor of the college after all.
> When students rejected college supervision and protection, the courts responded.
> And now when students ask for protection, but not supervision, the courts are
> responding again. Thus students may be able to shape the student-college re-
> lationship through the judicial system.

J. Szablewicz and A. Gibbs, "Colleges' Increasing Exposure to Liability: The New
In Loco Parentis," *Journal of Law and Education*, 16 (1987), 453–463. Zirkel and
Reichner, among others, have delivered the eulogy for higher education applications
of the doctrine: "The college context is the only one in which the *in loco parentis*
theory has undergone a clear rise and complete demise in our courts." "Is the In
Loco Parentis Doctrine Dead?" *Journal of Law and Education*, 15 (1986), 271–283.

In "The Non-Contractual Nature of the Student-University Contractual Relationship," Victoria Dodd showed how poorly contract theory fits between colleges and
students. She delineated

> the lack of a true bargaining and promise orientation in the student-university
> context, and hence, the intrinsically non-contractual nature of that relationship.
> Indeed, the myriad of individual student problems that can arise in a university
> situation would defy an attempt to embody in fair, written terms all of the
> "promises" inherent in such a situation.

The student-university relationship instead seems to fall more naturally into the realm of tort analysis. Tort liability generally is 'based upon the relations of persons with others; and those relations may arise generally, with large groups or classes of persons, or singly, with an individual.' The wrongs or injuries... flow from the relationship between student and university. Although this relationship is created by a contract of sorts through the payment of tuition, its survival extends beyond notions of contract. At least historically, too, one of the closest analogues to the student-university relationship has been the familial relationship. Perhaps that similarity helped to prevent the development of tort theory in education cases; the recognition of intra-familial tort liability is relatively recent.

Other, more modern tort analogues to the student-university relationship are found in the relationship between landlord and tenant, employer and employee, and common carrier and passenger. All are created by contract, yet the law imposes duties beyond those contemplated by the agreement. These areas can be distinguished from the educational setting because most of the additional tort duties in the former realms are primarily oriented toward the protection of persons and property from physical injury or damage. But the relevant concept is the law's infusion of tort notions into a contractual relationship. Courts have begun to move in this direction in the education area insofar as there is a growing tendency to impose tort liability on schools for failing to properly control third parties, for instance when a school fails to provide dormitories that are reasonably safe from crime. Perhaps this foreshadows a predilection toward tort analysis regarding the overall student-university relationship, for such problems could have readily been treated as a breach of contract under an implied contractual term of providing adequate living accommodations for students. In any event, it is hoped that this development will continue, and that contractual theories will be subjected to more probing scrutiny by both courts and education litigants in the future. *Kansas Law Review*, 33 (1985), 701–731.

In Loco Parentis and Due Process

Gott v. Berea College
156 Ky. 376, 161 S.W. 204 (1913)

NUNN, J. The appellant, J. S. Gott, about the 1st of September, 1911, purchased and was conducting a restaurant in Berea, Ky., across the street from the premises of Berea College. A restaurant had been conducted in this same place for quite a long while by the party from whom Gott purchased. For many years it has been the practice of the governing authorities of Berea College to distribute among the students at the beginning of each scholastic year a pamphlet entitled "Students Manual," containing the rules and regulations of the college for the government of the student body. Subsection 3 of this manual, under the heading "Forbidden Places," enjoined the students from entering any "place of ill repute, liquor saloons, gambling houses," etc. During the 1911 summer vacation, the faculty, pursuant to their usual practice of revising the rules, added another clause to this rule as to forbidden places, and the rule was announced to the student body at chapel exercise on the first day of the fall term, which began September 11th. The new rule is as follows: "(b) Eating houses and places of amusement in Berea, not controlled by the college, must not be entered by students on pain of immediate dismission. The institution provides for the recreation of its students, and ample accommodation for meals and refreshment, and cannot permit outside parties to solicit student patronage for gain."

Appellant's restaurant was located and conducted mainly for the profits arising from student patronage. During the first few days after the publication of this rule, two or three students were expelled for its violation, so that the making of the rule and its enforcement had the effect of very materially injuring, if not absolutely ruining, appellant's business because the students were afraid to further patronize it.

On the 20th day of September appellant instituted this action in equity and procured a temporary restraining order and injunction against the enforcement of the rule above quoted, and charging that the college and its officers unlawfully and maliciously conspired to injure his business by adopting a rule forbidding students entering eating houses. For this he claimed damages in the sum of $500. By amended petitions he alleged that in pursuance of such conspiracy the college officers had uttered slanderous remarks concerning him and his business and increased his prayer for damages to $2,000. The slanderous remarks were alleged to have been spoken at chapel and other public exercises to the student body as a reason for the rule, and were to the effect that appellant was a bootlegger, and upon more than one occasion had been charged and convicted of illegally selling whisky. Berea College answered and denied that any slanderous remarks had been made as to appellant, or that they had conspired maliciously or otherwise, or that the rule adopted was either unlawful or unreasonable. In the second paragraph the college affirmatively set forth that it is a private (incorporated) institution of learning, supported wholly by private donations and its endowment and such fees as it collects from students or parents of students who desire to become affiliated with said institution and abide by and conform to the rules and regulations provided by the governing authorities of the college for the conduct of the students; that every student upon entering said institution agrees, upon pain of dismissal, to conform to such rules and regulations as may be from time to time promulgated; that the institution aims to furnish an education to inexperienced country, mountain boys and girls of very little means at the lowest possible cost; that practically all of the students are from rural districts and unused to the ways of even a village the size of Berea; and that they are of very limited means. It is further alleged that they have been compelled from time to time to pass rules tending to prevent students from wasting their time and money and to keep them wholly occupied in study; that some of the rules prohibit the doing of things not in themselves wrong or unlawful, but which the governing authorities have found and believe detrimental to the best interest of the college and the student body. For these reasons the rule in question was adopted, but they say at the time that they had no knowledge that the plaintiff owned or was about to acquire a restaurant, and that the rule was in no way directed at the plaintiff. Upon motion the restraining order was dissolved, but, on account of allegations charging slanderous remarks, the lower court overruled demurrer to the petition. After filing of the answer, proof was heard, the case submitted and tried by the court with the result that the petition was dismissed, and Gott appeals to this court.

Passing the question as to whether an ordinary action can be joined with an equitable action for restraining order, there being no objection to it in the lower court, it is sufficient to say that on the question of uttering the slanderous words issue was joined, and the case submitted to the court without the intervention of a jury, and we are disposed to accept its finding against Gott since it is supported by sufficient evidence. The larger question, and the one we are called here to pass upon, is whether the rule forbidding students entering eating houses was a reasonable one and within the power of the college authorities to enact, and the further question whether, in that event, appellant Gott will be heard to complain. That the enforcement of the rule worked a great injury to Gott's restaurant business cannot well be denied; but, unless he can show that the college authorities have been guilty of a breach of some legal duty which they owe to him, he has no cause of action against them for the injury.

One has no right of action against a merchant for refusal to sell goods, nor will an action lie, unless such means are used as of themselves constitute a breach of legal duty, for inducing or causing persons not to trade, deal, or contract with another; and it is a well-established practice that, when a lawful act is performed in the proper manner, the party performing it is not liable for mere incidental consequences injuriously resulting from it to another.

College authorities stand in loco parentis concerning the physical and moral welfare and mental training of the pupils, and we are unable to see why, to that end, they may not make any rule or regulation for the government or betterment of their pupils that a parent could for the same purpose. Whether the rules or regulations are wise or their aims worthy is a matter left solely to the discretion of the authorities or parents, as the case may be, and, in the exercise of that discretion, the courts are not disposed to interfere, unless the rules and aims are unlawful or against public policy. Section 881 of the Kentucky Statutes, applicable to corporations of this character, provides that they may "adopt such rules for their government and operation, not inconsistent with law, as the directors, trustees, or managers may deem proper." The corporate charter of Berea College empowers the board of trustees to "make such by-laws as it may deem necessary to promote the interest of the institution, not in violation of any laws of the state or the United States." This reference to the college powers shows that its authorities have a large discretion, and they are similar to the charter and corporate rights under which colleges and such institutions are generally conducted.

Having in mind such powers, the courts have without exception held to the rule which is well settled: "A college or university may prescribe requirements for admission and rules for the conduct of its students, and one who enters as a student impliedly agrees to conform to such rules of government." The only limit upon this rule is as to institutions supported in whole or in part by appropriations from the public treasury. In such cases their rules are viewed somewhat more critically; but, since this is a private institution, it is unnecessary to notice further the distinction.

A further consideration of the power of school boards is found in Mechem on Public Officers, § 730, from which we quote: "There is no question that the power of school authorities over pupils is not confined to schoolroom or grounds, but to extend to all acts of pupils which are detrimental to the good order and best interest of the school, whether committed in school hours, or while the pupil is on his way to or from school, or after he has returned home." Of course this rule is not intended to, nor will it be permitted to, interfere with parental control of children in the home, unless the acts forbidden materially affect the conduct and discipline of the school.

There is nothing in the case to show that the college had any contract, business, or other direct relations with the appellant. They owed him no special duty; and, while he may have suffered an injury, yet he does not show that the college is a wrongdoer in a legal or any sense. Nor does he show that in enacting the rule they did it unlawfully, or that they exceeded their power, or that there was any conspiracy to do anything unlawful. Their right to enact the rule comes well within their charter provision, and that it was a reasonable rule cannot be very well disputed. Assuming that there were no other outside eating houses in Berea, and that there never had been a disorderly one, or one in which intoxicating liquors had been sold, still it would not be an unreasonable rule forbidding students entering or patronizing appellant's establishment. In the first place, the college offers an education to the poorest, and undertakes to offer them the means of a livelihood within the institution while they are pursuing their studies, and at the same time provides board and lodging for a nominal charge. Whatever profit was derived served to still further reduce expenses charged against the pupil. It stands to reason that when the plans of the institution are so prepared, and the support and maintenance of the students are so ordered, there must be the fullest co-operation on the part of all the students, otherwise there will be disappointment, if not failure, in the project. It is also a matter of common knowledge that one of the chief dreads of college authorities is the outbreak of an epidemic and against which they should take the utmost precaution. These precautions, however, may wholly fail if students carelessly or indiscriminately visit or patronize public or unsanitary eating houses. Too often those operating such places are ignorant of, or indifferent to, even the simplest sanitary requirements. As a safeguard against disease infection from this source, there is sufficient reason for the promulgation of the rule complained of.

But, even if it might be conceded that the rule was an unreasonable one, still appellant Gott is in no position to complain. He was not a student, nor is it shown that he had any children as students in the college. The rule was directed to and intended to control only the student body. For the purposes of this case the school, its officers and students, are a legal entity, as much so as any family, and, like a father may direct his children, those in charge of boarding schools are well within their rights and powers when they direct their students what to eat and where they may get it, where they may go, and what forms of amusement are forbidden.

* * *

[T]he mere fact that one's trade has been restrained, as Gott's admittedly has, gives him no ground to invoke the law, unless the means used to restrain it have been malicious and wrongful. And as above indicated the proof shows neither malice or wrong on the part of appellee.

Considering the whole case, the judgment of the lower court is affirmed.

Anthony v. Syracuse University
231 N.Y.S. 435 (1928)

SEARS, J. The defendant is an educational corporation incorporated under a special act of the Legislature of the state of New York (Laws 1887, c. 414), and conducts various departments for the higher education of men and women at Syracuse, N. Y. It is exempt from taxation. It is subject to visitation by the board of regents.

The plaintiff, from September 15, 1923, to October 6, 1926, was a student in the Department of Domestic Science or Home Economics of the defendant. This department is not shown to receive any financial aid from the state. On the day last mentioned she was dismissed from the defendant's institution by the officers without the assignment of any adequate cause for such action. She was simply advised that the authorities of the defendant had heard rumors about her; that they had talked with several girls "in the house"—that is, in the house of the Greek letter society of which she was a member—and found she had done nothing lately, but that they had learned that she had caused a lot of trouble in the house; and that they did not think her "a typical Syracuse girl."

In September, 1923, when the plaintiff was first received as a student at the University, she signed a registration card, which contained these words:

> "I agree in honor to comply with the regulations and requirements of Syracuse University and to co-operate with the University authorities and my fellow students in maintaining high standards of conduct and scholarship and in promoting the general welfare of the University. It is understood that I accept registration as a student in Syracuse University subject to the rule as to continuance therein found on page 47 of the University Catalogue."

The regulation referred to in the registration card as to continuance at the University, printed on page 47 of the University Catalogue, was as follows:

> "Attendance at the University is a privilege and not a right. In order to safeguard its scholarship and its moral atmosphere, the University reserves the right to request the withdrawal of any student whose presence is deemed detrimental. Specific charges may or may not accompany a request for withdrawal."

In September, 1924, and again in September, 1925, she signed similar registration cards. The regulation quoted above was slightly amended before the 1924 registration card was signed, and as printed in the catalogue, and referred to in the registration cards of 1924 and 1925, it was as follows:

> "Attendance at the University is a privilege and not a right. In order to safeguard those ideals of scholarship and that moral atmosphere which are in the very purpose of its founding and maintenance, the University reserves the right and the student concedes to the University the right to require the withdrawal of any student at any time for any reason deemed sufficient to it, and no reason for requiring such withdrawal need be given."

The plaintiff does not allege in the complaint that her dismissal was malicious, but simply that it was arbitrary and unjust and founds her action upon a contract which she claims to have existed between herself and the University for her continued attendance. In substance she seeks a specific performance of this contract. The defendant, on the other hand, relies on what it claims to be one of the terms of the contract, namely, that the plaintiff's continuance as a student at the University was strictly at the pleasure of that institution. No question is raised by the defendant as to the form of the action, or the right of the plaintiff to the judgment she obtained, if she is entitled to any judgment whatever.

Under ordinary circumstances and conditions a person matriculating at a university establishes a contractual relationship under which, upon compliance with all reasonable regulations as to scholastic standing, attendance, deportment, payment of tuition, and otherwise, he is entitled to pursue his selected course to completion, and receive the degree or certificate awarded for the successful completion of such course. The defendant, for the purpose of this litigation, concedes such to be the law. It rests its case upon the claim that an express contract between the parties takes this case out of the general rule stated, and that, under such express contract, a right to dismiss the plaintiff at any time for any cause whatever was granted to the defendant.

The regulation in force in 1923, assented to by plaintiff's signature to the registration card, did, doubtless, as claimed by the defendant, modify the ordinary rule, and this regulation continued to be a part of the contract between the parties throughout the term of the plaintiff's attendance at the University, except as it was modified in 1924. By signing the later registration cards, the plaintiff assented to the modification. Plaintiff argues that the regulation is not binding upon her, first, because at no time did she read the catalogue or have actual knowledge of the regulation printed in it; and, second, because the regulation is contrary to public policy. It is also suggested that it is not binding on her because she was an infant at the time all registration cards were signed. In my judgment none of these arguments is sound.

First, contracts must be enforced as they are written. The learned court at Special Term correctly stated in his opinion:

> "The fact that the plaintiff had no actual knowledge of the existence of this rule would not alter the situation, assuming that the rule of constructive knowledge be under the circumstances applicable."

The rule of constructive knowledge was applicable.

Second, the argument on public policy is based upon the theory that consent to such a regulation as was here printed in the catalogue amounts to a permission given the University authorities to do an act which would necessarily injure the reputation of the student. Such injury to reputation, however, if it occurred, would be merely incidental. As both parties argue, the relation between plaintiff and defendant was wholly contractual. It was voluntary in its inception on both sides. A student is not required to enter the University, and may in fact, after entry, withdraw without reason at any time. The University need not accept as a student one desiring to become such. It may, therefore, limit the effect of such acceptance by express agreement, and thus retain the position of contractual freedom in which it stood before the student's course was entered upon. I can discover no reason why a student may not agree to grant to the institution an optional right to terminate the relations between them. The contract between an institution and a student does not differ in this respect from contracts of employment.

Third, infancy is not material. The plaintiff relies upon a contract made when she was an infant. She cannot recover, except upon the contract. The only contract existing between the plaintiff and defendant embodied the regulation permitting the defendant to terminate the contractual relationship. If she repudiates her contract because of her infancy, she then becomes a stranger to the University. She cannot repudiate part and not repudiate all.

The construction of the regulation may be material. The regulation, in my judgment, does not reserve to the defendant an absolute right to dismiss the plaintiff for any cause whatever. Its right to dismiss is limited, for the regulation must be read as a whole. The University may only dismiss a student for reasons falling within two classes, one in connection with safeguarding the University's ideals of scholarship, and the other in connection with safeguarding the University's moral atmosphere. When dismissing a student, no reason for dismissing need be given. The University must, however, have a reason, and that reason must fall within one of the two classes mentioned above. Of course, the University authorities have wide discretion in determining what situation does and what does not fall within the classes mentioned, and the courts would be slow indeed in disturbing any decision of the University authorities in this respect.

When the plaintiff comes into court and alleges a breach of contract, the burden rests upon her to establish such breach. She must show that her dismissal was not for a reason within the terms of the regulation. The record here is meager on this subject. While no adequate reason was assigned by the University authorities for the dismissal, I find nothing in the record on which to base a finding that no such reason existed. She offered no testimony, either as to her character and relation with her college associates, or as to her scholarship and attention to her academic duties. The evidence discloses no reason for her dismissal not falling within the terms of the regulation. It follows, therefore, that the action fails. The judgment should be reversed on the law and the facts, with costs, and judgment granted to the defendant, dismissing the complaint, with costs. Certain findings of fact and conclusions of law disapproved and reversed, and new findings of fact made.

Hamilton v. Regents of University of California
293 U.S. 245 (1934)

Mr. Justice BUTLER delivered the opinion of the Court.

This is an appeal from a judgment of the highest court of California sustaining a state law that requires students at its university to take a course in military science and tactics, the validity of which was by the appellants challenged as repugnant to the Constitution and laws of the United States.

The appellants are the above-named minors, and the fathers of each as his guardian *ad litem* and individually. They are taxpayers and citizens of the United States and of California. Appellees are the regents constituting a corporation created by the State to administer the university, its president, and its provost. Appellants applied to the state supreme court for a writ of mandate compelling appellees to admit the minors into the university as students. So far as they are material to the questions presented here, the allegations of the petition are:

In October, 1933, each of these minors registered, became a student in the university and fully conformed to all its requirements other than that compelling him to take the course in military science and tactics in the Reserve Officers Training Corps, which they assert to be an integral part of the military establishment of the United States and not connected in any way with the militia or military establishment of the State. The primary object of establishing units of the training corps is to qualify students for appointment in the Officers Reserve Corps. The courses in military training are those prescribed by the War Department. The regents require enrollment and participation of able-bodied male students who are citizens of the United States. These courses include instruction in rifle marksmanship, scouting and patrolling, drill and command, musketry, combat principles, and use of automatic rifles. Arms, equipment and uniforms for use of students in such courses are furnished by the War Department of the United States Government.

These minors are members of the Methodist Episcopal Church and of the Epworth League and connected religious societies and organizations. For many years their fathers have been ordained ministers of that church. The Southern California Conference at its 1931 session adopted a resolution:

"With full appreciation of the heroic sacrifices of all those who have conscientiously and unselfishly served their country in times of war, but with the belief that the time has come in the unfolding light of the new day for the settlement of human conflicts by pacific means, and because we as Christians owe our first and supreme allegiance to Jesus Christ. Because the Methodist Episcopal Church in her General Conference of 1928 has declared: 'We renounce war as an instrument of national policy.' Because our nation led the nations of the world in signing the Paris Peace Pact, and the Constitution of the United States, Article 6, Section 2, provides that: 'This Constitution and the laws of the United States which shall be made in pursuance thereof and all treaties made under authority of the United States shall be the Supreme Law of the Land.' Thus making the Paris Pact the supreme law of the land which declares: 'The high contracting parties agree that the settlement of all disputes or conflict— shall never be sought except by pacific means.'

"Therefore we, the Southern California Conference, memorialize the General Conference which convenes in Atlantic City in May, 1932; to petition the United States Government to grant exemption from military service to such citizens who are members of the Methodist Episcopal Church, as conscientiously believe that participation in war is a denial of their supreme allegiance to Jesus Christ."

And in 1932 the General Conference of that Church adopted as a part of its tenets and discipline:

"We hold that our country is benefited by having as citizens those who unswervingly follow the dictates of their consciences ... Furthermore, we believe it to be the duty of the churches to give moral support to those individuals who hold conscientious scruples against participation in military training or military service. We petition the government of the United States to grant to members of the Methodist Episcopal Church who may be conscientious objectors to war the same exemption from military service as has long been granted to members of the Society of Friends and other similar religious organizations. Similarly we petition all educational institutions which require military training to excuse from such training any student belonging to the Methodist Episcopal Church who has conscientious scruples against it. We earnestly petition the government of the United States to cease to support financially all military training in civil educational institutions."

And the Southern California Conference at its 1933 session adopted the following:

"Reserve Officers' Training Corps—Recalling the action of the General Conference asking for exemption from military service for those members of our church to whom war and preparation for war is a violation of conscience, we request the authorities of our State University at Berkeley, Los Angeles and Tucson, to exempt Methodist students from the R.O.T.C. on the grounds of conscientious objection, and we hereby pledge the moral and official backing of this Conference, seeking such exemption, provided that it be understood that no conscientious objector shall participate in the financial profits of war. The Secretary of the Conference is asked to send copies of this paragraph to the governing boards of these institutions."

Appellants, as members of that church, accept and feel themselves morally, religiously and conscientiously bound by its tenets and discipline as expressed in the quoted conference resolutions; each is a follower of the teachings of Jesus Christ; each accepts as a guide His teachings and those of the Bible and holds as a part of his religious and conscientious belief that war, training for war, and military training are immoral, wrong and contrary to the letter and spirit of His teaching and the precepts of the Christian religion.

Therefore, these students, at the beginning of the fall term in 1933, petitioned the university for exemption from military training and participation in the activities of the training corps, upon the ground of their religious and conscientious objection to war and to military training. Their petition was denied. Thereupon, through that church's bishop in California, they and their fathers petitioned the regents that military training be made optional in order that conscientious and religious objectors to war, training for war and military training might not be confronted with the necessity of violating and foreswearing their beliefs or being denied the right of education in the state university to which these minors are entitled under the constitution and laws of the State of California and of the United States.

The regents refused to make military training optional or to exempt these students. Then, because of their religious and conscientious objections, they declined to take the prescribed course, and solely upon that ground the regents by formal notification suspended them from the university, but with leave to apply for readmission at any time, conditioned upon their ability and willingness to comply with all applicable regulations of the university governing the matriculation and attendance of students. The university affords opportunity for education such as may not be had at any other institution in California, except at a greater cost which these minors are not able to pay. And they, as appellees at the time of their suspension well knew, are willing to take as a substitute for military training such other courses as may be prescribed by the university.

* * *

[On] September 15, 1931, pursuant to the provisions of the organic act and constitution, the regents promulgated the following order:

"Every able-bodied student of the University of California who, at the time of his matriculation at the University, is under the age of twenty-four years and a citizen of the United States and who has not attained full academic standing as a junior student in the University and has not completed the course in military science and tactics offered to freshmen and sophomore students at the University shall be and is hereby required as a condition to his attendance as a student to enroll in and complete a course of not less than one and one-half units of instruction in military science and tactics each semester of his attendance until such time as he shall have received a total of six units of such instruction or shall have attained full academic standing as a junior student."

In the court below appellants assailed the laws and order above referred to as repugnant to specified provisions of the California constitution, and political code. And they adequately challenged the validity of the state constitution, organic act and regents' order, in so far as they were by the regents construed to require these students to take the prescribed course in military science and tactics, as repugnant to the Constitution and laws of the United States.

* * *

[W]e need only decide whether by state action the "liberty" of these students has been infringed.

There need be no attempt to enumerate or comprehensively to define what is included in the "liberty" protected by the due process clause. Undoubtedly it does include the right to entertain the beliefs, to adhere to the principles and to teach the doctrines on which these students base their objections to the order prescribing military training. The fact that they are able to pay their way in this university but not in any other institution in California is without significance upon any constitutional or other question here involved. California has not drafted or called them to attend the university. They are seeking education offered by the State and at the same time insisting that they be excluded from the prescribed course solely upon grounds of their religious beliefs and conscientious objections to war, preparation for war and military education. Taken on the basis of the facts alleged in the petition, appellants' contentions amount to no more than an assertion that the due process clause of the Fourteenth Amendment as a safeguard of "liberty" confers the right to be students in the state university free from obligation to take military training as one of the conditions of attendance.

Viewed in the light of our decisions that proposition must at once be put aside as untenable.

Government, federal and state, each in its own sphere owes a duty to the people within its jurisdiction to preserve itself in adequate strength to maintain peace and order and to assure the just enforcement of law. And every citizen owes the reciprocal duty, according to his capacity, to support and defend government against all enemies.

* * *

Plainly there is no ground for the contention that the regents' order, requiring able-bodied male students under the age of twenty-four as a condition of their enrollment to take the prescribed instruction in military science and tactics, transgresses any constitutional right asserted by these appellants.

The contention that the regents' order is repugnant to the Briand-Kellogg Peace Pact requires little consideration. In that instrument the United States and the other high contracting parties declare that they condemn recourse to war for the solution of international controversies and renounce it as an instrument of national policy in their relations with one another and agree that the settlement or solution of all disputes or conflicts which may arise among them shall never be sought except by pacific means. Clearly there is no conflict between the regents' order and the provisions of this treaty.

Affirmed.

Mr. Justice CARDOZO.

Concurring in the opinion I wish to say an extra word.

I assume for present purposes that the religious liberty protected by the First Amendment against invasion by the nation is protected by the Fourteenth Amendment against invasion by the states.

Accepting that premise, I cannot find in the respondents' ordinance an obstruction by the state to "the free exercise" of religion as the phrase was understood by the founders of the nation, and by the generations that have followed.

There is no occasion at this time to mark the limits of governmental power in the exaction of military service when the nation is at peace. The petitioners have not been required to bear arms for any hostile purpose, offensive or defensive, either now or in the future. They have not even been required in any absolute or peremptory way to join in courses of instruction that will fit them to bear arms. If they elect to resort to an institution for higher education maintained with the state's moneys, then and only then they are commanded to follow courses of instruction believed by the state to be vital to its welfare. This may be condemned by some as unwise or illiberal or unfair when there is violence to conscientious scruples, either religious or merely ethical. More must be shown to set the ordinance at naught. In controversies of this order courts do not concern themselves with matters of legislative policy, unrelated to privileges or liberties secured by the organic law. The First Amendment, if it be read into the Fourteenth, makes invalid any state law "respecting an establishment of religion or prohibiting the free exercise thereof." Instruction in military science is not instruction in the practice or tenets of a religion. Neither directly nor indirectly is government establishing a state religion when it insists upon such training. Instruction in military science, unaccompanied here by any pledge of military service, is not an interference by the state with the free exercise of religion when the liberties of the constitution are read in the light of a century and a half of history during days of peace and war.

*   *   *

Lansdale v. Tyler Junior College
470 F.2d 659 (1972)

CLARK, Circuit Judge, with whom MORGAN, Circuit Judge, joins:

Joe Richard Lansdale and two other young men attempted to register for the Fall 1970 Semester at Tyler Junior College, a public institution of the State of Texas. However, because their hair styles did not conform to a particular section of the "Dress Code," a comprehensive set of regulations governing student appearance adopted by the Board of Trustees shortly before the school term, they were not permitted to register. Subsequently, they brought suit in the court below, under 42 U.S.C.A. § 1983 and 28 U.S.C.A. § 1343, seeking to enjoin the operation and enforcement of the pertinent regulation against themselves and others similarly situated. They alleged, *inter alia*, that the enforcement of the regulation by college officials was arbitrary, unreasonable, and a violation of their right to equal protection of the laws guaranteed by the Fourteenth Amendment. The district judge granted the permanent injunctive relief prayed for. The college appeals. For the various reasons stated in separate concurring opinions, a majority of the court affirms.

Objectively viewed, there are few, if any, fundamental factual distinctions among the individual circumstances of each of the tens of thousands of college students on the hundreds of campuses in this circuit which should affect their respective constitutional statutes vis-a-vis the regulations of the educational institution in which they are enrolled. Thus, the part of Lansdale's collegiate life which can be constitutionally controlled by administrative edict would not be remarkably different if he were enrolled in any other junior or senior college in any other state. In like manner, students enrolled in a myriad of public school institutions in this circuit are, for any conceivable "Dress Code" regulatory purposes, similarly situated.

In the ultimate analysis, this sameness of the campus life in the respective grade and high school and collegiate environments means that judicial scrutiny of haircut regulations in these institutions almost never calls for what is truly an adjudication of facts. Except in a relative handful of cases where unique situations exist, it is a delusion and a pretense to imagine that the decision in hair length regulation cases can be based upon an objective determination gleaned from testimony by administrators, students or experts. Pragmatically and realistically, the result of the process embodies a particular judge's subjective selection among what he views as competing values. On the one hand, he attaches his own weight of merit and importance to the personal liberty of the student to wear his hair as he wills; then, on the other hand, he assesses his notion of the importance or "relevance" of the authoritarian prerogatives which school administrators have asserted they must exercise to achieve the aims of the particular educational institution. The most important tenet in my reasoning is that the decision either that hair must be cut if the student is to continue his education at the school because the regulation is deemed reasonably related to a legitimate state interest, or that the school must strike the regulation from its records because it has no rational basis and therefore arbitrarily infringes a valid constitutionally protected liberty, is wrongly cast if put in the mold of a determination of fact from record evidence.

So long as these ad hoc appraisals continue, the only hope that both students and school officials who are identically situated will receive meaningful and consistent adjudications of their constitutional positions lies in whatever compulsion for general conformity that may fortuitously exist among independent life-tenured federal judges. This is too faint an anticipation to be acceptable. The Fourteenth Amendment guarantees to the student of equal protection and due process, and the Tenth Amendment freedom of the public official to operate the school entrusted to his care in the manner he determines best, free of federal intrusion, each merits more certainty in the law. This need for more uniform treatment of litigants whose fact situations are really identical led the majority of this court in Karr to conclude that a per se rule should be adopted in high school haircut regulation litigation. That rule states that no number of experts opining on the wisdom or folly of such regulations, and no volume of student, parent or school board testimony as to events or motive should provoke a decision voiding a nonarbitrary regulation of hair length on constitutional grounds. Today's case asks that we extend the scope of that per se rule to the college campus. I refuse to do so, not because the college student has constitutional rights which his lesser-educated counterpart lacks, but because as a matter of law the college campus marks the appropriate boundary where the public institution can no longer assert that the regulation of this liberty is reasonably related to the fostering or encouragement of education. The value of the liberty hasn't changed, rather the setting in which it is to be exercised has.

Such line drawing may be attacked as arbitrary. Ofttimes three months, and sometimes only one week, separates the high school senior from the college freshman. It is likewise true that many high school students may find hair regulations so offensive as to prohibit their continued education, while an equal number of college students couldn't care less. But these are not controlling principles. The redeeming virtue of a per se rule, which far outweighs its shortcomings, is that it is more realistic and more equitable in its overall operation than random judicial "fact" fiats that treat one student one way and another virtually identically circumstanced student another. By differentiating between grade and high schools on the one hand and colleges on the other, we bring to academic regulation of hair style as much order as the inherent vagaries of a system of [judge-made] law will permit.

Basic also to today's decision is the premise that the state has no total right to regulate hair styles, either in general or within the entire framework of public education. There comes a time when its interest in teaching hygiene, instilling discipline, asserting authority and compelling uniformity all become so tenuous as to no longer be reasonably related to, nor effectively fostered by, a haircut regulation.

There are a number of factors which support the proposition that the point between high school and college is the place where the line should be drawn—the place where "the Law stops and just people starts." That place is the point in the student's process of maturity where he usually comes within the ambit of the Twenty-Sixth Amendment and the Selective Service Act, where he often leaves home for dormitory life, and where the educational institution ceases to deal with him through parents and guardians. From that day hence, only the presence of an unusual set of factors can justify regulating the length of his hair as a condition precedent to his right to continue to avail himself of public educational opportunities. There may be an extraordinary case where facts really could be produced to demonstrate that hair fetishes had become so distracting as to prevent collegiate scholastics from the normal pursuit of their learning. If it occurs and can be demonstrated, a different result would be warranted.

Today's decision should not be read as modifying the rationale of the majority opinion in *Karr*. *Karr* unqualifiedly includes the right of citizens to choose their mode of personal hair grooming within the great host of liberties protected by the Fourteenth Amendment from arbitrary state action. *Karr* nevertheless concludes that the regulation of that right by high school officials charged with the important state objective of educating young people does not lack a rational basis in a high school setting and therefore does not deprive such students of due process of law.

Thus, while we reaffirm that *Karr* is premised on an adjudication that the right of students to go into the world as they please is a constitutionally protected one, *Karr* is misinterpreted if it be read as providing that such a right is statically absolute throughout every educational experience. Of course it is not. Rather, like the measurement of time and space and like the even more explicit guarantees of the First Amendment, it must be relative. It functions in a variable equation, both with the need of the institution to regulate that right and with the maturity of the student involved. What is emphasized in today's decision is that the extent to which it is reasonable to invade personal liberty by the adoption of a haircut regulation changes with true variations between educational situations and types of students. For example, a post-graduate college or adult education classroom is not the same as a kindergarten or a 9th grade homeroom, just as certainly as the 24-year-old post-grad is twice the age of the 12-year-old sixth grader. The motives and motivations of each are entirely different. Today the court affirms that the adult's constitutional right to wear his hair as he chooses supersedes the State's right to intrude. The place where the line of permissible hair style regulation is drawn is between the high school door and the college gate.

If we reviewed the fact findings made by the district judge in the case at bar, we would find them to be free from clear error. But such a procedure would suffer from the same deficit I perceive in all other such "fact" adjudications as to this type regulation. If the "facts" on both sides have been adequately developed, a decision either way would doubtless have to be affirmed under this standard of review. Such variance in result is precisely what the rule of law we apply seeks to end. To avoid the erratic ad hoc results which either the varying abilities of individual parties to produce "proof" or the predilections of different district judges could impose on students and school officials otherwise similarly situated, the majority holds today that as a matter of law the college campus is the line of demarcation where the weight of the student's maturity, as compared with the institution's modified role in his education, tips the scales in favor of the individual and marks the boundary of the area within which a student's hirsute adornment becomes constitutionally irrelevant to the pursuit of educational activities.

In the absence of a showing that unusual conditions exist, the regulation of the length or style of a college student's hair is irrelevant to any legitimate college administrative interests and any such regulation creates an arbitrary classification of college students. Because no such unusual circumstances existed here, the regulation adopted in the instant case violates both the due process and equal protection provisions of the Fourteenth Amendment to the Constitution of the United States. The decision of the district court permanently enjoining the enforcement of a haircut regulation by Tyler Junior College is

Affirmed.

DYER, Circuit Judge, with whom GEWIN, COLEMAN, AINSWORTH and IN-GRAHAM, Circuit Judges, join, dissenting:

I dissent from the Court's conclusion that Lansdale has a Fourteenth Amendment right to wear his hair as long as he pleases, in violation of the College's "Dress Code." I has no authoritative support and, in my opinion, is contrary to the rationale of Karr v. Schmidt.

In *Karr* we said no less than five times that a substantial constitutional question was not presented in a haircut case.

> Believing, as did Mr. Justice Black, that appellee Karr's asserted right to be free of school regulations governing the length of his hair is one that is not cognizable in federal courts, we reverse with direction that the case be dismissed for failure to state a claim for which relief can be granted.

> Is there a constitutionally protected right to wear one's hair in a public high school in the length and style that suits the wearer? We hold that no such right is to be found within the plain meaning of the Constitution.

> It is our firm belief that this asserted freedom [to wear hair in school at the length that suits the student] does not rise to the level of fundamental significance which would warrant our recognition of such a substantive constitutional right.

> * * * [O]ur holding [is] that there is no substantial constitutional right to wear hair in the fashion that suits the wearer * * * .

> [Our decision] reflects recognition of the inescapable fact that neither the Constitution nor the federal judiciary it created were conceived to be keepers of the national conscience in every matter great and small.

What we said in *Karr* is equally applicable here. "By and large, public education in our Nation is committed to the control of state and local authorities. Courts do not and cannot intervene in the resolution of conflicts which arise in the daily operation of school systems and which do not *directly and sharply implicate basic constitutional values.*"

The Court is attempting to make law by a *coup de main* that articulates constitutional consequences dependent upon a line arbitrarily drawn between high schools and junior colleges in the face of contrary precedent.

RONEY, Circuit Judge (dissenting):

I dissent, first, because I see no distinction between high schools and junior colleges under the Karr v. Schmidt holding, which is now the law of this Circuit; and second, because I agree with the Karr v. Schmidt rationale except where school attendance is compelled by the state, which is not the case at Tyler Junior College.

The Texas community college system is nothing if not well groomed. In 1975, San Jacinto Junior College won the best-groomed-college award, after dismissing a bearded professor for refusing to shave. In *Hander v. SJCC*, 519 F.2d 273 (5th Cir. 1975), the Court held: "It is illogical to conclude that a teacher's bearded appearance would jeopardize his reputation or pedagogical effectiveness with college students."

Tort Theories

Tarasoff v. Regents of University of California
551 P.2d 334 (1976)

TOBRINER, Justice.

On October 27, 1969, Prosenjit Poddar killed Tatiana Tarasoff. Plaintiffs, Tatiana's parents, allege that two months earlier Poddar confided his intention to kill Tatiana to Dr. Lawrence Moore, a psychologist employed by the Cowell Memorial Hospital at the University of California at Berkeley. They allege that on Moore's request, the campus police briefly detained Poddar, but released him when he appeared rational. They further claim that Dr. Harvey Powelson, Moore's superior, then directed that no further action be taken to detain Poddar. No one warned plaintiffs of Tatiana's peril.

Concluding that these facts set forth causes of action against neither therapists and policemen involved, nor against the Regents of the University of California as their employer, the superior court sustained defendants' demurrers to plaintiffs' second amended complaints without leave to amend. This appeal ensued.

Plaintiffs' complaints predicate liability on two grounds: defendants' failure to warn plaintiffs of the impending danger and their failure to bring about Poddar's confinement pursuant to the Lanterman-Petris-Short Act. Defendants, in turn, assert that they owed no duty of reasonable care to Tatiana and that they are immune from suit under the California Tort Claims Act of 1963.

We shall explain that defendant therapists cannot escape liability merely because Tatiana herself was not their patient. When a therapist determines, or pursuant to the standards of his profession should determine, that his patient presents a serious danger of violence to another, he incurs an obligation to use reasonable care to protect the intended victim against such danger. The discharge of this duty may require the therapist to take one or more of various steps, depending upon the nature of the case. Thus it may call for him to warn the intended victim or others likely to apprise the victim of the danger, to notify the police, or to take whatever other steps are reasonably necessary under the circumstances.

In the case at bar, plaintiffs admit that defendant therapists notified the police, but argue on appeal that the therapists failed to exercise reasonable care to protect Tatiana in that they did not confine Poddar and did not warn Tatiana or others likely to apprise her of the danger. Defendant therapists, however, are public employees. Consequently, to the extent that plaintiffs seek to predicate liability upon the therapists' failure to bring about Poddar's confinement, the therapists can claim immunity under Government Code section 856. No specific statutory provision, however, shields them from liability based upon failure to warn Tatiana or others likely to apprise her of the danger, and Government Code section 820.2 does not protect such failure as an exercise of discretion.

Plaintiffs therefore can amend their complaints to allege that, regardless of the therapists' unsuccessful attempt to confine Poddar, since they knew that Poddar was at large and dangerous, their failure to warn Tatiana or others likely to apprise her of the danger constituted a breach of the therapists' duty to exercise reasonable care to protect Tatiana.

Plaintiffs, however, plead no relationship between Poddar and the police defendants which would impose upon them any duty to Tatiana, and plaintiffs suggest no other basis for such a duty. Plaintiffs have, therefore, failed to show that the trial court erred in sustaining the demurrer of the police defendants without leave to amend.

1. *Plaintiffs' complaints.*

Plaintiffs, Tatiana's mother and father, filed separate but virtually identical second amended complaints. The issue before us on this appeal is whether those complaints now state, or can be amended to state, causes of action against defendants. We therefore begin by setting forth the pertinent allegations of the complaints.

Plaintiffs' first cause of action, entitled "Failure to Detain a Dangerous Patient," alleges that on August 20, 1969, Poddar was a voluntary outpatient receiving therapy at Cowell Memorial Hospital. Poddar informed Moore, his therapist, that he was going to kill an unnamed girl, readily identifiable as Tatiana, when she returned home from spending the summer in Brazil. Moore, with the concurrence of Dr. Gold, who had initially examined Poddar, and Dr. Yandell, assistant to the director of the department of psychiatry, decided that Poddar should be committed for observation in a mental hospital. Moore orally notified Officers Atkinson and Teel of the campus police that he would request commitment. He then sent a letter to Police Chief William Beall requesting the assistance of the police department in securing Poddar's confinement.

Officers Atkinson, Brownrigg, and Halleran took Poddar into custody, but, satisfied that Poddar was rational, released him on his promise to stay away from Tatiana. Powelson, director of the department of psychiatry at Cowell Memorial Hospital, then asked the police to return Moore's letter, directed that all copies of the letter and notes that Moore had taken as therapist be destroyed, and "ordered no action to place Prosenjit Poddar in 72-hour treatment and evaluation facility."

Plaintiffs' second cause of action, entitled "Failure to Warn On a Dangerous Patient," incorporates the allegations of the first cause of action, but adds the assertion that defendants negligently permitted Poddar to be released from police custody without "notifying the parents of Tatiana Tarasoff that their daughter was in grave danger from Prosenjit Poddar." Poddar persuaded Tatiana's brother to share an apartment with him near Tatiana's residence; shortly after her return from Brazil, Poddar went to her residence and killed her.

Plaintiffs' third cause of action, entitled "Abandonment of a Dangerous Patient," seeks $10,000 punitive damages against defendant Powelson. Incorporating the crucial allegations of the first cause of action, plaintiffs charge that Powelson "did the things herein alleged with intent to abandon a dangerous patient, and said acts were done maliciously and oppressively."

Plaintiffs' fourth cause of action, for "Breach of Primary Duty to Patient and the Public," states essentially the same allegations as the first cause of action, but seeks to characterize defendants' conduct as a breach of duty to safeguard their patient and the public. Since such conclusory labels add nothing to the factual allegations of the complaint, the first and fourth causes of action are legally indistinguishable.

As we explain in part 4 of this opinion, plaintiffs' first and fourth causes of action, which seeks to predicate liability upon the defendants' failure to bring about Poddar's confinement, are barred by governmental immunity. Plaintiffs' third cause of action succumbs to the decisions precluding exemplary damages in a wrongful death action. We direct our attention, therefore, to the issue of whether plaintiffs' second cause of action can be amended to state a basis for recovery.

2. *Plaintiffs can state a cause of action against defendant therapists for negligent failure to protect Tatiana.*

The second cause of action can be amended to allege that Tatiana's death proximately resulted from defendants' negligent failure to warn Tatiana or others likely to apprise her of her danger. Plaintiffs contend that as amended, such allegations of negligence and proximate causation, with resulting damages, establish a cause of action. Defendants, however, contend that in the circumstances of the present case they owed no duty of care to Tatiana or her parents and that, in the absence of such duty, they were free to act in careless disregard of Tatiana's life and safety.

In analyzing this issue, we bear in mind that legal duties are not discoverable facts of nature, but merely conclusory expressions that, in cases of a particular type, liability should be imposed for damage done. As stated in *Dillon v. Legg*: "The assertion that liability must . . . be denied because defendant bears no 'duty' to plaintiff 'begs the essential question—whether the plaintiffs' interests are entitled to legal protection against the defendant's conduct . . . [Duty] is not sacrosanct in itself, but only an expression of the sum total of those considerations of policy which lead the law to say that the particular plaintiff is entitled to protection.' "

In the landmark case of *Rowland v. Christian,* Justice Peters recognized that liability should be imposed "for an injury occasioned to another by his want of ordinary care or skill" as expressed in section 1714 of the Civil Code. Thus, Justice Peters, quoting from *Heaven v. Pender* stated: " 'whenever one person is by circumstances placed in such a position with regard to another . . . that if he did not use ordinary care and skill in his own conduct . . . he would cause danger of injury to the person or property of the other, a duty arises to use ordinary care and skill to avoid such danger.' "

We depart from "this fundamental principle" only upon the "balancing of a number of considerations"; major ones "are the foreseeability of harm to the plaintiff, the degree of certainty that the plaintiff suffered injury, the closeness of the connection between the defendant's conduct and the injury suffered, the moral blame attached to the defendant's conduct, the policy of preventing future harm, the extent of the burden to the defendant and consequences to the community of imposing a duty to exercise care with resulting liability for breach, and the availability, cost and prevalence of insurance for the risk involved."

The most important of these considerations in establishing duty is foreseeability. As a general principle, a "defendant owes a duty of care to all persons who are foreseeably endangered by his conduct, with respect to all risks which make the conduct unreasonably dangerous." As we shall explain, however, when the avoidance of foreseeable harm requires a defendant to control the conduct of another person, or to warn of such conduct, the common law has traditionally imposed liability only if the defendant bears some special relationship to the dangerous person or to the potential victim. Since the relationship between a therapist and his patient satisfies this requirement, we need not here decide whether foreseeability alone is sufficient to create a duty to exercise reasonably care to protect a potential victim of another's conduct.

Although, as we have stated above, under the common law, as a general rule, one person owed no duty to control the conduct of another, nor to warn those endangered by such conduct, the courts have carved out an exception to this rule in cases in which the defendant stands in some special relationship to either the person whose conduct needs to be controlled or in a relationship to the foreseeable victim of that conduct. Applying this exception to the present case, we note that a relationship of defendant therapists to either Tatiana or Poddar will suffice to establish a duty of care; as explained in section 315 of the Restatement Second of Torts, a duty of care may arise from either "(a) a special relation . . . between the actor and the third person which imposes a duty upon the actor to control the third person's conduct, or (b) a special relation . . . between the actor and the other which gives to the other a right of protection."

Although plaintiffs' pleadings assert no special relation between Tatiana and defendant therapists, they establish as between Poddar and defendant therapists the special relation that arises between a patient and his doctor or psychotherapist. Such a relationship may support affirmative duties for the benefit of third persons. Thus, for example, a hospital must exercise reasonable care to control the behavior of a patient which may endanger other persons. A doctor must also warn a patient if the patient's condition or medication renders certain conduct, such as driving a car, dangerous to others.

Although the California decisions that recognize this duty have involved cases in which the defendant stood in a special relationship *both* to the victim and to the person whose conduct created the danger, we do not think that the duty should logically be constricted to such situations. Decisions of other jurisdictions hold that the single relationship of a doctor to his patient is sufficient to support the duty to exercise reasonable care to protect others against dangers emanating from the patient's illness.

* * *

Taking note of the uncertain character of therapeutic prediction, we held in *Burnick* that a person cannot be committed as a mentally disordered sex offender unless found to be such by proof beyond a reasonable doubt. The issue in the present context, however, is not whether the patient should be incarcerated, but whether the therapist should take any steps at all to protect the threatened victim; some of the alternatives open to the therapist, such as warning the victim, will not result in the drastic consequences of depriving the patient of his liberty. Weighing the uncertain and conjectural character of the alleged damage done the patient by such a warning against the peril to the victim's life, we conclude that professional inaccuracy in predicting violence cannot negate the therapist's duty to protect the threatened victim.

The risk that unnecessary warnings may be given is a reasonable price to pay for the lives of possible victims that may be saved. We would hesitate to hold that the therapist who is aware that his patient expects to attempt to assassinate the President of the United States would not be obligated to warn the authorities because the therapist cannot predict with accuracy that his patient will commit the crime.

Defendants further argue that free and open communication is essential to psychotherapy; that "Unless a patient ... is assured that ... information [revealed by him] can and will be held in utmost confidence, he will be reluctant to make the full disclosure upon which diagnosis and treatment ... depends." The giving of a warning, defendants contend, constitutes a breach of trust which entails the revelation of confidential communications.

We recognize the public interest in supporting effective treatment of mental illness and in protecting the rights of patients to privacy, and the consequent public importance of safeguarding the confidential character of psychotherapeutic communication. Against this interest, however, we must weigh the public interest in safety from violent assault. The Legislature has undertaken the difficult task of balancing the countervailing concerns. In Evidence Code section 1014, it established a broad rule of privilege to protect confidential communications between patient and psychotherapist. In Evidence Code section 1024, the Legislature created a specific and limited exception to the psychotherapist-patient privilege: "There is no privilege ... if the psychotherapist has reasonable cause to believe that the patient is in such mental or emotional condition as to be dangerous to himself or to the person or property of another and that disclosure of the communication is necessary to prevent the threatened danger."

We realize that the open and confidential character of psychotherapeutic dialogue encourages patients to express threats of violence, few of which are ever executed. Certainly a therapist should not be encouraged routinely to reveal such threats; such disclosures could seriously disrupt the patient's relationship with his therapist and with the persons threatened. To the contrary, the therapist's obligations to his patient require that he not disclose a confidence unless such disclosure is necessary to avert danger to others, and even then that he do so discreetly, and in a fashion that would preserve the privacy of his patient to the fullest extent compatible with the prevention of the threatened danger.

The revelation of a communication under the above circumstances is not a breach of trust or a violation of professional ethics; as stated in the Principles of Medical Ethics of the American Medical Association (1957), section 9: "A physician may not reveal the confidence entrusted to him in the course of medical attendance ... *unless he is required to do so by law or unless it becomes necessary in order to protect the welfare of the individual or of the community.*" We conclude that the public policy favoring protection of the confidential character of patient-psychotherapist communications must yield to the extent to which disclosure is essential to avert danger to others. The protective privilege ends where the public peril begins.

Our current crowded and computerized society compels the interdependence of its members. In this risk-infested society we can hardly tolerate the further exposure to danger that would result from a concealed knowledge of the therapist that his patient was lethal. If the exercise of reasonable care to protect the threatened victim requires the therapist to warn the endangered party or those who can reasonably be expected to notify him, we see no sufficient societal interest that would protect and justify concealment. The containment of such risks lies in the public interest. For the foregoing reasons, we find that plaintiffs' complaints can be amended to state a cause of action against defendants Moore, Powelson, Gold, and Yandell and against the Regents as their employer, for breach of a duty to exercise reasonable care to protect Tatiana.

* * *

We conclude, therefore, that the therapist defendants' failure to warn Tatiana or those who reasonably could have been expected to notify her of her peril does not fall within the absolute protection afforded by section 820.2 of the Government Code. We emphasize that our conclusion does not raise the specter of therapists employed by the government indiscriminately being held liable for damage despite their exercise of sound professional judgment. We require of publicly employed therapists only that quantum of care which the common law requires of private therapists. The imposition of liability in those rare cases in which a public employee falls short of this standard does not contravene the language or purpose of Government Code section 820.2.

This case (*Tarasoff* II) predictably generated much controversy, as its duty-to-warn holding has been followed in many other decisions. *Bradley Center v. Wessner*, 250 Ga. 199, 296 S.E.2d 693 (1982) (private physician owes duty to public at large to exercise reasonable control over mental patient with potential for violence). Even though Prosenjit Poddar had not named Tatiana Tarasoff as his intended victim, the court had noted that she was "readily identifiable" to Dr. Moore. In a later California case, with a disturbingly similar set of facts, a juvenile who threatened to kill an unidentified neighbor was released from a county facility; he killed a 5-year-old neighbor the day after his release. In *Thompson v. County of Alameda*, 167 Cal. Rptr. 70, 614 P.2d F28 (1980), the court distinguished *Tarasoff* II by indicating that the neighborhood child could not be identified or distinguished. Hence, there was no similar duty to unforeseeable victims. See G. Woods and C. Steadman, "*Bradley Center, Inc. v. Wessner*: The Psychotherapist's Duty to Protect," *Journal of College and University Law*, 10 (1983–84), 293–304.

Eiseman v. State

518 N.Y.S. 2d 608 (Ct. App. 1987)

KAYE, Judge.

This appeal from a negligence award focuses on the duty of the State, when an ex-felon with a history of drug abuse and criminal conduct, upon release from prison, is accepted into a special State college program for the disadvantaged, and thereafter rapes and murders a fellow student. We conclude that the State's alleged negligence involved no breach of duty owed to decedent, and the award to her estate must therefore be overturned.

Facts

Charged in three indictments with attempted murder, attempted assault, robbery, larceny, and criminal possession of weapons and drugs, on June 29, 1972, Larry Campbell—then 30 years old—pleaded guilty to criminal possession of dangerous drugs in the fourth degree in satisfaction of all the charges, and received a maximum prison sentence of six years. Campbell remained incarcerated at various correctional facilities until he was conditionally released on December 19, 1975—the statutorily mandated release date, calculated by applying both his "good behavior time" and his "jail time," or time served awaiting trial. Although a longtime heroin addict with a string of arrests, pleas and periods of incarceration for stealing and drug-related crimes beginning a decade or more earlier, this was Campbell's first extended prison confinement.

During his incarceration Campbell was at various times treated for mental disorders, and numerous psychiatric, psychological and parole evaluations were prepared. He was diagnosed as suffering from chronic schizophrenia, paranoid type, with a schizoid, impulsive/explosive personality, a high criminal potential, and a low rehabilitation potential; he was said to have a potential for killing, and was characterized as antisocial, temperamental, belligerent, unpredictable and disruptive, with a guarded prognosis. In his day-to-day prison life, Campbell apparently was comparatively well behaved. On a scale of 1 to 10 (1 being the best inmate), the Superintendent of the Auburn Correctional Facility—claimants' witness—graded Campbell at 2 1/2. He described Campbell as annoyingly litigious, but observed that he had few disciplinary infractions, none of a "serious" nature, and that he had participated in prison programs and pursued educational opportunities. While at Clinton Correctional Facility, Campbell obtained a high school equivalency diploma, and while at Eastern Correctional Facility took college-level courses.

Anticipating release, on January 20, 1975, Campbell applied for admission to the SEEK (Search for Education, Elevation and Knowledge) program at the State University College at Buffalo (the College), to begin September 1975. His application revealed his then residence at Albion Correctional Facility as well as prior incarceration elsewhere, and it was supported by several recommendations.

SEEK, created by the Legislature approximately 20 years ago, is part of a State-wide program conducted by public and private colleges and universities, to offer the opportunity for higher education to disadvantaged high school graduates. The statutory criteria for acceptance into the SEEK program are economic and educational—a high school diploma or its equivalent; the potential for completing a postsecondary program; and economic and educational disadvantage. The SEEK director at the College testified that applications there were evaluated solely on these three statutory criteria, and not on an applicant's prior criminal record or prior psychological history. Those admitted to the program were furnished tuition, room and board, and a stipend. Additionally, the statute provided for remedial courses and academic counseling.

As part of the acceptance package, the College sent Campbell a printed form entitled "Health Report and Physician's Certificate," a portion of it for completion by the prospective student and a portion by an examining physician. The purpose of this form was undisputedly to enable the College to offer follow-up care for its student, not as an admissions criterion. John P. Fernandez, a doctor at the Albion Correctional Facility, on May 12, 1975, completed the "Physical Examination" portion of the form. In response to the question, "Is there any evidence of any anxiety or other tension states or emotional instability?", Dr. Fernandez wrote, "No." In the portion of the form for the prospective student, the question, "Have you ever been under the care of a psychiatrist?", was left unanswered. Campbell's completed health report nowhere disclosed that he had been a heroin addict, or that he had a history of mental disorders, including several suicide attempts.

On July 22, 1975, Campbell left his temporary release job outside the prison, made an unauthorized trip into Buffalo, and was disciplined by the loss of "good time" and transfer from Albion (a low security facility) to Auburn Correctional Facility. While awaiting transfer, and after parole and early release had been denied, Campbell attempted suicide. He was sent to Fishkill Correctional Facility, from which he was admitted to Matteawan State Hospital for examination and treatment, and thereafter discharged back to the general prison population. From Fishkill, Campbell wrote to his SEEK counselor at the College, telling him of the suicide attempt and of his problems in prison. Campbell's request for a leave of absence was granted by the College, and he was advised that he would be expected for the spring semester.

On December 19, 1975 Campbell was conditionally released from prison. There is no indication that at the time of his release Campbell was addicted to drugs or in need of any treatment; no psychiatric treatment or medication was specified, and no special conditions were added to the printed "Conditions of Parole," which included supervision by a parole officer. During the spring semester, Campbell lived on campus and attended classes, and—despite an incident when he was visiting his mother in New York City during April 1976—was seemingly making a satisfactory adjustment at the College. His parole officer, testifying for claimants, said he regarded Campbell as a "high risk" case, and therefore placed him under "intensive supervision," meaning that he advised the SEEK liaison about Campbell, required biweekly visits and a curfew, worked closely with campus security, who the parole officer told to "let [him] know if Campbell sneezes," and checked on him during on-campus visits one or more times a week. During the spring semester Campbell arranged to continue attending classes for the summer and to live with the son of his SEEK counselor, a fellow student.

At the College, Campbell befriended Rhona Eiseman, Thomas Tunney, Teresa Beynard—all fellow students—and Michael Schostick, a nonstudent. Eiseman, Tunney, Beynard and Schostick shared an off-campus apartment. On June 9, 1976, at the apartment, Campbell murdered Tunney, raped and murdered Eiseman, and inflicted serious injuries on Schostick. Eiseman's estate and Schostick commenced suit claiming negligence on the part of the State in its release of Campbell, in failing to advise the College of his medical history, in admitting him to the College without appropriate inquiry, and in failing adequately to supervise him. The Court of Claims after trial dismissed Schostick's claim, on the ground that neither a duty of care nor a chain of causation linked the State to his injuries, but it held the State liable for Eiseman's death on two of the several theories propounded by claimants: that the State was negligent when its agent, the prison physician, failed to inform the College and its students of Campbell's medical history, and that the College was negligent in admitting him or failing to restrict his activity in accordance with the risk he presented, both of which were a proximate cause of injury. The Appellate Division affirmed. This court denied Schostick's motion for leave to appeal and, following a trial to assess damages, granted the State's motion. We now reverse the award and dismiss the claim.

Discussion

At the outset, it is helpful in narrowing the discussion to summarize certain matters resolved below relating to Campbell's release from prison and supervision while at liberty.

Although claimants initially cited Campbell's release as an act of negligence by the State, in fact his release from prison was required by law and was not an act upon which the State could be found negligent. As the Appellate Division noted, "The trial court correctly found that Campbell's release was statutorily mandated and that the Department of Correctional Services was without authority to deny Campbell's request for conditional release." Indeed, claimants no longer dispute that Campbell was entitled to release on December 19, 1975.

Similarly determined against claimants by the trial court, and affirmed by the Appellate Division, are assertions that the State was negligent in failing to impose additional restrictions on Campbell's release, or supervise him more closely, or revoke his release and return him to prison after evidences of violation of the conditions during April 1976. Setting the conditions of release was properly recognized as a discretionary function within the State's absolute immunity, foreclosed from judicial review. "The acts of the corrections officials and parole supervisors in monitoring Campbell's release involved the kinds of policy determinations which are of a discretionary or quasi-judicial nature and therefore insulated from liability." Moreover, as held below, even if immunity were for some reason inapplicable, the official actions in supervising Campbell and continuing his liberty had a rational basis and were nonnegligent; both lower courts were satisfied from the factual record that the State had acted reasonably in monitoring Campbell and allowing him to remain at liberty. Indeed, both courts observed that supervision of Campbell went beyond "reasonable": the trial court concluded that "even with benefit of hindsight there is no basis for a finding that [Campbell's parole officer] should have performed other than he did," and the Appellate Division observed "that he was supervised rather stringently." These affirmed factual findings have support in the record and are therefore beyond the scope of our review.

Claimants' assertions of negligence with respect to Campbell's release and supervision are now concentrated on one point: that Campbell's parole officer violated a statutory duty to revoke his conditional release as a result of the April 1976 New York City incident, and that this failure constituted negligence as a matter of law. In the factual circumstances found below, however, we agree with the conclusion of the lower courts that no statutory or regulatory duty was violated, and that the judgments made—if not shielded by absolute immunity—were nonnegligent.

Thus, what remains for determination is whether the State should be held answerable civilly in damages to the estate of decedent for the vicious acts of an ex-convict, while lawfully at liberty, (1) because of the prison physician's response to the health report, or (2) because of Campbell's enrollment at the College. We conclude that neither is a basis for liability, and do not reach the issue of causation.

Liability for Acts or Omissions of the Prison Physician

Both lower courts concluded that the prison physician inaccurately completed Campbell's health report—that in indicating there was no evidence of emotional instability he necessarily failed to examine Campbell's medical records and misled the College regarding Campbell's stability. With no citation of authority they held that the physician had thus breached a duty that ran to students of the College individually. In the judgment of the Appellate Division, if Campbell's medical history had been disclosed in the medical report, there could be little doubt that the College would have rejected him.

The human desire that there should be some recovery for this tragedy is understandable, as is the commonsense expectation that a health report would solicit a responsible medical history that would reveal prior instability and addiction. But before proceeding into the uncharted waters of the legal consequences of a physician's inaccurate responses to a health report—particularly the novel question whether his duty ran beyond the school, to consider whether there is any support in the record for the holding that by his responses the physician actually committed wrongdoing and misled the College.

Any finding of wrongdoing in the completion of the form must of course begin with scrutiny of the completed form upon which this holding hinges. Both courts specifically identified as wrongful the physician's negative response to the question, "Is there any evidence of anxiety or other tension states or emotional instability?" The trial court additionally referred to his failure to describe Campbell's medical history under "Personal History," and to respond to the question regarding prior psychiatric care. Dr. Fernandez was not himself called to testify by either party. There is, moreover, no suggestion that he withheld information personally known to him from any prior relationship with Campbell, or indeed that he had any prior relationship with Campbell; liability was predicated on the conclusion that the report imposed an affirmative duty on the prison physician to investigate Campbell's medical records.

The form was part of Campbell's postadmission acceptance package. The first page, including the "Personal History," asked "Have *you* ever been under the care of a Psychiatrist?" and "Do *you* have any drug, food or other allergies?" (emphasis added), obviously contemplating that responses would be made by the prospective student, not the physician. The second page, captioned "Physical Examination," was principally devoted to physical findings upon an examination, such as the condition of the patient's eyes, ears, glands, heart and lungs. It then asked, "Is this individual capable of unlimited physical activity (athletics, gym classes, swim?)"; "Is there any evidence of anxiety or other tension states or emotional instability?" (which, on the single line provided, the doctor answered "No"); "Do you recommend further investigation or treatment?" (left blank); and "If you wish any medical treatment carried out while the student is at College, please send separate detailed instructions to the College physician." The page concluded with the date, signature, address and telephone number of the "Examining Physician," and the following legend: "Examining Physician: Please detach along perforation and return this form to: Medical Director, State University College at Buffalo, 1300 Elmwood Avenue, Buffalo, New York 14222."

Wholly apart from its plain and undisputed intendment, this particular form on its face asked the doctor for a report of a physical examination, not a certified medical history; it did not call upon the physician to search and convey the contents of the prison medical records. While the State asserts that such an inquiry would have impermissibly sought confidential information, citing Mental Hygiene Law § 33.13, the fact remains that this form did not even request such information. Thus, there is no support for the predicate conclusions that the physician responded inaccurately, that he had a duty in completing this form to investigate Campbell's prison records, and that he misled the College.

Even assuming, however, that the physician's response was incomplete or inaccurate by reason of his failure to set forth Campbell's prior medical history, we disagree with the lower courts that the doctor's duty extended to all students of the College individually.

Embedded in the law of this State is the proposition that a duty of reasonable care owed by the tort-feasor to the plaintiff is elemental to any recovery in negligence. Foreseeability of injury does not determine the existence of duty. Unlike foreseeability and causation, both generally factual issues to be resolved on a case-by-case basis by the fact finder, the duty owed by one member of society to another is a legal issue for the courts. "While moral and logical judgments are significant components of the analysis, we are also bound to consider the larger social consequences of our decisions and to tailor our notion of duty so that 'the legal consequences of wrongs [are limited] to a controllable degree.' " While the Appellate Division in a single sentence disposed of the issue ("Fernandez was under a duty to respond accurately to the questionnaire, a duty which extended to the college community," we cannot agree that the physician completing a prospective college student's report of a physical examination owed a duty to each member of the college community to search out and disclose a patient's medical past.

Liability in negligence may of course rest on some form of written misrepresentation or nondisclosure on the part of defendant by which plaintiff or a third party is misled, resulting in injury or damage to plaintiff. The basis of liability is the fact that the misrepresentation or nondisclosure has led the person to whom it was made to forego action that might otherwise have been taken for the protection of the plaintiff. "Liability in such cases arises only where there is a duty * * * to give the correct information * * * There must be knowledge or its equivalent that the information is desired for a serious purpose; that he to whom it is given intends to rely and act upon it; that if false or erroneous he will because of it be injured in person or property. Finally, the relationship of the parties * * * must be such that * * * the one has the right to rely upon the other for information, and the other giving the information owes a duty to give it with care." Applying these standards in commercial actions for the negligent preparation of financial reports, we have further required actual privity, or something approaching privity, such as conduct on the part of defendant linking defendant to plaintiff which evinces defendant's understanding of plaintiff's reliance. We have limited the universe of permissible plaintiffs because a failure to do so would impose a duty of reasonable care enforceable by any member of an indeterminate class of persons, present and prospective, known and unknown, directly or indirectly injured by any negligence.

* * *

We therefore conclude that liability was erroneously imposed on the State for the conduct of the prison physician in completing Campbell's health report.

Liability for Acts or Omissions of the College

Independent of the physician's conduct, the courts below also found the College liable to claimants.

The trial court, while acknowledging the limited scope of judicial review of college admissions decisions, concluded that liability should be predicated on the College's failure to reject or restrict Campbell because of the unreasonable risk of harm and foreseeable danger he presented: "[the College's] duty, simply put, was not to subject its students to an unreasonable risk of harm from the conduct of one such as Campbell whom it knew or should have known posed such a risk. The Appellate Division found a breach of statutory duty to develop criteria for eligibility, concluding that if rational criteria had been established Campbell would not have been admitted. The Appellate Division, moreover, posited the College's duty of heightened inquiry on the fact that this was "an experimental program for the admission of convicted felons."

There is no basis for the conclusion first reached by the Appellate Division that the College breached a statutory duty when it accepted Campbell by simply applying the statutory standards, and without having formulated regulations establishing additional criteria for eligibility. We thus need not consider whether any duty to enact regulations, if it existed, would operate to permit recovery for damages for injury by one student to another.

Nor can we accept the conclusion below that, by participating in this special program, the College undertook either a duty of heightened inquiry in admissions, or a duty to restrict his activity on campus, for the protection of other students.

As noted earlier, the imposition of duty presents a question of law for the courts, resting on policy considerations of whether plaintiff's interests are entitled to legal protection against defendant's conduct. While both lower courts soundly disavowed the imposition of liability on the basis of the doctrine of in loco parentis—concluding that colleges today in general have no legal duty to shield their students from the dangerous activity of other students—the question before us today, in essence, is whether such a duty should nonetheless be recognized when a college admits an ex-felon such as Campbell as part of a special program. As claimants recognize, we have not previously imposed such a duty, and we see no justification for doing so now.

SEEK is an established program for the disadvantaged generally, which may include persons who have completed prison terms—and thus by definition persons with a history of antisocial, even dangerous behavior—but it does not include incarcerated felons. When he began his studies at the College, Campbell was not an incarcerated felon; he had served his prescribed punishment and was entitled to release, on conditions that did not include any continuing care or treatment. The SEEK admissions director at the College determined that—apart from his educational and economic qualifications—he had the "potential for the successful completion of a post secondary program." Consistent with his parole obligations, theoretically Campbell could have lived anywhere he chose, and otherwise enjoyed the rights of other citizens, including the right to be free of unfair discrimination by reason of prior arrests and imprisonment. His release and return to society at the age of 33—presumably with a long life still ahead of him—were mandated by law as well as by public policy, which have as their objectives rehabilitating and reintegrating former inmates in the hope that they will spend their future years productively instead of returning to crime. To this end, the value of education—both as an escape from society's underclass, and as a benefit to the public generally—is apparent.

These policy considerations are pertinent to our determination that, as a matter of law, a heightened duty of inquiry should not have been imposed on the College. Such a duty would run counter to the legislative policies embodied by the SEEK program as well as the laws and policies promoting the reintegration of former convicts into society. But even more fundamentally, the underlying premise that, once released, Campbell by reason of his past presumptively posed a continuing, foreseeable risk of harm to the community is at odds with the laws and public policy regarding the release of prisoners. Consistent with conditions of parole, an individual returned to freedom can frequent places of public accommodation, secure employment, and if qualified become a student. On any other theory, former inmates cannot be returned to society without imposing on those who open doors to them the risk of absolute liability for their acts.

Nor did the College have a duty to restrict Campbell, as a student, even assuming it had a right to control his contacts with other students. Publicly branding him on campus as a former convict and former drug addict would have run up against the same laws and policies that prevented discriminating against him. Moreover, the fact that Campbell had a criminal record was apparently known on campus, even to Eiseman and Schostick. In actual fact, Campbell was diligently monitored, as both lower courts found; until his brutal explosion, there was no complaint regarding his campus behavior. No greater restriction is even suggested that might have avoided this off-campus tragedy. As the college and university *amici* cogently contend, imposing liability on the College for failing to screen out or detect potential danger signals in Campbell would hold the college to a higher duty than society's experts in making such predictions—the correction and parole officers, who in the present case have been found to have acted without negligence.

Finally, it is apparent that there are profound social issues underlying this case. It therefore bears emphasis that the question before us for resolution is simply whether the College had a *legal duty* in the circumstances, that requires it to respond in damages for Campbell's rape and murder of a fellow student; we do not consider whether a college might or even should investigate and supervise its students differently. Moreover, while hindsight has a peculiar clarity and wisdom, the fact remains that the contemporaneous, nonreviewable judgments by which the College's actions must be evaluated were that Campbell, upon his release, needed no psychiatric care or other treatment, and further that he had a potential for success in college.

Accordingly, the judgment appealed from and order of the Appellate Division brought up for review should be reversed, with costs, and the claim dismissed.

Bradshaw v. Rawlings

612 F.2d 135 (1979), cert. denied, 446 U.S. 909 (1980)

ALDISERT, Circuit Judge.

The major question for decision in this diversity case tried under Pennsylvania law is whether a college may be subject to tort liability for injuries sustained by one of its students involved in an automobile accident when the driver of the car was a fellow student who had become intoxicated at a class picnic. Another question relates to the liability of the distributor who furnished beer for the picnic which led to the intoxication of the driver. Still another question concerns the tort liability of the municipality where the plaintiff's injuries occurred.

The district court permitted the question of negligence to go to the jury against the college, the beer distributor and the municipality. From an adverse verdict of

$1,108,067 each of the defendants has appealed, advancing separate arguments for reversal. The plaintiff has filed a conditional cross-appeal.

I.

Donald Bradshaw, an eighteen year old student at Delaware Valley College, was severely injured on April 13, 1975 in Doylestown, Pennsylvania, while a backseat passenger in a Saab automobile driven by a fellow student, Bruce Rawlings. Both were sophomores and had attended their class picnic at a grove owned by the Maennerchor Society on the outskirts of the borough. Returning to the college from the picnic, Rawlings drove through Doylestown on Union Street. Union Street is colloquially known as "Dip Street" because it was constructed with drainage dips, instead of sewers, to carry surface water runoff. While proceeding through one of the dips, Rawlings lost control of the automobile which then struck a parked vehicle. As a result of the collision Bradshaw suffered a cervical fracture which caused quadriplegia.

The picnic, although not held on college grounds, was an annual activity of the sophomore class. A faculty member who served as sophomore class advisor participated with the class officers in planning the picnic and co-signed a check for class funds that was later used to purchase beer. The advisor did not attend the picnic, nor did he get another faculty member to attend in his place. Flyers announcing the picnic were prominently displayed across the campus. They were mimeographed by the college duplicating facility and featured drawings of beer mugs. Approximately seventy-five students attended the picnic and consumed six or seven half-kegs of beer. The beer was ordered from Marjorie Moyer, trading as Sunny Beverages, by the sophomore class president who was underage.

The legal drinking age in Pennsylvania was, and is, twenty-one years, but the great majority of the students drinking at the picnic were sophomores of either nineteen or twenty years of age. Rawlings had been at the picnic for a number of hours. He testified that he had no recollection of what occurred from the time he left the picnic until after the accident. Bradshaw testified that Rawlings had been drinking and another witness, Warren Wylde, expressed his opinion that Rawlings was under the influence of alcohol when he left the picnic grove. That there was sufficient evidence on the question of Rawlings' intoxication to submit to the jury cannot be seriously questioned.

II.

On appeal, the college argues that Bradshaw failed to present sufficient evidence to establish that it owed him a duty for the breach of which it could be held liable in tort. The district court, apparently assuming that such a duty existed, submitted the question of the college's liability to the jury, stating:

> In any event, the college owes a duty to use due care under the circumstances to prevent an unreasonable risk of harm to sophomores who attend a class function. Restatement (Second) of Torts §§ 282 and 283 (1965) provide:
>
> § 282. Negligence Defined
>
> In the Restatement of this Subject, negligence is conduct which falls below the standard established by law for the protection of others against unreasonable risk of harm. It does not include conduct recklessly disregardful of an interest in others.
>
> § 283. Conduct of a Reasonable Man: The Standard

Unless the actor is a child, the standard of conduct to which he must conform to avoid being negligent is that of a reasonable man under like circumstances.

In its post-trial opinion, the district court attempted to justify this instruction by stating:

I submitted this case to the jury on the above concept. The College was permitted to argue to the jury that it was not negligent because it was powerless to control the habits of college sophomores in regard to drinking beer. The jury rejected the College's defense that it acted in a reasonable manner under the circumstances. It should be noted that the College's liability is predicated on the concept of want of due care which a reasonable man would exercise under the circumstances.

A.

The college's argument strikes at the heart of tort law because a negligence claim must fail if based on circumstances for which the law imposes no duty of care on the defendant. "Negligence in the air, so to speak, will not do." As Professor Prosser has emphasized, the statement that there is or is not a duty begs the essential question, which is whether the plaintiff's interests are entitled to legal protection against the defendant's conduct. " '[D]uty' is not sacrosanct in itself, but only an expression of the sum total of those considerations of policy which lead the law to say that a particular plaintiff is entitled to protection." Thus, we may perceive duty simply as an obligation to which the law will give recognition in order to require one person to conform to a particular standard of conduct with respect to another person.

These abstract descriptions of duty cannot be helpful, however, unless they are directly related to the competing individual, public, and social interests implicated in any case. An interest is a social fact, factor, or phenomenon existing independently of the law which is reflected by a claim, demand, or desire that people seek to satisfy and that has been recognized as socially valid by authoritative decision makers in society. Certainly, the plaintiff in this case possessed an important interest in remaining free from bodily injury, and thus the law protects his right to recover compensation from those who negligently cause him injury. The college, on the other hand, has an interest in the nature of its relationship with its adult students, as well as an interest in avoiding responsibilities that it is incapable of performing.

B.

Our beginning point is a recognition that the modern American college is not an insurer of the safety of its students. Whatever may have been its responsibility in an earlier era, the authoritarian role of today's college administrations has been notably diluted in recent decades. Trustees, administrators, and faculties have been required to yield to the expanding rights and privileges of their students. By constitutional amendment, written and unwritten law, and through the evolution of new customs, rights formerly possessed by college administrations have been transferred to students. College students today are no longer minors; they are now regarded as adults in almost every phase of community life. For example except for purposes of purchasing alcoholic beverages, eighteen year old persons are considered adults by the Commonwealth of Pennsylvania. They may vote, marry, make a will, qualify as a personal representative, serve as a guardian of the estate of a minor, wager at racetracks, register as a public accountant, practice veterinary medicine, qualify as a practical nurse, drive trucks, ambulances and other official fire vehicles, perform general fire-fighting duties, and qualify as a private detective. Pennsylvania has set eighteen as the age at which criminal acts are no longer treated as those of a juvenile, and eighteen year old students may waive their testimonial privilege protecting confidential statements to school personnel. Moreover, a person may join the Pennsylvania militia at an even younger age than eighteen and may hunt without adult supervision at age sixteen. As a result of these and other similar developments in our society, eighteen year old students are now identified with an expansive bundle of individual and social interests and possess discrete rights not held by college students from decades past. There was a time when college administrators and faculties assumed a role *in loco parentis*. Students were committed to their charge because the students were considered minors. A special relationship was created between college and student that imposed a duty on the college to exercise control over student conduct and, reciprocally, gave the students certain rights of protection by the college. The campus revolutions of the late sixties and early seventies were a direct attack by the students on rigid controls by the colleges and were an all-pervasive affirmative demand for more student rights. In general, the students succeeded, peaceably and otherwise, in acquiring a new status at colleges throughout the country. These movements, taking place almost simultaneously with legislation and case law lowering the age of majority, produced fundamental changes in our society. A dramatic reapportionment of responsibilities and social interests of general security took place. Regulation by the college of student life on and off campus has become limited. Adult students now demand and receive expanded rights of privacy in their college life including, for example, liberal, if not unlimited, parietal visiting hours. College administrators no longer control the broad arena of general morals. At one time, exercising their [parietal] rights and duties *in loco parentis*, colleges were able to impose strict regulations. But today students vigorously claim the right to define and regulate their own lives. Especially have they demanded and received satisfaction of their interest in self-assertion in both physical and mental activities, and have vindicated what may be called the interest in freedom of the individual will. In 1972 Justice Douglas summarized the change:

> Students—who, by reason of the Twenty-sixth Amendment, become eligible to vote when 18 years of age—are adults who are members of the college or university community. Their interests and concerns are often quite different from those of the faculty. They often have values, views, and ideologies that are at war with the ones which the college has traditionally espoused or indoctrinated.

Thus, for purposes of examining fundamental relationships that underlie tort liability, the competing interests of the student and of the institution of higher learning are much different today than they were in the past. At the risk of oversimplification, the change has occurred because society considers the modern college student an adult, not a child of tender years. It could be argued, although we need not decide here, that an educational institution possesses a different pattern of rights and responsibilities and retains more of the traditional custodial responsibilities when its students are all minors, as in an elementary school, or mostly minors, as in a high school. Under such circumstances, after weighing relevant competing interests, Pennsylvania might possibly impose on the institution certain duties of protection, for the breach of which a legal remedy would be available. But here, because the circumstances show that the students have reached the age of majority and are capable of protecting their own self interests, we believe that the rule would be different. We conclude, therefore, that in order to ascertain whether a specific duty of care extended from Delaware Valley College to its injured student, we must first identify and assess the competing individual and social interests associated with the parties.

III.

A.

In the process of identifying the competing interests implicated in the student-college relationship, we note that the record in this case is not overly generous in identifying the interests possessed by the student, although it was Bradshaw's burden to prove the existence of a duty owed him by the college in order to establish a breach thereof. Bradshaw has concentrated on the school regulation imposing sanctions on the use of alcohol by students. The regulation states: "Possession or consumption of alcohol or malt beverages on the property of the College or at any College sponsored or related affair off campus will result in disciplinary action. The same rule will apply to every student regardless of age." We are not impressed that this regulation, in and of itself, is sufficient to place the college in a custodial relationship with its students for purposes of imposing a duty of protection in this case. We assume that the average student arrives on campus at the age of seventeen or eighteen, and that most students are under twenty-one during the better part of their college careers. A college regulation that essentially tracks a state law and prohibits conduct that to students under twenty-one is already prohibited by state law does not, in our view, indicate that the college voluntarily assumed a custodial relationship with its students so as to make operative the provisions of § 320 of the Restatement (Second) of Torts.

Thus, we predict that the Pennsylvania courts would not hold that by promulgating this regulation the college had voluntarily taken custody of Bradshaw so as to deprive him of his normal power of self-protection or to subject him to association with persons likely to cause him harm. Absent proof of such a relationship, we do not believe that a prima facie case of custodial duty was established in order to submit the case to the jury on this theory.

B.

We next examine the facts adduced at trial to determine whether a special relationship existed as a matter of law, which would impose upon the college either a duty to control the conduct of a student operating a motor vehicle off campus or a duty to extend to a student a right of protection in transportation to and from off campus activities. We conclude that Bradshaw also failed to meet his burden of proving either of these duties. Bradshaw's primary argument is that the college had knowledge that its students would drink beer at the picnic, that this conduct violated a school regulation and state law, that it created a known probability of harm to third persons, and that knowledge by the college of this probable harm imposed a duty on the college either to control Rawlings' conduct or to protect Bradshaw from possible harm.

Although we are aware of no Pennsylvania decision that has addressed this precise issue, the supreme court of that state has held that a private host who supplies intoxicants to a visibly intoxicated guest may not be held civilly liable for injuries to third parties caused by the intoxicated guest's negligence. Only licensed persons engaged in the sale of intoxicants have been held civilly liable to injured parties, and the source of this liability derives from the common law, as well as from a violation of Pennsylvania's Dram Shop statute. Because the Pennsylvania Supreme Court has been unwilling to find a special relationship on which to predicate a duty between a private host and his visibly intoxicated guest, we predict that it would be even less willing to find such a relationship between a college and its student under the circumstances of this case.

The centerpiece of Bradshaw's argument is that beer-drinking by underage college students, in itself, creates the special relationship on which to predicate liability and, furthermore, that the college has both the opportunity and the means of exercising control over beer drinking by students at an off campus gathering. These contentions miss the mark, however, because they blur the distinction between establishing the existence of a duty and proving the breach thereof. Bradshaw does not argue that beer drinking is generally regarded as a harm-producing act, for it cannot be seriously controverted that a goodly number of citizens indulge in this activity. Our national public policy, insofar as it is reflected by industry standards or by government regulation of certain types of radio-television advertising, permits advertising of beer at all times of the day and night even though Congress has banned advertisement of cigarettes and the broadcasting industry has agreed to ban the advertisement of liquor. What we know as men and women we must not forget as judges, and this panel of judges is able to bear witness to the fact that beer drinking by college students is a common experience. That this is true is not to suggest that reality always comports with state and law college rules. It does not. But the Pennsylvania law that prohibits sales to, and purchases by, persons under twenty-one years of age, is certainly not a universal practice in other countries, nor even the general rule in North America. Moreover in New Jersey, the bordering state from which the majority of Delaware Valley College students come, the legal drinking age is eighteen. Under these circumstances, we think it would be placing an impossible burden on the college to impose a duty in this case.

Without explicating its rationale in detail, the state of New York has also refused to impose liability upon an institution of higher learning under somewhat similar circumstances.

Therefore, we conclude that Bradshaw failed to establish a prima facie case against the college that it should be charged with a duty of custodial care as a matter of law and that the district court erred by submitting the case to the jury.

IV.

Marjorie Moyer, the licensee who sold the beer to the minor students, is liable for injuries proximately resulting therefrom, unless she can demonstrate circumstances that remove her from the strictures of the general rule. She attempts to meet the task by arguing that there was insufficient evidence of Rawlings' intoxication to supply the causal link between the sale and the injury. Her argument must fail because, as we have previously concluded, there was sufficient evidence to submit the issue of the driver's intoxication to the jury. Witness Wylde testified that he, Rawlings, and Bradshaw were at the picnic all afternoon, were among the last to leave, and that in his opinion, Rawlings was "high." When directly asked whether Rawlings was under the influence of alcohol as he drove his car from the picnic grounds towards Union Street,

Wylde answered that he was. Also significant was Rawlings' testimony that although not seriously injured in the accident, he had no recollection of any of the events from sometime near the end of the picnic until after the collision occurred. We therefore conclude that no exception removed licensee Moyer from the Pennsylvania general rule imposing liability under the circumstances of this case, in which the beer was ordered by an underaged member of the sophomore class for use at a sophomore class picnic. Although the delivery was signed for by a student of legal age, the beer distributor had reason to know that the great majority of drinkers who would consume the beer were underage.

* * *

Doylestown further argues that any liability extending to it must be predicated on the theory that it was negligent in failing properly to warn of the existence of dips and that it cannot be held liable of this theory because there was proof that Rawlings had notice of the dips. This argument must also fail because failure to warn was only one of several alternative theories advanced by the plaintiff against the borough. Plaintiff argued and supplied sufficient evidence for the jury to find that Doylestown was negligent in creating and maintaining the dips, which presented an unreasonable risk of harm to the public. Evidence tended to show that simple culverts could have completely done away with the dangerous dips, that the borough failed to lower the speed limit on Union Street to a safer speed, and that it failed to place stop signs at the preceding intersection as an alternative safety measure.

* * *

VII.

The judgment of the district court will be affirmed in all respects except that part imposing liability against Delaware Valley College, which we reverse and direct that a judgment in favor of Delaware Valley College be entered. Accordingly, the judgment of the district court will be affirmed at Nos. 79–1409, 79–1410, and 79–1412; the judgment of the district court at No. 79–1411 will be reversed.

The law concerning liability as a result of student drinking is both common law and state law; half the states have enacted "dram shop" statutes to impose at least partial liability upon alcohol-providers, which may impose responsibility upon private or public institutions. See T. McLean, "Tort Liability of Colleges and Universities for Injuries Resulting from Student Alcohol Consumption," *Journal of College and University Law,* 14 (1987), 399–416.

In a California case, a visitor who drank heavily at a University of California staff party seriously injured himself when he fell off a campus balcony. The University was held to be partially liable, for its employees having continued to serve him alcohol after he was demonstrably intoxicated. *Zavala v. Regents of the University of California,* 125 Cal. App. 3d 646, 178 Cal. Rptr. 185 (1981).

If a fraternity contributes to the alcohol abuse, it can be held liable, particularly if its members fail to render aid. In *Ballou v. Sigma Nu,* 291 S.C. 140, 352 S.E.2d 488 (S.C. App. 1986), the court held that a fraternity could be held responsible for the death of a pledge who was intimidated into drinking so much liquor that he lapsed into unconsciousness and died. Due to the large number of injuries sustained by fraternity members during hazing, twenty seven states have enacted anti-hazing legislation. *Fraternal Law*, January, 1988, p. 6. See *Jeffery v. Furek*, 535 A.2d 408 (1987) (fraternity pledge injured when caustic oven cleaner poured on his head during hazing); *Fassett v. Delta Kappa Epsilon*, 807 F.2d 1150 (1986) (Pennsylvania fraternity members held to be "accomplices"); *Andres v. Alpha Kappa Lambda*, 730 S.W. 2d 547 (1987) (Missouri fraternity held to have "no liability as social hosts.")

Villalobos v. University of Oregon
Or. App., 614 P.2d 107 (1980)

WARREN, Judge.

This is an action under the Oregon Tort Claims Act, ORS 30.260 to 30.300, for the wrongful death of Ricardo Villalobos brought by his personal representative. Plaintiff appeals from a judgment in favor of defendant entered on defendant's demurrer in which the trial court ruled that the action was barred by the statute of limitations.

Decedent was enrolled in a high school equivalency program for minority students on the campus of defendant and was a resident in one of defendant's dormitories. Decedent was stabbed to death in the dormitory on February 11, 1977. On April 3, 1979, plaintiff filed a complaint entitled "Complaint (At Law) Wrongful Death." The first count is based on negligence and the second count on breach of an implied warranty of "habitability and safety." The theory of the second count is that decedent had surrendered control of his person and security to defendant, which thereafter breached an implied contractual duty, arising from the tenancy, to protect decedent from the criminal activities of third persons. The trial court sustained defendant's demurrer on the ground that the two-year period in which to bring the action under ORS 30.275(3) had expired before the complaint was filed. Plaintiff contends the applicable statute of limitations is ORS 12.080, providing that actions on express or implied contracts may be commenced within six years.

In *Securities-Intermountain, Inc. v. Sunset Fuel*, an action for damages against a provider of services, the Supreme Court after a historical review of the statutory and case law set forth the test for determining whether the statute of limitations for contract actions is applicable when a contract is pleaded but it is contended that the action is in reality one in tort to which a shorter statute of limitations applies:

> "Thus the statutes and the precedents leave us with several variations when an action for damages against one engaged to provide professional or other independent services is commenced after two years and is pleaded as a breach of contract. *If the alleged contract merely incorporates by reference or by implication a general standard of skill and care to which the defendant would be bound independent of the contract, and the alleged breach would also be a breach of this noncontractual duty, then ORS 12.110 applies.* Conversely, the parties may have spelled out the performance expected by the plaintiff and promised by the defendant in terms that commit the defendant to this performance without reference to and irrespective of any general standard. Such a defendant would be liable on the contract whether he was negligent or not, and regardless of facts that might excuse him from tort liability. Or the nature either of the defendant's default or of the plaintiff's loss may be of a kind that would not give rise to liability apart from the terms of their agreement. In such cases,

there is no reason why an action upon the contract may not be commenced for the six years allowed by ORS 12.080. Again, the scope of the damages demanded may characterize a complaint as founded in tort rather than in contract. But if the complaint nonetheless alleges the necessary elements of an action for breach of contract, including the alleged injury, nothing in the statutes prevents proceeding on that theory and limiting the damages accordingly."

We find the emphasized language in the above paragraph dispositive in the context of this case. The alleged contract here incorporates by implication a general standard of care to which defendant would be bound independent of any warranty. While the asserted contractual relationship between decedent and defendant may have provided the occasion for the alleged misfeasance, the claimed breach of warranty is essentially a breach of a duty to exercise reasonable care concerning security precautions. Defendant would not be liable to the decedent or his estate if, despite the exercise of reasonable care, the decedent sustained an injury. This can be seen by reference to the authority on which plaintiff relies to sustain her theory that the implied warranty of habitability and safety applies to this case.

Plaintiff relies upon the California case of *Duarte v. State*, which in turn relies upon the following language in *Kline v. 1500 Massachusetts Avenue Corp.*:

"There is implied in the contract between landlord and tenant an obligation on the landlord to provide those protective measures which are within his *reasonable* capacity."

The implied warranty itself is predicated upon an ordinary standard of reasonable care. Breach of the duty under the warranty theory would also be a breach of the duty to exercise reasonable care to which the defendant would be bound independent of the claim of warranty. The applicable statute of limitations is ORS 30.275(3) which the trial court properly applied.

Affirmed.

Mullins v. Pine Manor College

449 N.E. 2d 331 (Mass. 1983)

LIACOS, Justice.

The plaintiff, a female student at Pine Manor College (college), was raped on campus by an unidentified assailant who was never apprehended. She commenced this action against the college and its vice president for operations, William P. Person, to recover damages for injuries suffered. The case was tried before a jury in the Superior Court. The jury returned verdicts against the college and Person in the amount of $175,000. Pursuant to G.L. c. 231, § 85K, the trial judge reduced the amount of the judgment against the college to $20,000. The college and Person appeal from the denial of their motions for directed verdicts and for judgments notwithstanding the verdicts. We granted their applications for direct appellate review. We affirm the judgments.

There was evidence of the following facts. Pine Manor College is a four year college for women located in the Chestnut Hill section of Brookline. In 1977, approximately 400 students attended the school. The campus is surrounded on all sides by a six foot high chain link fence, except for an area on either side of the main entrance to the campus where the fence stands four feet tall. The college's dormitories are clustered together in three villages. Each village is comprised of a commons building and a number of separate dormitory buildings. The buildings are arranged to form a square. To gain access to a dormitory, a student must enter an enclosed courtyard through either the commons building or one of three exterior gates. Between 5 p.m. and 7 a.m., these gates and the door to the commons building are locked. Students enter their dormitory through locked doors which open directly into the courtyard. Each student had one key which unlocked the doors to her commons building, her dormitory building, and her individual room.

After 8 p.m., all visitors were admitted by a security guard at the main entrance to the campus. The guard would direct them to the appropriate commons building. At the entrance to the commons building, visitors would be stopped by a student on duty and would be registered.[3] The student hostess would be notified and was required to come to the commons building to act as the visitor's escort. No visitors were permitted anywhere on campus unescorted after 1 a.m. on weekends.

At the time of the rape, the college had two guards on duty after midnight. One guard was stationed in an observation post at the main entrance. The second guard was assigned to patrol the campus. He was responsible for making rounds to the villages every fifteen to thirty minutes to check the doors and gates to see that they were locked. The college had no formal system of supervising the guards. Rather, the director of security at the college would make random checks on their work.

Mullins was a first year student and, as required by the college, she lived on campus. Her dormitory housed thirty women. Under college regulations, male visitors were permitted to stay overnight. Mullins was assigned to a single room at the end of a corridor. Another student resided in a room located adjacent to hers. The doors to these two rooms were at a right angle to each other.

On December 11, 1977, Mullins returned to her dormitory at approximately 3 a.m. with two friends. It was a bitter cold night. They entered the village through one of the exterior gates to the courtyard. It was unlocked. They opened the door to their dormitory and proceeded to their rooms. After changing into her night clothes, Mullins, leaving the door to her room open, went to talk with a friend who resided in the room next door. They talked for a few minutes, apparently near the open door to the friend's room. Mullins returned to her room, locked her door, and went to sleep. Between 4 a.m. and 4:30 a.m., she was awakened by an intruder. He asked her where her car was located, and she responded that she did not have a car. The intruder then threatened her and placed a pillow case over her head. He led her out of the building and across the courtyard. They left the courtyard by proceeding under the chains of one of the exterior gates which was not secured tightly. They walked down a bicycle path toward the refectory, the college's dining hall. After marching about in front of the refectory, they entered the refectory through an unlocked door and spent several minutes inside. They proceeded out of the refectory and marched around in front. They then went back inside, and the assailant raped her. The entire

---

3. The record is unclear as to whether there was a student stationed at the entrance to the commons building after midnight. The process of registering visitors and ensuring that every visitor had an escort, however, was also performed by the guard at the main entrance to the campus.

incident lasted sixty to ninety minutes, and they were outside on the campus for at least twenty minutes.

Pine Manor is located in an area with relatively few reports of violent crime. In the years prior to this attack, there had been no incidents of violent crime on the campus. The record discloses, however, that one year before the attack a burglary had occurred in one of the dormitory buildings. Additionally, the evening before the rape, a young man scaled the outer fence around the campus and walked into the commons building of Mullins's village, which was the first building he saw. The door to the building was open. The college is also located a short distance from bus and subway lines which lead directly to Boston.

Additional facts, including the testimony of expert witnesses, will be discussed as they become relevant.

1. *Duty to protect against criminal acts.* The defendants argue that they owe no duty to protect students against the criminal acts of third parties. They rely on the general proposition that there is no duty to protect others from the criminal or wrongful activities of third persons. We conclude that this rule has little application to the circumstances of this case.

The duty of due care owed the plaintiff by the defendants in the present case can be grounded on either of two well established principles of law. First, we have said that a duty finds its "source in existing social values and customs." We think it can be said with confidence that colleges of ordinary prudence customarily exercise care to protect the well-being of their resident students, including seeking to protect them against the criminal acts of third parties. An expert witness hired by the defendant testified that he had visited eighteen area colleges, and, not surprisingly, all took steps to provide an adequate level of security on their campus. He testified also that standards had been established for determining what precautions should be taken. Thus, the college community itself has recognized its obligation to protect resident students from the criminal acts of third parties. This recognition indicates that the imposition of a duty of care is firmly embedded in a community consensus.

This consensus stems from the nature of the situation. The concentration of young people, especially young women, on a college campus, creates favorable opportunities for criminal behavior. The threat of criminal acts of third parties to resident students is self-evident, and the college is the party which is in the position to take those steps which are necessary to ensure the safety of its students. No student has the ability to design and implement a security system, hire and supervise security guards, provide security at the entrance of dormitories, install proper locks, and establish a system of announcement for authorized visitors. Resident students typically live in a particular room for a mere nine months and, as a consequence, lack the incentive and capacity to take corrective measures. College regulations may also bar the installation of additional locks or chains. Some students may not have been exposed previously to living in a residence hall or in a metropolitan area and may not be fully conscious of the dangers that are present. Thus, the college must take the responsibility on itself if anything is to be done at all.

Of course, changes in college life, reflected in the general decline of the theory that a college stands in loco parentis to its students, arguably cut against this view. The fact that a college need not police the morals of its resident students, however, does not entitle it to abandon any effort to ensure their physical safety. Parents, students, and the general community still have a reasonable expectation, fostered in part by colleges themselves, that reasonable care will be exercised to protect resident students from foreseeable harm.

The duty of care in this case can be grounded in another theory. It is an established principle that a duty voluntarily assumed must be performed with due care. Restatement (Second) of Torts § 323 (1965), states: "One who undertakes, gratuitously or for consideration, to render services to another which he should recognize as necessary for the protection of the other's person or things, is subject to liability to the other for physical harm resulting from his failure to exercise reasonable care to perform his undertaking, if (a) his failure to exercise such care increases the risk of such harm, or (b) the harm is suffered because of the other's reliance upon the undertaking."

Colleges generally undertake voluntarily to provide their students with protection from the criminal acts of third parties. The evidence warrants the conclusion that Pine Manor undertook such a duty. It is clear that this undertaking by Pine Manor was not gratuitous. Students are charged, either through their tuition or a dormitory fee, for this service. Adequate security is an indispensable part of the bundle of services which colleges, and Pine Manor, afford their students.

We recognize that the mere fact that Pine Manor had voluntarily undertaken to render a service is not sufficient to impose a duty. It must also be shown that either (a) the failure to exercise due care increased the risk of harm, or (b) the harm is suffered because of the students' reliance on the undertaking. As to the latter, it is quite clear that students and their parents rely on colleges to exercise care to safeguard the well-being of students. When students are considering enrolling in a particular college, they are likely to weigh a number of factors. But a threshold matter is whether the college has undertaken to provide an adequate level of security. Thus, prospective students and their parents who visit a college are certain to note the presence of a fence around the campus, the existence of security guards, and any other visible steps taken to ensure the safety of students. They may inquire as to what other measures the college has taken. If the college's response is unsatisfactory, students may choose to enroll elsewhere. The record indicates that Mullins visited several colleges, including Pine Manor, with her father during the summer before her senior year of high school. Thus, the jury could have found that students and their parents rely on the willingness of colleges such as Pine Manor to exercise due care to protect them from foreseeable harm.[11]

These two principles of law provide a sufficient basis for the imposition of a duty on colleges to protect their resident students against the criminal acts of third parties. Colleges must, therefore, act "to use reasonable care to prevent injury" to their students "by third persons whether their acts were accidental, negligent, or intentional."

We reject the argument advanced by the college and Person that the criminal attack here was not foreseeable. This contention is untenable in light of Person's testimony which admitted that he had foreseen the risk that a student at Pine Manor could be attacked and raped on campus. Indeed, the precautions which Pine Manor and other colleges take to protect their students against criminal acts of third parties would

---

11. Implicit in Pine Manor's requirement that freshmen live in dormitories provided by the college is the representation that the college believed that it could provide adequately for the safety and well-being of its students.

make little sense unless criminal acts were foreseeable. The director of student affairs testified that she warned students during freshman orientation of the dangers inherent in being housed at a women's college near a metropolitan area only a short distance from bus and train lines which lead directly to Boston. The risk of such a criminal act was not only foreseeable but was actually foreseen.

* * *

The jury also could have found that it was more likely than not that the assailant and Mullins would have been discovered had the defendants established an adequate system for supervising the guards and had employed three or four guards during the evening hours. The record is replete with evidence demonstrating that the guards did not carry out their duties. The guards were responsible for seeing that the gates to the village courtyards and the doors to the various buildings on campus were locked. One guard was assigned to patrol the campus every fifteen to thirty minutes and was required to check the gates and doors on each patrol. One of the guards on duty the night of the attack testified that if the gates to the courtyard were open, that fact would indicate that the guard had not performed those functions assigned to him. There was evidence that the gates were not locked and secured. Mullins testified that one gate to the courtyard was open at 3 a.m. when she returned to the village. She also testified that she and the assailant proceeded underneath the chains of another gate which was not adequately secured. Further, the door to the refectory was unlocked and, the evening before, the door to the commons room of Mullins's village was wide open. These facts warrant the conclusion that the guards had not made their rounds.

Second, the jury could have concluded that reasonable persons in the position of the defendants would have hired two additional guards. These additional guards would have permitted three guards to be patrolling the campus at any one time. A guard would have been beginning a round of the campus every five to ten minutes. Mullins testified that she and the assailant spent at least twenty minutes outside. The jury could have inferred that the actual period was longer. Mullins also testified that the assailant marched her back and forth in front of the refectory for a considerable period of time. From these facts, the jury could have concluded that it was more probable than not that, had the college deployed three guards, at least one of those guards would have seen Mullins, who had a pillow case over her head, and the assailant at some point during the march out of the dormitory, across the courtyard, down the bicycle path, and back and forth in front of the refectory.

The jury also could have considered the fact that the refectory should have been locked. Had it been locked, the assailant would have been faced with a choice. Given the bitter cold temperature, the rape most likely would not have been performed outdoors. The assailant most likely would have been compelled to either abandon his plan or begin a new search for some other sheltered location. The latter alternative would have required the assailant to march Mullins around the campus for a considerable period of time. The likelihood of discovery would have been increased, especially if three guards had been patrolling the campus. We conclude that the evidence warranted the conclusion that the defendants' negligence was a substantial cause of the attack.

c. *Proximate causation.* The college and Person next argue that the judge should have ruled, as matter of law, that the intervening criminal act of an unknown third person was a superseding cause which severed the chain of proximate causation. Our holding that the defendants had foreseen the risk of criminal attack largely disposes of the issue. The act of a third party does not excuse the first wrongdoer if such act was, or should have been, foreseen. There was no error in submitting the case to the jury.

3. *Liability of an officer of a charitable corporation in tort.* Person contends that he is entitled to the protection of the charitable immunity doctrine and that he cannot be held liable for mere negligence in the performance of a discretionary function. These questions were not raised below and, if we followed our usual practice, we would not consider them on appeal. However, because the questions presented are of some public importance and the result we reach is not changed by our consideration of them, we choose to state our views briefly.

The common law doctrine of charitable immunity provides that charitable institutions are immune from liability for their torts. The general rule, however, is that an agent is not entitled to the protection of his principal's immunity even if the agent is acting on behalf of his principal. In 1971, the Legislature abolished entirely the defense of charitable immunity from tort liability "if the tort was committed in the course of activities primarily commercial in character even though carried on to obtain revenue to be used for charitable purposes." "[I]f the tort was committed in the course of any activity carried on to accomplish directly the charitable purposes" of a charitable institution, liability may not exceed $20,000. This reflects a legislative determination to confine narrowly the doctrine of charitable immunity. We decline to ignore the wishes of the Legislature and expand the doctrine beyond its original boundaries.

We also reject the contention that an officer of a charitable institution may not be held liable for the negligent performance of a discretionary function without evidence of bad faith. Person relies primarily on our decision in *Whitney v. Worcester,* where we said that governmental entities and officials should be immune from liability when the conduct causing the injury involves the exercise of judgment and discretion. Our decision there rested on overriding considerations of public policy affecting the very quality and efficiency of government itself. These considerations are not present in the instant case.

Judgments affirmed.

———————

In a similar case, pleaded under the California Tort Claims Act, a public college was held to be liable for a failure to warn students of known dangers and to maintain clearer visibility near a campus parking lot and stair, where several assaults had occurred. The court held there was a "duty to exercise due care to protect students from reasonably foreseeable assaults on campus . . . [and the College] is not immune for failure to warn its students of known dangers posed by criminals on the campus." *Peterson v. San Francisco Community College District,* 205 Cal. Rptr. 842 (Cal. 1984).

In 1988, the Office for Civil Rights filed charges against Trenton (Missouri) Junior College, for failing to provide adequate security for black student athletes who were subjected to racial violence and harassment from the community. "College Violated Black Players' Rights by Dropping Basketball, U.S. Charges," *Chronicle of Higher Education,* 3 February 1988, p. A 36.

———————

University of Denver v. Whitlock
744 P.2d 54 (Colo. 1987)

LOHR, Justice.

Plaintiff Oscar Whitlock obtained a judgment against defendant University of Denver in the amount of $5,256,000, as a result of a jury trial in Denver District Court, for injuries suffered in a trampoline accident that rendered him a quadriplegic. The trial court ordered certain relief from this judgment based upon the University's motion for judgment notwithstanding the verdict. Whitlock appealed, and the University cross-appealed. The Colorado Court of Appeals rejected the University's argument that it owed no duty to Whitlock, reversed the trial court's order granting relief from the judgment, and directed that the jury's verdict be reinstated. The University then petitioned for certiorari, and we granted that petition.

The principal issue presented by this negligence case is whether the University of Denver owed a duty of care to Whitlock, who was a student at the University and a member of a fraternity, to take reasonable measures to protect him against injury resulting from his use of a trampoline under unsafe conditions when the trampoline was owned by the fraternity and was located on the front lawn of the house that the fraternity leased from the University. We conclude that the University had no such duty. Therefore, we reverse the judgment of the Colorado Court of Appeals, which recognized such a duty, and return the case to that court with directions to remand it to the trial court for dismissal of Whitlock's complaint against the University of Denver.

I.

The essential facts appear from the record of the jury trial in this case. On June 19, 1978, at approximately 10:00 p.m., plaintiff Oscar Whitlock suffered a paralyzing injury while attempting to complete a one-and-three-quarters front flip on a trampoline. The injury rendered him a quadriplegic. The trampoline was owned by the Beta Theta Pi fraternity (the Beta house) and was situated on the front yard of the fraternity premises, located on the University campus. At the time of his injury, Whitlock was twenty years old, attended the University of Denver, and was a member of the Beta house, where he held the office of acting house manager. The property on which the Beta house was located was leased to the local chapter house association of the Beta Theta Pi fraternity by the defendant University of Denver.

Whitlock had extensive experience jumping on trampolines. He began using trampolines in junior high school and continued to do so during his brief tenure as a cadet at the United States Military Academy at West Point, where he learned to execute the one-and-three-quarters front flip. Whitlock testified that he utilized the trampoline at West Point every other day for a period of two months. He began jumping on the trampoline owned by the Beta house in September of 1977. Whitlock recounted that in the fall and spring prior to the date of his injury, he jumped on the trampoline almost daily. He testified further that prior to the date of his injury, he had successfully executed the one-and-three-quarters front flip between seventy-five and one hundred times.

During the evening of June 18 and early morning of June 19, 1978, Whitlock attended a party at the Beta house, where he drank beer, vodka and scotch until 2:00 a.m. Whitlock then retired and did not awaken until 2:00 p.m. on June 19. He testified that he jumped on the trampoline between 2:00 p.m. and 4:00 p.m., and again at 7:00 p.m. At 10:00 p.m., the time of the injury, there again was a party in progress at the Beta house, and Whitlock was using the trampoline with only the illumination from the windows of the fraternity house, the outside light above the front door of the house, and two street lights in the area. As Whitlock attempted to perform the one-and-three-quarters front flip, he landed on the back of his head, causing his neck to break.

Whitlock brought suit against the manufacturer and seller of the trampoline, the University, the Beta Theta Pi fraternity and its local chapter, and certain individuals in their capacities as representatives of the Beta Theta Pi organizations. Whitlock reached settlements with all of the named defendants except the University, so only the negligence action against the University proceeded to trial. The jury returned a verdict in favor of Whitlock, assessing his total damages at $7,300,000. The jury attributed twenty-eight percent of causal negligence to the conduct of Whitlock and seventy-two percent of causal negligence to the conduct of the University. The trial court accordingly reduced the amount of the award against the University to $5,256,000.

The University moved for judgment notwithstanding the verdict, or, in the alternative, a new trial. The trial court granted the motion for judgment notwithstanding the verdict, holding that as a matter of law, no reasonable jury could have found that the University was more negligent than Whitlock, and that the jury's monetary award was the result of sympathy, passion or prejudice. The trial court alternatively ruled that if the court of appeals should find that the trial court's ruling on the defendant's motion for judgment notwithstanding the verdict was in error, a remittitur would be entered, reducing the jury's award to $4,000,000. As a third alternative, in the event that the court of appeals should also disapprove the remittitur, the trial court ordered a new trial.

A panel of the court of appeals reversed all three rulings by a divided vote. The court of appeals held that the University owed Whitlock a duty of due care to remove the trampoline from the fraternity premises or to supervise its use, and that it was improper for the trial court to order a remittitur or, in the alternative, a new trial. The case was remanded to the trial court with orders to reinstate the verdict and damages as determined by the jury. The University then petitioned for certiorari review, and we granted that petition.

II.

A negligence claim must fail if based on circumstances for which the law imposes no duty of care upon the defendant for the benefit of the plaintiff. Therefore, if Whitlock's judgment against the University is to be upheld, it must first be determined that the University owed a duty of care to take reasonable measures to protect him against the injury that he sustained.

Whether a particular defendant owes a legal duty to a particular plaintiff is a question of law. "The court determines, as a matter of law, the existence and scope of the duty—that is, whether the plaintiff's interest that has been infringed by the conduct of the defendant is entitled to legal protection." In *Smith v. City & County of Denver*, we set forth several factors to be considered in determining the existence of duty in a particular case:

Whether the law should impose a duty requires consideration of many factors including, for example, the risk involved, the foreseeability and likelihood of injury as weighed against the social utility of the actor's conduct, the magnitude of the burden of guarding against injury or harm, and the consequences of placing the burden upon the actor.

As the quoted language makes clear, this list was not intended to be exhaustive and does not exclude the consideration of other factors that may become relevant based upon the competing individual, public and social interests implicated in the facts of each case. A court's conclusion that a duty does or does not exist is "an expression of the sum total of those considerations of policy which lead the law to say that the plaintiff is [or is not] entitled to protection." "No one factor is controlling, and the question of whether a duty should be imposed in a particular case is essentially one of fairness under contemporary standards—whether reasonable persons would recognize a duty and agree that it exists."

We believe that the fact that the University is charged with negligent failure to act rather than negligent affirmative action is a critical factor that strongly militates against imposition of a duty on the University under the facts of this case. In determining whether a defendant owes a duty to a particular plaintiff, the law has long recognized a distinction between action and a failure to act—"that is to say, between active misconduct working positive injury to others [misfeasance] and passive inaction or a failure to take steps to protect them from harm [nonfeasance]." Liability for nonfeasance was slow to receive recognition in the law. "The reason for the distinction may be said to lie in the fact that by 'misfeasance' the defendant has created a new risk of harm to the plaintiff, while by 'nonfeasance' he has at least made his situation no worse, and has merely failed to benefit him by interfering in his affairs." Imposition of a duty in all such cases would simply not meet the test of fairness under contemporary standards.

In nonfeasance cases the existence of a duty has been recognized only during the last century in situations involving a limited group of special relationships between parties. Such special relationships are predicated on "some definite relation between the parties, of such a character that social policy justifies the imposition of a duty to act." Special relationships that have been recognized by various courts for the purpose of imposition of a duty of care include common carrier/passenger, innkeeper/guest, possessor of land/invited entrant, employer/employee, parent/child, and hospital/patient. The authors of the *Restatement (Second) of Torts* state that "[t]he law appears ... to be working slowly toward a recognition of the duty to aid or protect in any relation of dependence or of mutual dependence."

* * *

III.

The present case involves the alleged negligent failure to act, rather than negligent action. The plaintiff does not complain of any affirmative action taken by the University, but asserts instead that the University owed to Whitlock the duty to assure that the fraternity's trampoline was used only under supervised conditions comparable to those in a gymnasium class, or in the alternative to cause the trampoline to be removed from the front lawn of the Beta house. It is true that there is evidence in the record from which the jury could have found that the University possessed the authority to regulate the fraternity's use of the trampoline by enacting rules of student conduct. However, mere possession of such authority is not sufficient to establish that the University had the duty to exert such control with respect to the use of trampolines by fraternity members. If such a duty is to be recognized, it must be grounded on a special relationship between the University and Whitlock. According to the evidence, there are only two possible sources of a special relationship out of which such a duty could arise in this case: the status of Whitlock as a student at the University, and the lease between the University and the fraternity of which Whitlock was a member. We first consider the adequacy of the student-university relationship as a possible basis for imposing a duty on the University to control or prohibit the use of the trampoline, and then examine the provisions of the lease for that same purpose.

A.

The student-university relationship has been scrutinized in several jurisdictions, and it is generally agreed that a university is not an insurer of its students' safety. The relationship between a university and its students has experienced important change over the years. At one time, college administrators and faculties stood *in loco parentis* to their students, which created a special relationship "that imposed a duty on the college to exercise control over student conduct and, reciprocally, gave the students certain rights of protection by the college." However, in modern times there has evolved a gradual reapportionment of responsibilities from the universities to the students, and a corresponding departure from the *in loco parentis* relationship. Today, colleges and universities are regarded as educational institutions rather than custodial ones. "Their purpose is to educate in a manner which will assist the graduate to perform well in the civic, community, family, and professional positions he or she may undertake in the future." A university seeks to foster the maturation of its students. In a case involving injuries sustained by a student passenger in an automobile driven by a student who had become intoxicated by consuming alcoholic beverages in a college's residence hall and then had engaged in a speed contest, the California Court of Appeals stated:

> The transfer of prerogatives and rights from college administrators to the students is salubrious when seen in the context of a proper goal of postsecondary education—the maturation of the students. Only by giving them responsibilities can students grow into responsible adulthood. Although the alleged lack of supervision had a disastrous result to this plaintiff, the overall policy of stimulating student growth is in the public interest.

In today's society, the college student is considered an adult capable of protecting his or her own interests; students today demand and receive increased autonomy and decreased regulation on and off campus. The demise of the doctrine of *in loco parentis* in this context has been a direct result of changes that have occurred in society's perception of the most beneficial allocation of rights and responsibilities in the university-student relationship. By imposing a duty on the University in this case, the University would be encouraged to exercise more control over private student recreational choices, thereby effectively taking away much of the responsibility recently recognized in students for making their own decisions with respect to private entertainment and personal safety. Such an allocation of responsibility would "produce a repressive and inhospitable environment, largely inconsistent with the objectives of a modern college education."

The evidence demonstrates that only in limited instances has the University attempted to impose regulations or restraints on the private recreational pursuits of its students, and the students have not looked to the University to assure the safety of their recreational choices. Nothing in the University's student handbook, which contains certain regulations concerning student conduct, reflects an effort by the University to control the risk-taking decisions of its students in their private recreation. The testimony of the Assistant Dean of Student Life, whose office was in charge of the University's relationships with fraternities and sororities, reflects that, with the exceptions mentioned in footnote 5, the University did not attempt to regulate the recreational pursuits of members of the fraternities and sororities on campus. Indeed, fraternity and sorority self-governance with minimal supervision appears to have been fostered by the University. Aside from advising the Beta house on one occasion to put the trampoline up when not in use, there is no evidence that the University officials attempted to assert control over trampoline use by the fraternity members. We conclude from this record that the University's very limited actions concerning safety of student recreation did not give Whitlock or the other members of campus fraternities or sororities any reason to depend upon the University for evaluation of the safety of trampoline use. Therefore, we conclude that the student-university relationship is not a special relationship of the type giving rise to a duty of the University to take reasonable measures to protect the members of fraternities and sororities from risks of engaging in extra-curricular trampoline jumping.

The plaintiff asserts, however, that we should recognize a duty of the University to take affirmative action to protect fraternity members because of the foreseeability of the injury, the extent of the risks involved in trampoline use, the seriousness of potential injuries, and the University's superior knowledge concerning these matters. The argument in essence is that a duty should spring from the University's natural interest in the welfare and safety of its students, its superior knowledge of the nature and degree of risk involved in trampoline use, and its knowledge of the use of trampolines on the University campus. The evidence amply supports a conclusion that trampoline use involves risks of serious injuries and that the potential for an injury such as that experienced by Whitlock was foreseeable. It shows further that prior injuries resulting from trampoline accidents had been reported to campus security and to the student clinic, and that University administrators were aware of the number and severity of trampoline injuries nationwide.

The record, however, also establishes through Whitlock's own testimony that he was aware of the risk of an accident and injury of the very nature that he experienced. There is no evidence that the fraternity or Whitlock looked to the University for evaluation of the appropriateness of the use of a trampoline, or had reason to do so, or that they were unable to assess in an adequate though general way the dangers presented by trampoline use. We conclude that the relationship between the University and Whitlock was not one of dependence with respect to the activities at issue here, and provides no basis for the recognition of a duty of the University to take measures for protection of Whitlock against the injury that he suffered.

B.

We next examine the lease between the University and the fraternity to determine whether a special relationship between the University and Whitlock can be predicated on that document. The lease was executed in 1929, extends for a ninety-nine year term, and gives the fraternity the option to extend the term for another ninety-nine years. The premises are to be occupied and used by the fraternity "as a fraternity house, clubhouse, dormitory and boarding house, and generally for religious, educational, social and fraternal purposes." Such occupation is to be *under control of the tenant.*" The annual rental at all times relevant to this case appears from the record to be one dollar. The University has the obligation to maintain the grounds and make necessary repairs to the building, and the fraternity is to bear the cost of such maintenance and repair. The University has the right to inspect the building. The fraternity agrees that the building will not be used for unlawful or immoral conduct and that the occupants of the building are to "observe the reasonable rules of conduct therein and thereabout imposed from time to time on students of the University of Denver generally by the lessor." The lease can be terminated by the University for nonpayment of rental or for violation of the covenant against improper conduct, or upon notice after making provisions for a substitute facility. The lease is devoid of any other covenants limiting the activities of the fraternity or its members or giving the University the right to direct or control those activities. The University has promulgated no rules of conduct relating to private trampoline use. A lessor's reservation of rights to inspect the premises and make repairs is generally not sufficient control to give rise to liability of the lessor to the tenant or third parties for tort injuries.

The extent of control actually exerted by the University over the fraternity has been minimal. The University has supervised fire drills in the fraternity house and has required the fraternity to place a grid over one of its window wells because of an accident that had occurred. Also, a University representative once advised the Betas to take the trampoline down when not in use. Other than the suggestion made by the university official, which appears to have been only advisory as the fraternity failed to comply, the University's supervision has related primarily to fire protection, maintenance and repairs.

We conclude that the lease, and the University's actions pursuant to its rights under the lease, provide no basis of dependence by the fraternity members upon which a special relationship can be found to exist between the University and the fraternity members that would give rise to a duty upon the University to take affirmative action to assure that recreational equipment such as a trampoline is not used under unsafe conditions.

IV.

Considering all of the factors presented, we are persuaded that under the facts of this case the University of Denver had no duty to Whitlock to eliminate the private use of trampolines on its campus or to supervise that use. There exists no special relationship between the parties that justifies placing a duty upon the University to protect Whitlock from the well-known dangers of using a trampoline. Here, a conclusion that a special relationship existed between Whitlock and the University sufficient to warrant the imposition of liability for nonfeasance would directly contravene the competing social policy of fostering an educational environment of student autonomy and independence.

We reverse the judgment of the court of appeals and return this case to that court with directions to remand it to the trial court for dismissal of Whitlock's complaint against the University.

Contract Theories

Johnson v. Lincoln Christian College

501 N.E. 2d 1380 (Ill. App. 4 Dist. 1986);

app. den., 508 N.E. 2d 729 (1987)

Presiding Justice SPITZ delivered the opinion of the court:

Gregory Johnson filed suit against Lincoln Christian College (LCC) and Kent Paris, and both defendants filed motions to dismiss his complaint. These motions were allowed. Johnson appeals from the dismissal of his complaint.

When considering a motion to dismiss, a court is obligated to accept as true all well-pleaded facts and all reasonable inferences which could be drawn from those facts. Pursuant to section 2-612(b) of the Code of Civil Procedure "[n]o pleading is bad in substance which contains such information as reasonably informs the opposite party of the nature of the claim or defense which he or she is called upon to meet." Pursuant to section 2-603(c) of the Code of Civil Procedure "[p]leadings shall be liberally construed with a view to doing substantial justice between the parties." Furthermore, as this court stated in *Champaign National Bank v. Illinois Power Co.* "[i]f the facts alleged and any reasonable inferences capable of being drawn from those facts demonstrate a possibility of recovery, the pleading is not subject to dismissal." Consequently, our focus on review is whether any of the counts of Johnson's complaint "demonstrate a possibility of recovery," and, for the purpose of this appeal, we deem the following well-pleaded facts to be correct.

Johnson was a student at Lincoln Christian College from September 1976 to March 1981. He was enrolled in a five-year program to prepare him for a career teaching sacred music. Johnson has completed all of his course requirements and fully paid his tuition for each year; however, LCC has repeatedly refused to grant Johnson his diploma. LCC based its denial on a charge that Johnson might be homosexual.

The charge of homosexuality arose when, during Johnson's last semester at LCC, another student, Linda Heppner, told LCC's Dean of Students, Thomas Ewald, that Johnson might be homosexual. Solely in response to that student's accusation and without further investigation, LCC through Heppner, told Johnson that he would graduate only if he sought counseling from Kent Paris. Relying upon LCC's assurances that he would graduate if he sought counseling, and afraid that he would not graduate unless he complied with LCC's demand, Johnson repeatedly traveled between Lincoln and Champaign, where Paris' office was located, and attended private counseling sessions.

Throughout these counseling sessions, Johnson believed that anything he said, and any of Paris' resulting conclusions, would be held in confidence. Because he believed that the conversations were confidential, Johnson was willing to, and did, reveal many personal facts, some of which he had never told anyone else. He would not have given that information to Paris if he had suspected that Paris would discuss the information or his resulting conclusions with anyone else. Johnson never consented to the disclosure of any information about these counseling sessions, and Paris never in any way contradicted Johnson's faith in the confidentiality of their discussions; however, Paris reported to Ewald in March of 1981 that plaintiff had not changed and was not progressing.

As a result of that conversation, Ewald informed plaintiff that LCC would hold a hearing in less than 24 hours at which Johnson would be required to defend himself against the rumor that he was homosexual. Ewald told Johnson that he would be dismissed from LCC because of his alleged homosexuality, and that the reason for his dismissal would be stamped across his transcript. From that meeting, Johnson understood that he would be dismissed regardless of what happened at the hearing. Afraid that the accusation of homosexuality being imprinted on his transcript would destroy his career goal, Johnson withdrew from LCC. LCC held the threatened hearing in Johnson's absence. In addition, Ewald called Johnson's mother and told her that LCC was dismissing Johnson because he was homosexual. To this day, LCC refuses to grant plaintiff a diploma.

On November 29, 1984, Johnson filed a seven-count complaint against LCC and Paris in the circuit court of Champaign County. LCC filed a motion to transfer venue from Champaign County to Logan County, and Paris filed an affidavit in support of LCC's motion to transfer venue. On February 7, 1985, LCC's motion was allowed, and on May 7, 1985, an order to transfer venue to Logan County was filed in the circuit court of Champaign County.

Johnson's suit against Paris and LCC is based on several theories. With respect to LCC, plaintiff alleges: (1) LCC breached its college-student contract with plaintiff by arbitrarily and in bad faith denying him his diploma (count I); (2) LCC tortiously interfered with plaintiff's contract with Paris (count II); (3) LCC misused the confidential information that Paris divulged thereby violating the Mental Health and Developmental Disabilities Confidentiality Act (count III); and (4) LCC invaded plaintiff's privacy by publicly accusing him of homosexuality (count IV). With respect to Paris, plaintiff alleges: (1) Paris breached a contract with Johnson and violated the Mental Health and Developmental Disabilities Confidentiality Act (Ill. Rev. Stat. 1985, ch. 91 1/2, par. 801 *et seq.*) by disclosing information about his counseling sessions with plaintiff (count V); (2) Paris' disclosure of the confidential information tortiously interfered with plaintiff's college-student contract with LCC (count VI); and (3) Paris invaded plaintiff's privacy by disclosing confidential information (count VII).

Defendants filed seven separate motions to dismiss Johnson's complaint. Johnson filed a consolidated memorandum in opposition to defendants' motions to dismiss his complaint. On August 20, 1985, a hearing was conducted regarding the various motions to dismiss. On April 9, 1986 (nearly 8 months after the hearing), the circuit court issued a one-sentence ruling, stating that "[a]ll motions of the co-defendants heretofore heard in open Court and considered by the Court are allowed."

In count I of his complaint, Johnson alleged that (1) the terms of a college-student contract are implied by law; (2) the law implies in every college-student contract a duty that the college not arbitrarily, capriciously, or in bad faith prevent a student from graduating; (3) he fulfilled all of LCC's academic requirements and fully paid his tuition to LCC; and (4) by refusing to issue him a diploma, LCC breached its implied contract with Johnson and has acted arbitrarily, capriciously, and in bad faith by refusing to do so. Johnson also alleged that LCC told him he would be allowed to graduate if he sought professional help from Paris.

LCC argues that dismissal of count I was proper because count I failed to allege the terms of the contract between Johnson and LCC. LCC cites cases which involve contracts between a school and a student, and notes that in each of these cases, the student presented catalogues, bulletins, or other such material distributed by the school to establish the elements of the contract between the student and the school. Based on these cases, LCC argues that Johnson is obligated to provide some type of document to establish the elements of the contract between him and LCC. LCC's argument based on these cases is without merit. These cases simply stand for the proposition that documents distributed by a school are a *part* of the contract between the student and the school. It does not necessarily follow, or do any of the cases cited by LCC require, that a student must present such documents to establish the terms of an implied contract between the school and the student.

LCC also cites *McErlean v. Union National Bank of Chicago*, for the proposition that the allegations contained in count I of Johnson's complaint are "conclusory statements [which] are insufficient to adequately plead breach of contract absent supporting facts concerning the material terms of the contract." *McErlean* is a commercial case involving a partially oral and partially written contract to loan money in the future. There, the court stated that "[n]o allegations are expressly pleaded, nor can any be implied, in the instant complaint as to the material terms [of the contract] * * * particularly, interest, duration, and terms of repayment. In light of these significant omissions, we find no error in the dismissal of the amended complaint * * * ."

We believe that there is a valid distinction between a "commercial case" and a case involving an implied contract between a college and a student. In a commercial case such as *McErlean*, the material terms of an alleged contract are generally complex and unique to a particular set of circumstances, and cannot be implied. On the other hand, the traditional implied contract between a college and a student is much more standard and less complex than that which usually exists in a commercial setting.

The elements of a traditional contract are present in the implied contract between a college and a student attending that college, and are readily discernible. The student's tender of an application constitutes an offer to apply to the college. By "accepting" an applicant to be a student at the college, the college accepts the applicant's offer. Thereafter, the student pays tuition (which obviously constitutes sufficient consideration), attends classes, completes course work, and takes tests. The school provides the student with facilities and instruction, and upon satisfactory completion of the school's academic requirements (which constitutes performance), the school becomes obligated to issue the student a diploma. As this court stated in *Tanner v. Board of Trustees of University of Illinois*, a college "may not act maliciously or in bad faith by arbitrarily and capriciously refusing to award a degree to a student who fulfills its degree requirement."

LCC is well aware of what its own academic requirements are, and we fail to see how LCC can be surprised or prejudiced by the fact that Johnson does not allege these requirements with more specificity. Johnson alleged that he has met all of the academic requirements imposed by LCC in order to obtain a diploma, and if this allegation is not true, LCC should be easily able to present evidence to disprove Johnson's allegation in this regard. LCC was reasonably informed of the nature of the claim which it was called upon to meet, and pursuant to section 2-612(b) of the Code of Civil Procedure this count could not properly be dismissed. Consequently, we conclude that count I of Johnson's complaint states a valid cause of action for breach of an implied contract between Johnson and LCC, and the trial court erred in dismissing count I of the complaint.

In count V of his complaint, Johnson alleged that Paris violated sections 2, 3, and 5 of the Mental Health and Developmental Disabilities Confidentiality Act (Confidentiality Act) and also breached an implied-by-law contract by divulging confidential information disclosed to him by Johnson during private counseling sessions to LCC without Johnson's consent.

Section 3(a) of the Confidentiality Act provides that "[a]ll records and communications shall be confidential and shall not be disclosed except as provided in this Act." Section 5 of the Confidentiality Act provides that if a "recipient * * * is 18 years of age or older," records and "communications" may only be disclosed with his written consent.

* * *

Regarding Johnson's claim that Paris breached an implied contract, Paris argues that this claim was properly dismissed because Johnson failed to properly allege the elements of such a contract. We believe that Johnson's complaint adequately alleges a breach of contract by Paris. The complaint alleged that Paris offered his services and that Johnson agreed to accept them. The contract was allegedly formed in December of 1980, as is apparent from Johnson's allegation that he began the counseling sessions immediately following Heppner's December 1980 conversation with Ewald. Johnson alleged that he repeatedly drove from Lincoln to Champaign to attend these counseling sessions, and that he divulged confidential information to Paris in reliance upon Paris' obligation not to disclose this information. Johnson's detrimental reliance and his driving to and from Champaign constituted sufficient consideration to validate the contract. The terms of the contract were simply that Paris was to provide counseling services, and Johnson was to attend the sessions and accept the counseling. Furthermore, Johnson's complaint adequately specifies the breach of the contract. It alleges that the contractual relationship between Paris and Johnson obligated Paris not to disclose confidential information obtained as a result of that relationship, and that Paris breached the contract by disclosing that information. Count V adequately alleged a breach of contract by Paris and sufficiently informed Paris of the nature of the claim he was called upon to meet. Consequently, the circuit court erred by dismissing the breach of contract claim contained in count V of Johnson's complaint.

In count III of his complaint, Johnson alleged that LCC violated section 5 of the Confidentiality Act by redisclosing information learned from Paris to faculty members, students, and members of Johnson's family. LCC first argues that count III was properly dismissed because Paris' services were not covered by the Confidentiality Act. This argument is without merit because, as we have previously discussed, Paris' services were covered by the Confidentiality Act.

* * *

For the reasons stated herein, the order of the circuit court is hereby reversed in part, affirmed in part, and remanded to the circuit court for further proceedings consistent with the views expressed in this opinion.

Reversed in part, affirmed in part, and remanded.

AASE v. State, South Dakota Board of Regents
400 N.W. 2d 269 (S.D. 1987)

HEEGE, Circuit Judge.

This is one of a series of actions brought to test the legality of closing the University of South Dakota at Springfield (USD/S) and the affect of such closing on various individuals. The plaintiffs in this action are students who attended USD/S during the academic year 1983–84. The defendants include the members of the South Dakota Board of Regents, individually and in their capacity as regents. The trial court granted these defendants' motion for summary judgment and the plaintiffs appealed. We affirm.

In the spring of 1984 the South Dakota Legislature enacted Senate Bill 221, which was signed into law as an emergency measure on March 9, 1984. In pertinent part, the bill transferred control of the USD/S grounds and facilities from the Board of Regents to the Board of Charities and Corrections, effective May 1, 1984, and converted the school to a minimum security prison. The bill also permitted the students to finish out the 1983–84 academic year at the Springfield campus and required that the Board of Regents and the Board of Vocational Education take steps to give the students an opportunity to complete their courses of study in South Dakota through articulation agreements and by including a baccalaureate program of vocational education within one of the institutions under their control.

The students filed suit, alleging five counts in the amended complaint: (1) a claim for breach of contract; (2) a claim for injunctive relief to prevent closure of USD/S and a declaration that SB 221 is unconstitutional; (3) a claim for violation of civil rights under 42 U.S.C. § 1983 (1982); (4) a claim for invasion of individual constitutional rights; and (5) claims made under the South Dakota Deceptive Trade Practices and Consumer Protection Act.

We conclude, as did the trial court, that based on the record and as a matter of law the students had no enforceable contract rights against the Regents. As a general principle, the relationship between a university and a student is contractual by nature. However, the only contract formed between the student and the school which he is attending is for the term for which the tuition is paid. In the instant case the students were permitted to complete the academic year at the Springfield campus, so no rights of the students were impaired. Plaintiffs did not develop any other contract rights with the Board of Regents.

Plaintiffs claim the trial court erred in holding that SB 221 made impossible the performance of any contract with the Regents; they argue that the Regents could have performed their "contractual obligations" either at Springfield or at other institutions. We need not and do not reach this issue in view of our holding that no contract rights existed after the 1983–84 academic year.

The trial court was not required to determine, and we do not reach, the question of what rights the plaintiffs may have against the Board of Regents under the mandate from the legislature to "assure ... the opportunity to complete their course of study in South Dakota.... " We are compelled to reach this result because the plaintiffs made no claim against the Regents on that theory in their amended complaint. Moreover, it stands undisputed in the record that the Board of Regents gave the students the opportunity to complete their courses of study in South Dakota as required by SB 221.

With regard to the question of injunctive relief, it is clear that the students are not entitled to a mandatory injunction against closure of the Springfield campus. The constitutionality of SB 221 was previously established in *Kanaly*.

The trial court concluded, and we agree, that the Board of Regents is not a person within the meaning of 42 U.S.C. § 1983 (1982) and may not be sued under that section. Further, the trial court correctly held that the Regents in their individual capacities enjoy a qualified or good faith immunity which applies to the claims made in this action.

Finally, the trial court concluded, and we agree, that no constitutional rights of the students were invaded and no violation of SDCL ch. 37–24 was shown. Therefore, the trial court was correct in entering summary judgment within the strict standards set forth in *Wilson v. Great Northern Ry. Co.* The evidence viewed most favorably to the plaintiffs establishes that the Board of Regents, individually and in their official capacities, are entitled as a matter of law to judgment dismissing plaintiffs' amended complaint.

The judgment of the trial court is affirmed.

HENDERSON, Justice (dissenting).

Movant/State of South Dakota was not entitled to judgment as a matter of law.

A court must give the non-moving party the benefit of any doubt as to the propriety of granting summary judgment.

Be it a pleading, affidavit, or deposition, a court must give every reasonable inference which arises from said pleading, affidavit, or deposition, viewed most favorably, toward the non-moving party. In this instance, the students.

*   *   *

Students should have been permitted to phase out their educational programs. The majority of the programs offered at USD/S were not offered at other post-secondary institutions or institutions of higher education in South Dakota. Senate Bill 221 affected approximately 800 students enrolled in various educational programs. The educational rug was cut from under their feet. Now their legal rights are cut from under their feet. It is a tragedy of great dimension and unparalleled in South Dakota educational history. Prisoners in the State Penitentiary are now phased into students' classrooms and dormitories. USD/S was an outstanding junior college and technical/vocational school. To this end, degrees were awarded such as Associate of Arts, Associate of Science, Bachelor of Science and Technology, and Bachelor of Science and Education.

The plaintiffs and aforesaid students were enrolled in these programs and had invested their time and money in consuming college courses, admissions counselors, reading admission brochures for pre-enrollment use, and generally relying upon the representations of that institution's staff and faculty members regarding their educational programs. By Section 4 of Senate Bill 221, the Board of Regents and the Board of Vocational Education were directed to "take all necessary steps to insure that all students presently enrolled at the University of South Dakota at Springfield shall have the opportunity to complete their course of study in South Dakota at other public, post-secondary educational schools, public higher education institutions or a combination thereof through an articulation of agreements." Furthermore, the said Bill further mandated that "The Board of Regents shall include a baccalaureate program of vocational education within at least one of the institutions under its control." By Section 4 of this Act, the plaintiffs/students enrolled in various programs and courses of study were entitled to complete their course of instruction and the Legislature appropriated money to support the directive contained in said Senate Bill 221.

On June 30, 1984, a day in educational infamy, all educational programs were terminated at USD/S. There were hundreds of depositions taken of students and these reflect the composite/deep problems pressed upon these students: Many were forced to relocate out of South Dakota; some were transferred to other institutions and were forced to modify their academic programs which necessitated additional semesters of study; many students were unable to find an equivalent program and had to change their major; some were forced to discontinue their college education—altogether.

Traumatic, indeed, was Senate Bill 221 and now plaintiffs/students are told, before they ever have a chance to actually have their case heard in a court of law, that they have no case. In the depositions, most students testified that they were *never* provided an opportunity to continue the educational programs which they had begun at USD/S in the State of South Dakota.

It appears that hundreds of depositions were not considered by this trial court, for they were never transcribed in time for the trial court to consider them. Summary judgment should not have been granted in this case until *all* facts were sufficiently developed to enable the trial court to be reasonably certain that it was correct in its determination of the law.

Summary judgment should not be granted before discovery is completed. It was not completed here.

* * *

Vought v. Teachers College, Columbia University
511 N.Y.S. 2d 880 (A.D. 2 Dept. 1987)

MEMORANDUM BY THE COURT.

In an action to recover damages for breach of contract, fraud and negligence, the plaintiff appeals from an order of the Supreme Court, Nassau County dated May 29, 1986, which granted the defendant's motion for summary judgment and denied his cross motion for summary judgment.

ORDERED that the order is affirmed, with costs.

Based on an advertisement published by the defendant college, the plaintiff, an undergraduate student with 60 credits, became interested in the "Accel-A-Year" program offered by the defendant which would grant him a combined Bachelor of Science and Master of Arts degree after an additional two years of study, thereby saving him one year towards the latter degree. Thereupon, the plaintiff received an advisory statement from the defendant which referred to the prospective granting of a combined Bachelor of Science and Master of Arts degree solely in this manner: "Application is in process to Albany for approval of this program as a *combined* degree program of B.S./M.A." The plaintiff checked off the box marked "Master of Arts Degree" on his application for admission, and the defendant's letter of acceptance referred to his admission to a program leading to a Master of Arts degree. Furthermore, oral statements made during an interview to the plaintiff by an agent of the defendant also indicated that the program would lead to a Master of Arts degree, but that the application for a combined degree program had been made but was not yet approved. After six months of study, the defendant notified the plaintiff that the application was not going to be approved in time for him to receive the combined degree, and, therefore, he should consider returning to his undergraduate studies.

The plaintiff returned to his studies and the defendant granted him his Master of Arts degree in October 1982.

When a student is admitted to a university, an implied contract arises between the parties which states that if the student complies with the terms prescribed by the university, he will obtain the degree he seeks. The rights and obligations of the parties as contained in the university's bulletins, circulars and regulations made available to the student, become a part of this contract. Because the documents made available to the plaintiff herein by the university merely stated that he was entering a program which would lead to a Master of Arts degree, Special Term properly dismissed his breach of contract claim in which he alleged that he was promised the combined degree.

Since the plaintiff was made abundantly aware that the program would lead to a Masters of Arts degree, and that the defendant's application for approval of its combined-degree program had not been granted, his cause of action sounding in fraud must also fail because he cannot allege that he justifiably relied on the express statements in the advisory statement and advertisement to the effect that the program would result in a one-year saving in schooling. Furthermore, any oral statements that the application was expected to be granted were merely predictions and prophesies and were not misrepresentations of fact which would sustain a cause of action sounding in fraud.

Finally, Special Term also properly granted summary judgment in favor of the defendant on the plaintiff's negligence claim since the university decided not to continue its baccalaureate curricula in 1978, before it owed any duty to the plaintiff, and it was not reasonably foreseeable that the plaintiff would be injured thereby. Moreover, once a contractual relationship was entered into between the parties, that contract defined the scope of the duties owed to the plaintiff, and, without a special relationship out of which a separate and distinct legal duty sprang, the plaintiff cannot maintain a separate tort cause of action.

In unusual circumstances, equity courts will find a contractual or implied contractual relationship when a college discontinues a course of study, particularly if the deterioration of the program is substantially within the control of the institution. At a private college, PhD students at Vanderbilt were awarded damages because the University "hastily embarked upon a vague and ill-defined doctoral studies program when it knew or should have known that it did not have the resources to operate the program. Vanderbilt received [tuition] from these plaintiffs and gave little or nothing in return." Lowenthal v. Vanderbilt, Davidson County Chancery Court (unpublished opinion No. A8525, August, 1977).

At Ohio University, a public institution, the School of Architecture lost its accreditation, but "The staff of the college, as well as the dean, continued to convey the thought to these student plaintiffs that every effort would be made to again be accredited." Five years after the loss of accreditation, the University decided to close the School, leaving a number of students in the lurch; the Court of Appeals awarded damages to the stranded students, including "pecuniary loss due to delay" in the completion of studies. Behrend v. State, 379 N.E. 2d 617 (1978).

Student Admissions

Arizona Board of Regents v. Wilson
539 P.2d 943 (1975)

HOWARD, Chief Judge.

This is an appeal from the order to the trial court requiring appellants to admit appellee as a candidate for the degree of Master of Fine Arts and Studio Painting at the University of Arizona.

The appellee, a mature woman of the age of sixty, graduated from the College of Fine Arts of the University of Arizona, having majored in studio art. In addition to her studies at the University of Arizona, appellee took undergraduate courses in the art field at Columbia University, Southern Methodist University, and Washington University (Missouri). Her application for candidacy in the Graduate College Master of Fine Arts degree program was denied by Dr. Robert W. McMillan, head of the Art Department. The memorandum of rejection gave as a reason for denial the fact that the facilities were already committed but that she could re-apply in September of 1974 for possible admission in the second semester of the school year 1974–75. A further reason given as "Work seems already to be on professional level, but the committee feels that it does not appear to be particularly harmonious with the esthetic attitudes within the art department."

Persons who are interested in being admitted to the Graduate College are required by the Art Department to submit their applications before April 1 in order to enroll for the fall semester. These applications are to be accompanied by slides of their work for viewing by the faculty committee. The head of the Art Department has appointed a committee of five professors from his department to make the recommendations to him as to which applications should be granted. As the applications come in, they are broken down into sets of approximately eight applications. The candidates' slides are viewed by the faculty committee which votes upon whether the application should be granted. There is no "check list" or written set of standards which the faculty committee uses in judging the applicant's work. Each member of the committee uses his own standards and judgment in order to arrive at a decision as to whether there is potential in the student's work.

The Art Department does not wait until all of the applications are in before beginning its screening process, but instead considers the applications in the afore-mentioned group as they come in. It was explained that the reasons for doing this were that this is the system used by other colleges throughout the United States, and that if the Art Department waited until all the applications were in, it would not be able to compete with the other colleges and universities in selecting the most promising students. As it is, approximately two-thirds of the applications are denied.

Appellee's application was considered on the last day with thirteen other applications. Out of the fourteen applications, two were selected as candidates. The committee was unanimous in its rejection of appellee's application.

The trial court, in arriving at its decision, stated the following:

"The Court is particularly concerned about the following factors in the Art Department Graduate admission procedures:

1. The committee seems to have no agreed standards or even guidelines to follow. Of necessity, each committee member's evaluation of the applicant's

work must be subjective to a degree. However, each member of this committee seems to follow his own personal standard, idea or hunch as to whether the applicant should be admitted to the graduate program.

2. One of the reasons given for denial is 'Facilities committed.' The procedure used for arriving at this reason is unfair. The committee considered the applicants by groups, the groups being formed by chance, and the committee admitted applicants as it proceeded with each group. When the committee reached the last group of fourteen applicants, one of which was the plaintiff, evidently [its] facilities were almost entirely committed. It admitted only two of the fourteen applicants of the last group, whereas it admitted one out of four in the groups, overall. The fair way to have proceeded would be to defer the decisions until all applicants had been considered, then fill all available openings.

3. The only other reason given for denial was, 'work seems already to be on professional level, but the committee feels that it does not appear to be particularly harmonious with the esthetic attitudes within the Art Department.' The Court does not feel that this is sufficient reason for denial to the graduate college. The Court therefore finds that the Art Department's graduate admission procedures, both generally and as applied to the plaintiff, are unreasonable, arbitrary, capricious and discriminatory."

The members of the art committee which screened appellee's application testified that their main consideration was the creative efforts of appellee as evidenced by the sample of her work.

The main dispute in this case revolves around the statement made by the committee that "Work seems already to be on professional level, but the committee feels that it does not appear to be particularly harmonious with the esthetic attitudes within the art department." Appellee would have one believe that her rejection by the faculty committee was not unlike the rejection by the Salon of French Academie Royale of Manet's "Le Dejeuner sur L'Herbe." In other words, according to appellee's theory below, it was because she was different that she was rejected. Whereas Manet's painting was rejected because of his new revolutionary technique, Mrs. Wilson's problems seem to be the opposite. The testimony of Professor Wayne Enstice, a member of the faculty committee, is paraphrased as follows: Some amount of technical achievement was present but it was not used in any genuine original way in terms of form, composition or statement. Her paintings are cliches, formula written, of a pedestrian sort that one would find in a tourist situation. Her work was stagnant. Many of the same techniques and subject matter of appellee's painting can be seen in department stores and tourist establishments. The use of the words "professional level" as applied to Rubye Wilson meant that she had her paintings in various exhibitions and had done greeting cards, however, there are degrees of professional artists and Rubye Wilson's paintings are of the tourist establishment variety. Her paintings were "saccharin," and lacked any kind of formal invention or originality. The other members of the committee who remembered her work, testified to having had substantially the same impressions of it as did Professor Enstice.

Two of Mrs. Wilson's teachers testified. Mrs. Wilson took undergraduate work from Professor Dennison and also enrolled, while an undergraduate, in a graduate course in studio painting from which she later withdrew. Professor Dennison considered her unteachable by him. He stated that while she was in the graduate course most of his criticism ended up in an emotional dead-end. She wept and would leave class early in frustration. He did not consider her a potentially successful candidate for a Master of Fine Arts degree. His views were conveyed to the faculty committee.

Professor Scott, who is a member of the faculty committee and also taught her in an undergraduate course, considered her incapable of graduate work. He also stated that she could not take criticism nor would she cure any faults. He considered her unteachable.

Professor Croft, a member of the faculty committee, stated that when he viewed the work of the applicants, he looked for future promise. He tried to determine whether the candidate would succeed in the program. He stated that the kind of imagery that Mrs. Wilson was pursuing was pretty much a dead-end street. As far as he was concerned, there wasn't much anyone could do to work with her or help her improve something that is so commonplace that it seeks no further expression or seeks no further end.

Appellee presented no testimony by art instructors, art critics or art experts concerning her work. It was appellee's position below that since she had won awards in art exhibits, sold some of her work, and received good grades in undergraduate school, this was enough to require her admittance as a candidate for a Master of Fine Arts degree. As explained by members of the Art Department, there is not necessarily any correlation between undergraduate grades and the ability to complete the requirements for a Master of Fine Arts degree. Nor were the members of the faculty committee impressed with the fact that she had won prizes in art exhibits or sold her work. All members of the faculty committee stated that they based their decision on the slides that were presented to them which is a proper basis for their decision.

This case represents a prime example of when a court should not interfere in the academic program of a university. It was incumbent upon appellee to show that her rejection was in bad faith, or arbitrary, capricious or unreasonable. The court may not substitute its own opinion as to the merits of appellee's work for that of the members of the faculty committee who were selected to make a determination as to the quality of her work.

Although lawyers and the military may be fascinated by check lists, we do not believe that the lack of a check list or list of objective standards to be used by the members of the faculty committee renders their decision arbitrary, capricious or unreasonable. As was stated by Professor Littler, the chairman of the faculty committee who has been involved with check lists in the past and found them of no help:

> "To write them [standards] down as a list would be a distortion of our use of them, and also it would be a straight jacket for the action or any action had by the committee."

He stated that the standards would not clarify the committee's thinking since, "In a certain way the action of the committee is creative, a creative act. We go into the process of bringing as much of our own background and energy and understanding and perception as we possibly can. I think the other would be a poor substitute."

Indeed, the adoption of a set of "objective standards," even assuming that an art committee could agree as to what those standards would be, might lead to the rejection of a budding Monet or Kadinsky. Art cannot be created by any set of rules. In fact, one need only look at the works of Picasso to see that it is often the departure from the so-called rules that has created great art.

The method used by the university to select candidates, that is, the screening of applications as submitted and not in one large group, is not relevant in this case since it is clear that Mrs. Wilson would not have been selected as a candidate no matter when her application was processed. In any event, we find the method used by the appellants to have been rational and valid.

The judgment of the trial court is reversed and the trial court is ordered to enter judgment in favor of appellants and against appellee.

Steinberg v. Chicago Medical School
372 N.E. 2d 634 (1977)

DOOLEY, Justice:

Robert Steinberg received a catalog, applied for admission to defendant, Chicago Medical School, for the academic year 1974–75, and paid a $15 fee. He was rejected. Steinberg filed a class action against the school claiming it had failed to evaluate his application and those of other applicants according to the academic criteria in the school's bulletin. According to the complaint, defendant used nonacademic criteria, primarily the ability of the applicant or his family to pledge or make payment of large sums of money to the school.

The 1974–75 bulletin distributed to prospective students contained this statement of standards by which applicants were to be evaluated:

> "Students are selected on the basis of scholarship, character, and motivation without regard to race, creed, or sex. The student's potential for the study and practice of medicine will be evaluated on the basis of academic achievement, Medical College Admission Test results, personal appraisals by a pre-professional advisory committee or individual instructors, and the personal interview, if requested by the Committee on Admissions."

Count I of the complaint alleged breach of contract; count II was predicated on the Consumer Fraud and Deceptive Business Practices Act and the Uniform Deceptive Trade Practices Act; count III charged fraud; and count IV alleged unjust enrichment. This was sought to be brought as a class action. Accordingly, there were the customary allegations common to such an action.

The trial court dismissed the complaint for failure to state a cause of action. The appellate court reversed as to count I, the contract action, and permitted it to be maintained as a limited class action. It affirmed the circuit court's dismissal of the remaining counts II, III, and IV.

That the Consumer Fraud and Deceptive Business Practices Act is inapplicable is patent from the title of the Act: "An Act to protect consumers and borrowers and businessmen against fraud, unfair methods of competition and unfair or deceptive acts or practices in the conduct of any trade or commerce * * * ." A "consumer" is "any person who purchases or contracts for the purchase of merchandise * * * ." Obviously, plaintiff and those whom he represents were not consumers. The Uniform Deceptive Trade Practices Act is limited to goods or services. It is not relevant.

In equity a constructive trust may be imposed to redress unjust enrichment where there is either actual fraud or implied fraud resulting from a fiduciary relationship. Here there is no fiduciary relationship to support a constructive trust and the fraud charges are subsumed in count III. Accordingly, we affirm the appellate court's dismissal of counts II and IV.

The real questions on this appeal are: Can the facts support a charge of breach of contract? Is an action predicated on fraud maintainable? Is this a proper class-action situation?

On motion to dismiss we accept as true all well-pleaded facts. Count I alleges Steinberg and members of the class to which he belongs applied to defendant and paid the $15 fee, and that defendant, through its brochure, described the criteria to be employed in evaluating applications, but failed to appraise the applications on the stated criteria. On the contrary, defendant evaluated such applications according to monetary contributions made on behalf of those seeking admission.

A contract, by ancient definition, is "an agreement between competent parties, upon a consideration sufficient in law, to do or not to do a particular thing."

An offer, an acceptance, and consideration are basic ingredients of a contract. Steinberg alleges that he and others similarly situated received a brochure describing the criteria that defendant would employ in evaluating applications. He urges that such constituted an invitation for an offer to apply, that the filing of the applications constituted an offer to have their credentials appraised under the terms described by defendant, and that defendant's voluntary reception of the application and fee constituted an acceptance, the final act necessary for the creation of a binding contract.

This situation is similar to that wherein a merchant advertises goods for sale at a fixed price. While the advertisement itself is not an offer to contract, it constitutes an invitation to deal on the terms described in the advertisement. Although in some cases the advertisement itself may be an offer, usually it constitutes only an invitation to deal on the advertised terms. Only when the merchant takes the money is there an acceptance of the offer to purchase.

Here the description in the brochure containing the terms under which an application will be appraised constituted an invitation for an offer. The tender of the application, as well as the payment of the fee pursuant to the terms of the brochure, was an offer to apply. Acceptance of the application and fee constituted acceptance of an offer to apply under the criteria defendant had established.

Consideration is a basic element for the existence of a contract. Any act or promise which is of benefit to one party or disadvantage to the other is a sufficient consideration to support a contract. The application fee was sufficient consideration to support the agreement between the applicant and the school.

Defendant contends that a further requisite for contract formation is a meeting of the minds. But a subjective understanding is not requisite. It suffices that the conduct of the contracting parties indicates an agreement to the terms of the alleged contract. Williston, in his work on contracts, states:

> "In the formation of contracts it was long ago settled that secret intent was immaterial, only overt acts being considered in the determination of such mutual assent as that branch of the law requires. During the first half of the nineteenth century there were many expressions which seemed to indicate the contrary. Chief of these was the familiar cliche, still reechoing in judicial dicta, that a contract requires the 'meeting of the minds' of the parties."

Here it would appear from the complaint that the conduct of the parties amounted to an agreement that the application would be evaluated according to the criteria described by defendant in its literature.

Defendant urges *People ex rel. Tinkoff v. Northwestern University* controls. There the plaintiff alleged that since he met the stated requirement for admission, it was the obligation of the university to accept him. Plaintiff was first rejected because he was 14 years of age. He then filed a *mandamus* action, and subsequently the university denied his admission, apparently because of the court action. That decision turned on the fact that Northwestern University, a private educational institution, had reserved in its charter the right to reject any applicant for any reason it saw fit. Here, of course, defendant had no such provision in its charter or in the brochure in question. But, more important, Steinberg does not seek to compel the school to admit him. The substance of his action is that under the circumstances it was defendant's duty to appraise his application and those of the others on the terms defendant represented.

A medical school is an institution so important to life in society that its conduct cannot be justified by merely stating that one who does not wish to deal with it on its own terms may simply refrain from dealing with it at all.

As the appellate court noted in a recent case in which this defendant was a party:

> "A contract between a private institution and a student confers duties upon both parties which cannot be arbitrarily disregarded and may be judicially enforced.

Here our scope of review is exceedingly narrow. Does the complaint set forth facts which could mean that defendant contracted, under the circumstances, to appraise applicants and their applications according to the criteria it described? This is the sole inquiry on this motion to dismiss. We believe the allegations suffice and affirm the appellate court in holding count I stated a cause of action.

Count III alleges that, with intent to deceive and defraud plaintiffs, defendant stated in its catalogs it would use certain criteria to evaluate applications; that these representations were false in that applicants were selected primarily for monetary considerations; that plaintiffs relied on said representations and were each thereby induced to submit their applications and pay $15 to their damage.

These allegations support a cause of action for fraud. Misrepresentation of an existing material fact coupled with scienter, deception, and injury are more than adequate. *Roth* succinctly stated when a misrepresentation may constitute fraud:

> "A misrepresentation in order to constitute a fraud must consist of a statement of material fact, false and known to be so by the party making it, made to induce the other party to act, and, in acting, the other party must rely on the truth of the statement."

Plaintiff's allegations meet the test of common law fraud.

Not to be ignored is defendant's *modus operandi* as described in *DeMarco v. University of Health Sciences*:

> "An analysis of those exhibits shows that in 1970, at least 64 out of 83 entering students had pledges made in their behalves totalling $1,927,900. The pledges varied in amounts from $1400 to $100,000 and averaged $30,123. In 1971, at least 55 out of 83 students had pledges made in their behalves totalling $1,893,000. The pledges varied in amounts from $3000 to $100,000 and averaged $34,418. In 1972, at least 73 out of an entering class of 92 had contributions made in their behalves totalling $3,111,000. The pledges varied in amounts from $20,000 to $100,000 and averaged $42,603. In 1973, at least

78 out of 91 students had contributions made in their behalves totalling $3,749,000. The pledges varied in amounts from $10,000 to $100,000 and averaged $48,064. In addition, there were amounts pledged and partial payments made for students who did not enter or dropped out shortly after entering."

It is immaterial here that the misrepresentation consisted of a statement in the medical school catalog, referring to future conduct, that "the student's potential for the study and practice of medicine will be evaluated on the basis of academic achievement, Medical College Admission Test results, personal appraisals by a pre-professional advisory committee or individual instructors, and the personal interview, if requested by the Committee on Admissions." We concede the general rule denies recovery for fraud based on a false representation of intention or future conduct, but there is a recognized exception where the false promise or representation of future conduct is alleged to be the scheme employed to accomplish the fraud. Such is the situation here.

Here an action for fraud is consistent with the recognition of a contract action. The law creates obligations "on the ground that they are dictated by reason and justice." The right to recover on a "constructive contract," although phrased in contract terminology, is not based on an agreement between parties but is an obligation created by law. "Such contracts are contracts merely in the sense that [they] * * * are created and governed by the principles of equity." So here the facts of this situation mandate that equity imply an obligation by the defendant. We note this since the circumstances before us justify a contract action, as well as a fraud action, or, in the event no contract in fact can be proven, an action on an implied-in-law obligation of the defendant.

What about the propriety of a class action here? A class action is a potent procedural vehicle. Under its terms claims by multiple persons can be decided without the necessity of the appearance of each. A vindication of the rights of numerous persons is possible in a single action when for many reasons individual actions would be impracticable.

* * *

The legislature recently enacted section 57.2 of the Civil Practice Act (Pub. Act 80–809), setting forth the prerequisites for the maintenance of class actions. It provides:

"Prerequisites for the Maintenance of a Class Action.

(a) An action may be maintained as a class action in any court of this State and a party may sue or be sued as a representative party of the class only if the court finds:

(1) The class is so numerous that joinder of all members is impracticable.

(2) There are questions of fact or law common to the class, which common questions predominate over any questions affecting only individual members.

(3) The representative parties will fairly and adequately protect the interest of the class.

(4) The class action is an appropriate method for the fair and efficient adjudication of the controversy."

Since this statute is procedural in nature, it is applicable to pending litigation. Accordingly, we shall measure this action in terms of the statute.

That the class here is so numerous that joinder of all parties would be impracticable is obvious if for no reason other than economics. More than that, multiple separate claims would be an imposition on all litigants as well as the courts.

The statute simplifies with this language, "[t]here are questions of fact or law common to the class, which common questions predominate over any questions affecting only individual members," what had been a problem under Illinois case law. A community of interest in both the subject matter and the remedy was the original requisite.

*   *   *

So long as there are questions of fact or law common to the class and these predominate over questions affecting only individual members of such class, the statutory requisite is met. It would be needless to consider the variations in our case law on this aspect. With the advent of the statute many of the prior decisions have become corpses.

It is, of course, well established that the elemental determination that some members of a class are not entitled to relief because of some particular factor will not bar the class action.

Another requisite of the statute concerns adequate protection of the interest of the class by the representative party. Absentee class members must be so represented that their rights will receive adequate protection. Here plaintiff's interests are not antithetical to those of other members of the class, but are the same. This certainly does not appear to be a collusive or friendly action. As far as we can determine, representation by the plaintiff will afford protection to other members of the class who must be afforded due process.

*   *   *

Who constitutes the class Steinberg represents? The appellate court limited the class to those who applied to the medical school in the same year as Steinberg on the basis that the complaint was predicated on the standards described in the 1974–75 catalog. However, the complaint makes allegations broad enough to state a cause of action for all who applied and paid a fee predicated on a brochure containing the alleged misrepresentations. We hold that each of these can be members of this class. The commencement of the class action suspends the applicable statute of limitations as to all asserted members of the class who would have been parties had the suit continued as a class action.

On remand the trial court should, by a preliminary hearing, determine the following: (a) the proper members of the class; (b) whether the plaintiff will be able to adequately represent the class so that there will be no denial of due process; (c) whether notice is required to other members of the class and the character of such notice; and (d) other such pretrial findings proper to class action litigation.

The appellate court was correct in affirming the dismissal of counts II and IV of plaintiff's complaint and in reversing the dismissal of count I of the complaint. It erred in affirming the dismissal of count III and abbreviating the class represented by plaintiff.

The judgment of the appellate court is affirmed in part and reversed in part, and the judgment of the circuit court of Cook County is affirmed in part and reversed in part. The cause is remanded to the circuit court with directions to proceed in a manner not inconsistent with this opinion.

University of California Regents v. Bakke
438 U.S. 265 (1978)

Mr. Justice POWELL announced the judgment of the Court.

This case presents a challenge to the special admissions program of the petitioner, the Medical School of the University of California at Davis, which is designed to assure the admission of a specified number of students from certain minority groups. The Superior Court of California sustained respondent's challenge, holding that petitioner's program violated the California Constitution, Title VI of the Civil Rights Act of 1964, 42 U.S.C. § 2000d et seq., and the Equal Protection Clause of the Fourteenth Amendment. The court enjoined petitioner from considering respondent's race or the race of any other applicant in making admissions decisions. It refused, however, to order respondent's admission to the Medical School, holding that he had not carried his burden of proving that he would have been admitted but for the constitutional and statutory violations. The Supreme Court of California affirmed those portions of the trial court's judgment declaring the special admissions program unlawful and enjoining petitioner from considering the race of any applicant. It modified that portion of the judgment denying respondent's requested injunction and directed the trial court to order his admission.

For the reasons stated in the following opinion, I believe that so much of the judgment of the California court as holds petitioner's special admissions program unlawful and directs that respondent be admitted to the Medical School must be affirmed. For the reasons expressed in a separate opinion, my Brothers The Chief Justice, Mr. Justice STEWART, Mr. Justice REHNQUIST, and Mr. Justice STEVENS concur in this judgment.

I also conclude for the reasons stated in the following opinion that the portion of the court's judgment enjoining petitioner from according any consideration to race in its admissions process must be reversed. For reasons expressed in separate opinions, my Brothers Mr. Justice BRENNAN, Mr. Justice WHITE, Mr. Justice MARSHALL, and Mr. Justice BLACKMUN concur in this judgment.

Affirmed in part and reversed in part.

I

The Medical School of the University of California at Davis opened in 1968 with an entering class of 50 students. In 1971, the size of the entering class was increased to 100 students, a level at which it remains. No admissions program for disadvantaged or minority students existed when the school opened, and the first class contained three Asians but no blacks, no Mexican-Americans, and no American Indians. Over the next two years, the faculty devised a special admissions program to increase the representation of "disadvantaged" students in each Medical School class. The special program consisted of a separate admissions system operating in coordination with the regular admissions process.

Under the regular admissions procedure, a candidate could submit his application to the Medical School beginning in July of the year preceding the academic year for which admission was sought. Because of the large number of applications, the admissions committee screened each one to select candidates for further consideration. Candidates whose overall undergraduate grade point averages fell below 2.5 on a scale of 4.0 were summarily rejected. About one out of six applicants was invited for a personal interview. Following the interviews, each candidate was rated on a scale of 1 to 100 by his interviewers and four other members of the admissions committee. The rating embraced the interviewers' summaries, the candidate's overall grade point average, grade point average in science courses, scores on the Medical College Admissions Test (MCAT), letters of recommendation, extracurricular activities, and other biographical data. The ratings were added together to arrive at each candidate's "benchmark" score. Since five committee members rated each candidate in 1973, a perfect score was 500; in 1974, six members rated each candidate, so that a perfect score was 600. The full committee then reviewed the file and scores of each applicant and made offers of admission on a "rolling" basis. The chairman was responsible for placing names on the waiting list. They were not placed in strict numerical order; instead, the chairman had discretion to include persons with "special skills."

The special admissions program operated with a separate committee, a majority of whom were members of minority groups. On the 1973 application form, candidates were asked to indicate whether they wished to be considered as "economically and/ or educationally disadvantaged" applicants; on the 1974 form the question was whether they wished to be considered as members of a "minority group," which the Medical School apparently viewed as "Blacks," "Chicanos," "Asians," and "American Indians." If these questions were answered affirmatively, the application was forwarded to the special admissions committee. No formal definition of "disadvantaged" was ever produced, but the chairman of the special committee screened each application to see whether it reflected economic or educational deprivation. Having passed this initial hurdle, the applications then were rated by the special committee in a fashion similar to that used by the general admissions committee, except that special candidates did not have to meet the 2.5 grade point average cutoff applied to regular applicants. About one-fifth of the total number of special applicants were invited for interviews in 1973 and 1974. Following each interview, the special committee assigned each special applicant a benchmark score. The special committee then presented its top choices to the general admissions committee. The latter did not rate or compare the special candidates against the general applicants, but could reject recommended special candidates for failure to meet course requirements or other specific deficiencies. The special committee continued to recommend special applicants until a number prescribed by faculty vote were admitted. While the overall class size was still 50, the prescribed number was 8; in 1973 and 1974, when the class size had doubled to 100, the prescribed number of special admissions also doubled, to 16.

From the year of the increase in class size—1971—through 1974, the special program resulted in the admission of 21 black students, 30 Mexican-Americans, and 12 Asians, for a total of 63 minority students. Over the same period, the regular admissions program produced 1 black, 6 Mexican-Americans, and 37 Asians, for a total of 44 minority students. Although disadvantaged whites applied to the special program in large numbers, none received an offer of admission through that process. Indeed, in 1974, at least, the special committee explicitly considered only "disadvantaged" special applicants who were members of one of the designated minority groups.

Allan Bakke is a white male who applied to the Davis Medical School in both 1973 and 1974. In both years Bakke's application was considered under the general admissions program, and he received an interview. His 1973 interview was with Dr. Theodore C. West, who considered Bakke "a very desirable applicant to [the] medical school." Despite a strong benchmark score of 468 out of 500, Bakke was rejected. His application had come late in the year, and no applicants in the general admissions process with scores below 470 were accepted after Bakke's application was completed. There were four special admissions slots unfilled at that time, however, for which Bakke was not considered. After his 1973 rejection, Bakke wrote to Dr. George H. Lowrey, Associate Dean and Chairman of the Admissions Committee, protesting that the special admissions program operated as a racial and ethnic quota.

Bakke's 1974 application was completed early in the year. His student interviewer gave him an overall rating of 94, finding him "friendly, well tempered, conscientious and delightful to speak with." His faculty interviewer was, by coincidence, the same Dr. Lowrey to whom he had written in protest of the special admissions program. Dr. Lowrey found Bakke "rather limited in his approach" to the problems of the medical profession and found disturbing Bakke's "very definite opinions which were based more on his personal viewpoints than upon a study of the total problem." Dr. Lowrey gave Bakke the lowest of his six ratings, an 86; his total was 549 out of 600. Again, Bakke's application was rejected. In neither year did the chairman of the admissions committee, Dr. Lowrey, exercise his discretion to place Bakke on the waiting list. In both years, applicants were admitted under the special program with grade point averages, MCAT scores, and benchmark scores significantly lower than Bakke's.

After the second rejection, Bakke filed the instant suit in the Superior Court of California. He sought mandatory, injunctive, and declaratory relief compelling his admission to the Medical School. He alleged that the Medical School's special admissions program operated to exclude him from the school on the basis of his race, in violation of his rights under the Equal Protection Clause of the Fourteenth Amendment, Art. I, § 21, of the California Constitution, and § 601 of Title VI of the Civil Rights Act of 1964. The University cross-complained for a declaration that its special admissions program was lawful. The trial court found that the special program operated as a racial quota, because minority applicants in the special program were rated only against one another, and 16 places in the class of 100 were reserved for them. Declaring that the University could not take race into account in making admissions decisions, the trial court held the challenged program violative of the Federal Constitution, the State Constitution, and Title VI. The court refused to order Bakke's admission, however, holding that he had failed to carry his burden of proving that he would have been admitted but for the existence of the special program.

Bakke appealed from the portion of the trial court judgment denying him admission, and the University appealed from the decision that its special admissions program was unlawful and the order enjoining it from considering race in the processing of applications. The Supreme Court of California transferred the case directly from the trial court, "because of the importance of the issues involved." The California court accepted the findings of the trial court with respect to the University's program. Because the special admissions program involved a racial classification, the Supreme Court held itself bound to apply strict scrutiny. It then turned to the goals the University presented as justifying the special program. Although the court agreed that the goals of integrating the medical profession and increasing the number of physicians willing to serve members of minority groups were compelling state interests, it concluded that the special admissions program was not the least intrusive means of achieving those goals. Without passing on the state constitutional or the federal statutory grounds cited in the trial court's judgment, the California court held that the Equal Protection Clause of the Fourteenth Amendment required that "no applicant may be rejected because of his race, in favor of another who is less qualified, as measured by standards applied without regard to race."

Turning to Bakke's appeal, the court ruled that since Bakke had established that the University had discriminated against him on the basis of his race, the burden of proof shifted to the University to demonstrate that he would not have been admitted even in the absence of the special admissions program. The court analogized Bakke's situation to that of a plaintiff under Title VII of the Civil Rights Act of 1964. On this basis, the court initially ordered a remand for the purpose of determining whether, under the newly allocated burden of proof, Bakke would have been admitted to either the 1973 or the 1974 entering class in the absence of the special admissions program. In its petition for rehearing below, however, the University conceded its inability to carry that burden. The California court thereupon amended its opinion to direct that the trial court enter judgment ordering Bakke's admission to the Medical School. That order was stayed pending review in this Court.

* * *

The question of respondent's right to bring an action under Title VI was neither argued nor decided in either of the courts below, and this Court has been hesitant to review questions not addressed below. We therefore do not address this difficult issue. Similarly, we need not pass upon petitioner's claim that private plaintiffs under Title VI must exhaust administrative remedies. We assume, only for the purposes of this case, that respondent has a right of action under Title VI.

B

The language of § 601, 78 Stat. 252, like that of the Equal Protection Clause, is majestic in its sweep:

> "No person in the United States shall, on the ground of race, color, or national origin, be excluded from participation in, be denied the benefits of, or be subjected to discrimination under any program or activity receiving Federal financial assistance."

The concept of "discrimination," like the phrase "equal protection of the laws," is susceptible of varying interpretations, for as Mr. Justice Holmes declared, "[a] word is not a crystal, transparent and unchanged, it is the skin of a living thought and may vary greatly in color and content according to the circumstances and the time in which it is used." We must, therefore, seek whatever aid is available in determining the precise meaning of the statute before us. Examination of the voluminous legislative history of Title VI reveals a congressional intent to halt federal funding of entities that violate a prohibition of racial discrimination similar to that of the Constitution.

Although isolated statements of various legislators, taken out of context, can be marshaled in support of the proposition that § 601 enacted a purely color-blind scheme, without regard to the reach of the Equal Protection Clause, these comments must be read against the background of both the problem that Congress was addressing and the broader view of the statute that emerges from a full examination of the legislative debates.

The problem confronting Congress was discrimination against Negro citizens at the hands of recipients of federal moneys. Indeed, the color blindness pronouncements generally occur in the midst of extended remarks dealing with the evils of segregation in federally funded programs. Over and over again, proponents of the bill detailed the plight of Negroes seeking equal treatment in such programs. There simply was no reason for Congress to consider the validity of hypothetical preferences that might be accorded minority citizens; the legislators were dealing with the real and pressing problem of how to guarantee those citizens equal treatment.

In addressing that problem, supporters of Title VI repeatedly declared that the bill enacted constitutional principles.

* * *

In view of the clear legislative intent, Title VI must be held to proscribe only those racial classifications that would violate the Equal Protection Clause or the Fifth Amendment.

III

A

Petitioner does not deny that decisions based on race or ethnic origin by faculties and administrations of state universities are reviewable under the Fourteenth Amendment. For his part, respondent does not argue that all racial or ethnic classifications are *per se* invalid. The parties do disagree as to the level of judicial scrutiny to be applied to the special admissions program. Petitioner argues that the court below erred in applying strict scrutiny, as this inexact term has been applied in our cases. That level of review, petitioner asserts, should be reserved for classifications that disadvantage "discrete and insular minorities." Respondent, on the other hand, contends that the California court correctly rejected the notion that the degree of judicial scrutiny accorded a particular racial or ethnic classification hinges upon membership in a discrete and insular minority and duly recognized that the "rights established [by the Fourteenth Amendment] are personal rights."

En route to this crucial battle over the scope of judicial review, the parties fight a sharp preliminary action over the proper characterization of the special admissions program. Petitioner prefers to view it as establishing a "goal" of minority representation in the Medical School. Respondent, echoing the courts below, labels it a racial quota.

This semantic distinction is beside the point: The special admissions program is undeniably a classification based on race and ethnic background. To the extent that there existed a pool of at least minimally qualified minority applicants to fill the 16 special admissions seats, white applicants could compete only for 84 seats in the entering class, rather than the 100 open to minority applicants. Whether this limitation is described as a quota or a goal, it is a line drawn on the basis of race and ethnic status.

The guarantees of the Fourteenth Amendment extend to all persons. Its language is explicit: "No State shall...deny to any person within its jurisdiction the equal protection of the laws." It is settled beyond question that the "rights created by the first section of the Fourteenth Amendment are, by its terms, guaranteed to the individual. The rights established are personal rights." The guarantee of equal protection cannot mean one thing when applied to one individual and something else when applied to a person of another color. If both are not accorded the same protection, then it is not equal.

Nevertheless, petitioner argues that the court below erred in applying strict scrutiny to the special admissions program because white males, such as respondent, are not a "discrete and insular minority" requiring extraordinary protection from the majoritarian political process. This rationale, however, has never been invoked in our decisions as a prerequisite to subjecting racial or ethnic distinctions to strict scrutiny. Nor has this Court held that discreteness and insularity constitute necessary preconditions to a holding that a particular classification is invidious. These characteristics may be relevant in deciding whether or not to add new types of classifications to the list of "suspect" categories or whether a particular classification survives close examination. Racial and ethnic classifications, however, are subject to stringent examination without regard to these additional characteristics. We declared as much in the first cases explicitly to recognize racial distinctions as suspect:

> "Distinctions between citizens solely because of their ancestry are by their very nature odious to a free people whose institutions are founded upon the doctrine of equality."

> "[A]ll legal restrictions which curtail the civil rights of a single racial group are immediately suspect. That is not to say that all such restrictions are unconstitutional. It is to say that courts must subject them to the most rigid scrutiny."

The Court has never questioned the validity of those pronouncements. Racial and ethnic distinctions of any sort are inherently suspect and thus call for the most exacting judicial examination.

B

*   *   *

Because the landmark decisions in this area arose in response to the continued exclusion of Negroes from the mainstream of American society, they could be characterized as involving discrimination by the "majority" white race against the Negro minority. But they need not be read as depending upon that characterization for their results. It suffices to say that "[o]ver the years, this Court has consistently repudiated '[d]istinctions between citizens solely because of their ancestry' as being 'odious to a free people whose institutions are founded upon the doctrine of equality.' "

Petitioner urges us to adopt for the first time a more restrictive view of the Equal Protection Clause and hold that discrimination against members of the white "majority" cannot be suspect if its purpose can be characterized as "benign." The clock of our liberties, however, cannot be turned back to 1868. It is far too late to argue that the guarantee of equal protection to *all* persons permits the recognition of special wards entitled to a degree of protection greater than that accorded others. "The

Fourteenth Amendment is not directed solely against discrimination due to a 'two-class theory'—that is, based upon differences between 'white' and Negro.''

Once the artificial line of a "two-class theory" of the Fourteenth Amendment is put aside, the difficulties entailed in varying the level of judicial review according to a perceived "preferred" status of a particular racial or ethnic minority are intractable. The concepts of "majority" and "minority" necessarily reflect temporary arrangements and political judgments. As observed above, the white "majority" itself is composed of various minority groups, most of which can lay claim to a history of prior discrimination at the hands of the State and private individuals. Not all of these groups can receive preferential treatment and corresponding judicial tolerance of distinctions drawn in terms of race and nationality, for then the only "majority" left would be a new minority of white Anglo-Saxon Protestants. There is no principled basis for deciding which groups would merit "heightened judicial solicitude" and which would not.[36]

* * *

If it is the individual who is entitled to judicial protection against classifications based upon his racial or ethnic background because such distinctions impinge upon personal rights, rather than the individual only because of his membership in a particular group, then constitutional standards may be applied consistently. Political judgments regarding the necessity for the particular classification may be weighed in the constitutional balance, but the standard of justification will remain constant. This is as it should be, since those political judgments are the product of rough compromise struck by contending groups within the democratic process. When they touch upon an individual's race or ethnic background, he is entitled to a judicial determination that the burden he is asked to bear on that basis is precisely tailored to serve a compelling governmental interest. The Constitution guarantees that right to every person regardless of his background.

C

Petitioner contends that on several occasions this Court has approved preferential classifications without applying the most exacting scrutiny. Most of the cases upon which petitioner relies are drawn from three areas: school desegregation, employment discrimination, and sex discrimination. Each of the cases cited presented a situation materially different from the facts of this case.

* * *

We have held that in "order to justify the use of a suspect classification, a State must show that its purpose or interest is both constitutionally permissible and substantial, and that its use of the classification is 'necessary . . . to the accomplishment' of its purpose or the safeguarding of its interest." The special admissions program purports to serve the purposes of: (i) "reducing the historic deficit of traditionally disfavored minorities in medical schools and in the medical profession"; (ii) countering the effects of societal discrimination; (iii) increasing the number of physicians who will practice in communities currently underserved; and (iv) obtaining the educational

---

36. As I am in agreement with the view that race may be taken into account as a factor in an admissions program, I agree with my Brothers BRENNAN, WHITE, MARSHALL, and BLACKMUN that the portion of the judgment that would proscribe all consideration of race must be reversed.

benefits that flow from an ethnically diverse student body. It is necessary to decide which, if any, of these purposes is substantial enough to support the use of a suspect classification.

If petitioner's purpose is to assure within its student body some specified percentage of a particular group merely because of its race or ethnic origin, such a preferential purpose must be rejected not as insubstantial but as facially invalid. Preferring members of any one group for no reason other than race or ethnic origin is discrimination for its own sake. This the Constitution forbids.

The State certainly has a legitimate and substantial interest in ameliorating, or eliminating where feasible, the disabling effects of identified discrimination. The line of school desegregation cases, commencing with *Brown*, attests to the importance of this state goal and the commitment of the judiciary to affirm all lawful means toward its attainment. In the school cases, the States were required by court order to redress the wrongs worked by specific instances of racial discrimination. That goal was far more focused than the remedying of the effects of "societal discrimination," an amorphous concept of injury that may be ageless in its reach into the past.

We have never approved a classification that aids persons perceived as members of relatively victimized groups at the expense of other innocent individuals in the absence of judicial, legislative, or administrative findings of constitutional or statutory violations. After such findings have been made, the governmental interest in preferring members of the injured groups at the expense of others is substantial, since the legal rights of the victims must be vindicated. In such a case, the extent of the injury and the consequent remedy will have been judicially, legislatively, or administratively defined. Also, the remedial action usually remains subject to continuing oversight to assure that it will work the least harm possible to other innocent persons competing for the benefit. Without such findings of constitutional or statutory violations, it cannot be said that the government has any greater interest in helping one individual than in refraining from harming another. Thus, the government has no compelling justification for inflicting such harm.

Petitioner does not purport to have made, and is in no position to make, such findings. Its broad mission is education, not the formulation of any legislative policy or the adjudication of particular claims of illegality. For reasons similar to those stated in Part III of this opinion, isolated segments of our vast governmental structures are not competent to make those decisions, at least in the absence of legislative mandates and legislatively determined criteria. Before relying upon these sorts of findings in establishing a racial classification, a governmental body must have the authority and capability to establish, in the record, that the classification is responsive to identified discrimination. Lacking this capability, petitioner has not carried its burden of justification on this issue.

Hence, the purpose of helping certain groups whom the faculty of the Davis Medical School perceived as victims of "societal discrimination" does not justify a classification that imposes disadvantages upon persons like respondent, who bear no responsibility for whatever harm the beneficiaries of the special admissions program are thought to have suffered. To hold otherwise would be to convert a remedy heretofore reserved for violations of legal rights into a privilege that all institutions throughout the Nation could grant at their pleasure to whatever groups are perceived as victims of societal discrimination. That is a step we have never approved.

* * *

Petitioner simply has not carried its burden of demonstrating that it must prefer members of particular ethnic groups over all other individuals in order to promote better health-care delivery to deprived citizens. Indeed, petitioner has not shown that its preferential classification is likely to have any significant effect on the problem.

D

The fourth goal asserted by petitioner is the attainment of a diverse student body. This clearly is a constitutionally permissible goal for an institution of higher education. Academic freedom, though not a specifically enumerated constitutional right, long has been viewed as a special concern of the First Amendment. The freedom of a university to make its own judgments as to education includes the selection of its student body.

* * *

The atmosphere of "speculation, experiment and creation"—so essential to the quality of higher education—is widely believed to be promoted by a diverse student body. As the Court noted in *Keyishian*, it is not too much to say that the "nation's future depends upon leaders trained through wide exposure" to the ideas and mores of students as diverse as this Nation of many peoples.

Thus, in arguing that its universities must be accorded the right to select those students who will contribute the most to the "robust exchange of ideas," petitioner invokes a countervailing constitutional interest, that of the First Amendment. In this light, petitioner must be viewed as seeking to achieve a goal that is of paramount importance in the fulfillment of its mission.

It may be argued that there is greater force to these views at the undergraduate level than in a medical school where the training is centered primarily on professional competency. But even at the graduate level, our tradition and experience lend support to the view that the contribution of diversity is substantial. In *Sweatt v. Painter*, the Court made a similar point with specific reference to legal education:

> "The law school, the proving ground for legal learning and practice, cannot be effective in isolation from the individuals and institutions with which the law interacts. Few students and no one who has practiced law would choose to study in an academic vacuum, removed from the interplay of ideas and the exchange of views with which the law is concerned."

Physicians serve a heterogeneous population. An otherwise qualified medical student with a particular background—whether it be ethnic, geographic, culturally advantaged or disadvantaged—may bring to a professional school of medicine experiences, outlooks, and ideas that enrich the training of its student body and better equip its graduates to render with understanding their vital service to humanity.

Ethnic diversity, however, is only one element in a range of factors a university properly may consider in attaining the goal of a heterogeneous student body. Although a university must have wide discretion in making the sensitive judgments as to who should be admitted, constitutional limitations protecting individual rights may not be disregarded. Respondent urges—and the courts below have held—that petitioner's dual admissions program is a racial classification that impermissibly infringes his rights under the Fourteenth Amendment. As the interest of diversity is compelling in the context of a university's admissions program, the question remains whether the program's racial classification is necessary to promote this interest.

V

A

* * *

[R]ace or ethnic background may be deemed a "plus" in a particular applicant's file, yet it does not insulate the individual from comparison with all other candidates for the available seats. The file of a particular black applicant may be examined for his potential contribution to diversity without the factor of race being decisive when compared, for example, with that of an applicant identified as an Italian-American if the latter is thought to exhibit qualities more likely to promote beneficial educational pluralism. Such qualities could include exceptional personal talents, unique work or service experience, leadership potential, maturity, demonstrated compassion, a history of overcoming disadvantage, ability to communicate with the poor, or other qualifications deemed important. In short, an admissions program operated in this way is flexible enough to consider all pertinent elements of diversity in light of the particular qualifications of each applicant, and to place them on the same footing for consideration, although not necessarily according them the same weight. Indeed, the weight attributed to a particular quality may vary from year to year depending upon the "mix" both of the student body and the applicants for the incoming class.

This kind of program treats each applicant as an individual in the admissions process. The applicant who loses out on the last available seat to another candidate receiving a "plus" on the basis of ethnic background will not have been foreclosed from all consideration for that seat simply because he was not the right color or had the wrong surname. It would mean only that his combined qualifications, which may have included similar nonobjective factors, did not outweigh those of the other applicant. His qualifications would have been weighed fairly and competitively, and he would have no basis to complain of unequal treatment under the Fourteenth Amendment.

It has been suggested that an admissions program which considers race only as one factor is simply a subtle and more sophisticated—but no less effective—means of according racial preference than the Davis program. A facial intent to discriminate, however, is evident in petitioner's preference program and not denied in this case. No such facial infirmity exists in an admissions program where race or ethnic background is simply one element—to be weighed fairly against other elements—in the selection process. "A boundary line," as Mr. Justice Frankfurter remarked in another connection, "is none the worse for being narrow." And a court would not assume that a university, professing to employ a facially nondiscriminatory admissions policy, would operate it as a cover for the functional equivalent of a quota system. In short, good faith would be presumed in the absence of a showing to the contrary in the manner permitted by our cases.

B

In summary, it is evident that the Davis special admissions program involves the use of an explicit racial classification never before countenanced by this Court. It tells applicants who are not Negro, Asian, or Chicano that they are totally excluded from a specific percentage of the seats in an entering class. No matter how strong their qualifications, quantitative and extracurricular, including their own potential for contribution to educational diversity, they are never afforded the chance to compete with applicants from the preferred groups for the special admissions seats. At the same time, the preferred applicants have the opportunity to compete for every seat in the class.

The fatal flaw in petitioner's preferential program is its disregard of individual rights as guaranteed by the Fourteenth Amendment. Such rights are not absolute. But when a State's distribution of benefits or imposition of burdens hinges on ancestry or the color of a person's skin, that individual is entitled to a demonstration that the challenged classification is necessary to promote a substantial state interest. Petitioner has failed to carry this burden. For this reason, that portion of the California court's judgment holding petitioner's special admissions program invalid under the Fourteenth Amendment must be affirmed.

C

In enjoining petitioner from ever considering the race of any applicant, however, the courts below failed to recognize that the State has a substantial interest that legitimately may be served by a properly devised admissions program involving the competitive consideration of race and ethnic origin. For this reason, so much of the California court's judgment as enjoins petitioner from any consideration of the race of any applicant must be reversed.

VI

With respect to respondent's entitlement to an injunction directing his admission to the Medical School, petitioner has conceded that it could not carry its burden of proving that, but for the existence of its unlawful special admissions program, respondent still would not have been admitted. Hence, respondent is entitled to the injunction, and that portion of the judgment must be affirmed.

Opinion of Mr. Justice BRENNAN, Mr. Justice WHITE, Mr. Justice MARSHALL, and Mr. Justice BLACKMUN, concurring in the judgment in part and dissenting in part.

The Court today, in reversing in part the judgment of the Supreme Court of California, affirms the constitutional power of Federal and State Governments to act affirmatively to achieve equal opportunity for all. The difficulty of the issue presented—whether government may use race-conscious programs to redress the continuing effects of past discrimination—and the mature consideration which each of our Brethren has brought to it have resulted in many opinions, no single one speaking for the Court. But this should not and must not mask the central meaning of today's opinions: Government may take race into account when it acts not to demean or insult any racial group, but to remedy disadvantages cast on minorities by past racial prejudice, at least when appropriate findings have been made by judicial, legislative, or administrative bodies with competence to act in this area.

The Chief Justice and our Brothers STEWART, REHNQUIST, and STEVENS, have concluded that Title VI of the Civil Rights Act of 1964 prohibits programs such as that at the Davis Medical School. On this statutory theory alone, they would hold that respondent Allan Bakke's rights have been violated and that he must, therefore, be admitted to the Medical School. Our Brother POWELL, reaching the Constitution, concludes that, although race may be taken into account in university admissions, the particular special admissions program used by petitioner, which resulted in the exclusion of respondent Bakke, was not shown to be necessary to achieve petitioner's stated goals. Accordingly, these Members of the Court form a majority of five affirming the judgment of the Supreme Court of California insofar as it holds that respondent Bakke "is entitled to an order that he be admitted to the University."

We agree with Mr. Justice POWELL that, as applied to the case before us, Title VI goes no further in prohibiting the use of race than the Equal Protection Clause of the Fourteenth Amendment itself. We also agree that the effect of the California Supreme Court's affirmance of the judgment of the Superior Court of California would be to prohibit the University from establishing in the future affirmative-action programs that take race into account. Since we conclude that the affirmative admissions program at the Davis Medical School is constitutional, we would reverse the judgment below in all respects. Mr. Justice POWELL agrees that some uses of race in university admissions are permissible and, therefore, he joins with us to make five votes reversing the judgment below insofar as it prohibits the University from establishing race-conscious programs in the future.

* * *

[W]e need not rest solely on our own conclusion that Davis had sound reason to believe that the effects of past discrimination were handicapping minority applicants to the Medical School, because the Department of Health, Education, and Welfare, the expert agency charged by Congress with promulgating regulations enforcing Title VI of the Civil Rights Act of 1964, has also reached the conclusion that race may be taken into account in situations where a failure to do so would limit participation by minorities in federally funded programs, and regulations promulgated by the Department expressly contemplate that appropriate race-conscious programs may be adopted by universities to remedy unequal access to university programs caused by their own or by past societal discrimination. It cannot be questioned that, in the absence of the special admissions program, access of minority students to the Medical School would be severely limited and, accordingly, race-conscious admissions would be deemed an appropriate response under these federal regulations. Moreover, the Department's regulatory policy is not one that has gone unnoticed by Congress. Indeed, although an amendment to an appropriations bill was introduced just last year that would have prevented the Secretary of Health, Education, and Welfare from mandating race-conscious programs in university admissions, proponents of this measure, significantly, did not question the validity of voluntary implementation of race-conscious admissions criteria. In these circumstances, the conclusion implicit in the regulations—that the lingering effects of past discrimination continue to make race-conscious remedial programs appropriate means for ensuring equal educational opportunity in universities—deserves considerable judicial deference.

C

The second prong of our test—whether the Davis program stigmatizes any discrete group or individual and whether race is reasonably used in light of the program's objectives—is clearly satisfied by the Davis program.

It is not even claimed that Davis' program in any way operates to stigmatize or single out any discrete and insular, or even any identifiable, nonminority group. Nor will harm comparable to that imposed upon racial minorities by exclusion or separation on grounds of race be the likely result of the program. It does not, for example, establish an exclusive preserve for minority students apart from and exclusive of whites. Rather, its purpose is to overcome the effects of segregation by bringing the races together. True, whites are excluded from participation in the special admissions program, but this fact only operates to reduce the number of whites to be admitted in the regular admissions program in order to permit admission of a reasonable percentage—less than their proportion of the California population—of otherwise under-represented qualified minority applicants.

Nor was Bakke in any sense stamped as inferior by the Medical School's rejection of him. Indeed, it is conceded by all that he satisfied those criteria regarded by the school as generally relevant to academic performance better than most of the minority members who were admitted. Moreover, there is absolutely no basis for concluding that Bakke's rejection as a result of Davis' use of racial preference will affect him throughout his life in the same way as the segregation of the Negro schoolchildren in *Brown I* would have affected them. Unlike discrimination against racial minorities, the use of racial preferences for remedial purposes does not inflict a pervasive injury upon individual whites in the sense that wherever they go or whatever they do there is a significant likelihood that they will be treated as second-class citizens because of their color. This distinction does not mean that the exclusion of a white resulting from the preferential use of race is not sufficiently serious to require justification; but it does mean that the injury inflicted by such a policy is not distinguishable from disadvantages caused by a wide range of government actions, none of which has ever been thought impermissible for that reason alone.

In addition, there is simply no evidence that the Davis program discriminates intentionally or unintentionally against any minority group which it purports to benefit. The program does not establish a quota in the invidious sense of a ceiling on the number of minority applicants to be admitted. Nor can the program reasonably be regarded as stigmatizing the program's beneficiaries or their race as inferior. The Davis program does not simply advance less qualified applicants; rather, it compensates applicants who it is uncontested are fully qualified to study medicine, for educational disadvantages which it was reasonable to conclude were a product of state-fostered discrimination. Once admitted, these students must satisfy the same degree requirements as regularly admitted students; they are taught by the same faculty in the same classes; and their performance is evaluated by the same standards by which regularly admitted students are judged. Under these circumstances, their performance and degrees must be regarded equally with the regularly admitted students with whom they compete for standing. Since minority graduates cannot justifiably be regarded as less well qualified than nonminority graduates by virtue of the special admissions program, there is no reasonable basis to conclude that minority graduates at schools using such programs would be stigmatized as inferior by the existence of such programs.

D

We disagree with the lower courts' conclusion that the Davis program's use of race was unreasonable in light of its objectives. First, as petitioner argues, there are no practical means by which it could achieve its ends in the foreseeable future without the use of race-conscious measures. With respect to any factor (such as poverty or family educational background) that may be used as a substitute for race as an indicator of past discrimination, whites greatly outnumber racial minorities simply because whites make up a far larger percentage of the total population and therefore far outnumber minorities in absolute terms at every socio-economic level. For example, of a class of recent medical school applicants from families with less than $10,000 income, at least 71% were white. Of all 1970 families headed by a person *not* a high school graduate which included related children under 18, 80% were white and 20% were racial minorities. Moreover, while race is positively correlated with differences in GPA and MCAT scores, economic disadvantage is not. Thus, it appears that economically disadvantaged whites do not score less well than economically advantaged whites, while economically advantaged blacks score less well than do disadvantaged whites. These statistics graphically illustrate that the University's purpose to integrate its classes by compensating for past discrimination could not be achieved by a general preference for the economically disadvantaged or the children of parents of limited education unless such groups were to make up the entire class.

Second, the Davis admissions program does not simply equate minority status with disadvantage. Rather, Davis considers on an individual basis each applicant's personal history to determine whether he or she has likely been disadvantaged by racial discrimination. The record makes clear that only minority applicants likely to have been isolated from the mainstream of American life are considered in the special program; other minority applicants are eligible only through the regular admissions program. True, the procedure by which disadvantage is detected is informal, but we have never insisted that educators conduct their affairs through adjudicatory proceedings, and such insistence here is misplaced. A case-by-case inquiry into the extent to which each individual applicant has been affected, either directly or indirectly, by racial discrimination, would seem to be, as a practical matter, virtually impossible, despite the fact that there are excellent reasons for concluding that such effects generally exist. When individual measurement is impossible or extremely impractical, there is nothing to prevent a State from using categorical means to achieve its ends, at least where the category is closely related to the goal. And it is clear from our cases that specific proof that a person has been victimized by discrimination is not a necessary predicate to offering him relief where the probability of victimization is great.

E

Finally, Davis' special admissions program cannot be said to violate the Constitution simply because it has set aside a predetermined number of places for qualified minority applicants rather than using minority status as a positive factor to be considered in evaluating the applications of disadvantaged minority applicants. For purposes of constitutional adjudication, there is no difference between the two approaches. In any admissions program which accords special consideration to disadvantaged racial minorities, a determination of the degree of preference to be given is unavoidable, and any given preference that results in the exclusion of a white candidate is no more or less constitutionally acceptable than a program such as that at Davis. Furthermore, the extent of the preference inevitably depends on how many minority applicants the particular school is seeking to admit in any particular year so long as the number of qualified minority applicants exceeds that number. There is no sensible, and certainly no constitutional, distinction between, for example, adding a set number of points to the admissions rating of disadvantaged minority applicants as an expression of the preference with the expectation that this will result in the admission of an approximately determined number of qualified minority applicants and setting a fixed number of places for such applicants as was done here.

The "Harvard" program, as those employing it readily concede, openly and successfully employs a racial criterion for the purpose of ensuring that some of the scarce places in institutions of higher education are allocated to disadvantaged minority students. That the Harvard approach does not also make public the extent of the preference and the precise workings of the system while the Davis program employs a specific, openly stated number, does not condemn the latter plan for purposes of Fourteenth Amendment adjudication. It may be that the Harvard plan is more acceptable to the public than is the Davis "quota." If it is, any State, including California, is free to adopt it in preference to a less acceptable alternative, just as it is generally free, as far as the Constitution is concerned, to abjure granting any racial preferences in its admissions program. But there is no basis for preferring a particular preference program simply because in achieving the same goals that the Davis Medical School is pursuing, it proceeds in a manner that is not immediately apparent to the public.

V

Accordingly, we would reverse the judgment of the Supreme Court of California holding the Medical School's special admissions program unconstitutional and directing respondent's admission, as well as that portion of the judgment enjoining the Medical School from according any consideration to race in the admissions process.

Mr. Justice STEVENS, with whom The Chief Justice, Mr. Justice STEWART, and Mr. Justice REHNQUIST join, concurring in the judgment in part and dissenting in part.

It is always important at the outset to focus precisely on the controversy before the Court.[1] It is particularly important to do so in this case because correct identification of the issues will determine whether it is necessary or appropriate to express any opinion about the legal status of any admissions program other than petitioner's.

* * *

In this case, we are presented with a constitutional question of undoubted and unusual importance. Since, however, a dispositive statutory claim was raised at the very inception of this case, and squarely decided in the portion of the trial court judgment affirmed by the California Supreme Court, it is our plain duty to confront it. Only if petitioner should prevail on the statutory issue would it be necessary to decide whether the University's admissions program violated the Equal Protection Clause of the Fourteenth Amendment.

III

Section 601 of the Civil Rights Act of 1964, 78 Stat. 252, 42 U.S.C. § 2000d, provides:

> "No person in the United States shall, on the ground of race, color, or national origin, be excluded from participation in, be denied the benefits of, or be subjected to discrimination under any program or activity receiving Federal financial assistance."

---

1. Four Members of the Court have undertaken to announce the legal and constitutional effect of this Court's judgment. See opinion of Justices BRENNAN, WHITE, MARSHALL, and BLACKMUN. It is hardly necessary to state that only a majority can speak for the Court or determine what is the "central meaning" of any judgment of the Court.

The University, through its special admissions policy, excluded Bakke from participation in its program of medical education because of his race. The University also acknowledges that it was, and still is, receiving federal financial assistance. The plain language of the statute therefore requires affirmance of the judgment below. A different result cannot be justified unless that language misstates the actual intent of the Congress that enacted the statute or the statute is not enforceable in a private action. Neither conclusion is warranted.

Title VI is an integral part of the far-reaching Civil Rights Act of 1964. No doubt, when this legislation was being debated, Congress was not directly concerned with the legality of "reverse discrimination" or "affirmative action" programs. Its attention was focused on the problem at hand, the "glaring . . . discrimination against Negroes which exists throughout our Nation," and, with respect to Title VI, the federal funding of segregated facilities. The genesis of the legislation, however, did not limit the breadth of the solution adopted. Just as Congress responded to the problem of employment discrimination by enacting a provision that protects all races, so, too, its answer to the problem of federal funding of segregated facilities stands as a broad prohibition against the exclusion of *any* individual from a federally funded program "on the ground of race." In the words of the House Report, Title VI stands for "the general principle that *no person* . . . be excluded from participation . . . on the ground of race, color, or national origin under any program or activity receiving Federal financial assistance." This same broad view of Title VI and § 601 was echoed throughout the congressional debate and was stressed by every one of the major spokesmen for the Act.

Petitioner contends, however, that exclusion of applicants on the basis of race does not violate Title VI if the exclusion carries with it no racial stigma. No such qualification or limitation of § 601's categorical prohibition of "exclusion" is justified by the statute or its history. The language of the entire section is perfectly clear; the words that follow "excluded from" do not modify or qualify the explicit outlawing of any exclusion on the stated grounds.

The legislative history reinforces this reading. The only suggestion that § 601 would allow exclusion of nonminority applicants came from opponents of the legislation and then only by way of a discussion of the meaning of the word "discrimination." The opponents feared that the term "discrimination" would be read as mandating racial quotas and "racially balanced" colleges and universities, and they pressed for a specific definition of the term in order to avoid this possibility. In response, the proponents of the legislation gave repeated assurances that the Act would be "color-blind" in its application. Senator Humphrey, the Senate floor manager for the Act, expressed this position as follows:

> "[T]he word 'discrimination' has been used in many a court case. What it really means in the bill is a distinction in treatment . . . given to different individuals because of their different race, religion or national origin. . . .

> "The answer to this question [what was meant by 'discrimination'] is that if race is not a factor, we do not have to worry about discrimination because of race. . . . The Internal Revenue Code does not provide that colored people do not have to pay taxes, or that they can pay their taxes 6 months later than everyone else."

> "[I]f we started to treat Americans as Americans, not as fat ones, thin ones, short ones, tall ones, brown ones, green ones, yellow ones, or white ones, but as Americans. If we did that we would not need to worry about discrimination."

In giving answers such as these, it seems clear that the proponents of Title VI assumed that the Constitution itself required a colorblind standard on the part of government, but that does not mean that the legislation only codifies an existing constitutional prohibition. The statutory prohibition against discrimination in federally funded projects contained in § 601 is more than a simple paraphrasing of what the Fifth or Fourteenth Amendment would require. The Act's proponents plainly considered Title VI consistent with their view of the Constitution and they sought to provide an effective weapon to implement that view. As a distillation of what the supporters of the Act believed the Constitution demanded of State and Federal Governments, § 601 has independent force, with language and emphasis in addition to that found in the Constitution.

As with other provisions of the Civil Rights Act, Congress' expression of its policy to end racial discrimination may independently proscribe conduct that the Constitution does not. However, we need not decide the congruence—or lack of congruence—of the controlling statute and the Constitution since the meaning of the Title VI ban on exclusion is crystal clear: Race cannot be the basis of excluding anyone from participation in a federally funded program.

In short, nothing in the legislative history justifies the conclusion that the broad language of § 601 should not be given its natural meaning.

* * *

The University's special admissions program violated Title VI of the Civil Rights Act of 1964 by excluding Bakke from the Medical School because of his race. It is therefore our duty to affirm the judgment ordering Bakke admitted to the University.

Accordingly, I concur in the Court's judgment insofar as it affirms the judgment of the Supreme Court of California. To the extent that it purports to do anything else, I respectfully dissent.

In the decade since *Bakke* was decided, it has been widely cited, both for its institutional right-to-choose holding, and for its striking-down-quotas result. Thus, the University of Michigan was allowed to dismiss Scott Ewing after he failed his exams, while the University of North Carolina's practice of setting aside places in the student government for black students was struck down, both citing *Bakke*. *Regents v. Ewing*, 474 U.S. 214 (1985); *Uzzell v. Friday*, 592 F. Supp. 1502 (1984). The literature on the *Bakke* case includes an extraordinary outpouring; among the most thoughtful include M. Clague, "The Affirmative Action Showdown of 1986: Implications for Higher Education," *Journal of College and University Law*, 14 (1987), 171–257; D. Days, "Minority Access to Higher Education in the Post-*Bakke* Era," *University of Colorado Law Review*, 55 (1984), 491–514; and "A Symposium," *California Law Review*, 67 (1979).

McDonald v. Hogness
598 P.2d 707 (1979)

WRIGHT, Justice.

Frederick N. McDonald, an unsuccessful applicant to the University of Washington (U.W.) School of Medicine, seeks admission to the school and damages. In the trial court he alleged that in denying his application for the 1976 entering class the school discriminated against him racially in violation of the Fourteenth Amendment, Title 6 of the 1964 Civil Rights Act and 42 U.S.C. § 1983. He also asserted that the school's admission process is arbitrary and capricious as was the treatment of his application. The trial judge dismissed the action after McDonald rested his case. McDonald appealed. The Court of Appeals, Division One, certified the case to this Court.

There are two major questions. First, does a state medical school's admission policy deny equal protection when it considers race as a factor in evaluating applications? Second, are the admission standards and procedures of the U.W. medical school arbitrary and capricious, and did their application to McDonald constitute arbitrary and capricious action?

For the 1976 year, 1,703 individuals applied, and 175 could be admitted. Of the 175 positions, 50 were earmarked for qualified residents of Alaska, Montana and Idaho under the Washington, Alaska, Montana and Idaho (WAMI) program, a system of regional medical education. Another two seats were earmarked for another special program. Selection factors were set forth in Medical School Admissions Requirements 1976–77, at page 304, as follows:

> Candidates are considered comparatively on the basis of academic performance, medical aptitude, motivation, maturity, and demonstrated humanitarian qualities. Extenuating background circumstances are considered as they relate to these selection factors.

Medical school personnel believe grade-point average (GPA) is the best measure of academic performance, while the Medical College Admissions Test (MCAT) score is the best measure of medical aptitude. Noncognitive criteria—motivation, maturity and demonstrated humanitarian qualities—are assessed from the applicant's file and the interview. McDonald, a Washington resident, had a cumulative undergraduate GPA of 3.58 out of 4.0 at the time he applied. He allegedly scored in the top five percent nationally on the MCAT. Though the trial court found McDonald qualified, it said his overall credentials were comparatively average.

The medical school's selection process was aptly summarized by the trial court:

> [T]he Committee on Admissions functions simultaneously at three levels. . . . Generally, the paper credentials of each applicant are reviewed independently by two members of the Admissions Committee. . . . [C]andidates considered potentially competitive . . . are invited to meet with an interview-conference committee. . . . Interview-conference committees evaluate the candidates' paper credentials and the candidates . . . and forward their evaluations to the Executive Committee [EXCOM] of the Committee on Admissions as a part of each . . . application. . . . [The EXCOM], which reviews applicants in the context of the total applicant pool, makes final determinations. . . .

The "first screen" score calculated upon receipt of an application is based on GPA and MCAT. It is the "bright-line" test for referral to the admissions committee and is considered later by admissions committee application readers and interview-conference committee members. Of the 1,703 applicants, 816 were referred to the reading committee. Interviews were granted to 546 applicants considered potentially competitive by reading committee analyses.

The interview-conference committee evaluates the candidate and his paper credentials in terms of published selection factors and identifies strengths and weaknesses. Before each interview-conference, each committee member reviews a copy of the candidate's application file, including letters of recommendation. Members are provided at each session with written guidelines and forms for comments. After the 20-30 minute interview the candidate is excused and each member independently places the applicant in one of four categories: (1) Unacceptable (specific deficiencies); (2) Possible (with comparative deficiencies academically and/or with regard to noncognitive features); (3) Acceptable (no deficiencies that are not balanced by other abilities, would be an average medical student); and (4) Outstanding (no apparent deficiencies, high probability of making an excellent physician and scholar). Following each interview-conference, committee staff calculate an average of the individual committee members' ratings based on a scale of 4 for "outstanding" downward through 1 for "unacceptable." The average is entered on the interview-conference summary.

The Skeletal Consideration List (SCL) serves as a rough agenda for EXCOM selection meetings. Placement is determined by one's total score—first screen score plus interview-conference score—grouped again in categories 4, 3, 2 and 1. Placement in category 2 or 1 nearly always leads to application denial. McDonald averaged 2.17 on the interview and was placed in category 2. His SCL position was at the number 237 level. When corrected for "ties" of 546 candidates interviewed for 175 slots, more than 300 placed higher than McDonald. However, every Black, Chicano and American Indian placing higher than McDonald on the SCL had a lower "first screen" score than he did. On April 30, 1976, EXCOM voted that all candidates not otherwise acted upon, which included McDonald, be considered noncompetitive for the 1976 class, and his application was denied.

The first question is whether using race as a positive factor in a state medical school's admission policy and process violates the equal protection clause of the Fourteenth Amendment and § 601, Title 6 of the 1964 Civil Rights Act (42 U.S.C. § 2000d). We conclude that it does not.

At the outset, we note that the evidence shows McDonald would not have been admitted into the E-76 class even absent the six minority persons accepted and without any consideration of race. This alone is justification for denying relief on equal protection grounds. However, because of the public importance of the issue and the likelihood of its recurrence, we will consider the broader question. Under the Supreme Court majority's analysis in *Regents of the University of California v. Bakke*, if the admission program does not violate the Fourteenth Amendment, it does not violate § 601 of Title 6. Accordingly, we shall emphasize the equal protection issue.

McDonald states that the U.W. medical school's practice is to admit all qualified minority persons because of race, but not all qualified nonminority individuals. Nonminority candidates are forced to compete with one another for the remaining seats, a "competitive disadvantage." The organizational focus of McDonald's criticism is the interview-conference committee, which purportedly puts the minority applicant with basic credentials (adequate MCAT and GPA) in a position on the SCL which "assures ultimate acceptance." Nonminority individuals with better "first screen" scores than some minority persons are denied "extra points" afforded minority applicants which would place them in favored SCL categories. "If Fred McDonald were Black, he would have gotten a higher score on the interview," appellant declares.

First, McDonald inaccurately describes the U.W. system. As respondent points out and as the record shows, not all qualified minority persons are admitted by the medical school. Seven minority persons ranked higher than McDonald on the 1976 Skeletal Consideration List and were not offered admission. Approximately 30 minority applicants in the interview-conference pool were not offered admission.

Furthermore, analysis of *Regents of the University of California v. Bakke*, shows the school of medicine's admission policies and procedures do not violate the equal protection clause of the Fourteenth Amendment. In *Bakke*, the Medical School of the University of California at Davis had two admission programs for the entering class of 100 students—the regular and special programs. A separate committee operated the special program, and selected only minority applicants to fill 16 positions reserved for them.

Bakke, a white male, applied to the Davis medical school in both 1973 and 1974. His application was considered by the general admission program and he was interviewed in both years. In 1973 he had a strong "benchmark" or overall score of 468 out of 500 but no applications with scores below 470 were accepted after Bakke's was completed. In both years, Bakke was denied admission while applicants were admitted under the special program with grade-point averages and MCAT scores significantly lower than Bakke's.

Bakke sued, seeking admission. He alleged the special admission program excluded him on a racial basis, in violation of his rights under the equal protection clause of the Fourteenth Amendment, the state privileges and immunities clause and § 601, Title 6 of the 1964 Civil Rights Act (42 U.S.C. § 2000d). The trial court held the program violative of both the constitutional and statutory provisions. Ignoring the state constitutional and statutory grounds, the California Supreme Court held the program violated the equal protection clause of the Fourteenth Amendment.

Five members of the United States Supreme Court voted to affirm the judgment of the California court ordering that respondent Bakke be admitted to Davis. Mr. Justice Powell based his decision to affirm on a finding the program violated the equal protection clause. Mr. Chief Justice Burger and Justices Stewart, Rehnquist and Stevens avoided the constitutional issue we confront here, holding instead that the university excluded Bakke from participation in its medical education program because of his race in violation of § 601, Title 6 of the 1964 Civil Rights Act (42 U.S.C. § 2000d). Four justices, Brennan, White, Marshall and Blackmun, dissenting, found the admission program valid on the constitutional ground.

Appellant argues that *Bakke* supports his position because here all qualified minority applicants are admitted while nonminority applicants are forced to compete among themselves as in *Bakke* for the remaining seats. But this admission program significantly differs from that at Davis. Appellant concedes that a quota or target number of minority applicant admissions is not involved. Further, there is not a separate admission system isolating minority persons from competition with nonminority persons as in *Bakke*; the university "gave no separate consideration or separate treatment" to Black, Chicano and American Indian applicants interviewed.

Separate consideration of minority applicants is discouraged by Mr. Justice Powell in his *Bakke* opinion. Under Mr. Justice Powell's opinion, the use of race is impermissible where one group is cut off solely on a racial basis from competition with others. On the other hand, Powell considers the use of race in admissions permissible if it is (1) designed to promote a compelling state interest, and (2) does not insulate an applicant from competition with remaining applicants.

In applying his test, Mr. Justice Powell characterizes the goal of the attainment of a diverse student body as compelling, stressing that the freedom to select a student body is an element of academic freedom, a special First Amendment concern. He explains that this diversity encompasses a broad array of qualifications and characteristics of which racial origin is a single element. He concludes from the experience of other university admission programs which take race into account in achieving diversity that the assignment of a fixed number of places to a minority group is not necessary.

In *dicta,* Mr. Justice Powell indicates that the Harvard admission plan, which like the plan here employs race as an admission factor, furthers a compelling state interest in diversity of the student body. Justices Brennan, White, Marshall and Blackmun also found the Harvard plan constitutional under their approach. Thus, a majority of the court find constitutional a plan without a quota or separate consideration for minority groups but where race may be a beneficial factor. The University of Washington School of Medicine's admission policies and procedures have the same redeeming characteristics.

McDonald argues there is no finding the classification here serves a compelling or substantial interest, or is necessary to realize such an interest. As respondent emphasizes, however, both in seeking diversity and in fulfilling the *DeFunis* mandate of "promoting integration in public education," the school of medicine has a compelling state interest permitting consideration of race. The Washington plan also fulfills the second element of Mr. Justice Powell's test. The system assures competition among applicants, thereby avoiding "denial of individualized consideration," the principal evil of the Davis plan.

In the second *Bakke* opinion which supports the U.W. medical school on this issue, Justices Brennan, White, Marshall and Blackmun pronounce the Davis program constitutionally valid. In their opinion, the state need only show the racial criteria (1) serves an important, articulated purpose, (2) does not stigmatize any discrete group, and (3) is reasonably used in light of the program's objectives. The Brennan group believes Davis' goal of admitting students disadvantaged by effects of past discrimination is sufficiently important. They reasonably read Mr. Justice Powell's opinion as agreeing this can constitute a compelling purpose.

In *DeFunis v. Odegaard,* this court rejected the argument that a state law school violated equal protection rights by denying plaintiff admission, yet accepting minority applicants with lower objective indicators than plaintiff. We stressed gross underrepresentation in law schools and the legal profession in finding an overriding interest in promoting integration in public education. We held the interest in eliminating racial imbalance within public legal education is compelling.

In the instant case the trial court determined the school had decided that in order to serve the educational needs of the school and the medical needs of the region, the school should seek greater representation of minorities "where there has been serious underrepresentation in the school and in the medical profession." Thus, the program furthers a compelling purpose of eliminating racial imbalance within public medical education.

Furthermore, the program here meets the additional elements of the Brennan group's test. The racial classification does not stigmatize any discrete group and is reasonably used in light of its objectives.

As noted by Mr. Justice Powell in *Bakke* and by this court in *DeFunis*, it is not enough that a state can show that its purpose is substantial or compelling. The use of race, a suspect classification, must be necessary to the accomplishment of its purpose. Though the Davis plan failed this element of Powell's test in *Bakke*, he indicated that a program under which a race is but one factor in achieving diversity would survive it. In addition, this court found necessary in *De Funis* a law school admissions policy which provided that minority applicants were compared to one another but not with nonminority applicants. Since the program here does not involve consideration of minority applicants apart from others, it appears to meet both the Powell *Bakke* and *DeFunis* standards of necessity.

The University of Washington School of Medicine's admissions program survives both the Powell and Brennan group tests. Moreover, a majority of the *Bakke* court stated race may be a factor in a state medical school's admissions program. Justice Powell joined the Brennan group in reversing the portion of the California court's judgment enjoining Davis from considering the race of any applicant. Thus, the *Bakke* majority followed the lead of this court which held in *DeFunis* that "consideration of race as a factor in the admissions policy of a state law school is not a per se violation of the equal protection clause of the Fourteenth Amendment."

Finally, McDonald asserts that Mr. Justice Stevens' opinion, in which Mr. Chief Justice Burger, and Justices Stewart and Rehnquist joined, would not even permit "racial discrimination" under the Harvard plan. By implication, in appellant's view the Stevens opinion condemns the U.W. medical school's program, which also uses race as one of many admission factors. As indicated earlier, however, a majority said the Harvard approach is constitutional. Stevens relied exclusively on the federal statute, avoiding the constitutional issue. The Stevens group held only that the Davis medical school excluded Bakke from its program of medical education in violation of § 601, Title 6 of the 1964 Civil Rights Act (42 U.S.C. § 2000d). We think the substantial differences between the Davis and U.W. programs render the Stevens holding inapplicable. Here, there was not a quota excluding McDonald from competing for a certain group of seats.

The University of Washington School of Medicine's admission policies and procedures survive the *Bakke* Powell and Brennan equal protection test, using race as an admission factor in a manner permitted under both *Bakke* and *DeFunis*. Accordingly, we hold that the use of race in these policies and procedures does not offend the equal protection clause of the Fourteenth Amendment of the United States Constitution.

McDonald's second major argument is that the medical school's admission policies and procedures are arbitrary and capricious and that their application to him constituted arbitrary and capricious action. As part of this argument, he urges that the delegation of authority to the Board of Regents to set admission requirements denies due process and violates equal protection rights under U.S. Const. Amend. 14 and Const. art. 1, § 12 because it contains no standards prescribing how that authority is to be exercised. Under *Barry and Barry, Inc. v. Department of Motor Vehicles*, and subsequent cases, the delegation survives our scrutiny.

In *Barry and Barry*, this court found a constitutional delegation in authority given to the director of the Department of Motor Vehicles to approve fee schedules and set maximum employment agency fees. Discarding the requirement of specific legislative standards, we held:

> [T]he delegation of legislative power is justified and constitutional and the requirements of the standards doctrine are satisfied, when it can be shown (1) that the legislature has provided standards or guidelines which define in general terms what is to be done and the instrumentality or administrative body which is to accomplish it, and (2) that *procedural safeguards exist to control arbitrary administrative action and any administrative abuse of discretionary power.*

Applying the first part of the test, the court concluded that RCW 19.31.070—which provides for the director's issuance of reasonable rules and regulations to enforce the Employment Agency Act—was clear in indicating the rules could be issued administratively, and specifically by the director of the Department of Motor Vehicles. As to the second element, we found adequate procedural safeguards in Administrative Procedure Act provisions providing that interested parties will be heard before rule adoption and for judicial review to protect against arbitrary and capricious administrative action. Noting the power delegated did not admit of precise standards, we held that the Director-promulgated schedule of employment agency maximum fees was a valid and constitutional delegation of legislative power.

* * *

Here a review of medical school practices shows procedural safeguards. First, basic admission criteria are published and applied at all levels of the process. Competitive applicants are subject to three-tiered review involving a minimum of several admissions committee members. At the interview-conference level, interviewers are trained and familiarized with applicant files beforehand. They are provided with guidelines, including the admission criteria, and evaluation sheets to ensure some consistency in the manner in which interviews are conducted and appraised. These and other school of medicine procedures described below support our holding there are sufficient procedural safeguards to avoid arbitrary administrative action and abuse of discretion.

We now turn from the standards issue to the broader question of whether the admission policies and procedures are arbitrary and capricious and whether the process leading to the denial of McDonald's application was the same. In *DeFunis*, plaintiff similarly contended law school admissions procedures constituted arbitrary and capricious action. We applied the longstanding test:

> Arbitrary and capricious action of administrative bodies means willful and unreasoning action, without consideration and in disregard of facts or circumstances. Where there is room for two opinions, action is not arbitrary or capricious when exercised honestly and upon due consideration, even though it may be believed that an erroneous conclusion has been reached.

Plaintiff must carry the burden of proof on this issue.

McDonald first states that the published selection criteria do not provide a standard for admission or rejection. He singles out for criticism the subjective factors, motivation, maturity and demonstrated humanitarian qualities; he argues these are not definable, meaningful concepts which can be reasonably applied. *DeFunis* indicates, however, that consideration of subjective factors, or factors involving judgmental evaluation, is permissible in state professional school admissions.

Contrary to McDonald's assertion, the findings adequately support the trial court's conclusion the selection process is not arbitrary and capricious. As in *DeFunis*, the record indicates both the admissions committee and the interview-conference committee employ predetermined standards and procedures for selection. Before participating in an interview-conference, each admissions committee member serves on the reading committee to acquire experience in evaluating application files. Application readers work from a "screening" worksheet, and spend approximately 20-30 minutes evaluating several aspects of each application: (1) the difficulty of the applicant's undergraduate program; (2) MCAT variables; (3) outside activities; (4) motivation for medicine; (5) maturity; (6) letters of recommendation; (7) special considerations, including extenuating circumstances.

Before participating in an interview-conference, admissions committee members also attend a training session conducted by admissions committee chairman Belknap. During this session they are provided with copies of the Association of American Medical Colleges Medical School Requirements book, the School of Medicine bulletin, a screening worksheet, guidelines for interviews and a completed application to review at that session. They also are instructed on evaluating application files. If a committee member is absent, an individual meeting is scheduled with Dr. Belknap which lasts more than an hour.

At the interview-conference level, each trained interviewer is required to read his or her personal copy of each application including the letters of recommendation, before the interview-conference. Each member spends approximately 30 minutes per review and makes notes on the application regarding areas for inquiry during the interview-conference. Guidelines given to each interviewer at each interview-conference session include: (1) a list of selection criteria; (2) MCAT and GPA mean averages for the previous year's entering class; (3) suggested guidelines for evaluation of motivation, maturity, humanitarian qualities and candidate strengths and weaknesses; (4) MCAT-suggested areas of noncognitive assessment; (5) suggested areas for discussion; (6) suggested areas for observation. The members of the interview-conference committee rate the candidate comparatively on the basis of the selection criteria, the application file and the interview.

McDonald's application was read by Dr. Belknap and a student committee member and was rated competitive by both. Subsequently, McDonald was interviewed for 22 minutes by an interview-conference committee comprised of two faculty members and one student. Each interviewer independently placed McDonald in category 2, indicating he was a possible candidate "with comparative deficiencies academically and/or with regard to noncognitive features." The interview-conference committee forwarded McDonald's application to the executive committee. That committee at its April 30, 1976 meeting voted that all candidates not acted upon be considered noncompetitive, subject to Chairman Belknap's review of the applications of interviewed candidates remaining. Belknap reviewed the remaining applications, including McDonald's. He reported to the committee that in his judgment there were not any applicants the committee would be likely to consider more competitive than those previously admitted, or made alternates, based upon committee guidelines. A May 10, 1976 letter notified McDonald his application was denied.

The foregoing standards and procedures consistently utilized and also used in evaluating McDonald's application cannot be characterized as "willful and unreasoning, without consideration," or as exercised without "due consideration."

It is further argued that McDonald would have been admitted based on his combined GPA and MCAT ("first screen") score but was not because of his score in an interview with no demonstrated validity in measuring the three remaining selection factors. As respondent notes, the plaintiff's claims in *DeFunis* were similar. There plaintiff contended that using subjective, nonmathematical factors and weighing them differently for different applicants arbitrarily denied admission. This court declared that the exercise of judgment in evaluating an applicant's file is not arbitrary and capricious action. We explained:

> The fallacy of plaintiff's argument is the assumption that, but for the special consideration given minority applicants, selection decisions by the committee would have been based solely upon objective, measurable mathematical projections of the academic performance of applicants. Actually, although the PFYA [based on GPA and LSAT] was a very important factor, it was not the sole determinative factor for any group of students. Rather, the committee utilized the PFYA as a starting point in making its judgment....

Here, like in *DeFunis*, the score based on GPA and MCAT is not the sole criteria but instead is a starting point for consideration. Relevant subjective criteria—motivation, maturity and demonstrated humanitarian qualities—are specified in the medical school admissions book. As in *DeFunis*, letters of recommendation and the difficulty of an applicant's undergraduate program also are considered. Outside activities and extenuating circumstances are factors. The information in each applicant's file is evaluated by interview-conference committee members in light of the specified criteria and is included in their ratings. In *DeFunis* this court said: "Law school admissions need not become a game of numbers; the process should remain sensitive and flexible, with room for informed judgment in interpreting mechanical indicators." In short, the fact some qualified applicants are rejected and nonmathematical factors are weighed differently by different interview committee members does not show arbitrary and capricious conduct.

The university has broad discretion in admission decisions and may use subjective, noncognitive criteria. The Board of Regents alone is given authority that it may delegate to set admission requirements. Regulations and policies relating to admissions are exempt from rulemaking provisions of the State Higher Education Administrative Procedure Act. Thus, it is evident that the legislature intended to vest broad discretion in the university on admission matters. Other courts have found a university's broad discretion in admission decisions and also justified nonintervention by analogy to cases involving academic standards. Like the Montana court's stance in *State ex rel. Bartlett v. Pantzer*, we generally favor nonintervention in admission decisions but never the less will continue to review them for arbitrary and capricious action and abuse of discretion.

Finally, McDonald argues that since racially discriminatory criteria are used, the university must demonstrate that the selection process is a valid predictor of the qualities sought (the published criteria) and that these criteria are a valid index to a successful physician. He relies on two cases interpreting Title 7 of the 1964 Civil Rights Act, which are concerned with discriminatory employment tests. There is no basis for applying these Title 7 cases here. As respondent points out, they are concerned with employment and do not set standards for arbitrary and capricious action in medical school admissions.

McDonald has not shown that the policies and procedures of the University of Washington School of Medicine are arbitrary and capricious. There has not been willful and unreasoning action, without consideration and in disregard of facts or circumstances.

Because McDonald is not entitled to relief, the question of whether the trial court erred in concluding he is not entitled to monetary damages has not been addressed.

The decision of the trial court is affirmed.

In an admissions case that became a chapter from *Bleak House,* an applicant to medical school was accorded the right to sue under Title IX of the Education Amendments of 1972, designed to eradicate sex discrimination. In *Cannon v. University of Chicago,* 441 U.S. 677 (1979), the U.S. Supreme Court rejected the suggestion that "this kind of litigation is burdensome" and held that there was a private federal remedy in the statute:

> Respondents' principal argument against implying a cause of action under Title IX is that it is unwise to subject admissions decisions of universities to judicial scrutiny at the behest of disappointed applicants on a case-by-case basis. They argue that this kind of litigation is burdensome and inevitably will have an adverse effect on the independence of members of university committees.
>
> This argument is not original to this litigation. It was forcefully advanced in both 1964 and 1972 by the congressional opponents of Title VI and Title IX, and squarely rejected by the congressional majorities that passed the two statutes. In short, respondents' principal contention is not a legal argument at all; it addresses a policy issue that Congress has already resolved.

Justice Stevens may have spoken too soon. Although Cannon won her right to sue, she never was admitted to medical school. In 1986, after 13 appeals, the court held that they were groundless, and that the litigation was frivolous. She was held liable for court costs and defendants' legal fees. *Cannon v. Loyola University of Chicago,* 784 F.2d 777 (7th Cir. 1986). As noted elsewhere, the *Grove City* case limited the reach of Title IX, although Congress enacted the Civil Rights Restoration Act in 1988, to extend the reach of Title IX.

In a 1987 admissions matter, the University of Rochester withdrew an offer of admission to a student, when officials from the Eastman Kodak Co. protested that the student's participation in classes with their employees would expose him to Kodak proprietary information or trade secrets; he was an employee of Fuji Photo Film Co., a Kodak competitor. Kodak is a major financial supporter of the University of Rochester. After much adverse publicity, the University readmitted the student to the business school. "U. of Rochester Cancels Admission of Employee of a Kodak Competitor," *Chronicle of Higher Education,* 9 September 1987, pp. A1, 30; "U. of Rochester Readmits Employee of Kodak Competitor," *Chronicle of Higher Education,* 16 September 1987, pp. A1, 34.

Grades

It should surprise no reader of education law to discover no case in which a student sued successfully to change a grade given in a course. Any number of arbitrary or wrongly-awarded grades may have been arbitrated, overturned internally, or ordered changed through an adjudication short of litigation, but grading has proven to be a central protection afforded teachers, absent any evidence of wrongdoing on the part of the professor. (For example, if a grade were traded for a sexual relationship) *Naragon v. Wharton,* 737 F.2d 1403 (1984). Professors have been dismissed over grading practices, at least in part, as was evident in *Parate v. Isibor* (in Chapter II), and the refusal to alter grading practices is not always a constitutionally protected activity of an untenured professor. *Hillis v. Stephen F. Austin State University,* 665 F.2d 547 (5th Cir. 1982).

In a case tried in a Massachusetts Superior Court, David Keen brought an equity claim in 1984, claiming that Western New England College of Law had violated his rights as a student by denying him the chance to retake an exam which he had failed, by refusing to assign the grade he requested in another course, and by assigning a letter grade rather than a numerical grade in a third course. The judge dismissed the complaint, and the Appeals Court affirmed the decision. *Keen v. Western New England College,* 23 Mass. App. Ct. 84, 499 N.E. 2d 310 (1986).

While there have been very few cases in which grades or exam conditions were actually litigated, there have been many near-misses. In one highly publicized instance, a student at the University of Southern California film school threatened to sue when he didn't get to show his full, 33 minute film project; the course requirement had limited the films to 20 minutes. The USC film faculty, which sees the entire process as one encouraging extraordinary entrepreneurial skills and discipline, backed down and relented after the student hired a lawyer.

"Hollywood Discovers Film Schools"
Robert Goldberg, *Premiere,* November, 1987, pp. 47–51.
Reprinted with permission

* * *

The USC School of Cinema-Television may well be, as director Zemeckis puts it, the Harvard Business School of the movies. Established in 1932, it is certainly the oldest cinema school in the nation (with programs in filmmaking, criticism, writing, and producing—the last a master's degree unique to USC). The list of USC alumni is arguably the most distinguished in the country, if not the world. Over the past 25 years, at least one USC graduate has been an Oscar nominee every year.

When it comes to high tech, USC is also a leader. It is, in fact, the highest of tech—the first school in the country to have 70mm projection facilities, the first to have the revolutionary THX sound system. USC's new $15 million facility, opened in 1984, has everything from computer graphics systems to specially designed editing chairs with advanced back support, from a black-and-white film processing lab to the Steven Spielberg Scoring Stage, a facility so advanced there's almost no use for it. As USC's Miura says, the school is a "self-service bank," with everything necessary to make a film from storyboard to release print. The students have nicknamed the complex "the Death Star."

If anything, the rap against USC is that its equipment overwhelms its filmmaking— that its tutoring in camera work, sound, and editing far outstrips its ability to teach students to write or to direct actors. "Our weak point was that the conceptual was not on the same level as the craft part," admits new dean Frank Daniel (formerly cochair of Columbia's film program and head of Czechoslovakia's national film institute, FAMU, and founding dean of the American Film Institute's Center for Advanced Film Studies). "That's what I'm trying to change as fast as possible." (Daniel recently added renowned drama teacher Nina Foch to the staff.)

Central to the USC experience for both graduate and undergraduate students is a demanding program of film production with a rigid structure of prerequisites. In addition to courses in sound, camera work, editing, film history, and critical studies, students must make five super-8 color films, two 16mm color films (one as director, one as camera-person), and crew on one twenty-minute 16mm color film with synchronized sound (called a 480).

Then students try to get a 480 of their own to direct. It's not a requirement for graduation, but everyone knows that if you want to show Hollywood you can direct, you have to have a 480. It's a professional-caliber film and a calling card to the industry. The rub is, because USC completely finances these $5,000 to $15,000 films, there's only enough money to make five or six a semester, ten to twelve a year. With 450 undergraduates and 200 graduate students vying for these few slots, that means a lot of people who have laid out a lot of tuition are bound to be disappointed.

Competition is the key throughout "the 480 experience," as students call it. "It's very grueling," recalls alum Phil Joanou. "Everyone's going for that golden carrot." A hundred scripts are submitted, and the faculty chooses the ones to be produced. Then 20 to 25 would-be directors come in and pitch to a committee of professors for the five or six available directing slots. This is no simple case of asserting "I can really relate to this material." The students bring in storyboards, complete budgets, and day-by-day breakdowns of the shooting. Some haul in photos or videos of the actors they plan to cast and tapes of music for the sound-track. Some, like Joanou, even shoot a 16mm trailer.

As the students wait for the final selections to be thumbtacked to a bulletin board, the tension is cruel. "This is it," Joanou recalls. "If Universal rejects your script, you can go across the street to Paramount. But if you lose here, you don't get to go over to UCLA and pitch. It's over." It's over, that is, unless you pay tuition for one more semester and try again. One student who made the semi-finals two semesters in a row with the same screen-play and was not chosen threatened suit. Another student is considering hiring a lawyer to stop his classmates from directing a screenplay he had written and submitted in the hopes of directing it himself. Accusations of "subjective," even "unfair," have haunted the 480 process (which dean Daniel is working hard to improve). The students who are shut out are certainly bitter. Why all the fuss? "Well, one guy who waited three semesters and finally got a 480 got development deals at Fox and Orion," says Joanou. "Those who left without one are still looking for work." Joanou, on the other hand, is directing a film for Spielberg, and his first feature, *Three O'Clock High*, will be released this fall by Universal.

Once a student is granted a 480 project of his or her own, the competition begins all over again. Shooting over six weekends while attending classes, pulling two to three all-nighters a week for the month of postproduction, students take to wearing buttons that proclaim "Sleep Is for Sissies." The pace is compounded by strict limits on the raw footage: 80 minutes of stock to shoot a twenty-minute film, for a skimpy four-to-one ratio. The footage allotment is one of many rules designed—in the interest of fairness—to ensure that all directors are working under the same conditions. Other rules stringently prescribe production time, access to equipment, and the length of finished films. To insure that no student gets "creative" and sneaks in extra footage (Joanou notoriously snuck thirteen extra minutes into his student film, *Last Chance Dance*), the negatives and stock are now kept under lock and key, and the physical cutting is done by an independent off-campus negative cutter.

As the student directors scramble along, their uncut dailies are shown in weekly meetings to students and faculty and are roundly criticized, "It's like a session in a studio," says USC's professor Miura. "The faculty is acting as producers, executives. If you screw up, everyone's gonna know."

Some students, like Joanou, get pretty steamed about the process: "These guys are armchair quarterbacks. You shoot your ass off for three days, you work 48 hours straight, and these guys say, 'How come you didn't get more coverage?' In front of a hundred people, they tear apart your dailies—that's public humiliation. I used to get in big arguments with them." In fact, Joanou's epic battles with the faculty almost escalated into a legal case. "They didn't submit my film to any film festivals," he says. "I had to submit it myself to the FOCUS awards, which I won." Faculty members say that the competitive framework is created on purpose: "It really puts pressure on the students," says Miura. "If the student isn't devoted, he's not going to make it. We are very competition-driven, but that's the secret to our success." Some graduates question the harshness of the training. Richard Lewis, a recent alum, says: "They throw you in the pool, and you either swim or drown. It's not a real positive learning experience."

After limiting the ranks of its directors, USC tries to impose a measure of fairness on the process by enforcing equal working conditions on all student films. Many students chafe under the USC rules—which have become increasingly strict since Joanou's time—and see them as a kind of totalitarian effort to enforce mediocrity when all they want to do is make the best films they can. Those who choose to break the rules purchase extra film stock, rent expensive professional equipment, employ outside sound editors to mix their films, and end up with a better-looking calling card. Cheating at USC is not like cheating on a math test; it takes a lot of money to rent cranes—about $100 an hour. While it seems ludicrous for teachers to be locking students out of editing rooms and limiting their access to equipment they are desperate to use, there is a certain democratic method to this madness. Director Ken Kwapis, a USC alum whose second film, *Vibes*, with Cyndi Lauper, will open next spring, defends the principle, but with a caveat. "It's in the interest of academic independence in the long run. What the faculty would argue is that it's a *class*. And we're not letting students direct films *in order* to get jobs. Therefore, everyone should play by a certain set of ground rules.

"I defend that idea," says Kwapis, "but I don't defend the idea of a faculty arbitration board to decide what kinds of films are made at all. That's where the real mediocrity happens; the faculty knows that its reputation is based entirely on producing successful, mainstream Hollywood directors. I was just invited to show my film in a 'best of USC for the past twenty years' program as part of the opening of a new movie theater. And what was on the list? All the predictable films by all the people who had gone on to be Hollywood successes: Randal Kleiser, George Lucas, Phil Joanou. Does anyone know that James Ivory went to USC, or Les Blank? USC disowns them, in effect, because they aren't mainstream successes. What's more, they are filmmakers who didn't come into their own until later, and what USC is doing is celebrating instantaneous success.

"I think it's very telling that the students would nickname the school the Death Star," Kwapis continues, "because the whole ethos of George Lucas, which in its inception was an avant-garde impulse, has become in students' minds the establishment. People like Lucas scrounged together their films in a department that looked like a stable. Now the department is as big as a small studio."

* * *

This pattern of pressure occurs regularly in professional curricula, with architecture students completing a project, law students preparing moot court briefs, engineering students building engines or robots, or students rushing to complete a major paper. The persistence paid off, as Joanou went on to work for Amblin Enterprises, Steven Spielberg's production company. See also, J. Kearney, "Behind The Scenes: Amazing Story," *American Film*, September, 1987. The opposite also happened at USC, when in 1988 a film student sued to prevent another student from directing a movie from his screenplay. *Perspectives*, May 1988, p. 3. See "Hollywood Sends Talent Scouts to (Film) School," *New York Times*, 19 May 1988, p. C 23.

Harris v. Blake
798 F.2d 419 (10th Cir. 1986)

SEYMOUR, Circuit Judge.

Henry Harris brought this action under 42 U.S.C. § 1983 (1982), alleging that his rights to procedural and substantive due process were violated when he was required to withdraw from a program of graduate study. The district court granted summary judgment in favor of all defendants. We affirm.

I.

Summary judgment is inappropriate unless there is no genuine issue of material fact and the moving party is entitled to judgment as a matter of law. On appeal, the record is properly viewed in the light most favorable to the nonmoving party. Viewed according to this standard, the record reflects the following facts.

In the spring of 1979, Harris was a part-time graduate psychology student in the University of Northern Colorado's Center for Special and Advanced Programs (CSAP), a master's degree program designed for off-campus students. Harris enrolled in a counseling course taught by Professor Margaret Blake. In order to attend classes, he had to commute daily from Boulder to Greeley. His car broke down after four classes, and he could not arrange for other transportation. He left several telephone messages with Blake's office, explaining his absences and ultimately notifying her that he would have to withdraw from the course. He did withdraw in early May.

It is unclear what happened during the four classes he did attend. Blake was present for two of those sessions, neither of which seems to have been exceptional in any way. When she was away at a convention, the class was taught by a graduate assistant, who supervised the students' counseling of volunteer clients. Harris failed to obtain a client of his own and to provide a videotape cassette, both of which were required. His counseling of a volunteer client supplied by another student was observed by the graduate assistant and other members of the class. Among other things, Blake asserts that Harris could not maintain a conversation with the client. Harris responds that he followed instructions not to speak excessively. After his car broke down, he failed to notify the client that he was unable to keep a scheduled appointment. He also missed at least one conference with Blake, although it may have been scheduled to take place after he stopped attending class.

Dissatisfied with Harris' performance, Blake expressed her concerns to Professor Gimmestad, chairman of the psychology department. Subsequently, Harris attempted to obtain Blake's permission to withdraw from the class, but she refused to authorize it. When Harris withdrew via proper administrative channels, Blake consulted with the CSAP Advisory Committee because she wanted the opportunity to evaluate his performance. Professor Ellis Copeland chaired this committee in his capacity as CSAP academic coordinator. Although Blake testified that the committee recommended she put her concerns in writing, Copeland does not recall a formal recommendation. Blake also states that she was instructed to institute proceedings to "oust" Harris from CSAP.

On May 16, Blake wrote the letter which ultimately led to this lawsuit. Addressed "To Whom It May Concern," the text reads as follows:

> "This letter concerns when Henry Harris was registered for and his with-drawal from my Introductory Practicum in Counseling, PCG 612, during Spring Quarter of 1979. Mr. Harris was allowed to withdraw by the Dean of Students, long after the drop date and after he had exhibited specific behaviors of being incompetent and unethical in his supervised practicum.

> "It is my belief that Henry should not be allowed to register for a practicum and that if he does, the practicum should be aware of his past performance."

The May 16 letter became a part of Harris' academic file and was disseminated among some of CSAP's instructors and administrative personnel.

After the May 16 letter was written, the Advisory Committee met to consider the case. The committee determined that no action should be taken to remove Harris from CSAP but that future instructors should be informed of his performance in Blake's course. Although Copeland had read the letter, the committee did not review it or decide that it would serve as the means of informing other instructors.

Copeland called Harris in late May or early June. Harris had registered for another counseling course, and Copeland notified him that he would instead have to take the course at a different location with Professor H. Dan Smith. Smith was associated with the University of Fresno in California and had been hired by CSAP as a visiting professor. During that conversation, Copeland mentioned the May 16 letter and told Harris that Blake had several concerns about him.

Harris enrolled in the course indicated by Copeland. Smith had somehow received a copy of the May 16 letter but did not mention this to Harris. The course consisted of two weekend-long sessions, which proved unusual in that Smith repeatedly confronted half of the fourteen-person class about drinking and other disruptive conduct. Harris claims that Smith did not work with him at any point and that Smith's graduate assistant disparaged him without cause. He also claims that he completed all requirements but nonetheless received a "D" as his final grade.

Harris previously had received an "incomplete" in a CSAP course taught by Copeland. He fulfilled the outstanding requirements by the spring or early summer of 1979, and Copeland gave him a "C" as his final grade. He had been doing "B" work in the first half of the course, and the final paper he wrote was never returned to him. He had earned A's and B's in the other CSAP courses he had taken. One or both of the grades Harris received from Smith and Copeland lowered his average below the required minimum and effectively compelled his withdrawal from CSAP.

During the summer or early fall, Harris tried unsuccessfully to obtain a copy of Blake's letter by mail. At the beginning of October, he went with his father to the CSAP office, where Copeland gave him a copy. After speaking with Copeland, they proceeded to Professor Gimmestad's office and insisted upon seeing him. Their conversation was heated, and Harris demanded to know how and why the letter had been placed in his file. At Harris' request, Gimmestad obtained an explanatory letter from Blake. That letter, dated October 9, explained her original use of the terms "incompetent" and "unethical" as follows:

"Incompetence: Inability to verbalize his own and others' perceptions. Lack of attentive behavior, paucity of listening skills. No warmth, genuineness, respect or empathy in his interactions with client or fellow classmates. No confrontive skills. Language inadequacy.

Unethical: Failure to arrange for client contact; lack of follow-through in meeting client. No appearance at feedback session; no contact then or later with professor. Failure to take responsibility for taping; no tape recorder, tapes, or video tape for feedback."

The letter also detailed the basis for these conclusions, including Harris' failure to provide his own client and his subsequent failure to inform the client he "borrowed" that he would not be able to attend the next scheduled session.

Harris was not satisfied with Blake's explanation. Pursuing channels within the administration, Harris ultimately persuaded Arthur Partridge, Dean of the College of Education, to have the May 16 letter removed from his file. Partridge's written directive stated that the letter should not have been placed in Harris' file. After referring to the threat of legal action and requesting all copies of the May 16 letter, the Dean concluded:

"If Dr. Blake had a reasonable factual basis for accusing Mr. Harris of being unethical and incompetent, she should have filed some sort of charge. That, I think, would have been proper procedure. I believe, however, that this sort of memorandum with no supporting data and no specification of charges is most inappropriate."

Harris also lodged an official grievance with the school's Academic Appeal Board. He challenged the grades he had received from both professors who had seen the May 16 letter as well as the conduct of Blake and Copeland concerning the letter. After a hearing in which Harris participated, the Appeal Board upheld the grades and declined to rule on the other charges since the letter had been expunged.

One year after the May 16 letter was written, Harris filed this lawsuit and a related action in state court. His federal complaint essentially alleged that he was deprived of a property interest in continued enrollment and a liberty interest in his ability to pursue a career in psychology. He claimed that the conduct of Blake, Copeland, and Gimmestad denied him both procedural and substantive due process and that the Board of Trustees was liable for these violations. In granting defendants' motion for summary judgment, the district court characterized Blake's evaluation as academic rather than disciplinary and ruled that no hearing was required under *Board of Curators v. Horowitz*. The court also held that any claim of defamation was foreclosed by *Paul v. Davis*. Finally, the court found no indication of arbitrariness, capriciousness, or bad faith to support the alleged violation of substantive due process.

II.

The Due Process Clause applies when government has deprived an individual of an interest in liberty or property. In *Gaspar v. Bruton*, we held that an individual's place in a post-secondary nursing program constitutes a protected property interest. We relied in part upon *Goss v. Lopez*, which recognized a property interest in public education. In *Goss*, the State of Ohio had entitled its residents to a primary and secondary education. Colorado has created the basis for a similar claim of entitlement to an education in its state college system, which includes the University of Northern Colorado. The legislature has directed that these colleges "shall be open...to all persons resident in this state" upon payment of a reasonable tuition fee. The actual payment of tuition secures an individual's claim of entitlement. Accordingly, Harris had a property interest in his CSAP enrollment which entitled him to procedural due process.

"The very nature of due process negates any concept of inflexible procedures universally applicable to every imaginable situation." The Supreme Court has emphasized that less stringent procedural requirements attach when a school makes an academic judgment about a student than when it takes disciplinary action. In *Horowitz*, a medical student challenged her school's failure to provide a hearing before her dismissal. The student had been informed of deficiencies in her academic performance and, in addition, had received numerous reviews of her work and opportunities to improve. The Court held that the process she received, notice followed by a careful and deliberate determination, satisfied the requirements of due process.

Harris contends that placing the May 16 letter in his file was disciplinary rather than academic in nature, arguing that it was done to punish him because he missed classes and later withdrew. Like the district court, however, we believe that the decisions affecting Harris were academic rather than disciplinary. The evidence is undisputed that attendance at each class session was critical because the course was a practical one in counseling methods, involving actual participation and observation. The students were so informed and were told they could not be absent. Attendance was thus an academic requirement. Blake's explanatory letter of October 9 clarifies that her concerns were academic, not disciplinary. Although the May 16 letter may have been prompted by Harris' withdrawal, there is no dispute on this record that Blake's purpose was to ensure that he would be evaluated for his actual performance in class notwithstanding his withdrawal. Harris was thus entitled only to the minimal procedures discussed in *Horowitz*.

Arguably, both the May 16 letter and the poor grades Harris received were not careful evaluations in the sense intended by *Horowitz*. Although the letter pertained to academic matters, it may nonetheless have been ill-considered. Dean Partridge flatly termed it "most inappropriate" for an academic evaluation. Harris charges that the grades which forced his withdrawal were not the product of careful deliberation or even inadvertence but rather were foregone conclusions based upon the improperly written letter. Under *Horowitz*, however, the procedures Harris received were more than adequate to protect his property interest in continued enrollment. CSAP provided an established appeals procedure which culminated in a hearing before the school's Academic Appeal Board. Harris employed that procedure and participated personally in the hearing to challenge his grades. Independent review confirmed the propriety of the grades and further demonstrated that the ultimate decision concerning his case was a careful one.

Harris urges that he was entitled to challenge the initial placement of the May 16 letter in his academic file. Due process, however, required that CSAP protect only against the deprivation of Harris' constitutionally protected interest in continued enrollment. That interest was not necessarily jeopardized by an unfavorable letter of evaluation.

Even if CSAP were constitutionally required to take action with respect to Blake's evaluation, the procedures followed were sufficient. Harris was notified of the letter's existence and nature. Although Harris was unable to obtain a copy by mail, Copeland gave him one when asked in person to do so. Gimmestad obtained an explanatory letter for him from Blake. Harris then appealed until the letters were removed from his file. In short, he received several opportunities to present his position to responsible school officials. It is also uncontroverted that Harris was entitled to place his own explanatory letter in the file and that the Appeal Board was prepared to consider any charges concerning the May 16 letter had it not already been expunged. The requirements of procedural due process were therefore satisfied with respect to Blake's evaluation as well as the challenged grades.

III.

The Due Process Clause not only provides a procedural safeguard against deprivations of life, liberty, and property but also protects substantive aspects of those interests from unconstitutional restrictions by government. We have already held that Harris had a property interest in his post-graduate education. He contends further that defendants' actions which resulted in his dismissal from the program were so arbitrary that they denied him substantive due process.

In *Regents of the University of Michigan v. Ewing*, a student was dismissed from a medical program when he did not pass a required examination. He alleged that his dismissal was arbitrary and capricious because he was denied permission to retake the test although other failing students were routinely allowed to do so. The Court assumed without deciding that a graduate student's interest in continued enrollment constitutes a property interest warranting substantive protection. In assessing Ewing's claim, the Court pointed out that the procedures used by the university had been fair, and that the university had not concealed nonacademic or constitutionally impermissible reasons for dismissal.

* * *

The Court's approach in *Ewing* is dispositive of Harris' claim. He does not assert that the CSAP procedures he used to appeal his grades were unfair. Moreover, there is no evidence in this record that any of the CSAP personnel who were involved harbored nonacademic or unconstitutional motives for effecting his withdrawal. As in *Ewing*, the essence of Harris' claim is that defendants misjudged his fitness to remain a student. We must therefore review the record to determine whether the evidence, viewed most favorably to Harris, unmistakably demonstrates that defendants' decision was "made conscientiously and with careful deliberation," or whether the record shows "such a substantial departure from accepted academic norms as to demonstrate that the person or committee responsible did not actually exercise professional judgment."

The record reveals that a fact issue exists over whether Blake's actions in writing the May 16 letter and placing it in Harris' file were appropriate academic procedures. A fact issue also exists concerning whether the letter affected the grades given to Harris by Smith and Copeland. However, Harris was given the opportunity to challenge the letter and the grades before the Academic Appeal Board. It is the Board's decision that ultimately resulted in Harris' forced withdrawal, and Harris has failed to show that this decision was not made with conscientious deliberation through the exercise of professional judgment. It is undisputed that unbiased faculty members have considered Harris' case and have exercised their own judgment concerning the propriety of the grades that compelled his withdrawal. Accordingly, Harris has failed to support the alleged denial of substantive due process.

The judgment of the district court is affirmed.

Academic Dismissals

Absent extraordinary circumstances of faculty misconduct or institutional negligence, students do not win their academic dismissal cases. For examples of the legal theories under which such cases have been brought, see *Mauriello v. University of Medicine and Dentistry on New Jersey*, 781 F.2d 46 (3rd Cir. 1986) (substantive due process); *Morin v. Cleveland Metropolitan General Hospital School of Nursing*, 516 N.E.2d 1257 (Ohio App. 1986) (procedural due process); *North v. State of Iowa*, 400 N.W.2d 566 (Iowa 1987) (breach of contract, tortious interference with business opportunity); *Cuddihy v. Wayne State University*, 413 N.W.2d 692 (Mich. App. 1987) (promissory estoppel); *Hankins v. Temple University*, 829 F.2d 437 (3rd Cir. 1987) (racial and sex discrimination); *Hammond v. Auburn University*, 669 F. Supp. 1555 (M.D. Ala. 1987) (equal protection).

In a case filed in San Francisco County Superior Court in 1986, Steven Mosher sued Stanford University officials for his dismissal from the Anthropology Ph.D. program. Following his field work in the People's Republic of China, Mosher was accused of academic improprieties, in connection with his U.S. government funded dissertation research. This *cause célébre* has a political cast, because Mosher alleged that the PRC population programs included widespread forced abortions and sterilizations. Mosher's suit alleges breach of contract, tortious interference with contract and prospective economic advantages, negligence, fraud, libel and slander, and violation of civil rights. Brief for Plaintiff, No. 864701, 29 September 1986. For a review of the controversy, see "Politics and Scholarship Mix in China Researcher's Long Battle with Stanford," *Chronicle of Higher Education*, 14 January 1987, pp. 1, 8–9;

"Rebuttal to the Allegations Made by Stanford University and the People's Republic of China," Steven Mosher Defense Committee, Montclair, California, November, 1985.

Board of Curators of the University of Missouri v. Horowitz
435 U.S. 78 (1978)

Mr. Justice REHNQUIST delivered the opinion of the Court.

Respondent, a student at the University of Missouri-Kansas City Medical School, was dismissed by petitioner officials of the school during her final year of study for failure to meet academic standards. Respondent sued petitioners under 42 U.S.C. § 1983 in the United States District Court for the Western District of Missouri alleging, among other constitutional violations, that petitioners had not accorded her procedural due process prior to her dismissal. The District Court, after conducting a full trial, concluded that respondent had been afforded all of the rights guaranteed her by the Fourteenth Amendment to the United States Constitution and dismissed her complaint. The Court of Appeals for the Eighth Circuit reversed, and a petition for rehearing en banc was denied by a divided court. We granted certiorari, to consider what procedures must be accorded to a student at a state educational institution whose dismissal may constitute a deprivation of "liberty" or "property" within the meaning of the Fourteenth Amendment. We reverse the judgment of the Court of Appeals.

I

Respondent was admitted with advanced standing to the Medical School in the fall of 1971. During the final years of a student's education at the school, the student is required to pursue in "rotational units" academic and clinical studies pertaining to various medical disciplines such as obstetrics-gynecology, pediatrics, and surgery. Each student's academic performance at the School is evaluated on a periodic basis by the Council on Evaluation, a body composed of both faculty and students, which can recommend various actions including probation and dismissal. The recommendations of the Council are reviewed by the Coordinating Committee, a body composed solely of faculty members, and must ultimately be approved by the Dean. Students are not typically allowed to appear before either the Council or the Coordinating Committee on the occasion of their review of the student's academic performance.

In the spring of respondent's first year of study, several faculty members expressed dissatisfaction with her clinical performance during a pediatrics rotation. The faculty members noted that respondent's "performance was below that of her peers in all clinical patient-oriented settings," that she was erratic in her attendance at clinical sessions, and that she lacked a critical concern for personal hygiene. Upon the recommendation of the Council on Evaluation, respondent was advanced to her second and final year on a probationary basis.

Faculty dissatisfaction with respondent's clinical performance continued during the following year. For example, respondent's docent, or faculty adviser, rated her clinical skills as "unsatisfactory." In the middle of the year, the Council again reviewed respondent's academic progress and concluded that respondent should not be considered for graduation in June of that year; furthermore, the Council recommended that, absent "radical improvement," respondent be dropped from the school.

Respondent was permitted to take a set of oral and practical examinations as an "appeal" of the decision not to permit her to graduate. Pursuant to this "appeal," respondent spent a substantial portion of time with seven practicing physicians in the area who enjoyed a good reputation among their peers. The physicians were asked to recommend whether respondent should be allowed to graduate on schedule and, if not, whether she should be dropped immediately or allowed to remain on probation. Only two of the doctors recommended that respondent be graduated on schedule. Of the other five, two recommended that she be immediately dropped from the school. The remaining three recommended that she not be allowed to graduate in June and be continued on probation pending further reports on her clinical progress. Upon receipt of these recommendations, the Council on Evaluation reaffirmed its prior position.

The Council met again in mid-May to consider whether respondent should be allowed to remain in school beyond June of that year. Noting that the report on respondent's recent surgery rotation rated her performance as "low-satisfactory," the Council unanimously recommended that "barring receipt of any reports that Miss Horowitz has improved radically, [she] not be allowed to re-enroll in the . . . School of Medicine." The Council delayed making its recommendation official until receiving reports on other rotations; when a report on respondent's emergency rotation also turned out to be negative, the Council unanimously reaffirmed its recommendation that respondent be dropped from the school. The Coordinating Committee and the Dean approved the recommendation and notified respondent, who appealed the decision in writing to the University's Provost for Health Sciences. The Provost sustained the school's actions after reviewing the record compiled during the earlier proceedings.

II

A

To be entitled to the procedural protections of the Fourteenth Amendment, respondent must in a case such as this demonstrate that her dismissal from the school deprived her of either a "liberty" or a "property" interest. Respondent has never alleged that she was deprived of a property interest. Because property interests are creatures of state law respondent would have been required to show at trial that her seat at the Medical School was a "property" interest recognized by Missouri state law. Instead, respondent argued that her dismissal deprived her of "liberty" by substantially impairing her opportunities to continue her medical education or to return to employment in a medically related field.

The Court of Appeals agreed, citing this Court's opinion in *Board of Regents v. Roth*. In that case, we held that the State had not deprived a teacher of any liberty or property interest in dismissing the teacher from a nontenured position, but noted:

> "[T]here is no suggestion that the State, in declining to re-employ the respondent, imposed on him a stigma or other disability that foreclosed his freedom to take advantage of other employment opportunities. The State, for example, did not invoke any regulations to bar the respondent from all other public employment in state universities."

We have recently had an opportunity to elaborate upon the circumstances under which an employment termination might infringe a protected liberty interest. In *Bishop v. Wood,* we upheld the dismissal of a policeman without a hearing; we rejected the theory that the mere fact of dismissal, absent some publicizing of the reasons for the action, could amount to a stigma infringing one's liberty:

> "In *Board of Regents v. Roth,* we recognized that the nonretention of an untenured college teacher might make him somewhat less attractive to other employers, but nevertheless concluded that it would stretch the concept too far 'to suggest that a person is deprived of "liberty" when he simply is not rehired in one job but remains as free as before to seek another.' This same conclusion applies to the discharge of a public employee whose position is terminable at the will of the employer when there is no public disclosure of the reasons for the discharge.

> "In this case the asserted reasons for the City Manager's decision were communicated orally to the petitioner in private and also were stated in writing in answer to interrogatories after this litigation commenced. Since the former communication was not made public, it cannot properly form the basis for a claim that petitioner's interest in his 'good name, reputation, honor, or integrity' was thereby impaired."

The opinion of the Court of Appeals, decided only five weeks after we issued our opinion in *Bishop,* does not discuss whether a state university infringes a liberty interest when it dismisses a student without publicizing allegations harmful to the student's reputation. Three judges of the Court of Appeals for the Eighth Circuit dissented from the denial of rehearing en banc on the ground that "the reasons for Horowitz's dismissal were not released to the public but were communicated to her directly by school officials." Citing *Bishop,* the judges concluded that "[a]bsent such public disclosure, there is no deprivation of a liberty interest." Petitioners urge us to adopt the view of these judges and hold that respondent has not been deprived of a liberty interest.

B

We need not decide, however, whether respondent's dismissal deprived her of a liberty interest in pursuing a medical career. Nor need we decide whether respondent's dismissal infringed any other interest constitutionally protected against deprivation without procedural due process. Assuming the existence of a liberty or property interest, respondent has been awarded at least as much due process as the Fourteenth Amendment requires. The school fully informed respondent of the faculty's dissatisfaction with her clinical progress and the danger that this posed to timely graduation and continued enrollment. The ultimate decision to dismiss respondent was careful and deliberate. These procedures were sufficient under the Due Process Clause of the Fourteenth Amendment. We agree with the District Court that respondent

> "was afforded full procedural due process by the [school]. In fact, the Court is of the opinion, and so finds, that the school went beyond [constitutionally required] procedural due process by affording [respondent] the opportunity to be examined by seven independent physicians in order to be absolutely certain that their grading of the [respondent] in her medical skills was correct."

In *Goss v. Lopez,* we held that due process requires, in connection with the suspension of a student from public school for disciplinary reasons, "that the student be given oral or written notice of the charges against him and, if he denies them, an explanation of the evidence the authorities have and an opportunity to present his side of the story." The Court of Appeals apparently read *Goss* as requiring some type of formal hearing at which respondent could defend her academic ability and performance. All that *Goss* required was an "informal give-and-take" between the student and the administrative body dismissing him that would, at least, give the student "the opportunity to characterize his conduct and put it in what he deems the proper context." But we have frequently emphasized that "[t]he very nature of due process negates any concept of inflexible procedures universally applicable to every imaginable situation." The need for flexibility is well illustrated by the significant difference between the failure of a student to meet academic standards and the violation by a student of valid rules of conduct. This difference calls for far less stringent procedural requirements in the case of an academic dismissal.

Since the issue first arose 50 years ago, state and lower federal courts have recognized that there are distinct differences between decisions to suspend or dismiss a student for disciplinary purposes and similar actions taken for academic reasons which may call for hearings in connection with the former but not the latter. Thus, in *Barnard v. Inhabitants of Shelburne*, the Supreme Judicial Court of Massachusetts rejected an argument, based on several earlier decisions requiring a hearing in disciplinary contexts, that school officials must also grant a hearing before excluding a student on academic grounds. According to the court, disciplinary cases have

> "no application. . . . Misconduct is a very different matter from failure to attain a standard of excellence in studies. A determination as to the fact involves investigation of a quite different kind. A public hearing may be regarded as helpful to the ascertainment of misconduct and useless or harmful in finding out the truth as to scholarship."

A similar conclusion has been reached by the other state courts to consider the issue. Indeed, until the instant decision by the Court of Appeals for the Eighth Circuit, the Courts of Appeals were also unanimous in concluding that dismissals for academic (as opposed to disciplinary) cause do not necessitate a hearing before the school's decisionmaking body. These prior decisions of state and federal courts, over a period of 60 years, unanimously holding that formal hearings before decisionmaking bodies need not be held in the case of academic dismissals, cannot be rejected lightly.

Reason, furthermore, clearly supports the perception of these decisions. A school is an academic institution, not a courtroom or administrative hearing room. In *Goss*, this Court held that suspensions of students for disciplinary reasons have a sufficient resemblance to traditional judicial and administrative factfinding to call for a "hearing" before the relevant school authority. While recognizing that school authorities must be afforded the necessary tools to maintain discipline, the Court concluded:

> "[I]t would be a strange disciplinary system in an educational institution if no communication was sought by the disciplinarian with the student in an effort to inform him of his dereliction and to let him tell his side of the story in order to make sure that an injustice is not done.
>
> . . . .
>
> "[R]equiring effective notice and informal hearing permitting the student to give his version of the events will provide a meaningful hedge against erroneous

action. At least the disciplinarian will be alerted to the existence of disputes about facts and arguments about cause and effect."

Even in the context of a school disciplinary proceeding, however, the Court stopped short of requiring a *formal* hearing since "further formalizing the suspension process and escalating its formality and adversary nature may not only make it too costly as a regular disciplinary tool but also destroy its effectiveness as a part of the teaching process."

Academic evaluations of a student, in contrast to disciplinary determinations, bear little resemblance to the judicial and administrative factfinding proceedings to which we have traditionally attached a full-hearing requirement. In *Goss*, the school's decision to suspend the students rested on factual conclusions that the individual students had participated in demonstrations that had disrupted classes, attacked a police officer, or caused physical damage to school property. The requirement of a hearing, where the student could present his side of the factual issue, could under such circumstances "provide a meaningful hedge against erroneous action." The decision to dismiss respondent, by comparison, rested on the academic judgment of school officials that she did not have the necessary clinical ability to perform adequately as a medical doctor and was making insufficient progress toward that goal. Such a judgment is by its nature more subjective and evaluative than the typical factual questions presented in the average disciplinary decision. Like the decision of an individual professor as to the proper grade for a student in his course, the determination whether to dismiss a student for academic reasons requires an expert evaluation of cumulative information and is not readily adapted to the procedural tools of judicial or administrative decisionmaking.

Under such circumstances, we decline to ignore the historic judgment of educators and thereby formalize the academic dismissal process by requiring a hearing. The educational process is not by nature adversary; instead it centers around a continuing relationship between faculty and students, "one in which the teacher must occupy many roles—educator, adviser, friend, and, at times, parent-substitute." This is especially true as one advances through the varying regimes of the educational system, and the instruction becomes both more individualized and more specialized. In *Goss*, this Court concluded that the value of some form of hearing in a disciplinary context outweighs any resulting harm to the academic environment. Influencing this conclusion was clearly the belief that disciplinary proceedings, in which the teacher must decide whether to punish a student for disruptive or insubordinate behavior, may automatically bring an adversary flavor to the normal student-teacher relationship. The same conclusion does not follow in the academic context. We decline to further enlarge the judicial presence in the academic community and thereby risk deterioration of many beneficial aspects of the faculty-student relationship. We recognize, as did the Massachusetts Supreme Judicial Court over 60 years ago, that a hearing may be "useless or harmful in finding out the truth as to scholarship."

"Judicial interposition in the operation of the public school system of the Nation raises problems requiring care and restraint. . . . By and large, public education in our Nation is committed to the control of state and local authorities." We see no reason to intrude on that historic control in this case.

III

In reversing the District Court on procedural due process grounds, the Court of Appeals expressly failed to "reach the substantive due process ground advanced by

Horowitz." Respondent urges that we remand the cause to the Court of Appeals for consideration of this additional claim. In this regard, a number of lower courts have implied in dictum that academic dismissals from state institutions can be enjoined if "shown to be clearly arbitrary or capricious." Even assuming that the courts can review under such a standard an academic decision of a public educational institution, we agree with the District Court that no showing of arbitrariness or capriciousness has been made in this case. Courts are particularly ill-equipped to evaluate academic performance. The factors discussed in Part II with respect to procedural due process speak *a fortiori* here and warn against any such judicial intrusion into academic decisionmaking.

The judgment of the Court of Appeals is therefore

Reversed.

Mr. Justice MARSHALL, concurring in part and dissenting in part.

I agree with the Court that, "[a]ssuming the existence of a liberty or property interest, respondent has been awarded at least as much due process as the Fourteenth Amendment requires." I cannot join the Court's opinion, however, because it contains dictum suggesting that respondent was entitled to even less procedural protection than she received. I also differ from the Court in its assumption that characterization of the reasons for a dismissal as "academic" or "disciplinary" is relevant to resolution of the question of what procedures are required by the Due Process Clause. Finally, I disagree with the Court's decision not to remand to the Court of Appeals for consideration of respondent's substantive due process claim.

* * *

IV

While I agree with the Court that respondent received adequate procedural due process, I cannot join the Court's judgment because it is based on resolution of an issue never reached by the Court of Appeals. That court, taking a properly limited view of its role in constitutional cases, refused to offer dictum on respondent's substantive due process claim when it decided the case on procedural due process grounds. Petitioners therefore presented to us only questions relating to the procedural issue. Our normal course in such a case is to reverse on the questions decided below and presented in the petition, and then to remand to the Court of Appeals for consideration of any remaining issues.

Rather than taking this course, the Court here decides on its own that the record will not support a substantive due process claim, thereby "agree[ing]" with the District Court. I would allow the Court of Appeals to provide the first level of appellate review on this question. Not only would a remand give us the benefit of the lower court's thoughts, it would also allow us to maintain consistency with our own Rule 23 (1)(c), which states that "[o]nly the questions set forth in the petition or fairly comprised therein will be considered by the court." By bypassing the courts of appeals on questions of this nature, we do no service to those courts that refuse to speculate in dictum on a wide range of issues and instead follow the more prudential, preferred course of avoiding decision—particularly constitutional decision—until " 'absolutely necessary' " to resolution of a case.

I would reverse the judgment of the Court of Appeals and remand for further proceedings.

Mr. Justice BLACKMUN, with whom Mr. Justice BRENNAN joins, concurring in part and dissenting in part.

The Court's opinion, and that of Mr. Justice MARSHALL, together demonstrate conclusively that, assuming the existence of a liberty or property interest, respondent received all the procedural process that was due her under the Fourteenth Amendment. That, for me, disposes of this case, and compels the reversal of the judgment of the Court of Appeals.

I find it unnecessary, therefore, to indulge in the arguments and counterarguments contained in the two opinions as to the extent or type of procedural protection that the Fourteenth Amendment requires in the graduate-school-dismissal situation. Similarly, I also find it unnecessary to choose between the arguments as to whether respondent's dismissal was for academic or disciplinary reasons (or, indeed, whether such a distinction is relevant). I do agree with Mr. Justice MARSHALL, however, that we should leave to the District Court and to the Court of Appeals in the first instance the resolution of respondent's substantive due process claim and of any other claim presented to, but not decided by, those courts.

Accordingly, I, too, would reverse the judgment of the Court of Appeals and remand the case for further proceedings.

University of Texas Health Science Center v. Babb
646 S.W. 2d 502 (Tex. App. 1 Dist. 1982)

PRICE, Justice.

This appeal is from an order granting Joy Ann Babb, appellee, a temporary injunction permitting her to resume classes and to complete her degree requirements without any interference from the University of Texas School of Nursing.

Appellee entered the Nursing school in Houston, Texas, in January 1979, under the admission requirements of the school's 1978–1979 catalog. At that time the school was conducting classes under the semester system. The pertinent provisions of that catalog are:

> If at the end of any long-session semester or summer session, a student's grade-point average for the total number of hours undertaken in the School of Nursing falls below 2.0 he will be placed on scholastic probation.

> If a student repeats a course which he has failed in the School of Nursing, his official grade is the last one made.

> A student may obtain a degree from the School of Nursing according to the requirements in the catalog under which he enters the School, or the catalog governing any subsequent year in which he is registered in the School, provided that he completes the work for the degree within six years of the date of the catalog. The student will submit to the Dean a written request for readmission. The request will be reviewed by the Dean, Chairperson of the Undergraduate Curriculum Council, and the faculty of the course to which the student is requesting re-admission. An interview may be requested. The Dean or her delegate, will advise the student in writing of the decision.

Prior to the end of the fall term, 1979, appellee was notified that she was failing one of her 12-hour courses. Her school counselor advised her to withdraw from the semester program, send a letter asking for readmission, and re-enter the school the following January under the School's newly organized quarter program. Appellee did this and was re-admitted but received the grade WF (withdrew failing) for her Fall, 1979 semester's grades. Appellee successfully completed a total of six 3-hour courses under the quarter system in order to make up the "WF" grade placed on her record while she was under the semester system.

However, the 1979–1981 catalog, under which the appellee re-entered the school, contained a restriction that was not in the 1978–1979 catalog. That statement was: "A student with more than two D's in the program will be required to withdraw."

During the course of appellee's progress through the quarter system, she received two "D's." She subsequently received official notification from the School that she was being terminated from the program because school policy so required of any student with a total of three "D's," "F's" or "WF's." Appellee then tried to talk with the Dean about her expulsion, but she was repeatedly denied an interview.

Finally, appellee brought this suit, contending that the 1979–1981 catalog, with its "no more than two D's" requirement, should not apply to her since she originally entered the School under the 1978–1979 catalog. The resulting injunction is the order from which the appellants appeal.

Appellants' first point of error contends that the trial court erred in overruling their plea in abatement. Appellants maintain that because they are a part of the State's university system, they share in governmental immunity and cannot be sued without legislative consent or statutory authorization.

We agree with appellants that a party must have legislative consent or statutory authorization before it can maintain a suit and recover a judgment which will operate to control State action, or subject the State to liability, or which would affect the State's property rights and interests. However, it is equally well settled that an entity or person whose rights have been violated by the unlawful action of a State official may bring suit to remedy the violation or prevent its occurrence, and such suit is not a suit against the State requiring legislative or statutory authorization. Therefore, we hold that appellee may maintain this suit for injunctive relief to determine if the action of the school officials in dismissing appellee is unauthorized. We overrule point of error number one.

Appellants' second point of error alleges that the trial court erred in overruling their plea of privilege, because venue was not proper in Harris County. We have searched the record and find no plea of privilege or any indication that one was filed. Further, the record is devoid of any controverting plea or any evidence on this issue. Finding nothing in the record to support appellants' claim, we overrule their second point of error.

Appellants contend, in their third point of error, that the trial court erred in issuing its order granting the temporary injunction because it is impracticable and self-contradictory, and purports to abolish all academic standards as applied to appellee. Our attention is directed toward the contradictory terms of provisions 5 and 9 of the injunctive order. Provision 5 of the order calls for adjusting appellee's grade from the semester to the quarter system, whereas provision 9 provides for correcting the quarter system grades to semester grades.

Except for this conflict, the injunctive order is clear and precise and adequately informs appellants of acts they are restrained from doing. This conflict is remedied, however, by modifying the order, by deleting the provisions of section 5.

In addition to the contradictory provisions, appellants contend that the injunction is overly broad and exaggerated, arguing that the injunction would prevent the University from expelling appellee regardless of how many failing grades she received. We disagree. If the appellee receives too many failing grades, she cannot graduate because she will not have maintained the 2.0 GPA required under the 1978–1979 catalog.

We overrule the third point of error.

The fourth point of error alleges that the trial court erred in issuing its order granting a temporary injunction because the injunction is in effect a mandamus compelling state officers to perform certain acts, and exclusive jurisdiction for the insurance of such a writ is in the Supreme Court of Texas. Appellants rely on Art. 1735, Tex.Rev.Civ.Ann., which indicates that only the Supreme Court can issue a writ of injunction or mandamus against any of the officers of the executive departments of this State's government.

This statute and its application were discussed in *Malone v. Rainey*. The Supreme Court held that, in a suit to compel admission to a State University, the School officials are not officers of this State within the meaning of Article 1735. Consequently, this statute does not apply to the present case and we overrule the appellants' fourth point of error.

Appellants next contend that the trial court erred in finding that a valid contract existed between appellants and appellee that would blind the former to anything more than impartial evaluation of appellee's academic work. They maintain that principles of contract law should not be strictly applicable in construing provisions of a student manual. However, appellants further assert that if the manual is a contract, then it should not be binding and unchangeable so that modification would be impossible. The University, in order to properly exercise its educational responsibility, should be able to modify the catalog as it becomes necessary.

The appellee agrees that a School has the right to change its catalog, but argues that there was an express promise by the University in the 1978–1979 catalog to allow a student who begins school under a certain catalog to continue through the program under that same catalog. Any rule change would not apply retroactively to a student electing to be bound under a previous catalog.

We hold that a school's catalog constitutes a written contract between the educational institution and the patron, where entrance is had under its terms. Therefore, in the instant case, the appellee, upon entering the nursing school under the 1978–79 catalog, had a right to rely on its terms. This catalog permitted a student to complete the degree requirements under its terms, within a six-year period, regardless of the school's later amendments to the catalog. Further, the 1978–1979 catalog did not permit the school to dismiss a student based on the number of bad grades that that student made; it only required a student to maintain a 2.0 GPA.

Appellants next contend that even under the 1978–1979 catalog, appellee fell below the 2.0 minimum GPA with the "WF" she received, and that she would have been expelled anyway under the semester system. This, however, is contrary to the provisions of the 1978–1979 catalog which dictates scholastic probation for such conduct.

The University did allow her to make up these courses, and appellee made a "C" or better in all of them. The school's effort to dismiss appellee was based on the number of bad grades and not on her falling below the minimum GPA standards.

The appellants' fifth point of error is overruled.

Appellants contend, in their sixth and final point of error, that the trial court erred in issuing the temporary injunction, because appellants' First Amendment right to academic freedom allows it to set academic standards as it will, unimpeded by the continuing oversight of the courts. Appellants argue that for a student to have a cause of action, the student would have to show arbitrary and capricious conduct on the part of University officials. We disagree.

Appellee never suggests that the standards of the University are unreasonable, or that the University cannot change the standards. Neither does she dispute that if a student fails to maintain the prescribed scholastic rating, the dismissal would be justified. Appellee only questions her right to be judged under the scholastic rating prescribed in the 1978–1979 catalog, rather than that contained in the 1979–1981 catalog.

The sixth point of error is overruled.

An order granting a temporary injunction should not be reversed unless an abuse of discretion is shown. We find no abuse of discretion. The judgment of the trial court, as modified, is affirmed.

Regents of University of Michigan v. Ewing
474 U.S. 214 (1985)

Justice STEVENS delivered the opinion of the Court.

Respondent Scot Ewing was dismissed from the University of Michigan after failing an important written examination. The question presented is whether the University's action deprived Ewing of property without due process of law because its refusal to allow him to retake the examination was an arbitrary departure from the University's past practice. The Court of Appeals held that his constitutional rights were violated. We disagree.

I

In the fall of 1975 Ewing enrolled in a special 6-year program of study, known as "Inteflex," offered jointly by the undergraduate college and the medical school. An undergraduate degree and a medical degree are awarded upon successful completion of the program. In order to qualify for the final two years of the Inteflex program, which consist of clinical training at hospitals affiliated with the University, the student must successfully complete four years of study including both premedical courses and courses in the basic medical sciences. The student must also pass the "NBME Part I"—a 2-day written test administered by the National Board of Medical Examiners.

In the spring of 1981, after overcoming certain academic and personal difficulties, Ewing successfully completed the courses prescribed for the first four years of the Inteflex program and thereby qualified to take the NBME Part I. Ewing failed five of the seven subjects on that examination, receiving a total score of 235 when the passing score was 345. (A score of 380 is required for state licensure and the national mean is 500.) Ewing received the lowest score recorded by an Inteflex student in the brief history of that program.

On July 24, 1981, the Promotion and Review Board individually reviewed the status of several students in the Inteflex program. After considering Ewing's record in some detail, the nine members of the Board in attendance voted unanimously to drop him from registration in the program.

In response to a written request from Ewing, the Board reconvened a week later to reconsider its decision. Ewing appeared personally and explained why he believed that his score on the test did not fairly reflect his academic progress or potential. After reconsidering the matter, the nine voting members present unanimously reaffirmed the prior action to drop Ewing from registration in the program.

In August, Ewing appealed the Board's decision to the Executive Committee of the Medical School. After giving Ewing an opportunity to be heard in person, the Executive Committee unanimously approved a motion to deny his appeal for a leave of absence status that would enable him to retake Part I of the NBME examination. In the following year, Ewing reappeared before the Executive Committee on two separate occasions, each time unsuccessfully seeking readmission to the medical school. On August 19, 1982, he commenced this litigation in the United States District Court for the Eastern District of Michigan.

II

Ewing's complaint against the Regents of the University of Michigan asserted a right to retake the NBME Part I test on three separate theories, two predicated on state law and one based on federal law. As a matter of state law, he alleged that the University's action constituted a breach of contract and was barred by the doctrine of promissory estoppel. As a matter of federal law, Ewing alleged that he had a property interest in his continued enrollment in the Inteflex program and that his dismissal was arbitrary and capricious, violating his "substantive due process rights" guaranteed by the Fourteenth Amendment and entitling him to relief under 42 U.S.C. § 1983.

The District Court held a 4-day bench trial at which it took evidence on the University's claim that Ewing's dismissal was justified as well as on Ewing's allegation that other University of Michigan medical students who had failed the NBME Part I had routinely been given a second opportunity to take the test. The District Court described Ewing's unfortunate academic history in some detail. Its findings reveal that Ewing "encountered immediate difficulty in handling the work," and that his difficulties—in the form of marginally passing grades and a number of incompletes and make-up examinations, many experienced while Ewing was on a reduced course load—persisted throughout the 6-year period in which he was enrolled in the Inteflex program.

Ewing discounted the importance of his own academic record by offering evidence that other students with even more academic deficiencies were uniformly allowed to retake the NBME Part I. The statistical evidence indicated that of the 32 standard students in the Medical School who failed Part I of the NBME since its inception, all 32 were permitted to retake the test, 10 were allowed to take the test a third time, and 1 a fourth time. Seven students in the Inteflex program were allowed to retake the test, and one student was allowed to retake it twice. Ewing is the only student who, having failed the test, was not permitted to retake it. Dr. Robert Reed, a former Director of the Inteflex program and a member of the Promotion and Review Board, stated that students were "routinely" given a second chance. Ewing argued that a promotional pamphlet released by the medical school approximately a week before the examination had codified this practice. The pamphlet, entitled "On Becoming a Doctor," stated:

> "According to Dr. Gibson, everything possible is done to keep qualified medical students in the Medical School. This even extends to taking and passing National Board Exams. Should a student fail either part of the National Boards, an opportunity is provided to make up the failure in a second exam."

The District Court concluded that the evidence did not support either Ewing's contract claim or his promissory estoppel claim under governing Michigan law. There was "no sufficient evidence to conclude that the defendants bound themselves either expressly or by a course of conduct to give Ewing a second chance to take Part I of the NBME examination." With reference to the pamphlet "On Becoming A Doctor," the District Court held that "even if [Ewing] had learned of the pamphlet's contents before he took the examination, and I find that he did not, I would not conclude that this amounted either to an unqualified promise to him or gave him a contract right to retake the examination.

With regard to Ewing's federal claim, the District Court assumed that Ewing had a constitutionally protected property interest in his continued enrollment in the Inteflex program and that a State University's academic decisions concerning the qualifications of a medical student are "subject to substantive due process review" in federal court. The District Court, however, found no violation of Ewing's due process rights. The trial record, it emphasized, was devoid of any indication that the University's decision was "based on bad faith, ill will or other impermissible ulterior motives"; to the contrary, the "evidence demonstrate[d] that the decision to dismiss plaintiff was reached in a fair and impartial manner, and only after careful and deliberate consideration." To "leave no conjecture" as to his decision, the District Judge expressly found that "the evidence demonstrate[d] no arbitrary or capricious action since [the Regents] had good reason to dismiss Ewing from the program."

Without reaching the state-law breach-of-contract and promissory-estoppel claims, the Court of Appeals reversed the dismissal of Ewing's federal constitutional claim. The Court of Appeals agreed with the District Court that Ewing's implied contract right to continued enrollment free from arbitrary interference qualified as a property interest protected by the Due Process Clause, but it concluded that the University had arbitrarily deprived him of that property in violation of the Fourteenth Amendment because (1) "Ewing was a 'qualified' student, as the University defined that term, at the time he sat for NBME Part I"; (2) "it was the consistent practice of the University of Michigan to allow a qualified medical student who initially failed the NBME Part I an opportunity for a retest"; and (3) "Ewing was the only University of Michigan medical student who initially failed the NBME Part I between 1975 and 1982, and was not allowed an opportunity for a retest." The Court of Appeals therefore directed the University to allow Ewing to retake the NBME Part I, and if he should pass, to reinstate him in the Inteflex program.

We granted the University's petition for certiorari to consider whether the Court of Appeals had misapplied the doctrine of "substantive due process." We now reverse.

III

In *Board of Curators, Univ. of Mo. v. Horowitz*, we assumed, without deciding, that federal courts can review an academic decision of a public educational institution under a substantive due process standard. In this case Ewing contends that such review is appropriate because he had a constitutionally protected property interest in his continued enrollment in the Inteflex Program. But remembering Justice Brandeis' admonition not to " 'formulate a rule of constitutional law broader than is required by the precise facts to which it is to be applied,' " we again conclude, as we did in *Horowitz*, that the precise facts disclosed by the record afford the most appropriate basis for decision. We therefore accept the University's invitation to "assume the existence of a constitutionally protectible property right in [Ewing's] continued enrollment," and hold that even if Ewing's assumed property interest gave rise to a substantive right under the Due Process Clause to continued enrollment free from arbitrary state action, the facts of record disclose no such action.

As a preliminary matter, it must be noted that any substantive constitutional protection against arbitrary dismissal would not necessarily give Ewing a right to retake the NBME Part I. The constitutionally-protected interest alleged by Ewing in his complaint, and found by the courts below, derives from Ewing's implied contract right to continued enrollment free from arbitrary dismissal. The District Court did not find that Ewing had any separate right to retake the exam and, what is more, explicitly "reject[ed] the contract and promissory estoppel claims, finding no sufficient evidence to conclude that the defendants bound themselves either expressly or by a course of conduct to give Ewing a second chance to take Part I of the NBME examination." The Court of Appeals did not overturn the District Court's determination that Ewing lacked a tenable contract or estoppel claim under Michigan law, and we accept its reasonable rendering of state law, particularly when no party has challenged it.

The University's refusal to allow Ewing to retake the NBME Part I is thus not actionable in itself. It is, however, an important element of Ewing's claim that his dismissal was the product of arbitrary state action, for under proper analysis the refusal may constitute evidence of arbitrariness even if it is not the actual legal wrong alleged. The question, then, is whether the record compels the conclusion that the University acted arbitrarily in dropping Ewing from the Inteflex program without permitting a re-examination.

It is important to remember that this is not a case in which the procedures used by the University were unfair in any respect; quite the contrary is true. Nor can the Regents be accused of concealing nonacademic or constitutionally impermissible reasons for expelling Ewing; the District Court found that the Regents acted in good faith.

Ewing's claim, therefore, must be that the University misjudged his fitness to remain a student in the Inteflex program. The record unmistakably demonstrates, however, that the faculty's decision was made conscientiously and with careful deliberation, based on an evaluation of the entirety of Ewing's academic career. When judges are asked to review the substance of a genuinely academic decision, such as this one, they should show great respect for the faculty's professional judgment. Plainly, they may not override it unless it is such a substantial departure from accepted academic norms as to demonstrate that the person or committee responsible did not actually exercise professional judgment.

Considerations of profound importance counsel restrained judicial review of the substance of academic decisions. As Justice WHITE has explained:

"Although the Court regularly proceeds on the assumption that the Due Process Clause has more than a procedural dimension, we must always bear in mind that the substantive content of the Clause is suggested neither by its language nor by preconstitutional history; that content is nothing more than the accumulated product of judicial interpretation of the Fifth and Fourteenth Amendments. This is ... only to underline Mr. Justice BLACK's constant reminder to his colleagues that the Court has no license to invalidate legislation which it thinks merely arbitrary or unreasonable."

Added to our concern for lack of standards is a reluctance to trench on the prerogatives of state and local educational institutions and our responsibility to safeguard their academic freedom, "a special concern of the First Amendment." If a "federal court is not the appropriate forum in which to review the multitude of personnel decisions that are made daily by public agencies," far less is it suited to evaluate the substance of the multitude of academic decisions that are made daily by faculty members of public educational institutions—decisions that require "an expert evaluation of cumulative information and [are] not readily adapted to the procedural tools of judicial or administrative decision-making."

This narrow avenue for judicial review precludes any conclusion that the decision to dismiss Ewing from the Inteflex program was such a substantial departure from accepted academic norms as to demonstrate that the faculty did not exercise professional judgment. Certainly his expulsion cannot be considered aberrant when viewed in isolation. The District Court found as a fact that the Regents "had good reason to dismiss Ewing from the program." Before failing the NBME Part I, Ewing accumulated an unenviable academic record characterized by low grades, seven incompletes, and several terms during which he was on an irregular or reduced course load. Ewing's failure of his medical boards, in the words of one of his professors, "merely culminate[d] a series of deficiencies. . . . In many ways, it's the straw that broke the camel's back." Moreover, the fact that Ewing was "qualified" in the sense that he was eligible to take the examination the first time does not weaken this conclusion, for after Ewing took the NBME Part I it was entirely reasonable for the faculty to reexamine his entire record in the light of the unfortunate results of that examination. Admittedly, it may well have been unwise to deny Ewing a second chance. Permission to retake the test might have saved the University the expense of this litigation and conceivably might have demonstrated that the members of the Promotion and Review Board misjudged Ewing's fitness for the medical profession. But it nevertheless remains true that his dismissal from the Inteflex program rested on an academic judgment that is not beyond the pale of reasoned academic decision-making when viewed against the background of his entire career at the University of Michigan, including his singularly low score on the NBME Part I examination.

The judgment of the Court of Appeals is reversed and the case is remanded for proceedings consistent with this opinion.

———

Haberle v. University of Alabama at Birmingham

803 F. 2d 1536 (11th Cir. 1986)

HILL, Circuit Judge:

FACTS

Appellant Frederick J. Haberle was admitted to graduate school at the University of Alabama at Birmingham in July, 1979, to pursue a Ph.D. in chemistry. The requirements to obtain that degree are set out in a document entitled "Requirements for Degree in Chemistry." Generally it shows that the requirements for a Ph.D. in chemistry are completion of course work, demonstration of competence in two foreign languages, successful completion of the qualifying examination, presentations at two seminars, and the completion of a dissertation. Mr. Haberle was given a copy of this document soon after he entered the program. During his time as a student in the chemistry department, Haberle completed his course work, demonstrated his competency in two foreign languages, and made a presentation at one graduate seminar.

Mr. Haberle completed his course work in the fall of 1981. He registered for his dissertation in research in the winter term of 1980–81 and continued with it through the summer term of 1983–84. In July of 1981, the graduate committee supervising Mr. Haberle's studies met to discuss his curriculum and the qualifying (or "comprehensive") examination requirement. At this meeting the committee listed remaining course requirements, and planned to meet again in order to consider a research proposal and set a date for the qualifying examination. However, the committee did not meet again until January of 1984. At that time the committee noted that Haberle had never taken the qualifying examinations, and suggested he do so promptly. Mr. Haberle objected, stating that he should have taken the exam before beginning his dissertation research three years prior. However, the committee insisted that he take the qualifying exam.

The exam is divided into two portions, a written portion and an oral portion. Mr. Haberle passed the written portion by one point, and failed the oral portion. He was given the choice between accepting a master's degree or retaking the qualifying examination. He chose to take the exam again, and he failed again. He was then dismissed from the Chemistry Ph.D. program.

After his dismissal Mr. Haberle complained to Dr. Blaine Brownell, who was then co-dean of the graduate school. He was advised to ask the committee members to reconsider their decision. They refused to do so. Mr. Haberle then addressed a grievance to the two deans of the graduate school, Kenneth J. Roozen and Blaine Brownell, and Peter O'Neal, Dean of the School of Natural Sciences and Mathematics.

O'Neal, along with the dean of the graduate school, decided that O'Neal would appoint an impartial committee to review Mr. Haberle's grievance. O'Neal appointed Professors Joseph Gauthier and Daniel Bearce to review the matter. They had never had any dealings with Mr. Haberle. Haberle was given the opportunity to submit additional information to the committee; he declined the opportunity to do so. The reviewing committee decided that the graduate committee had acted reasonably and that Mr. Haberle had been treated fairly. Their decision was then reviewed by the dean of the graduate school, who concurred.

Soon after, Mr. Haberle filed suit in federal district court, claiming that his dismissal and the procedures used to procure it violated his substantive and procedural due process rights. Haberle objected to the procedure used in disposing of his grievance on the following grounds: (1) the procedures were established on an ad hoc basis, (2) nowhere along the line did any of the administrators review Mr. Haberle's grades, and (3) the procedures did not follow those described in the graduate school bulletin. He also argued that his dismissal was arbitrary and thus a violation of substantive due process.

On summary judgment motion, the district court found that, as a matter of law in the Eleventh Circuit, the right to pursue a degree in the public school system was a constitutionally protectable interest. The court then dismissed the procedural due process claims, finding that all the procedures used were constitutionally adequate. After the Supreme Court's decision in *Regents of the University of Michigan v. Ewing*, the district court *sua sponte* reconsidered its motion for summary judgment and dismissed the substantive due process claims as well.

I.

With respect to the procedural due process claim, the legal standard governing academic dismissals was enunciated in the Supreme Court's decision *Board of Curators, University of Missouri v. Horowitz*. The court emphasized that academic dismissals were not easily adapted to traditional review, and that the standards governing academic dismissals were not as strict as those required in disciplinary actions. Formal hearings are not required in academic dismissals. Rather, the Supreme Court held that the decision-making process need only be "careful and deliberate."

The district court found that under the *Horowitz* standard, the procedures used in dismissing Mr. Haberle were adequate. The court noted:

1. Plaintiff had several discussions with members of the graduate committee during which he expressed objections to taking the preliminary exam.

2. He was given two opportunities to take the exam.

3. He had discussions with the co-dean of the graduate school, further consideration by the graduate committee, and further consideration by the Dean of the School of Natural Sciences and Mathematics.

4. An impartial committee was appointed to review his complaint, and he was given an opportunity to submit further information to the committee.

Obviously Mr. Haberle was given substantial opportunity to complain to all relevant decision-makers. The fact that the procedures used were ad hoc does not violate the *Horowitz* standard; no formal hearing is required. In fact, University officials testified that the procedures afforded Haberle far exceeded the grievance procedure outlined in the University bulletin. There is no reason to reverse the district court's finding that procedural due process requirements were met in this case.

II.

We now turn to the substantive due process issue. In *Ewing*, the Supreme Court laid out a very narrow standard of substantive review over academic decisions.

* * *

Ewing makes it plain that, in the absence of an improper motive, an academic dismissal must be "such a substantial departure from accepted academic norms as to demonstrate that the faculty did not exercise professional judgment," before it will be overturned on substantive due process grounds.

Appellant contends that Mr. Haberle's dismissal was arbitrary because he was required to take the qualifying exam "for no reason." Theoretically the qualifying exam is given to a student before embarking upon dissertation research, to test one's competency and ability to carry out extensive research in one's chosen specialty. Mr. Haberle felt that his three years of dissertation research had already demonstrated his capacity to do extensive research, and that the examination was therefore a totally arbitrary, unnecessary intrusion into his academic career. However, the professors at the Department of Chemistry all felt, as a matter of professional judgment, that such an exam is necessary to test the caliber of one who would enter the company of scholars.

A summary chart submitted to the district court proved that no student had ever been awarded a Ph.D. without having to take the qualifying exam. In fact, the same evidence proved that it was not at all out of the ordinary for a student to take his or her qualifying exam after registering to begin dissertation research. The court found that requiring Mr. Haberle to take it four years after the normal time (i.e. before beginning one's dissertation research) was not such a substantial departure from academic norms as to amount to an arbitrary deprivation of property.

Appellant objects to the admission of the summary chart, noting that a similar chart was excluded in *Ewing*. However, in *Ewing* it was used to show that the dismissed individual's academic performance was as bad as other students who had also been dismissed. In the instant case, the chart did not attempt to prove that these students were similarly situated; rather, it merely indicated that the exam had never been waived, and that other students had been required to take it late in their academic career. In other words, the chart was used to demonstrate the academic norms of the Chemistry Department of the University of Alabama, and was therefore admissible.

Mr. Haberle also argues that the graduate committee "waived" the exam requirement for him by not requiring that he take the exam before beginning his dissertation research. This argument is purely fallacious. While it may have been unfortunate for the committee to allow him to do three year's worth of dissertation research, in fact no one ever told Mr. Haberle that the exam had been waived, and the exam has never been waived for anyone.

Appellant's attempts to distinguish himself from the plaintiff in *Ewing* do not help him. It is true that in *Ewing* the student was dismissed because of a generally poor academic performance. His failure to pass his medical boards was merely the crowning blow. In the instant case, Mr. Haberle's performance in the classroom was very good. However, as appellee points out, the qualifying exam is used to probe one's in-depth knowledge of one's chosen specialty. Only one of the five faculty members who examined Haberle felt that he possessed the overall knowledge of the subject and academic talent necessary for advanced graduate study. Professor Larry K. Krannich, Chairman of the Department of Chemistry, testified in his deposition that, while it is routine to allow a student who fails a qualifying exam a second opportunity to pass, no student has ever been given a third opportunity to take the exam. After two attempts Mr. Haberle was dismissed in accordance with the department's normal procedure.

It may be unfortunate to spend years studying a discipline only to discover that one's capabilities do not pass academic muster. However, the academic community requires a general comprehensive examination to determine whether or not a student is properly qualified for doctoral accomplishments. Had Mr. Haberle learned earlier that he did not have the comprehensive qualifications in chemistry to make him a suitable candidate for a doctoral degree, he might not have pursued the narrow research studies leading towards his dissertation for quite so long. Nevertheless, this is an academic question. The comprehensive exam is a prerequisite to the doctorate. Mr. Haberle failed the exam. There is no dispute about that. Therefore, he is not entitled to continue to pursue the doctorate. There is nothing arbitrary about such a requirement. The courts should not interfere with this academic decision.

Accordingly, the decision of the district court is

AFFIRMED.

Cosio v. Medical College of Wisconsin
407 N.W. 2d 302 (Wis. App. 1987)

SULLIVAN, Judge.

Jose Cosio appeals a summary judgment which dismissed his amended complaint against the Medical College of Wisconsin, Inc. (MCW). Cosio's amended complaint alleged that his academic dismissal from MCW constituted (1) a breach of express and implied contract; (2) gross negligence; and (3) an arbitrary and capricious act. Cosio also pled promissory estoppel and a violation of his rights under 42 U.S.C.A. sec. 1983. We will not address these last two issues since Cosio did not brief them on appeal; they are deemed abandoned. We affirm the judgment.

Cosio enrolled for the 1981–82 academic year in MCW's Doctor of Medicine program. Under MCW's academic policies, he was required to repeat his first year because of "marginal" and "unsatisfactory" grades. After he completed his repeated first year, he was advanced to the second year of study. He continued to have academic problems and was granted a leave of absence before the end of the term. He was allowed to repeat his second year of study under academic conditions, which he failed to meet. MCW dismissed Cosio on June 4, 1985. Cosio filed a complaint in the circuit court. The court granted summary judgment against Cosio, finding that he failed to establish the existence of fact issues relating to breach of contract or MCW's duty of care owed to him, or to show arbitrary conduct on MCW's part. We agree.

In reviewing Cosio's appeal, this court applied summary judgment standards in the same manner as the trial court. We must determine whether MCW is entitled to judgment as a matter of law. We give no deference to the trial court's conclusions on matters of law. We apply the following methodology in determining whether summary judgment was properly granted to MCW:

> The first step is to examine the pleadings to determine whether a claim has been stated and whether a genuine issue of fact is presented. If the complaint states a claim and the pleadings show the existence of factual issues, the second step is to examine the moving party's affidavits and other proof to determine whether the party has made a prima facie case for summary judgment. To make a prima facie case, a moving defendant must show a defense which would defeat the plaintiff. If the moving party has made a prima facie case, the third step is to examine the affidavits and other proof of the opposing party to determine whether there exist disputed material facts or undisputed material facts from which reasonable alternative inferences may be drawn, sufficient to entitle the opposing party to a trial.

MCW has the burden to establish that no fact issue exists and that it is entitled to judgment.

BREACH OF CONTRACT

Cosio's first cause of action is based on breach of contract, including breach of implied warranty of good faith. MCW breached, Cosio claims, by failing to provide competitive examinations which decided scholastic promotion. Instead, Cosio argues, MCW knew of widespread cheating by numerous students on examinations. MCW breached its covenant of good faith contract performance by its tolerance of cheating which, Cosio maintains, caused his failure and the promotion of those who cheated. We reject this argument because the contract provided a means of addressing students' unethical behavior which Cosio failed to use.

An uncontroverted affidavit of the senior associate dean and director of student affairs at MCW averred that Cosio received a 1981–82 Bulletin and Handbook when he was interviewed and when he registered. These documents were contractual in nature and spelled out part of the relationship between Cosio and MCW.

The handbook provided a comprehensive student honor system to deal with student's unethical behavior. It provided, *"All alleged honor violations are to be reported to a member of the Student Affairs Committee (S.A.C.) of the class to which the alleged offender belongs."* The handbook contained detailed provisions for creation of a committee to consider violations, for a preliminary hearing, for a final hearing before SAC, and for determination of violations and sanctions. It mandated notice and opportunity to be heard for the violator at each step. The handbook required written SAC findings and provided for rehearing in the event of newly discovered evidence and for appeal to the appeals subcommittee of the Executive Committee of the Faculty.

It is without dispute that Cosio never used this procedure. In an uncontroverted affidavit, the associate dean for student affairs asserted that in the spring of 1982 Cosio reported cheating to her. She made a photocopy of the handbook honors provisions and offered to assist him in proceeding against the offenders. Cosio did not pursue the matter. Later the associate dean saw Cosio and inquired whether he wanted to proceed. He said he did not.

Cosio's amended complaint alleges that MCW had a duty to monitor examinations. No such duty is found in the bulletin or handbook. No duty will be read into an unambiguous contract on summary judgment. We conclude that the pleadings and affidavits fail to raise a fact issue as to any contractual breach on the part of MCW.

ARBITRARY DISMISSAL

Cosio maintains that his dismissal was arbitrary because MCW tolerated widespread cheating on examinations. MCW's reason for Cosio's dismissal, however, was his unsatisfactory academic performance.

MCW's bulletin contained provisions regulating dismissals. This power was vested in the Committee on Academic Standing, which weighed departmental evaluations and sought advice from faculty members and the director of student affairs. The bulletin states that the appeals procedure can be obtained at the dean's office. A review of Cosio's academic performance, found in uncontroverted affidavits on summary judgment, showed that MCW continuously monitored his scholastic performance. The committee permitted Cosio to repeat his first and second academic years.

Cosio was aware of the committee's consideration of his work and other personal circumstances. The committee advised Cosio that any grade less than passing in his second repeated year would be grounds for dismissal. When Cosio failed to meet this condition, the committee dismissed him, stating its reasons and advising him of his appeal rights.

Cosio argues that MCW acted arbitrarily because while dismissing him, it permitted others, who engaged in cheating, to graduate. We reject this argument. The test for arbitrary or capricious dismissal is whether the dismissal is based on sufficient reasons; if a school has sufficient reasons for dismissal, as MCW did, the court will not interfere.

NEGLIGENCE

Cosio's amended complaint charges MCW with negligence in failing to monitor examinations. Essentially, it alleges that MCW was negligent in the performance of its contract with him. As a result, Cosio claims, those who cheated received grades of passing and the grade curve was thereby skewed to his disadvantage. Because we have determined that MCW had no duty to monitor examinations under its contractual arrangement with Cosio, we reject this argument.

In summary, we hold that the trial court providently granted summary judgment because (1) no issue of fact is presented relating to MCW's breach of contract or warranty of good faith because Cosio failed to use the remedy provided by contract to correct unethical student behavior; (2) Cosio's dismissal was not arbitrary because MCW's reason to dismiss him, unsatisfactory scholastic performance, was undisputed in the record; and (3) MCW was not negligent because it owed Cosio no duty to monitor examinations.

Judgment affirmed.

Disciplinary Dismissals

The line between academic behavior and disciplinary actions is not always clear. In his dissent to *Horowitz*, Justice Marshall suggested that judgment of students' clinical behavior and patient interaction were disciplinary in nature: many dismissals for "conduct" occur in mixed academic/behavior settings, such as laboratories, libraries, or clinics. Even when pre-*Horowitz* courts have conceded mixed-performance settings, students lost because the process afforded them was usually held to constitute their due. See *Sofair v. SUNY*, 388 N.Y.S.2d 453 (App. Div. 1976) (grades may represent a "complex variety of skills that make up professional competence"). Steven Mosher's conduct included allegations that he failed to abide by exchange-scholar guidelines in the PRC; Carol North was diagnosed as a schizophrenic; Diane Mauriello's research errors caused her adviser to lose confidence in the quality of her research skills; Ben Hammond's grade point average was too low to continue, even though the college raised its standards once he was already enrolled in the program. Similarly, many instances of cheating involved mixed academic/behavior fact patterns.

The cases selected for this Section include students dismissed for a variety of behaviors, some of which have little bearing on their fitness for remaining in an academic program (such as a harmless radio prank or posing for *Playboy*), while others have a clearer connection between their fitness to remain in college and the behavior. At West Point, an A student was dismissed for failing two "military development" courses, in which hazing by upper-class student occurs and military discipline is inculcated. The institution upheld his dismissal: "while cadet Edwards achieved considerable academic success at West Point, under the 'whole man' concept he was in other endeavors a marginal cadet." "Review of West Point's Verbal Hazing Policy is Ordered," *Houston Chronicle*, 26 April 1988. As often as these cases occur, more often the student simply moves to another school (as did Picozzi).

Dixon v. Alabama State Board of Education
294 F.2d 150 (1961)

RIVES, Circuit Judge.

The question presented by the pleadings and evidence, and decisive of this appeal, is whether due process requires notice and some opportunity for hearing before students at a tax-supported college are expelled for misconduct. We answer that question in the affirmative.

The misconduct for which the students were expelled has never been definitely specified. Defendant Trenholm, the President of the College, testified that he did not know why the plaintiffs and three additional students were expelled and twenty other students were placed on probation. The notice of expulsion which Dr. Trenholm mailed to each of the plaintiffs assigned no specific ground for expulsion, but referred in general terms to "this problem of Alabama State College."

The acts of the students considered by the State Board of Education before it ordered their expulsion are described in the opinion of the district court, from which we quote:

> "On the 25th day of February, 1960, the six plaintiffs in this case were students in good standing at the Alabama State College for Negroes in Montgomery, Alabama * * * On this date, approximately twenty-nine Negro students, including these six plaintiffs, according to a prearranged plan, entered as a group a publicly owned lunch grill located in the basement of the county courthouse in Montgomery, Alabama, and asked to be served. Service was refused; the lunch-room was closed; the Negroes refused to leave; police authorities were summoned; and the Negroes were ordered outside where they remained in the corridor of the courthouse for approximately one hour. On the same date, John Patterson, as Governor of the State of Alabama and a chairman of the State Board of Education, conferred with Dr. Trenholm, a Negro educator and president of the Alabama State College, concerning this activity on the part of some of the students. Dr. Trenholm was advised by the Governor that the incident should be investigated, and that if he were in the president's position he would consider expulsion and/or other appropriate disciplinary action. On February 26, 1960, several hundred Negro students from the Alabama State College, including several if not all of these plaintiffs, staged a mass attendance at a trial being held in the Montgomery County Courthouse, involving the perjury prosecution of a fellow student. After the trial these students filed two by two from the courthouse and marched through the city approximately two miles back to the college. On February 27, 1960, several hundred Negro students from this

school, including several if not all of the plaintiffs in this case, staged mass demonstrations in Montgomery and Tuskegee, Alabama. On this same date, Dr. Trenholm advised all of the student body that these demonstrations and meetings were disrupting the orderly conduct of the business at the college and were affecting the work of other students, as well as work of the participating students. Dr. Trenholm personally warned plaintiffs Bernard Lee, Joseph Peterson and Elroy Embry, to cease these disruptive demonstrations immediately, and advised the members of the student body at the Alabama State College to behave themselves and return to their classes. * * *

"On or about March 1, 1960, approximately six hundred students of the Alabama State College engaged in hymn singing and speech making on the steps of the State Capitol. Plaintiff Bernard Lee addressed students at this demonstration, and the demonstration was attended by several if not all of the plaintiffs. Plaintiff Bernard Lee at this time called on the students to strike and boycott the college if any students were expelled because of these demonstrations."

As shown by the findings of the district court, just quoted, the only demonstration which the evidence showed that *all* of the expelled students took part in was that in the lunch grill located in the basement of the Montgomery County Courthouse. The other demonstrations were found to be attended "by several if not all of the plaintiffs." We have carefully read and studied the record, and agree with the district court that the evidence does not affirmatively show that *all* of the plaintiffs were present at any but the one demonstration.

*   *   *

The evidence clearly shows that the question for decision does not concern the sufficiency of the notice or the adequacy of the hearing, but is whether the students had a right to any notice or hearing whatever before being expelled.

*   *   *

It is not enough to say, as did the district court in the present case, "The right to attend a public college or university is not in and of itself a constitutional right." That argument was emphatically answered by the Supreme Court in the Cafeteria and Restaurant Workers Union case, when it said that the question of whether " * * * summarily denying Rachel Brawner access to the site of her former employment violated the requirements of the Due Process Clause of the Fifth Amendment * * * cannot be answered by easy assertion that, because she had no constitutional right to be there in the first place, she was not deprived of liberty or property by the Superintendent's action. 'One may not have a constitutional right to go to Bagdad, but the Government may not prohibit one from going there unless by means consonant with due process of law.' " As in that case, so here, it is necessary to consider "the nature both of the private interest which has been impaired and the governmental power which has been exercised."

The appellees urge upon us that under a provision of the Board of Education's regulations the appellants waived any right to notice and a hearing before being expelled for misconduct.

"Attendance at any college is on the basis of a mutual decision of the student's parents and of the college. Attendance at a particular college is voluntary and is different from attendance at a public school where the pupil may be required to attend a particular school which is located in the neighborhood or district in which the pupil's family may live. Just as a student may choose to withdraw from a particular college at any time for any personally-determined reason, the college may also at any time decline to continue to accept responsibility for the supervision and service to any student with whom the relationship becomes unpleasant and difficult."

We do not read this provision to clearly indicate an intent on the part of the student to waive notice and a hearing before expulsion. If, however, we should so assume, it nonetheless remains true that the State cannot condition the granting of even a privilege upon the renunciation of the constitutional right to procedural due process.

* * *

The precise nature of the private interest involved in this case is the right to remain at a public institution of higher learning in which the plaintiffs were students in good standing. It requires no argument to demonstrate that education is vital and, indeed, basic to civilized society. Without sufficient education the plaintiffs would not be able to earn an adequate livelihood, to enjoy life to the fullest, or to fulfill as completely as possible the duties and responsibilities of good citizens.

There was no offer to prove that other colleges are open to the plaintiffs. If so, the plaintiffs would nonetheless be injured by the interruption of their course of studies in mid-term. It is most unlikely that a public college would accept a student expelled from another public college of the same state. Indeed, expulsion may well prejudice the student in completing his education at any other institution. Surely no one can question that the right to remain at the college in which the plaintiffs were students in good standing is an interest of extremely great value.

Turning then to the nature of the governmental power to expel the plaintiffs, it must be conceded, as was held by the district court, that that power is not unlimited and cannot be arbitrarily exercised. Admittedly, there must be some reasonable and constitutional ground for expulsion or the courts would have a duty to require reinstatement. The possibility of arbitrary action is not excluded by the existence of reasonable regulations. There may be arbitrary application of the rule to the facts of a particular case. Indeed, that result is well nigh inevitable when the Board hears only one side of the issue. In the disciplining of college students there are no considerations of immediate danger to the public, or of peril to the national security, which should prevent the Board from exercising at least the fundamental principles of fairness by giving the accused students notice of the charges and an opportunity to be heard in their own defense. Indeed, the example set by the Board in failing so to do, if not corrected by the courts, can well break the spirits of the expelled students and of others familiar with the injustice, and do inestimable harm to their education.

The district court, however, felt that it was governed by precedent, and stated that, "the courts have consistently upheld the validity of regulations that have the effect of reserving to the college the right to dismiss students at any time for any reasons without divulging its reason other than its being for the general benefit of the institution." With deference, we must hold that the district court has simply misinterpreted the precedents. We are confident that precedent as well as a most fundamental constitutional principle support our holding that due process requires notice and some opportunity for hearing before a student at a tax-supported college is expelled for misconduct.

For the guidance of the parties in the event of further proceedings, we state our views on the nature of the notice and hearing required by due process prior to expulsion from a state college or university. They should, we think, comply with the following standards. The notice should contain a statement of the specific charges and grounds which, if proven, would justify expulsion under the regulations of the Board of Education. The nature of the hearing should vary depending upon the circumstances of the particular case. The case before us requires something more than an informal interview with an administrative authority of the college. By its nature, a charge of misconduct, as opposed to a failure to meet the scholastic standards of the college, depends upon a collection of the facts concerning the charged misconduct, easily colored by the point of view of the witnesses. In such circumstances, a hearing which gives the Board or the administrative authorities of the college an opportunity to hear both sides in considerable detail is best studied to protect the rights of all involved. This is not to imply that a full-dress judicial hearing, with the right to cross-examine witnesses, is required. Such a hearing, with the attending publicity and disturbance of college activities, might be detrimental to the college's educational atmosphere and impractical to carry out. Nevertheless, the rudiments of an adversary proceeding may be preserved without encroaching upon the interests of the college. In the instant case, the student should be given the names of the witnesses against him and an oral or written report on the facts to which each witness testifies. He should also be given the opportunity to present to the Board, or at least to an administrative official of the college, his own defense against the charges and to produce either oral testimony or written affidavits of witnesses in his behalf. If the hearing is not before the Board directly, the results and findings of the hearing should be presented in a report open to the student's inspection. If these rudimentary elements of fair play are followed in a case of misconduct of this particular type, we feel that the requirements of due process of law will have been fulfilled.

The judgment of the district court is reversed and the cause is remanded for further proceedings consistent with this opinion.

Reversed and remanded.

CAMERON, Circuit Judge (dissenting).

The opinion of the district court in this case is so lucid, literate and moderate that I cannot forego expressing surprise that my brethren of the majority can find fault with it. In this dissent I shall try to avoid repeating what the lower court has so well said and to confine myself to an effort to refute the holdings of the majority where they do attack and reject the lower court's opinion.

* * *

Certainly I think that the filing of charges, the disclosure of names of proposed witnesses, and such procedures as the majority discusses are wholly unrealistic and impractical and would result in a major blow to our institutions of learning. Every attempt at discipline would probably lead to a *cause célébre,* in connection with which federal functionaries would be rushed in to investigate whether a federal law had been violated. I think we would do well to bear in mind the words of Mr. Justice Jackson:

" * * * no local agency which is subject to federal investigation, inspection, and discipline is a free agency. I cannot say that our country could have no central police without becoming totalitarian, but I can say with great conviction that it cannot become totalitarian without a centralized national police."

I think, moreover, that, in these troublous times, those in positions of responsibility in the federal government should bear in mind that the maintenance of the safety, health and morals of the people is committed under our system of government to the states. More than a hundred year ago Chief Justice Marshall stated the principle in these words:

> "The power to direct the removal of gunpowder is a branch of the police power, which unquestionably remains, and ought to remain, with the states."

I dissent.

Goss v. Lopez
419 U.S. 565 (1975)

Mr. Justice WHITE delivered the opinion of the Court.

This appeal by various administrators of the Columbus, Ohio, Public School System (CPSS) challenges the judgment of a three-judge federal court, declaring that appellees—various high school students in the CPSS—were denied due process of law contrary to the command of the Fourteenth Amendment in that they were temporarily suspended from their high schools without a hearing either prior to suspension or within a reasonable time thereafter, and enjoining the administrators to remove all references to such suspensions from the students' records.

* * *

The proof below established that the suspensions arose out of a period of widespread student unrest in the CPSS during February and March 1971.

Two named plaintiffs, Dwight Lopez and Betty Crome, were students at the Central High School and McGuffey Junior High School, respectively. The former was suspended in connection with a disturbance in the lunch-room which involved some physical damage to school property. Lopez testified that at least 75 other students were suspended from his school on the same day. He also testified below that he was not a party to the destructive conduct but was instead an innocent bystander. Because no one from the school testified with regard to this incident, there is no evidence in the record indicating the official basis for concluding otherwise. Lopez never had a hearing.

* * *

On the basis of this evidence, the three-judge court declared that plaintiffs were denied due process of law because they were "suspended without hearing prior to suspension or within a reasonable time thereafter," and that Ohio Rev. Code Ann. § 3313.66 (1972) and regulations issued pursuant thereto were unconstitutional in permitting such suspensions. It was ordered that all references to plaintiff's suspensions be removed from school files.

Although not imposing upon the Ohio school administrators any particular disciplinary procedures and leaving them "free to adopt regulations providing for fair suspension procedures which are consonant with the educational goals of their schools and reflective of the characteristics of their school and locality," the District Court declared that there were "minimum requirements of notice and a hearing prior to suspension, except in emergency situations." In explication, the court stated that relevant case authority would: (1) permit "[i]mmediate removal of a student whose conduct disrupts the academic atmosphere of the school, endangers fellow students, teachers or school officials, or damages property"; (2) require notice of suspension proceedings to be sent to the student's parents within 24 hours of the decision to conduct them; and (3) require a hearing to be held, with the student present, within 72 hours of his removal. Finally, the court stated that, with respect to the nature of the hearing, the relevant cases required that statements in support of the charge be produced, that the student and others be permitted to make statements in defense or mitigation, and that the school need not permit attendance by counsel.

The defendant school administrators have appealed the three-judge court's decision. Because the order below granted plaintiffs' request for an injunction—ordering defendants to expunge their records—this Court has jurisdiction of the appeal pursuant to 28 U.S.C. § 1253. We affirm.

II

At the outset, appellants contend that because there is no constitutional right to an education at public expense, the Due Process Clause does not protect against expulsions from the public school system. This position misconceives the nature of the issue and is refuted by prior decisions. The Fourteenth Amendment forbids the State to deprive any person of life, liberty, or property without due process of law. Protected interests in property are normally "not created by the Constitution."

* * *

Here, on the basis of state law, appellees plainly had legitimate claims of entitlement to a public education. Ohio Rev. Code Ann. §§ 3313.48 and 3313.64 (1972 and Supp. 1973) direct local authorities to provide a free education to all residents between five and 21 years of age, and a compulsory-attendance law requires attendance for a school year of not less then 32 weeks. It is true that §§ 3313.66 of the Code permits school principals to suspend students for up to 10 days; but suspensions may not be imposed without any grounds whatsoever. All of the schools had their own rules specifying the grounds for expulsion or suspension. Having chosen to extend the right to an education to people of appellees' class generally, Ohio may not withdraw that right on grounds of misconduct, absent fundamentally fair procedures to determine whether the misconduct has occurred.

Although Ohio may not be constitutionally obligated to establish and maintain a public school system, it has nevertheless done so and has required its children to attend. Those young people do not "shed their constitutional rights" at the schoolhouse door. "The Fourteenth Amendment, as now applied to the States, protects the citizen against the State itself and all of its creatures—Boards of Education not excepted." The authority possessed by the State to prescribe and enforce standards of conduct in its schools although concededly very broad, must be exercised consistently with constitutional safeguards. Among other things, the State is constrained to recognize a student's legitimate entitlement to a public education as a property interest which is protected by the Due Process Clause and which may not be taken away for misconduct without adherence to the minimum procedures required by that Clause.

The Due Process Clause also forbids arbitrary deprivations of liberty. "Where a person's good name, reputation, honor, or integrity is at stake because of what the government is doing to him," the minimal requirements of the Clause must be satisfied. School authorities here suspended appellees from school for periods of up to 10 days based on charges of misconduct. If sustained and recorded, those charges could seriously damage the students' standing with their fellow pupils and their teachers as well as interfere with later opportunities for higher education and employment. It is apparent that the claimed right of the State to determine unilaterally and without process whether that misconduct has occurred immediately collides with the requirements of the Constitution.

Appellants proceed to argue that even if there is a right to a public education protected by the Due Process Clause generally, the Clause comes into play only when the State subjects a student to a "severe detriment or grievous loss." The loss of 10 days, it is said, is neither severe nor grievous and the Due Process Clause is therefore of no relevance. Appellants' argument is again refuted by our prior decisions; for in determining "whether due process requirements apply in the first place, we must look not to the 'weight' but to the *nature* of the interest at stake." Appellees were excluded from school only temporarily, it is true, but the length and consequent severity of a deprivation, while another factor to weigh in determining the appropriate form of hearing, "is not decisive of the basic right" to a hearing of some kind. The Court's view has been that as long as a property deprivation is not *de minimis*, its gravity is irrelevant to the question whether account must be taken of the Due Process Clause.

A 10-day suspension from school is not *de minimis* in our view and may not be imposed in complete disregard of the Due Process Clause.

A short suspension is, of course, a far milder deprivation than expulsion. But, "education is perhaps the most important function of state and local governments," and the total exclusion from the educational process for more than a trivial period, and certainly if the suspension is for 10 days, is a serious event in the life of the suspended child. Neither the property interest in educational benefits temporarily denied nor the liberty interest in reputation, which is also implicated, is so insubstantial that suspensions may constitutionally be imposed by any procedure the school chooses, no matter how arbitrary.

III

"Once it is determined that due process applies, the question remains what process is due." We turn to that question, fully realizing as our cases regularly do that the interpretation and application of the Due Process Clause are intensely practical matters and that "[t]he very nature of due process negates any concept of inflexible procedures universally applicable to every imaginable situation."

*   *   *

At the very minimum, therefore, students facing suspension and the consequent interference with a protected property interest must be given *some* kind of notice and afforded *some* kind of hearing. "Parties whose rights are to be affected are entitled to be heard; and in order that they may enjoy that right they must first be notified."

It also appears from our case that the timing and content of the notice and the nature of the hearing will depend on appropriate accommodation of the competing interests involved. The student's interest is to avoid unfair or mistaken exclusion from the educational process, with all of its unfortunate consequences. The Due Process Clause will not shield him from suspensions properly imposed, but it disserves both his interest and the interest of the State if his suspension is in fact unwarranted. The concern would be mostly academic if the disciplinary process were a totally accurate, unerring process, never mistaken and never unfair. Unfortunately, that is not the case, and no one suggests that it is. Disciplinarians, although proceeding in utmost good faith, frequently act on the reports and advice of others; and the controlling facts and the nature of the conduct under challenge are often disputed. The risk of error is not at all trivial, and it should be guarded against if that may be done without prohibitive cost or interference with the educational process.

* * *

We do not believe that school authorities must be totally free from notice and hearing requirements if their schools are to operate with acceptable efficiency. Students facing temporary suspension have interests qualifying for protection of the Due Process Clause, and due process requires, in connection with a suspension of 10 days or less, that the student be given oral or written notice of the charges against him and, if he denies them, an explanation of the evidence the authorities have and an opportunity to present his side of the story. The Clause requires at least these rudimentary precautions against unfair or mistaken findings of misconduct and arbitrary exclusion from school.

There need be no delay between the time "notice" is given and the time of the hearing. In the great majority of cases the disciplinarian may informally discuss the alleged misconduct with the student minutes after it has occurred. We hold only that, in being given an opportunity to explain his version of the facts at this discussion, the student first be told what he is accused of doing and what the basis of the accusation is.

* * *

We stop short of construing the Due Process Clause to require, countrywide, that hearings in connection with short suspensions must afford the student the opportunity to secure counsel, to confront and cross-examine witnesses supporting the charge, or to call his own witnesses to verify his version of the incident. Brief disciplinary suspensions are almost countless. To impose in each such a case even truncated trial-type procedures might well overwhelm administrative facilities in many places and, by diverting resources, cost more than it would save in educational effectiveness. Moreover, further formalizing the suspension process and escalating its formality and adversary nature may not only make it too costly as a regular disciplinary tool but also destroy its effectiveness as part of the teaching process.

On the other hand, requiring effective notice and informal hearing permitting the student to give his version of the events will provide a meaningful hedge against erroneous action. At least the disciplinarian will be alerted to the existence of disputes about facts and arguments about cause and effect. He may then determine himself to summon the accuser, permit cross-examination, and allow the student to present his own witnesses. In more difficult cases, he may permit counsel. In any event, his discretion will be more informed and we think the risk of error substantially reduced.

Requiring that there be at least an informal give-and-take between student and disciplinarian, preferably prior to the suspension, will add little to the factfinding function where the disciplinarian himself has witnessed the conduct forming the basis for the charge. But things are not always as they seem to be, and the student will at least have the opportunity to characterize his conduct and put it in what he deems the proper context.

We should also make it clear that we have addressed ourselves solely to the short suspension, not exceeding 10 days. Longer suspensions or expulsions for the remainder of the school term, or permanently, may require more formal procedures. Nor do we put aside the possibility that in unusual situations, although involving only a short suspension, something more than the rudimentary procedures will be required.

IV

The District Court found each of the suspensions involved here to have occurred without a hearing, either before or after the suspension, and that each suspension was therefore invalid and the statute unconstitutional insofar as it permits such suspensions without notice or hearing. Accordingly, the judgment is

Affirmed.

Picozzi v. Sandalow
623 F. Supp. 1571 (D.C. Mich. 1986)

Feikens, J.

* * *

I. FACTS

During his second year at the University of Michigan Law School, Picozzi leased room K-33 in the Lawyers Club, the law school student residence. At about 4:00 a.m. on March 8, 1983, fire broke out in his room. Picozzi alleges that he awoke and attempted to leave the room and that because flames blocked the doorway to the hall, he used the third floor window to exit the room. He says he attempted initially to stay on the windowsill, but eventually either jumped or fell to the ground. As a result, he sustained burns and a fractured vertebra. He was treated at the University of Michigan Hospital from March 8 to April 2, 1983; he then transferred to the University of Pittsburgh Hospital in order to be closer to his family. He remained hospitalized until sometime in May, 1983, and in a body cast until October, 1983.

By April, 1983, it appeared that Picozzi would be physically unable to return to school during the 1983 Winter Term. On April 1, 1983, Associate Dean Eklund informed Picozzi's father that Picozzi had been disenrolled for the remainder of the 1983 Winter Term. [Dean] Sandalow maintains, as recited in Dean Eklund's letter, that Picozzi was disenrolled at the request of Picozzi's father, in order to facilitate tuition and lease rebates. Although Picozzi denies that either he or his father ever requested disenrollment, it is clear that his father at least sought information regarding tuition adjustments for students absent from school for an extended period for medical reasons. I note that this factual dispute is not material to resolution of the case.

The fire aroused concern within the Law School community. In its March 16, 1983, edition, the Law School newspaper, *Res Gestae*, carried a front page story on the fire and its aftermath. The story included Sandalow's statement expressing distress over the incident and urging that rumors be quelled. On April 4, 1983, Sandalow again addressed the Law School community in an effort to calm the understandable anxiety created by acts of violence, including the fire within the dormitory.

Both public statements alluded to an ongoing police investigation of the fire. That investigation led the Ann Arbor Police Department to conclude almost immediately that the fire had been deliberately set. The investigators also concluded that Picozzi himself had likely set the fire. Nonetheless, the Washtenaw County Prosecutor's Office declined to prosecute the case.

On May 13, 1983, Sandalow wrote Picozzi informing him that he would not be allowed to re-enroll at the Law School unless he either took and passed a polygraph test conducted by the police department or prevailed at an administrative hearing. Sandalow noted that "the Law School and the University have an independent interest in determining the identity of the person responsible, especially because the continuing presence of that individual within the community would create a serious risk to its members." On June 29, 1983, Sandalow again wrote to Picozzi asking for a prompt reply in the interest of resolving the matter prior to the beginning of the 1983 Fall Term.

Picozzi responded to Sandalow's letters on July 18, 1983, stating that he was "not yet prepared to give a full response to [defendant's] ultimatum." Although Sandalow replied on July 29, 1983, his letter was returned unclaimed. In any event, the matter was not resolved prior to the 1983 Fall Term.

On November 7, 1983, Picozzi requested a letter from Sandalow regarding his academic status at the Law School. On November 16, 1983, Sandalow responded:

> I am writing in response to your letter of November 7, 1983 requesting a statement regarding your academic standing and a copy of your transcript. A copy of your transcript is enclosed.
>
> My understanding is that you are currently on a leave of absence from the Law School, having withdrawn while in good academic standing. A question remains regarding your eligibility to re-enroll. As I wrote on May 13, 1983 and again on June 29, 1983, information that we have received from the police has raised a question regarding your responsibility for the fire in your room on March 8. My hope, as I have previously written, is that the question of your responsibility might be resolved by your taking a polygraph examination as requested by the Ann Arbor Police. Were you to take and pass such an examination, under the circumstances stated in my earlier letters, you would of course be eligible to re-enroll at the Law School. If, however, you decide against taking the examination or if you fail to pass it, a hearing would be necessary to determine your eligibility to re-enroll.

On November 23, 1983, Picozzi asked Sandalow to write to James Thomas, Dean of Yale Law School, informing him that Picozzi is "currently on leave of absence from the University of Michigan Law School, having withdrawn while in good academic standing." On November 29, 1983, Sandalow replied that "it would be misleading for me to [write the requested letter] without a further statement indicating that there is a question regarding your eligibility to re-enroll at the Law School." On December 5, 1983, Picozzi repeated his request for an unqualified letter. Sandalow replied on December 13, 1983, with a proposed letter to Dean Thomas including an explanation regarding Picozzi's conditional eligibility to re-enroll. Picozzi rejected the proposed letter. This ended the parties' communications with each other.

On July 30, 1984, Picozzi's counsel demanded that Sandalow write an unqualified letter of good standing. Sandalow refused. On August 24, 1984, Picozzi filed this lawsuit against the Regents of the University of Michigan, President Shapiro, and Dean Sandalow.

His complaint contains five counts. Count I alleges that defendant deprived plaintiff of liberty and property without due process of law. Count II alleges that defendant violated plaintiff's right to equal protection of the laws by conditioning his re-enrollment on successful completion of a polygraph exam or an administrative hearing. Count III alleges that defendant unconstitutionally conditioned the enjoyment of plaintiff's liberty and property upon plaintiff's waiver of his privilege against self-incrimination. Count IV summarily alleges that an "*ex parte* and *ultra vires* adjudicative mechanism" violated plaintiff's rights to equal protection of the law. Count V alleges that defendant breached a contract with plaintiff.

II. PROCEDURAL DUE PROCESS

Picozzi's core claim is that Sandalow denied him procedural due process by detrimentally altering his status at the University without first affording him a hearing. Procedural due process claims require a two-step analysis. First, I must determine whether Sandalow deprived Picozzi of any liberty or property interest Second, assuming I so find, I must determine whether the deprivation occurred without due process. In resolving these issues I note that both parties seek Summary Judgment, and that there are no material facts that are controverted.

A. Deprivation of Protected Interest

The first question I must decide is whether Sandalow deprived Picozzi of a protected interest. I hold that he did. The gravamen of Picozzi's claim is that Sandalow altered his good standing at the Law School, making it impossible for him freely to pursue his studies there or at any other accredited law school. Picozzi could not return to his studies at the University of Michigan because of conditions imposed upon his re-enrollment. He could not complete his studies at any other accredited law school because no such law school would accept him as long as his status at the University of Michigan was less than unqualifiedly good.

A public university student has a protected interest in continuing his studies. This is as it should be. Education is the key—or at least the prerequisite—to many successful careers, including a career in law. When the government provides professional graduate education, it should do so within the constraints of due process.

Sandalow does not directly contest this point, but he contends vigorously that Picozzi has no protected interest at stake in this case. He argues that Picozzi has pleaded a protected interest in only a letter of unqualified good standing and not in a general right to continue his studies. He asserts that Picozzi has no protected interest in such a letter. Of course, if Picozzi has not been deprived of a protected interest, no due process concerns arise.

Sandalow's argument construes the complaint too narrowly. Count I does allege a property deprivation in terms of a letter of good standing. Sandalow refused to issue such a letter because he had previously altered Picozzi's status at the Law School by conditioning his re-enrollment. In other words, the controversy over the letter reflected an underlying dispute over Sandalow's action temporarily and preliminarily restricting Picozzi's ability to continue his studies. Picozzi's allegation that Sandalow's actions "in denying plaintiff a letter of good standing . . . deprived plaintiff of property without due process of law," broadly construed, includes not only the controversy over the letter itself, but also the underlying dispute over Picozzi's status at the University.

The case Sandalow cites to support his argument on this point involve interests dissimilar to the protected interest asserted by Picozzi. Picozzi has not claimed a protected interest in a letter of recommendation. He asked only for a letter confirming his good standing at the Law School. Sandalow refused the letter because Picozzi's status was not unqualifiedly good. Sandalow's action in altering Picozzi's status from "good" to something less than that, thus temporarily interfering with his ability to pursue his studies, is ultimately what this lawsuit tests. Cases dealing with performance evaluations and letters of recommendation simply have no relevance.

Before evaluating the adequacy of process employed, I must find not only that Picozzi has a protected interest at stake, but also that Sandalow deprived him of the interest. Although I have already held that there was a deprivation, its precise nature requires some definition.

Mathews v. Eldridge helps define the deprivation in this case. In *Mathews,* the Court tested Social Security procedures for terminating a person's disability payments. The procedures included an evidentiary hearing prior to final termination of benefits. But the procedures also included a preliminary step permitting termination of benefits without an evidentiary hearing. At the preliminary step, the Court defined a claimant's interest as "the uninterrupted receipt of [disability payments] pending final administrative decision on his claim." The Court held that a claimant could properly be deprived of this limited interest without a prior evidentiary hearing.

In this case, the deprivation was similarly limited. Sandalow neither imposed nor sought formal disciplinary sanctions. Neither did he permanently and finally bar plaintiff's access to legal education. He simply placed a temporary and preliminary hurdle in Picozzi's path, *pending the outcome of an administrative hearing.* He made it clear to Picozzi that the University was ready to move ahead with a hearing at his convenience. Picozzi resisted the hearing. Even as late as August 30 and 31, 1984, during a hearing on his Motion for Preliminary Injunction, Picozzi continued to oppose a hearing.

Although limited, the deprivation in this case is enough to trigger due process protection. Application of due process does not depend upon the weight of the interest, but upon the nature of the interest. I have already held that Picozzi had a protected interest in continuing his studies at the University. By burdening this interest, Sandalow triggered due process protections for plaintiff.

B. Adequacy of Process

Although the weight of the protected interest is not relevant in triggering application of due process, it is an important factor in determining the precise procedure due in a particular case. To guide [a] decision of what process is due in a particular case, the Court has articulated broad principles of due process. In general, the decision involves balancing government interests with private interests. More specifically, the Court stated:

> [I]dentification of the specific dictates of due process generally requires consideration of three distinct factors: First, the private interest that will be affected by the official action; second, the risk of an erroneous deprivation of such interest through the procedures used, and the probable value, if any, of additional or substitute procedural safeguards; and finally, the Government's interest, including the function involved and the fiscal and administrative burdens that the additional or substitute procedural requirement would entail.

I now apply these principles to this case and hold that defendant fully complied with the requirements of due process.

1. Pre-deprivation Hearing

The first question I must decide is whether Picozzi was entitled to a hearing prior to Sandalow's action depriving him of his interest in continuing his education pending the outcome of a full administrative hearing. I hold that he was not entitled to a hearing prior to deprivation of this limited interest. In *Goss*, the Court applied procedural due process principles to an analogous, although more severe, situation of formal school discipline. The Court held that high school students facing ten-day suspensions are ordinarily entitled to some kind of hearing prior to suspension. The Court noted that the hearing required need not involve any more than an informal discussion between the student and the disciplinarian immediately following the incident leading to discipline. Based on this assumption of informality, the Court concluded "that as a general rule notice and hearing should precede removal of the student from school." However, the Court stopped short of rigidly requiring a pre-suspension hearing in all cases. The Court stated:

> We agree with the District Court ... that there are recurring situations in which prior notice and hearing cannot be insisted upon. Students whose presence poses a continuing danger to persons or property or an ongoing threat of disrupting the academic process may be immediately removed from school. In such cases, the necessary notice and rudimentary hearing should follow as soon as practicable, as the District Court indicated.

This case falls squarely within the *Goss* provision for situations not requiring a pre-suspension hearing. Sandalow's first letter to Picozzi following the fire specifically grounded Sandalow's actions in concern for the safety of the law school community. In an earlier memorandum addressed to the law school community, Sandalow addressed a rising anxiety among the community's members over various incidents of violence, including the fire, within the community. Such anxiety disrupts academic calm. This is precisely the situation in which *Goss* permits suspension without a prior hearing.

Even if Sandalow had not complied with *Goss*, I would hold that under *Mathews* Picozzi received all the process to which he was entitled. This case does not involve formal suspension or any other school discipline. At stake in this case is a preliminary and temporary interference with Picozzi's interest in continuing his education *pending the outcome of an administrative hearing* to be held at plaintiff's convenience. Although even this limited deprivation might in some cases inevitably delay a student's progress, in this case Picozzi could have promptly accepted Sandalow's offer of a hearing and cleared up his status at the Law School prior to the first date on which he was physically able to return to class, further diminishing the severity of the deprivation. Under *Mathews*, the weight of the private interest affected is the first factor I must consider in determining the procedural protection required by due process. Because Picozzi's interest in this case is less weighty than the interest at stake in *Goss*, less procedural protection is due him than was due the plaintiffs in *Goss*.

Moreover, strong public interests, a second factor in *Mathews*' balance, supported Sandalow's action. First, he had a duty to protect the security of the law school community. He discharged his duty by conditioning Picozzi's re-enrollment on his clearing up the suspicion that naturally surrounded him as the subject of an unexplained arson fire. Second, Sandalow had a duty not to mislead other schools into thinking Picozzi was in unqualified good standing at the Law School. If Picozzi's theory of the case prevails, Sandalow could be compelled to certify a student's unqualified good standing, even though the student was subject to suspicion, simply because the school had not yet been able to conduct a formal hearing. Dean Sandalow, and others in his position, must have in such cases the authority to take prompt and reasonable preliminary action that preserves the school's interest without finally and permanently depriving a student of his interest in continuing his education. This is precisely what his action accomplished in this case.

Neither the specific dictates of *Goss* nor the general principles of *Mathews* entitled Picozzi to a hearing prior to Sandalow's action conditioning Picozzi's re-enrollment on his successful completion of a polygraph test or an administrative hearing.

2. Law School Handbook

Picozzi also argues that Sandalow denied him due process by using procedures other than those outlined in the Law School Handbook for "investigating and reporting student conduct bearing upon character and fitness for the practice of law." Although I doubt whether Picozzi has sufficiently pleaded this claim as a due process deprivation (he has pleaded the matter as a contract claim), I will address it only to say that Picozzi's claim, assuming it is properly pleaded, is legally untenable. Due process is a matter of federal constitutional law; failure to comply with state procedures does not, by itself, violate due process.

The only question for me is whether Picozzi received *constitutionally* adequate notice and hearing. I have already discussed and passed upon the constitutional adequacy of the hearing procedure. In addition, I hold that Picozzi received constitutionally adequate notice of the basis for defendant's action. "The fundamental requisite of due process of law is the opportunity to be heard." Constitutionally adequate notice is that which provides a person with sufficient information to make the eventual hearing meaningful. Already in his first letter to Picozzi, Sandalow made it clear that the purpose of conditioning Picozzi's re-enrollment was to determine his responsibility for the fire. ("The information available to us had led me to conclude that I would not be warranted in permitting you to re-enroll without a close examination of the question whether you are the person responsible for setting the March 8 fire"). This is precisely the question that the 1985 administrative hearing finally adjudicated. Picozzi had official notice of it during May, 1983. Even if Sandalow had not made this perfectly clear by letter, I cannot believe anyone in Picozzi's position could have been unaware of the basis for the Dean's action.

3. Timing of the Administrative Hearing

Finally, Picozzi argues that the administrative hearing ultimately held should have taken place sooner than it did, even if not prior to Sandalow's preliminary action. Picozzi relies upon *Goss*, which permits suspension in some cases without a presuspension hearing, but requires in those cases that a hearing follow suspension "as soon as practicable." Picozzi argues that Sandalow failed to satisfy this requirement. I reject this argument.

First, Sandalow had no duty in this case to satisfy the strictures of *Goss*. Second, Picozzi himself is responsible for the delay in the hearing's commencement. In both his first and second letters to Picozzi, Sandalow urged prompt reply. In his second letter, Sandalow expressed his hope that the entire matter could be resolved prior to the beginning of 1983 Fall Term. Unfortunately, Picozzi's medical condition prevented such an early disposition of the matter. But even after he recovered, Picozzi—not Sandalow—resisted holding a hearing. Picozzi cannot now complain of the delay he occasioned.

C. Qualified Immunity

Even if Sandalow did violate Picozzi's procedural due process rights, and I hold he did not, I also hold that Sandalow is entitled on the facts of this case to qualified immunity. Qualified immunity seeks to provide state and federal officials, acting reasonably, with the authority to make difficult decisions and to exercise discretion without fear of being held to answer in damages. In the words of the Supreme Court:

> Even defendants who violate constitutional rights enjoy a qualified immunity that protects them from liability for damages unless it is further demonstrated that their conduct was unreasonable under the applicable standard.

It is now clear that qualified immunity shields officials from damage liability as long as their conduct "does not violate clearly established statutory or constitutional rights of which a reasonable person would have known."

In this case, Sandalow's action was objectively reasonable because it did not violate a clearly established right of which a reasonable person would have known. Neither *Goss, Mathews*, nor any other federal law clearly requires a hearing prior to the preliminary action Sandalow took in this case. He faced a situation calling for prompt action and requiring reliance on information supplied by other people, precisely the situation in which *Wood* calls for application of the qualified immunity doctrine. ("As with executive officers faced with instances of civil disobedience, school officials, confronted with student behavior causing or threatening disruption, also have an 'obvious need for prompt action, and decisions must be made in reliance on factual information supplied by others.' "). He responded by altering Picozzi's status pending the outcome of a polygraph test, or a full administrative hearing. Even if this action violated Picozzi's constitutional right, Sandalow cannot be held liable for damages because the right violated was not clearly established at the time he took the action.

III. OTHER MATTERS

A. Equal Protection

Counts II and IV of the complaint allege that Sandalow denied Picozzi equal protection by treating him differently than other students at the University. It is true that Sandalow conditioned the re-enrollment rights of Picozzi only. But he rightfully treated Picozzi differently than other students because Picozzi was not similarly situated with any other student. The unexplained arson fire took place in Picozzi's room, and no one else's room. No other student was seen near Picozzi's room at the time of the fire. In fact, the Ann Arbor Police Department informed Sandalow that they considered Picozzi the primary, if not the only, suspect. These factors provided a rational basis for his action with respect to Picozzi. Since Picozzi is not alleging denial of a fundamental right or a classification based on suspect class lines, this is all equal protection requires.

B. Self-Incrimination

Picozzi alleges in Count III that Sandalow deprived him of his privilege against self-incrimination. Although the complaint does not articulate a theory for this cause of action, he argues in his brief that Sandalow deprived him of his privilege by asking him to submit to a polygraph test. In Picozzi's words:

> This request imposed an unconstitutional choice upon Mr. Picozzi. He either had to waive his right to silence ... or he had to request an administrative hearing at which his failure to take the examination was to be considered substantive evidence of his guilt.

I hold that Picozzi was not deprived of his privilege against self-incrimination by Sandalow's request that plaintiff take a polygraph test.

Sandalow never conditioned Picozzi's re-enrollment rights on a polygraph test. He presented the polygraph test to Picozzi as an option to accept or reject. In fact, if Picozzi submitted to a polygraph test and failed, Sandalow would still have permitted him to go through an administrative hearing. ("If, however, you decide against taking the examination or if you fail to pass it, a hearing would be necessary to determine your eligibility to re-enroll"). That Picozzi's refusal to take the test might be used at the administrative hearing as evidence that he set the fire does not threaten his privilege. In the first place, the refusal would have virtually no probative value because Sandalow gave him the option of a polygraph or a hearing. I do not think this point would escape the attention of a qualified hearing officer. Furthermore, even though a person may assert the privilege against self-incrimination during a civil proceeding, the privilege protects a person from only criminal exposure. The administrative hearing was a civil proceeding.

C. Contract

Count V of Picozzi's complaint alleges that he entered into a contract with the University upon enrollment at the Law School, and that the terms of this contract were contained in the Law School Handbook. He alleges that Sandalow breached this contract by failing to use the disciplinary procedures contained in the handbook. I reject this claim because I hold as a matter of law that Picozzi never entered into a contract to be governed by the procedures contained in the Law School Handbook. Even if he did enter into such a contract, I hold that Sandalow did not breach it in the manner alleged because Sandalow never sought to discipline Picozzi. Furthermore, *Pennhurst* forbids me from exercising pendent jurisdiction over a state law claim against state officials for the purpose of ordering state officials to comply with state law, or of assessing damages against state officials for violation of state law.

D. Defendant Shapiro

Plaintiff's counsel stated before me on the record that he was retaining defendant Shapiro solely to preserve a motion for § 1988 attorney fees arising out of the Preliminary Injunction hearing and the administrative hearing. Although Picozzi has not presented the Court with a formal motion for fees, I *sua sponte* consider the matter now.

Under 42 U.S.C. § 1988, attorney fees are available to civil rights claimants. But no such fees may be awarded unless I find the party seeking fees to be a prevailing party. I hold that Picozzi was not a prevailing party at the Preliminary Injunction hearing. He wanted me to order defendants to issue an unqualified letter of good standing on his behalf. I did not enter such an order. Instead, the parties agreed after two mornings of discussion to conduct an administrative hearing to determine Picozzi's responsibility for the fire. Although defendants pressed for the hearing, Picozzi initially resisted it. As is evident from the transcript of the hearing, Picozzi was not a prevailing party. Accordingly, he is not entitled to § 1988 fees for the Preliminary Injunction hearing.

Picozzi did prevail at the administrative hearing conducted pursuant to the parties' agreement. But that outcome, although important to him, does not make him the prevailing party on his underlying civil rights cause of action. On the contrary, I have just held that his civil rights were not violated. Accordingly, the administrative hearing cannot support § 1988 fees.[12]

There being no reason for Shapiro to remain a defendant in this case, I order that he be dismissed with prejudice.

IV. DISPOSITION

For the reasons given in this opinion, defendant Sandalow's Motion for Summary Judgment is GRANTED on all counts, and plaintiff Picozzi's Motion for Partial Summary Judgment is DENIED on all counts. In addition, defendants Shapiro and Board of Regents are DISMISSED with prejudice.

IT IS SO ORDERED.

"Trial by Fire"

Trustman Senger, *Rolling Stone*, 24 September 1987, pp. 111–113, 163–164, 167–168. Reprinted with permission.

Law students everywhere will tell you they were burned out after two years of school. Few could say it with as much justification as James Picozzi, a University of Michigan law student whose second-year studies were abruptly ended in the early morning of Tuesday, March 8th, 1983, as he crawled out of his third-floor dorm window and clung briefly to the sill, engulfed by the black smoke pouring out of his gasoline-doused room.

When Picozzi's blackened body hit the ground, his back was broken and his nightmare was only beginning. Suspected of arson by the Ann Arbor Police Department but never prosecuted for the crime, Picozzi would feel it necessary to sue Terrance Sandalow, the dean of the University of Michigan Law School, before going on to complete his legal studies. He would have to hire the New York lawyers William Kunstler and Alan Silber, as well as his own detective, before discovering that critical evidence being used against him was totally undermined by a police report that, although filed, had disappeared.

---

12. On August 24, 1984, Picozzi filed a verified complaint seeking a preliminary injunction ordering Sandalow to issue a letter of unqualified good standing on behalf of Picozzi. During a hearing on Picozzi's Motion for Preliminary Injunction, the parties agreed to resolve through an administrative hearing the questions of Picozzi's responsibility for the March 8, 1983 fire, and of his standing at the Law School. The Hearing Officer issued his decision "that the University of Michigan has not, by clear and convincing evidence, established that James M. Picozzi started the fire in Room K-33 at the University of Michigan Law School on March 8, 1983" on August 22, 1985. Pursuant to this decision, Sandalow issued a letter of good standing on August 23, 1985. After presenting this letter, Picozzi was accepted by Yale Law School, where he is currently enrolled.

Lying on the ground outside his dorm at 4:30 in the morning, Picozzi began his alternative legal education by telling police officers he thought someone had poured gasoline into his room. "Someone in a uniform, a police officer, security guard, someone of that nature," Picozzi recalled later, "looked at me and said, 'Is there anyone who doesn't like you?' And I said, 'Yeah, there's a lot of people.' "

First-year law students endure a unique form of torture. The same group of students is herded from room to room and forced to listen to a handful of students who speak at length in every class, every day, for the entire year. Dubbed "gunners" at the University of Michigan and "assholes" everywhere else, the representatives of this breed are immediately recognized and rarely forgotten. "I was a law student thirty years ago in another school, and I can still remember their names," Dean Sandalow admits with a chuckle.

Jim Picozzi was certainly a gunner. But there were many others among his classmates. "I think I can name at least another dozen people, myself included, who talked as frequently as he did and, depending on your perspective, were at least as, if not more, obnoxious than he was," says Ned Miltenberg, his most vocal adversary.

During his first semester at Michigan, Picozzi went to see the assistant to Susan Eklund, the dean of students. He presented his right hand, which was missing part of two fingers as a result of a childhood lawn-mower accident, and arranged to get twenty minutes added to each of his three-hour exam periods.

To many people the prospect of having exams lengthened by twenty minutes might seem more of a punishment than a privilege. But to law students, whose job prospects are largely determined by their first-year grades, extra minutes take on heightened significance. This is perhaps uniquely true at the University of Michigan Law School. As a state school with a national reputation, the opportunities for students at the top of the class are vastly superior to the opportunities for those at the bottom. The stakes are high, and the pressures intensify in what is already a competitive environment.

Just before Picozzi's first exam, he notified his contracts professor that the outline he had prepared for the exam had been stolen; he requested permission to take the exam at a later time. Next, Picozzi had an altercation with Ned Miltenberg minutes before the property exam, when Picozzi found Miltenberg studying notes he had given to another member of Miltenberg's study group. Finally, Picozzi interrupted his property exam to report having seen someone with the stolen contracts outline; he was given a four-hour break to go back to his room and cool off.

Picozzi began his second semester with two A's and two B pluses, but it was clear that he wasn't going to win any awards for popularity. He was hissed in class. Students made snide comments as they passed him in the hallway. And Miltenberg had no trouble finding an appreciative audience for his imitation of Picozzi's voice and mannerisms. At the advent of spring exams Picozzi was already receiving repeated late-night phone calls and having trouble studying, which prompted him to switch rooms. Students began placing bets on whether or not he would show up for exams on time.

Picozzi made several visits to Dean Eklund's office to complain about such treatment. Eklund, who acknowledges that law students do not "tend to be the nicest or kindest people," says she spent an inordinate amount of time attempting to resolve Picozzi's difficulties. "I offered him a great deal of advice during his first year," she says, "most of which he did not take."

Meanwhile, Miltenberg's interest in Picozzi apparently increased. "He made law school incredibly fun," Miltenberg says. "It was a soap opera in our midst." The two men had a confrontation in the library. Miltenberg asked Picozzi about the rumors that he had been given extra exam time and who it was he had seen with the stolen contracts outline. Miltenberg then called professor and Dean Sue - as Eklund was called by the law students - to find out how much extra time Picozzi had received. He confronted Picozzi again. He wondered what "scam" Picozzi would try next.

The first exam in the spring of 1982 was contracts. No one saw Picozzi in the exam room. Yet later that night he sat at a dinner table where the exam was allegedly discussed. He was spotted the next day still carrying his contracts textbook. Rumors reached a fever pitch. "People were concerned about what he was going to get away with," Miltenberg said. So Miltenberg and a group of four other students decided to approach Picozzi in the library and ask him when he had taken the exam. Picozzi stood up, announced he didn't have to answer any questions and slammed his briefcase shut. According to Miltenberg, Picozzi told the people around him to write down the names of the inquiring students and said that they were going to be brought up on charges. Then he told Miltenberg to crawl back under the rock where he came from and stormed out of the library.

The next morning Miltenberg visited Dean Sue to explain what happened. Picozzi's attorney Alan Silber has characterized his client's behavior during his first year as "reasonably appalling," but he is even more amazed by the "whiny little tattletales" in Picozzi's class. "What a sniveling crew of assholes," Silber says before breaking into a falsetto: " 'Dean Sue! Dean Sue! He did this! Dean Sue! He got twenty minutes on the exams! Dean Sue!' Jesus. And she was a birdbrain. I mean, really, how did she put up with that shit?"

Picozzi decided to try to leave this environment. As a *cum laude* graduate of Yale, he had applied to Yale Law School but had been rejected. Near the end of his first year at Michigan he reactivated his application to Yale, explaining that he was the object of "repeated harassment."

"During the spring finals period," Picozzi wrote in his application, "[when] I entered the library, I was promptly assaulted by five of my classmates. That assault left me unable to study for several days and hence can be directly linked to my unusually low grade in Civil Procedure."

Picozzi went to some of his professors and asked them to change his grades. They refused. At least one of them responded by firing Picozzi as a research assistant. None of them would provide favorable recommendations to Yale, which eventually rejected his application.

Clearly, Picozzi had a lot to think about that summer. He apparently thought about his behavior during his first year of law school and the response to it. "I tried to stretch the rules my first year," he has said. "Call it immaturity, call it selfishness, call it lack of ethical standards. I'm not too proud of that. But I learned some important things from it...My behavior was pretty petty. I would not characterize myself as being victimized. I got what I deserved." But Picozzi's second year at Michigan was another matter entirely.

Picozzi returned to school in the fall of 1982 intent on maintaining a low profile and securing a good job for the following summer. He also wanted to try again to transfer to Yale. He rarely spoke in class. He had no contact with Miltenberg. But for Miltenberg and the other students who disliked him, Picozzi remained a favorite topic of discussion. "Any time anything would happen," Miltenberg said, "people would wonder if it was Picozzi who was behind it."

During the last week of January 1983, Miltenberg heard that Picozzi had bragged to several students—including David Berger, Kathy Rakowsky and Tom Good—about what he had got away with in law school. Tom Good, who was friends with Picozzi his first year but began spending time with his foes the second year, told David Berger he had once seen Picozzi with a gun.

The next Sunday, as Miltenberg and Berger sat in a pizza parlor, Miltenberg read a newspaper article about a man with two artificial arms who had bowled a 300. "I showed it to David," Miltenberg recall, "and I said, 'I wonder how much extra time he had." David said, 'Don't say that too loud, Picozzi might shoot you.' I said, 'What do you mean by that?' He said, 'Picozzi has a gun.' I said, 'What?' "

Miltenberg checked the story with Good, and the next morning headed for Dean Sue's office with his report. Eklund apparently spoke to Good, then called Diane Nafranowicz, the director of the law-school dorms, and told her she had had reports from several students of a gun in Picozzi's room. Eklund asked Nafranowicz to follow up on the reports without revealing Eklund's role to Picozzi. Picozzi was called in and told that Nafranowicz had received a note reporting that a gun had been spotted in his possession. Picozzi asked to see the note, leading an embarrassed Nafranowicz to lie further by saying that it had been destroyed.

Picozzi was asked if he would consent to a search of his room. He calmly agreed, saying he didn't have a gun, but asked that the search be done immediately to avoid claims that he had disposed of the weapon before the search. No gun was found. Less than two weeks later Good and Berger hung posters depicting a submachine-gun-wielding cherub with Picozzi's face. The caption read, A FISTFUL OF FIRE-POWER! THE ST. VALENTINE'S DAY MASSACRE FEATURING JIM (MR. SEARCH & SEIZURE) PICOZZI. Miltenberg rushed to assure Dean Sue that he had nothing to do with the prank. When she asked who was responsible, he gave her Berger's name.

Picozzi's detective, Josiah Thompson, is still incredulous after two years. "It was just so gratifying to learn that in training all these young lawyers, the University of Michigan saw it as absolutely central that one of the most important principles for any young lawyer is to rat on your friend at the earliest opportunity."

Not long after Valentine's Day, the students left for spring break. Picozzi had received offers for summer employment from nine law firms. He had again reactivated his application to Yale after his room had been searched and had been successful in obtaining two letters of recommendation from new professors. The first two nights back from spring break he told his friends he was optimistic about being accepted at Yale. But by the end of the third night he was in intensive care, unsure if he would ever walk again. And he was soon to be the Ann Arbor Police Department's sole suspect in a felony investigation.

Detective David Jachalke arrived at the scene of the crime on Tuesday morning, about two hours after Picozzi had been taken to University of Michigan Hospital. He spoke to fire investigators and university security personnel who were already there and learned that the carpet and a five-volume set of the Internal Revenue Code and IRS regulations, lying on the floor of Picozzi's room to the left of the door, had been doused with liquid fuel. A trail of gasoline leading from the books to the door had been poured on the carpet and lighted.

Jachalke and other investigators conducted an extensive search of Picozzi's room and the surrounding area for a container that could have been used to transport gasoline to the room. Jachalke testified that every bottle, can and mug in the room was sniffed during the search. No container was found. No other students' rooms were searched, the Ann Arbor police say, because they did not have probable cause to do so.

Silber, who affectionately refers to his client as Sparky, says a subtle prejudice was already at work in the investigation. He believes the police and the university officials were eager to quell fears on campus by solving the case quickly. And Picozzi was an easy target. "There was clearly that feeling by the second year that Sparky was the rotten apple in the barrel," he says. "And part of that is that they didn't think he was wrapped too tight."

Jachalke says that after looking at "the physical evidence of the room . . . the type of fire, the intensity of the heat," he felt Picozzi had set the fire. "There was no way somebody else could have done it and gotten away." At the hospital Jachalke asked Picozzi if he had any idea who might have set the fire. Picozzi responded that he wasn't sure, that Miltenberg "made no secret he doesn't like me, but I never expected something like this."

Thursday morning, Jachalke's supervisor, Sergeant John Atkinson, took over the case. Silber describes Atkinson as "a hotshot in the best sense of television detectives. He's lawyer who wears a three-piece suit that definitely costs more than mine." At 10:00 a.m. Atkinson and Jachalke requested a search warrant for Picozzi's jeans and boots. Tests could indicate the presence of gasoline on the clothing, which might yield evidence that Picozzi set the fire.

The two cops headed over to the hospital. As Jachalke described it, Picozzi "had an oxygen mask on. He was obviously under some type of medication, the standard tubes, et cetera. He was on a special type of bed due to his back injury. . . . His burns were still wrapped or dressed." They asked Picozzi to sign a release form giving them access to his hospital records. The nature of the burns might indicate that Picozzi set the fire. Picozzi complied with their request and told them where his boots and jeans were.

Thomas Nolan, a former policeman and fire investigator hired by Picozzi to testify at his hearing, was astounded by the investigation. "They got a man, lying in a hospital, burned, suffers a broken back, and they go back to the scene, and they investigate as if he did the thing," Nolan said. "That 's ridiculous. That's [tantamount] to you going to an [attempted] homicide, a [person] sitting with a gunshot wound, bleeding, and you say, 'Why did you shoot yourself?' "

Well, not exactly. Experienced policeman and firemen acknowledge that arsonists are often burned while setting fires, a fact that helps in the solution of many arson cases. Picozzi was the only person burned by the fire in his room. "There's no question that Picozzi did it," says Atkinson. "The fire investigator said this fire was started from inside the room."

Jachalke went to collect Picozzi's clothes; Atkinson went to the Amoco station two blocks from the school to determine if anyone had purchased a small quantity of gas before the fire. The police report states that the cashier, Claire Lathrop, told him a white male had bought four cents of gas in a jelly jar on Tuesday night, at approximately eight. "She was certain it was Tuesday night," the police report reads, "because she did not work on Monday night, March 7th." Of course, on Tuesday at 8:00 p.m., Picozzi was in the intensive-care unit at University of Michigan Hospital.

The next day, armed with this "identification," which Silber calls "suspicious, idiotic and completely off the wall," Atkinson returned to the hospital with Jachalke. They asked Picozzi to repeat in detail his account of the fire. Picozzi complied. Atkinson informed him that the doctors had said his burns were consistent with his having set the fire. In fact, the doctors had said the burns were also consistent with Picozzi's account of the fire. Atkinson pushed to see if Picozzi would confess and deliberately avoided reading him his rights. "I didn't light the fire, I really didn't," Picozzi said. Asked if he would submit to a polygraph exam, Picozzi said he would consider it after his surgery.

That afternoon Atkinson returned to the Amoco station with Jachalke and spoke to Brian Myers, who had been on duty the night of the fire. Myers told them that on Monday night he had sold a small amount of gasoline to a white male in his mid-twenties who was wearing a dark-blue parka with a furlike collar (Picozzi had no such jacket.) He said the man was short, about five feet nine or ten (Picozzi is about five four). For the detectives it could have been another dry hole. But Myers also said the man was missing two fingers on his right hand. Bingo.

The police showed Myers two pages of the Michigan law-school handbook; there were thirty-two pictures, including those of twenty-one white male students. Myers was asked if the purchaser was among them. Myers said he couldn't be sure but pointed to Picozzi's picture and said the man looked something like that.

Then something strange happened. Atkinson, a real go-getter of a cop, had just turned up a critical piece of evidence. Did he try to discover Picozzi's where-abouts at the time Myers reported having seen him? No. Did he rush to the district attorney's office, brandishing his evidence, requesting that Picozzi be charged with the crime? No. He effectively dropped out of the case. (Atkinson says this was because his help was no longer need. His role had been simply to assist in the investigation for a few days.)

And Jachalke, who now had a key witness, appeared to do nothing for two days; after a couple of more interviews he then spoke to Miltenberg, Berger and Good for the first time. Over thirty students had been questioned by the police before they spoke to Picozzi's enemies.

Jachalke learned there were no traces of gasoline on Picozzi's boots. He tried one more time, unsuccessfully, to get Picozzi to confess. And then, almost three weeks after he had talked to Myers, Jachalke went to the Washtenaw County Prosecutors' Office, presented his evidence and asked the office to issue a complaint charging Picozzi with arson. The office refused. "There was just no evidence to show that he set the fire," says prosecutor William Delhey.

Picozzi knew nothing about Brian Myers or the results of the police investigation. He had more important matters on his mind. Four days after the prosecutor's office declined to press charges, he was transferred by air ambulance to a hospital near his parents in Pittsburgh. Two metal rods were inserted into his spine and fused in place with a bone graft. He was placed in a full-body cast that would not be removed for seven months.

In May, Picozzi received a letter from Dean Sandalow requesting that he submit to a polygraph test. Acknowledging that no criminal charges had been filed, Sandalow wrote that the university had an "independent interest" in determining who set the fire. "If you do take a polygraph test administered or arranged by the Ann Arbor police," Sandalow wrote, "and if that test indicates that you are not responsible for the March 8 fire, you would of course be permitted to return to the Law School in the fall term.

"With regret, I must also inform you that unless you take a polygraph test, an administrative proceeding will be required.... The necessity for such a proceeding would, of course, be obviated if you were to take and pass a polygraph test, and I of course hope that you will pursue that course."

Silber believes the missive from Sandalow was an inappropriate way to handle the situation, regardless of Picozzi's guilt or innocence. "I mean, why didn't the University of Michigan simply follow its own rules?" he says. "Send him a letter saying, 'We think you set the fire. We're scheduling a disciplinary hearing on such and such a date. Get your lawyer and show up.'"

Sandalow explains that he proceeded in this manner because of an obligation to the students and the university "to be sure people are not subjected to undue risk." In addition, he says, "it was not clear... whether Picozzi ever planned to return to the university."

Sandalow repeated his request on June 29th. Picozzi answered in a letter dated July 18th that he was "not yet prepared to give a full response to your ultimatum." On November 7th, Picozzi wrote to Sandalow asking for a copy of his transcript and a letter stating his academic standing at the school. "My understanding is that you are currently on a leave of absence from the Law School, having withdrawn while in good academic standing," Sandalow responded.

"A question remains regarding your eligibility to re-enroll," Sandalow added, then repeated the "ultimatum." Picozzi, who still hoped to transfer to Yale, requested that Sandalow reiterate his statement that Picozzi was in good standing and send it to James Thomas, the dean of admissions at Yale Law School. Sandalow refused to do so without raising the issue of Picozzi's eligibility to reenroll. It "would have been essentially deceitful," he says. Although it was Yale's decision to make "they were entitled to the full and accurate record."

Picozzi refused to accept a letter from the dean that included his characterization of the police investigation and the request for a lie-detector test. "To be perfectly frank, sir," Picozzi had written, "I have never understood either the adversary situation you have created between us or what you hope to gain by it. Right now, I am attempting to give you a gentleman's way out. I sincerely hope you take it. The alternative, for both parties, would be much more painful—but, I believe, more damaging for you. If nothing else, I would think I have proven, in more ways than one, that I do not die easily."

After discovering that members of the Michigan bar were less than enthusiastic about the prospect of taking on the University of Michigan, Picozzi persuaded the famous civil-rights attorney William Kunstler to represent him. In July 1984, Kunstler fired off a blistering letter to Sandalow, demanding that the law school issue the letter of good standing by August 10th to enable Picozzi to meet Yale's deadline for matriculation in September 1984. Sandalow was in Europe, and two other university officials refused to handle the matter.

In a letter to Kunstler dated August 14th, Sandalow repeated his refusal and the reasons for it, noting that "information we have received from the Ann Arbor police raises a serious question about Mr. Picozzi's responsibility for the fire." He did not say what that information was.

On August 24th, Picozzi filed suit against Sandalow and others in federal district court in Michigan, alleging violations of his constitutional right to due process. He requested a preliminary injunction compelling the dean to issue the letter, $7 million in compensatory and punitive damages, reasonable attorneys' fees and a public apology.

In a subsequent court hearing both parties agreed to resolve the question of Picozzi's responsibility for the fire and his standing in the law school at an administrative hearing to be held at the law school and open to the public. The lawyers battled over the choice of a hearing officer; the hearing was finally scheduled to begin on February 18th, 1985, almost two years after the fire.

Soho criminal-defense lawyer Alan Silber agreed to represent Picozzi at the hearing. Silber quickly called San Francisco detective Josiah Thompson, author of *Six Seconds in Dallas*, which attacked the single-gunman theory of the Warren Commission. At age forty Thompson had left a tenured position at Haverford College and put his Yale Ph.D. to good use as a gumshoe. The two men read the police report and flew to Ann Arbor the week before the hearing.

Silber admits that he and Thompson thought Picozzi was guilty after reading the police report. But there was one sentence in the police description of the interview with Brian Myers that intrigued them. "Mr. Myers did confirm he had been spoken to earlier by another officer believed to be Sgt. G. Miller concerning this matter," it read, "however, at that time he was shown no photographs."

Thompson and Silber knew that they had to talk to Sergeant Miller, but their hopes weren't high; they assumed that university counsel Peter Davis had already spoken to Miller. Indeed, in a prehearing memorandum written a week before the hearing, Davis had indicated that he planned to use the eyewitness testimony of both gas-station attendants. Thompson and Silber assumed Claire Lathrop would testify that she made her four-cent sale on Monday at 8:00 p.m., despite the assertion in the police report that it was made on Tuesday night. They were curious about what Miller would say about Myers, but, Thompson recalls, "we all expected that Miller would simply buttress the other side's case."

Thompson met with Miller and was thunderstruck to discover that on the day before Myers identified Picozzi for Atkinson and Jachalke, Myers had told Miller that he had *not* sold any small quantities of gasoline on the night of the fire or any time immediately prior to that date. "I asked him specifically," Miller said, "about an individual that came in, who was missing some fingers on the right hand, rather short in stature, to see if he recalled anyone like that being in there. He said . . . he did not."

Sergeant Miller had *told* Brian Myers that the suspect the police were looking for was short and missing parts of some fingers on the right hand the day *before* Myers appeared to volunteer the same information to Sergeant Atkinson. Late Wednesday night Myers said he had seen no such person. On Friday he said he had.

Miller told Detective Jachalke about his discussion with Myers after Jachalke and Atkinson interviewed Myers. Miller then filed a report detailing his interview with Myers. "It was clear that [Jachalke] knew that Brian Myers was full of shit from the day he talked to Miller," Silber says. Yet there was nothing in Jachalke's report about what Myers told Miller.

And Miller's report disappeared.

"Coincidental, wouldn't you say?" Silber asks with a snicker.

Silber became even more incredulous about the police explanation of the fire when Claire Lathrop, the gas-station cashier, refused to talk to Thompson before the hearing and had him thrown out of the store where she worked. Silber's theory is that Atkinson may have used information about Lathrop and Myers as leverage to get them to make the identifications he needed to wrap up his case. Atkinson, who doesn't remember his meeting with Lathrop, emphatically denies this. "I had never dealt with either of them before," he says. "I certainly wouldn't pressure someone to say anything that wasn't true."

As for Miller's missing report, Atkinson explains that the Ann Arbor Police Department files over 60,000 reports each year. If only one of several identification numbers appears incorrectly on a document, it is attached to the wrong report and lost in the files. Silber is wiling to concede this possibility but refuses to believe it was also coincidental that Jachalke left out of his report any details of his discussion with Miller.

Silber theorizes that "Atkinson told Jachalke to keep it out of the report altogether, and Jachalke, being somewhat straight up, stuck the one line [about Sergeant Miller] in." Atkinson says he doesn't know why the information did not appear in Jachalke's report. But he is adamant that it is not because of anything he said. "As an officer of the court, I would never stoop so low as to suppress any evidence favorable to the defendant," Atkinson says.

Silber is also troubled about the extent of the university's knowledge of what he believes was "a deliberately false ID." University counsel Peter Davis didn't speak to Sergeant Miller until the day of the hearing, even though he knew Miller had interviewed Myers.

"We knew about that," Davis said, referring to Miller's talk with Myers. "But [Miller] didn't show [Myers] any photographs, and the next day he picked [Picozzi] out of all those faces before he was told that this is the guy."

Miller didn't show Myers any photographs, but Atkinson probably showed them to Lathrop, because Myers testified that he first learned he had selected Picozzi's picture after talking to Lathrop. "The police told her who it was," Myers said.

Peter Davis remains convinced of the validity of Myers's identification. "There is no doubt in [Myers's] mind that Picozzi is the man who came in to buy gasoline," he says.

The hearing officer found Myers's testimony to be "inconsistent and contradictory" and accorded it no weight. Davis says he decided not to call Lathrop as a witness as soon as he discovered she worked on a night other than that of the fire. "I hadn't talked to her," he explains, "when I listed her" as a witness the week before the hearing began. At the hearing Jachalke testified that Lathrop's only involvement was to have referred Atkinson to Myers as the person on duty the night before the fire.

Her initial statement to the police describing a four-cent sale of gas and her ability to tell Myers he had selected Picozzi's picture remain unexplained.

In any event, Sam Dimon, a friend of Picozzi's from the Christian Law Students Association, who recently completed a two-year clerkship with Supreme Court Justice Byron White, testified that he spent most of Monday morning and afternoon with Picozzi. Dimon, who spoke to Picozzi around nine on Monday night after Picozzi had returned from a two-hour class, described his friend's mood as "upbeat" and "cheerful." Dimon visited Picozzi in the hospital eight times. "I think if he had started the fire himself," Dimon testified, "he would have been much more uncomfortable around me than he was."

At the start of the hearing a throng of law students crowded into the University of Michigan Law School's moot-court room to witness the final act in what had become a three-year, three-ring circus. Silber, a self-confessed child of the Sixties, was shocked by the atmosphere. "It never occurred to me that they wouldn't be cheering Sparky on," he says. "But they were there for the hanging, and you could just see, you know, by the third or fourth day, it was like disappointed people coming in."

University counsel Peter Davis, who is "still convinced that [Picozzi] set the fire," says his role at the hearing was to establish, by clear and convincing evidence, that Picozzi set the fire. He even went so far as to try to introduce into evidence the activity of Picozzi's heart monitor while the cops were interrogating him, claiming the monitor was a "sort of crude polygraph machine." Even the results of actual lie-detector tests are generally inadmissible in court. (Davis says that he tried to introduce this evidence because "it was a civil case, and in this district in Michigan, lie-detector tests frequently are admissible.") The hearing officer sustained Silber's objection to this tactic the first time Davis tried it. The second time the hearing officer himself objected.

Davis's theory is that Picozzi set the fire because he "had a burning desire to go to Yale." According to Davis, Picozzi intended to set a small fire in his room and put it out to make himself look like a hero and to convince the university that he was in danger so they would facilitate his transfer to Yale.

What clear and convincing evidence did Davis have? "Our expert witness was 100 percent certain Picozzi set the fire," Davis says. Maybe so, but Picozzi's expert witnesses were also certain that he did not set the fire. And after extensive testimony from the experts about Picozzi's burns, the pour pattern on the rug and the fire damage to the room, the hearing officer judged the battle of the experts a draw.

Davis argued that Picozzi was the only one with the opportunity to light the fire, that it is inconceivable that anyone other than Picozzi could have entered the locked door to the dorm, known that the door to Picozzi's room would be unlocked and counted on not being seen coming or going with a container of gasoline at 4:00 a.m. It would have been even more difficult for someone to open the door while Picozzi was in his room sleeping, splash gasoline on the floor, pour a trailer to the door, light it and close the door without waking him and without being burned.

In fact, many students had keys to the dorm, and several students testified about incidents in which unauthorized visitors had entered dorm rooms late at night. Davis argued that the fastidious Picozzi would never have gone to bed leaving his door unlocked. But Picozzi said that on the night of the fire, he had left the door unlocked after a late-night trip to the bathroom so that the noisy bolt would not awaken a student across the hall who had spent the night struggling to overcome a cough. Davis argued that no one else could have known that the door would be unlocked. Of course, someone could have been planning to light the fire outside the door, then changed his mind after trying the knob and discovering that it was unlocked.

As for other evidence implicating Picozzi, much was made at the hearing of the fact that no one trapped in a burning room would have or take the time to put on jeans and boots before escaping, even if they were wearing only underwear. Yet Picozzi's coughing neighbor opened the door to this room, saw the fire, closed the door, took off his pajamas and got dressed before leaving the building.

Underlying all this circumstantial evidence was a feeling by many at the university that Picozzi had exhibited erratic behavior, that therefore he was nuts and that because whoever set the fire was nuts, Picozzi must have set the fire. "The leap here is of Kierkegaardian proportion," say Silber.

Silber's theory is that the torching of Picozzi's room was yet another in a series of increasingly serious pranks carried out by students who disliked Picozzi. "Frankly," Silber said in his closing argument, "I went to law school in New York, and in New York City, we would have burned him out in the second day, not waiting to the second year."

Where were Picozzi's enemies—dubbed the *contras* by Silber—on the night of the fire? The student rumored to have made the harassing phone calls to Picozzi was never interviewed by the police, even though he was seen at the time of the fire calling a friend into his room to watch the smoke pour out of Picozzi's window. Miltenberg, who rushed to assure Dean Sue he had had nothing to do with the fire on March 8th, told police a week afterward that he didn't remember where he had been on Tuesday morning. He told the police he would submit to a lie-detector test if Picozzi did. On the stand two years later Miltenberg at first testified that he didn't remember where he had spent the evening, then said, "I was home alone in bed."

Tom Good, who lived on the floor above Picozzi, spent most of his evening with David Berger and Kathy Rakowsky. The trio, who frequently liked to discuss how much they disliked Picozzi, had gone to a movie, then out for pizza and beer, before returning to the dorm around 2:00 a.m. Good testified that Berger lived at an off-campus address and that he and Rakowsky, who both lived in the dorms, walked back to the quad together. Rakowsky, who was never interviewed by the police, says that both Good and Berger walked back to the law quad with her. This would have meant that all three of them were in the law quad roughly two hours before the fire. Berger, who had told police he would submit to a polygraph examination at any time, refused comment for this article.

Rakowsky says she never left her room after the fire alarm went off. Sara Allen, a former girlfriend of Picozzi's who lived in the dorms, testified that Good was "shaking like a leaf" outside the dorm after the fire. Isn't it possible that the barefoot, pajama-clad Good was cold? "It was very obvious that he was nervous," Allen said. In any event, Good refused to walk around the building to see Picozzi on the ground.

"I do not think Tom Good set the fire," Silber says, "because I don't think that he would have the gall."

On August 22nd, 1985, the hearing officer decided that the university had failed to prove by clear and convincing evidence that Jim Picozzi set the fire. In reaching his decision, the hearing officer was persuaded by the fact that no container was located in Picozzi's room. The experts agreed that the fire would have to have been lighted within a minute after the gasoline was poured. So if Picozzi set the fire, the container would have been in his room. It is possible that he washed it out in seconds or that the investigators missed it, but the hearing officer found these possibilities to be unlikely. The hearing officer stated that he did not believe Good's account that he had sighted a gun in Picozzi's room—but he also stated that he was not suggesting that any of "those who testified... or were mentioned at the hearing," meaning the *contras*, were involved in the starting of the fire.

At any time before the conclusion of the hearing, Picozzi would have been willing to drop his lawsuit against Dean Sandalow in exchange for a letter of good standing. Once the hearing officer delivered his ruling, however, Picozzi was no longer willing to settle his suit. The next day Dean Sandalow directed Dean Sue to issue the following letter:

> To whom it may concern:
>
> James Picozzi is a student in good standing at the University of Michigan Law School and is eligible to return.

Needless to say, he did not.

Instead, Picozzi submitted the letter in support of his applications for admission to Yale, Stanford, Columbia, Cornell, the University of Virginia and the University of Pennsylvania law schools. He was accepted at Pennsylvania and at Yale. His lawsuit against Dean Sandalow was dismissed by Judge John Feikens, a University of Michigan alumnus, on Sandalow's motion for summary judgment. The case is on appeal in the United States Court of Appeals for the Sixth Circuit. By the time a decision is reached, Dean Sandalow, who stepped down after serving a ten-year term, will be Professor Sandalow.

Picozzi, who had the personality traits of a good litigator and now had the experience as well, enrolled at Yale Law School in September of 1985. He was, according to Dean Thomas, "a good student and a good citizen." He became an editor of *The Yale Law Journal* by writing a note for the journal on the due-process implications of university disciplinary proceedings. The note will be published just after his case is argued in the Sixth Circuit. But he wasn't totally successful in putting his past behind him.

While applying for full-time jobs with many different law firms, Picozzi ran into more of what Silber dubbed the "subtle prejudice" that plagued him at Michigan. Alumni and past associates working at various firms were convinced either of his guilt or of his obnoxiousness and did their best to ensure that he wasn't hired. Finally, with a recommendation from Silber, for whom he had worked as a law clerk, Picozzi was offered a job as an associate at the New York firm of Fried, Frank, Harris, Shriver and Jacobson.

In May, Jim Picozzi graduated from Yale Law School, with Silber to cheer him on. "It was a very, very good moment," says Silber, his eyes shining. And Silber, a man not easily impressed by institutions, was, well, impressed. "You know, no mistake about it," he says, "a law school taking Sparky at that point, even with a letter of good standing, was taking a chance.... One of the things that makes Yale a great law school is to right this kind of wrong and to take this kind of chance."

Yale Law School apparently believed what it taught its students about the presumption of innocence and due process. "The hearing officially cleared him," says Dean Thomas. "And as far as we were concerned, that was enough. . . . And he proved us right." Thomas, who considers himself a friend of Picozzi's, admits that "it did help that he came from [Yale] originally and had friends here."

Silber believes that the fire and the trial had a positive effect on Picozzi. "I think Sparky learned a whole lot about life," he says. "Ten years from now, when he looks back on it, I think he'll say he would've been somebody different if this hadn't happened. Somebody not as good."

James Picozzi's student article, mentioned in the *Rolling Stone* story, appears in the July, 1987 *Yale Law Journal*: "University Disciplinary Process: What's Fair, What's Due, and What You Don't Get," *Yale Law Journal*, 96 (1987), 2132–2161.

Stone by Stone v. Cornell University
510 N.Y.S. 2d 313 (A.D. 3 Dept. 1987)

HARVEY, Justice.

Appeal from an order of the Supreme Court at Special Term (Ellison, J.), entered October 11, 1985 in Tompkins County, which dismissed the complaint.

During the summer of 1985, plaintiff, a 16-year-old high school student, attended the Cornell University Summer College Program operated by defendant. Prior to completion of the program, plaintiff was questioned by the program's residential director regarding information he had received indicating that drugs and alcohol were being used by students in the program. Plaintiff admitted smoking marihuana and consuming alcohol while in attendance at the program. As a result of these admissions, she was expelled from the program and informed that no appeal from this expulsion was available.

Claiming that her expulsion without an administrative hearing violated her right to due process under the Cornell Campus Code of Conduct (hereinafter Campus Code) and N.Y. Constitution, article I, § 6, plaintiff commenced this action seeking an order directing defendant to provide her with a hearing as provided by the Campus Code and permitting her to complete her classwork. Pending the hearing and determination of this action, plaintiff was permitted to complete her courses pursuant to an order to show cause signed on August 8, 1985.

By decision dated September 26, 1985, Special Term dismissed the complaint finding no basis for plaintiff's request for an administrative review of her expulsion. On appeal, plaintiff seeks release of her transcript so that she might receive academic credit for the courses she completed in the Summer College Program.

A college or university must substantially adhere to its own rules regarding the procedures to be followed prior to expelling a student. Defendant's Summer College Code of Conduct (hereunder Summer College Code) provided that "[c]onsumption or possessions of alcohol and other drugs is grounds for immediate dismissal." Plaintiff and her mother subscribed their signatures to a document indicating their acceptance of this and the other provisions of the Summer College Code. Since plaintiff admits that she used marihuana and consumed alcohol, we find defendant's decision to expel plaintiff entirely consistent with the rules and procedures articulated in its Summer College Code.

We find no merit in plaintiff's contention that her conduct should come under the provisions of the Campus Code rather than the Summer College Code. The Summer College Code is designed to cover high school students in the Summer College Program whereas the Campus Code governs conduct of the older, college students. The particular problems caused by having younger, high school students on campus requires a more stringent code which, among other things, imposes curfew requirements, restricts visits of guests in the dormitories, prohibits use of motor vehicles and requires parental authorization for overnight time away from campus. Here, it is undisputed that plaintiff was not a matriculated college student, but merely a high school student at defendant's campus solely for the Summer College Program. Accordingly, we hold that plaintiff's conduct was governed by the Summer College Code and, under the provisions of that code, expulsion was authorized upon plaintiff's admission to the use of marihuana and the consumption of alcohol.

Finally, we reject plaintiff's assertion that she was denied due process as guaranteed by N.Y Constitution, article I, § 6. A threshold requirement to invoking the State's constitutional due process provision is a showing that "the State has in some fashion involved itself in what, in another setting, would otherwise be deemed private activity." Although defendant receives some financial assistance from the State, this alone does not constitute a sufficient degree of State involvement so as to allow an intrusion into defendant's disciplinary policies. We conclude that plaintiff has failed to allege sufficient State involvement to invoke the requirements of constitutional due process.

Order affirmed, with costs.

Fussell v. Louisiana Business College of Monroe
519 So. 2d 384 (La. App. 2 Cir. 1988)

MARVIN, Judge.

In this action for breach of contract, plaintiff, Ms. Fussell, appeals a judgment rejecting her demands on the finding that the defendant business college was justified in suspending her from its business college.

In an earlier review, we held that plaintiff made a prima facie case of breach of contract by the defendant by showing that her status as a student at the school was terminated [and that] it was . . . incumbent upon the defendant to show by competent evidence that the breach was that of plaintiff, rather than its own, and to show that the plaintiff's dismissal was justified.

We remanded for that purpose.

The issue in this appeal is whether the defendant met its burden of proving on remand that its suspension of plaintiff was justified. On remand the trial court held that

> if the defendant breached its contract to give plaintiff a course of study by suspending her, it was because [plaintiff] had breached her contractual responsibilities to conduct herself as a responsible adult by creating and/or exacerbating the turmoil which could not be tolerated in academic surroundings.

The record does not support the trial court's conclusion. Defendant did not prove plaintiff disrupted the scholastic program of the college.

We reverse and render judgment for plaintiff.

FACTS

On February 7, 1983, defendant contracted under an "enrollment contract" to train plaintiff for a position as a legal secretary for $3,600 in tuition. Within four months, on May 26, 1983, plaintiff was suspended for being a "disruptive influence." The college refused to readmit plaintiff unless she signed a document admitting she had been a disruptive influence, agreeing to a future suspension if she again became a disruptive influence, and agreeing that the evaluation of her future conduct was to be left to the sole discretion of the school administrator. Plaintiff refused to sign the statement and instead brought this action.

The evidence at the first hearing and on remand shows that many students and teachers at the college in May 1983 became discontented with the administration. The husband of one of the teachers prepared a petition addressed to the district attorney, which was signed by 21 students, including plaintiff. The petition reflected the concern of some students and teachers that the school's administration was overcharging students and misappropriating government loans and grants that had been assigned by students to the college. A newspaper article on May 18, 1983, outlined these complaints. The article also contained allegations that some instructors were unqualified, that the school had a poor job placement record, and that an admissions policy to boost enrollment allowed unqualified students to enter the school. Many students left the school because of discontent and enrollment declined.

Two former teachers at the school and a former student testified at plaintiff's request. Ms. Hicks, the former student, testified that she had suggested the petition. Hicks was suspended but was readmitted when she signed the document that plaintiff was requested to sign to gain readmission. Ms. Hicks later graduated. No other students were suspended.

The two ex-teachers, one of whom voluntarily quit and the other of whom was terminated in May 1983, testified that plaintiff was an excellent student with a 3.57 GPA and that she was not at all disruptive. Both ex-teachers said that other students often complained about the school administration.

The trial court initially concluded that plaintiff's admissions at the first hearing (that she had signed the petition and had complained to others) were sufficient to establish the school's burden of proving that plaintiff was a disruptive influence. We disagreed and remanded to require the school to prove its justification.

On remand, several members of the school's administration and one former student testified at the request of the school. The former student, Ms. Zaunbrecker, had presented a hand-written complaint about plaintiff to the school's administration in May 1983 which the school used as its primary justification for suspending plaintiff. This "complaint" reads somewhat ambiguously as follows:

> Maria Fussell and Patti Hicks are asking Bruce Easterling about his GED and when he will be finishing his courses. And that he better past (sic) retake courses because the school will charge them for extras after graduating time is up for his course.

> I feel that they are putting doubts in other student's minds.

s/Debora Zaunbrecker

5/26/83

Ms. Zaunbrecker did not state that the "complaint" disrupted her, any other student, or any classroom of students.

The school administrators were repeatedly asked, on both direct and cross-examination, to specify the behavior of plaintiff which led to her suspension. Ms. Evans, the academic dean and administrator, was unable to provide specific information:

Q. Specifically what made you decide to suspend these two students?

A. There had to be an end—there had to be an end to what was going on ... once it becomes obvious that someone is undermining your goals, then you just have to take some steps to eliminate that...

Ms. Schultz, the president and owner of the school, also did not specifically detail how plaintiff had been disruptive:

Q. Do you know the reason for their suspension?

A.... they were instigating unrest in our student body and stopping my staff from doing their job...

THE DEFENDANT-COLLEGE'S BURDEN OF PROOF

The remand hearing produced little specific information to support the school's conclusion or contention that plaintiff was disruptive.

The conversation between plaintiff and Bruce Easterling, as described by Ms. Zaunbrecker, did not occur during a study or classroom session and cannot be characterized as disruptive conversation. It was established that plaintiff, on one occasion, briefly allowed a tape recorder to play in a classroom. The recording was described as being a transcription of an earlier meeting between some of the discontented students and school officials. Plaintiff and another witness testified that the tape was only accidentally turned on and was then immediately turned off. The teacher of that class testified, however, that the incident did not disrupt her or the class.

No teacher was called by the college to testify. The *only teachers*, the two called by plaintiff, stated that plaintiff was an excellent student who did not disrupt class. Defendant's contentions that plaintiff was "putting doubts in other students' minds" and "instigating unrest" related mainly to fiscal policies of the administration. Grumbling by college students must be of a greater degree than is shown here to reach the status of being legally disruptive of the scholastic program.

The defendant failed to meet the burden of proof we required in our first review of this case. We must conclude that the trial court's finding that plaintiff's suspension was justified is clearly wrong.

The school administration obviously lost the trust and confidence of some of its students and teachers even before plaintiff enrolled in February before she was suspended in May. The fact that no teacher or student testified about any classroom or study disruption by plaintiff is particularly significant. Plaintiff is shown to have attended classes, behaved herself in the general sense, and made excellent grades. The fact that plaintiff casually voiced suspicions, whether or not unfounded, that she and others had about the administration to a newspaper reporter and to other students was not a breach of plaintiff's obligation to avoid disruptive behavior to the scholastic program. We cannot agree that plaintiff's behavior justified her suspension.

DAMAGES

Plaintiff sought damages for monetary loss, the delay of her education, and mental anguish. Courts of appeal may award damages where the trier of fact erroneously fails to do so, and where the record contains sufficient proof of damages.

Damages for the breach of a contract are designed to put the plaintiff in the position she would have been in had the defendant not breached the contract.

The defendant itemized the plaintiff's account as follows:

70 percent of $3,600 tuition	$2,520.00
Enrollment fee	50.00
Books	449.93
Total amount of debt	$3,019.93
Less guaranteed student loan payment	(1,187.50)
Less federal grant (Pell grant)	(900.00)
Total amount paid by plaintiff	$2,087.50
Amount owed	$932.43

The college apparently contends that plaintiff owed 70 percent of the tuition under the withdrawal provision of the enrollment contract:

I understand that *withdrawal* after the commencement of classes, the refund policy shall be: * * *

4. During the second 25% of the course the college will retain 70% of the stated course price. (Emphasis added.)

This provision does not provide for involuntary and unjustified suspensions. Plaintiff contracted for about a year's course of instruction that would prepare her for employment as a legal secretary. Despite the fact that plaintiff successfully completed about four months of the course, defendant did not prepare plaintiff to qualify for a position as a legal secretary. Plaintiff received no academic credits and nothing of scholastic value. Accordingly, the defendant is liable to return the $2,087.50 it received for plaintiff's tuition.

Plaintiff's secretarial training and prospects for employment were delayed by the defendant's breach. Although the precise monetary loss brought about by this delay cannot be calculated, plaintiff is nevertheless entitled to compensation.

Where there is a legal right of recovery but the amount cannot be determined precisely, the court has reasonable discretion to assess an amount based upon all the facts and circumstances.

Ms. Throckmorton, an employee of the state job placement office and an expert in vocational job placement, testified that a beginning legal secretary with the one year of training that plaintiff contracted for could expect to earn between $600 and $750 per month. Plaintiff enrolled at Northeast Louisiana University in January 1984, about eight months after she was suspended by defendant. The delay attributable to defendant is the four months plaintiff was enrolled in defendant's college. Exercising our discretion, we shall award plaintiff $1,500 general damages.

Even if plaintiff proved mental anguish damages, which we find she did not, these damages can be awarded only in limited circumstances. Defendant's obligation to provide *vocational* training was not intended to "gratify a nonpecuniary interest."

DECREE

The judgment of the trial court is reversed and there is judgment against defendant-college and in favor of plaintiff for $2,087.00 in tuition and for $1,500 in damages, with legal interest from the date of defendant's active breach of the contract (May 26, 1983). All costs are assessed to defendant.

REVERSED AND RENDERED.

HBU Student Suspended for Radio Prank

Houston Chronicle, 11 December 1987, Sec. 6, pp. 1, 12

It started as a joke, but not everyone is laughing. KKBQ Radio employee Elliot Segal wanted to play a prank on his mother, but his actions have had serious disciplinary repercussions.

Segal was suspended indefinitely Wednesday by Houston Baptist University for an on-air prank he played last month.

The 18-year-old freshman, who works part time at KKBQ (92.9 FM, 790 AM), had an idea for one of the morning pranks that program director and disc jockey John Lander plays. For the radio jokes, which Lander calls "zoogurizations," listeners call in with tricks they want to play on their friends. Lander assumes another identity, calls the subject of the prank, and carries out the put-on. If the "victims" don't catch on, Lander tells them it's all a joke, and they have been zoogurized. Lander then puts the taped conversations on the air.

Lander says zoogurizations have been one of the more popular features of the Q-Zoo, which airs 6-10 a.m. weekdays. But this time the joke backfired.

Lander called Segal's mother, Phyllis Witt, who lives in Phoenix, Ariz., Nov. 9. He pretended to be Dr. James Massey, dean of student affairs at HBU. He told her that he had found an 8-foot inflatable condom hanging from the flagpole and that he had traced it to her son; he said Segal's fraternity had been involved with hazing.

Witt was not happy, and she assured Lander that it was not the way her son was brought up. Lander said they would either have to expel Segal or she would have to pay $6,200, because her son's scholarship had been revoked. When she was thoroughly upset, Lander informed her she had been zoogurized. The "zoogurization" first aired Nov. 11.

But they weren't laughing at HBU. Segal has been told he can appeal his case in February, [1988] but cannot attend the university until the matter is resolved.

"A student's records are private, confidential communications, so we cannot comment on any of the proceedings of the action," said Sharon Saunders, director of university relations of HBU.

"I feel terrible about what's happened," said Segal. "It was all very innocent. I didn't mean any harm by it, and my mom thought it was funny."

"This has been going on for a month, but the actual suspension just took place on Wednesday. I went to a due process court and was told I could have counsel, but he had to come from HBU, so I was at their mercy. What happened has been blown out of context."

Segal said he has been suspended for "impugning the character of the university." He had a full scholarship at HBU and had wanted to stay in Houston because he could combine academics with his radio work.

"I don't come from a wealthy family, so it was an ideal situation because I could get a good education and get experience working for a radio station," he said.

"I have a hard time understanding why HBU is taking this so seriously," Lander said. "It was a joke, and the situation was imaginary. Elliot didn't actually do what I told his mother, which we explained on the air. I called (HBU) president (E.D.) Hodo and offered to take that bit off the air if they would drop the charges."

Lander says the station has received numerous calls supporting Segal and they will continue to fight the case.

Reprinted with permission.

Academic Misconduct

As several of these cases reveal, students can perpetrate extremely sophisticated frauds, which may be detected years later through serendipity or subsequent evidence. But academic misconduct and degree revocation are not a strictly modern occurrence: in Bentley's Case (*The King v. The University of Cambridge*), a degree was revoked in 1723. Dr. Richard Bentley had his degree revoked, due to a debt of four pounds, six shillings owed to Dr. Coniers Middleton. When the demand for payment was issued by the Cambridge University court (the equivalent of an ecclesiastical and civil proceeding), he "spoke contemptuous words of the court, for which he was de-graded,and from which no appeal would lie.... " After establishing that Dr. Bentley had certain rights ("Neither shall it be said, that where a corporation has admitted a man willingly to his freehold, that they shall have power to disfranchise him because they do not like him; neither can the Universities give degrees to whom they please, and take them away *ad libitum*"), they defined the contours of due process and notice ("How can a man be said to be contumacious to a court when he did not know when and where they assembled as a court?"), and held that he indeed had received notice ("Upon the whole matter, the Doctor knows he is degraded, and for what cause, and he ought to have made his submission before he moved for a [dismissal]; and if that had been done, he might have no occasion to apply himself to this court.") Two of the Justices dissented:

> Fortescue, Justice. The words are "a contempt to the court," for which he ought to have been committed if he had been present in court; and if not, he ought to have been bound to his good behavior. I do not see how a deprivation for this cause is agreeable to reason or justice: many customs of the University have been adjudged void. It is a rule, that all customs shall be certain. Now this custom to deprive *pro contumacia* is uncertain as to the meaning of the word "contumacy," whether it means contumacy to the congregation, to the vice chancellor, to this court, or to the University; whether to Dr. Gooch as head of the college, or as judge of the inferior court.

Pratt, Chief Justice (as to this matter). The words are improper and indecent: we should punish all persons who should speak so disrespectfully of our process, and might bind them to their good behavior; but the authorities seem too strong to allow a power to remove a person from his freehold [i.e., his degree] for such words.

(K.B. 1723), 8 Modern Rep. (Select Cases) 148, 2 Ld. Raym. 1334. [edited for modern usage] See also, B. Reams, "Revocation of Academic Degrees by Colleges and Universities," *Journal of College and University Law*, 14 (1987), 283–302.

University of Houston v. Sabeti

676 S.W. 2d 685 (Tex. App. 1 Dist. 1984)

COHEN, Justice.

The sole question before us is whether a student permanently expelled from a state university was denied due process of law because his counsel was not allowed to speak during the expulsion hearing.

In April of 1983, the appellee was charged with violating the university's rules by misrepresenting as his own work certain papers which were prepared by another. Under the school's policies regarding academic dishonesty, a hearing was held by the engineering department, followed by another hearing before the college honesty board, and an appeal to the university provost. The departmental hearing took place on April 25, 1983, the appellee was found guilty, and the department chairman recommended a permanent expulsion because the appellee was a second offender, having previously been accused of cheating on an exam. There is no issue before this court concerning the procedures followed at the first hearing before the engineering department.

The second step in the process, a hearing before the college honesty board, was held on May 4, 1983, before a panel of two faculty members and three students. The hearing was presided over by a faculty member appointed by the dean.

The appellee was assisted by his counsel of choice, a law student. This counsel attended the hearing and advised the appellee during the hearing; however, he was not allowed to speak, argue or question witnesses during the hearing. The appellee, speaking for himself, was allowed to testify and to make opening and closing statements, but was not permitted to question witnesses directly. All questions were directed to the hearing officer, who would ask the question directly of the witness. The hearing officer asked some, but not all the questions requested by the appellee. No attorney or other counsel represented the university.

The appellee was found guilty and was permanently expelled. He then exercised his final administrative remedy by appealing unsuccessfully to the Provost.

The appellee then sued to have his expulsion set aside because the procedure followed in the hearing before the college honesty board denied him due process of law in that his counsel was not permitted to question witnesses and make statements. The district court agreed with these contentions. The court's conclusions of law state:

> 6. Procedural due process requires that the student subject to permanent suspension must be provided a hearing at which the student could be represented

by counsel, and, *through counsel*, present witnesses on his own behalf, and cross-examine adverse witnesses.

7. The prohibition against representation of plaintiff by and *through counsel* was a violation of plaintiff's right to due process.

The court permanently enjoined the university from giving effect to the expulsion and required that the appellee be allowed to enroll in classes; it ordered the university to remove all language regarding the expulsion from the appellee's transcript and to remove all grades of F given as a result of the expulsion; and it enjoined any rehearing of charges against the appellee without prior court approval of the procedures to be followed in the hearing.

The issue before us has divided courts for years. Several United States Circuit Courts of Appeal have held that the fourteenth amendment to the United States Constitution does not require confrontation and cross-examination of witnesses by the accused, much less by counsel, in expulsion proceedings. In *Wasson v. Trowbridge*, the Court upheld the expulsion of a student from the United States Merchant Marine Academy and rejected a contention that he was entitled to counsel:

> "Where the proceeding is non-criminal in nature, where the hearing is investigative and not adversarial and the government does not proceed through counsel, where the individual concerned is mature and educated, where his knowledge of the events . . . should enable him to develop the facts adequately through available sources, and where the other aspects of the hearing taken as a whole are fair, due process does not require representation by counsel."

The *Wasson* Court held that the hearing was "not adversarial" even though the student was permanently expelled. It compared the circumstances to *Dixon*, which upheld the expulsion of students from a non-military college.

> "It is significant that in the *Dixon* case where the balancing of government and private interest favored the individual far more than here, the Court did not suggest that a student must be represented by counsel in an expulsion proceeding."

In *Greenhill v. Bailey*, the Court, as in *Dixon v. Alabama State Board*, held that, although a reversal was required because lack of notice deprived the college student of due process, "the presence of attorneys or the imposition of rigid rules of cross-examination at a hearing for a student . . . would serve no useful purpose, notwithstanding that the dismissal in question may be of permanent duration."

Several federal district courts have also declined to impose such a requirement.

High school students do not shed their constitutional rights at the school-house gate, nor do students forfeit their constitutional rights by attending a state university. We have come a long way in the opposite direction since Mr. Justice Holmes, faced with a due process claim, concluded that, "The petitioner may have a constitutional right to talk politics, but he has no constitutional right to be a policeman." Attendance at a state university is an interest protected by the due process clause of the fourteenth amendment; however, "once it is determined that due process applies, the question remains what process is due."

In *Goss v. Lopez*, the Supreme Court held that due process did not require confrontation and cross-examination of witnesses or representation by counsel to support the suspension of high school students for ten days. The Court declined to impose these requirements even though it held unconstitutional an Ohio statute which failed to give notice and a right to be heard to the suspended students. Although the Court stated that longer suspensions or expulsions might require "more formal procedures," it declined to impose them. Four justices, all of whom are on the court today, dissented even from the limited holding of *Goss*. Nevertheless, several federal courts both before and after *Goss* have held that representation by counsel is required.

One court has held that due process requires that counsel be present to advise the student at the hearing and that the student, not the counsel, may question witnesses against him. This procedure was followed in the instant case.

In *Texarkana Independent School District v. Lewis*, a court of three judges announced three opinions, including a dissenting opinion. The court held that the right to cross-examination and confrontation is not always mandatory. However, the court also held that a high school student has the right to be represented by counsel

> "where the school district proceeds through counsel, and particularly when the school intends to expel the student; it is not necessary to notify the student of his right to counsel ... when the school district does not elect to proceed through counsel and does not intend to expel the student."

The *Lewis* case was never reviewed or approved by the Texas Supreme Court. The holding quoted above relied for authority upon *Madera v. Board of Education*. However, neither case made such a holding. *Madera* reversed an injunction which required that attorneys be allowed to participate in junior high school guidance conferences. It was not an expulsion case, and the only issue to be decided at the guidance conference which the attorney was barred from attending was whether the child would be reinstated in the same school and class or transferred to another school. The court stated:

> "What due process may require before a child is expelled from public school or is remanded to a custodial school or other institution which restricts his freedom to come and go as he pleases is not before us."

Wasson v. Trowbridge expressly rejected any requirement of counsel such as the court found in *Lewis*.

We further observe that *Lewis* involved high school students, who were minors. Minors may be more in need of counsel's participation than would an adult with greater education, such as the appellee.

We hold that due process of law guaranteed by the fourteenth amendment to the U.S. Constitution was not violated by the facts in this case. The appellant has not claimed that he received no notice, late notice, or vague notice of the charges. He has not complained that he was denied the right to have an attorney or other counsel present at the proceedings. He was assisted at the hearing by his counsel of choice, a law student, acting without fee as a "student defender," pursuant to the university's policy to provide such assistance. The appellee testified fully. A form of cross-examination was allowed. The university had no advantage over the appellee in this respect because it had no counsel, attorney or otherwise, at the hearing. None of the factors listed in *Wasson v. Trowbridge* as favoring counsel were present: 1) the proceeding was not criminal; 2) the government did not proceed through counsel; 3) the student was mature and educated; 4) the student's knowledge of the events enabled him to develop the facts adequately; and 5) the other aspects of the hearing, taken as a whole, were fair.

The record shows that a fair hearing was conducted which gave the appellee fair opportunity to defend himself against his accusers. The basic elements of due process, notice and a right to be heard, were afforded the appellee. The due process clause requires only fundamental fairness; it does not require that every dispute with a government agency be resolved as a lawsuit would be. Due process "negates any concept of inflexible procedures applicable to every imaginable situation." It is a flexible concept that may be reflected in many different methods of dispute resolution other than the judicial model, as long as the method used provides reasonable notice and fair hearing, as it did under the facts in this particular case.

Points of error one and two are sustained. The judgment of the district court is reversed. Judgment is hereby rendered in favor of the appellant setting aside the injunction and denying all relief sought by the appellee.

Expulsion is not always the only option. In *Napolitano v. Princeton University*, 453 A.2d 263 (N.J. Super. A.D. 1982), Princeton's one year suspension of a graduating senior who plagiarized a Spanish paper was upheld. The Court held for the University, and noted,

> One last observation. Plaintiff claims that the penalty is supposed to provide something educative in its imposition. She argues that the penalty here is improper because there is no educational value to be found in it. Perhaps plaintiff's self-concern blinds her to the fact that the penalty imposed on her, as a leader of the University community, has to have some educative effect on other student members of the community. In addition, to paraphrase the poet, "the child is mother to the woman," we believe that the lesson to be learned here should be learned by Gabrielle Napolitano and borne by her for the rest of her life. We are sure it will strengthen her in her resolve to become a success in whatever endeavor she chooses.

In another case involving Princeton, the institution's honor code and its procedures were upheld. *Clayton v. Princeton University*, 608 F. Supp. 413 (D.N.J. 1985).

Abalkhail v. Claremont University Center
No. B014012 (Cal. Ct. App. Feb. 27, 1986),
cert. denied, 107 S. Ct. 186 (1986)

Spencer, P.J.

Plaintiff Sulaiman S. Abalkhail appeals from an order of dismissal entered after the trial court denied his petition for writ of mandate and sustained demurrers to his remaining three causes of action, alleging breach of contract, intentional infliction of emotional distress and negligent infliction of emotional distress, plaintiff thereafter failing to amend within the 30 days allowed.

STATEMENT OF FACTS

Plaintiff, a citizen of Kuwait, enrolled in Claremont Graduate School, one of six independent colleges comprising Claremont University Center, in August 1977. He completed all required courses satisfactorily in pursuit of a Ph.D. in Government and submitted a doctoral dissertation entitled "Public Enterprise and Development in Kuwait." Following the approval and acceptance of plaintiff's dissertation, he was awarded a Ph.D. in Government in 1979.

In April 1980, Abdulla M. Ali (Ali), also a citizen of Kuwait and director of the Arab Planning Institute, wrote to the president of Claremont Graduate School asserting that plaintiff's doctoral dissertation was copied from a paper written by a fellow member of the Arab Planning Institute, Dr. Muhammad T. Sadik (Sadik), entitled "Public Enterprises and Development in the Arab Countries." Ali indicated that Sadik's paper thereafter had been published in 1978 as chapter one of a book of the same title. Approximately two weeks later, Ali sent a similar letter to Abdlatif Al-Hamad (Al-Hamad), a trustee of the Arab Planning Institute and alumnus of Claremont McKenna College. Al-Hamad forwarded this letter to Claremont Graduate School on April 22, 1980.

No similar situation previously had arisen or been foreseen in the experience of Claremont Graduate School. Consequently, the Graduate School did not maintain a standing committee or rules and regulations for the investigation and determination of charges brought against its degree holders who might merit disciplinary action. After receiving the letters, the Graduate School appointed a three-member subcommittee to investigate the charges concerning plaintiff's doctoral dissertation. The subcommittee's "investigation" consisted of a detailed comparison of plaintiff's doctoral dissertation and the first chapter of Sadik's book. Upon completing this comparison, the subcommittee conferred and concluded that approximately 75 percent of the material in the two documents was identical. Based on that conclusion, the subcommittee reported that there may have been a breach of the canons of academic honesty.

On the basis of the subcommittee's report, Paul A. Albrecht, Dean of the Graduate School, wrote to plaintiff in Kuwait on December 16, 1980. The letter states in pertinent part: "we are sad and disturbed to report that you are accused of plagiarizing substantial parts of your 1979 doctoral dissertation: *Public Enterprise and Development in Kuwait,* from a document published in 1978 by the International Center for Law in Development, New York, entitled *Public Enterprises and Development in the Arab Countries* (Cat. No. 78–1165 copyright, 1977). According to the preface of this volume its chapters are 'based on papers presented to a Seminar on Public Enterprises and Development in the Arab Countries, held in Kuwait, March 22–25, 1976.' The seminar was cosponsored by the Arab Planning Institute and the International Legal Center (the successor organization being the International Center for Law and Development).

"In response to this charge, I appointed a faculty committee, three professors (from Government, Philosophy and Education) to review the charges. That committee has reviewed the matter and has concluded unanimously that there may have been a breach of academic honesty.

"A formal hearing on this matter will be held in the near future to determine the validity of the charge. Evidence in your behalf may be presented in writing and/or orally by yourself and/or attorney and/or other representative. This hearing will be scheduled at a time convenient for your appearance or representation. If you do not respond to this notice, the formal hearing will be held on Monday, February 9, 1981 at 1:30 p.m. in the Treanor Room at Claremont Graduate School.

"At this hearing, the evidence presented will be recorded and a certified transcript of the proceedings provided for you. The formal hearing committee will determine the validity of these allegations and recommend to me and the graduate faculty what action should be taken. Upon receipt of these findings, the recommended action will be referred to the graduate faculty and the Board of Trustees for final action. You will receive a final notification of that action.

"The hearing committee, after receiving all the evidence, may find that a) the allegations are not sustained, or b) sustained to a substantial degree. If the latter finding is made, your degree may be revoked by Claremont Graduate School."

Subsequently, plaintiff requested and received a delay in the proceedings of two months in order to prepare his defense. The three-member subcommittee, comprised of Professors Jordan, Louch and Drew, conducted a formal hearing on May 5 and 6, 1981. A court reporter was in attendance and prepared a complete transcript of the proceedings. Also present were an associate dean of the Graduate School, the school's legal counsel and plaintiff.

Plaintiff was given a copy of Ali's letter of complaint and given an opportunity to explain the similarity between his dissertation and Sadik's work. He testified that he had worked for Sadik in 1975 as a researcher at the Arab Planning Institute, himself writing substantial portions of Sadik's paper; Sadik had combined plaintiff's work and that of other researchers, presenting the result to a seminar and later publishing it, without mentioning plaintiff's name as a contributor. Since the work was his own and Sadik had not mentioned plaintiff's contribution, plaintiff believed he could base his dissertation on this work without referencing Sadik's publication. According to plaintiff, Ali had made the accusation of plagiarism out of jealousy and factionalism; Sadik, a Palestinian, was under Ali's thumb and would say anything Ali requested.

The hearing subcommittee also received testimony from a member of plaintiff's dissertation committee and permitted plaintiff to question this witness. At this point, plaintiff was given the opportunity to ask additional questions and was invited to suggest any additional procedure he deemed necessary to ensure a fair hearing. Plaintiff made no comments directed at the conduct of the hearing, expressing only a concern with any possible influence exerted by Al-Hamad; he was assured that Al-Hamad had no involvement in either the investigation or the decision to be made. Stating he felt he had been fairly treated, plaintiff declined to present any further evidence. In conclusion, the subcommittee members explained that they might wish to obtain additional information, given the substantial contradictions in plaintiff's testimony and the accusations made. If further information were obtained, plaintiff would be furnished with copies of that evidence and would have an opportunity to challenge and rebut it.

At the direction of the subcommittee, legal counsel wrote to Ali on May 18, 1981, requesting additional information in possible corroboration of plaintiff's testimony. Ali responded by letter on May 30. He states that plaintiff worked for the Department of Public Administration & Industrial Management, an organization independent from the Arab Planning Institute, until 1975. The letter continues, "during the time when Mr. Sadik's paper was prepared and submitted to the Conference, [plaintiff] was not in Kuwait. He was studying in the United States from the 28th of April 1975 to 1st of June 1977. He came to Kuwait on the 14th of June and stayed until the 20th of August 1977 and then he went back to the U.S.A. for further studies.... [T]he records show that he was not in Kuwait at anytime during the Conference or during the year before the Conference and he did not come after the Conference for another year."

Legal counsel again sought further information from Ali on January 31, 1982. Ali responded by telex on February 1, referencing his letter of May 30, 1981. The telex states: "[Plaintiff] never worked with Mr. Sadik as research assistant or trainee.... Our records, which leaves no doubt, shows [plaintiff] never did any research related to the topic of his dissertation or any other topic, in Arabic or English, except a paper entitled "The Growth of Pubic Expenditure in Kuwait" (in Arabic) which he prepared in partial fulfilment (sic) of the requirement for the graduate diploma of Institute's course on development planning, when he was working at the Ministry of Planning in Kuwait, in June 1974.

"Furthermore, [plaintiff] joined the Department of Public Administration and Industrial Management as a research assistant in October 1974 and left for the U.S.A. for further studies in April 1975 and he never returned back to the Institute until 2 June 1979. Please be advised that the Conference on Public Enterprises and Development in the Arab Countries was held in Kuwait, March 22–23, 1976. Sadik's paper was presented to this conference in English and never being translated into any other language until this—. Sadik prepared this paper upon request of the Institute and did the field work during the summer of 1975....

"I will call on you when I pass through Los Angeles around mid-February."

The hearing subcommittee decided to meet with Ali in mid-February in the offices of legal counsel. During that meeting on February 16, the subcommittee members questioned Ali concerning the relationship between the Department of Public Administration and Industrial Management and the Arab Planning Institute, plaintiff's involvement with each organization and his employment during the relevant time periods. In addition, Ali presented the subcommittee with a memorandum detailing plaintiff's educational and employment record, which had been prepared by Dr. Abdulhadi Alawadi, assistant director of the Department of Public Administration and Industrial Management. In the interim between Ali's February 1 telex and the February 16 meeting, Ali had forwarded a copy of plaintiff's paper, "The Growth of Public Expenditure in Kuwait."

On March 1, 1982, subcommittee member Professor A.R. Louch wrote to plaintiff, enclosing a copy of Dr. Alawadi's memorandum and summarizing Ali's additional evidence. The letter states in pertinent part: "Specifically, [Ali] denies that you worked at any time as a researcher for Mr. Sadik, or that you filed a copy of your dissertation at the Institute. The only research paper submitted by you to the Institute was "The Growth of Public Expenditure in Kuwait," as required for your diploma in Development Planning. That paper has been reviewed by the committee, and appears to be unrelated to your dissertation or the material in Mr. Sadik's paper."

Professor Louch invited plaintiff to respond, stating: "If there is any evidence you can offer to substantiate your claim to have contributed a research paper to Mr. Sadik on Public Enterprise and Development in Kuwait, or to refute other aspects of the account of your education and employment record with the Department of Public Administration and Industrial Management you should get in touch with Dean Ellner as soon as possible and no later than March 22, 1982. The committee will soon complete its investigation in the matter of charges of plagiarism against you, and it is in the interest of all parties that a decision be reached as soon as possible."

Subsequently, the hearing subcommittee in the person of Professor Louch received a letter from Sadik, written March 16, 1982. Sadik states: "I deeply regret to have to inform you that [plaintiff] never worked with me directly or indirectly while I was engaged on preparing the study on Public Enterprises or any other activity. He did not serve as my research assistant in 1975."

Since plaintiff had not responded to Professor Louch's letter of March 1, 1982, legal counsel again wrote to him on April 6. The letter warns plaintiff: "By his letter of March 1, Professor Louch invited you to respond to the statements made by Mr. Ali and asked that you do so on or before March 22, 1980 (sic). The Committee has construed your silence as a decision not to respond to Mr. Ali's assertions." The letter continues, informing plaintiff of the contents of Sadik's March 16 letter and concludes with yet another invitation to present a defense: "Inasmuch as the Committee intends to commence its final deliberations in this matter within the next several weeks, it is anxious to give you an unfettered opportunity to respond in writing to the statements made by both Mr. Ali and Mr. Sadik. If you would like to take advantage of this opportunity, please send your written response to Dean Carolyn Ellner of the Graduate School within the next few weeks but in no event later than April 23, 1982. In addition, if you plan on making the submission . . . , would you kindly advise me by telex on or before Friday, April 16, 1982." Plaintiff did not respond.

On April 12, after thorough deliberations, the hearing subcommittee submitted its report to the members of the Graduate Council. The report recounts and weighs the evidence in detail, concluding that the charges of plagiarism have been substantiated, and recommends that plaintiff's Ph.D. in Government be revoked. The Graduate Council voted to accept the recommendation.

On May 12, 1982, plaintiff belatedly responded to the letters of March 1 and April 6, submitting a memorandum. The hearing subcommittee reviewed the memorandum, which more or less repeated plaintiff's hearing testimony, but concluded its contents did not warrant additional deliberations or a change in the recommendation made. Following the Graduate Council review, the hearing subcommittee's recommendation was accepted successively by the Graduate Faculty of the Claremont Colleges, the Claremont Graduate School Committee of the Board of Fellows and the Board of Fellows of Claremont University Center. Plaintiff's degree was revoked in October 1982; he was informed of this action by letter dated February 1, 1983. The instant action followed.

CONTENTS

I

Plaintiff contends the trial court erred in denying his petition for writ of mandate, in that it is established as a matter of law that he did not receive those due process protections to which he was entitled and, hence, did not have a fair hearing.

II

Plaintiff asserts the trial court erred in sustaining the demurrer to his second cause of action for breach of contract, in that the complaint clearly alleges an actionable breach.

III

Finally, plaintiff avers the trial court erred in sustaining the demurrers to his third and fourth causes of action for intentional and negligent infliction of emotional distress, in that the complaint clearly states each cause of action.

DISCUSSION

I

Plaintiff contends the trial court erred in denying his petition for writ of mandate, in that it is established as a matter of law that he did not receive those due process protections to which he was entitled and, hence, did not have a fair hearing. We cannot agree.

An educational institution's decisions concerning its students are subject only to very limited judicial review. With respect to academic matters, because educators are uniquely qualified to assess the capability of students, their discretion is absolute. Accordingly, a student dismissal for academic reasons will be set aside only for an abuse of discretion, i.e., where it appears to be arbitrary, capricious or undertaken in bad faith. In contrast, dismissals for disciplinary reasons turn on objective questions of fact and thus will be subject to more searching review.

Whenever the deprivation of a significant interest is at issue, the holder of that interest is entitled to procedural fairness. The right to pursue a profession is such a significant interest and the right to pursue an education is an interest of corollary significance. In the instant matter, defendants sought to deprive plaintiff of the fruits of his education, i.e., his degree. That is a vital interest connected with the pursuit of one's livelihood; hence, plaintiff was entitled to procedural fairness prior to the revocation of his degree.

However, he was not—as he claims—entitled to full-blown procedural due process. Rather, he was entitled only to the minimum requisites of procedural fairness, to be provided with "adequate notice of charges and a 'fair opportunity... to present his position.'" This entails neither "formal proceedings with all the embellishments of a court trial...nor adherence to a single mode of process." Indeed, the courts have recognized "the practical limitations on the ability of private institutions to provide for the full airing of disputed factual issues."

Plaintiff asserts he was denied procedural fairness in the following respects: (1) defendants failed to provide adequate notice of the charges; (2) plaintiff was not permitted to confront and cross-examine all adverse witnesses; (3) the committee which initially investigated whether further consideration should be given to the charge was the same committee which ultimately held a hearing and rendered factual determinations, thereby denying plaintiff a fair hearing; and (4) defendants improperly yielded to outside influences. Whether a hearing comports with the standards of procedural fairness is a question of fact. Hence, on appeal, the trial court's determination must be upheld if supported by substantial evidence. In assessing the sufficiency of the evidence, a reviewing court must view the evidence in the light most favorable to the trial court's judgment, indulging every legitimate inference necessary thereto.

What procedure will afford a party a fair hearing is determined by the facts and circumstances presented. At a minimum, a fair hearing requires adequate notice of the charges, a reasonable opportunity to respond and an impartial hearing panel. However, since private entities such as defendants have no subpoena power, procedural fairness does not encompass the right to confront and cross-examine adverse witnesses unless, of course, those witnesses testify at a hearing which the subject of the inquiry attends. Moreover, the hearing body is prohibited from considering ex parte communications only when the affected party is unaware of their contents and has no opportunity to respond.

Plaintiff claims the notice provided to him was deficient, in that it did not include the names of his accusers and thus prevented him from gathering evidence pertinent to his defense prior to the hearing. Adequate notice of the charges includes the specific accusation made and a statement of the consequences which may follow if the charges are found true. There is no requirement that notice include the names of adverse witnesses. It is sufficient if, at the hearing, the affected party is informed of the names and evidence of nonappearing witnesses and afforded an opportunity to respond to the facts thus presented.

Plaintiff was provided with detailed information concerning the publication he was accused of plagiarizing in preparing his doctoral dissertation, including the author, title and publication date. In addition, he was told the nature of the hearing to be held, given a proposed date, invited to present evidence, made aware he could seek the assistance of and have an attorney present at the hearing, told the composition of the hearing committee and informed of the likely consequence that his degree would be revoked if the committee found the charges to be true.

It is obvious plaintiff not only had adequate notice of the charges and possible consequences, but also of the general procedure to be followed in determining the issue and his basic rights. Indeed, plaintiff evinced his understanding of this by requesting and obtaining a substantial continuance of the hearing date in order to prepare his defense. The notice provided plaintiff exceeds the minimum requirements of fair procedure; hence, he was not denied a fair hearing on this ground.

Plaintiff also complains he was not permitted to confront and cross-examine all adverse witnesses. As noted *ante,* private institutions such as defendants have no subpoena power; consequently, procedural fairness does not per se include the right to confront and cross-examine adverse witnesses. In the instant matter, the complaining witnesses were citizens of Kuwait who were not present in the United States during the initial investigation of the charges or at the time of plaintiff's hearing. He was given their names and provided with the evidence they had submitted to the hearing subcommittee. In the circumstances, procedural fairness required no more.

At the conclusion of two days of hearings, during which plaintiff did cross-examine the sole witness other than himself who testified before the subcommittee, the subcommittee informed plaintiff there was a sufficient conflict in the evidence to prompt further investigation. He knew the subcommittee would be seeking additional evidence from the complaining witnesses and he was invited to submit further evidence in his defense. Approximately nine months later, counsel for the subcommittee learned one of the witnesses, Ali, would be in the United States in less than two weeks and desired to meet with the subcommittee. At the time, plaintiff was in Bahrain. The subcommittee did meet with Ali, questioning him in detail concerning aspects of plaintiff's defense. Thereafter, the committee informed plaintiff of the evidence given by Ali and forwarded a copy of a memorandum which Ali had submitted as evidence; plaintiff was invited to respond.

Given the time constraints and the distance involved, the dictates of fair procedure required no more. While the subcommittee received Ali's evidence ex parte, plaintiff was informed of its contents and had every opportunity to respond. Accordingly, the procedure employed was not repugnant to the concept of fair procedure.

Plaintiff argues that the initial investigation of the charges against him by the same subcommittee which ultimately held a hearing and rendered a factual determination denied him a fair hearing. An impartial adjudicatory panel is integral to a fair hearing. However, the combining of investigatory and adjudicatory functions does not necessarily violate concepts of fair procedure. The affected party has been denied a fair hearing only if "the facts of a case show foreclosure of fairness as a practical or legal matter."

In *Applebaum,* the court held the affected party had been denied a fair hearing where there not only was an overlap of investigatory and adjudicatory functions, but the complaining party was a member of both bodies and members of the adjudicatory body also were members of the reviewing body. In addition, the complaining party was one of only two persons involved in this process who had expertise in the area of investigation.

It is also noteworthy that the investigation in *Applebaum* included the taking of testimony and the gathering of expert opinion. In contrast, the only "investigation" undertaken in the instant matter was the examination of plaintiff's doctoral dissertation and comparison with the purportedly plagiarized document to ascertain whether there were enough similarities to pursue the matter further. No evidence was taken until the subcommittee convened a hearing. At that time, the members received testimony concerning the process by which plaintiff's dissertation was approved and his explanation of the similarities and his asserted right to use the material without attribution. Further, once the hearing committee reached a decision, it made a recommendation to a full adjudicatory board which included *no* member of the hearing committee. In these circumstances, the small overlap of function had no tendency to foreclose fairness either as a practical or as a legal matter. Accordingly, plaintiff was not thereby denied a fair hearing.

Finally, plaintiff urges that defendants improperly yielded to outside pressures from Ali-Hamad in reaching their decision. While plaintiff presents evidence in the form of his declaration that this is so, there is ample evidence to the contrary. The trial court's conclusion that plaintiff received a fair hearing implies a finding that defendants reached their decision free from improper outside influences. Inasmuch as the record contains substantial evidence to support such a finding, this court is bound by it on appeal. In sum, it is abundantly clear the trial court's conclusion plaintiff received a fair hearing is well-founded.

II

Plaintiff asserts the trial court erred in sustaining the demurrer to his second cause of action for breach of contract, in that the complaint clearly alleges an actionable breach. The assertion lacks merit.

Since even the decisions of an educational institution as to academic fitness must not be arbitrary, capricious or undertaken in bad faith, it is clear that a covenant of good faith and fair dealing is implied in the educator-student relationship. There is no authority suggesting a party may not state a claim for the breach of this covenant.

Doubtlessly, plaintiff's second cause of action adequately alleges on its face the existence of a contractual relationship and its breach by the revocation of his doctoral degree without first affording him a fair hearing. However, the merits of his petition for a write of mandate were considered and decided before the demurrer was considered. In denying the petition, the trial court specifically found plaintiff had received a fair hearing.

Although sufficient on its face, a complaint nonetheless will be subject to demurrer if it appears defective by reference to facts which may be judicially noticed. A court may take judicial notice of any court records, including its own records in a particular matter. A court's power of judicial notice extends to the truth of facts asserted in findings of fact, orders and judgments. Once judicial notice is taken of the finding plaintiff received a fair hearing, included in the order denying the petition for writ of mandate, the second cause of action becomes defective; it no longer adequately alleges the breach of any contractual relationship.

III

Finally, plaintiff avers the trial court erred in sustaining the demurrers to his third and fourth causes of action for intentional and negligent infliction of emotional distress, in that the complaint clearly states each cause of action. Again, we perceive no merit in the averment.

Plaintiff's third and fourth causes of action suffer from the same defect as his second cause of action. While each adequately alleges either the intentional or the negligent infliction of emotional distress on its face, each asserts the act resulting in emotional distress is the revocation of plaintiff's doctoral degree without first affording him a fair hearing. Again, once judicial notice is taken of the finding he received a fair hearing, the third and fourth causes of action no longer adequately allege any act amounting to outrageous conduct or actionable negligence. Accordingly, the trial court correctly sustained the demurrer to these causes of action as well as to the second cause of action.

The order is affirmed.

Crook v. Baker
813 F.2d 88 (6th Cir. 1987)

*   *   *

Before dealing with the district court's conclusion that Crook was denied procedural due process in all possible respects, it is necessary that we outline somewhat more fully the facts leading up to the University's proceedings and the proceedings resulting in the revocation.

Crook was awarded a degree of Master of Science in Geology and Mineralogy by the University on April 30, 1977. His thesis, submitted to meet a requirement for a master's degree, purported to describe a theretofore unknown mineral, which Crook called "texasite." Crook stated that he had discovered this new mineral while on a field trip in Texas. Available at the University was an electron microprobe, and Crook represented in his thesis that, with this microprobe, he had produced data which, when processed there with a computer program called EMPADR, showed that the chemical composition of "texasite" was such that it was indeed a previously unknown, naturally occurring mineral.

In the latter part of 1978, after receiving an allegation that Crook had, after leaving the University, fabricated data in evaluating a mineral, professors in the Geology and

Mineralogy department investigated and tentatively determined that Crook had not actually carried out the electron microprobe-*cum*-computer analysis as represented in his master's thesis. One reason for this suspicion was that the time log upon which a record of the use of the microprobe was kept indicated that Crook had not used the microprobe nearly enough, the professors thought, to have developed the data that were presented in the thesis. Another reason was that the thesis data as claimed by Crook were, upon reflection, really too good to be true in that the figures were so precise as to indicate that they were a product of working backward from a desired result. The department members also suspected that this "texasite," claimed by Crook to be a natural mineral, was in fact synthetic; the basis of this suspicion was, among other things, that the claimed chemical composition of the allegedly new, natural mineral was so close to that of a synthetic material which had been produced in a laboratory at the University, and a sample of such synthetic material, which had been available to Crook, was now missing. There were other questions raised concerning the validity of the thesis, but these turned out not to be the determinative ones before the hearing Committee.

The department invited Crook to return to the University to rerun his electron microprobe data on a computer using an improved EMPADR program. Crook purported to do this in February of 1979, and he delivered the results to the department. However, his work on the computer was, unknown to him, monitored on another computer. This showed that, contrary to his representation, he had simply put data into the computer that he wanted it to give back. Upon his being confronted with this deception, Crook admitted that he had delivered to the department EMPADR "results" that were not developed by the computer from his electron microprobe data. The department concluded that Crook's thesis' contention that his "texasite" was a new, natural mineral was false and that the data in the thesis represented by him to support this claim were fabricated.

On April 10, 1979, the Dean of the Graduate School informed Crook by letter that the Department of Geology and Mineralogy was charging him with fabrication of the data claimed by him in the thesis to have been developed by him. Specifically, the letter charged, *inter alia*, that the analytical results were uniformly so highly precise as to be suspect, that the time consumed by Crook in the analysis was insufficient to support the claimed results, and that the "texasite" claimed in the thesis to be a new, natural mineral was in fact a synthetic analogue. The letter explained that an Ad Hoc Disciplinary Committee of faculty members had been appointed to hear the matter. Procedures were outlined and later amended. Crook was warned that if the charges were proved, his master's degree might be revoked. The date of the hearing was initially set for May 14, 1979.

Crook almost immediately employed an experienced trial attorney, John Dethmers, of Lansing, Michigan who represented Crook throughout the proceedings at the University up to and including an appearance before and argument to the Board of Regents when it voted to revoke the degree. Shortly after he was employed, he obtained a continuance of the hearing to September 22, 1979.

On the Committee to hear the charges were four faculty members, none of whom were from the Department of Geology and Mineralogy, and three of whom were in science or engineering fields; the fifth member, Rosberg, a law professor and a non-voting member unless there was a tie, was designated as chairman.

On June 20, 1979, the department filed with the Committee and served on Crook a much more complete and scientific statement of charges with supporting documents; and, within a couple of weeks, the department served two additional documents when they became available. Although it was contemplated that Crook would respond by August 1, he did not file his response until September 7. The department then filed some rebuttal documents on September 19. The hearing was held on September 22, 1979.

At the hearing, in addition to the Committee, were Crook, his wife, his parents, and his lawyer, Dethmers. Also present were professors in the Geology Department, other persons who would likewise make statements, and Roderick Daane, who was general counsel of the University. At the request of Dethmers, all persons who were expected to and who did testify or make statements were sworn by the court reporter at the inception of the hearing. Opening statements were made by Professor Kelly, chairman of the department, Daane, Crook and his attorney, Dethmers.

It was a part of the procedure that had been established that while Crook was entitled to be represented by counsel, his counsel would not be allowed to examine and cross-examine witnesses. Neither Daane, for the department, nor Dethmers, for Crook, was allowed to do this, although the record reflects that Dethmers did in fact pose a few questions and make some statements during the proceeding.

The record reflects that the procedure followed by the Committee was an informal one. The Committee asked questions and the participants, including Crook, made statements and asked questions. Both the department and Crook were allowed to make submissions after the hearing and to comment on the submissions of the other. The hearing consumed eight hours, all in one day.

In its report, filed on March 7, 1980, the Committee stated that the burden was on the department to prove its charges by "clear and convincing" evidence. The report then carefully reviewed the evidence in great detail and found that the department had so proved that Crook had fabricated his thesis data submitted to prove that "texasite" was a new, natural mineral. The report further stated that the Committee felt that it was not competent to determine whether the material that had been the subject of the thesis was a natural mineral or was synthetic material that had been produced by another in a laboratory at the University. The Committee did not make a recommendation as to what action should be taken as a result of the fraud it found.

The Executive Board of the Graduate School, after considering Crook's response to the Committee's report, on May 7, 1980, unanimously voted to recommend rescission of Crook's degree. This recommendation was then to be reviewed by the Vice President of Academic Affairs, Dr. Alfred Sussman, who, however, recused himself because he had drafted the original charges. In his stead, the recommendation was reviewed by Vice President Dr. Charles G. Overberger, a scientist in charge of scientific research, who had not been involved in the matter. On July 18, 1980, Dr. Overberger sent a memorandum to the Regents stating that he had reviewed the Committee's report and recommended that the Regents rescind Crook's degree.

On October 16, 1980, the Regents had the question of the rescission of Crook's degree on their agenda. The report of the Committee and the recommendation of the Executive Board of the Graduate School and Dr. Overberger were before them. Crook's attorney, Dethmers, argued his client's case to the Regents. The Regents voted to rescind the degree.

The district court concluded that Crook's master's degree constituted an important property interest and that, in revoking the degree for fabrication of thesis data, an important liberty interest was also implicated. Since the Regents do not contend, at least on this appeal, the contrary, we assume these propositions, *arguendo*, and accept them as givens.

The district court found that Crook was denied a due process right to notice and an opportunity to be heard.

In *Goss v. Lopez*, cited and relied upon by the district court, the Court held that a student suspended for ten days from a public high school for misconduct was entitled to "oral or written notice of the charges against him and, if he denies them, an explanation of the evidence the authorities have and an opportunity to present his side of the story" either before or within a reasonable period of time after the suspension. While pointing out the difference between a disciplinary and an academic decision, the Regents acknowledge that their decision rescinding this degree had some aspects of both and therefore do not argue that Crook was not entitled to the notice contemplated by *Goss*.

As heretofore stated, the Committee determined that Crook had fabricated the thesis data on which he based his finding that "texasite" was a newly-discovered, natural mineral, and this was the only basis for the rescission of the degree. The question then becomes: did Crook have notice of this charge and the evidentiary basis for this charge? It appears to us beyond peradventure that Crook did have such notice. The letter sent to Crook on April 10, 1979 by the Dean of the Graduate School stated, *inter alia*, that thesis data fabrication was charged and that the time consumed by Crook in the analysis was insufficient to support the claimed results. Then, on June 30, 1979, the department served on Crook a much more complete statement of charges, supported by documents, which again made this charge. That Crook understood this charge and the basis for the charge is made clear by Crook's repeating the charge in his response filed on September 7, 1979. We quote: "Mr. Crook did not have sufficient time on the microprobe to have analyzed all the samples reported in the thesis, and therefore must have fabricated analyses which appear in his thesis."

With respect to Crook's opportunity to be heard, it is without dispute that, in addition to the abundant notice we have just described, he had counsel from the beginning who dealt with the University, he had the opportunity to and did file a response to the charges that was supplemented after the hearing, he had the opportunity to present witnesses and to have an expert with him at the hearing, he and his counsel both made opening statements at the hearing and his counsel was free to advise him, and he made statements and asked questions of the other witnesses. Moreover, Crook filed exceptions to the Committee's findings and his attorney argued his case before the Regents. Though the district court in its opinion described the hearing presided over by Professor Rosberg as a "circus-like free-for-all," the full transcript that is in the record makes clear that it simply was an informal rather than a trial-type hearing.

We therefore conclude, in sum, that the district court's determinations that Crook was denied procedural due process in that he did not have notice and an opportunity to be heard were clearly erroneous.

The district court also determined that Crook was denied procedural due process because his attorney, Dethmers, was not allowed to examine and cross-examine witnesses.

Although Crook's attorney stated at the inception of the hearing: "No way do I want to try to turn this into a courtroom proceeding," the Regents do not contend that the right to examine and cross-examine witnesses was waived. And although Dethmers did ask a few questions and make some comments other than his opening statement, the Regents do not deny that he was not afforded the right to examine and cross-examine. The ground rules that had been established for the hearing clearly proscribed such activity by counsel for either side.

The district court found Crook's procedural due process right to have counsel examine and cross-examine witnesses in *Goldberg v. Kelly*. There, the Court held that welfare recipients are entitled to a hearing before their benefits are cut off and that, if they have counsel, they have a right to have counsel cross-examine adverse witnesses. In reaching this result, the Court pointed out that such recipients would be in dire circumstances once their welfare benefits are improperly withdrawn and that, therefore, fairness required that the right of cross-examination be afforded to reduce the incidence of illegal withdrawal of benefits. The Court distinguished the plight of blacklisted government contractors, discharged government employees, and taxpayers denied tax exemptions as being less serious than that of the eligible welfare recipient whose benefits are withdrawn.

The district court was aware of and discussed the opinion of this court in *Frumkin v. Board of Trustees,* which held that a tenured college professor, who was discharged for stated reasons that adversely reflected upon him, was not entitled to have his counsel examine and cross-examine witnesses at the hearing that resulted in such findings. In reaching this result, this court discussed *Goldberg v. Kelly*, and stated:

> We cannot, however, accept appellant's contention that we should rule in his favor on the basis of an analogy between the problems which beset an unrepresented welfare recipient confronted with an administrative court and the position of a professional academic who, under the direction of his attorney, presents his case to a panel of fellow faculty members.

This court in *Frumkin* then discussed and applied the balancing test as set out in *Mathews v. Eldridge,* and concluded, as stated, that Frumkin did not have a procedural due process right to have his attorney examine and cross-examine witnesses.

While there are differences between the case before us and that presented in *Frumkin*, we conclude that there are very important similarities and that the instant case is much closer to *Frumkin* than it is to *Goldberg v. Kelly*. In both *Frumkin* and here, we have academic decisions being made in academic surroundings. While Crook's loss of his master's degree on the basis of fraud meant the loss of an important property interest and implicated injury to a liberty interest, the same can be said of the loss of a tenured professorship on findings that severely attacked the professor's character and competence. Both in *Frumkin* and here the parties asserting the right to have their counsel examine and cross-examine witnesses are themselves highly educated persons with expertise in the fields that were the subject of the investigation.

We conclude, therefore, that the district court was in error in determining that Crook was denied procedural due process because his attorney was not allowed to examine and cross-examine witnesses.

Although the district court determined that Crook, himself, did not have a reasonable opportunity to cross-examine at the hearing, we believe that the record clearly shows that he did have such opportunity with respect to the question whether he had used the microprobe enough to have developed the data submitted in his thesis.

The district court, under a heading in its opinion styled, enigmatically, "Evidence To The Decision Maker," holds that Crook was denied procedural due process because he was denied an opportunity to make an oral presentation to the decision maker. The court relied on a holding in *Goldberg v. Kelly*, that due process in that context required an opportunity to make an oral presentation to the person who made the decision to withdraw welfare benefits. In this case, however, without dispute Crook's counsel, Dethmers, made an oral argument to the Board of Regents at the time the Regents voted to revoke his degree. Moreover, under the holding of this court in *Bates v. Sponberg*, due process did not require that the Regents, who had the Committee's report, review the transcript of the hearing. Accordingly, we conclude that there was not a due process deprivation here.

The district court, under a heading styled "Decision Based on Evidence," again relying on *Goldberg v. Kelly*, held that Crook had been denied procedural due process in still another respect. It is unclear whether the district court intended to hold that the defect was the consideration of hearsay evidence or was the consideration of evidence to which Crook had no opportunity to respond, or both. It is clear that admission of hearsay evidence is not a denial of procedural due process. That case involved the familiar situation of the admission in evidence of medical reports in Social Security cases. It is true that submissions were made to the Committee by both sides and copies exchanged after the formal hearing, and the chairman, with the knowledge and consent of Crook, after the hearing contacted certain persons suggested by Crook in an effort to rebut the strong case that had been presented to the Committee that Crook had indeed fabricated thesis data. However, and in any event, as will be seen in the discussion, of the substantive due process issue, the evidence upon which the Committee determined that Crook had fabricated thesis data was presented prior to and at the hearing, and Crook had an opportunity to attack all of it. Moreover, Crook's attorney stated at the hearing that there was no objection to such documentary evidence as being hearsay. There was no denial of procedural due process here.

The district court, after citing cases holding that the decision maker must be impartial (with which proposition the Regents do not disagree), concludes that Crook was denied procedural due process because: "Here, the 'decision' was cast by persons whose impartiality has been impugned, and adopted by defendants without hearing." Even if the decision was made "by persons whose impartiality has been impugned," that is nothing more than a finding that their impartiality has been assailed. It is not a finding that these persons were not impartial. In any event, at the opening of the Committee's hearing, Rosberg, the chairman, stated that there had been no challenges to the members of the Committee and, after invitation, no challenges were made then. Moreover, while Rosberg, prior to the hearing, had read the materials that had been submitted and felt that the department had a strong case, there is no evidence in the record that Rosberg or the other members of the Committee were partial, or that the Executive Committee of the Graduate School was partial, or that Vice President Overberger was partial, or that the Regents were partial.

Accordingly, the finding that the "decision maker" was not impartial, if that was the intent of the district court, is clearly erroneous.

Substantive Due Process

The district court held that, in rescinding Crook's degree, Crook was also denied substantive due process in that "there was no rational basis" for the rescission.

The basis for the revocation was, of course, a finding by the Committee that Crook had fabricated the thesis data which, Crook claimed, showed that his "texasite" was a new, natural mineral.

* * *

The Regents in the instant case argue, in resolving the substantive due process issue, that the standard so applied in *Ewing* is precisely applicable in this case. However, we do not need to decide whether this standard is so applicable here because we find that the Committee not only exercised professional judgment but also that the evidence of fabrication was such that the determination by the Committee was not arbitrary or capricious and therefore substantive due process was not denied.

Upon reviewing the materials submitted to the Committee by the parties prior to its hearing, which were available to both sides and to the Committee, and upon reviewing the transcript of the hearing and the Committee's report finding the thesis data to be fabricated, we conclude that not only was the finding not arbitrary or capricious or lacking in a rational basis, but rather the finding was supported by clear and convincing evidence.

To have obtained the data from use of the microprobe as claimed by Crook, it would have consumed at least 200 to 400 hours of use. Crook testified at the hearing that he thought it would take 400 to 600 hours. However, from the logs upon which use of the microprobe was recorded and testimony of the parties in position to have knowledge of this use, the proof is overwhelming that Crook did not come close to using the microprobe to that extent.

While it was department policy and proper scientific practice to retain the original data from the microprobe work and the use of the EMPADR program, of which Crook was aware, he could produce none of this. Further, as the Committee found, Crook's explanations for not having these materials were not believable, and Crook admitted that he had lied when he stated he had rerun the microprobe data with the EMPADR program when he returned to Ann Arbor in February of 1979.

Crook, in order to show that he had used the microprobe more than the log would indicate, contended he often signed the name of another on the log, but there was no apparent reason for such deception if, in fact, Crook did practice it. The graduate student whose name Crook claimed he signed denied that this was so. Moreover, even if Crook had signed the name of others as he claimed, it was clear, nevertheless, that he had not used the microprobe nearly enough to have developed the data that he reported in the thesis.

There is much additional support in the record and set out in the Committee's report for the conclusion of the Committee that Crook had fabricated thesis data, but the foregoing should be sufficient to demonstrate that the Committee's findings were not arbitrary or capricious.

We, therefore, conclude that the finding by the district court that Crook was denied substantive due process is clearly erroneous.

CONCLUSION

In the covering letter with which the Committee forwarded its report to the Graduate School, it was suggested that, while the Department of Geology must assume its graduate degree candidates to be honest, this unfortunate occurrence might not have happened if the department had exerted somewhat closer oversight over its graduate students and more care in reviewing their theses. It was suggested that "further inquiry into the Department's program is warranted."

This case does indeed present an unfortunate and sad occurrence, which may well have been avoided with closer supervision and repetition of which should be avoided. However, we are satisfied that the Regents of the University of Michigan had the authority to revoke Crook's degree and that, in doing so, they did not deprive him of due process law under the federal Constitution.

The judgments of the district court declaring the rescission of the degree to be a nullity, enjoining the Regents to restore the degree, and granting attorney fees are VACATED and the cause is REMANDED with instructions to dismiss this action.

Mr. Crook's second fraud (the rerun of his data) was detected because of the Department's monitoring of his computer runs. More often, the misconduct occurs in plagiarizing a paper (the *Sabeti* case), cheating in an examination [*Nash v. Auburn University,* 812 F.2d 655 (11th Cir. 1987)], or in falsifying credentials for admissions [the *Waliga* case or *Merrow v. Goldberg,* 672 F. Supp. 766 (D. Vt. 1987)]. The problems are substantial ones, and with increasingly sophisticated techniques, loom as a larger issue. See American Association of Collegiate Registrars and Admissions Officers, *Misrepresentation in the Marketplace* (D.C.: AACRAO, 1987).

Waliga v. Board of Trustees of Kent State University
488 N.E. 2d 850 (Ohio 1986)

George A. Waliga and Kent L. Taylor, plaintiffs-appellees, received Bachelor of Arts degrees from the Board of Trustees of Kent State University, defendants-appellants ("university"), in 1966 and 1967, respectively. In 1978 and 1982, the university received information concerning discrepancies in the official academic records ("records") of appellees and, subsequently, after conducting an examination of the records, the university determined that the records were incorrect and that appellees had failed to complete the substantive degree requirements to obtain their respective degrees.

The university notified appellees by letter that as a result of the grade discrepancies, it was contemplating revocation of their degrees; that appellees would have the opportunity to review the documentation and present their evidence at a hearing to be held before the College Advisory Council of the College of Arts and Sciences ("CAC"); but that appellees could not be represented by counsel at said hearing. After conducting a hearing which appellees did not attend, CAC recommended to the university that appellees' degrees be revoked.

Prior to any action being taken on said recommendation by the university, appellees on May 23, 1983 brought an action seeking declaratory relief regarding the authority of the university to revoke degrees previously conferred upon appellees by the university and injunctive relief to prevent the university from revoking their degrees. At a hearing on the merits before the trial court, appellees dismissed their request for injunctive relief and the matter proceeded for declaratory judgment.

The trial court posed the issues involved as follows: (1) "May the present Board of Trustees of Kent State University revoke a degree issued some 15 years prior?" and (2) "[i]f the Board has the authority, what procedure should be followed, who has the burden of proof, and are the plaintiffs entitled to legal representations in all stages of that [sic] proceedings?"

The trial court answered the first question in the negative, stating that the university "possesses only the authority conferred upon it by the legislature," and that authority "does not include any right to revoke degrees issued in the past." The trial court further stated that, "with this conclusion it is not necessary for this Court to address the other issues presented in the case."

The court of appeals affirmed the trial court's judgment. While the appellate court opined that the university has the power to revoke a degree once granted, the court nevertheless held that "[t]he trial court was correct in its decision as it refers to the appellees herein * * * [because] [t]heir rights were taken away from them by committees or persons in the university having no right or authority to do so."

The university filed a motion to reconsider, asserting that the court of appeals had relied on an erroneous assumption that appellees' degrees had actually been revoked when in fact they never had been revoked. The court of appeals overruled this motion. Judge Cook dissented, stating that "[u]pon reconsideration, we should find that the Board of Trustees of Kent State University does have the inherent power to revoke degrees for just cause after affording the degree holder due process."

The cause is now before this court pursuant to the allowance of a motion to certify the record.

WISE, Judge.

The sole issue raised by this case is whether the university has the authority and power to revoke improperly awarded degrees. The procedural issues before the trial court were not addressed, and hence are not before this court.

Kent State University, by virtue of R.C. Chapter 3341, and specifically R.C. 3341.05, "may confer such * * * academic degrees as are customarily conferred by colleges and universities in the United States." R.C. 3341.04 provides, in part, that the universities "shall do all things necessary for the proper maintenance and successful and continuous operation of such universities."

We consider it self-evident that a college or university acting through its board of trustees does have the inherent authority to revoke an improperly awarded degree where (1) good cause such as fraud, deceit, or error is shown, and (2) the degree-holder is afforded a fair hearing at which he can present evidence and protect his interest. Academic degrees are a university's certification to the world at large of the recipient's educational achievement and fulfillment of the institution's standards. To hold that a university may never withdraw a degree, effectively requires the university to continue making a false certification to the public at large of the accomplishment of persons who in fact lack the very qualifications that are certified. Such a holding would undermine public confidence in the integrity of degrees, call academic standards into question, and harm those who rely on the certification which the degree represents.

Any action which is necessary for the proper maintenance and successful operation of a state university is authorized, unless it is prohibited by statute. In the event that a degree is procured through fraud, or a degree is awarded erroneously, it is certainly within the implied authority of the university to revoke it. A power of a state agency may be fairly implied from an express power where it is reasonably related to the duties of the agency. The power to confer degrees necessarily implies the power to revoke degrees erroneously granted.

* * *

Modern courts have also traditionally refused to interfere with fundamental university functions, such as the granting and withdrawing of academic degrees, except to require that good cause be shown and that a fair hearing procedure be made available.

A degree-holder possesses a property right in and to his degree and that substantial right cannot be taken away "except pursuant to constitutionally adequate procedures."

We hold that the university board of trustees does have the authority to revoke previously granted academic degrees for proper cause after affording the degree-holder constitutionally adequate procedures.

Based on the foregoing, the judgment of the court of appeals is reversed.

Judgment reversed.

Recognition of Student Organizations

The growth of student organizations has led to some large colleges having hundreds of official student groups on their campuses. Litigation in this area tends to reflect administrators' fear that student organizations will reflect badly on their institutional image (in many instances, a concededly-correct concern), will lead to institutional liability for a group's actions, or will espouse an unpopular or inappropriate ideology—one antithetical to an institution's mission. For these reasons, several cases have been selected for their references to socially unpopular causes—politics (*Healy*), homosexuality (*Gay Student Services* and *Gay Rights Coalition*), and minorities (*Ad-Hoc Committee*). Other similar cases appear throughout the book, in the consideration of religion, institutional claims to academic freedom, higher education and the state, and affirmative action.

Healy v. James
408 U.S. 169 (1972)

Mr. Justice POWELL delivered the opinion of the Court.

This case, arising out of a denial by a state college of official recognition to a group of students who desired to form a local chapter of Students for a Democratic Society (SDS), presents this Court with questions requiring the application of well-established First Amendment principles. While the factual background of this particular case raises these constitutional issues in a manner not heretofore passed on by the Court, and only infrequently presented to lower federal courts, our decision today is governed by existing precedent.

As the case involves delicate issues concerning the academic community, we approach our task with special caution, recognizing the mutual interest of students, faculty members, and administrators in an environment free from disruptive interference with the educational process. We also are mindful of the equally significant interest in the widest latitude for free expression and debate consonant with the maintenance of order. Where these interests appear to compete the First Amendment, made binding on the States by the Fourteenth Amendment, strikes the required balance.

I

We mention briefly at the outset the setting in 1969–1970. A climate of unrest prevailed on many college campuses in this country. There had been widespread civil disobedience on some campuses, accompanied by the seizure of buildings, vandalism, and arson. Some colleges had been shut down altogether, while at others files were looted and manuscripts destroyed. SDS chapters on some of those campuses had been a catalytic force during this period. Although the causes of campus disruption were many and complex, one of the prime consequences of such activities was the denial of the lawful exercise of First Amendment rights to the majority of students by the few. Indeed, many of the most cherished characteristics long associated with institutions of higher learning appeared to be endangered. Fortunately, with the passage of time, a calmer atmosphere and greater maturity now pervade our campuses. Yet, it was in this climate of earlier unrest that this case arose.

Petitioners are students attending Central Connecticut State College (CCSC), a state-supported institution of higher learning. In September 1969 they undertook to organize what they then referred to as a "local chapter" of SDS. Pursuant to procedures established by the College, petitioners filed a request for official recognition as a campus organization with the Student Affairs Committee, a committee composed of four students, three faculty members, and the Dean of Student Affairs. The request specified three purposes for the proposed organization's existence. It would provide "a forum of discussion and self-education for students developing an analysis of American society"; it would serve as "an agency for integrating thought with action so as to bring about constructive changes"; and it would endeavor to provide "a coordinating body for relating the problems of leftist students" with other interested groups on campus and in the community. The Committee, while satisfied that the statement of purposes was clear and unobjectionable on its face, exhibited concern over the relationship between the proposed local group and the National SDS organization. In response to inquiries, representatives of the proposed organization stated that they would not affiliate with any national organization and that their group would remain "completely independent."

In response to other questions asked by Committee members concerning SDS' reputation for campus disruption, the applicants made the following statements, which proved significant during the later stages of these proceedings:

> "Q. How would you respond to issues of violence as other S.D.S. chapters have?

> "A. Our action would have to be dependent upon each issue.

"Q. Would you use any means possible?

"A. No I can't say that; would not know until we know what the issues are.

"Q. Could you envision the S.D.S. interrupting a class?

"A. Impossible for me to say."

With this information before it, the Committee requested an additional filing by the applicants, including a formal statement regarding affiliations. The amended application filed in response stated flatly that "CCSC Students for a Democratic Society are not under the dictates of any National organization." At a second hearing before the Student Affairs Committee, the question of relationship with the National organization was raised again. One of the organizers explained that the National SDS was divided into several "factional groups," that the national-local relationship was a loose one, and that the local organization accepted only "certain ideas" but not all of the National organization's aims and philosophies.

By a vote of six to two the Committee ultimately approved the application and recommended to the President of the College, Dr. James, that the organization be accorded official recognition. In approving the application, the majority indicated that its decision was premised on the belief that varying viewpoints should be represented on campus and that since the Young Americans for Freedom, the Young Democrats, the Young Republicans, and the Liberal Party all enjoyed recognized status, a group should be available with which "left wing" students might identify. The majority also noted and relied on the organization's claim of independence. Finally, it admonished the organization that immediate suspension would be considered if the group's activities proved incompatible with the school's policies against interference with the privacy of other students or destruction of property. The two dissenting members based their reservation primarily on the lack of clarity regarding the organization's independence.

Several days later, the President rejected the Committee's recommendation, and issued a statement indicating that petitioners' organization was not to be accorded the benefits of official campus recognition. His accompanying remarks, which are set out in full in the margin, indicate several reasons for his action. He found that the organization's philosophy was antithetical to the school's policies, and that the group's independence was doubtful. He concluded that approval should not be granted to any group that "openly repudiates" the College's dedication to academic freedom.

Denial of official recognition posed serious problems for the organization's existence and growth. Its members were deprived of the opportunity to place announcements regarding meetings, rallies, or other activities in the student newspaper; they were precluded from using various campus bulletin boards; and—most importantly—nonrecognition barred them from using campus facilities for holding meetings. This latter disability was brought home to petitioners shortly after the President's announcement. Petitioners circulated a notice calling a meeting to discuss what further action should be taken in light of the group's official rejection. The members met at the coffee shop in the Student Center ("Devils' Den") but were disbanded on the President's order since nonrecognized groups were not entitled to use such facilities.

Their efforts to gain recognition having proved ultimately unsuccessful, and having been made to feel the burden of nonrecognition, petitioners resorted to the courts. They filed a suit in the United States District Court for the District of Connecticut, seeking declaratory and injunctive relief against the President of the College, other administrators, and the State Board of Trustees. Petitioner's primary complaint centered on the denial of First Amendment rights of expression and association arising from denial of campus recognition. The cause was submitted initially on stipulated facts, and, after a short hearing, the judge ruled that petitioners had been denied procedural due process because the President had based his decision on conclusions regarding the applicant's affiliation which were outside the record before him. The court concluded that if the President wished to act on the basis of material outside the application he must at least provide petitioners a hearing and opportunity to introduce evidence as to their affiliations. While retaining jurisdiction over the case, the District Court ordered respondents to hold a hearing in order to clarify the several ambiguities surrounding the President's decision. One of the matters to be explored was whether the local organization, true to its repeated affirmations, was in fact independent of the National SDS. And if the hearing demonstrated that the two were not separable, the respondents were instructed that they might then review the "aims and philosophy" of the National organization.

Pursuant to the court's order, the President designated Dean Judd, the Dean of Student Affairs, to serve as hearing officer and a hearing was scheduled. The hearing, which spanned two dates and lasted approximately two hours, added little in terms of objective substantive evidence to the record in this case. Petitioners introduced a statement offering to change the organization's name from "CCSC local chapter of SDS" to "Students for a Democratic Society of Central Connecticut State College." They further reaffirmed that they would "have no connection whatsoever to the structure of an existing national organization." Petitioners also introduced the testimony of their faculty adviser to the effect that some local SDS organizations elsewhere were unaffiliated with any national organization. The hearing officer, in addition to introducing the minutes from the two pertinent Student Affairs Committee meetings, also introduced, *sua sponte*, portions of a transcript of hearings before the United States House of Representatives Internal Security Committee investigating the activities of SDS. Excerpts were offered both to prove that violent and disruptive activities had been attributed to SDS elsewhere and to demonstrate that there existed a national organization that recognized and cooperated with regional and local college campus affiliates. Petitioners did not challenge the asserted existence of a National SDS, nor did they question that it did have a system of affiliations of some sort. Their contention was simply that their organization would not associate with that network. Throughout the hearing the parties were acting at cross purposes. What seemed relevant to one appeared completely immaterial to the other. This failure of the hearing to advance the litigation was, at bottom, the consequence of a more basic failure to join issue on the considerations that should control the President's ultimate decision, a problem to which we will return in the ensuing section.

Upon reviewing the hearing transcript and exhibits, the President reaffirmed his prior decision to deny petitioners recognition as a campus organization. The reasons stated, closely paralleling his initial reasons, were that the group would be a "disruptive influence" at CCSC and that recognition would be "contrary to the orderly process of change" on the campus.

After the President's second statement issued, the case then returned to the District Court, where it was ordered dismissed. The court concluded, first, that the formal requisites of procedural due process had been complied with, second, that petitioners had failed to meet their burden of showing that they could function free from the

National organization, and, third, that the College's refusal to place its stamp of approval on an organization whose conduct it found "likely to cause violent acts of disruption" did not violate petitioner's associational rights.

Petitioners appealed to the Court of Appeals for the Second Circuit where, by a two-to-one vote, the District Court's judgment was affirmed. The majority purported not to reach the substantive First Amendment issues on the theory that petitioners had failed to avail themselves of the due process accorded them and had failed to meet their burden of complying with the prevailing standards for recognition. Judge Smith dissented, disagreeing with the majority's refusal to address the merits and finding that petitioners had been deprived of basic First Amendment rights. This Court granted certiorari and, for the reasons that follow, we conclude that the judgments of the courts below must be reversed and the case remanded for reconsideration.

II

At the outset we note that state colleges and universities are not enclaves immune from the sweep of the First Amendment. "It can hardly be argued that either students or teachers shed their constitutional rights to freedom of speech or expression at the schoolhouse gate." Of course, as Mr. Justice Fortas made clear in *Tinker*, First Amendment rights must always be applied "in light of the special characteristics of the... environment" in the particular case. And, where state-operated educational institutions are involved, this Court has long recognized "the need for affirming the comprehensive authority of the States and of school officials, consistent with fundamental constitutional safeguards, to prescribe and control conduct in the schools." Yet, the precedents of this Court leave no room for the view that, because of the acknowledged need for order, First Amendment protections should apply with less force on college campuses than in the community at large. Quite to the contrary, "[t]he vigilant protection of constitutional freedoms is nowhere more vital than in the community of American schools." The college classroom with its surrounding environs is peculiarly the " 'marketplace of ideas,' " and we break no new constitutional ground in reaffirming this Nation's dedication to safeguarding academic freedom.

Among the rights protected by the First Amendment is the right of individuals to associate to further their personal beliefs. While the freedom of association is not explicitly set out in the Amendment, it has long been held to be implicit in the freedoms of speech, assembly, and petition. There can be no doubt that denial of official recognition, without justification, to college organizations burdens or abridges that associational right. The primary impediment to free association flowing from nonrecognition is the denial of use of campus facilities for meetings and other appropriate purposes. The practical effect of nonrecognition was demonstrated in this case when, several days after the President's decision was announced, petitioners were not allowed to hold a meeting in the campus coffee shop because they were not an approved group.

Petitioners' associational interests also were circumscribed by the denial of the use of campus bulletin boards and the school newspaper. If an organization is to remain a viable entity in a campus community in which new students enter on a regular basis, it must possess the means of communicating with these students. Moreover, the organization's ability to participate in the intellectual give and take of campus debate, and to pursue its stated purposes, is limited by denial of access to the customary media for communicating with the administration, faculty members, and other students. Such impediments cannot be viewed as insubstantial.

* * *

The opinions below also assumed that petitioners had the burden of showing entitlement to recognition by the College. While petitioners have not challenged the procedural requirement that they file an application in conformity with the rules of the College, they do question the view of the courts below that final rejection could rest on their failure to convince the administration that their organization was unaffiliated with the National SDS. For reasons to be stated later in this opinion, we do not consider the issue of affiliation to be a controlling one. But, apart from any particular issue, once petitioners had filed an application in conformity with the requirements, the burden was upon the College administration to justify its decision of rejection.

It is to be remembered that the effect of the College's denial of recognition was a form of prior restraint, denying to petitioners' organization the range of associational activities described above. While a college has a legitimate interest in preventing disruption on the campus, which under circumstances requiring the safeguarding of that interest may justify such restraint, a "heavy burden" rests on the college to demonstrate the appropriateness of that action.

III

These fundamental errors—discounting the existence of a cognizable First Amendment interest and misplacing the burden of proof—require that the judgments below be reversed. But we are unable to conclude that no basis exists upon which nonrecognition might be appropriate. Indeed, based on a reasonable reading of the ambiguous facts of this case, there appears to be at least one potentially acceptable ground for a denial of recognition. Because of this ambiguous state of the record we conclude that the case should be remanded, and, in an effort to provide guidance to the lower courts upon reconsideration, it is appropriate to discuss the several bases of President James' decision. Four possible justifications for nonrecognition, all closely related, might be derived from the record and his statements. Three of those grounds are inadequate to substantiate his decision: a fourth, however, has merit.

A

From the outset the controversy in this case has centered in large measure around the relationship, if any, between petitioners' group and the National SDS. The Student Affairs Committee meetings, as reflected in its minutes, focused considerable attention on this issue; the court-ordered hearing also was directed primarily to this question. Despite assurances from petitioners and their counsel that the local group was in fact independent of the National organization, it is evident that President James was significantly influenced by his apprehension that there was a connection. Aware of the fact that some SDS chapters had been associated with disruptive and violent campus activity, he apparently considered that affiliation itself was sufficient justification for denying recognition.

Although this precise issue has not come before the Court heretofore, the Court has consistently disapproved governmental action imposing criminal sanctions or denying rights and privileges solely because of a citizen's association with an unpopular organization.

In these cases it has been established that "guilt by association alone, without [establishing] that an individual's association poses the threat feared by the Government," is an impermissible basis upon which to deny First Amendment rights. The government has the burden of establishing a knowing affiliation with an organization possessing unlawful aims and goals, and a specific intent to further those illegal aims.

Students for a Democratic Society, as conceded by the College and the lower courts, is loosely organized, having various factions and promoting a number of diverse social and political views, only some of which call for unlawful action. Not only did petitioners proclaim their complete independence from this organization, but they also indicated that they shared only some of the beliefs its leaders have expressed. On this record it is clear that the relationship was not an adequate ground for the denial of recognition.

B

Having concluded that petitioners were affiliated with, or at least retained an affinity for, National SDS, President James attributed what he believed to be the philosophy of that organization to the local group. He characterized the petitioning group as adhering to "some of the major tenets of the national organization," including a philosophy of violence and disruption. Understandably, he found that philosophy abhorrent. In an article signed by President James in an alumni periodical, and made a part of the record below, he announced his unwillingness to "sanction an organization that openly advocates the destruction of the very ideals and freedoms upon which the academic life is founded." He further emphasized that the petitioners' "philosophies" were "counter to the official policy of the college."

The mere disagreement of the President with the group's philosophy affords no reason to deny it recognition. As repugnant as these views may have been, especially to one with President James' responsibility, the mere expression of them would not justify the denial of First Amendment rights. Whether petitioners did in fact advocate a philosophy of "destruction" thus becomes immaterial. The College, acting here as the instrumentality of the State, may not restrict speech or association simply because it finds the views expressed by any group to be abhorrent. As Mr. Justice Black put it most simply and clearly:

> "I do not believe that it can be too often repeated that the freedoms of speech, press, petition and assembly guaranteed by the First Amendment must be accorded to the ideas we hate or sooner or later they will be denied to the ideas we cherish."

C

As the litigation progressed in the District Court, a third rationale for President James' decision—beyond the questions of affiliation and philosophy—began to emerge. His second statement, issued after the court-ordered hearing, indicates that he based rejection on a conclusion that this particular group would be a "disruptive influence at CCSC." This language was underscored in the second District Court opinion. In fact, the court concluded that the President had determined that CCSC-SDS' "prospective campus activities were likely to cause a disruptive influence at CCSC."

If this reason, directed at the organization's activities rather than its philosophy, were factually supported by the record, the Court's prior decision would provide a basis for considering the propriety of nonrecognition. The critical line heretofore drawn for determining the permissibility of regulation is the line between mere advocacy and advocacy "directed to inciting or producing imminent lawless action and ... likely to incite or produce such action." In the context of the "special characteristics of the school environment," the power of the government to prohibit "lawless action" is not limited to acts of a criminal nature. Also prohibitable are actions which "materially and substantially disrupt the work and discipline of the school." Associational activities need not be tolerated where they infringe reasonable campus rules, interrupt classes, or substantially interfere with the opportunity of other students to obtain an education.

The "Student Bill of Rights" at CCSC, upon which great emphasis was placed by the President, draws precisely this distinction between advocacy and action. It purports to impose no limitations on the right of college student organizations "to examine and discuss *all* questions of interest to them." But it also states that students have no right (1) "to deprive others of the opportunity to speak or be heard," (2) "to invade the privacy of others," (3) "to damage the property of others," (4) "to disrupt the regular and essential operation of the college," or (5) "to interfere with the rights of others." The line between permissible speech and impermissible conduct tracks the constitutional requirement, and if there were an evidential basis to support the conclusion that CCSC-SDS posed a substantial threat of material disruption in violation of that command the President's decision should be affirmed.

The record, however, offers no substantial basis for that conclusion. The only support for the view expressed by the President, other than the reputed affiliation with National SDS, is to be found in the ambivalent responses offered by the group's representatives at the Student Affairs Committee hearing, during which they stated that they did not know whether they might respond to "issues of violence" in the same manner that other SDS chapters had on other campuses. Nor would they state unequivocally that they could never "envision ... interrupting a class." Whatever force these statements might be thought to have is largely dissipated by the following exchange between petitioners' counsel and the Dean of Student Affairs during the court-ordered hearing:

> Counsel: "...I just read the document that you're offering [minutes from Student Affairs Committee meeting] and I can't see that there's anything in it that intimates that these students contemplate any illegal or disruptive practice."
>
> Dean: "No. There's no question raised to that, counselor...."

Dean Judd's remark reaffirms, in accord with the full record, that there was no substantial evidence that these particular individuals acting together would constitute a disruptive force on campus. Therefore, insofar as nonrecognition flowed from such fears, it constituted little more than the sort of "undifferentiated fear or apprehension of disturbance [which] is not enough to overcome the right to freedom of expression."

D

These same references in the record to the group's equivocation regarding how it might respond to "issues of violence" and whether it could ever "envision ... interrupting a class," suggest a fourth possible reason why recognition might have been denied to these petitioners. There remarks might well have been read as announcing petitioner's unwillingness to be bound by reasonable school rules governing conduct.

The College's Statement of Rights, Freedoms, and Responsibilities of Students contains, as we have seen, an explicit statement with respect to campus disruption. The regulation, carefully differentiating between advocacy and action, is a reasonable one, and petitioners have not questioned it directly. Yet their statements raise considerable question whether they intend to abide by the prohibitions contained therein.

As we have already stated in Parts B and C, the critical line for First Amendment purposes must be drawn between advocacy, which is entitled to full protection, and action, which is not. Petitioners may, if they so choose, preach the propriety of amending or even doing away with any or all campus regulations. They may not, however, undertake to flout these rules. Mr. Justice BLACKMUN, at the time he was a circuit judge on the Eighth Circuit, stated:

"We ... hold that a college has the inherent power to promulgate rules and regulations; that it has the inherent power properly to discipline; that it has power appropriately to protect itself and its property; that it may expect that its students adhere to generally accepted standards of conduct."

Just as in the community at large, reasonable regulations with respect to the time, the place, and the manner in which student groups conduct their speech-related activities must be respected. A college administration may impose a requirement, such as may have been imposed in this case, that a group seeking official recognition affirm in advance its willingness to adhere to reasonable campus law. Such a requirement does not impose an impermissible condition on the students' associational rights. Their freedom to speak out, to assemble, or to petition for changes in school rules is in no sense infringed. It merely constitutes an agreement to conform with reasonable standards respecting conduct. This is a minimal requirement, in the interest of the entire academic community, of any group seeking the privilege of official recognition.

Petitioners have not challenged in this litigation the procedural or substantive aspects of the College's requirements governing applications for official recognition. Although the record is unclear on this point, CCSC may have, among its requirements for recognition, a rule that prospective groups affirm that they intend to comply with reasonable campus regulations. Upon remand it should first be determined whether the College recognition procedures contemplate any such requirement. If so, it should then be ascertained whether petitioners intend to comply. Since we do not have the terms of a specific prior affirmation rule before us, we are not called on to decide whether any particular formulation would or would not prove constitutionally acceptable. Assuming the existence of a valid rule, however, we do conclude that the benefits of participation in the internal life of the college community may be denied to any group that reserves the right to violate any valid campus rules with which it disagrees.

IV

We think the above discussion establishes the appropriate framework for consideration of petitioners' request for campus recognition. Because respondents failed to accord due recognition to First Amendment principles, the judgments below approving respondents' denial of recognition must be reversed. Since we cannot conclude from this record that petitioners were willing to abide by reasonable campus rules and regulations, we order the case remanded for reconsideration. We note, in so holding, that the wide latitude accorded by the Constitution to the freedoms of expression and association is not without its costs in terms of the risk to the maintenance of civility and an ordered society. Indeed, this latitude often has resulted, on the campus and elsewhere, in the infringement of the rights of others. Though we deplore the tendency of some to abuse the very constitutional privileges they invoke, and although the infringement of rights of others certainly should not be tolerated, we reaffirm this Court's dedication to the principles of the Bill of Rights upon which our vigorous and free society is founded.

Reversed and remanded.

Gay Student Services v. Texas A&M
737 F. 2d 1317 (1984)

JOHN R. BROWN, Circuit Judge:

Today we address the issue whether a state supported university violates the First Amendment rights of this gay student organization and three of its members by refusing to afford it official recognition. The District Court found that the University's refusal to recognize the group was not based on the content of the group's ideas about homosexuality. Instead, the trial court found that the group had been denied recognition due to the University's long standing policy of refusing to recognize fraternal organizations whose principal purpose is to hold social gatherings to encourage friendship and personal affinity. Finally, the Court held that the University had not created a forum open to fraternal or social groups. Thus, on appeal, the University contends that it never created a generally open forum for First Amendment expression. For these reasons, the District Court concluded and the University argues that there was no constitutional deprivation. We think those findings and conclusions are clearly erroneous and reverse. We affirm, however, the Court's conclusion that recovery of monetary damages is prohibited by the Eleventh Amendment.

Facts and Procedural History

In April of 1976, a group of students on the Texas A&M University (TAMU) campus met with Dr. John Koldus, the University's Vice President for Student Affairs, to discuss with him the possibility of using University facilities to conduct the business of a group they had formed, Gay Student Services (GSS). The students informed Koldus that they did not at that time seek official recognition, but merely wished to post notices on school bulletin boards, meet on campus, and have access to the student newspaper and radio. Their reasons for not seeking official recognition included their wish to maintain the anonymity of some of their members as well as their understanding that the group's existence might pose an "uncomfortable" problem in the conservative TAMU community.

Koldus advised the students that no form of limited recognition was available and referred them to Dr. Carolyn Adair, Director of Student Affairs, to receive information regarding the requirements for official recognition. Dr. Adair advised the students to apply for recognition as a service group rather than a political or social group because there would be fewer problems. Accordingly, the goals and purposes reflected on GSS's application were service-related. The application, dated April 5, 1976, stated the following goals and purposes:

> 1) To provide a referral service for students desiring professional counseling including psychological, religious, medical, and legal fields.

2) To provide to the TAMU community information concerning the structures and realities of gay life.

3) To provide speakers to classes and organizations who wish to know more about gay lifestyles.

4) To provide a forum for the interchange of ideas and constructive solutions to gay people's problems.

Dr. Koldus directed Dr. Adair to forward GSS's application directly to him rather than to the Student Organization Board, which is ordinarily the first step in attaining recognition. Koldus, who is responsible for the final decision regarding recognition, stated that this was his usual procedure when dealing with applications presenting special problems. Sherri Skinner, one of the group's founding members, testified that Koldus had informed the students at the initial meeting that the University would deny their application.

On May 4, 1976, the student representatives of GSS again met with Koldus, who told them that he had written a response to their application. Koldus stated that University officials had asked him to delay release of the response until Jack Williams, President of the University, and the University legal staff had had an opportunity to study the request. A memorandum dated May 28, 1976 from Williams to Koldus indicated that Koldus had provided information regarding other Texas universities' treatment of similar situations. Furthermore, Williams' memo stated that TAMU would not recognize GSS "until and unless we are ordered by higher authority to do so." The students met with Koldus in June and September of 1976, again requesting action on their application. Finally, Dr. Koldus issued a letter denying recognition on November 29, 1976.

Dr. Koldus' denial was premised on two points. First, Koldus asserted that because homosexual conduct was illegal in Texas at that time, it would be inappropriate for TAMU officially to support an organization likely to "incite, promote and result" in homosexual activity. Second, Koldus stated that the TAMU staff and faculty, not TAMU student organizations, were responsible for providing referral services, educational information, and speakers to students and the larger public. Thus, Koldus concluded that the stated purposes and goals of TAMU were not "consistent with the philosophy and goals" of TAMU. Nowhere in the letter did Koldus assert that denial of recognition was premised on the fraternal nature of GSS.

This lawsuit, seeking declaratory, injunctive and compensatory relief under 42 U.S.C. § 1983, was filed in February of 1977. In November of 1977, the District Court granted TAMU's motion to dismiss without stating its reasons for doing so, and GSS appealed. We vacated and remanded, finding that none of the asserted bases for dismissal were proper. The District Court held a bench trial in November of 1981. The evidence presented at trial consisted almost solely of medical testimony from specialists in human sexuality regarding the effect the presence of a homosexual student group might have on a university campus. The defense in particular centered on statistics and opinion documenting increased crime rates and severe emotional problems found within the homosexual community. The defense presented no testimony at trial regarding whether GSS functioned as a purely social organization.

On May 19, 1982, the District Court entered a final judgment for TAMU, along with findings of fact and conclusions of law. On appeal, GSS asserts that these findings and conclusions were erroneous and require reversal. We agree, for the reasons that follow.

The Nature of GSS

In its findings of fact, the District Court found that TAMU "did not and has not to the time of trial in this case, recognized fraternal organizations, i.e. student groups whose principal if not sole purpose is to hold social gatherings to encourage friendships and personal affinity." The record shows that in October 1977, Dr. Koldus denied recognition to Sigma Phi Epsilon, a national social fraternity, by stating the following policy:

> For over one hundred years, Texas A&M has chosen not to include the national social fraternity and sorority system as an official part of its educational program. The University has supported the premise that its social character was developed in the concept of togetherness in that all students were Aggies and that a social caste system would detract from this most important concept which welded together the students that attended Texas A&M.
>
> *   *   *
>
> As an administrator, it is my responsibility to attempt to perpetuate these traditions which have added not only to the character of the institution but to its strength. It is upon this premise that I deny official university recognition of Sigma Phi Epsilon.

At the heart of the findings and conclusions of the District Court was its decision that GSS was merely a "fraternal or social" group "whose message is mere friendship and personal affinity." This led the Court to conclude that GSS was not denied recognition "based upon the content of [its] ideas about homosexuality, since the group is not trying to convey any message about homosexuality," but rather because GSS was a "fraternal" organization subject to TAMU's traditional ban. We think this factual finding was clearly erroneous, for several reasons.

Such a finding is utterly at odds with the asserted purposes of GSS, which sought recognition to provide services and information regarding gay issues to gay persons and to the general public. Moreover, Dr. Koldus' asserted reasons for denying recognition were clearly based on his perception that the organization *would* attempt to convey ideas about homosexuality. Nowhere in his letter of November 29 does Koldus state that the University's refusal to recognize GSS was based on anything other than reasons tied to the homosexual nature of the group. Further evidence of TAMU's opposition to recognizing a gay student group is found in a resolution passed by the TAMU Board of Regents following the filing of this lawsuit in 1977. The minutes of the Board's meeting of March 22, 1977 state that the following "policy position" was approved:

> So-called "gay" activities run diabolically [*sic*—diametrically?] counter to the traditions and standards of Texas A&M University, and the Board of Regents is determined to defend the suit filed against it by three students seeking "gay" recognition and, if necessary, to proceed in every legal way to prohibit any group with such goals from organizing or operating on this or any other campus for which this Board is responsible.

Moreover, TAMU presented no evidence at trial regarding the "fraternal" nature of GSS. Such a theory for denying recognition was never advanced in the case until

TAMU filed its post-trial brief. Indeed, the sole evidence alleged to support the theory was advanced by GSS itself, in its attempt to show that GSS was a "normal" student group rather than a hotbed of deviant homosexuals anxious to influence the morals of impressionable TAMU students at on-campus meetings. TAMU relies, for example, on the testimony of Dr. Kenneth Nyberg, who agreed to become GSS's faculty advisor and attended some of its early meetings. Dr. Nyberg stated:

> Theirs was a quintessent typical student group.... What you are talking about are students so their interests are those of students.... How do you, you know, how do you get registered? What person to take for a class, what person not to take for a class. What did you do last week? It was mostly concerning... student issues.

* * *

> They reflect most of the same goals and aspirations and concerns almost all my students did. They subsequently looked into most of the same issues. The singular exception was, of course, the homosexual aspect.

It later became clear that GSS elicited such testimony from Dr. Nyberg in order to contravene a later opinion by defense witness Dr. Cameron, who opined that in light of statistical evidence regarding homosexual behavior, "it would be a shock really, if there were not homosexual acts engaged in at or immediately after" a meeting of a homosexual student organization.

Apparently relying upon the testimony of Dr. Sherri Skinner, the District Court also found that GSS was a fraternal group that was "not trying to convey any message about homosexuality" because it was "not organized for political advocacy" and had "no official position regarding repeal of Tex. Penal Code Ann., § 21.06, which makes homosexual conduct a misdemeanor." Dr. Skinner's testimony, like that of Dr. Nyberg, was elicited by GSS for the express purpose of showing that GSS was a typical student service group deserving recognition rather than a substitute for a gay singles bar. Moreover, Dr. Skinner emphasized that any political or social goals GSS may have had were intentionally eliminated from the application for recognition because Dr. Adair had advised the students to seek recognition as a service-type group. What Dr. Skinner actually said, in the context of emphasizing the service-related purposes of GSS, was that while the individual members of GSS would probably support repeal of the anti-homosexuality laws, "the organization itself has been very careful to keep clear of political action or activism, per se." In light of the fact that TAMU recognizes more service-related student organizations than it does political ones, we simply cannot agree that GSS's failure to organize as a political group renders it a social or fraternal group subject to the TAMU ban.

Finally, we point out that recognition was denied before GSS ever had the opportunity to function as the service-type group it sought to become. The Court's determination regarding the nature of the group was based on how it functioned as an off campus group that had been denied the benefits and privileges of official recognition. The minutes of GSS's meetings reveal that much of the group's meeting time was consumed by discussion of the pending lawsuit. We think evidence concerning how GSS functioned as an off campus group is irrelevant to the determination whether GSS, as it sought to exist, was entitled to official recognition.

For all the foregoing reasons, we conclude that the District Court's factual findings with regard to the nature of GSS were clearly erroneous. We think it clear from the facts that TAMU refused officially to recognize GSS based upon the homosexual content of the group's ideas—which it sought to convey through implementing its stated goals and purposes.

* * *

In *Healy* the Court stated that there "can be no doubt that denial of official recognition, without justification, to college organizations burdens or abridges" the First Amendment freedom of association. The university bears the burden of justifying its decision rejecting the application for recognition. Although university authorities have a legitimate interest in prohibiting student activities intended to and likely to incite or produce imminent lawless action or those that materially and substantially disrupt the work and discipline of the school, the record in *Healy* disclosed only an unsubstantiated fear or apprehension that recognition of the group would produce such a result. Thus, the Court found the University's asserted reasons for denying recognition insufficient to meet its "heavy burden" of justifying the infringement on the students' right to freedom of expression.

We think that the standards enunciated in *Healy* are precisely on point in this case. We therefore turn to TAMU's asserted reasons for denying recognition to GSS to determine their constitutionality under *Healy*.

Asserted Justifications

In his letter denying GSS official recognition, Dr. Koldus stated that GSS's goals and purposes were not consistent with the philosophy and goals of TAMU. This alone as a reason for denying recognition is clearly forbidden by *Healy*, where the Court specifically rejected for constitutional purposes the college president's statement that SDS's philosophies of destruction, violence and disruption were " 'counter to the official policy of the college.' " The Court held that:

> The mere disagreement of the President with the group's philosophy affords no reason to deny it recognition. As repugnant as these views may have been . . . , the mere expression of them would not justify the denial of First Amendment rights. Whether petitioners did in fact advocate a philosophy of 'destruction' thus becomes immaterial. The College, acting here as the instrumentality of the State, may not restrict speech or association simply because it finds the views expressed by any group to be abhorrent.

Dr. Koldus proffered two additional, more specific reasons for denying recognition to GSS. First, he stated that because homosexual conduct was illegal in Texas, it would be inappropriate for TAMU to recognize a group likely to "incite, promote, and result" in homosexual acts. Second, he stated that student organizations did not have the "educational experience, the responsibility or the authority to educate the larger public." The District Court did not reach these issues because its findings of fact precluded analysis under any form of heightened scrutiny.

As to TAMU's asserted interest in preventing expression likely to "incite, promote, and result" in then-illegal homosexual activity, we emphasize that while Texas law may prohibit certain homosexual practices, no Texas law makes it a crime to *be* a homosexual. Furthermore, there is no evidence that any illegal activity has taken place as a result of GSS's existence in the past, nor is there any evidence that GSS is an organization devoted to advocacy and incitement of imminent illegal, specifically proscribed homosexual activity. Consistent with *Healy*, we cannot conclude that the "critical line . . . between advocacy and action" has been violated in this case.

We are not alone in reaching this conclusion. In *Gay Students Organization of the University of New Hampshire v. Bonner*, the University suspended its earlier recognition of a gay group (GSO) and ordered a strict ban on the group's social functions after a GSO sponsored dance resulted in unfavorable media coverage and criticism by the Governor of New Hampshire. The First Circuit held that the asserted interest in preventing illegal deviate sex acts was insufficient to justify impairment of the group's First Amendment rights because there were neither allegations nor evidence of any illegal or improper acts at GSO's social functions. The Court stated that mere " 'undifferentiated fear or apprehension' of illegal conduct . . . is not enough to overcome First Amendment rights, and speculation that individuals might at some time engage in illegal activity is insufficient to justify regulation by the state."

Similarly, in *Gay Alliance of Students v. Matthews*, the Fourth Circuit concluded that because there was no evidence that the gay group in that case was "an organization devoted to carrying out illegal, specifically proscribed sexual practices," the University's argument that recognition of the group would increase the opportunity for illegal homosexual contact was insufficient to justify the infringement on First Amendment rights. Finally, in *Gay Lib v. University of Missouri*, the District Court had held that nonrecognition of Gay Lib was justified by medical testimony showing that "recognition of Gay Lib would probably result in . . . violations of Missouri [sodomy] law." The Eighth Circuit reversed, holding that even "accepting the opinions of defendants' experts at face value, we find it insufficient to justify a governmental prior restraint on the right of a group of students to associate for the purposes avowed in their statement . . . of purposes."

With regard to Koldus' assertion that GSS lacked the experience to educate the public or provide referral services, we point out that even if Koldus was correct in arguing that the University faculty and staff are better equipped to perform these functions, "the state and its agents are forbidden from usurping the students' right to choose." At the heart of the freedom guaranteed by our Constitution is the freedom to choose—even if that choice does not accord with the state's view as to which choice is superior. In *Gay Students Organization,* the First Circuit held that the gay group's efforts to organize the homosexual minority, "educate" the public as to its plight, and obtain for it better treatment from individuals and from the government thus represent but another example of the associational activity unequivocally singled out for protection in the very "core" of association cases decided by the Supreme Court.

More important, TAMU presented no evidence, nor did the District Court find, that such a goal would "infringe reasonable campus rules, interrupt classes, or substantially interfere with the opportunity of other students to obtain an education."

We therefore conclude that none of the reasons for nonrecognition proffered by Dr. Koldus are sufficient to justify the infringement on appellants' First Amendment rights. At trial, however, TAMU asserted yet another alleged justification. It claimed that recognition of GSS would encourage more homosexual conduct, resulting in an increase in the number of persons with the psychological and physiological problems TAMU's experts claimed were more prevalent among homosexuals than among heterosexuals. Thus TAMU argued that denial of recognition was justifiable as an appropriate means of protecting public health. The District Court stated that this testimony was "credible" although it declined to rely on the evidence, pointing out that the University did not offer such a rationale as a basis for Koldus's decision in 1976.

This asserted justification must fail for the same reasons the others did: TAMU has simply not proven that recognition will indeed imminently result in such dire consequences. The speculative evidence offered by the defendants' experts "for which no historical or empirical basis is disclosed," cannot justify TAMU's content-based refusal to recognize GSS. We think that on this record TAMU's public health argument is precisely the kind of "undifferentiated fear or apprehension" that the Supreme Court has repeatedly held "is not enough to overcome the right to freedom of expression."

In *Gay Lib,* the Eighth Circuit concluded that denying recognition to a gay group "smacks of penalizing persons for their status [as homosexuals] rather than their conduct, which is constitutionally impermissible." We similarly conclude that none of TAMU's asserted justifications are sufficient to overcome the violation of GSS's rights under the First Amendment.

This leaves TAMU's final argument: that because it never created a forum open for First Amendment discourse, no First Amendment violation has taken place.

Public Forum

The District Court found that TAMU had not "created a forum that is generally open to student groups" because it had traditionally refused to recognize fraternal organizations. Finding that GSS was such a fraternal group, the Court concluded that GSS failed to come within the class of student groups entitled to First Amendment protection under *Widmar v. Vincent.* This conclusion was erroneous. As we have already found, GSS was not merely a fraternal group and was not denied recognition on that basis. Rather, we think that GSS is similar to many other student groups that have received recognition in the TAMU forum—except, of course, for the pro-homosexual nature of its message.

Moreover, we do not agree that by virtue of its traditional exclusion of social fraternities, TAMU may escape the constitutional dictates of *Widmar.* In *Widmar* the Supreme Court held that where a state supported university opens its facilities for use by student groups, it may not exclude a particular group based on the content of the group's intended speech absent a compelling state interest and proof that the interest would not be served by a less restrictive alternative. As we interpret it, one of TAMU's arguments on appeal is that because it has traditionally refused to recognize fraternal groups, it has not created a "generally open forum" within the meaning of *Widmar;* thus it can refuse to recognize *any* group—not merely fraternal or social groups. In support of this argument, TAMU relies upon *Perry Education Association.* Although we have grave doubt that this really presents an arguable contention in view of TAMU's recognition of so many other similar groups, we assume that *Perry* requires us to reach the issue and proceed to determine whether *Perry* compels reversal or remand—or both.

*   *   *

More important, and in our opinion dispositive, is the fact that *Perry* squarely held that if the selective access policy adopted by the *Perry* schools functioned to "discourage one viewpoint and advance another," strict scrutiny would apply "regardless of whether a public forum [was] involved." The five member majority concluded that the schools' denial of access to all but one union was based on the unions' "status," i.e., rival unions as opposed to exclusive bargaining unit, not their views. Concluding that the access policy was viewpoint neutral, the Court questioned only whether the restriction was "reasonable in light of the purpose which the forum at issue serves." Contrastingly, in this case TAMU admits and the District Court found that TAMU allows other views of homosexuality to be presented on this campus. Moreover, the record shows that TAMU recognized other groups that sought acceptance and integration of their particular lifestyle in the University community. We think that the denial of recognition to a student group wishing to express its own views on the same or similar subjects is clearly the sort of viewpoint based discrimination forbidden by *Perry* in any type of public forum.

This leads us to consider whether any of the asserted reasons for the denial of recognition constitute a sufficiently narrow and compelling state interest to uphold the denial under the public forum analysis we have discussed. We reach and decide the issue for the same reasons discussed. As already determined, all of TAMU's asserted reasons for nonrecognition were insufficient to justify infringement of GSS's rights under the straightforward First Amendment analysis. For the same reasons, they are insufficient to state a compelling interest for content-based regulation in TAMU's forum.

Damages

GSS also asserts that the District Court erred in finding that any award of damages was barred by the Eleventh Amendment. Appellants urge us to "carefully craft" a judgment wherein monetary damages would come from bookstore profits or from student service fees, neither of which funds are kept in the state treasury. They cite, however, no authority that convinces us that a federal court should exercise any such power to avoid the proscription of the Eleventh Amendment. We are convinced that the District Court properly applied Supreme Court precedent in *Zentgraf v. Texas A&M University*, a sex discrimination suit brought against TAMU. After examining the legal relationship between the state and TAMU, the Court concluded that because TAMU was an alter ego of the State of Texas, "any suit against the University or its officials for monetary relief is a suit against the state and thereby barred by the Eleventh Amendment."

Conclusion

TAMU's refusal to recognize GSS as an on-campus student organization impermissibly denied appellants their First Amendment rights. The judgment of the District Court is therefore reversed and the case is remanded for the entry of appropriate injunctive and declaratory relief in accordance with this opinion.

REVERSED AND REMANDED.

Gay Rights Coalition v. Georgetown University
536 A. 2d 1 (D.C. App. 1987)

MACK, Associate Judge:

In the District of Columbia, the Human Rights Act prohibits an educational institution from discriminating against any individual on the basis of his or her sexual orientation.[1] Two student gay rights groups contend that Georgetown University

---

1. D.C. Code § 1–2520 (1987) provides:

violated this statutory command by refusing to grant them "University Recognition" together with equal access to the additional facilities and services that status entails. The University, relying on the trial court's factual finding that Georgetown's grant of "University Recognition" includes a religiously guided "endorsement" of the recipient student group, responds that the Free Exercise Clause of the First Amendment protects it from official compulsion to "endorse" an organization which challenges its religious tenets. Upholding the asserted constitutional defense, the trial court entered judgment in favor of Georgetown. The student groups appeal.

Our analysis of the issues differs from that of the trial court. At the outset, we sever the artificial connection between the "endorsement" and the tangible benefits contained in Georgetown's scheme of "University Recognition." With respect to the University's refusal to grant the status of "University Recognition," we do not reach Georgetown's constitutional defense. Contrary to the trial court's understanding, the Human Rights Act does not require one private actor to "endorse" another. Thus, Georgetown's denial of "University Recognition"—in this case a status carrying an intangible "endorsement"—does not violate the statute. Although affirming the trial court's entry of judgment for the University on that point, we do so on statutory rather than constitutional grounds.

We reach a contrary conclusion with respect to the tangible benefits that accompany "University Recognition." While the Human Rights Act does not seek to compel uniformity in philosophical *attitudes* by force of law, it does require equal *treatment*. Equality of treatment in educational institutions is concretely measured by nondiscriminatory provision of access to "facilities and services." Unlike the "endorsement," the various additional tangible benefits that accompany a grant of "University Recognition" are "facilities and services." As such, they must be made equally available, without regard to sexual orientation or to any other characteristic unrelated to individual merit. Georgetown's refusal to provide tangible benefits without regard to sexual orientation violated the Human Rights Act. To that extent only, we consider the merits of Georgetown's free exercise defense. On that issue we hold that the District of Columbia's compelling interest in the eradication of sexual orientation discrimination outweighs any burden imposed upon Georgetown's exercise of religion by the forced equal provision of tangible benefits.

Thus, on statutory rather than constitutional grounds, we affirm the trial court's conclusion that Georgetown need not grant "University Recognition" to—and

---

It is an unlawful discriminatory practice... for an educational institution:

(1) To deny, restrict, or to abridge or condition the use of, or access to, any of its *facilities and services* to any person *otherwise qualified, wholly or partially, for a discriminatory reason, based upon* the race, color, religion, national origin, sex, age, marital status, personal appearance, *sexual orientation,* family responsibilities, political affiliation, source of income or physical handicap of any individual....

Section 1–2501 provides:

It is the intent of the Council of the District of Columbia, in enacting this chapter, to secure an end in the District of Columbia to discrimination for any reason other than that of individual merit, including, but not limited to, discrimination by reason of [various characteristics including sexual orientation].

Section 1–2502 (28) provides:

"Sexual orientation" means male or female homosexuality, heterosexuality and bisexuality, by preference or practice.

thereby "endorse"—the student groups. The Human Rights Act does, however, mandate that the student groups be given equal access to any additional "facilities and services" triggered by that status. Georgetown's asserted free exercise defense does not overcome the Human Rights Act's edict that the tangible benefits be distributed without regard to sexual orientation. We affirm in part, reverse in part, and order the trial court to enter judgment accordingly.

I
FACTUAL BACKGROUND

A. *Georgetown University*

In 1789, the year in which the Constitution was ratified and the federal government created, Georgetown University was established. Its founder was John Carroll, a Jesuit priest, a friend of George Washington and later, as Bishop of Baltimore, the first Roman Catholic prelate in the nation. "On this academy," he declared, "rests all my hope for the flourishing of our holy religion in the United States."

In 1805 Georgetown College, as it was then known, was formally committed to the control and guidance of the Society of Jesus. In 1815, Congress bestowed on Georgetown College the first university charter to be granted by the federal government. This charter was signed by James Madison as president of the United States. By decree of the Holy See in 1833, Georgetown College was given the status of a Pontifical University. This grant from the Pope empowered the University to confer the highest ecclesiastical degrees in Philosophy and Sacred Theology. To this day, Georgetown remains one of only two universities in the nation with this distinction. In 1844, Georgetown College was incorporated by a special Act of Congress. Its charter was amended in 1966 to allow it to operate as a nonprofit corporation and to adopt the name Georgetown University.

Today, approaching the bicentennial it shares with the ratification of our Constitution, the college Carroll founded on the banks of the Potomac is a major private, co-educational university and the oldest Roman Catholic institution of higher learning in the United States. Its enrollment consists of roughly 10,000 students in several undergraduate, graduate and professional schools. Georgetown University also runs a hospital and sponsors research institutes and other educational endeavors.

B. *Georgetown's Religious Tradition*

Through two centuries of growth, Georgetown University has been guided by the religious hope of its founder, John Carroll. All of its forty-six presidents have been Roman Catholic clergymen. On four occasions, the University has been headed by a bishop. In particular, Georgetown has continued a close relationship with the Jesuits. Since about 1825, without exception, members of that order have filled the presidential office.

At trial, Reverend Timothy S. Healy, S.J., Georgetown's president and a defendant in this case, testified that "until 1969 the general understanding was that the Society of Jesus owned the University and its property." In that year, the president and directors of Georgetown University signed an agreement with its Jesuit Community. With a few exceptions, the Jesuits relinquished their rights to University property. They also undertook to make periodic contributions to the University. Other provisions of the 1969 agreement sought to "guarantee the continued and effective presence of the Jesuits at Georgetown University." Among these were promises by the Jesuit Community to make themselves available for religious services, residential duties and teaching positions, and to take steps to ensure that highly qualified members of their order be assigned to the campus community. The agreement specified the desirability, "in order to preserve the Jesuit traditions of Georgetown University," that the University president be a member of the Society. Without confining deanships to their ranks, it was agreed that "qualified members of the Society of Jesus will be regularly appointed to such of those positions as may be practical." The office of University Chaplain was reserved for a Jesuit. In the words of President Healy, the 1969 agreement represented a "clear understanding that the University would continue to keep a very close affiliation with the Society of Jesus, to guarantee their presence at the University and to guarantee the meaning of the University in Jesuit terms that have existed up until that formal contract was drawn."

President Healy testified that throughout its existence Georgetown has invariably defined itself as a Roman Catholic institution. This perception is illustrated by some of the opening words in its undergraduate bulletin: "Georgetown is committed to a view of reality which reflects Catholic and Jesuit influences.... As an institution that is Catholic, Georgetown believes that all men are sons of God, called to a life of oneness with Him now and in eternity." Georgetown University, University Bulletin—Undergraduate Schools 1 (1980–81) (hereinafter "Undergraduate Bulletin"). According to its Law Center bulletin, "Georgetown's religious heritage is a cherished part of its distinctive quality." Georgetown University, Law Center Bulletin 31 (1980–81) (hereinafter "Law Center Bulletin"). The Faculty Handbook describes "Georgetown University as an American, Catholic, Jesuit institution of higher learning," seeking to "uphold, defend, propagate, and elucidate the integral Christian and American cultural heritage" through "certain established principles, specific ideals, and definite traditions." Georgetown University, Faculty Handbook vi (1971) (hereinafter "Faculty Handbook"). The "established principles" are "the demonstrated philosophical truths about the nature of man, the universe and God; the truths of Christian revelation and their crystallization through the centuries...." Among the "specific ideals" are "the perfectibility of society through the acquisition and practice by its members of the theological, intellectual, moral virtues and their derivatives [and] the value of service to the community as an expression of Christian democratic ideals." And the "definite traditions" include "the Christian culture and conduct having their source and inspiration in the teachings and example of Christ...."

Georgetown University is a member of several associations of Roman Catholic educational institutions. As a Pontifical University, it is one of only two American universities entered in the Annuario Pontificio, an annual listing by the Holy See of all such institutions throughout the world. Chapels are scattered throughout its properties and Masses offered several times each day. Almost all of its directors are Catholic, although there is no formal requirement that they be so. During a five-year period just prior to trial, Jesuits made up between one third and one half of the board. Faculty members must "maintain a sympathetic attitude towards Catholic beliefs and practices...." Georgetown has the largest number of ministers in residence among the Jesuit colleges and universities in the United States.

Roman Catholic doctrine influences some of Georgetown's policy decisions. Abortions and other proscribed procedures are not performed in the University hospital. Student newspapers may not carry advertisements for abortion clinics. Birth control devices may not be sold in the student stores. Cohabitation is forbidden between single students in the dormitories. In 1981, Georgetown returned a gift of $750,000 to the Libyan government due to the conflict between Roman Catholic teachings and that nation's perceived links with terrorist activity. Religious considerations, the trial court found, influenced Georgetown's denial of "University Recognition" and accompanying tangible benefits to the student groups.

C. *Georgetown's Secular Educational Role*

Despite its historical identification with the Roman Catholic Church, Georgetown University's professed intention is to provide a secular education, albeit one that is informed by Christian values. Its founder, John Carroll, insisted from the very beginning that the college be open to students of every religious persuasion. Religious belief plays no role in admissions, graduation, class attendance, participation in sports or other student activities, or eligibility for financial aid, placement facilities, awards or honors programs. The Undergraduate Bulletin declares that Georgetown "imposes no religious creed on any faculty member or any student, but it expects them to respect the religious convictions of each person." The University motto is "Making of One—Jew and Gentile." Although undergraduate students must attend two courses in the Theology Department, neither need be taught from the Catholic perspective. Faculty members are not required to be Catholic, nor are they asked to propagate the Catholic faith or indoctrinate students with Catholic philosophy.

D. *The Relationship between Georgetown's Religious Tradition and its Secular Educational Role*

From the foregoing, and from Georgetown's published materials, it appears that the University perceives itself as fulfilling a secular educational role without abandoning its religious heritage. This view is expressed in its Undergraduate Bulletin. While Georgetown reflects its Catholic and Jesuit influences,

> [i]t neither wishes nor expects all its members to be Catholic, but it does assume that all of them share a basic, widely accepted view of humankind. It sees all men as essentially equal, as endowed with a human dignity always to be respected.... It seeks to open its arms, in the fullest sense of ecumenism, to those of all beliefs and all races.

A similar idea is expressed by the Law Center: "The Law Center welcomes students of all religious beliefs and does not proselytize. On the other hand, Georgetown's religious heritage is a cherished part of its distinctive quality."

President Healy has described the interrelationship between Georgetown's secular educational role and its spiritual objectives:

> Theology no longer has the sway in the University that it once had, nor can we any longer talk about it as the organizing base of the other academic disciplines. What we can talk about is a religious tradition which after 200 years must condition what the University is and does. Any university is a creature of time and is by its nature secular. Our job is to discover what impact the habit of belief in God has on the secular reality of a university, on its teaching, its learning, its research and its service.

In a later report, President Healy voiced similar thoughts: "... Georgetown has the imperatives of its own secular being, but the Church reinforces, strengthens, and personalizes them." Also, he notes, "[e]ducation remains principally a secular business, and the university is a secular entity with a clear secular job to do. The Church, however, can deeply influence how that secular job is done."

E. *The Recognition Criteria*

On October 13, 1977, the gay students of Georgetown University held a public meeting in a room on campus. Sometime later, the group chose a name, Gay People of Georgetown University (GPGU), and adopted a constitution. After its formation, GPGU met weekly, its activities including lectures, discussions, film shows and social events.

Around the same time, a similar development occurred at the Law Center. There, a group known as the Gay Rights Coalition (GRC) of Georgetown University Law Center formed and adopted a constitution. Unfortunately, in contrast to GPGU, the record is relatively barren with regard to GRC's origins and subsequent activities.

After a time, both student groups decided to seek the formal status and attendant privileges enjoyed by many other campus organizations. On the main campus, where GPGU is based, the procedures for doing so were established by written guidelines. When GPGU first initiated the recognition process, during academic year 1978–79, these criteria were contained in a document issued by the Student Activities Commission (SAC) under the name "What Your Club Needs to Know." This document was superseded in the fall of 1979 by another, more specific set of guidelines known as "Recognition Criteria: Student Clubs and Organizations" (hereinafter "Recognition Criteria"). This later document primarily clarified and expanded upon the criteria set forth in the earlier one; the two were not inconsistent. Hence, although GPGU in fact made two unsuccessful applications in successive academic years, one under each set of guidelines, we make no distinction between their applications and treat both as though they were governed by "Recognition Criteria." Also because the guidelines do not conflict, we reject the student groups' claim that "Recognition Criteria"—the later and more explicit of the two—is a "self-serving," pretextual document, adopted in response to GPGU's first application and designed to close the door on its second one.

"Recognition Criteria" sets forth a tiered system of support available to undergraduate student groups: "This support, in order to reach all the members of the community, is offered on three different levels." Applications are initially submitted to SAC, an advisory body of the undergraduate student senate. The different levels of support are defined as follows:

> "*Student Body Endorsement*": SAC grants this recognition representing the interest of the Student Government and the entire student body.

> "*University Recognition*": SAC makes recommendations concerning this recognition. Final approval is granted through the University's Director of Student Activities.

> "*University Funding*": is recognition in a monetary form.

The three tiers of recognition are listed in declining order of accessibility. The most accessible, "Student Body Endorsement," does not depend on approval by the University administration. It is available to any group which satisfies basic requirements as to size and composition and whose activities are "within the scope of the student body interest and concern, serving an educational, social, or cultural purpose."

The more elusive "University Recognition," the status at issue in this case, requires approval by the University administration and may only be sought by groups that have already obtained "Student Body Endorsement." In order to obtain "University Recognition," such organizations have to satisfy two further conditions. They must:

(1) "be successful in aiding the University's educational mission in the tradition established by its founders (as outlined in the University's Statement of Educational Goals and Objectives)"; and

(2) "provide a broad service to the University community in the sense that the activities of the group may not be of an immediate and/or special interest."

"Recognition Criteria" describes "University Recognition" as Georgetown's "endorsement of the various co-curricular activities undertaken by a specific club."

"University Funding," the third and least accessible tier of recognition, may be sought only by groups that have already obtained "University Recognition." Such groups, however, have no automatic right to direct financial support. Lastly, and only implicitly, a fourth tier exists outside the scheme established by "Recognition Criteria"—that occupied by completely unrecognized campus groups, operating without even "Student Body Endorsement."

More than status is at stake. The facilities and services afforded to a student group by the University are dependent upon its level of recognition within this three-tiered scheme. A group with "Student Body Endorsement," but without "University Recognition," may:

(a) use University facilities;

(b) apply for lecture fund privileges;

(c) receive financial counseling from the SAC comptroller;

(d) use campus advertising; and

(e) petition to receive assistance from Student Government.

"University Recognition" entitles a group to four additional benefits. They may

(f) use a mailbox in the SAC office and request one in Hoya Station;

(g) use the Computer Label Service;

(h) use mailing services; and

(i) apply for funding.

Success in obtaining direct financial support, a discretionary decision by the University, elevates a student group to "University Funding," the highest tier established by "Recognition Criteria."

No written guidelines such as "Recognition Criteria" were issued at the Law Center, where GRC was located. The University's treatment of GPGU's and GRC's respective applications was, however, indistinguishable. More importantly, the student groups do not suggest that any alternative criteria were ever in force at the Law Center. We have no basis on which to conclude that the eligibility factors to be applied to GRC are significantly different from the written guidelines set forth in "Recognition Criteria" at the main campus.

F. *The Student Groups' Attempts to Gain "University Recognition"*

GPGU made two attempts to gain "University Recognition." The first was in academic year 1978–79 and the other immediately afterwards in the following academic year. On both occasions it obtained only "Student Body Endorsement." George-town refused to grant it "University Recognition" or the accompanying tangible benefits.

SAC first considered and approved GPGU's application on January 30, 1979. The same day, SAC issued the following statement:

> The SAC has granted a charter to the [GPGU] for the purpose of providing a forum where all students of Georgetown may come to understand the concerns of Gay Students.

> The recommendation for a charter does not mean that the SAC is making any statement on the rightness or wrongness of homosexuality or is implying that the University is making such a statement.

Within a week the Student Senate ratified both the action of SAC in approving a "Student Government Charter" and the statement that accompanied it.

The following day William C. Schuerman, Associate Dean of Student Affairs, informed the Student Government that GPGU would not be recognized as an "official" activity of Georgetown University. He wrote:

> The administration recognizes that the issue is both an educational and pastoral one. It is an issue that the University has addressed in an understanding manner. The University has been and will continue to be sensitive to the concerns of its gay students and the problems they face on the campus and in our society. . . .

> The University has acknowledged in a supportive way its gay students. These students may continue to organize, to express opinions, to publicize education-ally related events. Gay students may use University facilities for educationally related purposes such as meetings, discussion groups, speakers, etc. The office and services of the Director of Student Activities are available to gay students for help and assistance in planning educationally related programs. All academic personnel and educational support services in the University are open and available to gay students for assistance and advice.

> It is the position of the University that this access by gay students to University resources:

> (1) Makes possible an atmosphere in which gay people as members of this University community can develop a sense of pride, self-worth and awareness.

> (2) Provides for the dissemination of educational information that may encourage understanding and dialogue between gay and non-gay people.

> (3) Allows for forums and open expression of opinions helpful in the development of responsible sexual ethics consonant with individual personal beliefs.

> (4) Allows students to gather together in an educational setting to share common interests and beliefs.

> *The University, however, will not endorse the [GPGU] as an "official" activity of its Student Affairs Programs.* The University will not contribute to the support of this organization:

> (1) Through a grant of University funds.

> (2) By providing subsidized office space, telephone service, office supplies, and equipment.

(3) By granting authorized use of the name Georgetown University.

Georgetown University is a private University with a history and tradition which is specifically Catholic. University administrators must often make decisions in light of the conscience and value system identified with this tradition. The University, in terms of this responsibility cannot concur with the argument of its Student Government in this particular case, that official acknowledgment would not imply endorsement.

This situation involves a controversial matter of faith and the moral teachings of the Catholic Church. "Official" subsidy and support of a gay student organization would be interpreted by many as *endorsement of the positions taken by the gay movement on a full range of issues.* While the University supports and cherishes the individual lives and rights of its students it will not subsidize this cause. *Such an endorsement would be inappropriate for a Catholic University.*

GPGU appealed Dean Schuerman's decision to the Dean of Student Affairs, William R. Stott, Jr., and met with him for that purpose. Dean Stott upheld the decision to "den[y] endorsement to the [GPGU] as an official activity of the University's Student Affairs Program." He continued:

The fact that *the University has chosen not to grant endorsement to the [GPGU]* as an approved student activity, does not indicate a lack of concern, a lack of sympathy for the Gay Student in particular, or students in general. It simply means that after the facts have been considered and discussion has taken place, *there remains a point of disagreement as to whether endorsement of the [GPGU] as a student activity is appropriate for a Catholic University.* The University's decision, therefore, is not a reflection on or a judgment of the personal choices of its members, but rather represents a judgment of what is appropriate for Georgetown as an institution.

GPGU again appealed, this time to Reverend Aloysius P. Kelley, S.J., Executive Vice President for Academic Affairs. Taking issue with the equation of "recognition" and "endorsement," GPGU wrote:

We think it important to emphasize at the start that *what we are seeking is recognition, not endorsement, as Dean Stott's response seems to imply.* It is our belief, as well as that of the student government, that *official recognition of our organization would not be construed as an endorsement of homosexual activity.* Since this seems to be the major concern of the administration, we ask: "Is it not possible for the administration to issue a statement saying that, in granting recognition to our group, it is *not* endorsing such activity?"

After meeting with GPGU representatives, Reverend Kelley denied its appeal. He relied upon the position taken by Deans Schuerman and Stott, and then added:

As I tried to explain when we talked, I believe that our goals are essentially the same, but that the means to arrive at them are different. Georgetown will continue to show support for Gay Students but in a way which is deemed appropriate for this University. You mentioned that there may be additional ways in which the Administration could be supportive short of official recognition and I suggested that you discuss these with Mr. Schuerman.

Reverend Kelley's denial of GPGU's appeal ended its attempt to gain "University Recognition" in academic year 1978–79.

GPGU renewed its efforts early in the following academic year. This time it made separate visits to SAC to request a "Student Government Charter" and, later, "University Recognition." SAC approved GPGU's request for a "Student Government Charter" on November 13 and its decision was ratified by the Student Senate on November 18, 1979. SAC accompanied its approval with the following statement:

> The [GPGU] convinced the SAC, with both their written constitution and their oral presentation, that they represent a distinct group of students on this campus whose existence we as student representatives are bound to acknowledge. Furthermore, by enumeration of their educational functions (e.g. answering questions in nursing classes, enlightening RAs, etc.) the [GPGU] depicted itself as, to borrow from the criteria, "a positive force within the University community."

As had happened the previous year, Dean Schuerman wrote immediately to the Student Government to point out that the administration did not accept the action of SAC as giving "official recognition" to GPGU. The reasons he gave were essentially borrowed from his letter of the previous year.

Undaunted, GPGU again appeared before SAC two weeks later and requested "University Recognition" to add to the "Student Body Endorsement" it had already received. Both SAC and the Student Senate voted in favor of GPGU despite the administration's recent announcement that it would not accede to this request. At the end of 1979, therefore, GPGU was waiting the University's reaction to the favorable response it had won from the Student Government.

On January 15, 1980, in an effort to clarify its position, GPGU requested the administration to furnish it with a statement as to the group's status. This was provided by the Director of Student Activities, Debbie L. Gottfried. After repeating the administration's previous reasons for denying "University Recognition," she added:

> As I have told you and other gay students, the services of my office are available to you for help and assistance in planning educationally related programs. I cannot stress to you enough the sincerity behind this offer. I cannot offer any possibility of the University's changing its position on *what it feels would be interpreted as endorsement and official support of the full range of issues associated with this cause.*

Both GPGU and the Student Government requested that this decision be reconsidered. As had happened the previous year, GPGU met with Dean Schuerman, but failed to persuade him that "University Recognition" was appropriate. Dean Schuerman wrote:

> In my judgment, *official recognition by the University of a gay student organization would be interpreted by many as endorsement, support, and approval of the positions taken by the gay movement on a full range of issues.* This would be inappropriate for a Catholic University. While I recognize your disagreement with this position, I was not dissuaded by your argument that the University could on the one hand grant official recognition (defined by Student Government's recently updated criteria as "endorsement of the various co-curricular

activities undertaken by a specific club") and on the other hand, disclaim *"endorsement" of the major activities which, by definition, are associated with a gay organization.*

    ... [T]he University does not recognize the [GPGU] as an official activity of the Student Affairs program and will not subsidize this cause.

Continuing in the pattern set the previous year, GPGU unsuccessfully appealed Dean Schuerman's decision to Dean Stott and Reverend Donald Freeze, S.J., Vice President for Academic Affairs and Provost. This time it appealed, without success, all the way to President Healy. The day after President Healy's ultimate denial of "University Recognition," this action was filed in Superior Court.

By then, a similar chain of events had taken place at the Law Center. On December 6, 1979, GRC had submitted its application to become a "recognized" student activity to the Law Center Committee on Student and Faculty Life (CSFL). Its petition was approved by CSFL on February 14, 1980. Two weeks later, David J. McCarthy, Jr., Dean of the Law Center, told CSFL that he would not "implement either recognition or funding of the proposed organization." Dean McCarthy's reasons for denying GRC "official recognition" were couched in terms almost identical to those Dean Schuerman had given GPGU. After this action had been filed, President Healy informed Dean McCarthy that his earlier decision denying GPGU "University Recognition" on the main campus applied equally and for the same reasons to GRC at the Law Center. ("The University's decision is not a reflection on or a judgment of the personal choices of its individual members but rather reflects a judgment of what is appropriate for Georgetown as an institution"). A letter to the same effect was sent to the Chancellor of the Medical Center, Georgetown University's one remaining campus, although no similar group there had sought "University Recognition."

Thus, at the time this action was filed, GPGU had obtained "Student Body Endorsement" at the Main Campus and GRC had obtained its apparent equivalent at the Law Center. Neither group had been successful in its attempts to obtain "University Recognition" or the additional benefits that status carries with it.

II
THE TRIAL COURT PROCEEDING

The two gay student groups and twenty individual members brought suit against Georgetown University, its president, and the dean of its Law Center. They alleged that the denial of "University Recognition," together with the increased access to facilities and services that status entails, violated the Human Rights Act. Georgetown defended itself by insisting that its denial of "University Recognition" was not "on the basis of" the sexual orientation of the students, but rather on account of the "purposes and activities" of the particular organizations they had formed. Georgetown also asserted that even if its actions were taken on the basis of sexual orientation, they were protected by the Free Exercise Clause of the First Amendment.

The student groups moved for summary judgment. On March 9, 1981, the trial court partially granted their motion. Judge Leonard Braman found that Georgetown's denial of "University Recognition" violated the Human Rights Act. On the statutory issue as to whether Georgetown had discriminated on the basis of sexual orientation, he held, no material factual issue was in genuine dispute and the student groups were entitled to judgment as a matter of law. Judge Braman ordered that the only issue set for trial would be the validity of the University's claimed free exercise defense.

In so doing, Judge Braman found immaterial to the statutory discrimination issue Georgetown's claim that a grant of "University Recognition" would constitute an unwilling "endorsement" of the student groups.

Discrimination on the basis of sexual orientation having been found, and a statutory violation therefore established, the case proceeded to a nonjury trial on Georgetown's free exercise defense. After seven days of testimony, Judge Sylvia Bacon held that the statute was unconstitutional as applied to the facts of this case: "the District of Columbia Human Rights Act must yield to the Constitutional guarantee of religious freedom."

Judge Bacon made several findings of fact. She described the three levels of recognition available to campus organizations and found that the student groups had achieved "Student Body Endorsement," together with its attendant tangible benefits, but had been denied "University Recognition" and the additional tangible benefits which accompany that status.

Judge Bacon also found that "Georgetown University is a religiously affiliated educational institution which serves both sectarian and secular purposes." In denying "University Recognition," Judge Bacon determined that Georgetown's administrators had applied the moral or normative teachings of the Roman Catholic Church, as these were established at trial through expert testimony and Church documents. Under Catholic doctrine, sexual function has its true meaning and moral rectitude only in heterosexual marriage. Homosexual acts—as distinguished from a homosexual orientation—are morally wrong and must be viewed as "gravely evil and a disordered use of the sexual faculty." Persons of homosexual orientation have an obligation to "try as is reasonably possible to change if they find themselves in such orientation" and must in any event conform their conduct to the normative teachings on human sexuality. No believer affiliated with the Roman Catholic Church may condone, endorse, approve or be neutral about homosexual orientation, homosexual lifestyle or homosexual acts.

Judge Bacon found that "the major purpose of '[U]niversity [R]ecognition' is official endorsement, an endorsement which the University believes will conflict with the normative teachings of the Church on homosexuality." However, Judge Bacon acknowledged that, in addition to the "endorsement," a grant of "University Recognition" allows a student group access to additional facilities and services.

Judge Bacon also found that Georgetown's denial of "University Recognition" was based on its view, one not without foundation, that "the gay student organizations, as evidenced by their charters and their activities, were participating in and promoting homosexual life styles," and that Georgetown was religiously opposed to this type of group activity. University administrators acted upon a sincerely-held religious belief that official recognition of the two groups "would be inconsistent with Church normative teachings and with the basic obligation not to undermine the normative teachings of the Church." Finally, Judge Bacon found that without "University Recognition" clubs may be formed, meetings held on campus, and application made for lecture funds, and that in the District of Columbia there are other off-campus opportunities available to gay students.

In addition to her findings of fact, Judge Bacon made several conclusions of law. She held that Georgetown University is not so pervasively secular that it cannot separate secular and sectarian activities and that its receipt of federal funds for secular purposes neither required it to abandon its sectarian activities nor put it in violation of the Establishment Clause of the First Amendment. Moreover, its status as a church-affiliated educational institution allowed it to raise and rely on First Amendment guarantees of religious freedom. The religious beliefs in issue are sincerely held and central to the Roman Catholic faith and they impose affirmative commands upon its adherents. Judge Bacon held that enforcement of the Human Rights Act in this case would require Georgetown to act in a manner "inconsistent with its duties as a Catholic institution" and would therefore place a burden on the free exercise of religion. On the other hand, because there is no "national" policy requiring state intervention in matters relating to sexual orientation, the Human Rights Act does not further any "compelling" governmental interest which could outweigh the burden on religious exercise. In the circumstances of this case, she held, the Human Rights Act is "a local enactment of well-motivated purpose but impermissible reach." Upholding Georgetown's free exercise defense, Judge Bacon dismissed the student groups' complaint.

III
THE HUMAN RIGHTS ACT VIOLATION

In granting partial summary judgment, Judge Braman found that Georgetown's denial of "University Recognition" and the attendant tangible benefits violated the Human Rights Act. At trial on the free exercise defense, Judge Bacon therefore proceeded from the premise of an established statutory violation. Without challenging the underlying finding of a Human Rights Act violation, Georgetown asks this court to affirm Judge Bacon's conclusion that the Human Rights Act is unconstitutional as applied.

"If there is one doctrine more deeply rooted than any other, it is that we ought not to pass on questions of constitutionality . . . unless such adjudication is unavoidable." Thus, "if a case may be decided on either statutory or constitutional grounds, [the courts], for sound jurisprudential reasons, will inquire first into the statutory question." A constitutional issue is presented in this case only if Judge Braman correctly concluded that the statute was violated. Before considering Judge Bacon's later ruling on the free exercise defense, we must ask ourselves whether the Human Rights Act was properly construed by Judge Braman.

The deeply rooted doctrine that a constitutional issue is to be avoided if possible informs our principles of statutory construction. We do not needlessly pit a statute against the Constitution. Insofar as its language permits, the Human Rights Act must be construed in a manner which projects its constitutionality. Moreover, it should be read, if it can be, so as to avoid difficult and sensitive constitutional questions concerning the scope of the First Amendment.

On the facts of this case, as found by Judge Bacon after trial, the particular scheme of "University Recognition" operating at Georgetown includes a religiously guided institutional "endorsement" of recipient student groups. Contrary to Judge Braman's earlier construction, the Human Rights Act does not require one private actor to "endorse" the ideas or conduct of another. The trial court's interpretation would defeat the plain language of the statute and simultaneously transform the Human Rights Act into a patent invasion of the First Amendment. The statute would be rendered both practically and legally unenforceable. Because the Human Rights Act does not require Georgetown to "endorse" the student groups, its denial of "University Recognition" did not violate the statute.

While the Human Rights Act does not require any "endorsement"—and therefore does not require the type of "University Recognition" offered by Georgetown—it does require equal access to the "facilities and services" attendant upon that status. In this case the student groups have been denied four tangible benefits that also come with a grant of "University Recognition": officially approved use of a mailbox, use of the Computer Label Service, mailing services, and the right to apply for (but not necessarily to receive) funding. All of these tangible benefits, unlike an "endorsement," are "facilities and services" within the meaning of the Human Rights Act; the record supports Judge Braman's conclusion that they were denied on the basis of sexual orientation. Tangible benefits having been denied upon an impermissible basis, we affirm, to that extent only, Judge Braman's finding that the Human Rights Act was violated; we reverse his holding that the denial of "University Recognition" was of itself a statutory violation.

A. *Judge Bacon's Factual Finding that "University Recognition" at Georgetown Includes an "Endorsement"*

Judge Bacon found as a fact that under the Georgetown scheme "University Recognition" benefits a student group in two ways. "The major purpose of "[U]niversity [R]ecognition' is official endorsement. . . . ", an "endorsement" which Georgetown tenders in accordance with the normative teachings of the Roman Catholic Church. "University Recognition" also gives a student group access to certain tangible benefits. Unless "clearly erroneous," these factual findings are binding upon us for purposes of this appeal.

Specifically, the student groups urge us to disregard as clearly erroneous Judge Bacon's factual finding that "University Recognition" at Georgetown includes an "endorsement." They point out that other groups with "University Recognition" occupy a broad range of the political, social and philosophical spectrum, and argue that Georgetown cannot claim that all of these organizations are strictly Roman Catholic in outlook. In particular, the student groups refer us to the recognized existence of such diverse bodies as the Jewish Students Association, the Organization of Arab Students, the Young Americans for Freedom, and the Democratic Socialist Organizing Committee.

At trial, the student groups challenged President Healy with evidence concerning the University's willingness to extend "University Recognition" to organizations whose members adhere to religions other than Catholicism. President Healy responded:

> It is the understanding of the Roman Catholic Church that faiths other than the Roman Catholic Church are, to put it in the technical terms, carriers of grace and as such are good. The Roman Catholic Church would feel that they are incomplete, but in the context of a complex university, it is the clear and stated purpose of the Roman Catholic Church that those of other faiths receive the same pastoral and intellectual sustenance in their faith as far as it is possible for the University to grant it, given the multiplicity, as Catholic students receive from a Catholic university.

The student groups also sought to undermine Georgetown's claim of "endorsement" by pointing to views on artificial birth control, abortion, divorce and lesbianism associated with members of the Women's Rights Collective (WRC) and the Women's Political Caucus (WPC). However, one of their witnesses, Sister Mary K. Liston, stated that WPC, another campus group of which she was a member, had not and could not take a pro-abortion position "[b]ecause of the stand of the Catholic Church on the issue of abortion." Sona Jean Vandall, a representative of WRC, acknowledged that the only formally stated purpose of that organization is the eradication of policies and practices which alienate and discriminate against women. She further testified that views contrary to Roman Catholic teachings were carried in none of WRC's published information and that no such positions had been voted on by its membership. Referring to an occasion when WRC posted other organizations' notices concerning artificial birth control and abortion, President Healy testified that he referred the matter to a committee to "determine whether [these incidents were] an isolated instance or whether [they were] an essential part of the collective activity." After discussion with the various parties, he regarded the incidents in question as "such minor instances of activity as not to be of serious concern to the University." He concluded, on that basis, that withdrawal of WRC's "University Recognition" would not be appropriate.

With regard to the plaintiff student groups, President Healy saw the matter differently. He testified that the University does not distinguish between students on the basis of their sexual orientation and said that group activity merely promoting the legal rights of gay people would present no religious conflict. But, according to President Healy and other Georgetown representatives, including its theological expert, the purposes set forth in the GPGU Constitution described an organization for which "University Recognition" would be inappropriate for a Catholic institution.

"The statement that stopped me most," said President Healy, was GPGU's stated commitment to "the development of responsible sexual ethics consonant with one's personal beliefs." Under Roman Catholic doctrine, as expert testimony established, responsible sexual ethics are not a question of personal belief. "The University cannot make that statement about any area of front line morality without insisting upon the objectivity of moral fact and that it is not left strictly to individual determination within any context which can reasonably be read as Catholic." Under Roman Catholic doctrine, contrary to GPGU's suggestion, sexual ethics are the subject of an absolute and unyielding moral law, one laid down by God.

President Healy also testified that GPGU's expressed intention to "establish a program of activities which reflect the above purposes," was "open-ended enough to involve the University in a host of positions and activities which together or singly it would find inappropriate." He had similar reservations about GRC's stated commitment to the provision of information to gay and lesbian law students concerning "Washington's gay community, including educational, cultural, religious, social and medical services." According to President Healy, GRC's association with the range of activities engaged in by the Washington gay community would "involve Georgetown University in positions it would not wish publicly to adopt."

Roman Catholic teachings establish "moral norms" which prevent believers from recognizing homosexual conduct, as distinguished from homosexual orientation, as anything other than sinful. President Healy added that the duty to obey these "moral norms" would be more binding upon institutions, which have to act publicly and where there is an added moral consideration of leading others astray or giving scandal in the technical sense of the word, so that the binding authority of Roman Catholic teaching on an institution would, at least in that dimension, be greater than it would be on an [individual].

Reverend Richard J. McCormick, S.J., Georgetown's theological expert, testified to the same effect. He said that a Roman Catholic university "has a duty to act in a way consistent with those teachings and not to undermine them in its public policies." Thus, "in its public policies and public acts," the University "ought not to adopt a public policy of explicit endorsement or implicit endorsement" of, for example, abortion, premarital intercourse, or homosexual conduct. Georgetown should not "in its public actions, policies, decisions, take a position that would equivalently establish another normative lifestyle equally valid with the one that is in a normative position." According to President Healy, a grant of "University Recognition" to GPGU and GRC would conflict with Georgetown's duty not to undermine the Roman Catholic teaching that "human sexuality can be exercised only within marriage. . . . "

The trial court did not define precisely what it meant by "endorsement." For President Healy, "a position that the Church was *either neutral or approving* of the range of homosexual activities is unacceptable." This statement reveals what we understand to be at stake. An official "endorsement," as symbolized by Georgetown's grant of "University Recognition," would express religious approval of or neutrality towards the student groups. Under the Georgetown scheme, "University Recognition" is reserved for groups that do not fundamentally challenge the "moral norms."

We cannot characterize as "clearly erroneous" Judge Bacon's finding that the scheme of "University Recognition" offered by Georgetown includes the type of "endorsement" just described. "Recognition Criteria" described it as an "endorsement." Georgetown administrators repeatedly testified that they understood it to have that effect. From the outset of its dealings with GPGU and GRC, Georgetown equated "University Recognition" with an "endorsement." Neither "Recognition Criteria" nor any evidence adduced at trial indicates that "University Recognition" is an automatic right. That status was granted in the University's discretion and some application of Roman Catholic doctrine was involved in the recognition process.

Our required deference to Judge Bacon's factual finding is not undercut by Georgetown's willingness to "endorse" a wide range of groups with extremely diverse goals and activities. For those whose common interest is a non-Catholic religious belief system, Georgetown's "endorsement" appears to have been granted in the spirit of ecumenism. For others, including WRC, the evidence permitted Judge Bacon to conclude that no "essential part of the collective activity" contravened Roman Catholic doctrine, and that the administration would withdraw "University Recognition" if there were more than "isolated instances" of unofficial activity inconsistent with those teachings. The trial court was therefore entitled to conclude that the University adopted an approving or at least neutral position towards all of the existing groups because it did not perceive them to be incompatible with its religious obligations. This comports with our understanding of what "endorsement" means in this case.

An appellate court may not usurp the role of the factfinder. We cannot label "clearly erroneous" Judge Bacon's "endorsement" finding, i.e., that "University Recognition" at Georgetown contains an expression of religious approval or neutrality towards a student group obtaining that status.

B. *The "Endorsement" Distinguished from the Tangible Benefits*

The distinction between the "endorsement" and the other benefits contained in Georgetown's scheme of "University Recognition" is fundamental. It is so from both a statutory and a constitutional perspective. In this case, the separateness of the benefits at issue is obscured by the fact that they are bundled together into a single package known as "University Recognition." Because the "endorsement" and the tangible benefits contained in that package are fundamentally distinct, we must sever the artificial connection between them in order to analyze the true issues.

The "endorsement" contained in "University Recognition" is an intangible. To a student group, it is no more than an expression of official approval or neutrality, a statement of Georgetown's tolerance towards organizations that pose no fundamental challenge to the "moral norms." The "endorsement" is a symbolic gesture, a form of speech by a private, religiously affiliated educational institution, an entity free to adopt partisan public positions on moral and ethical issues. In speaking out on human sexuality, Georgetown is guided by a religious mission undertaken along with secular educational functions. The "endorsement" contained in "University Recognition" assists the student group only by giving it Georgetown's imprimatur or, at least, nihil obstat. Quite different are the tangible benefits associated with "University Recognition." Unlike the "endorsement," the tangible benefits are "facilities and services," and not an abstract expression of the University's moral philosophy. Their distinct characteristics are disguised only because both the "endorsement" and the additional tangible benefits are included in one package known as "University Recognition."

As amicus The Governor's Council on Lesbian and Gay Issues of the State of Wisconsin points out, "such a structure unnecessarily ties the University's religious beliefs to extension of benefits." We agree. While the "endorsement" and the tangible benefits may be one for Georgetown's administrative purposes, they are not so in the eyes of the Human Rights Act, nor are they so in the eyes of the First Amendment. "The constitutionality of the statute," as the District of Columbia remarks, "cannot depend on the [U]niversity's internal linkages. We open up the package of "University Recognition" and examine its contents separately.

C. *Applying the Human Rights Act to the "Endorsement" Element of "University Recognition"*

The Human Rights Act does not require one private actor to "endorse" another. Georgetown's denial of "University Recognition" to the student groups did not violate the statute.

There are two reasons why, as a matter of statutory construction, the Human Rights Act cannot be read to compel a regulated party to express religious approval or neutrality towards any group or individual. First, the statute prohibits only a discriminatory denial of access to "facilities and services" provided by an educational institution. An "endorsement" is neither. The Human Rights Act provides legal mechanisms to ensure equality of *treatment*, not equality of *attitudes*. Although we fervently hope that nondiscriminatory attitudes result from equal access to "facilities and services," the Human Rights Act contains nothing to suggest that the legislature intended to make a discriminatory state of mind unlawful in itself. Still less does the statute reveal any desire to force a private actor to express an idea that is not truly held. The Human Rights Act demands action, not words. It was not intended to be an instrument of mind control. Judge Braman's construction of the statute, as requiring an insincere expression of opinion, conflicts with its literal meaning.

Second, as we have already pointed out, unless the language of the statute is plainly to the contrary, we must construe it so as to uphold its constitutionality. To read into the Human Rights Act a requirement that one private actor must "endorse" another would be to render the statute unconstitutional. The First Amendment protects both free speech and the free exercise of religion. Its essence is that government is without power to intrude into the domain of the intellect or the spirit and that only conduct may be regulated. Interpreting the Human Rights Act so as to require Georgetown to "endorse" the student groups would be to thrust the statute across the constitutional boundaries set by the Free Speech Clause and also, where sincere religious objections are raised, the Free Exercise Clause. Nothing in the statute suggests, let alone requires, such a result.

Because similar interests are often implicated, the Supreme Court has relied on both the Free Speech Clause and the Free Exercise Clause to protect against government intrusion into the inner domain. The Court has made clear that the state is without power to regulate the intellect or the spirit; its rule is over actions and behavior only. In its initial decision interpreting the Free Exercise Clause, the Court described the division between opinion and action as "the true distinction between what properly belongs to the Church and what to the State." With the adoption of the Free Exercise Clause, "Congress was deprived of all legislative power over mere opinion, but was left free to reach actions which were in violation of social duties or subversive of good order." The Court quoted with approval a statute drafted by Thomas Jefferson to protect religious freedom in Virginia: "[i]t is time enough for the rightful purposes of civil government for its officers to interfere when principles break out into overt acts against peace and good order. "[T]o suffer the civil magistrate to intrude his [or her] powers into the field of opinion, and to restrain the profession or propagation of principles on supposition of their ill tendency, is a dangerous fallacy which at once destroys all religious liberty." The Court concluded, as a matter of constitutional principle, that "[l]aws are made for the government of actions, and while they cannot interfere with mere religious belief and opinions, they may with practices."

That principal has been emphatically reaffirmed in a later free exercise case: "the Amendment embraces two concepts,—freedom to believe and freedom to act. The first is absolute but, in the nature of things, the second cannot be. Conduct remains subject to regulation for the protection of society."

*   *   *

In sharp contrast to the threatened "endorsement" here, the *Prune Yard* Court had stressed the unlikelihood that the pamphleteers' views would be identified with those of the shopping center owner and also emphasized that no specific message was being dictated by the government in that case. But Georgetown's scheme of "University Recognition" cannot be analogized to a public forum, nor can its campus be equated with "a business establishment that is open to the public to come and go as they please."

Far from *Prune Yard*'s required accommodation of another's speech, this case raises the specter of compelled expression in violation of the First Amendment. A grant of "University Recognition" by Georgetown includes an "endorsement" of student groups it considers broadly compatible with Roman Catholic doctrine. To that extent, "University Recognition" is speech. Government compulsion to grant "University Recognition" would threaten both the free speech and free exercise guarantees of the First Amendment. Although a compelling state interest may justify regulation of religiously motivated conduct, nothing can penetrate the constitutional shield protecting against official coercion to renounce a religious belief or to endorse a principle opposed to that belief. "The very purpose of a Bill of Rights is to withdraw certain subjects from the vicissitudes of political controversy, to place them beyond the reach of majority and officials and to establish them as legal principles to be applied by the courts." Georgetown's right to express opinions based on Roman Catholic teachings includes the right to do so by way of granting "University Recognition" to groups it regards as consonant with that belief system. Individuals will not always agree with Georgetown's choices as to what groups are deserving of its approval, but its right to freely express its views is nonetheless protected by the First Amendment.

Freedom of expression is a right to which we all lay equal claim, irrespective of the content of our message. This is easily illustrated. Suppose that the Gay University of American (GUA) is established as a private educational institution. Part of its mission is to win understanding and acceptance of gay and bisexual persons in an intolerant society. Although open to everyone, regardless of sexual orientation, GUA does expect its faculty, staff and students to maintain a sympathetic attitude towards gay practices and the philosophies that support them. GUA has, as the trial court finds, a system of "University Recognition" through which it expresses its approval or tolerance of various student groups desiring that status. But the GUA administration refuses to grant "University Recognition" to the Roman Catholic Sexual Ethics Association (RCSEA). In that situation, the Human Rights Act's ban on discrimination based on religion could not avail the Catholic student group, for the simple reason that the statute does not require GUA to give expression of approval or tolerance. Insincere statements of opinion are not what the Human Rights Act requires. On the other hand, the statute would require equal distribution of any attendant tangible benefits if GUA's denial of these was based on the religion of RCSEA members. Georgetown's protection against compelled expression is no more and no less.

The trial court's construction of the Human Rights Act would transform the statute into a violation of the First Amendment. It would compel Georgetown to "endorse" the student groups despite the Supreme Court's warning that a religious actor may not be forced to "say ... anything in conflict with [its] religious tenets." This construction of the Human Rights Act is required neither by its language nor by its purpose of ensuring equal *treatment*—treatment concretely measured by access to "facilities and services," not by the educational institution's expressed approval of the "purposes and activities" of recipient student groups.

Georgetown's obligation under the statute is not to express a particular point of view. It is to make tangible benefits available to its students without regard to their sexual orientation. The Human Rights Act does not require Georgetown to grant "University Recognition" and its accompanying intangible "endorsement" to the student groups.

D. *Applying the Human Rights Act to the Tangible Benefits Contained in "University Recognition"*

Although the student groups were not entitled to summary judgment on the ground that Georgetown's denial of "University Recognition"—including an "endorsement"—violated the Human Rights Act, the statute does require Georgetown to equally distribute, without regard to sexual orientation, the tangible benefits contained in the same package. If discrimination appears from the record, this court may sustain the statutory ruling "on a ground different from that adopted by the trial court." Our review of the record reveals no genuine dispute that the tangible benefits were denied on the basis of sexual orientation. The Human Rights Act was violated to that extent.

The Human Rights Act cannot depend for its enforcement on a regulated actor's purely subjective, albeit sincere, evaluation of its own motivations. "Bias or prejudice is such an elusive condition of the mind that it is most difficult, if not impossible, to always recognize its existence. . . . " It is particularly difficult to recognize one's own acts as discriminatory. Apart from organizations that failed to meet purely technical requirements such as a minimum membership, the record shows that Georgetown never denied "University Recognition" to a student group that was not mainly composed of persons with a homosexual orientation. Where, as here, those possessing characteristics identified by the legislature as irrelevant to individual merit are treated less favorably than others, the Human Rights Act imposes a burden upon the regulated actor to demonstrate that the irrelevant characteristic played no part in its decision. Georgetown failed to present facts that could show it was uninfluenced by sexual orientation in denying the tangible benefits.

One nondiscriminatory reason asserted by Georgetown for its denial of the tangible benefits contained in "University Recognition" was that it could not give its accompanying "endorsement" to the student groups without violating its religious principles. But as the Human Rights Act, properly construed, requires no direct, intangible "endorsement," Georgetown cannot avoid a finding of discrimination on that ground. The remaining nondiscriminatory reasons asserted by Georgetown may be summarized as follows: the "purposes and activities" of the student groups fell outside the boundaries set by "Recognition Criteria," rendering them ineligible for the tangible benefits they sought and not "otherwise qualified" within the meaning of the statute; and, in any event, the denial of tangible benefits was based on the "purposes and activities" of the student groups, not on the homosexual status of their members, so that the sexual orientation of the students involved played no part in the decision-making process.

In this case, the nondiscriminatory reasons asserted by Georgetown have the effect of fusing together what would normally be two separate inquiries—are the student groups "otherwise qualified" for the tangible benefits they seek, and, if so, did Georgetown deny those tangible benefits due to the sexual orientation of their members? Here, because the answer to both of those distinct questions is determined by objective reference to the "purposes and activities" of the student groups, what are normally two separate inquiries collapse into one: did the homosexual orientation of the group members cause them to be treated differently from other applicants?

We are not bound by Georgetown's subjective perception of the "purposes and activities" to which it objected. Georgetown must view the "purposes and activities" of a student group in a way which is free from impermissible reliance upon factors unrelated to individual merit. Accordingly, if the homosexual status of group members entered into Georgetown's assessment of the "purposes and activities" of the student groups, albeit unconsciously, the denial of tangible benefits was itself based on sexual orientation. Put differently, it would be irrelevant that Georgetown saw itself as doing nothing more than applying neutral guidelines established by "Recognition Criteria" if sexual orientation had in fact influenced how those standards were applied.

In denying GPGU's application for "University Recognition" Georgetown adverted to that group's expressed purpose (one of four) to "provide a forum for the development of responsible sexual ethics consonant with one's personal beliefs." That purpose is at odds with Roman Catholic teachings. But GRC's constitution contained no comparable statement; Georgetown's stated objection was to GRC's much broader intention to "[p]rovide lesbians and gay men entering the Law Center with information about Washington's gay community, including educational, cultural, religious, social and medical services." Because GRC's purposes include an asexual commitment to serving the broad range of needs experienced by homosexual students, but no statement as to the propriety of homosexual conduct, Georgetown's objection to that organization must to some extent have been prompted by the sexual orientation of its members.

That Georgetown's treatment of the gay student groups was not exclusively influenced by a specific objection to "purposes and activities" inconsistent with Roman Catholic dogma was further evidenced by Debbie Gottfried, the University's Director of Student Activities. In clarifying GPGU's status after it had obtained "Student Body Endorsement," but had failed to obtain "University Recognition," Gottfried wrote that the University would not change its position "on what it feels would be interpreted as endorsement and official support of *the full range of issues associated with this cause*." At no time has Georgetown defined what it meant by "the full range of issues" associated with the gay student groups, despite its insistence that Roman Catholic doctrine favors the provision of equal civil and political rights to homosexually oriented persons and that its religious objection was directed only to the promotion of homosexual conduct.

It is apparent from this correspondence, all of which was before Judge Braman when he granted summary judgment on the discrimination issue, that Georgetown's denial of tangible benefits was not closely tied to specific "purposes and activities" of the student groups promoting the homosexual conduct condemned by Roman Catholic doctrine. The conclusion is inescapable that the predominantly gay composition of the student groups played at least some role in their treatment by Georgetown. By objecting to the student groups' assumed connection, "by definition," to a "full range of issues" associated with the "gay movement," rather than to specific "purposes and activities" inconsistent with its Roman Catholic tradition, Georgetown engaged in the kind of stereotyping unrelated to individual merit that is forbidden by the Human Rights Act. In short, the record reveals no genuine doubt that Georgetown's asserted nondiscriminatory basis for its action was in fact tainted by preconceptions about gay persons. Georgetown did not apply "Recognition Criteria" on an equal basis to all groups without regard to the sexual orientation of their members.

Judge Braman's finding that Georgetown discriminated on the basis of sexual orientation is further supported by his express reliance on another provision of the Human Rights Act. The effects clause provides that "[a]ny practice which has the effect or consequence of violating any of the provisions of this chapter shall be deemed to be an unlawful discriminatory practice."

A Human Rights Act violation was established with regard to Georgetown's denial of the tangible benefits. The evidence before Judge Braman may not permit the conclusion that Georgetown consciously denied benefits due to the sexual orientation of the student groups involved. It is nonetheless evident that the University allowed the homosexual orientation of the individuals involved—not just the "purposes and activities" of their student organizations—to creep into its decisionmaking. By failing to confine its objections to "purposes and activities" which it found offensive for reasons *independent* of the sexual orientation of these students, Georgetown discriminated. The position that "a gay organization" is "by definition" associated with a "full range of issues" reveals that sexual orientation was a factor in Georgetown's denial of tangible benefits. That statement established an intentional violation; and, in any event, under the effects clause the Human Rights Act also prohibits unintentional discrimination. Finally, none of the Human Rights Act's narrowly drawn exceptions avails Georgetown here.

The Human Rights Act having been violated with respect to the tangible benefits, we proceed to Georgetown's free exercise defense.

IV
GEORGETOWN'S FREE EXERCISE DEFENSE

Georgetown claims that the Free Exercise Clause of the First Amendment exempts it from the Human Rights Acts' edict that it distribute the tangible benefits equally without regard to sexual orientation. We disagree.

In the trial court, due to Judge Braman's prior statutory construction, Judge Bacon premised her free exercise analysis on the mistaken belief that compliance with the Human Rights Act would require Georgetown to provide a religious "endorsement" as well as tangible benefits. The true issue is a much more limited one. It is whether the forced distribution of various tangible benefits without regard to sexual orientation, severed from the direct "endorsement" required by a compelled grant of "University Recognition," imposes an unconstitutional burden on Georgetown's exercise of religion. The answer is no.

* * *

We consider that the Council of the District of Columbia acted on the most pressing of needs when incorporating into the Human Rights Act its view that discrimination based on sexual orientation is a grave evil that damages society as well as its immediate victims. The eradication of sexual orientation discrimination is a compelling governmental interest.

D. *Balancing the Compelling Governmental Interest against the Burden on Religious Exercise*

Given that the District of Columbia has a compelling governmental interest in eradicating sexual orientation discrimination, we must determine whether that interest outweighs the burden enforcement of the Human Rights Act would impose on Georgetown's religious exercise.

In this case, compelling equal access to the tangible benefits, without requiring the intangible "endorsement" contained in "University Recognition," imposes a relatively slight burden on Georgetown's religious practice. As Georgetown itself concedes, "[the only tangible benefits plaintiffs could receive by the grant of official recognition are relatively insignificant—such as mailing and computer labeling services." It then argues that "[s]uch minor perquisites cannot outweigh the substantial burden on the University's religious liberty that would follow from compelled recognition of the student groups." But its argument fails because the "substantial burden" to which it refers—compulsion to grant the intangible "endorsement" contained in "University Recognition"—is not required by the Human Rights Act. By Georgetown's own admission, what the Human Rights Act actually does require—equal distribution of the tangible benefits—is considerably less burdensome.

Our conclusion that the burden on religious liberty does not outweigh the District's compelling interest receives additional support from the facts that Georgetown voluntarily gives the student groups the fewer tangible benefits that come with "Student Body Endorsement" and that it has never objected to the student groups meeting on campus. Without inference from the Georgetown administration, the student groups are an active force in the university community. GPGU, for example, has held campus meetings almost weekly, hosting discussions, speakers, and educational and social events. Finally, the burden imposed upon Georgetown's religious exercise is further diminished by the parties' representations that GPGU has already been given a mailbox, one of the tangible benefits theoretically in dispute.

E. Enforcement of the Human Rights Act is the Least Restrictive Means Available

Finally, even though the District of Columbia's compelling interest in eradicating sexual orientation discrimination outweighs the burden that compliance with the Human Rights Act would impose on Georgetown's religious exercise, the statute can be enforced only if it is the least restrictive means of attaining that goal.

Here, that condition is met. To tailor the Human Rights Act to require less of the University than equal access to its "facilities and services," without regard to sexual orientation, would be to defeat its compelling purpose. The District of Columbia's overriding interest in eradicating sexual orientation discrimination, if it is ever to be converted from aspiration to reality, requires that Georgetown equally distribute tangible benefits to the student groups. Other than compelling the equal provision of tangible benefits, there are no available means of eradicating sexual orientation discrimination in educational institutions that would be less restrictive of Georgetown's religious exercise.

V
CONCLUSION

The Human Rights Act does not require a grant of "University Recognition" because, in the particular scheme at Georgetown University, that status includes a religiously based "endorsement" of the recipient student group. But the Human Rights Act does demand that Georgetown make its "facilities and services" equally available without regard to sexual orientation. Those "facilities and services" include the tangible benefits that come with "University Recognition." Georgetown denied tangible benefits on the basis of sexual orientation and in so doing violated the Human Rights Act. The University's free exercise defense does not exempt it from compliance with the statute, because the District of Columbia's compelling interest in eradicating sexual orientation discrimination outweighs any burden that equal provision of the tangible benefits would impose on Georgetown's religious exercise. On statutory rather than constitutional grounds, we therefore affirm the trial court's holding that Georgetown is not required to grant the student groups "University Recognition." We reverse the trial court's ruling that the Free Exercise Clause relieves Georgetown from its statutory obligation to provide the tangible benefits without regard to sexual orientation. We order the trial court to enter judgment accordingly.

The *Georgetown* case, as noted, wended its way through a number of involved procedural hurdles. In addition, while it was precluded from using D.C. bond funds, Georgetown sought to finance its facilities through neighboring Maryland's bond program. "D.C.'s Georgetown U. Seeks Bonds from Maryland," *Chronicle of Higher Education*, 1 April 1987, p. 22. After the D.C. Court of Appeals decision required Georgetown to accord all "tangible benefits" to the student groups, President Healy instructed G.U. officials to comply with the order; however, the trustees then decided to secure a stay and to appeal. A preliminary stay was granted on January 11, 1988 (108 S. Ct. 688), and on January 25, 1988, the Supreme Court denied the stay. 108 S. Ct. 768. After reconsideration, the University decided not to pursue its appeal. "SBA Funds LAGA," *Georgetown Law Weekly*, 8 February 1988, pp. 1, 7.

In a March 28, 1988 letter to Georgetown faculty and alumni, President Healy noted:

> "The conclusion of the Board was that we had a very weak case to present to the court for the following reasons:
>
> 1) The decision granted the University what it said it wanted, and the court manifestly regarded the "tangible benefits" as minor. That perception was justified by the University's own brief.
>
> 2) In order to make a successful appeal, we were advised that we would have to attack the statute itself, as well as plead our rights of free exercise and free speech. The Board felt that a Catholic institution would have difficulty attacking the statute, which while it was perhaps over-inclusive, at the same time addressed a real problem and constituted a reasonable exercise of the District's police powers.
>
> 3) All the members of the Board felt that having treated our gay students during the long course of the trial with sympathy and understanding made it possible for the other side to urge that we sought now to refuse what we had all along freely granted.
>
> 4) Everyone felt that the reaction of the Supreme Court when we asked for a stay in execution indicated that it was not sympathetic to the University's position. As best we can determine the denial of the stay was 7-to-0.
>
> 5) Judge Antonin Scalia recused himself from the discussion of the stay and thus from the case. He is not obliged to give a reason and he did not. The press speculated that as an alumnus of Georgetown he did not wish to be involved in the case. Even with the addition of Judge Kennedy, this left us facing an eight-judge court, and everyone felt that this was not an ideal way to approach the Supreme Court.
>
> 6) As the decision now stands, its binding authority is limited to the District of Columbia and is based on a broadly drafted statute peculiar to the District. If the case were taken by the Supreme Court (many on the Board felt it would not be) and if the court decided against us, a national precedent would be set which could cause much mischief.

For all of these reasons, the Board voted unanimously that it would be best to work out an agreement with the plaintiffs in the case, so that the trial court in issuing its order would take into account those aspects of its work and life that the University sought most to protect. The Board instructed the University to seek such an agreement, and only to appeal to the Supreme Court if it became clear that the agreement would not be forthcoming or that there was little chance of the judge incorporating it into her order.

In the days that followed, an acceptable agreement was reached. It protected the essential elements I have described above, and it was accepted by the judge. Following the instructions of the Board, the University has allowed the last day on which it could appeal for *certiorari* from the Supreme Court to pass without an appeal." *Letter from President Healy.*

The District of Columbia is one of few cities that has such an ordinance prohibiting discrimination on the basis of sexual orientation. In Chapter One, it was seen that a similar ordinance in Philadelphia, prohibiting Temple University Law School from allowing the military to recruit students for employment, was struck down on preemption grounds. *U.S. v. City of Philadelphia*, 798 F.2d 81 (3rd Cir. 1986).

Ad-Hoc Committee v. Bernard M. Baruch College
835 F.2d 980 (2nd Cir. 1987)

MESKILL, Circuit Judge:

This is an appeal from an order entered in the United States District Court for the Southern District of New York, dated December 15, 1986, dismissing plaintiffs-appellants' complaint pursuant to Fed. R. Civ. P. 12(c). Plaintiffs are alumni of Bernard M. Baruch College (Baruch College or the College), a branch of the City University of New York. They seek to form an alumni association dedicated to the concerns of minority students and alumni of Baruch College which will be incorporated and officially recognized as the Bernard M. Baruch Black and Hispanic Alumni Association (Black and Hispanic Alumni Association). Plaintiffs are collectively known as the Ad-Hoc Committee of the Baruch Black and Hispanic Alumni Association (Ad-Hoc Committee). They have brought a class action alleging that Baruch College's selective refusal to grant recognition to their group, while having granted official recognition to another alumni association, the Bernard M. Baruch Alumni Association, Inc. (Baruch Alumni Association), violated among other things the First Amendment and the Equal Protection Clause of the Fourteenth Amendment. We hold that the district court erred in dismissing the action at this point in the proceedings. We therefore vacate the district court's order and remand the case to the district court for further proceedings.

BACKGROUND

In recent years, increasing numbers of Black and Hispanic students have enrolled at Baruch College. For example, in the freshman class entering the College in the fall of 1983, 417 students were Caucasian, 395 were Black, 176 were Hispanic and 157 were Asian. The plaintiffs desire to form an alumni association that will address the particular interests of minority students and alumni of Baruch College, including job opportunities and the high dropout rate among minority students. Under the proposed by-laws of the Black and Hispanic Alumni Association, membership would be open to all graduates of Baruch College, students in the senior class, faculty and staff, without regard to race or ethnic origin.

In November 1982 the Ad-Hoc Committee by letter informed Joel Segall, the President of Baruch College, of its intent to form the Black and Hispanic Alumni Association. Segall responded by letter in December 1982, stating that he was pleased that the group was forming, but adding that another alumni association already had been established. He noted that although the existing alumni association's activities "would not bar your group from forming to serve purposes and needs that are special to you and perhaps not within the broader purview of the Alumni Association," he hoped that the plaintiff's group would "ally itself actively" with the existing alumni association.

Plaintiffs proceeded to prepare a certificate of incorporation for the Black and Hispanic Alumni Association, but they were unable to file the certificate without the approval of Segall. In April 1984, members of the Ad-Hoc Committee met with Segall and other members of the college administration to discuss formal recognition of the Black and Hispanic Alumni Association. At this meeting, Segall asserted that he would only support the group if it became a part of the existing alumni association. A member of the Baruch College administration later suggested that the plaintiffs form a "presidential advisory committee" rather than an officially sanctioned alumni association, but the plaintiffs rejected that proposal.

Because of its status as an unrecognized association, the Ad-Hoc Committee was denied access by the defendants to meeting rooms on campus; officially recognized associations, such as the Baruch Alumni Association, are permitted to use campus facilities for their activities. In addition, plaintiffs learned that the Dean of Students of the College encouraged students not to sponsor rooms on campus for meetings with the Ad-Hoc Committee.

The plaintiffs brought this class action suit contending that the defendants' refusal to treat their group in the same manner as the other alumni association violated 42 U.S.C. § 1983 (1982), the First Amendment, the Fifth Amendment, the Thirteenth Amendment and the Fourteenth Amendment. After defendants had answered the complaint and plaintiffs had moved for class certification, defendants moved to dismiss the action for failure to state a claim upon which relief can be granted.

On December 15, 1986, the district court granted the defendants' motion and dismissed the complaint under Fed.R.Civ.P. 12(c), stating that plaintiffs did not "cite activities by defendants which could even arguably be construed as violative of such constitutional rights. On the contrary, the complaint shows that plaintiffs have met freely with each other, have formed an association, and have spoken out on issues they regard as important." The court concluded that the closest the plaintiffs came to stating a claim was an argument based on *Healy v. James*, in which the Supreme Court unanimously held that a state-supported college had violated the First Amendment rights of students who sought to form a local chapter of Students for a Democratic Society by denying them official recognition as a campus organization. The court distinguished *Healy*, correctly noting that an alumni group rather than a student group was involved in the instant case. It concluded that as there already was a recognized alumni association that was open to all, the College's denial of official separate recognition to the plaintiffs' group did not result in the "chilling" of plaintiffs' rights to speak and organize. The district court added that because the existing alumni association was open to all, the defendants had not violated the Equal Protection Clause.

On appeal, the Ad-Hoc Committee contends that the district court erred in dismissing the complaint.

DISCUSSION

In this case, the defendants moved to dismiss the complaint for failure to state a claim after they had answered the complaint. The district court granted the motion pursuant to Fed.R.Civ.P. 12(c); no matters outside the pleadings were considered and thus this motion was not converted into one for summary judgment under Fed.R.Civ.P. 56. Although the motion was dismissed under Fed.R.Civ.P. 12(c), the same standards that are employed for dismissing a complaint for failure to state a claim under Fed.R.Civ.P. 12(b)(6) are applicable here. Under these standards, a court must accept the allegations contained in the complaint as true. In addition, a court should not dismiss a complaint for failure to state a claim "unless it appears beyond doubt that the plaintiff can prove no set of facts in support of his claim which would entitle him to relief."

We conclude that under these standards, the district court dismissed the plaintiffs' complaint prematurely. The allegations in the complaint should be construed liberally in favor of the plaintiffs. When so construed, it does not appear beyond doubt that plaintiffs will be unable to present any set of facts to support their claims that their constitutional rights have been violated. For example, it is possible that plaintiffs could demonstrate that the College's selective denial of official recognition to their alumni association was improperly motivated by discrimination based on political viewpoint or race. It is important to examine the proffered justifications for a college's selective denial of recognition to an organization. Mere disagreement with the group's philosophy is not an adequate ground for denial of First Amendment rights because a state college cannot "restrict speech or association simply because it finds the views expressed by any group to be abhorrent." " '[T]he freedoms of speech, press, petition and assembly guaranteed by the First Amendment must be accorded to the ideas we hate or sooner or later they will be denied to the ideas we cherish.' " In this case, the College has not yet offered any justification for its denial of recognition to the Black and Hispanic Alumni Association, and thus it is impossible to determine at this stage whether this action was motivated by a desire to "discourage one viewpoint and advance another" in violation of the First Amendment.

Moreover, as the Supreme Court noted in *Village of Arlington Heights v. Metropolitan Housing Development Corp.*, the determination whether an action is motivated by an invidious racially discriminatory purpose and therefore is in violation of the Equal Protection Clause "demands a sensitive inquiry into such circumstantial and direct evidence of intent as may be available." No such inquiry was conducted in the instant case.

We thus conclude that the district court erred in dismissing the plaintiffs' complaint at this preliminary point in the proceedings without any record establishing the College's justifications for its denial of official recognition to the Black and Hispanic Alumni Association. Accordingly, the district court's order dismissing the complaint for failure to state a claim is vacated, and the case is remanded to the district court for further proceedings consistent with this opinion. In remanding, we express no opinion as to the merits of the plaintiffs' constitutional claims.

———

Student Fees

As a corollary to students' rights to organize, they gain access to funds, usually by participating in the institution's money generated by a system of student fees and a distribution scheme. The usual practice is to reserve a pool of money earmarked for student activities, with access for approved student groups on an application basis. The cases in this Section include issues of mandatory fee structures, acceptable restrictions on student fee-funded activities, and First Amendment guidelines for expenditures. In Chapter 2, a companion case was included for its student First Amendment references. *Brown v. University of Nebraska*, 640 F. Supp. 674 (D. Neb. 1986).

For a review of the complex issues presented here, see A. Gibbs and G. Crisp, "The Question of First Amendment Rights vs. Mandatory Student Activity Fees," *Journal of Law and Education*, 8 (1979), 185–196; and C. Steele, "Mandatory Student Fees at Public Universities: Bringing The First Amendment within the Campus Gate," *Journal of College and University Law*, 13 (1987), 353–374.

———

Erzinger v. Regents of the University of California
187 Cal. Rptr. 164 (App. 1982)

GERALD BROWN, Presiding Justice.

Plaintiffs Susan Erzinger, et al., appeal a judgment favoring the Regents of the University of California on the plaintiffs' third amended complaint.

The plaintiffs' third amended complaint alleges: Plaintiffs are students at the University; the University collects a registration fee from all students; the registration fee is used to provide health services to students at facilities on and off campus; such health services include abortion counseling, abortion referral and abortion; plaintiffs have refused to pay the portion of their registration fees used to pay for abortion counseling, abortion referral and abortion; plaintiffs have offered to pay all of the required fees except such amounts paid for abortion counseling, abortion referral and abortions; the University has not accepted partial payments of the required registration fees; the University has violated plaintiffs' rights under the First and Fourteenth Amendments to the United States Constitution and Article I, section 4, and Article IX, section 9 of the California Constitution by cancelling plaintiffs' enrollments at the University; the University's collecting from plaintiffs fees used to pay for abortions would force plaintiffs to violate their religious beliefs as a condition for attending the University. The plaintiffs asked the superior court to declare unconstitutional the University's policy requiring all students to pay compulsory registration fees and allotting a portion of such fees to pay for abortions without a pro rata exception or exemption for plaintiffs. The plaintiffs also asked the court to enjoin the University from implementing such policy and discriminating against plaintiffs and others sharing their beliefs about abortion and abortion-related services.

Pending litigation the University permitted plaintiffs to deposit the disputed fees into a trust fund.

The University asked the court to specify as without substantial controversy:

(1) the University's using mandatory student fees to provide student health services including abortion services and pregnancy counseling does not infringe plaintiffs' rights to free exercise of religion; and

(2) the University's Regents have legal authority to assess mandatory student fees and use such fees to benefit the student population even when such fees are not used directly to support the cost of specific educational programs or services.

The plaintiffs opposed the University's motion and filed their own motion for summary judgment, asserting as a matter of law they were entitled to judgment on all issues in their third amended complaint.

After hearing, the court denied plaintiffs' motion for summary judgment and granted the University's motion to specify issues as without substantial controversy. The court said:

> "In order for an individual to show that he has been prohibited from the free exercise of his religion, he must demonstrate that he has been coerced in his religious beliefs or that the government has unreasonably interfered with his practice of religion. In this case I see no coercion. The individuals who are students at the University of California are not required to submit to abortions. They are not required to, themselves, advocate abortions. They are not required, themselves, to advocate birth control. . . . Medical care is provided to students in the universities to enable the student to be as free as possible to devote themselves to their studies so that they will not have to worry about problems in connection with their health. . . . Merely because a student is required to pay "X" number of dollars at the beginning of each semester or each quarter does not mean that that student is endorsing abortions. . . . I know of no authority for the proposition that refusal to pay government taxes or fees is an activity protected by the First Amendment and no case has been cited to that effect. . . . [The Regents] possess virtually exclusive power with regard to the internal regulation of the universities, and certainly this broad discretion extends to their ability and the right to be able to set mandatory student fees. . . . The health services that have been afforded to students of the University of California are really nondiscriminatory and they are religiously neutral and they are consistent with the educationally related objectives."

After plaintiffs voluntarily dismissed other causes of action, the court entered judgment for the University on plaintiffs' third amendment complaint.

Plaintiffs contend the court erred in finding the University's using mandatory student fees to provide student health services including abortion services and pregnancy-related counseling does not infringe their rights to free exercise of religion; they assert they should be exempt from paying the proportion of such fees the University uses to provide services they deem objectionable on religious grounds. However, to prevail on their First Amendment claim, the plaintiffs must allege and prove the University coerced their religious beliefs or unreasonably interfered with their practice of religion. Plaintiffs do not show the University's collecting mandatory student fees and using portions of such fees to provide services they deem objectionable in any way coerced their religious beliefs. Plaintiffs do not allege or show the University's collecting and using the fees coerced them from holding or expressing their views against abortion. They do not allege or show the University coerced them to advocate a position on abortion contrary to their religious views. They do not allege or show the University forced them to join any pro-abortion organization. They do not allege or show the University forced them to use the student health service programs, receive pregnancy counseling, have abortions, perform abortions or endorse abortions. Plaintiffs make no showing the University denied them enrollment because of their religious beliefs opposing abortion; instead, the University cancelled their enrollment because they did not pay mandatory student fees. Further, plaintiffs do not show the University's collecting mandatory student fees and using portions of such fees to provide services plaintiffs deem objectionable violates their First Amendment right to practice their religion. Plaintiffs' answers to the University's interrogatories assert their religious beliefs require them not to pay those portions of student fees the University uses to provide abortion-related services; they allege in their third amended complaint the University should exempt them from paying such portions of the fees. However, the right to free exercise of religion does not justify refusal to pay taxes: "nothing in the Constitution prohibits the Congress from levying a tax upon all persons, regardless of religion, for support of the general government. The fact that some persons may object, on religious grounds, to some of the things that the government does is not a basis upon which they can claim a constitutional right not to pay a part of the tax." Similarly, the First Amendment does not prohibit the University from requiring all students, regardless of religion, to pay fees for general student support services; the fact plaintiffs may object on religious grounds to some of the services the University provides is not a basis upon which plaintiffs can claim a constitutional right not to pay a part of the fees.

Under Article IX, section 9(a) of the California Constitution, the Regents have full powers to organize and govern the University. Plaintiffs concede the University has power to assess mandatory student fees generally as a condition of enrollment but assert they should not pay the portion of such fees representing the portion of the University's services they deem objectionable. However, under Article IX, section 9(f) of the California Constitution, the Regents are "vested with the legal title and the management and disposition" of University property. Once the University collects mandatory student fees, such funds become University property. The Regents, not plaintiffs, have exclusive authority to decide how to spend University funds; allowing plaintiffs to withhold portions of mandatory student fees would effectively impair such authority. In asking the superior court to specify issues as without substantial controversy, the University submitted declarations asserting providing comprehensive student health services is a proper University function serving the education-related purpose of minimizing the detrimental effects of students' health conditions on their academic performance. Plaintiffs offered no evidence to the contrary. Given such evidence, the superior court properly found "as a matter of law the Regents have the legal authority to assess mandatory student fees and utilize those fees for the benefit of its student population, even when those fees are not used directly to support the cost of specific education programs or services." In light of this finding, the allegations of the third amended complaint and plaintiffs' interrogatory answers, the superior court properly found the University's "use of mandatory student fees to provide student health services, which include abortion services and pregnancy-related counseling, does not infringe plaintiffs' free exercise of religious rights protected under the First Amendment to the United States Constitution."

Plaintiffs contend the judgment should be reversed because the University violated 42 U.S.C. section 300a-7(d). While this statute did not exist when the complaint was filed, it would apply to discrimination occurring after its effective date, September 29, 1979. The statute was raised in plaintiffs' superior court brief and pursued here. We shall consider the issue.

The statute was intended to protect persons opposing abortion on religious or moral grounds. However, the statute is limited in scope.

The statute prohibits denying admission or discriminating against any applicant for study because of the applicant's reluctance to "assist or in any way participate in the performance of abortions or sterilizations." The crucial words are "performance of abortions or sterilizations." The proscription applies only when the applicant must participate in acts related to the actual performance of abortions or sterilizations. Indirect or remote connections with abortions or sterilizations are not within the terms of the statute. We believe Congress did not intend to prevent the University from requiring its students to participate in a comprehensive health insurance program which includes cost benefits for persons desiring abortions or sterilizations. A health program containing benefits for procedures which others might choose does not mean the applicant is involved in the "performance" of those procedures.

The judgment is affirmed.

Galda v. Rutgers
772 F.2d 1060 (1985)

WEIS, Circuit Judge.

The plaintiff students contend that a mandatory fee imposed on them by a university for the specific purpose of supporting an independent organization whose aims they oppose is an infringement on their First Amendment rights. The district court held that the funding procedure was permissible because the outside organization contributed to the education of its student members. We conclude that because the educational component is only incidental to the organization's ideological objectives, the educational benefits are not adequate to overcome the constitutional objections. Consequently, we will vacate the district court's judgment and direct that collection of the mandatory fee be enjoined.

In an earlier appeal in this litigation we reversed a summary judgment in favor of defendants. On remand, the district court held a two week bench trial. After filing extensive findings of fact and conclusions of law, the court entered judgment for the defendants.

This suit for injunctive relief was brought under 42 U.S.C. § 1983 by current and former students at Rutgers Camden College of Arts and Sciences, a unit of Rutgers, the State University of New Jersey. Plaintiffs asserted that their First Amendment rights were violated by the University's imposition of a mandatory, refundable fee for the specific purpose of supporting the New Jersey Public Interest Research Group (PIRG).

The New Jersey PIRG has members at a number of other college campuses in New Jersey. It is an independent, non-profit corporation, controlled by a board of student representatives at the state-wide level. It maintains a paid staff consisting of a director, one part-time and six full-time employees.

PIRG is politically nonpartisan, but participates in state legislative matters and actively engages in research, lobbying and advocacy for social change. Its staff and student members have lobbied for a federal student assistance act, the Equal Rights Amendment, a nuclear weapons freeze, and the enactment of the Pine Lands Preservation Act. PIRG also opposed the construction of the Tocks Island Dam on the Delaware River.

In addition, members of the organization drafted proposed legislation mandating a study of energy production in New Jersey and testified in opposition to an increase in utility rates before an administrative agency. PIRG members have researched and published documents on a number of other consumer and environmental issues. The organization also provides internships for students who receive academic credit for the work they perform.

Because PIRG is an organization independent of the University, it is ineligible to receive money from the general student activities fee. It has, however, qualified for financial support under the Rutgers "neutral funding policy." To do so PIRG was required to submit a "concept plan" to the University outlining the organization's educational value. Following administration approval, the next step was to participate in an election where PIRG was required to obtain the vote of at least 25% plus one of the student body on a particular campus. The neutral funding policy also requires that the votes must represent a majority of the ballots actually cast.

PIRG's concept plan has received the University's approval in each of the three-year periods in which it was submitted, and it has been successful in securing the necessary affirmative votes in most of the student referenda.

As a result of PIRG's qualification under the Rutgers' funding procedures, each student enrolled at a particular campus must pay a mandatory fee of $3.50 to PIRG. In a twelve year period, the organization received more than $800,000 in this fashion and currently receives over $100,000 per year from the mandatory assessment. A student who does not wish to support PIRG is required to request a refund, which is generally returned several months later.

In the first proceeding, without exploring the plaintiffs' contentions, the district court granted summary judgment for defendants, holding that since the fee was refundable, there had been no constitutional infringement. On appeal from that ruling, we held that the refund provision was not adequate and on that record even a temporary exaction of the PIRG fee from plaintiffs could not be justified. We remanded because there was a genuine issue of material fact on whether assessment of the fee infringed the plaintiffs' constitutional rights.

At trial PIRG's organizational structure was developed in some detail. In essence, the court found that the group's policies were made by the state board of student directors, which also had the authority to hire and discharge the salaried executive director. In addition to an executive director, PIRG hires a paid staff that manages the day-to-day operations of the organization.

Plaintiffs produced three expert witnesses who testified that PIRG operates as a political action group and its purpose is to "pursue change in the political process." One expert opined that PIRG "consistently represents and adheres to a liberal ideology and views American society as covertly oppressive." Another of the plaintiffs' experts conceded that the "could not quantify PIRG's political and non-political activities" and that many of its projects were non-ideological.

Defendants produced four experts, including the President of Rutgers, who testified to what they believed were the educational benefits to the students participating in PIRG. These included "learning to advocate and thoroughly learning their adversary's position in order to rebut them," forcing students to "publicly campaign and promote an organization," providing an opportunity "to investigate, research, write, and advocate their positions before governmental agencies," providing "students with leadership opportunities," and "teaching students to function as citizens."

A number of faculty members as well as current and former students testified about their participation in PIRG activities. The students noted that their experiences included public speaking, learning the use of a law library, and developing interest in a public service, governmental career which some followed after graduation. The faculty members talked favorably about the opportunity for, and close supervision of, internships.

One faculty member spoke especially about the "stream walking" phase of the environmental project for clean streams. In this activity, participants walked along water courses in search of illegal polluters who were then reported to the Environmental Protection Agency. The court found this to be a major activity. Faculty members testified that the stream walking program was valuable because of the students' opportunity to learn about the environment and governmental process.

The defense witnesses did not dispute that PIRG took positions on political as well as ideological issues and worked actively to advance them. An examination of PIRG's financial documents by a certified public account as well as an independent review by the district court established that it was not possible to "numerically quantify 'political' and 'educational' components of PIRG."

The district court found that Rutgers "has made a carefully reasoned decision that PIRG is a valuable educational adjunct to the more traditional classroom activities." PIRG had "engaged in projects that can be objectively characterized as both 'educational' and 'political.' Because of the fact that some activities ostensibly political are also inherently educational, it is impossible to neatly quantify PIRG's activities into these simplistic categories."

In passing on the experts' testimony, the court stated that to the extent the parties differ "about the nature of PIRG and its contributions to the university community, the court finds there exists some difference of opinion in the academic community." But, the court concluded, "PIRG has a very substantial educational component, and its presence at Rutgers significantly enhances the educational opportunities available for students at that institution." The court therefore found that "plaintiffs have failed to overcome the presumptive validity of the University's judgment and have thus failed to make out a prima facie case that their constitutional rights have been violated." Accordingly, judgment was entered for defendants.

Preliminarily, it is helpful to briefly review the nature of the constitutional right at stake. Plaintiffs assert that they may not be compelled to contribute to an organization which espouses and promotes ideological causes they oppose. The contours of this right are still in the developmental stage. Frequently cited as the seminal case is *Board of Education v. Barnette*, where the Court recognized an individual's right to refuse on religious grounds to participate in the traditional flag salute. The Court described the right as freedom from "a compulsion of students to declare a belief."

The *Barnette* rationale was extended to the forced payment of "union shop" or "agency shop" fees, portions of which were used for purposes not germane to collective bargaining activities.

In *Abood*, the Court found "meritorious" the argument that employees "may constitutionally prevent the Union's spending a part of their required service fees to contribute to political candidates and to express political views unrelated to its duties as exclusive bargaining representatives."

* * *

In short, what *Abood* holds objectionable is the "compulsory subsidization of ideological activity" by those who object to it. Commentators have debated the basis supporting this right. It may be a broad concept of "individual freedom of mind," or a ban on coerced affirmation of distasteful views, or a right not to be subjected to a limitation on freedom of conscience, or perhaps a right to maintain silence in the face of a governmental pronouncement. We resist the temptation to expound on these absorbing theories because whatever the source or underlying rationale, the Supreme Court's precedents establish to our satisfaction that plaintiffs have presented a valid constitutional interest for consideration.

Although the jurisprudential underpinnings for the constitutional right are complex, the issue here is a narrow one and may perhaps best be explained by eliminating what is not at stake. This case does not address the problem presented by a state university's allocation of a mandatory non-refundable student activity fee. We are not concerned here with the question whether an organization with PIRG's philosophic outlook may be funded through the general activities fund as are other campus organizations representing diverse views.

In short, we do not enter the controversy on whether a given campus organization may participate in the general activities fee despite the objections of some who are required to contribute to that fund.

And, although we are reluctant to belabor the obvious, it apparently must be made absolutely clear that in no way does this case present the issue of whether PIRG or any other organization may be restricted in the expression of its views on campus or elsewhere. Nor does this case in any way question PIRG's right to finance its operations by voluntary contributions from those who agree with its objectives.

As *Galda I* emphasized, there is a distinction between PIRG and student organizations that are funded through the student activity fee. We noted that the student activity fee is used to subsidize a variety of student groups, and therefore that assessment can be "perceived broadly as providing a 'forum' for a diverse range of opinion." In contrast, "PIRG does not provide a forum for the expression of differing views" but is a "group." Moreover, the PIRG fee is segregated from other charges listed on the students' bills and supports only that "group."

The question here is limited to whether a state university may compel students to pay a specified sum, albeit refundable, to an independent outside organization that espouses and actively promotes a political and ideological philosophy which they oppose and do not wish to support.

In *Galda I*, we noted that "considerable deference" should be accorded the university's judgment that the organization was "an appropriate participant in the total university forum." In order to "overcome the presumptive validity of the university's judgment and to make out a prima facie case that exaction of the fee conflicts with the mandate of First Amendment," plaintiffs must establish that PIRG "functions essentially as a political action group with only an incidental educational component." In addition, we stated that the university is free to "counter the plaintiff's showing or to otherwise demonstrate a compelling state interest by establishing the importance of the challenged group's contribution to the university forum."

In speaking of a prima facie case, *Galda I* referred to the "exaction of the fee," referring to the mandatory assessment of the payment to PIRG. The elements of compulsion and payment to an outside organization with which the plaintiffs disagree are the significant factors that trigger the inquiry in this case. Whether the compulsion occurred through unilateral decision of university officials or only after the vote of a majority of the students does not diminish the infringement on the plaintiffs' right to withhold their support to an organization whose aims they find repugnant.

At trial plaintiffs presented evidence that PIRG, in at least some, if not a majority, of its activities is an entity devoted to political and ideological objectives. Defendants did not dispute that fact, but instead focused on the educational benefits associated with participation in the PIRG program. As noted earlier, these include observing governmental agencies in action, public speaking, research, leadership development, and other factors which may ordinarily be obtained from the "hands-on" training common to any large organization and particularly one that has some contacts with government.

The educational advantages described in the testimony do not differ from those that might be obtained by working with, or for, an independent organization such as the Republican or Democratic Party, or a clearly religious group which has undertaken an active and vigorous proselytizing program. As we have said, "it could not be seriously contended that student fees could be funneled to such a group." Yet, the educational component that the University presents here as justification would be precisely the same were the recipient group one that clearly could not receive affirmative state support.

PIRG's efforts are primarily devoted to changing conditions outside the University. For example, its interest in environmental and energy concerns focuses on state-wide or national issues. Similar in scope is its commitment to enactment of an equal rights amendment, reform of tenants rights, and a nuclear weapons freeze. While such matters may affect the general public, those causes are not particularly germane to students of the University qua students.

Although such issues as educational loans and consumer protection reports on businesses near campus may come closer to direct student interests, they do not minimize the group's activities of a broader scope. In this respect, PIRG's programs and purposes are quite unlike a service organization, such as a bar association, which in the course of promoting the specialized interests of the group may at times take positions opposed by various members.

Although the training PIRG members may receive is considerable, there can be no doubt that it is secondary to PIRG's stated objectives of a frankly ideological bent. To that extent the educational benefits are only "incidental"—arising from or accompanying the principal objectives—and subordinate to the group's function of promoting its political and ideological aims.

It is not quantity that determines whether the benefit is incidental in circumstances such as these. That assessment is made by examining the nature of the group and its primary function. *Galda I* made that point in noting that in the procedural posture of the case, the court had to assume "at least one of PIRG's functions is purely political, and non-educational in nature." The district court in reciting PIRG's history stated, "Under the students' proposal, PIRG was to be a non-partisan, non-profit corporation which would research and lobby for social change." Those functions have continued to be PIRG's raison d'etre as a review of its programs and activities confirms.

The experience gained from lobbying activities as well as advocacy, leadership, public speaking, and research might just as readily be obtained by membership in the University sponsored Legislative Action Committee, by participation in internships in various governmental agencies also available to Rutgers students, and through the work of other campus organizations.

Moreover, it must be recognized that because the plaintiffs are opposed to PIRG's ideological aims, the educational benefits flowing from PIRG's activities will not be available to them. Their beliefs exclude them from access to the programs that offer the educational opportunities. Despite that bar to participation, plaintiffs must nevertheless pay to support the organization.

We conclude that defendants did not overcome the caution we raised in our first opinion—the educational component cannot obscure the underlying substance of the plaintiffs' complaint that they were compelled to finance a political entity whose function is to attain certain fixed ideological objectives.

* * *

Generally, when an activity fund comes into existence, all student groups on campus are free to compete for a fair share. That is not the situation here where the mandated contribution is earmarked for only one organization, an organization which has no obligation to use any part of the fund for the benefit of a group which pursues a different philosophy.

The University appears to argue that the neutral funding policy supplies the requisite opportunity for equal access, but it is no answer to say that opponents may utilize the "neutral funding" policy to support a vehicle of their own. For example, the opponents may be small in number, as is apparently true here, and unable to attract the necessary student support. No extended discussion is required to explain the basic concept that the First Amendment protects the views of a minority as well as those of the majority.

Moreover, even if the opponents succeed in achieving mandatory contributions for their own organization, they are not relieved from the obligation to pay a fee to a group with which they disagree. For example, if the university compelled a student to make separate contributions to both the Democratic and Republican National Committee, the evil is not undone; it is compounded. Adherents to each party would be forced to pay a fee to the other political group, a clearly unconstitutional exaction.

The objection to funding an outside entity through the "neutral funding" procedure is that the result achieved is not neutral and does not achieve equal access. The process offers an opportunity for a majoritarian group to compel support from minorities in circumstances where no compelling state interests justifies the limitation on First Amendment rights.

The situation is quite different than that which would be presented if the outside organization, for example, were a well equipped museum or symphony society where the university had no comparable facilities to enhance its teaching capacity. Nothing in the record here demonstrates that in its ordinary operations the University is unable to offer students the opportunity to learn about environmental or consumer concerns or similar matters advocated by PIRG.

The University has thus failed to show any compelling state interest that would justify overriding the plaintiffs' First Amendment rights.

It follows, therefore, that the district court erred in concluding that plaintiffs had failed to make out a prima facie case. They presented credible evidence that PIRG was an outside independent, ideologically-oriented organization whose activities they opposed but were nevertheless compelled to support directly through a mandatory fee. Those facts were not disputed, and by presenting that evidence plaintiffs established a prima facie case.

The University relied on the deference to be given its judgment as to PIRG"s educational value. But as has been discussed, that judgment was not supported by evidence of an educational component other than that incidental to, and inherent in, the ideological activities. Moreover, the district court did not make any findings to demonstrate a compelling state interest that would justify utilization of PIRG as a vehicle for the incidental educational benefits in preference to a campus, or another outside organization, which did not require the compelled support of plaintiffs.

Defendants did not produce any evidence that would allow an advance proration of the mandatory fee, and we have previously found the rebate procedures unsatisfactory. Hence, the exaction of a compulsory fee payable to PIRG cannot continue. We, of course, make no judgment as to a voluntary contribution program.

Accordingly, the judgment of the district court will be vacated and the case will be remanded to the district court for the entry of an order enjoining the assessment of the mandatory fee payable to PIRG.

Student Government v. Trustees, University of Massachusetts

676 F. Supp 384 (D. Mas. 1987)

TAURO, District Judge.

This action for declaratory and injunctive relief was brought by three student groups and three individual students at the University of Massachusetts at Amherst against the Board of Trustees of the University and four University officials. The complaint alleges that the defendants conspired and acted to violate plaintiffs' First Amendment rights to speak and associate freely, and to petition the government with grievances. Presently at issue is defendants' motion for summary judgment.

I.

The University of Massachusetts ("UMass") is a part of the Massachusetts system of public institutions of higher education, established by the Massachusetts General Laws. The board of regents of higher education governs the higher education system. Each institution within the system, including UMass, has its own board of trustees. The UMass board of trustees (the "Board") manages the University's two campuses, in Boston and Amherst.

In 1974, the Board established the Legal Services Offices (the "LSO") as an administrative unit of the University. The LSO consisted of several attorneys and various administrative and clerical staff. It provided legal advice, representation, referral services and educational services to UMass students.

As originally created, the LSO did not have authority to represent students in litigation against UMass or in criminal matters. On October 1, 1975, however, the Board authorized the LSO "to represent students in criminal matters and to engage in litigation against the University on their behalf" for the duration of the then current fiscal year. Nine months later, on June 2, 1976, the Board authorized the LSO to continue indefinitely the extended representation authorized in 1975. The LSO's authority to represent students in criminal matters and in suits against UMass, as granted in the 1976 vote, continued uninterrupted for more than ten years.

During the past two years, the Board has twice acted to remove the added authority it had granted the LSO in 1975 and 1976. The Board's efforts in this direction sparked the instant litigation. On August 6, 1986, the Board rescinded the 1975–76 grants of authority to represent students in criminal matters and in suits against UMass. One year later, on August 31, 1987, the Board rescinded "all prior votes of the Board of Trustees concerning the Legal Services Office," effectively eliminating the LSO altogether.

At the same time the Board abolished the LSO in August of 1987, it created a new entity, the Legal Services Center (the "LSC"). The LSC was granted no authority to represent students in any litigation or to negotiate with the University. The LSC is authorized only to provide students with primary legal advice and legal education.

Plaintiffs filed this action on November 21, 1986, after the Board first rescinded the LSO's authority to represent students in criminal matters and in suits against UMass, but before the Board's subsequent decision to abolish the LSO and to establish the LSC. Defendants, in the motion under consideration, move for summary judgment on four grounds, one of which asserts that plaintiffs have suffered no constitutional injury.

II.

In deciding defendants' summary judgment motion, the court must view the evidence presented by the parties in the light most favorable to the non-movant, the plaintiffs here. The resolution of defendants' summary judgment motion hinges on whether plaintiffs suffered a constitutional injury. This inquiry raises two interrelated issues: 1) whether the LSO services constituted a public forum, and 2) whether the Board's decisions with respect to the LSO were content-based.

III.
A.

A state government may not restrict access to a public forum without the requisite governmental interest. The degree of government interest the state must demonstrate depends on the type of forum it is regulating. There are three types of fora: traditional public; limited public; and nonpublic. The more a vehicle for expression resembles a public forum, the greater an interest the government must prove to justify restricted access. Conversely, the state may deny access to a nonpublic forum, even if it presents only a reasonable justification, as long as there are alternative means of communication open to the excluded individual.

In all but traditional public fora, the state may eliminate the forum altogether and, by so doing, legitimately restrict the exercise of speech. In other words, merely because the state provides a limited public forum, it does not have a continuing obligation to keep it open.

Here, the threshold inquiry concerns the kind of forum LSO legal services constituted. "A facility is a public forum only if it is designed to provide a general public right of access to its use, or if such public access has historically existed and is not incompatible with the facility's primary activity." Factors to consider in evaluating whether a facility or forum is public are the government's policy and practice with respect to access to the facility, the nature of the essential purpose of the facility, and its normal use or capability of accommodating expressive activity.

The services LSO provides to UMass students do not constitute a public forum. Traditionally, public fora include sidewalks, parks, and other places where the public, typically or historically, has had access and an expectation that their freedom to speak will be tolerated. The LSO did not meet that test. It was never open to the general public. Rather, LSO services were available only to UMass students who paid a mandatory activities fee.

The LSO, however, may be considered what has become known as a "limited public forum." A non-traditional, or limited, public forum is a government facility, not typically used for expressive activities, but which the government has opened to the public for expressive activities. Here, the University opened the LSO's services to UMass students for expressive activity. Although LSO services were not available to the general public, they were uniformly offered to UMass students.

The student's access to the LSO, however, was restricted in several ways. The LSO's resources were limited. There were, at most, four lawyers working for the LSO at any one time. Presumably, some students would have been denied legal aid, if a large number simultaneously requested LSO services. Further, these services were a benefit that UMass conferred on its students for an undetermined period of time. The University had no obligation to provide them in the first place, and it made no commitment to provide them permanently.

The LSO services, therefore, may fairly be deemed not to have been a public forum in the classic sense.

B.

The key question defendants' summary judgment motion presents is whether the University's actions are a content-based restriction of the students' exercise of First Amendment activities. A regulation is content-based if it "is in fact an attempt to suppress content because of its message." A content-based regulation infringes upon First Amendment rights because it singles out and prohibits a certain message. A content-neutral regulation of access to a limited public or nonpublic forum, on the other hand, does not violate the First Amendment.

Here, the Board's termination of LSO services was content-neutral and, therefore, constitutional. The Board's 1986 decision was to rescind LSO's authority to represent students in criminal matters *and* in suits against UMass. This was not content-based action. To the contrary, it was a non-selective withdrawal of an entire gratuitous grant of authority made in 1975–76. In 1975–76 the Board gave the LSO authority to represent students in two ways—in criminal cases and in suits against the University. In 1986, the Board ended that authority with respect to both types of suits. The

Board did not merely eliminate suits against the University. The 1975–76 grants of such authority were not permanent. To hold that the University's subsequent attempt to withdraw such authority was a First Amendment violation would be tantamount to concluding that the Board could never change its mind after granting students a service or a privilege.

Plaintiffs question defendants' motive for eliminating the LSO's authority to represent students. But, in the absence of a constitutional injury, defendants' motive is irrelevant. In other words, if the Board's action is content-neutral, even an improper motive will not render it unconstitutional.

Because it was content-neutral, the Board's action would be constitutionally sound no matter what kind of forum the LSO services provided. As discussed, UMass' grant of LSO services to its students created at most a non-traditional and at least a nonpublic forum. In order to justify limitation of access to a nontraditional forum, UMass must only demonstrate that its action was content-neutral or, if it was content-based, that it was supported by a compelling state interest and narrowly tailored to achieve that interest. To limit access to a nonpublic forum, the state must give a reasonable justification and there must exist alternative means of communicating the speakers' message.

Finally, the students who have lost access to the LSO services have alternative means for litigating their disputes with the University and for obtaining representation in criminal matters. The fact that some of the students are indigent or that alternative services may not be as readily available as LSO services is not a matter of constitutional significance.

Conclusion

Although the LSO provided a vehicle through which UMass students expressed themselves, it was not a traditional public forum and the University had the right to regulate access to its services and, indeed, eliminate the forum entirely. Here, the rescission of both services, granted together, was content neutral, and did not violate the UMass students' First Amendment rights. Having failed to allege a First Amendment injury, the plaintiffs claims must fall. The defendants' motion for summary judgment is, therefore, granted.

Swope v. Lubbers

560 F. Supp. 1328 (1983)

HILLMAN, District Judge.

Presently before the court are plaintiffs' requests for declaratory and injunctive relief pursuant to Fed.R.Civ.P. 65. Plaintiffs allege that the rights secured them by the First Amendment, and their Fourteenth Amendment rights to due process of law have been violated, and accordingly bring suit under 42 U.S.C. § 1983. Jurisdiction is alleged under 28 U.S.C. §§ 1331 and 1343(3) and (4).

Plaintiffs are students at Grand Valley State College ["Grand Valley"], a publicly-funded state college, and members of the Student Senate of the College. The defendants are, besides the College, members of Grand Valley's "Board of Control," Arend Lubbers, the President of the College, and Linda Johnson, Dean of Students.

The dispute arises out of the proposed showing of an "X"-rated film on the Grand Valley campus located near Grand Rapids. Each semester, at registration, Grand Valley students pay a "general service fee" of $15.00. This money is commingled with other college funds. Each year, the Grand Valley Student Senate is allocated $60,000 to be spent for extra-curricular student activities, such as the showing of motion pictures. A "Programming Committee" is formed by Student Senate members, and in the fall of 1982 it conducted a survey among Grand Valley students to assess interest in activities the Programming Committee could bring to campus. In the survey, ten categories of movies were listed (western, science fiction, etc.). The top three in order were "comedy," which received 179 votes; "adventure," 128 votes and "X-rated," 108 votes.

Typically, in the fall, a proposed schedule of films is presented by the Student Senate to the administration. Some time before a particular film is scheduled to be shown, a student on behalf of the Student Senate would write to Ms. Johnson or one of her assistants and request that funds be issued for the activity in question. Ms. Johnson or a staff member would then direct the college's Purchasing Department to issue a check to the vendor of the particular activity. The purchase order typically indicated that the money was spent on request of the Student Senate. If a film had been ordered, it was delivered to Ms. Johnson's office. Prior to February of 1983, no official guidelines had been adopted to guide defendant Johnson on what films she could or could not order.

In the fall of 1982, the Student Senate responded to the student interest reflected in the survey. Twenty-five films were selected. The schedule included only one X-rated film entitled "Inserts."[2] "Inserts" is a United Artists production starring Richard Dreyfus. Set in the 1930s, the film is about the crisis in the life of a man who had been a famous director of silent motion pictures. With the onset of "talkies" in the 1930s, the demand for silent films quickly evaporated. The film portrays how the director turned to the making of "pornographic" movies. The film was rated "X" on the scale of "suggested guidelines" promulgated by the Motion Picture Association of America. Plaintiffs were subsequently told by defendant Johnson, and one of her administrative assistants, that funds would not be transferred to allow the ordering of "Inserts."

The College does not have a system in effect that ensures prompt judicial determination of the constitutional status of films requested for Student Senate activities.

During the ensuing months, the issue of whether or not Grand Valley would allocate $250.00 for the rental of "Inserts" was much debated between plaintiffs and defendants. Plaintiffs repeatedly requested that defendants put their views about "Inserts" in writing, and sought the transfer of funds for "Inserts" again on or about February 14, 1983. The transfer request was again denied. In late February, the Grand Valley Board of Control passed a resolution tacitly addressing the showing of "Inserts." The Board resolved that, while the College would not "ban" the showing of "X"-rated films on campus, "no institutional funds of this College shall be used by student organizations for the acquisition of X-rated films. . . . The Administration is directed

---

2. Among the other films requested at that time were "Excalibur" (rated "PG"), "Dragonslayer" (also rated "PG"), "Some Kind of Hero" ("R" rating), "The Corpse Grinders" ("R"), "Star Wars" ("PG"), and the "Three Stooges Film Festival" ("G").

to review and authorize the expenditure of institutional funds in accordance with this policy."

Plaintiffs state that April 22 is the last possible date on which "Inserts" may be shown this school year. In order to obtain the film in time for the April 22 screening, the rental order must be placed by April 8th. To meet this deadline, plaintiffs filed suit on March 28th, requesting that defendants be enjoined from "refusing to allow" the transfer of funds sufficient to order "Inserts," and from otherwise interfering with the ordering or showing of the film.

* * *

Defendants argue that this is only a "funding" case, and that, as such, it involves no First Amendment rights. The sole issue, in defendants' view, is whether the Student Senate has the authority to require Grand Valley administrators to disburse funds when the administration has elected not to.

Plaintiffs characterize the dispute very differently. At issue here, they claim, is whether the First and Fourteenth Amendment rights of Grand Valley students should continue to be violated by College administrators. They argue that the practice of selectively disbursing funds set aside for extracurricular student entertainment constitutes a prior restraint that does not pass constitutional muster.

In support of the argument that this is a "funding" case, defendants would analogize the instant dispute to the so-called abortion cases: *Maher v. Roe, Harris v. McRae,* and *Poelker v. Doe.* In each case, plaintiffs unsuccessfully contested whether a state entity could, in effect, refuse to fund plaintiffs' decisions to abort a pregnancy. Defendants stress that the right to have an abortion is constitutionally guaranteed after *Roe v. Wade.* Here, they argue, the College has made a decision similar to that made by the government authorities in *Roe, Harris,* and *Poelker: e.g.,* a decision against funding an activity determined by the authorities to be against the best interests of the institution and those affiliated with it.

If in fact the instant case is a "funding" case like *Roe* and *Poelker,* the conduct of the defendants would meet constitutional requirements if it is "rationally" based. In *Harris* and *Maher,* the Supreme Court held that the governmental decision against funding abortions would be invalidated only if it rested on grounds "wholly irrelevant" to the achievement of a "legitimate" governmental objective.

Defendants advance several reasons to establish a rational basis for their decision not to fund the showing of "Inserts." Initially, they argue that if they do not fund the rental of "X"-rated films such as "Inserts," they will better fulfill their responsibilities of maintaining the "quality" of campus activities. This is because defendants have concluded that movies with such a rating, as a group, generally do not meet their standards of the "quality" of activity they want promoted on the Grand Valley campus. Additionally, they note that using the Motion Picture Rating of a film as the criterion for funding is "rational" because it serves the administration's legitimate interest of saving time and effort over funding decisions, and it also benefits the students because the funding decision is not based on the subjective determination of a campus official.

Whether the defendants' decision to withhold funds from "X"-rated films is "rationally" based is not an issue here. This is because I find that the cases relied upon by defendants are inapposite. True, funds are at issue in this dispute, but that does not make this a "funding" case. To regard this dispute as a "funding" case would entail ignoring a large body of precedential case law erected to safeguard the First Amendment rights of persons such as these plaintiffs.

A fundamental tenet of constitutional analysis is "ranking" of constitutional rights. Over 20 years ago one scholar explained this ranking of rights as follows:

> "Freedom of expression is so vital in its relationship to the objectives of the Constitution that inevitably it must stand in a preferred position. In looking toward the fulfillment of that objective, there are a variety of [doctrinal] devices, to be employed separately or in combination, which enable the courts to express the constitutionally mandated preference for freedom of speech and thought."

Defendants would ignore the settled view that constitutional rights are ranked in a hierarchy, and that differently-ranked rights are protected by rules derived from wholly separate doctrines. The "funding" cases concern the "lower-valued" rights originally said to derive from the "penumbra" of rights expressly guaranteed by the Constitution. In the view of the Supreme Court, because the rights implicated in abortion funding cases have a relatively low constitutional status, they may be regulated by rules that meet the "lower" standard of being only "rationally" based.

First Amendment rights, however, have long been regarded as among the most precious. As one court stated, "[i]t needs no citation to suggest that first amendment liberties have been considered among the most important guaranteed to citizens in the Bill of Rights."

As a correlative of that "preferred" status, governmental conduct regulating the exercise of First Amendment rights is constitutionally sound only if it passes "strict scrutiny." As the Supreme Court recently stated, "First Amendment rights are entitled to special constitutional solicitude. Our cases have required *the most exacting scrutiny* in cases in which a State undertakes to regulate speech."

It is my conclusion that this case does in fact involve First Amendment rights. Films convey ideas, and the right to receive the thoughts of others is a right protected by the First Amendment. Here, by the withholding of funds defendants have effectively ensured that a movie of which they disapprove will not be seen by the students of Grand Valley. The device of stopping funds has kept the film off campus since the fall of 1982 to this day. The label may be "funding," but the demonstrated effect is censorship. This conclusion is buttressed by comparing this case to factually similar cases.

In *Joyner v. Whiting*, for example, the United States Court of Appeals for the Fourth Circuit prohibited the President of North Carolina Central University from withdrawing all funds from the student-run newspaper. At the time of the lawsuit, NCCU was principally a black institution. The university president cut the funding for a student paper after the paper ran articles "questioning" the increasing number of white students on campus. The newspaper editor and the president of the university student association brought suit for alleged violation of their First and Fourteenth Amendment rights. As in the case at bar, the university did not ban the student publication, and made no objection to its being distributed on the campus. It simply objected to being asked to fund what it believed to be offensive and repugnant material.

The Fourth Circuit Court of Appeals rejected the "funding only" argument advanced by the university, saying:

"Fortunately, we travel through well charted waters to determine whether the permanent denial of financial support to the newspaper because of its editorial policy abridged the freedom of the press. The First Amendment is fully applicable to the states... and precedent establishes 'that state colleges and universities are not enclaves immune from [its] sweep.' A college acting 'as the instrumentality of the State, may not restrict speech... simply because it finds the views expressed by any group to be abhorrent.'... It may well be that a college need not establish a campus newspaper, or, if a paper has been established, the college may permanently discontinue publication for reasons wholly unrelated to the First Amendment. But if a college has a student newspaper, its publication cannot be suppressed because college officials dislike its editorial comment.... This rule is but a simple extension of the precept that freedom of expression may not be infringed by denying a privilege....

The principles reaffirmed in *Healy* have been extensively applied to strike down every form of censorship of student publications at state-supported institutions. Censorship of constitutionally protected expression cannot be imposed by suspending the editors, suppressing circulation, requiring imprimatur of controversial articles, excising repugnant material, withdrawing financial support, or asserting any other form of censorial oversight based on the institution's power of the purse."

First Amendment principles apply even though the instant defendants have not totally banned the showing of "Inserts" on the Grand Valley campus. *Joyner* did not treat an absolute ban of the expression of segregationist views from the NCCU campus, but only the termination of funds for the student-run paper that had expressed such views. Similarly, in *Widmar v. Vincent, supra,* the defendant university sought to keep a religiously-oriented student group from using campus facilities for the group's meetings. The group was not barred from expressing its views elsewhere on the campus, and no sanctions were aimed at the members. The defendants in *Widmar* decided not to "subsidize" the religious group by allowing it the free use of facilities granted other student groups. Even though the restraint placed on the *Widmar* plaintiffs was not a total ban, the Supreme Court held that the restriction violated the First Amendment rights of the religious group members. Similarly, the cut of funding for the student newspaper at issue in *Joyner* was not a total ban. The paper in fact continued to appear for a time after the university stopped funding it. The "partial" ban effected in *Joyner* was nonetheless deemed to violate the First Amendment. As the bar of funds in the instant case constitutes a similar "partial" ban, it too must be tested under the First Amendment.

* * *

Defendants have conceded that their procedure does not satisfy the prior restraint requirements of *Bantam Books* or *Southeastern Promotion, Ltd. v. Conrad*. It is obvious that defendants have not undertaken judicial proceedings to test the constitutional status of "Inserts," or that the denial of funds has constituted only a brief ban on the showing of the film. Nor is there any system followed by the college that ensures a prompt, final, judicial resolution of the question here at issue. In fact, there is no system at all, and judicial consideration of the "merits" of "Inserts" hinges still on the initiative of persons other than defendants. As defendants' treatment of "Inserts" does not satisfy *Bantam Books'* or *Southeastern Promotions'* requirements, only one other argument could possibly save their conduct from being deemed an illegal prior restraint.

Since the controversy arose, defendants have passed a "Resolution" that flatly prohibits the College from funding the showing of all "X"-rated movies on campus. If the "X" rating was a short-hand label for judicially-defined pornography, then defendants' content-based discrimination against funding such films could be deemed lawful. This argument must fail, however, since it is well-established that the Motion Picture ratings may not be used as a standard for a determination of constitutional status.

* * *

The last factor to consider is whether the public interest will be advanced by granting the requested relief. I find that it will, principally because the relief here requested is to safeguard the rights traditionally valued so highly by our society.

In sum, plaintiffs have fulfilled the requirements of injunctive relief by showing that they will probably succeed with their substantive claim of violation of their First Amendment rights; that the impending harm is irreparable in nature; that the harm they will suffer absent injunctive relief is greater than that defendants will bear when it is granted; and that the public interest will be helped, not hurt, by granting a preliminary injunction in the case at bar. Consequently, an Order will issue directing the defendants to allocate the $250.00 before the passage of the April 8th deadline on the ordering of "Inserts."

CONCLUSION

We are reminded that originally freedom to speak was deemed a gift from heaven and the Founding Fathers talked about it as a "natural" right of man. This, of course, was in the era of town meetings. A century later, however, Justices Holmes and Brandeis gave the concept a new connotation —the right to hear. "For only by the free flow of ideas does society become enriched. Only by the back and forth of controversy do we gain that capacity for critical analysis which tends to correct errors."

While I find that defendants must be directed forthwith to allocate $250 for the ordering of the movie, "Inserts," by the Grand Valley Student Senate, it is appropriate to note certain issues that are not before the court. At issue here was the constitutional validity of defendants' decision to block or impede the exercise of First Amendment activity, on the basis of its content, without any reference to the standards governing prior restraints. Whether the film "Inserts" is pornographic, within the meaning of *Miller v. California,* was not an issue in this case. In fact, as far as the court is aware, the movie has never been seen by the students seeking the funds nor by any college officials who have denied those funds. I have reached my conclusion about the system of regulation, not about the constitutional status of a particular movie affected by that system. Whether "Inserts" could or should be banned under the *Miller* standard has neither been raised nor litigated; consequently, that determination, should it be raised, awaits another day.

The Student Press and Distribution on Campus

Notwithstanding the First Amendment protection afforded student-edited newspapers, institutions continue to exert significant control over the student press. A

1987 study of student newspapers found widespread censorship and substantial increases in control. "University Efforts to Censor Newspapers Are on the Increase, Student Editors Say," *Chronicle of Higher Education,* 22 April 1987, 35–37. In a review of student press cases, T. D. Buckley has noted, "ordinary first amendment analysis is inadequate in most student press disputes.... The reason for the conceptual difficulties is that the student press is a form of expression that is paid for by the state, while the first amendment's role historically has been to protect the citizen against the state; the courts have tried to decide the student press cases without taking the fact of state subsidization into full account." "Student Publications, The First Amendment, and State Speech," *Cleveland State Law Review,* 34 (1985–86), 267–309.

According to Buckley, the student press should "be recognized as a form of 'state speech,' which enjoys constitutional protection, but which as a form of state action is also subject to special constitutionally mandated constraints." He characterizes student press issues as "the clash between student editors and school administrators ... [and] as an intra-governmental freedom of expression dispute in which one branch, the [subsidized] student publication, is in conflict with another branch, the school administration.... The state speech approach thus makes the nature of the state enterprise claiming first amendment protection an important issue, and asks what kind of government component should get first amendment protection." The cases in this chapter pose these issues in terms of students as publishers and as distributors (*Papish* and *Texas Review Society*), newspaper fees and retaliation (*Stanley*), and censorship of high school newspapers (*Hazelwood*).

Papish v. Board of Curators of the University of Missouri
410 U.S. 667 (1973)

PER CURIAM.

Petitioner, a graduate student in the University of Missouri School of Journalism, was expelled for distributing on campus a newspaper "containing forms of indecent speech" in violation of a bylaw of the Board of Curators. The newspaper, the Free Press Underground, had been sold on this state university campus for more than four years pursuant to an authorization obtained from the University Business Office. The particular newspaper issue in question was found to be unacceptable for two reasons. First, on the front cover the publishers had reproduced a political carton previously printed in another newspaper depicting policemen raping the Statue of Liberty and the Goddess of Justice. The caption under the cartoon read: "... With Liberty and Justice for All." Secondly, the issue contained an article entitled "M-----f----- Acquitted," which discussed the trial and acquittal on an assault charge of a New York City youth who was a member of an organization known as "Up Against the Wall, M-----f-----." [sic]

Following a hearing, the Student Conduct Committee found that petitioner had violated Par. B. of Art. V of the General Standards of Student Conduct which requires students "to observe generally accepted standards of conduct" and specifically prohibits "indecent conduct or speech." Her expulsion, after affirmance first by the Chancellor of the University and then by its Board of Curators, was made effective in the middle of the spring semester. Although she was then permitted to remain on campus until the end of the semester, she was not given credit for the one course in which she made a passing grade.

After exhausting her administrative review alternatives within the University, petitioner brought an action for declaratory and injunctive relief pursuant to 42 U. S. C. § 1983 in the United States District Court for the Western District of Missouri. She claimed that her expulsion was improperly premised on activities protected by the First Amendment. The District Court denied relief and the Court of Appeals affirmed, one judge dissenting. Rehearing *en banc* was denied by an equally divided vote of all the judges in the Eighth Circuit.

The District Court's opinion rests, in part, on the conclusion that the banned issue of the newspaper was obscene. The Court of Appeals found it unnecessary to decide that question. Instead, assuming that the newspaper was not obscene and that its distribution in the community at large would be protected by the First Amendment, the court held that on a university campus "freedom of expression" could properly be "subordinated to other interests such as, for example, the conventions of decency in the use and display of language and pictures." The court concluded that "[t]he Constitution does not compel the University ... [to allow] such publications as the one in litigation to be publicly sold or distributed on its open campus."

This case was decided several days before we handed down *Healy v. James,* in which, while recognizing a state university's undoubted prerogative to enforce reasonable rules governing student conduct, we reaffirmed that "state colleges and universities are not enclaves immune from the sweep of the First Amendment." We think *Healy* makes it clear that the mere dissemination of ideas—no matter how offensive to good taste—on a state university campus may not be shut off in the name alone of "conventions of decency." Other recent precedents of this Court make it equally clear that neither the political cartoon nor the headline story involved in this case can be labeled as constitutionally obscene or otherwise unprotected. There is language in the opinions below which suggests that the University's action here could be viewed as an exercise of its legitimate authority to enforce reasonable regulations as to the time, place, and manner of speech and its dissemination. While we have repeatedly approved such regulatory authority, the facts set forth in the opinions below show clearly that petitioner was expelled because of the disapproved *content* of the newspaper rather than the time, place, or manner of its distribution.

Since the First Amendment leaves no room for the operation of a dual standard in the academic community with respect to the content of speech, and because the state University's action here cannot be justified as a nondiscriminatory application of reasonable rules governing conduct, the judgments of the courts below must be reversed. Accordingly the petition for a writ of certiorari is granted, the case is remanded to the District Court, and that court is instructed to order the University to restore to petitioner any course credits she earned for the semester in question and, unless she is barred from reinstatement for valid academic reasons, to reinstate her as a student in the graduate program.

Reversed and remanded.

Texas Review Society v. Cunningham

659 F. Supp. 1239 (W.D. Tex. 1987)

NOWLIN, District Judge.

The above-styled case came on for trial before the Court on December 10, 1986. The Court, having considered the evidence and argument presented at the trial, the post-trial briefs submitted by the parties, as well as all of the pleadings on file in this case, enters the following findings of fact and conclusions of law.

I. INTRODUCTION

Plaintiffs are the publishers of a student newspaper at The University of Texas at Austin (UTA). They have brought suit against the President and Board of Regents of UTA, in their official capacities. The Plaintiffs seek a permanent injunction preventing the Defendants from enforcing a university rule that prohibits the Plaintiffs from personally distributing their newspaper on campus. The suit centers around one small portion of the UTA campus: an area known as the West Mall. Plaintiffs originally brought suit under both the First and Fourteenth Amendments of the U.S. Constitution (and parallel provisions of the Texas Constitution), arguing both that (1) the rule at issue is not a reasonable time, place and manner restriction, and (2) that UTA treats the Texas Review differently than it treats the Daily Texan, a competing student newspaper. At trial, the Plaintiffs abandoned the latter claim, and therefore this suit concerns only First Amendment issues (as well as issues under certain parallel provisions of the Texas Constitution). Thus, the sole question presented by this case is whether the First Amendment of the U.S. Constitution or Article 1, §§ 8 or 27 of the Texas Constitution prohibits UTA from enacting a rule disallowing "solicitation" on the West Mall of the UT campus.

The Court has jurisdiction over this case pursuant to 28 U.S.C. § 1331, as the case arises under the Constitution of the United States. The case was tried to the Court, as no party demanded a jury.

II. FINDINGS OF FACT

A. The following facts are not in genuine dispute or are established by the pleadings or by stipulations or admissions of counsel:

1. The Texas Review Society is a registered student organization as that term is defined in the Institutional Rules on Student Services and Activities of the University of Texas at Austin, Texas.

2. UTA is a public educational institution organized under the laws of the State of Texas and is a part of the University of Texas System.

3. The Regents of the University of Texas are the duly appointed officers who govern the University of Texas System.

4. The Texas Review Society has a properly authorized organization table located on the West Mall of the University campus. The table is a location from which the Texas Review Society recruits new members and where organization members engage in debate and dialogue with other students.

5. The most popular distribution location (except during registration) for all student organizations at UTA is the West Mall of the UTA campus.

6. The West Mall is an area on the UTA campus bounded on the west by Guadalupe Street, on the north by Texas Union and the Academic Center, on the east by the

Main Building and on the south by Goldsmith Hall and Battle Hall. The West Mall is an area in which student organizations are permitted to maintain tables from which they can distribute literature and engage in dialogue with passersby. Here, students may partake of a genuine marketplace of ideas.

7. The Texas Review Society is a student organization which attempts, through its newspaper, to give expression to conservative political and social thought at the UTA campus. In its own words, the *Review* is "Texas' conservative student journal of opinion." The Texas Review is published, authored and edited by the student members of the Texas Review Society.

8. Student interactions fueled by dialogue with organization members and supported by distribution of The Texas Review at the West Mall organization table location are a source of new membership for the Texas Review Society.

B. From the evidence presented at trial, the Court makes the following additional findings of fact:

1. The Board of Regents of the University of Texas System has declared that

> The campuses of the component institution of The University of Texas System are not open for assembly and expression of free speech as are the public streets, sidewalks and parks. The responsibility of the Board of Regents to operate and maintain an effective and efficient system of institutions of higher education requires that the time, place, and manner of the exercise of the right of assembly and free speech on the grounds and in the buildings and facilities of the various component institutions be regulated.

Pursuant to this decision, the Regents have enacted a rule prohibiting "solicitation" on campus. That rule defines "solicitation" as

> the sale or offer for sale of any property or service, whether for immediate or future delivery; the receipt of or request for any gift or contribution; and the request that a vote be cast for or against a candidate, issue, or proposition appearing on the ballot at any election held pursuant to state or federal law.

The rule goes on to state that certain activities are not solicitation. Among those is:

> The sale or offer for sale of any newspaper, magazine, or other publications by means of a vending machine in an area designated in advance by the chief administrative officer or his delegate for the conduct of such activity.

The rule does not prohibit a student organization from endorsing a candidate for political office, or from giving out information about a candidate.

2. Pursuant to these rules, the administration of UTA has enacted very similar polices regarding the UTA campus. The UTA rules define solicitation identically to the Regents' Rules, contain the same exception for newspapers set out above, and the same policies regarding political candidates. Based upon these rules, UTA officials have told the Texas Review Society that on campus, and specifically on the West Mall, its members may not personally hand out copies of the Texas Review which contain paid advertisements.

3. On the West Mall, distribution of periodicals or other literature containing advertising which solicits business for enterprises not affiliated with the University is

limited to two areas: 1) the sidewalk beside Guadalupe Street bordering the mall on the west; and, 2) a space in the center of the south end of the Mall, between Goldsmith Hall and Battle Hall, opposite the Academic Center. In these areas, such literature containing solicitation for off-campus enterprises must be distributed from unmanned racks or vending machines.

4. Since at least the time this lawsuit was filed, the Review has contained advertisements. The ads range from solicitations for subscriptions for other conservative journals to ads that simply solicit patronage of a product (*e.g.*, Cody's Nightclub and Coors Beer). The Review usually fills two pages of a twelve-page issue with ads.

5. It has been the Review Society's practice to distribute their newspaper on the West Mall by personally handing out copies of the Review to passersby. The Society does not charge for the paper. During the pendency of this case, the Society has continued to distribute the Review on the West Mall in this manner.

6. The University has interpreted its Rules to allow members of the Texas Review Society to have personal copies of its newspaper at its West Mall organization table. This copy may be shown to other students; but, the University's interpretation of the Rules will not permit the free-of-charge distribution of the Texas Review Society's newspaper from the West Mall organization table location because of the paid advertisements contained therein.

7. The Texas Review attempts to publish approximately six issues every school year. The Review has had a difficult time meeting its financial requirements. The two main sources of income to the Review are donations and advertising revenue. If the Review stopped running ads in order to comply with the solicitation rule, the decrease in income would limit the number of pages and frequency of issues the Review could afford to publish. The Review is free, and the managing editor of the Review testified that the free cost of the paper encourages some students to read the paper who might otherwise not read it.

8. Using the method of handing out the papers to students passing through the West Mall, the Review has been able to "get rid of" up to 100 issues per hour, the managing editor testified. The UTA administration has designated a rack on the West Mall from which the Review could be distributed in compliance with the solicitation rule. The rack is adjacent to a rack currently used by the Daily Texan, UTA's other student newspaper. The Plaintiffs conducted a "test" of the effect of the University's rule by complying with the rule during two-hour periods on two separate days. On both days the Plaintiffs did not distribute the papers by handing them to passersby, but rather placed them in the designated rack, and referred students who asked for a Review to the rack. On the first day, a Wednesday, the test was run from 1:30 p.m. to 3:30 p.m. During that period, six issues were picked up from the rack. On the second day, a Friday, the test was run from 1:00 p.m. to 3:00 p.m. Only two issues were taken from the rack on that day.

9. The results of Plaintiffs' tests are of dubious value, however, because they were conducted at low traffic times.

* * *

17. There are approximately 600 student organizations at UTA. A rule that allowed student organizations to freely distribute advertising on campus would significantly affect the West Mall area, and would detract from the free marketplace of ideas in that area. UTA's rule that material containing advertising be distributed from un-

manned receptacles is directly related to its desire to prevent commercial hawking on campus, and it is a reasonable means of accomplishing that goal.

18. The other student newspaper, the Daily Texan, distributes its papers on the West Mall by placing copies in the designated racks. The Texan distributes approximately 1000 copies per day from that location. The Texan has a daily circulation (Monday through Friday) in excess of 43,000 copies. Copies are distributed on campus free of charge.

III. CONCLUSIONS OF LAW

As noted at the outset of this opinion, the only issue before the Court is whether the Defendants' rule regarding solicitations as applied to the West Mall, violates the First Amendment to the United States Constitution or Article 1, §§ 8 or 27 of the Texas Constitution. There are no equal protection issues before the Court, as the Plaintiffs abandoned those claims at trial.

A. *First Amendment*

The First Amendment provides, in relevant part, that "Congress shall make no law ... abridging the freedom of speech, or of the press; or of the right of the people peaceably to assemble...." U.S. CONST. amend. I. The First Amendment is binding on the states through application of the Fourteenth Amendment. Although the First Amendment prohibits a state from abridging freedom of speech, the Amendment does not prohibit all regulation of expressive activities. Likewise, although the distribution of a newspaper is protected by the free press and speech provisions of the First Amendment, the Amendment does not prohibit all regulation of distribution. Accordingly, First Amendment rights may be regulated by limitations on the time, place, and manner of their exercise. For a time, place and manner restriction to be valid, it must be content-neutral, and must be narrowly tailored to serve a significant governmental interest, providing for ample alternative channels of communication.

The extent of the permissible regulation is dependent in part upon the place to be regulated. If the place is one that is a "public forum," then few restrictions on the use of the area will be tolerated. The University of Texas System has stated in its Regents' Rules that "the campuses of the component institutions of the University of Texas System are not open for assembly and expression of free speech as are the public streets, sidewalks and parks." Thus, the Defendants have not created a traditional public forum on the UTA campus. The testimony at trial showed, however, that UTA *has* created a public forum on the West Mall insofar as student organizations are concerned. This is consistent with the Supreme Court's conclusion in *Widmar v. Vincent*, that the "campus of a public university, at least for its students, possesses many characteristics of a public forum." Thus, although the Supreme Court

> has long recognized 'the need for affirming the comprehensive authority of the states and of school officials, consistent with constitutional safeguards, to prescribe and control conduct in the schools'..., the precedents of th[e] Court leave no room for the view that, because of the acknowledged need for order, First Amendment protections should apply with less force on college campuses than in the community at large.

In order to prevail in this case, therefore, the Defendants must show that the rule at issue is a content-neutral rule, narrowly tailored to serve a significant governmental interest, and that it leaves open ample alternative channels for communication.

Plaintiffs make much of the fact that some of the advertisements published by the Review are not "pure" commercial speech. This point is not terribly important to the outcome of this case, however. First, Plaintiffs do no deny that some of their ads *are* purely commercial, for example the "Coors" and the "Cody's" ads. These ads alone would support the University's conclusion that the Review contains advertisements which fall within the definition of solicitation. Moreover, the Plaintiffs do not deny that while some of the "less-than-commercial" ads do attempt to communicate political messages, they nevertheless solicit purchases or donations. The question presented by this case is whether or not the university may regulate the distribution of a student newspaper which contains solicitations by third parties. The fact that some of the third parties are soliciting funds for politically oriented essays rather than beer does not alter the fact that solicitation is occurring. On the other hand, the fact that some of the ads are purely commercial does not alter the standard the Court will apply here. The Defendants' rule clearly impacts the Plaintiffs' First Amendment rights to publish non-commercial speech, and whether the rule is permitted by the First Amendment must be judged by the rule set out above. Whether the ads are purely commercial or not does not affect the standard of review applied here.

There is no question in this case that the rule at issue is content-neutral. The rule evenhandedly prohibits solicitation on campus. The undisputed testimony at trial also showed that the officials of UTA have not applied the rule in this case based on the content of the Plaintiffs' paper, but rather have focused solely on the fact that the paper contains advertising. The rule has been applied with equal force to the Daily Texan, a student newspaper of opposing political views, which has been required to distribute its papers from an unmanned receptacle on the West Mall. By its terms, the rule would apply to any student organization that wished to distribute a document containing paid advertisements.

There is also little doubt that the rule is intended to serve a significant governmental interest. Supreme Court cases recognize that First Amendment rights must be viewed "in light of the special characteristics of the school environment."

* * *

The Defendants have shown that the solicitation rule is content-neutral, is narrowly tailored to serve a significant governmental interest, and leaves open ample alternative channels of communication. The rule is therefore a valid time, place and manner restriction, and does not violate the Plaintiffs' First Amendment rights to freedom of speech or freedom of the press.

The Plaintiffs also purport to make an argument that the solicitation rule violates their First Amendment right to freedom of association. The argument appears to be based upon the contention that the solicitation rule will adversely affect the Review's circulation, which in turn will decrease the number of members the Society is able to recruit. This, they argue, abridges their right to association. There is no question that the First Amendment protects the right of individuals to associate to further their political beliefs. Although the First Amendment does not make this explicit, the Supreme Court has long held that the right is implicit in the freedom of speech, assembly and petition.

The Court is of the view that Plaintiffs have simply failed to establish that the rule abridges their freedom to associate. There is no evidence that the university has denied the Plaintiffs the use of any facilities or buildings in which they may meet. Moreover, the evidence indicates that the university allows the Plaintiffs to set up a table on the West Mall from which they may recruit members and engage in discussion and debate. More importantly, the Plaintiffs' argument that they would not be able to recruit members if they could not distribute their paper hand-to-hand is based upon an assumption that their tests were accurate reflections of the impact the rule will have on distribution. The Court has already noted that Plaintiffs' test results are not entitled to much weight. Particularly as they relate to this issue, the Court finds those results of no value. Plaintiffs offered no evidence of the correlation between distribution of the paper and recruitment of members, except to say that the paper is an important tool in recruitment. Moreover, the publisher of the Review testified that the type of person who would become a member of the Review Society is also the type of person who would be interested enough in reading Plaintiffs' paper that he would walk to the designated rack to obtain a copy. Thus, the prohibition against hand-to-hand distribution should have no impact upon the recruitment of members. Because the Plaintiffs have utterly failed to carry their burden of persuasion on their claim that the university rule abridges their ability to associate, this claim too must fail.

* * *

Again, the Court is of the view that, based on the lack of Texas authority to the contrary, and the similarity of the provisions, the Courts of Texas would treat Article 1 § 27 as coextensive with the parallel provisions of the First Amendment. The Court has already found that the Plaintiffs have wholly failed to prove a denial of their right to association, and thus any claim under Article 1 § 27 must also fail.

IV. CONCLUSION

The solicitation rule created by the Regents of the University of Texas System, and adopted by UTA, is a permissible time, place and manner restriction. The rule does not therefore violate the First Amendment rights of the Plaintiffs, nor does it violate their rights under the Texas Constitution. ACCORDINGLY, the Court will enter a judgment this day that Plaintiffs take nothing on their claims against Defendants. The Court need not reach the issue of Plaintiffs' attorneys fees, as Plaintiffs have not prevailed on their claim. The parties shall bear their own costs.

———————

The University of Texas case reflects the rise of alternative, conservative student newspapers, most prominently the Dartmouth *Review*. For more information on the *Texas Review* and Dartmouth *Review*, see "View from the Right at UT," *Texas Observer*, 4 April 1986, 13–14; "Dartmouth President Blasts Conservative Campus Paper in 'Poisoning' the College's Intellectual Atmosphere," *Chronicle of Higher Education*, 6 April 1988, A27–28; "4 Conservative Students at Dartmouth Say They'll Appeal Penalties Imposed After Incident with Black Professor," *Chronicle of Higher Education*, 23 March 1988, p. A34.

The *Student Press Law Center Report* regularly reviews various legal issues concerning student newspapers. See also, R. Keiter, "Judicial Review of Student First Amendment Claims," *Missouri Law Review*, 50 (1985), 25–84; J. Okamoto, "Prior Restraint and the Public High School Student Press: The Validity of Administrative Censorship of Student Newspapers Under the Federal and California Constitutions," *Loyola of Los Angeles Law Review*, 20 (1987), 1055–1165; "Editor of Brooklyn College Paper Caught in Imbroglio Over Content," *New York Times*, 19 May 1988, p. B9.

Stanley v. McGrath
719 F.2d 279 (1983)

ARNOLD, Circuit Judge.

At the end of the 1978–79 school year, the *Minnesota Daily*, the student newspaper of the Twin Cities campuses of the University of Minnesota, published an especially controversial issue. The Board of Regents, the governing body of the University, later changed the method of funding the newspaper. In the past, a compulsory fee had been exacted from every student to support the *Daily*. The Board voted to allow students to obtain a refund of this fee. Its stated reason was solicitude for students who objected to buying a newspaper they did not want. Our study of the record, however, leaves us with the definite and firm conviction that this change in funding would not have occurred absent the public hue and cry that the *Daily*'s offensive contents provoked. Reducing the revenues available to the newspaper is therefore forbidden by the First Amendment, as made applicable to the states by the Fourteenth, and the *Daily* is entitled to an injunction restoring the former system of funding.

I.

In June 1979 the "Finals Week" edition or "Humor Issue" of the *Minnesota Daily*, styled in the format of sensationalist newspapers, contained articles, advertisements, and cartoons satirizing Christ, the Roman Catholic Church, evangelical religion, public figures, numerous social, political, and ethnic groups, social customs, popular trends, and liberal ideas. In addressing these subjects, the paper frequently used scatological language and explicit and implicit references to sexual acts. There was, for example, a blasphemous "interview" with Jesus on the Cross that would offend anyone of good taste, whether with or without religion. No contention is made, however, that the newspaper met the legal definition of obscenity.

This issue generated vehement criticism. Members of the Board of Regents and University administrators received numerous letters deploring the content of the "Humor Issue" from church leaders, members of churches, interested citizens, students, and legislators, who in many cases were responding to the complaints of constituents. On June 8, 1979, the Regents unanimously passed a resolution stating that they were "compelled to deplore the content of the June 4–9, 1979 issue of the Minnesota Daily." University President C. Peter Magrath sent this resolution to the acting president of the Board of Student Publications, stating that "the Regents will want some accounting as to what corrective action is contemplated in response to their resolution."

In another resolution passed unanimously on July 13, 1979, the Regents stated that the issue in question was "flagrantly offensive" and established an ad hoc committee "to review with the President the concerns expressed and the recommendations of the President regarding the Minnesota Daily." Among other things, the Regents directed the special committee to consider the "appropriate mechanism for circulation and financial support for the Minnesota Daily."

At a meeting of the Regents in August 1979, the ad hoc committee made its report. The committee recommended that the Regents not take any action at that time to change the funding of the paper. In support of its recommendation, committee members stated that the fees issue should be left to the normal funding procedure, under which student committees and the administration would make recommendations on which the Board would vote in May 1980. They also offered the opinion of the University attorney that changing the fees immediately following the "Humor Issue" could be viewed as punitive action in violation of the First Amendment. The committee's resolution was passed, although several Regents expressed their unhappiness with waiting until May of the next year to take action on changing the funding.

Meanwhile, both houses of the Minnesota Legislature held committee hearings regarding the "Humor Issue." The Senate Committee on Education met on June 25, 1979, and the House Education Committee, Higher Education Division met on November 14, 1979. In December, the House committee chairman wrote the chairman of the Board of Regents stating that the vast majority of the Division recommended that the "Regents allow students a means to withdraw their individual financial support from the *Daily*."

In March of 1980, the Student Services Fees Committee, composed of elected students, faculty members, and administrators, recommended by a 6–5 vote that a refund system not be instituted and in addition that the Board of Publications Fees be increased by 11.6%. In April, the President sent the Regents his recommendation in favor of a refundable fee. Following the release of this recommendation, the Twin Cities Campus Assembly voted 99–7 against changing to a refundable fee.

On May 9, 1980, the Board of Regents passed, by an 8–3 vote, a resolution that instituted a refundable fee system for a one-year trial period, allowing objecting students to obtain a refund of that part of the service fee allotted to the Board of Student Publications. The resolution also increased the Board of Student Publications fee from $1.80 to $2.00 for the 1980–81 school year. In May of 1981 and again in May of 1982, the Board voted in favor of retaining the refund system and on both occasions also raised the Board of Student Publications fee, from $2.00 to $2.12 in 1981 and from $2.12 to $2.56 in 1982.

Catherine M. Stanley, Jeffrey A. Goldberg, Michael Douglas, and Christopher Isom, former editors of the *Daily*, the *Daily* itself, and the Board of Student Publications then brought this suit against the President of the University and the Members of the Board of Regents in their individual and official capacities. They claimed, among other things, that the Regents' change of policy affected the *Daily* adversely and that it was motivated by public opposition to the contents of the "Humor Issue." After trial to the court, the complaint was dismissed. The District Court's key finding was that "[o]ne of the motivations for establishment of the refundable fee system was to respond to the concerns of those students who objected to being coerced into giving financial support to the Daily." It added that the Regents' action was "rational," and held that the First Amendment had not been violated. This appeal followed.

II.

Plaintiffs claim that the Regents' decision to institute the refundable fee system for the Board of Student Publications was in response to the content of the "Humor Issue" and hence violates the First Amendment. A public university may not constitutionally take adverse action against a student newspaper, such as withdrawing or reducing the paper's funding, because it disapproves of the content of the paper. Thus, to prevail on their First Amendment claim, the plaintiffs must show that the Regents' decision was adverse and that the decision was substantially motivated by the content of the newspaper.

The District Court emphasized at several points that the refund system, when considered in the context of the simultaneous increases in the amount of the publications fee, did not reduce the total amount of the *Daily*'s fee support. The Court reached this conclusion by comparing the amount received from student fees in the year prior to the funding change (1979–80) to the amount received in the year following the funding change (1980–81). Despite the money lost due to refunds, the amount received in 1980–81 was $15,826.22 greater than the amount received in 1979–80, because the Regents had raised the Board of Student Publications fee from $1.85 to $2.00. In addition, the amount received in 1981–82 was $14,914.57 greater than that received in 1980–81, because of a further increase in the fee.

We conclude nevertheless that the *Daily* has suffered an injury in fact. Although the total amount of fee support has risen, it has concededly risen less because of the change to refundability. The beginning point for the Regents' action was the recommendation of the Student Service Fee Committee that the fee be increased to $2.00 and that no refund system be adopted. The Regents then voted to increase the fee but to change the compulsory funding mechanism. No one testified at trial that the fee increase was intended to make up for losses that refundability would cause, nor does the Regents' resolution adopting a refund feature make any such claim.[4] The amount of money lost is beside the point. If any measurable loss has occurred, and if the motivation of those inflicting the loss is forbidden by the First Amendment, plaintiffs have a right to judicial relief.

Furthermore, apart from the economic effect of the Regents' decision, it is clear that it conveyed the impression that the *Daily* would be losing funds as a result of the fee change. One of the reasons that President Magrath offered to the Regents in support of the refund system was that the threat of losing financial support from students would promote responsible journalism. As stated in the District Court's opinion, this effect was acutely felt by the plaintiff editors, who on several occasions altered the content of the paper out of fear of further reprisals by the Regents. Since the Regents' decision as its natural result caused this chilling effect, the decision must be considered adverse to the plaintiffs.

III.

As to whether the Regents' decision was substantially motivated by the content of the "Humor Issue," the District Court found that the Regents did not intend to punish the plaintiffs or deprive them of any constitutional rights and that "[o]ne of the motivations for establishment of the refundable fee system was to respond to the concerns of those students who objected to being coerced into giving financial support to the Daily." We assume for present purposes that this is a constitutionally permissible motivation. On the other hand, it is clear that the First Amendment prohibits the Regents from taking adverse action against the *Daily* because the contents of the paper are occasionally blasphemous or vulgar.

---

4. Indeed, President Magrath's statement to the Regents clearly anticipates that the *Daily* would suffer some financial loss.

In all probability, (this is speculative, of course) the proposal will not cripple the *Daily*'s financial base, which is an important consideration if we want to preserve it as a viable student newspaper.

We have here a case of mixed motives. The Supreme Court has laid down the rule for such cases in *Mt. Healthy School Dist. v. Doyle. Doyle* was an employment case— discharge of a public employee allegedly in retaliation for the exercise of First Amendment rights—but its analytical framework is useful here. If the Board of Regents would have changed the funding mechanism simply because of students' objections, it should prevail here, even if opposition to the *Daily*'s contents was also in the Board's collective mind. But on this question of fact the Board has the burden of proof. It must show by a preponderance of the evidence that the permissible motive would have produced the adverse result, even in the absence of the impermissible motive. This allocation of the burden favors the party asserting First Amendment rights, and we think properly so. Once a plaintiff has come forward with some substantial evidence of illegal retaliation, it should be difficult for a defendant to prevail; placing the burden of proof on the defendant is the law's way of creating this difficulty.

The District Court found that one of the Board's motives was an objective we assume to be legitimate. It did not find what the Board's other motive or motives were. In this posture, we should ordinarily remand this case for further findings by the trier of fact. Here, however, we think a finding either that the Board had no improper motivation, or that its proper motivation alone would have produced the adverse action, would be clearly erroneous. Remand is therefore not necessary.

Evidence of the Regents' improper motivation was clearly brought out in the testimony. Several Regents testified that one of the reasons that they voted in favor of the resolution was that students should not be forced to support a paper which was sacrilegious and vulgar. The enormous political pressure that was brought to bear and the Regents' two resolutions which deplore the contents of the "Humor Issue" also furnish strong evidence that the Regents were reacting to the contents of the paper and to the disapproval that others expressed of those contents.

Finally, it is significant that the Regents did not move to establish a refund system at the Duluth, Morris, or Waseca campuses of the University. Testimony at trial showed that the student-funded newspapers at each of these campuses regularly published articles of a partisan nature, took stands on controversial subjects, and endorsed candidates for office on all levels, from college positions to the Presidency of the United States. If the Regents had truly been motivated by the principle that a student ought not be forced to support a newspaper that espouses views the student opposes, then one would expect that they would have taken some action in regard to the newspapers at the other campuses. Yet in 1980 when the refund system was instituted, the Regents took no such action. No motion was even made that the Board conduct a study of the feasibility of instituting the refund system at the other schools. In 1981, a motion to institute the refund system at these other schools was made and defeated.

IV.

Having found that the District Court erred in denying the plaintiff's First Amendment claim, we must now consider the defendants' argument that the Regents' decision to establish the refund system is a legislative act and hence that they are immune from § 1983 liability under the doctrine of legislative immunity. We reject this argument. The Regents do not qualify as legislators within the meaning of the legislative-immunity doctrine. Although the Regents are given the power "to enact laws for the government of the university" they are essentially administrators who oversee the operation of a state educational institution. Their rule-making powers are limited solely to the regulation of that institution. That state law may characterize their activity as "legislative" for some purposes is not controlling in the interpretation of a federal statute such as 42 U.S.C. § 1983.

There are instances in which the members of bodies other than state legislatures may have legislative immunity from suit under § 1983. The governing body of a state-supported institution of higher learning, we think, cannot qualify for such protection. Such a rule would leave such bodies too free to violate the Constitution. For example, if defendants' argument is accepted, they could adopt a rule forbidding the admission of any Baptists, and no § 1983 suit could do anything about it. The argument proves too much. "To state [the proposition]," as Mr. Chief Justice White was fond of remarking, "is to answer it."

The judgment of the District Court is reversed, and the cause is remanded for issuance of appropriate injunctive relief consistent with this opinion.

Hazelwood School District v. Kuhlmeier
108 S.Ct. 562 (1988)

Justice WHITE delivered the opinion of the Court.

This case concerns the extent to which educators may exercise editorial control over the contents of a high school newspaper produced as part of the school's journalism curriculum.

I

Petitioners are the Hazelwood School District in St. Louis County, Missouri; various school officials; Robert Eugene Reynolds, the principal of Hazelwood East High School, and Howard Emerson, a teacher in the school district. Respondents are three former Hazelwood East students who were staff members of Spectrum, the school newspaper. They contend that school officials violated their First Amendment rights by deleting two pages of articles from the May 13, 1983, issue of Spectrum.

Spectrum was written and edited by the Journalism II class at Hazelwood East. The newspaper was published every three weeks or so during the 1982–1983 school year. More than 4,500 copies of the newspaper were distributed during that year to students, school personnel, and members of the community.

The Board of Education allocated funds from its annual budget for the printing of Spectrum. These funds were supplemented by proceeds from sales of the newspaper. The printing expenses during the 1982–1983 school year totaled $4,668.50; revenue from sales was $1,166.84. The other costs associated with the newspaper—such as supplies, textbooks, and a portion of the journalism teacher's salary—were borne entirely by the Board.

The Journalism II course was taught by Robert Stergos for most of the 1982–1983 academic year. Stergos left Hazelwood East to take a job in private industry on April 29, 1983, when the May 13 edition of Spectrum was nearing completion, and petitioner Emerson took his place as newspaper adviser for the remaining weeks of the term.

The practice at Hazelwood East during the spring 1983 semester was for the journalism teacher to submit page proofs of each Spectrum issue to Principal Reynolds for his review prior to publication. On May 10, Emerson delivered the proofs of the May 13 edition to Reynolds, who objected to two of the articles scheduled to appear in that edition. One of the stories described three Hazelwood East students' experiences with pregnancy; the other discussed the impact of divorce on students at the school.

Reynolds was concerned that, although the pregnancy story used false names "to keep the identity of these girls a secret," the pregnant students still might be identifiable from the text. He also believed that the article's references to sexual activity and birth control were inappropriate for some of the younger students at the school. In addition, Reynolds was concerned that a student identified by name in the divorce story had complained that her father "wasn't spending enough time with my mom, my sister and I" prior to the divorce, "was always out of town on business or out late playing cards with the guys," and "always argued about everything" with her mother. Reynolds believed that the student's parents should have been given an opportunity to respond to these remarks or to consent to their publication. He was unaware that Emerson had deleted the student's name from the final version of the article.

Reynolds believed that there was no time to make the necessary changes in the stories before the scheduled press run and that the newspaper would not appear before the end of the school year if printing were delayed to any significant extent. He concluded that his only options under the circumstances were to publish a four-page newspaper instead of the planned six-page newspaper, eliminating the two pages on which the offending stories appeared, or to publish no newspaper at all. Accordingly, he directed Emerson to withhold from publication the two pages containing the stories on pregnancy and divorce. He informed his superiors of the decision, and they concurred.

Respondents subsequently commenced this action in the United States District Court for the Eastern District of Missouri seeking a declaration that their First Amendment rights had been violated, injunctive relief, and monetary damages. After a bench trial, the District Court denied an injunction, holding that no First Amendment violation had occurred.

The District Court concluded that school officials may impose restraints on students' speech in activities that are " 'an integral part of the school's educational function' "—including the publication of a school-sponsored newspaper by a journalism class—so long as their decision has " 'a substantial and reasonable basis.' " The court found that Principal Reynolds' concern that the pregnant students' anonymity would be lost and their privacy invaded was "legitimate and reasonable," given "the small number of pregnant students at Hazelwood East and several identifying characteristics that were disclosed in the article." The court held that Reynolds' action was also justified "to avoid the impression that [the school] endorses the sexual norms of the subjects" and to shield younger students from exposure to unsuitable material. The deletion of the article on divorce was seen by the court as a reasonable response to the invasion of privacy concerns raised by the named student's remarks. Because the article did not indicate that the student's parents had been offered an opportunity to respond to her allegations, said the court, there was cause for "serious doubt that the article complied with the rules of fairness which are standard in the field of journalism and which were covered in the textbook used in the Journalism II class." Furthermore, the court concluded that Reynolds was justified in deleting two full pages of the newspaper, instead of deleting only the pregnancy and divorce stories or requiring that those stories be modified to address his concerns, based on his "reasonable belief that he had to make an immediate decision and that there was no time to make modifications to the articles in question."

The Court of Appeals for the Eighth Circuit reversed. The court held at outset that Spectrum was not only "a part of the school adopted curriculum," but also a public forum, because the newspaper was "intended to be and operated as a conduit for student viewpoint." The court then concluded that Spectrum's status as a public forum precluded school officials from censoring its contents except when " 'necessary to avoid material and substantial interference with school work or discipline . . . or the rights of others.' "

The Court of Appeals found "no evidence in the record that the principal could have reasonably forecast that the censored articles or any materials in the censored articles would have materially disrupted classwork or given rise to substantial disorder in the school." School officials were entitled to censor the articles on the ground that they invaded the rights of others, according to the court, only if publication of the articles could have resulted in tort liability to the school. The court concluded that no tort action for libel or invasion of privacy could have been maintained against the school by the subjects of the two articles or by their families. Accordingly, the court held that school officials had violated respondents' First Amendment rights by deleting the two pages of the newspaper.

We granted certiorari, and we now reverse.

II

Students in the public schools do not "shed their constitutional rights to freedom of speech or expression at the schoolhouse gate." They cannot be punished merely for expressing their personal views on the school premises—whether "in the cafeteria, or on the playing field, or on the campus during the authorized hours," unless school authorities have reason to believe that such expression will "substantially interfere with the work of the school or impinge upon the rights of other students."

We have nonetheless recognized that the First Amendment rights of students in the public schools "are not automatically coextensive with the rights of adults in other settings," and must be "applied in light of the special characteristics of the school environment." A school need not tolerate student speech that is inconsistent with its "basic educational mission," even though the government could not censor similar speech outside the school. Accordingly, we held in *Fraser* that a student could be disciplined for having delivered a speech that was "sexually explicit" but not legally obscene at an official school assembly, because the school was entitled to "disassociate itself" from the speech in a manner that would demonstrate to others that such vulgarity is "wholly inconsistent with the 'fundamental values' of public school education." We thus recognized that "[t]he determination of what manner of speech in the classroom or in school assembly is inappropriate properly rests with the school board," rather than with the federal courts. It is in this context that respondents' First Amendment claims must be considered.

A

We deal first with the question whether Spectrum may appropriately be characterized as a forum for public expression. The public schools do not possess all of the attributes of streets, parks, and other traditional public forums that "time out of mind, have been used for purposes of assembly, communicating thoughts between citizens, and discussing public questions." Hence, school facilities may be deemed to be public forums only if school authorities have "by policy or by practice" opened those facilities "for indiscriminate use by the general public," or by some segment of the public, such as student organizations. If the facilities have instead been reserved for other intended purposes, "communicative or otherwise," then no public forum has been created, and school officials may impose reasonable restrictions on the speech of students, teachers, and other members of the school community. "The government does not create a public forum by inaction or by permitting limited discourse, but only by intentionally opening a nontraditional forum for public discourse."

The policy of school officials toward Spectrum was reflected in Hazelwood School Board Policy 348.51 and the Hazelwood East Curriculum Guide. Board Policy 348.51 provided that "[s]chool sponsored publications are developed within the adopted curriculum and its educational implications in regular classroom activities." The Hazelwood East Curriculum Guide described the Journalism II course as a "laboratory situation in which the students publish the school newspaper applying skills they have learned in Journalism I." The lessons that were to be learned from the Journalism II course, according to the Curriculum Guide, included development of journalistic skills under deadline pressure, "the legal, moral, and ethical restrictions imposed upon journalists within the school community," and "responsibility and acceptance of criticism for articles of opinion." Journalism II was taught by a faculty member during regular class hours. Students received grades and academic credit for their performance in the course.

School officials did not deviate in practice from their policy that production of Spectrum was to be part of the educational curriculum and a "regular classroom activit[y]." The District Court found that Robert Stergos, the journalism teacher during most of the 1982–1983 school year, "both had the authority to exercise and in fact exercised a great deal of control over Spectrum." For example, Stergos selected the editors of the newspaper, scheduled publication dates, decided the number of pages for each issue, assigned story ideas to class members, advised students on the development of their stories, reviewed the use of quotations, edited stories, selected and edited the letters to the editor, and dealt with the printing company. Many of these decisions were made without consultation with the Journalism II students. The District Court thus found it "clear that Mr. Stergos was the final authority with respect to almost every aspect of the production and publication of Spectrum, including its content." Moreover, after each Spectrum issue had been finally approved by Stergos or his successor, the issue still had to be reviewed by Principal Reynolds prior to publication. Respondents' assertion that they had believed that they could publish "practically anything" in Spectrum was therefore dismissed by the District Court as simply "not credible." These factual findings are amply supported by the record, and were not rejected as clearly erroneous by the Court of Appeals.

* * *

Instead, they "reserve[d] the forum for its intended purpos[e]," as a supervised learning experience for journalism students. Accordingly, school officials were entitled to regulate the contents of Spectrum in any reasonable manner. It is this standard, rather than our decision in Tinker, that governs this case.

B

The question whether the First Amendment requires a school to tolerate particular student speech—the question that we addressed in *Tinker*—is different from the question whether the First Amendment requires a school affirmatively to promote particular student speech. The former question addresses educators' ability to silence a student's personal expression that happens to occur on the school premises. The latter question concerns educators' authority over school-sponsored publications, theatrical productions, and other expressive activities that students, parents, and members of the public might reasonably perceive to bear the imprimatur of the school. These activities may fairly be characterized as part of the school curriculum, whether or not they occur in a traditional classroom setting, so long as they are supervised by faculty members and designed to impart particular knowledge or skills to student participants and audiences.

Educators are entitled to exercise greater control over this second form of student expression to assure that participants learn whatever lessons the activity is designed to teach, that readers or listeners are not exposed to material that may be inappropriate for their level of maturity, and that the views of the individual speaker are not erroneously attributed to the school. Hence, a school may in its capacity as publisher of a school newspaper or producer of a school play "disassociate itself," not only from speech that would "substantially interfere with [its] work . . . or impinge upon the rights of other students," but also from speech that is, for example, ungrammatical, poorly written, inadequately researched, biased or prejudiced, vulgar or profane, or unsuitable for immature audiences. A school must be able to set high standards for the student speech that is disseminated under its auspices—standards that may be higher than those demanded by some newspaper publishers or theatrical producers in the "real" world—and may refuse to disseminate student speech that does not meet those standards. In addition, a school must be able to take into account the emotional maturity of the intended audience in determining whether to disseminate student speech on potentially sensitive topics, which might range from the existence of Santa Claus in an elementary school setting to the particulars of teenage sexual activity in a high school setting. A school must also retain the authority to refuse to sponsor student speech that might reasonably be perceived to advocate drug or alcohol use, irresponsible sex, or conduct otherwise inconsistent with "the shared values of a civilized social order," or to associate the school with any position other than neutrality on matters of political controversy. Otherwise, the schools would be unduly constrained from fulfilling their role as "a principal instrument in awakening the child to cultural values, in preparing him for later professional training, and in helping him to adjust normally to his environment."

Accordingly, we conclude that the standard articulated in *Tinker* for determining when a school may punish student expression need not also be the standard for determining when a school may refuse to lend its name and resources to the dissemination of student expression. Instead, we hold that educators do not offend the First Amendment by exercising editorial control over the style and content of student speech in school-sponsored expressive activities so long as their actions are reasonably related to legitimate pedagogical concerns.

This standard is consistent with our oft-expressed view that the education of the Nation's youth is primarily the responsibility of parents, teachers, and state and local school officials, and not of federal judges. It is only when the decision to censor a school-sponsored publication, theatrical production, or other vehicle of student expression has no valid educational purpose that the First Amendment is so "directly and sharply implicate[d]," as to require judicial intervention to protect students' constitutional rights.

III

We also conclude that Principal Reynolds acted reasonably in requiring the deletion from the May 13 issue of Spectrum of the pregnancy article, the divorce article, and the remaining articles that were to appear on the same pages of the newspaper.

* * *

In sum, we cannot reject as unreasonable Principal Reynolds' conclusion that neither the pregnancy article nor the divorce article was suitable for publication in Spectrum. Reynolds could reasonably have concluded that the students who had written and edited these articles had not sufficiently mastered those portions of the Journalism II curriculum that pertained to the treatment of controversial issues and personal attacks, the need to protect the privacy of individuals whose most intimate concerns are to be revealed in the newspaper, and "the legal, moral, and ethical restrictions imposed upon journalists within [a] school community" that includes adolescent subjects and readers. Finally, we conclude that the principal's decision to delete two pages of Spectrum, rather than to delete only the offending articles or to require that they be modified, was reasonable under the circumstances as he understood them. Accordingly, no violation of First Amendment rights occurred.

The judgment of the Court of Appeals for the Eighth Circuit is therefore

Reversed.

Although *Hazelwood* was limited to high school newspapers, it was immediately employed by several colleges to reorganize their student newspapers (e.g, California State University at Los Angeles and Western Kentucky University) and to censor a college magazine. At San Jacinto College, a public two year institution in Texas, the Chancellor ordered a student play removed from the campus literary magazine: "It's an excellent play. Good work. But I had a real problem with the harsh language. I'm the publisher and it's sold to students and the community we serve." The one-act play had won the 1987 Excellence in Play Writing Award at the American College Theater Festival, a national competition. "San Jac Officials Pull Plug on Play," *Houston Chronicle*, 8 April 1988, Sec. 1, p. 22; "Campus Censorship Made Easy," *Los Angeles Times,* 9 April 1988, pt. 1, p. 10. For additional detail on the Hazelwood case, see "From Hazelwood to the High Court," *New York Times Magazine,* 13 September 1987, 100–105. For another 8th Circuit case concerning a high school publication, see *Bystrom v. Fridley High School,* 822 F.2d 747 (8th Cir. 1987) (distribution regulations permitting prior restraint on student papers permissible). It is not only administrators who "pull the plug." In *Mississippi Gay Alliance v. Goudelock,* a student editor refused to accept paid advertising from a gay group. The decision was held to be an acceptable editorial decision. 536 F.2d 1073 (1976).

The College as an Open Forum for Students

Free speech on campus comes in many guises, as has been evident in the cases involving religion, academic freedom, the student press, and several other issues. In this Section, the cases include dimensions of religious worship in campus facilities, solicitation in dormitories, erection of shanties on campus, sit-ins in university buildings, and heckling of speakers. This Section could treat many additional dimensions of the topic, including campus police practices, athletic and cultural event access issues, or the status of transients on campus, but the cases represent the major open forum issues that arise on modern campuses.

Two major cases that undergird the rights of free speech on campus include *Tinker v. Des Moines*, the case which held that students have the right to wear arm bands in class as protests, provided that their conduct was not disruptive ("It can hardly be argued that either student or teachers shed their constitutional rights at the schoolhouse gate") 393 U.S. 503 (1969), and *State of New Jersey v. Schmid*, 84 N.J. 535, 423 A. 2d 615 (1980), which held that the New Jersey Constitution could subject private campuses to reasonable access requirements, if the campuses held themselves out for public uses. *Schmid* appears in Chapter 2. Since *Schmid*, many campuses have enacted trespass statutes with time, place, and manner restrictions. If they are reasonably related to maintaining order, do not restrict all speech, and are applied evenhandedly, courts will find them acceptable. See *City of Parma v. Manning*, 514 N.E.2d 749 (Ohio App. 1986) (five-week advance permit requirement for campus distributing is constitutional, in light of shorter period regularly employed); *Esteban v. Central Missouri State College*, 415 F.2d 1077 (1969) (reviews reasonable administrative procedures).

Several cases have bearing upon solicitation on campus, particularly in the commercial context. The complex *American Future Systems v. Pennsylvania State University* cases held that universities may enjoin commercial solicitation in dormitories by reasonably restricting the time, place, and manner of these practices. 618 F.2d 252 (3d Cir. 1980); 688 F.2d 907 (3d Cir. 1982). However, the regulations cannot be so broadly drawn as to prevent sales demonstrations in dorm rooms if individual students invite the sales representative to their rooms. 553 F. Supp. 1268 (M.D. Pa. 1982); 568 F. Supp. 666 (M.D. Pa. 1983). See also *Brush v. Penn State University*, 414 A.2d 48 (Pa. 1980) (university can reasonably restrict canvassers attempting "to influence student opinion, [to] gain support, or [to] promote a particular cause").

The unusual situation of students residing in college housing has had interesting consequences in search and seizure cases. Students have been found to have reasonable expectations of privacy in their dorm rooms. *Piazzola v. Watkins*, 442 F.2d 284 (5th Cir. 1971) (warrantless searches unconstitutional except in narrowly-tailored situations); *State v. Pi Kappa Alpha Fraternity*, 491 N.E. 2d 1129 (Ohio, 1986) (liquor control agents who employed fictitious story to enter fraternity house did not properly search). However, in a seizure of student drugs, it has been held that a police officer has the right to accompany a suspect into his room, even if the arrest takes place outside the dormitory. *Washington v. Chrisman*, 455 U.S. 1 (1982).

Chapman v. Thomas
743 F. 2d 1056 (1984)

JAMES DICKSON PHILLIPS, Circuit Judge:

Scott Chapman, a student at North Carolina State University (NCSU), appeals from a judgment of the United States District Court for the Eastern District of North

Carolina granting the defendant's motion for summary judgment. The district court held that NCSU's policy prohibiting door-to-door solicitation in its dormitories did not unconstitutionally interfere with the exercise of Chapman's first amendment rights. Finding no error, we affirm the judgment of the district court.

I

The undisputed facts are as follows. Prior to June of 1980 the University Solicitation Policy (the Policy) imposed a total prohibition on door-to-door solicitation in university dormitories. The policy was revised in the spring of 1980 to establish a narrow exception for some student government office candidates. Under the revised policy, candidates for the student government offices of president, president of the senate, and treasurer were allowed to campaign door-to-door during a two-week period prior to the elections. The revised policy went into effect in June of 1980. This exception was removed from the policy in December of 1980 when a total ban on solicitation was reinstated. Because the student elections for the 1980 academic year were held prior to the effective date of the revised policy excepting student politicians, the challenged exception was never actually implemented.

While a student at NCSU, Chapman was a member of the Church of Christ, a fundamentalist, evangelical Christian church. In the summer of 1980, Chapman, in accordance with the tenets of his faith, sponsored a series of Bible discussions on the NCSU campus. In order to encourage attendance, Chapman went from door to door in various dormitories informing fellow students of the planned Bible discussions. After receiving complaints from several students, NCSU officials informed Chapman that his activities violated the policy prohibiting door-to-door solicitation by anyone except certain student candidates for campus offices. When Chapman refused to cease solicitation, he was threatened with expulsion and subjected to an action initiated by the NCSU judicial system. Because witnesses produced by the University failed to identify Chapman as one of the solicitors, the charges were dismissed.

Chapman commenced the present action under 42 U.S.C. § 1983 in November of 1980 claiming, in part, that the policy violated his first amendment rights of freedom of speech and religion on the grounds that it granted candidates for student government offices the right to campaign door-to-door in student dormitories while prohibiting door-to-door solicitation for religious purposes. The district court granted summary judgment for the defendants. This appeal followed.

II

In *Perry Education Association v. Perry Local Educators' Association*, the Supreme Court held that "[t]he existence of a right of access to public property and the standard by which limitations upon such a right must be evaluated differ depending on the character of the property at issue." In determining the constitutionality of state restrictions on the exercise of first amendment rights on public property, three categories of public property, each subject to a different standard, must be considered.

The first category includes traditional public forums such as streets and parks "which by long tradition or by government fiat have been devoted to assembly and debate. . . . " The state's power to restrict first amendment activities in public forums is severely limited. All communicative activity may not be prohibited. "For the state to enforce a content-based exclusion it must show that its regulation is necessary to serve a compelling state interest and that it is narrowly drawn to achieve that end."

Content-neutral time, place, and manner restrictions may be enforced if significant government interests are served, the restrictions are narrowly drawn, and ample alternative channels of communication are provided.

Public property not in the first category that is, however, opened to the public by the state as a forum for expressive activity comprises the second category. Although the state is not constitutionally required to open such facilities to the public, if it chooses to do so, the state then "is bound by the same standards as apply in a traditional public forum."

The third category consists of public property which is neither a traditional nor a designated public forum. These nonpublic forums are governed by different standards. Not only may the state enforce reasonable time, place, and manner restrictions, but "the state may [also] reserve the forum for its intended purposes, communicative or otherwise, as long as the regulation on speech is reasonable and not an effort to suppress expression merely because the public officials oppose the speaker's view." In *Perry*, the Court held that

> Implicit in the concept of nonpublic forum is the right to make distinctions in access on the basis of subject matter and speaker identity. These distinctions may be impermissible in a public forum but are inherent and inescapable in the process of limiting a nonpublic forum to activities compatible with the intended purpose of the property. The touchstone for evaluating these distinctions is whether they are reasonable in light of the purpose which the forum at issue serves. [W]hen government property is not dedicated to open communication the government may—without further justification—restrict use to those who participate in the forum's official business.

We now turn to the application of these principles to the present case.

III

The public property at issue here, residential areas of dormitories located on the campus of a state institution of higher learning, which has not by tradition or designation ever constituted a public forum for communicative purposes must be placed in the category of nonpublic forums. This being so, the standard by which the university's policy between June and December of 1980 banning door-to-door solicitation with a narrow exception for candidates for the three highest student government positions must be evaluated is one of reasonableness. The issue is whether, in light of the purpose which these residential areas serve, the distinction between religious and political solicitation is reasonable and "not an effort to suppress expression merely because [of opposition to] the [religious] speaker's view." For the reasons that follow, we conclude that the university's selective solicitation policy was reasonable, and therefore, the appellant's constitutional rights were not violated.

First off, there can be no doubt that the university had a legitimate interest in protecting students in its residential dormitories from unwanted, indiscriminate door-to-door solicitation by whoever might chose to descend uninvited upon them at whatever time and for whatever purpose. The question goes only to the selectivity of the policy adopted to further this undoubtedly legitimate general interest.

Looking to the selectivity feature, and focusing upon the ultimate distinction it made between political and religious solicitation as put in direct issue by plaintiff's challenge, we find the policy a constitutionally reasonable one. It reflected a more particularized legitimate interest of the university in promoting student participation in student government. That interest is real, not fanciful, and goes far beyond mere indulgence in another voluntary extracurricular student activity. Student government by law and custom on this state university campus has an important structural role in the state's administration of this important agency. Student government is a mandatory student organization, the only one that includes every student. The student government organization has legal authority to process student disciplinary actions and to impose sanctions, including a recommendation of expulsion, upon students. Further, the student body president, as a matter of statute, sits on the university board of trustees.

To further this legitimate interest in encouraging responsible and effective participation in student government political activity, the challenged exception was narrowly drawn both in terms of those freed up from the general ban on solicitation and in terms of the time period in which it could be invoked. Only those candidates for the three highest positions in student government, president, president of the senate, and treasurer, were covered by the exception. Door-to-door campaigns by those candidates could be engaged in for only a two-week period prior to the election.

The university's selective solicitation policy did not prohibit all solicitation by appellant within residence halls. Solicitation in the lobbies and waiting parlors of the dormitories and fraternity houses was permitted by the policy. Upon express invitation, the appellant could also carry on his activities in the individual rooms of students.

We, therefore, conclude that the selective solicitation policy was reasonable and not aimed at suppressing appellant's speech merely because of opposition to his views. The judgment of the district court is therefore affirmed.

Rosenfeld v. Ketter
820 F.2d 38 (2d Cir. 1987)

WINTER, Circuit Judge:

Alan Rosenfeld appeals from a grant of summary judgment dismissing his complaint against three officials of the State University of New York at Buffalo ("SUNYAB" or "University"). Rosenfeld's complaint sought declaratory relief and damages pursuant to 42 U.S.C. § 1983 (1982) for alleged deprivations of his due process and first amendment rights as a result of disciplinary action taken against him. We affirm.

BACKGROUND

The facts are essentially undisputed. In February 1982, Rosenfeld was a third-year law student at SUNYAB. Students had scheduled a rally for the evening of February 26 to protest the University's plan to convert the student union, known as Squire Hall, into a facility for the dental school. The students planned to remain in Squire Hall past its 2:00 a.m. closing time. Rosenfeld and other students intended to be present at the rally as "legal observers" to witness any arrests and prevent violence.

On the afternoon of February 26, Rosenfeld described his plans to Ronald Stein, assistant to University President Robert Ketter. Stein informed him that the building would be closed at 2:00 a.m. the next morning and that anyone who remained after being told to leave would be arrested pursuant to President Ketter's instructions. Stein stated that no exceptions would be made for "legal observers." Stein relayed Rosenfeld's plans to Ketter, who reiterated his instructions to arrest anyone who did not leave the building. Stein then conveyed Rosenfeld's plans and Ketter's instructions to Lee Griffin, director of public safety at SUNYAB, and Griffin's assistant, John Grela.

That evening, Rosenfeld attended the Squire Hall rally. At approximately 2:00 a.m. on February 27, Griffin announced to those in the building that they no longer had permission to remain and that they had ten minutes to leave. He further stated that those who did not leave would be arrested and that if they were students, they would also be suspended. Rosenfeld concedes that Griffin's general announcement was repeated several times and that Griffin and Grela personally told him that he too would be arrested if he remained in the building. At some point thereafter, Rosenfeld attempted "once again" (in his words) to explain to Griffin that he was present not as a participant in the rally, but only as a witness to the arrests and would voluntarily leave the building after the arrests were completed. Griffin told Rosenfeld that he would not be allowed to observe because he would be arrested if he did not leave the building.

At about 2:40 a.m., Rosenfeld, then the sole "legal observer" remaining in the building, was arrested and charged with third-degree criminal trespass. Following his arrest, he was served with a notice indicating that he had been "temporarily suspended immediately as a student," which meant that all of his "rights and privileges as a University student [w]ere suspended" and that he was "barred from participating in any University activity or entering onto or being in any property owned or operated by [SUNYAB]." The notice did not state the duration of the temporary suspension, but the attached summons did indicate that a formal hearing before the Hearing Committee for the Maintenance of Public Order was scheduled for March 20.

Rosenfeld was released from custody sometime before 4:00 a.m. on February 27. Later that day, he requested and received an informal hearing before President Ketter concerning his suspension. At the hearing, Ketter concluded that Rosenfeld might continue to disrupt the orderly operations of SUNYAB and therefore declined to remove the temporary suspension. Two days later, on March 1, Rosenfeld received a second informal hearing before Steven Sample, who had replaced Ketter as president earlier that day. Sample lifted Rosenfeld's temporary suspension on March 3.

The formal hearing, originally scheduled for March 20, was held on March 13. The Hearing Board found that Rosenfeld had violated University Rule 535.3g, which prohibits persons from refusing to leave a building after being told to do so by an authorized administrative officer. Rosenfeld was therefore placed on disciplinary probation for the remainder of the spring 1982 semester.

On July 1, 1982, Rosenfeld commenced this action pursuant to 42 U.S.C. § 1983 seeking declaratory relief and damages. On December 10, 1986, Judge Elfvin granted summary judgment against him. On appeal, Rosenfeld limits his arguments to two claims: first, that his suspension on the morning of February 27 without a predeprivation hearing violated his right to due process; and, second, that the provisions of the suspension order prohibiting him from entering SUNYAB property violated his first amendment rights. Finding these claims to be without merit, we affirm.

DISCUSSION

(1) Due Process Claim

Relying on *Goss v. Lopez*, Rosenfeld argues that he was denied due process because he was not afforded a hearing before he was suspended from February 27 to March

3. In *Goss*, the Supreme Court held that a high school student facing temporary suspension "of 10 days or less" must "be given oral or written notice of the charges against him and, if he denies them, an explanation of the evidence the authorities have and an opportunity to present his side of the story." A formal hearing is unnecessary. "In the great majority of cases the disciplinarian may informally discuss the alleged misconduct with the student minutes after it has occurred." While this requirement "add[s] little to the factfinding function where the disciplinarian himself has witnessed the conduct forming the basis for the charge[,] . . . things are not always as they seem to be, and the student will at least have the opportunity to characterize his conduct and put it in what he deems the proper context."

The conceded facts plainly reveal that Rosenfeld was afforded all of the process required by *Goss*. Rosenfeld remained in Squire Hall after being asked to leave, and there was thus no doubt as to the relevant facts. His conversation with Stein on the afternoon before the demonstration afforded him an opportunity to air his claim of immunity as a "legal observer" with a university official. Moreover, just before Rosenfeld's arrest and suspension, Griffin warned him to leave, Rosenfeld "once again" argued his claim of immunity, and he was told that it would not be accepted. These discussions afforded Rosenfeld the opportunity required by *Goss* to characterize his conduct, put it in the proper context and urge that University rules not be enforced against him. An additional or more formal hearing would have been wholly redundant.

(2) *First Amendment Claim*

Rosenfeld argues that the terms of the suspension order, which prohibited him from participating in any University activity or entering any University property, violated his first amendment rights. He contends that those restrictions deprived him of the opportunity to participate in the cultural and political activities at the University that are open to students and the general public. We find this claim to be entirely without merit.

The suspension order did not prevent Rosenfeld from participating in any political activity, speaking on any subject or assembling with any group. The order merely barred him from doing those things, or anything at all, *at the University*. Rosenfeld has not argued that this restriction was not reasonably related to the University's interests in punishing him and preventing further disruption—interests that are unrelated to the suppression of speech. The Supreme Court has held that in circumstances such as these "an incidental burden on speech is no greater than is essential, and therefore is permissible . . . , so long as the neutral regulation promotes a substantial government interest that would be achieved less effectively absent the regulation." We will not second-guess the University's view that excluding Rosenfeld from campus was the most appropriate method of promoting the University's interests in this case. Given the virtually unlimited opportunities for free expression that remained available to Rosenfeld, he simply has not stated a valid claim under the first amendment.

The decision of the district court is therefore affirmed.

University of Utah Students Against
Apartheid v. Peterson

649 F. Supp. 1200 (D. Utah 1986)

ALDON J. ANDERSON, Senior District Judge.

I. INTRODUCTION

This action involves a dispute between student groups and the University of Utah over the existence and extent of the groups' right to protest the South African apartheid system and the university's investment policy through the use of physical structures resembling shanties (hereinafter "shanties"). The university gave the students a permit to display the shanties beginning in February, 1986. In late July, 1986, however, university officials determined that the shanties would have to be removed from campus. Attempts to negotiate failed and the student groups brought this action in this court seeking a temporary restraining order and permanent injunctive relief.

After a hearing, the court issued a temporary restraining order dated August 11, 1986, prohibiting the defendants from removing or destroying the displays until a full hearing could be held on the issue of injunctive relief. A hearing on the request for injunctive relief was held on August 29, 1986, at which time the parties stipulated that the hearing would serve as a final trial on the merits pursuant to Fed.R.Civ.P. 65(a)(2). The day long trial included the examination of a number of witnesses and the introduction of documentary evidence. At the conclusion of the trial, the court ruled from the bench, granting the plaintiffs' motion for a permanent injunction with several conditions attached, and reserving the right to file a written opinion, articulating its ruling in further detail.

II. FACTS

On February 24, 1986, a student organization, University of Utah Students Against Apartheid, erected several protest displays resembling "shanties." These displays were located on a grass area a short distance from the student union building. The students allege, and the university does not dispute, that the shanties were erected to represent the oppressive conditions suffered by blacks in South Africa. The displays were initially constructed without university approval but approval was subsequently obtained in a meeting between Richard Christensen, a member of the university administration, and Connie Spencer, a member of the student protest group.

Testimony given at the trial and sworn statements provided through affidavits indicate that dialogue and interchange on apartheid and University divestiture occurred almost daily at the display site. The shanties resulted in considerable press attention, both supportive and critical of the student protest. Further evidence indicated that a lecture series on the South African situation was held near the displays and that other more spontaneous discussions occurred at the site.

From February 24 to the date of the trial, from one to three shanties existed at the display site. The university does not claim that the displays obstruct pedestrian traffic or otherwise disrupt the regular educational function of the university. Rather, the university contends that the existence of the shanties causes the university considerable expense and exposes the university to large potential liability. As support for this argument, the university points to several violent and potentially dangerous incidents resulting from the existence of the shanties. On two occasions part or all of the shanties were destroyed in nighttime attacks. On another occasion one shanty was set on fire. On a final occasion a Molotov Cocktail was thrown in the vicinity of the shanties. Although no injuries were sustained in these attacks, it forced the university to increase police protection of the shanties and increased the university's estimated potential liability. The university introduced evidence that as a result insurance through the State Risk Management Pool, a form of state government self-insurance, was cancelled with respect to any liability resulting from the existence of the shanties.

The administration allowed the shanties to remain for approximately six months before informing the students that it was considering requiring their removal. During this time President Peterson gave support to the right of the students to speak to the issue through use of the shanties. On July 14, 1986, the university's Institutional Council voted against divestiture. On July 17, 1986, President Peterson requested a meeting with the protesting students. A meeting was subsequently held on August 6, 1986, in which President Peterson informed the students that the shanties had to come down. Apparently, the parties made some attempt to negotiate. The plaintiffs stated they would provide their own insurance and security. They further offered to use only one portable shanty and display it only during daytime hours. President Peterson disputed student testimony regarding the exact content of the offers but stated that he told the students that they could display the shanties if they would make them portable and bring them on campus only on limited occasions as permitted by the administration. Upon failing to reach an agreement, the students initiated this action, alleging that the university's removal of the shanties would violate their right to freedom of speech under the first amendment.

III. DISCUSSION

A. *The Scope of the First Amendment*

The initial inquiry for the court in this case is to determine whether the shanties themselves come within the scope of the fist amendment's protection of free expression. It has long been clear that "speech" within the meaning of the first amendment's guarantee of "freedom of speech" includes more than mere verbal or written communication. Despite distinctions between some types of conduct not typically involving speech and what has been labeled "pure speech," protected speech under the first amendment can include expressive and symbolic conduct. Various forms of nonverbal expression have been extended first amendment "free speech" protection by the Supreme Court. Expressive conduct, including demonstrating, picketing, marching and conducting "sit-ins," has received first amendment protection. Other expressive conduct of a more symbolic nature, including wearing armbands, desecrating an American flag and displaying a red flag to advocate the overthrow of the government, has also received protection.

Of course, the free speech protection extended to nonverbal expression is not without limits. Chief Justice Warren, writing for the majority in *United States v. O'Brien*, said:

> We cannot accept the view that an apparently limitless variety of conduct can be labeled "speech" whenever the person engaging in the conduct intends thereby to express an idea.

Although the speech/conduct dichotomy was identified in *O'Brien*, not until *Spence v. Washington*, did the Court attempt to articulate standards which could be applied to other forms of symbolic expression or conduct. In *Spence*, a college student was prosecuted for violating a Washington statute which prohibited attaching extraneous material to a United States flag. Spence had attached a large peace symbol to a flag and then hung the flag upside down out of his apartment window. Three police officers viewed the flag from the street and arrested Spence. In reviewing the case, the Supreme Court reiterated its caution in *O'Brien* that not all conduct can be labeled speech. The Court ruled, however, that under the circumstances in *Spence*, the display of the flag was symbolic expression protected under the first amendment. In reaching this conclusion, the Court stated:

> [T]he nature of the appellant's activity, combined with the factual context and environment in which it was undertaken, lead to the conclusion that he engaged in a form of protected expression.... In many of their uses flags are a form of symbolism comprising a "primitive but effective way of communicating ideas...," and "a short cut from mind to mind."... Moreover, the context in which a symbol is used for purposes of expression is important, for the context may give meaning to the symbol. [The appellant's act] was a pointed expression of anguish by appellant about the then-current domestic and foreign affairs of his government. An intent to convey a particularized message was present, and in the surrounding circumstances the likelihood was great that the message would be understood by those who viewed it.

The Court in *Spence* focused on two aspects of a symbolic expression to determine its status as protected speech. The first factor focused on the actor: is there an intent to convey a particularized message? The second factor focused on observer understanding: is there a substantial likelihood that the message will be understood by those who view it? Application of the approach taken by the Court in *Spence* to the displays in this case makes it clear to this court that the shanties represent symbolic expression which is protected by the first amendment.

There is little doubt that the students intended to convey a particularized message through construction and display of the shanties. The photographs introduced as evidence by the plaintiffs reveal the unique nature of the displays and the clear intent by their builders to communicate a message. The structures themselves have few, if any, nonexpressive benefits. They are not like a table, booth, kiosk or other temporary structure from which protected speech can be disseminated; rather, they effectively serve as the speech itself. Further, on all outside walls of the shanties, words and drawings serve to explain the anti-apartheid/pro-divestiture message of the protesters. Although only the shanties themselves are at issue in this case, it is instructive to note that the students themselves maintained a constant vigil at the shanties to discuss the apartheid/divestiture issue and to further communicate their ideas to others. The defendants have not argued that the plaintiffs had any other purpose in displaying the shanties and the court is convinced that the shanties themselves make their creators' intention to communicate self-evident.

The second factor set forth in *Spence*, the likelihood that the message will be understood by those who observe it, is similarly satisfied in this case. Indeed, it is hard to imagine a more effective transmission of a message than that which has occurred by using the shanties to protest apartheid. Shanties, as structures, have come to symbolize the poverty, oppression and homelessness of South African blacks and have been used by student groups throughout the United States to convey this same message. Much like a flag, a cross, or the black armbands used during the Vietnam War, the shanties are now understood to represent a strong statement condemning apartheid and protesting university investment in South Africa. As the Supreme Court found in *Spence*, "in the surrounding circumstances the likelihood was great that the message would be understood by those who viewed it." Similarly, "the nature of the [plaintiffs'] activity, combined with the factual context and environment in which it was undertaken, lead to the conclusion that [they] engaged in a form of protected expression."

Other courts have applied the *Spence* test to symbolic expression and found such expression to be within the scope of the first amendment. In *Monroe v. State Court*, the Eleventh Circuit held that a woman's burning of an American flag during a public demonstration protesting the United States' involvement in Iran was "symbolic expression within the purview of the first amendment." The court found that the protester-intent and observer-understanding requirements of *Spence* were satisfied under the circumstances surrounding the flag burning.

In *United States ex rel. Radich v. Criminal Court*, the court applied *Spence* to a claim that the disfigurement of the American flag as part of several sculptures was protected speech under the first amendment. The court permitted the use of the flag in the sculptures, finding that the use was intended to be communicative and would be understood as such by visitors to the gallery where the sculptures were displayed.

In a pre-*Spence* decision, the Court of Appeals for the District of Columbia found that a three dimensional display containing eleven styrofoam tombstones commemorating those who died in Southeast Asia was entitled to some degree of first amendment protection. The court stated:

> It may be true that erection of a display is not what one would call prototypical First Amendment activity or precisely the mode of expression which the framers of the Bill of Rights envisioned. But it is a vehicle for expression of views nonetheless and, hence, entitled to a degree of First Amendment protection.

The *Spence* analysis distinguishes the shanties from other conduct or symbolism which may arguably fall outside of first amendment protection. For instance, the defendants in their trial brief compare the shanties to jogging without wearing a shirt, discussed in *DeWeese v. Town of Palm Beach*. In *DeWeese*, the plaintiff claimed that "by refusing to wear a shirt, he communicate[d] a philosophy to members of the public who observe him about health, fitness and the oneness of mind and body." Even if it is assumed that DeWeese intended to communicate a message by jogging without a shirt, it is difficult to identify his message as "particularized." Further, it is doubtful that there was a "great likelihood" that others would understand it. Male joggers are frequently seen without shirts. It is unlikely that many of them intend to convey a particularized message, nor probable that onlookers would attribute a special message to such conduct.

Other forms of expressive conduct are similarly ambiguous and courts have been reluctant to bring them within the purview of the first amendment.

* * *

The cases discussed above illustrate the differences between the shanties involved in this case and other types of symbolic expression that pose more difficult questions. The intent in erecting the shanties is clear and observer understanding indisputable.

As a result, a *Spence* analysis compels this court to hold that the shanties are symbolic expression protected under the first amendment.

B. *Validity of the Order to Remove the Displays*

Having concluded that the shanties are a form of speech, however, does not mean that any infringement on the right to display them would be unconstitutional. The first amendment does not offer absolute protection to all speech under all circumstances and in all places.

1. *Character of the University as a Public Forum*

Even protected speech is not equally permissible in all places and at all times. "Nothing in the Constitution requires the Government freely to grant access to all who wish to exercise their right to free speech on every type of government property without regard to the nature of the property or to the disruption that might be caused by the speaker's activities." In this case we are confronted with a situation where students and recognized student groups are conducting a protest on a state university campus at an outdoor location near the student union building.

*   *   *

In *Perry Educ. Ass'n v. Perry Local Educators' Ass'n*, the Supreme Court held that the existence of a right of access to public property for the exercise of free speech rights depends on the character of the property at issue. The Court identified three categories of public forums: the "quintessential" public forum, the limited public forum and the nonpublic forum. In discussing these categories, the Court explained: "A second category consists of public property which the State has opened for use by the public as a place for expressive activity." In describing this type of forum the court noted: "A public forum may be created for a limited purpose such as use by certain groups, *e.g., Widmar v. Vincent* (student groups). . . . "

In the case at hand the evidence reveals that, as to students and student groups, the university campus is at least a limited public forum. Section 2.02 of the university-enacted Student Bill of Rights states:

> Students shall have the right to freedom of speech and assembly without prior restraint or censorship, subject only to clearly stated reasonable and nondiscriminatory rules and regulations regarding time, place, and manner.

The Student Code is "officially sanctioned by the Institutional Council of the University." Testimony indicates that, in fact, the university has granted permits to student groups conducting rallies and demonstrations. The evidence before the court is sufficient to find that the university campus is available to students as a public forum.

2. *University Regulation of the Protected Expression*

The university does have authority to regulate student expression. It can "enforce regulations of the time, place, and manner of expression which are content-neutral, are narrowly tailored to serve a significant government interest, and leave open ample alternative channels of communication." As applied to symbolic expression, the Court has stated:

> Symbolic expression of this kind [sleep] may be forbidden or regulated if the conduct itself may constitutionally be regulated, if the regulation is narrowly

drawn to further a substantial governmental interest, and if the interest is un-related to the suppression of free speech.

The Court further stated that "[e]xpression, whether oral or written or symbolized by conduct, is subject to reasonable time, place, and manner restrictions." As pointed out earlier, the university itself has enacted a student code which, consistent with constitutional standards, allows it to regulate student free speech only through "clearly stated reasonable and nondiscriminatory rules and regulations regarding time, place, and manner."

The university's determination that the shanties would have to be removed was not based on the application of any specific university regulations. Rather, the university administration concluded that it would be in the best interests of the university to require their removal. This approach, however, is not appropriate as a means of limiting or prohibiting the exercise of free speech rights. Although the university can regulate free speech interests through clearly stated, narrowly tailored regulations enacted to further substantial government interests, in this case the university had not enacted such regulations. Formally drawn regulations are necessary to insure that restrictions on free speech are content-neutral. They also serve as guidelines which enable students and student groups to plan and develop their free speech activities in a way that will be effective for the students and yet acceptable to the administration.

The cases cited by the university in support of its right to order the removal of the shanties involved alleged violations of formally enacted regulations. The history of the CCNV case is particularly instructive. In the initial case, the circuit court ruled that the National Park Service had applied regulations to the expressive sleeping which did not in fact apply to the sleeping. Since the court concluded that the activity did not violate the regulation, it affirmed the district court's order allowing the protesters to sleep in Lafayette Park as part of their protest. The Park Service then formally revised its regulations to expressly proscribe sleeping. Once specific regu-lations were in place and a violation of those regulations was alleged, the court could rule on whether the regulations were a constitutionally permissible infringement on free speech rights. Ultimately, the Supreme Court held that they were a permissible restriction.

In the hearing before this court, President Peterson cited a number of reasons for requiring the removal of the shanties. "Major," and "predominant" reasons included overall cost, difficulty and expense in obtaining liability insurance, risk of physical harm, potential university liability and aesthetic concerns. However substantial these interests are, they cannot be used in their present form to circumscribe the students' speech interests. The court encourages the university to use the reasons set out above as a basis for enacting "clearly stated reasonable and nondiscriminatory rules and regulations regarding time, place and manner" which are not content related that will enable the university to protect its interests while allowing the maximum possible exercise of student expression.

The court reaffirms its earlier ruling, denying the defendants' motion for summary judgment and granting the plaintiffs' motion for an injunction. The court is aware of the further trouble which has occurred at the site since the oral order.

At the hearing it was suggested that the shanties be made portable and be removed at night. The court has broad authority to mold an equitable remedy in a fashion that will serve the interests of all involved. The Supreme Court has stated:

Moreover, in constitutional adjudication as elsewhere, equitable remedies are a special blend of what is necessary, what is fair, and what is workable. . . .

In equity, as nowhere else, courts eschew rigid absolutes and look to the practical realities and necessities inescapably involved in reconciling competing interests, notwithstanding that those interests have constitutional roots.

Exercising its equitable powers, the court further orders that pending the enactment of the university's rules and regulations the shanties be made portable and be removed at night. Testimony from the University of Utah Chief of Police and others revealed that the acts of violence all occurred at night. Further, the bulk of the alleged increase in police protection costs were incurred during night shifts. Finally, the free speech interests of the students do not appear to be furthered by nighttime display. Certainly, requiring nightly removal of the displays represents an increased burden on the students, but the burden is incidental to the free speech interest itself.

If the parties are unable to agree on other problems that arise relating to the imposition of the injunction, they may request the court's further assistance. This memorandum opinion and the accompanying injunction fully resolve the issues before the court and obviate the necessity of considering any other relief requested by the parties.

Students may pay dearly for their actions. In addition to suspension from school (the case in *Rosenfeld*), students can receive criminal sentences (3 to 6 months, in a 1987 Texas case). "Judge Metes out Harsh Sentences to Texas Anti-Apartheid Protesters." *Chronicle of Higher Education*, 2 December 1987, p. A35. Many states have enacted statutes to govern campus disruptions, such as the Texas Education Code, which provides:

Sec. 4.30 DISRUPTIVE ACTIVITIES

(a) No person or group of persons acting in concert may wilfully engage in disruptive activity or disrupt a lawful assembly on the campus or property of any private or public school or institution of higher education or public vocational and technical school or institute.

(b) For the purposes of this section, disruptive activity means:

(1) obstructing or restraining the passage of persons in an exit, entrance, or hallway of any building without the authorization of the administration of the school;

(2) seizing control of any building or portion of a building for the purpose of interfering with any administrative, educational, research, or other authorized activity;

(3) preventing or attempting to prevent by force or violence or the threat of force or violence any lawful assembly authorized by the school administration;

(4) disrupting by force or violence or the threat of force or violence a lawful assembly in progress; or

(5) obstructing or restraining the passage of any person at an exit or entrance to said campus or property or preventing or attempting to prevent by force or violence or by threats thereof the ingress or egress of any person

to or from said property or campus without the authorization of the administration of the school.

(c) For the purpose of this section, a lawful assembly is disrupted when any person in attendance is rendered incapable of participating in the assembly due to the use of force or violence or due to a reasonable fear that force or violence is likely to occur.

(d) A person who violates any provision of this section, is guilty of a misdemeanor and upon conviction is punishable by a fine not to exceed $200 or by confinement in jail for not less than 10 days nor more than 6 months, or both.

(e) Any person who is convicted the third time of violating this section shall not thereafter be eligible to attend any school, college, or university receiving funds from the State of Texas for a period of two years from such third conviction.

(f) Nothing herein shall be construed to infringe upon any right of free speech or expression guaranteed by the Constitutions of the United States or the State of Texas. V.T.C.A. Sec. 4.30 (Education Code)

In the wake of 1968 student unrest, Congress denied eligibility for student federal loans for two years to any student convicted of a crime involving force or disruption of an institution. P.L. 90–575. In addition, P.L. 90–557 enacted a provision in the Labor/HEW Appropriations Bill for FY 1969, specifying that none of the legislation's funds could be awarded to a student convicted of employing force to disrupt an institution. See also J.S. Kunen, *The Strawberry Statement: Notes of a College Revolutionary* (NY: Random House, 1969); M. Dickstein, "Columbia Recovered," *New York Times Magazine*, 15 May 1988, pp. 32–35, 64–68.

Students Against Apartheid Coalition v. O'Neil
671 F. Supp. 1105 (W.D. Va 1987)

TURK, Chief Judge.

This case comes before the court on plaintiff's Motion for Preliminary Injunction and defendants' Motion for Summary Judgment. At issue is the University of Virginia's amended Lawn Use Policy. Plaintiffs contend that defendants' enforcement of these regulations violates their first amendment rights. For the reasons set forth below, the court has determined that the amended regulations are constitutional and that defendants' motion is granted.

Several months ago, these parties were before this court presenting similar issues. In that decision, this court found the University of Virginia's Lawn Use Policy to be unconstitutional. The policy regulating plaintiffs' freedom of speech was unconnected to the University's professed esthetic interest. The policy was also unconstitutionally vague, failing to alert students of the scope of the policy. Since that time, the University amended its regulations in an attempt to address the unconstitutional areas. A revised Lawn Use Policy was promulgated by defendant Robert M. O'Neil, President of the University of Virginia, on May 25, 1987. Specifically, the changes defined the term "structure" and omitted the ambiguous phrase "extended presence."

On May 28, 1987, during a scheduled meeting of the University of Virginia's Board of Visitors, the plaintiffs held a demonstration protesting apartheid in South Africa. As part of the protest, plaintiffs erected a shanty in front of the University's Rotunda. The Rotunda is part of the historic Lawn area, originally designed by Thomas Jefferson. Minutes after the shanty was built, University personnel removed the shanty pursuant to the new Lawn Use Policy. The demonstrators were not disturbed. Plaintiffs now seek to enjoin enforcement of the University's revised Lawn Use Policy.

Plaintiffs contend the revised policy is, in essence, no different from the prior unconstitutional policy and seek to bar defendants from relitigating the issue under the doctrine of collateral estoppel. This court finds that the University's revisions, although minor in appearance, substantively change the Lawn Use Policy and warrant a new constitutional analysis of the amended policy.

In their complaint, plaintiffs incorporate by reference the Stipulation of Facts agreed to by both parties in the earlier case. Defendants, in failing to object, agree to the facts stipulated in the prior suit. The only material differences are the outlined changes in the Lawn Use Policy.

The initial step in the first amendment analysis is to determine if the plaintiffs' expression in the form of a shanty, is constitutionally protected. The Supreme Court, in *Spence v. Washington*, identified two factors that determine protected symbolic expression or conduct. The first factor, whether a party intended his symbolic expression to convey a particularized message, is not disputed by these parties. In the Stipulation of Facts, the parties state that shanties are "symbolic and evocative lifesize representations, for illustrative, educative, and persuasive purposes, of the dwellings of black South Africans in the ghettoes of apartheid."

The second factor, whether the message will be understood by viewers, has previously been answered in the affirmative by this court.

As constitutionally protected expression, plaintiffs' speech remains subject to reasonable time, place, and manner restrictions. Such restrictions are valid provided that they are content-neutral, are narrowly tailored to serve a significant governmental interest, and leave open ample alternative channels for communication. Defendants' new Lawn Use Policy meets these constitutional requirements. Plaintiffs do not contend, nor do the facts suggest, that the challenged Lawn Use Policy is directed at the subject matter of the expression. Nor do plaintiffs argue that the defendants' policy was applied in a discriminatory manner. The court therefore concludes the Lawn Use Policy is content neutral.

As to the interest of defendants in regulating expressive conduct, this court recognized in *SAAC* that the University has a valid interest in preserving the "esthetic integrity" of its historic grounds. Regulations of speech based on esthetic concerns alone have been found constitutional.

Content neutral regulations based on a proper interest must still be narrowly tailored to focus on this interest. The degree of requisite narrowness is a legal question. The court's role is not to determine this degree, nor to substitute its judgment for that of the University. Rather, the court must determine if the new Lawn Use Policy lies within the "zone of constitutionality" prescribed by the first amendment.

The specific esthetic concern of the University is the architectural value of the Lawn area. A Lawn Use Policy which prohibits certain types of expressive conduct must exhibit a cognizant relationship between the policy and "the ends it was designed to serve."

The defendants' new Lawn Use Policy regulates only "structures." A structure is defined and confined to those physical objects which would interrupt the architectural lines of the historic area. The policy restricts structures from only a small section of the historic area, namely the south side of the Rotunda. Plaintiffs believe the "contrast" between the shanty and Rotunda is essential to their message. However, the facts do not indicate only the south side of the Rotunda will effectively communicate plaintiffs' message to the Board of Visitors. Plaintiffs are free to erect structures on the remaining three sides of the Rotunda, which are highly visible from the access roads.

Another indication of the University's efforts to tailor its policy to fit the constitutional mold is the omission of the ambiguous phrase "extended presence." A "common sense" reading of "extended" and "presence" might refer to time or the size of a student demonstration. Without this phrase, the policy focuses solely on architecture, reinforcing the nexus between the University's concern and the regulation. Thus, the new Lawn Use Policy restricting structures is narrowly tailored to achieve the University's professed esthetic interest in preserving the Lawn's architectural purity.

Because the policy is of requisite narrowness, alternate means of communication are available to plaintiffs. Structures are but one form of communication. In disallowing only "structures" as defined in the policy, defendants implicitly allow the wide range of expressive modes not listed. For example, the new policy does not prohibit demonstrations, sit-ins, marches, hand-held signs or other forms of protest. As evidence of permissible uses of the Lawn, when the University enforced its new policy, only the shanty was removed. The demonstrators were permitted to continue their protest on the Lawn. While the alternatives may not be plaintiffs' first choice of expression, "the First Amendment does not guarantee the right to communicate one's views at all times and places or in any manner that may be desired."

The court found the University's Lawn Use Policy was also unconstitutional on grounds of vagueness. The defendants revised their Lawn Use Policy to address specifically this failing. The new policy defines a structure to include "props and displays, such as coffins, crates, crosses, theater, cages, and statues; furniture, and furnishings, such as desks, tables . . . book cases, and cabinets; shelters, such as tent, boxes, shanties and other enclosures; and other similar physical structures." Anticipating questions of this definition, the new policy also defines what are not structures: "chairs, signs held by hand, bicycles, baby carriages, and baby strollers temporarily placed in, or being moved across the lawn; and wheelchairs and other devices for the handicapped." In addition, the University removed the unclear phrase "extended presence," eliminating any difficulty in interpreting its meaning. Every statute or regulation may be faulted for vagueness as any number of hypothetical interpretations may be proposed. The Lawn Use Policy must be read with common sense. Similarly, the policy must be enforced with common sense. This court finds the revised policy sufficiently clear.

The University of Virginia may regulate the symbolic speech of its students to preserve and protect the Lawn area as an architectural landmark. To be constitutionally permissible, the regulation must be reasonable in time, place and manner. The revised Lawn Use Policy lies within the constitutional boundaries of the first amendment. The new policy is content-neutral, precisely aimed at protecting the University's esthetic concern in architecture, and permits students a wide array of additional modes of communication. The new policy is also sufficiently detailed to inform students as to the types of expression restricted on the Lawn. Because the revised Lawn Use Policy does not offend constitutional protections of free speech, defendants' motion for summary judgment is granted.

Students Against Apartheid Coalition v. O'Neil
838 F.2d 735 (4th Cir. 1988)

Before WIDENER, SPROUSE and WILKINS, Circuit Judges.

PER CURIAM.

The Students Against Apartheid Coalition and the National Lawyers Guild, University of Virginia Chapter (Student Groups) appeal the entry of summary judgment in favor of University of Virginia officials in their 42 U.S.C. § 1983 action seeking injunctive relief from the enforcement of a school regulation prohibiting display of symbolic shanties on the Lawn of the Rotunda building at the University. We affirm.

The Student Groups, in an effort to convince the University Board of Visitors to change its policy of investing in South African corporations, constructed shanties on the Lawn outside the Rotunda where the Board meets. The shanties were wooden structures erected to illustrate the living conditions of black South Africans under apartheid.

In September 1986, the University enacted a Lawn use regulation prohibiting "structures" or an "extended presence" on the Lawn within 700 feet of the Rotunda. The district court invalidated this regulation on the ground that it was unconstitutionally vague and not narrowly tailored to achieve the University's interest in aesthetics.

In May 1987, the University enacted a revised regulation defining the term "structure" and deleting the ambiguous phrase "extended presence." On the present challenge to the revised regulation, the district court granted summary judgment for the University, finding that the regulation was not vague and constituted a reasonable time, place and manner restriction of the Student Groups' expression.

As noted by the district court, the validity of the University regulation depends on whether it is content neutral, narrowly tailored to meet a significant government interest and leaves open other channels of communication. The Student Groups concede that the regulation is content neutral. The interest sought to be protected by the regulation is the preservation and integrity of the Lawn, described in the regulation as "the geographical and spiritual heart of the University." It is now well established that aesthetic concerns alone constitute a permissible government interest under the *Clark* test. The revised regulation is narrowly drawn to ensure maintenance of the architectural integrity of the upper Lawn, which is part of a National Historic Landmark designed by Thomas Jefferson.

Finally, the regulation prohibits the erection of shanties only to the south of the Rotunda. The areas to the north, east and west immediately surrounding the Rotunda, along its access routes, and areas throughout the entire campus are not restricted. We agree with the analysis of the district court that the regulation meets the *Clark* test. We therefore affirm on the reasoning of the district court.

Many divestment protests and campus vigils have been prompted by the treatment of Black South Africans by the white government, particularly its racist apartheid policies. For controlling dissent on South African campuses, the government has promulgated new criteria for student misconduct. These include the Internal Security Act of 1982, and a 1987 regulation. "South Africa Issues Stiff Rules to Check Unrest on Campuses," *Chronicle of Higher Education*, 28 October 1987, pp. A1, 45.

Albert v. Carovano
824 F.2d 1333 (2d Cir. 1987)

Before OAKES and WINTER, Circuit Judges, and METZNER, District Judge.

OAKES, Circuit Judge:

On November 14, 1986, J. Martin Carovano, president of Hamilton College, a private institution in Clinton, New York, suspended a group of twelve students for engaging in a three-day sit-in of the college's administration building following their unsuccessful attempt to meet with Carovano to discuss the college's alleged insensitivity to various racial and gender issues. The suspended students filed suit in the United States District Court for the Northern District of New York against Carovano, the college, and the dean of students, Jane Jervis. The suit sought equitable relief on the basis of several causes of action, including one premised on the college's alleged failure to satisfy the Due Process clause of the Fourteenth Amendment and another on its alleged discrimination against the students. In an opinion delivered from the bench, the court denied the students' request for a preliminary injunction and dismissed their complaint, finding that their claims did not meet the "under color of" state law requirement of 42 U.S.C. § 1983.

On appeal, the students argue that their suspensions amounted to action under color of state law because the college's rules for "Maintenance of Public Order" were promulgated by the faculty in 1969 for the express purpose of complying with New York Education Law § 6450, which mandates that colleges adopt and file with the State a set of disciplinary rules that must include the possibility of suspension for breaches of public order. Under any one of several theories of color of state law, appellants argue, their claims meet the requirements of a section 1983 cause of action.

In essence, this case presents us with a veritable rerun of *Coleman v. Wagner College*, in which we held that under certain circumstances the State of New York's involvement in college discipline pursuant to section 6450 might be sufficient to allow us to classify as "state action" certain disciplinary decisions made by private colleges. The seventeen years that have passed since *Coleman* have seen significant doctrinal developments in the concepts of "state action" and "under color of state law"—not the least of which is that the concepts are not synonymous, in that while state action is action under color of law, conduct under color of law is not necessarily state action. Nevertheless, we feel that *Coleman* has retained its validity and directly governs the issues raised in this case. Accordingly, we reverse the district court's dismissal of the students' claims, and remand for further proceedings.

FACTS

The events leading up to the appellants' suspension on November 14, 1986, are disputed. According to the "declaration" of appellant Melamede, the sit-in at Buttrick Hall was spurred by what the students saw as the college's inadequate response to several racist and sexist incidents on campus the previous year. These incidents, including slurs against black women students and repeated death threats against one of the appellants, were exacerbated in the students' minds by the college's policies regarding divestment of South African holdings and the establishment of an African-American Studies program. Apparently perceiving that the college as a whole would benefit from improved dialogue on these issues, the college began the 1986–87 school year by holding an alumni symposium on discrimination on November 7, 1986, and a debate on divestment on November 10. These programs backfired, however, as a group of students felt that remarks by an alumnus at the symposium and by President Carovano at the debate merely highlighted the Hamilton administration's insensitivity to racial and gender issues.

In the two days following the debate, members of several student organizations agreed that a group of students would attempt to meet with Carovano to discuss his remarks at the debate, the possibility of another symposium on prejudice, and the African-American study program. On Wednesday, November 12, 1986, approximately fifty to sixty students and faculty went to Buttrick Hall, where Carovano has his office. They found the building essentially unoccupied because Carovano was out of town and Dean Jervis had sent the staff home early in anticipation of the demonstration. The students and faculty then congregated in the hallway of the building, where they sang songs and, at some point, decided to remain in the building until they were allowed to meet with Carovano. Despite Dean Jervis's request that they leave, the students stayed past the building's 4:30 closing time. About twenty to forty students stayed overnight in Buttrick, coming and going throughout the night. President Carovano returned to Clinton at around 9:00 p.m. and was apprised by Dean Jervis of the situation at Buttrick.

At 8:30 the next morning Dean Jervis announced to the group that pursuant to the college's rules on maintenance of public order, Buttrick had been declared off limits to students and that the college would seek a court injunction ordering them to leave. The students chose to remain. At about 1:20 p.m., the students were served with a temporary restraining order obtained by the college from the Supreme Court of New York. The students nonetheless remained in Buttrick (apparently believing that they were not in violation of the order). Dean Jervis returned and again instructed the students to leave. She stated that letters warning of disciplinary action were being sent to students and their parents. Dean Jervis also maintains that she informed the students that Carovano would meet with them, but only if they left the building. Four of the appellants, however, state that they were unaware of this possibility. Some twenty to thirty students again camped out in Buttrick overnight.

At about 11:00 a.m. on Friday Dean Jervis returned to Buttrick and read a notice stating that the students were violating the court order, that Hamilton would initiate contempt of court and possibly trespass charges against the students, and that students who did not leave immediately would be suspended. After some discussion, several students left. At 1:00 p.m., after meeting with Carovano, Jervis went again to Buttrick and informed the remaining students—the twelve appellants—that they were immediately suspended for the remainder of the academic year. Letters to this effect were sent to the students and their parents. The appellants nonetheless remained in the building until 7:00 p.m. After they left Buttrick, two professors met with Jervis and arranged for some of the students to meet with Carovano on the following Monday.

On Monday morning, November 17, Carovano revised the suspension so it would become effective on December 20, 1986, the final day of the fall semester. On that same day, by a vote of 96 to 24, with one abstention, the faculty adopted a resolution calling for the suspensions to be withdrawn in order to allow the students to be disciplined according to the procedures set out in the student handbook, discussed below. No action was taken on this resolution, but Carovano did write to each of the appellants to suggest that if there were "extraordinary circumstances" that made the suspension unjust in a particular case, the student could submit a written statement for consideration by the trustees at their December 5–6 meeting. Only one student responded, and at no time did Carovano further modify the suspensions.

In Carovano's affidavit, he states that his decision to suspend the appellants "was based solely upon the conduct of the [appellants] and the disciplinary options which were available" to him. He bases his disciplinary authority on the college's *A Guide to the Policies and Procedures of Hamilton College* (1986), which states in its discussion of student discipline that "[t]he right of the President to decide finally on any student disciplinary matter is not precluded by the provisions outlined below." The "provisions" referred to in this statement present a detailed outline of the college's "judicial system," including a description of the student-faculty Judiciary Board and the procedures by which the Board is to operate. The *Guide* expressly states that "certain minor infractions" may be adjudicated by the dean of students in an administrative proceeding; other infractions are to be "presented to the Judiciary Board for disposition."

Another section of the *Guide,* entitled "Freedom of Expression/Maintenance of Public Order at Hamilton College," sets out additional rules, regulations, and procedures governing conduct at Hamilton. This section defines "disruptions of public order" as including "physical possession of a building which denies the right of authorized persons to enter and to work in it" and "undue noise or other interference which disrupts the carrying out of an academic or noncurricular activity of the College." This section also details specific steps to be taken by the president of the college to restore order following a disruption, including the seeking of a court-ordered injunction, and states that the disciplinary procedures for students who disrupt public order "shall be those set forth under 'Student Discipline,' and may result in disciplinary action of the most severe kind, including suspension or expulsion."

As the *Guide* itself states, these provisions for "maintenance of public order" were promulgated by Hamilton "in compliance with" New York Education Law § 6450. Section 6450, which was adopted by the legislature in 1969 in response to various incidents of student unrest in New York State, requires chartered colleges to adopt rules and regulations for the maintenance of public order on campus and to file these regulations with the board of regents and the commissioner of education. Specifically, the statute states that "[t]he penalties for violations of such rules and regulations shall be clearly set forth therein and shall include provisions for . . ., in the case of a student or faculty violator his suspension, expulsion or other appropriate disciplinary action." Prior to adoption of section 6450, Hamilton's student handbook had simply stated, "Conduct becoming a gentleman is expected of Hamilton men at all times." According to the 1967 handbook, conduct in violation of this standard was subject to discipline by the Judiciary Board, with the penalty of suspension reserved for "extremely serious misconduct."

PROCEEDINGS BELOW

The twelve suspended students commenced this action on November 26, 1986, in the United States District Court for the Northern District of New York before Judge Cholakis. Their complaint, which sought only injunctive relief, stated three causes of action allegedly "aris[ing] under" the Due Process clause of the Fourteenth Amendment and 42 U.S.C. § 1983. The first cause of action alleges that Carovano's suspension of the students without a hearing falls short of due process, that Hamilton was induced by section 6450 "to adopt a more severe attitude to campus disruption and to impose harsher sanctions on unruly students," and that the students would be irreparably injured by their suspension. It notes faculty votes supporting resolutions that the failure to provide a hearing violated Hamilton's own procedures. The second cause of action charges Hamilton with failing to follow the disciplinary procedures set out in the *Guide,* a claim that the parties agree states a cause of action under state law. Finally, the third cause of action contends that the college violated the Fourteenth Amendment's Equal Protection and Due Process clauses by "selectively enforcing" Hamilton's rules against the students "because they are black, Latin or gay; supportive of the rights of blacks, Latins and gays and without old family ties to Hamilton."

The court moved quickly on the students' request for a preliminary injunction by issuing an order to show cause. After the defendants countermoved for dismissal under Fed.R.Civ.P. 12(b)(1) and 12(b)(6) and affidavits were submitted, the court heard oral argument on December 19, 1986. Sua sponte, the court scheduled an evidentiary hearing on the issue of "state action" for December 23. At this hearing the court heard testimony and reviewed exhibits submitted by both parties. In an oral opinion, the court found, first, that there would be irreparable harm to the students if an injunction did not issue and, second, that "it appears that the President may not have followed the proper procedure in suspending" the appellants. Nevertheless, the court concluded that the first and third causes of action, both of which it characterized as section 1983 claims, must be dismissed because New York did not "[intrude] into the workings of Hamilton College, or any other College within the State of New York to the extent that such activities by the President or the Dean of Students could be or would be considered State action, or action under color of State Law or authority." The court then dismissed the pendent state law claim.

The students appealed this decision on January 9, 1987, and moved for an injunction pending appeal. We granted a limited injunction to allow the students to attend classes and participate in academic activities at Hamilton pending oral argument. Upon motion by the parties, we extended this stay pending the issuance of this opinion.

* * *

Our inquiry is thus whether the action taken by Carovano and Jervis, concededly private individuals, and by Hamilton, a private college, in suspending the twelve appellants can be considered "state action" for purposes of the Fourteenth Amendment. In *Lugar,* the Court described the state action requirement as ensuring "that the conduct allegedly causing the deprivation of a federal right be fairly attributable to the State."

Turning to the first part of *Lugar's* standard, the students claim that section 6450 amounts to a state-imposed rule of conduct. They argue it was intended to be, and has been applied as, a command to colleges to adopt a particular system of regulation of conduct on campuses and other college property. We addressed this very same argument in *Coleman*. The majority in *Coleman* noted that section 6450 on its face does not require colleges to secure approval of the rules drafted and filed pursuant to the section, to proscribe specific activities as violations of public order, or to designate any penalty, though it does require college officials to provide for the sanction of ejection and, in the case of students and faculty members, for "appropriate disciplinary action," including suspension and expulsion. Even so, the *Coleman* majority remanded on the theory that while section 6450 did not appear to enact substantive rules of conduct for colleges, it may in fact have been "intended or applied as a command to the colleges of the state to adopt a new, more severe attitude toward campus disruption and to impose harsh sanctions on unruly students." Essentially, whether action taken upon the impetus of section 6450 could be considered state action was seen as a factual question. One factor going to the state action issue was said to be the "actions of the state officials with whom the rules and regulations are to be filed," for example, whether they believe themselves empowered to look into substantive inadequacies or otherwise to exert influence upon the content of the rules and regulations. Another factor was the attitude of college administrators, particularly whether they had a wide-spread belief that they were required by the statute or by state officials to adopt a particular stance toward campus demonstrators.

On the whole, we find sufficient evidence in the record at least to raise a significant factual issue as to the state's responsibility for the substantive content of the regulations adopted by Hamilton in order to comply with section 6450. The fact that there has been a considerable lapse of time since passage of section 6450 and the adoption of Hamilton's regulations is by no means dispositive; what is important is that the rule of conduct embedded in the regulations may well have been established as a result of the statute, and is looked to by beleaguered administrators for support. At the same time, we are not persuaded by the appellees' clever argument that Carovano's suspension of the students could not have been pursuant to a state-imposed rule of conduct because Carovano did not follow the rules prescribed in the *Guide*. As the appellants point out, when the college's decision to discipline students is made pursuant to a state-imposed rule of conduct, the fact that the college allegedly failed to accord the students the requisite procedural protections afterward does not make the original decision any less a product of state action.

This bring us to the second part of *Lugar*'s test for state action, the requirement that "the party charged with the deprivation [of a protected right] must be a person who may fairly be said to be a state actor." In *Lugar*, the Court recognized that a determination of when a private party can be characterized as a "state actor" under one of the various tests articulated by the Court is "necessarily [a] fact-bound inquiry." Reviewing the evidence presented here, we find that the appellants have raised sufficient factual issues as to the appellees' status as state actors to survive a motion for summary judgment.

To recapitulate, we find that the district court erred by dismissing the appellants' claims for failure to show that the appellees' conduct could be considered state action. We find that the evidence presented by the students shows that there is a genuine dispute over the material issues of whether the decision to suspend the students is "fairly attributable" to the State under *Coleman* and whether the State "substantially encouraged" the disciplinary action taken by Carovano.

The appellants next challenge as error the court's dismissal of its third cause of action alleging discriminatory and selective enforcement of Hamilton's disciplinary rules. The district court rather summarily rejected the students' argument that this cause of action stated a claim under 42 U.S.C. § 1981, and instead treated the claim as one under section 1983, which it then dismissed for lack of conduct under color of state law. Appellants now argue, and we agree, that the third cause of action contained in their complaint does state a valid section 1981 claim. Although the complaint does not specifically mention section 1981, it does state in part that "because [the students] are black, Latin or gay," the college had selectively enforced its disciplinary rules, and that "[t]his selective enforcement of the College's rules violates the Fourteenth Amendment's equal protection and due process clauses." This statement, coupled with the other facts alleged in the complaint, amounts to more than the mere "naked assertions" which we have in the past found inadequate to state a section 1981 claim. And, as we recognized in *DeMatteis v. Eastman Kodak Co.*, a white person who suffers reprisals as a result of efforts to vindicate the rights of nonwhites has standing to sue under section 1981. Accordingly, we reverse the district court's dismissal of the third cause of action and remand for fuller consideration of the claim.

In addition, having reversed the district court's dismissal of the students' first and third claims, we also reverse the dismissal of the second, pendent state-law claim and remand for further consideration of that claim.

Finally, appellants ask that this court grant their earlier motion for a preliminary injunction, basing their request on the district court's statements that it appeared that Carovano had failed to follow proper procedures and that the students would be irreparably harmed by the suspension. We decline to do so, however, and instead remand to the district court for full consideration of the propriety of a preliminary injunction here in light of this opinion and the standards set out in *Jackson Dairy, Inc. v. H.P. Hood & Sons, Inc.*

Reversed and remanded.

WINTER, Circuit Judge, dissenting:

The sweeping opinion in this case subjects to federal judicial review virtually every decision disciplining students for disruption by a private college or university in the State of New York. Additionally, the opinion creates unprecedented rights of action against colleges and universities in the circuit under Section 1981. Because I believe that: (1) even if the fourteenth amendment applies, these plaintiffs were afforded all the procedural protection that due process requires; (2) under clearly established precedent, the action of Hamilton College's administrators and Board of Trustees do not constitute "state action" and therefore do not implicate the fourteenth amendment; and (3) under clearly established precedent, the plaintiffs' complaint does not allege a claim under Section 1981, I respectfully dissent.

* * *

Albert v. Carovano
839 F.2d 871 (2d Cir. 1987)

ORDER ON PETITION FOR REHEARING

In respect to the third cause of action alleged in the complaint, we are in accord with Judge Winter that 42 U.S.C. § 1981 is directed toward racial or ethnic discrimination. We also agree that section 1981 does not cover discrimination based on sexual orientation or on relationships to college alumni or on the content of all protests. But, while not artfully pleaded, as we view the complaint insofar as it alleges discrimination against blacks or Latins or against white persons suffering reprisal as a result of efforts to vindicate the rights of nonwhites, it is sufficient. True, as our original opinion noted, the complaint must contain more than mere "naked assertions." This complaint, by virtue of reallegation in Paragraph 34 of earlier allegations of the complaint, alleges (Paragraph 7) "repeated expressions of racist... prejudice on the Hamilton College [campus], including racial slurs directed to black women students and death threats directed at one black women student" and refers to "*racism, sexism and other forms of prejudice at Hamilton*" and that certain events scheduled at the college as well as the remarks of the defendant Carovano were "insensitive and offensive to *blacks* and women" (emphasis added).It is in light of these allegations that Paragraph 35 alleges selective enforcement of the college rules on student conduct against plaintiffs because of their criticisms of *racism*, sexism, and other prejudices at Hamilton and "the Administration's indifference to and toleration of such prejudice and because they are *black, Latin* or gay; *supportive of the rights of blacks, Latins* and gays and without old family ties to Hamilton" (emphasis added). Paragraph 36 spells out why the college rules on student conduct were being selectively enforced since it alleges that the defendants failed to discipline or even admonish white students who insulted, harassed, and threatened students engaged in lawful protest against college policy on continued investment in South Africa; failed to discipline or investigate students who made derogatory racial and sexual slurs to black women students; and only reluctantly and belatedly undertook an investigation of death threats against a black women student active in protesting the college's South African policy.

It would be preferable on remand were leave to amend the complaint granted so as to focus on permissible section 1981 claims. The complaint, filed November 26, 1986, was dismissed on December 23 after receipt of exhibits, affidavits, and an evidentiary hearing in a brief oral opinion, the court simply noting that "[i]nsofar as the Court is concerned, the third claim does not plead a 1981 claim. At best, if anything it pleads a 1983 claim." Thus its holding that there was no state action ended the matter. The December 24 order dismissing the complaint, we note, did not afford plaintiffs the opportunity to replead.

State v. Brand

Ohio App., 442 N.E. 2d 805 (1981)

BLACK, Judge.

The defendant-appellant, James Brand, seeks reversal of his conviction by a jury of disturbing a lawful meeting in violation of R.C. 2917.12, alleging two assignments of error: (1) that the court erred in not granting his motions for dismissal and acquittal; and (2) that the court erred in its instructions to the jury. We find merit in the second assignment.

I

On May 16, 1980, the defendant was one of a crowd of people gathered on Fountain Square in Cincinnati for a Mental Health Association rally featuring then First Lady Rosalyn Carter among the speakers. During the course of Mrs. Carter's brief address, the defendant shouted statements supporting the Iranian revolution and condemning the Carter administration's policies toward Iran. The defendant persisted in this behavior for approximately one minute, despite three separate requests by a police officer to be quiet. The defendant was arrested and continued to "yell and scream" as he was escorted through the crowd and placed in a police cruiser. The sentence of thirty days was stayed on posting of a $1,000 bound pending disposition of this case on appeal.

II

Defendant's first assignment of error alleges that the court erred in failing to grant his motions for dismissal and acquittal because (A) R.C. 2917.12 is on its face unconstitutionally vague and overbroad, (B) the statute is unconstitutional as applied in this case and (C) the verdict was against the weight of the evidence. We disagree. We find that the statute is constitutional and that the conviction is supported by sufficient evidence.

A

It is basic principle of due process that an enactment is void on its face for vagueness if it " * * * fails to give a person of ordinary intelligence fair notice that his contemplated conduct is forbidden by the statute. * * * " We believe that the statute *sub judice* is clear and unequivocal; it gives fair notice of what is forbidden. Its plain meaning is that it prohibits any person from acting with a purpose to prevent or disrupt a lawful gathering and from succeeding in that effort by actually obstructing or interfering with its due conduct. We find no imprecision in the statutory language that would prevent a person of ordinary intellect from knowing what is and what is not proscribed.

B

The invalidation of a statute because it is facially overbroad is an exception to the traditional rule that the challenger of a statute must have standing; that is, in the one instance of a challenge against a statute for an overbroad regulation of free speech, the challenger may assert that the statute would be unconstitutional when and as applied to others. The effect of holding a statue to be facially overbroad is that enforcement is " * * * totally forbidden until and unless a limiting construction * * * so narrows it as to remove the seeming threat or deterrence to constitutionally protected expression. * * * " Under this rubric, we find R.C. 2917.12 may reasonably be limited and narrowed in its application so as to meet the constitutional requirement that legislation affecting free speech shall not be overbroad.

R.C. 2917.12 is not the Ohio legislature's first attempt to prohibit the disruption of lawful assemblies. Its predecessor was R.C. 3761.11, which was upheld against a challenge of facial overbreadth in *State v. Schwing*. Therein the Ohio Supreme Court found, first, that because the statute as written made no distinction between nondisruptive interruptions of a lawful assemblage on the one hand, or on the other hand, disruptions that block the business of the assemblage, the statute was facially overbroad. The court then proceeded to validate the statute by restricting it so that it could be applied only against constitutionally unprotected activity. The court held that the following two types of willful interferences are not constitutionally protected: " * * * those which cause a lawful assemblage to terminate in an untimely manner * * * " and " * * * those which substantially impair the conduct of the assemblage * * * ." The court limited the statute to the prohibition of those two types of willful interference.

The *Schwing* decision was rendered after the repeal of R.C. 3761.11 and after the enactment of R.C. 2917.12, which replaced it. We believe that the Supreme Court's limiting construction must apply to the new statute, thereby saving it from unconstitutional overbreadth.

C

Defendant next asserts that R.C. 2917.12 is unconstitutional as applied because it is contrary to the First and Fourteenth Amendments. We reject the assertion. The statute is designed to preserve the free speech of those conducting a lawful meeting by preventing others from disrupting it. The statute does not regulate the context of any person's speech, but it applies to his conduct and the act of speaking when the actor's intent is not to facilitate the exchange of ideas but rather to disrupt or prevent either an exchange or the legitimate expression of ideas by others.

Clearly a state legislature may regulate both conduct and speech which is antagonistic to legitimate public interests by placing reasonable restrictions on the time, place and manner of expressive activity. The interests of free people are served by legislation which balances in a reasonable way the First Amendment rights of those desiring to express opposing points of view. As construed and as applied in this case, the language *sub judice* is not unconstitutional.

D

Defendant also asserts in his first assignment of error that his conviction was against the weight of the evidence because his conduct amounted to no more than the brief heckling of a public figure that did not substantially impede the conduct of the gathering. We disagree. While the testimony was in conflict, one of the defense witnesses testified that Mrs. Carter stopped talking for as long as forty-five seconds and only resumed after the defendant was led away. We find that there was ample probative evidence from which reasonable minds could conclude that the defendant acted with the purpose to disrupt a lawful meeting and that his shouts and screams substantially obstructed the due conduct of the meeting.

The first assignment of error is overruled.

III

In his second assignment of error, the defendant raises four issues about the court's instructions to the jury. We find merit in one of his contentions.

A

He first maintains that the court erred in charging the jury that R.C. 2917.12 is constitutional, claiming that this suggested to the jury that all interrupting speech can be constitutionally prohibited. We find no merit in this argument. An instruction that the statue is constitutional does not direct a jury that any particular statement of the defendant was made with the requisite purpose to obstruct the meeting or had that desired effect.

Instructions about the validity of criminal statutes are, in general, completely unnecessary, because questions of validity are matters of law for the court to decide, not the jury. We hold, however, that the instruction about constitutionality was not prejudicial error in this case.

B

Defendant argues that the court committed prejudicial error when it defined "disrupt" as follows: "to intercept or impede progress of something." He contends that this diminished the state's burden to prove an element of the offense. The error, if any, was cured shortly thereafter when the court charged that "before you can find him guilty, you must find that he did some act which substantially interfered with the due conduct of the gathering in question." The jury was properly told that only substantial interference is a violation of the statute. The argument has no merit.

C

Defendant alleges that the court erred in failing to make available to the jury a means of viewing a television videotape of the incident that had been offered by defendant and admitted in evidence as an exhibit. In addition, defendant contends that the court unfairly commented on its evidentiary value. Just before the jury retired to deliberate, the court said:

"There's not much that you'll be able to do with that television tape. I don't know of any way you'll be able to review it, because there's no equipment to do it with. But, since it is an exhibit, we're going to send it out with you and it should be retained in the possession of the foreman until you announce your verdict in open court."

Defendant argues that the court erred by foreclosing the possibility of the jury's reviewing the tape and by denigrating its probative value. We disagree.

During the course of the trial, at defendant's initiative, the jury had been driven to a local television studio where they viewed the videotape which had been admitted as an exhibit in evidence, but the defendant failed to supply any equipment to enable the jury to view it during deliberations. That was his obligation, not the court's. We hold that the court's ruling was not erroneous.

As to the court's comment that there was not much the jury could do with the exhibit, we believe that the court was making the obvious observation that, without the proper equipment in the jury room, they could not see and hear it again. We do not believe the court intended to say that the exhibit had no probative value; nor do we believe that reasonable minds would so construe the comment.

D

Defendant contends that the court erred in its definition of the term "substantial." We agree with him. In keeping with the statutory construction from *State v. Schwing*, and as previously noted, the court properly instructed the jury that before they could find guilt, they must find that the defendant substantially interfered with the due conduct of the meeting. The court, however, defined "substantial" as follows:

" * * * a strong possibility as contrasted with a remote or insignificant one that a certain result may occur or that certain circumstances may exist."

This was derived from the definition of "substantial risk" found in R.C. 2901.01(H), the only section containing any definition that includes the adjective "substantial." The use of this definition was, we believe, erroneous because "substantial risk" looks to the future, to the prospective consequences of some present act. The statute *sub judice* prohibits conduct that has the immediate effect of substantially obstructing the due conduct of the meeting. The proscription is not against creating strong possibilities of some result in the future, but against the actual, concurrent result, *in praesenti*.

The adjective "substantial" has a number of meanings as it is generally used, but as used in the statute *sub judice*, it is a relative term designating the degree or the extent of the disruption. In this sense it means major, consequential, effective or significant; it means that the offending act is of considerable quantity or dimension, or of solid effect. Any act that brings the meeting to an early termination obviously constitutes a substantial interference, but the statute also reaches conduct that effectively impairs, interferes with or obstructs its due conduct in a major, consequential, significant or considerable manner. The statute is designed to protect the right of free speech of those conducting a lawful meeting against the conduct of others that terminates the meeting or that impedes its conduct to a degree effectively preventing the exercise of that constitutional right.

In this one respect, the second assignment of error has merit.

IV

We reverse the judgment below and remand this cause for further proceedings.

Judgment reversed and cause remanded.

In an earlier heckling case, the California Supreme Court noted that heckling was "as old as American and British politics." *In re Kay*, 83 Cal. Rptr. 686, 464 P.2d 142 (1970). In a more recent and highly publicized incident at Harvard Law School, Nicaraguan leader Adolfo Calero was attacked by a student from another institution, leading to the cancellation of the speech. "Attack at Harvard on Contra Leader Sparks Debate Over Speakers' Rights," *National Law Journal*, 26 October 1987, p. 4. For a review of cases on this issue and an analysis of the competing rights, see E. Wagner, "Heckling: A Protected Right or Disorderly Conduct," *University of Southern California Law Review*, 60 (1986), 215–237.

Widmar v. Vincent
454 U.S. 263 (1981)

Justice POWELL delivered the opinion of the court.

This case presents the question whether a state university, which makes its facilities generally available for the activities of registered student groups, may close its facilities to a registered student group desiring to use the facilities for religious worship and religious discussion.

I

It is the stated policy of the University of Missouri at Kansas City to encourage the activities of student organizations. The University officially recognizes over 100 student groups. It routinely provides University facilities for the meetings of registered organizations. Students pay an activity fee of $41 per semester (1978–1979) to help defray the costs to the University.

From 1973 until 1977 a registered religious group named Cornerstone regularly sought and received permission to conduct its meetings in University facilities. In 1977, however, the University informed the group that it could no longer meet in University buildings. The exclusion was based on a regulation, adopted by the Board of Curators in 1972, that prohibits the use of University buildings or grounds "for purposes of religious worship or religious teaching."[3]

Eleven University students, all members of Cornerstone, brought suit to challenge the regulation in the Federal District Court for the Western District of Missouri. They alleged that the University's discrimination against religious activity and discussion violated their rights to free exercise of religion, equal protection, and freedom of speech under the First and Fourteenth Amendments to the Constitution of the United States.

Upon cross-motions for summary judgment, the District Court upheld the challenged regulation. It found the regulation not only justified, but required, by the Establishment Clause of the Federal Constitution. Under *Tilton v. Richardson*, the court reasoned, the State could not provide facilities for religious use without giving prohibited support to an institution of religion. The District Court rejected the argument that the University could not discriminate against religious speech on the basis of its content. It found religious speech entitled to less protection than other types of expression.

The Court of Appeals for the Eighth Circuit reversed. Rejecting the analysis of the District Court, it viewed the University regulation as a content-based discrimination against religious speech, for which it could find no compelling justification. The court held that the Establishment Clause does not bar a policy of equal access, in which facilities are open to groups and speakers of all kinds. According to the Court of Appeals, the "primary effect" of such a policy would not be to advance religion, but rather to further the neutral purpose of developing students' " 'social and cultural awareness as well as [their] intellectual curiosity.' "

We granted certiorari. We now affirm.

II

Through its policy of accommodating their meetings,the University has created a forum generally open for use by student groups. Having done so, the University has assumed an obligation to justify its discriminations and exclusions under applicable constitutional norms. The Constitution forbids a State to enforce certain exclusions from a forum generally open to the public, even if it was not required to create the forum in the first place. The University's institutional mission, which it describes as providing a *"secular* education" to its students, does not exempt its actions from constitutional scrutiny. With respect to persons entitled to be there, our cases leave

---

3. The pertinent regulations provide as follows:

"4.0314.0107 No University buildings or grounds (except chapels as herein provided) may be used for purposes of religious worship or religious teaching by either student or nonstudent groups.... The general prohibition against use of University buildings and grounds for religious worship or religious teaching is a policy required, in the opinion of The Board of Curators, by the Constitution and laws of the State and is not open to any other construction. No regulations shall be interpreted to forbid the offering of prayer or other appropriate recognition of religion at public functions held in University facilities....

"4.0314.0108 Regular chapels established on University grounds may be used for religious services but not for regular recurring services of any groups. Special rules and procedures shall be established for each such chapel by the Chancellor. It is specifically directed that no advantage shall be given to any religious group."

no doubt that the First Amendment rights of speech and association extend to the campuses of state universities.

Here UMKC has discriminated against student groups and speakers based on their desire to use a generally open forum to engage in religious worship and discussion. These are forms of speech and association protected by the First Amendment. In order to justify discriminatory exclusion from a public forum based on the religious content of a group's intended speech, the University must therefore satisfy the standard of review appropriate to content-based exclusions. It must show that its regulation is necessary to serve a compelling state interest and that it is narrowly drawn to achieve that end.

III

In this case the University claims a compelling interest in maintaining strict separation of church and State. It derives this interest from the "Establishment Clauses" of both the Federal and Missouri Constitutions.

A

The University first argues that it cannot offer its facilities to religious groups and speakers on the terms available to other groups without violating the Establishment Clause of the Constitution of the United States. We agree that the interest of the University in complying with its constitutional obligations may be characterized as compelling. It does not follow, however, that an "equal access" policy would be incompatible with this Court's Establishment Clause cases. Those cases hold that a policy will not offend the Establishment Clause if it can pass a three-pronged test: "First, the [governmental policy] must have a secular legislative purpose; second, its principal or primary effect must be one that neither advances nor inhibits religion . . . ; finally, the [policy] must not foster 'an excessive government entanglement with religion.' "

In this case two prongs of the test are clearly met. Both the District Court and the Court of Appeals held that an open-forum policy, including nondiscrimination against religious speech, would have a secular purpose and would avoid entanglement with religion. But the District Court concluded, and the University argues here, that allowing religious groups to share the limited public forum would have the "primary effect" of advancing religion.

The University's argument misconceives the nature of this case. The question is not whether the creation of a religious forum would violate the Establishment Clause. The University has opened its facilities for use by student groups, and the question is whether it can now exclude groups because of the content of their speech. In this context we are unpersuaded that the primary effect of the public forum open to all forms of discourse, would be to advance religion.

We are not oblivious to the range of an open forum's likely effects. It is possible— perhaps even foreseeable—that religious groups will benefit from access to University facilities. But this Court has explained that a religious organization's enjoyment of merely "incidental" benefits does not violate the prohibition against the "primary advancement" of religion.

We are satisfied that any religious benefits of an open forum at UMKC would be "incidental" within the meaning of our case. Two factors are especially relevant.

First, an open forum in a public university does not confer any imprimatur of state approval on religious sects or practices. As the Court of Appeals quite aptly stated, such a policy "would no more commit the University ... to religious goals" than it is "now committed to the goals of the Students for a Democratic Society, the Young Socialist Alliance," or any other group eligible to use its facilities.

Second, the forum is available to a broad class of nonreligious as well as religious speakers; there are over 100 recognized student groups at UMKC. The provision of benefits to so broad a spectrum of groups is an important index of secular effect. If the Establishment Clause barred the extension of general benefits to religious groups, "a church could not be protected by the police and fire departments, or have its public sidewalk kept in repair." At least in the absence of empirical evidence that religious groups will dominate UMKC's open forum we agree with the Court of Appeals that the advancement of religion would not be the forum's "primary effect."

B

Arguing that the State of Missouri has gone further than the Federal Constitution in proscribing indirect state support for religion, the University claims a compelling interest in complying with the applicable provision of the Missouri Constitution.

The Missouri courts have not ruled whether a general policy of accommodating student groups, applied equally to those wishing to gather to engage in religious and nonreligious speech, would offend the State Constitution. We need not, however, determine how the Missouri courts would decide this issue. It is also unnecessary for us to decide whether, under the Supremacy Clause, a state interest, derived from its own constitution, could ever outweigh free speech interests protected by the First Amendment. We limit our holding to the case before us.

On one hand, respondents' First Amendment rights are entitled to special constitutional solicitude. Our cases have required the most exacting scrutiny in cases in which a State undertakes to regulate speech on the basis of its content. On the other hand, the state interest asserted here—in achieving greater separation of church and State than is already ensured under the Establishment Clause of the Federal Constitution—is limited by the Free Exercise Clause and in this case by the Free Speech Clause as well. In this constitutional context, we are unable to recognize the State's interest as sufficiently "compelling" to justify content-based discrimination against respondents' religious speech.

IV

Our holding in this case in no way undermines the capacity of the University to establish reasonable time, place, and manner regulations. Nor do we question the right of the University to make academic judgments as to how best to allocate scarce resources or "to determine for itself on academic grounds who may teach, what may be taught, how it shall be taught, and who may be admitted to study." Finally, we affirm the continuing validity of cases, that recognize a university's right to exclude even First Amendment activities that violate reasonable campus rules or substantially interfere with the opportunity of other students to obtain an education.

The basis for our decision is narrow. Having created a forum generally open to student groups, the University seeks to enforce a content-based exclusion of religious speech. Its exclusionary policy violates the fundamental principle that a state regulation of speech should be content-neutral, and the University is unable to justify this violation under applicable constitutional standards.

For this reason, the decision of the Court of Appeals is

Affirmed.

Student Athletes

Of the variety of student athlete topics and cases, only two issues and three cases are included in this Section: the legal status of student athletes (*Hall* and *Colorado Seminary*) and the legality of mandatory drug testing (*Levant*); other cases do appear in the text, in the context of sex discrimination and institutional autonomy. There is a rapidly growing body of scholarly literature concerned with the many legal issues that have arisen. L. Greene, "The New NCAA Rules of the Game: Academic Integrity or Racism?" *St. Louis University Law Journal*, 28 (1984), 101–137; B. Porto, "Balancing Due Process and Academic Integrity in Intercollegiate Athletics: The Scholarship Athlete's Limited Property Interest in Eligibility," *Indiana Law Journal*, 62 (1986–87), 1151–1180; H. Appenzeller and T. Appenzeller, *Sports and the Courts* (Charlottesville: Michie, 1980); "Symposium on Athletics in Higher Education," *Journal of College and University Law*, 8 (1981–82); J. Weistart and C. Lowell, *The Law of Sports* (Charlottesville: Michie, 1979).

That college athletics have legal implications is inarguable. In an extraordinary document issued by a Special Committee of Methodist Bishops, concerning illegal payments to athletes and numerous violations of NCAA regulations by Southern Methodist University, detailed evidence of substantial wrongdoing was made public in 1987. The Report included a pattern of rules violations, recruiting abuses, cash payments to athletes, NCAA sanctions, collusion by trustees and administrators to "keep the lid on," decisions by the President of the Board (who resigned to become Texas Governor) to continue illegal payments, an agreement to bribe a disgruntled former employee who threatened to go public, public disclosures of the payments, deceptions towards the faculty NCAA representative, a "strategy of containment and cover-up," a plan for one person to become the scapegoat, and other improprieties that the Bishops termed "embarrassing and offensive in many instances." A Trustee said in 1985,

> members of the Board would have been naive not to have known that SMU players were being paid. [The trustee] was right. The evidence was everywhere. It was abundant and it was longstanding. But the Board of Governors members were content to win football games, to trust the leadership and look the other way. The institutional attitude and response to the NCAA allegations and investigations were symptomatic of the Board of Governors' attitude toward football in general: "Whatever was happening in the SMU football program was no better but no worse than what was happening in every other major college program." They told themselves that the other schools in the Southwest Conference and the NCAA were after SMU. They reasoned that SMU had been down so long, its competitors simply could not stand to see SMU win. "Everybody's doing it, why pick on SMU?"—that was the Board of Governors' stance. That translated into a combative, adversarial relationship with the NCAA and

its investigation. The Board of Governors was guilty of more than neglect. Their attitude was one of acquiescence in the actions of a small group of leaders on the Board. As with many of the active participants in this drama, the other members of the Board were able, through their passivity, to deny direct knowledge or direct participation in wrong-doing. The entire Board of Governors, as a Board, was at fault. All members of that Board share some measure of responsibility for the payments to players at SMU and the consequences of that course of action. *The Bishop's Committee Report on SMU*, June 19, 1987.

See also, R. Smith, "The National Collegiate Athletic Association's Death Penalty: How Educators Punish Themselves and Others," *Indiana Law Journal*, 62 (1986–87), 985–1059.

Mark D. Hall v. University of Minnesota

530 F. Supp. 104 (1982)

MILES W. LORD, Chief Judge.

This Court is presented with a serious and troubling question concerning the academic standing and athletic eligibility of a University of Minnesota varsity basketball player. The plaintiff in this action is a 21 year old black senior at the defendant University of Minnesota. He is also a formidable basketball player who, up to this season, played for the defendant University of Minnesota men's intercollegiate varsity basketball team. He is before the Court seeking an injunction ordering the University to admit him to a degree program, a prerequisite to the athletic eligibility he lost.

Because this Order must be issued prior to January 4, 1982, to be of benefit to the plaintiff, this Court does not have the luxury of setting forth an extensive discussion of the voluminous evidence that has been presented in support of and in opposition to this motion. The Court has reviewed all of the depositions and affidavits and has considered the arguments advanced by both parties during their oral presentation. This Order reflects the findings of fact and conclusions of law made by this Court.

The plaintiff was enrolled in a non-baccalaureate degree program at the defendant University's General College. His program terminated upon the accumulation of approximately 90 credits. Once his program terminated, the plaintiff attempted to enroll in a "degree program" at the University Without Walls (hereafter UWW), a college within the defendant University, and at the General College. The plaintiff was denied admission twice at UWW and once at the General College. By failing to enroll in a "degree program," the plaintiff lost his eligibility to play on the defendant University's basketball team according to Charles Liesenfelt, Director of Registration, Records & Scheduling. Liesenfelt contends that in order for the plaintiff to remain eligible to participate on the basketball team, he must be a "candidate for a degree" under Rule 1, § 1, A. Part Two, of the "Big Ten Handbook."

The plaintiff does meet the Big Ten eligibility standards with respect to grade point average and credit accumulation, but unless he is enrolled as a "candidate for a degree," he is ineligible to practice or play on the defendant University's basketball team. According to the coach of the University basketball team, the plaintiff is the only player he has known who has met the grade and credit criteria of the Big Ten but has been refused admission into a degree program.

The plaintiff filed this action on December 15, 1981, alleging that the defendants rejected his two applications to the UWW without affording him due process and in bad faith in an arbitrary and capricious manner. The plaintiff makes various other claims, but for the purpose of this motion, he relies primarily on the claim noted above. The plaintiff and the defendant agreed to expedite discovery and the plaintiff deposed nine individuals associated with the defendant University and the defendants deposed the plaintiff. On December 29, 1981, the plaintiff moved this Court for a preliminary injunction compelling his admission to a degree program. Unless the plaintiff is declared eligible for intercollegiate basketball competition on January 4, 1982, he will be ineligible to participate on the basketball team for all of the winter quarter of 1982 which comprises all but two or three games of the remaining season.

According to the evidence, if the plaintiff is accorded the opportunity to represent the University of Minnesota in intercollegiate varsity basketball competition during winter quarter of 1982, his senior year, he will have a significant opportunity to be a second round choice in the National Basketball Association draft this year, thereby acquiring a probable guarantee of his first year's compensation as a player in the National Basketball Association. If the plaintiff is denied the opportunity to participate in intercollegiate basketball competition on behalf of the University of Minnesota during winter quarter 1982, his chances for a professional career in basketball will be impaired; and it will be extremely unlikely that his compensation as a first year player in the National Basketball Association will be guaranteed. The evidence indicates that without an opportunity to play during the winter quarter of 1982, the plaintiff would likely be a sixth round choice in the National Basketball Association draft.

This Court has no hesitation in stating that the underlying reason for the plaintiff's desire to be enrolled in a degree program at the defendant University is the enhancement of his chances of becoming a professional basketball player. The plaintiff will probably never attain a degree should he be admitted to a degree program since the National Basketball Association draft occurs in April of 1982, well before the plaintiff could accumulate sufficient credits for a degree. The plaintiff was a highly recruited basketball player out of high school who was recruited to come to the University of Minnesota to be a basketball player and not a scholar. His academic record reflects that he has lived up to those expectations, as do the academic records of many of the athletes presented to this Court.

The plaintiff applied for admission to the UWW twice, once in August of 1981 and once in October of 1981. In each case, the UWW admissions committee determined, based on the plaintiff's application, that he should be admitted to the UWW introductory program. In each case, the directors of the program (further up in the hierarchy of the UWW) intervened in the admissions process and effectively directed the admissions committee to reject plaintiff's application. This interference by the directors never occurred in any other case as to any other student.

Prior to the intervention of the directors, one of the UWW directors contacted Dean Lupton of the General College concerning the plaintiff. The director summarized the information conveyed by Dean Lupton in a confidential memorandum regarding the plaintiff. The memorandum noted that the following factors bore on the plaintiff's application:

1. The "political aspects" of admitting plaintiff;

2. Plaintiff's "substantial" travel record (one weekend trip to Chicago in fall quarter 1981);

3. The plaintiff had earned "A's" in courses he was not eligible to be in;

4. The General College had found it necessary to monitor plaintiff's work through a Professor Harris;

5. The plaintiff improperly turned in work on Regent's letterhead stationary [sic];

6. The plaintiff turned in work done by others as his;

7. That every "W" (withdrawal) on plaintiff's transcript was originally an "N" (equivalent to an "F");

8. That within four weeks of the commencement of classes, plaintiff typically had earned a grade of "N"; and

9. That plaintiff had put through fake approval forms on more than one occasion.

Most of these allegations are attributed (in the memorandum) to Dean Lupton of the General College. The memorandum further states that Dean Lupton indicated that the plaintiff would not be accepted into a degree program at the General College, even though the plaintiff had not even applied at the time.

After receiving the above information, the director contacted another director and they in turn conveyed this information to the admissions committee and effectively instructed the committee to reject the plaintiff's application. Until plaintiff's case arose, the UWW admissions committee decision to admit had been considered final.

This memorandum was passed on to a successor director who, after the plaintiff reapplied and was again accepted by the admissions committee, effectively vetoed the decision of the admissions committee.

Opposed to the procedures set forth above used in processing the plaintiff's two applications to the UWW, the UWW distributed a pamphlet explaining the policies and procedures of admission. This pamphlet notes the following:

1. The *information you present* in your application will determine whether you are admitted to UWW.

2. *Admissions decisions are based on your responses to the application form* which appears at the back of this booklet.

3. *Your application will be reviewed and acted upon by an admissions committee* made up of UWW advisors. You will be notified in writing of the committee's decision. If you are not accepted, *the reasons for the decision will be explained....*

4. *The admissions committee will determine which applicants will be admitted* for enrollment in the Introductory Period.

With regard to items 1 and 2 above, the UWW's Faculty Director testified that these statements were the correct policy with respect to processing UWW admission applications. He further stated that applicants to the UWW are supposed to be judged *solely* on the basis of their application form.

It seems apparent that the plaintiff was not judged solely on the basis of his applications and the information therein. Each time the admissions committee reviewed the plaintiff's application, they recommended that he be admitted. After the intervention of the directors and the communication of the information outlined in the above-mentioned memorandum, the plaintiff was denied admission. However, in both of the rejection letters sent to the plaintiff, none of the allegations noted in the memorandum were listed as reasons for the plaintiff's failure to gain admission to the UWW.

The plaintiff asserts that he has been denied his right to due process of law arising under the Fourteenth Amendment. Due process protects life, liberty and property. Protected property interests are usually created and defined by sources such as state laws. A student's interest in attending a university is a property right protected by due process. The defendant asserts that while in cases of expulsion, public education may be a property right, in cases of nonadmission, public education is but a mere privilege, citing *Davis v. Southeastern Community College*. However, the right versus privilege distinction has long been abandoned in the area of due process. And in any event, even though the plaintiff was denied admission, the circumstances of this case make it more like an expulsion case than a non-admission case. The plaintiff lost existing scholarship rights; he cannot enroll in another college without sitting out one year of competition under athletic rules; and although he has attended the defendant University for several years, he may no longer register for day classes at the defendant University.

But to say that due process applies in the area of a student's interest in attending a university does not finish the analysis. One must answer the question of what process is due. "Due process is flexible and calls for such procedural protection as the particular situation demands." Factors balanced to determine what process is due are: 1) the private interest affected by the action; 2) the risk of an erroneous deprivation of such interest through the procedures used and the value of additional procedural safeguards; and 3) the government's interest involved, including fiscal and administrative burdens.

The private interest at stake here, although ostensibly academic, is the plaintiff's ability to obtain a "no cut" contract with the National Basketball Association. The bachelor of arts, while a mark of achievement and distinction, does not in and of itself assure the applicant a means of earning a living. This applicant seems to recognize this and has opted to use his college career as a means of entry into professional sports as do many college athletes. His basketball career will be little affected by the absence or presence of a bachelor of arts degree. This plaintiff has put all of his "eggs" into the "basket" of professional basketball. The plaintiff would suffer a substantial loss if his career objectives were impaired.

The government's interest, i.e., the defendant University's interest, is the administrative burden of requiring a hearing or other due process safeguards for every rejection of every student who applies to the University. This burden would be tremendous and this Court would not require the defendant University to shoulder it.

The key factor in this case which weighs heavily in the plaintiff's favor is the risk of an erroneous deprivation given the nature of the proceedings used in processing the plaintiff's application. This Court is aware that in the area of academic decisions, judicial interference must be minimal. However, an academic decision is based upon established academic criteria. In this case, the plaintiff's applications to the UWW were treated very differently than all other applications. The directors intervened in the process and provided the admissions committee with allegations concerning the plaintiff's conduct, a facet of the proceedings that taints this "academic" process and turns it into something much like a disciplinary proceeding. Given this aspect of the proceedings, it would appear that the plaintiff should have at least been notified that allegations had been made regarding his conduct so that he could have presented evidence in his own behalf. Without this safeguard, there exists a chance that the plaintiff may have been wrongfully accused of actions which then form the basis for his rejection.

This is not to say that all applicants who are rejected by the defendant University must be given an opportunity to rebut evidence used in evaluating a college application; however, if the defendant University intends to interject evidence concerning allegations of improper conduct of the applicant into the admissions process, it must provide the applicant an opportunity to give his or her side of the story.

Finally, one must consider all that has occurred in light of the standards utilized by the Courts in this Circuit in evaluating the propriety of issuing a preliminary injunction. Four factors determine whether a preliminary injunction should issue. They are: (1) the threat of irreparable harm to the moving party, (2) the state of balance between that harm and the injury that granting the injunction will inflict on other parties, (3) the public interest, and (4) the probability that the movant will succeed on the merits of the claim.

With respect to the first factor, if the plaintiff is not eligible to play basketball by January 4, 1982, he will not play his senior year. This poses a substantial threat to his chances for a "no cut" contract in the National Basketball Association, according to his coach, and his overall aspirations regarding a career as a professional basketball player. It would be difficult indeed to measure the loss to the plaintiff in terms of dollars and cents. The injury is substantial and not really capable of an accurate monetary prediction. Thus, it would be irreparable.

The harm to the other parties, i.e., the defendant University, is difficult to assess. On the one hand, this Court doubts that the University men's intercollegiate varsity basketball team and coaching staff would characterize the reinstatement of the plaintiff to the team in terms of "harm." But the defendant University academic wing argues that if this Court orders the plaintiff into a degree program, its academic standards and integrity would be undermined. The plaintiff and his fellow athletes were never recruited on the basis of scholarship and it was never envisioned they would be on the Dean's List. Consequently we must view with some skepticism the defendant University's claim, regarding academic integrity. This Court is not saying that athletes are incapable of scholarship; however they are given little incentive to be scholars and few persons care how the student athlete performs academically, including many of the athletes themselves. The exceptionally talented student athlete is led to perceive the basketball, football, and other athletic programs as farm teams and proving grounds for professional sports leagues. It well may be true that a good academic program for the athlete is made virtually impossible by the demands of their sport at the college level. If this situation causes harm to the University, it is because they have fostered it and the institution rather than the individual should suffer the consequence.

It appears from the record that there is a "tug of war" going on over this plaintiff. The academicians are pulling toward higher standards of achievement for all students while the athletic department must tug in the direction of fielding teams who contribute to paying a substantial share of the university's budget. In this tug of war the academic department will suffer substantially no ill effects if it loses. On the other hand, the athletic department, directors, coaches and personnel under this system are charged with the responsibility of at least maintaining and fielding teams which are capable of competing with the best in their conference or in the nation. This Court is not called upon to determine any long term solution to the dilemma posed. It is called upon to determine if the rights of an individual caught up in the struggle have been violated.

The only perceivable harm to the defendant University would result from the fact that the National Collegiate Athletic Association (NCAA), of which the defendant University is a member, has rules which permit certain sanctions to be leveled upon the defendant University should a player be declared eligible under a court order which is later vacated, stayed, reversed, etc. This rule defines sanctions including the vacation of the athlete's records for the period for which the athlete played, the forfeiture of games by the team, the declaration of ineligibility of the team for post-season tournaments, to the return of television receipts for games that the athlete played in. However, in this regard, the defendant University's destiny is in its own hands. The University does not have to appeal this Order if it is fearful of the sanctions which might be imposed by the NCAA. And the defendant University's lawyer is of the opinion that the NCAA could not force an appeal. Therefore, an appeal with all of the usual uncertainties accompanying it is not mandated. It would be the defendant University's choice whether it wants to risk these sanctions at this time. Presumably some impartial arbitrator at the defendant University will make the decision of whether the defendant University will risk these potential sanctions.

The public interest is difficult to assess. It depends on whether the public prefers highly-tuned athletes who devote most of their waking hours to honing their athletic skills or whether it wants an individual with the plaintiff's athletic abilities to be required to make substantial scholastic achievement. There is no doubt that the public does have an interest but until the universities themselves clarify their position on the matter, the Court must assume that the public interest is equally ambivalent.

The fourth factor concerns the probability that the plaintiff will succeed ultimately on his suit. During the two weeks since this suit was filed, the plaintiff has revealed some disturbing facts regarding the defendant University's handling of the plaintiff's applications to the UWW and the General College. Besides the unusual procedures at the UWW, which forms the basis of this injunction and which has already been discussed, this Court has considered the Dean of the General College's testimony regarding the plaintiff's application to the General College. Dean Lupton testified that the plaintiff's summer school credits were not good evidence in determining whether the plaintiff has "shown progress" in his academic career because these courses were not General College courses. During the summer of 1981, the plaintiff enrolled in 30 credits of classes at the defendant University and successfully completed 26. The plaintiff received three "A's," four "B's" and one "C," and one "satisfactory." Dean Lupton and the defendants' other witnesses were unable to satisfactorily explain to this Court why the plaintiff's most recent academic endeavor would not be good evidence in assessing his capabilities and present attitudes or why they did not evidence "progress in his academic career." Although these courses were not the most esoteric in their nature, they were offered for credit by the defendant University.

The defendant University academic wing argues that, during the two quarters prior to applying to the General College, the plaintiff only completed 48% of the credits he attempted. If the General College would have considered the plaintiff's summer scholastic activity, his completion rate for the two quarters prior to his application would have been 72%.

This Court is of the opinion that the plaintiff has shown a substantial probability of success on at least his claim regarding the UWW. It is conceivable that the UWW may have had reason to deny the plaintiff admission to its degree program. However, the manner in which the UWW processed the plaintiff's application strongly suggests that he has been treated disparately and in a manner violative of due process. The plaintiff was given no notice nor any opportunity to answer the allegations leveled against him by the Dean of the General College. It is equally conceivable that the plaintiff would have had a "good answer" to these charges had he been given an opportunity to respond.

Balancing all of the above factors, this Court concludes that an injunction should issue requiring the defendant University to admit the plaintiff into a degree program on January 4, 1982 and to declare him eligible to compete in intercollegiate varsity basketball competition.

NOW, THEREFORE, IT IS ORDERED That during the pendency of this action, or until the final determination thereof, or until the Court shall otherwise Order, the defendant Regents, defendant Marieneau, defendant Lupton and defendant Leyasmeyer, and said defendants' agents, servants and employees, are enjoined and restrained from:

1. Preventing plaintiff's registration as a bona fide matriculated, registered and regularly enrolled resident candidate for a degree in the General College or the University Without Walls of the defendant University at the option of the defendant University.

2. Preventing plaintiff from enrolling for a full work load as defined by the regulations of the defendant University and certified by the University to the Big Ten Conference pursuant to eligibility Rule 4, Section 1, B of the July 1, 1981 Handbook of the Intercollegiate (Big Ten) Conference ("The Big Ten Handbook");

3. Failing to certify to the Big Ten Conference that plaintiff is eligible to compete in intercollegiate varsity basketball competition as a representative of the University, unless:

a. Plaintiff fails to satisfy the applicable cumulative grade average requirement set forth in Eligibility Rule 3, Section 3, B of the Big Ten Handbook, or

b. Plaintiff, after having been given a reasonable opportunity to do so, fails to register for a full work load as a student of the defendant University at or before the commencement of each University term during the pendency of this injunction.

4. Withholding distribution of scholarship proceeds due and payable to plaintiff for winter and spring quarters of 1982 under the grant-in-aid tendered plaintiff by the defendant University in the summer of 1981.

Colorado Seminary (University of Denver) v. N.C.A.A.
570 F.2d 320 (1978)

PER CURIAM.

This action was brought by the University of Denver and by several of its student athletes to enjoin the National Collegiate Athletic Association from imposing sanctions against the hockey team and other DU athletic teams. The trial court denied the plaintiffs' motion for summary judgment and granted a like motion of the defendants with some exceptions. The plaintiffs have taken this appeal.

The trial court held that the interest of the student athletes in participating in intercollegiate sports was not constitutionally protected, and that no constitutionally protected right of the University had been violated. We agree with these conclusions, and we agree with the Memorandum Opinion of the trial court.

The facts are described in the trial court's Memorandum, and need not be repeated here. It is sufficient to say that the dispute began between the University and the NCAA as to the eligibility of several hockey players, and culminated with the NCAA placing the hockey team on a two-year probation with no post season participation in NCAA events, and also the probation of all other University athletic teams for a one-year period with similar consequences.

We conclude that this appeal is controlled by our decision in *Albach v. Odle*, and *Oklahoma High School Athletic Ass'n v. Bray*. These two cases, of course, concerned high school athletics, but the same considerations are applicable here. The arguments as to the difference between high school athletic programs and those in the universities have been examined. We have also considered the point that college athletic scholarship arrangements may create a distinction. But all considered, we find no more than a difference in degree. The fundamental positions are the same, the goals are the same, the stakes are pretty much the same. The same relationship also exists between the primary academic functions of the schools in each category and the athletic programs. The differences in degree or magnitude do not lead to a different result. In each, the athletic program is very important, as are the many other diverse functions, programs, and activities not within the academic core. As we held in *Albach v. Odle*:

> " ... The educational process is a broad and comprehensive concept with a variable and indefinite meaning. It is not limited to classroom attendance but includes innumerable separate components, such as participation in athletic activity and membership in school clubs and social groups, which combine to provide an atmosphere of intellectual and moral advancement. We do not read *Goss* to establish a property interest subject to constitutional protection in each of these separate components."

It is obvious that the relative importance of the many school "activities" to each other, and to the academic core, depends on where you sit. The "educational process" is indeed a bundle of diverse situations to which the students are subjected by varying degrees of compulsion, both officially and by their peers. This is basically the *Goss v. Lopez* assumption. It is then to be applied with the significant conclusion therefrom reached in *Albach v. Odle*, quoted above, to the effect that if one stick in the bundle is removed, it does not necessarily mean that a constitutionally protected right of a student has thereby been violated.

As we said in *Oklahoma High School Athletic Ass'n v. Bray*, as to the [plaintiffs'] claim:

> " ... In the case at bar, once the pleadings were pierced at pretrial, it became apparent that Bray's grievance with the Athletic Association lay only with the application of its residence rule, the Board's refusal to grant an exception for hardship, and a general attack upon the amount of power delegated by the high schools to the Association. Such complaints are not within federal cognizance,

are not subject to review in federal court, and, indeed, are not subject to review in the state courts of Oklahoma. Had this case not been voluntarily dismissed by plaintiff it would have been the duty of the trial court, upon the present record, to have dismissed it for lack of a federal question."

The same conclusion was there reached as to the complaint of the school itself against the association.

Thus here also we must hold that there is present no substantial federal question.

The equal protection argument, as the trial court observes, is answered by *San Antonio Independent School Dist. v. Rodriguez*. There is here no valid argument based on classification. In the final analysis, the NCAA reacted to the position taken by the University as a member and in response to the NCAA pronouncements. The matter resulting in the probation sanction became removed from the issue of eligibility of the several hockey players.

AFFIRMED in all respects.

For a case brought under a tort theory by a student athlete against his football coach, see *Rutledge v. Arizona Board of Regents, Frank Kush, et al.*, 600 F.2d 1345 (1981) (scholarship athlete's allegations of humiliating treatment by football coach do not constitute Sec. 1983 claim, even if coach "went beyond the usual verbal lashings common to football practice fields"). One reason college coaches may be anxious to win is the increasingly-high stakes collegiate game. For a review of the commercial issues involved, see J. Graves, "Coaches in the Courtroom: Recovery in Actions for Breach of Employment Contracts," *Journal of College and University Law*, 12 (1986), 545–559. The Appendix to this article details damages claimed by coach F.C. "Pepper" Rodgers, the football coach at Georgia Tech, fired with two years remaining on his contract. In addition to traditional breach of contract claims, he also sought damages on his lost opportunities (his radio and television shows) and various perquisites (tickets, memberships, etc.). The eventual settlement included an agreement not to reveal its terms. See *Rodgers v. Georgia Tech Athletic Ass'n.*, 166 Ga. App. 156, 303 S.E.2d 467 (1983).

In an unpublished California State Court opinion, the judge struck down Stanford's drugtesting plan, as applied to an intercollegiate diver; the NCAA has appealed the Superior Court decision in *LeVant*. In *O'Halloran v. University of Washington*, a U.S. District Court judge held, "The invasion of her privacy interest by the specimen collection procedures of the drug-testing program are outweighed by the compelling interest of the University and NCAA in protecting the health of student-athletes, reducing peer pressure and temptations to use drugs, ensuring fair competitions . . . and educating about and deterring drug abuse in sports competition." (C87-1024 M, McGovern, J., April, 1988). A random drug testing plan for high school athletes and cheerleaders was upheld in *Schaill v. Tippecanoe County School* (U.S. District Court, Northern Indiana, L-87-0090 February 1, 1988, Sharp, J.). For a review of drug testing issues, see M. Rothstein, "Drug Testing in the Workplace: The Challenge to Employment Relations and Employment Law," *Chicago-Kent Law Review*, 63 (1987), 683–743. Although his analysis flows from an employment setting, his conclusions have relevance for the student or student-athlete context:

> Drug abuse in America and drug abuse in American workplaces are complicated problems. Drug abuse will not be eliminated or even brought under control

simply through law enforcement, military action, public relations campaigns, rehabilitation, legalization of certain drugs, or prohibiting any current drug user from obtaining private or public employment. Similarly, a facile solution to the problem of workplace drug abuse will not be found in a specimen jar or a million specimen jars.

At best, drug testing is a sometimes-necessary evil that is part of a comprehensive program to insure the public health and safety. At worst, it is an unholy alliance of politics, profiteering, unrestrained technology, and heedless personnel policies.

The efficacy and desirability of drug testing in the workplace will continue to be weighed by judges, legislators, and policy makers in the public and private sectors. In making these decisions, it is essential to consider the limits of technology, the inability of drug testing to resolve the underlying problem of drug abuse, and the human and organizational costs of implementing drug testing programs. Drug testing must be considered in the light of established employment law principles, such as equal opportunity, job-related decisionmaking, and reasonable accommodation. Drug testing also must be viewed in the larger context of a society that is built on values of autonomy, privacy, and dignity.

See also J. Scanlan, "Playing the Drug-Testing Game: College Athletics, Regulatory Institutions, and the Structures of Constitutional Argument," *Indiana Law Journal*, 62 (1986–87), 863–983; "Drug Testing Decisions Starting to Come Down," *Perspectives*, May 1988, pp. 3–5.

Student Residency Requirements

To students in private institutions there is little stake in whether or not they are classified as residents or non-residents, at least not for the sake of determining tuition charges. Public institutions distinguish between residents and non-residents, on the theory that tax supported, public institutions should be available at lower cost to those taxpayers (and their families) whose money supports the colleges. As a corollary, non-residents (or state non-taxpayers) can be required to pay a higher share of the costs.

The charge to students attending public institutions as non-residents can be exceedingly high: for instance, in some states, the differential can be a factor of 10. A variety of court cases, dating back to 1882, has established that states may charge nonresidents extra fees for attending state institutions and may determine who is entitled to be classified as a resident. In most situations, this procedure works well enough, as state institutions spell out the basic residency requirements and students seem to understand the rules.

There is an intuitive, appealing symmetry to this arrangement, one that recognizes the important benefit available to those who pay for it, however indirectly. Realizing that a mix of in-state and out-of-state students is a public good, officials in some states have made it possible for students to cross borders and to migrate, as long as their higher tuition costs "equalize" the tax burden upon residents. This presumption, too, seems fair, especially in a country with highly decentralized postsecondary state systems. The balance properly favors resident taxpayers yet does not fence out those

who wish to change locations and attend schools without having made a tax contribution to that state's coffers. This arrangement also distributes students and acts as
an incentive for states to establish strong postsecondary sectors. It does so by preventing a mass migration to states with lower charges, and engendering loyalties, both
political and academic, to state institutions. By means of compacts and state consortia
agreements, it can also distribute scarce places in highly specialized and expensive
curricula, such as optometry, pharmacy, and veterinary medicine.

In a surprisingly large number of situations, applicants or students have presented
increasingly sophisticated claims to residency, where residency practices (either laws
or regulations) had not envisioned such claims. When persons live in a state for many
years and attend a state institution, it is easy to consider such students as residents;
conversely, if a student moves from State A to State B solely for the purpose of attending
B state college, it is equally clear that he or she is a nonresident, at least at first. The
wide space between these two scenarios, however, is the rub. As a general rule, states
will allow a person who "moves" to a state to become reclassified as a resident after
a specified period of time. This time period ranges from 90 days (e.g., the District
of Columbia) to 12 months (a period employed by nearly all the states). No state
with a durational test currently employs a waiting period of more than 12 months,
and in several states (e.g., New York and Tennessee), it is possible to become reclassified immediately upon arrival. Absent other complications, when the specified time
passes, states with a simple durational requirement will allow a student to pay the
lower tuition as a resident. Domicile, however, is another matter, usually requiring
establishment of a "true, permanent, fixed abode."

Frame v. Residency Appeals Committee
675 P. 2d 1157 (Utah 1983)

STEWART, Justice:

Appellants are out-of-state students who were denied resident status for tuition
purposes by Utah State University. After the University's denial, appellants filed this
suit. They challenge the constitutionality of the rules by which the University determines residency, and allege that the University's decision was arbitrary and capricious.
On cross motions for summary judgment, the trial court upheld both the rules and
the University's decision. We affirm.

The parties agree, as evidenced by their motions for summary judgment, "that
there is no genuine issue as to any material fact." Appellants George and Lori Frame
met and were married in California in 1970 or 1971. At that time, George was
temporarily stationed by the military in California, and Lori was a resident of California. Prior to being stationed in California, George had been a resident student in
Alaska.

In the spring of 1971, the couple moved to Logan, Utah, and George Frame immediately enrolled at Utah State University. The Frames allege that during the next
year they rented an apartment in Logan, opened an account with a local bank,
registered to vote in Utah, and George obtained a Utah driver's license. During that
year appellants did not apply for resident status at the University.

In June, 1972, appellants moved to Tanzania, Africa, to do wildlife research for
thesis and dissertation requirements at Utah State. While in Tanzania appellants

opened a bank account there, but stored some of their personal belongings in Utah and gave as their mailing address the Cooperative Wildlife Research Unit at Utah State.

In February, 1978, appellants returned to Logan. In March, 1978, both appellants registered at Utah State for classes beginning the following September. From March to September, 1978, appellants spent most of their time outside Utah visiting their families and traveling through several states to further their employment as lecturers, free lance writers, and photographers. During this time appellants continued to store some belongings in Utah; they listed the Wildlife Science Department as their mailing address; and George obtained a New Jersey driver's license.

In September, 1978, appellants returned to Logan to recommence their schooling. They again rented local living quarters, opened a local bank account, registered to vote, and George obtained a Utah driver's license and automobile registration.

Toward the end of that month appellants applied to Evan J. Sorenson, the Assistant Director of Admissions and Records, for Utah resident status so that they might pay the lower Utah resident tuition. Applying the State Board of Regents' rules governing residency for tuition purposes, Sorenson ruled that appellants did not qualify for resident status because they had not lived continuously in Utah for one year prior to the quarter for which resident status was sought, and because they had come to Utah primarily to attend an institution of higher learning, and could not demonstrate by objective facts that Utah was their domicile. Appellants appealed that decision to the University's Residency Appeals Committee, which affirmed Sorenson's decision for essentially the same reasons.

In April, 1979, appellants again applied for resident status on the ground that over one year had elapsed since their March, 1978, registration at the University. Because appellants had been absent from the state for more than thirty days during the summer of 1978, Sorenson again denied their request on the ground that appellants had not resided continuously in the state for one year. On appeal, the Residency Appeals Committee affirmed.

Having exhausted their administrative remedies, appellants filed suit in the district court in August, 1979, to compel the University to classify them as residents for tuition purposes. Appellants argue that it is a violation of due process and equal protection to deny resident status to them because they were absent for more than thirty days during the one-year period. Appellants also contend that the University's reliance on their acceptance of out-of-state, "nontemporary" employment and their failure to purchase property in Utah as indicia of intent to establish permanent domicile in the state, violates the Equal Protection Clause. Finally, they contend that the Appeals Committee decisions should be reversed because it was arbitrary and capricious.

I. REGENTS' RULES

U.C.A., 1953 § 53–34–1 authorizes the Board of Regents to charge higher college tuition to nonresident students than to resident students. Section 53–34–2.2 defines "resident student" for tuition purposes:

(1) The meaning of the word "resident" for the purposes of this act shall be determined by reference to the general law on the subject of domicile, except that the following rules shall be observed:

(2) An adult who has come to Utah and established residency here for the purpose of attending an institution of higher education must maintain continuous Utah residency status for one full year prior to the beginning of the academic period for which registration as a resident student is sought, and, in each case, must demonstrate by additional objective evidence the establishment of a domicile in Utah and that the student does not maintain a residence elsewhere.

Pursuant to subsection (7) of this section, the State Board of Regents has promulgated supplementary rules and regulations to assist institutions of higher education in classifying students as residents or nonresidents. Appellants challenge the constitutionality of these rules, which closely parallel the language of § 53–34–2.2. Rule I.A. sets forth the basic requirements for resident student status, including the statutory one-year residence requirement:

I. ADULTS—(Married students and single students 18 years and over)

A. In order to qualify as a resident student,

1. an adult must establish by objective evidence an intent to establish a permanent domicile in Utah; and

2. an adult student who has come to Utah for the primary purpose of attending an institution of higher education must reside in Utah for at least one continuous year prior to the beginning of the academic period for which registration as a resident student is sought.

Rule I.D. permits a thirty-day absence from the state without disqualifying a student from complying with the one-year residency requirement. That rule states:

D. *Year's Continuous Residency*

A person who lives in the state for one year will not qualify as a resident unless the other requirements of paragraph A are satisfied. Short absences from the state, i.e., less than 30 days, will not break the running of the required one-year residence. Extended absences, i.e., longer than 30 days, especially if during such an absence the student works out of state or returns to the prior home of record for an extended duration, will break the running of the continuous year.

It is established law that a state may charge a higher tuition for nonresident students. It is also established that a one-year period of residency may be imposed to qualify for resident tuition.

Appellants do not attack any of the above propositions. Rather, they focus their challenge on the rule which precludes the establishment of residency if a student is absent from the state more than thirty days during the one year. They assert (1) that the thirty-day rule irrebuttably presumes, in violation of due process, that students who must travel outside the state for more than thirty days at a time are nonresidents; and (2) that the rule violates equal protection because there is no rational basis for distinguishing nonresident students who travel outside the state for more than thirty days from resident students.

II. DUE PROCESS

Rule I.A.1 requires that an adult seeking to qualify as a resident student "must establish by objective evidence an intent to establish a permanent domicile in Utah." The evidence of permanent domicile may include evidence of any of the several factors listed in Rule I.E.,[4] which are typically utilized in determining domiciliary status. If,

---

4. Rule I.E. describes the type of evidence relevant to a determination of residency. It states:

however, an adult comes to Utah primarily for the purpose of attending an institution of higher education, he is presumed to be a nonresident. As to such a person, Rule I.A.2 imposes the additional requirement that he establish one year's continuous residency prior to the academic year for which he applies for residency status. Because of the difficulty in determining a student's domiciliary intent when he applies for residency after coming to this state for the purpose of attending an institution of higher learning, the law establishes a rebuttable presumption that a person who enrolls in college "within a year after entering Utah from out of state" has entered the state primarily for academic reasons and therefore lacks domiciliary intent. This presumption may be rebutted either through one continuous year of residence or by "[clearly demonstrating] that the move to Utah was not academically motivated." Rule I.D. provides that short absences from the state of not more than a total of thirty days do not disqualify one from meeting the one-year requirement.

Appellants contend that the thirty-day rule creates an irrebuttable presumption of nonresidence in violation of *Vlandis v. Kline*. That case ruled that where a state is concerned with the factual question of residency, the state may not make the determination of the question turn on a permanent irrebuttable presumption. The Court held a Connecticut law unconstitutional which provided that (1) a student was presumed to be a nonresident for tuition purposes if his "legal address for any part of the one-year period immediately prior to his application for admission" to the state university system was outside the state, and (2) that a student's status "as established at the time of his application for admission... [was, as a matter of law, his] status for the entire period of his attendance at [school]." In holding that the irrebuttable presumption violated due process, the Supreme Court stated:

> In sum, since Connecticut purports to be concerned with residency in allocating the rates for tuition and fees in its university system, it is forbidden by the Due Process Clause to deny an individual the resident rates on the basis of a permanent and irrebuttable presumption of nonresidence, when that presumption is not necessarily or universally true in fact, and when the State has reasonable alternative means of making the crucial determination. Rather, standards of due process require that the State allow such an individual the opportunity to present evidence showing that he is a bona fide resident entitled to the in-state rates. Since [the law] precluded the appellees from ever rebutting the presumption that they were nonresidents of Connecticut, that statue operated

---

An applicant for resident status must furnish evidence of personal intent to remain indefinitely by establishing significant legal and other ties or contacts within the State of Utah during the year's required residence, and by terminating reasonably terminable ties out of state. *Significant ties and contacts may include, among other matters, the purchase of property; acceptance of non-temporary employment*; establishment of banking relationships; qualification for Utah driver's license; registration of a motor vehicle; registration to vote; membership and participation in off-campus political, social, religious, fraternal and civic associations; marriage to a Utah resident; or the existence of compelling non-academic reasons for coming to Utah and leaving the previous domicile, such as health needs, divorce, or offer of permanent employment. The following factors may be ground for denying resident status:
1. Out-of-state voter registration
2. Out-of-state motor vehicle registration
3. Out-of-state driver's license
4. Out-of-state support to such an extent that the student would probably have to leave the State of Utah if that support were withheld. [Emphasis added.]

to deprive them of a significant amount of their money without due process of law.

Vlandis does not control the instant case. The law that *Vlandis* invalidated established an irrebuttable presumption of nonresidency that lasted the entire period that a student attended school. Under Utah law, by contrast, an out-of-state resident may, at any time after his arrival in the state, establish himself as a bona fide resident or domiciliary of the state by overcoming the rebuttable presumption of nonresidency. In this case, appellants could, by living continuously in the state for one year and by meeting the other tests for determining domicile, establish themselves as residents.

The requirement that the one year may not be interrupted by more than thirty days of absence is not prohibited by *Vlandis*. Since a flat one-year presumption of nonresidency is valid, it follows that the thirty-day grace period must necessarily be valid.

III. EQUAL PROTECTION
A.

Both appellants and the University agree that the thirty-day rule neither jeopardizes a fundamental right nor creates a suspect classification. Therefore, equal protection of the laws requires only that the classification created by the rule bear a rational relationship to a legitimate state purpose. Since the Board of Regents may legitimately distinguish between residents and nonresidents by charging the latter a higher tuition, and may also impose a one-year residency requirement to assist in making that distinction, the issue is whether the state, in determining whether the one-year requirement has been met, may rationally distinguish between students who reside outside the state for a period of more than thirty days during the one year, and those who do not.

Appellants contend that their education-related research and temporary employment are legitimate reasons for extended absences from the state, and that it is "unfair [and] totally illogical to strip all persons who leave the state for more than thirty days of resident student status." The argument is not valid. It is not the thirty-day absence rule that precludes residency status; it is appellants' failure to rebut the presumption of nonresidency arising from a failure to establish physical presence in the state for one year (less a thirty-day grace period).

Under Rules I.A. and I.D., appellants' motivation for leaving the state each summer is immaterial. Although motivation may be relevant in determining residency or domiciliary status in a different context, the purpose of the instant rules is to distinguish between those whose attachment to the state is sufficient to justify charging resident tuition and those who have a lesser detachment and are therefore less likely to contribute to their tax-subsidized education by the payment of taxes. In establishing general rules for distinguishing between residents and nonresidents for tuition purposes, the state must be reasonable in the classifications created by the rules. The classifications in this case rationally distinguish between those who come to this state solely for attendance at an institution of higher learning during the school year, and those who come with the intention of residing here for purposes other than enrolling at a state educational institution for an indefinite period of time.

The authority to draw lines that discriminate is necessary if government is to act in the many areas of human conduct where the shades of human activity do not lend themselves to precise categories. When some legislative line must be drawn, it is no objection to the rule that some cases will fall closer to the line than others and thus may individually have more merit and greater claim to being treated differently than those that fall farther away. That objection will exist in virtually all cases. Such a determination provides no basis for holding a rule unconstitutional as long as the classifications are reasonable. The classification in this case is rationally based and imposes no invidious discrimination, even though the lines drawn by the rules may traverse gray areas.

Appellants would also have us alter the thirty-day rule to allow tacking of twelve nonconsecutive months of residency. This Court has no such power. The prerogative and power to draw such lines belongs to bodies invested with the power to legislate or to make rules under legislative authority.

In sum, the thirty-day rule as written does not unlawfully discriminate and is not unconstitutional.

B.

Appellants also contend that the University's reliance on "nontemporary" employment and the purchase of property in Utah, as indicia of intent to establish permanent domicile, is a violation of equal protection. These two factors are among several set forth in Rule I.E. of the Board of Regents' rules. The specific issue here is whether these factors are reasonably indicative of domiciliary intent.

Appellants cite *Kelm v. Carlson*, to support their argument that nontemporary employment may not be considered in determining domiciliary intent. *Kelm* invalidated a university regulation that required acceptance of post-graduate employment within the state in order to acquire resident-student status. Under the rules in the instant case, acceptance of nontemporary employment, before or after graduation, is not a requirement for resident status, but only one of several criteria to be considered in determining "personal intent to remain indefinitely."

Both employment and acquisition of property may provide some evidence of intent to remain indefinitely. Of course, a student with no actual intent to establish residency might purchase a home and obtain apparent permanent employment. Since, however, such actions are not likely taken solely to establish resident-status for tuition purposes, those factors have traditionally been used in determining whether one has an attachment to the state that is indefinite in duration and hence indicative of domiciliary intent.

The Equal Protection Clause, in the circumstances of this case, requires only that similarly situated persons be treated similarly and that any differences in treatment be reasonably and fairly related to a legitimate governmental purpose. Reliance upon employment and acquisition of property as evidence of one's intent to establish a domicile is not unreasonably related to the purpose of the statute.

IV. REASONABLENESS OF THE UNIVERSITY'S RULING

Finally, appellants argue that the decision of the Residency Appeals Committee denying them resident status was arbitrary and capricious. Both parties agree that our scope of review is whether the University acted arbitrarily or capriciously. Since neither party disputes that proposition, we shall assume that to be the proper scope of review.

The Committee's decision was supported by substantial evidence. Appellants first came to Utah in 1972, left in 1973, and returned in 1978, when they again enrolled as students at Utah State University. They applied for resident status in September,

1978, but clearly had not satisfied the one-year residency rule because of their sojourn of six years in Africa, followed by a summer of travel throughout this country. During the summer of 1978, George Frame held a New Jersey driver's license. When they reapplied in April, 1979, they still had not satisfied the one-year residency requirement and did not establish that this state constituted their domicile. The Cache County clerk's office had no record of appellants' having registered to vote or having voted by absentee ballot, as claimed in their application. When out of state, they gave as their permanent address the Department of Wildlife Science. They did not have a Utah driver's license or car registered in their name in this state, and there is no record that they had ever filed Utah State income tax returns. It may be that the Committee could have ruled the other way, as the dissent contends it should have, but the ruling was not arbitrary or capricious.

Affirmed. No costs.

HALL, C.J., and OAKS, J., concur.

HOWE, Justice (dissenting):

I dissent. The appellants proffered substantial evidence (most of which was not controverted by the University) that they had been Utah residents since 1971. It was therefore error to grant summary judgment against them. I would reverse for an evidentiary trial on the question.

The University in denying their application gave as its reasons that appellants had not complied with Rules I.D. and I.E. As I will attempt to demonstrate, those rules are flawed because they introduce as tests of residency factors which cannot be properly relied upon to deny a student residency status.

I. RULE I.D.

The Board of Regents in promulgating Rule I.D. seriously deviated from the authority given to it by the Legislature to promulgate supplementary rules and regulations to assist institutions in classifying students as residents or non-residents. Contrary to the statement in the majority opinion, Rule I.D. does not "closely parallel" the language of § 53–34–2.2. It is at odds with that section. Moreover, Rule I.D. cannot be lightly dismissed, as does the majority opinion, by characterizing its effect as "simply provid[ing] some reasonable flexibility to the one year rule."

I have no quarrel with the statement in Part I of the majority opinion that a state may charge higher tuition for non-resident students than it does for resident students and that it may require a student to be a resident for one year before he qualifies for the lower rate. The cases cited there support that proposition. However, none of them deal with the problem now confronting us, which is whether absence from the state for more than 30 days necessarily breaks the running of the continuous one year residency period.

The basic error of the majority opinion is that it misperceives the meaning of § 53–34–2.2 which defines a "resident" student. The majority opinion erroneously ascribes to that section the requirement that the student must physically remain within the borders of Utah for one year to qualify. On the basis of that erroneous interpretation, the majority opinion then justifies Rule I.D. as an "amelioration" of the stringent one year requirement by extending the student 30 days of grace. I do not agree with that analysis.

Section 53–34–2.2 is very explicit in its direction as how to determine whether a student is a "resident" for tuition purposes. Subsection (1) directs that the meaning of the word "resident" shall be determined by reference to the "general law on the subject of domicile." Subsection (2) adds three requirements, however, which must be observed in so doing:

> An adult who has come to Utah and established residency here for the purpose of attending an institution of higher education (1) must maintain continuous Utah *residency status* for one full year ... and ... (2) must demonstrate by additional objective evidence the establishment of a *domicile* in Utah and (3) that the student does not maintain a residence elsewhere. [Italics and numbers added.]

Subsection (7) authorizes the Board of Regents to make rules and regulations "*not inconsistent with the provisions of this section*" concerning the definition of resident and non-resident students, and establishing procedures for classifying and reclassifying students and criteria for judging claims of residency, domicile, emancipation, abandonment and other related matters. In my view, Rule I.D. is inconsistent with the statute in that contrary to subsections (1) and (2) it introduces an additional and arbitrary requirement, viz., that a student may not leave the borders of the state, irrespective of his intent in so doing, for more than 30 days without losing his Utah residency. This requirement is imposed even where the student leaves in order to work during summer vacation.

A. Certainly there is nothing in the "general law on the subject of domicile" which subsection (1) directs us to follow that would give basis for such a rule. Under the general law on the subject of domicile, an adult couple, such as the appellants here, who leave the state during the summer to lecture and to collect materials and photographs in pursuit of their vocation but always maintain the intent to return for the resumption of school in the fall, would not lose their residency status. In 25 Am.Jur.2d Domicil § 31 (1966) it is written:

> A domicil, once established, is not lost by by an absence from it for months or even years, for the purpose of business or pleasure or the like, if during such absence there exists an intent to be absent merely temporarily and an intent to resume residence in the place of domicil following the completion of the purpose of the absence.

It should be emphasized that in the instant case we are not dealing with a student who is single, who has never severed ties with the home of his parents, who comes to Utah for the school year and returns home during the summer vacation. We have here students who are a married couple. Years ago each of them left the state where his (or her) parents reside. When they left Utah during the summer of 1978 it was not to return to be under the roof of the parents of either of them. Rather, it was to travel in pursuit of earning their living. The appellants support themselves by their free-lance writing and photography. The fact that they may have visited Mr. Frame's parents briefly during the summer is inconsequential. They did not move back with parents nor did they move to a former residence of their own. The Restatement (Second) Of Conflict Of Laws, § 18 (1971) recognizes this critical distinction in Illustrations 13 and 14:

> 13. A, a young man aged twenty one, leaves his father's home to enter the X university. A returns to his father's home for vacations. These facts tend to show

that A does not intend to make his home near the university and that his domicil remains unchanged.

14. A, a young man just graduated from college, definitely leaves his former home, marries and goes with his wife to state X where he enters a professional school. He takes a house there, intending to live there until he secures his professional degree. These facts tend to show that A intends to make his home in X and has acquired a domicil of choice there.

In sum, Rule I.D. does violence to the general law of domicile which as pointed out above is that a person does not lose his residency by being temporarily out of the state in pursuit of his employment or career when he intends to return to the state after that sojourn ends. Thousands of people, including lecturers, artists, entertainers and athletes spend many months away from their domicile without losing it. This principle has been recognized by our Legislature in respect to residency for voting purposes. In § 20–2–14(d) it is provided that:

A person must not be considered to have lost his residence who leaves his home to go into a foreign country or into another state or precinct within the state for temporary purposes merely with the intention of returning; provided, he has not exercised the right to elective franchise in such state or precinct.

The Legislature has not shown any intent to deny resident students the same latitude and Rule I.D. should not be permitted to rob them of it.

B. Furthermore, Rule I.D. is inconsistent with subsection (2) which requires only the "residency status" or "domicile" to be maintained for one full year. (The two words are used interchangeably there). It does not state that the student must dwell in or have his abode in the state for one year, in which case it could be contended that he must remain within the borders of the state for that time. The statute clearly focuses on the *status* or *domicile* of the student, which is not affected by his temporary absence from the state while in pursuit of his career.

C. Rule I.D. also is out of harmony with subsection (2) because it provides for the loss of residency by a student who is outside the borders of the state even though there is no evidence that during that time he established residency outside of Utah. The appellants here have demonstrated that they do not maintain "a residence elsewhere" as the statute requires. The majority opinion has completely ignored this part of the statute and has failed to mention and give emphasis to the fact that there is no evidence whatever that the appellants had a residence elsewhere. If the appellants did in fact lose their Utah residency by being outside of this state for more than 30 days, then it follows that they had to establish a residency somewhere else. The Restatement (Second) Of Conflict Of Laws, § 19 (1971) states:

A domicil once established continues until it is superseded by a new domicil.

Neither the University nor the majority opinion has suggested where the appellants' residency might have been. A person's residency cannot be floating but must be fixed at some location. Before it can be concluded that the appellants lost their Utah residency by leaving the state during the summer, it should be decided where their residency was during that period of time. Was it in New Jersey where Mr. Frame lived with his parents before 1964 and where the appellants spent part of the summer in a vacation cottage on the seashore? Was it in California where Mrs. Frame resided with her parents prior to her marriage? Was it in Alaska where Mr. Frame lived when he entered the Army?

II. RULE I.E.

In addition to the fact that the appellants were not physically present in the State of Utah for 11 of the 12 months, the University gave as a second reason for denying their application "that they had not met the requirement of showing objective evidence of intent to remain in Utah as described in [Rule I.E.] such as purchasing property, acceptance of non-temporary employment or other evidences that would be of a nature to show that they in fact intended to remain in the state after graduation." The denial of appellants' application for this second reason is equally erroneous. In the first place, Rule I.E. does not require evidence that the student intends to remain in the state after graduation. Indeed, college graduates traditionally know that they must go where employment opportunities open. This applies to native born Utahns as well as to students who move here from out of state to attend a university such as the appellants. It cannot be seriously contended that this eventual possibility prevents them from being residents while they are here attending college. Restatement (Second) Of Conflicts Of Laws, § 18 (1971) states:

> To acquire a domicil of choice in a place, a person must intend to make that place his home *for the time at least.*

In the comment which follows in the Restatement, it is stated that:

> If there is an intention to make a home *at present*, the intention is sufficient although the person whose domicil is in question intends to change his home upon the happening of some future event.

As illustrations, the Restatement furnishes the following:

> 5. A, after graduation from college, leaves his father's house, teaches for several years and then comes to the law school of a university. His expenses are paid partly from his own money and partly from money borrowed from his father which he is under obligation to repay. He has a domicil in the university town if he intends to make his home there while attending the university.

> 6. A leaves his father's home, establishes another dwelling place, and earns his own living for several years. He comes to a university to attend the undergraduate department. He has a domicil in the university town if he intends to make his home there while attending the university.

We recently held in *Bustamante v. Bustamante*, that an alien who does not know whether he may be accorded the right to remain indefinitely or permanently in our country, may nevertheless establish the requisite residency necessary to bring a divorce action in this state. We stated that under those conditions the alien may have a dual intent—an intent to remain if that may be accomplished, and at the same time an intent to leave if the law so commands.

Furthermore, *Kelm v. Carlson*, cited in the main opinion invalidated a university regulation that required acceptance of post-graduate employment within the state in order to acquire resident student status. Therefore, in my opinion the reliance of the University on the fact that the appellants had not shown evidence that they intended to remain in Utah after graduation was ill-placed and violated its own rule.

The only evidence proffered to the trial court as to the plans for the appellants after their graduation from the University came from the deposition of Mr. Frame, wherein he stated that he wanted to stay in Utah upon graduation and become employed as a wildlife ecologist and continue his free-lance writing and photography on the side. The University did not dispute this intent. It was therefore improper for the University to deny appellants' application on the ground that they had not proved that they intended to remain in Utah after graduation.

The University's reliance upon the fact that the appellants had not accepted non-temporary employment in Utah is equally fallacious. The appellants are full-time students seeking to become wildlife ecologists. Until they finish their university work they do not intend to seek employment in that field. While students, they have chosen to be self-employed by their free-lance writing and photography. The University's insistence that they accept non-temporary employment by a Utah employer makes little sense in their case.

The remaining reason for the University's rejection of appellants' application was that they had not shown evidence that they had purchased "property." Rule I.E. does not specify what kind of property the student should purchase. It suffices to say that thousands of native born Utahns who have resided here all of their lives have not and do not own real property. No one can seriously contend that the lack of ownership of real property should be a disqualification to attaining residency. This test, like acceptance of employment from a Utah employer, is arbitrary and unreasonable.

III.

Having answered the University's reasons for denying residency status to the appellants in Part I and Part II of this dissenting opinion, I turn to an analysis of the evidence proffered by the appellants to prove their Utah residency. The majority opinion does not seem to dispute that the appellants became Utah residents when they returned here from Africa in March of 1978 and registered at the University. From that month until September when their classes began, they were away from Utah. First, they delivered a lecture at the Philadelphia Academy of Natural Sciences. Following that, they spent time in New Jersey and Pennsylvania collecting materials and photographs of the animals of the Atlantic tidal marshes—something they could not accomplish in Utah. Mr. Frame spent some time in the Philadelphia Academy of Natural Sciences researching materials on cheetahs for his Ph.D. degree. During two of the months they lived in a seaside vacation cottage on the coastline in New Jersey.

Before returning to Utah to attend classes, they purchased an automobile which they drove here and registered here upon arrival. From 1971 to 1975, Mr. Frame had a Utah driver's license which expired while appellants were in Africa. He therefore obtained a temporary New Jersey driver's license in order to drive the automobile to Utah. The New Jersey license expired on October 23, 1978, at which time he acquired a permanent Utah driver's license.

The appellants claimed to have registered to vote in Utah in 1971, 1978 and 1980 and to have voted by absentee ballot in either 1972 or 1976, and voted in person in 1978. They did not register to vote nor did they vote in any state other than Utah from 1971 to 1979.

Appellants continuously maintained a bank account in a Logan, Utah bank from 1971 to the present time. In addition, they claimed to have filed Utah State income tax returns for 1976, 1978 and 1979. (They were not required to file for the other years because of insufficient income). Except while they were in Africa, they have used no other address than their address at Utah State University since 1971. They likewise attended no other university during that period of time. Both of them deposed that they came to Utah in 1971 with the intent to live here primarily because of this state's wilderness areas. As heretofore noted in this opinion, there was no evidence that they had any ties to any other place. Mr. Frame deposed that he had not lived with his parents nor been dependent on them since 1964. He had obtained a B.S. degree from the University of Alaska and had worked in that state as an oceanographer until he was drafted into the Army. While stationed with the Army in California, he met Mrs. Frame; and, following his discharge from the Army, they married and came directly to Utah. While the University did dispute the appellants' claim of voting and filing income tax returns, it proffered no evidence that since appellants arrived in this state in 1971 they have had a residency elsewhere. Nor did it proffer evidence of any other residency from March 1978 to March 1979, which is the crucial period here under examination.

Rule I.E. authorizes the University to deny residency status to a student who registers to vote out of state, registers a motor vehicle out of state, obtains an out of state driver's license or receives significant out of state support. The appellants did none of the above except that Mr. Frame obtained a temporary two-month New Jersey driver's license in order to drive his newly purchased automobile to Utah.

At the very minimum, appellants made a substantial showing that they meet most of the indicia of residency listed in Rule I.E. I would reverse the summary judgment and remand for a trial.

DURHAM, J., concurs in the dissenting opinion of HOWE, J.

———————

Residency requirements are one of the few areas where student litigants win as often as they lose. Alien students have a particularly good record of winning, on grounds of preemption [*Toll v. Moreno*, 458 U.S. 1 (1982) (G-4 aliens allowed to establish postsecondary residency)], due process [*Leticia "A" v. University of California*, California Superior Court, June 10, 1985, No. 588–982–5) (undocumented college students entitled to establish residency)], and equal protection [*Plyler v. Doe*, 457 U.S. 202 (1982) (undocumented children cannot be charged tuition in public schools)]. The judge in *Leticia "A"* reviewed the State's residency practices, and concluded: "The policies underlying the immigration laws and regulations are vastly different from those relating to residency for student fee purposes. The two systems are totally unrelated for purposes of administration, enforcement and legal analysis. The use of unrelated policies, statutes, regulations or case law from one system to govern portions of the other is irrational. The incorporation of policies governing adjustment of status for undocumented aliens into regulations and administration of a system for determining residence for student fee purposes is neither logical nor rational."

For a review of residency requirement issues, see M. Olivas, "*Plyler v. Doe, Toll v. Moreno*, and Postsecondary Admissions: Undocumented Adults and 'Enduring Disability,'" *Journal of Law and Education*, 15 (1986), 19–55; P. Lines, "Tuition Discrimination: Valid and Invalid Uses of Tuition Differentials," *Journal of College and University Law* 9 (1982–83), 241–161; M. Olivas, "Administering Intentions: Law, Theory, and Practice of Postsecondary Residency Requirements," *Journal of Higher*

Education, 59 (1988), 263–290. For a review of the unique problems posed by residency requirements for Native American students, see J.Y. Henderson, "The Question of Nonresident Tuition for Tribal Citizens," *American Indian Law Review*, 4 (1976), 47–70.

Chapter 5
Affirmative Action

The cases in this chapter are, in many respects, the most significant in the field of higher education law, for litigation against racism in the academy has included the most profound, and profoundly difficult issues. Systematic racism, exclusionary practices, and the legacy of institutional resistance to change have exacted a great toll, one that continues in the mistrust of minority communities toward predominantly white institutions and in the considerable effort expended at providing equal access. In large part, the legalization of the academy came about as a means of integrating higher education, a process that is evident in the widespread legislation, regulation, and litigation. The cases selected here could have taken on dozens of dimensions, more fully articulating one large issue (for instance, the "desegregation" of higher education, or sexism in the academy), but consistent with the comprehensive approach of each of the chapters, several issues are treated in moderate depth.

Each of the three sections (Institutions, Students, and Faculty) includes several cases concerning matters of discrimination on the basis of race, national origin, gender, and handicap. In several instances, different levels of important cases are included to show how the issue changed over time (and over different federal administrations), and the full range of institutional wins and losses is revealed. Several key cases are summarized rather than included (*Brown, Grove City, Firefighters Local Union No. 1784*), as circumstances have either changed or commentary provides sufficient treatment. In addition, numerous cases incorporated elsewhere in the book have arisen as a result of race or gender issues. This approach both highlights discriminatory practices and infuses all the dimensions of higher education law with their consideration. It also elucidates acceptable institutional behavior and allows readers to consider the contours of what is desirable and what is possible.

Affirmative Action and Institutions

What constitutes the race of a college? What is a racially-isolated institution? As the cases in this Section reveal, the answers to these seemingly-obvious questions are neither easy nor agreed upon. It is clear that public white institutions resisted efforts by black students to enroll. In 1936, the first legal efforts leading to the 1954 *Brown* decision challenged the exclusion of blacks from the University of Maryland. *Pearson v. Murray*, 168 Md. 478, 182 A. 590 (1936). In 1938, the Supreme Court invalidated a Missouri plan that denied admission but paid the tuition for black residents who attended law school outside the state; Georgia and other states had similar programs. *Missouri ex rel. Gaines v. Canada*, 305 U.S. 377 (1938). In 1948, the Supreme Court required Oklahoma to enroll a black law student, as the State had no separate black law school. *Sipuel v. Board of Regents*, 332 U.S. 631 (1948). Oklahoma then admitted blacks, but literally roped black students off in the corner of classrooms and school

"Negro Attends First Class at University of Oklahoma

G. W. McLaurin, 54-year-old negro, nearest camera, watches from an anteroom as Dr. Frank Balyeat instructs the first class ever attended by a negro at the University of Oklahoma. The class was in educational sociology. The negro is taking five classes totaling 12 hours in his studies for a doctor's degree in education. The University has also assigned McLaurin a special desk in the library and a special room in the student union building where he can eat his meals." New York Times, 14 October 1948.   © New York Times, reprinted with permission.

facilities; in *McLaurin v. Oklahoma State Regents*, the Supreme Court held this practice to be unconstitutional. 339 U.S. 637 (1950); see also *McKissick v. Carmichael*, 187 F.2d 949 (4th Cir. 1951). In Texas, the State went so far as to establish a separate black law school (Texas State, later Texas Southern University) to keep blacks from enrolling at the University of Texas, but in *Sweatt v. Painter*, the Supreme Court held that there was such a substantial differential in the two schools that the practice could not be countenanced: "What is more important, the University of Texas Law School possesses to a far greater degree those qualities which are incapable of objective measurement but which make for greatness in a law school." 339 U.S. 629 (1950). South Carolina also established a black law school rather than accord admissions to black students at white colleges. *Wrighten v. University of South Carolina*, 72 F. Supp. 948 (E.D.S.C., 1947).

As most students know, the Supreme Court struck down separate but equal practices in *Brown v. Board of Education*, 347 U.S. 483 (1954); see also 349 U.S. 294 (1955) (duty to proceed with all "deliberate speed"). Additional cases continued to reveal the intransigence of college and state officials in Florida, Georgia, Alabama, Mississippi, and other states. As the *Adams* and *Geier* cases reveal, the issues have not been fully resolved. For a review of higher education's resistance to minorities, see G. Kujovich, "Equal Opportunity in Higher Education and the Black Public College: The Era of Separate But Equal," *Minnesota Law Review*, 72 (1987), 29–172; J. Entin, "*Sweatt v. Painter*, the End of Segregation, and the Transformation of Education Law," *The Review of Litigation*, 5 (1986), 3–71; J. Preer, *Lawyers v. Educators: Black Colleges and Desegregation in Public Higher Education* (Westport, Connecticut: Greenwood Press, 1982); L. Morris, *Elusive Equality* (D.C.: Howard University Press, 1979); M. Olivas, *The Dilemma of Access* (D.C.: Howard University Press, 1979).

Adams v. Richardson

356 F. Supp. 92 (1973)

JOHN H. PRATT, District Judge.

This cause came before this Court upon plaintiffs' motion for summary judgment and defendants' combined motion to dismiss and cross-motion for summary judgment. Upon the entire record before this Court including the pleadings, depositions and affidavits, and upon the Memorandum Opinion of this Court dated November 16, 1972, it is hereby ORDERED that plaintiffs' motion is granted, defendants' motions are denied and plaintiffs are granted the following declaratory and injunctive relief on each of the six separate causes of action:

I. HEW's Functions Under Title VI of the Civil Rights Act of 1964
Concerning Public Higher Education

A. Declaratory Judgment

(1) In January, 1969 HEW concluded that the State of Louisiana was operating a racially segregated system of higher education in violation of Title VI of the Civil Rights Act of 1964 (42 U.S.C. § 2000d et seq.). Between January, 1969 and February, 1970, HEW made the same administrative determination regarding the systems of higher education of the states of Mississippi, Oklahoma, North Carolina, Florida,

Arkansas, Pennsylvania, Georgia, Maryland and Virginia. In letters to the ten states, HEW requested each of them to submit a desegregation plan within 120 days or less.

(2) The states of Louisiana, Mississippi, Oklahoma, North Carolina and Florida have totally ignored HEW's requests of three to four years ago and have never submitted a desegregation plan.

(3) Although the other five states, Arkansas, Pennsylvania, Georgia, Maryland and Virginia, submitted to HEW between 24 and 38 months ago desegregation plans which were found unacceptable, HEW has failed formally to comment on any of these submissions in the intervening years.

(4) HEW has not commenced an administrative enforcement action against any of these ten states. Nor have these matters been submitted to the Justice Department for the filing of suits against any of the ten states.

(5) HEW has advanced and continues to advance Federal funds in substantial amounts for the benefit of institutions of higher education in the ten states.

(6) HEW has attempted to justify its failure to commence enforcement action on the grounds that negotiations with the ten states are still pending, the desegregation of state-wide systems is complex, and the Supreme Court standard of desegregation "at once" does not apply to public higher education.

(7) The time permitted by Title VI of the Civil Rights Act of 1964 to delay the commencement of enforcement proceedings against the ten states for the purpose of securing voluntary compliance has long since passed. The continuation of HEW financial assistance to the segregated systems of higher education in the ten states violates the rights of plaintiffs and others similarly situated protected by Title VI of the Civil Rights Act of 1964. Having once determined that a state system of higher education is in violation of Title VI, and having failed during a substantial period of time to achieve voluntary compliance, defendants have a duty to commence enforcement proceedings.

B. *Injunction*

(1) Defendants, their successors, agents and employees, are required and enjoined within 120 days from the date of this Order to commence enforcement proceedings by administrative notice of hearing, or to utilize any other means authorized by law, in order to effect compliance with Title VI by the states of Louisiana, Mississippi, Oklahoma, North Carolina, Florida, Arkansas, Pennsylvania, Georgia, Maryland and Virginia.

(2) Defendants, their successors, agents and employees, are required and enjoined to provide in verified form the following data to counsel for the plaintiffs on the dates indicated:

a. Within 150 days of the date of this Order, a report of all steps they have taken to comply with the injunctive provision set forth in the preceding paragraph, including a description of what action the Justice Department has taken in any public higher education violation defendants may have referred to that Department.

b. Every sixth month after the issuance of this Order for a period of three years, so as to permit evaluation of the reasons for any delays by defendants in bringing enforcement proceedings:

1. A description of each complaint (without identification of complainants) or other information of racial segregation or discrimination in public higher education received by defendants;

2. Whenever within 120 days of receipt of such complaint or other information no administrative determination as to racial segregation or discrimination was made by HEW, an explanation of the specific reasons for the failure to make such determination;

3. Based on each such complaint or other information, any findings by defendants as to the presence or absence of racial segregation or discrimination and the specific reasons therefor;

4. Whenever enforcement proceedings have not been commenced within 90 days of an HEW finding of racial segregation or discrimination, the specific reasons for the failure by defendants to commence such proceeding.

* * *

Plaintiffs are awarded the costs of this action, including the costs of the depositions taken therein. Plaintiffs are entitled to an attorney's fee as part of the costs, in an amount to be specified by further Order of this Court after appropriate proceedings.

APPENDIX A
Public Higher Education Compliance Efforts

State	Date of HEW Letter Requesting Desegregation Plan Within 120 Days or Less	Date State Plan Submitted (Latest Submission if Plan Revised)	Date of HEW Comment on State's Latest Submission
Louisiana	January 1969	None	
Mississippi	March 1969	None	
Oklahoma	February 1970	None	
North Carolina	February 1970	None	
Florida	February 1970	None	
Arkansas	January 1969	October 1969	None
Pennsylvania	March 1969	November 1969	None
Georgia	February 1970	May 1970	None
Maryland	March 1969	December 1970	None
Virginia	December 1969	December 1970	None

Adams v. Bennett

675 F. Supp. 668 (D.D.C. 1987)

JOHN H. PRATT, District Judge.

* * *

I. Background

It is appropriate at this point, before we begin our consideration of the Article III concerns raised by the Court of Appeals, to set forth briefly the relevant history of this case. This litigation has its roots in the distant past. Several actions have been joined to give it its present shape and form.[1] The common thread underlying each of

---

1. The original *Adams* litigation presented a challenge to the Department of Health, Edu-

the several complaints in this litigation, however, is the alleged improper grant of federal funds in violation of various statutes and regulations. These statutes and regulations include Title VI of the Civil Rights Act of 1964, as amended (Title VI), 42 U.S.C. § 2000d et seq. (1982), Title IX of the Education Amendments of 1972 (Title IX), 20 U.S.C. § 1681 et seq. (1982), Executive Order No. 11246, as amended by Executive Order 11375, and § 504 of the Rehabilitation Act of 1973, 29 U.S.C. § 794 (1982). Plaintiffs also present a constitutional challenge to defendants' conduct.

The original *Adams* case presented a challenge to HEW's policy of non-enforcement of Title VI with regard to claims of racial discrimination. In 1976 additional groups and individuals were allowed to intervene in the *Adams* litigation on the basis of HEW's representation that the Title VI enforcement obligations previously imposed by this court made it impossible to devote sufficient resources to the review and processing of Title IX sex discrimination and Title VI national origin discrimination complaints. In October 1977, the National Federation of the Blind also intervened, complaining of lack of enforcement of § 504 of the Rehabilitation Act of 1973 and § 904 of the Education Amendment Act of 1972 with respect to discrimination based on handicap. Thus, the entry of these plaintiff-intervenors in the *Adams* suit greatly expanded the statutory scope of the litigation.

As an indication of the breadth of this extensive and protracted litigation, it is significant to note that the current *Adams* plaintiffs consist of forty (40) individuals, eight (8) individual plaintiff-intervenors and five (5) plaintiff-intervenor organizations. The current *WEAL* plaintiffs consist of two (2) individuals and six (6) organizations.

A. *Court of Appeals Pronouncements*

In the original *Adams* case filed in 1970, we held that the Department of Health, Education and Welfare and its Director of the Office of Civil Rights did not have further discretion but were under an affirmative duty to commence enforcement proceedings against public educational institutions to ensure compliance with Title VI where efforts towards voluntary compliance were not attempted or successful. Subsequently, we ordered the agency to take certain corrective measures. With minor modifications not here relevant the Court of Appeals, sitting *en banc*, affirmed this court's decision ["*Adams I*"]. Although our order directed that the commencement of enforcement proceedings take place within certain time frames, the appellate court was careful to emphasize that:

> the order merely requires *initiation of a process* which, excepting contemptuous conduct, will then pass *beyond the District Court's continuing control and supervision.*

---

cation & Welfare's policy of nonenforcement of Title VI of the Civil Rights Act of 1964, as amended, 42 U.S.C. §§ 2000d et seq. (1982), with respect to seventeen (17) southern and border states. In 1975 a similar suit was filed against HEW alleging that the agency was failing to enforce Title VI in thirty three (33) northern and western states as well. Judge Sirica found HEW in default of its statutory obligations. Relief in that case was for the most part consolidated with *Adams* in the December 29, 1977 order. The 1977 Consent Decree also expanded the scope of the litigation by including a separate suit brought by the Women's Equity Action League in 1974. In that complaint, WEAL alleged that the Department of Health, Education & Welfare (HEW) and the Department of Labor (DOL) had both failed to meet their obligation to enforce Executive Order 11246 with respect to institutions of higher education, and that HEW had failed to comply with its Title IX obligations.

A further interpretation of the boundaries of our 1973 order arose later in another context. In March, 1979, the Department of Education (DE), which had succeeded to HEW's jurisdiction, rejected the State of North Carolina's desegregation plans, and subsequently commenced enforcement proceedings against the State. In response, North Carolina filed suit in federal court in North Carolina to enjoin the administrative hearing and to prevent the DE from deferring grant payments. The North Carolina court enjoined the deferral of payments but permitted the enforcement proceeding to continue. After the Department had completed the presentation of its case in chief, after several months of hearings, the parties entered into a consent settlement, which the North Carolina court approved. At this juncture, the *Adams* plaintiffs, who were not parties to the North Carolina suit, sought injunctive relief from this court to enjoin the Department from acceding to the proposed consent settlement. We declined to grant the requested relief, for reasons of comity as well as limitations in the scope of our original 1973 order. The Court of Appeals for this Circuit, again sitting *en banc*, affirmed our decision ["*Adams II*"]. It found that the purpose of the 1973 decree was to require the Department to meet its responsibilities under Title VI by the commencement of formal proceedings or through voluntary compliance, and that our decree did not extend to details of particular enforcement programs, including the supervision of the Department's settlement with North Carolina.

The opinions of the appellate court in *Adams I* and *Adams II* are the only Court of Appeals decisions concerning the proper reach and meaning of our original order. They both affirm the original direction of this litigation, and emphasize the limited nature of our intervention.

We turn now to the events leading up to the 1977 Consent Decree, the validity of which was indirectly challenged in the appeal in *WEAL*.

B. *The 1977 Consent Decree*

In 1975, in response to plaintiffs' suit alleging delays in the administrative processing of complaints in elementary and secondary education cases, we ordered the agency to proceed against defaulting school districts and imposed time frames controlling future enforcement activities by the agency. This consent order was negotiated by the parties and served to supplement our original February 16, 1973 order. It came to be known as the First Supplemental Order, and was the first of a series of orders establishing time frames for each stage of the administrative process. Part F of this order directed attention for the first time to future Title VI enforcement activities, setting time limitations for the handling of future complaints and compliance reviews. Part F of the First Supplemental Order was modified by an unpublished June 14, 1976 order of this court which established separate guidelines for the administrative processing of Title VI and Title IX complaints, compliance reviews, and Emergency School Aid Act cases. A so-called Second Supplemental Order concerning the acceptable ingredients for the desegregation of higher education in the states was issued on April 1, 1977.

In mid-1977, the *Adams* plaintiffs were again before this court seeking further relief for noncompliance with the 1975 order referred to above and with that portion of the 1973 order relating to special purpose and vocational schools. Plaintiffs sought compliance with previously imposed time frames and other administrative requirements. The court, after an extensive hearing, directed the parties to enter into negotiations. These negotiations resulted some months later in the 1977 Consent Decree issued on December 29, 1977.

The 1977 Decree was more extensive than the orders entered previously and differed from them in several respects. First, the Decree broadened the court's review of HEW enforcement activities to include all fifty states. Second, in addition to Title VI, it applied to complaints and compliance reviews under Title IX, Executive Order No. 11246, and § 504 of the Rehabilitation Act of 1973. Third, it set forth a number of additional procedural steps to be performed following receipt of a completed complaint.

It is a fair summary to state that the emphasis in the original order of 1973 stemmed from defendants' abdication of their statutory responsibility in pursuing a conscious policy of non-enforcement. The 1973 order, as stated previously, rejected the agency claim that it had almost unfettered discretion in this area, and, instead, directed that enforcement proceedings be commenced within certain limited time frames. These time frames have become more detailed with the issuance of each new order, in part because of defendants' chronic delays and in part because of the asserted necessity for these delays during the various stages of the administrative proceedings. The Consent Decree of December 29, 1977 was a culmination of this process and attempted to address these difficulties in a single document fifty-four (54) pages in length comprised of eighty-eight (88) separately numbered paragraphs. Limitations of space prevent a detailed catalogue of these provisions. It is sufficient to say that the parties, in good faith, made a serious attempt to settle all outstanding differences existing between them.

In August 1982 defendants moved to vacate the 1977 Consent Order asserting changes in fact and law, as well as the need for a deeper consideration of the facts in light of experience. We denied defendants' motion to vacate on March 11, 1983. On the same day, in response to Motions for Orders to Show Cause filed by the *Adams* and *WEAL* plaintiffs, we entered a detailed order of thirty-seven (37) pages modifying the 1977 Consent Order as it applied to the DE and the DOL. On March 24, 1983, in response to Plaintiffs' Renewed Motion for Further Relief Concerning State Systems of Higher Education, we entered a separate order, in which we found that five southern states had defaulted in their commitments under previously accepted desegregation plans in violation of Title VI. We ordered defendants to require these states, with the exception of Virginia, which had recently submitted a provisionally approved plan, to submit further plans within a limited time frame or to commence formal enforcement proceedings no later than September 15, 1983. Injunctive relief was also granted requiring defendants to take similar action with respect to Pennsylvania and Kentucky, and was denied with respect to Texas, West Virginia, Missouri and Delaware.

Defendants appealed from this court's denial of their motion to vacate the 1977 Consent Decree and from the March 24, 1983 order relating to statewide systems of higher education. It is this appeal which is the subject of the Court of Appeals remand of September 14, 1984.

II. *Discussion*

Because the remand raised issues of standing and mootness, defendants were given an opportunity to engage in and complete discovery on these issues. After extensive discovery, defendants filed a Motion to Dismiss on the grounds that (1) plaintiffs lack standing; (2) the doctrine of separation of powers defeats standing as a matter of law and (3) the claims of the plaintiffs in *WEAL* and the plaintiff-intervenors in the *Adams* litigation are moot. The *Adams* plaintiffs, in opposition to defendants' Motion to Dismiss, assert (1) that plaintiffs are suffering concrete personal injuries; (2) that these injuries are fairly traceable to defendants' conduct and (3) that such injuries are likely to be redressed by a decree of this court. After distinguishing *Allen v. Wright*, they contend that defendants' separation of powers argument is lacking in substance. They point to the necessity of time frames to meet defendants' chronic delays in the enforcement of defendants' obligations under Title VI and other statutes and the fact that the time frames were consented to by the appropriate officials of two different political administrations. Oppositions to defendants' Motion to Dismiss have been filed on behalf of WEAL, as well as other *Adams* intervenors.

* * *

1. *Injury*

Plaintiffs' basic contention is that defendants have granted and are continuing to grant federal assistance to educational institutions and political entities in violation of the rights of the plaintiffs under various statutes and under the Fifth Amendment of the Constitution. They assert that this is an injury separate and apart from the harm inflicted by the educational institutions in which they are enrolled, or by the states in which they reside.

The individual *Adams* plaintiffs, some 40 in all reside in various states and attend a variety of state educational institutions. Many of the plaintiffs can be placed in one of the following categories. (1) Three are students at Virginia State University (VSU), a predominantly black institution. They complain of unequal and inadequate facilities, equipment and programs. VSU is not in accord with the time frames set in our March 11, 1983 order. (2) Four of the plaintiffs are students at the University of Arkansas at Fayetteville (UAF), a traditionally white institution. According to the July 8, 1985 findings by OCR, UAF had failed to reach its black student, faculty and administrator goals for 1984–85, as required by its statewide desegregation plan.[16] Defendants have not denied this allegation. (3) Three of the plaintiffs are students in Dillon County, South Carolina School District No. 2 (Dillon), who are enrolled in segregated classrooms. Since 1977, Dillon has been found by OCR to be in violation of Title VI on three different occasions. The matter was referred to the Department of Justice on June 23, 1983, following our order of March 11, 1983. Almost one year later it was returned by the Department of Justice to OCR, where it is still "under review." These facts are not challenged. (4) Five of the plaintiffs are students in Halifax County, Virginia, alleging racially discriminatory action in connection with events which occurred on a County school bus. OCR investigated the report and issued a letter of finding that Halifax County had not violated Title VI.

* * *

There is no doubt but that Congress designed Title VI to put an end to discrimination in the administration of Federal programs, and thereby to promote the national

---

16. Arkansas' performance has not improved. *See* House Committee on Government Operations, 100th Cong., 1st Sess., Report on Failure and Fraud in Civil Rights by the Department of Education. In this Report, the Committee states that Arkansas and nine other southern and border states have failed in their commitments to reduce racial discrimination in their colleges and universities.

policy of non-discrimination. The same national policy is reflected in the passage of several statutes following on the heels of Title VI, *i.e.*, Title VII (discrimination in employment) and Title IX (discrimination based on sex). But the above statements of purpose and intent do not alone solve the problem of whether plaintiffs' injury, which we hold to be judicially cognizable, is "fairly traceable" to the challenged conduct of defendants.

It is defendants' basic position that the educational institutions themselves and the political entities, both state and local, are "the direct causation of the discrimination of which plaintiffs complain." They claim that it is the conduct of these independent institutions and political entities, and not the action or inaction of defendants, which has caused plaintiffs' injury. Accordingly, they assert that the causal relationship between defendants' actions and plaintiffs' injury is too indirect and attenuated to supply the indispensable link of causation.

* * *

[T]he decisions of educational and political institutions in response to the threatened or actual cut-off of funds in this context cannot be predicted with certainty. To believe that strict enforcement of time frames in the administrative processing of complaints or of time frames for compliance with state plans would redress the injury of which plaintiffs complain, is to indulge in speculation. The connection between plaintiffs' injury and defendants' action or inaction is too indirect to provide a proper nexus.

It should not be forgotten that the discriminatory practices of which plaintiffs' complain existed long before the passage of the Civil Rights Act of 1964. They were not caused by defendants. They have been continued, and maintained to the extent they presently exist, not by defendants, but by the schools and states themselves, where these practices have unfortunately long been customary. Any effect plaintiffs suffer as a result of the grant of federal assistance to these separate and independant entities is similar to the effect of the refusal to deny Section 501(c)(3) tax exempt status discussed in *Allen*. It is indirect, attenuated and speculative. In no sense is such injury "fairly traceable" to defendants' conduct.

3. Redressability

As is frequently the case, the concepts of causation and redressability are closely related. This is especially so in the instant action. Since the injury of which plaintiffs complain is not sufficiently linked to the action or inaction of defendants, it is also speculative to predict that the close monitoring of the day-to-day affairs of two arms of the Executive Branch, the DE and DOL, would remedy or even attenuate this injury. The effect of terminating, or threatening to terminate, federal aid to institutions continuing discriminatory practices, is even more speculative. This is especially so in the area of higher education.

a. Higher Education

The most difficult problems in educational desegregation exist in the area of higher education. This was recognized long ago, when the Court of Appeals in *Adams I* affirmed the injunctive relief provided by this court with one single exception. With regard to institutions of higher education, the Appeals Court extended the period of compliance with Title VI by lengthening to 120 days the time within which a state was required to submit a plan for eventual desegregation, and, if an acceptable plan had not been submitted within 180 days, the initiation of compliance procedures. The court recognized the problems of integrating higher education when it noted:

> Perhaps the most serious problem in this area is the lack of state-wide planning to provide more and better trained minority group doctors, lawyers, engineers and other professionals. A predicate for minority access to quality post-graduate programs is a viable, coordinated state-wide higher education policy that takes into account the special problems of minority students and of Black colleges. As *amicus* points out, these Black institutions fulfill a crucial need and will continue to play an important role in Black higher education.

We stressed this thought in our Second Supplemental Order of April 1, 1977. That order addressed the failure of certain southern states to submit acceptable plans for desegregation, and ordered defendants within 90 days to promulgate the ingredients of an acceptable higher education desegregation plan, and within 60 days thereafter to require the states of Arkansas, Florida, Georgia, North Carolina, Oklahoma, and Virginia to submit revised plans. At the same time, we stated:

> The process of desegregation must not place a greater burden on Black institutions or Black students' opportunity to receive a quality public higher education. The desegregation process should take into account the unequal status of the Black colleges and the real danger that desegregation will diminish higher education opportunities for Blacks. Without suggesting the answer to this complex problem, it is the responsibility of HEW to devise criteria for higher education plans which will take into account the unique importance of Black colleges and at the same time comply with the Congressional mandate.

The lack of integration in higher education remains despite the passage of more than a decade, and was the focus of our March 24, 1983 order presently under review. The explanations are easily found and may be judicially noticed. First, there is the inherent difficulty of increasing Black enrollment in predominantly white public institutions, stemming at least in part from current admissions standards, which many Blacks, because of inferior secondary education, find difficult to meet. It is no secret that many of the Black eligibles with proper academic qualifications are persuaded to attend private out-of-state institutions offering scholarships and other financial aid. Extensive recruiting efforts have not been entirely successful. Second, white enrollment in predominantly Black institutions has also lagged but for different reasons, among them the diminished academic quality of these institutions and their poorer facilities. In order to bring Black institutions up to equality and make them competitive with white institutions state legislatures will have to act to supply the needed funds for the hiring of faculty and the expansion of physical plant and facilities.

These conditions long antedated the passage of Title VI in 1964 and are conditions over which defendants have no control. They were not caused by any action of defendants and are not "fairly traceable" to anything defendants have done or have failed to do. It is overly sanguine to believe that the enforcement of time frames or the defendants' ultimate weapon of cutting off funds will achieve the desired results of substantial compliance. In the case of Black institutions, in addition to being ineffective, the effect of cutting off federal funds might well be devasting. Funding from state and local sources is already in short supply. The record in this case indicates that many of the 104 Black colleges would have serious difficulty surviving if federal funding were eliminated. The injury of which plaintiffs complain, particularly in the case of state institutions of higher learning, is not redressible by the relief which plaintiffs seek.

The orders of March 11, 1983 and March 24, 1983 not only go well beyond the initiation of the enforcement process, but, through the detailed imposition of precise time frames governing every step in the administrative process, seek to control the way defendants are to carry out their executive responsibilities. The fact that the government for the most part consented to these burdens is of no consequence. More importantly, plaintiffs do not claim that defendants have abrogated their statutory responsibilities, but rather that, in carrying them out, they do not always process complaints, conduct investigations, issue letters of findings, or conduct compliance reviews as promptly or expeditiously as plaintiffs would like. As was said in *Laird v. Tatum*:

> Carried to its logical end, [respondents'] approach would have the federal courts as virtually continuing monitors of the wisdom and soundness of Executive action; such a role is appropriate for Congress acting through its committees and the 'power of the purse'; it is not the role of the judiciary, absent actual present or immediately threatened injury resulting from unlawful governmental action.

Thus, entirely apart from plaintiffs' failure to meet the causation and redressability elements of standing, the orders under review intrude on the functions of the Executive branch and violate the doctrine of separation of powers, which is the basic core of standing.

* * *

A detailed analysis of each of defendants' claims of mootness with respect to each of the multitude of matters raised by the *WEAL* plaintiffs and the plaintiff-intervenors in *Adams* is difficult on the basis of the record before us. In view of our treatment of the issue of standing, we prefer to avoid this unnecessary and possibly indecisive exercise and make no determination concerning defendants' claims of mootness.

III. *Conclusion*

For all of the reasons set forth above, it is our holding that all of the plaintiffs and intervenors in *Adams*, as well as all of the plaintiffs in *WEAL*, lack standing to continue this litigation.

Accordingly, we grant defendants' motion to dismiss.

APPENDIX
PARTIAL CHRONOLOGICAL INDEX OF RELEVANT DECISIONS AND ORDERS

★ *Adams v. Richardson*, 480 F. 2d 1159 (D.C. Cir. 1973) [*Adams I*], affirming 356 F. Supp. 92 (D.D.C. 1973).

★ *Adams v. Weinberger*, 391 F. Supp. 269 (D.D.C. 1975) [First Supplemental Order].

★ *Adams v. Califano*, 430 F. Supp. 118 (D.D.C. 1977) [Second Supplemental Order] (Modified unpublished order of March 14, 1975).

★ *Adams v. Califano* No. 3095–70 (D.D.C. December 29, 1977) [Consent Decree] (basis for March 11, 1983 and March 24, 1983 Orders).

★ *North Carolina v. Department of Education* No. 79–217–CIV–5 (E.D.N.C. July 17, 1981) (Approved consent settlement between the Department of Education and the State of North Carolina).

★ *Adams v. Bell*, 711 F. 2d 161 (D.C. Cir. 1983) [*Adams II*] (affirming this court's refusal to enjoin the Department of Education from entering into a consent settlement with the State of North Carolina).

★ *Adams v. Bell*, No. 3095–70 (D.D.C. March 11, 1983) (Order modifying the terms of the 1977 Consent Decree).

★ *Adams v. Bell*, No. 3095–70 (D.D.C. March 11, 1983) (Order denying defendants' motion to vacate the December 29, 1977 Consent Decree).

★ *Adams v. Bell*, No. 3095–70 (D.D.C. March 24, 1983) (Order modifying 1977 Consent Decree with respect to issues pertaining to state-wide systems of higher education).

———

Judge Pratt's ruling included a reference (Footnote 16) to a Congressional *Report on Failure and Fraud in Civil Rights by the Department of Education*. It was revealed in 1987 that OCR staff had fraudulently backdated official responses to make it appear that the Department had complied with Judge Pratt's earlier orders. "OCR Discloses Backdating of Documents In Its Civil Rights Investigations," *Education Daily*, 31 March 1987, pp. 1–3. See also, "ED Ends Higher ED Desegregation Requirements for Four Southern States," *Education Daily*, 11 February 1988, pp. 1, 8. After the Civil Rights Restoration Act was enacted, by an override of President Reagan's veto, the Justice Department refiled charges in Alabama. "Justice Dept. to Use New Civil-Rights Law to Press Segregation Charge Against Alabama's Colleges," *Chronicle of Higher Education*, 6 April 1988, pp. A1, 22.

———

Geier v. Blanton
427 F. Supp. 644 (1977)

GRAY, Chief Judge.

* * *

This action was originally filed by the plaintiffs, both white and black citizens of the State of Tennessee, to enjoin the proposed construction and expansion of the University of Tennessee-Nashville Center. The plaintiffs alleged, *inter alia*, that Tennessee Agricultural and Industrial State University, now Tennessee State University (hereinafter referred to as TSU), was originally established under State statute as a State public higher education institution for the education of blacks, which statute was prima facie evidence of racial discrimination; that TSU was being maintained by State officials as a segregated black institution contrary to the Fourteenth Amendment to the Constitution of the United States; that appropriations for TSU were not provided on a basis equal to those of the State's predominantly white institutions; and that the new construction and expansion of the predominantly white University of Tennessee-Nashville Extension Center would serve to perpetuate TSU, also located in Nashville, as a segregated black institution which would ensure the continued existence of a dual system of public higher education in Tennessee. Based on the foregoing reasons, and others, the plaintiffs requested that the State be enjoined from

expanding the Nashville Extension Center, from providing unequal educational facilities, and from maintaining racially segregated institutions of higher education in
Nashville.

Subsequently, the United States moved to intervene in the action. The United States
joined the plaintiffs in their allegations and requested relief, and, in addition, the
United States requested that the State officials be required to formulate and submit
to the Court a plan of desegregation designed to eliminate the dual system of public
higher education in Tennessee. On July 22, 1968, the Court granted the motion of
the United States for leave to intervene as a party plaintiff.

After a hearing conducted on August 19, 20 and 21, 1968, the Court delivered an
opinion from the Bench, which opinion was followed by an Order on August 22,
1968, denying the requests of the plaintiffs and plaintiff-intervenor, the United States,
to enjoin the proposed construction and expansion of the University of Tennessee-
Nashville Center (hereinafter referred to as UT-N), but requiring the defendants to
formulate and submit to the Court, by April 1, 1969, a plan designed to dismantle
the dual system of higher education in Tennessee, with particular attention to TSU.
In its opinion, filed in written form on August 23, 1968, the Court found that a dual
system of higher education had been established by law in Tennessee and that it had
not been dismantled; that progress toward desegregating the traditionally white institutions in the eight years of an open-door policy had been slow as shown by the
percentages of black enrollment ranging from .6 percent to about 7 percent at the
individual universities; that TSU still had a black enrollment in excess of 99 percent;
and that the record at that time did not indicate that the proposed construction and
operation of UT-N would necessarily perpetuate a dual system of higher education.

* * *

Today, over 60 years after the State's establishment of TSU as an institution for
negroes and over 8 years after the Court's initial mandate to desegregate, TSU's
student population is still overwhelmingly black. The February 1976 Progress Report
reveals that the enrollment at TSU in fall, 1975, was about 85 percent black and
about 12.2 percent white. However, the proportion of whites on the main campus
had not changed since the previous year and remained at about 7 percent, leading to
the conclusion that a great number of the white students enrolled at TSU were actually
taking courses in off-campus centers, since over 80 percent of the students in these
centers were white. Progress was reported in the area of faculty recruitment, as black
faculty at TSU dropped to 68.84 percent of the total. By way of contrast, since the
filing of this suit, while UT-N has grown from a small extension program of the
University of Tennessee at Knoxville to a degree-granting institution with full campus
status (from 1,788 students to 5,828 students), UT-N has remained predominantly
white with 12.7 percent total black enrollment in the fall, 1975. Black faculty at UT-
N did not advance in 1975; the percentage dropped from 4.3 percent in 1974 to 4.1
percent in 1975 with the number of black faculty members remaining at five.

The Court now finds that the existence and expansion of predominantly white UT-
N alongside the traditionally black TSU have fostered competition for white students
and thus have impeded the dismantling of the dual system.

The competition for white students between the two four-year degree-granting
institutions was recognized early by the Tennessee Higher Education Commission in
a report filed on July 31, 1972, which stated in part:

"The only successful large scale desegregation of formerly black institutions has come by attracting adult, largely part-time commuting students, mostly enrolling in evening classes. This is the type of students that U.T. Nashville has been developed to serve, and U.T. Nashville provides the biggest competition to Tennessee State in its efforts to attract white students."

The best evidence of the competitive nature of the Nashville situation is found in the similar programs offered by both institutions. These programs have remained predominantly one-race at each institution. For example, in the fall of 1976, TSU's Department of Arts and Sciences had a total enrollment of 1,629 students, of which 1,590, or 97.6 percent, were black; UT-N's Division of Arts and Sciences had a total enrollment of 1,895 students, of which 1,521 or 80.3 percent, were white. For the same period, TSU's Department of Business Administration enrolled 800 students, of which 785, or 98.1 percent, were black; UT-N's Division of Business Administration enrolled 2,098 students, of which 1,828, or 87.1 percent, were white.

The defendants have sought repeatedly to show that the two schools are not competing institutions because UT-N was established to serve working adults who wish to attend college on a part-time basis after 4:00 p.m., while TSU was established as a land-grant institution to serve the traditional younger college student. In deciding this case, the Court must recognize that, up to this date, the pattern of student enrollment in Nashville has been that white students have overwhelmingly enrolled at UT-N, as part-time evening students, and that black students have overwhelmingly enrolled at TSU as daytime students. This pattern of enrollment does not appear to be just coincidental but appears to be a vestige of the former state-imposed dual system of public higher education in the State of Tennessee. Moreover, even if the average student profile at UT-N shows that those students are older and are employed, these are the kind of white students that TSU must attract if it is to prosper.

The competition for students between UT-N and TSU is roughly paralleled by the situation in Memphis several years ago which was described extensively by Dr. Cecil Humphreys, former president of Memphis State University (hereinafter referred to as MSU). About the same time that the University of Tennessee Board of Trustees initiated its Nashville Center, it opened a comparable extension center in Memphis, where courses were offered during the evenings primarily for working adults, which courses could be used for credit at an accredited institution. In the 1950's, MSU, which had been operating prior to the initiation of the UT-Memphis Center, began to offer evening programs at its own campus, located four to five miles from the UT Center. At the hearing, Dr. Humphreys stated that MSU and the UT Center were in competition for students and that MSU was handicapped in its ability to compete because a UT degree had greater prestige. As was stated in a history of the later established Joint University Center: "For reasons unknown to many but understandable by a few, many University of Tennessee downtown students drove past the Memphis State University Campus to take classes." In the 1960's MSU established a center downtown close to the UT Center and was able to thwart the granting of resident center status to UT, which would have made the center more attractive to students. Concern was expressed about the duplication of programs offered at the two institutions, which concern eventually resulted in the establishment of a Joint University Center in which MSU plays the primary role.

It is clear from the above discussion that the growth of UT in Memphis was cut off by MSU's efforts to attract a large part of the evening students in Memphis. The

Court expresses no opinion as to whether TSU officials were at fault in not expanding their programs to compete with UT-N, as did MSU, or as to whether UT-N's existence kept TSU from so expanding. However, the fact remains that UT-N and TSU are in competition for students just as were MSU and the UT-Memphis center. With TSU's black history and UT's prestige, this competition inevitably fosters dualism.

In its 1972 opinion, the Court charged the defendants with the responsibility of allocating programs to TSU which would ensure a substantial "white presence on the campus." Specifically, the Court pointed toward the duplicative nursing program at UT-N and the UT School of Social Work then housed at UT-N as examples of programs to consider. Furthermore, the Court recognized that the foregoing action would not result in the adequate desegregation of TSU and ordered the defendants to consider additional methods for desegregation, including the feasibility of merger and of curriculum consolidation of the Nashville institutions. After finding that the defendants' interim plans ordered by the Court in its previous opinions had not been effective in desegregating TSU, the Court, on February 15, 1974, directed the defendants to file a new interim plan for 1974–1975 and a long range plan for the State. All of these orders were, for the most part, attempts by the Court to do something about the competition for white students in the Nashville area. The Court now finds that, with respect to the Nashville area, the defendants' plans have not produced the desired result.

From the first plan filed by the defendants through the Long Range Plan now in effect, the defendants have sought to achieve the ordered progress at TSU by utilizing certain joint and cooperative programs between UT-N and TSU (sometimes also Middle Tennessee State University and Austin Peay), and by providing exclusive program assignments for the two Nashville institutions. The record clearly shows that this approach "has not worked and, indeed, appears to contain no prospect of working."

It appears appropriate for the Court to review the record with respect to the success or lack of success of the joint, cooperative and exclusive programs which have been implemented.

The Long Range Plan defines a joint program as one leading to a joint degree in which some of the course work must be done at one institution and some at another, and in which the faculty of both institutions are involved in planning and teaching. Only two programs included in the Long Range Plan meet this definition.

The first of these programs, the joint degree in general engineering between UT-N and TSU, is admittedly a failure. The program was put into effect in 1971 and was reevaluated in 1976. The report, prepared by the Ad Hoc Committee on the TSU/UT-N Joint Engineering Program and presented to the Monitoring Committee on September 13, 1976, concluded that the program had not attracted significant numbers of TSU students, and was, therefore, never effective in enhancing the white presence on that campus. The Committee attributed the program's failure to the differences in clienteles at the two institutions and the differences in academic calendars between TSU and UT-N (TSU is on the semester system while UT-N is on the quarter system). The Committee recommended that the program be terminated.

The only other joint program as defined in the Long Range Plan is a joint masters in public administration between UT-N, TSU and MTSU. At the hearing it was learned that the first class had been enrolled for Fall, 1976, with TSU being designated as the first coordinating institution. Although this program is new and cannot therefore be evaluated fully as to its impact, the Court must take notice of the problems encountered with the joint engineering program discussed previously. These two problems are present with any joint program involving UT-N and TSU, so the Court must find that the prospects for the program's success are not good.

Cooperative programs are defined by the Long Range Plan as programs which make it easier but do not require students to take work on both campuses, by facilitating student exchange of credits. In these programs the institutions may also agree to cooperate in other ways such as in the exchange of faculty. Although these programs are defined, no cooperative academic credit programs involving both UT-N and TSU are identified. The February 1976 Progress Report discusses several proposed noncredit programs such as inservice-type programs for teachers, career education conferences, workshops, and the like, but the Report does not describe these programs with specificity or show how these programs have contributed or will contribute to the desegregation of either campus. The record thus shows that the joint or cooperative programs have had no appreciable impact on the desegregation of TSU.

* * *

Thus, the Court finds that two programs account for the majority of TSU's white enrollees: the exclusive graduate education program and the off-campus centers program. As noted above, the February 1976 Progress Report states that the percentage of white students on campus remained at 7 percent in the fall of 1975, while the total number of whites enrolled increased to 12.2 percent in 1975. This conclusion that most of TSU's whites are still in the off-campus centers can also be drawn from TSU's tentative enrollment figures for 1976.

From the foregoing discussion, it appears to the Court that the State's approach utilizing joint, cooperative and exclusive program planning has not eliminated the competition between UT-N and TSU, and past failures leave little hope for future progress. The hope for future progress is further dimmed by the historical inability of the defendants to agree among themselves as to the proper course of action, and by the reluctance of the politically powerful University of Tennessee to take significant steps to eradicate dualism in Nashville.

Both the division between the boards governing UT-N and TSU and the power of the University of Tennessee System is demonstrated at the outset by counsel for the defendants. From the beginning, the University of Tennessee and its Board of Trustees have retained their own counsel. In the initial stages of the action, UT was represented by in-house counsel; in the latter stages, private counsel was retained by the System. The remaining defendants, including the Board of Regents as the governing board of TSU (before 1972, the Board of Education), and the Tennessee Higher Education Commission (the central governing board) have been represented by the Attorney General for the State of Tennessee, whose duties include, *inter alia*, the defense of "any and all suits . . . in any of the district courts of the United States held in the state of Tennessee, in which suit or suits the state may be a party, or in which the state has or may have interests of a pecuniary nature."

The division among the defendants appeared most destructive after the Court's 1972 opinion requiring the allocation of courses to TSU that would ensure a white presence on campus, and a feasibility study of merger and curriculum consolidation.

THEC filed a report on July 31, 1972, suggesting that, while merger was not appropriate at that time, the competition for white students between TSU and UT-N could be ameliorated by assigning all teacher education in Nashville exclusively to TSU. TSU filed a separate statement on the same date calling for merger under TSU, while UT filed a statement on August 1, 1972, rejecting merger under either institution and suggesting cooperative-type programs as the primary means for achieving desegregation.

In April, 1974, the disagreements were heightened by the submission of separate interim plans. Reporting that it could not resolve differences about the role of UT in Nashville, THEC suggested that undergraduate engineering, undergraduate education, or graduate education be moved exclusively to TSU by Court Order. The University of Tennessee also filed an interim plan which rejected merger as an alternative and said of the exclusive program allocation proposed by THEC:

> "However, proposals for such assignments advanced by the THEC staff have placed the entire burden of desegregation on UT-N, without regard to other middle Tennessee institutions."

On April 10, 1974, the University of Tennessee espoused further its opinions on exclusive program allocation:

> "The University of Tennessee does believe that the allocation of *new* programs between or among middle Tennessee institutions is a promising way to promote further desegregation....
>
> "The University of Tennessee stands ready to work with the Tennessee Higher Education Commission and the State Board of Regents in developing a plan for assignment of future exclusive programs ... but does not accept the discontinuance of existing programs at the University of Tennessee at Nashville as a viable method for desegregating the TSU campus."

Thus, although the agreement has been reached to implement the Long Range Plan and a spirit of greater cooperation among the defendants was apparent at the recent hearing of this case, the Court takes notice that program allocations have, for the most part, followed the wishes expressed by the University of Tennessee. Although the graduate teacher education program assigned to TSU by the Court Order has been the most successful program in terms of racial impact, the Long Range Plan does not contemplate any proposal for similar allocations in the other areas proposed by THEC.

Most importantly, when a disagreement occurs among the institutions or governing boards, THEC has no power to resolve it.

* * *

In the foregoing discussion, the Court has found that the defendants' approach to eliminating the effects of State-imposed segregation in the Nashville area institutions has not worked and that it offers no real hope for further progress in that direction. Therefore, the Court finds that "more radical remedies are required."

The only approach proposed by the parties plaintiff is the merger of TSU and UT-N. The defendant THEC addressed this possibility in its report filed July 31, 1972, which stated: "[A] merger of Tennessee State and U.T. Nashville does not appear to be feasible *at the present time [1972], although this may be necessary at some time in the future to complete the desegregation process and to eliminate duplication and overlapping of programs."* [Emphasis supplied.] Although rejecting merger for the moment, THEC recognized in its report that UT-N was engaged in competition with TSU for white students, which competition this Court has previously found to exist. THEC's proposals at that time were basically the same as those in the Long Range Plan. Since joint, cooperative and exclusive programming has not resulted in progress toward eliminating the dual system in Nashville, while Tennessee's predominantly white institutions on a statewide basis are making genuine progress towards that end, the Court finds at this time that the only reasonable alternative is the merger of TSU and UT-N into a single institution under a single governing board.

Expert testimony in the record, including some testimony by the defendants' own experts, shows that merger is the best long range solution for desegregating the Nashville area.

* * *

In summary, when the record is considered regarding alternative approaches of desegregating the Nashville area, two things become apparent. First, the expert witnesses all believe that merger is an acceptable approach for desegregating the Nashville area, with most of the expert witnesses believing that merger is the best long range solution. Second, most of the expert witnesses and several of the defendant officials believe that eventually there will be one institution in Nashville. Consequently, the evidence overwhelmingly supports merging the two Nashville institutions under one governing board.

As to which governing board should operate the merged institution, the record contains little testimony in support of merger under UT-N. Neither the record nor the historical facts would support placing the merged institution under the UT Board of Trustees. TSU is a land-grant university with a 60-year history. UT-N is a newly created branch of the UT system which has become a degree-granting campus during the period of this litigation. For the Board of Trustees of UT to take over the merged institution would mean the elimination of TSU as an educational institution with all the concomitant losses entailed therein.

The Court is further of the opinion that merger under the Board of Regents should provide additional advantages with respect to the goal of desegregation since the other three State institutions of higher education in Middle Tennessee are under this Board. Any problems of competition or duplicative programs can obviously best be handled by one governing board.

The Court rejects the proposal of plaintiff-intervenors Richardson, *et al.*, that immediate merger should be directed, feeling that such precipitate action might well result in needless disruption and possibly the temporary loss of some educational services to the Nashville area.

The Court finds that merger under the Board of Regents, with UT-N supporting TSU during the transition period, offers the best prospect for success. It further finds that the merger should be completed within three (3) years from July 1, 1977.

Although this Court finds that merger is the best solution to the Nashville area problem, the remedy of merger is admittedly a radical remedy. In light of recent Supreme Court decisions limiting federal remedial powers in desegregation cases, the Court finds it necessary to briefly comment on merger in the context of one of these opinions.

In *Austin Independent School District v. United States,* the Supreme Court reversed the Fifth Circuit Court of Appeals approval of a requirement of extensive cross-town busing to achieve a certain degree of racial balance in every school. In reversing, the Supreme Court determined that the Court had abused its remedial powers, which may only be used in the face of a constitutional violation and which, if used, may not exceed the effect of the constitutional violation. In the initial stages of this case, the first criterion was met: the establishment by State statute of a dual system of higher education was a blatant constitutional violation. The second criterion has also been met: merger does not exceed what is necessary to eliminate the effect of the statutory scheme. Eight years under the State's method is proof that a stronger remedy is required. Certainly, it cannot be argued that TSU would be overwhelmingly black today if it had not been established as an institution for negroes. Merger is a drastic remedy, but the State's actions have been egregious examples of constitutional violations.

SUMMARY OF CONCLUSIONS

Nashville is a metropolitan center with a demonstrated need for a State institution of higher education offering a broad curriculum to both day and evening students. It now has two State universities which have in the past, are now, and will under the State's Long Range Plan, compete for students. This competition has lessened, to some extent, as a result of Court orders in this case, but it can be expected to increase if TSU follows the Plan and increases its evening offerings.

Desegregation at TSU, except for faculty, has been minimal and, to the extent that statistics indicate otherwise, due almost exclusively to the allocation of graduate education courses to it by order of the Court.

Prospects for effective cooperation between the Board of Trustees of the University of Tennessee and the State Board of Regents, insofar as it may affect the Nashville scene, are very poor. The political prowess of the University, so frequently evidenced in the past, serves to bolster its apparent resolve to offer only minimal cooperation in the efforts necessary to achieve the system of higher education in the Nashville area.

There is no reason why one university in the Nashville area could not effectively utilize both the home campus of TSU and the downtown campus now occupied by UT-N. The record shows that both are now operating some so-called off-campus centers, and witnesses supporting the Long Range Plan advocated an increase of this activity by TSU.

The two universities in Nashville, TSU and UT-N, must, in order to remedy the constitutional violations discussed herein, be merged under the governance of the State Board of Regents.

Progress by the defendants in the dismantling of a dual system of higher education in Tennessee, outside the Nashville area, has been slow, but the Court does not find that it has been so slow and devoid of good-faith effort as to show that it constitutes, at this time, a violation of constitutional requirements. The Long Range Plan, as it applies to such matters, appears to be a promising step forward and, under the careful supervision of the Monitoring Committee, should result in further progress.

The Court recognizes that the representation of blacks in the higher administrative positions in the State system and on the governing boards is minimal and should be increased. It rejects, however, the proposal that the Court should arbitrarily order the appointments of blacks to either the administrative positions or the governing boards, feeling that such action would be an improper exercise of the judicial function.

This opinion constitutes the findings of fact and conclusions of law required by Rule 52, Federal Rules of Civil Procedure.

An appropriate judgment will be submitted by counsel to the Court within twenty (20) days after the filing of this opinion. Such judgment will, of course, include the time limit of July 1, 1980, for the completion of all facets of the merger approved herein and will provide for retention of jurisdiction by the Court. In the event counsel cannot agree on a form of judgment, separate judgments may be submitted to the Court for consideration.

JUDGMENT

FRANK, GRAY, Jr., Chief Judge.

The court issued a memorandum opinion in this action on January 31, 1977, pursuant to its consideration of the entire record herein including the evidence adduced during the month-long evidentiary hearing (September 20 to October 20, 1976) and the proposed findings of fact, or statement in lieu thereof, submitted by the parties. The opinion of January 31, 1977, constitutes the findings of fact and conclusions of law required by Rule 52, Federal Rules of Civil Procedure, and is incorporated herein by reference. Based on these findings of fact and conclusions of law and the entire record, the court ADJUDGES, ORDERS and DECREES as follows:

A. The University of Tennessee-Nashville (UT-N) and Tennessee State University (TSU) shall be merged as a single institution under the governance of the State Board of Regents, such merger to be completed by July 1, 1980. The State Board of Regents will formulate a plan for the merger and its implementation and, in the development of such plan, shall have the assistance of an advisory committee consisting of six persons, three to be named by the President of TSU and three by the Chancellor of UT-N. In addition, all defendants herein are directed to provide necessary assistance to the Board of Regents in the planning and implementation of the merger. The plan for merger will be formulated and filed within seventy-five (75) days after the entry of this Judgment.

B. The Monitoring Committee set up under the Long Range Plan of defendants will oversee the continued desegregation of the predominantly white institutions of higher education, calling to task any institution which does not make steady progress.

C. Jurisdiction of this case is retained by the court for the enforcement of this Judgment.

Geier v. Alexander
801 F. 2d 799 (6th Cir. 1986)

LIVELY, Chief Judge.

The United States, an intervenor in an action seeking desegregation of public institutions of higher learning in Tennessee, appeals from a consent decree containing affirmative action provisions. The original plaintiffs, intervening individual plaintiffs, and their successors and the State of Tennessee defendants signed the consent decree and agreed to its entry. Of the parties remaining in the case after more than 15 years of litigation, only the United States objected to the consent decree. In approving the consent decree the district court found that there was a compelling interest in eliminating the residual effects of *de jure* segregation in Tennessee's higher education system, that less drastic remedial orders had failed to achieve this result, and that the order was designed to achieve the goal of "a system of higher education in Tennessee tax supported colleges and universities in which race is irrelevant, in which equal protection and equal application of the laws is a reality."

I.

This action began with a complaint by several individuals seeking to enjoin the University of Tennessee from constructing a new facility to expand its program at a non-degree granting "center" in Nashville. The reasoning of the plaintiffs was that any expansion of the University of Tennessee in Nashville (UT-N) would affect the efforts of Tennessee A & I State University, a predominantly black institution, to desegregate its student body and faculty. The United States intervened in the action as a plaintiff pursuant to Title IX of the Civil Rights Act of 1964, 42 U.S.C. § 2000h-2 (1982). The intervening complaint of the United States went beyond the request for an injunction and requested the court to "order the State defendants to present a plan calculated to produce meaningful desegregation of the public universities of Tennessee."

The district court found that six years elapsed after *Brown v. Board of Education* before racial requirements for admission to Tennessee's public universities and colleges were abolished. Although all institutions were following a policy of open-door admissions by 1968, the district court found that "the dual system of education created originally by law has not been effectively dismantled." Upon concluding that the University of Tennessee had no intention of converting its Nashville center into a degree-granting institution, the district court denied the original plaintiffs' request for an injunction. However, relying principally on *Green v. County School Board*, the district court stated it was "convinced that there is an affirmative duty imposed upon the State by the Fourteenth Amendment to the Constitution of the United States to dismantle the dual system of higher education which presently exists in Tennessee." In accordance with this conclusion the district court ordered the defendants (all of whom are state officials, agencies or institutions) to submit a plan "designed to effect such desegregation of the higher educational institutions in Tennessee, with particular attention to Tennessee A & I State University, as to indicate the dismantling of the dual system now existing." The defendants did not appeal.

The defendants submitted a plan to the court which relied primarily on the efforts of individual predominantly white institutions to expand and intensify efforts to recruit black students and faculty. The plan called for Tennessee State University (TSU), the former Tennessee A & I State University, to seek to recruit white students and faculty and to develop and publicize academic programs that would attract white as well as black students from the Nashville area. The individual plaintiffs and the United States filed objections to the plan and after a hearing the district court found that the plan lacked specificity. Instead of disapproving the plan, the district court directed the defendants to file a report showing what had been done to implement each individual component of the plan.

The defendants filed a report which showed some progress in attracting black students to the formerly all-white institutions, but little improvement in the number of black faculty at those schools and virtually no progress in desegregating TSU. The individual plaintiffs filed a motion for further relief, contending that the plan and report failed to offer a scheme for dismantling the dual system of public higher education as ordered by the court. While this motion was under consideration a new report showed that TSU remained 99.7% black and that its entering class in the fall of 1970 was 99.9% black. The district court found that so long as TSU remained overwhelmingly black it could not be found that the Tennessee defendants had dismantled the dual system or that they were "in any realistic sense, on their way toward doing so."

The district court found that an "open door policy, coupled with good faith recruiting efforts,... is sufficient *as a basic requirement*" in cases involving the desegregation of institutions of higher learning. However, when this basic requirement fails to accomplish the goal of eliminating identifiably "white" and "black" institutions, something more is required. In determining what the court should require of the defendants to comply with their affirmative duty to dismantle the dual system, the district judge stated that he would rely on traditional equitable principles, balancing the various interests involved, considering the workability of any proposed remedy and tailoring the "gravity" of the relief required to the "gravity" of the situation to be remedied. The defendants were directed to present a plan to the court by March 15, 1972 that would provide for substantial desegregation of the TSU faculty and for allocation of programs to TSU to ensure a substantial white presence on the TSU campus.

The defendants submitted several plans and amendments in ensuing years, and the district court ordered that some courses and fields of study be offered exclusively in the Nashville area at TSU. Contrary to the district court's earlier expectations the University of Tennessee did convert UT-N into a degree-granting institution and this exacerbated TSU's problems in attracting white students. All plaintiffs, including the United States, proposed a merger of TSU and UT-N with TSU as the surviving institution. The district court held a month-long evidentiary hearing on this proposal in 1976. After considering voluminous records and a great deal of testimony the district court found steady, but slow progress in attracting black students and faculty to the former white institutions, but, as before, little or no progress in converting TSU from a one-race university. The court concluded that the plans used over the eight years that this litigation had been in progress had not worked and showed no prospect of working. In light of this conclusion the district court ordered the merger of TSU and UT-N into a single institution under the Board of Regents, a body that governed all regional state institutions of higher learning in Tennessee as well as TSU. The district court chose this "drastic remedy" because "the State's actions have been egregious examples of constitutional violations."

This court affirmed the district court, and the Supreme Court denied certiorari. In affirming, this court agreed with the district court's original conclusion that the *Green v. County School Board* pronouncement of an affirmative duty to remove all vestiges of state-imposed segregation applies to public higher education as well as to education at lower levels. We rejected the argument that *Green* applies only to elementary and secondary education, agreeing with the holding of a three-judge court in the Fourth Circuit that " 'the state's duty is as exacting' to eliminate the vestiges of state-imposed segregation in higher education as in elementary and secondary school systems; it is only the means of eliminating segregation which differ." Thus we recognized the intrinsic differences in the degree of control which local school boards and institutions of higher learning can exercise over the make-up of student bodies. Such affirmative acts as busing and adjustment of attendance zones are not available to desegregate higher education. Nevertheless, we affirmed that the duty to remove all vestiges of *de jure* segregation is the same.

This court also held that the findings upon which the district court based its decision were not clearly erroneous, and that the remedy ordered was within the traditional bounds of equitable relief, properly related to a condition found to offend the Constitution.

We have detailed the history of this litigation in order to show the setting in which all of the original parties and the intervening individual plaintiffs finally reached agreement on a plan to achieve the goal of a unitary system of public higher education in Tennessee. Further, the plan embodied in the consent decree was the culmination of long hours and days of negotiations in which all parties, including the United States, participated.

II.
A.

Although the "Stipulation of Settlement," which became the consent decree when approved by the district court, imposed a broad range of affirmative obligations on the defendants, all defendants agreed to its entry. As the only objecting party the United States has limited its objection on appeal to the provisions of Part II(N):

> N. Defendants will coordinate the development of a cooperative program to increase the number of black students who enroll in and graduate from professional programs. Every spring beginning in 1985 and for five years, 75 black sophomore students who are Tennessee residents enrolled in Tennessee public institutions will be selected by committees representing the faculties of all state-supported professional schools and all other public universities in the state for pre-enrollment in the state's schools of law, veterinary medicine, dentistry, pharmacy and medicine. There shall be representation by black faculty members on these committees, to the extent available. The professional schools will counsel these students, assist in planning their pre-professional curricula, provide summer programs at the end of their junior and senior years and agree to their admission as first year professional students if they successfully complete their undergraduate work and meet minimum admissions standards. Defendants will consult with other states that have developed similar programs [*e.g.,* Kentucky] and complete development of the program described in this paragraph II, (N), including a proposed budget and projected source of funds, within 180 days.

The decree imposed no obligation on the United States.

In its opening brief in this court the United States articulated its objection to Part II(N) as follows:

> The ground for our objection was that the provision both exceeds the scope of judicial remedial power and violates the Equal Protection Clause by using an express racial criterion and by according preferential treatment to blacks who, by definition, have never been victims of discrimination in professional school admissions.

The United States also claimed error in the failure of the district court to hold an evidentiary hearing on its objections "to determine whether the proposed relief was necessary and/or permissible."

B.

Virtually the entire argument by the Department of Justice in the district court was built upon the theory of "victim specificity." This theory holds that a court may order affirmative action only to benefit individuals who have been identified as actual victims of past or ongoing acts of illegal discrimination. This argument was recently rejected by the Supreme Court in two cases brought under Title VII of the Civil Rights Act of 1964, 42 U.S.C. § 2000e et seq. (1982). In *Local 28 of the Sheet Metal Workers' International Ass'n v. Equal Employment Opportunity Commission*, the union, supported by the United States as amicus curiae, sought to reverse an affirmative action order that contained a "membership goal" on the ground, inter alia, that § 706(g) of the 1964 Act "authorizes a district court to award preferential relief only to the actual victims of unlawful discrimination." This plurality of four Justices rejected the argument that a court may not order benefits to be extended except to identified victims. Justice Powell concurred in the judgment and wrote that the remedy in the case violated neither Title VII nor the Equal Protection Clause of the Constitution.

In *Local No. 93, International Ass'n of Firefighters, etc. v. City of Cleveland*, also decided July 2, 1986, a union and the United States as amicus curiae sought to overturn a consent decree that imposed promotion goals on the city. As in the present case, all of the original parties to the suit agreed to an affirmative action plan. The union, as an intervening defendant, and the United States objected to the "quotas" and argued that the district court exceeded its authority under Title VII in approving the consent decree. Specifically, the union and the Department of Justice argued that § 706(g) precluded the entry of a consent decree that might benefit some minority individuals who were not identified as actual victims of unlawful discrimination. While deciding the case on other grounds the Court stated:

> The Court holds today in *Sheet Metal Workers v. EEOC* that courts may, in appropriate cases, provide relief under Title VII that benefits individuals who were not the actual victims of a defendant's discriminatory practices.

C.

In view of these pronouncements of the Supreme Court, the Department of Justice did not press its "victim specificity" theory in oral argument before this court. Although both *Sheet Metal Workers v. EEOC* and *Firefighters v. City of Cleveland* determined only that Title VII does not require victim specificity, the Department of Justice does not argue that these decisions are inapplicable to the present case which arose under the Fourteenth Amendment. In view of the long line of school desegregation cases in which affirmative action plans have been upheld without regard to whether each beneficiary was an identifiable victim of discrimination, it would be futile to argue that remedies under the Equal Protection Clause are limited by the theory of victim specificity.

The Department of Justice makes the broader argument that the use of "racial quotas" to prefer minority students in this case deprived non-minority students of equal protection. There are three facets to this argument. In the first place, it is claimed that cases such as *Green v. County School Board*, which require all vestiges of past discrimination to be eliminated "root and branch," do not control litigation concerned with segregation in public higher education. The Department of Justice argues that since higher education is a voluntary activity, a state satisfies the Constitution by putting an end to discriminatory practices, and has no obligation to eliminate the vestiges of past discrimination. According to this contention, the only justification for approving affirmative action decrees in school cases lies in the fact that school attendance is compulsory at the elementary and secondary levels and a state cannot require pupils to attend segregated schools. Thus since attendance at colleges and universities is voluntary, the state had no compelling interest in embarking on additional remedial action after it had established "neutral admissions standards." As its second argument the appellant maintains that the former dual system of higher education was effectively dismantled by the prior decrees in this case. Finally, the Department of Justice argues that even if an affirmative order is permissible in a higher education case the remedy included in the consent decree was not "narrowly tailored" to embody the least restrictive method for curing the condition sought to be corrected.

1.

The principal authority cited in support of the first equal protection argument was *Bazemore v. Friday*, in which a majority of the Supreme Court held that the North Carolina Agricultural Extension Service fulfilled its constitutional obligation by adopting a wholly neutral admissions program for local 4-H and Homemaker Clubs that had been segregated prior to 1965. In response to the Civil Rights Act of 1964 the extension service discontinued its past practice of maintaining separate white and black clubs. Nevertheless, there continued to be many all-white and all-black clubs. In *Bazemore* the district court found no evidence of discrimination after the clubs were opened to members of all races and concluded that any remaining racial imbalance in the clubs resulted from wholly voluntary choices of the individual members.

The Supreme Court affirmed the finding that there is no current violation of the Fourteenth Amendment because club membership is voluntary. Distinguishing the *Green* requirement of affirmative steps to end dual school systems, the Court stated:

> While school children must go to school, there is no compulsion to join 4-H or Homemaker Clubs, and while School Boards customarily have the power to create school attendance areas and otherwise designate the school that particular students may attend, there is no statutory or regulatory authority to deny a young person the right to join any Club he or she wishes to join.

We believe the Department of Justice reads too much into *Bazemore*. While no one is compelled to enter a profession, in order to do so a person must attend a university offering courses of study leading to a degree in the profession selected. The State of Tennessee offers this professional training at public institutions that were formerly segregated by law. The district court found that the present disparity between black and white enrollment in professional studies resulted from the long history of denial of equal educational opportunities to generations of black Tennesseans. The district court also found that the disproportionately low black enrollment in all areas of higher education at the beginning of this litigation resulted from decades of separate and unequal education of black students at every level in Tennessee. It appears fallacious to attempt to extend *Bazemore* to any level of education. While membership in 4-H and Homemaker Clubs offers a valuable experience to young people and families, particularly in rural areas, it cannot be compared to the value of an advanced education. The importance of education to the individual and the interest of the state in having its young people educated as completely as possible indicate clearly that the holding in *Green* rather than that of *Bazemore* applies.

It was established as the law of the case in the present litigation more than 15 years ago that *Green* applies to the desegregation of public higher education, and the United States did not argue to the contrary before the district court. In the only previously appealed decision, this court held that "the *Green* requirement of an affirmative duty applies to public higher education as well as to education at the elementary and secondary school levels." Nothing in the *Bazemore* decision, where the compelling interest of a state in the education of its citizenry was not involved, requires us to reexamine these holdings.

Four years before its decision in *Brown v. Board of Education* the Supreme Court held that the Fourteenth Amendment precludes a state from requiring black law students and graduate students to attend separate professional and graduate schools from those attended by white students. The remedy prescribed in *Sweatt* was that the black applicant be admitted to the University of Texas Law School. No later case has held, or even hinted that affirmative remedies are not available to remove the vestiges of past unlawful segregation in public higher education.

2.

The Department of Justice asserts that the illegal condition of segregation in public higher education in Tennessee was cured by adoption of an open-admissions policy and compliance with the district court's prior decrees, and thus the state had no compelling interest in embarking on additional remedial action. This position is contrary to specific findings of the district court in decisions that became final without appeal. In the first *Geier* decision the district court found that fourteen years after *Brown v. Board of Education* nothing had been done to dismantle effectively the dual system of higher education in Tennessee. Four years later the district court concluded that the affirmative duty to dismantle the dual system remained despite an open-door policy of admissions and good faith recruitment efforts. In 1977 the district court found that plans adopted in over eight years of litigation had not worked and showed no prospect of working. In ordering a "drastic remedy" the court found that the state's actions "have been egregious examples of constitutional violations." In approving the consent decree the district court relied on these earlier findings and its own determination that the residual effects of past discrimination have not been eliminated. The United States participated fully in all stages of the proceedings leading to these decisions. We think the record in this case establishes without question that a "compelling governmental interest" is involved. The United States has not denied that the state has such an interest in providing equal educational opportunities at all levels to all its residents.

3.

We also believe that Part II(N) of the consent decree was "narrowly tailored" to the achievement of this goal. Since Part II(N) does contain percentage goals, we examine it further in light of the four factors Justice Powell prescribes in considering race-conscious hiring remedies, though there are differences between hiring goals and goals related to the selection of undergraduate students for possible post-graduate professional training. The first factor is the efficacy of alternative remedies. The record in this case demonstrates conclusively that sixteen years of alternative efforts failed to remove the vestiges of *de jure* segregation. The second factor is the planned duration of the remedy. The duration in this case is five years—a reasonable time by any yardstick. The third factor is whether the goal is related to the percentage of minority group numbers in the relevant population. The goal of 75 black candidates for professional education each year for five years in Tennessee's public universities is modest by any standard and certainly does not exceed the size of the relevant pool of minority prospects for such education. The final factor is whether waiver provisions are available in the event the goal is not met. In approving the consent decree the district court pointed out that its "numerical references" are clearly defined as objectives only and went on to state: "Whether or not the goal is reached or exceeded will only be one of many indicia of the good faith efforts of all the parties to achieve a unitary system. . . ." This statement, referring to all of the goals in the consent decree, indicates sufficient flexibility to satisfy the fourth factor.

The Department of Justice proposed a preferential admissions program open to disadvantaged students of all races in lieu of the program contained in the stipulation of settlement. Such a program would certainly be commendable, but it would not be tailored to the problem with which the district court had been wrestling for more than 15 years. Given the record in this case we cannot find an abuse of discretion in the district court's acceptance of the program agreed to by the parties most directly involved rather than the less specifically directed one proposed by the intervenor.

The most telling feature with respect to the narrowness of Part II(N) is that it does not guarantee that any black student chosen during his or her sophomore year will ever be enrolled in a professional school. The professional schools are required to admit these students only "if they successfully complete their undergraduate work and meet minimum admissions standards." This plan does no more than offer remedial aid to apt black students to help them throw off the disadvantages attendant to a long history of discrimination. It is merely a catch-up provision. The percentage goals of Part II(N) are just a modest step toward the larger goal of a Tennessee system of higher education in which no component is identifiable by race. They do not impose the same serious consequences on members of the majority race as the protections from layoff stuck down in *Wygant v. Jackson Board of Education*. They are much more like the hiring goals approved in *Sheet Metal Workers v. EEOC* and *Firefighters v. City of Cleveland* in their impact on individual members of the majority.

III.
A.

The final contention of the appellant is that it was an abuse of discretion for the district court to approve the consent decree without conducting an evidentiary hearing on the Department of Justice's objections.

It has been noted that the United States intervened in this action in 1968 and participated in every phase of the case thereafter, including many evidentiary hearings as well as the negotiations that produced the consent decree. The record is filled with evidence which supports the district court's several findings that the vestiges of state-imposed segregation had not been removed. The Department of Justice argues, however, that it was entitled to an evidentiary hearing in order to demonstrate that the low minority enrollment in professional schools is not a vestige of the dual system.

The district court conducted three hearings at which it heard arguments on the objections to the consent decree. At the first hearing Mr. Douglas, representing the Department of Justice, stated that he was concerned that there was no foundation for the numerical goals in the decree, but acknowledged that he was not then asking for an evidentiary hearing. Without mentioning the professional school program specifically, he argued it would be better to have a plan based on "strategies" for desegregation rather than to have essentially arbitrary numerical goals. The district judge asked that the objections be made more specific, and set the matter for a later hearing.

Following the second hearing, which centered primarily on conditions at TSU, the district court directed the attorney for the United States to file detailed written objections to the consent decree, and set the matter for a third hearing. The heart of the written objections is found in Part II, captioned "A Court's Remedial Authority To Order Affirmative Equitable Relief Is Limited to those Measures Necessary to 'Make Whole' Actual Victims of Unlawful Discrimination." There follows a recitation of the arguments put forward by the Department of Justice in many cases in recent years where it has sought to limit affirmative action according to its theory of "victim specificity." The same arguments were made to the Supreme Court and rejected in *Sheet Metal Workers v. EEOC* and *Firefighters v. City of Cleveland*.

At the third hearing, following submission of the written objections, Assistant Attorney General William Bradford Reynolds appeared for the United States. Mr. Reynolds argued that an evidentiary hearing was required to determine the basis for the latest report showing that the 1984 entering class at TSU was still 90% black. He stated that it was not at all clear to him that this figure resulted from discrimination or that there had been a failure to dismantle the dual system. In further colloquy Mr. Reynolds said he thought the state should have an opportunity to prove that it was in full compliance with the previous decree before the court entered the consent decree imposing additional duties. The court then reminded the Assistant Attorney General that the state had agreed to the consent decree and did not seek an evidentiary hearing. Then, speaking only for the United States, Mr. Reynolds stated:

> What I'm suggesting is that this Court's ability in the absence of the consent of all parties to enter a modification of the decree is—I would say something that this Court lacks the authority to do unless you can show that there's been a change in the operational law as it was at the time the decree was entered which I would submit is not the case. Or you can show on a factual record that there has been a sufficient change in the factual situation to warrant modification.

In response to the district judge's question, Mr. Reynolds agreed that a third ground for the court's authority to approve the consent decree would arise from the court's duty to monitor its previous decree, but he insisted that an evidentiary hearing would be required before this authority could be exercised.

The Department of Justice never made a proffer of evidence, and never indicated that there was any evidence in existence that contradicted the statistical evidence in the record upon which the court relied. This evidence disclosed that despite the implementation of several programs seeking to increase black enrollment in professional studies, very little progress had been made. Tennessee's population is 15.8% black. In 1984 black enrollment in the state's professional schools was 4.2%. The case had been set for trial on July 30, 1984 and after the original parties reached a settlement the hearings on objections to the consent decree took place on July 30, August 2 and August 13, 1984. Thus, at the time of the hearings, the Department of Justice should have known what proof, if any, it had to support its position.

* * *

C.

All of the parties directly involved in this case agreed to settle it after sixteen years of litigation. In the early years it was the United States that exhorted the court to broaden its remedial orders while the state sought to restrict them. At the very time the state became convinced that its earlier efforts had failed to eliminate the vestiges of its past discriminatory practices, the Department of Justice was urging the court to pull back—a truly ironic situation. The district court did not abuse its discretion when, after considering the intervenor's detailed written objections and conducting three hearings, it approved a settlement agreed to by all the original parties to the action.

A statement by the Second Circuit in regard to an intervenor's objection to settlement of a class action seems appropriate here:

> In general the position taken by the objectors is that by merely objecting, they are entitled to stop the settlement in its tracks, without demonstrating any factual basis for their objections and to force the parties to expend large amounts of time, money and effort to answer their rhetorical questions, notwithstanding the copious discovery available from years of prior litigation and extensive pre-trial proceedings. To allow the objectors to disrupt the settlement on the basis of nothing more than their unsupported suppositions would completely thwart the settlement process. On their theory no class action would ever be settled, so long as there was at least a single lawyer around who would like to replace counsel for the class and start the case anew. To permit the objectors to manipulate the distribution of the burden of proof to achieve such an end would be to permit too much. Although the parties reaching the settlement have the obligation to support their conclusion to the satisfaction of the District Court, once they have done so, they are not under any recurring obligation to take up their burden again and again *ad infinitum* unless the objectors have made a clear and specific showing that vital material was ignored by the District Court. There is no need for the District Court to hold an additional evidentiary hearing on the propriety of the settlement. Its conclusion appears to have been reached only after a thorough investigation of all relevant facts.

The district court rejected the argument that it could not properly conclude from the record that the low minority enrollment in Tennessee's public professional schools resulted from past discriminatory practices. The district court was fully justified in making this determination. Applicants do not arrive at the admissions office of a professional school in a vacuum. To be admitted they ordinarily must have been students for sixteen years. Students applying for post-graduate schooling in the 1983–84 school year would have begun school at age six in 1967 and would have entered college in 1979. The district court had made consistent findings between 1968 and 1984 that the public colleges and universities of Tennessee had not eliminated the vestiges of their years of operation under state-imposed segregation. The district court could also take judicial notice of findings by the district courts and this court that those vestiges had not been eliminated from many of the public school systems of Tennessee, all of which were operated under the same state-imposed system of separate schools for the two races.

The consent decree in this case does not seek to remedy some amorphous "societal" wrong. It is directed solely at the continuing effects of past practices that adversely affected black Tennesseans as they moved through the public school systems and the higher education system of the state. The consent decree imposes no obligations on the United States, and the state defendants have agreed to assume those that it imposes upon them. It represents the first agreement of substance in this long and sometimes bitter litigation. The district court did not abuse its discretion in entering the consent decree without the approval of one intervening party.

The judgment of the district court is affirmed.

State-College Desegregation, the Courts, and the U.S. Government: a Chronology

1970: The NAACP Legal Defense and Educational Fund sues the U. S. Department of Health, Education, and Welfare, charging that H.E.W.'s Office for Civil Rights had failed to enforce Title VI of the Civil Rights Act because it had not started proceedings to cut off federal aid to public colleges in states that it had found to be maintaining segregated systems of higher education. The 10 states are: Arkansas, Florida, Georgia, Louisiana, Maryland, Mississippi, North Carolina, Oklahoma, Pennsylvania, and Virginia.

1973: U.S. District Judge John H. Pratt rules that H.E.W. must begin enforcement proceedings against states that do not submit to the Office for Civil Rights an acceptable plan for desegregating their higher-education systems.

1974: H.E.W. accepts desegregation plans from all of the states involved except Louisiana and Mississippi. It refers Louisiana, which refused to submit a plan, and Mississippi, which submitted an unacceptable plan, to the U. S. Department of Justice for enforcement.

1977: Judge Pratt finds that the plans accepted by H.E.W. have not been effective and orders H.E.W. to develop specific criteria for new desegregation plans.

1978: After H.E.W. publishes new criteria for plans, it accepts new five-year plans from Arkansas, Florida, Georgia, Oklahoma, and the North Carolina community-college system.

1978: The U. S. Department of Education is created and assumes responsibility for the cases.

1979: The Department of Education accepts a five-year plan from Virginia.

1980: Judge Pratt requires the Education Department to obtain desegregation plans from eight other states. The states covered by this order are: Alabama, Delaware, Kentucky, Missouri, Ohio, South Carolina, Texas, and West Virginia.

1981: The Department of Education accepts five-year plans for desegregating the University of North Carolina system and public colleges in Delaware, Mississippi, South Carolina, and West Virginia. The Department of Education refers Alabama and Ohio to the Department of Justice for enforcement.

1982: The Department accepts a five-year desegregation plan from Kentucky.

1983: Júdge Pratt orders the Education Department to negotiate additions to the six desegregation plans it accepted in 1977.

1983: The department accepts additions to the 1977 plans from the six states, and new five-year plans from Pennsylvania and Texas.

1985: Desegregation plans expire in Arkansas, Florida, Georgia, and Oklahoma, and for North Carolina community colleges. The Education Department accepts a new five-year plan from Maryland.

1986: Desegregation plans expire in Delaware, Missouri, South Carolina, Virginia, and West Virginia, and for the University of North Carolina system.

1987: Desegregation plan expires in Kentucky.

1987: Judge Pratt dismisses the case, saying that the Legal Defense and Educational Fund lacks the legal right to continue the suit, and that it has failed to prove that action against the Education Department will bring changes to the public colleges involved in the case.

1988: The Education Department says that Arkansas, North Carolina, South Carolina, and West Virginia are in compliance with Title VI. The department says six other states—Delaware, Florida, Georgia, Missouri, Oklahoma, and Virginia—have made progress toward desegregation, but must take further steps to desegregate by 1989 or face a possible cutoff of federal funds to their public colleges.

Chronicle of Higher Education, 17 February 1988, p. A 24.

Reprinted with permission.

Although there remain more than 100 public and private historically or traditionally Black institutions, there are very few historically Hispanic institutions. For a review of these institutions, see M. Olivas, "Indian, Chicano, and Puerto Rican Colleges: Status and Issues," *Bilingual Review*, 9 (1982), 36–58; M. Olivas, "Federal Higher Education Policy: The Case of Hispanics," *Educational Evaluation and Policy Analysis*, 4 (1982), 301–310.

There are more than three dozen public and private Indian colleges, including Bureau of Indian Affairs (BIA) institutions. In 1978, Congress enacted the Tribally Controlled Community College Assistance Act to provide resources for the tribal institutions. For a review of the extensive problems with the government's administration of the TCCCAA, see M. Olivas, "The Tribally Controlled Community College Assistance Act of 1978: The Failure of Federal Indian Higher Education Policy," *American Indian Law Review*, 9 (1981), 219–251; "In a Barren Land, a Tribal College Flourishes," *Chronicle of Higher Education*, 6 April 1988, pp. A1, 16–17; "Government Settles Suit Against D-Q University," *Chronicle of Higher Education*, 23 March 1988, p. A2.

In *Indian Tribes v. University of Michigan*, descendants of several tribes unsuccessfully sued the University of Michigan in 1981, claiming that the Treaty of Ft. Meigs (1817) had created a "trust" responsibility:

> Some of the Ottawa, Chippewa, and Potawatomy Tribes, being attached to the Catholick [sic] religion, and believing they may wish some of their children hereafter educated, do grant to the rector of the Catholick church of St. Anne

of Detroit, for the use of the said church, and to the corporation of the college at Detroit, for the use of the said college, to be retained or sold, as the said rector and corporation may judge expedient, each, one half of three sections of land, to contain six hundred and forty acres, on the river Raisin, at a place called Macon, and three sections of land not yet located, which tracts were reserved, for the use of the said Indians, by the treaty of Detroit, in one thousand eight hundred and seven; and the superintendent of Indian affairs, in the territory of Michigan, is authorized, on the part of the said Indians, to select the said tracts of land.

The Court found no trust existed, and dismissed the case without imposing a constructive trust: "It is clear to the Court that 'college' here means a school such as Spring Hill's School rather than a large university in the modern context." 104 Mich. App. 482 (1981). See also R. Barsh and J.Y. Henderson, *The Road: Indian Tribes and Political Liberty* (Berkeley: University of California Press, 1980).

When Judge Pratt rendered his decision in December, 1987, Hispanic plaintiffs in Texas, dissatisfied with slow progress by that State in its *Adams* consent decree, filed suit in Texas State District Court, alleging disparities in the State's expenditures for minority postsecondary students, historical practices of segregating minority students though geographical placement of institutions, and violations of the State's constitutional guarantees of equal rights. *LULAC v. Clements*, filed in Cameron County, 2 December 1987. The case is a postsecondary corollary to the case of *Edgewood Independent School District v. Kirby*, a Texas K-12 school finance decision that in 1987 found the disparities between rich and poor districts to be unconstitutional under the Texas Constitution: "The facts I have recited and found indicate that our financial system, which includes the combination of State and local funds as they currently act in tandem, do not yet meet the requirements of our constitution. With all due respect to history and to the legislature for its recent generous and thoughtful efforts to rectify this situation, by order of this Court the current system will be set aside." Harley Clark, District Judge (1987), 250th Dist. Ct., Travis County, TX.

Mississippi University for Women v. Hogan
458 U.S. 718 (1982)

Justice O'CONNOR delivered the opinion of the Court.

This case presents the narrow issue of whether a state statute that excludes males from enrolling in a state-supported professional nursing school violates the Equal Protection Clause of the Fourteenth Amendment.

I

The facts are not in dispute. In 1884, the Mississippi Legislature created the Mississippi Industrial Institute and College for the Education of White Girls of the State of Mississippi, now the oldest state-supported all-female college in the United States. The school, known today as Mississippi University for Women (MUW), has from its inception limited its enrollment to women.

In 1971, MUW established a School of Nursing, initially offering a 2-year associate degree. Three years later, the school instituted a 4-year baccalaureate program in nursing and today also offers a graduate program. The School of Nursing has its own faculty and administrative officers and establishes its own criteria for admission.

Respondent, Joe Hogan, is a registered nurse but does not hold a baccalaureate degree in nursing. Since 1974, he has worked as a nursing supervisor in a medical center in Columbus, the city in which MUW is located. In 1979, Hogan applied for admission to the MUW School of Nursing's baccalaureate program. Although he was otherwise qualified, he was denied admission to the School of Nursing solely because of his sex. School officials informed him that he could audit the courses in which he was interested, but could not enroll for credit.

Hogan filed an action in the United States District Court for the Northern District of Mississippi, claiming the single-sex admissions policy of MUW's School of Nursing violated the Equal Protection Clause of the Fourteenth Amendment. Hogan sought injunctive and declaratory relief, as well as compensatory damages.

Following a hearing, the District Court denied preliminary injunctive relief. The court concluded that maintenance of MUW as a single-sex school bears a rational relationship to the State's legitimate interest "in providing the greatest practical range of educational opportunities for its female student population." Furthermore, the court stated, the admissions policy is not arbitrary because providing single-sex schools is consistent with a respected, though by no means universally accepted, educational theory that single-sex education affords unique benefits to students. Stating that the case presented no issue of fact, the court informed Hogan that it would enter summary judgment dismissing his claim unless he tendered a factual issue. When Hogan offered no further evidence, the District Court entered summary judgment in favor of the State.

The Court of Appeals for the Fifth Circuit reversed, holding that, because the admissions policy discriminates on the basis of gender, the District Court improperly used a "rational relationship" test to judge the constitutionality of the policy. Instead, the Court of Appeals stated, the proper test is whether the State has carried the heavier burden of showing that the gender-based classification is substantially related to an important governmental objective. Recognizing that the State has a significant interest in providing educational opportunities for all its citizens, the court then found that the State had failed to show that providing a unique educational opportunity for females, but not for males, bears a substantial relationship to that interest. Holding that the policy excluding Hogan because of his sex denies him equal protection of the laws, the court vacated the summary judgment entered against Hogan as to his claim for monetary damages, and remanded for entry of a declaratory judgment in conformity with its opinion and for further appropriate proceedings.

On rehearing, the State contended that Congress, in enacting § 901(a)(5) of Title IX of the Education Amendments of 1972, Pub. L. 92–318, 86 Stat. 373, 20 U.S.C. § 1681 *et seq.*, expressly had authorized MUW to continue its single-sex admissions policy by exempting public undergraduate institutions that traditionally have used single-sex admissions policies from the gender discrimination prohibition of Title IX. Through that provision, the State argued, Congress limited the reach of the Fourteenth Amendment by exercising its power under § 5 of the Amendment. The Court of Appeals rejected the argument, holding that § 5 of the Fourteenth Amendment does not grant Congress power to authorize States to maintain practices otherwise violative of the Amendment.

We granted certiorari, and now affirm the judgment of the Court of Appeals.

II

We begin our analysis aided by several firmly established principles. Because the challenged policy expressly discriminates among applicants on the basis of gender, it is subject to scrutiny under the Equal Protection Clause of the Fourteenth Amendment. That this statutory policy discriminates against males rather than against females does not exempt it from scrutiny or reduce the standard of review. Our decisions also establish that the party seeking to uphold a statue that classifies individuals on the basis of their gender must carry the burden of showing an "exceedingly persuasive justification" for the classification. The burden is met only by showing at least that the classification serves "important governmental objectives and that the discriminatory means employed" are "substantially related to the achievement of those objectives."

Although the test for determining the validity of a gender-based classification is straightforward, it must be applied free of fixed notions concerning the roles and abilities of males and females. Care must be taken in ascertaining whether the statutory objective itself reflects archaic and stereotypic notions. Thus, if the statutory objective is to exclude or "protect" members of one gender because they are presumed to suffer from an inherent handicap or to be innately inferior, the objective itself is illegitimate.

If the State's objective is legitimate and important, we next determine whether the requisite direct, substantial relationship between objective and means is present. The purpose of requiring that close relationship is to assure that the validity of a classification is determined through reasoned analysis rather than through the mechanical application of traditional, often inaccurate, assumptions about the proper roles of men and women. The need for the requirement is amply revealed by reference to the broad range of statutes already invalidated by this Court, statutes that relied upon the simplistic, outdated assumption that gender could be used as a "proxy for other, more germane bases of classification," to establish a link between objective and classification.

Applying this framework, we now analyze the arguments advanced by the State to justify its refusal to allow males to enroll for credit in MUW's School of Nursing.

III
A

The State's primary justification for maintaining the single-sex admissions policy of MUW's School of Nursing is that it compensates for discrimination against women and, therefore, constitutes educational affirmative action. As applied to the School of Nursing, we find the State's argument unpersuasive.

In limited circumstances, a gender-based classification favoring one sex can be justified if it intentionally and directly assists members of the sex that is disproportionately burdened. However, we consistently have emphasized that "the mere recitation of a benign, compensatory purpose is not an automatic shield which protects against any inquiry into the actual purposes underlying a statutory scheme." The same searching analysis must be made, regardless of whether the State's objective is to eliminate family controversy, to achieve administrative efficiency, or to balance the burdens borne by males and females.

It is readily apparent that a State can evoke a compensatory purpose to justify an otherwise discriminatory classification only if members of the gender benefited by the classification actually suffer a disadvantage related to the classification. We considered such a situation in *Califano v. Webster*, which involved a challenge to a statutory classification that allowed women to eliminate more low-earning years than men for purposes of computing Social Security retirement benefits. Although the effect of the classification was to allow women higher monthly benefits than were available to men with the same earning history, we upheld the statutory scheme, noting that it took into account that women "as such have been unfairly hindered from earning as much as men" and "work[ed] directly to remedy" the resulting economic disparity.

A similar pattern of discrimination against women influenced our decision in *Schlesinger v. Ballard*. There, we considered a federal statute that granted female Naval officers a 13-year tenure of commissioned service before mandatory discharge, but accorded male officers only a 9-year tenure. We recognized that, because women were barred from combat duty, they had had fewer opportunities for promotion than had their male counterparts. By allowing women an additional four years to reach a particular rank before subjecting them to mandatory discharge, the statute directly compensated for other statutory barriers to advancement.

In sharp contrast, Mississippi has made no showing that women lacked opportunities to obtain training in the field of nursing or to attain positions of leadership in that field when the MUW School of Nursing opened its door or that women currently are deprived of such opportunities. In fact, in 1970, the year before the School of Nursing's first class enrolled, women earned 94 percent of the nursing baccalaureate degrees conferred in Mississippi and 98.6 percent of the degrees earned nationwide. That year was not an aberration; one decade earlier, women had earned all the nursing degrees conferred in Mississippi and 98.9 percent of the degrees conferred nationwide. As one would expect, the labor force reflects the same predominance of women in nursing. When MUW's School of Nursing began operation, nearly 98 percent of all employed registered nurses were female.

Rather than compensate for discriminatory barriers faced by women, MUW's policy of excluding males from admission to the School of Nursing tends to perpetuate the stereotyped view of nursing as an exclusively woman's job. By assuring that Mississippi allots more openings in its state-supported nursing schools to women than it does to men, MUW's admissions policy lends credibility to the old view that women, not men, should become nurses, and makes the assumption that nursing is a field for women a self-fulfilling prophecy. Thus, we conclude that, although the State recited a "benign, compensatory purpose," it failed to establish that the alleged objective is the actual purpose underlying the discriminatory classification.

The policy is invalid also because it fails the second part of the equal protection test, for the State has made no showing that the gender-based classification is substantially and directly related to its proposed compensatory objective. To the contrary, MUW's policy of permitting men to attend classes as auditors fatally undermines its claim that women, at least those in the School of Nursing, are adversely affected by the presence of men.

MUW permits men who audit to participate fully in classes. Additionally, both men and women take part in continuing education courses offered by the School of Nursing, in which regular nursing students also can enroll. The uncontroverted record reveals that admitting men to nursing classes does not affect teaching style, that the presence of men in the classroom would not affect the performance of the female nursing students, and that men in coeducational nursing schools do not dominate the classroom. In sum, the record in this case is flatly inconsistent with the claim that excluding men from the School of Nursing is necessary to reach any of MUW's educational goals.

Thus, considering both the asserted interest and the relationship between the interest and the methods used by the State, we conclude that the State has fallen far short of establishing the "exceedingly persuasive justification" needed to sustain the gender-based classification. Accordingly, we hold that MUW's policy of denying males the right to enroll for credit in its School of Nursing violates the Equal Protection Clause of the Fourteenth Amendment.

*   *   *

IV

Because we conclude that the State's policy of excluding males from MUW's School of Nursing violates the Equal Protection Clause of the Fourteenth Amendment, we affirm the judgment of the Court of Appeals.

It is so ordered.

Chief Justice BURGER, dissenting.

I agree generally with Justice POWELL's dissenting opinion. I write separately, however, to emphasize that the Court's holding today is limited to the context of a professional nursing school. Since the Court's opinion relies heavily on its finding that women have traditionally dominated the nursing profession, it suggests that a State might well be justified in maintaining, for example, the option of an all-women's business school or liberal arts program.

Although there are several dozen private women's colleges, MUW was, at the time its admissions practice was held unconstitutional, the only such public college not to admit men. Texas Women's University had admitted men for years. See *TWU v. Chayklintaste*, 521 S.W. 2d 949 (1975) (TWU cannot allow men but not women to live off campus). For an analysis of the *Hogan* case, see M. Olivas and K. Denison, "Legalization in the Academy: Higher Education and the Supreme Court," *Journal of College and University Law*, 11 (1984), 1–50.

Other special-mission institutions include private colleges for the deaf, such as Gallaudet University, which became embroiled in a major civil rights dispute in 1988, leading to the appointment of its first deaf president. When his predecessor, a non-deaf administrator, was named to the position, the students held widely publicized protests. The hearing woman named by the board resigned after 36 hours, following a student strike, which closed the D.C. campus. " 'Deaf President Wow!' How 4 Students Kept Control of Gallaudet Movement," *Chronicle of Higher Education*, 23 March 1988, pp. A13–14.

Affirmative Action and Students

Cases brought by students or against students constitute the majority of cases in this book. In this Section, several cases involving affirmative action are included, including issues of race, national origin, sexual harassment, and physical handicaps in admissions. Suits brought before *Bakke* and after *Bakke* are included, for that litigation remains the major case in student affirmative action. Although race discrimination cases will undoubtedly continue in large numbers, sexual harassment and handicapped cases promise to increase substantially.

Lucy v. Adams
224 F. Supp. 79 (1963)

GROOMS, District Judge.

This matter came on for hearing at this time upon the request of petitioner, Hubert E. Mate, in his capacity as Dean of Admissions of the University of Alabama, for construction of the present efficacy of the judgment rendered in this cause on July 1, 1955 wherein it was decreed as follows:

> "1. That the defendant, William F. Adams, his servants, agents, assistants and employees, and those who might aid, abet, and act in concert with him, are hereby permanently enjoined and restrained from denying the plaintiffs and others similarly situated the right to enroll in the University of Alabama and pursue courses of study thereat, solely on account of their race or color."

William F. Adams, who was the Dean of Admissions of the University of Alabama, resigned effective February 3, 1961. Since the first day of October, 1961, petitioner, Hubert E. Mate, has occupied the position of Dean of Admissions of the University of Alabama.

Rule 65(d), Federal Rules of Civil Procedure, provides that an injunction

> "is binding only upon the parties to the action, their officers, agents, servants, employees, and attorneys, and upon those persons in active concert or participation with them who receive actual notice of the order by personal service or otherwise."

Amended Rule 25(d), (1) and (2), effective July 19, 1961, provides as follows:

> "(1) When a public officer is a party to an action in his official capacity and during its pendency dies, resigns, or otherwise ceases to hold office, the action does not abate and his successor is automatically substituted as a party. Proceedings following the substitution shall be in the name of the substituted party, but any misnomer not affecting the substantial rights of the parties shall be disregarded. An order of substitution may be entered at any time, but the omission to enter such an order shall not affect the substitution.

> "(2) When a public officer sues or is sued in his official capacity, he may be described as a party by his official title rather than by name; but the court may require his name to be added,"

* * *

It is the general rule "that one who succeeds to the interest of a party to whom the injunction is directed and who has notice of the injunction, is bound by the judgment and punishable for contempt for disobedience." 43 C.J.S.

In Chanel Industries, Inc. v. Peirre Marche, Inc., it was stated:

"Successors and assigns, not parties to the enforcement order, may become part of it and subject to its prohibitions when they become instrumentalities by which parties–defendant seek to escape and thereby be in active concert or participation in the violation of the injunction.

There appears to be no question as to petitioner's knowledge of the writ issued in this case. The Court is, therefore, of the opinion that the injunction issued on July 1, 1955, is binding upon petitioner herein, in his capacity as Dean of Admissions of the University of Alabama, and upon all of those connected with the University who have knowledge of such decree.

The rights of black students had been secured in Alabama only after protracted litigation, the calling-out of the National Guard, public race-baiting by then-Governor George Wallace, and even after black plaintiffs had won, it required the 1963 *Lucy* case to hold the Dean of Admissions at the University of Alabama to a court order rendered in 1955: the order had required the University's Dean to admit blacks. When he resigned in 1961, his successor argued that the 1955 order did not bind him, and that he would not obey his predecessor's order. This disingenuity also led southern states to argue, albeit unsuccessfully in most cases, that *Brown v. Board of Education* was limited to public elementary and secondary schools, since its facts arose in the K-12 setting.

In a fascinating footnote to these cases, a predominantly white men's basketball team was to play Loyola of Chicago in the 1963 NCAA championship tournament. Loyola's team, the eventual 1963 NCAA champions, included a number of black players. When Mississippi State University's all-white team drew its turn to play Loyola, a state senator secured a court order enjoining the team from leaving the state (the game was to be played in Michigan). The team had to sneak out of town and employ surreptitious means to fly to the game. Final score: Loyola 61, MSU 51. "Another Blow to Jim Crow," *Sports Illustrated,* 18 November 1987, p. 113.

Chance v. Board of Examiners
330 F. Supp. 203 (1971)

MANSFIELD, Circuit Judge.

The fairness and validity of competitive examinations, once described by Gilbert and Sullivan as the means of attaining "a Duke's exalted station," have frequently been challenged in courts and elsewhere. We are here called upon to decide whether those examinations which have been prescribed and administered by the Board of Examiners of the City of New York (the "Board" herein) to candidates seeking licenses for permanent appointment to supervisory positions in the City's school system (principals, assistant principals, administrative assistants, etc.) are unconstitutional. We conclude that a sufficient showing has been made of violation of the Equal Protection Clause of the Fourteenth Amendment to warrant the issuance of preliminary injunctive relief.

The two named plaintiffs, who are respectively Black and Puerto Rican, have brought this purported class action on behalf of themselves and all other persons similarly situated pursuant to federal civil rights laws, 42 U.S.C. §§ 1981 and 1983.

They allege that the competitive examinations, which must be passed by a candidate before he or she can qualify for licensing and appointment, discriminate against persons of Black and Puerto Rican race, and have not been validated or shown fairly to measure the skill, ability and fitness of applicants to perform the duties of the positions for which the examinations are given, with the result that success on the examination does not indicate in any way that the candidate will succeed as a supervisor. This racial discriminatory effect, coupled with lack of justification or predictive value as measurements of abilities required to perform the jobs involved, is alleged to violate not only plaintiffs' federal constitutional rights but also (based on pendent jurisdiction) Art. 5, § 6 of the New York State Constitution, and §§ 2590-j(3) (a) (1), 2569 (1), and 2573 (10) of the New York Education Law.

Plaintiffs seek a preliminary injunction under Rule 65, F. R. Civ. P., prohibiting the alleged violations of these laws. They also seek declaratory relief pursuant to 28 U.S.C. § 2201. We have jurisdiction under 28 U.S.C. §§ 1331 and 1343(3).

The Board of Education has not actively opposed the motion for preliminary injunction, and it agrees that plaintiffs have presented triable issues of fact. The Board of Examiners ("Board" herein), however, has vigorously opposed the motion.

In reaching our decision we have had the benefit of a plethora of lengthy affidavits and exhibits, a hearing at which oral testimony was taken, a series of arguments, and extensive briefing of the law and facts by the parties. In addition the following organizations have appeared as amici and filed briefs supporting plaintiffs: New Association of Black School Supervisors and Administrators, ASPIRA of America, Inc., and the Public Education Association.

An applicant for permanent appointment to a supervisory position in the New York City School System must, in addition to meeting state requirements for the position, obtain a New York City license. First, each such candidate must have met minimum education and experience requirements established by the City's Board of Education and the Chancellor, Harvey B. Scribner, who is the Chief Administrator of the School District of the City of New York. For instance, a candidate for principal of a day elementary school must, among other things, have had (1) four years' experience teaching in day schools under regular license and appointment as a teacher, and (2) two years' experience of supervision in day schools under license and appointment, or meet various alternative experience requirements.

Next the candidate must pass an examination procedure prepared and administered by the Board for the particular type or classification of supervisory post desired, which may take as long as two years to complete. If the candidate successfully completes the testing procedure, he or she is granted a license and placed on a list of those eligible for assignment to the type of supervisory position involved. The appropriate school governing authority—either a central board of education or a community school board under New York City's present decentralized system—then selects the person it wishes from the eligible list to fill an open position. Since appointments of permanent supervisory personnel in the New York City School System must be made from lists of eligibles who have passed examinations, the Board from time to time announces and conducts examinations for particular supervisory posts (of which there are more than 50 different types) following which the number of persons eligible for appointment are supplemented by promulgation of lists of those who passed the latest examination. If a successful candidate, after being listed as eligible for appointment, is not appointed within four years, he or she is dropped from the list and must again pass the qualifying examinations to be listed as eligible.

Only in the cities of Buffalo and New York does state law provide for examinations in addition to *state* certification, N.Y. Education Law § 2573 (10-a), and only the New York City School District maintains a Board of Examiners and the specific examination and licensing procedure here under attack. The Board has described itself as "a highly select group with broad professional background in education and related fields chosen through the most objective and impartially searching examination given under civil service."

Were it not for New York City's special examination and licensing procedure, plaintiffs Chance and Mercado would have been appointed permanent elementary school principals. Both have been certified by the *state* for that position, and both are specially trained to be principals, having graduated from a year-long Fordham University Instructional Administrators and Principals Internship Program in Urban Education.

Plaintiff Boston M. Chance has been employed in the New York City public school system for the last 15 years and is acting principal of P.S. 104, an elementary school in the Bronx. Chance, who is of the Black race, possesses all of the basic qualifications of education and experience established by law and by the Board of Education and the Chancellor of the New York City School District for the position of principal of an elementary school. However, he lacks a *city* license as elementary school principal and therefore is barred at present from securing a permanent position as principal. In September, 1968, Chance took the examination given by the Board for the position of Assistant Principal, Junior High School, but he failed it and thus was not placed on the eligibility list and was not issued a license entitling him to permanent appointment.

Plaintiff Louis Mercado, a Puerto Rican who also holds a New York State license as a principal, has been serving the New York City school system for the last 12 years. He is presently acting principal of P.S. 75, an elementary school in Manhattan, but he is barred from permanent appointment because he does not have a New York City license as an elementary school principal. Mercado is in a somewhat different position from Chance in that he does not allege that he has ever taken the relevant Board of Examiners' Supervisory Examination. While the present motion was pending—and while the parties were collecting statistical information pursuant to our order—the Board conducted their November, 1970 series of examinations for elementary school principal. Mercado withdrew from this examination and refused to take it on the grounds that the "Board of Examiners is not the appropriate agency for qualifying school personnel" and "the examination is not relevant * * * ."

Both Chance and Mercado were selected for their present acting principalships by their respective community school boards, in accordance with New York City's decentralized system. In some instances such local school boards found, after interviewing licensed principals listed as eligible by the Board, that persons not so licensed were more qualified to serve as principals than those interviewed and that they performed their duties in a superior manner.

There are approximately 1,000 licensed Principals of New York public schools of varying levels (e.g., elementary day, junior high school, high school, etc.), of whom some act as the heads of schools and others function in administrative positions. Of the 1,000 only 11 (or approximately 1%) are Black and only 1 is Puerto Rican. Furthermore, of the 750 licensed Principals of New York elementary schools only 5 (or less than 1%) are Black, and none is Puerto Rican. Of the 180 high school administrative assistants, none is Black or Puerto Rican.

Of the 1,610 licensed Assistant Principals of New York City junior high and elementary schools, only 7% are Black and only .2% are Puerto Rican. When the list for the position of Principal, elementary school, was originally promulgated, only 6 out of the 340 persons (or about 1.8%) were Black and none was Puerto Rican; and when the list for Principal, high school, was promulgated, none of the 22 licensed people was Black or Puerto Rican. The promulgated list of licensed Assistant Principals for junior high schools reveals that only 55 out of 690 persons (or 8%) were Black and none was Puerto Rican.

Plaintiffs contend that the written and oral examinations of the Board are the major factor accounting for this extremely low percentage of Black and Puerto Rican supervisors in a school system where 55% of the students are Black or Puerto Rican. Plaintiffs summarize their basic argument as follows:

> "[T]hese tests place a premium on familiarity with organizational peculiarities of the New York City school system which, while having little to do with educational needs, are largely gained through coaching and assistance from present, predominately white, supervisory personnel. [sic]

> *   *   *

> "The testing procedures do not indicate a candidate's ability to do the job being tested for. There is no evidence that they measure merit or fitness, they have never been validated, and they are unreliable psychological instruments."

Rather than risk the endless delay that would be encountered while the parties obtained this essential evidence through pretrial discovery procedures, we directed the parties, in view of the importance of the issue, to use their best efforts to agree on a procedure whereby the Board of Examiners and the Board of Education would compile the necessary racial statistics. All parties cooperated fully and at considerable effort in working out almost all of the details of the procedure to be followed. Such differences as existed were resolved by court order. The result has been that after months of research we have been presented with the pass-fail statistics for the relevant racial and ethnic groupings of candidates for 50 supervisory examinations given over the past few years. In view of plaintiffs' claims that the examinations had a "chilling effect" inhibiting Blacks and Puerto Ricans from becoming candidates, this statistical survey ("the Survey") also includes figures as to those candidates who "Did Not Appear" to take the written test, which commenced the examination process, or who "Withdrew," i.e., took the written test but did not appear for subsequent parts of the examination.

All parties and amici have submitted briefs as to the relevance of the statistics thus adduced and the inferences that may be drawn from them. The parties also submitted affidavits by statistical experts. A hearing was held, at which each side's expert testified and was subject to cross-examination; and we heard more oral argument on the statistical data. After declining the opportunity to examine and cross-examine any other witnesses, including those presented by affidavit, both sides rested on the record thus adduced.

Upon the evidence thus presented we find that the examinations and testing procedures prepared and administered by the Board for the purpose of determining which candidates will be licensed as supervisory personnel have the effect of discriminating against Black and Puerto Rican candidates.

The Survey reveals that out of 6,201 candidates taking most of the supervisory examinations given in the last seven (7) years, including all such examinations within the last three (3) years, 5,910 were identified by race. Of the 5,910 thus identified, 818 were Black or Puerto Rican and 5,092 were Caucasian. Analysis of the aggregate pass-fail statistics for the entire group reveals that only 31.4% of the 818 Black and Puerto Rican candidates passed as compared with 44.3% of the 5,092 white candidates. Thus on an overall basis, white candidates passed at almost 1 1/2 times the rate of Black and Puerto Rican candidates. These overall figures, however, tell only part of the story.

*   *   *

Thus white candidates passed the examination for Assistant Principal of Junior High School at almost double the rate of Black and Puerto Rican candidates, and passed the examination for Assistant Principal of Day Elementary School at a rate one-third greater than Black and Puerto Rican candidates. The gross disparity in passing rates on these two examinations is of particular significance not only because they were taken by far more candidates than those taking any other examinations conducted in at least the last seven years, resulting in licensing of the largest number of supervisors, but also because the assistant principalship has traditionally been the route to and prerequisite for the most important supervisory position, Principal. To the extent that [Blacks] and Puerto Ricans are screened out by the examination for Assistant Principal they are not only prevented from becoming Assistant Principals but are kept out of the pool of eligibles for future examinations for the position of Principal as well. The fact that the process involves a series of examinations and that to reach the top one must pass several examinations at different times in his or her career serves to magnify the statistical differences between the white and non-white pass-fail rates.

*   *   *

Plaintiffs offered the testimony of Dr. Jacob Cohen, an expert in the field of statistics, in support of the validity and significance of the Survey results. The Board, in turn, adduced the testimony of Dr. Nathan Jaspen, an expert in the same field, in opposition. Both witnesses possess outstanding qualifications. After reviewing their testimony and appraising them as witnesses, we are more persuaded by the testimony of Dr. Cohen with respect to certain crucial matters affecting the significance of the figures for present purposes.

Turning first to the gross aggregate pass-fail statistics, which reveal that the overall pass rate of white candidates (44.3%) was almost half again as high as the non-white rate (31.4%), Dr. Cohen testified that on the basis of such a large sample (5,910 out of 6,201 candidates), the test results were especially valuable and formed a sound basis for drawing valid statistical conclusions as to the difference in passing rates between the ethnic groups involved. In analyzing the statistics he used the Chi-Square Test (Yates-corrected), which is a method using formulas generally accepted by statistical experts to determine whether an observed difference in any given sample is greater than that which would be expected on the basis of mere chance or probability.

He found with respect to the aggregate test that by "the Chi-Square (Yates-corrected) statistical test, the probability of the difference being a chance result not related to the factor of race is determined as *less than one in one billion*." (Emphasis added)

In an effort to rebut Dr. Cohen's analysis the Board, after first dismissing the aggregate figures as insignificant on the ground that the "examinations are discrete competitions related to widely-varied, particular supervisory examinations" offered Dr. Jaspen's testimony that he did not compute probabilities on the basis of the gross aggregate figures because of the possibility of "overlap," i.e., the taking of more than one test by the same persons. We reject this excuse for several reasons. In the first place, the Board, although it had the data as to any overlap within its control and was afforded the opportunity to adduce any relevant evidence, chose not to do so. Under such circumstances we cannot assume any significant overlap. Secondly, if a "random" overlap existed (i.e., one where the number of persons repeating an examination because of a previous failure approximates those taking a second, more advanced examination after passing the first), it would not substantially affect the probabilities. Dr. Jaspen conceded, for instance, that a random overlap of as much as 50% would not substantially affect the significance of the observed difference between the white and non-white pass rates. Lastly, Dr. Cohen (plaintiffs' expert) testified that because of the large Chi-Square value an overlap would not significantly affect the probability data. In other words, the observed difference between the aggregate pass-fail rates of whites and non-whites was too great to be a mere matter of chance, unrelated to race (the chance of such an occurrence being less than one in a billion) so that even if the probability were reduced somewhat because of overlap, the figure would still be significant, e.g., one in one million, or one in 500,000, and if the overlap were no greater than 15%, the statistical results would not be affected at all.

* * *

Plaintiffs also argue that discrimination may be inferred from the fact that the percentage of Black and Puerto Rican Principals and Assistant Principals in New York City schools (1.4% and 7.2%, respectively) is far below the percentage of the total student body who are Black and Puerto Rican (55.8%) and when compared with similar figures for the five largest school systems in the country (New York, Los Angeles, Chicago, Detroit, and Philadelphia) constitutes not only the lowest minority representation in the supervisory ranks, but also the lowest ratio of such minority group supervisors to minority group students. We reject this contention. Supervisors are drawn from the pool of qualified teachers, most of whom attended elementary and high school long ago, and not from present-day students. Undoubtedly the low number of minority teachers eligible to take the supervisory examinations prescribed by the Board has been due in part to the fact that the percentage of minority students who 10 or 15 years ago went on to college and qualified for a teaching career, and thus provided the source of today's minority teachers, was much smaller than the number of white students following such a course, with the result that a larger pool of qualified white graduates entered the teaching profession. In addition the minority student population in New York City has increased during the same period, with the effect of increasing the racial imbalance between teachers and students. Current efforts to promote higher educational opportunities for minority groups will not produce qualified teachers for some years. But statistics as to the current dearth of qualified minority teachers do not have probative value with respect to the question before us, which is whether New York City's examination system discriminates against *minority candidates who have already qualified as licensed teachers.*

For the same reasons we are unimpressed with plaintiffs' comparisons between (1) the percentage of Black and Puerto Rican members of the general population in New York City, and (2) the percentage of Black and Puerto Rican Principals and Assistant Principals found in the City's total school supervisory personnel. Statistical comparisons to the general racial population of the community may be relevant in determining whether there is discrimination in job opportunities that are supposed to be open to the general public, in the selection of teachers from a pool of those already qualified and eligible for appointment, or in qualification of voters or jurors. But we are here dealing with candidates who must meet preliminary eligibility requirements as to education and experience that are not possessed by most of the general population. Where the education of our children is at stake, such insistence upon the highest possible quality in our teachers is a salutary and lawful objective, provided it does not result in racial discrimination between candidates who are otherwise eligible, which is the case here.

Notwithstanding the introduction of some evidence thus found irrelevant, the evidence establishes to our satisfaction that the examinations prepared and administered by the Board for the licensing of supervisory personnel in New York City schools do have the *de facto* effect of discriminating significantly and substantially against qualified Black and Puerto Rican applicants. However, the existence of such discrimination, standing alone, would not necessarily entitle plaintiffs to relief. The Constitution does not require that minority group candidates be licensed as supervisors in the same proportion as white candidates. The goal of the examination procedures should be to provide the best qualified supervisors, regardless of their race, and if the examinations appear reasonably constructive to measure knowledge, skills and abilities essential to a particular position, they should not be nullified because of a *de facto* discriminatory impact. We accordingly pass on to the question of whether the examinations under attack can be validated as relevant to the requirements of the positions for which they are given, i.e., whether they are "job-related."

The parties disagree as to which side bears the burden of proving that the examinations are job-related. Plaintiffs contend that once a discriminatory impact is shown the burden is on the Board to show a compelling necessity or justification for tests having an unintended discriminatory effect.

Most of these decisions arise under Title VII of the 1964 Civil Rights Act, which embodied an express Congressional policy directed toward the consequences of certain employment practices, regardless of the employer's motive or interest, and interpreted by the Supreme Court as placing on the employer the burden of showing that any given testing mechanism or requirement has a manifest function in measuring a candidate's capability of performing the employment in question. Since we are here concerned, however, with whether the Board's examinations meet the requirements of the Equal Protection Clause rather than those of a specific Congressional enactment, the foregoing authorities, while relevant, are not controlling.

The Board contends that in a Constitutional framework plaintiffs must show that there is no rational relationship between the examinations and the requirements of the supervisory positions for which they are given.

Although the "rational relationship" standard has been applied to practices attacked as causing commercial or economic harm, we are here dealing with racial, not economic, discrimination, where even reputed strict constructionists have joined in the view that a more stringent standard must be applied. Where official conduct discriminates as to race, it is "constitutionally suspect," regardless of lack of intent to discriminate racially. In a closely parallel situation arising under Title VII of the 1964 Civil Rights Act, 42 U.S.C. § 2000e et seq. in Griggs v. Duke Power the Supreme Court pointed out that "good intent or absence of discriminatory intent does not redeem employment procedures or testing mechanisms that operate as 'built in headwinds' for minority groups and are unrelated to measuring job capability. * * * "

We are satisfied that where, as here, plaintiffs show that the examinations result in *substantial* discrimination against a minority racial group qualified to take them, a strong showing must be made by the Board that the examinations are required to measure abilities essential to performance of the supervisory positions for which they are given.

Before considering the evidence with respect to the validity, reliability and objectivity of the examinations conducted by the Board, a few general principles must be stated. It seems to be generally accepted that before an examination will be recognized as a reliable instrument for measuring the fitness and ability of a candidate to perform tasks demanded by a given position, the examination should be validated, i.e., shown to be reasonably capable of measuring "what it purports to measure." The first step toward this basic objective is to insure that as to subject matter the examination will elicit from the candidate information that is relevant to the job for which it is given. If so, it is described as having "content validity." Otherwise the examination could be a useless and misleading tool. For instance, an examination eliciting information required to perform a bus-driver's job would hardly be relevant in determining a candidate's capacity to perform the duties of a policeman, lawyer or accountant.

In constructing an examination that will have "content validity," the preferred course is first to have an empirical analysis made of the position for which it is given, usually by experts or professionals in the field. Such an analysis requires a study to be made of the duties of the job, of the performance by those already occupying it, and of the elements, aspects and characteristics that make for successful performance. Questions are then formulated, selective procedures established, and criteria prepared for examiners that should elicit information enabling them to measure these characteristics, skills and proficiency in a candidate and determine his capacity to do the job satisfactorily.

As Professor R.L. Thorndike has observed:

> "Whenever a test is being tried for selection of personnel for some job specialty, it is most desirable that it be validated empirically. Experimental evidence is called for to show that the test is in fact effective in discriminating between those who are and those who are not successful in a particular job. Though it may be necessary under the press of an emergency to rely upon the professional judgment of the psychologist to establish the value of a test for personnel selection, this must be recognized as a stopgap."

To a lesser extent the validity of an examination as a means of selecting candidates best suited for a position may also be checked or verified empirically by comparing the relative examination scores of successful candidates with their later performance on the job. If there is a significant correlation between test scores and later perfor-mance, the examination has "predictive validity." Predictive validity is of greater significance in evaluating aptitude tests than proficiency tests. Furthermore it often takes a long time to establish such validity and even then the evaluation depends upon the reliability and fairness of the field appraisal of performance on the job.

Lastly, an examination must, of course, be administered objectively, free from bias or prejudice in favor of or against particular candidate or group, if it is to be a useful selection tool.

At the outset of the hearings, being inexperienced in the field of examinations generally, we indicated doubt as to whether examinations could be constructed that would be valid for selection of Principals and other supervisory personnel, since we viewed their duties as being executive and complex in nature, with the success of a Principal in a given school depending not so much on his knowledge of duties and educational content of courses given by his subordinates as on such intangible factors as leadership skill, sensitivity to the feelings and attitudes of teachers, parents and children, and ability to articulate, to relate, to organize work, to establish procedures, to promote good community relations, to induce subordinates to accept directions, to work cooperatively, to criticize without creating unnecessary animosity or ill-will, to analyze and evaluate administrative problems, to take decisive action when required, to operate under stress, to initiate and promote new programs, and to instill a feeling of confidence. In short we questioned whether tests that might be valid for purposes of determining a candidate's knowledge of the duties of a position or of detailed educational information would be valid for purposes of determining his judgment and ability as an executive, particularly since the candidate, being a licensed teacher, has already demonstrated his or her technical skills in certain fields of education, including ability to read, write and speak English.

Notwithstanding our doubt, both sides in this dispute agree that while examination procedures may have weaknesses in testing for higher level executive positions, such procedures (including use of written tests) are essential tools in selecting supervisory personnel. However, they differ as to the areas of weakness. Plaintiffs, for instance, state that "content validity is of limited utility in selecting persons for fairly sophis-ticated or complex job" because of the difficulties faced in preparing tests that fairly sample the job and accurately predict a candidate's performance. According to plain-tiffs, examinations for such positions are useful only if they have predictive validity, since content validity is primarily relevant for the purpose of determining whether a candidate has learned a defined body of knowledge rather than for the purpose of determining how he will use and apply that knowledge on the job. The Board, on the other hand, takes the view that content validity is more important in determining a candidate's proficiency or capacity to perform the duties of a Principal, and that predictive validity should be de-emphasized in judging the utility of such tests because predictive validity is more relevant to aptitude for learning than to achievement or proficiency for satisfactory performance on the job. The Board further points out that follow-up studies used to determine predictive validity are not generally used in licensing of doctors, lawyers, or other professionals.

*   *   *

[T]he Board's methods and procedures seem reasonable enough to one lacking expertise in the field of educational testing, and normally we would be prepared to accept the Board's views on the subject. Indeed, there appear to be few differences between the procedures advocated by the Board and by plaintiffs' expert, Dr. Richard S. Barrett. The basic aims of both are the same (to achieve validity, reliability and objectivity), with the parties differing as to the need for and importance of predictive validity in administration of supervisory examinations. However, a major stumbling block—and in our view a fatal weakness in the Board's system—lies in the methods used by the Board to implement the techniques and procedures adopted in principle and approved by independent experts. As is often the case in such difficult and complex matters, theory is one thing, practice may be another. Despite its professed aims the Board has not in practice taken sufficient steps to insure that its examinations will be valid as to content, much less to predictiveness.

* * *

It also appears that Harvey B. Scribner, the Chancellor of the New York City School District, a distinguished and fearless educator, does not share the Board's confidence in the validity of its examinations. In a memorandum to the Board of Education dated October 13, 1970, Dr. Scribner noted that he was "pressed to evaluate whether the present examination and licensing system, which dictates specific limitations of employment and promotion of staff for the public schools, is a help or a hardship [in the efforts of community boards to operate] * * * ." He recommended that in lieu of current employment practices the Board adopt New York State certification.

* * *

"For the reasons outlined in this position paper, my position with regard to the Chance and Mercado case is that I prefer not to defend myself against the action. To do so would require that I both violate my own professional beliefs and defend a system of personnel selection and promotion which I no longer believe to be workable. We are facing a future in education which leaves no alternative to the selection of the most creative teachers; the most talented supervisors; the most able principals and other administrators who possess the highest level of leadership qualities possible from wherever they may be found and as area available at any given time."

Digging deeper, we find to our dismay that the Board's position does not appear to be supported by most of the research reports submitted by it as demonstrating the content validity of its supervisory examinations.

* * *

With respect to the question of the *objectivity* of the examinations, adequate precaution appear to have been taken by the Board to assure objectivity in the conduct of the written examinations. As for the oral interviews, we are not persuaded by vague and speculative hearsay statements that members of the examining committees intentionally discriminate against Black or Puerto Rican candidates because of their color, use of "southernisms," or the like. Since each candidate has already been licensed as a teacher and has received New York State certification for a supervisory position, the examiners are dealing with a group of well educated applicants. On the other hand, the hard, cold facts are that all members of the Board of Examiners are white, the great majority of the oral examiners or examination assistants are white, and white candidates have passed the combined oral and written tests at a much higher rate than Black and Puerto Rican candidates, resulting in *de facto* discrimination against the latter. This raises a "serious and substantial question" as to whether discrimination against Blacks and Puerto Ricans is not being *unconsciously* practiced by white interview examiners.

CONCLUSION

The evidence reveals that the examinations prepared and administered by the Board of Examiners for the licensing of supervisory personnel, such as Principals and Assistant Principals, have the *de facto* effect of discriminating significantly and substantially against Black and Puerto Rican applicants.

Despite the fact that candidates for such positions are licensed teachers who have satisfied prerequisites as to education and experience established by the Board of Education for supervisory positions and have already been certified by the State of New York for the positions sought, a survey of the results of examinations taken by 5,910 applicants (of whom 818 were Black or Puerto Rican) reveals that white candidates have received passing grades at almost 1 1/2 times the rate of Black and Puerto Rican candidates and that on one important examination given in 1968 for the position of Assistant Principal, Junior High School, white candidates passed at almost double the rate of Black and Puerto Rican candidates. The discriminatory effect in the latter case is aggravated by the fact that the Assistant Principalship has traditionally been an essential prerequisite to the more important supervisory position of Principal.

The existence of such *de facto* racial discrimination is further confirmed by the fact that only 1.4% of the Principals, and 7.2% of the Assistant Principals in New York City schools are Black or Puerto Rican, percentages which are far below those for the same positions in the four other largest city school systems in the United States. For example, the percentage of Black and Puerto Rican Principals in each of the cities of Detroit and Philadelphia is 16.7%, or 12 times as high as that in New York.

Such a discriminatory impact is constitutionally suspect and places the burden on the Board to show that the examinations can be justified as necessary to obtain Principals, Assistant Principals and supervisors possessing the skills and qualifications required for successful performance of the duties of these positions. The Board has failed to meet this burden. Although it has taken some steps towards securing content and predictive validity for the examinations and has been improving the examinations during the last two years, the Board has not in practice achieved the goals of constructing examination procedures that are truly job-related. Many objectionable features remain, with the result that some 37 minority Acting Principals and 131 minority Acting Assistant Principals, who are considered fully qualified and are desired for permanent appointment by the community school boards, are rendered ineligible for such permanent appointment. A study of the written examinations reveals that major portions of them call simply for regurgitation of memorized material. Furthermore, the oral examination procedure leaves open the question of whether white candidates are not being favored—albeit unconsciously—by committees of examination assistants who have been entirely or predominantly white.

There appears to be a strong likelihood that plaintiffs will prevail on the merits at trial. It further appears that plaintiffs would suffer greater harm from denial of preliminary injunctive relief than defendants would suffer from the granting of relief. Denial of relief would perpetuate existing racial discrimination, depriving plaintiffs and others similarly situated of an equal opportunity for permanent appointment and licensing as supervisors. During the long period before the case would finally be adjudicated on the merits, permanent appointments would be made from lists promulgated by the Board, which would have the effect of threatening the continued employment of those holding acting appointments, since New York law requires vacancies to be filled from the eligibility lists if such lists exist.

For the foregoing reasons a preliminary injunction will issue restraining defendants from (1) conducting further examinations of the type found to be unconstitutionally discriminatory against Blacks and Puerto Ricans, and from (2) promulgating eligible lists on the basis of such examination procedures.

The foregoing shall constitute our findings of fact and conclusions of law as required by Rule 52(a), F.R.Civ.P.

We take this opportunity to express appreciation to the parties for their thorough papers, and to the amici for their briefs, which were of assistance in resolving the difficult and complex issues.

Settle order on notice.

Although the *Chance* case involved the employment setting, its discussion of testing generally remains one of the most sophisticated in the context of minorities and psychometrics. Discrimination litigation requires extraordinary statistical evidence, particularly regression equations and other sophisticated methodological techniques, to measure inequities and to isolate discriminatory effects. S. Bombey and B. Saltzman, "The Role of Statistics in Employment Discrimination Litigation—A University Perspective," *Journal of College and University Law*, 9 (1982–83), 263–278; G. Bodner, "Analyzing Faculty Salaries in Class Action Sex Discrimination Cases," *Journal of College and University Law*, 10 (1983–84), 305–323. For a review of these statistical issues in race litigation, see *Bazemore v. Friday*, 478 U.S. 385 (1986) (plaintiff in Title VII suit "need not prove discrimination with scientific certainty," but with preponderance of evidence).

Gonzalez v. Southern Methodist University
536 F. 2d 1071 (1976)

TJOFLAT, Circuit Judge:

Guadalupe Gonzalez, a Mexican-American, applied to the School of Law of Southern Methodist University (SMU), a private educational institution, seeking admission to the class entering in the fall of 1975. Her application was denied. She then filed this suit alleging that SMU had discriminated against her because of her race in violation of Title 42, United States Code, Sections 1981, 1982, and 1983. She moved for a preliminary injunction to enjoin SMU from denying her admission to the fall 1975 class; she also sought a determination that the suit should proceed as a class action. Since the beginning of the fall term was imminent, the district court began, on September 5, a hearing which lasted for several days. At the conclusion of that hearing, the court denied Gonzalez' motion for a preliminary injunction and determined that the suit should not proceed as a class action. Gonzalez now appeals from these rulings. We affirm.

This court has outlined four prerequisites for a preliminary injunction: (1) there must be a substantial likelihood of success on the merits; (2) there must be a threat of irreparable injury to the plaintiff which (3) outweighs the threatened harm to the defendants; and (4) the injunction must not disserve the public interest. The district court found that Gonzalez had failed to prove the existence of these four prerequisites, and we agree.

The record indicates little likelihood that Gonzalez would eventually succeed on the merits of her case. The trial court correctly decided that Gonzalez could not have prevailed under Title 42, United States Code, Sections 1982 or 1983. It is well settled that Section 1983 does not provide a remedy for private acts of racial discrimination. And even though Section 1982 may reach private discriminatory action, we see no property interest here which would bring this case within the scope of that statute.

On the other hand, Gonzalez' complaint does state a claim under Section 1981. She alleges that SMU discriminated against her because of her race, and thereby denied her (in the words of the statute) "the same right . . . to make and enforce [contracts] . . . as is enjoyed by white citizens. . . . " The Supreme Court has recently held that Section 1981 reaches discriminatory conduct in the context of private education. Thus Gonzalez would be entitled to relief if she could adduce the facts necessary to show race-based discrimination against her by SMU.

Such facts simply do not exist, however, on the record before us. The record shows absolutely no evidence of race-based discrimination against Gonzalez or any other minority applicant. SMU had a policy of fully reviewing the application of any minority student whose undergraduate grades and LSAT score failed to gain him automatic admission. The point of this review was to examine the record of the minority applicant in order to determine that applicant's merit in light of a broader view of his record, thus vitiating the effects of any possible "cultural bias" in the LSAT testing. Gonzalez' own application was subjected to this procedure which, if anything, gave her some advantages over the non-minority applicant. In short, there is more than ample evidence in the record as it now exists to support the trial court's finding that Gonzalez "has not been denied admission to the SMU law school on the basis of sex, race, color, ethnic background or national origin." Gonzalez thus fell far short of demonstrating any likelihood of success on the merits.

We also affirm the trial court's refusal to allow this suit to proceed as a class action. The standard of review on that determination is whether the trial court abused its discretion. In this case the trial court made its ruling after four days of hearings on Gonzalez' preliminary injunction; it was fully aware of the facts of the case, and found that Gonzalez had failed to establish the necessary prerequisites to maintain a class action. Our review of the record indicates that the trial court's ruling was well within its discretion.

For the reasons stated above, the trial court's order denying the plaintiff's motions for a preliminary injunction and for leave to proceed as a class action is AFFIRMED.

———————

Although Ms. Gonzalez did not convince the court that her case warranted their intervention, there is a growing body of statistical studies measuring the differential predictive validity of tests taken by Latino students and by whites. In "Prediction of Hispanics' College Achievement," Psychologist Richard Duran found a significant difference in the ability of standardized test scores to predict first year college performance. The review of data "indicate[s] that combining information about high school grades and admissions test scores in ethnic specific regression equations [a common college admissions practice] leads to less accurate prediction of Hispanics' college grades. In terms of the college grade-point average variance accounted for, Hispanics' college grades were predicted 9 to 10 percent less accurately than were whites' grades." In M. Olivas, *Latino College Students* (NY: Teachers College Press, 1986), pp. 221–245. In another chapter in the book, Maria Pennock-Roman reviewed the literature on "test fairness," and concluded,

> Not all of the unresolved issues are methodological, however. How discrepant must an item be before it is flagged for inspection? By what criteria should we judge whether the content of a discrepant item is related to the trait being measured and is, therefore, "fair"? Questions of this sort cannot be settled by psychometric research alone, because they involve values. A societal consensus is required. The inescapable fact is that fairness in all aspects of testing is ultimately a question of values.

"Research on Spanish-Language Tests and Test Item Bias," pp. 193–220.

In a recent case, the use of ACT scores for admissions purposes was held not to be racially discriminatory; the State of Mississippi's institutions had adopted the "extremely modest" standards for the general public good. *Ayers v. Allain*, 674 F. Supp. 1523 (N.D. Miss. 1987). See also *U.S. v. LULAC*, 793 F. 2d 636 (5th Cir. 1986) (overturning preliminary order that barred use of teacher certification examination). For a review of postsecondary testing issues, see D. Greer, "Legal Issues in Truth-in-Testing Legislation," *Review of Higher Education*, 7 (1984), 321–356.

Alexander v. Yale University

459 F. Supp. 1 (1977)

NEWMAN, District Judge.

The Ruling of the Magistrate is hereby adopted as the decision of the Court. Because of the significance of the issue concerning Title IX of the Education Amendments of 1972, the Ruling is set forth in full as Appendix A.

APPENDIX A

ARTHUR H. LATIMER, Magistrate.

RULING ON MOTION TO DISMISS

The appropriateness of immediate federal judicial relief is at issue in the instant civil action seeking redress for purported sex discrimination at Yale University. Plaintiffs are a male faculty member and several women students or former students who fundamentally contend that the defendant university's purported

> "failure to combat sexual harassment of female students and its refusal to institute mechanisms and procedures to address complaints and make investigations of such harassment interferes with the educational process and denies equal opportunity in education."

In requesting corrective measures "to be designed and implemented under the supervision of this Court", plaintiffs assert a right to relief individually and on behalf of a proposed class under Title IX of the Education Amendments of 1972, which provides in pertinent part in 20 U.S.C. § 1681(a) that "[n]o person in the United States shall, on the basis of sex, be excluded from participation in, be denied the benefits, of, or be subjected to discrimination under any education program or activity receiving Federal financial assistance...."

In express terms, Title IX calls for administrative enforcement of that prohibition against sex discrimination, with funding cut-off a potential sanction when "compliance cannot be secured by voluntary means", but plaintiffs have not attempted resort to the responsible enforcing agency, the Department of Health, Education and Welfare. The statute contains no explicit grant of private suit rights other than through ultimate judicial review of H.E.W.'s actions, and in moving to dismiss defendant chiefly argues that no right to sue can be properly "implied".

It is of course settled that no express statutory reference to a right of action is required to enable federal courts "to provide such remedies as are necessary to make effective the congressional purpose", and judicial remedies accordingly have been thought appropriately "implied" when "congressional purposes are likely to be undermined absent private enforcement" by those "intended to be protected by the statute". The general inquiry prompted by defendant's pending motion then is "whether the creation by judicial interpretation of the implied cause of action asserted ... is necessary to effectuate Congress' goals."

That "need" inquiry here involves distinct aspects. A logical prerequisite is that there be a sufficiently defined wrong under the statute invoked, and claims for relief adequately presented by the parties plaintiff. In this regard, it should be stressed at the outset that while the complaint deserves generous reading, the question is not so much the customary one on motion to dismiss—whether plaintiffs could conceivably prove facts calling into play an established right of action—as instead whether any circumstance depicted genuinely impels judicial creation of a new suit right. Such an approach is surely also consistent with Title IX's aims, for the statute is clearly addressed to specific practices of exclusion, inequitable resource allocation and similar concrete abuses. So viewed, most claims advanced in this action are tenuous indeed.

The complaint is founded on alleged instances of sexual harassment of women students by male faculty members or administrators, and the principal claim for relief is for an order "requiring defendant to institute and continue a mechanism for receiving, investigating and adjudicating complaints of sexual harassment", with plaintiffs asserting in conclusory fashion that their reported experiences are somehow

"the result of a pattern, practice, and policy of defendant, its officers, agents, and employees, of neglecting and refusing to consider seriously complaints of sexual harassment of women students, with the effect of actively condoning continued sexual harassment of female students by male faculty members and administrators."

Before considering the university's possible responsibility, however, it must be observed that in any event a number of the proposed plaintiffs simply advance no persuasive claim that they have been deprived of cognizable Title IX rights. Plaintiff John Winkler, a member of the classics department, believes his teaching effort to have been hampered by an "atmosphere of distrust [of] male professors"; plaintiff Lisa Stone, a current student, speaks of "great emotional distress" on learning that another woman student was "the subject of sexual pressures and attentions from" a male university employee; plaintiff Ann Olivarius, a recent Yale graduate, relates that she had occasion as an officer of the Undergraduate Women's Caucus when at Yale to discuss with other students their complaints of sexual harassment, and allegedly met rebuff or indifference in attempting to press such complaints herself. None of these claims is of personal exclusion from a federally funded education program or activity, or of the personal denial of full participation in the benefits of such a program or activity in any measurable sense. No judicial enforcement of Title IX could properly extend to such imponderables as atmosphere or vicariously experienced wrong, and the claims just mentioned are untenable on their face.

Since any underlying claim that she was herself denied Title IX rights in unsuccessfully pursuing others' complaints does not merit recognition, there is no need to examine the propriety otherwise of the lone request for damages, plaintiff Olivarius' incidental prayer for $500 as compensation for asserted expenditure of "time, effort and money in investigating complaints herself, preparing them to be presented to responsible officials... and attempting to negotiate the complexities of *ad hoc* 'channels.' " Moreover, her graduation seems to have rendered moot her claim for equitable relief, which would appear to be the case as well for plaintiff Ronni Alexander—a graduate in 1977 before suit was commenced—absent sheer conjecture that the latter may in the future wish to resume study in a field allegedly abandoned at Yale because of "sexual demands" by her tutor.

Currently at Yale are two other women students who—like plaintiff Alexander—complain of a direct, personal experience of sexual harassment. Plaintiff Margery Reifler speaks in general terms of humiliation, distraction from studies and denial of recognition resulting from alleged harassment by a coach when she was manager of an athletic team; she "wanted to complain to responsible authorities" but did not. Plaintiff Pamela Price asserts that she received a poor grade in a course in her major field of study, not due to any "fair evaluation of her academic work", but as the consequence of her rejecting a professor's outright proposition "to give her a grade of 'A' in the course in exchange for her compliance with his sexual demands." Price represents that she did complain promptly after that alleged incident only to be "told by responsible officials of defendant that nothing could be done to remedy her situation"; plaintiff further alleges that long after the ensuing course mark was given, she was asked to re-submit her complaint, but then "no investigation of the incident" was made and Yale officials have indicated that "nothing further will or can be done about her complaint". Plaintiff Price is a senior, in the process of applying to law schools, and expresses immediate concern that a clearly improper low grade "could materially damage... likelihood of admission."

A critical difference between these two claims is that plaintiff Reifler concededly made no complaint on which Yale could act, while plaintiff Price did complain to the university and supposedly met rebuff. The former's artfully drafted but conclusory assertion that general university inertia should be equated with policy and has "the effect of actively condoning... sexual harassment" is simply not adequate to show that Yale acted to deny her any right, and the concept of mere *respondeat superior* appears ill-adapted to the question of Title IX sex discrimination based on harassment incidents. This is not to say either that sexual harassment is never of concern under Title IX, or that a university may properly ignore the matter entirely. In plaintiff Price's case, for example, it is perfectly reasonable to maintain that academic advancement conditioned upon submission to sexual demands constitutes sex discrimination in education, just as questions of job retention or promotion tied to sexual demands from supervisors have become increasingly recognized as potential violations of Title VII's ban against sex discrimination in employment. When a complaint of such an incident is made, university inaction then does assume significance, for on refusing to investigate, the institution may sensibly be held responsible for condoning or ratifying the employee's invidiously discriminatory conduct.

But may any such private suit be entertained? The only reported appellate decision is contrary to plaintiffs' position, the Court of Appeals for the Seventh Circuit having held in the context of sex discrimination alleged by a disappointed medical school applicant that

"it would be an unwarranted exercise of federal judicial power to imply a private right of action in the face of a sophisticated scheme of administrative enforcement and judicial review that, if given an opportunity to work, may well prove itself adequate to the task for which Congress designed it."

On careful study of the factors pertinent to any such conclusion, however, this Court is unable to agree that the private claim may be summarily dismissed without further inquiry into actual need.

As pointed out initially, the overall question is whether the federal court should recognize or fashion a new suit right because "necessary to effectuate Congress' goals". The commonly accepted approach to the question of implying a judicial remedy, seemingly still valid, has been to examine four specific factors identified as relevant in *Cort v. Ash*:

"First, is the plaintiff 'one of the class for whose *especial* benefit the statute was enacted,' that is, does the statute create a federal right in favor of the plaintiff? Second, is there any indication of legislative intent, explicit or implicit, either to create such a remedy or to deny one? Third, is it consistent with the underlying purposes of the legislative scheme to imply such a remedy for the plaintiff? And finally, is the cause of action one traditionally relegated to state law, in an area basically the concern of the States, so that it would be inappropriate to infer a cause of action based solely on federal law?

It is clear that plaintiff Price is within the class Title IX was designed to protect and that the claim is in no realistic sense more appropriate for state court action. Title IX's legislative history does not unequivocally show an express congressional intent to permit or preclude a private right of action, and although the history of subsequent passage of the Attorney's Fees Award Act of 1976, may perhaps be read to indicate that the latter statute's mention of Title IX was but prudent inclusion in the event courts did thereafter imply a private remedy, plaintiff's resort to this Court is certainly not ruled out. Indeed, H.E.W. has further urged here and in *Cannon* that private suit enforcement would promote Title IX's purpose. The *Cannon* panel concluded that leave to sue "would be inconsistent with the legislative intent and underlying purposes of the statutory scheme", that court discerning "implicit" intent in the stress on the administrative process and expressing concern lest "private parties . . . circumvent the remedial scheme created by Congress", with the "remedies available" not shown "wholly inadequate".

One difficulty with following *Cannon* is that the decision may yield substantially different enforcement rights to victims of sex discrimination than to those subjected to discrimination in federally assisted programs "on the ground of race, color, or national origin" in violation of Title VI of the Civil Rights Act of 1964, although Title IX was obviously patterned after Title VI, including its enforcement provisions. It seems plain enough that Title VI violations are actionable, and it is hard to understand why all Title IX claims should be less favorably regarded. It naturally has been suggested that such Title VI cases have been against "public" defendants and therefore strictly rest on the Civil Rights Act's grant of the right to sue for a deprivation under color of state law "of any rights... secured by the Constitution and laws". If so, it could hardly be a principled distinction that one student would be at Yale and another at the University of Connecticut; if the state college student can secure judicial relief under § 1983, the more reason to imply a suit right for the identically situated private university student.

More importantly, perhaps, the issue of need for the remedy merits additional probing. While the Supreme Court has remarked that "express statutory provision for one form of proceeding ordinarily implies that no other means of enforcement was intended by the Legislature" the observation has been made in the context of either clearer legislative intent than is provided by Title IX's ambiguous history—a statute based on Title VI and curiously followed by subsequent legislative mention of attorney's fees which are not evident for all possible Title IX claims. It is obviously significant that the enforcing agency urges recognition of private suit rights, particularly since H.E.W.'s position that private enforcement is at least a helpful supplement is a reasonable one. In view of that stance, it may be improvident either hastily to infer an unexpressed legislative "intent" to bar any such suit, or merely to assume inconsistency between remedies.

As *amici curiae*, the Women's Equity Action League Educational and Legal Defense Fund and the National Organization for Women Legal Defense Fund contend in further support of plaintiffs that it is already patent under Title IX that "the remedies available have proven to be wholly inadequate to the task of protecting those rights". To the extent factual and concerned with delayed and circumscribed administrative enforcement, the argument cannot be accepted outright without opportunity for reply by defendant. In the light of H.E.W.'s long delay even in promulgating enforcing regulations, however, the contentions advanced are surely not insubstantial, and it seems unsound to dismiss this complaint in its entirety at the outset on sheer assumption that administrative enforcement may prove adequate while refusing to allow a threshold showing purporting to demonstrate the contrary.

For similar reasons, plaintiff Price's complaint may not be dismissed on its face despite failure to seek any administrative recourse whatsoever, since ordinarily beneficial and fair requirements of administrative exhaustion should not be imposed absent realistic possibility of a meaningful remedy. Although H.E.W. could hardly evince indifference to what amounts to a claim that Yale has not complied with the basic implementing regulation calling for Title IX "grievance procedures", 45 C.F.R. § 86.8(b), and while under the Title VI regulations also made applicable in Title IX matters, 45 C.F.R. § 86.71, an individual may make a written complaint which would at least obligate H.E.W. to make initial "prompt investigation" if the information provided "indicates a possible failure to comply" with Title IX duties, 45 C.F.R. § 80.7(b)-(c), there is good reason to believe that to leave Price to her administrative remedy would be an empty exercise. Putting to one side unconceded representations that the enforcement system is grossly deficient in actual operation, it is not realistic to expect even that "prompt" first-step administrative action—much less any multistage proceedings—could yield an effective remedy to one claiming imminent injury, with only a short interval between Yale's supposed abandonment of her complaint and the law school application process. Beyond the prayer for a court-ordered complaint mechanism, plaintiff Price has specifically requested investigation and a transcript notation in the interim that the disputed grade is under review, which clearly are potentially effective measures. Whether any such relief is proper is of course not the issue on the motion to dismiss, but can be immediately tested on plaintiff's now-pending motion for preliminary injunction.

As far as this plaintiff is concerned, defendant's attendant jurisdictional objection lacks compelling force. If the federal statutory claim may not rest on the jurisdictional grant extending to suits for relief "under any Act of Congress providing for the protection of civil rights", the Court cannot hold with requisite certainty in this instance that the amount in controversy is inadequate to support proceedings under the general federal question grant of 28 U.S.C. § 1331. Defendant has also suggested that Title IX may be unconstitutional if construed to allow private suit, but advances no convincing authority for that contention in the situation presented.

For the reasons stated above, the instant motion to dismiss is accordingly hereby granted as to plaintiffs Alexander, Olivarius, Reifler, Stone and Winkler, and denied as to plaintiff Price.

Tayyari v. New Mexico State University
495 F. Supp. 1365 (1980)

CAMPOS, District Judge.

This case is before the Court on application by Plaintiffs for a declaratory judgment and permanent injunction. Money damages are not sought. Plaintiffs are 15 Iranian citizens, students at New Mexico State University (NMSU), and in good standing with the Immigration and Naturalization Service (INS) in respect to visa status. Defendants are NMSU, the Board of Regents of NMSU (Regents) and the five individual members of the Board of Regents. By letter of August 6, 1980 to the United States Attorney for New Mexico, I invited the United States to intervene or to participate as *amicus curiae*. I was concerned about the importance of this case as it may relate to United States foreign policy or immigration policy. The United States declined to intervene, but moved for leave to appear as *amicus curiae*. Leave was granted.

This controversy arises out of action taken by Regents designed to rid the campus of Iranian students. For the reasons discussed below, the Court concludes that such action must be declared unconstitutional and that defendants must be permanently enjoined from implementing that action.

The essential facts are not in dispute. On May 9, 1980 Regents passed the following Motion:

> ... that any student whose home government holds, or permits the holding of U.S. citizens hostage will be denied admission or readmission to New Mexico State University commencing with the Fall 1980 semester unless the American hostages are returned unharmed by July 15, 1980.

To clarify its original action, Regents passed a Substitute Motion on June 5, 1980, which reads:

> Any student whose home government holds or permits the holding of U.S. citizens hostage will be denied subsequent enrollment to New Mexico State University until the hostages are released unharmed. The effective date of this motion is July 15, 1980.

It is this Substitute Motion whose validity is now at issue.

At the court hearing on July 16, 1980, the parties agreed to the entering of a preliminary injunction pending final decision on the merits. Defendants have been enjoined from enforcement of their motion as it applies to the Plaintiffs during the pendency of this action.

Another stipulation made at the hearing is that only in Iran are United States hostages held with permission of the home government. To date one hostage has been released for medical reasons.

Two plaintiffs are "immigrant aliens." They are in this country on permanent residency status and are eligible for naturalization after five years of residence here. The rest of Plaintiffs are "nonimmigrant aliens" who are admitted for a fixed period of time for a specific purpose, in this case on student visas to attend school. The Substitute Motion on its face affects both types of aliens.

Before discussing the merits of Plaintiffs' contentions, I must consider some jurisdictional and other preliminary matters raised by Defendants.

*   *   *

[T]here is federal jurisdiction to consider Plaintiffs' Title VI claim.

Defendants next argue that there exists no case or controversy here that is ripe for judicial decision because Plaintiffs have not yet been denied enrollment. They argue that the case may become moot if the hostages are released unharmed before enrollment is actually denied, or if individual Plaintiffs are ineligible for some other reason, such as nonpayment of fees. It is true that enrollment for the Fall semester had not commenced at the time of the hearing in this case. I conclude, however, that the threat of being denied enrollment is sufficiently real and imminent to make this case ripe for decision at this time. If Plaintiffs were denied enrollment, they would have to make other plans for school attendance because their student visas are conditioned upon attendance at an American school. It would be improvident to make Plaintiffs wait until actual denial of enrollment to bring this action. Nor has release of the hostages ever seemed likely to come about soon. The difference between a hypothetical or abstract question and a "case or controversy" is one of degree. The basic inquiry is whether the "conflicting contentions of the parties ... present a real, substantial controversy between parties having adverse legal interests, a dispute definite and concrete, not hypothetical or abstract." Plaintiffs have demonstrated a realistic danger of sustaining direct injury as a result of enforcement of Regents' Substitute Motion, thus the questions presented to me are not abstract or hypothetical.

As for the potential ineligibility of some Iranian students for enrollment at NMSU on a basis other than Regents' Substitute Motion, this argument is precluded by a stipulation entered into between Plaintiffs and Defendants at the hearing. That stipulation was to the effect that these Plaintiffs would be eligible for reenrollment but for the Motion adopted by Regents. Therefore, the Court may proceed to the merits of Plaintiffs' contentions.

Plaintiffs claim they are being denied equal protection of the laws and due process rights guaranteed to them under the Constitution of the United States. They seek a judicial declaration that the action of the Regents in adopting the Motion denying Plaintiffs subsequent enrollment at NMSU is unconstitutional. Also, they pray for an injunction permanently enjoining Defendants from implementing the challenged Motion.

EQUAL PROTECTION. The first inquiry in an equal protection analysis is into the nature of the classification involved in the challenged action. This is important for it establishes the Court's standard of review of that action. The classification here is along lines of both alienage and national origin. Regents' motion distinguishes between aliens and United States citizens because it is directed at students with a home government other than the United States. At the hearing, Defendants further refined the alienage classification by stating that the motion would not be applied against the two immigrant alien Plaintiffs. Thus, the class against which Regents' action is directed is nonimmigrant aliens. No rationale has been presented by Defendants for distinguishing among aliens according to their immigrant status except that Defendants admit they believe the Motion could not constitutionally be applied to these immigrant aliens.

Aliens residing in our land have long enjoyed protection of the United States Constitution. The Fourteenth Amendment protects not only citizens, but also "any person" within a state's jurisdiction, from unequal treatment at the hands of the state.

Alienage has been treated under modern equal protection analysis as a suspect classification, thus invoking strict judicial scrutiny of a state's challenged action. While states may deny aliens the right to vote, a traditional badge of citizenship, they may not deny aliens welfare benefits, competing for certain civil service jobs, membership in the Bar, or engineering jobs. In this line of cases, the one most on point for our purposes is *Nyquist v. Mauclet.* In that case, the Supreme Court found an equal protection violation where the State of New York denied aliens the right to receive state financial assistance for higher education. Plaintiffs argue that if a state cannot deny aliens financial assistance for a college education, *a fortiori* it cannot deny them the education itself.

Defendants argue that alienage is not always a suspect classification. While *Graham v. Richardson* and its progeny have never been expressly overruled, Defendants cite recent cases in which the Supreme Court has applied a lesser standard, that of rationality, to the challenged state action involving aliens.

Foley and *Ambach* relied on language in *Sugarman* that left open the door for a ban on employment of aliens for certain positions in state government. *Sugarman* used strict scrutiny, and looked to "the substantiality of the State's interest in enforcing the statute in question, and to the narrowness of the limits within which the discrimination is confined." In *Sugarman*, the statute in question did not pass consti-tutional muster primarily because the statute, barring aliens from all competitive civil service jobs, was "neither narrowly confined nor precise in its application." The Court recognized as legitimate and substantial, however, the State's interest in having loyal citizens as civil servants to formulate and execute government policy. It stated that its scrutiny would be less demanding when dealing with matters related to a state's self-government, "a State's constitutional prerogatives."

Foley involved a challenge against a New York statute limiting state police jobs to United States citizens. The Court upheld the statute, finding a rational relationship between the interest sought to be protected (state self-government by loyal employees executing governmental policy) and the limiting classification. The reason for not employing strict judicial scrutiny was that the police function "involves discretionary decisionmaking, or execution of policy, which substantially affects members of the political community."

The Court in *Ambach* applied the rational basis test to a New York statute restricting public elementary and secondary school teaching positions to citizens and noncitizens intending to become citizens. Use of this standard was again justified on the basis of the discretionary role of public school teachers in teaching political values to children. The Court found public school teachers to fulfill a "governmental function" so as to invoke less demanding judicial scrutiny.

The distinguishing factor, then, between this case and the situations present in *Foley* and *Ambach*, is that students attending a state university do not perform any discretionary function implicating the state's right to self-government. Thus, the gov-ernmental function exception to the general rule that alienage is a suspect classification requiring strict judicial scrutiny, is not called into play here. *Graham* and *Nyquist* control.

Alienage is not the only suspect classification involved here. Even though no nation is named in the Substitute Motion, the classification is necessarily based on national origin. A student with a home government other than the United States is a student from a foreign country. If that country permits the holding of United States hostages, then students from that country, and only students from that country, are affected. Not only is the effect so limited, but testimony and exhibits at the hearing show the clear purpose of Regents was to exclude only students of one nationality: Iranian. Nationality is another suspect classification calling for strict judicial scrutiny. Even Justice Rehnquist, who believes the Fourteenth Amendment should only protect against racial discrimination, seems to look askance at a state statute discriminating against aliens on the basis of nationality. In *Sugarman*, he said:

> The state statute that classifies aliens on the basis of country of origin is much more likely to classify on the basis of race, and thus conflict with the core purpose of the Equal Protection Clause, than a statute that . . . merely distin-guishes between alienage as such and citizenship as such.

Defendants' final argument against use of strict judicial scrutiny is based on *Narenji v. Civiletti*. In that case, the court of appeals applied the rational basis test and upheld a regulation promulgated by the Attorney General at the direction of President Carter. The regulation required all Iranian students of higher education who are nonim-migrant aliens to clear their status with INS or risk deportation proceedings. That case involved not state action but action by the executive branch of the federal government. The decision rested on principles of separation of powers: the President is vested with authority over foreign affairs. That authority sometimes requires distinctions to be drawn along lines of alienage and national origin. It is not the province of the judicial branch to closely scrutinize actions by the President which bear some rational relationship to his authority over foreign affairs. But here we do not deal with presidential action, we are dealing with state action. No credible policy reason has been advanced by Defendants to support their contention for relaxed scrutiny as applied to Regents' action.

None of the reasons offered by Defendants for their action rises to that level of compelling state interest which withstands strict scrutiny. Their first justification is financial: credit is extended to Iranian students and they might not pay their bills. If they don't pay their bills it wouldn't be fair to make the citizens of New Mexico pick up all the fees for Iranian students while financing all other students only partially. And if the Iranian students don't pay, it wouldn't be fair to let them stay in student housing since there is a shortage and students who would pay should be given housing. Finally, if the Iranian students don't pay their bills it might be difficult to collect amounts owing because the Iranian embassy in the United States has been closed.

The action taken by Regents—barring all Iranian students from enrolling at NMSU—sweeps too broadly and too indiscriminately if their true concern is financial. If Regents' true concern be financial, they have, in a figurative sense, thrown out the baby with the bath water.

First of all, Regents have come up with a financial justification rather late in the game. This was a wobbly afterthought first articulated at the hearing. No such concerns were publicly expressed prior to the hearing. Notably, the only mention of finances in the Regents' minutes of May 9, 1980, is that the taxpayers shouldn't have to support Iranian students at NMSU. The reasoning given for that proposition at the time had nothing to do with whether Iranian students could or would pay their bills. It was that Iran had become an enemy of the United States and that Americans are angry and fed up with Iranians and, therefore, Iranian students shouldn't get any benefits from New Mexico taxpayers. I find that concerns about finances at NMSU did not underlie Regents' action.

Second, even if finances were a true concern of Regents, Defendants have utterly failed to demonstrate any fiscal danger posed by Iranian students. Evidence admitted at the hearing showed only that some Iranian students owed the school money in May 1980. Apparently, credit is extended to students for school expenses. As of the date of the hearing, only two Plaintiffs were in arrears, for a total of $930.00. Several others still owed money but were not in arrears. Three were paid up. It should be noted that a fiscal policy at NMSU applies to all students:

> (A)ll fees and bills owed NMSU must be paid in full before a student may enroll in any subsequent Fall or Spring semester. These bills include payment of library fees, payment of dormitory and residence fees, and payment of all bills incurred for such items as those purchased from the University Book Store and the University Cafeteria.

Presumably, tuition is one of the "fees" which must be paid in full prior to reenrollment. Since no student can enroll if his or her payments are in arrears, there seems no present danger of large bills going unpaid by Iranian students. Moreover, it was not demonstrated that Iranian students are any less likely to pay than other students.

Exclusion of all Iranian students because some of them may in the future end up owing money seems misdirected and extreme.

This post-hoc fiscal rationale is certainly insufficient to justify the action taken by Regents. Even if Regents' action had been more rationally related to fiscal concerns, such as requiring Iranian students to pay more tuition than other students or to pay all their expenses in advance, they would have to show a compelling need for it. No showing at all was made in this Court, beyond mere speculation about the future, that Iranian students are poor credit risks. In Mississippi, recently, a federal district court granted a preliminary injunction restraining the State's Board of Trustees from enforcing an appropriation bill raising tuition for students whose home government does not have diplomatic relations with the United States and against which the United States has economic sanctions. [*Shabani v. Simmons*] That bill was struck down, at least preliminarily, even though it is finely focused on fiscal considerations. *Nyquist* controls both cases and instructs that in this case Regents' action is impermissible.

Another rationale advanced by Defendants for Regents' action is safety. They are assertedly concerned that if Iranian students are allowed to remain on campus, some physical harm may come to them, to others on campus, and to campus buildings. Regents perceive their duty to protect these people and things as being discharged by their Substitute Motion. I do not agree. Again, the action sweeps too broadly and indiscriminately.

* * *

DUE PROCESS. Plaintiffs claim their right to procedural and substantive due process has been violated by Regents' summary action. With respect to their procedural due process claim, Plaintiffs point out the Substitute Motion was adopted without notice to them or an opportunity to be heard. Yet the Motion denies Plaintiffs the right to continue their education at NMSU. In support of their substantive due process claim, Plaintiffs allege Regents' Motion amounts to arbitrary, unreasonable and capricious action which fulfills no proper Board function.

A violation of due process can be found only if Plaintiffs have demonstrated they possess a liberty or property right or interest in being allowed to continue their education at NMSU. No effort was expended at the hearing to establish such a right or interest on the part of these Plaintiffs. It does seem that some university officials present at the May 9, 1980 meeting of the Board of Regents thought Plaintiffs did have at least a contract or property right to continue at NMSU. It has been university practice to apply the same rules and regulations to a student throughout his or her attendance at NMSU as were in effect when that student was admitted.

I am of the view that serious questions of a due process violation have been raised by Regents' action. However, I decline to rest my decision on this ground. Even if Plaintiffs had been afforded notice and an opportunity to be heard, Regents' action cannot withstand constitutional attack on equal protection grounds. Nor, in the absence of more proof do I find it necessary to address more fully the substantive due process issue.

* * *

PREEMPTION. Plaintiffs and the United States as *amicus curiae* urge that Regents' Substitute Motion be struck down for another reason, that it interferes with federal immigration policy and federal foreign policy. The focus shifts, then, from the rights of Plaintiffs to the superior right of the federal government to exercise exclusive power and control over aliens and to dictate foreign policy without interference from the states. Defendants argue that they did not intend to enter the area of immigration policy or foreign policy, and that in any event their Substitute Motion will not interfere with federal policy. Even if Regents' Motion did not violate Plaintiffs' Fourteenth Amendment rights, I conclude that its potential effect on this nation's management of immigration and foreign affairs would dictate its demise.

It is evident from the record in this case that Regents' true purpose in enacting the Substitute Motion was to make a political statement. Individual Regents had been under pressure because of their own personal reactions to the hostage crisis and from New Mexico taxpayers to "do something" about the Iranian students on campus. Anger and frustration about the hostage situation sought an accessible scapegoat. Iranian students on campus receive the benefits of a higher education subsidized by money from the State tax coffers. Regents decided to retaliate against Iran and the Iranian students, the latter as a class, by depriving the students of the right to continue to receive an education at NMSU.

In view of Regents' purpose, the Court's role becomes more clear. Strong negative reactions to the hostage situation have become commonplace. Hostility towards those responsible for the continued crisis has risen to the level of xenophobia directed against all Iranians without regard to their affiliations as to the present regime in Iran. The anger being expressed against the government of Iran is understandable and completely justified in the face of the hostile and illegal action taken against our citizens in that foreign land. This crisis tests our country's patience. It also tests our country's commitment to its fundamental principles of liberty expressed in the Constitution. In my view, Regents have gone beyond personal expression of their anger and frustrations in a permissible way. Their action is cloaked with the power of the State, and they have entered the arenas of foreign affairs and immigration policy, interrelated matters entrusted exclusively to the federal government.

* * *

I conclude that the action by Regents of NMSU imposes an impermissible burden on the federal government's power to regulate immigration and conduct foreign affairs. As such, it must be invalidated.

One of America's great radicals expressed an idea which deserves at least momentary reflection by all parties in this case as well as by anyone else who might be interested in this litigation—those in this country as well as those in the Islamic Republic of Iran. Incidentally, the name of that loved and admired American is also subscribed to the United States Constitution which has been before me today. To Mr. Benjamin Franklin of Pennsylvania are attributed these thoughts:

> God grant that not only the love of liberty, but a thorough knowledge of the rights of man may pervade all the nations of the earth so that a philosopher may set his foot anywhere on its surface and say, "this is my country."

These noble sentiments may indeed rest at dizzying heights of naiveté. From the practical and pragmatic perspective not much may realistically be claimed for them. But even conceding this, I suggest that the ideal is as civilized and as civilizing today as when Mr. Franklin articulated it about two hundred years ago.

International students continue to be singled out for "special" treatment. In 1987,

Massachusetts passed legislation to charge higher tuition to foreign students than to Massachusetts residents or residents of other states. The bill's sponsor indicated that his legislation was intended to remove subsidies to "students from nations that practice terrorism, such as Iran." An immediate showdown was averted by grandparenting all foreign students enrolled at the time (Fall and Spring, 1987–88), but the legislation is being challenged in court and legislators are moving to consider repealing the law, which was tacked onto a supplemental appropriations measure. "Nationwide Repercussions Feared from Mass. Law Linking Foreign-Student Fees to Cost of Education," *Chronicle of Higher Education,* 12 August 1987, pp 19–20; "Lawmakers Say They Goofed on Hike of Foreigners' Tuition," *Boston Globe,* 8 October 1987, p. 1.

In a case also related to the Iran hostage situation, it was held that Iranian college students could be required to obey a Presidential Order that they report their status to the INS; a small percentage was found to be out of status. *Narenji v. Civiletti,* 617 F. 2d 745 (D.C. Cir. 1979), 481 F. Supp. 1132 (D.D.C. 1979), *cert. denied,* 446 U.S. 957 (1980).

Southeastern Community College v. Davis
442 U.S. 397 (1979)

Mr. Justice POWELL delivered the opinion of the Court.

This case presents a matter of first impression for this Court: Whether § 504 of the Rehabilitation Act of 1973, which prohibits discrimination against an "otherwise qualified handicapped individual" in federally funded programs "solely by reason of his handicap," forbids professional schools from imposing physical qualifications for admission to their clinical training programs.

I

Respondent, who suffers from a serious hearing disability, seeks to be trained as a registered nurse. During the 1973–1974 academic year she was enrolled in the College Parallel program of Southeastern Community College, a state institution that receives federal funds. Respondent hoped to progress to Southeastern's Associate Degree Nursing program, completion of which would make her eligible for state certification as a registered nurse. In the course of her application to the nursing program, she was interviewed by a member of the nursing faculty. It became apparent that respondent had difficulty understanding questions asked, and on inquiry she acknowledged a history of hearing problems and dependence on a hearing aid. She was advised to consult an audiologist.

On the basis of an examination at Duke University Medical Center, respondent was diagnosed as having a "bilateral, sensori-neural hearing loss." A change in her hearing aid was recommended, as a result of which it was expected that she would be able to detect sounds "almost as well as a person would who has normal hearing." But this improvement would not mean that she could discriminate among sounds sufficiently to understand normal spoken speech. Her lipreading skills would remain necessary for effective communication: "While wearing the hearing aid, she is well aware of gross sounds occurring in the listening environment. However, she can only be responsible for speech spoken to her, when the talker gets her attention and allows her to look directly at the talker."

Southeastern next consulted Mary McRee, Executive Director of the North Carolina Board of Nursing. On the basis of the audiologist's report, McRee recommended that respondent not be admitted to the nursing program. In McRee's view, respondent's hearing disability made it unsafe for her to practice as a nurse. In addition, it would be impossible for respondent to participate safely in the normal clinical training program, and those modifications that would be necessary to enable safe participation would prevent her from realizing the benefits of the program: "To adjust patient learning experiences in keeping with [respondent's] hearing limitations could, in fact, be the same as denying her full learning to meet the objectives of your nursing programs."

After respondent was notified that she was not qualified for nursing study because of her hearing disability, she requested reconsideration of the decision. The entire nursing staff of Southeastern was assembled, and McRee again was consulted. McRee repeated her conclusion that on the basis of the available evidence, respondent "has hearing limitations which could interfere with her safely caring for patients." Upon further deliberation, the staff voted to deny respondent admission.

Respondent then filed suit in the United States District Court for the Eastern District of North Carolina, alleging both a violation of § 504 of the Rehabilitation Act of 1973, and a denial of equal protection and due process. After a bench trial, the District Court entered judgment in favor of Southeastern. It confirmed the findings of the audiologist that even with a hearing aid respondent cannot understand speech directed to her except through lip-reading, and further found:

> "[I]n many situations such as an operation room intensive care unit, or post-natal care unit, all doctors and nurses wear surgical masks which would make lipreading impossible. Additionally, in many situations a Registered Nurse would be required to instantly follow the physician's instructions concerning procurement of various types of instruments and drugs where the physician would be unable to get the nurse's attention by other than vocal means."

Accordingly, the court concluded:

> "[Respondent's] handicap actually prevents her from safely performing in both her training program and her proposed profession. The trial testimony indicated numerous situations where [respondent's] particular disability would render her unable to function properly. Of particular concern to the court in this case is the potential of danger to future patients in such situations."

Based on these findings, the District Court concluded that respondent was not an "otherwise qualified handicapped individual" protected against discrimination by § 504. In its view, "[o]therwise qualified, can only be read to mean otherwise able to function sufficiently in the position sought in spite of the handicap, if proper training and facilities are suitable and available." Because respondent's disability would prevent her from functioning "sufficiently" in Southeastern's nursing program, the court held that the decision to exclude her was not discriminatory within the meaning of § 504.

On appeal, the Court of Appeals for the Fourth Circuit reversed. It did not dispute the District Court's findings of fact, but held that the court had misconstrued § 504. In light of administrative regulations that had been promulgated while the appeal was pending, the appellate court believed that § 504 required Southeastern to "reconsider plaintiff's application for admission to the nursing program without regard to her hearing ability." It concluded that the District Court had erred in taking respondent's handicap into account in determining whether she was "otherwise qualified" for the program, rather than confining its inquiry to her "academic and technical qualifications." The Court of Appeals also suggested that § 504 required "affirmative conduct" on the part of Southeastern to modify its program to accommodate the disabilities of applicants, "even when such modifications become expensive."

Because of the importance of this issue to the many institutions covered by § 504, we granted certiorari. We now reverse.

II

As previously noted, this is the first case in which this Court has been called upon to interpret § 504. It is elementary that "[t]he starting point in every case involving construction of a statute is the language itself." Section 504 by its terms does not compel educational institutions to disregard the disabilities of handicapped individuals or to make substantial modifications in their programs to allow disabled persons to participate. Instead, it requires only that an "otherwise qualified handicapped individual" not be excluded from participation in a federally funded program "solely by reason of his handicap," indicating only that mere possession of a handicap is not a permissible ground for assuming an inability to function in a particular context.

The court below, however, believed that the "otherwise qualified" persons protected by § 504 include those who would be able to meet the requirements of a particular program in every respect except as to limitations imposed by their handicap. Taken literally, this holding would prevent an institution from taking into account any limitation resulting from the handicap, however disabling. It assumes, in effect, that a person need not meet legitimate physical requirements in order to be "otherwise qualified." We think the understanding of the District Court is closer to the plain meaning of the statutory language. An otherwise qualified person is one who is able to meet all of a program's requirements in spite of his handicap.

The regulations promulgated by the Department of HEW to interpret § 504 reinforce, rather than contradict, this conclusion. According to these regulations, a "[q]ualified handicapped person" is, "[w]ith respect to postsecondary and vocational education services, a handicapped person who meets the academic and technical standards requisite to admission or participation in the [school's] education program or activity. . . . " An explanatory note states:

> "The term 'technical standards' refers to *all* nonacademic admissions criteria that are essential to participation in the program in question."

A further note emphasizes that legitimate physical qualifications may be essential to participation in particular programs. We think it clear, therefore, that HEW interprets the "other" qualifications which a handicapped person may be required to meet as including necessary physical qualifications.

III

The remaining question is whether the physical qualifications Southeastern demanded of respondent might not be necessary for participation in its nursing program. It is not open to dispute that, as Southeastern's Associate Degree Nursing program currently is constituted, the ability to understand speech without reliance on lip-reading is necessary for patient safety during the clinical phase of the program. As the District Court found, this ability also is indispensable for many of the functions that a registered nurse performs.

Respondent contends nevertheless that § 504, properly interpreted, compels South-eastern to undertake affirmative action that would dispense with the need for effective oral communication. First, it is suggested that respondent can be given individual supervision by faculty members whenever she attends patients directly. Moreover, certain required courses might be dispensed with altogether for respondent. It is not necessary, she argues, that Southeastern train her to undertake all the tasks a registered nurse is licensed to perform. Rather, it is sufficient to make § 504 applicable if respondent might be able to perform satisfactorily some of the duties of a registered nurse or to hold some of the positions available to a registered nurse.

Respondent finds support for this argument in portions of the HEW regulations discussed above. In particular, a provision applicable to postsecondary educational programs requires covered institutions to make "modifications" in their programs to accommodate handicapped persons, and to provide "auxiliary aids" such as sign-language interpreters. Respondent argues that this regulation imposes an obligation to ensure full participation in covered programs by handicapped individuals and, in particular, requires Southeastern to make the kind of adjustments that would be necessary to permit her safe participation in the nursing program.

We note first that on the present record it appears unlikely respondent could benefit from any affirmative action that the regulation reasonably could be interpreted as requiring. Section 84.44(d)(2), for example, explicitly excludes "devices or services of a personal nature" from the kinds of auxiliary aids a school must provide a handicapped individual. Yet the only evidence in the record indicates that nothing less than close, individual attention by a nursing instructor would be sufficient to ensure patient safety if respondent took part in the clinical phase of the nursing program. Furthermore, it also is reasonably clear that § 84.44(a) does not encompass the kind of curricular changes that would be necessary to accommodate respondent in the nursing program. In light of respondent's inability to function in clinical courses without close supervision, Southeastern, with prudence, could allow her to take only academic classes. Whatever benefits respondent might realize from such a course of study, she would not receive even a rough equivalent of the training a nursing program normally gives. Such a fundamental alteration in the nature of a program is far more than the "modification" the regulation requires.

Moreover, an interpretation of the regulations that required the extensive modifi-cations necessary to include respondent in the nursing program would raise grave doubts about their validity. If these regulations were to require substantial adjustments in existing programs beyond those necessary to eliminate discrimination against otherwise qualified individuals, they would do more than clarify the meaning of § 504. Instead, they would constitute an unauthorized extension of the obligations imposed by that statute.

The language and structure of the Rehabilitation Act of 1973 reflect a recognition by Congress of the distinction between the evenhanded treatment of qualified hand-icapped persons and affirmative efforts to overcome the disabilities caused by hand-icaps. Section 501(b), governing the employment of handicapped individuals by the Federal Government, requires each federal agency to submit "an affirmative action program plan for the hiring, placement, and advancement of handicapped individ-uals...." These plans "shall include a description of the extent to which and methods whereby the special needs of handicapped employees are being met." Similarly, § 503(a), governing hiring by federal contractors, requires employers to "take affirmative action to employ and advance in employment qualified handicapped individuals...." The President is required to promulgate regulations to enforce this section.

Under § 501(c) of the Act, by contrast, state agencies such as Southeastern are only "encourage[d]... to adopt and implement such policies and procedures." Section 504 does not refer at all to affirmative action, and except as it applies to federal employers it does not provide for implementation by administrative action. A comparison of these provisions demonstrates that Congress understood accommodation of the needs of handicapped individuals may require affirmative action and knew how to provide for it in those instances where it wished to do so.

Although an agency's interpretation of the statute under which it operates is entitled to some deference, "this deference is constrained by our obligation to honor the clear meaning of a statute, as revealed by its language, purpose, and history." Here, neither the language, purpose, nor history of § 504 reveals an intent to impose an affirmative-action obligation on all recipients of federal funds. Accordingly, we hold that even if HEW has attempted to create such an obligation itself, it lacks the authority to do so.

IV

We do not suggest that the line between a lawful refusal to extend affirmative action and illegal discrimination against handicapped persons always will be clear. It is possible to envision situations where an insistence on continuing past requirements and practices might arbitrarily deprive genuinely qualified handicapped persons of the opportunity to participate in a covered program. Technological advances can be expected to enhance opportunities to rehabilitate the handicapped or otherwise to qualify them for some useful employment. Such advances also may enable attainment of these goals without imposing undue financial and administrative burdens upon a State. Thus, situations may arise where a refusal to modify an existing program might become unreasonable and discriminatory. Identification of those instances where a refusal to accommodate the needs of a disabled person amounts to discrimination against the handicapped continues to be an important responsibility of HEW.

In this case, however, it is clear that Southeastern's unwillingness to make major adjustments in its nursing program does not constitute such discrimination. The uncontroverted testimony of several members of Southeastern's staff and faculty established that the purpose of its program was to train persons who could serve the nursing profession in all customary ways. This type of purpose, far from reflecting any animus against handicapped individuals, is shared by many if not most of the institutions that train persons to render professional service. It is undisputed that respondent could not participate in Southeastern's nursing program unless the standards were substantially lowered. Section 504 imposes no requirement upon an educational institution to lower or to effect substantial modifications of standards to accommodate a handicapped person.

One may admire respondent's desire and determination to overcome her handicap, and there well may be various other types of service for which she can qualify. In this case, however, we hold that there was no violation of § 504 when Southeastern concluded that respondent did not qualify for admission to its program. Nothing in the language or history of § 504 reflects an intention to limit the freedom of an educational institution to require reasonable physical qualifications for admission to a clinical training program. Nor has there been any showing in this case that any action short of a substantial change in Southeastern's program would render unreasonable the qualifications it imposed.

V

Accordingly, we reverse the judgment of the court below, and remand for proceedings consistent with this opinion.

Pushkin v. Regents of the University of Colorado
658 F.2d 1372 (1981)

WILLIAM E. DOYLE, Circuit Judge.

This is an appeal by the defendants-appellants consisting of the Regents of the University of Colorado; the University of Colorado Hospital, also known as University of Colorado Health Science Center; the University of Colorado Psychiatric Hospital; and Douglas Carter, M.D. The action was brought by Joshua R. Pushkin, M.D., the plaintiff-appellee in this court, pursuant to § 504 of the Rehabilitation Act of 1973, 29 U.S.C. § 794, and 42 U.S.C. § 1983.

The decree in question is an injunction directing that plaintiff-appellee be admitted to the next class at the University of Colorado Psychiatric Residency Program; the judgment awarded plaintiff attorneys fees and costs. The plaintiff had sought monetary damages as well. This request has been denied and no appeal is taken from this denial.

Dr. Pushkin is a medical doctor who alleges that the University of Colorado wrongfully denied him admittance to the Psychiatric Residency Program because he suffers from multiple sclerosis. As a result of this disease Dr. Pushkin is confined to a wheelchair, and is disabled in his abilities to walk and to write. The court found that Dr. Pushkin was an otherwise qualified handicapped individual who had been excluded from a program receiving federal financial assistance solely by reason of his handicap, and that the University was in violation of § 504 of the Rehabilitation Act which provides in pertinent part:

> No otherwise qualified handicapped individual in the United States as defined in § 706(6) of this Title, shall, solely by reason of his handicap, be excluded from participation in, be denied the benefits of, or be subjected to discrimination under any program or activity receiving federal financial assistance.…

It is undisputed that the program in question is receiving federal financial assistance. The district court recognized this and further ruled that the statute was violated because the plaintiff was excluded from participation in or denied the benefits of or subjected to discrimination under a program receiving such funds within the meaning of the statute. The court also held that Dr. Pushkin was an otherwise qualified individual in spite of his handicap, in accord with the Supreme Court's ruling in *Southeastern Community College v. Davis*, and thus was entitled to admittance to the program. Pursuant to the injunction, Dr. Pushkin was admitted to the residency program on July 1, 1981 and he is actually taking part in the program at the present time. We have expedited the appeal in an effort to reach an early resolution of the controversy. As already noted defendants have not disputed that Dr. Pushkin is handicapped within the meaning of the statute, that the Psychiatric Residency Program is a program or activity receiving federal financial assistance within the meaning of the statute and that defendants were acting under color of state law within the meaning of § 1983 in taking the position which they took.

Defendants appeal the trial court's ruling on three grounds. They maintain that: 1) no private cause of action exists under § 504; 2) plaintiff has failed to exhaust his administrative remedies prior to filing this lawsuit; and 3) the trial court erroneously decided the merits of the case. Each of these contentions will be taken up in this review.

* * *

THE FINAL ANALYSIS

Unquestionably plaintiff has established a prima facie case by showing that he is a handicapped person who is qualified for the residency program apart from his handicap and that he was rejected from the program under circumstances which support a finding that his rejection was based solely on his handicap. As to his qualifications, plaintiff met the requisite academic standards of the program in that he held an M.D. degree and had obtained a satisfactory "dean's letter." Plaintiff also presented a letter from Dr. Wong, his supervisor during one year of residency in psychiatry at the Menninger Foundation in Topeka, Kansas. In this letter Dr. Wong stated:

> Doctor Pushkin is a hard-working, thorough, reliable and efficient physician, showing remarkable patience and perseverance and more than the average understanding for his patients. His supervisors did not feel that his medical illness presented any emotional impairment in his work in the field of psychiatry and felt that he had great potential for a future in psychiatry. He has a pleasing personality, works well with his colleagues and is able to handle the most difficult case in a satisfactory manner. He was an inspiration to his colleagues, to faculty and staff.

Furthermore, plaintiff had been practicing medicine with an emphasis on psychiatry at the time that he applied for the program in question.

The position of the University is that Dr. Pushkin was denied admittance to the residency program on the basis of the interview reports of four members of the program faculty: Drs. Carter, Weissberg, Scully and Barchilon. Dr. Pushkin's mean interview ratings, when computed by scores granted by the four interviewers, were held to be too low. In addition to the grades given by the interviewers each made comments expressing their views about Pushkin's capabilities. Dr. Carter stated that Dr. Pushkin "is teachable, but to face the devastation, guilt, pity and rage that can be stirred up in his patients by his physical condition appears to be too much to ask of his patients or of him."

Dr. Weissberg's report noted that while Dr. Pushkin is bright and has terrific drive, that it was doubtful that Dr. Pushkin would be able to work full time.

Dr. Scully's report noted that Pushkin had multiple sclerosis with significant physical defects, that prognosis is unclear, and that Dr. Pushkin has a lot of anger due to his multiple sclerosis that he is "either unaware of or cannot deal with at this time." Dr. Scully stated in his report that Dr. Pushkin is "able to talk about how his illness might be an issue in psychotherapy," that the effect on his classmates is unclear, and that, clearly, Dr. Pushkin "is a risk."

Dr. Barchilon's report indicates concern that the emotional stress of treating patients may be too much for Dr. Pushkin, and that he might not be able to stand the stress and strain of on call duty due to his disease.

*   *   *

There was testimony also from Dr. Gordon Farley, Dr. Pushkin's psychiatrist and a psychiatrist at the University of Colorado Health Center. Dr. Farley expressed anxiety about being subpoenaed as a witness since his patient was suing his employer. He was apprehensive about testifying in opposition to his employers. Also to be noted is that Dr. Farley participates as an interviewer of potential residents at the University of Colorado, but that he was not one of Dr. Pushkin's interviewers. Farley testified that Dr. Pushkin's emotional responses were "within the range of normal," and that from Dr. Pushkin's discussions of his work with his patients, Dr. Pushkin had "treated those patients appropriately," "has had good emotional accessibility" to his patients, and has "reasonably well understood their feelings toward him." Dr. Farley said that Dr. Pushkin is "quick mentally," that he "exercises good judgment in his care of patients," and that he is a "responsible, reasonable, reasoned and conscientious physician." Dr. Farley said that Dr. Pushkin's mentation had not been affected by either the medications that he was taking or by the disease itself. He testified that having observed Dr. Pushkin for four years he had never observed any delirium in him, any disabled sensorium, or any noticeable effect from either the steroids or from the disease. Dr. Farley further testified that Dr. Pushkin "does as well as he can with his illness as any human being could," and that he is "well within the norm of emotional control and behavior." According to Dr. Farley, Dr. Pushkin would make an "exceptional" psychiatrist.

The reports of the interviewers and the testimony of the other witnesses indicates that on the basis of 45 minute interviews and discussions by some of the interviewers with Dr. Bernstein, the admissions committee made certain assumptions regarding his handicap, such as:

1) That Dr. Pushkin was angry and so emotionally upset due to his MS that he would be unable to do an effective job as a psychiatrist; and

2) That Dr. Pushkin's MS and use of steroids had led to difficulties with mentation, delirium and disturbed sensorium; and

3) That Dr. Pushkin would be unable to handle the work involved in the residency because of his MS; and

4) That Dr. Pushkin would miss too much time away from his patients whereby they would suffer.

The testimony of the Pushkins and Dr. Farley and the letter from Dr. Wong rebut all these assumptions. Dr. Farley, who actually counseled Dr. Pushkin, and has done so for over a long period of time and was not merely reaching conclusions on the basis of his observations in the interview, stated that after four years of observing Pushkin closely he could not agree that any of the assumptions made by the admissions committee regarding MS applied to Dr. Pushkin.

It is within the power of the trier of the facts, here the trial court, to weigh the evidence and to determine the credibility of the witnesses. The trial judge found that the assumptions made by the admissions committee were rebutted by other evidence, and thus Dr. Pushkin could not be held to be unqualified due to his handicap. When the trial court's decision is supported by substantial evidence in the record, we are not free to reverse that decision. It boils down to that factor. We fully understand also why the trial court would find that the evidence on behalf of Pushkin was the more persuasive. In short, in the absence of a clearly erroneous decision by the trial court, this court is not going to substitute its judgment for that of the trial court.

It is argued that the judgment of Dr. Farley may not be used as a substitute for the judgment of the admissions committee, who are solely responsible for admissions decisions. We do not disagree with this but feel that the defendants' argument misses the point. The trial court did not substitute Dr. Farley's judgment for that of the admissions committee. That witness was offered to rebut the University's articulated reasons for maintaining that Dr. Pushkin was not qualified for the program despite his handicap. The witnesses on behalf of the University, and the reports of the interviewers, alleged that Dr. Pushkin's handicap would preclude him from doing a good job as a psychiatrist. Thus Dr. Farley was offered as a witness to show that, after four years of observing Dr. Pushkin, he believed the University's assumptions to be based on incorrect factual premises. We see no more effective way for Dr. Pushkin to rebut the University's assumptions or unduly restrictive beliefs as to Dr. Pushkin's capabilities when considered in relation to multiple sclerosis. To preclude this kind of evidence would be to preclude individual plaintiffs from ever rebutting the reasons articulated by a defendant for the actions which it has taken. Indeed it would preclude relief under § 504.

An attempt was made by some of the interviewers to say that Dr. Pushkin was not rejected solely because of his handicap, but that he would have been rejected anyway even if he had not been handicapped. The trial court found that this evidence was overshadowed by the contrary evidence, including the interviewers reports, showing that Pushkin was rejected from the residency program solely on the basis of his handicap. The record fully supports the trial court's decision that their conclusions at the interview were centered on the multiple sclerosis. It was only when the interviews reached the trial stage that they sought to expand their reasoning.

Dr. Barchilon testified that Dr. Pushkin was not of the caliber of people usually interviewed for the residency program and that Dr. Pushkin overidentified with his patients. However, Dr. Barchilon testified that he had not communicated any of those thoughts to any of the committee members prior to the time the decision to reject Dr. Pushkin was made. That doctor further testified that on the basis of such a brief interview of Dr. Pushkin, his assessment was merely an "educated guess." Furthermore, Dr. Barchilon indicated that he was irritated with the procedure which was followed with regard to Dr. Pushkin's application.

Dr. Scully also stated at trial that Dr. Pushkin was not of the caliber of residents usually admitted to the program. This is in conflict with the testimony of Dr. Bernstein, who indicated that Dr. Scully was primarily concerned with the fact that Dr. Pushkin had MS. Moreover, Dr. Scully's testimony indicated uncertainty as to factors other than MS causing Dr. Pushkin's rejection, since he stated further that he thought Dr. Pushkin "had more issues going on than his MS or whatever; I wasn't quite sure."

In addition, Dr. Weissberg stated that Dr. Pushkin was not up to the usual quality of applicants to the program. He also stated, however, that he had not made that observation in his interview report.

As noted before, however, the trial court weighed the credibility of the conflicting evidence and rejected the after the fact testimony that Dr. Pushkin was not qualified for the program apart from his handicap. We are disinclined to substitute our judgment for that of the trial court, since that court's conclusion is supported by the record. We have evaluated the evidence and considered the findings and have approved the trial court's action. The conclusions of the examining board rest on psychologic theory. Our reaction is that these are weak and inadequate threads where, as here, the entire future of the plaintiff is at stake. We also hold that he applied the proper tests in determining whether defendants' articulated reasons for finding Dr. Pushkin unqualified on the basis of his handicap were legitimate or whether those reasons were based upon incorrect assumptions or inadequate factual grounds. Based upon the weighing of all the evidence the trial court held that the latter applied and since the decision is supported by the record, this court cannot reach its own factual conclusion and determine otherwise.

Viewing the record as a whole we conclude that the judgment of the district court is affirmed.

Russell v. Salve Regina College
649 F. Supp. 391 (D.R.I. 1986)

SELYA, District Judge.

*   *   *

I. BACKGROUND

Salve is a religiously affiliated college located in Newport, Rhode Island, administered by the Sisters of Mercy of the Roman Catholic Church. Russell was admitted to the College by early decision in the winter of 1981–82. She began her studies in September 1982. Russell's interest in a nursing career antedated her matriculation: she had applied only to colleges with nursing programs and had expressed her intention to pursue such a course of study both in her original application to Salve and in her admissions interview. She commenced her academic endeavors at the College with the avowed intention of gaining admittance to Salve's program of nursing education.

During her inaugural year at the College, there is rather fragile evidence that Russell sought some treatment for obesity. At various times during that school year, her 5'6" frame recorded weights between 306 and 315 pounds according to data on file at the College's health services unit. It is plain that, although she achieved no meaningful weight loss during her freshman year, Russell was considerably more successful as a student. Her work in liberal arts courses was adequate and her grades were respectable. Consequently, Russell was admitted to the nursing program, effective at the start of her sophomore year. She was given a copy of the "Nursing Handbook" (Handbook) issued by the College, and clearly understood that the Handbook set out the requirements for successful completion of the degree in nursing.

The fabric of Russell's aspirations began to unravel in the fall of 1983, when she entered her sophomore year (her first as a nursing student per se). The parties have presented an intricate (and sometimes conflicting) history of the interaction between the plaintiff and her sundry academic supervisors. It would serve no useful purpose at this juncture fully to recapitulate those events, or to attempt to reconcile every conflict. After all, the mechanism of Rule 56 does not require that there be no unresolved questions of fact; it is sufficient if there are no genuine issues remaining as to any *material* facts.

It suffices for the moment to say that there were myriad problems along the way: the agonizing search for uniforms and scrub gowns that would fit a woman of Russell's girth; a tendency on the part of faculty members to employ Russell in order to model hospital procedures incident to the care of obese patients; prolonged lectures and discussions about the desirability of weight loss; and so on and so forth. Indeed, the record reveals a veritable smorgasbord of verbal exchanges characterized by one side as "torment" or "humiliation" and by the other as "expressions of concern" or "forthright statements of school policy." (It takes little imagination to decipher which litigants are wont to apply which epithets to which actions.)

The court recognizes, of course, that sadism and benevolence—like beauty—often reside principally in the eye of the beholder. And, the court has neither the need nor the means to attempt to discern the subjective motives of myriad actors on the cold, fleshless record of a Rule 56 motion. For the purposes at hand, it is enough to acknowledge that an array of such incidents occurred and that, by the end of her sophomore year, Russell's size had become a matter of concern for all of the parties.

In her junior year, the plaintiff executed a contract (Contract) purporting to make her further participation in the College's nursing curriculum contingent upon an average weight loss of two pounds per week. The Contract was a singular sort of agreement. (It is reproduced in full as an appendix to this opinion). Notwithstanding the signing of the Contract, Russell proved unable to meet the commitment, or even closely to approach it. Her body weight never fell appreciably below 300 pounds. Though the circumstances are complex, she seems to have made—and invariably to have broken—a series of promises in this regard. Predictably, an escalating level of tension began to characterize dealings between Russell and certain of the individual defendants.

The climax occurred on or about August 23, 1985. The plaintiff received a letter from the coordinator of the nursing program, defendant Chapdelaine, advising that she had been dismissed from the nursing department and from the College. Russell's education was concededly interrupted at that point (though, after a year's hiatus, she resumed her studies in nursing at another institution).

II. STATEMENT OF THE CASE

Russell's complaint, as noted above, contains an octet of claims. Two of these supposed causes of action—Counts VI and VII—allege "federal" claims. Count VI charges the defendants with a denial of due process and an unconstitutional inter- ference with the plaintiff's protectible liberty and property interests. Count VII alleges handicapped discrimination in derogation of 29 U.S.C. § 794.

The remaining six counts implicate state law, and the parties (who agree on little else) concur that Rhode Island law governs in this diversity case. The state law claims possess a variety of characteristics. Two of these initiatives are contract-based: Count I alleges nonperformance of an agreement to educate and Count II asserts breach of an implied covenant of good faith and fair dealing. Three of the remaining state law initiatives are tort-based: Counts III and VIII posit intentional and negligent infliction of emotional distress, respectively; and Count IV remonstrates against a perceived invasion of Russell's privacy. Count V—which seeks redress for wrongful dismissal— is a contract/tort hybrid.

It is alleged throughout that the plaintiff lost a year of prospective employment in a job which she claims to have been offered contingent upon successful completion of her nursing degree. Russell seeks compensatory damages for this delay and for the physical and emotional trauma which she purportedly suffered as a result of what she views as the callous, humiliating, and wrongful conduct of the several defendants. The plaintiff also prays for exemplary damages, counsel fees, and costs.

The court will first address the impact of the pending Rule 56 motion on the federal law claims, and will thereafter turn to a consideration of the other (state law) counts.

III. FEDERAL CLAIMS

Both of the claims which arise under federal law founder on essentially the same reefs and shoals: the College is not a "state actor," and its nursing curriculum is not a federally funded "program or activity" within the meaning of the Rehabilitation Act of 1973, 29 U.S.C. § 794. The court need not tarry overlong in putting these claims to rest.

A. *Due Process*

With respect to what the plaintiff envisions as an utter disregard for the niceties (or even the basics) of due process, the court has no need to reach the hotly-debated questions of whether Russell enjoyed any constitutionally protected interest, created by the terms of the Handbook or distilled from any other source. The fifth and fourteenth amendments to the Constitution apply only to the federal government and to the state, respectively—and derivatively, to those whose actions can fairly be attributed to federal or state government. Even where an institution admittedly discriminates in its membership policies, there is no deprivation of due process unless the action in question sufficiently implicates the state so as to make the conduct "state action."

To be sure, if the government plays the role of enforcer for privately originated discrimination, then the government may be forbidden to exercise its police power in furtherance of the discriminatory activity. Or when the web of interconnection between the government and private bigotry is spun tightly enough to conclude that the government agency has "insinuated itself into a position of interdependence" with a discriminatory actor, then the challenged conduct must be subjected to fifth or fourteenth amendment scrutiny. Those maxims do not, however assist this plaintiff. The requirement of "state action" demands more than some (modest) interplay between the public and private sectors.

* * *

These scraps of evidence, combined, do not turn the state action corner; and the record contains aught else. Though what little has been adduced must be construed in the light most favorable to the plaintiff, it utterly fails to demonstrate the slightest glimmer of the requisite governmental involvement. Accordingly, Count VI cannot stand.

B. *Handicapped Discrimination*

In respect to the plaintiff's statement of claim under the Rehabilitation Act, 29 U.S.C. § 794, the teachings of the Supreme Court in *Grove City College v. Bell* are controlling. In *Grove City*, the Court held that a college which received federal funding only indirectly (that is, through tuition subsidies to students) was not subject in all its departments to the provisions of federal antidiscrimination law. A private institution of higher education which, like Salve, receives federal monies exclusively through its students, is subject to federal antidiscrimination laws only with respect to its financial aid program. And, it is well to note that, in this case, Russell does not charge that Salve discriminated against her in respect to scholarship assistance or other financial aid.

The plaintiff, although mouthing the empty conclusion that the College's nursing curriculum is a "program or activity receiving Federal financial assistance" as required by 29 U.S.C. § 794, has failed to call the court's attention to any evidentiary fact which is capable of bearing the weight of that averment. The law is transparently clear: the Supreme Court has decided the point in *Grove City* and has since cited that opinion with approval in the context of the very statute at issue here. Absent proof that federal funding or financial assistance of any kind was involved in the College's nursing program, Russell can mount no cause of action against these defendants under 29 U.S.C. § 794. That being so, the difficult issue of whether Russell's obesity can be considered to be an "impairment" (handicapping condition) within the meaning of 29 U.S.C. § 706(7)(B) need not be reached—and the court expresses no opinion thereon. The lack of any showing of the requisite federal subsidization necessitates the grant of *brevis* disposition in the defendants' favor on Count VII of the complaint.

IV. STATE LAW CLAIMS

Conceptually, the plaintiff's claims for wrongful discharge (Count V) and for the transgression of a theoretical (implied) covenant of good faith and fair dealing (Count II) are linked by common ties in the relevant caselaw. So, the court proposes to deal with these initiatives ensemble. The same sort of approach will be taken with respect to the claims for infliction of emotional distress—intentional (Count III) and negligent (Count VIII), respectively—which likewise lend themselves to collective scrutiny. The remaining two state law causes of action will be treated individually.

A. *Dismissal*

The plaintiff's remonstrance in Count V of the complaint, which apparently seeks to draw sustenance from an analogy to the employment relationship, postulates that even a collegian who has no contractual claim to a continuing place in the student body cannot be expelled without just cause. To be sure, some jurisdictions have evidently created such an open-ended cause of action in favor of at-will employees who have been peremptorily dismissed from their jobs. As an ultimate matter, the plaintiff's claim teeters because of her failure to discover *any* case in *any* jurisdiction from which it might be inferred that such a cause of action (if it existed at all) can— or should—be extended to the university/student context. But in this case, there is no need to speculate upon such a far-reaching extension of the at-will employment doctrine—for the underlying doctrine itself simply does not occupy a place in Rhode Island law.

* * *

There is, under Rhode Island law, no independently actionable covenant of good faith or fair dealing implicit in the university/student relationship. And, Russell has shown nothing which would enhance her case so as to extricate it from the operation of this general principle. The defendant's Rule 56 motion for summary judgment has merit insofar as it pertains to Count II, and must be granted.

* * *

Whether the conduct of a given defendant surpasses the bounds of decency is a function of three factors: (i) the conduct itself, (ii) in light of the particular relationship of the parties, (iii) having in mind the known (or knowable) susceptibility of the aggrieved party to emotional injury. These can best be assayed, in this case, in the inverse order of their appearance. Russell was a known quantity. Despite her evident sensitivity to weight-related emotional trauma, and her documented history of precarious emotional balance and tenuous self-esteem, the individual defendants—well-educated professionals all—plowed ahead. Given the full panoply of the circumstances, the proposition that they acted in reckless disregard of the probability that an obese youngster's psychic equilibrium could easily be knocked askew seems fairly debatable. This conclusion is fortified by a glimpse of the middle factor. The student stands in a particularly vulnerable relationship vis-a-vis the university, the administration, and the faculty. She is away from home, subject to the authority and discipline of the institution, and under enormous pressure to succeed. The relationship of these parties was such that the defendants could fairly be expected to have acted maturely—and even with some tenderness and solicitude—toward the plaintiff.

Seen in this context, the defendants' conduct, as the plaintiff has portrayed it, cannot be said as a matter of law to stumble on the threshold of outrageousness. To be sure, the law does not shield a person from words or deeds which are merely inconsiderate, insulting, unflattering, or unkind. The courts possess no roving writ which warrants intervention whenever someone's feelings are hurt or someone has been subjected to a series of petty indignities. And, there must be room for some lack of courtesy and finesse in interpersonal relations. In *Champlin*, for example, the state court ultimately declined to impose liability because of the need to afford a creditor "reasonable latitude in the manner in which it seeks to collect overdue notes, even though there may be times when these methods might cause some inconvenience or embarrassment to the debtor."

Yet, the behavior challenged here, viewed in the light most favorable to the plaintiff's case, seems to be shaped of sterner stuff. Although a private college must be afforded wide discretion in enforcing its scholastic standards and in disciplining its students, there is no justification for debasement, harassment, or humiliation. The academic mise en scene, in any reasoned view, is considerably more civilized than the debtor-creditor environment, and there is correspondingly less play for roughness. Given the trust implicit in the student's selection of a college, and the peculiar vulnerability of undergraduates, the facts set forth by the plaintiff, if ultimately proven, comprise a scenario which is far more conscience-provoking than the *Champlin* counterpart. The indignities which Russell asserts have been practiced on her are arguably offensive in the extreme, perhaps repugnant to the norms which one would expect to flourish in the academic world. Taken from the plaintiff's coign of vantage, the behavior in question, if it is shown to be as obnoxious as the plaintiff in her Rule 56 opposition suggests, might well be thought by a properly-instructed jury to be so atrocious as to be actionable. As a general matter, the plaintiff appears to have raised sufficient doubt as to the quality of the defendant's actions to blunt the summary judgment ax.

C. *Right to Privacy*

Count IV of the complaint posits a supposed invasion of Russell's privacy. No such cause of action was recognized at common law in Rhode Island. The General Assembly, however, filled this perceived void in 1980 by the enactment of a statute which is now codified at R.I. Gen. Laws § 9–1–28.1 (1985 Reenactment) (Privacy Act). The Privacy Act, which established a "right to be secure from unreasonable intrusion upon one's physical solitude or seclusion," must necessarily inform this court's determination of the motion sub judice insofar as the fourth count of the complaint is concerned.

*   *   *

Yet, the case at bar arises in a far different—and more urbane—sort of institutional context, one which conduces toward reading R.I. Gen. Laws § 9–1–28.1(a)(1) exactly as it was written, thereby providing a remedy for "unreasonable intrusion upon one's physical solitude or seclusion (that)...was or is offensive or objectionable to a reasonable man." The relationship is such that Russell could reasonably have expected to be granted a considerable degree of privacy as to intimate, personal matters. Thus, a literal reading of the Privacy Act reaches the perimeter of this claim. The court so holds.

Once it has been determined that Count IV states an actionable claim, the record reflects the presence of facts adequate to preclude summary judgment. Section 9–1–28.1(a)(1) does not speak in terms of the "publication" of a private fact, but rather in terms of "an invasion of something that is entitled to be private or would be expected to be private." To be sure, there was nothing private or confidential about Russell's corpulence (it was there to be seen at the most casual glance), so drawing attention to her girth would not, in and of itself, be actionable as an invasion of privacy under Rhode Island law. Yet, there was considerably more here: the continual inquiry into the progress of the plaintiff's diet, the scrutiny of her personal weight loss records, the exaggerated interest in what forbidden morsels Russell ingested, and the preoccupation with her perceived lack of self-discipline, to name but a few variations on the intrusive theme which the defendants played. These provocations coalesce to fit comfortably within the species of conduct which a trier of fact could reasonably find offensive or objectionable. And, this is especially true inasmuch as few things are more personal or private to a young, single person than weight and one's efforts to control it. Accordingly, the Rule 56 motion misfires as to this statement of claim.

D. Implied Contract

The final issue to be addressed is the contract claim asserted in Count I. It is accepted law that the relationship between student and university is contractual in nature. Concededly, the specific character of this sort of contractual relationship is somewhat amorphous. The contract is " 'not an integrated agreement, the standard is that of reasonable expectation—what meaning the party making the manifestation, the university, should reasonably expect the other part to give it.' "

If a contract existed, it came into being when Russell matriculated at Salve, and she and the College, as the contracting parties, would be the real parties in interest. The nisi prius roll shows clearly that no express agreement embodied the kind of terms which the plaintiff alleges permeated the relationship. Thus, the court must ascertain whether the implied agreement between the College and its (former) pupil arguably extended far enough to support Russell's present litigation. Upon close perscrutation, the court finds that the disputed facts surrounding the terms of the "contract" provide sufficient grist to warrant turning the mill of jury deliberation.

The record is not so clear as to entitle Salve to summary judgment on Count I at this state of the proceedings.

Salve formulates a variety of positions in its search to justify *brevis* disposition of the flagship count of the plaintiff's complaint. In the first place, the institutional defendant asseverates that the scales of "reasonable expectation" should be tipped by the provisions of the Handbook, a pamphlet which admittedly affirms the important parallel between a nursing student's health status and the health of the patients whom the nurse hopes to serve. The Handbook requires each student to inform the clinical coordinator of particular health problems; indeed, nursing students must sign a form for the clinical placement program each semester that vouchsafes full disclosure of all medical abnormalities. And, the Handbook reserves to the coordinator discretion to determine whether a student's participation in the clinical program is contraindicated because of health. The standardized form signed by all students states: "I will accept the decision of the Clinical Agency Coordinator and Department Chairman as final as to whether or not I can function in the Clinical Area." The College has an obvious interest in ensuring that a student poses no health risk to herself or otherwise as she proceeds into a clinical placement. But, howsoever rational the College's generalized requirements might be, the application of those requirements in Russell's case is another matter.

Contagion was not legitimately at issue—after all, there is no allegation of communicable corpulence here—nor have the defendants essayed any showing that clinical work would have jeopardized Russell's own wellbeing.

The only possible bases for prohibiting the plaintiff from clinical training were either (i) that her obesity would impede satisfactory performance of her duties, or (ii) that her appearance would be a poor example for patients.

The college cannot plausibly argue, however, that Russell was bound unconditionally to accept the decision to exclude her from further participation in the clinical placement program, regardless of how arbitrary or irrational that decision might have been. As a matter of Rhode Island law, "[t]here is no doubt that ordinarily if one exacts a promise from another to perform an act the law implies a counter promise against arbitrary or unreasonable conduct on the part of the promisee." And, at the very least, the reasonableness of either of the possible lines of thought limned above is open to serious question.

In the circumstances at bar, there are competing inferences which can be drawn. There is evidence which, if credited, tends to show that Russell's girth did not reduce her proficiency. The argument that her overweight condition was deleterious to patients as a matter of example rests, at this point, on sheer speculation. Accordingly, the decision to expel Russell, insofar as it prescinds from the Handbook, must be tried to determine whether it was the product of reason or caprice. Summary judgment would be an inappropriate means of resolving the conflict.

The second morsel in Salve's Count I cupboard is equally unavailing. In a nutshell, the College argues that Russell failed one of the courses prerequisite to completion of her nursing degree, thereby justifying her dismissal and eliminating the need for further inquiry. Yet, there is evidence that the instructor admitted that all of Russell's deficiencies in this course were "directly related" to the claimant's obesity. On this record, a genuine question exists as to whether adiposis was, in Russell's case, a legitimate impediment to due fulfillment of the clinical requirements of the nursing program (as Salve maintains), or whether the College's evaluation was tainted by an unreasonable aversion to obesity or by a desire to expel Russell because she did not conform to the "Salve image."

There is considerable evidence in the record attesting to the plaintiff's competence as a student and as a nurse, notwithstanding her one negative evaluation by the defendant Lavin. On August 20, 1985, just one day before Chapdelaine's billet-doux was authored, the plaintiff's supervisor at Hartford Hospital, Patricia Reilly, wrote that she "looked and acted in a very professional manner. Her attendance was excellent and her performance very good. I would be most pleased to hire her as a professional nurse. In fact, I expect to be able to offer her a position for June of 1986." After her dismissal from the College, Russell was promptly admitted to the nursing program at St. Joseph's College (also operated by the Sisters of Mercy). She completed the program there without incident.

While the court is sensitive to the importance of academic freedom and recognizes that deference must be accorded to the reasonable judgment of responsible College officials, the question of reasonableness is in too precarious a balance here to permit summary disposition. Faced with contrary opinions from qualified health care professionals and particularized allegations of personal animosity born of obesophobic obsession, this issue, viewed in the manner most hospitable to the plaintiff's case, survives Fed.R.Civ.P. 56 scrutiny.

The same sort of reasoning applies to the claim that Russell, having signed a document which pledged a weight loss of two pounds per week as a condition of continuing her studies in the College's nursing department, was open to ouster for her failure to abide by her written promise. (After all, the Contract itself provided that a failure to achieve the stated goal would result in "voluntary and immediate withdrawal from the nursing program at Salve Regina College.") But, though it is beyond dispute that the plaintiff did not shed the required poundage, issues of material fact exist as to duress, coercion, and her state of mind, generally, upon the execution of the document. Moreover, as the plaintiff notes, there was no readily ascertainable consideration for her promise. If certain (arguably plausible) inferences are drawn in the manner least favorable to the movant, the weight loss covenant can be seen not as an avenue of defense, but as a product of the invidiously discriminatory course of conduct which the defendants displayed in Russell's case. Finally, the oxymoronic concept of a student essaying a "voluntary withdrawal" against her will itself stirs doubts.

In sum, the Contract is at best a useful piece of evidence to assist in constructing the jigsaw of contractual terms, and at worst a piece of paper which is meaningless except as proof of the defendants' malevolence. In any event, it is not dispositive, as a matter of law, of the merits of Count I. It is impossible to apply the standard of "reasonable expectation" to Russell's situation without the aid of precisely the sort of factfinding which battens the Rule 56 hatch. Inasmuch as the viability of Russell's breach of contract claim will depend on the resolution of questions of disputed fact, *brevis* disposition must be withheld on this count.

V. CONCLUSION

The problems presented by this lawsuit are weighty in every sense of the word. The case emphasizes the uncertain configuration of the boundaries which surround important, but markedly different, values: the necessarily broad freedom which academic administrators must possess in order to operate institutions of higher learning, the rights of a student of tender years to be sheltered from gratuitous debasement or intrusiveness (or worse, from malicious conduct which offends fundamental notions of human decency), the standards of behavior which a university and an undergraduate can reasonably expect from each other. At this relatively early stage of the instant litigation, it remains somewhat unclear as to precisely where on this dimly-lit terrain the College's conduct vis-a-vis Russell falls. So, the illumination of further factfinding seems essential in order to clarify certain of the issues and to map the rights and liabilities of the parties more exactly.

In summary, the court holds that the defendants, and each and all of them, have demonstrated an entitlement to summary judgment in their favor on Counts II, V, VI, VII, and VIII of the complaint. There are, as to these initiatives, no genuine questions of material fact. For the reasons stated, the defendants deserve to prevail thereon as a matter of law. Conversely, the motion for summary judgment must be denied as to Counts I, III, and IV of the complaint. Russell has shown enough steel to put the defendants to their mettle on these claims.

The motion for summary judgment is *granted in part and denied in part*, as outlined above. As to those counts upon which the defendants have prevailed, entry of final judgment shall be withheld pending disposition of the remaining claims.

It is so ordered.

APPENDIX
CONTRACT

I, Sharon Russell, agree to the following conditions for continuing in Nursing 312 during the Spring 1985 Semester. I understand that failure to meet any and all of these conditions will result in my voluntary and immediate withdrawal from the Nursing Program at Salve Regina College thus making me ineligible for Nursing 411.

1. Maintain a minimum weight loss of 2 pounds per week effective immediately.

2. Report to Mrs. Chapdelaine or Faculty Secretary weekly (every Friday morning) with evidence of progress in weight loss program. This will commence January 25, 1985.

NB—Report January 22nd for first accounting after the holiday.

3. Maintain academic standing as required.

Additionally, I will be aware of all requirements listed in the Nursing Department Handbook, 1983–85 Edition.

/s/ Sharon Russell

Sharon Russell

Dec. 18, 1984

s/ Catherine E. Graziano, RN

Witness

———————

For a review of issues concerning the handicapped on campus, see L. Rothstein, "Section 504 of the Rehabilitation Act: Emerging Issues for Colleges and Universities," *Journal of College and University Law*, 13 (1986), 229–265; L. Rothstein, *Rights of Physically Handicapped Persons* (Colorado Springs: Shepard's/McGraw-Hill 1984), with cumulative supplements. See also, *Handicapped Persons' Rights Under Federal Law* (DC: Office for Civil Rights, 1987).

Affirmative Action in Employment

The cases chosen for inclusion in this Section do not constitute a scientific sample of all the possible cases in college employment law, for in truth, the law in this area draws from employment law generally, from equal opportunity law generally, and from cases specifically involving colleges, universities, and school systems. They do include cases won and lost by faculty litigants in race, national origin, and gender contexts, and draw from a variety over the last fifteen years. Several of the cases in this Section and elsewhere are detailed in G. La Noue and B. Lee, *Academics in Court* (Ann Arbor: University of Michigan Press, 1987), including *Kunda* and *Scott* in Chapter 3, and *Mecklenberg*.

Bazemore v. Friday

478 U.S. 385 (1986)

PER CURIAM.

These cases present several issues arising out of petitioners' action against respondents for alleged racial discrimination in employment and provision of services by the North Carolina Agricultural Extension Service (Extension Service). The District Court declined to certify various proposed classes and, after a lengthy trial, entered judgment for respondents in all respects, finding that petitioners had not carried their burden of demonstrating that respondents had engaged in a pattern or practice of racial discrimination. The District Court also ruled against each of the individual plaintiff's discrimination claims. The Court of Appeals affirmed. We hold, for the reasons stated in the opinion of Justice BRENNAN, that the Court of Appeals erred in holding that under Title VII of the Civil Rights Act of 1964, as amended, the Extension Service had no duty to eradicate salary disparities between white and black workers that had their origin prior to the date Title VII was made applicable to public employers; that the Court of Appeals erred in disregarding petitioners' statistical analysis because it reflected pre-Title VII salary disparities, and in holding that petitioners' regressions were unacceptable as evidence of discrimination; that the Court of Appeals erred in ignoring evidence presented by petitioners in addition to their multiple regression analyses; that, on remand, the Court of Appeals should examine all of the evidence in the record relating to salary disparities under the clearly erroneous standard; that the reasons given by the Court of Appeals for refusing to certify a class of black employees of the Extension Service do not support a decision not to certify such a class; and that the Court of Appeals was correct in refusing to certify a class of defendant counties. We further hold, for the reasons stated in the opinion of Justice WHITE, that neither the Constitution nor the applicable Department of Agriculture regulations require more than what the District Court and the Court of Appeals found the Extension Service has done in this case to disestablish segregation in its 4-H and Extension Homemaker Clubs. Accordingly, the judgment of the Court of Appeals is affirmed in part, vacated in part and remanded for further proceedings consistent with this opinion.

It is so ordered.

Justice BRENNAN for a unanimous Court, concurring in part.

I

A

The purpose of North Carolina's agricultural extension program, administered through the North Carolina Agricultural Extension Service (Extension Service), is to aid in the dissemination of "useful and practical information on subjects relating to agriculture and home economics." The Extension Service is a division of the School of Agriculture and Life Sciences at North Carolina State University (NCSU). It is headed by a Director who exercises authority over District Extension Chairmen responsible for administering all Extension Service programs within the State's six Extension Service districts. The District Extension Chairmen, in turn, supervise the 100 County Extension Chairmen who are responsible for developing and coordinating all Extension Service activities within their respective counties. The County Extension Chairmen also report to their respective Board of County Commissioners (Board), a unit of local government, on extension programs and on matters relating to budgeting and personnel.

The Extension Service operates in four major areas: home economics, agriculture, 4-H and youth, and community resource development. In both the home economics and 4-H areas, one of the Extension Service's methods entails the establishment of clubs to educate the club members in home economics and other useful and practical skills. The agricultural program educates and encourages farmers to adopt scientific methods and to adjust to changing economic circumstances. The community resource development program emphasizes group action through citizen groups and organizations. Each of these programs is implemented by local agents who are selected for employment jointly by the Extension Service and the county Boards. Agents are divided into three ranks: full agent, associate agent and assistant agent. "While the three ranks of agents perform essentially the same types of tasks, when an agent is promoted his responsibilities increase and a higher level of performance is expected of him."

The salaries of all workers are determined jointly by the Extension Service and the Boards. The federal, state and county governments all contribute to these salaries. The Boards and the Extension Service determine jointly the proportionate share of salaries to be paid by the State and by the county. Moreover, all county extension hirings and firings are decided " 'jointly between the North Carolina Agricultural Extension Service and the Board of County Commissioners.' "

The Extension Service has overall responsibility for establishing qualifications for employment in the Service and for screening applicants before recommending qualified applicants to the county commissioners for appointment to vacant or new positions. The Extension Service also prepares and submits an annual budget request to the Board of Commissioners for the county's share of funds for salaries.

Each Board of County Commissioners reviews the budget requests from the Extension Service each year and confers with and advises the District and County Extension Chairman concerning Extension Service programs. The Board furnishes the county's share of salaries for extension personnel. In addition, it provides office space and equipment, utilities, telephone, demonstration materials, etc.

Prior to August 1, 1965, the Extension Service was divided into two branches: a white branch and a "Negro branch." Only the "Negro branch" had a formal racial designation. The "Negro branch" was composed entirely of black personnel and served only black farmers, homemakers and youth. The white branch employed no blacks, but did on occasion serve blacks. On August 1, 1965, in response to the Civil Rights Act of 1964, the State merged the two branches of the Extension Service into a single organization. However, as the District Court subsequently found, "[the] unification and integration of the Extension Service did not result immediately in the elimination of some disparities which had existed between the salaries of white personnel and black personnel...."

B

The private petitioners include employees of the Extension Service, recipients of its services, members of Extension Homemaker Clubs, and parents of 4-H Club youths. They brought this action in 1971 alleging racial discrimination in employment and in the provision of services on the part of the Extension Service in violation of the First, Fifth, and Fourteenth Amendments to the Constitution, 42 U.S.C. §§ 1981, 1983 and 2000d, and 7 U.S.C. § 341 et seq. The defendants, respondents here, were William C. Friday, President of the University of North Carolina, and various officials associated with the University and its school of Agriculture. In addition, County Commissioners from Alamance, Edgecomb, and Mecklenburg Counties were also named as defendants.

On April 7, 1972, the United States intervened under § 902 of Title IX and §§ 601 and 602 of Title VI of the Civil Rights Act of 1964, 42 U.S.C. §§ 2000h-2, 2000d, and 2000d-1. The United States subsequently amended its complaint in intervention to include allegations that defendants had also violated §§ 703 and 706 of Title VII of the Civil Rights Act of 1964, as amended, 42 U.S.C. §§ 2000e-2, 2000e-5. The United States' complaint essentially tracked the claims made by the private petitioners. Private petitioners were permitted on the eve of trial to amend their complaint to add a claim under Title VII as well.

On two occasions prior to trial the District Court was asked, but declined, to certify the action as a class action. Near the close of trial the plaintiffs again requested the court to certify four classes of plaintiffs and one class of defendants. However, the District Court once again declined to do so, and this decision was subsequently upheld by the Court of Appeals. On the merits, the trial explored allegations of racial discrimination in virtually every aspect of the Extension Service's employment practices and provision of services. The District Court ruled in favor of respondents in all respects. On most issues it concluded that petitioners had failed to carry their burden of proof. As a general proposition, the District Court was of the view that the Extension Service had conducted itself in a nondiscriminatory manner since it became subject to Title VII and since the merger of the black and white branches in 1965. Both private petitioners and the United States limited their appeals to the claims that the District Court erred in considering the evidence before it regarding salaries and promotions to chairmen, and in concluding that the Extension Service had not discriminated against blacks with respect to salaries and promotions to County Chairmen. The United States also claimed that the system used to determine merit pay increases violated Title VII. Private petitioners also appealed the rejection of their claim that respondents were unlawfully providing services and materials to segregated

4-H and Extension Homemaker Clubs, and the District Court's refusal to certify the case as a class action. The Court of Appeals affirmed the District Court in all respects.

II

The first issue we must decide is whether the Court of Appeals erred in upholding the District Court's finding that petitioners had not proved by a preponderance of the evidence that the respondents had discriminated against black Extension Service employees in violation of Title VII by paying them less than whites employed in the same positions. The Court of Appeals reasoned that the Extension Service was under no obligation to eliminate any salary disparity between blacks and whites that had its origin prior to 1972 when Title VII became applicable to public employers such as the Extension Service. It also reasoned that factors, other than those included in the petitioners' multiple regression analyses, affected salary, and that therefore those regression analyses were incapable of sustaining a finding in favor of petitioners.

A

Both the Court of Appeals and the District Court found that before the black and white Extension Service branches were merged in 1965, the Extension Service maintained two separate, racially-segregated branches and paid black employees less than white employees. The Court of Appeals also acknowledged that after the merger of the Extension Service, "[s]ome pre-existing salary disparities continued to linger on," and that these disparities continued after Title VII became applicable to the Extension Service in March 1972 and after this suit was filed. Indeed, the Court of Appeals noted that "the Extension Service admits that, while it had made some adjustments to try to get rid of the salary disparity resulting on account of pre-Act discrimination, it has not made all the adjustments necessary to get rid of all such disparity." The court interpreted petitioners' claim on appeal to be that "the pre-Act discriminatory difference in salaries should have been affirmatively eliminated but has not." Relying on our cases in *Hazelwood School District v. United States*, and *United Air Lines, Inc. v. Evans*, it concluded, "[w]e do not think this is the law."

The error of the Court of Appeals with respect to salary disparities created prior to 1972 and perpetuated thereafter is too obvious to warrant extended discussion: that the Extension Service discriminated with respect to salaries *prior* to the time it was covered by Title VII does not excuse perpetuating that discrimination *after* the Extension Service became covered by Title VII. To hold otherwise would have the effect of exempting from liability those employers who were historically the greatest offenders of the rights of blacks. A pattern or practice that would have constituted a violation of Title VII, but for the fact that the statute had not yet become effective, became a violation upon Title VII's effective date, and to the extent an employer continued to engage in that act or practice, he is liable under that statute. While recovery may not be permitted for pre-1972 acts of discrimination, to the extent that this discrimination was perpetuated after 1972, liability may be imposed.

Each week's pay check that delivers less to a black than to a similarly situated white is a wrong actionable under Title VII, regardless of the fact that this pattern was begun prior to the effective date of Title VII. The Court of Appeals plainly erred in holding that the pre-Act discriminatory difference in salaries did not have to be eliminated.

The Court of Appeals' conclusion that pre-Act salary discrimination did not have to be eliminated undermines the rest of its analysis of the District Court opinion.

Having rejected the effect of pre-Act discrimination, the court considered solely whether the Extension Service discriminated with respect to the application of quartile rankings which, according to the Court of Appeals, were "the only aspect of salary computation in which the Extension Service exercised any discretion." Because, as we have explained, the Extension Service was under an obligation to eradicate salary disparities based on race that began prior to the effective date of Title VII, the Court of Appeals erred in concentrating its analysis solely on the issue of whether there was racial discrimination in the ranking system.

B

We now turn to the issue of whether the Court of Appeals erred in upholding the District Court's refusal to accept the petitioners' expert statistical evidence as proof of discrimination by a preponderance of the evidence. In a case alleging that a defendant has engaged in a pattern and practice of discrimination under § 707(a) of the Civil Rights Act of 1964, 42 U.S.C. § 2000e-6(a), plaintiffs must "establish by a preponderance of the evidence that racial discrimination was the company's standard operating procedure—the regular rather than the unusual practice." Further, our decision in *United Postal Service Board of Governors v. Aikens*, although not decided in the context of a pattern and practice case, makes clear that if the defendants have not succeeded in having a case dismissed on the ground that plaintiffs have failed to establish a *prima facie* case, and have responded to the plaintiffs' proof by offering evidence of their own, the factfinder then must decide whether the plaintiffs have demonstrated a pattern or practice of discrimination by a preponderance of the evidence. This is because the only issue to be decided at that point is whether the plaintiffs have actually proved discrimination. This determination is subject to the clearly erroneous standard on appellate review.

At trial, petitioners relied heavily on multiple regression analyses designed to demonstrate that blacks were paid less than similarly situated whites. The United States' expert prepared multiple regression analyses relating to salaries for the years 1974, 1975, and 1981. Certain of these regressions used four independent variables—race, education, tenure, and job title. Petitioners selected these variables based on discovery testimony by an Extension Service official that four factors were determinative of salary: education, tenure, job title, and job performance. In addition, regressions done by the Extension Service itself for 1971 included the variables race, sex, education, and experience; and another in 1974 used the variables race, education, and tenure to check for disparities between the salaries of blacks and whites.

The regressions purported to demonstrate that in 1974 the average black employee earned $331 less per year than a white employee with the same job title, education, and tenure, and that in 1975 the disparity was $395. The regression for 1981 showed a smaller disparity which lacked statistical significance.

> The Court of Appeals stated that the "district court refused to accept plaintiffs' expert testimony as proof of discrimination by a preponderance of the evidence because the plaintiffs' expert had not included a number of variable factors the court considered relevant, among them being the across the board and percentage pay increases which varied from county to county. The district court was, of course, correct in this analysis."

The Court of Appeals thought the District Court correct for essentially two reasons: First, the Court of Appeals rejected petitioners' regression analysis because it "contained salary figures which reflect the effect of pre-Act discrimination, a consideration not actionable under Title VII...." Second, the court believed that "[a]n appropriate regression analysis of salary should...include *all* measurable variables thought to have an effect on salary level." In particular, the court found that the failure to consider county to county differences in salary increases was significant. It concluded, noting that "both experts omitted from their respective analysis variables which ought to be reasonably viewed as determinants of salary. As a result, the regression analysis presented here must be considered unacceptable as evidence of discrimination." The Court of Appeals' treatment of the statistical evidence in this case was erroneous in important respects.

1

The Court of Appeals erred in stating that petitioners' regression analyses were "unacceptable as evidence of discrimination," because they did not include "all measurable variables thought to have an effect on salary level." The court's view of the evidentiary value of the regression analyses was plainly incorrect. While the omission of variables from a regression analysis may render the analysis less probative than it otherwise might be, it can hardly be said, absent some other infirmity, that an analysis which accounts for the major factors "must be considered unacceptable as evidence of discrimination." Normally, failure to include variables will affect the analysis' probativeness, not its admissibility.

Importantly, it is clear that a regression analysis that includes less than "all measurable variables" may serve to prove a plaintiff's case. A plaintiff in a Title VII suit need not prove discrimination with scientific certainty; rather, his or her burden is to prove discrimination by a preponderance of the evidence. Whether, in fact, such a regression analysis does carry the plaintiffs' ultimate burden will depend in a given case on the factual context of each case in light of all the evidence presented by both the plaintiff and the defendant. However, as long as the court may fairly conclude, in light of all the evidence, that it is more likely than not that impermissible discrimination exists, the plaintiff is entitled to prevail.

2

In this case the Court of Appeals failed utterly to examine the regression analyses in light of all the evidence in the record. Looked at in its entirety, the petitioners offered an impressive array of evidence to support their contention that the Extension Service engaged in a pattern or practice of discrimination with respect to salaries. In addition to their own regression analyses described above, petitioners offered regressions done by the Extension Service for 1971 and 1974 that showed results similar to those revealed by petitioners' regressions. Petitioners also claim support from multiple regressions presented by respondents at trial for the year 1975. Using the same model that the petitioners had used, and similar variables, respondents' expert obtained substantially the same result for 1975, a statistically significant racial effect of $384. Indeed, respondents also included in their analysis, "quartile rank" as an independent variable, and this *increased* the racial effect to $475.

Petitioners also presented evidence of pre-Act salary discrimination, and of respondents' ineffectual attempts to eradicate it. For example, the petitioners submitted evidence, and the District Court found, that blacks were paid less than whites in comparable positions prior to the merger of the black and white services in 1965. Moreover, in 1971, the respondents acknowledged that substantial salary differences between blacks and whites existed. In addition, evidence was offered to show that the efforts by the Extension Service to equalize those salaries in 1971 were insufficient to accomplish the goal.

* * *

Finally, and there was some overlap here with evidence used to discredit the county to county variation theory, the petitioners presented evidence consisting of individual comparisons between salaries of blacks and whites similarly situated. Witness testimony, claimed by petitioners to be unrebutted, also confirmed the continued existence of such disparities.

Setting out the range of persuasive evidence offered by the petitioners demonstrates the error of the Court of Appeals in focusing solely on the characteristics of the regression analysis. Although we think that consideration of the evidence makes a strong case for finding the District Court's conclusion clearly erroneous, we leave that task to the Court of Appeals on remand which must make such a determination based on the "entire evidence" in the record.

* * *

In another 1986 case involving black Agricultural Extension Service agents, the U.S. Supreme Court held that unreviewed state administrative proceedings did not have a preclusive effect on Title VII claims, but did have such a preclusive effect upon Section 1983 claims. *University of Tennessee v. Elliott*, 478 U.S. 788 (1986).

In cases against black institutions, non-black employees have won with more frequency than have black litigants suing white colleges. In two cases that arose from the same dismissal action, two white professors were ordered reinstated and reimbursed after being wrongfully dismissed from Howard University. *Planells v. Howard University*, 35 EPD (CCH) ¶ 34, 669, 34 FEP (BNA) 66 (D.D.C. 1984); *Turgeon v. Howard University*, 571 F. Supp. 679 (1983) ("In sum, plaintiff had demonstrated that she was discharged from Howard University because she is a white woman.") When historically black Alabama State University argued that its black-preference hiring policy was justified under a Title VII "business necessity" exception, the Court held for the white employee, under a "disparate impact" analysis. *Craig v. Alabama State University*, 804 F. 2d 682 (11th Cir. 1986). ASU had earlier been found guilty of engaging in a pattern and practice of favoring blacks over whites in employment. *Craig v. Alabama State University*, 451 F. Supp. 1207 (M.D. Ala. 1978).

Abrams v. Baylor College of Medicine
581 F. Supp. 1570 (1984)

DeANDA, District Judge.

This cause having been tried upon the facts without a jury, the Court hereby enters the following Findings of Fact and Conclusions of Law, pursuant to Rule 52(a), F. R. Civ. P.

FINDINGS OF FACT

The Plaintiffs are licensed physicians who have been employed by the Defendant Baylor College of Medicine ("Baylor") as anesthesiologists during periods of time which are material to this lawsuit.

Plaintiff Lawrence Abrams ("Abrams") began employment for Baylor at the Fondren-Brown Cardiovascular Unit of the Methodist Hospital ("Fondren-Brown") on July 16, 1978. Abrams resigned from this position effective October 30, 1980. Since that time, he has held employment as an Associate Professor of Clinical Anesthesiology and Director of Cardio-Thoracic Anesthesiology at the State University of New York, Downstate Medical Center, Brooklyn, New York.

Plaintiff Stuart Linde ("Linde") began employment for Baylor at Fondren-Brown on September 1, 1979, and is still employed by Baylor as an anesthesiologist.

Both Plaintiffs have been employed by Defendant under the title of Assistant Professor, Department of Anesthesiology while working for Baylor at Fondren-Brown.

Baylor is a large non-profit, private medical institution located in Houston, Texas, which employs several hundred people, including physicians and support staff personnel.

Baylor provides anesthesiology staffing at four hospital facilities in Houston, namely Ben Taub Hospital, Jefferson Davis Hospital, the Veterans Administration Hospital, and Fondren-Brown. All anesthesiologists assigned to these hospitals hold faculty positions at Baylor.

Fondren-Brown is among the world's foremost cardiovascular surgical units. Such cardiovascular luminaries as Dr. Michael DeBakey perform advanced techniques, including open-heart surgery, at Fondren-Brown. Of the four hospitals staffed by Baylor, the level of cardiovascular work is most intense at Fondren-Brown.

A typical operating room team for cardiovascular surgery at Fondren-Brown consists of a surgeon, an assistant surgeon, scrub and circulating nurses, an anesthesiologist, an assistant anesthesiologist, and if a heart-lung machine is in use, a perfusionist. The surgeons, anesthesiologists, and perfusionists are Baylor employees while the nurses are employees of Methodist Hospital who are subject to the direction and supervision of Baylor faculty.

The surgery performed at Fondren-Brown is fee-generating. Baylor anesthesiologists receive a portion of these fees as part of their overall compensation. The precise ratio of "regular" salary and fee-sharing for individual anesthesiologists is set by the Chairman of the Baylor Anesthesiology Department, subject to the approval of Baylor's President.

In the summer of 1976, members of the Baylor faculty, including Dr. Michael DeBakey, were approached by the Hospital Corporation International ("HCI") regarding a rotation program in which Baylor would send cardiovascular surgical teams to the King Faisal Specialist Hospital and Research Center ("King Faisal") located in Riyadh, Saudi Arabia.

A study group of Baylor faculty, including Drs. Arthur Beall (a surgeon) and Sharon Storey (an anesthesiologist), conducted a feasibility study regarding the King Faisal program. This study included an on-site inspection and eventually gave rise to extended negotiations which ultimately culminated in a Memorandum of Agreement, dated October 1, 1977, between Baylor and the King Faisal hospital ("the Agreement").

The King Faisal hospital is owned by the Kingdom of Saudi Arabia and has been managed during all material time periods by HCI.

Under the Agreement, Baylor received a cash advance to initiate the program and hire replacements for personnel who would be absent due to the rotations. Baylor began sending cardiovascular surgical teams to King Faisal on a rotating basis shortly thereafter. The first such rotation lasted from May 15, 1978 to August 15, 1978.

The rotating teams consist of surgeons, anesthesiologists and various operating room personnel (similar to a typical surgical team at Fondren-Brown).

No specific salaries for the Baylor team members are set by the Agreement. Instead, Baylor sets these compensation levels based on what appear (to Baylor administrators) to be sufficient amounts of pay to induce adequate participation in the program.

The Agreement provides maximum amounts which are to be reimbursed to Baylor by the Saudis. These amounts are comprised of three categories of reimbursement: (1) "direct costs,' which include salaries and benefits; (2) "reimbursables," which include air travel expenses, travel allowances and a per diem schedule for travel time; and (3) "indirect costs," which represent a large percentage of the costs incurred by Baylor in maintaining and administering the program. Under the terms of the Agreement, as amended, the maximum amounts paid by the Saudis to Baylor have increased by 10% for each twelve-month period, beginning with the October, 1981—October, 1982 period. In essence, the Saudis have provided the source of funding for the King Faisal program, and based on the evidence adduced at trial, this funding has been forthcoming in handsome amounts.

Participants in the King Faisal program must travel and remain in Saudi Arabia for at least three consecutive months. Participants must secure entry and exist visas from the Kingdom of Saudi Arabia.

The salary levels set by Baylor for its anesthesiologists who participate in the program are attractive. The initial salary level for the senior anesthesiologist position was set by Dr. Arthur Beall, who was designated by Dr. DeBakey (President of Baylor at that time) to administer and oversee the King Faisal program. Dr. Beall set the salary levels based largely on the recommendations of Dr. Sharon Storey. Dr. Storey's figures were predicated on the lowest compensation amounts that would induce a substantial number of Baylor anesthesiology faculty members to take rotations in the program. In fact, the annualized salary levels for anesthesiologists participating in the program have been at least twice the salary levels for anesthesiologists working for Baylor in Houston.

The annualized compensation level for anesthesiologists participating in the King Faisal program in 1978 was approximately $250,000. In 1979, this level rose to $300,000. By 1981, the level of compensation had risen to $350,000, and by 1982, the level of pay was $400,000.

As alluded to above, travel expenses of participants are reimbursed by the Saudis. Further, each participant receives ten days of paid administrative leave from Baylor as a fringe benefit. While in Saudi Arabia, Baylor personnel are provided modest but adequate living quarters at a guarded compound near the King Faisal hospital. Baylor personnel are afforded transportation to and from the hospital, if they choose to utilize it. All personnel are free to come and go while residing in the compound.

In addition to the monetary benefits associated with participation in the King Faisal program, the program provides valuable clinical experience. In particular, the professional horizons of anesthesiologists are substantially expanded due to the markedly higher incidence of congenital and heart-valve (rheumatic fever) diseases which are treated at King Faisal. By contrast, cardiovascular treatments at Baylor predominantly involve coronary artery disease, so that working in the rotation program heightens a physician's experience in dealing with pediatric patients and with patients suffering from the ravages of rheumatic fever.

The Agreement contains no criteria or requirements regarding which persons are eligible to serve as anesthesiologists in the rotation program other than provisions such as "Baylor will provide...a senior cardiac anesthesiologist, who will be responsible for overall supervision of the anesthesia portion" of the program. Baylor has established its own criteria for the position of senior cardiac anesthesiologist.

The objective criteria established by Baylor for participation in the program (regarding anesthesiologists) are that (1) the person must be a member of the Baylor Department of Anesthesiology faculty; and (2) that the person must be certified by the American Board of Anesthesiology or hold an equivalent foreign certification recognized by the American Board of Anesthesiology.

The evidence clearly establishes that both Plaintiffs met the objective criteria set forth immediately above during times material to this lawsuit.

In addition to the objective criteria, Baylor has posited what may be labelled as the "team player criteria" as being necessary to qualify for the program. (We note that this "team player" qualification was raised at trial but was not put before the EEOC.) The Court is not convinced that a requirement of being a "team player" is in any way objective in nature. "Team player" requirements are innately subjective and amorphous. As such, the Court finds that the "team player criteria" are not objective occupational requirements.

The responsibility for designating the anesthesiologists who are to participate in the program is exercised by the Chairman of the Anesthesiology Department, who currently is Dr. Dean Morrow. Formerly, Dr. Lawrence Schuhmacher served as Chairman. Once the physicians (and other rotation participants) have been designated, Baylor provides them with various forms to complete, including a visa application card supplied by HCI. The completed forms are returned to Ms. Dorothy Hosely, administrative secretary to Dr. Beall, who oversees the program.

The visa application card contains a line for indicating a person's religious preference. The applications are eventually forwarded to the Saudi government for approval. Ms. Hosely testified that every line of the applications must be completed prior to processing the applications, and that in the past, when persons indicated "no preference" under "Religion," the persons were required to name a preference.

Ms. Hosely testified that the Saudi visas were usually issued within 24 hours of submission. Further, problems arising out of visa applications for Baylor employees have been quite rare and have been resolved expeditiously. When problems have arisen, either Dr. Beall or Dr. DeBakey has interceded and has been successful in obtaining the visa. It is therefore fairly apparent that the Saudi government has been very cooperative in dealing with visa applications for Baylor personnel who are designated to participate in the King Faisal program.

The evidence shows that no qualified medical personnel employed by Baylor who are Jewish have been afforded any rotation in the King Faisal program.

In particular, Dr. Lewis Coveler, currently Chief of Anesthesiology Services at Ben Taub Hospital and an Associate Professor at Baylor, had been led to believe that he would participate in the program but was never designated to do so by the Chairman. Dr. Coveler is qualified to participate, and he is Jewish. Dr. Coveler was informally assured of a spot on the rotations by Dr. Schuhmacher prior to the first rotation's departure for Saudi Arabia. As was required by Baylor policy, Dr. Coveler attended an orientation meeting in April, 1978, held jointly by Baylor and HCI. The orientation was held for all Baylor personnel who were designated to participate in the program. Although Dr. Coveler had agreed to participate, his name had been removed from the list of designees by the time of the meeting.

Dr. Coveler subsequently took up this matter with Dr. Schuhmacher, who was Chairman of Anesthesiology at that time. Very shortly thereafter, Drs. Schuhmacher, Beall and Coveler met to discuss the matter. The subject of Judaism arose, and Dr. Schuhmacher stated that he would ascertain whether Jews could be included in the rotations to Saudi Arabia, since the Saudis have an apparent hostility to Jews.

Dr. Schuhmacher took part in the first rotation to King Faisal. Although he did not speak with Saudi officials regarding the matter, he concluded that Jews would not be allowed entry visas into Saudi Arabia. He relayed these conclusions to Dr. Morrow and to other Baylor faculty.

Dr. Beall and Dr. Morrow have stated that they are of the opinion that Jews could not participate in the King Faisal program because they believe the Saudi government would not allow Jews to enter their country. Dr. Morrow expressed this opinion to various members of the Baylor anesthesiology faculty on a number of occasions. Moreover, Dr. Morrow told Plaintiff Abrams that he felt it was dangerous for Jews to go to Saudi Arabia. Dr. Sharon Storey, who participated in preparing the lists of designees, stated that his concern for the safety of Jews in Saudi Arabia was a factor in his opinion that Jews should not participate in the program.

It is apparent that these views, expressed by the various doctors who were in charge of different phases of the program, were widely disseminated among Baylor faculty and became a frequent topic of discussion among Baylor employees who were interested in the King Faisal program.

It is worth note at this juncture to point out that Baylor has never had any express agreement or understanding with the Saudis to the effect that Baylor would not send Jews on the rotation program. Further, Baylor has never been given any notification by the Saudi government that Jews would not be allowed to participate in the program. While there appears to have been some discussion of this issue on the part of Baylor officials and HCI personnel, this discussion occurred sometime between the signing of the Agreement and the date of the first rotation. The exact nature of the discussion and the conclusions which flowed from it, if any, are not clear. The issue was not discussed during the negotiation meetings which led to the Agreement.

Dr. Morrow expressed his views regarding the inability of Jews to participate in the program to Dr. Allen Hyman while Morrow was engaged in recruitment efforts for Baylor. In October, 1978, Dr. Morrow stated to Dr. Hyman (a Jewish anesthesiologist at Columbia University) that Jews and women were not eligible for the King Faisal program. When pressed for details by Dr. Hyman, Morrow's response was that he "could not accept Jews" for the rotations.

Dr. Abrams first learned of the King Faisal program at a meeting with Dr. Morrow, held a few days before Dr. Abrams first reported for duty at Baylor. Dr. Morrow knew that Abrams is Jewish and advised him that this fact would preclude his participation in the program. Later, Dr. Schuhmacher told Abrams that the Saudis did not want Jews to visit their country.

Dr. Abrams eventually became a spokesman for Baylor personnel who were protesting the marked inequities in compensation between faculty members who went on rotations to King Faisal and faculty members who did not. Dr. Storey resented Dr. Abrams' protests and Dr. Abrams was later transferred, over his objections, from Fondren-Brown to Ben Taub Hospital. The Court finds that this transfer resulted from official displeasure with Dr. Abrams' protestations, and that this transfer had a deleterious impact on his research project.

Dr. Abrams persisted in his desire to participate in the program, even after his transfer to Ben Taub Hospital. As noted above, Dr. Abrams was fully qualified to participate in the King Faisal program. Further, he possesses an outstanding *curriculum vitae* and has received glowing letters of recommendation, including one written by Dr. George Noon, Professor of Surgery at Baylor.

The Court finds that if Baylor had permitted Dr. Abrams to participate in the King Faisal program, he would have done so. Moreover, based on the evidence we heard regarding the mechanics of the rotation program and based on the length of his tenure at Baylor, the Court finds that Dr. Abrams would have participated in at least three rotations to King Faisal. (For example, Dr. Beall has taken five rotations during the time of the program and various other physicians have each taken three or four rotations.)

The Court finds that the only reason that Dr. Abrams did not participate is because the Baylor physicians who administered the program (excluding Dr. DeBakey, who did not actively engage in the administration process) repeatedly made it clear that Jews were not eligible for the program.

Dr. Linde first learned of the King Faisal program from Dr. Abrams, shortly after he (Linde) began working at Fondren-Brown. Dr. Linde discussed the program with Dr. Storey, who confirmed the fact that Jews were not eligible. Dr. Storey expressed his regrets and sympathy to Linde about this state of affairs, as did Dr. Morrow at a later time.

Shortly after his arrival at Fondren-Brown, Dr. Linde became fully qualified for the King Faisal program. A South African anesthesiologist who has worked with Dr. Christian Barnard, Dr. Linde has received a South African Fellowship in anesthesiology, which is recognized as an equivalent to certification by the American Board. Dr. Linde possesses outstanding professional qualifications.

The Court finds that if Baylor had allowed Dr. Linde to participate in the King Faisal program, he would have done so. Further, the Court finds that Dr. Linde would have participated in four rotations in the King Faisal program.

The Court finds that, as was true of Dr. Abrams, the sole reason for Dr. Linde's non-participation in the program is because Baylor administrators made it clear that Jews could not participate in the rotations.

The Court finds that Baylor has not established any bona fide justification for excluding Jews from the King Faisal program. These exclusionary practices were undertaken unilaterally by Baylor's administrative officials. There is no evidence to show that Baylor officials took any appropriate steps to determine the actual policy of the Kingdom of Saudi Arabia toward Jews participating in the program. Moreover, Baylor took no steps to alleviate or rectify the effects of any perceived discriminatory practices and policies on the part of the Saudis.

The ready acquiescence of Baylor officials in furthering the perceived Saudi exclusion of Jews is in stark contrast to the non-discriminatory policies which were implemented by two other institutions engaged in programs similar to the King Faisal rotations. Officials of both the University of Colorado Medical School and the University of Washington Medical School insisted that non-discrimination clauses be included in the agreements they entered into with the Saudis and that those clauses would be enforced. There is no reason to conclude that Baylor would have been unable to achieve the same results if it had only attempted to do so.

The Court finds that the discrimination against Jews was intentional, and that there was indifference and insensitivity on the part of the Baylor officials who actually administered the King Faisal program regarding the issue of whether Jews could participate in that program.

The Court finds that the "factual bases" (or motives) on which these administrators decided that Jews were to be excluded include (1) informal conversations in Riyadh and various gleaned impressions to the effect that the Saudis did not want any Jews in their country; and (2) a paternalistic "concern" for the safety of Jews traveling to Arab lands. Furthermore, an examination of the totality of the evidence leaves this Court with the firm impression that the implicit reason behind Baylor's exclusion of Jews from the program was the desire to avoid "rocking the boat" vis-a-vis the Saudis. The Baylor officials were utterly indifferent to the clearly discriminatory effects which the exclusionary practices imposed on their Jewish employees.

Dr. Michael DeBakey, who is director of the program but who was not involved in the details of overseeing and administering it, testified that if he had known a Baylor employee could not participate in the program because of his or her race or religion, he would have corrected the problem or ended the Agreement. Dr. DeBakey stated that, as Chancellor of Baylor, he would cancel any program where Jews were excluded and that his staff is aware of his views regarding such discriminatory practices. Unfortunately, the problem of Jews participating in the program was never brought to Dr. DeBakey's attention by his subordinates who administered the program. If only his administrators (Drs. Morrow, Beall, et al.) had shared Dr. DeBakey's commitment to non-discriminatory policies and practices, then we would not have this lawsuit before us.

Dr. Linde filed a charge of discrimination with the EEOC on February 18, 1982. Baylor has sent teams on rotation to King Faisal (including anesthesiologists) within 180 days preceding the filing of his charge and every three months since his charge was made. As noted earlier, Dr. Linde has been continuously employed by Baylor since September 1, 1979.

Dr. Abrams filed a charge of discrimination with the EEOC on November 7, 1980, and amended his charge on November 29, 1980. Baylor sent rotation teams to King Faisal within 180 days preceding the filing of the charge. Dr. Abrams was employed by Baylor from July 16, 1978 until October 30, 1980.

Both Plaintiffs received notices of the right to sue from the EEOC and timely brought their actions in federal court.

The Court finds that the discriminatory actions taken by Baylor deprived the Plaintiffs of substantial employment opportunities and that these actions resulted in monetary losses to the Plaintiffs, based on entitlement to back pay and lost benefits.

Dr. Abrams' actual earnings from Baylor during the material times are as follows:

Budget Year	Baylor Salary	Patient Fees	Actual Earnings
1978–1979	$47,916.59	$33,329.75	$81,246.34
1979–1980	51,969.84	35,930.04	87,899.88
1980–1981	25,316.06	6,458.38	31,774.44

Dr. Abrams' annualized rate of compensation was:

$$1978–1979 = \$84,367.60$$
$$1979–1980 = 87,899.88$$
$$1980–1981 = 95,323.32$$

Based on all the evidence presented at trial, the Court finds that Dr. Abrams would have participated in a total of three rotations which would have been compensated at annualized rates of $250,000 for the first rotation and $300,000 (each) for the other two. After making the appropriate deductions for receipt of Baylor salaries and fee-sharing compensation, and after making calculations based on the quarterly nature of each rotation, the Court finds that Dr. Abrams is entitled to $145,602.30 in back pay for the periods in question. Moreover, Dr. Abrams is entitled to recover for the various days of administrative leave which he would have received as part and parcel of the rotations. Assuming three rotations, the amount of recovery for lost leave is $11,238.00. The total amounts of these awards to Plaintiff Abrams is $156,840.30.

* * *

Based on all the evidence presented at trial, the Court finds that Dr. Linde would have participated in a total of four rotations which would have been compensated at annualized rates of $300,000 (each) for the first two rotations and $400,000 (each) for the other two. After performing the calculations discussed above (regarding Abrams' losses), the Court finds that Dr. Linde is entitled to back pay in the amount of $229,326.08. His award for lost administrative leave is $19,656.00. The total amount of Dr. Linde's awards is $248,982.08.

The Plaintiffs have argued that they should be entitled to recover compensatory damages for the mental anguish and humiliation they suffered because of Defendant's discriminatory actions. The Court finds that such a recovery would not be proper in this case simply because the proffered evidence on this element is insufficient to support a finding of humiliation and mental anguish.

The discriminatory actions of Baylor were, as noted above, the result of intentional discrimination, together with indifference and insensitivity. However, the Court does not find that the conduct was so wilfully malicious and egregious as to support the imposition of punitive damages.

Conclusions of Law

1. This Court has jurisdiction of this action pursuant to Title VII of the Civil Rights Act of 1964, 42 U.S.C. § 2000e-5(f); 28 U.S.C. §§ 1331, 1337, 1343, 2201, and 2202; and 50 U.S.C.App. § 2407 *et seq.*

A. The Title VII Claims

2. Defendant Baylor College of Medicine is an "employer" within the meaning of 42 U.S.C. § 2000e *et seq.*, which employed the Plaintiffs during times material to this lawsuit.

3. The Court concludes that the Plaintiffs' EEOC charges were timely filed. The facts of this case place it within the ambit of *Perez v. Laredo Junior College*, wherein the court held that where the statutory violation occurs as a result of a continuing policy, itself illegal, then the statute of limitations does not foreclose an action aimed at the defendants' continuing enforcement of the illegal policy. Moreover, every time the Defendant selected a rotation team and that selection process excluded Jews from the team, a new and continuing violation occurred.

4. The Defendants have argued that the Plaintiffs' cause must fail because they never applied for participation in the King Faisal program. This argument is ill-founded for two reasons. First, the Supreme Court held in *International Brotherhood of Teamsters v. United States*, that where the act of formal application would be futile, the fact that a plaintiff never applied does not preclude recovery. For example:

> If an employer should announce his policy of discrimination by a sign reading "Whites Only" on the hiring door, his victims would not be limited to the few who ignored the sign and subjected themselves to personal rebuffs. The same message can be communicated to potential applicants more subtly but just as clearly by an employer's actual practices ... When a person's desire for a job is not translated into a formal application solely because of his unwillingness to engage in a futile gesture he is as much a victim of discrimination as is he who goes through the motions of submitting an application.

In this case, the repeated message to Baylor employees was "Non-Jews Only." Hence the Court concludes that *Teamsters* applies and that the Plaintiffs are not precluded from recovery. But for Baylor's overt discrimination, the Plaintiffs would have "applied." The second reason why Defendant's argument cannot be sustained is because the facts show that there was no formal application process. Rather, Baylor's administrators of the program designated team members. Information regarding who was interested in participating as designees was spread by word-of-mouth. The facts show that the desire of the Plaintiffs (and of other Jewish employees) to participate in the program was informally communicated to those in charge of designating the members of the rotation teams. This is sufficient, under the facts, to defeat Baylor's argument.

5. The Plaintiffs have established, by a preponderance of the evidence, that (1) they sought positions in the King Faisal program; (2) they were fully qualified to participate in the program; (3) their requests to participate in the program were denied because they are Jews; and (4) that following these denials, Baylor persisted in designating non-Jewish participants. Therefore, they have established a *prima facie* case.

6. Baylor has failed to establish legitimate business reasons for its discriminatory actions. The decision to exclude Jews was based on stereotyped impressions of a religious (or racial) class, namely, persons who are Jewish. As such, their posited business reasons are obviously pretextual as a matter of law.

7. The patronizing, paternalistic "concerns" of Baylor for the safety of Jews in Saudi Arabia is not a defense to the Plaintiffs' Title VII actions. Rather, such behavior is clearly violative of Title VII. Moreover, the reasons behind the exclusion of Jews do not qualify as a bona fide occupational qualification ("BFOQ").

8. The Court concludes the exclusion of Jews from the King Faisal program was not justified by either a business necessity or by a BFOQ.

9. In any event, the Court concludes that the Plaintiffs have amply met their burden of showing discrimination *vel non*, which is the ultimate issue in a Title VII case.

10. The Plaintiffs are entitled to recover back pay awards which completely redress the economic injury which has resulted from the unlawful discrimination. The Court therefore concludes that the Plaintiffs are entitled to recover the amounts set forth above in the Findings of Fact.

* * *

15. The Court concludes that the Plaintiffs are not entitled to any further relief, based upon their Title VII claims, other than that which has been set forth above.

B. The Export Administration Act

16. In addition to their Title VII claims, the Plaintiffs have alleged a cause of action for violation of the Export Administration Act of 1979, as amended, 50 U.S.C. App. § 2401 *et seq.* ("EAA") which relate to foreign boycotts. The threshold question regarding this asserted cause of action is to determine whether an implied private cause of action exists under the EAA. Prior to trial, the Court held that, based on an application of the factors enumerated in *Cort v. Ash* to the instant dispute, there is an implied private cause of action. The Defendant has continued to challenge this ruling, but the Court concludes that we should adhere to the initial decision for reasons which are set forth below.

* * *

25. The above example of conduct which violates the EAA so closely parallels the conduct of the Defendant in this case that the Court concludes that the Defendant has violated the EAA. This conclusion rests not only on the example itself but on the terms of the EAA, the policies underlying it, and the regulations promulgated pursuant to it as they are applied to the instant facts. All necessary elements, including boycott intent, have been established. Finally, most if not all of the proscribed activity of the Defendant occurred after the effective date of the anti-boycott amendments to the EAA.

* * *

Judge James De Anda's decision in *Abrams* was upheld, although the Fifth Circuit ordered a remand on the issue of the award of attorney's fees. The Court of Appeals called Baylor College of Medicine's assertions "A Theoryless Theory":

> One of the chief difficulties in this case is that Baylor simply never arrived at a theory of its case. There was at least a theoretical possibility that Baylor could assert that "non-Jewishness" was a bona fide occupational qualification (BFOQ) for the Faisal Hospital rotation program, notwithstanding the fact that the exclusion of Jews as Jews would normally be prohibited from discrimination under Title VII. Baylor just danced all around this; it never zeroed in on this as a BFOQ. In order to substantiate that defense though, Baylor would have to prove that the official position of the Saudi government forbad or discouraged the participation of Jews in the program. That would have meant that Baylor would have to obtain formally an authoritative statement of the position of the Saudis. Yet [Baylor President and Heart Surgeon Dr. Michael] DeBakey testified that it was not until 1983, more than a year after suit was instituted, that Baylor attempted to obtain such a statement. While the failure to seek or obtain such a critical determination is puzzling—and goes a long way toward knocking the props from under the BFOQ defense—a good explanation may well be the

District Court's finding that Baylor's inaction was motivated, in part, by its desire not to "rock the boat" of its lucrative Saudi contributors.

Worse than that, Baylor's own witnesses went a long way toward destroying the BFOQ defense. Both Dr. Abrams and Dr. Linde were informed, by various Baylor officials, that there were problems securing visas for Jews. Yet, Baylor never attempted to substantiate the "problem," and the veracity of those assertions is called seriously into question by the following testimony of Dr. DeBakey:

> May I indicate to you that one of the reasons that I had not asked for a policy before was because we never had a problem. It has never come up before, and I have on occasions had Jewish physicians go [to Saudi Arabia] to see special patients I wanted them to see. And we had no difficulty getting visas for them.

In 1987, the Supreme Court treated an Iraqui professor and Jewish plaintiffs as eligible to sue under Reconstruction-era civil rights statutes, including Sec. 1981: "Jews and Arabs were among the peoples then considered to be distinct races and hence [are included] within the protection of the statute[s]." *St. Francis College v. Al-Khazraji*, 107 S. Ct. 62 (1987); *Shaare Tefila Congregation v. Cobb*, 107 S. Ct. 2019 (1987). In *Manzanares v. Safeway Stores*, the Tenth Circuit Court of Appeals held: "The measure is group to group, and plaintiff has alleged that the "group" to which he belongs—those he describes as of Mexican American descent—is to be measured against the Anglos as the standard. . . . In this holding we consider that Mexican American, Spanish American, Spanish-surname individuals, and Hispanos are equivalents, and it makes no difference whether these are terms of national origin, alienage, or whatever. It is apparent that a group so described is of such an identifiable nature that the treatment afforded its members may be measured against that afforded the Anglos." 593 F. 2d 968, 970 (10th Cir. 1979).

Pime v. Loyola University of Chicago
803 F.2d 351 (7th Cir. 1986)

FAIRCHILD, Senior Circuit Judge.

Appellant Jerrold S. Pime brought suit against Loyola University of Chicago under Title VII of the Civil Rights Act of 1964, 42 U.S.C. § 2000e-2(a), for religious discrimination in the hiring of tenure track professors in Loyola's College of Arts and Sciences, Department of Philosophy. The Department of Philosophy had passed a resolution reserving the next three vacancies in tenure track teaching positions for Jesuits, members of the Society of Jesus.

Loyola asserted two affirmative defenses. First, it claimed that it could require its employees to be Jesuits (and thus Catholics) under 42 U.S.C. § 2000e-2(e)(2) (hereafter (e)(2)). Subsection (e)(2) permits an educational institution to employ persons of a particular religion if the institution is "in whole or in substantial part, owned, supported, controlled, or managed . . . by a particular religion or by a particular religious corporation, association, or society." It also claimed it could require those employees to be Jesuits according to 42 U.S.C. § 2000e-2(e)(1) (hereafter (e)(1)). Subsection (e)(1) permits an employer to employ an individual "on the basis of his religion, sex, or national origin in those certain instances where religion, sex, or national origin is a bona fide occupational qualification reasonably necessary to the normal operation of that particular business or enterprise." [BFOQ]

The district court judge, after a bench trial, granted judgment in favor of Loyola after finding that being a Jesuit was a BFOQ. Plaintiff Pime challenges the finding of a BFOQ. Defendant Loyola challenges Judge Leighton's conclusion that Loyola could not rely on subsection (e)(2).

I. BACKGROUND

The Society of Jesus is a religious order of the Roman Catholic Church. Its members, who are, with few exceptions, priests, are called Jesuits. The order has been characterized by interest and particular energy in the promotion of education, and has established twenty-eight universities in the United States. Jesuits are required to complete a protracted course of training and to make perpetual vows. Once they accept positions as professors they continue to incorporate their religious mission into their professional work.

Loyola University of Chicago has a long Jesuit tradition. Since 1909 its legal entity has been an Illinois not-for-profit corporation. Until 1970, it was governed by a Board of Trustees, all members of which were Jesuits. It has become a large university, consisting of ten schools and colleges, a medical center and a hospital. Presently 93% of academic administrators are non-Jesuit, as are 94% of the teaching staff.

In 1970, apparently to respond to the needs of growth, the Board amended the By-laws, enlarging the Board to 23, but requiring that one more than one-third must be Jesuits. The majority are in fact non-Jesuit. Amendment of the By-laws requires a two-thirds vote. The By-laws provide, however, that the president, who is the principal executive officer, must be a Jesuit.

Every undergraduate must take three Philosophy courses. About 75% of the students come from Catholic backgrounds. There was testimony by the President that, "I'm convinced that of all the things we say about Loyola, the most effective single adjective in attracting students and alumni support and benefactors is its Jesuitness."

In the fall of 1978, there were 31 tenure track positions in the Philosophy Department. Seven had been held by Jesuits, but one had resigned and two more retirements were imminent. On October 12, the department chairman reported to a meeting of the department faculty as follows:

> We anticipate 3 full-time faculty openings in the Philosophy Department beginning September 1979. They are the position of Fr. Dehler and those of Fr. Grant and Fr. Loftus after they retire at the end of the current academic year. There are two different kinds of departmental needs which seem to bear heavily on the decision as to the kind of persons we should seek to hire for these openings.
>
> 1. The first is a need which the Chairman voiced two years ago just after Fr. Dehler's resignation. That is, the need for an adequate Jesuit presence in the Department. We are a Philosophy Department in a University with a Jesuit tradition. It is mainly by reason of this tradition that philosophy has the importance it does in the education of Loyola undergraduates. Therefore, it behooves us, however strongly we may feel about "the autonomy of philosophy," to acknowledge our association with this tradition. One very basic and obvious way of making such acknowledgment is by insisting upon an adequate Jesuit

presence in the faculty of the Department. With the retirement of Father Grant and Father Loftus, we shall be left with 4 out of 31 faculty positions occupied by Jesuits. 4 out of 31 is not an adequate Jesuit presence in the Department. In the judgment of the Chairman, it would be highly desirable to fill all three openings with professionally competent Jesuit philosophers. And it is his recommendation that we do so if we can.

2. The second kind of departmental need is for faculty especially qualified to teach courses in the following areas: a. Applied ethics, especially medical ethics. There is an increasing student demand for such courses and for additional undergraduate course offerings at the Medical School. b. Philosophy of Law. This is one of the most popular of our 300-level course offerings. It needs to be offered annually both at Lake Shore Campus and Water Tower Campus and there seems to be some desire that we offer it annually in the Law School. c. Logic. There is an exceedingly heavy student enrollment at both Lake Shore Campus and Water Tower Campus. Additional sections of courses in logic should be offered on each campus.

Consequently, we should seek persons who have special competence and interest in teaching courses in these areas. The Chairman's recommendation is that we seek to hire persons who will help teach in these areas.

These two kinds of needs are different though not incompatible. The Chairman's recommendations as to hiring is the following:

> That for each of these 3 positions we seek to hire a professionally competent Jesuit philosopher—preferably a young Jesuit with competence to teach in one or several of the areas mentioned above.

At the November 30 meeting, the following resolution was adopted:

> That for each of the 3 positions we seek to hire a professionally competent Jesuit philosopher—preferably a young Jesuit with competence to teach in one or several of the following areas: a) applied ethics, especially medical ethics; b) philosophy of law; and c) logic; and that if we should be unable to hire such, we hire temporary full-time person(s) with special competence to teach in one or several of these areas.

Plaintiff Pime, a Jew, had been employed in 1976 as a part-time lecturer in the department. He taught several courses. He expected to receive his doctorate in June, 1979 and had received indications of approval of his work. He knew of the resolution of November 30, and asked the department chairman when there would be a full-time tenure track position for him. The chairman said he saw nothing in the way of a position for Pime in the next three or four years. Disappointed, Pime left Loyola after the spring semester.

He filed a timely charge of employment discrimination with EEOC and received notice of his right-to-sue. Then he filed this action.

There is no hint of invidious action against Pime on account of his religion. The faculty resolution excluded every non-Jesuit from consideration, whether of the Catholic faith or otherwise. We shall assume, however, that because Pime's faith would prevent his being a Jesuit, he has a claim of discrimination on account of religion.

II. BFOQ

42 U.S.C. § 2000e-2(e)(1) provides:

> (e) [I]t shall not be an unlawful employment practice for an employer to hire and employ employees, . . . on the basis of his religion, sex, or national origin in those certain instances where religion, sex, or national origin is a bona fide occupational qualification reasonably necessary to the normal operation of that particular business or enterprise.

The BFOQ involved in this case is membership in a religious order of a particular faith. There is evidence of the relationship of the order to Loyola, and that Jesuit "presence" is important to the successful operation of the university. It appears to be significant to the educational tradition and character of the institution that students be assured a degree of contact with teachers who have received the training and accepted the obligations which are essential to membership in the Society of Jesus. It requires more to be a Jesuit than just adherence to the Catholic faith, and it seems wholly reasonable to believe that the educational experience at Loyola would be different if Jesuit presence were not maintained. As priests, Jesuits perform rites and sacraments, and counsel members of the university community, including students, faculty, and staff. One witness expressed the objective as keeping a presence "so that students would occasionally encounter a Jesuit."

It is true that it has not been shown that Jesuit training is a superior academic qualification, applying objective criteria, to teach the particular courses. It is also true that in looking at claims of BFOQ, courts have considered only the content of the particular job at issue. Yet it seems to us that here the evidence supports the more general proposition that having a Jesuit presence in the Philosophy faculty is "reasonably necessary to the normal operation" of the enterprise, and that fixing the number at seven out of 31 is a reasonable determination.

Judge Leighton found as follows:

> Clearly, religion, the fact that the three full-time vacancies were reserved for Jesuits, persons who were Catholics, was the basis for the decision which the tenured faculty made on October 12, 1978, at the general meeting of the Department of Philosophy. In good faith, Loyola, through its tenured faculty in the Department of Philosophy, decided that being a Jesuit, again a matter of religion, was to be required of those who were to fill the three vacancies. This was a *bona fide* determination of qualification for the position. Finally, the full-time faculty determined that it was necessary for the future of the department, and for Loyola, that a "Jesuit presence" in the university be maintained, and that the designated areas of teaching be done by competent Jesuit philosophers. Therefore, Loyola qualifies for the [BFOQ] exemption. . . .

The finding is not clearly erroneous.

The judgment appealed from is AFFIRMED.

POSNER, Circuit Judge, concurring.

I agree that Pime must lose this Title VII case. But my ground is different from and narrower than my brethren's ground, and although not emphasized by the defendant is sufficiently argued that we need not treat it as waived.

Pime was turned down for a tenure-track position in Loyola's philosophy department not because he is a Jew, not because he is not a Catholic, but because he is not a member of the Jesuit order. I therefore do not think he has been deprived of an employment opportunity because of his religion. 42 U.S.C. § 2000e-2(a). It is true that you cannot be a Jesuit if you are not a Catholic; but only a tiny fraction of Catholics are Jesuits. If Pime were a Catholic but not a Jesuit he would be just as ineligible for the position as he is being a Jew, yet it would be odd indeed to accuse Loyola of discriminating against Catholics because it wanted to reserve some positions in its philosophy department for Jesuits, thus excluding most Catholics from consideration. Not only is Pime's being Jewish an adventitious circumstance in this case but so is the fact that Loyola is a Catholic school. It is hard to believe that the philosophy department of the University of Chicago—or of Brandeis University— would be guilty of a prima facie violation of Title VII if it reserved a few slots for Jesuits, believing that the Jesuit point of view on philosophy was one to which its students should be exposed; and Loyola should have the same right. To take another example, suppose Loyola reserved a slot for a rabbi, to teach Jewish theology; would this be a prima facie violation of Title VII? I cannot believe it would be; and if this conclusion is right it casts doubt on my brethren's assumption that the mere fact of reserving one or more slots for members of a religious order establishes a prima facie case.

Of course my argument would fall to the ground if the Jesuit order were itself a religion within the meaning of Title VII. But the statute seems to use the term in its ordinary sense, see 42 U.S.C. § 2000e(j) ("The term 'religion' includes all aspects of religious observance and practice, as well as belief"), and in ordinary language Jesuits are a Catholic order, not a separate religion.

*   *   *

If I am wrong in thinking that Loyola is not guilty of prima facie discrimination, I would give serious consideration to interpreting the defense of bona fide occupational qualification broadly enough to reach what Loyola has done, for it seems so remote from any concern that Congress had when it passed Title VII. But it is not necessary to decide whether Loyola has made out this defense and I think it would be the better part of valor to forgo reliance on it and place decision on the narrower ground. For reasons having nothing to do with antipathy to Jews or other non-Catholics, Loyola wants to have a certain proportion of its philosophy professors drawn from a particular religious order to which, as I have said, most Catholics do not belong and could not belong, because they would be either unable to satisfy the demanding entrance requirements or unwilling to take the vows of poverty, chastity, and obedience. In giving a modest and thoroughly understandable preference to members of this order, in circumstances that rebut any inference of invidious discrimination, Loyola is not discriminating against members of any religious faith within the meaning of Title VII.

For completeness I will address the other defense pressed by Loyola, the religious-employer defense, which so far as applicable to this case is available to a university that "is, in whole or in substantial part, owned, supported, controlled, or managed by a particular religion or by a particular religious corporation, association, or society." 42 U.S.C. § 2000e-2(e)(2). That is an apt description of Loyola as of its founding as St. Ignatius College in 1870. But for many years now Loyola has not been owned by the Jesuit order. It is incorporated not as a religious corporation but as an ordinary nonprofit corporation, and financial contributions from the Jesuit order provide only one-third of one percent of the university's income. Although three-fourths of the students are Catholic, the university does not require students to take any courses in Catholic theology (it does require each student to take three courses in theology, however), does not have a seminary (though it has a theology department), and offers a full range of secular instruction. It is no longer a religious or sectarian school in the narrow sense. All this would matter not at all if it were clear that the board of trustees was controlled by Jesuits, for control in whole or substantial part is all the statute requires. But only a minority of the board are Jesuits. The university's by-laws require that at least one-third plus one of the trustees be Jesuits (in fact 40 percent of the trustees are Jesuits)—enough to block amendments to the by-laws, since such amendments require the approval of two-thirds of the board—and that the president of the university, who has the normal powers of a chief executive officer (the by-laws describe him as the university's "principal executive officer"), be a Jesuit.

Is the combination of a Jesuit president and nine Jesuit directors out of 22 enough to constitute substantial control or management by the Jesuit order? There is no case law pertinent to this question; the statute itself does not answer it; corporate-control and state-action analogies are too remote to be illuminating; and the legislative history, though tantalizing, is inconclusive. The exemption originated in an amendment offered by Congressman Purcell and extensively debated. The focus of the debate, however, was on the merits rather than the scope of the exemption. One thing that seems reasonably clear from a remark by Congressman Purcell is that the exemption is not limited to schools chartered as religious corporations: "most church-related schools are chartered under the general corporation statutes as nonprofit institutions for the purpose of education." Moreover, this and other references to "church-related" and "church-affiliated" schools indicate that Congress did not intend to limit the exemption to schools formally owned by religious bodies—but that is anyway apparent from the language of the exemption. However, the debates did not focus on the question, at what point does the relation between the religious body and the school become so attenuated that the exemption ceases to be available? The suggestion by an opponent of the exemption that any schools "that were connected in the beginning or are still connected with some particular denomination of the Christian faith" would be within the exemption seems deliberately exaggerated. Although Congress seems to have been aware that the degree of religious involvement in universities popularly considered to be religiously affiliated is highly variable, neither the statute nor the legislative history indicates where in the continuum Congress wanted to make the cut.

If the governance arrangements of Loyola are typical of those of Catholic universities, then I would have little doubt that Loyola was within the protection of the religious-employer exemption, but the record contains no information on the matter. They may not be typical; a recent decision concerning a Catholic university in Puerto Rico noted that the university's by-laws required that a majority of the board of trustees as well as the university's president had to be members of the Dominican order. If Loyola, perhaps in order to attract financial or other support from non-Catholic sources has attenuated its relationship to the Jesuit order far beyond that of other Catholic universities, there would be a serious problem in holding that it could nevertheless discriminate freely in favor of Catholics; for remember that the exemption allows the religious employer to confine all hiring to members of one religious faith. But the record is as I have said silent on these questions, which makes me as leery about using this case to determine the scope of the religious-employer exemption as about using it to determine the scope of the exemption for religion as a bona fide occupational qualification. I would avoid both defenses, and place decision on the ground that there was no prima facie violation of Title VII, given the lack of evidence of either discriminatory intention or discriminatory effect.

Faro v. New York University
502 F.2d 1229 (1974)

MOORE, Circuit Judge:

Plaintiff, Maria Diaz Faro, a doctor of philosophy, Ph.D. in anatomy, not a medical doctor (referred to herein as Dr. Faro), appeals from an order of the District Court denying her application for a preliminary injunction in an action brought under Title VII of the Civil Rights Act of 1964, 42 U.S.C. § 2000e *et seq.*, wherein she sought an injunction against defendant from allegedly changing her employment status in the New York University Medical Center (for brevity usually referred to as "NYU"), pending action by governmental agencies with which she had filed complaints alleging discrimination against her because she is a woman.

After a three-day hearing, the court denied the preliminary injunction, concluding that it was "thoroughly unconvinced that the defendant University was motivated by sex bias or discrimination in refusing to create a special position for plaintiff and to give that job to her" and, since "the plaintiff has failed to show either irreparable harm or the likelihood of success on the merits," that no injunction should issue.

To appraise the merits of Dr. Faro's claim, the facts relating to her coming to NYU and her position and work there since that time should be reviewed.

Dr. Faro came to NYU in early 1965 from Puerto Rico as one of some fourteen members of a research staff of the Laboratory of Perinatal Physiology, a group brought to NYU by Dr. William F. Windle and which was engaged in primate studies. She was given the status of a research scientist as an Instructor of Experimental Rehabilitation Medicine. Her compensation was from special funds. In 1968 her grade was changed to Assistant Professor and in September 1972 to Associate Professor.

The Department of Rehabilitation Medicine of NYU is frequently referred to as the Rusk Institute because of its founder and chairman, Dr. Howard A. Rusk. The grant under which Dr. Windle and his staff were conducting their research was not a grant in perpetuity. Dr. Windle advised his staff that his grant would terminate in February 1971 and that he was departing about that time. Apparently, all other members of the research group except two women, Dr. Faro and Dr. Barker, left. To aid Dr. Faro in continuing her research, NYU arranged to have her participate in teaching a course in Gross Anatomy in the Department of Cell Biology on a temporary basis in the Spring of 1971 and again from September 1971 to February 1972. In addition, Dr. Rusk was able to secure some funds from private foundations to support Dr. Faro's research activities for a further limited period.

In the summer of 1971, Dr. Rusk wrote to eleven employees of his Department including Dr. Faro, terminating their appointments as of August 31, 1972, and offering new appointments without tenure possibilities but with continuation of current salary and fringe benefits. All except Dr. Faro accepted. Dr. Faro chose to regard this as a "demotion" and requested consideration for a tenured position which she was subsequently advised NYU's financial and academic situation precluded. NYU's financial condition (large deficits having been incurred) forced it to terminate Dr. Faro's employment as of December 31, 1973. Dr. Faro sought other academic employment but without success. She decided to attempt to remedy this situation by filing alleged employment discrimination charges with the U.S. Equal Employment Opportunity Commission and the New York City Commission on Human Rights. Because of the anticipated delays before these Commissions, Dr. Faro brought this suit and moved for a preliminary injunction. Primarily her claim is, and of necessity must be, that the action taken by NYU in her case was of a discriminatory nature because she is a woman.

The district court did not dispose of the motion on the affidavits alone but granted a protracted hearing (three days) in which Dr. Faro and Drs. Sabatini (Chairman of the Cell Biology Department), Rusk (Director of the Institute of Rehabilitation Medicine and Chairman of the Department of Rehabilitation Medicine), Potter (Associate Dean of the Medical Schools) and Goodgold (Professor of Rehabilitation Medicine and Director of Research and Training in the Institute of Rehabilitation Medicine); all testified. The court's conclusion that there was no discrimination against Dr. Faro is amply supported by the proof—in fact, it is the only conclusion which could be properly adduced therefrom. In argument, Dr. Faro points to the hiring of other medical professors who are male but the proof shows no professional comparison between these professors, their experience, skills and purposes for which they were hired, and Dr. Faro.

Dr. Faro also argues that the district court applied a too stringent standard of proof in denying the preliminary injunction; that the court was in error in stating that she must show a strong likelihood of ultimate success on the merits; that she has shown irreparable injury; and that the issues here, legal and factual, are complex.

Dr. Faro, in effect, envisions herself as a modern Jeanne d'Arc fighting for the rights of embattled womanhood on an academic battlefield, facing a solid phalanx of men and male faculty prejudice. She would compare herself and her qualifications with all recent appointees to the NYU medical faculty and asserts that she is just as competent as they are. In particular, she selects three doctors for comparison. She states that she was offered $4,000 for the same job for which a Dr. Alves was paid $23,000. Of course, as the district court found and the record substantiates, it was not the same job. Analysis of the proof clearly shows that the experience possessed by such male professors as have been hired is not comparable to the limited teaching and research background of Dr. Faro.

By this suit, Dr. Faro seeks a teaching job in any department of the Medical School which keeps her in the tenure chain and provides her with a full-time salary. The fact that, for a person of Dr. Faro's qualifications, there is no such job available apparently is inconsequential.

The faculty selection process has been described by Dr. Rusk as follows:

> Recommendations come from the chairman of the department and then there is a promotions committee within the department made up of senior faculty members who discuss, approve or disapprove these recommendations. From there it goes to the medical center executive committee where it is reviewed by

a special promotions committee and then it comes back for approval or disapproval by the subcommittee as a whole.

No one other than the department chairman makes such recommendations.

Of all fields, which the federal courts should hesitate to invade and take over, education and faculty appointments at a University level are probably the least suited for federal court supervision. Dr. Faro would remove any subjective judgments by her faculty colleagues in the decision-making process by having the courts examine "the university's recruitment, compensation, promotion and termination and by analyzing the way these procedures are applied to the claimant personally." All this information she would obtain "through extensive discovery, either by the EEOC or the litigant herself." This argument might well lend itself to a *reductio ad absurdum* rebuttal. Such a procedure, in effect, would require a faculty committee charged with recommending or withholding advancements or tenure appointments to subject itself to a court inquiry at the behest of unsuccessful and disgruntled candidates as to why the unsuccessful was not as well qualified as the successful. This decision would then be passed on by a Court of Appeals or even the Supreme Court. The process might be simplified by a legislative enactment that no faculty appointment or advancement could be made without the committee obtaining a declaratory judgment naming the successful candidate after notice to all contending candidates to present their credentials for court inspection and decision. This would give "due process" to all contenders, regardless of sex, to advance their "I'm just as good as you are" arguments. But such a procedure would require a discriminating analysis of the qualifications of each candidate for hiring or advancement, taking into consideration his or her educational experience, the specifications of the particular position open and, of great importance, the personality of the candidate.

In practically all walks of life, especially in business and the professions, someone must be charged with the ultimate responsibility of making a final decision—even as are the courts. The computer, highly developed though it be, is not yet qualified to digest the punch cards of an entire faculty and advise the waiting and expectant onlookers of its decision as to hiring or promotion. Even were it so capable, a new rule would have to be added to appellate rules entitled "Appeal from a Computer."

As to "irreparable harm," Dr. Faro is in no way different from hundreds of others who find that they have to make adjustments in life when the opening desired by them does not open. This situation is not confined to medical schools. Of a hypothetical twenty equally brilliant law school graduates in a law office, one is selected to become a partner. Extensive discovery would reveal that the other nineteen were almost equally well qualified. Fifty junior bank officers all aspire to become a vice-president—one is selected. And, of course, even judges are plagued by the difficulty of decision in selecting law clerks out of the many equally well qualified.

Dr. Faro apparently is convinced "of the sex-bias in higher educational institutions" and that she "must fight the sexism in other institutions of higher learning." A certain well-known Governor of New York frequently and wisely said. "Let's look at the record." So looking, we find that the district court did not confine itself to any one limited set of standards but rather considered all, likelihood of success, irreparable damage, "substantial and difficult" issues and balance of hardships. After considering the law and the facts it found that it was "forced to conclude that the defendant University had treated Dr. Faro fairly and in a manner that was above reproach".

The record supports this conclusion. The Court said, "The University's Medical School is presently going through a period of difficult financial strain and officials have explained this to plaintiff [Dr. Faro], pointing out that the circumstances require the termination of her research." After analyzing the facts, it is obvious that "The defendant has been far from heartless in its termination of Dr. Faro. Various officials of the University have attempted to aid her in her search for a position at another institution but to no avail."

The reasons for the termination of Dr. Faro's research project are clear but even clearer is the conclusion that no violation of any provision of Title VII was involved therein.

Order affirmed.

Mecklenberg v. Montana State Board of Regents
13 EPD ¶ 11, 438 (1976)

MURRAY, D.J.: This cause came on for trial August 11, 1975. The court having heard the evidence, finds the facts and states the conclusions of law as follows:

Findings of Fact

The defendant Montana State University is a state institution of higher education and an agent of the State of Montana.

The Montana Board of Regents of Higher Education is charged by the Montana Constitution (Art. X, § 9) with full power, responsibility and authority to supervise, coordinate, manage, and control the Montana State University System which includes Montana State University, located in Bozeman, Montana. Carl W. McIntosh is the President of Montana State University.

Montana State University is an "employer" within the definitions of 42 U.S.C. § 2000e and 29 U.S.C. § 203(d) and the business activities of the university are performed for a common business purpose and constitute an "enterprise" within the meaning of 29 U.S.C. § 203(r). The university is also an "employer" under the amended version of section 41–1301 of the Revised Codes of Montana (1947).

The named defendants in this lawsuit are Montana State University, the Montana Board of Regents of Higher Education and President Carl W. McIntosh. The Montana State Board of Education is no longer a party defendant; it was dropped by virtue of the plaintiff's motion which was unopposed by the defendants.

Neither the Regents nor Dr. McIntosh were named in the charges filed with the Equal Employment Opportunity Commission by the plaintiffs in this action. The EEOC charges complain of sex discrimination in a variety of forms, and the evidence in this case demonstrates a direct or indirect involvement by the Regents and President McIntosh in many of the policies complained of. The EEOC was therefore apprised in general terms that the alleged discriminatory parties included the President and the Regents or could have so determined in an investigation growing out of the discrimination charges.

The named plaintiffs in this action are Bette A. Lowery, Ellen Kreighbaum, Helen Mecklenberg, Jeanne J. Claus, and Eleanor R. Pratt. They are all faculty members who are currently employed or were employed in the past on the teaching staff of

Montana State University. Plaintiffs have filed this action charging the defendant with maintaining policies and practices of discrimination against females as a class, specifically with regard to the underutilization of women in certain departments, salaries, promotions, and the representation of women on prominent university committees and in important administrative and policy making positions.

The named plaintiffs in this action also represent all females who have suffered from the alleged discriminatory policies of the defendants.

(A) The class of women included as plaintiffs in this action are so numerous that joinder of all members is impracticable. There are at least one hundred and five (105) women on the faculty at Montana State University who are included in the class; in actuality the class is larger because it encompasses former female employees who may have been discriminated against, and women who may in the future suffer because of unequal treatment, as well as those who were never hired because of discriminatory policies of the defendants.

(B) There are questions of law or fact common to the class. Although the type of discriminatory activity affecting each member of the class and each individual's qualifications may differ, the common issue of law and fact is the question of discrimination on the basis of sex.

(C) The claims and defenses of the representative parties are typical of the claims and defenses of the class. A number of EEOC administrative charges in evidence reflect this "typicality." It is also demonstrated by a comparison of the named individual plaintiffs' complaints with the statistical evidence suggesting discrimination.

(D) The representative parties fairly and adequately represent the class. The plaintiffs' counsel are qualified and capable of conducting this litigation and the plaintiffs do not have interests antagonistic to those of the class.

(E) The defendants have acted on grounds generally applicable to the class, thereby making final injunctive and declaratory class relief appropriate; the predominate relief sought by the class is such injunctive and declaratory relief.

Each of the named plaintiffs have filed charges with the Equal Employment Opportunity Commission alleging discrimination on the basis of sex. Two of these plaintiffs have received "right to sue" letters from the Department of Justice. Dr. Kreighbaum filed her complaint on March 9, 1973, charging, "[m]ales paid higher salaries than females for similar work." The charge was amended on June 28, 1974 to include retaliation, discrimination in promotion, underutilization of women on the university faculty, and underrepresentation by females as deans, vice presidents, and on faculty committees. The amendments thus alleged additional acts constituting unlawful employment practices directly related to or growing out of the subject matter of the original EEOC charges. On July 18, 1974, the right to sue letter was issued to Dr. Kreighbaum by the Civil Rights Division of the Department of Justice. Dr. Lowery filed her complaint on March 9, 1973, charging:

> Unequal pay for equal education and equal work, males received higher salaries for similar work. In addition to what is already there Montana State University has established wage and promotional skill systems which have in the past and which continue to limit the wage scale and promotional opportunities of female employees as opposed to the wages paid to and promotions given to male employees of Montana State University.

Dr. Lowery's charge was amended by the same letter as that of Dr. Kreighbaum on June 28, 1974, and her "right to sue" letter was issued on July 18, 1974. The evidence indicates that Dr. Mecklenberg's charge of discrimination on the basis of promotion was forwarded to Montana State University on March 8, 1974, and the defendants have not denied receipt of notice of charges for Doctors Kreighbaum and Lowery.

The testimony indicated there are no women vice presidents or deans at Montana State University, nor are there any female assistant deans representing the various colleges at the university according to the Affirmative Action Plan.

Montana State University underutilizes women as department heads, and in many departments, too few women have been employed in faculty instructional positions. The Engineering College underutilizes women; in fact, there are no women in any of the six departments. The College of Letters and Sciences has an inadequate representation of women—one half of the twelve departments with faculty have no female instructional members. Women are underrepresented in earth sciences, life sciences, social sciences, modern languages, and history, government, and philosophy. In the professional schools, women are underutilized in the arts (architecture, art, film and television production and music). The "availability" figures (percentages of qualified women available for academic instructional positions) used by the university in its Affirmative Action Plan are very conservative in that they are based on the percentage of doctorates earned by women. Exhibit #25 shows that well over one third of the faculty at Montana University does not possess a doctorate degree. There are some fields for which a master's is considered a "terminal" degree.

The defendants contend that Montana State University is underapplied to by women and hence the defendants are not to blame for any underutilization of women; this conclusion is not supported by the evidence. The "availability" figures used by the Affirmative Action Plan were based on the "average percentage ... of *all degrees* [bachelor's, master's, and doctor's] earned by women...." These availability statistics are totally inconsistent with the availability figures used by the university in determining whether women were "underutilized" in instructional positions. At any rate, the explanations (*e.g.*, climate, geographical isolation) given by witnesses testifying for the university and suggested in the Affirmative Action Plan are totally speculative.

The promotional decisions at Montana State University reflect the defendant's implementation of a nonstandardized merit system. There are a great number of variables which those in the promotion review process are allowed to consider. In addition, the various academic departments at the university may weigh these factors differently. Thus those who play a role in the promotion process may apply a number of vague and subjective standards, and there are no safeguards in the procedure to avert sex discriminatory practices.

Recommendations for individual faculty promotions are initiated at the department level; the department head plays a primary role in making decisions which lead to promotions. These recommendations are then passed to the appropriate dean of the particular college involved, who in turn, transfers them to the Promotion and Tenure Committee. The Promotion and Tenure Committee relays its recommendations to the Personnel Committee which approves or denies the applications. They then go to the President for review; he conveys them to the Board of Regents for final approval. In the great majority of cases, there will be no women involved in this entire promotional procedure, for there are only two female department heads out of thirty five and there are no women deans, there are no women on the Promotion and Tenure Committee nor the Personnel Committee, and the President is also a male.

Dr. Jack Gilchrest, a sociologist and statistician, utilized information stored in the personnel data bank at Montana State University in determining how promotion is affected by sex at the university. Dr. Gilchrest testified that a comparison of males and females by degree at Montana State University shows a larger percentage of males reach the rank of professor and associate professor than do females. For example, of the females with doctorates at Montana State University, 15% are full professors and 25% are associate professors, compared to 38% of the males achieving the full professor rank and 36% achieving the rank of associate professor. Of the females with master's degrees, 2.9% achieve the rank of full professor while 24.5% of the males with master's attain the title of full professor.

This comparison of the disparate percentages of men and women in the higher ranks at Montana State University occurs even though females have the same relative experience as males. In Gilchrest's study of those individuals with common degrees and sixteen or more years of experience (allowing all individuals ample time to attain the rank of full professor), 79% of the male doctorates are full professors, while only 42% of the females achieve that title. Of the males with masters, 41% reach the full professor rank, while only 5% of the women succeed to that rank.

The faculty handbook for Montana State University indicates that the normal minimum time required in rank before promotion is three years as instructor and five years each for assistant and associate professors. Exhibit numbers 27 through 29 (based on information from the Affirmative Action Plan) show that males [consistently] spend less time in rank than is stipulated as "minimal" for each rank in the faculty handbook. Women on the other hand, spend more time in rank than the handbook requires for each rank. The disparity between male and female "time in rank" is significant. Women spend almost twice as long as men in rank at the associate level, 1.69 times as long at the assistant level, and 1.45 times as long in the instructor rank.

From Table #19 of the Affirmative Action Plan, the defendants conclude that a higher percentage of females eligible for promotion were promoted as compared to the percentage of males. That result is based only upon promotions effective for the year 1974-75. The cumulative effects of past discrimination have not been taken into consideration, nor have there been adjustments for the longer times that women spend in rank before promotion.

The defendants' explanations for the discrepancies in the promotions of men and women at Montana State University (*e.g.*, assertions that women's careers are more limited by family obligations or that women are less ambitious than men) are wholly conjecture.

One of the measures by which faculty members are evaluated for purposes of promotion and salary increases is the ability to garner grant money from state or federal granting agencies. Although the evidence indicated that many more males than females had been awarded such grants, these grants were concentrated primarily in the physical, biological, and agricultural sciences—all fields which are heavily dominated by men at Montana State University.

The tenure policy at Montana State University has also resulted in disproportionately fewer women achieving tenure than men. Tenure at Montana State University has been automatic after three years of service at the rank of associate professor or professor, and thus promotion to those ranks was a critical aspect of achieving tenure. Since the promotion analyses indicate that it has been more difficult for women to move up to those ranks, presumably it would be more difficult for them to achieve tenure status. The statistics in the Affirmative Action Plan bear out this conclusion. During the 1973-74 academic year, 25 females and 240 males were tenured faculty. When considering the total numbers of male and female faculty approximately 68% of the men have tenure, while only 27% of the women do. The new tenure policy which emphasizes time of service rather than rank should largely remove sex discriminatory treatment in tenure, although the past efforts of discrimination may be relevant in determining damages.

Dr. Gilchrest's analysis of how sex is related to salary at Montana State University (based on information from the university personnel data bank) revealed that female faculty members were likely to earn substantially less money than comparable males. In his study, Gilchrest controlled several variables which might ordinarily be expected to affect salary, including "department," years of experience, and type of degree held. Thus the vast majority of quantitative variables which were used in the study conducted by Dr. Tiahrt were included directly or indirectly in the Gilchrest analysis. Dr. Gilchrest intentionally eliminated "rank" (and rank related variables, such as "tenure," "number of promotions," etc.) in his salary analysis. This was done because Gilchrest's preliminary studies (dealing with promotion) suggested such variables were sex dependent; that is, a comparison of salaries within a particular rank could not detect any sex discriminatory policies in the promotional system itself. The salary differences for the individual women at the university were compared to reference salaries (males in the same department with comparable experience and educational level) and then noted as positive or negative deviations. Dr. Gilchrest concluded in his comparison of salaries, that it would take a total of $222,776 to bring the females up to the level of the males for the year 1974-75.

Dr. Kenneth Tiahrt, professor of statistics at Montana State University, used a "multiple regression" technique in his analysis of salaries at the university; the results of this examination appear in the Affirmative Action Plan. The Tiahrt study sought to determine which of a number of variables were the most significant salary predictors. Based on the numerous quantitative factors he considered, Dr. Tiahrt reasoned that he could not conclude that there was a pattern of salary differential with regard to sex at Montana State University.

Nevertheless, using the sex factor, the Tiahrt analysis shows that there have been inequities at certain ranks in particular years; the sex variable appeared as a salary predictor, especially at the assistant professor and instructor levels. Furthermore, one of the other variables used in the Tiahrt approach was "nursing." At Montana State University, all nurses are female and nearly half of the female instructional faculty are nurses. As Dr. Gilchrest pointed out, it is simply impossible to conclude that any disparity in salaries due to the "nursing" variable was attributable to the fact that the individuals involved were nurses or that they were female. "Nursing" appeared as a variable both in the associate professor and instructor ranks.

The Tiahrt analysis was done "within rank"; it also included variables which the statistics relating to promotion and tenure suggest are sex dependent. Because the Tiahrt salary study was done within each rank, it was impossible to "catch" any discriminatory salary treatment resulting from inequities in promotions. For example, a female assistant professor may be getting a salary comparable to her fellow male assistant professor. But, if she rightfully should be an associate professor and is not because of discriminatory treatment, she should have been earning more money. The Tiahrt approach was not designed to ascertain that problem; thus it cannot contradict the results obtained from Gilchrest's salary analysis.

In both the Tiahrt and Gilchrest salary studies, qualitative variables (*e.g.*, teaching ability, research contributions, community contributions, etc.) were not considered. Therefore, no conclusions as to how such factors affect men and women dissimilarly can be drawn. Although some witnesses referred to "market conditions" and how they may affect salaries within a given year and field, there is no evidence that would indicate *within a department* (the level incorporated in the Gilchrest salary analysis) there is reason to suspect that women have specialities more or less valuable than men.

Tables 11 through 16 of the Affirmative Action Plan compare the predicted salaries of the Tiahrt analysis with the actual salaries of the male and female instructional faculty at Montana State University, to determine what percentages are below or above the predicted salary. These tables show that a greater percentage of females are under the predicted salary in the instructor, assistant professor and associate professor levels. The converse is also true—a greater percentage of men (in all but the full professor level) have actual salaries greater than the predicted level.

Eleanor Pratt's part-time salary study at Montana State University showed large discrepancies between the average salaries of men and women. The salary summary is inaccurate, however, because the data included other than truly part-time faculty members, such as full-time summer session faculty, retired faculty teaching full-time in selected quarters, and faculty teaching less than a full load. Due to this error, it is impossible to conclude that part-time salaries are affected by sex discrimination.

Evidence relating to the percentage of male and female applicants who were granted "sabbatical" and "educational" leaves does not support the conclusion of sex discrimination at Montana State University with regard to leaves. The faculty handbook indicates that "sabbatical" and "educational" leaves may be accompanied by pay, while other types of leaves are not. Although there was testimony suggesting that the percentage of males on leave who received pay was far greater than the percentage of females who were paid while on leave, it is impossible to conclude that these disparities were not due to a higher percentage of women than men applying for nonpaying leaves.

Women at Montana State University as a class have little or no leadership roles on important committees which relate to promotion and tenure and those committees advising the President on matters concerning budgets, personnel, long-range planning and major policy developments. When all boards, standing committees, and councils at Montana State University are considered, the Affirmative Action Plan concludes that women are inadequately represented. Women constitute only a little more than half of the committee representation that they should.

With regard to the individual named plaintiffs, the following facts have been established:

(A) Dr. Helen Mecklenberg is an assistant professor in the biology department who received her doctorate during the year 1972-73. Dr. Mecklenberg was recommended for promotion by her department head, Dr. Pickett in the academic year 1973-74; the promotion recommendation, however, was rejected at the Personnel Committee level. Dr. Mecklenberg contends that she was denied the promotion because of her activities on behalf of women. Dr. Mecklenberg's recommendation for promotion was denied by the Personnel Committee on April 18, 1974, after she had filed a charge of discrimination against the university on February 14, 1974, which was forwarded to the university by the EEOC on March 8, 1974. Although there is testimony denying a discriminatorily motivated denial of Dr. Mecklenberg's promotion, this court finds such explanations merely a "pretext." Dr. Pickett testified that Dr. Mecklenberg's rank in the biology department was low due to her meager research productivity and the fact that her teaching was only average. Yet, these conclusions are incongruous with Dr. Pickett's recommendation for the Mecklenberg promotion. In addition Dr. Mecklenberg was given a merit raise of over $3,000 by her department head without a promotion. Finally, Dr. Mecklenberg was never supplied with a written statement from her department head stating the reasons for the denial of her promotion as is required by § 404 of the faculty handbook; thus there was a departure from what appears to be normal due process in the plaintiff's case.

(B) Both Dr. Kreighbaum and Dr. Lowery are members of the physical education department. Kreighbaum has been employed at the university for ten years and her salary is now $13,600 and Lowery has been employed for thirteen years and her salary is $13,500. Both complained of sex discrimination with regard to salary. Dr. Lowery testified that she was only given a salary increase of $350 for completing her doctorate, whereas Joel LaPray, who received his Ph.D. in the same year received a $500 increase. In 1973, Niles Humphrey received a larger salary increase than Kreighbaum for attaining his Ph.D. and was awarded an additional increase for his promotion from instructor to assistant professor. Neither Kreighbaum nor Lowery received any salary increases for promotions in rank. Other members of the department with higher salaries than the plaintiffs include Mr. Agocs, who has a salary $4,375 higher than Lowery and $4,275 higher than Kreighbaum; Dr. Evans makes $3,500 more than Lowery and $3,400 more than Kreighbaum; Mr. Lambert makes $3,840 more than Lowery and $3,740 more than Kreighbaum; and Dr. Morris, employed last year, was hired at a salary greater than Kreighbaum's and slightly less than Lowery's.

Although there is evidence to the effect that Lowery and Kreighbaum received very large percentage increases in their salaries in the past few years, they are still thousands of dollars below their male counterparts. At any rate, percentage increases are meaningless when utilized in comparisons. For example 85% of a small salary may be less than 40% of a salary that was much larger to begin with.

The defendants have rebutted the above salary comparison with a number of comparisons of their own, concluding that some men were paid more because of coaching duties, more experience, graduate studies responsibilities, or degree specialties. Yet it was admitted that Dr. Kreighbaum's Ph.D. (biomechanics) is an area for which there is high demand. The head of the physical education department testified that both Kreighbaum and Lowery were very competent first rate faculty members. Some of the males the plaintiffs compared themselves with did not have doctorate degrees, one had far less experience, and one had given up his coaching responsibilities long ago. Mr. Lambert has no coaching duties and no doctorate and yet he was still paid considerably more than the plaintiffs. The court finds the excuses for the salary disparities given by the defendants in rebuttal are merely a pretext for discriminatory treatment of Dr. Lowery and Dr. Kreighbaum.

(C) Eleanor Pratt is a former part-time faculty member of the language department at Montana State University who was refused an appointment to a part-time position in the fall of 1974 because her department head objected to her activities on behalf of women.

There is further evidence of retaliation against Ms. Pratt in that a part-time position in French was advertised in the fall of 1975, but when she inquired about it with the department head, she was told that Ms. Franklin was being offered the job. It is rather incongruous that the university should advertise a position which was previously filled by one particular individual (who was already a full time employee) but when Ms. Pratt inquired, state that the position was being filled by that same individual.

(D) Jeanne Claus has been employed by Montana State University since 1958. She holds a master's degree and was an assistant professor for 16 years until her promotion to associate professor for 1975-76. Ms. Claus complains that she was never informed of the requirements for promotion or that she was eligible for promotion.

The court finds that the evidence with regard to Jeanne Claus does not support the discrimination charged. Ms. Claus was aware or should have been aware of other associate professors in the nursing department who only had a master's degree. In addition, the promotion policy of the university is printed in the faculty handbook.

Conclusions of Law

This court has jurisdiction over the subject matter of this suit and the parties involved under 42 U.S.C. 2000e-5(f)(3), 28 U.S.C. § 1343, 42 U.S.C. § 1983 and § 1981, 29 U.S.C. § 206, and 28 U.S.C. §§ 2201 and 2202. The court also has pendent jurisdiction over a state equal pay claim provided for in Revised Codes of Montana (1947), § 41-1307.

It is "hypertechnical" to insist on absolute compliance with the formal pleading requirements of EEOC administrative charges. "It is sufficient that the EEOC be apprised, in general terms, of the alleged discriminating parties and the alleged discriminatory acts." Therefore the Board of Regents and President McIntosh in addition to Montana State University are proper party defendants in this action.

In addition to the complaints of discriminatory policies with regard to salaries and promotions, the charges of retaliation, underutilization of women on the faculty, and discriminatory policies preventing women from becoming deans, vice presidents or members of important committees were properly before this court. All of those complaints were included in an amendment to the EEOC administrative charges and such amendment relates back to the original filing date of the charge.

The named plaintiffs have standing as individuals and on behalf of the women who have been affected by the discriminatory policies of the defendants.

* * *

Statistics alone may establish a prima facie case of discrimination against a class. "In many cases, the only available avenue of proof is the use of racial statistics to uncover clandestine and covert discrimination by the employer. . . . "

Studies that show experience requirements are sometimes waived for males, but never for females suggest discrimination.

The evidence shows discrimination against women as a class by the defendants at Montana State University in that females are underutilized as deans, vice presidents, department heads and as instructional faculty in many departments of the University.

Women have also been discriminated against as a class in the areas of promotion, tenure, salary, and appointment to important university committees.

The evidence does not support a finding of sex discrimination by the defendants with regard to part time salaries and faculty "leaves."

In the private individual Title VII [42 U.S.C. 2000e, et seq.] suit, the plaintiff must carry the initial burden of establishing a prima facie case of discrimination. The burden then shifts to the employer to articulate some "legitimate, nondiscriminatory reason for the employee's rejection." Then the plaintiff must be afforded an opportunity to show that the defendant's stated reason for the rejection was in fact a pretext. Included among the types of evidence which may be used to establish "pretext" is *statistical evidence reflecting a general pattern of discrimination.*

The evidence shows discrimination on the basis of sex against the named individuals as follows:

A) Helen Mecklenberg has suffered discriminatory retaliation in the area of promotion;

B) Ellen Kreighbaum and Bette Lowery have been discriminated against in the area of salary;

C) Eleanor Pratt has suffered retaliatory discrimination in the form of hiring.

Nonrenewal of even an untenured teacher may not be predicated on his exercise of First or Fourteenth amendment rights.

The evidence shows no discrimination on the basis of sex against Jeanne Claus with regard to promotion.

Pursuant to Title 41, § 1307 of the Revised Codes of Montana (1947), the plaintiffs as individuals and as a class are entitled to equal pay for equal work and the defendants have failed to comply with said provisions.

The plaintiffs are entitled as a class to damages under 42 U.S.C. 2000e-5(g). Damages in this case, however, have been bifurcated from the issues of liability, and will be determined at a later date, to be set upon the agreement of the parties and the court.

The defendants are enjoined from further discrimination against the named plaintiffs as individuals and the class of women they represent. More particularized equitable relief may be ordered by the court at the time the questions regarding damages are resolved.

In *Academics in Court*, La Noue and Lee recounted the Mecklenberg case and its interesting history. The case has been relatively unknown, for it was not published by Judge Murray in a Federal Reporter. They note that if her attorney had not been invited to submit the decision to CCH for its commercial publication, "The *Mecklenberg* opinion might have been the legal equivalent to the Zen riddle of whether a tree makes a noise when it falls deep in the forest where no one can hear it."

Fields v. Clark University
817 F.2d 931 (1st Cir. 1987)

BOWNES, Circuit Judge.

In this opinion we consider both the plaintiff's and defendant's appeals from a district court order in a suit brought under Title VII of the Civil Rights Act of 1964,

42 U.S.C. §§ 2000e to e-17 (1982). The court found that the process by which plaintiff was denied tenure at Clark University was tainted with sexual discrimination. It did not order that she be granted tenure, however, because the court also found that she failed to prove she was so entitled. It ordered that plaintiff be reinstated for a two-year probationary period and then reconsidered for tenure, and awarded her back pay, attorney's fees, and costs. We hold that the court erred in its allocation of the burdens of proof, and, therefore, vacate the court's order and remand the case for a new trial.

I. BACKGROUND

In 1972, Clark University hired Rona Fields as a full-time associate professor in the sociology department. She was considered for tenure after her second year of teaching. At the initial stage of the review process, six members of the sociology department, all male, voted unanimously to recommend that she not be given tenure. Fields contested this decision. She submitted additional materials on her own behalf at subsequent meetings, but on review the members of the department unanimously affirmed their decision, and the president of the university was notified of the outcome.

The departmental vote was referred to the committee on personnel, which is charged with advising the university's president on evaluations of the faculty's professional credentials. The committee reviewed the file on which the faculty relied, which was supplemented by materials Fields submitted. It also obtained additional student evaluations of her teaching. The committee voted twice—each time unanimously—to accept the faculty's recommendation, and it forwarded this decision to the board of trustees. The committee denied a request for reconsideration by Fields.

On May 9, 1975, the board of trustees voted to give Fields a one-year terminal appointment ending August 31, 1976. She asked the university to form a faculty review committee to examine the decision, alleging a number of procedural irregularities and charging sexual bias. Such a committee was appointed in June 1975; it convened in January 1976 and held a number of meetings. It reported that there was no evidence Fields was denied tenure because of sexual bias, and concluded that the sociology department, the committee on personnel, and the board of trustees had adequately considered her case.

Fields filed charges with the Equal Employment Opportunity Commission and the Massachusetts Commission Against Discrimination, claiming that the tenure decision constituted unlawful discrimination. The Equal Employment Opportunity Commission found reasonable cause to believe the allegations and issued a right to sue letter. Fields subsequently instituted this action in district court.

The allegations of sexual discrimination focused on the all-male sociology department. According to Fields, the members of the department subjected her to "a continuous course of sexual harassment, sexual innuendo and denigration of her professional status." She claims an associate professor who had just been awarded tenure made sexual advances toward her, and when she rejected them, he warned that her refusal "was no way to get tenure." This associate professor later participated in the departmental vote recommending that Fields be denied tenure.

The university, on the other hand, claims that the sociology department's negative recommendation, and the university's decision not to grant Fields tenure, were made because she was a poor teacher. To substantiate its claim, the university relied principally on student evaluations and the comments of other professors, some solicited by Fields, which criticized her teaching.

After a nonjury trial, the district court found that the sociology department "was generally permeated with sexual discrimination of which the plaintiff was in fact a victim." It did "not find any evidence of improper bias in the subsequent review procedure or on the part of the ultimate deciding authority, the board of trustees." It concluded that the departmental recommendation "was the most significant step in the tenure process," and that she had "proved by a preponderance of the evidence" that the sociology department's sexual bias rendered the tenure decision "impermissibly infected with sexual discrimination, and accordingly, she is entitled to relief under Title VII."

The court also said, however, that Fields had "not proved that on this record she is entitled to tenure." It found that "the record raises substantial questions as to the plaintiff's capacity as a teacher." It noted testimony that student evaluations of her teaching were unusually negative. There was evidence that a female tenured faculty member said she could not recommend that Field be granted tenure. The female dean of women also gave a negative recommendation, and she reported many complaints about the way Fields taught. The court ordered the university to reinstate Fields for a two-year probationary period and to reconsider her for tenure afterward "under circumstances free of sexual discrimination." She was also awarded $25,000 back pay and $75,697.72 in attorney's fees and costs.

Fields argues that the court misallocated the burdens of proof. According to her, she was entitled to reinstatement with tenure and full back pay. She also claims the court erred in reducing the hourly rate at which her lead counsel's attorney's fees were computed. The university cross-appeals, also claiming that the burdens of proof were incorrectly applied and that it was entitled to a verdict. Additionally, the university claims that the court erred by allowing an associate professor, who was hired in the sociology department after Fields left, to testify about sexual harassment occurring four years after Fields was denied tenure. Lastly, Clark alleges that the damage award and the computation of attorney's fees were flawed in various respects.

II. BURDENS OF PROOF

Fields claims the court's ruling that the tenure decision was "impermissibly infected with sexual discrimination" meant that she carried her burden of persuasion. She argues that the burden then shifted to the university to prove that, even if there had been no discrimination, she would not have been granted tenure. The university claims that the burden of persuasion remained at all times on Fields, and that the court's conclusion that she failed to prove she was entitled to tenure required a defendant's verdict.

Title VII prohibits employers from discriminating on the basis of race, color, religion, sex, or national origin in hiring and with respect to the privileges and conditions of employment. 42 U.S.C. § 2000e-2(a). A plaintiff does not have to present direct proof of discriminatory motive to prevail in a Title VII suit. A plaintiff can establish a prima facie case of discrimination if she "prove[s] by a pr[e]ponderance of the evidence that she applied for an available position for which she was qualified, but was rejected under circumstances which give rise to an inference of unlawful discrimination." The Supreme Court set out the order and allocation of the burdens of proof for such a case in *McDonnell Douglas Corp. v. Green*:

First, the plaintiff has the burden of proving by the preponderance of the evidence a prima facie case of discrimination. Second, if the plaintiff succeeds in proving the prima facie case, the burden shifts to the defendant "to articulate some legitimate, nondiscriminatory reason for the employee's rejection." Third, should the defendant carry this burden, the plaintiff must then have an opportunity to prove by a preponderance of the evidence that the legitimate reasons offered by the defendant were not its true reasons, but were a pretext for discrimination.

When an adverse employment decision has been made under circumstances that raise an inference of discriminatory treatment, the employee is entitled "to an explanation from the defendant-employer for whatever action was taken." This court has applied the *McDonnell Douglas* approach in a line of Title VII cases arising in an academic setting.

The burden of proving a prima facie case can be met "by showing that a qualified applicant, who was a member of a [protected class], had unsuccessfully sought a job for which there was a vacancy and for which the employer continued thereafter to seek applicants with similar qualifications." The district court did not rule specifically on whether Fields made out a prima facie case under the *McDonnell Douglas* approach. To show that she was qualified for tenure and satisfy the second step of the prima facie case, Fields must have shown that her qualifications were such that a decision granting tenure would have been a reasonable exercise of discretion. Even if Fields did so, "[t]he burden on the defendant is only to rebut the plaintiff's prima facie case; the burden of persuasion rests at all times with the plaintiff." The defendant need only "articulate some legitimate, nondiscriminatory reason" for its decision. The university articulated such a reason—poor teaching—and produced evidence, chiefly in the form of student evaluations and faculty recommendations, to substantiate it. Under *McDonnell Douglas*, the burden would then be on Fields to prove by a preponderance of the evidence that this reason was a mere pretext for sexual discrimination. The district court did not go through this analysis, and it is unclear what its finding would have been on the question of pretext, for while the court found that "the record raises substantial questions as to the plaintiff's capacity as a teacher," the court also found that "two male faculty members with poor teaching evaluation, ...one with less scholarly achievement than the plaintiff, were accorded tenure after a favorable vote from the department."

The question here, however, is not how *McDonnell Douglas* should be applied, but whether it should be applied at all. The court did not grant a verdict for the defendant because it found "strong evidence of a pervasively sexist attitude on the part of the male members of the sociology department." If this meant Fields had proved by direct evidence that sexual discrimination was a motivating factor in the decision to deny her tenure, the court was correct in not following the *McDonnell Douglas* test. It erred, however, in its subsequent rulings.

The Supreme Court has instructed that the shifting burdens of proof set forth in *McDonnell Douglas* are "inapplicable where the plaintiff presents direct evidence of discrimination."

Nevertheless, a plaintiff who has established that unlawful discrimination was a motivating factor in an employment decision is not necessarily entitled to relief under Title VII. The statute forbids the courts to "require the...hiring, reinstatement, or promotion of an individual as an employee, or the payment to him of any back pay, if such individual was refused admission, suspended, or expelled, or was refused employment or advancement or was suspended or discharged *for any reason other than discrimination*." 42 U.S.C. § 2000e-5(g). Therefore, before the court could order that Fields be reinstated or paid back salary, the cause of the tenure decision had to be determined. She is not entitled to such relief solely on the basis that the decision was infected with discrimination. But discrimination need not be the sole reason for an adverse job decision for a plaintiff to be entitled to Title VII relief; "no more is required to be shown than that [it] was a 'but for' cause."

The question, which is one of first impression in this circuit, is whether a plaintiff who has proved by direct evidence that unlawful discrimination was a motivating factor in the employment decision must also prove that it was a 'but for' cause. Based on our review of the law, we conclude that the *McDonnell Douglas* format should not be slavishly followed and that, after such proof by the plaintiff, the defendant must prove that the same decision would have been made absent the discrimination.

The logic of such an approach is inescapable. The employer is in the best position to prove which of its motives were determinative. As Justice Scalia said while on the District of Columbia Circuit, "it is unreasonable and destructive of the purposes of Title VII to require the plaintiff to establish in addition the difficult hypothetical proposition that, had there been no discrimination, the employment decision would have been made in his favor." Furthermore, as the Supreme Court has explained in the context of unfair labor practices,

> [t]he employer is a wrongdoer; he has acted out of a motive that is declared illegitimate by the statute. It is fair that he bear the risk that the influence of legal and illegal motives cannot be separated, because he knowingly created the risk and because the risk was created not by innocent activity but by his own wrongdoing.

* * *

We hold that when a plaintiff has proved by direct evidence that unlawful discrimination was a motivating factor in an employment decision, the burden is on the employer to prove by a preponderance of the evidence that the same decision would have been made absent the discrimination. We recognize that some courts have required the defendant to carry its burden of proof by "clear and convincing" evidence. Others require proof by a preponderance of the evidence. Because of the difficulties inherent in proving what might have been done in a hypothetical situation, we think the test usually applied in civil cases—preponderance of the evidence—is the appropriate one. Moreover, this is the test employed by the Supreme Court in *Mt. Healthy*, a case in which constitutional rights were at stake, and the Court fashioned the procedure by which a defendant could prove "that it would have reached the same decision as to respondent's reemployment even in the absence of the protected conduct." We see no reason to adopt a more demanding test in this context.

The district court's finding that sexual discrimination "impermissibly infected" the decision not to grant Fields tenure appears to us to be the equivalent of a finding that she proved by direct evidence that discrimination was a motivating factor in the decision. This finding cannot be reconciled with the court's putting the burden on Fields to prove that she was entitled to tenure. Therefore, the court erred in its allocation of this burden of proof. The court also erred by reinstating Fields for two years and awarding back pay without finding that the university, after having been afforded the opportunity to prove Fields would not have been granted tenure absent discrimination, failed to carry its burden of proof. We, therefore, remand the case for a new trial on all issues by another district court judge.

Vacated and remanded for proceedings consistent with this opinion.

No costs.

After a 1986 ruling, Professor Fields had returned to Clark University, 10 years after she had left. During her first semester back on the job (Spring 1987), the Appeals Court ruled against her and remanded for a new trial. She left Clark once again. "Former Professor Doggedly Pursues Sex-Bias Charges 13 Years After She Was Denied Tenure at Clark U.," *Chronicle of Higher Education*, 9 December 1987, A 15-16.

Denny v. Westfield State College
669 F. Supp. 1146 (D. Mass. 1987)

FINDINGS OF FACT
A. Parties

Plaintiff Leah Stern is a female who was employed by defendants from August 1973 to August 1977 in the Philosophy Department of Westfield State College.

Plaintiff Marilyn Denny is a female who was employed by defendants from December 1971 to August 1977 in the Sociology Department of Westfield State College.

Plaintiff Catherine Dower is a female who has been employed by defendants since 1956 in the Music Department of Westfield State College.

Defendants Westfield State College and the Board of Regents of Higher Education are agencies of the Commonwealth of Massachusetts, and are "employers" within the meaning of 42 U.S.C. § 2000e.

B. Evidence of Discrimination

Prior to trial, the parties entered a stipulation providing:

> The job requirements for all teachers, within ranks, are substantially equal in terms of skill, effort, and responsibility and are performed under similar working conditions.

> However, the parties acknowledge that different teachers may have different professional qualifications including different skills, experience, education, and disciplinary and technical backgrounds. Nothing contained in this stipulation shall be deemed to mean that the college could not properly have taken these factors into consideration when fixing initial salaries, entitlements to promotions and other benefits affecting the rates of compensation of faculty members, provided that whether the college considered such factors or the legitimacy of the method used to consider such factors are the issues to be determined at trial.

Plaintiffs' evidence at trial consisted of the testimony of plaintiff Dower and Arlene S. Ash, Ph.D., a Professor of Statistics. Dr. Ash undertook a statistical study of wages at WSC, the results of which were admitted at trial. Defendants' evidence consisted of the testimony of Ernest T. Kendall, Ph.D., a labor economist, who also performed a statistical study of WSC's system of compensation, and Jean Regan, formerly an employee in the personnel office of the Board of Regents of Higher Education (successor to the Board of Trustees of State Colleges).

1. Statistical Evidence

Both Dr. Ash and Dr. Kendall used a statistical method known as multiple regression analysis to produce their different opinions. Briefly put, multiple regression analysis is a computer-assisted statistical method by a which a variety of factors ("explanatory variables") are considered at one time to determine their combined effect on another variable such as salary ("outcome variable"). In this case, Drs. Ash and Kendall set out to determine how factors such as seniority, departmental affiliation, and prior experience, affected the salaries of WSC faculty members. The theory goes: to the extent salaries at WSC are not fully explained by these factors, an impermissible factor, such as sex, may account for the discrepancy. Moreover, assuming the proper variables are selected and that the result of the analysis is "statistically significant," the amount of salary differential due to sex discrimination may be estimated.

Though both Drs. Ash and Kendall used this basic method, they actually used two different types of regression analysis. Dr. Kendall used what is known as the "dummy variable" technique whereas Dr. Ash performed "men only" regressions. Each criticized the other's chosen methodology, but generally agreed that neither approach is demonstrably superior to the other.

a. Dr. Ash's Regression Analysis

Relying on data supplied by defendants during discovery, Dr. Ash coded information for all full-time faculty members at WSC during the years 1974 through 1984. Dr. Ash used the following explanatory variables: departmental grouping, seniority at WSC, years of prior tenure-track teaching experience, years of other relevant prior experience, current rank, and the number of years since a terminal degree (e.g. Ph.D. or M.F.A.) was obtained. Using this model, Dr. Ash reported that she was able to "explain" over seventy percent of variation in men's salaries at WSC in every year studied except one. However, in the latter years of her study, Dr. Ash's results tended to provide less explanation of salary variance among male faculty members.

* * *

[c. Dr. Kendall's Regression Analysis]

Dr. Kendall "explained" the statistically significant findings in the latter years by attempting to demonstrate that the sex differentials could be accounted for by differences in starting salaries of new faculty members in two particularly competitive fields—business.administration and computer sciences. To reach this result, defendants begin with a basic assumption: "Sex-related differentials in salary could have arisen at Westfield State College during the period in question through one or more of four possible avenues. Males could have been favored in (1) promotions, (2) starting salaries, (3) distinguished service awards, or (4) starting salaries." From there, they analyze data concerning each of these four factors and conclude that "[a]nalysis of the first three have revealed absolutely no evidence that males were given preferential treatment with respect to any of these determinants of salary...." This suggests, according to defendants, that the source of salary differential must be starting salaries in the period 1980 to 1984.

Defendants state:

> It was during this period that Westfield State College sought to expand its program in computer science and business administration. Between 1980 and 1984, the College hired a total of 48 new faculty members, 21 of whom were in the fields of computer science and business. Of these 21 new faculty, only 2 were women. In contrast 14 of the 27 faculty hired into the other departments were women.
>
> What happened at Westfield is now readily understood. Faculty in the computer science and business administration are in two fields where the competition for qualified personnel is very strong, both inside and outside of academia. In order to staff these two growing departments, it was necessary for the College to add substantial market adjustments to starting salaries in order to compete in a market-place that is dominated by private industry. Because most of those hired were males, many males were given substantial salary adjustments in response to these market forces; as a direct result the average male starting salary rose substantially above that of females.

At first glance, this appears to be a persuasive explanation for the seemingly discriminatory wage structure at WSC. Closer scrutiny belies this, however. For one thing, the Court does not find that an adequate foundation was laid for these results. As defendants elsewhere argue

> "because of the sophistication and complexity of many of the statistical models being used in discrimination cases by professional econometricians, courts must give 'close scrutiny [to the] empirical proof' on which the models are erected ...in order to guard against the use of statistical data that may have been 'segmented and particularized and fashioned to obtain a desired result.'"

By looking at these four factors in isolation, perhaps defendants are guilty of the very segmenting and particularizing they caution against. Defendants have not shown that these analyses are based on anything but gross statistics of particular variables, the relationship of which to the entire data set is unclear at best.

Apart from this general criticism, even assuming Dr. Kendall was correct that every valid explanation for wage disparity could be eliminated except for starting salaries in two departments, this approach hardly accounts for the entire variance revealed in the studies of Drs. Ash and Kendall. Thus, whatever may have occurred in the period in which WSC was attempting to "beef up" its business administration and computer science departments, this does not explain the statistically significant results Dr. Ash uncovered for pre-1980 years. It is also misleading to assume that the special cases of the business administration and computer science departments are relevant for the entire period of 1980 to 1984 because, as plaintiffs state, no bonuses were given in the business administration department in the years 1980, 1981 and 1982 and none given in the computer science department in 1980 and 1981.

In addition, defendants seem to be double counting the computer science department. As plaintiffs note, Residual R-1 already contains a marker for a professor's membership in the computer science department. Having already accounted for the effect of service in this department in his regression, Dr. Kendall cannot also point to . . . computer science to explain statistically significant results his analysis revealed.

2. Non-Statistical Evidence

Through the evidence at trial consisted mostly of statistical evidence, both sides presented some non-statistical evidence to prove or rebut discrimination.

Plaintiff Dower testified that in 1967 she had a conversation with Dr. Leonard Savignano, then President of Westfield State. Plaintiff Dower approached Dr. Savignano because she felt her salary was low compared to comparable males at WSC. Dr. Savignano reportedly told Dr. Dower that men needed higher salaries than women because they had families to support and that the only way she could improve her salary was by getting her Ph.D. so she could be promoted from assistant professor to the rank of associate professor. Based on this conversation, plaintiff Dower eventually obtained her Ph.D. and was promoted. According to Jean Regan, an employee of the Board of Regents of Higher Education, the requirement of a Ph.D. for promotion to associate professor had in fact been adopted by the Board of Trustees of State Colleges in 1967. Thus, even if one assumes that Dr. Savignano did make the discriminatory statement, his advice to Dr. Dower seems to have been quite legitimate.

Dr. Regan also testified to the effect that the Board of Regents of Higher Education or any of its previous incarnations had the final say on the question of faculty salaries. Though this was literally true, it seems that the recommendation from a president of one of the state colleges was accorded great weight.

The remainder of the evidence was of the pseudo-statistical variety comparing each one of the plaintiffs to one or another of the male faculty members. This evidence not only swings both ways but it is also singularly unconvincing. The Court, therefore, gives it very little weight.

III. CONCLUSIONS OF LAW

* * *

In order to make out a claim for disparate impact in a traditional Title VII case, plaintiffs must first establish a prima facie case of discrimination by a preponderance of the evidence. The burden then shifts to the defendants to articulate a legitimate, nondiscriminatory reason for their challenged actions. If defendants do so, plaintiffs are then given an opportunity to establish by a preponderance of the evidence that the reasons asserted by the defendants are a mere pretext for unlawful discrimination. However, "[t]he ultimate burden of persuading the trier of fact that the defendant intentionally discriminated against the plaintiff . . . 'remains at all times with the plaintiff.' "

Though this action was tried solely as a Title VII case, plaintiffs argue that the burdens of proof applicable to actions under the Equal Pay Act of 1963, 29 U.S.C. § 206(d) ("EPA"), should govern.

> The Equal Pay Act provides as follows:
>
> No employer having employees subject to any provisions of this section shall discriminate, within any establishment in which such employees are employed, between employees on the basis of sex by paying wages to employees in such establishment at a rate less than the rate at which he pays wages to employees of the opposite sex in such establishment for equal work on jobs the performance

of which requires equal skill, effort, and responsibility, and which are performed under similar working conditions, except where such payment is made pursuant to (i) a seniority system; (ii) a merit system; (iii) a system which measures earnings by quantity or quality of production; or (iv) a differential based on any further factor other than sex.

Generally, EPA is a narrower remedial statute than Title VII. Unlike Title VII, EPA does not prohibit discrimination in hiring, firing or promoting employees and it is applicable to a much narrower range of employers. However, because of the way burdens of proof are allocated in an Equal Pay Act case, a plaintiff may be able to prevail under that Act where she could not under Title VII. This is because, unlike an ordinary Title VII case, the defendant in an Equal Pay Act has the burden of persuasion as well as production on the four enumerated defenses.

Attempts at "integrating" Title VII and EPA have their origin in the so-called Bennett Amendment to Title VII. Section 703(h) of the Civil Rights Act of 1964, 42 U.S.C. § 2000e-2(h). The amendment provides:

> It shall not be an unlawful employment practice under this title for an employer to differentiate upon the basis of sex in determining the amount of the wages or compensation paid or to be paid to employees of such employer if such differentiation is authorized by the provisions of section 6(d) of the Fair Labor Standards Act as amended (29 U.S.C. § 206(d)).

In *County of Washington v. Gunther,* the Court explained to what degree the Bennett Amendment actually limited a Title VII plaintiff. In *Gunther,* the Court considered whether, by virtue of the Bennett Amendment, EPA's "equal work" requirement was applicable to Title VII plaintiffs. After reviewing the legislative history, the Court concluded it did not. The Court held that "only differentials attributable to the four affirmative defenses of the Equal Pay Act are 'authorized' by that Act within the meaning of [the Bennett Amendment]." The Court left unanswered questions about "how sex-based wage discrimination litigation under Title VII should be structured to accommodate" the affirmative defense of EPA.

Relying on *Gunther,* the Ninth Circuit in *Kouba v. Allstate Insurance Co.,* held that EPA's order of proof was applicable to Title VII claims. As the court stated:

> [E]ven under Title VII, the employer bears the burden of showing that the wage differential resulted from a factor other than sex. . . . Nothing in *Burdine* converts this affirmative defense which the employer must plead and prove under *Corning Glass,* into an element of the cause of action, which the employee must show does not exist.

This approach is rejected in *EEOC v. Sears, Roebuck & Co.* In that case the district court analyzed the legislative history to the Bennett Amendment and concluded that "Congress did not intend the Bennett Amendment to impose Equal Pay Act burdens and elements of proof to pay claims brought under Title VII."

To date, the First Circuit has not ruled on the question of whether EPA's burdens of proofs are applicable to Title VII equal pay claims. The issue was discussed in *Marcoux v. State of Maine,* in which the district court adopted the *Kouba* approach, but because neither party had raised an objection below, the Court of Appeals declined to rule.

This Court concludes that *Kouba* and its progeny (which constitute the clear weight of authority) represent the better view. The Equal Pay Act and Title VII "are in *pari materia* and must be construed in harmony with one another." The Supreme Court's holding in *Gunther* demonstrates that the Bennett Amendment is not simply, as *Sears, Roebuck* would have it, a "protect[ion to] employers in Title VII cases by requiring them to meet a greater burden of proof." Rather, the Bennett Amendment is a device intended to harmonize the protections of two, somewhat overlapping statutory schemes by incorporating EPA's four affirmative defenses into Title VII. Indeed, the very notion of an "affirmative defense" strongly suggests that, as with other affirmative defenses, the party claiming its benefit has the burden, not just of pleading, but also of persuading the trier of fact by a preponderance of the evidence that the party should prevail on the defense. Accordingly, the Court will proceed to analyze plaintiffs' claim under the EPA approach.

In light of this conclusion, plaintiffs are required initially to establish that they received lower salaries than men for comparable work. Once this is established, defendants have the burden of persuading the Court, by a preponderance of evidence, that the wage disparity was the result of (i) a seniority system; (ii) a merit system; (iii) a system which measures earnings by quantity or quality of production; or (iv) a differential based on any further factor other than sex.

The Court concludes plaintiffs have established their initial burden of demonstrating a *prima facie* case. The parties have stipulated to the comparable nature of the work performed by male and female faculty members at WSC. Plaintiffs have also established discriminatory wage differentials by a preponderance of the evidence through the statistical analyses presented at trial. Such evidence alone is sufficient to establish plaintiffs' *prima facie* case. Though the Court has expressed criticism for some aspects of Dr. Ash's report, on the whole the Court finds that the report is sufficient to demonstrate that female faculty members at WSC received significantly lower salaries than male faculty members given equivalent experience, rank, years since receiving doctorate and departmental affiliation.

In Title VII terms, defendants have articulated a legitimate, non-discriminatory reason for the salary differential at WSC; in EPA terms, defendants have come forward with some evidence to sustain the defense that female faculty members at WSC received lower salaries than equivalent males because of "a differential based on any further factor other than sex," 29 U.S.C. § 206(d)(1)(iv): according to defendants' expert, Dr. Kendall, the salary differential uncovered by Dr. Ash can be explained by two variables not fully accounted for in Dr. Ash's study—market forces as reflected in departmental affiliation and exceptional performance as reflected in distinguished service awards. However, as the Court noted above, apart from serious statistical short-comings in defendants' argument, defendants are unable to account for salary discrepancies in all years studied.

The Court finds, however, that while defendants have satisfied their burden of production, they have failed to sustain their burden of proving, by a preponderance of the evidence, that the salary differentials for faculty members at WSC in the years studied were due to factors other than sex.

IV. CONCLUSION

The Court finds that the named plaintiffs have sustained their burden of proving a violation of 42 U.S.C. §§ 2000e, *et seq.*, with respect to their claim that they received lower salaries than similarly situated males at WSC, and that this differential was due to illegal sex discrimination. Moreover, the Court finds that plaintiffs are entitled to an award of backpay limited by the periods in which the administrative complaints were filed as measured by the extent of the wage disparities discovered in Dr. Ash's results. The parties are ordered to attempt to stipulate to a proposed form of judgment within thirty days. Should stipulation prove impossible, the parties may submit separate proposed judgments within this time period.

The Equal Pay Act of 1963 was amended in 1972 to apply to colleges and universities. Since that time, male and female plaintiffs have sued their institutions over disparities in pay. In *Board of Regents of the University of Nebraska v. Dawes*, the salary equalization plan was challenged by male faculty, who "established that the members of the class [males who made less than the females' new formula amount] were unlawfully discriminated against." 522 F. 2d 380 (1975), *cert. denied*, 424 U.S. 914 (1976).

Subsequent EPA cases have to reckon with *United Steelworkers of America v. Weber*, a Supreme Court case that upheld racial affirmative plans entered into voluntarily. Under Title VII, private, voluntary race-conscious plans are permissible, provided they are narrowly drawn for the purpose of opening employment opportunities for minorities, and do not bar whites entirely from participation or require the discharge of whites. 443 U.S. 193 (1979). In *Lyon v. Temple University*, the District Court held that a *Dawes*-like plan could not be permitted even after the *Weber* decision because it placed the male professors at an unnecessarily permanent disadvantage. 543 F. Supp. 1372 (E.D. Pa. 1982); See also *Hein v. Oregon College of Education*, 718 F. 2d 910 (1983). In *Ende v. Board of Regents of Northern Illinois University*, the Court followed the *Weber* reasoning and allowed a *Dawes*-like plan that only adjusted women's salaries: "The *Lyon* Court, in our opinion, reads *Weber* too narrowly." 565 F. Supp. 501 (1983). Even where a college's plan is "relatively weak" or "flawed and inadequate," if it is implemented in good faith, it will be found acceptable. *Ottaviani v. SUNY at New Paltz*, 45 EPD 37, 720 (1988). For a review of the literature on equal pay and its corollary doctrine, comparable worth, see K. Weeks, "Equal Pay: The Emerging Terrain," *Journal of College and University Law,* 12 (1985), 41-60; K. Weeks and J. Organ, "Educational Institutions and Comparable Worth: A Doctrine in Search of Applications," *Journal of Law and Education*, 15 (1986), 207–228.

Johnson v. University of Wisconsin-Milwaukee
783 F.2d 59 (7th Cir. 1986)

CUMMINGS, Chief Judge.

This case involves an age discrimination suit brought by plaintiff Edna Johnson ("plaintiff"), pursuant to the provisions of the Age Discrimination in Employment Act of 1967, as amended, 29 U.S.C. §§ 621 *et seq.* ("ADEA"), against the defendant University of Wisconsin-Milwaukee ("defendant"). Plaintiff appeals from the district court's order denying plaintiff's motion for judgment notwithstanding the verdict ("JNOV") or for a new trial. For the reasons set out below, we affirm.

I

Plaintiff was born April 17, 1922, and was hired by defendant November 11, 1965. She initially worked for defendant as a secretary for several years. Around 1973 or 1974, she began to work in defendant's Fringe Benefits Office, and in 1978 became a retirement counselor. She was working as a payroll and benefit staff counselor when she was terminated on September 17, 1981.

Plaintiff contested her termination through the arbitration procedure afforded by her state employment contract. Not surprisingly, plaintiff and defendant disagreed as to the reasons for her termination. Defendant contended that plaintiff was terminated because she was unable to complete routine work assignments, attempted to avoid work, and performed work incorrectly. Plaintiff argued that her discharge was in retaliation for the legal action taken by her son, who was terminated by the University in September 1980, against certain University officials. The arbitrator found that plaintiff was not terminated because of age or handicap discrimination, retaliation against her son's legal actions against certain University officials, or nepotism. The arbitrator further decided that plaintiff was not discharged for just cause, but ruled that there was just cause for a ten-week suspension without pay, and ordered that she be reinstated with back pay less pay for the ten-week suspension and less earnings from other employment during the period since her discharge.

Plaintiff also applied for unemployment compensation benefits after her termination. The matter proceeded to a contested hearing before the Appeal Tribunal of the State of Wisconsin Department of Industry, Labor and Human Relations, which ruled that plaintiff was not terminated for "misconduct" within the meaning of Wis. Stat. § 108.04(5) (1974), and hence was entitled to unemployment compensation benefits. As part of his findings, the hearing examiner stated that although there is some evidence that plaintiff committed errors and failed to perform certain aspects of her job, plaintiff "for the last several months of her employment . . . had been beset by her immediate supervisors with a concerted program of formal disciplinary proceedings, a substantial amount of which was specious or contrived." The hearing examiner did not state the motivation for this concerted program of specious disciplinary hearings.

Plaintiff subsequently brought this age discrimination suit in federal district court. Plaintiff moved for partial summary judgment, arguing that the decisions of both the arbitrator and the Wisconsin appeal tribunal should preclude defendant from raising the defense that plaintiff was terminated as the result of a legitimate business decision. The court denied plaintiff's motion. During the jury trial that ensued, plaintiff attempted through various means to introduce evidence that plaintiff was discharged in retaliation for her son's legal action. However, the court refused to admit the appeal tribunal's decision into evidence, and rejected as irrelevant the testimony of plaintiff and another witness that defendant terminated plaintiff in retaliation for her son's legal action. The court did admit the arbitrator's decision and award into evidence, and allowed the parties to stipulate that plaintiff had to sue in order to collect unemployment compensation benefits. The jury found that plaintiff's age was not a determining factor in her termination. The court denied plaintiff's motion for JNOV or for a new trial. At no time did plaintiff move for a directed verdict.

II

At the outset, we must untangle several procedural knots created by plaintiff before we can reach the merits of this case.

*   *   *

[N]either the arbitrator's determination nor the Wisconsin appeal tribunal's decision precludes defendant from proffering a legitimate, nondiscriminatory reason for terminating plaintiff.

The second issue on appeal is whether evidence of defendant's retaliatory motive against plaintiff for plaintiff's son's legal action against various officials of the University was wrongfully excluded as irrelevant to the issue of whether defendant's proffered reason for terminating plaintiff was pretextual. To answer this question, the various methods of proof in an age discrimination suit must be reviewed.

In an age discrimination suit, the employee-plaintiff has two methods in which he may prove his case against the employer-defendant. He may use the direct method of proof and present direct or circumstantial evidence that age was a determining factor in his discharge. Alternatively, he may use the indirect method of proof as set out by the Supreme Court in *Texas Department of Community Affairs v. Burdine* and *McDonnell Douglas Corp. v. Green*. The indirect method is by far the more common method of proof, and the circuits have agreed that this indirect method, while originally formulated for Title VII cases, nevertheless applies equally well to age discrimination cases under the ADEA. This indirect method features shifting burdens of production. The employee must first prove a prima facie case of discrimination, which he does by showing that: (1) he was in the protected class, (2) he was doing his job well enough to meet his employer's legitimate expectations, (3) in spite of his performance he was discharged, and (4) the employer sought a replacement for him. If the employee is successful, this creates a rebuttable presumption of discrimination, and the burden of production shifts to the employer to articulate a legitimate, nondiscriminatory reason for the employee's discharge. If the employer is successful, the presumption dissolves, and the burden shifts back to the employee to show that the employer's proffered reasons are a pretext. The employee may show this in one of two ways: (1) that the employer was more likely motivated by a discriminatory reason, or (2) that the employer's proffered reason is unworthy of credence. The burden of persuasion remains with the employee at all times. Moreover, the employee may anticipate the employer's justification and introduce evidence of pretext in his case-in-chief, as plaintiff did in the case at bar.

Against this background, the issue raised by plaintiff is as follows: when defendant offers a legitimate, nondiscriminatory reason for defendant's discharge or her (that plaintiff was not doing her work correctly), is evidence that defendant's true reason for terminating plaintiff was different and less honorable but still nondiscriminatory (evidence that defendant terminated plaintiff in retaliation for her son's legal action against various University officials) relevant? We conclude that such evidence is not relevant. It must be noted that when the burden of production shifts back to plaintiff under the indirect method of proof, plaintiff must show that defendant's proffered reason is not just a pretext, but a pretext for discrimination. It is one matter if plaintiff shows such pretext by showing that defendant's proffered reason is unworthy of credence; such a showing is fully consistent with the conclusion that defendant has discriminated against plaintiff. It is an entirely different matter if plaintiff demonstrates pretext by showing that defendant's true reason was another nondiscriminatory reason; this does not show that defendant's proffered reason was a pretext for discrimination, and is not consistent with the conclusion that defendant discriminated against plaintiff. As support for our conclusion, suppose defendant stole plaintiff's argument and stated that the true reason defendant terminated plaintiff was because plaintiff's son was a trouble-maker, rather than waiting for plaintiff to argue that this was the true reason for her termination. While defendant would not be deserving of praise, this "bad' reason proffered by defendant would still constitute a nondiscriminatory reason that satisfies defendant's burden under the indirect method of proof in an age discrimination case. Given this result, in our case where defendant proffers a "good" but allegedly false nondiscriminatory reason, plaintiff cannot show that defendant's proffered reason is a pretext for discrimination by showing that the true reason was a "bad" but also nondiscriminatory reason.

The case of *Douglas v. Anderson*, provides support for this result. In that age discrimination suit, the defendant showed that the plaintiff was terminated because of the plaintiff's financial mismanagement of the defendant's bookstore. The plaintiff argued that the real reason for his discharge was his criticism of certain financial transactions conducted by the defendant which the plaintiff discovered. The court concluded that this does not show that defendant's proffered reason is a pretext for discrimination, "but merely presents an alternate reason not based on age." As the Ninth Circuit aptly summarized, "[t]he reason for a business decision need not meet the unqualified approval of the judge or jury, so long as it is not based on age." The same can be said for the case at bar.

For the above-stated reasons, we affirm the judgment in favor of defendant.

As the *Johnson* case reveals, it will be difficult to prove discrimination under the federal statute, and in several states, there is applicable state legislation governing mandatory retirement. This issue will likely have an enormous impact upon higher education, as Congress in 1986 outlawed mandatory retirement on account of age; a window was accorded colleges to exempt them until 1994, but after that date, as a recent AAUP report put it, "ADEA trumps all outstanding obligations to retire at a certain age." *Academe,* July-August 1987, pp. 45-48. See also "Study on Ban on Mandatory Retirement is Delayed; AAUP Will Not Resist End to Academe's Exemption," *Chronicle of Higher Education,* 5 August 1987, pp. 9, 12; *Retirement Ages for College and University Personnel* (NY: Commission on College Retirement, 1986); H. Eglit, "The Age Discrimination in Employment Act's Forgotten Affirmative Defense: The Reasonable Factors Other Than Age Exception," *Boston University Law Review,* 66 (1986), 155-226.

Title IX of the Education Amendments of 1972 has undergone significant change in the years since its enactment. It provides: "No person in the United States shall, on the basis of sex, be excluded from participation in, be denied the benefits of, or be subjected to discrimination under any education program or activity receiving Federal financial assistance...." 86 Stat. 373, 20 U.S.C. Sec. 1681. The statute was used to strike down athletic programs and other educational practices that excluded women, aided in part by *Cannon v. University of Chicago,* 441 U.S. 677 (1979), which held that there was a private right of action under the statute ("Not only the words and history of Title IX, but also its subject matter and underlying purposes, counsel implication of a cause of action in favor of private victims of discrimination.") On the remand in *Cannon,* the 7th Circuit held that intentional discrimination must be proved under Title IX. 648 F.2d 1104, *cert. denied,* 102 S. Ct. 981 (1981). In addition, Cannon was so persistent that an exasperated court admonished her to "discontinue this endless stream of redundant and meritless pleadings" or face sanctions. 116 F.R.D. 244 (N.D. Ill. 1987). See R. Salomone, "Title IX and Employment Discrimination: A Wrong in Search of a Right," *Journal of Law and Education*, 9 (1980), 433-447.

As the jurisprudence of Title IX developed, the relief offered by *Cannon* never fully materialized in women's options for litigating sex discrimination. *Cannon* itself was limited on remand, while *Lieberman v. University of Chicago* held that Title IX did not contain an implied right of action for damages. 660 F. 2d 1185 (7th Cir. 1981). In *North Haven v. Bell* the Supreme Court held that Title IX's language covered employment discrimination, but was restricted to persons "subjected to discrimination under" education *programs* receiving federal funds. 456 U.S. 509 (1982). Although *program* was not defined, its contours became clear in *Grove City v. Bell*, in which the Supreme Court held that a college's receipt of federal student aid funds constituted "financial assistance," but that the "program or activity" was to be considered narrowly as the office receiving and administering the money. 465 U.S. 555 (1984). In *Grove City*, then, the financial aid office was reached by Title IX, but not the institution as a whole ("We conclude that the receipt of BEOGs by some of Grove City's students does not trigger institution-wide coverage under Title IX. In purpose and effect, BEOGs represent federal financial assistance to the college's own financial aid program, and it is that program that may properly be regulated under Title IX.")

In 1988, Congress acted to expand Title IX by the Civil Rights Restoration Act, and overrode a presidential veto. The broadened definition of "program" also affects other similarly-worded civil rights statutes, including Title VI, Section 504, and the Age Discrimination Act. Until the revised Title IX becomes a more certain path for women who bring sex discrimination or sexual harassment suits, Title VII or state statutes will likely be the vehicles for this litigation. For example, Marie Best was able to establish a sexual harassment pattern under a District of Columbia law prohibiting sexual harassment: "Thus, we hold that a plaintiff establishes a prima facie case of sexual harassment upon demonstrating that unwelcome verbal and/or physical advances of a sexual nature were directed at him/her in the workplace, resulting in a hostile or abusive working environment. The test to determine whether the plaintiff has met her burden is essentially a balancing test, in which the trier of fact should consider, inter alia, the amount and nature of the conduct, the plaintiff's response to such conduct, and the relationship between the harassing party and the plaintiff. In other words, the totality of the circumstances must be considered." *Howard University v. Best*, 484 A. 2d 958 (D.C. App. 1984). A 1986 case brought by a woman bank employee clarified what courts will consider as sexual harassment: plaintiffs may establish a Title VII claim if they can prove that sex discrimination created a "hostile or abusive work environment." *Meritor Savings Bank v. Vinson*, 477 U.S. 57 (1986). See also *Johnson v. Transportation Agency*, 107 S. Ct. 1442 (1987) (county may use affirmative action preference plan for promoting women employees). See C. MacKinnon, *Sexual Harassment of Working Women* (Cambridge: Harvard University Press, 1979); M. Greenberger and C. Beier, *Federal Funding of Discrimination: The Impact of Grove City College v. Bell* (D.C.: National Women's Law Center, 1984); R. Schneider, "Sexual Harassment and Higher Education," *Texas Law Review*, 65 (1987), 525–583.

Faculty who are denied tenure, lose their jobs, or who perceive that prejudice detrimentally affects the quality of their working conditions will continue to press cases against institutions. Far more often than not, colleges will prevail due to the extraordinary costs of bringing suits, the statistical and legal proofs required to prevail, and the significant psychic toll that litigation exacts. In some settings, preventive actions render the problems less significant, as when consent decrees are entered into, pledging an administration to a course of action. See La Noue and Lee, *Academics in Court* (Ann Arbor: University of Michigan Press, 1987), especially Chapter 7; "Women Professors Pressing to Close Salary Gap; Some Colleges Adjust Pay, Others Face Lawsuits," *Chronicle of Higher Education*, 15 July 1987, pp 1, 14; *Lilia Melani v. Board of Higher Education of the City of New York, Notice of Preliminary Approval of Consent Decree* (May 15, 1984); *Lucy Peng-Fei Chang v. University of Rhode Island, Notice of Proposed Settlement of Class Action* (January, 1986); *Lamphere v. Brown University*, 798 F. 2d 532 (1st Cir. 1986) (sex discrimination case arising from consent decree); *Rajender v. University of Minnesota*, 20 EPD ¶ 30, 225 (1979).

While the changing terrain of this area of law has required colleges to prove their cases, and while new laws no longer completely exempt higher education from their reach (e.g., Age Discrimination in Employment Act), many of the issues litigated evolve from deeply held convictions. Many faculty continue to feel that ethnic studies or women's studies are less creditworthy than are more traditional fields, which may lead to substantial problems for some women or minority faculty at tenure time. See *Lynn v. Regents of the University of California*, 656 F. 2d 1337 (9th Cir. 1981) ("A disdain for women's issues, and a diminished opinion of those who concentrate on those issues, is evidence of a discriminatory attitude towards women.") In "The Id, the Ego, and Equal Protection: Reckoning with Unconscious Racism," Charles Lawrence argues:

> Traditional notions of intent do not reflect the fact that decisions about racial matters are influenced in large part by factors that can be characterized as neither intentional—in the sense that certain outcomes are self-consciously sought—nor unintentional—in the sense that the outcomes are random, fortuitous, and uninfluenced by the decisionmaker's beliefs, desires, and wishes.

> Americans share a common historical and cultural heritage in which racism has played and still plays a dominant role. Because of this shared experience, we also inevitably share many ideas, attitudes, and beliefs that attach significance to an individual's race and induce negative feelings and opinions about nonwhites. To the extent that this cultural belief system has influenced all of us, we are all racists. At the same time, most of us are unaware of our racism. We do not recognize the ways in which our cultural experience has influenced our beliefs about race or the occasions on which those beliefs affect our actions. In other words a large part of the behavior that produces racial discrimination is influenced by unconscious racial motivation. *Stanford Law Review*, 39 (1987), 317–388.

Both racism and sexism, or prejudice in general, may be unwitting or unexamined. One lesson from these cases is that colleges may be called to account for actions, in which instances any prejudice that substantially figured in the triggering incidents will not remain unexamined.

There is a voluminous literature reviewing affirmative action in employment, particularly in higher education. See, for example, M. Clague, "The Affirmative Action Showdown of 1986: Implications for Higher Education," *Journal of College and University Law*, 14 (1987), 171–257; G. Rutherglen and D. Ortiz, "Affirmative Action

Under the Constitution and Title VII: From Confusion to Convergence," *UCLA Law Review*, 35 (1988), 467–518; H. Edwards, *Recent Supreme Court Decisions and Implications for Higher Education* (Houston: IHELG, 1987, Monograph 87–8); "Symposium: Affirmative Action," *Iowa Law Review*, 72 (1987). While the many cases may strike some readers as bloodless, they clearly reflect great investments by all parties involved. The Chapter ends with an incident that did not end up in court, but which reflects a reality in modern U.S. higher education.

The Price and Pain of Racial Perspective
by Derrick Bell

All now agree that what happened was wrong. "Outrageous" is the term most frequently used by those Stanford Law faculty members who have offered me their apologies. They are embarrassed that a few of their colleagues, in an action that may be without precedent in law school history, listened to, concurred with, and acted on expressions of dissatisfaction registered by some first-year students in my Constitutional Law course.

What was Done?

Without consulting me, a few faculty members, with some degree of approval from the administration, organized a series of "enrichment lectures" intended to supplement coverage of my course. So that I would not feel excluded, officers of the Law Forum, a student-run speakers group, were enlisted to invite me to give one of the lectures. I accepted. I was not told the real purpose of the series, but now understand that some teachers who agreed to participate did so only after being told that I would take part.

In fact, I was totally unaware of the project's real purpose until members of the Stanford Black Law Students Association (BLSA) came to my office and shared with me the protest statement they planned to read before the first lecture. Even some weeks after the event, I am unable to rationally express the range of my feelings— from abject humiliation to absolute outrage. Here were black students, some of whom had hailed my visit as a real gain for them, forced to bring me the news that even as I taught my courses, walked through the halls, attended meetings, and generally participated in the life of this community, a large percentage of students knew that the administration had approved a program organized and specifically designed to compensate for student-reported teaching inadequacies. It was by a considerable margin, the worst moment of my professional life.

The BLSA protest led both to the cancellation of the lecture series and the slow but steady return to my Constitutional Law class of perhaps two dozen students who, disregarding their assignments, were attending one of the other two Constitutional Law Sections.

Why Did the School Do It?

Some in the Stanford community have questioned the BLSA assertion that there was a racial component to both the negative reaction of some students to my course and the faculty response to the student criticism. As is usually the case in contemporary racial issues, it is possible to identify non-racial factors that may have contributed to the student resistance I noticed from almost the first day. I am a visitor and unknown to most first-year students, many of whom were disappointed that a number of nationally-known faculty members were not teaching Constitutional Law this year. Then too, I am using a text that is quite innovative, and one that can be difficult for new students.

These difficulties are not unusual and I was surprised when they did not resolve themselves after the first few weeks. After all, I thought, Stanford students are not that different from those to whom over the years I have taught Constitutional Law at Oregon, Harvard, Emory, Illinois, the University of Washington, and Florida State.

At none of those schools had faculty members intervened in the adjustment process and encouraged the misgivings of students during the early adjustment process so familiar to every black teacher. The question is why did it happen at Stanford? I may have been a stranger to the first-year students, but I was certainly known to the faculty. Obviously, I did not favorably impress some students in those first few weeks, but I have searched diligently for reasons not influenced by race that would enlarge first-year law student complaints, no matter how lurid, into a crisis for faculty colleagues well aware of my reputation.

And there, I fear, is the problem. When I entered teaching after a dozen years in civil rights work, I determined that I would try to bring to my classrooms and my scholarship both my legal skills and my experience and perspective as a black man in this country. In my view, neither the students, nor my life-long commitment to the racial struggle, would be well served if I simply sought to emulate the teaching approach and the scholarly outlook of my white counterparts.

This, for me, did not mean every subject had to be infused with race. But it did mean that when race played a role in the development of an area of law, it should be explored rather than, as so often has been the case, ignored. As the text co-authored by Professor Paul Brest makes clear, issues of race and slavery played a much larger role in the formulation of the Constitution than most history books report and most Americans realize.

Understanding why the Framers compromised their principles and built slavery into the Constitution, and recognizing the importance of property rights in their thinking, are essential elements in a course on this country's basic law. Without this background, the later chapters devoted to contemporary racial issues are not coherent. They seem on the periphery of the constitutional pattern of which they may be the most important part.

The other two Constitutional Law sections also used Paul Brest's book, but both chose to reorganize the materials so as to enable their students to experience doctrinal development much earlier in the course than is possible if the chapters are taken in order, as I decided to do. This choice was not likely welcomed by some students who were obviously displeased with my Charles Beard-influenced interpretation of the Framers' motivations.

In a word, the interpretation and my presentation of it was as threatening to some students as my [writings] are unnerving for many of my law teacher colleagues. When the student complaints were reported to faculty members, I believe that the content of my course was translated into a competency problem to which response became important. This explanation, if correct, explains why no one thought it necessary to discuss the material with me. Even Constitutional Law teachers as renowned as those on this faculty would not attempt to teach the basic Constitutional Law course in a series of lectures. But I suggest the felt need was not to convey information, but to provide equal time.

Actually, if I am correct and those who were concerned about the "balance" of my teaching had honestly spoken to me about that, I might have agreed to a series of public discussions with other teachers so that all students could compare my perspectives with others on this faculty. This was done recently on a current issue in school desegregation, and I think everyone profited from the exchange.

I realize that my conclusions are based less on any hard proof than on my 55 years living as a black person in this society. A degree of racial paranoia is an unavoidable part of that life. But I submit that had I come here with a political outlook comparable to the black neo-conservatives now receiving so much undeserved media attention, and had my teaching of Constitutional Law been in that mold, either the student complaints would have been less virulent or the faculty response would have been more in keeping with the usual practices, which is to say students would have been urged to be patient and talk over their problems with the teacher.

Assessing Damages

Few outside the black community may agree with my evaluation of this incident, and yet it makes little difference whether I am right or wrong on the causes of what happened. The fact of my exclusion from the dialogues that must have taken place before so radical a remedy for student upset was adopted was a denial of my status as a faculty member and my worth as a person every bit as demeaning and stigmatizing to me as the Jim Crow signs I helped remove from public facilities across the South two decades ago.

Trying to recover from this experience, I find myself remembering with feelings approaching fondness the occasional Southern judge, who, to insure that I did not miss his disdain for both my competence and my cause, swiveled his chair and faced the wall when I approached the bench to argue a civil rights case. Back then, the racial hostility was patent and the insult expected. Here, quite frankly, I accepted the invitation to visit Stanford as something of a reward for a decade and a half of "proving myself worthy" to teach at a prestigious school that has been less than lavish in its job offers to black law teachers. As a guest welcomed with smiles at the door, I must confess that I simply was not prepared for what happened after I thought myself safe among friends.

Dean John Ely tells me that he feels awful about his failure to get more involved in the matter, and a number of white students have been at pains to offer their apologies both personally and on behalf of their school. I have accepted all apologies in the spirit in which they were made. For me, they are like condolences, expressions of sympathy for a years-in-the-making reputation that will never be quite the same. Unavoidably altered as well is the facade of collegiality and acceptance that all people of color operating at the upper echelons of white society carefully need to construct as an insulation against the dilemma of their difference.

It is a universal need. What happened to me here in my 17th year as a law professor and a former law school dean was dramatically damaging to my public reputation and hardly helpful to the sense of personal competence so critical to the effective functioning of every teacher. And yet there are few black people, including even those of us in the highest reaches of our professions, who do not suffer, and suffer frequently, similar and similarly painful reminders that race in America is isolating and that those who are not white must strive always and in vain for the presumption of conventionality, competence, and acceptance our white associates receive from this society as a matter of course.

My salvation, for not the first time, were the black students. They acted with a firm but fair maturity in this matter that everyone has quite rightly praised. I owe them my public thanks. They responded responsibly and forthrightly to the insult inherent in the lecture series when even those faculty members who were experiencing growing misgivings about the plan remained silent. I regret though that black students for whom I consider myself a special model, an advisor, and, in a symbolic way, a protector, had to come to my rescue, had to do for me what they had every right to expect that I would be doing for them.

Probably out of kindness, no black student has asked whether if on such shabby evidence, a person in my position can be so humiliated, what can they expect either here or out in the larger world? Had they asked, I would have no answer more clear than the experience from which they rescued me. They deserve better as do all associated with this great law school.

Searching for a Remedy

A remedy is not obvious. Perhaps none is possible. But it is clear that the law school and I would have been spared this harrowing experience were there more black teachers on this faculty. Their visible presence would have quieted the concerns of those students who, aware of the dearth of teachers of color here, viewed me as a token, visiting presence of questionable competence and unacceptable politics. And any black teacher who learned of the lecture series plan would have quickly and vigorously protested the all-too-apparent implications of this scheme, and predicted the unhappy consequences of going ahead . . . as, finally, the black students did. . . .

© The Stanford Law School Journal, 1986. Reprinted with permission.

This incident chronicled by Professor Bell led to a great outcry of protest. In Fall, 1987, Paul Brest, the new Stanford dean, invited Professor Bell back to Stanford and offered a public apology.

Appendix I

Sensitive Compartmented Information Nondisclosure Agreement

An Agreement between _____ and the United States
(Name—Printed or Typed)

1. Intending to be legally bound, I hereby accept the obligations contained in this Agreement in consideration of my being granted access to information known as Sensitive Compartmented Information (SCI). I have been advised and am aware that SCI involves or derives from intelligence sources or methods and is classified or classifiable under the standards of Executive Order 12356 or under other Executive order or statute. I understand and accept that by being granted access to SCI, special confidence and trust shall be placed in me by the United States Government.

2. I hereby acknowledge that I have received a security indoctrination concerning the nature and protection of SCI, including the procedures to be followed in ascertaining whether other persons to whom I contemplate disclosing this information have been approved for access to it, and that I understand these procedures. I understand that I may be required to sign subsequent agreements as a condition of being granted access to different categories of SCI. I further understand that all my obligations under this Agreement continue to exist whether or not I am required to sign such subsequent agreements.

3. I have been advised and am aware that direct or indirect unauthorized disclosure, unauthorized retention, or negligent handling of SCI by me could cause irreparable injury to the United States or could be used to advantage by a foreign nation. I hereby agree that I will never divulge such information unless I have officially verified that the recipient has been properly authorized by the United States Government to receive it or have been given prior written notice of authorization from the United States Government Department or Agency (hereinafter Department or Agency) last granting me either a security clearance or an SCI access approval that such disclosure is permitted.

4. I further understand that I am obligated to comply with laws and regulations that prohibit the unauthorized disclosure of classified information. As used in this Agreement, classified information is information that is classified under the standards of E. O. 12356, or under any other Executive order or statute that prohibits the unauthorized disclosure of information in the interest of national security.

5. In consideration of being granted access to SCI and of being assigned or retained in a position of special confidence and trust requiring access to SCI and other classified information, I hereby agree to submit for security review by the Department or Agency

last granting me either a security clearance or an SCI access approval all materials, including works of fiction, that I contemplate disclosing to any person not authorized to have such information, or that I have prepared for public disclosure, which contain or purport to contain:

(a) any SCI, any description of activities that produce or relate to SCI, or any information derived from SCI;

(b) any classified information from intelligence reports or estimates; or

(c) any information concerning intelligence activities, sources, or methods.

I understand and agree that my obligation to submit such information and materials for review applies during the course of my access to SCI and at all times thereafter. However, I am not required to submit for review any such materials that exclusively contain information lawfully obtained by me at a time when I have no employment, contract, or other relationship with the United States Government, and which are to be published at such time.

6. I agree to make the submissions described in paragraph 5 prior to discussing the information or materials with, or showing them to, anyone who is not authorized to have access to such information. I further agree that I will not disclose such information or materials unless I have officially verified that the recipient has been properly authorized by the United States Government to receive it or I have been given written authorization from the Department or Agency last granting me either a security clearance or an SCI access approval that such disclosure is permitted.

7. I understand that the purpose of the review described in paragraph 5 is to give the United States a reasonable opportunity to determine whether the information or materials submitted pursuant to paragraph 5 set forth any SCI or other information that is subject to classification under E. O. 12356 or under any other Executive order or statute that prohibits the unauthorized disclosure of information in the interest of national security. I further understand that the Department or Agency to which I have submitted materials will act upon them, coordinating with the Intelligence Community or other agencies when appropriate, and substantively respond to me within 30 working days from date of receipt.

8. I have been advised and am aware that any breach of this Agreement may result in the termination of any security clearances and SCI access approvals that I may hold; removal from any position of special confidence and trust requiring such clearances or access approvals; and the termination of my employment or other relationships with the Departments or Agencies that granted my security clearances or SCI access approvals. In addition, I have been advised and am aware that any unauthorized disclosure of SCI or other classified information by me may constitute a violation or violations of United States criminal laws, including the provisions of Sections 641, 793, 794, 798, and 952, Title 18, United States Code, the provisions of Section 783(b), Title 50, United States Code and the provisions of the Intelligence Identities Protection Act of 1982. I recognize that nothing in this Agreement constitutes a waiver by the United States of the right to prosecute me for any statutory violation.

9. I hereby assign to the United States Government all royalties, remunerations, and emoluments that have resulted, will result, or may result from any disclosure, publication, or revelation not consistent with the terms of this Agreement.

10. I understand that the United States Government may seek any remedy available to it to enforce this Agreement including, but not limited to, application for a court order prohibiting disclosure of information in breach of this Agreement.

11. I understand that all information to which I may obtain access by signing this Agreement is now and will forever remain the property of the United States Government. I do not now, nor will I ever, possess any right, interest, title, or claim whatsoever to such information. I agree that I shall return all materials which have or may come into my possession or for which I am responsible because of such access, upon demand by an authorized representative of the United States Government or upon the conclusion of my employment or other relationship with the Department or Agency that last granted me either a security clearance or an SCI access approval. If I do not return such materials upon request, I understand that this may be a violation of Section 793, Title 18, United States Code, a United States criminal law.

12. Unless and until I am released in writing by an authorized representative of the United States Government, I understand that all conditions and obligations imposed upon me by this Agreement apply during the time I am granted access to SCI and at all times thereafter.

13. Each provision of this Agreement is severable. If a court should find any provision of this Agreement to be unenforceable, all other provisions of this Agreement shall remain in full force and effect.

14. I have read this Agreement carefully and my questions, if any, have been answered to my satisfaction. I acknowledge that the briefing officer has made available to me Sections 641, 793, 794, 798, and 952 of Title 18, United States Code, Section 783(b) of Title 50, United States Code, the Intelligence Identities Protection Act of 1982, and Executive Order 12356 so that I may read them at this time, if I so choose.

15. I make this Agreement without mental reservation or purpose of evasion.

Signature   Date

Social Security Number   Organization
(see notice below)

The execution of this Agreement was witnessed by the undersigned, who, on behalf of the United States Government, agreed to its terms and accepted it as a prior condition of authorizing access to *Sensitive Compartmented Information*.

WITNESS and ACCEPTANCE:

Signature   Date

Organization

Notice: The Privacy Act, 5 U.S.C. 552a, requires that federal agencies inform individuals, at the time information is solicited from them, whether the disclosure is mandatory or voluntary, by what authority such information is solicited, and what uses will be made of the information. You are hereby advised that authority for soliciting your Social Security Number (SSN) is Executive Order 9397. Your SSN will be used to identify you precisely when it is necessary to 1) certify that you have access to the information indicated above, 2) determine that your access to the information indicted has terminated, or 3) certify that you have witnessed a briefing or debriefing. Although disclosure of your SSN is not mandatory, your failure to do so may impede the processing of such certification or determinations.

Appendix II

Proposed Schema for a Pontifical Document on Catholic Universities

From the Congregation for Catholic Education

VII. Opportuneness of Some Fundamental Norms for Catholic Universities

45. With the apostolic constitution *Sapientia Christiana* on April 15, 1979, norms for ecclesiastical universities and faculties were issued. These are the academic centers concerned with the study and teaching of the sacred sciences and the subjects of study connected with them. The time is now opportune for the provision of a new pontifical document for the issuing of analogous norms for Catholic universities and faculties, by which are meant centers of secular studies, including those that also have faculties of ecclesial studies.

46. It is necessary to point out that the situation of Catholic universities differs from region to region. The religious, political and social conditions of the nations in which they exist differ. Civil university legislation similarly differs; it is necessary to take this into account so that Catholic universities can be recognized and so that the academic degrees which they confer can have civil value. Also, the ecclesial conditions of Catholic universities differ from place to place. Some in fact have been canonically erected and approved, and others, though being really Catholic, do not have such a juridical status.

47. Furthermore, there exist Catholic universities that contain faculties or institutes of secular studies only, and others which as well as such studies also contain ecclesiastical faculties, erected in accordance with the constitution *Sapientia Christiana*.

48. In such diversity of situation a precise law for application uniformly to all Catholic universities appears impossible.

49. However, some elements necessarily common by virtue of Catholic identity do exist and can be emphasized. It is precisely this which involves the possibility of establishing norms concerning the nature and purposes of Catholic universities and the indispensable means for accomplishing them.

50. For this reason the present pontifical document on Catholic universities, including autonomous faculties and institutes and higher schools which confer degrees and titles, treats them inasmuch as they are *Catholic* and establishes the necessary requirements so that they can be truly such and can be clearly recognized as such.

51. The document does not therefore treat them inasmuch as they are universities, because under this aspect the same laws apply to them as apply to every university.

NORMS
Chapter 1
Nature and Objectives of the Catholic University

Article 1.1. The Catholic university, as "Catholic," is a university which by reason of its constitutional bond or by a common decision between those concerned animates its research and teaching, as well as its other activities, with a genuine Catholic spirit.

1.2 The Catholic university is distinguished by the following characteristics:

a) Its Christian inspiration not only of individuals but of the university community as such.

b) A continuing reflection in the light of the Catholic faith upon the growing treasury of human knowledge, to which it seeks to contribute by its own research.

c) Fidelity to the Christian message as it comes to us through the church in conformity with the magisterium.

d) An institutional commitment to the service of the people of God and of the human family in their pilgrimage to the transcendent goal which gives meaning to life.

Article 2.0. In view of the particular nature of the faculties, the objectives of the Catholic university are principally the following:

2.1 To promote scientific investigation in seeking and disseminating truth. In order to achieve this the Catholic university:

a) Shall evaluate the achievements of the various disciplines through philosophical and theological reflection in order to come to a clearer understanding of the meaning of life, of mankind and of the world.

b) Shall dedicate itself to the structuring of a vital synthesis of the various disciplines in order to promote and illustrate the concept of man in his wholeness.

c) Shall bring to bear the principles of the Gospel and the results of experience in the debates on contemporary questions.

d) Shall seek ways and means of bringing out into the open the truths and ethical values to be found in a study of various cultures.

2.2. To educate men and women so that after completing their higher studies they will duly undertake their professions, tasks and services and in so doing be authentic witnesses of the Catholic faith.

2.3 To offer appropriate aid to the church primarily in spreading the message of Christ in the world of culture.

2.4 To create in its midst an environment permeated with the evangelical spirit, thanks to which all the members of the university community may be helped to perfect their personal and spiritual development and each, according to his or her condition, may enrich with Catholic values the knowledge of the world, of life and of man which one is acquiring or gradually deepening.

Article 3. The statutes or other equivalent document shall establish in every Catholic university the manner in which these objectives shall be sought and attained, in accordance with this present document.

Chapter II
The Catholic University Within the Church

Article 4. The church has the right to establish and govern universities, which serve to promote the deeper culture and fuller development of the human person, and to complement the church's own teaching office.

Article 5.1. The Catholic university touches the church herself, and hence it cannot be considered as a purely private institution. It is for this reason that the relationship between the Catholic university and the church as a whole, and with its pastors, must be seen as an internal requirement of the university insofar as it is Catholic, i.e., to the degree that this component distinguishes and animates the whole activity of the university.

5.2. This relationship should be constantly fostered in order to protect the identity of the Catholic university for the good of both the university and the church.

Article 6. No university, even if it is in fact Catholic, may bear the title "Catholic university" except by the consent of the competent ecclesiastical authority.

Article 7. A Catholic university may be honored by the Congregation for Catholic Education with the designation "pontifical" in special circumstances.

Article 8.1. Episcopal conferences and diocesan bishops shall foster and assist Catholic universities in view of their importance so that they may contribute ever more to the good of the church. Episcopal conferences, then, should create an episcopal commission for such universities.

8.2. On their part Catholic universities shall maintain strict and faithful relations with diocesan bishops and episcopal conferences, because this communion with the pastors of the church is required of its nature for the attainment of their goals.

Article 9.1. The episcopal conferences and the diocesan bishops concerned have the duty and the right of seeing to it that in these universities the principles of Catholic doctrine are faithfully observed.

9.2. Should problems arise concerning the Catholic identity of the university, whether doctrinal or disciplinary, the ecclesiastical authority will confer with the authorities at the university in order to find satisfactory solutions taking into account the university's statutes or equivalent document.

9.3. If the Catholic character of the university continues to be compromised in a serious way the competent ecclesiastical authority may declare the university to be no longer Catholic.

Article 10.1. The autonomy proper to universities belongs also to Catholic universities. This autonomy is never absolute but is inspired and disciplined by truth and the common good.

10.2. Likewise due freedom in research, in accordance with the norms of Vatican II, shall be recognized in order that genuine progress may be made.

Chapter III
Various Types of Catholic University

Article 11. There are universities which are Catholic because they have been erected or approved by the Holy See.

Article 12. This erection or approval requires on the part of the Congregation for Catholic Education the approbation of the statutes and the establishment of the office of chancellor.

Article 13.1. The chancellor is the ordinary prelate on whom the university depends unless the Holy See otherwise decrees.

13.2. If the chancellor is not the local ordinary, norms shall be drawn up so that the chancellor and the ordinary may be able to carry out their respective responsibilities in mutual accord and to ensure that the rights of the local ordinary are fully respected.

Article 14. The chancellor:

14.1. Represents the Holy See in relations with the university and the university vis-a-vis the Holy See,

14.2. Fosters the preservation and progress of the university,

14.3 Defends and promotes the Catholic character of the university and facilitates its close links with the local and universal church.

Article 15. In the case of a canonically erected or approved university the nomination of rector/president needs to be confirmed by the Holy See or by another ecclesiastical authority delegated by it.

Article 16.1. There are also universities which are Catholic because they are approved by episcopal conferences in accord with the norms drawn up by the Holy See.

16.2. This approbation shall be given in the form of a written document, especially in the case of a university that wishes to include the term "Catholic" in its name.

Article 17. There are universities which are Catholic because they depend on or are administered by a religious family or some other canonical entity.

Article 18. There are universities which are Catholic by reason of a common decision by those concerned on condition that these universities have a juridical connection with the diocesan ordinaries concerned.

Article 19. All the universities referred to here shall define accurately their Catholic identity in their statutes or in some equivalent document in such a way that all that has been prescribed in this pontifical document is clearly indicated and applicable.

Article 20.1. There are also various kinds of Catholic institutes of higher studies legally equivalent to universities either in their full structure or in part thereof.

20.2. What is decreed in this pontifical document concerning Catholic universities shall have congruous application to such institutes.

Article 21. Every five years Catholic universities and other Catholic institutes of higher education shall send to the Congregation for Catholic Education a statistical report and information on their academic state and educational activity.

Article 22. "Ecclesiastical faculties" within Catholic universities shall be governed by the apostolic constitution *Sapientia Christiana* and its annexed norms.

Chapter IV
The Academic Community

Article 23. As a university constitutes a community of persons, all who belong to this community, whether considered as individuals or as members of academic moral bodies, shall accept responsibility—according to each one's situation—both for the common good and for the Catholic identity of the university, and therefore they shall cooperate diligently in their efforts to assist the university to attain its proper goals.

Article 24.1. To encourage this sense of co-responsibility all those involved in the university should share the same vision of man and of the world, should be animated by the same spirit of love and shall share reciprocally in a sincere dialogue.

24.2. In a special way spiritual values in relation to the person and the Christian community must be coherently shared and properly fostered by all members of the university community.

24.3. The authorities of the university shall render effective this co-responsibility by appropriate means such as participation in the councils of the university, consultations with members of the university community and the creation of suitable university associations.

Article 25. The rector of the university, who shall be chosen and named in accordance with the university's statutes, shall be a Catholic and shall possess those qualities that will enable him or her to promote the academic life of the university and its Catholic identity.

Article 26.1. All teachers who are to be chosen, nominated and promoted in accordance with the statutes are to be distinguished by academic and pedagogic ability as well by doctrinal integrity and uprightness of life so that they may cooperate effectively to achieve goals of the university.

26.2. Teachers who lack these requirements are to be dismissed, observing the procedures established in the statutes or equivalent document.

26.3. In accordance with Article 19 of these norms, every Catholic university shall establish such a juridical procedure.

Article 27.1. Catholic teachers and researchers shall carry out their tasks faithfully observing the principles of Catholic doctrine.

27.2. In view of their accepting appointments to teach in Catholic universities non-Catholic teachers shall loyally respect the Catholic character of the universities.

Article 28.1. Catholic students shall be educated in such a way that their learning and general development as well as their continuing formation are always marked by sound Catholic doctrine and practices so that they be evident in their everyday lives.

28.2. Non-Catholic students shall be expected to respect the Catholic character of their university, and opportunities shall be provided for them to learn about the Catholic faith while their freedom of conscience shall be always fully respected.

Chapter V
Catholic Orientation of the Curriculum

Article 29.1. Scientific research and academic teaching shall be carried out according to methods and principles that are properly scientific.

29.2. The research and teaching shall always take Catholic teaching into account.

Article 30.1. The competent ecclesiastical authority is to ensure that in Catholic universities there is established a faculty or institute or at least a chair of theology in which lectures are given to lay students also, so that they may deepen their understanding of Catholic doctrine.

30.2. There are also to be lectures on the theological questions particularly connected with the sciences and disciplines cultivated in the university, and in which both the Christian vision of the world and of man, and the professional ethic, will be expounded so that the students will be prepared to exercise rightly their future professions.

30.3. In the measure of their importance, ecumenical questions are also treated, according to the norms of the competent ecclesiastical authority; relations with non-Christian religions and the problems arising from modern atheism should also be treated.

Article 31. Those who teach theological subjects in any institute of higher studies must have a mandate from the competent ecclesiastical authority.

Article 32. In conferring the doctorate *honoris causa* on persons for scientific, cultural or ecclesial merits, the Catholic character of the university is to be taken into account.

Chapter VI
University Pastoral Care

Article 33.1. Very special attention shall be given to the pastoral care of the university so that the Christian life may be promoted and practiced.

33.2. Suitable opportunities shall be provided for teachers and students to deepen their understanding of the word of God and to participate in the sacraments.

33.3. Free initiatives are to be encouraged to help to deepen Christian life and its free exercise in a manner consonant with contemporary mentality.

33.4. A zealous apostolic spirit shall be encouraged among the members of the university community in order to foster a genuine Christian community spirit in the university milieu.

34.1. In view of serious social problems facing human society, possibilities to know the social teaching of the church are to be offered.

34.2. Suitable various initiatives inspired by a true Christian spirit and directed toward helping those in need, both within the university milieu and more particularly among the masses of deprived and impoverished people in society at large, shall be encouraged and facilitated.

Article 35.1. Diocesan bishops in accord with the competent university authorities shall promote pastoral care within the university.

35.2. To achieve this, appropriate initiatives are to be taken such as the setting up of various associations and even of the establishment of a university parish if there be need.

35.3. The university pastoral apostolate shall always be carried on in harmony with the church's pastoral ministry on the local and universal levels in order that, in reciprocal coordination, apostolic action may be efficaciously accomplished in society.

Article 36. Chaplains and other pastoral collaborators who are full of zeal, experts in pastoral care, capable of dialogue with teachers and students and of outstanding valiant helpers from among them, shall be appointed by agreement between the local ordinary and the university authorities.

Article 37. Wherever Catholic universities are situated in non-Catholic countries or areas, the university pastoral apostolate shall take due account of the local religious situation.

Chapter VII
Planning and Cooperation

Article 38. Due attention shall be taken to ensure that Catholic universities are well-distributed in various parts of the world through well-informed planning.

Article 39.1. It is primarily the responsibility of the episcopal conferences to carry out this plan, because they know effectively the apostolate needs and financial possibilities of their region, it is also the responsibility of religious orders dedicated to the university apostolate.

39.2. The Congregation for Catholic Education, assisted by experts, presides over the planning.

Article 40. Cooperation on the national and international levels between Catholic universities shall be promoted in order that through mutual help the desired goals may be more easily attained.

Article 41. To achieve this cooperation the following forms of collaboration shall be used:

a) Exchange of information, academic initiatives, publications, etc.

b) Exchange and interchange of teachers and students.

c) Sponsoring conferences in various academic fields.

d) Collaboration in research on various problems of interest to the church and society.

Article 42. Cooperation shall be encouraged with other universities, including non-Catholic universities, first through associations of teachers and through contacts with organizations that are not university based, especially to accomplish interdisciplinary research, in order to study important issues of society and to apply humanely the fruits of knowledge.

Article 43.1. In order to facilitate the cooperation and collaboration it is useful to have university associations functioning on the national, regional and international levels.

43.2. First the International Federation of Catholic Universities, erected by the Holy See for a more effective pursuit of their aims, is to be promoted.

Chapter VIII
Other Ecclesial Activities in the University and Cultural Milieu

Article 44. A harmonious form of pastoral care of intellectuals (*pastoralis intelligentiae*) shall also be encouraged and extended throughout the world of culture. This kind of apostolate shall be regarded as of prime importance and urgent need in today's world.

Article 45. Other kinds of Catholic institute of higher studies which will have a salutary influence on education and on the cultural apostolate shall be established.

Article 46.1. Eminent Catholic scholars are to be encouraged to undertake scientific research and teaching in non-Catholic universities.

46.2. Special interest should be taken in very talented students, whether Catholic or not, who show evidence of being well-suited to research or teaching, so that they be qualified to undertake various university appointments.

Article 47. Where it is possible, faculties of Catholic theology or institutes or chairs of Catholic theology should be established in non-Catholic universities too, on condition that orthodoxy of teaching be safeguarded.

Article 48. Special care is to be taken of Catholic students in non-Catholic universities or institutes. To this end, it will be helpful to establish at or near such universities or institutes residences or colleges in which well-chosen and qualified priests and laity offer spiritual assistance to the students as well as doctrinal and civil advice.

Article 49. Opportunities should be available to university students for financial support in the form of bursaries, accommodation, social security, etc.

Reprinted with permission.

Appendix III

Statement on Academic Freedom, Southern Baptist Convention*

The concern of the Seminary for freedom in teaching and learning arises from the Christian faith, with its promise of freedom in Christ to know the truth which is from God, which judges all human forms and institutions, and which shall set men free (John 8:32). The Seminary must strive to be a community of teaching and learning in which freedom of mind and spirit is accepted as fundamental under the Lordship of Jesus Christ.

The academic freedom in a theological seminary rests upon the Gospel itself as it creates a community in which the spirit of Christ informs and judges all human activities and becomes the source of all genuine freedom.

The following assertions are fundamental to a Christian view of academic freedom:

(1) The Christian faith directs all thought and life toward God who is the source of truth, the judge of all human thoughts, and the ultimate end of all theological inquiry.

(2) The freedom of the Christian always involves a commensurate responsibility toward God and neighbor. It is never the freedom merely to be left alone or to ignore basic obligations.

(3) Christian freedom exists within the confession of Christian faith. As stated under qualifications, every elected member of the faculty at the Seminary shall be a member of a Baptist church in active affiliation with the Southern Baptist Convention and shall be an active participant in the worship and work of that church. All persons accepting faculty responsibility in the Seminary shall be considered by such acceptance as engaging to teach in accordance with, and not contrary to, that statement which reads:

"The Articles of Faith of this Seminary shall be the statement on the Baptist Faith and Message adopted by the Southern Baptist Convention in 1963."

(4) While freedom must ultimately be realized through the spirit and loyalties of men, it must take form and be protected by concrete standards of institutional practice.

Every statement of such standards moves somewhat in the sphere of law and regulations. It is recognized that the effectiveness of stated principles depends finally upon the dedication within the Christian theological school to a genuine concern for liberty of mind and spirit in theological training.

---

* Based upon statement adopted by the Association of Theological Schools, June 16, 1960, and further developed by faculty and trustees of Southwestern Baptist Theological Seminary. Reprinted with permission.

Index